The Essential Reference

Vegetables

from Amaranth *to* Zucchini

Other books by Elizabeth Schneider

Uncommon Fruits & Vegetables: A Commonsense Guide

Ready When You Are: Made-Ahead Meals for Entertaining

Dining in Grand Style (with Dieter Hannig)

Better Than Store-Bought (with Helen Witty)

The Essential Reference

Vegetables

from Amaranth to Zucchini

500 Recipes *and* 275 Photographs

Elizabeth Schneider

Photographs by Amos Chan

WM

WILLIAM MORROW
75 YEARS OF PUBLISHING
An Imprint of HarperCollins*Publishers*

HarperCollins books may be purchased for educational, business, or sales promotional use. For information please write: Special Markets Department, HarperCollins Publishers Inc., 10 East 53rd Street, New York, NY 10022.

FIRST EDITION

Designed by Ralph Fowler

Printed on acid-free paper

Library of Congress Cataloging-in-Publication Data
Schneider, Elizabeth
    Vegetables from amaranth to zucchini : the essential reference /
Elizabeth Schneider.—1st ed.
        p.   cm.
    Includes index.
    ISBN 0-688-15260-0
    1. Cookery (Vegetables)   2. Vegetables.   I. Title.
TX801 .S353   2001
641.6'5—dc21

                                                            2001030423

02 03 04 05 / IMSP 10 9 8 7 6 5 4 3 2

I often reflect upon the variety of good things to eat which have been
introduced into this noble country [England] . . . over the last fifty years. The
vast influx of so many refugees . . . has led to the introduction of delights
previously considered inedible, worthless or even poisonous.

—A *Brief Account of the Fruit, Herbs & Vegetables of Italy,*
Giacomo Castelvetro, 1614

The greatest service which can be rendered any country is,
to add an useful plant to its culture. . . . One service of this kind rendered
to a nation is worth more to them than all the victories of the most
splendid pages of their history, and becomes a source of exalted
pleasure to those who have been instrumental in it.

—*Thomas Jefferson's Garden Books,*
1766–1824

O, mickle is the powerful grace that lies
In plants, herbs, stones, and their true qualities.
For nought so vile, that on the earth doth live.
But to the earth some special good doth give.

Romeo and Juliet, c. 1595,
—William Shakespeare

Contents

Acknowledgments

This book is enriched by the experience of hundreds of people in dozens of professions. Whether they work from state-of-the-art kitchens or cubbyhole home galleys, vast fields or backyard gardens, chilly laboratories or trailers in the tropics, these dedicated individuals have made produce fruitful terrain for me and for you.

Chefs and Other Food Professionals

Chefs, caterers, restaurant consultants, restaurants, teachers, and cookbook authors have been unstinting with recipes, practical advice, and encouragement. In part because the "Produce Pro" series I write for *Food Arts* keeps me in regular contact with these professionals, this book's culinary picture is painted in colors contributed from their diverse palettes (and palates). Their names follow alphabetically with the most current affiliations I was able to determine. My apologies if press time did not match career changes. Other culinary authorities whose written words are cited are listed in the bibliography.

Jody Adams, Rialto, Cambridge, Mass.; **Rashmi Aggarwala; Mark Allen; Anthony Ambrose,** Ambrosia on Huntington, Boston; **Helene An,** Crustacean, San Francisco and Beverly Hills; **Elizabeth Andoh; Robert Bagli,** Café Botanica, New York City; **Lidia Matticchio Bastianich,** Felidia and Becco restaurants, New York City; **Mario Batali,** Babbo, Lupa, and Esca restaurants, New York City; **Rick Bayless,** Topolobampo and Frontera Grill restaurants, Chicago; **Philippe Bertineau,** Payard Pâtisserie & Bistro, New York City; **Paul Bertolli,** Oliveto, Berkeley; **Scott Bieber,** Eli's Restaurant, New York City; **Jan Birnbaum,** The Catahoula Restaurant & Saloon, Calistoga, Calif., and Sazerac, Seattle; **Rob Boone,** Bambú, Miami; **Philippe Boulot,** Heathman Hotel, Portland, Ore.; **Catherine Brandel; Roy Breiman,** Ocean House Restaurant, Dennisport, Mass.; **Terrance Brennan,** Picholine, New York City; **Ed Brown,** Sea Grill, New York City; **Daniel Bruce,** Rowes Wharf Restaurant, Boston; **Jeff Buben,** Vidalia and Bis restaurants, Washington, D.C.; **Floyd Cardoz,** Tabla, New York City; **Bill Cardwell,** Cardwell's, St. Louis; **Antoine Cedicci,** Pane Caldo, Chicago; **James Chew,** Asian Culinary Society, New York City; **Cecilia Chiang,** founder, Mandarin restaurants, Beverly Hills and San Francisco; **Philippe Chin; Terry Choi,** Hangawi, New York City; **Sam Choy,** Sam Choy's, Honolulu; **Michael Cimarusti,** Water Grill, Los Angeles; **John**

Claussen; **Scott Cohen**, Las Canarias, San Antonio; **Tom Colicchio**, Gramercy Tavern and Craft, New York City; **Beth Collins**; **Jesse Cool**, Flea Street Café, Menlo Park, Calif.; **Matt Costello**, The Dahlia Lounge, Seattle; **Jack Czarnecki**, The Joel Palmer House, Dayton, Ore.; **Charles Dale**, Renaissance and R Bistro, Aspen, Colo.; **Marcel Desaulniers**, The Trellis, Williamsburg, Va.; **Rocco DiSpirito**, Union Pacific, New York City; **Fernando Divina**; **Roberto Donna**, Galileo, Vivo!, and II Radicchio restaurants, Washington, D.C.; **Romy Dorotan**, Cendrillon, New York City; **Jeff Drew**, Coyote Café, Santa Fe; **Alain Ducasse**, Louis XV, Monaco, and Alain Ducasse au Plaza Athénée, Paris, and Alain Ducasse at the Essex House, New York City; **Matthew Dunn**, Star Canyon, Dallas; **Troy Dupuy**; **Curtis Eargle**, Maryland Club, Baltimore; **Odette Fada**, San Domenico, New York City; **Gianni Fassio**, Palio d'Asti, San Francisco; **Rene Fieger**; **Jim Fobel**; **Susanna Foo**, Susanna Foo, Philadelphia; **Diane Forley**, Verbena, New York City; **Mark Franz**, Farallon, San Francisco; **Bill Fuller**; **Robert Gadsby**; **Michelle Gayer**, Charlie Trotter's, Chicago; **Chris Gesualdi**; **Anne Gingrass**, Désirée, San Francisco; **Joyce Goldstein**; **Laurent Gras**, Fifth Floor, San Francisco; **Tom Gray**; **Vincent Guerithault**, Vincent's on Camelback, Phoenix, Ariz.; **P. G. Gustafsson**, One C.P.S., Plaza Hotel, New York City; **Rick Hackett**; **Fatéma Hal**, Mansouria, Paris; **Alan Harding**, Petite Crevette, Brooklyn; **Chris Hastings**, Hot and Hot Fish Club, Birmingham, Ala.; **Reed Hearon**, Black Cat and Rose Pistola restaurants, San Francisco; **Kerry Heffernan**, Eleven Madison Park, New York City; **Lee Hefter**, Spago, Beverly Hills; **Maria Helm**; **Alejandro Heredia**, Hacienda de los Morales, Mexico City; **Greg Higgins**, Higgins, Portland, Ore.; **Bruce Hill**, Oritalia, San Francisco; **Peter Hoffman**, Savoy, New York City; **Josefina Howard**, Rosa Mexicano, New York City; **Todd Humphries**, Martini House, St. Helena, Calif; **Morgen Jacobson**; **Madhur Jaffrey**; **Erling Jensen**, Erling Jensen, The Restaurant, Memphis, Tenn.; **Jean Joho**, Everest, Chicago, Brasserie Jo, Boston and Chicago, and Eiffel Tower, Las Vegas; **Hubert Keller**, Fleur-de-Lys, San Francisco; **Loretta Keller**, Bizou, San Francisco; **Sarah Belk King**; **Barbara Kirshenblatt-Gimblett**; **Randy Kliewer**, Glissandi, Resort at Squaw Creek, Olympic Valley, Calif.; **Gray Kunz**; **Myung Ja Kwak**, Dok Suni and Dō restaurants, New York City; **Christer Larsson**, Christer's, New York City and Alta, Greenwich, Conn.; **Rémi Lauvand, Alex Lee**, Daniel, New York City; **Roland Liccioni**, Les Nomades, Chicago; **Susan McCreight Lindeborg**, Majestic Café, Alexandria, Va.; **Anita Lo**, Annisa, New York City; **Eileen Yin-Fei Lo**; **Eric Maillard**; **Waldy Malouf**, Beacon, New York City; **Francesco Martorella**, Pod, Philadelphia; **Cory Mattson**, Fearrington House Restaurant, Pittsboro, N.C.; **Tony May**, San Domenico, New York City; **Jay McCarthy**; **Peter Merriman**, Merriman's, Hula Grill, and Bamboo Bistro restaurants, Hawaii; **Carlo Middione**, Vivande Ristorante, San Francisco; **Rick Moonen**, Oceana, New York City; **Thomas Moran**, The Mayflower Inn, Washington, Conn.; **Masaharu Morimoto**, Morimoto, Philadelphia; **Bruce Naftaly**, Le Gourmand, Seattle; **Fortunato Nicotra**, Felidia, New York City; **Michel Nischan**, Heartbeat, New York City; **Wayne Nish**, March, New York City; **Andrew Nordby**, Heathman Hotel, Portland, Ore.; **Nancy Oakes**, Boulevard, San Francisco; **Andrew O'Connell**; **Patrick O'Connell**, The Inn at Little Washington, Va.; **Paul O'Connell**, Chez Henri, Brookline, Mass.; **Kazuhiro Okochi**, Kaz Sushi Bistro, Washington, D.C.; **Kenneth Oringer**, Clio, Boston; **Louis Osteen**; **Michael Otsuka**, Verbena, New York City; **Jean-Louis Palladin**; **Gary Palm**, La Posada de Santa Fe,

Santa Fe; **Sinclair Philip,** Sooke Harbour House, Sooke Harbour, B.C.; **Odessa Piper,** l'Etoile, Madison, Wisc.; **Sylvain Portay,** The Dining Room, Ritz-Carlton, San Francisco; **Nora Pouillon,** Restaurant Nora and Nora Asia, Washington, D.C.; **Maricel Presilla,** Zafra, Hoboken, N.J.; **Stephen Pyles,** Star Canyon and Starfish restaurants, Dallas; **Patricia Quintana,** Restaurant Izod, Mexico City; **Alois Raidl; Jan Raven,** Hilton International, Antwerp; **Stefano Riccioletti,** Alfredo of Rome, New York City; **Eric Ripert,** Le Bernadin, New York City; **Jacky Robert,** Locke-Ober Cafe, Boston; **Hans Röckenwagner,** Beverly Hills; **Douglas Rodriguez,** Chicama, New York City; **Michael Romano,** Union Square Café, New York City; **Anne Rosenzweig,** Inside, New York City; **Rosa Lo San Ross; David Ruggerio; Richard Sandoval,** Maya, New York City; **Lorna Sass; Charles Saunders; Jimmy Schmidt,** The Rattlesnake Club, Detroit; **Cory Schreiber,** Wildwood Restaurant, Portland, Ore.; **Joseph Schultz,** India Joze, Santa Cruz, Calif.; **Amaryll Schwertner,** Stars Bar & Dining, San Francisco; **Jamie Shannon; Ken Snapp,** Typhoon Brewery, New York City; **Katy Sparks; Barbara Spiegel; Sarah Stegner,** The Ritz-Carlton, Chicago; **John Martin Taylor,** Hoppin' John's Culinary Web site; **Jeffrey Tomchek; Sylvia Thompson; Corinne Trang; Jerry Traunfeld,** The Herbfarm, Woodinville, Wash.; **Charlie Trotter,** Charlie Trotter's, Chicago; **Patrick Vaccariello,** Maloney & Porcelli, New York City; **Jean-Georges Vongerichten,** Jean George, Vong, and Jo Jo restaurants, New York City; **Seiji Wakabayashi,** Ondine, Sausalito, Calif.; **James Walt; David Waltuck,** Chanterelle and Le Zinc restaurants, New York City; **Jeffrey Weiss; Brian Whitmer; Paul Wildermuth,** Red Light, Chicago; **Patricia Williams; Tina Wilson; Alan Wong,** Alan Wong's Restaurant and The Pineapple Room, Honolulu; **Stephen Wong; Irene Khin Wong,** Saffron 59, New York City; **Geoffrey Zakarian,** Town, New York City; **Peter Zimmer,** Zen World Cuisine, Santa Fe.

Scientists and Scholars

Authorities in diverse fields who helped abundantly and often, and whose wisdom is expressed frequently in their words and mine, are: **Peter Crisp,** director of Crisp Innovar Ltd., Norfolk, England, bountiful correspondent and vegetable gold mine; **Alan Davidson,** whose pivotal publications have long inspired my work and whose appreciative words have encouraged it; **Stephen Facciola,** author of *Cornucopia II,* a treasured resource; **Stanley J. Kays,** of the Department of Horticulture, University of Georgia, Athens, who kindly reviewed numerous entries; **Joy Larkcom,** author of *Oriental Vegetables* and other invaluable reference books; **Gary Lincoff,** educator about all things wild and edible, and munificent mushroom identifier; **Franklin Martin,** plant geneticist and horticulturist, retired—except when he corrected my tropical tuber entries; **Maricel Presilla,** author, educator, restaurateur—wonder woman; **Paul Williams,** spirited brassica champion, the Crucifer Genetics Cooperative and Wisconsin Fast Plants, University of Wisconsin, Madison.

Specialists who fielded queries about specific vegetables, language, etymology, and taxonomy: **Chokechai Aekatasanawan,** National Corn and Sorghum Research Center of Kasetsart University, Thailand; **Thomas Andres,** The Cucurbit Network, Bronx, N.Y.; **David Astley,** Horticulture Research International, Wellesbourne, England; **Brian Benson,** California Asparagus Seed & Transplants, Davis, Calif.; **Jim Brewbaker,** University of Hawaii at Honolulu; **Blair Buckley,** Louisiana State Agricultural Center, Calhoun; **Ronald A. Bunch,** D'Arrigo Bros., Salinas, Calif.; **Thomas E. Carter, Jr.,** Agricultural Research Service, USDA, Raleigh, N.C.; **Michael Castellano,** USDA Forestry Sciences, Corvallis, Ore.; **Katie Chafin,** Going Bananas Nursery, Homestead, Fla.; **Ronald Christ,** Lumen Books, Santa Fe; **Malcolm Clark,** Gourmet Mushrooms, Sebastopol, Calif.; **Marie-Christine Daunay,** Centre de Recherche Agronomique d'Avignon, France; **Deena Decker-Walters,** The Cucurbit Network, Miami; **Geoffrey R. Dixon,** University of Strathclyde & GreenGene International, Ayrshire, Scotland; **Glenn Drowns,** Curator of Vine Crops, Seed Savers' Exchange, Decorah, Iowa; **James A. Duke,** Distinguished Economic Botanist and consultant, Herbal Vineyard, Fulton, Md.; **Brian Ford-Lloyd,** School of Biosciences, University of Birmingham, England; **Clifford Foust,** University of Maryland, College Park; **Peter Fraissinet,** L.H. Bailey Hortorium, Cornell University, Ithaca, N.Y.; **Walton C. Galinat** (retired), University of Massachusetts, Waltham; **Jim Gerritsen,** Wood Prairie Farm, Bridgewater, Maine; **Irwin Goldman,** University of Wisconsin, Madison; **Andy Grant,** Grant Family Farms, Wellington, Colo.; **Arthur Greathead,** farm adviser (retired), University of California, Watsonville; **Richard Hall; Michael J. Havey,** University of Wisconsin, Madison; **Charles B. Heiser, Jr.,** Indiana University, Bloomington; **Marite Hirshkoff; Jim Hollyer,** University of Hawaii, Honolulu; **Robert L. Johnston,** Johnny's Selected Seeds, Albion, Maine; **Adel Kader,** University of California, Davis; **David Karp; Robert Kourik; Marcel Le Nard,** l'Institut National de la Recherche Agronomique, Plougoulm, France; **Richard Lester,** University of Birmingham, England; **Gary Lucier,** USDA Economic Research Service; **Dale E. Marshall,** Michigan State University, East Lansing; **Jim McFerson; Gene Mero,** PetoSeed Company, Saticoy, Calif.; **John Mickel,** New York Botanical Garden, Bronx, N.Y.; **Carol A. Miles,** Washington State University, Chehalis; **Teddy Morelock,** University of Arkansas, Fayetteville; **James R. Myers,** Oregon State University, Corvallis; **Ellen and Shepherd Ogden,** The Cook's Garden, Londonderry, Vt.; **Stephen K. O'Hair,** Tropical Research and Education Center, University of Florida, Homestead; **Jack Olsen,** San Mateo County Farm Bureau, Calif.; **Andrew Paterson,** University of Georgia, Athens; **Ken Pecota,** North Carolina State University, Raleigh; **Robert Pemberton,** Agricultural Research Service, USDA Aquatic Plant Management Laboratory, Fort Lauderdale; **Leonard Pike,** Vegetable & Fruit Improvement Center, Texas A & M University, College Station; **David Pilz,** Forestry Sciences Laboratory, Corvallis, Ore.; **Taweesak Pulam,** Novartis, Thailand; **William Randle,** University of Georgia, Athens; **George Richter,** George Richter Farm; **Joel Reiter,** Territorial Seed Company, Cottage Grove, Ore.; **Richard W. Robinson,** Cornell University, Ithaca, N.Y.; **Vincent Rubatzky** (retired), University of California, Davis; **Bill Schaefer,** C-Brand Tropicals, Gould, Fla.; **R. H. Sciaroni,** San Mateo Cooperative Extension Service, Calif.; **Adam Schneider; Annette Simonson,** Northwest Mycolocial Consultants; **Gérard Sparfel,** l'Institut National de Recherche Agronomique, Ploudaniel, France; **William F. Tracy,** University of Wisconsin, Madison; **Jim Trappe,** Oregon State University, Corvallis; **John Trestrail,** Spectrum Health Regional Poison Center, Grand Rapids, Mich.; **Arthur Tucker,** Delaware State University, Dover; **Nancy J. Turner,** University of Victoria, B.C.;

Sherry Vance, L.H. Bailey Hortorium, Cornell University, Ithaca, N.Y.; **Marisa Wall,** New Mexico State University, Las Cruces; **William Woys Weaver,** author, historian, and gardener, who maintains the Roughwood Seed Collection, Devon, Pa.; **Tod C. Wehner,** North Carolina State University, Raleigh; **Norman Welch,** farm adviser, University of California, Watsonville; **John H. Wiersema,** University of Maryland, College Park; **David W. Wolfe,** Cornell University, Ithaca, N.Y.

Produce Distributors and Growers

Distributors and growers of fine produce form the root system that fed this book—with both vegetables and expert information. **Baldor Specialty Foods, Inc.,** Bronx, N.Y., has been paramount, thanks to Kevin Murphy and his attentive staff, who supplied a wealth of select vegetables despite hail, drought, strikes, and crop failures. Lee Jones and the Jones family of **Chef's Garden,** Huron, Ohio, offered a rainbow of flavor-rich samples from their exceptional farm.

Phenomenal fungus came from **Gourmet Mushrooms,** Sebastopol, Calif.; **Hans Johansson's Mushrooms and More,** White Plains, N.Y.; **Marché aux Délices,** New York City; and **Phillips Mushrooms,** Kennett Square, Pa.; Rosario Safina, **Urbani USA,** Long Island City, N.Y., ensured a high-quality truffle crop from around the world.

Difficult-to-find produce was also supplied or located by: **Frieda's Finest,** Los Alamitos, Calif.; **Japan California Products,** Los Angeles; **JFC International,** Brooklyn, N.Y.; **Indian Rock Produce,** Quakertown, Pa.; Joel Patraker, **Union Square Greenmarket,** New York City; **RD Produce,** Edam, Netherlands; **Sid Wainer & Son,** New Bedford, Mass.

Specialized growers and associations helped out with their crops: artichokes from the **California Artichoke Advisory Board,** Castroville, Calif.; Asparation and bunching onions from **Sanbon Co.,** El Centro, Calif.; avocados from **C-Brand Tropicals,** Gould, Fla., and **Calavo Growers,** Tustin, Calif.; beets and radishes from **Underwood Ranches,** Somis, Calif.; Belgian (or California) endive from **California Vegetable Specialties,** Rio Vista, Calif.; Chinese vegetables from **Sang Lee Farms,** Peconic, N.Y.; kiwano and yacon (the latter no longer available—and, sadly, cut from this book) from **Swift Subtropicals,** Los Osos, Calif.; palm hearts from **Wailea Agricultural Group,** Honomu, Hawaii, and **Rock Garden South,** Miami; potatoes from **Wood Prairie Farm,** Bridgewater, Maine, **Irish Eyes & Garden City Seeds,** Thorp, Wash., **Potato Patch,** Halstad, Minn., and **Catskill Family Farms;** radicchio and puntarelle from **European Vegetable Specialties Farms,** Salinas, Calif.; rhubarb from **George Richter Farm,** Puyallup, Wash.; salicornia (Seaphire) from **Planetary Design Corporation,** Phoenix, Ariz.; squashes of all types from **Grant Family Farms,** Wellington, Colo.; sweet/mild onions from the **National Onion Association,** Greeley, Colo., **Keystone Fruit Marketing,** Greencastle, Pa., and **Saven Corp.,** Sylvan Lakes, Mich.; sweetpotatoes from **Virginia Eastern Shore Development Corp.,** Belle Haven, Va., and **Livingstone Farmers' Cooperative,** Livingstone, Calif.; watercress from **B & W Quality Growers,** Fellsmere, Fla.; wild (and semi-wild) greens from **Honey Locust Farm House,** Newburgh, N.Y.

Others Who Helped Cultivate This Book

For assistance in the kitchen, at the market, and at the computer during the early part of this book's development, thanks to Sandra Strachan, an eager and able graduating student from the Natural Gourmet Cookery School. Rosemary Serviss, the placement director, kindly recruited other interested students to try out recipes. Pupils from Peter Kump's Cooking School volunteered to do the same. Among the pupils from both schools are Kay Chun, Sara Kuntz, Michele Owings, Kate Potter, and Elizabeth Zipern. Others who tried recipes or assisted in the market are Nathaniel and Rebecca Herz, Didi Hunter, Yongja Kim, Richard Kowall, Edward Maloney, Van Luc and Ben Saelim.

Michael and Ariane Batterberry of *Food Arts* magazine, and Nahum Waxman of Kitchen Arts & Letters, New York City, have championed my work for as long as I have written about food. My gratitude for their past and present support grows with the years.

At William Morrow, Pam Hoenig was the first to find this project worthy of cultivation. Harriet Bell took over and sped the monumental manuscript to fruition with the participation of editorial gardeners Ann Cahn and Susan Gamer (most careful planters and pruners), Judith Sutton, and Karen Ferries. Thanks to Leah Carlson-Stanisic for overseeing the design, to Karen Lumley for production, and to Roberto de Vicq de Cumptich for the jacket. Ralph Fowler developed the interior landscape to display the vegetable garden. Carrie Weinberg will spread the word.

Amos Chan contributed even more than is evident in his pristine photographs. For four years, he went miles and hours beyond the call of duty (often on bicycle) to literally lighten my vegetable load and keep the perishables in shape to meet his perfectionist standards.

Ronald Christ, Dennis Dollens, Richard Kowall, Edward Maloney, and Lorna Sass helped in countless ways on so many days.

Barbara Spiegel, recipe adviser, critical tester and taster, and dearest friend, is a category unto herself: sine qua non.

Last and most is Seth Shulman, supreme helpmate, chief forager, and wildlife refuge. *Et maintenant, il faut cultiver notre jardin!*

Main Vegetable Entries

Recipes by Category

MAIN DISHES

With Meat and Seafood

Vegetable-Based

VEGETABLE SIDES

CONDIMENTS, SAUCES, AND SEASONINGS

The Essential Reference

Vegetables

from Amaranth *to* Zucchini

Introduction

Vegetable Discoveries

At the start of the 21st century, it is my good fortune to live at one of the earth's great vegetable crossroads: New York City. A short subway ride takes me to one county, Queens, where the most diverse population in the United States is represented by over 167 nationalities and 116 languages—and more vegetables than those two numbers combined. On Main Street in Flushing, I pluck ivory lotus, fuzzy gourds, and Chinese broccoli from overflowing bins as varied as Taipei's. Nearby, on Northern Boulevard, I find fragrant chrysanthemum and water celery in the Korean supermarkets. In Jackson Heights, where Indian and Bangladeshi shops cluster, I gather up curry-scented fenugreek greens and tiny, crunchy tindora. At a bodega a block away, I bag cushcush yams, sweet boniato, and arracacha.

Vegetables eaten here connect immigrants to their lands of birth. Plants reveal the roots of a community; they remind us that culture is contained in agriculture. Across the United States, the diversity of Queens exists on a smaller scale, with different specifics. In New Orleans, Seattle, and Kansas City, Vietnam's culinary influence sizzles pea vines and water spinach in the cities' woks. In Miami and Jersey City, Cuban cooks stir malanga, calabaza, and yuca into the melting pot.

Vegetables from Amaranth to Zucchini: The Essential Reference includes some 350 vegetables, common and exotic, that can be found (some easily, some with much digging) in markets in the United States today. In essence, the work chronicles the emergence of a multinational vegetable vocabulary from seed to recipe, from geneticist to chef. Discoveries from authorities in many fields (theoretical and earthbound) form the root system of this book. As this book grew, the experts involved began to explore each other's worlds: Geneticists spoke with produce managers in local groceries and found out which vegetables *really* reach the consumer; farmers asked me how to cook vegetables they grow, which some then tasted for the first time; distributors discussed with mycologists the safety of certain wild mushrooms, and cut some from their lists; chefs visited farmers to learn about the source of their ingredients, and then to commission custom crops.

Research scientists in genetics, horticulture, taxonomy, plant pathology, and agronomy have been generous beyond measure—and a source of delight. They seem surprised that their work has a bearing beyond the scientific community. Yet without their help I could not have written even the first entry—which Robert

Pemberton made possible by identifying dried leaves from a market in Queens as an unusual green amaranth. Lacking that identification, *I* might enjoy "Nameless Green" with Wheat, Scallions, Garlic, and Spices, but I could not tell *you* what to buy for the recipe. Orzo Risotto with Shiitake and Wild Mallows would not be here either, had Pemberton not checked out the mallow specimen I sent.

A fast-moving squadron of researchers in France cleared up the alias of a mislabeled onion in New York by delivering product, government decrees, and a library of botanical references within days of my call for help (see échalion, page 558). The British breeder Peter Crisp faxed many delicious musings, including ones that solved the mystery of the "Chinatown Green Thing" (see Chinese garlic stems, page 204) and the problem of pinning brassicas to the page long enough to get the book in print (their classifications seem to change with each improved microscope). A brassica breeder, Gene Mero, assured me that Broccoflower and broccoli Romanesco are green cauliflowers with old pedigrees, not the "hot new vegetables" promised by the popular press. Gary Lincoff listened to my praise for gyromitra soup savored at a French restaurant, then advised me to tell everyone to stay clear of that deadly mushroom (see page 302).

Farmers, foragers, and produce distributors braved hail, drought, and the disfavor of some national marketing groups (who consider minor crops and cultivar names taboo). I learned from Bill Schaefer that some 60 kinds of avocado are still grown in Florida for commerce, but that none of these juicy, low-fat salad types can be purchased by name. Nevertheless, gleaming, mature tagged samples arrived at my door "because you need to understand the big picture anyway" (a corner of which appears on page 39). Lee Jones introduced me to New Zealand spinach and proved that salad greens grown in Ohio fields at Thanksgiving had more flavor than any hothouse leaf I'd ever tasted. Daniel Bruce, a chef and forager in Boston, tenderly packed puffballs, chicken of the woods, and honey mushrooms that his New York–based mother-in-law toted to my home so that I could appreciate the beauty and flavor of East Coast specimens.

Chefs were the final stage in my seed-to-table learning process, but they were the first to show me, decades ago, that there are few "trade secrets" among those who do their jobs well. The most committed and often most celebrated chefs want to share what they know; they do not hide it. Along with her recipe ideas for ramps, Lidia Bastianich told me how her family foraged in Istria—and how and where she still forages in Queens. Jean Joho, who is cited often in these pages, taught me to refrigerate porcini and morels on a white cloth overnight—to get a bug count and to gauge usability. Jean-Georges Vongerichten shared tips for the preparation of nettles and recalled how he had learned the perils and pleasures of the plant on his first day as an apprentice in the kitchen of Paul Bocuse. These culinary leaders and close to 200 more (see Chefs and Other Food Professionals, page ix) took time to explain how they choose and cook the vegetables here.

Recipes, the last stop on the discovery route for each vegetable, are my domain. The first thing I do in the kitchen is try to *forget* all I've learned about cooking. I steam, boil, bake, sauté, simmer in broth, microwave each subject—unadorned, peeled and not, stemmed and not, whole and sliced—to find its culinary raison d'être. This not only reveals the flavors and textures, naked and real, but helps dispel preconceptions based on food fashions. Thirty years of developing recipes for a dozen magazines (as distinct as *Gourmet* and *Family Circle*) have given me a healthy skepticism about "what's hot and what's not." Tasting vegetables plain also frees the conceptual palate from ethnic type-casting. Tomatillos are as lively with dill or tarragon as with the usual cilantro. Mustard greens and turnip greens need no pork seasoning to shine. Flowering (Chinese) chives are elegant with butter and wine.

The start-from-scratch approach also entails reexamining techniques we take for granted. Comparison-testing tells me that few mushrooms are best sautéed, that salting does little to de-bitter eggplants and bitter gourds, and that none of the methods "guaranteed" to remove okra's slipperiness works—which is fortunate, for okra is luscious just as nature made it. My goal is to give each vegetable (which is, with a few exceptions, an evolved, ancient plant) a timeless (yet timely!) taste or look. Often, I find it.

I spend extra time working with the most exotic vegetables so that they will feel at home, familiar—which is what will happen naturally, over the years, as they become assimilated. When I was researching my previous book, *Uncommon Fruits & Vegetables: A Commonsense Guide,* in the early 1980s, arugula, chilli, cilantro, and radicchio were little more than curiosities in most of the United States.

I've also had a fresh look at oldies and goodies. I've confirmed that potatoes benefit dramatically from a cold start—not boiling water. That beets individually long-baked with whole spices in foil are melting perfection, but that partially cooked ones are best for salad. That beet stems, as well as radish greens and peels, make dandy dishes. That a microwave is just the tool needed to cut a tough pumpkin down to size. I like to sauté cucumbers, poach (not boil) shell beans, and roast green asparagus—but boil purple asparagus, steam sweetpotatoes, and simmer radicchio in risotto. Recipes (500 plus) are ready and waiting for you. Tasting is believing.

That's the map for the territory I explore in the pages that follow.

What's *not* here? Plants that play primary roles as seasonings rather than as vegetables are absent. Sprouts and "microgreens," produced from just about anything that grows from seed, are not included, because of their sheer number—and because they're almost all used in salad. Nor will you find some of the most common vegetables or vegetables already well represented in many other books: bell pepper, cabbage, corn, tomatoes, lettuces and other familiar salad greens, and spinach. If I could not discover something fresh to say about a vegetable, then it's not here.

Untangling the Terms

COMMON NAMES are a can of worms in the vegetable patch, starting with "vegetable," another word for a plant—no less, no more. It does not have botanical significance. When the context is culinary, "vegetable" means something edible grown in the ground and not likely to show up as dessert. Seeds and grains are considered another culinary category. Plants used primarily as seasoning (lemon grass, horseradish, ginger, tarragon) are called herbs and aromatics, not vegetables. Mushrooms begin to push this imprecise vegetable category over the edge: Mushrooms are not plants. They grow not in the ground but in things that are in the ground. Still, at the table, they are vegetables. It is not until you oppose "vegetable" with "fruit" that the can of worms overflows. That is because "fruit" has both botanical and common meanings. It specifies a seed-bearing organ, which is how it relates to vegetables. When we eat a seed-bearing part of a plant, it is the fruit. Botanically, cucumber, tomato, and mushrooms are fruits. Culinarily, they are vegetables.

An individual vegetable may have six common names in English alone, names that arise naturally from different sources and local usage. Common names vary from one region to another and from one city, distributor, farmer, or seed company to another. Rocket on the West Coast is arugula on the East. Lima beans are butter beans in the South—and have half a dozen other names as well.

"Foreign" common names overlap or are additional. In this book they are not treated as foreign (they are not italicized). They are simply the names in specified markets. If you want burdock in a Japanese market, you'll ask for gobo. For taro leaves in a West Indian market, try callaloo. For Chinese broccoli anywhere, gai lan should work. Some non-English names are sole or primary: bok choy, jícama, mizuna, porcini, radicchio, shiitake, tomatillo, and yuca.

MARKETING NAMES usually land on top of and in addition to naturally occurring common names. They are names superimposed to make generic foods into brands—and often confuse. If you do not know that Broccoflower is a cauliflower, you may think you are buying a different vegetable altogether. If you do want a cauliflower (a green one), you may not realize that you should buy Broccoflower. Marketing names are also given to genuinely distinct products developed by a single company—such as Cinnamon Cap mushrooms, a special strain; or Asparation (also sold as Broccolini), a broccoli–Chinese broccoli hybrid. Sugar snap peas, which have become a generic category of edible-podded peas, originally designated a single cultivar (see below) called Sugar Snap, a pea refined and named by one breeder, Calvin Lamborn.

BOTANICAL NAMES get close to the truth on paper. About the only way to be fairly sure you're talking about the same vegetable as someone else is to use the Linnaean binomial system in which genus and then species are given in Latin, an international language that transcends all others for identifying a plant. *Tuber melanosporum* means only one particular truffle, no matter what language you speak at breakfast. In English, you would call it a black truffle, a meaningless term in any other language—or even in English, which includes at least three species commonly called black.

In writing, if another species of the same genus follows in the text, the convention is to abbreviate the species to its first letter: Thus, the white truffle (of the same genus, *Tuber*) would follow as *T. magnatum*. Sometimes further explanations are appended to genus and species in the form of variety (var.), subspecies (subsp.), or Group. But none of these are fixed either, not even the family classification! Taxonomy changes with technology and individual opinion. As this book was being written, species were being modified and some are still questionable (and so indicated).

CULTIVAR NAMES are what most people refer to as "varieties," a term that also has another meaning (above). The term "cultivar," first proposed in 1923 by the great American botanist and horticulturist Liberty Hyde Bailey, elides "cultivated" and "variety." It denotes a botanical category subordinate to a species that has originated and persisted under cultivation. In technical works, a cultivar is usually capitalized and set off by single quotes. I have chosen to capitalize only. Often, we know vegetables by their cultivar names without realizing it: Hass avocado, Jalapeño chilli, Buttercup and Sweet Dumpling squash, and Yukon Gold potato.

POLITICALLY CORRECT NAMES are a new category. The word "Oriental" poses a problem at present but "American" and "Hispanic" are not far off. The blanket term "Asian" has supplanted "Oriental" as the noun that describes the inhabitants of the Far East nations of Asia and their descendants. But the adjective "Oriental" is still used to distinguish the vegetables (and carpets, cuisines, markets, etc.) of China, Japan, North and South Korea, Taiwan, and Hong Kong (and sometimes additional areas) from the vegetables of other parts of Asia. Cucumbers and eggplants, for example, are divided into both Oriental and Asian categories. If you want chrysanthemum greens, it won't do you much good to look for an "Asian" market unless it is Chinese, Japanese, or Korean (in other words, Oriental). If you go to an Asian market that is Indian or Middle Eastern, you've wasted a trip.

With such a tangle of terms, how do you find anything in this book? For the big picture, check under one of the 134 main encyclopedic entry heads in the text, which represent the most common market names in the United States: Bok Choy or Chanterelle Mushrooms or Beans, Snap. If you specifically want Shanghai bok choy or yellowfoot chanterelle or haricot vert (or French or filet bean—you'll find them under all three names), go straight to the Index of Vegetables by Their Common and Botanical Names. Similarly, go to the Index if you're seeking a vegetable name in Spanish, verifying a Latin classification, or trying to locate a vegetable by its marketing name. The Index includes names in all the categories above—common, foreign, marketing, trademarked, Latin, and cultivar—as well as some incorrect ones (which send you to the right name). Or you can follow a long, pleasurable route and flip through Amos Chan's lucid photographs until you find what you're after.

How Each Entry Is Organized

- Vegetable name(s): One or two names, usually the name or names most common in markets in the mainland United States

- Botanical name(s) in Latin

- Additional common names: Colloquial, vernacular, "foreign," and marketing names you're likely to see, followed parenthetically by a generalized description (Chinese, Latin American, West Indian) of the market that carries the vegetable by that name

- Photo: Vegetables in their usual market form, usually shown cut to display the interior; a few are depicted in stages of preparation

- Background: Why the vegetable is included, a physical profile, and a brief history and etymology

- Basic use: My suggestions for general use, and descriptions of traditional use, when helpful. (I have stayed with methods common to American kitchens. Sun-drying, salt-pickling, and baking in ashes are not described even if typical for the vegetable in question.)

- Selection: Availability and detailed criteria for choosing the vegetable in peak form

- Storage: Advice about ripening and handling; preferred storage methods

- Preparation: How best to wash, peel, cut, seed, slice, precook

- Recipes: Each recipe is chosen to exemplify a technique I believe best presents the vegetable's essence; if a recipe for, say, steaming or roasting is lacking, it is because I did not find that the method enhanced the vegetable's best characteristics.

- Pros Propose: Recipe sketches from chefs (and other culinary professionals) too lengthy, complex, or exotic to include in full. Some treat technical areas not covered by the basic recipes. Others describe interesting uses not suitable for American kitchens.

Amaranth (*Amaranthus* species)

Also Chinese spinach, vegetable amaranth, Joseph's coat, tampala;
yin choy and variations (Chinese), callaloo and variations (Caribbean),
quelite and quintonil (Mexican), bledo blanco (Latin American), chaulai
and bhaji (Indian), pirum (or birum) namul (Korean)

¼ **actual size**

In the United States, forms of amaranth are more familiar in flamboyant decorative plantings—where their brilliant multicolored leaves and magenta chenille tassels create dramatic displays—than they are in stewpots. Amaranth seeds show up in the natural food larder—puffed into breakfast cereal, baked in bread, or cooked as a grain.

Curiously, although most amaranths originated in the American tropics, were known to early Native Americans, and have long been established in much of the world (they are among the most important leaf vegetables of the African and Asian tropics), it is just lately that their edible greens (and purples and pinks) have brightened produce stalls—thanks largely to Far Eastern and Caribbean immigrants.

Because the closely related species vary considerably in size, color, and shape, amaranth is tricky to identify. Pretty bite-size, bicolor leaves pop up in salad mixes. Or you might see waist-high spruce green bunches, as I do on Flatbush Avenue in Brooklyn in Jamaican and Haitian markets. Fuchsia-splashed smaller bouquets are the norm in Chinese shops, while smooth, basil green amaranth appears to be preferred in Korean ones.

For those uninitiated in the culinary ways of the Caribbean, confusion reigns when the word "callaloo" (calalú, calaloo, callilu, etc.) appears, for it can signify many species of amaranth *or* of taro (page 655), *or* it can designate a soup or stew made with either—or without. For simplicity, let me say only that "amaranth" is one meaning of "callaloo." Mexican "quelite" also causes confusion: The word can be applied to a number of Mexican greens (notably lamb's quarters, page 351, and other *Chenopodium* as well as *Amaranthus* species). Or it may signal any one or all of them in the way of "greens"—coming, as it does, from the Nahuatl "quelitl" meaning "greens of any sort" (*America's First Cuisines* by Sophie Coe).

Given the plethora of common names, it is not surprising that the word "amaranth" itself has tangled roots. According to Alan Davidson, "it is derived from the Greek *amarantos* (unfading) because of an ancient belief that it was immortal. However, a false idea arose that the name meant 'love flower' (Latin *amor,* love, and Greek *anthos,* flower) and its name thus acquired a final 'h.' Vernacular names such as love-lies-bleeding and florimer (flor-amor) suggest this misunderstanding" (*The Oxford Companion to Food*).

Although the term "amaranth" refers to several species, the flavor of the leafy greens is fairly constant: earthy and spinachy, not sharp or bitter. Some types are rather assertive, in the manner of beet greens, while many are milder. Some have fine stems, some are as thick as collards. Although they look forbiddingly fibrous, these stems usually cook quickly to a tender, slightly slippery texture reminiscent of asparagus.

BASIC USE: For salad, use the tiniest leaves, in small quantities, mixed with mild and aromatic greens.

Amaranth is at its best cooked, when it is almost as versatile as spinach and can be used in similar ways. For the simplest treatment, steam amaranth stems, then leaves, then toss with oil and lemon. For soup, stir leaves into broth to turn it a warm pink and to add an earthy edge. Braise stems and leaves in a thick vegetable stew with beans and pumpkin. Chop leaves and stems, blend with grains and spices, cover tightly, and cook over lowest heat. Or sauté leaves with garlic or shallots, tomato dice, and a touch of chillis. For seasonings, you can head to Mexico, Italy, the Far East, or India with equal success. If the earthiness is too pronounced for your taste, combine amaranth with a brightening and lightening vegetable or two, such as red bell pepper or corn.

SELECTION: In the United States, amaranth can be found erratically during all but the coldest months (and even then some may show up). The magenta-sprinkled medium size pictured here is most common in Chinese and Indian markets. Korean and Mexican markets may offer a slightly larger all-green type; Caribbean markets display even larger green forms.

STORAGE: Wrap stem bases in wet paper and enclose the bunch in plastic. Store briefly—for just a day or two. For longer keeping (4 or 5 days) or to perk up tired leaves, trim stalk base, then soak plants for a few minutes in a sink filled with lukewarm water. Shake off most water, then pack amaranth in an airtight container.

PREPARATION: Cut off roots, if any. Discard dried, wilted, slippery, or yellow leaves. Drop amaranth into a huge amount of tepid water. Dunk up and down, then lift out gently so debris falls to the bottom. Drain, then repeat several times so that no sand remains. Do not be tempted to stop with one washing.

Cut leaves (but not leaf-stems, which are tougher and require longer cooking along with the stalks) from stalks and set aside. Trim very heavy base, if any, from stalks. Cut large leaves to bite size. If leaves are very large, remove the central veins—unless you'll be chopping, long-cooking, or both.

Basic Steamed Amaranth

Amaranth stems, which look alarmingly tough, cook quickly to a tender asparagus-like texture. The flavor, too, hints of asparagus, with a touch of artichoke. Amaranth leaves are more earthy—rather like mild beet greens. If too earthy for your taste, combine with other mild vegetables. For a crunchy, sweet finish, top either of the following recipes with Oven-Toasted Shallot Crisps (page 561).

About 1¼ pounds amaranth
Full-flavored olive oil
Coarse sea salt or fleur de sel
Slim lemon wedges

1. Cut off roots and/or very heavy stalk base, if any, from amaranth. Dip amaranth into several changes of water, lifting from bath so that sand sinks. Cut leaves

(not stems) from stalks; set aside. If there are very large leaves, cut them to manageable mouthfuls.

2. Spread stalks (with their attached leaf-stems) on steamer rack over boiling water. Cover and cook until almost tender, 3 to 6 minutes. Timing will vary with thickness of stems and type of steamer used.

3. Add all leaves. Steam until tender, 2 to 5 minutes.

4. Transfer leaves to serving dish and stalks to cutting board. Cut stalks into bite-size pieces, add to leaves. Serve hot or at room temperature, with a cruet of oil, a dish of salt, and lemon wedges.

Serves 4

Variation

Steamed Amaranth with Chilli Oil, Soy Sauce, and Sesame

Season the steamed amaranth with ½ teaspoon chilli oil or Asian (dark) sesame oil and 1 tablespoon soy sauce. Sprinkle with 1 tablespoon toasted sesame seeds.

Amaranth-Hominy Soup with Chili and Cheddar

A bowlful of South America (where amaranth, chilli, and corn originate) is an appealing vegetarian alternative to pasta with greens. If you have time to prepare it, the chewiness of fresh-cooked hominy (posole) is special—but so is the speed with which the dish can be whipped together using the canned. To match the quick assembly, use a chili powder blend rather than separate spices. The power of these blends varies: Adjust to suit your heat threshold.

About 1 pound amaranth
1 large onion
2 large garlic cloves
1 tablespoon olive oil
1 teaspoon dried oregano
1 tablespoon blended chili powder
3 cups vegetable, pork, or beef broth
About 3 cups fresh-cooked hominy (or two
    15-ounce cans), plus 1 cup of the cooking
    liquid or water
About 1 cup shredded sharp Cheddar cheese

1. Dip amaranth into several changes of water, until no sand remains. Cut leaves (not stems) from stalks; set aside. Cut stalks with stems into small pieces. Dice onion. Mince garlic.

2. Heat olive oil in heavy pot over moderately low heat. Add onion and stir until slightly softened. Add garlic, oregano, and chopped amaranth stalks. Cover and cook 2 minutes. Add chili powder and stir a few moments, until fragrant. Add broth, hominy, and cooking liquid; bring to a boil.

3. Bunch together amaranth leaves; slice thin, then chop. Add to soup. Simmer until tender, about 5 minutes. Season. Ladle into bowls and add cheese.

Serves 4

Amaranth with Wheat, Scallions, Garlic, and Spices

The toasty taste of bulgur wheat blends warmly with amaranth rather than contrasting with it, and the Moroccan spicing is gentle. Because the chopped greens contain so much moisture, little additional water is required, and the resulting flavors are full, undiluted. To prevent drying and scorching, choose a heavy pot with a tight-fitting lid that is just large enough to hold the ingredients.

Any type of full-grown leafy amaranth (whether called bledo or callaloo or birum namul, whether all-green, purplish, or mixed) will work. Enjoy as both vegetable and starch accompaniment to chicken or lamb. For a meatless meal, serve the wheat and greens with baked tomatoes and summer squash.

About ¾ pound amaranth
1 to 2 bunches scallions (green onions)
2 large garlic cloves
¾ teaspoon caraway seeds
½ teaspoon ground cinnamon
¼ teaspoon chilli flakes
¼ teaspoon coarse-ground or cracked
    pepper
1¼ teaspoons kosher salt
¾ cup water
2 tablespoons olive oil
1 cup medium or coarse bulgur wheat

Optional: 12 oil-cured black olives, pitted
and sliced
Orange or mandarin wedges

1. Dip amaranth into several changes of water, lift-ing up from bath so that sand sinks to bottom. Trim heavy bases as needed. Bunch amaranth and slice thin, then chop. Trim scallions, slice, then coarse-chop enough to yield about 1½ cups.

2. In suribachi or mortar, crush together garlic, car-away, cinnamon, chilli, pepper, and salt to form a paste. Add water and olive oil and blend well.

3. Combine scallions, bulgur, and amaranth in heavy pot with tight-fitting lid. Add spice mixture and blend well. Cut a piece of waxed paper or parchment to lie flat against mixture to completely cover it. Set over moderate heat until you hear simmering sounds. Cover tightly with lid, then reduce to lowest heat. Cook 20 minutes.

4. Toss amaranth and bulgur gently. Replace paper and cover tightly. Cook until bulgur is tender and greens soft, 10 to 15 minutes longer. Remove from heat and let stand 5 minutes. Scoop into a serving dish.

5. Serve at room temperature, with optional olives stirred in and orange wedges for diners to squeeze over each portion.

Serves 4 to 6 as a side dish

Garlicky Sauté of Amaranth and Tomatoes, Cuban Style

Maricel Presilla, Latin American culinary historian, calls this dish *ensalada de bledo blanco,* explaining that so-called "sweated salads" were popular in Cuba around 1900. Although it is lightly cooked and fresh in color and taste, its texture is more stewy than salad in con-temporary terms; but, as in salad, only the leaves are used. Serve with grilled steak or chops, or with a toss of rice, beans, and corn for a meatless meal.

Maricel Presilla's traditional recipe calls for 6 more garlic cloves and a large onion, but I am an allium wimp and have modified it for my taste. Cumin, allspice, and sesame are inspired seasonings that subtly underscore the amaranth. Do not be tempted to omit them.

1 hefty bunch amaranth (about 1½ pounds)
1 pound plum tomatoes (6 medium)
6 medium scallions (green onions)
2 garlic cloves
4 tablespoons olive oil
1 teaspoon kosher salt
Pepper
¼ teaspoon ground allspice
½ teaspoon ground cumin
1 to 2 teaspoons balsamic vinegar
1 tablespoon toasted sesame seeds

1. If amaranth leaves are large, cut from leaf-stems, then halve, removing central vein (discard stalks and stems). If small, strip leaves from stalks, then trim leaf-stems. Drop into water, swish vigorously, and lift out. Repeat until no sand remains. Drain well.

2. Peel, seed, and dice tomatoes in any way you like. (My preference is the method described in the Note below.)

3. Slice scallions lengthwise, then cut into thin slices. Mince garlic. In very large skillet, heat 3 table-spoons oil over fairly low heat. Add garlic and stir until light golden. Add scallions, tomatoes, salt, pepper, all-spice, and cumin. Raise heat to moderately high and sauté until tomatoes are juicy and tender but not soft—about 2 minutes.

4. Add amaranth leaves. With tongs, turn to mix evenly with tomato mixture. Stir and twist leaves con-stantly until they barely wilt, a minute or two. Turn off heat. Add remaining 1 tablespoon oil and 1 teaspoon vinegar. Taste and add more vinegar and pepper if needed.

5. Scoop into dish. Sprinkle with sesame seeds and serve hot.

Serves 4 to 5 as a side dish

Note: Pierce tomato with long-handled fork and hold in flame until skin splits in several places—less than a minute. Repeat with remaining tomatoes. When all tomato skins are split, slip them off and discard. Halve tomatoes, scoop out seeds, then cut flesh into small dice.

Pros Propose

Paula Wolfert's appreciation for the honest flavors of *Mediterranean Grains and Greens* shines from her book, as here, in the dish of greens called horta by Greeks and Cypriots, "simply boiled greens dressed with vinegar or lemon juice and best-quality olive oil. Some cooks will add a little *rigani* (a type of oregano) or thicken the greens with some grated zucchini or garnish them with a few crumbles of briny feta cheese, but no matter the variation the dish retains its elegant simplicity." One of her favorite hortas is **Amaranth and Sheep's Milk Cheese:** Rub amaranth with salt; let stand ½ hour or more. Wash in several changes of water. Cut off thick stem bases. Boil in meat broth and water until tender. Drain and mix at once with Greek extra-virgin olive oil and both grated sharp sheep's milk cheese (such as kefalotyri) and mild sheep's milk cheese (such as kasseri). Season and serve warm.

Similar to horta in concept is Korean namul, boiled greens that are usually seasoned with chilli and sesame and served as a condiment or add-on to any meal. Equally apt and simple is a Chinese dish described in *Charmaine Solomon's Encyclopedia of Asian Food,* **Amaranth with Flowering Chives:** Trim lower stems from stalks and cut tender stems and leaves into bite-size pieces. Trim lower stems from chives and cut into bite-size lengths. Combine vegetables in heatproof dish. Set on a rack over boiling water. Steam over low heat until wilted but still deep green, about 7 minutes. Combine dark sesame oil, light soy sauce, and a little sugar and drizzle over.

Chef Jay McCarthy and his coauthor Robb Walsh discovered whimsically titled **Callallo Rundown on Fried Plantains** at the Try-all Golf, Tennis and Beach Club in Montego Bay: Boil coconut milk to reduce by half, stirring. Add thyme, diced onion and tomato, chopped scallions, chopped Scotch bonnet chilli, and stemmed and chopped callaloo (amaranth). Cook until thick, 5 to 10 minutes. Deep-fry ripe plantain slices cut ½ inch thick; drain. Top with callaloo mixture. Heat through in a high oven (from *Traveling Jamaica with Knife, Fork & Spoon*).

On his annual pilgrimage to Mexico, Chef Rick Bayless unearths authentic flavors such as this complex beans-greens stew, **Quelites con Frijoles, Estilo Veracruzano:** Gently cook dried black beans, partly covered, until creamy-tender. Briefly toast stemmed dried chipotle chiles in a dry skillet. Open and flatten stemmed, seeded ancho chiles and do the same. Cover both with hot water and rehydrate ½ hour. Drain. Combine in food processor with garlic, onion, and enough water to make a puree. Strain through medium sieve. Cook in lard until thickened. Add to beans and simmer ½ hour longer. Prepare small dumplings of masa dough, cilantro, and crumbled queso fresco. Drop into the gurgling broth and simmer 5 minutes. Very gently stir in plenty of stemmed, sliced amaranth and cook until tender. Ladle into bowls and sprinkle with cilantro. Serve with tortillas.

Back in the United States, chef Bruce Naftaly prepares a simple soup based on celeriac, a vegetable that he chooses both to add body and to smooth and deepen the flavor of leafy greens. To prepare **Amaranth and Celeriac Soup:** Combine sliced celeriac with chicken stock and cook until very soft. Add cleaned, sliced amaranth greens and cook until tender. Puree and strain, "for a gorgeously green soup." Season with salt, pepper, and nutmeg. Garnish with snips of chickweed and chives.

Arracacha, Apio *(Arracacia xanthorrhiza)*

Also arracha, Peruvian carrot, Peruvian parsnip,
apio amarillo (Hispanic Caribbean)

Combine aspects of carrot, celeriac, and root parsley; add a dose of tropical tubers; and you have a hint of the range of tastes and textures of the rather elusive vegetable called arracacha or apio in U.S. markets. The tropical side expresses itself with subtle savors of plantain, yuca, and coconut, combined. Its texture and color, too, hint at plantain and yuca, with their special sweet stickiness, and plantain's warm golden hue. (In its original area of distribution—the Andes from Venezuela to Bolivia—and in areas later cultivated, from the highlands to Central America, apio grows in brighter, deeper colors than what comes to us, which is mainly from Costa Rica.) Whatever the comparison, arracacha seems to measure up to and exceed expectations, even for those tasting it for the first time.

"Apio" is also the Spanish word for celery, itself a member of the family of Apiaceae (or Umbelliferae)—as are arracacha and the three root vegetables mentioned above. This may be one reason why some publications have misidentified celeriac as arracacha, causing confusion among unwary grocers and shoppers. In common with celeriac, apio presents a scruffy surface, hides a sweetly aromatic interior, and shows us only a portion of itself in its marketed form. But in the case of apio, it is not just the leafy branches that are missing but what many in Latin American consider the vegetable itself, which has two distinct parts: a stumpy "neck" and carrot-like "fingers." According to those who have eaten the whole vegetable, the fingers are smoother, more tender, and less concentrated in flavor than the neck we see in North American groceries. Judging from the perishability of that seemingly sturdy part, my guess is that the torpedo-shape roots may have an even more fleeting shelf life. Or perhaps it is the climatic requirements and tricky growing procedures that prevent it from being raised in the United States? Two horticultural adventurers, the indefatigable and insatiably curious messieurs Paillieux and Bois, recorded one of their rare defeats when they wrote in *Le potager d'un curieux* (a fact-filled gem as original today as when

diameter of slices: 2-3 inches

it was first published in 1892) that apio "showed itself to be rebellious to every attempt at cultivation."

So we are fortunate that a fresh flock of immigrants has demanded this vegetable in their new home and that others can sample its creamy, tacky, sweetish, herbal deliciousness.

BASIC USE: Imagine that you could make celeriac-potato soup with just one vegetable and give it the color of golden rutabaga puree and the smoothness of banana cream, and you'll know what arracacha can do. A starch in texture, an herb in aroma, it can play both roles in soups and purees. Or peel and chunk and include it with other starchy vegetables in thick vegetables stews. Or simply serve it steaming hot and sliced for a starchy-sweet side dish that suggests a blend of corn, plantain, and yuca. For a more typical and rich treatment, mash boiled apio and blend with cream or butter. In Puerto Rico, the starchy roots are boiled, pureed, blended with eggs and baking powder, and deep-fried to make fritters or crullers (buñuelos). In *Mi cocina, a la manera de Caracas,* Armando Scannone describes tiny fritters made from a similar batter enriched with firm white cheese and served with hot clove–spiced brown sugar syrup.

Be warned that arracacha/apio must be served hot. Cold, it turns clunky and heavy. Do not cook by microwaving, which destroys its texture.

SELECTION AND STORAGE: For ease of preparation and minimal waste, choose large arracacha with comparatively few gnarls and protuberances. Arracacha is very perishable, turning soft and slimy in a few days. Refrigerate in a paper bag or newspaper—not in plastic, which hastens spoilage—for as short a time as possible.

PREPARATION: Cut apio into large chunks, then peel closely, dropping into water as you proceed. Although the flesh has a touch of the characteristic tropical tackiness, it does not discolor as dramatically as true yam or yautía, although it does darken. If there are any small protrusions or dark areas or soft spots, trim these.

Basic Arracacha (Apio)

Simply boiled or steamed (for a tad more sugar and scent), arracacha makes a lovely side dish, at once starchy and vegetably. Both cooking methods yield flavorful, surprisingly pretty, warm yellow-gold slices. The aroma and taste suggest potato, corn, and apple; the texture is slightly tacky and dense, but not heavy. For fragrant variations, substitute fresh-ground coriander or grated nutmeg for the pepper.

> 1½ to 2 pounds arracacha
> About 1½ tablespoons hazelnut, pecan, walnut, or olive oil
> Salt and white pepper

1. Peel arracacha, leaving pieces whole. If they are very different in size, cut large ones to match the smallest so they'll cook in the same time. If you're boiling the roots, halve them lengthwise; if steaming, quarter lengthwise.

2. *Either* boil in salted water until tender but not falling apart, about 20 minutes. *Or* set on rack over boiling water, cover, and steam for about the same time.

3. Cut arracacha into thin slices. Toss in heated serving dish with oil and seasoning. *Or* heat oil in skillet, add sliced tubers, and toss gently until heated through. Season. Serve at once.

Serves 4

Smooth Arracacha (Apio) Soup with Paprika

With few ingredients and little time, obliging arracacha is transformed into a silky, light-textured, pumpkin-colored "cream" soup, although it contains no cream. Serve to open a meal for four or as a generous supper for two. For the latter, garnish with toasted, chopped cashews and minced celery leaves. Crunchy corn bread is the perfect accompaniment.

> 1 medium onion
> 3 medium celery stalks
> 1 tablespoon mild oil, such as corn, safflower, or grapeseed
> About 1½ pounds arracacha
> 2 teaspoons hot paprika (or add ⅛ teaspoon hot pepper to 2 teaspoons sweet paprika)
> ½ teaspoon ground ginger
> About 4 cups vegetable broth
> 1 teaspoon kosher salt (omit if broth is salted)
> 1 orange, quartered

1. Dice or chop onion and celery. Warm oil in medium saucepan over moderately low heat. Add onion and celery and cook until softened, about 5 minutes. Meanwhile, halve arracacha and trim small protrusions. Peel, then cut into rough ¾-inch dice.

2. Add paprika and ginger to saucepan and stir a minute. Add arracacha, 4 cups broth, and salt and bring to a boil. Lower heat and simmer, partly covered, until arracacha is tender, about 20 minutes.

3. Cool soup slightly. Puree in food processor or blender until entirely smooth. Season assertively.

4. To serve, reheat soup gently, stirring. Add more broth if soup is too thick. Squeeze in orange juice to taste, a section at a time.

Serves 4 as a first course, 2 as a main course

Aromatic Arracacha (Apio) Puree

When simmered with spices, pressed through a mill, and then whipped with seasoned stock, the gnarled beastie arracacha turns soufflé-soft. Suave, spoonable, light-bodied, the yellow puree can take the place of winter squash dishes—although it is quite different.

Maricel Presilla, who kindly loaned this recipe from her forthcoming book about the foods of Latin America, lightly underscores the vegetable's mysterious savor with sweet spices. She likes it best with venison and sauce, but she allows that any roast with gravy or natural juices would do nicely. Tiny fragrant Caribbean peppers, ajíes dulces, are usually found in the same markets as apio. If they are not available, green peppers make a surprisingly effective substitute. The dish is lightest when freshly made, but it can be heated in a microwave.

> About 3½ pounds arracacha
> 1 small cinnamon stick, broken in half
> 6 peppercorns
> 4 cloves
> 1 star anise "flower"
> 1 tablespoon brown sugar
> About 1½ teaspoons kosher salt
> 1 cup rich vegetable or chicken broth
> White parts of 6 scallions (green onions), sliced
> Optional: 1 shallot, sliced
> 6 ajíes dulces or ½ small green bell pepper, sliced
> 5 whole allspice berries
> 2 coriander (cilantro) stalks
> About 1 tablespoon olive oil or butter

1. Halve arracacha. Peel closely and cut away any dark or soft areas. Rinse. Cut into 2-inch chunks (you should have about 6 cups).

2. Combine arracacha in saucepan with water to cover, cinnamon, pepper, cloves, star anise, sugar, and 1 teaspoon salt. Bring to a boil. Lower heat, cover, and simmer until fork-tender, about 20 minutes.

3. While arracacha cooks, combine broth in small saucepan with scallions, optional shallot, ajíes dulces, allspice, and coriander. Bring to a boil, covered. Lower heat and simmer 5 minutes. Uncover and boil until liquid is reduced to ½ cup. Pour into a fine sieve and press hard to extract all liquid.

4. Drain arracacha and pick out spices. While still hot, press through medium disc of food mill into mixing bowl. Heat broth if necessary. Gradually beat broth into puree, using a wooden spoon. Add oil or butter and salt to taste. Serve hot.

Serves 4 as a side dish

Pros Propose

Maricel Presilla rearranges authentic ingredients in original ways that preserve their integrity. Traditionally, arracacha is pureed, but "it has such a lovely color and texture that I like to cut it up and show it," she says. The Cuban sauce *mojo agrio,* which usually acts as dressing for starchy tubers, becomes her cooking medium. To prepare sautéed arracacha in garlic sauce, **Arracacha Salteada con Mojo:** Crush garlic and salt to a paste. Mix with sour orange juice. Slice small white onions, separate into rings, and cook slightly in olive oil. Stir in juice mixture and heat through; reserve. Peel arracacha and cut into large equal chunks. Boil until just tender. Cut into 1-inch dice, more or less, as form dictates. Reheat mojo in skillet. Add arracacha and cook until slightly golden. "Serve with anything! People are crazy about it. If it weren't so difficult to peel and so perishable, I'd probably serve it with every dish I make."

In *Rice and Beans and Tasty Things* by Dora Romano, a useful guide to Puerto Rican food, the author describes a type of layered "shepherd's pie" or **Pastelón de Apio:** To prepare stuffing: Render fatback or heat olive oil. Sauté ground beef and minced ham in it. Reserve meat; drain fat. Add chopped onion, tomato, and bell peppers to pan; cook 5 minutes. Add garlic, chopped green olives and capers, oregano, tomato sauce, and raisins and simmer briefly. Add meat and cook until thick. Meanwhile, boil 2-inch cubes of peeled apio until soft. Mash, then mix with annatto oil, butter, and beaten eggs. Line bottom and sides of loaf pan with some of mixture. Spread stuffing in center and cover with remaining apio. Bake in moderate oven 15 minutes. Brush with butter and bake until browned.

In Venezuela, as in Puerto Rico, arracacha is called apio and is a favored soup ingredient. Three apio-based soups appear in *Mi cocina, a la manera de Caracas* by Armando Scannone, including **Crema de Apio con Espinacas (Apio Puree with Spinach):** Boil white part of leek, halved onion, and large chunks of peeled apio in meat broth until soft. Discard onion and leek. Puree apio with broth. Return to pot with cooked, chopped spinach. Add white pepper, cilantro, and mint sprigs and bring to a boil. Remove herbs and add butter.

Arrowhead (primarily *Sagittaria sagittifolia*)

Also Chinese arrowhead, Chinese potato, swamp potato, and
kuwai (Japanese); ci gu, chi ku, and variations (Chinese)

Water cress, rice, and wild rice are the only water-grown vegetables that bob up regularly in North American kitchens. But there are others, cultivated in tropical and temperate climates as both edible and decorative plants. Lotus (page 372), water chestnut (page 694), water celery (page 691), and arrowhead have surfaced in Chinese-American markets in recent years.

Among these plants of Asian origin, arrowhead is more a pleasant curiosity than a potential staple. Cooked, the winter specialty, which resembles an enlarged, ivory water chestnut, tastes rather like sunchoke crossed with potato, but more bitter.

Arrowhead plays a small role in regional Chinese dishes but a more ubiquitous one in Japanese. In the few Chinese recipes I have been able to locate, the arrowhead is either stir-fried with pork or cooked in stock. In his *Dictionary of Japanese Food,* a useful little reference, Richard Hosking explains that arrowhead (kuwai) "is often served as nimono and features in the New Year o-sechi-ryori," food collectively referred to as New Year cuisine. Elizabeth Andoh, an American journalist based in Tokyo, notes that "kuwai are often carved—in the shape of a bell (to resemble the temple bells that ring out the old year) or tortoise (symbol of longevity)—then simmered in dashi stock seasoned with sake, sugar, and soy sauce," and that sometimes fresh kuwai is thin-sliced and deep-fried to make chips.

Although it is more likely that someone interested in sampling arrowhead will find it in an Oriental market, the North American species, *Sagittaria latifolia* and *S. cuneata* (which forager friends tell me are much like the cultivated species), are there for the picking. But picking this native arrowhead (wapato, wapatoo, or duck potato by name) is no picnic. According to Euell Gibbons in his groundbreaking book on foraging, *Stalking the Wild Asparagus,* "The Indian method of harvesting wapatoo was to wade in the mud and pull off the tubers with their bare toes. At the time of year when the tubers are mature, this is apt to be a chilly

½ **actual size**

business." Nevertheless, these species, found at the edges of swamps, ponds, and streams throughout most of North and Central America, "were eaten by American Indian tribes from coast to coast, sometimes forming their chief vegetable food."

In *Wild Food,* Roger Phillips writes that the American explorers Lewis and Clark were familiar with wapato. He cites William Clark's description (1804) of a visit to an Indian lodge where he was given "roundish roots about the size of a small Irish potato which they roasted in the embers until they become soft." Clark records that "this root they call Wap-pat-to the bulb of which the chinese cultivate in great quantities called the Sa-gitti folia or common arrow head . . . has an agreeable taste and answers verry well in place of bread. We purchased about 4 bushels of this root and divided it to our party."

BASIC USE: Were it not for their unpredictable bitterness, I would recommend cooking arrowheads as you would sunchokes (Jerusalem artichokes). But because of it, I have limited their use to soup (in which any bitterness is mellowed by plenty of liquid) and salad (in which it is masked by a sharp, sweet vinaigrette). Serve the salad with cold smoked meats or seafood, or add these to the dressed arrowhead. When sliced thick and sautéed slowly, arrowhead cooks to a nicely crunchy texture, but its blandness makes it seem hardly worth the bother of peeling. Monitor cooking so that the arrowhead does not turn from crunchy and mild to overcooked, starchy, and dull. Incidentally, if bitterness is present, I have not found that blanching modifies it.

SELECTION: Palp each corm to be sure it is solid—with the exception of the center of the base, which is spongy. Sprouts, if any, should be small. Choose the palest, largest specimens, which are easiest to peel, taste freshest, and have the smallest amount of waste.

STORAGE: Refrigerate arrowhead in a bowl of water, which should be changed every few days. It will last more than a week.

PREPARATION: Rinse arrowhead corms. With a sharp knife, trim off any shoot and spongy base. Remove the outer layer with a swivel peeler, applied lightly.

Creamy Arrowhead Soup

Subtle and sweetish, this milky ivory-beige soup serves as a mild opener to a multicourse meal. At once starchy, vegetably, and fruity, arrowhead mixes the characteristics of potato, water chestnut, and apple—and tastes all its own. Choose the largest arrowhead corms you can find, to minimize the labor of peeling.

> 1 large white onion
> 1 large celery stalk
> 1 tablespoon butter
> 1 pound arrowhead
> 1 teaspoon kosher salt
> ¼ teaspoon dried dill, crumbled to powder

> ½ teaspoon ground mace or grated nutmeg
> ¼ teaspoon fine-ground white pepper
> 1 large apple, such as Rome or Cortland
> About 1½ cups vegetable or light meat broth
> 1½ cups whole milk
> Minced fresh dill

1. Slice onion. Zip strings from celery and slice stalk. Melt butter in heavy casserole over moderately low heat. Stir in sliced vegetables. Cook, covered, stirring now and then, until softened, about 5 minutes.

2. Rinse arrowhead. With sharp knife, trim off shoots and spongy bases. Remove outer layer with peeler. Slice or chop. Add to casserole with salt, dried dill, mace, and pepper. Quarter, peel, and slice apple. Add with 1½ cups broth and milk.

3. Simmer gently, covered, until all is very tender—about ½ hour.

4. Puree mixture in blender or food processor to achieve a smooth texture. Reheat gently. Season and thin with broth as desired. Ladle into small bowls and sprinkle with dill.

Serves 4 as a first course

Salad of Shrimp, Arrowhead, and Mandarins

Peachy pink, ivory, and clear orange illustrate the flavor tone of this dish, which is light and gentle with a bright edge. The sweetness of the mandarin, honey, and shrimp is balanced by the bitterness of arrowhead, citrus rind, and frisée or endive—all enveloped in a creamy dressing sharpened by the zing of ginger juice. Clementine is a particularly tender small type of seedless mandarin, but others (including those confusingly called tangerines) are all fine. Use any of these or small blood oranges. Serve as an appetizer or main-course lunch or brunch salad.

> ¾ pound arrowhead
> 1 to 2 tablespoons grated ginger, as needed
> 2 tablespoons champagne vinegar or rice vinegar
> ½ teaspoon kosher salt
> 1 tablespoon honey
> 2 tablespoons whole-milk yogurt

2 tablespoons mild vegetable oil, such as grapeseed or canola

¾ pound cooked, shelled, and deveined medium shrimp

3 Clementines (or other small seedless mandarins)

1 medium head frisée or 2 medium Belgian endives.

2 tablespoons minced inner celery stalk

2 tablespoons very thin sliced small scallion (green onion) tops

1. Rinse arrowheads. With sharp knife, trim off shoots and bases. Remove outer layers with peeler. Halve.

2. Drop arrowheads into a large pot of boiling salted water (plenty of water helps remove some bitterness, if present). Cook just until corms lose their raw taste but not their crunch, about 2 minutes. Refresh in cold water, then drain. Spread on a plate to dry. Chill.

3. Meanwhile, squeeze 1 heaping tablespoon ginger in cloth or press in fine sieve to extract juice. You should have at least 1 tablespoon. Squeeze more grated ginger if needed. Combine with vinegar, salt, and half the honey, blending well. Whisk in yogurt, then oil.

4. Slice arrowheads quite thin. Toss with dressing and shrimp. Cover and refrigerate an hour or more, or until serving time.

5. With swivel peeler, remove zest from 1 Clementine. Cut enough hair-thin strips to make 1 heaping tablespoon. Drop into boiling salted water and boil 1 minute; drain. Toss with remaining honey; reserve.

6. Cut base from frisée (or Belgian endives) and separate leaves. Cut into manageable bite-size pieces. Rinse and spin-dry. Arrange on plates.

7. Pare pith from the Clementine from which zest was removed. Cut all rind and pith from remaining 2 Clementines. Halve each through "poles." Lay cut side down and slice across to form thin semicircles. Arrange with greens. Toss dressed shrimp and arrowhead with celery, scallions, and reserved rind mixture. Taste, season, and mound on plates.

Serves 4 as a first course, 2 as a main course

Artichoke, Globe Artichoke (*Cynara scolymus*)

Including **"baby" artichokes**

½ **actual size**

Tiny artichokes simmered in white wine, rosemary, thyme, and other aromatics, à la provençale; artichoke slices bathed in garlicky lemon oil and grill-seared, Barcelona style; tender hearts stewed with lamb and sweet spices in a Moroccan tagine; artichokes plumped with dill-scented rice, Turkish fashion; wedges braised with leeks and mint, à la grecque; and whole flattened miniatures, their flower-like forms fried leafy brown and dusted with coarse salt, alla giudia (Italian Jewish style).

Then there are raw artichokes: bittersweet crescent cuts in vinaigrette with croutons, walnuts, tomatoes, mint, and parsley, in fresh California style. But the en-

joyment of raw artichoke is no modern invention. Giacomo Castelvetro, gardener to Lucy Countess of Bedford, explained to her in 1614 that "we eat them raw or cooked. When . . . about the size of a walnut they are good raw, with just salt, pepper, and some mature cheese to bring out the flavour" (*The Fruit, Herbs & Vegetables of Italy,* translated by Gillian Riley).

In 1699, the English memoirist John Evelyn wrote of "artichaux" in *Acetaria: A Discourse of Sallets,* "In Italy they sometimes broil them, and as the Scaly Leaves open, baste them with fresh and sweet *Oyl* [and] they eat them with the Juice of *Orange* and *Sugar.*"

So how has it come to pass that in the United States

we cling to big boiled artichokes, that the beautiful bud is—as often as not—large and sodden, little more than a butter holder? The large artichokes we cultivate in the United States are virtually all the Green Globe variety, descended from rootstock planted by Italian immigrants at the end of the 19th century. (Italy is known as home to the plant, but it is likely that it was developed in North Africa—from the cardoon.) While visually striking (a bouquet of artichokes makes a fabulous centerpiece), these are not the tender eat-it-all buds of the Mediterranean, which have few prickles and little to no chokes and cook quickly enough to be bought on a whim for a work-night dinner.

But we are beginning to modify our "big is beautiful" philosophy. If we do not yet grow the gamut of varieties that enlivens the tables of Italy, France, Spain, Greece, Turkey, Egypt, and North Africa, we can at least find "babies" grown in North America's artichoke belt, a swath of the central California coast with headquarters in Castroville.

"Baby artichokes" are not, in fact, babies. An artichoke, when mature, attains a size that depends on its placement on the plant. Artichokes at the top of the plant, for example, can be enormous, while those at the base, shaded by the dense, silvery, sueded leaves, may grow no larger than a Ping-Pong ball. And once an artichoke's petals (technically, bracts) begin to open, it is over the hill, whatever its size.

My goal here is to remind readers about artichoke "parts" and small artichokes, to urge them to experiment with techniques for preparing and cooking (and not cooking) them, and to encourage growers to plant multiple varieties, as is done in other artichoke-growing countries. It's time we caught up with the Old World.

SELECTION: High-quality artichokes are usually compact and heavy for their size. The bracts are tightly furled in the center, exceptionally crisp, and a brisk, clear green. Squeezed, a fresh artichoke protests with a noisy squeak; a flabby one barely mumbles. The thickness of each stalk should correspond to the size of the artichoke (thin stalks signal dehydration). Fresh stalks are firm, without "give."

California supplies markets year-round, but the peak season is March through May, with a secondary harvest in October. Blistered or brown spots on otherwise fine winter artichokes indicate exposure to cold, not poor quality. The California Artichoke Advisory Board promotes these "winter-kissed" artichokes as superior, but no one seems to have compared them for flavor.

A wider range of sizes is sold for the foodservice industry than the retail market—measured in counts of 18, 24, 30, 36, 48, 60, and 72 to the case, or loose-packed for even tinier artichokes. Although purple-shaded varieties are usual in Europe, American growers have told me that "purple has a negative image" in this country and has been bred out of the vegetable.

STORAGE: Artichokes remain fairly constant in appearance for weeks, but flavor and tone are adversely affected from the moment they are cut from the stalk. For maximum taste and tenderness, cook them as soon as possible; do not stock up.

If you do store: Trim a slice from the stem, wrap the artichoke in wet paper towel, and store in the vegetable crisper. When you have a large quantity, arrange them close together in the crisper, topped with moist newspaper.

In a restaurant, keep artichokes in the coldest part of the walk-in, preferably at 34° to 38° F, away from the blower. If the artichokes are displayed, keep the stems in a bed of ice and mist often.

PREPARATION: To get the most out of artichokes, small or big, careful trimming is called for. Time invested in preparation is more than compensated for by an increase in the repertoire of cooking methods and a decrease in cooking time. Keep in mind that the goal is a tender vegetable that will cook through evenly—not preservation of as much artichoke as possible! Be swift and ruthless when removing tough, fibrous, and otherwise undesirable parts.

Preliminary cleaning: Rap artichoke forcefully against work surface to open up "petals." Soak in lukewarm water while you prepare other ingredients, then rinse well. (Most artichokes are sprayed with pesticides throughout the growing cycle.)

Stem sense: The stem is a continuation of the artichoke bottom (or crown, or *fond* in French) and can be equally choice—so do not remove it automatically. To check, pare until you reach the stem's pale core: taste. If very bitter, remove (see below). If not, peel and keep intact or slice for sautés or stuffing.

To remove stem: Lay artichoke on its side and hold it with one hand. With the heel of the other hand, forcefully press down on the stem to break it off. Some stems resist and must be cut. Pare base.

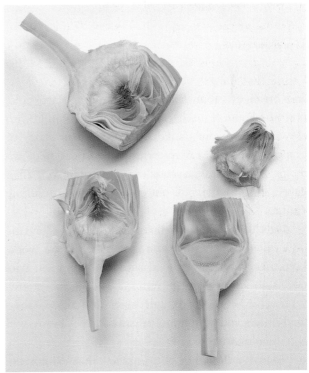

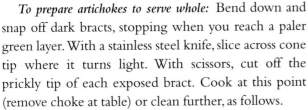

above and top: to prepare artichokes to cook whole

above and top: to prepare hearts from small artichokes

To prepare artichokes to serve whole: Bend down and snap off dark bracts, stopping when you reach a paler green layer. With a stainless steel knife, slice across cone tip where it turns light. With scissors, cut off the prickly tip of each exposed bract. Cook at this point (remove choke at table) or clean further, as follows.

To remove choke: Rap trimmed artichoke top hard against work surface to open it wide, then open further with fingers. With melon ball cutter or grapefruit spoon, scoop out choke and prickly parts.

To prepare hearts from medium-to-large artichokes: Bend down and snap off bracts until you reach the tender yellow-green core. Slice off most of remaining

cone tip. (Any tender yellow "petals" that remain can be cut into fine strips and added to the dish.) Pare stem, if desired; or snap it off and trim base. This is now an artichoke heart. For most dishes, cut quarters, sixths, or eights, as size dictates; then, cutting each wedge from its pointed toward its wide end, slice out choke. Cook as is, or slice smaller.

To prepare hearts from small artichokes: Snap off bracts until you reach the paler interior. Trim stem, if needed. Halve artichoke lengthwise. Remove prickly purple leaves; small chokes are edible.

To prepare crowns (bottoms) from medium-to-large artichokes: Proceed as for hearts, but slice off entire cone

to prepare crowns

and break off stem, leaving only rounded artichoke bottom. Reserve tender yellow bracts to cook with crowns. Scrape out choke with melon ball cutter or grapefruit spoon. Leave crowns whole, or cut up to suit recipe. (Alternatively, cook whole artichokes, then gently lift off cone, pull out choke, and trim resulting crown.)

About discoloration: Artichokes discolor—dramatically but normally. To lessen darkening as you work, keep them in water acidified with lemon juice. If tartness is not desirable, plain water does a fair job of preventing browning (although water browns). Carbon steel knives and aluminum or cast-iron cookware will also discolor artichokes.

No matter how they're treated beforehand, most artichokes cook to similar taupe tones—with one striking exception: Every now and then, one will turn an alarming turquoise, quite unlike any other natural food color. Granville Perkins, retired general manager of Artichoke Industries, a processing company in Castroville, explains: "When water is unusually alkaline (hard), artichokes, like litmus paper, will change color. But they have no harmful effects. However, water-soluble vitamins are lost, so it is best to add some acid to all cooking water, both for color and vitamin retention."

To prepare crowns of uniform color: When paleness is desired, precook or cook crowns in the traditional French way, *à blanc:* In a non-aluminum saucepan whisk together 3 to 4 tablespoons flour with a little water. Gradually add about 2 quarts more water, the

juice of a lemon, a drop of oil, and a little salt. Bring to a boil, then add artichoke bottoms and cook to desired stage of doneness.

To Cook Whole Artichokes: The Basics

If whole artichokes are your choice, try *not* boiling them for a change. Handsome and sleek, they beg to be "undressed" at table, a job as delicious as it is amusing if they are flavorful and tender. Once cooked, they adapt amiably to being served at a wide range of temperatures with an even wider range of accompaniments. Before proceeding with any of the methods below, please see "To prepare artichokes to serve whole," page 21.

To pressure cook: P.c. wizard Lorna Sass, who has written numerous books on cooking under pressure, won me over with this method: In cooker, combine a cup of water with coriander seeds, bay leaves, a garlic clove, and a few lemon slices. Set trimmed artichokes on pot rack. Lock top and bring to full pressure. Cook from 4 minutes (for the smallest) to 12 (for largest). Quick-release pressure. Strain and reduce cooking liquid; season and enrich with fresh herbs and olive oil for a savory, succinct sauce.

To steam: Set trimmed artichokes stem end up on steamer rack over boiling water (seasoned or not with lemon grass and ginger, or garlic cloves and rosemary or thyme branches). Cover; cook until tender to the tooth, 30 to 45 minutes, depending upon size.

To steam-bake: Place seasonings or stuffing in trimmed artichoke. Rub sparingly with olive oil. Set on a square of foil large enough to enclose amply. Twist foil firmly closed. Set in pan; bake in 375°F oven until tender, 35 to 60 minutes, depending on size.

To microwave: Although this method is less successful than others, it works adequately if time is tight and you lack a pressure cooker: Set artichokes in a microwavable dish, sprinkle with a little water; cover dish with plastic. Cook on high until base dents with a finger's pressure. Check microwave chart for timing, which varies dramatically depending on size and number of artichokes. (Artichoke hearts, which take just minutes to cook, *are* delicious microwaved.)

Salad of Crunchy Artichoke and Endive with Honeyed Lemon

A subtle bittersweet combination, this unusual dish intrigues as a starter for an elegant meal. Or, for a light main dish, surround with poached or grilled seafood. When you are going to prepare citrus zest, purchase organically raised fruit. If it is not available, scrub the fruit with a brush under warm running water before paring.

> 1 lemon
> ¼ teaspoon kosher salt
> ⅛ teaspoon fine ground white pepper
> 2 tablespoons olive oil
> 4 medium-to-large (or 8 small) artichokes
> 1 tablespoon honey
> 4 small Belgian endives, bases trimmed and
>   leaves separated
> 2 tablespoons roasted, salted, and chopped
>   pumpkin seeds
> 1 tablespoon snipped chives

1. With citrus stripper, channel knife, or vegetable peeler, remove yellow zest from lemon; reserve. Halve lemon and squeeze juice. Blend 1 tablespoon with salt, pepper, and olive oil. Pour remainder of juice into a bowl of water.

2. Prepare medium-to-large artichokes as for crowns (see page 21), leaving ½ inch of bracts attached. Reserve tender yellow bracts, stack them, and cut into thin diagonal strips. Drop into the lemon water. (For small artichokes, prepare quartered artichoke hearts, see page 21.)

3. Drain artichokes and drop into lightly salted boiling water. Boil just until the raw taste—but not the crunch—disappears, 2 to 3 minutes.

4. Drain artichokes and spread out to cool briefly. Press with towel to absorb moisture. Quarter crowns, then, cutting from point of each toward wide end of wedge, slice away just enough to remove choke, which will pull out easily with a tug of the adjacent petals. Cut into ⅛-inch slices. (For small hearts, cut into ¼-inch slices.) Toss at once with dressing; reserve.

5. Stack a few pieces of lemon zest; cut into finest strips. Repeat with the remaining zest. Drop into boiling water and boil 2 minutes; drain. Return to a boil with fresh water and cook until tender, about 10 minutes. Drain and mix with honey.

6. Arrange endive spears spoke-fashion on four plates. Mound artichoke slices in center, then sprinkle with honeyed zest, pumpkin seeds, and chives. Drizzle over any dressing that remains.

Serves 4 as a first course

Herb-Scented Little Artichokes in Packets

No mess, no fuss, no pots and pans—this is a dandy way to make friends with the "babies," if you haven't yet done so. Pick them up on a whim to perk up a plain meal. Season to taste, customizing flavors for each diner's fragrant packet.

FOR EACH SERVING/PACKET

> 2 little artichokes (2 to 3 ounces each)
> 2 teaspoons olive oil
> 1 small garlic clove, halved
> 2 small thyme, rosemary, or savory sprigs, or
>   ½ teaspoon coriander seeds, or ¼ teaspoon
>   fennel seeds
> Salt and pepper

1. Turn oven to 375°F. Snap off artichoke bracts until you reach paler green ones. Slice off about 1 inch of the artichoke tip. Pare stems. Halve artichokes lengthwise. Rinse and pat dry.

2. Set the halves on a square of foil large enough to enclose amply. Rub each artichoke half with oil. Nestle ½ garlic clove each in two of the halves and place an herb sprig (or ¼ teaspoon coriander seeds or ⅛ teaspoon fennel seeds) on top. Season with salt and pepper. Top each seasoned half with an unseasoned one to form a whole. Close foil tightly. Set in baking pan. Bake until tender (open one to check), about ½ hour.

3. Serve hot, in the foil. Or unwrap, arrange on platter, and serve warm or at room temperature, with a little extra olive oil and some lemon wedges alongside.

Pasta with Woodsy Artichoke-Mushroom Sauce

Brown and savory, this sauce looks and tastes meaty but more subtle—because it's artichoke and dried porcini. If porcini do not fit your budget, any dried mushrooms will do—even generic supermarket ones. The mixture is equally good over soft polenta.

About ⅓ ounce (⅓ cup) dried porcini or
    other dried mushrooms
1 cup hot water
5 medium-to-large artichokes
    (or 8 smaller ones)
1½ tablespoons olive oil
½ teaspoon kosher salt
4 garlic cloves, thin-sliced
⅓ cup dry vermouth
1 tablespoon red wine vinegar
1 pound Italian rotini or other imported
    curly pasta
1 tablespoon butter
Pepper
1 cup grated Pecorino Romano or aged
    Provolone cheese

1. Combine porcini and water; soak while you prepare other ingredients.

2. Prepare artichoke hearts (see page 21).

3. Lift mushrooms gently from water to avoid stirring up debris. Slowly pour liquid into a clean cup, leaving dirt behind. Rinse mushrooms lightly if they seem sandy, then coarse-chop.

4. Drain artichokes. Set on cutting board and blot dry with towel.

5. Set medium sauté pan over moderately low heat and add oil. Cut artichoke pieces lengthwise into thin slices, tossing into pan as you go. Add salt and sauté until artichokes are lightly browned, about 5 minutes. Add garlic and toss until barely colored. Add mushrooms and toss.

6. Add vermouth and vinegar; raise heat and stir to evaporate. Add mushroom liquid and bring to a boil. Reduce heat. Simmer, covered, until artichokes are almost tender, about 5 minutes. Simmer, uncovered, a few minutes longer, until tender.

7. Meanwhile, boil pasta in a large pot of salted water until almost done; drain.

8. Return pasta to pot, add artichoke mixture and toss a few minutes over low heat, until most of liquid has been absorbed. Off heat, stir in butter and pepper.

9. Divide among four heated shallow bowls. Serve with cheese alongside.

Serves 4

Artichoke Ragoût with Olives

A toothsome Mediterranean ragoût, messy but nice, as is the way of artichoke dishes. *Copine* and culinary confidante Barbara Spiegel, who devised this, observes that "even if some of the little artichokes have a bit of fluff inside, there is no need to clean them out beforehand. Nor is there a need to remove orange peel, parsley, thyme sprigs, garlic, and bay leaves from this rustic sort of dish." She serves it as a first course, in shallow bowls, with fork and knife to handle the juicy graygreen mélange—brightened with carrot-and-celery confetti. Or serve as a side to roasted veal, lamb, or chicken.

Choose French, Italian, or other mild-cured green olives—not the sharp Spanish style.

12 small artichokes (2 to 3 ounces each)
3 tablespoons olive oil
1 cup minced carrots
1 cup minced celery
3 medium garlic cloves, halved
½ orange (organic or well scrubbed)
6 parsley sprigs
3 bay leaves
6 thyme sprigs (or 1 teaspoon dried thyme)
1 teaspoon kosher salt
⅔ cup pitted, coarse-chopped green olives

1. Break off artichoke bracts until you reach the yellowish layer. Peel stems and pare bottom "scales." Cut about an inch from each cone tip.

2. Heat oil in non-aluminum saucepan or sauté pan large enough to hold artichokes in a single layer. Add carrots, celery, and garlic; cook over moderate heat, stirring occasionally, until softened, about 5 minutes.

Meanwhile, with peeler, remove zest from orange half in 3 or 4 strips.

3. Add artichokes and just enough water to pan to almost cover (about 2 cups). Add parsley, bay, thyme, salt, and orange zest. Bring to a boil, then reduce heat and simmer, covered, until artichokes can be easily pierced with a knife, about 20 minutes. Stir in olives.

4. Serve with a slotted spoon—hot, warm, or at room temperature. (Alternatively, for a more concentrated, less soupy effect, strain liquid from artichokes. Boil down to just a few spoonfuls, then add to artichokes with chopped olives.)

Serves 4 to 6

Pros Propose

Each year, the California Artichoke Advisory Board sponsors a "Chefs' Summit" in the vicinity of Castroville, "artichoke center of the world." At one such event, chef Tina Wilson presented this **Artichoke Salad with Walnut Croutons:** Prepare vinaigrette of grapeseed, walnut, and olive oils, lemon juice, sherry vinegar, garlic, shallots, thyme, and pepper. Toss cubes of country walnut bread in olive and walnut oils: oven-toast. Combine parsley, mint, tomato slices, walnut halves, and mizuna. Thin-slice trimmed small artichokes. Add to greens with bread cubes and vinaigrette. Top with crumbled aged goat cheese.

Raw artichokes also appear in **Sliced Artichoke and Prosciutto Salad,** one of many appealing recipes from the Provence-inspired *At Home with Patricia Wells:* Toss paper-thin slices of raw artichoke hearts with lemon juice, olive oil, salt, and pepper. Shave long strips of Parmesan over and toss. Add julienne of prosciutto and stemmed arugula leaves and toss again.

Cooked artichokes at their simplest star in **Artichoke and Pink Grapefruit Salad,** from *Chez Panisse Vegetables* by Alice Waters: Cut cooked artichoke hearts into half-moon slices. Alternate on plates with pink grapefruit sections. Drizzle with very flavorful olive oil and season. Scatter chervil sprigs over.

Brick-Flattened Fried Artichokes, a traditional Italian delicacy, are included in Faith Willinger's lively *Red, White & Greens:* Cook trimmed small artichokes gently in olive oil in a wide pan, turning to gild. Turn "petal"-side up and continue cooking until bases are well browned. Drain: cool upside down. Turn over, spread petals, and flatten gently. Set in heated non-stick pan with a little oil and top with a pan to flatten. Brown well. Serve hot with coarse salt.

Arugula, Rocket *(Eruca sativa)*

Also garden rocket, rocket salad; rucchetta, rughetta,
and rucola (Italian); roquette (French)
Including **wild rocket** (or wild arugula)

Despite arugula's trendy position atop paper-thin pizzas and under little goat cheese discs, it did not burst onto the American scene with the Mediterranean restaurant boom. Rocket (a name now more common on the West Coast than the East Coast) was planted during colonial times and has been in and out of our culinary and medicinal vocabulary ever since.

Nor is rocket a horticultural greenhorn elsewhere. In a recent monograph on the plant's use in Israel, Yaniv, Schafferman, and Amar wrote, "The name rocket . . . is well documented in the old literature of the Holy Land. . . . Most scientists agree that this is the garden vegetable mentioned in the Bible . . . as 'Oroth.' Many sources are mentioned in the Mishna and the Talmud (a Jewish manuscript from the first to fifth centuries) about rocket's uses in the Holy Land during the Hellenistic period, as a spice, a food, and a medicine." Specifically, they cite its use as a treatment for eye infections, an aphrodisiac, a deodorant, a protection against dog bites, a digestive aid, a garden pest deterrent, and finally a culinary subject: salad green and spice (the seeds were treated as mustard).

What *is* new and noteworthy is arugula's widespread presence in the American marketplace. The national passion for Italian food and a growing interest in salad greens have moved this member of the vast family of Brassicaceae (also known as Cruciferae) from the tables of neighborhood restaurants to supermarket shelves nationwide.

What is also relatively new is rocket's curious American name, arugula. Although it probably derives from Italian, none of the language or plant experts I consulted could verify if, when, or how. Perhaps, as with many vegetables, the name was arrived at in error by a farmer, distributor, or grocer and just stuck.

Whatever its name, the tender, mustard-sharp, bitterish

left to right: **standard size, small greenhouse type, and wild arugulas**

¼ **actual size**

green is standard fare throughout the Mediterranean, where it is used primarily as the old herbals specified, "as a seasoning leaf" for salad. A relative of the radish, arugula resembles these leaves in flavor and appearance. Like water cress, another family member, it is more intense than most leafy green vegetables but less so than herbs.

Wild rocket (or wild arugula), a term previously used to distinguish the foraged variety from the garden-grown, now refers to another garden species, *Diplotaxis erucoides,* which has a slimmer, sharper form and a fiercer flavor. Called Sylvetta and sometimes rucola selvatica (which also refers to another species), it is common in Europe but shows up only occasionally in American farmers' markets and seed catalogues.

In 1853, the chef Alexis Soyer wrote in *The Pantropheon* that rocket "enjoyed some reputation among the ancients, who mixed the wild and the garden rocket together, so as to temper the heat of the one by the coldness of the other." Today, the superchef Alain Ducasse does the same for his salad, "les jumelles ruchetta et rucola" (see Pros Propose, page 29).

BASIC USE: Raw, arugula is a punctuating leaf par excellence. Vervy and shapely—an oakleaf-dandelion decoupage—it transforms any mild mélange of salad greens. In Italy, it is commonly contrasted with red chicory and pale lettuces. In Provence, it plays a leading role in the celebrated mesclun salad, a toss of baby lettuces, bitter greens, and herbs. It balances sweet (figs, pomegranates, dried tomatoes, raisins), sharp (blue cheese or goat cheese), salty (olives, capers, and prosciutto), rich (creamy and mild cheeses, nuts, avocado), acid (grapefruit, lemon, wine vinegar), or bland (eggs, potatoes, beans).

When rocket is particularly pungent, chewy, or both, it warms to contact with hot foods, softening slightly and becoming less sharp. Slice and toss with hot, sauced pasta or sautéed summer squash. Cooked arugula loses its bite but develops a pleasant bitter-green depth. Sauté momentarily with garlic, then toss with hot pasta, beans, or potatoes. Or cook with potatoes and puree for a subtle soup, hot or chilled.

SELECTION: Available year-round, arugula varies markedly in size, tenderness, and bite. Hydroponically grown leaves and "babies" are usually relatively soft and mild. Other forms vary in heat and size with season and temperature: Hot weather makes for hot leaves. Arugula is usually sold in bunches, with roots attached. Avoid bunches that are bruised, waterlogged (a major problem with current supermarket produce-handling methods), or yellowed. A little limpness is no problem. Smaller leaves, which can be left whole, will look prettier than large leaves, which must be cut apart to be manageable in the mouth.

STORAGE: Arugula is very perishable, so do not buy much in advance of use. Remove whatever device holds the bunch together and pull out any over-the-hill pieces. Wrap roots in damp toweling, then enclose all in plastic. Or proceed as for preparation (below), then pack in a plastic container. Refrigerate for no more than a day or two.

Ethylene gas, formed during ripening, adversely affects green leafy vegetables, causing yellowing and hastening decay. Avoid storage near fruits, some of which continue to ripen after harvesting.

PREPARATION: Rocket leaves hide sand no matter how clean they may appear. Do not be tempted to rinse casually under running water. Instead, cut off the roots, then swish the leaves in plenty of lukewarm water. Let stand a moment, then gently lift them out so that sand is left at the bottom. Repeat as needed—usually twice more. Spin-dry leaves, then wrap in toweling and chill until serving time.

Salad of Arugula, Radicchio, and Fresh Goat Cheese

For a salad with a fancy feel that can be assembled with little effort, try this simple version of a combo that has come to signify California cuisine: sharp arugula, bittersweet radicchio, creamy fresh goat cheese, and toasty walnuts. Choose mild American or French goat cheese that is soft but not mushy for the colorful toss. Heated dressing slightly softens firm radicchio to meld the leafy elements better.

2 medium bunches arugula (about ½ pound)
1 small round red radicchio (about 6 ounces)
1 tiny red onion, diced
¼ cup lightly toasted, coarse-chopped walnuts
2 tablespoons sherry vinegar or red wine vinegar
½ teaspoon sugar
¼ teaspoon kosher salt

¼ cup walnut or roasted peanut oil
About ¼ pound fresh goat cheese, cut into
    ½-inch cubes

1. Cut roots from arugula. Dunk leaves up and down in water, let stand a moment, and then lift out gently. Repeat until no sand remains. Spin-dry. Cut into large bite-size pieces if necessary. Place in mixing bowl (do not refrigerate).

2. Core and halve radicchio. Cut into very fine strips, like slaw. Rinse and spin-dry. Add to arugula. Add onion and walnuts.

3. In small pan, mix vinegar, sugar, and salt. Add oil and bring to a boil, stirring. Pour over salad and toss lightly. Distribute among four plates, interspersing cheese pieces. Serve immediately.

Serves 4 as a first course

Chilled Arugula-Potato Soup with Buttermilk

This smooth soup has definite arugula character, thanks to a two-step procedure: First, leaves are simmered with leeks and potatoes to make a mellow, thick base; then raw leaves pureed with buttermilk are added for bright color and a light mustardy nip. Serve on a summer's eve to precede a meal of cold meat, cucumbers, tomatoes, and dark bread.

    2 medium leeks
    1 tablespoon mild vegetable oil, such as
        grapeseed or corn
    1 garlic clove, peeled
    2 large floury potatoes, such as russets
        (1 pound)
    5 cups water
    About 1½ teaspoons kosher salt
    1 pound arugula (about 3 medium-large
        bunches, for 8 cups trimmed)
    Hot pepper sauce
    About a dozen small red radishes
    About 1½ cups buttermilk

1. Trim roots and heaviest green tops from leeks. Halve stalks and slice. Wash several times, lifting out of water to let debris sink.

2. Heat oil in large pot. Add leeks and garlic; cook over moderately low heat, stirring often, until leeks are somewhat softened, about 5 minutes. Meanwhile, peel potatoes; cut ¾-inch slices.

3. Add potatoes to pot with water and salt. Simmer 15 minutes, covered.

4. Meanwhile, trim off arugula roots and any very heavy stems. Wash leaves in several changes of water, lifting out to let sand sink. Reserve 3 packed cups and refrigerate.

5. Slice remaining arugula casually; add to soup. Simmer, partly covered, until potatoes are very soft and arugula stems are tender, about 15 minutes. Cool soup to lukewarm.

6. Pour soup into container of food processor and puree until quite smooth. Season assertively with pepper sauce and salt. Chill thoroughly.

7. To serve, trim radishes. Slice a couple for each bowl. Combine reserved arugula leaves with 1 cup buttermilk in food processor. Whiz to a fine puree. Whisk into chilled soup. Add more buttermilk and cold water if needed for desired consistency. Season. Ladle into bowls and top with radishes.

Serves 6 to 7 as a first course

Pasta with Arugula and Tomato-Olive Compote

Pasta shells are studded with snippets of intense flavor—more condiment than sauce: salty olives, sweet dried tomato bits, and onion dice. These are briefly simmered with vinegar, oregano, and chilli, then tossed with arugula leaves wilted in garlicky oil. If your dried tomatoes are less tender than mine (plump and slightly moist halves that are best stored in the freezer), cook longer, adding a few spoons of water if necessary to prevent sticking.

    1 very small red onion
    About 8 dried tomato halves
    About 12 tender oil-cured olives
    ¼ cup cider vinegar or red wine vinegar
    ¼ cup water
    ⅛ to ¼ teaspoon chilli flakes
    ¼ teaspoon dried oregano
    1 teaspoon brown sugar

2 medium bunches arugula (about ½ pound)
½ pound imported Italian pasta shells or
    butterflies (farfalle)
2 tablespoons olive oil
1 large garlic clove, minced

1. Cut onion into ¼-inch dice. Cut dried tomatoes into ½-inch squares. Pit olives and quarter lengthwise.

2. In small, heavy saucepan, combine onion, vinegar, water, chilli flakes, oregano, and sugar. Bring to a boil. Then reduce heat and simmer 2 minutes. Add tomatoes and olives, cover, and simmer gently until tomatoes are tender, about 5 minutes (just a very little liquid should remain).

3. Meanwhile, cut roots and any heavy stems from arugula. Dunk leaves up and down in water, let stand a moment, and then gently lift out so sand is left behind. Repeat until no sand remains. Spin-dry. Bunch arugula together and slice into 1-inch sections, more or less (about 4 cups, lightly packed).

4. Cook pasta in boiling salted water until just al dente. Drain.

5. Meanwhile, as pasta finishes cooking, heat olive oil and garlic over moderate heat in large wide skillet. As garlic starts to turn golden, add arugula and toss just until it begins to wilt—less than 1 minute. Remove from heat.

6. Add pasta and tomato mixture and toss to mix. Divide between two heated bowls. Serve at once.

Serves 2 as a main course

Pros Propose

Both wild and cultivated forms of rocket play peppery parts in the salad that chef and author Alain Ducasse calls **The Twins, Ruchetta and Rucola:** Trim, wash, spin-dry, and chill wild "ruchetta" (or cultivated Sylvetta) and garden rocket. Prepare vinaigrette of red wine, salt, pepper, and olive oil. Using one per person, sprinkle Rocamadour cheeses (or other slightly aged goat cheese buttons) with fresh thyme leaves. Grill as many slices of rustic bread as cheeses. At the same time, set cheeses in microwave oven just to warm and soften—*not* to become runny—about 15 seconds. Toss greens and dressing. Divide among plates and eat at once, while cheese and toast are warm (from *Méditer-ranées: Cuisine de l'essentiel*).

A Mediterranean salad of favored Sicilian ingredients, **Arugula with Pine Nuts and Pomegranate,** is quick to make and glows in tricolor: Sauté pine nuts in olive oil until golden; drain. Combine red wine vinegar, mustard, and minced shallot; whisk in olive oil and seasoning. Sprinkle pine nuts and pomegranate seeds over arugula and toss with dressing. Arrange on plates. Top with more pomegranate (from *La Cucina Siciliana di Gangivecchio* by Wanda and Giovanna Tornabene with Michele Evans).

Rocket salad with an Asian lilt comes from chefs Ellen Greaves and Wayne Nish via their elegant little book, *Simple Menus for the Bento Box*. For **Arugula Salad with Parmesan and Pickled Shiitake:** Combine rice vinegar, white wine vinegar, sugar, salt, and water in a small pot; bring to a simmer. Add trimmed fresh shiitake caps, remove from heat, and cool in liquid. Blend some cooking liquid with olive oil for dressing. Shave long Parmesan curls. Toss arugula leaves with dressing. Arrange on plates and top with shiitake and Parmesan.

For **Spaghetti con Rucola e Ricotta,** popular British chefs and authors Rose Gray and Ruth Rogers prepare pesto from cooked and raw greens: Wash and spin-dry about 2 pounds of arugula for each pound of pasta. Chop and reserve half. In a large skillet, heat chopped garlic in olive oil until golden. Add basil leaves and the whole arugula, cover, and wilt. Transfer to food processor and chop. Add half the reserved chopped arugula and blend to combine. Add seeded, chopped fresh red chillis, salt, pepper, and olive oil. Combine cooked spaghetti and sauce in skillet and turn gently to coat over low heat. Fold in lightly beaten ricotta and remaining chopped arugula. Season and serve with Parmesan (from *The Cafe Cookbook*).

"Arugula—*roka* to the Greeks—grows wild all over the countryside," writes Diane Kochilas in *The Greek Vegetarian*. "Although most cuisines call for arugula to be eaten raw . . . in Greek kitchens it is often cooked, the way all wild greens are. Cooking changes the taste quite dramatically; all the pepperiness of the arugula becomes pleasantly bitter," as in **Navy Beans Stewed with Arugula:** Gently cook chopped red onion in olive oil until tender. Add minced garlic and stir momentarily. Add soaked dried navy beans, chopped plum tomatoes, and then trimmed, chopped arugula (about 1 pound to each cup of dried beans). Add water to cover and simmer until beans are soft. Stir in sherry vinegar and salt to taste. Serve warm or at room temperature.

Chef Charlie Trotter's complex dishes are focused, original, and demanding to prepare. **Arugula Noodles with Smoked Tomato Sauce, Olives, and Roasted Garlic Puree** (from *Charlie Trotter's Vegetables*) points up arugula in three forms: flavored oil, pasta dough, and fresh. For pasta, prepare like spinach fettuccine, using semolina flour, eggs, and stemmed, blanched arugula. For the oil, puree arugula that has been stemmed, blanched, and refreshed in cold water, with grapeseed and olive oils. Refrigerate 24 hours. Strain and refrigerate another day, then decant. Prepare sauce: Peel and quarter yellow tomatoes and smoke over hickory chips until heavily flavored. Soften diced onion in butter. Add smoked tomatoes and cook gently until liquid is reduced. Puree until smooth: season. To assemble: Cook noodles al dente. Toss with stemmed, chopped arugula. Season. Spread a circle of sauce on each plate. With long fork, twist noodles into a central mound on each. Around this, arrange quartered oil-cured olives and chopped oven-dried tomatoes. Spoon arugula oil and a touch of roasted garlic puree around plate. Grind over pepper.

Asparagus, White and Purple

and some thoughts on Green (all are *Asparagus officinalis*)

In the United States, white is the "other asparagus." In Belgium, France, Holland, Germany, and Spain, the "other asparagus" would be green. Most people reading this will know something about green asparagus, but little about white and purple. So please consider this a supplement to your knowledge of green asparagus, not a comprehensive entry about all asparagus. (While green asparagus needs no introduction, those who have not roasted and microwaved it might look at page 36 for these non-traditional cooking methods.)

White asparagus is no mere blip on the specialty produce screen. According to the proceedings of the Ninth International Asparagus Symposium (1997) as reported by Brian Benson, president of California Asparagus Seed and Transplants in Davis, in the 61 asparagus-producing countries of the world (with an estimated total production area of 218,335 hectares), 55 percent of the asparagus grown is white. China, with 55,000 hectares, grows the most (virtually all for export and canning), followed by Spain (about 20,000 hectares) and France and Germany, each with about 12,000.

Just what is white asparagus? In brief, "white asparagus or blanched asparagus is harvested from plants whose spears have not seen the light of day," says Benson. It is naturally green-colored asparagus grown in the dark. "By harvesting the spears from either highly ridged soil covering the asparagus plant or by any other device (black plastic tunnels, etc.) used to exclude light . . . the chlorophyll [green-producing] and anthocyanin [purple-producing] pigments are not formed and the spear remains white." The labor required to achieve this is "four times what it takes to produce green asparagus," and white asparagus is, as a consequence, very expensive—just one reason to devote attention to its purchase.

Anyone who has been in Europe in April knows that white asparagus is a cause for celebration. In the following paragraph from *A Taste of Alsace,* Sue Styles is writing about France, but she could be describing any number of regions in Europe: "It is difficult to convey to anyone who has never been to Alsace in the spring the quasi-religious fervour inspired by the great

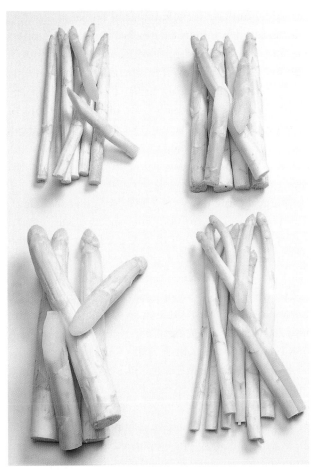

length: 6-9 inches

god asparagus." Asparagus is "cut at crack of dawn each day before any tips have a chance to emerge [from the soil] and take colour." Restaurants in the asparagus-growing areas base their entire reputation on the vegetable, she says, and open only from mid-April until Saint John's Day (June 24th).

Why then is the magnificent, pearlescent (and laughably phallic—hold one up to the uninitiated and listen to the response) springtime pride of Europe virtually unknown in North America? The sad truth is that until very recently, white asparagus grown in the Americas—North, South, and Central—was totally inedible: a bitter, fibrous, watery, nasty look-alike. But there are now notable exceptions, and there may be more by the time you read this.

The German-born chef Hans Röckenwagner, whose eponymous restaurants in Santa Monica and Beverly Hills annually showcase white asparagus, is more diplomatic: "I am a big fan of American products. But these are the big exception. It is only the white asparagus from Europe which are wonderful—the ones from Germany, France, and Holland. Nothing I have tasted from anywhere else is worth considering." He has nurtured his local clientele on European imports and won them over. "It is not until you taste the real thing that you understand how they can become a cult. It took three years of educating and of losing money on asparagus—and now, people call ahead and ask when they're coming in. They are incredibly expensive and worth every penny, provided they're the real thing."

The real thing tastes very little like green asparagus. The big smooth spears combine aspects of salsify, palm hearts, and artichoke, but they're milder. And even the finest and best have a flavor Americans associate with canned asparagus—which they love or don't.

So why can't Americans grow the real thing? Brian Benson explains that "the main slip-up place is the post-harvest handling. No matter how great asparagus may be to begin with, fiber forms quickly in the vascular bundles and the spears become tough or fibrous if they are not quickly cooled down to 34°F and kept there pretty much until you cook them." As with many crops, the largest increase in production has been in warm climates, "in countries in the Southern Hemisphere . . . with low labor rates where they can produce spears relatively cheaply," Benson says. "Few countries or small companies have the hydrocooling capabilities to cool them down or the equipment to keep them cooled."

Some do, however. Bill Schaefer, president of C-Brands Tropicals in Homestead, Florida, a company with asparagus fields in Peru, says that "asparagus quality depends upon fast, cold, moist post-harvest handling. The fields must be right near the packing house so the asparagus can be cut, hydrocooled, and packed within hours. We estimate that for every hour lost between cutting and chilling, a day of shelf life is lost. There is no margin for error."

A taste test of several sizes of European and Peruvian asparagus confirmed that there has been a considerable improvement in quality since I last tasted (and rejected) American produce. Unfortunately, however, California

and Mexican asparagus was as I remembered. Miniature white asparagus (120 to the pound—as compared with 4 per pound for large Dutch asparagus), grown in several states, is crisp and cute and tastes rather like soybean sprouts.

BASIC USE: Peel white asparagus and cook until truly tender, not al dente. Traditionally, the spears are simmered in a small amount of water with sugar and salt, in a tall pot that holds them upright and protects the tender tips from damage. Or asparagus of the same size can be bundled, trimmed, and tied with string, then boiled in water to cover. When tender (leave one loose for sampling), they can be lifted out of a pot of water by hitching a fork around the string.

In countries that love white asparagus, it is often served with an egg-butter sauce (hollandaise being the best known) or herb mayonnaise. Fat is the supreme finish for these mild spears. In Alsace and parts of Germany they are typically offered with slices of cooked ham, raw smoked ham, and a choice of three sauces: vinaigrette, mayonnaise, and hollandaise (according to *La gastronomie alsacienne* by François Voegeling).

In untraditional American style, Röckenwagner's annual asparagus menu includes white asparagus with house-smoked salmon and scallion pancakes, jumbo green and white asparagus in roasted shallot-porcini oil vinaigrette with honey-cured ham, white asparagus soup with portobello mushroom caviar, and a main course of "the traditional one pound of steamed white asparagus with new potatoes, herbed vinaigrette, and house-made mayonnaise."

NOTE ON SERVING: In countries that wait for the asparagus season, the vegetable is grasped with the fingers to be nibbled whole. It is sacrilege to hack it up. The British writer E. S. Dallas lamented that "the greatest defect of the English arrangement of dinner is that almost always vegetables are of no account save as adjuncts," but rejoiced in the exception made for artichokes and asparagus. He wondered "whether this exception is due to a pure admiration of the vegetable, or to the circumstance that, having to be eaten with the fingers, it is necessary to put down either knife or fork in order to seize the vegetable" (*Kettner's Book of the Table,* 1877).

SELECTION: White asparagus from Europe and the United States appears from March into May. South American spears may appear at any time. Buy from markets where asparagus is kept chilled—not displayed in a warm area. The spears should show no evidence of shrinking or wrinkling and should be pearly, shiny, and free of ridges. Do not bother with them if they look stringy at the base or are pitted, bruised, or dented. They must be firm and juicy. Ask to cut a bare slice from the base to be sure they're clean and smooth. If there is fiber sticking out, forget it. The tips should be totally closed (no sign of opening) and all white—except, perhaps, for a touch of pink or lilac at the top.

Bigger is definitely better. Not only is there less waste and less labor (white asparagus must be peeled completely) but for the most part big spears are also sweeter, juicier, and smoother-textured.

STORAGE: Don't keep white asparagus. If you won't use it within a day or two, don't buy it. Store in the coldest part of the refrigerator. You can keep up appearances and perhaps add a day to asparagus spears if you trim the bases and set them upright in a little water in the refrigerator; but they will still lose their freshness and turn fibrous.

PREPARATION: Unlike most green asparagus, the white ones *must be totally peeled*—and this takes care, as the spears are extremely brittle. Hans Röckenwagner says that while "the apprentices can trim green asparagus, it is the chef who prepares the white—or there is too much expensive loss." Rinse asparagus. Holding each spear flat against a work surface and turning so that it remains that way as you work, lightly peel stalk with swivel peeler. Then go over the stalk again to pare more toward the middle of the stalk and even more toward the base. Trim an inch or two from the bottom, depending upon how fibrous it is.

Asparagus, Purple

The purple spears pictured here were (every last one was eaten) among the most sweet, juicy, tender, and tasty asparagus I have ever eaten. So was the purple asparagus I sampled last year, and a year earlier.

Although a range of purple-hued asparagus is common in European markets, it is fairly rare in ours. For now, it seems to be represented by one commercial cultivar, Purple Passion. Brian Benson, who developed

purple asparagus

length: 7-9 inches

the seed from Violetto de Albinga, an Italian asparagus, says that it has not yet taken hold in the marketplace.

Even when purple asparagus is munched raw, the fiber is nil and the flavor and sugar are prominent. Uncooked, the exceptionally solid stalks are violet to lilac to dusky mauve, green-tinged beneath the skin and white inside. Simmered briefly in salted water, the bracts turn a pretty lavender and the spears a deep, rich green—almost spruce. The tips are fleshy and sweet; the stalk is meaty and totally fiber-free. Jumbo and large spears are juicier and sweeter than slim ones.

BASIC USE: Boil or steam large and standard spears, then serve as you would the finest green asparagus: to eat with your fingers, whole, with sauce for dipping. The color and flavor are not enhanced by roasting, stir-frying, or microwaving. Diagonally cut pencil-size spears remain crisp and firm in stir-fries, soups, or frittatas.

SELECTION: Choose bright, solid spears without a trace of shriveling or pitting. The base should snap as cleanly as a green bean, with no visible fiber. Larger spears are sweeter and juicier.

STORAGE: Although not as sensitive as white asparagus—and never as fibrous—purple asparagus swiftly loses its charm in storage. Asparagus is not a vegetable for keeping.

PREPARATION: Fresh purple asparagus should need no more than a sliver trimmed from the base. If the spears are elderly, bend them at the base to break off any fibrous part and lightly peel the thick bottom.

Asparagus peelings: Green asparagus trimmings make great broth. White trimmings are too bitter and should be tossed out. Purple peelings barely exist because the skin is so tender. But if you do have purple trimmings, use them in a dark soup or stock because they turn the water brown. They're good with dried mushrooms for a risotto.

Basic White Asparagus

White asparagus must be fully peeled and cooked until truly tender to reveal its secrets. Do not steam, microwave, roast, stir-fry, or cook briefly, or you will wind up with a mouthful of bitter fibers. Chef Hans Röckenwagner, who recommends the following method,

warns that "it may take a little time to appreciate white asparagus, but once you have tasted a good one, you will understand why there is such a hoopla made over this vegetable."

How much you serve depends on the size of the asparagus (bigger is better), your budget, and your guests' appetites. Large to super-jumbos (I don't recommend small ones) run from 22 to 4 per pound—quite a range. Remember that there is plenty of waste.

Offer asparagus warm as a first course with classic hollandaise or another butter-egg sauce, or with lemony or herbed mayonnaise, or with a mild vinaigrette.

FOR 1½ POUNDS WHITE ASPARAGUS

6 cups water, or to cover asparagus by
  several inches
1 tablespoon lemon juice
2 teaspoons kosher salt
2 teaspoons sugar
1 tablespoon butter
Sauce of choice

1. Rinse asparagus. Holding each spear flat against work surface and turning so that it remains flat as you work, lightly peel entire stalk with swivel peeler or knife, starting just below the tip. Then pare away more toward the middle of each stalk and even more toward base. Do not leave any peel. You may need to cut an inch or more from each base.

2. Combine water, lemon juice, salt, sugar, and butter in sauté pan or deep skillet. Add asparagus. Boil gently until truly tender—not crisp. Asparagus will bend when lifted with tongs and will appear almost translucent—like alabaster, not white and opaque. Timing varies dramatically but will always be more than for green. Super-jumbos can take 15 to 25 minutes, while standards or large can take 8 to 15. The only way to be sure is to cut off a piece and taste.

3. Carefully lift out asparagus with tongs, tamping with a towel to dry slightly. Serve hot with sauce.

Warm White Asparagus and Potatoes in Lemon-Oil Dressing

If you can find perfect white asparagus and *if* you can find perfect new potatoes (see page 500) or waxy potatoes, together they are a feast for cognoscenti. But use only superior vegetables, for there is no cover-up, just a gentle lemony dressing. Lemon zest processed with grapeseed oil produces an unusually light sauce—just slightly tart and richly perfumed. While butter-and-egg sauces are the classic accompaniments, they are not in tune with the health concerns of the moment. This version is no compromise at all.

> 3 large lemons, preferably organically grown
> ⅔ cup grapeseed oil
> 2 teaspoons minced shallot
> About 1 tablespoon kosher salt
> 2 teaspoons Dijon mustard
> ⅛ teaspoon fine-ground white pepper
> About 4 dozen large white asparagus spears (about 3 pounds)
> About 12 to 20 medium waxy potatoes (about 3 pounds), scrubbed
> 1 tablespoon sugar
> 1 tablespoon butter
> About 2 tablespoons thin-sliced chives
> Fleur de sel or other crisp sea salt

1. Scrub and rinse 1 lemon; pat dry. Remove yellow zest with peeler or paring knife (wrap and refrigerate lemon). Combine in blender or food processor with oil. Whiz until zest is chopped into granules. Pour into jar and scrape in all zest. Cover and leave overnight.

2. Pour contents of jar into a fine sieve (do not wash jar or remove stray lemon bits—they're fine in the dressing). Press zest to extract oil; discard zest in sieve. Halve the peeled lemon and squeeze the juice. Squeeze more from a second lemon, if needed, to make 2 tablespoons. Blend in the oil jar, with shallot, ¼ teaspoon salt, mustard, and pepper. Add lemon oil, cover, and shake to emulsify. Adjust seasoning.

3. Rinse asparagus. Holding each spear flat against work surface, peel lightly to remove all skin. Then pare more deeply toward middle and end of spear. Trim an inch or two of base.

4. Set potatoes on steamer rack over boiling water. Cover, and steam until tender, 15 to 20 minutes. Set aside on cutting board.

5. Meanwhile, squeeze juice from remaining lemons. Combine with remaining salt and the sugar in very large deep sauté pan or skillet. Add water to cover asparagus generously. Bring to a boil. Taste the water—it should be distinctly salty, lemony, and a little sweet. Adjust as needed.

6. Add butter and asparagus. Boil gently until fully tender: Asparagus will bend when lifted with tongs and will have no white center but will be slightly translucent throughout. Timing varies considerably. Cut off pieces to taste.

7. Meanwhile, peel potatoes. Return to steamer for a minute to heat through if needed.

8. Lift asparagus onto towel. Slice potatoes and arrange on warmed plates. Arrange asparagus alongside. Shake or whisk dressing to emulsify again and divide over potatoes and asparagus. With tongs, gently twist asparagus to coat with dressing. Sprinkle over chives. Serve at once, with fleur de sel.

Serves 4 as a main course

Basic Purple Asparagus

The purple asparagus available at this writing (pictured) are luscious when they are simply boiled—not roasted, microwaved, steamed, or stir-fried (except the skinny ones, which *are* good stir-fried). I like the heightened sweetness and richness of a little sugar and butter in the water, but they are not necessary. Serve the drained hot asparagus with butter-egg sauces, a mustard vinaigrette, or herbed mayonnaise. Or just serve straight, with citrus wedges and crisp salt.

The size of the asparagus, the role they play in the meal (solo, or as side dish), and your appetite for them will determine how much you need. Figure that 9 jumbos, 20 standards, or 50 pencil-size weigh about 1 pound, and go from there. Bigger ones are juicier and sweeter.

FOR ABOUT 1½ POUNDS PURPLE ASPARAGUS

About 6 cups water, or to cover asparagus
   by a few inches
2 teaspoons kosher salt
Optional: 1 teaspoon sugar
Optional: 1 tablespoon butter

1. Rinse asparagus and trim bases. (Unless they have been kept too long or poorly stored, there should be no need to peel.)

2. Combine water, salt, sugar, and butter in large skillet and bring to a boil. Add asparagus. Boil gently until tender but not soft (these asparagus are nice a bit al dente): about 6 minutes for larger ones, about 5 for standard. Cut a piece to test.

3. Lift out with tongs, tamping with towel to dry slightly. Serve hot.

Basic Microwaved Green Asparagus

Just in case you have not yet tried it, this remarkably fuss-free and mess-free approach gets asparagus on the table in minutes and requires little cleanup. For a quick meal, the ease of preparation can't be beat—although flavor and texture are not as well developed as when asparagus are roasted, steamed, or boiled. Water is not needed if the dish holds the vegetable closely. Do not cook the asparagus completely, but let it "rest" to finish cooking. As a final touch, the delicate French fleur de sel is ideal, but other crisp forms of salt will do the job.

1 pound medium asparagus (16 to 20 spears)
Fleur de sel or other crisp sea salt
Lemon wedges

1. Bend base of each asparagus spear to snap off fibrous part. Lightly peel stalks. Fit into microwavable dish with little room to spare. Cover dish with plastic wrap.

2. Microwave for 2 minutes. Shake dish to redistribute stalks. Cook 2 minutes longer. With sharp knife tip, prick through plastic into asparagus to test doneness. If almost done, let stand a minute or so (do not cook fully). If too firm, cook another minute and test

again. Be sure to allow for resting time, or asparagus will become flabby.

3. After resting, serve hot with salt and lemon. Or spread out to cool, then chill, to serve with vinaigrette.

Serves 2

Basic Roasted Green Asparagus

If you've never roasted asparagus, you're in for a treat. This method, which produces a very different effect than boiled or steamed, underscores the firmness and nuttiness of the vegetable and deepens the color. The scent is also quite different—big and sweet, rather like garden peas.

Accent the savory spears with no more than a flick of coarse salt and spritz of both orange and lemon—at the table (not beforehand, or you risk sogginess). For an Asian lilt, substitute a touch of oyster sauce, soy, or fish sauce for the salt.

1 pound medium green asparagus
   (16 to 20 spears)
About 1 tablespoon olive oil
Fleur de sel or other crisp sea salt
Lemon and orange wedges

1. Preheat oven to 500°F. Bend base of each asparagus spear to snap off fibrous part. Lightly peel stalks.

2. Choose a roasting pan that holds asparagus closely. Drizzle 1 tablespoon oil over them, then shake pan until asparagus is coated. Add more oil as needed to finely film spears, shaking to distribute evenly.

3. Roast in center of oven 5 minutes. Shake pan vigorously to turn stalks. Roast until tender, about 5 minutes more. Serve at once, with salt and citrus alongside.

Serves 2

Pros Propose

To add new perspectives to the green asparagus repertory, there are these thoughts from two extraordinary French craftsmen. "I use meat juices—thick, smooth essences . . . to heighten the flavors of vegetables," says Alain Ducasse. For his **Roasted Asparagus with Meat Juice and Black Olives:** Cook large green asparagus in heavily salted boiling water for 3 minutes; drain. Refresh in cold water and drain. Spread on towels. Heat butter in skillet and cook asparagus in a single layer until done. Heat meat juices from roast beef or chicken. Add pitted Taggiasche or Niçoise olives, lemon juice, white pepper, and salt. Add butter to make the sauce velvety. Spread asparagus in a gratin dish and nap with sauce. Heat briefly in a hot oven (from *Méditerranées: Cuisine de l'essentiel*).

Skewered Grilled Asparagus, another unusual take, comes from *Roger Vergé's Vegetables in the French Style,* truly a treasure chest. The ever-curious chef writes, "I ate asparagus grilled on skewers for the first time in Japan; I learned that grilling spotlights its mild bitterness and heightens its flavor. The olive oil keeps the asparagus from drying out, and the fresh savory is like a burst of sunshine." To prepare: Peel thick green asparagus spears. Cut tips to about 4 inches in length (reserve remaining stalks for soup). Spread tips on plate and sprinkle with salt to make them less brittle. Align in groups of 5 and pierce through each group with two bamboo skewers about an inch apart. Drizzle with olive oil. Broil or grill about 3 minutes. Turn and cook another few minutes. Meanwhile, warm olive oil with savory sprigs in skillet. When asparagus is cooked, dip both sides in the scented oil. Arrange skewers on platter, season with pepper, and garnish with savory.

For white asparagus, butter and eggs are the favored additions, whether as separate elements or combined in hollandaise sauce, perhaps the most revered accompaniment (along with its sister maltaise, made with oranges). **Asperges à la flamande** is among the most long-lived and luscious of traditional treatments: Boil peeled asparagus upright, their tips out of the water, 5 minutes. Add water to cover tips and continue cooking until completely tender, 5 to 15 minutes longer, depending on size. Salt the water, then drain. "Set on napkin on porcelain rack surrounded by halved hard-cooked eggs and chopped parsley. On the side serve melted butter to which lemon juice has been added. Eggs are mashed with butter sauce and parsley on the plate and the tip of the asparagus is dipped into the mixture while left hand holds end of vegetable" (from *A Belgian Cookbook* by Juliette Elkon).

A version of the same dish appears in the *Everybody Eats Well in Belgium Cookbook* (by Ruth Van Waerebeek with Maria Robbins): Bunch peeled white asparagus, tie with string, and simmer, covered, in plenty of salted water until tender, 15 to 30 minutes depending upon their thickness. Remove and drain on a towel. Mash hard-cooked eggs in a bowl with a fork. Add plenty of warm melted butter (4 ounces for 3 eggs). Add lemon juice, minced parsley, salt, pepper, and nutmeg. Arrange warm asparagus on plates and spread sauce over all but tips. Serve at once.

Van Waerebeek's grandmother served the first asparagus of the season with eggs and butter in a simpler form. The large warm white stalks were served in a porcelain dish "alongside of which were a sauceboat filled with melted butter and little silver dishes holding soft-cooked eggs. We ate with our fingers (a rare and delightful treat), dipping the asparagus first in the melted butter and then in the creamy egg yolks. Pure heaven and a very sensuous experience!"

Avocado (*Persea americana*)

Also avocado pear, alligator pear, aguacate (Spanish)
Including **avocadito (mini-avocado)** and **avocado leaves**

Not all avocados are created equal. Two types may be as different from each other as Idaho russet and Peruvian purple fingerling potatoes. An avocado may taste nutty to fruity, savory to sweet. The skin may be thick and pebbly, thin and smooth, shiny or dull; it may be colored spruce, burgundy, grass-green, or black. The flesh, ocher to chartreuse, may be creamy to dense, juicy to relatively dry. Some avocados turn brown once cut; most do not. Some avocados tip the scales at one-half pound, some at five. Perhaps most telling on the tongue is oil content, which can range from 3 to 30 percent and which affects the character of the fruit dramatically.

But as varied as they are, all avocados derive from three races, all probably indigenous to Mexico. The great American plant explorer, Wilson Popenoe, wrote in his invaluable *Manual of Tropical and Subtropical Fruits* (1920) that in 1653, Bernabe Cobo, a priest who had traveled widely in tropical America, first described "the three groups of cultivated avocados recognized at the present time by horticulturists under the names of West Indian, Guatemalan, and Mexican." ("West Indian" is a misnomer assigned when Europeans discovered the fruit in Jamaica in 1696, for it had been cultivated in Central and South America long before their arrival.) All avocados stem from these forebears, whether bred in the Americas, the Philippines, India, Australia, or South Africa—to name a few of the many lands in which they thrive.

"The correct name of this fruit in English at present [and still, in 2001] is recognized to be avocado," Popenoe wrote. "This is undoubtedly a corruption of the Spanish ahuacate or aguacate, which in turn is an adaptation of the Aztec ahuacatl," the word both for the fruit and for a testicle, picturesquely enough. The word "avocado," perhaps more acceptable to some churchly chronicler, was probably first published in 1696 by Sir Hans Sloane, in his catalogue of the plants of Jamaica, according to Popenoe.

In the United States, Guatemalan avocados and Guatemalan-Mexican crosses grow primarily in California; West Indian and West Indian–Guatemalan crosses grow in Florida. Commercially, these are usually referred to as California and Florida avocados, indicating their main growing areas—and, by association, the types grown.

To generalize: California-grown fruit is rich in oil (from 18 to 30 percent), dense, relatively small, quite sturdy, and tastes nutty and buttery. As with many agricultural products, the vast majority of the commercial crop is represented by one cultivar: the very rich, solidly shippable, green-black Hass (pronounced like "pass" and named after Rudolph Hass, a mailman from Wisconsin who retired to Pasadena and patented the tree in 1935). In addition to California, the Hass is imported from Mexico and Chile. Other commercial California varieties sometimes specified are Fuerte, Gwen, Reed, Bacon, Zutano, and Pinkerton.

Florida avocados are comparatively juicy, not buttery; with just 3 to 5 percent oil, they contain roughly 25 to 50 percent less fat than California fruit. Their flavor is relatively mild, more fruity than nutty, more creamy than oily (in fact, sometimes watery). The skin does not darken but stays bright green when the avocados are ripe (with the exception of the eggplant-dark Hardee). These brighter, larger fruits are generally favored by the Hispanic population for salads; the richer Guatemalan types are reserved for guacamole and other sauces.

Sadly, none of the 60-odd avocado varieties grown in Florida arrive with name tags. "There are no varietal specifications on avocados from Florida," says Bill Schaefer, president of C-Brand Tropicals in Homestead, Florida. "They are sold by size. They arrive in seasonal order, in small and large lots. It would be impossible to handle the volume of names."

Occasionally you may come upon a batch of tiny avocados about the size of cornichons or baby carrots. These **avocaditos**, also called cocktail, cuke, or mini-avocados, occur unpredictably as a result of a variety of genetic factors and sudden changes in climate. The seedless oblong fruit is particularly prevalent in Fuerte

avocados from
California

top, left to right: Fuerte,
Pinkerton, Hass
bottom, left to right:
Bacon, Zutano
length: 4-6 inches

avocados from Florida

top, left to right:
Tower 2, Simmonds, Miguel
bottom, left to right: Beta, Pol-
lack, Nesbitt
length: 5-8 inches

avocados. While difficult to peel, they are cute and tasty sliced into rounds as a tidy garnish or canapé-topper, or floated in soup. Halve and arrange "petals" on a salad; or halve (without peeling), scoop out the flesh, combine with diced marinated seafood or vegetables in vinaigrette, return to the shells, and serve as an hors d'oeuvre.

Avocado leaves from trees of the Mexican race have a basil-anise scent, sometimes full-blown, sometimes faint. (Avocado is kin to bay leaf, cinnamon, and other popular aromatics of the Lauraceae family.) These can serve as a bed for steaming fish or chicken, or to scent in the manner of bay leaves; or toast and grind for flavoring. They are available in Latin American shops or can be picked directly from unsprayed trees in California.

BASIC USE: A fruit that plays vegetable and is as rich as a dairy product, that is as suitable for soup as for dessert, and is at home in a tiny taqueria or deluxe dining room—avocado defies categorization and offers a wealth of culinary possibilities.

Most important is choosing the right avocado for the right role. The richer California avocados make luscious sauces, pureed soups, and satisfying main courses for vegetarian meals. The lighter sliceable Florida types are a natural for salads, salsas, sandwiches, and garnishes. Rather than describe their general use, which is familiar to most people, I've supplied particular suggestions in Pros Propose.

SELECTION: Hass, the primary commercial cultivar, is available year-round from California, Chile, and Mexico (for states north of the frost line). It should not only become tender but darken to inky green-black when ripe. Other Guatemalan types appear intermittently. Florida fruit is in season from June through January, more or less, and the Florida varieties are complemented by shipments from the Dominican Republic from September to March.

Choose fruit that is uniform in color and feel—whether tender, with just a little "give," or hard to the touch. Inconsistent texture indicates potential ripening problems. To determine its condition, do not squeeze avocado with the fingers, which will leave bruises when the fruit ripens. Instead, turn it slowly and palp with your palm.

RIPENING: Avocados must be at "room temperature" (roughly 68° to 71°F) to soften properly. The amount of time needed to reach a pleasing eating consistency varies with the season. Because avocado does not ripen fully until cut from the tree, the tree is used as a storehouse. Hanging fruit does not ripen, but it does continue to mature. Thus, at the start of the season, when new fruit is picked, it ripens gradually; but toward the end, fruit held on the tree can ripen very quickly. Keep watch on your "hatching" fruit. To hurry it along, place an apple in a bag with the avocado to release ethylene gas and speed up the process.

Foodservice note: Before ripening at room temperature, California fruit can be held at a chilly 38° to 40°F, Florida fruit at 50° to 55°F. (Ideally, however, avocado is not refrigerated.) Some chefs, like Rick Bayless, who uses four to five cases daily, work with small purveyors who ripen the avocado to order. Because Bayless uses the fruit at once, there is no need to refrigerate it. In order to have a regular supply of ready-to-eat fruit, some large restaurants and chains request fruit that has been "speed-ripened" with higher concentrations of ethylene than occur in the normal course of events. These can be stored for a shorter period than usual, at 36°F.

PREPARATION: When you halve an avocado, the pit may slip out easily. If it doesn't, smack a heavy knife blade directly into it to embed firmly. Twist the knife to pull out the pit, still attached to the blade. Slice the fruit as desired, then strip off the peel.

Florida fruit slices nicely and can be prettily and neatly fanned: Halve avocado, remove seed, halve again; pull off peel. Trim each wedge to eliminate the central cavity so that the fruit rests flat on a cutting board. Slice crosswise (not lengthwise), then slide apart.

Readers are warned about browning when avocado is mentioned in print, but of the 30 types I cut and left at room temperature for an hour or more, only two looked splotchy. If you have chosen one that does brown, scrape off the imperfection. No big deal! It tastes just fine. Or coat with lime, lemon, or vinegar to maintain color. Forget about leaving the pit in the guacamole; this does no good.

Guacamole from Rosa Mexicano

Why tamper with a classic? When Josefina Howard shared this recipe with me in 1985, it was a popular menu item at her restaurant Rosa Mexicano in New York City. When I spoke with her about it again in 2000, it was even more so. At the restaurant, waiters prepare the guacamole tableside in beautiful Mexican mortars of black volanic stone (*molcajetes*). The two-step operation is essential—as is a fully ripe oil-rich type of avocado.

SEASONING PASTE

1 teaspoon minced Serrano chilli (with seeds and ribs)
1 tablespoon minced white onion
1 tablespoon chopped cilantro (coriander) leaves
¼ teaspoon kosher salt
½ California avocado, such as Hass or Fuerte

GUACAMOLE

¼ cup hard-ripe tomato dice (¼ to ½ inch)
About 3 tablespoons diced white onion
About 1 tablespoon chopped cilantro (coriander) leaves
Remaining ½ avocado
Minced Serrano chilli
Salt

1. Prepare seasoning paste: Combine chilli, onion, cilantro, and salt in mortar. With pestle, smash mixture to a paste. Peel avocado and roughly dice. Add to paste and crush to a rough texture.

2. For guacamole: Add tomato, 2 tablespoons onion, and 1 tablespoon cilantro to seasoning paste, mixing lightly. With butter knife, score avocado flesh into ½-inch squares, cutting down to skin. Run knife around flesh as close to skin as possible to release cubes into mixture. Fold together. Taste and add onion, cilantro, chilli, and salt.

Serves 3 to 4 as a condiment

Salad of Avocado, Spinach, and Carambola (or Orange)

Here is a showcase for the bright, sliceable West Indian-type avocado grown in Florida. Small carambola (aka star fruit) is a perfect tart-sweet mate. If it isn't to be had, substitute two small blood oranges or navel oranges. Pretty, unusual, and easy.

About 1 pound small-leafed bunched spinach or about 10 ounces cleaned small spinach leaves
1 Florida avocado (about ¾ pound; or use part of a larger one)
2 yellow-ripe carambolas, 3 to 4 ounces each (or 2 oranges)
2 tablespoons peanut or corn oil
1 teaspoon ground cumin
2 tablespoons chopped red onion
1½ tablespoons brown sugar
Dash of ground hot pepper
⅓ cup rice vinegar
½ tablespoon shoyu (Japanese soy sauce)

1. Dunk spinach into several changes of water, lifting out gently so sand sinks. Nip leaves from stems: spin-dry. Halve avocado, strike seed with knife, and lift out. Quarter avocado lengthwise, then peel. Cut crosswise into ¼-inch slices. Halve carambola (or peeled oranges) lengthwise, and then slice ⅛ inch thick.

2. Heat oil in small heavy non-aluminum saucepan over moderate heat. Stir in cumin and cook briefly until fragrant. Add onion and stir 1 minute. Add brown sugar, hot pepper, vinegar, and soy, stirring to blend.

3. Pour three-quarters of the dressing over spinach and toss. Divide among four plates. Arrange carambola and avocado on spinach. Spoon over the remaining dressing.

Serves 4

Avocado "Mayonnaise" with Lime and Basil

A satiny sauce, the color of pistachio cream, to dress chilled salmon, shrimp, or white fish fillets. Or spoon dollops over asparagus, snap beans, or even corn on the cob—messy but yummy. Or garnish chilled soups with the pretty topping and a scattering of snipped basil and chives. Scoop into pita and add sprouts. Offer as a dip on a vegetable platter. Buttermilk replaces the usual oil to give the sauce a tart edge, light and creamy texture, and enough acid to keep the bright fresh color. Use rich California-grown avocados, such as Hass, Fuerte, or Zutano.

¾ teaspoon kosher salt
1 teaspoon sugar
⅛ teaspoon fine-ground white pepper
About 3 tablespoons lime juice
1 or 2 ripe rich avocados (to equal ¾ pound)
1 tablespoon sliced chives
1 tablespoon thin-sliced basil leaves
About ¾ cup buttermilk
Optional: additional chives and basil for garnish

1. Stir together salt, sugar, white pepper, and 3 tablespoons lime juice.

2. Peel and chunk avocado. Combine with chives and basil in food processor container. Add lime juice mixture. Whiz to a smooth puree. With motor running, gradually add buttermilk until desired flavor and consistency are achieved. Season assertively.

3. Scoop into a dish, cover, and refrigerate an hour or more (up to about 24 hours) to mellow and chill.

4. To serve, add minced chives and thin-sliced basil leaves, if desired.

Makes 1½ to 2 cups

Pros Propose

At its ripest and best, avocado needs little or no adornment. Serve halves with no more than a spoon, lime wedges, and a little fleur de sel. Restaurateur Nora Pouillon says, "I'd love to see people go back to the old standard, avocado vinaigrette. The slow scooping out of the buttery flesh is one of my fondest early food memories. Now I'd even do without dressing—maybe just a touch of really fine aged balsamic. Sometimes the simplest is really the most delicious."

I find nothing as perfect with avocado as warm corn tortillas, their original and eternal complement. But avocado crostini make a pretty amazing second choice for an impromptu appetizer, snack, or light lunch: Grill slices of rustic white bread. Top with avocado slices and press gently with a fork to cover the surface completely (leaving no exposed bread to burn). Run under flame until hot. Sprinkle with crisp salt grains. To gild the lily (laurel, in fact), add toasted, crushed coriander seeds or ground sumac, or chives and basil, or lime and cilantro. Serve at once.

Maricel Presilla, Latin American food authority, urges cooks to "believe in the beauty of unadulterated avocado, whether as salad, garnish, or complementary ingredient. There is nothing more sensuous than eating it pure—floating a thin slice in clear soup," she says. "Or play its simple creaminess against spicy, sweet, sour, or crunch." She shows off the West Indian–type avocados preferred in her native Cuba in **Consommé with Avocado:** Season clear rich chicken broth with cilantro and Jalapeño. Deep-fry malanga (yautía) matchsticks. Stack in center of soup and surround with Florida avocado cubes.

Tart fruits such as carambola, tomato, or citrus underscore the richness of avocado, whether sliced for a salad or diced to a rough salsa. Or taste the beautiful balance of Maricel Presilla's **Avocado and Grilled Pineapple Salad:** Cube pineapple. Sprinkle with brown sugar and run under broiler to caramelize. Mix with diced Florida avocado, queso fresco dice, and julienne of red onions. Arrange on water cress dressed with Seville orange juice, Habanero peppers, cumin, and olive oil—and serve plenty of Cuban bread on the side.

Avocado's ability to instantly change from satiny solid to smooth liquid makes soup an easy goal—starter or entrée, sliced or pureed, hot or chilled. From chef Patricia Williams comes **Avocado Soup with Tomato Ice:** Puree Hass avocados with chilled and skimmed chicken broth, creme fraîche, and lime juice. Serve with a chunk of granita made from fresh tomato juice, diced tomatoes, Jalapeño, and cilantro.

A more elaborate **Chilled Cream of Avocado and**

Chèvre Soup with Chèvre Quenelles comes from Jean-Louis Palladin: Combine avocados with vegetable broth in food processor. Add soft fresh goat cheese, cream, a little oil, and lemon juice and process just to blend. Chill. For quenelles: Combine soft goat cheese with cream and olive oil. Season. To serve: halve avocado lengthwise, pit, and peel. Cut crosswise into ¼-inch slices. Arrange 4 slices in each bowl to rest on rim with ends in center. Using teaspoons, form ovals of cheese and set one against each avocado arch. Cut triangles from some remaining avocado slices and set one on each quenelle. Thin soup as needed with consommé. Ladle into bowls, and garnish with dill sprigs (from *Jean-Louis: Cooking with the Seasons*).

Some find avocado too rich for starters. When it replaces meat, poultry, or dairy foods, it makes an unusually satisfying entree. In fact, it deserves more attention in special diets, as it is nutrient-rich, easily digested, and agreeably mild. For **Avocado, Grapefruit, and Arugula with Ginger Vinaigrette,** the "avocado is the 'meat,' so cut it into large pieces—thick bâtonnets," explains chef Peter Zimmer. Combine with sections of ruby grapefruit and arugula, with a dressing of rice vinegar, grated ginger, and sesame oil. Toss with mint and cilantro leaves. Garnish with fried rice wafers.

Chef Rick Bayless is not fond of avocado soups, "which resemble sauces and are too rich for a first course," he says. But he makes an exception for **Avocado Beef Soup,** "which is sturdy enough to be a main course." To prepare: Puree roasted garlic, avocado, fat-free rich beef stock, Serrano chilli, salt and pepper. Serve cold with grilled scallions, cilantro leaves, and shredded crisp-fried beef brisket.

"We know little about how avocados . . . were eaten in pre-Columbian America," writes Sophie Coe in *America's First Cuisines.* "The one recipe that we may be sure of is the Aztec *ahuaca-mulli,* or avocado sauce, familiar to all of us today as guacamole." Following is a trio of guacamoles—all best prepared with rich California fruit.

Here are instructions from chef Rick Bayless for guacamole (as prepared twice daily at his Chicago restaurants): "With a knife—never a machine—chop tomatoes, Serranos, and cilantro. With a potato masher, slowly crush Hass avocados—that have not been refrigerated—to a coarse puree. Add tomato mixture. Chop white onions very fine. Rinse and dry. Add to guacamole with lime juice and salt. Cover closely with plastic and let rest about an hour. Do not refrigerate. To serve, sprinkle with cilantro and a little more rinsed onion. Surround with radish, hothouse cucumber, and jícama slices."

Tomatillos have just the right acid note and color to balance oily avocados in this guacamole from *Madhur Jaffrey's World Vegetarian:* Combine tomatillos with water to cover; simmer until tender. Drain and cool, then peel and mash. Coarsely crush avocado. Add tomatillos, minced onion, minced green chillis, chopped cilantro, crushed garlic, lime juice, and salt.

Grande dame of Mexican cookery Diana Kennedy surprises with this novel **Guacamole Chamacuero** from Señora Leticia Sanchez: Crush minced white onion, minced Serrano chillis, and salt to a paste. Stir in roughly crushed avocado pulp, peeled and diced firm-ripe peaches, halved seedless grapes, lime juice, and pomegranate seeds. Mix well and top with more pomegranate (from *My Mexico*).

Bamboo Shoots (primarily *Phyllostachys* species and *Bambusa* species)

Also chuk sun, tung sun (winter bamboo), chun sun (spring bamboo)
in Chinese markets; takenoko (Japanese)

Some people think of bamboo as one type of plant, but its multiplicity is mind-boggling. Some taxonomists count as many as 1,250 species. The two most common genera called bamboo, *Bambusa* and *Phyllostachys,* contain at least 175 species. Most bamboos have edible shoots. The size, shape, and quality of bamboo depend not only on the species but also on the time of year when it is harvested. Spring bamboo shoots, according to *Charmaine Solomon's Encyclopedia of Asian Food,* are chunky and pale, while winter shoots are "a daintier, more elongated shape, finer in texture, deeper in colour, and have a distinctive flavour."

I hope this complexity will explain why I do not know how to describe different species or compare their characteristics—or even identify what is pictured here! I do know that those shoots averaged 1 pound before cleaning, were grown in Costa Rica, and are harvested year-round. I can also say that they seemed less like vegetables than like the furry tusks of some mythological beast, and that once trimmed, the crisp ivory interior smelled fresh and sweet, but strange—quite unlike any other edible except perhaps taro. Although I smelled them, I did not taste them, because most bamboo shoots contain toxic hydrocyanic acid, which cooking dispels. Once bamboo is cooked, its texture becomes very special: dense, slightly chewy, very crisp and firm but at the same time meaty. Despite all statements to the contrary, I do not find that high-quality processed bamboo shoots are similar to fresh ones, which are well worth trying.

There is simply no way to know which bamboo you have unless you grow it yourself—a very good idea, given how delicious it is, how easy to cultivate, and how difficult to find in the market. But do not go out and adventurously pick your own from unfamiliar patches. "Powerful herbicides are used to control and eradicate bamboo," writes Rosalind Creasy in *The Gardener's Handbook of Edible Plants.* "Do not accept friendly offers of young shoots unless you know their

length: 10 inches

history!" If you want to start your own little forest, please see the bibliography for information about Creasy's books and Stephen Facciola's *Cornucopia II,* which provides numerous sources for bamboo—and any other edible plant you would ever grow.

BASIC USE: All bamboo sold in North American markets must be peeled and cooked before eating. Once cooked, it can be used in recipes that call for canned bamboo, or for jícama, or water chestnuts. However you use it, bamboo retains a nice crunch—so don't worry about overcooking. Cut slices, sticks, cubes, diamonds, or julienne. If you have the narrow cylindrical type, you'll cut rings. Add bamboo to stir-fries or sautés with colorful complements such as red and yellow bell peppers or snow peas. Add it, for crunch, to tuna or chicken salad, or to relishes. Toss with fried rice or noodles. Stir into poultry, seafood, or vegetable braises or stews, such as curries or tofu hot-pots. Cook in soup. Add to scrambled eggs, tofu, or tempeh. Shred to fill omelets and spring rolls or dumplings.

Bamboo shoots are traditionally limited to Eastern cookery—for no reason I understand, since they flourish all over the globe. But the seasoning palette of Asia does seem to suit them particularly well.

SELECTION: Bamboo shoots are available, though erratically, all year, from some Asian markets and specialty produce suppliers. Choose comparatively solid, heavy bamboo shoots without any sign of softening, mold, or cracks. Sniff deeply to be sure there is absolutely no hint of fishiness or sourness. If there is, forget it.

STORAGE: Wrap whole shoots individually in paper and refrigerate. If in good shape, they last for several weeks.

PREPARATION: Whether the bamboo is the large cone shapes pictured or the slim, graduated cylindrical shoots, the outer layers must be completely removed to leave just the creamy core. Follow directions for Basic Bamboo Shoots for peeling and precooking. Fresh bamboo shoots must be cooked to become edible.

Note: In a chapter entitled "How to Avoid Being Vulgar," A. Zee, the cryptically named author of *Swallowing Clouds,* devotes 15 delightful pages to bamboo, pages that depend upon eloquently explained ideograms that cannot be reproduced here. Find the book to enjoy them.

Basic Bamboo Shoots

Because bamboo shoots vary dramatically in size (from a few ounces to over a pound apiece), I cannot give hard and fast timing or predictable yield. I can just tell you that for this basic recipe I used one large bamboo shoot. Once you have cooked the slices, you can cut them to suit the desired textural effect: hair-thin strips, brunoise, triangles, julienne, dice—whatever will enhance the dish to come.

If you have slim bamboo shoots, they can be husked almost as easily as corn. Trim off all the covering so that only the creamy central core—a hollow tower of graduated cylinders—remains. Then cut into ¼-inch rings.

1 pound bamboo shoots
About 2 quarts water
1 tablespoon salt
1 tablespoon rice

1. Using a very sharp knife, start at wide end of (each) shoot and slit, then unwrap successive layers until you reach the pale edible core. When you have all pale, solid core, cut off the green pointed, furled tip. Pare off remaining covering, leaving a pale cone. Cut off the dry fibrous base as necessary. Rinse cone.

2. Cut off top part of cone where it naturally separates from the wide base. Halve top lengthwise. Halve base, then cut into ⅛- to ¼-inch slices, as desired for recipe.

3. Combine bamboo, water, salt, and rice in pot and bring to a full boil, stirring occasionally. Boil 5 minutes, then taste. If crunchy-tender and not bitter, remove from heat. If bitter, boil 5 minutes longer and taste again. If necessary, boil 5 minutes longer. Drain and rinse rice from bamboo. Cover and refrigerate.

Makes about 1½ cups (6 to 8 ounces)

Sautéed Bamboo Shoots and Snow Peas with Sherry and Dill

Western flavors (dill, Madeira, and butter) turn vegetables with an Eastern accent into a vivid international garnish that brightens simply prepared seafood of any origin. Lightly cooked scallops, shrimp, or fish fillets become a complete and colorful meal when tossed or topped with this slightly sweet, double-crisp duo.

6 ounces snow peas
About 6 ounces Basic Bamboo Shoots
½ teaspoon sugar
½ teaspoon kosher salt
½ tablespoon grapeseed or other mild oil
2 tablespoons Madeira or medium-dry sherry
½ tablespoon butter
About 1 tablespoon minced dill

1. Break stem end from each snow pea and slowly zip off the thicker "backbone" (the side to which peas

attach) as needed (some types do not require string-ing). Test the other side of a few pods in case the batch needs double duty. Cut pods into ¾-inch sections. Cut bamboo into ¼-inch diamonds or dice. Toss both with sugar and salt.

2. Heat oil in wide pan over moderately high heat. Add vegetables and toss until slightly browned and crisp-tender, about 5 minutes. Add Madeira and stir to evaporate completely.

3. Off heat, toss with butter and dill. Season and serve hot.

Serves 3 to 4

Sweet-Tart Rice Noodles, Bamboo Shoots, and Eggs

This light and fluffy stir-fry acts as both starch and veg-etable complement to broiled chicken, roasted pork, or sautéed seafood. Deceptively monochromatic, the peachy noodles hide crunchy bamboo strands and creamy egg morsels. To serve as a vegetable meal for two, add another egg and top with roasted, salted, chopped almonds.

½ pound thin dried rice noodles (vermicelli)
About ½ pound Basic Bamboo Shoots
1 tablespoon tomato paste
3 tablespoons fish sauce
2 tablespoons sugar
3 tablespoons distilled vinegar
4 medium scallions (green onions)
2 eggs
1 teaspoon Asian (dark) sesame oil
2 tablespoons plus 1 teaspoon peanut or
   vegetable oil
1 small garlic clove, minced
3 to 4 tablespoons slivered cilantro (coriander)
   or basil leaves

1. Soak noodles in warm water to cover until flexi-ble and tender but still too springy to eat, about 20 minutes.

2. Meanwhile, cut prepared bamboo shoots into long thin strips. Blend tomato paste, fish sauce, sugar, and vinegar. Cut pale part of scallions into thin slices;

set aside. Cut greens at an angle into very thin strips. Whisk eggs with sesame oil.

3. Drain noodles. With scissors, cut into shorter lengths, as desired. Toss with 1 tablespoon peanut oil.

4. Heat wok over high heat. Add 1 tablespoon peanut oil and tip to coat pan. Spread bamboo shoots in single layer in wok and brown, tossing occasionally, about 3 minutes. Add pale scallion parts and toss 1 minute. Reduce heat to moderate.

5. Add garlic and noodles and toss a moment. Add seasoning liquid and scallion greens. Toss until shoots and pale part of scallions are evenly colored.

6. Push contents of wok to one side. Spoon in re-maining 1 teaspoon oil, then eggs, spreading in a thin layer. When nearly set, gently fold and break up into noodles to mix evenly, adding cilantro during last few folds. Scoop into warmed dish.

Serves 4 as a side dish

Variation

Stir-Fried Noodles with Pork (or Chicken) and Bamboo Shoots

Heat wok over high heat. Add ½ tablespoon peanut or vegetable oil. Spread ½ pound thin pork (or chicken) strips in wok and sear, tossing to whiten and half-cook, 2 to 3 minutes. Scoop out and re-serve. Continue recipe as above, increasing both fish sauce and vinegar to ¼ cup and returning meat to wok with noodles.

Pros Propose

Bamboo shoots are used extensively in Buddhist meals. Among the many recipes for them in *Good Food from a Japanese Temple* by Soei Yoneda are bamboo shoots dressed with vinegar and miso, shoots simmered with konbu, sushi in which the bamboo is the container for the rice, and this **Bamboo Shoot Tempura:** Cut bam-boo shoots into ⅜-inch-thick half-moons. Combine in small saucepan with water, shoyu, sake, sugar, and salt. Bring to a boil, then simmer, partly covered, for 5 min-utes. Drain and dry. Prepare tempura batter. Coat slices with batter. Deep-fry at 340°F until pale tan, not browned. Serve hot.

Chef Michael Otsuka serves **Glazed Bamboo Shoots** as an appetizer for a multicourse vegetarian meal: Boil trimmed bamboo chunks in the water left from washing rice. When tender, drain and chill. Cut into neat, uniform bite-size wedges. Sauté in grapeseed and sesame oils. Deglaze pan with tamari sauce, grated ginger, shichimi togarashi (7-spice chilli seasoning), and rice vinegar. Serve hot.

Another all-vegetable dish with Japanese origins is a colorful toss of fine strips of **Hijiki, Shiitake, and Bamboo Shoots:** Soak rinsed hijiki in warm water: Lift out and rinse. At same time, soak dried shiitake. When rehydrated, remove stems and cut caps into ⅛-inch strips. Sauté these with the hijiki, julienne-cut parboiled bamboo shoots, and julienne-cut carrot for 1 minute. Add dashi, salt, sugar, mirin, and shoyu. Cover and simmer gently 10 minutes. Uncover and boil for a moment to evaporate liquid if necessary (from *Madhur Jaffrey's World-of-the-East Vegetarian Cooking*).

Beef with Bamboo Shoots is a staple of Vietnam. Sri Owen, authority on Asian cooking, writes in the *Classic Asian Cookbook* that "you can find Indonesian, Malaysian, Singaporean, and Filipino variations of the classic Southeast Asian dish." To prepare: Blend fish sauce, crushed garlic, minced red chilli, and lime juice; reserve. Stir-fry thin strips of rump steak in peanut oil; set aside. Stir-fry long thin strips of parboiled bamboo shoots 1 minute. Add thin-sliced scallion diagonals and toss. Stir in reserved seasoning mixture and stir-fry 30 seconds. Return beef to pan with roasted, crushed sesame seeds. Toss and serve hot.

Banana Bud (*Musa* species)

Also banana flower, banana blossom

The tropical vegetable pictured is not common in North American food shops, but immigrants from Southeast Asia—the banana's land of origin—have coaxed it into their neighborhoods. If you should chance upon it, you'll probably want to know what on earth it could be. And if you're curious about new foods, you'll probably try it. If you do so without guidance, you may be as frustrated and disappointed as I was when I did. For if you follow recipes from the few cookbooks that include it, you risk choking—an apt word, for a banana "bud" (technically, the inflorescence) is about as edible as artichoke fuzz.

Whether or not the banana buds in Asia are entirely different from the ones here, I cannot say. Or perhaps those who prepare them are already familiar with the preliminaries and need no instruction. But after cooking them six ways, I can state firmly that *cleaning* correctly is the primary goal.

Here is what I learned from *bitter* experience: To render this majestic maroon torpedo edible, you must ruthlessly remove its royal robe and male parts. According to Katie Chafin, a co-owner of Going Bananas Nursery in Homestead, Florida, each colorful capsule contains female, neuter, and male flowers, and each opens up to produce baby bananas—except one, the large terminal bud that hangs down from a ripening bunch of bananas. This cornucopia of all-male flowers has no bananas and is the one served up as vegetable—much in the way of artichokes, which, once cooked, it slightly resembles in form, flavor, texture, and color.

Of the hundreds of banana varieties that flourish in the tropics, those chosen to play the role of a vegetable are more tender and less bitter than most here, Asian chefs tell me. "Those who know bananas seem to prefer the Saba, a Filipino cooking banana; and the Rajapuri, an Indian dessert banana," says Katie Chafin, who grows both. Trimmed and thin-sliced, they are tossed in aromatic condiment salads, stewed in coconut milk or cream, and stir-fried with spicy noodles. Some are merely sliced, seasoned in dipping sauce, and nibbled raw (in the manner of the cardoons of Italy

length: 10 inches

which—unlike their bitter American counterparts—are sufficiently tender and mild to be eaten uncooked).

BASIC USE: Outside the tropics, banana buds must be tenderized by heavy salting, rinsing, the addition of acid, long cooking, or all of these. Forceful flavors, intense aromatics, or rich mellowing sauces are needed to balance their bitterness. Hot, sour, spicy, sweet, and salty all suit—in pairs, trios, or concert. Coconut milk or cream is the traditional cooking agent, and it really does the trick.

SELECTION AND STORAGE: Look for large banana blossoms (which have relatively less waste) in Southeast Asian and some Chinese markets somewhere between year-round and never. I know of no predictable seasons. Ranging from about 12 ounces to 2 pounds, banana buds should be tightly furled and bright, with no blackening. "Check under a few bracts to be sure the buds are fresh, not browning," advises Chafin. Refrigerated, banana buds will last for several days or more.

PREPARATION: Slice off and discard bud tip. Pull off and discard red bracts and encircling fringe of yellow flowers or "fingers"—which have a sweet, green-banana scent—until you reach the paler, more tender edible innards. Cut each pale bract free from the base and unwrap from the head, trying to keep it whole. Discard the "fingers" (all horribly astringent) between the layers. Stack several bracts at a time and roll a tight "cigar"; slice thin.

Banana Buds in Coconut Milk

Despite its lilting name, the banana blossom is a big, meaty hunk of vegetable leaves best suited to stewing, as in this traditional Philippine dish. The rich concoction, which suggests a mix of onions, artichokes, and cabbage, is typically served with meat or fish as a sauce or condiment—as it was at Cendrillon, the New York restaurant where I saw it prepared. I prefer to leave the sauce rather soupy (reduce it only slightly), sharpen it with lime juice, and serve it over red or black rice sprinkled with fresh coriander.

> Two 1-pound banana buds
> About ¾ cup kosher salt
> One 13- to 15-ounce can coconut milk
> 4 garlic cloves, chopped
> 2 or more very hot small fresh chillis

1. Slice off and discard banana bud tips. Remove and discard several layers of red bracts and encircling yellow "fingers" until you reach paler, more tender core. Cut each bract free from base and unwrap from head. Discard all "fingers" (which are horribly astringent) as you proceed. Stack several bracts at a time, rolling to form a tight cigar; slice thin.

2. Combine slices with salt, kneading it in, mashing and squeezing banana buds forcefully for several minutes so salt penetrates and is completely incorporated. Crush mercilessly. A handful at a time, squeeze out as much bitter juice as possible. Set in a colander and crush and mash under running water to remove salt and more bitter liquid; drain.

3. Heat coconut milk in heavy saucepan with garlic. Simmer to reduce by one-quarter to one-third. Add chillis and sliced banana buds. Boil gently until only a little soupy sauce remains and leaves are very tender, about 15 minutes or more.

Makes about 2 cups, to serve 4 as a side dish or condiment

Garlicky and Aromatic Banana Bud Salad

Turn simple steamed or grilled fish or poultry into an exotic meal with a bed of this intense, crunchy, fragrant condiment salad that combines elements of Cambodian, Thai, Vietnamese, and Malaysian cuisines.

> Juice of 1 lemon
> 2½ teaspoons kosher salt
> 3 cups plus 3 tablespoons lukewarm water
> 1 banana bud (1 to 1¼ pounds)
> 1 small garlic clove
> 1 small shallot, sliced
> 3 tablespoons sugar
> 3 tablespoons fish sauce
> ¼ cup lime juice
> ⅛ to ¼ teaspoon ground hot pepper
> ½ cup lightly packed mint leaves
> 1 cup lightly packed basil leaves
> 1 small red bell pepper
> 1 European (greenhouse) cucumber
> 1 very small banana
> ½ cup roasted, salted peanuts

1. Combine lemon juice, 2 teaspoons salt, and 3 cups water in a bowl. Slice off and discard tip of banana bud. Remove and discard several layers of red bracts and yellow flowers or "fingers" until you reach paler, more tender core. Cut each bract free from base, then unwrap from head, trying to keep whole. Discard all "fingers" as you proceed. Stack several bracts at a time, rolling to form a tight cigar, and then slice thin. Stir into lemon water.

2. Prepare dressing: Crush garlic and shallot to a paste with pestle in suribachi or mortar. Combine sugar, remaining 3 tablespoons water, and ½ teaspoon salt in a tiny pan and bring to a boil. Blend with garlic mixture; cool. Add fish sauce, 3 tablespoons lime juice, and hot pepper.

3. Drain banana bud and combine with dressing. Chill.

4. Rinse and spin-dry mint and basil leaves. If small, leave whole; if large, bunch and slice. Mince red pepper. Halve cucumber lengthwise. Scoop out seeds, preferably with melon ball cutter. Halve again lengthwise, then cut into thin slices. Dice banana. Toss with remaining 1 tablespoon lime juice.

5. Drain banana bud, reserving dressing. Toss with cucumber, red pepper, herbs, and banana to distribute evenly. Taste, then add seasoning or some reserved dressing or both. Sprinkle with peanuts.

Serves 4 to 6 as a side condiment salad

Pros Propose

In Southeast Asia, banana buds carry more weight than one might guess. Charmaine Solomon offers four recipes for these—and just three for cauliflower—in her hefty *Encyclopedia of Asian Food*. For **Thai Soup with Banana Flower:** Remove outer layers of banana bud. Boil bud 15 minutes. Cool, quarter lengthwise, and thin-slice, discarding any flowers ("fingers"). Combine with water, salt, thin-sliced lemon grass, lime leaves, galangal, chillies, and chopped garlic. Cover and simmer until bud is tender. Stir in thick coconut milk, fish sauce, and lime juice. Garnish with chopped coriander and scallion greens.

Banana Blossom Salad (from *Classic Thai Cuisine* by David Thompson) seems more a rich appetizer than a salad—particularly with its "chilli jam," a fierce flavoring that counters the banana astringency. To prepare the jam: Deep-fry shallot and garlic slices to brown; drain, then place in blender. Deep-fry dried chillis and dried shrimp 30 seconds. Drain and add to blender. Puree. For the salad: Quarter trimmed banana bud and discard flowers. Thin-slice bud. Soak in acidulated water. Boil coconut cream. Add chilli jam to taste, fish sauce, and palm sugar, stirring to dissolve. Bring to a boil, add shelled shrimp, and cook through. Add drained banana bud, lime juice, and roasted, coarse-ground peanuts. Serve hot with minced cilantro.

A more salad-like chicken-enriched **Banana Blossom Salad** comes from *The Elephant Walk Cookbook* by Longteine de Monteiro and Katherine Neustadt, which *does* teach about cleaning the bud. I only wish it had been published before I conducted my fruitless experiments! Make dressing: Caramelize sugar in small pan. Add water, more sugar, and salt. Cool, then add vinegar and minced garlic. Clean and slice banana buds as in Preparation (see page 49). Combine with cooked, shredded chicken breast, basil and mint leaves, mung bean sprouts, sliced red bell pepper, ground peanuts, and dressing.

Basella, Malabar Spinach (*Basella alba*)

Also Ceylon spinach, Malabar nightshade, slippery vegetable, saan choi
and variations (Chinese), poi (Indian), brèdes (French Caribbean)

Phooey on the whole mess of common names! Or phooi, which is another name I find on bins of basella in the Indian shops I frequent in Queens. Nightshade—but isn't that deadly? And spinach—modified by Indian, Surinam, Ceylon, climbing, vine, and Malabar (the most common). Open up a cookbook that mentions the vegetable, and you'll read that it is a strain of spinach. But it is *not* related to spinach, and if you expect it to be, you'll be taken aback when you eat it. The plant is distinct enough to have its own family, Basellaceae; spinach belongs to the Chenopodiaceae.

Basella is a love-it or leave-it vegetable, like okra—and for the same reason: sliminess. There! The truth is out, and you can stop right here if you hate sticky stuff. The Chinese name, saan choi, usually translated as "slippery vegetable," comes close. Martha Dahlen and Karen Phillipps write in *A Popular Guide to Chinese Vegetables* that "a better translation of . . . 'saan' is not slippery, but mucilaginous, and this second adjective quite accurately describes the eating texture of this vegetable."

The basella pictured here, from New York City's Chinatown, has fleshy, rubbery—yet crisp—leaves that are as juicy as purslane (page 513) and as mucilaginous as cactus pads (page 139). They taste earthy and tart, like a gentle blend of Swiss chard and sorrel. This green-leafed species (confusingly called *alba,* white, supposedly to distinguish it from the red-streaked *rubra*—a more logical name in this case) is one of three. All probably originated in India or Madagascar and are now cultivated in the tropics worldwide, with China, Africa, and India the major growers. It is people from these lands who demand basella in the United States, although it is not new here, having been introduced in seed catalogues of the early 19th century. Clearly, it was not a big hit. Perhaps a new wave of immigrants will teach us ways to appreciate it.

BASIC USE: Gardening books treat this plant as a salad green. Either the fresh-picked plant is very differ-

length: 11 inches

ent from the market bunches I have bought, or gardeners are very different from this taster. What I have sampled raw was out of the question.

Cooked, it is another—and delicious—matter. Basella is a wonderful soup subject, whether as the base for a slurpy stew or floated in clear broth. For the latter, the leaves feel and look like brilliant green egg noodles crossed with spinach, and the stems have the texture of well-cooked asparagus, minus the fiber.

Steam, drain, and chop basella; then include in the same kind of dishes as spinach (at this point it is comparable in use, if not taste and texture): quiches, soufflés, and casseroles.

SELECTION AND STORAGE: Basella is available in Asian, Chinese, and some Caribbean markets erratically during the year, with best volume and quality during the summer. Choose very firm, dry leaves with no trace of slipperiness. In good condition, the vegetable can be refrigerated up to a week in perforated plastic.

PREPARATION: Trim off and discard any very heavy base parts. Dunk vegetable in a sink filled with water. Lift out, letting sand sink. Repeat until no grit remains. For most dishes, you'll separate stems and leaves to cook. How you cut them will depend upon the recipe.

Sweet-Hot Basella Broth

Fast and simple, this gingery soup is for lovers of hot-sweet savors and slithery textures. As the leaves wilt, they exude a very thin gel that lends light, slippery body to the broth—primarily pineapple juice—which has just the right fruity-sour edge to balance the earthy basella. Prepare the tart soup at the last minute, or color and texture turn nasty.

Note that when the soup begins to heat up, it may be almost gelatinous. As it begins to simmer, it thins to the right texture. After that, it thins too much and the leaves turn drab—so don't overcook.

About ½ pound basella (Malabar spinach)
2 teaspoons vegetable oil
1 medium shallot, minced
Optional: 1 small garlic clove, minced
¼ to ½ teaspoon ground hot pepper
1 teaspoon curry powder or garam masala
2½ cups water or vegetable broth
1 teaspoon kosher salt
4 teaspoons very fine ginger julienne
About 1½ cups pineapple juice
1 to 3 teaspoons sugar
Lime wedges

1. Trim only the heaviest base from basella. Wash as many times as necessary, lifting out to let sand settle. Bunch together and slice lengthwise a few times, then crosswise into very thin strands.

2. Heat oil in saucepan over moderate heat. Stir in shallot, optional garlic, hot pepper, and curry. Stir a moment, then add water, salt, and half the ginger; bring to a boil. Reduce heat, cover, and simmer 5 minutes.

3. Return to a boil. Add basella and 1½ cups pineapple juice. Stir just until leaves lose their raw taste and broth thickens very slightly—a minute or two. Add remaining ginger, sugar, and pineapple juice to taste.

4. Ladle at once into small bowls. Serve with lime wedges—a must.

Serves 4 as a first course

Basella Raita

Steamed Malabar spinach creates a succulent base for an Indian-style sauce/salad that is both light and full-bodied—and slippery. Tart, earthy, roundly spoonable, the bright white and spruce green mix makes an attractive complement to grilled fish or lamb. But do not prepare it more than a few hours before serving, or both color and flavors fade. It's just lightly garlic-tinged: garlic lovers may prefer to add a sting of the raw bulb. I like the rounded flavor of full-fat or some low-fat yogurts; nonfat is too chalky and sharp for this.

1½ cups yogurt (preferably whole-milk)
½ pound basella (Malabar spinach)
3 medium garlic cloves, sliced
½ to 1 teaspoon grated lemon zest
½ to 1 teaspoon grated orange zest
¼ teaspoon kosher salt
¼ teaspoon pepper
1 to 2 tablespoons lemon juice

1. Scoop yogurt into a sieve lined with cheesecloth or paper towel. Drain while you prepare the remaining ingredients, or about ½ hour.

2. Trim only the heaviest base stems from basella. Dunk greens in plenty of water. Lift out. Repeat until no grit remains. Nip leaves from stems, stack or roll, and slice thin. Cut stems very thin.

3. Spread the greens on a rack over boiling water, top with garlic. Cover and steam until tender, about 10 minutes. Transfer to a colander. Cool slightly.

4. Press greens gently to squeeze out some liquid. Combine on cutting board with ½ teaspoon each lemon and orange zest, and the salt and pepper. Chop and blend. Combine in bowl with the drained yogurt and blend well. Add 1 tablespoon lemon juice.

5. Chill for an hour or two. Before serving, taste and season with additional salt, pepper, citrus zest, and lemon juice.

Makes 1½ cups, to serve 4

Mussel and Basella Gumbo

Basella replaces okra in this light soup-stew. Unlike traditional gumbos, this one derives its rich flavor from the strength of quick-cooked mussel broth, the deep green Malabar spinach savor, and a modicum of hot sausage, rather than from hours of cooking. The slippery finish associated with okra or filé powder, its usual sources, comes instead from the basella. Serve as a main course with baguettes and Fennel, Orange, and Green Olive Salad (page 277). Prepare the soup ahead of time if you like, up to the final addition of greens.

1 large onion
2 garlic cloves
2 tablespoons olive oil
½ cup dry sherry
2 pounds cultivated mussels
1 cup water
¾ pound basella (Malabar spinach)
3 medium celery stalks with leaves
1 green bell pepper
1 medium bunch scallions (green onions)
¼ pound hot garlic sausage, such as
   andouille or kielbasa
1 teaspoon kosher salt
¼ to ½ teaspoon ground hot pepper
1 teaspoon paprika
1 teaspoon dried thyme
½ teaspoon dried oregano
1 bay leaf, crumbled fine
1 fairly small parsley bunch

1. Dice or chop onion. Mince garlic. Heat 1 tablespoon oil in deep sauté pan or Dutch oven over moderate heat. Add garlic and half the onion; stir until softened. Add sherry and bring to a boil. Add mussels and water. Cover, bring to a boil, and cook until mussels just open, a matter of a few minutes.

2. With slotted spoon, lift mussels into a bowl. Pour broth into a 2-quart measure. Add water as needed to make 5 cups. Rinse and dry pan.

3. Trim off only heaviest base from basella. Rinse greens in plenty of water, lifting out to leave debris behind. Repeat until no grit remains in sink or bowl. Nip off leaves and slice thin. Chop remaining stems. Dice celery, reserving leaves. Dice green pepper. Trim scallions. Cut apart light and dark parts and thin-slice both. Cut sausage into small dice.

4. Heat remaining 1 tablespoon oil in same pan. Cook sausage over moderate heat to render fat. Add remaining onion, basella stems, diced celery, bell pepper, and light part of scallions. Cook, stirring often, until slightly browned, about 10 minutes. Add salt, hot pepper, paprika, thyme, oregano, and bay leaf; stir a minute or two.

5. Add mussel broth and half the basella leaves. Simmer, covered, until vegetables are soft, about 15 minutes.

6. Meanwhile, set aside 8 to 12 mussels. Remove others from their shells. Cut parsley leaves from stems, rinse, and chop coarse. Combine in a bowl with the scallion greens and remaining basella leaves. (Can be prepared ahead to this point. Chill mussels, greens, and soup separately.)

7. To serve, heat soup base to simmering. Add greens and bring to a boil, stirring. Add mussel meats and heat through. Meanwhile, heat mussels in shell in small pot. Mince celery leaves.

8. Season soup and ladle into wide shallow bowls. Garnish with mussels in the shell and sprinkle over celery leaves.

Serves 4 as a main course

Pros Propose

Soup is the place to put basella, or Malabar spinach, or slippery vegetable—or whatever you decide to call it. When Rosa Lo San Ross cleans what she calls slippery vegetable, she advises using tepid water with a little oil to help remove dirt. She says it is then unnecessary to add more oil to her **Slippery Vegetable–Chicken Soup:** Cut slippery vegetable into manageable pieces. Slice boneless, skinless chicken breasts into thin strips. Simmer unsalted chicken stock with ginger until flavored; discard ginger. Bring stock to a boil and stir in chicken, quickly and thoroughly separating pieces. When chicken whitens, add slippery vegetable, soy sauce, and black pepper. Simmer until greens are tender to taste. Season. Add minced scallions and cilantro leaves. Off heat, immediately stir in beaten egg, using a fork to make shreds (from *Beyond Bok Choy*).

For a thick pottage, there is **Potato and Spinach Soup** from Yamuna Devi, who finds that "Indian Malabar spinach . . . has a lemony bite, something like spring sorrel." To prepare: Melt ghee or butter in large saucepan. Stir in ground cardamom, coriander, and shredded coconut and toss briefly. Add trimmed Malabar spinach and thin-sliced peeled potatoes; toss for 2 minutes. Add vegetable stock and boil. Reduce heat and simmer until potatoes are soft. Add whole milk. Puree in batches until smooth. Season. In small pan, toast brown mustard seeds, partially covered, until they pop. Remove from heat. Add ghee or butter, and grated lemon zest. Pour into soup. Serve sprinkled with hot pepper or paprika (from *The Vegetarian Table: India*).

Beans, Shelling or Shell Beans

"Shellies" is an old-time Southern term for shelling beans—legumes with seeds that are plucked from their pods to be cooked fresh, not dried. I am borrowing the affectionate sobriquet to describe a diverse bowlful of pod-dwellers that would require a chapter of explanation to group accurately.

Just as fresh-shelled English peas have become an endangered species, so have fresh limas, cranberry beans, blackeye peas, and their kin. Once ordinary home fare, shellies are now delicacies for devotees who prize their gentle savor, tender texture, and *almost* American seasonality (few are imported). As with fresh green peas, careful cooking and simple presentation do more for these beans than wildly creative cuisine.

Shellies that have disappeared from the market have done so for the same reason: labor costs—whether for growing, harvesting, transporting, or shelling them. "Bean counters" do not approve of these beans. In a bottom-line era, cleaning limas on the porch until dusk is not a cost-efficient concept for restaurants. Nor does it fit a two-job family. Like many fine, simple foods, shellies are now limited to the plainest traditional meals (which they never left) and the most sophisticated dining rooms (where they're being discovered).

Before discussing distinctions, here are some similarities to help define shellies in general.

SELECTION: Fresh shell beans are mainly a summer treat, but some (notably favas) appear in spring as well. Look for plump, filled-out pods: Immature seeds are difficult to impossible to extract. Check for punctures or stains, indicating insect damage. Avoid "blanks" or "rattails" where beans have not developed. A hint of yellow is normal, but yellow pods are overmature; brown pods are over the hill. For colorful horticultural beans, such as Vermont Cranberry or Dragon Tongue, look for pods with subdued—not brilliant—hues, which are likely to be more tender and sweet.

STORAGE: Shellies are highly perishable. If they must be stored, refrigerate them no more than a few days at most, in baskets or paper bags—not plastic. Do not keep in the coldest area, but at 40° to 45°F if possible. Fluff them up every day to redistribute.

For longer storage, freeze them, as does chef Jeff Buben, a Southerner who cherishes a year-round supply: "At the end of the season, I buy as many coolers of shelled beans as come to the farmers' markets. I blanch them for 2 minutes with 3 parts sugar to 1 part salt for color and flavor. Then I drain them, cool them on sheet pans, and freeze in zipper-lock bags."

YIELD: There is great variability here. Very roughly, figure on 50 percent shell-out: 1 pound of cleaned beans for 2 pounds in the pod (less for limas and favas, more for most horticultural beans).

Warning: "Shell beans should not be used raw," cautions James Myers, a bean geneticist at Oregon State University in Corvallis. "They interfere with digestive processes and some have been known to cause more serious problems. Eating just a few raw mature seeds of common beans has been reported to kill small children." (Soybeans and favas, however, are not in this category.)

TO COOK: With the exception of favas and green soybeans, shellies need gentle cooking. Whether cooked stove-top or baked, near-simmering produces beans of uniform smoothness and prevents breakage; boiling blurs individuality and toughens texture. When it comes to seasoning shellies, restraint is best. "Fresh shell beans' texture and flavor are so special that the less you do to change them, the better," says chef Jody Adams. "Dried beans need their flavor punched up. Fresh ones need to be left alone."

Common Bean (*Phaseolus vulgaris*)

Also haricot or kidney bean

The common bean of commerce, the native American *Phaseolus vulgaris,* is not just a bean but a world of beans, embracing almost everything we call "bean"—from yellow wax to black turtle, from green (snap or string bean) to dried. The remarkable scope and multiple forms of this New World bean have made it among the most difficult plants to classify in either scientific or common terms.

For the common terms, one simplified example from *The Oxford Companion to Food* should suffice. As Alan Davidson recounts, when Europeans arrived in America, countless varieties of *Phaseolus vulgaris* with local names had already been cultivated for millennia in North and South America. But the "first samples . . . to reach Europe, in the 16th century, were of a dark red, kidney-shaped variety, so giving rise to the common English name kidney beans." In France, the bean landed with its "Aztec name, *ayecotl,* [which] was soon corrupted to haricot, a name which already had another meaning (a meat ragout) and another deriva-

tion (from *harigoter,* to cut up). This usage spread to England, with curious consequences; in the 18th century a dish might be called 'arrico of kidney beans.' "

Sticking with the shelly form of common beans to be had in the United States today narrows the field considerably (happily for some readers, unhappily for posterity; for bean diversity—indeed, crop diversity—dwindles daily). Just a few are harvested at an intermediate stage to be eaten fresh. They are represented here and there by green-podded Kentucky Wonder, Romano, and White Marrow. More often, there is a type generically referred to as **horticultural or cranberry or borlotto** beans.

Tongue of Fire, Vermont Cranberry, and French Horticultural are three examples of this type—all stunning. Their yellow green-to-cream pods are mottled or marbled with rose, wine, or scarlet; the tightly packed beans may be cream to pink, splashed with a range of reds similar to the pods.

Horticultural beans are starchy-sweet and mild, more neutral than other shellies—easy to eat, versatile, uncomplicated. Taut, smooth skins give way to creamy, floury interiors. They are usually a cinch to shell. Do not be seduced by the bird-of-paradise hues that many flaunt when mature; they change to those of house

horticultural (cranberry) beans

length: 5-6 inches

sparrows when cooked—beige with occasional brown or mauve speckles.

Basic Shell Beans

Slow, gentle cooking rather than boiling produces beans with a uniform texture and prevents skin breakage. Cooled in the cooking liquid, they remain moist and plump, with tight-fitting coats. If firmer beans with a dry texture and slightly more colorful skin are your preference (some like them this way in salads), boil the beans in unsalted water until just tender. Add salt to taste, then drain. For pronounced flavor, cook beans in broth with aromatics.

> 3 cups shelled fresh beans
> Optional: savory or thyme sprigs and/or
>   bay leaves
> 1 to 2 tablespoons butter, olive oil, or pork
>   or goose fat
> Salt

1. In heavy saucepan, combine beans, optional herbs, butter, and cold water to just cover. Bring to a boil.

2. Reduce heat to very low. Cover and cook until beans are uniformly tender, monitoring heat to keep below a simmer to prevent breakage. Timing varies: Small or thin beans may take 15 minutes, while larger beans may take 30. Taste often.

3. When beans are tender, add salt and other seasonings, if desired. Uncover and allow to cool in liquid. Remove herb sprigs or bay leaves.

Serves 4

Variations for Cooked Shell Beans

Add meat juices from a roast to the cooked beans with some of their cooking liquid. Or stir heavy cream into the drained beans; simmer until liquid reduces slightly and beans are creamy. Or cook minced shallots in butter; add the drained beans and minced fresh herbs. For a warm salad, drain beans and toss with olive oil or nut oil, lemon juice, and minced parsley and scallion greens, then serve at room temperature, with sliced chicory. Or gently cook chopped onions in butter, add drained beans

and equal parts cooked snap beans and cooked corn kernels, and heat through.

Baked Fresh Cranberry Beans and Escarole

Plump and shiny beans star in a main course perfumed with Provence. The bittersweet escarole softens and melts, thickening the broth and adding depth. Serve as a Sunday supper, with a platter of olives, fennel strips, radishes, and goat cheese. Although cranberry beans' sweet starchiness makes a fine foil for the dark greens, other shelling beans or southernpeas can be substituted for a different effect.

> 1 teaspoon fennel seeds
> 1½ teaspoons fresh thyme leaves
> 1½ teaspoons fresh rosemary leaves
> 1 medium head escarole (flat-leaf endive),
>   about 1¼ pounds
> 2 medium tomatoes
> 3 tablespoons olive oil
> 1 large garlic clove, sliced
> 1 teaspoon kosher salt
> ⅛ to ¼ teaspoon chilli flakes
> 3 cups shelled cranberry beans (about
>   2½ pounds in the pod)
> 2½ cups vegetable, duck, ham, or chicken broth
> 2 tablespoons thin-sliced scallion (green
>   onion) tops
> Fleur de sel or other crisp sea salt
> Pepper

1. Heat oven to 350°F. Mince together fennel seeds, thyme, and rosemary. Reserve one-third for garnish. Trim escarole. Quarter lengthwise, then cut each quarter crosswise into 1-inch strips. Rinse thoroughly in several changes of water; drain. Cut tomatoes into ¼-inch dice.

2. Heat 2 tablespoons olive oil in heavy ovenproof pot large enough to hold all ingredients. Stir in minced herbs, garlic, salt, and chilli flakes. Add escarole and half the tomato dice. Raise heat to high, and stir to wilt escarole and evaporate most liquid.

3. Add beans and broth. Spoon over remaining 1 tablespoon olive oil. Bring to a simmer. Cover and

bake until beans are creamy inside but still intact, about 50 minutes (but timing can vary from ½ hour to more than an hour, depending upon the type of bean).

4. Uncover. Fold in remaining tomato dice. Continue to bake, uncovered, until liquid reduces to slightly stewy consistency, about 15 minutes. Stir in reserved herbs and the scallions.

5. Ladle into serving bowls. Sprinkle each serving with crisp salt grains and pepper.

Serves 4

Pros Propose

"I think shell beans are well worth any work. I try to have them on the menu every day, and always fresh in season," says chef Scott Bieber (who comes from Kentucky, where beans take pride of place). "For the most part, I like fresh shell beans on their own, whether as a starter or main course." For **Borlotto Beans with Tuscan Kale:** Soften diced fennel, leek, onion, and minced garlic in olive oil. Add beans, a bundle of thyme and rosemary, and cold water. Simmer until about half cooked. Add fairly large pieces of Tuscan kale leaves and simmer to make a rather thick soup. To serve, shave Prince de Claverolle (or another sheep cheese) over each bowl; grind over black pepper.

Cheese finds its way into many bean dishes, hot and cold, such as a salad from chef Mario Batali, **Cranberry Bean Salad with Shallot Pickles and Cacio:** Combine red wine vinegar, water, sugar, salt, and fresh beet juice. Submerge sliced shallots in this. Refrigerate 24 hours or more. Boil shelled cranberry beans (Batali boils them to keep the color) in salted water until just barely al dente. Drop into ice water. Drain and spread on towels to dry. Toss with the pickled shallots, frisée pieces, and olive oil. Divide among chilled plates. Shave shards of Cacio di Roma or another firm sheep's milk cheese onto each.

Chef Fortunato Nicotra prepares **Cranberry Bean and Olive Puree** as a savory spread for thin crackers: Combine celery, onion, carrot, parsley, tomato, and cranberry beans; add water to cover, and simmer until tender. Pick out and discard vegetables. Drain beans. Whiz to a paste with garlic, lemon and orange zests, and pitted Gaeta olives. Gradually add olive oil, making a fairly coarse, thick puree.

In an elegant departure from Mediterranean olive oil or the pork flavoring typical of the South, Alsatian-born chef Jean Joho seasons legumes with luxury shellfish. For **Fricassee of Lobster and Cranberry Beans:** Combine beans with light lobster stock and bake, uncovered, until not quite done ("beans develop more flavor when you reheat them to finish cooking"). Let cool. To serve, reheat beans in their stock with big lobster chunks. Spoon into individual oval gratin dishes, spread over a light coating of whipped cream, and add a touch of Parmesan. Bake at 450°F until golden, about 5 minutes.

Lima Bean/Butter Bean

(*Phaseolus lunatus*)

Also "baby" lima, sieva (and variations, below), butter pea

Limas are one of those rare foods with a common name that makes sense. Early examples (7000 to 5000 B.C., depending upon the authority cited) *were* unearthed in Peru (although Brazil may be home to the very earliest), and Europeans *did* discover them in Lima. Although there are lima beans of strikingly different form, color, and size, they are usually grouped as one species, *Phaseolus lunatus;* but some distinguish the larger ones as *Phaseolus limensis*. Limas are found in markets from Africa to Madagascar to Myanmar to the Philippines, but few fresh ones can be found in the United States, where dried and frozen lima beans are the norm. Dried, we have white-seeded, marbled, and multicolored types: huge pale Gigantes; chestnut and calico beans; and Christmas limas, among others. Frozen, they are lima bean green.

Fresh lima beans, if you can locate them (farmers' markets are the best bet) are usually the same varieties as frozen, but they taste dramatically different. In the South, where shellies are a passion and an art, you'll find a wider range. Called butter beans there, they have other names, and forms, distinct from those in the rest

lima (butter) beans   length: 3-6 inches

of the country. Large ones are green or speckled—the latter having an unusually creamy texture and a sharp earthy flavor quite unlike the pale green ones. Small ones are known in different Southern regions as Carolina bean or civet, seewee, and sivvy—all corruptions of sieva bean, a name for small limas. So-called dwarf butter beans or butter peas, white and speckled, even smaller than sieva beans, are also limas.

Succulent, smooth, and elegant, these fresh legumes deserve prominent positions. Small ones may be less starchy than larger ones, but both types are vivid and vegetably—closer to fresh favas than to horticultural beans—and require less cooking than common shell beans. Put them in starring roles, as you would favas: Float them in Asian broths, toss with small shrimp or lobster bits; simmer with butter or cream, fleck with chives and chervil, and serve in a little china dish. Toss warm limas with olive oil and lemon, or top with ground sumac.

Shelling limas can be tricky. The more tender and full the pods, the easier to handle. Most heavy-podded limas are best cut open with scissors to extract the seeds. For small limas, destring and press open, and pop out the beans.

Warning: Do not nibble raw lima beans. They contain linamarin, which releases a cyanide compound (deactivated by cooking) when the bean's seed coat is ruptured.

Creamy Lima Beans with Horseradish

Limas can be cooked as Basic Shell Beans (page 57), but they are particularly pleasing in cream. Like horticultural beans, they require gentle cooking to keep the interior smooth and skins intact. Also like horticultural beans, limas are more luscious if cooled in their cooking liquid, then reheated, rather than being served freshly cooked. Spoon alongside roasted veal, lamb, chicken, or pheasant.

> 3 to 3½ cups shelled fresh limas
>   (about 2½ pounds in the pod)
> About ⅔ cup heavy cream
> Salt and sugar
> About 2 teaspoons prepared horseradish

1. In heavy 2-quart saucepan combine beans, ½ cup cream, and cold water to barely cover beans. Bring to a simmer. Cover, reduce heat, and maintain near a simmer until beans are not yet creamy-tender, but cooked. Timing varies, but 15 minutes is likely for medium limas. Check now and then to be sure beans are not boiling and to stir.

2. Uncover and simmer gently, stirring often with rubber spatula until interior of beans is almost puree-tender and cream has thickened a bit. Again, timing varies, but 15 to 20 minutes is fairly likely. Add a big pinch each of salt and sugar.

3. Remove saucepan from heat and let cool completely. Refrigerate until serving time.

4. To serve, heat gently, partly covered. Add cream for desired consistency, if necessary. Stir in 1½ teaspoons horseradish. Gradually add more to taste, as well as salt and sugar.

Serves 4

Variation

Creamy Baby Lima Beans

If you have delicate little limas (which are less starchy and have a brighter flavor), cook for a shorter time and serve as a pure and simple first course—without horseradish. Instead, add more cream in step 4. Season with salt, sugar, and white pepper. Spoon into small bowls and sprinkle sparingly with slivered chives and chervil.

Pros Propose

The much missed chef Felipe Rojas-Lombardi, whose Ballroom Restaurant and Tapas Bar introduced sophisticated Latin American flavors to New York City, was born in Peru, where limas are a birthright. **Baby Lima**

Beans Braised in Lemon is typical of his eclectic and aromatic recipes: Heat butter and olive oil: Stir in minced Jalapeño, roasted pine nuts, limas, a little water, lemon juice, and salt. Simmer, stirring occasionally, until beans are barely tender and have absorbed the liquid. Stir in butter mashed with grated lemon rind, thin-sliced green onions, and plenty of shredded fresh mint leaves (from *The Art of South American Cooking*).

Ronni Lundy, a Kentuckian, loves beans enough to to title her paean to the South *Butter Beans to Blackberries*. For a homey brunch, she likes **Mixed Beans with Coddled Eggs:** Combine butter beans with just enough water to cover and simmer until tender. Add an equal amount of green beans cut into bite-size pieces, plenty of butter, and water if needed. Simmer, covered, 10 minutes. Add minced onions and simmer until limas are creamy and green beans very tender. Transfer to individual baking dishes. Form an indentation in each and break an egg into it. Top with melted butter. Bake until whites turn translucent. Serve with warm buttered toast.

Newfangled corn and beans, as **Swirled Succotash Soup,** comes from Virginia food and wine writer Sarah Belk King: In two covered pots, separately simmer fresh small limas and an equal amount of corn kernels in chicken broth to not quite cover until tender. Puree limas and broth until smooth in food processor, then press through sieve back into pot. Do same to corn. Stir a little crème fraîche into each mixture and heat through. Season. Half-fill warmed soup bowls with lima puree, add corn puree, and swirl with a spoon. Sprinkle with julienned dry-cured country ham.

Lima lovers are not limited to the Americas. For a sweet and spicy approach, try **Lima Beans with Golden Raisins** from *Lord Krishna's Cuisine* by Yamuna Devi: Add shelled fresh limas to boiling water. Reduce heat to low and cook until not quite tender. Add ghee or unsalted butter and a small amount each of ground paprika, mustard, and turmeric. Stir in golden raisins, jaggery or brown sugar, lime or lemon juice, salt, chopped fresh coriander, and a little water. Simmer, partly covered, until beans are tender. Uncover, raise heat, and reduce liquid to a glaze.

Southernpea, Cowpea

(*Vigna unguiculata*)

Also blackeye or black-eyed pea, field pea

Of African, not American, origin, the southernpea does not belong to the genus *Phaseolus,* as do common and lima beans. It is still grown widely in Africa, as well as Asia, India, and the Caribbean. In the United States, it is cultivated in and associated with the South—even more so than the beans discussed here—primarily because of the plant's need for a long, hot growing season. In fact, few legume lovers outside Southern states have sampled this group of deeply flavorful peas (also called beans) in their fresh form.

Generally, southernpeas exhibit more assertive personalities than the starchier, milder, softer common beans and limas. Firm and nutty, some are closer in texture and flavor to the yard-long bean (page 718), a subspecies grown extensively in China and Southeast Asia for its fresh green pods rather than its seeds. To help make order of the diverse southernpeas, Blair Buckley, a breeder at the Calhoun Research Center at Louisiana State University, puts them into the following groups, beginning with the most delicate and winding up with the most intense.

Cream or lady pea type: Slim, pale yellow-greenish pods, some dappled with mauve, hold small pearly peas without an apparent apparent "eye" (the hilum, the point where the pea is attached to the pod). Cooked, they are fresh and light in color and flavor. Tender yet almost crisp, they are a graceful accent to mild meats, seafood, or pasta. Go easy on seasoning: butter or cream and a touch of sugar and salt should suffice.

Pinkeye purple hull type: Burgundy to green pods (with marbled variations between) contain peas that vary from small to large and are drab green to pinkish-tan with rose eyes. While more pronounced in flavor than common beans, they are closer in texture and application to these than other cowpeas are. Plump and full when cooked, they are high-yield, easy to handle, all-purpose, with a very slight sweetness almost like a dried bean. They take to the same seasonings as kidney beans or blackeyes—such as salty, porky, and herbal backdrops, whether Southern or Italian style.

Blackeye type: Yellow-green pods contain tightly packed, green to tan, small to large peas that do indeed

southernpeas or cowpeas: pinkeye purple hull (*left*) and cream or lady pea types length: 7-10 inches

southernpeas or cowpeas: blackeye (*left*) and another pinkeye purple hull   length: 7-10 inches

have a brown to black eye at each hilum. Cooked, they are smooth and floury, with a taste akin to oily yard-long beans, but lighter, a bit mushroomy, without sweetness. Traditional Southern smoky-porky seasonings complement them, as do spices, coconut milk, and other Asian ingredients. Do not be shy with seasoning, but do not overwhelm the beans.

Crowder type: Green- to gray-podded crowder peas are truly crowded with peas—so much so that they are misshapen. Cooked, the tan to gray-green peas yield deep-brown juices and develop flavor as intense as the hues. They seem to be the most love-it or leave-it of Southern legumes—and a strong regional favorite.

Shelling southernpeas takes time. Although some leap from the pod in merry profusion, some hang back and refuse to be extracted. The variations are from batch to batch and pod to pod—not type to type. I asked chef Louis Osteen, of Charleston, how anyone could shell enough cowpeas to make a meal. He responded, in de-lib-er-ate-ly slow cadence: "You set on the front porch and shell until the sun goes down—or you buy 'em shelled, the way I do, and pay more."

Warning: Do not believe the particulars above about southernpeas! There are so many different col-

ors, shapes, styles, and flavors that all generalizations are suspect—mine included.

Warm Southernpea, Fennel, and Tomato "Salad"

Not exactly a salad or a side dish, this mélange plays both roles. (For a more salad-like look, serve on small mustard and spinach leaves.) Cowpeas are tossed with a mix of barely wilted fennel strips, tomato, and red onion, and sharpened with mustard seeds. When the dish is freshly made, the peas contrast with the crisp vegetables; reheated, the textures and colors become more uniform and the effect is more starchy, less vegetably—but just as tasty.

1 pound blackeye, pinkeye, or other cowpeas
    (1½ cups shelled)
2 to 3 tablespoons olive oil
About 1 teaspoon kosher salt
3 medium tomatoes
1 small fennel bulb with greens

1 medium red onion

2 teaspoons mustard seeds

½ teaspoon fennel seeds

2 tablespoons cider vinegar or red wine vinegar

½ teaspoon sugar

1. Shell peas. Combine with cold water to barely cover in heavy pot. Add ½ tablespoon oil and bring to a boil. Reduce heat to lowest point, cover, and cook until peas are fully tender, about 25 minutes (but timing varies). Add ½ teaspoon salt, then cool in liquid. (Can be made ahead and refrigerated.) Drain, saving liquid for soup or sauce.

2. Meanwhile, flame-peel tomatoes (see Note, page 10, for method). Halve, seed, and dice. Toss in a sieve with ¼ teaspoon salt; let drain.

3. Cut off fennel greens and reserve. Cut off stalks and heavy outer layer and cut out core (save for broth). Cut fennel bulb into thin julienne strips about an inch long. Dice onion.

4. In large skillet, heat 1½ tablespoons oil. Add mustard and fennel seeds and stir and shake over moderate heat until they pop wildly (keep a cover at hand to prevent escapees), about 1 minute. Add fennel and red onion and toss 1 minute, just to lose their raw crunch. Add vinegar, sugar, and tomatoes; toss to heat through. Add drained peas and toss to just heat. Remove from heat.

5. Chop enough reserved fennel greens to yield about ¼ cup. Stir into peas with salt and oil to taste. Serve warm or at room temperature.

Serves 4 as a side dish

Pros Propose

For the ultimate combination of haute and humble, there's **Foie Gras Sauté with Blackeye Peas** from The Inn at Little Washington, Virginia. "In the 1980s, the great food editor, Craig Claiborne—who came here every year for his birthday—wrote about the dish in *The New York Times*," says Patrick O'Connell, chef and co-owner, "and we've kept it on the menu ever since." To prepare: Combine ham skin and fat, bay leaves, chopped onion, lots of thyme, and peppercorns in cheesecloth bag. Combine with blackeye peas, water

to cover, and a little balsamic vinegar; simmer gently until tender. Drain; discard bag. While still warm, combine peas with tarragon vinaigrette. Spoon onto plate. Surround with lightly dressed small greens. Top each with a small, thin slice of cooked country ham, then seared foie gras. Deglaze pan with minced shallot, garlic, and balsamic. Spoon over foie gras and top with sliced green onion.

Chef Jeff Buben's more traditional **Southernpea Ragoût** serves as a base for pork chops or squab: Score streak o' lean bacon. Brown and render, keeping fat. Sweat trimmed halved leeks, whole destringed celery, halved peeled onion, and peeled carrot briefly in fat. Add pinkeye purple hulls; a sachet of thyme, bay leaves, peppercorns, and chicken broth. Cover and simmer gently until peas are tender, tasting often. Strain, reserving broth. Spread vegetables, bacon, and peas on sheet pan and chill. To serve, cut vegetables and bacon into fine dice. Add to beans and heat through with reserved broth.

Chef Louis Osteen's rich **Tomato Stuffed with Late Summer Succotash** contains cream peas (both White Acre and Zipper Cream) and pinkeye purple hulls, simmered with the typical pork backdrop: Boil fatback with water in three pots. When tasty, add one kind of peas to each, top up with chicken stock, and simmer until "tender—not soft and not al dente." Drain broth from all and combine; reduce as much as possible without its becoming too salty. Combine peas and reduction. Add corn kernels cooked in butter and cream, minced shallot, chives, and parsley. Peel, core, and remove pulp (save for another dish) from "really ripe really big" tomatoes; season, add butter, and bake to soften slightly. Fill with pea mixture "and bake until real nice and tender, a little collapsed."

Chef Cory Mattson prefers peas al dente. He considers the firm texture of blackeyes to be their most distinct asset and has his own views on how to best display it: "Do not salt while cooking; simmer just until barely tender; and chill as soon as cooked." He prefers aromatics to Southern pork seasoning for **Baked Goat Cheese on Blackeye Pea Salad:** Combine peas, onion, garlic cloves, bay leaves, and water to cover. Simmer until al dente. Drain, spread on sheet pan, and chill. Prepare tart marinade of mustard powder, dried oregano, olive oil, and red wine vinegar. Combine with grilled red onion slices; marinate, then dice. Make basil dressing: Blend cider vinegar and basil to slush, adding as much basil as possible. Add olive oil; season. Dice unpeeled Granny Smith apple and skinned, seeded tomato; mix with peas, onions, and basil dressing. Coat goat cheese logs with minced basil, chive blossoms, oregano, and thyme. Cut slices; bake to soften. Let stand 5 minutes to firm. Spoon salad onto greens; top with cheese.

Peas are fired up and sweetened in an Indian-inspired dish from *Yamuna's Table* by Yamuna Devi. For her simple, spicy **Warm Black-Eyed Peas:** Heat olive oil in sauté pan. Add chopped Serrano chillis, grated ginger, and cumin seeds; sauté until seeds darken a little. Add a generous quantity of diced yellow bell pepper and sauté a few minutes. Add maple syrup, lime juice, cooked and drained black-eyed peas, and chopped cilantro. Heat through and season.

Fava Bean (*Vicia faba* and *Faba vulgaris*)

Also broad bean, English bean

length: 3-7 inches

This venerable mainstay of the Old World has been cultivated for so long that its wild ancestors and place of origin are no longer traceable. While favas are common fare from China to England (as broad beans), Iran to Spain, and Africa to South America, it is their association with Provence and parts of Italy that probably accounts for their current renaissance in the United States. Although the beans were introduced to North America at the start of the 1600s, they fell out of favor toward the mid-1800s. Thanks to the present-day passion for Mediterranean cuisines, upper echelon restaurants now offer what is one of the kitchen's most labor-intensive fancy legumes in fashion—for it can no longer be considered a staple.

Like artichokes, favas demand considerable trimming (shelling, blanching, and peeling) to get to the edible parts, and they produce more waste than comestible parts. Like artichoke hearts, they yield subtly bittersweet nuggets of flesh. But once skinned, the nutty favas—unlike artichokes—require no further preparation and offer a uniquely verdant primavera presentation (although the green form in our markets is but one of many varieties cultivated worldwide).

Fresh fava beans are more an accent vegetable than other legumes. Blanched and skinned, they taste less like starch than like green vegetable plus nut. A distinct personality to be savored alone or with a few choice ingredients, fava must not be hidden or overcooked. "The less you do to them, the more beautiful they are," says chef Jody Adams. "I feel they are one of those foods that should be treated with almost ritualistic simplicity."

ABOUT SHELLING AND SKINNING FAVAS: For some dishes, such as rustic stews and thick purees, fava skin lends a pleasing chewy texture and cheesy flavor. Generally, though, it is too coarse and bitter. Most beans sold in the United States must be shelled and skinned. To do this: Cut tips from the pod, then press open the seam. Pull the fat beans from the plush where they nestle, nipping off any stems or sprouts. Drop into boiling salted water. Return to a boil; cook 30 to 60 seconds depending on size—but no more, or they may squish when you skin them. Drain; drop into ice water (some chefs let them cool naturally). With your fingernails, pinch off a strip of skin at the top of each bean where it attaches to the pod. With the other hand, squeeze skin at the bottom to pop out the bean (projecting it from the skin without touching it). The yield is minimal; the eating pleasure is maximal.

Note: Robert Meyer, owner of Stoney Plains Farm in Tenino, Washington, who has has grown fresh favas and sold them in farmers' markets for a dozen years, claims that "you don't need to double-peel favas that are grown properly and really fresh. The skin is nearly transparent, like cellophane. Chefs should work directly with farmers if they want favas in top shape."

Warning: Fava beans should be avoided by anyone taking antidepressants of the MAO-inhibitor type. In addition, the beans can cause severe anemia in a small number of people of Mediterranean origin (and some Africans, Arabs, and Asians) who suffer from glucose-6-phosphate dehydrogenase deficiency, an inherited imbalance. One hopes they know who they are before they sit down to your table.

Fava and Avocado Crostini

For this dish, the unpeeled beans are braised, then pureed for a chunky, chewy toast topping. Avocado replaces the customary olive oil, offering color, creaminess, and sweetness. The effect is more complex than you might expect—as if herbs and cheese had been added. For variation, add a modicum of slivered mint or basil leaves or both.

> 3 pounds fava beans
> 2 tablespoons olive oil
> 2 large garlic cloves, crushed
> About 1 teaspoon kosher salt
> 1 small, very rich avocado, such as Hass or Fuerte
> About 1½ tablespoons lemon juice
> Hot pepper sauce
> About 2 dozen slices cut from a baguette or narrow ciabatta
> Optional: olive oil to brush on crostini

1. Preheat oven to 400°F. Shell favas. Drop into boiling water, return to a boil and cook 30 seconds. Drain, drop into cold water, and drain again. Set aside about one-quarter of the beans.

2. Combine remaining favas in heavy saucepan with olive oil, garlic, and 1 teaspoon salt. Cover and simmer gently until garlic is soft and fava skin fairly tender, about 10 minutes, crushing and stirring so flavors penetrate.

3. Meanwhile, with fingernails, break skin of each reserved fava, then press to pop out bean, working carefully to avoid breakage. Slide apart the two seed halves. Reserve.

4. Transfer fava-garlic mixture to food processor. Chop fine, scraping sides often. Scoop into mixing bowl. Halve, seed, peel, and dice avocado. Add to bowl with 1 tablespoon lemon juice. Crush to coarse texture. Fold in peeled favas, hot pepper sauce, and lemon juice and salt to taste.

5. Toast bread on baking sheet in 400°F oven until crunchy on the outside but still slightly chewy within. (For richer crostini, brush top side lightly with olive oil before toasting.)

6. Spread fava mixture on warm crostini. Serve at once.

Makes about 1½ cups spread for about 2 dozen crostini; serves 5 to 6 as an hors d'oeuvre

Risotto of Favas, Country Ham, and Savory

I was delighted with this springtime risotto laced with pink ham bits and bright green favas—until I discovered that despite my effort to be original, I had developed a similar recipe for *Uncommon Fruits & Vegetables: A Commonsense Guide*. Some recipes are just meant to be! This version is milder (no smoky bacon and strong sage), to better showcase the favas. Serve as a main course, followed by Salad of Treviso, Enokitake, Water Cress, and Hazelnuts (page 519).

> 2 to 2½ pounds fava beans
> About 6 large scallions (green onions) or 3 or 4 medium bulbing spring onions
> One 2-ounce slice prosciutto or Smithfield-type country ham
> 1 garlic clove
> 1½ tablespoons olive oil
> 1½ cups Italian rice for risotto
> ¼ cup very dry sherry
> 6 cups unsalted or very lightly salted vegetable and/or chicken broth

About 1 tablespoon minced summer savory
leaves
About ¾ cup grated Parmesan or Pecorino
Romano cheese
Salt and white pepper

1. Shell, blanch, and peel favas as described on page
64. You should have a generous cup or so.

2. Thin-slice scallions (or spring onions) to yield
about 1 cup (for larger spring onions, halve bulbs before slicing). Cut prosciutto into ¼-inch squares (do
not trim fat). Mince garlic.

3. In heavy saucepan, heat oil over moderate heat.
Add prosciutto and stir until lightly browned. Reduce
heat slightly, add scallions and garlic, and stir until softened but not browned. Add rice and stir 2 minutes.
Add sherry, stirring to evaporate.

4. Meanwhile, heat broth to not-quite-simmering
in another pan. Ladle ¾ cup into rice. Adjust heat so
that rice simmers in a lively fashion but does not stick,
stirring often, until liquid is almost absorbed. Continue
adding broth in ½-cup increments and stirring as
needed until each is almost absorbed.

5. In 13 to 15 minutes or so (depending upon the
type of rice), the grains will be nearly done—still firm,
but no longer hard in the center. At this point, add
favas, 2 teaspoons savory, and more broth. In a few
minutes, the risotto should be properly tender.

6. Stir in enough broth to make a creamy, slightly
soupy mixture. Stir in ¼ cup cheese and salt, white
pepper, and savory to taste. Spoon into heated bowls.
Serve at once, with remaining cheese on the side.

Serves 4 as a main course, 6 to 8 as a first course

Favas and Pearl Onions with Olives and Herbs

Favas cooked in their skins are yellowy green and chewy-
starchy rather than apple green and smooth. Preparing
the dish this way gives a higher yield, adds subtle fermented flavor, and saves considerable preparation time.
Choose favas that are not overmature, or the skins will be
tough. Open a pod or two to check that the beans show
no black seams where they attach to the pod.

Offer as a room temperature appetizer, with tiny
sweet tomatoes and bread sticks. Or serve hot with
braised or roasted lamb or pork and a side of baked
tomatoes. For vegetarians, stuff the tomatoes, and add
some sautéed greens. The duo of herbs adds depth but
is not strictly necessary; one will do.

About ¾ pound pearl (baby or mini) onions
2½ to 3 pounds fava beans
3 to 4 tablespoons flavorful olive oil
1 large garlic clove, bruised
½ cup water
1 teaspoon sugar
About 2 teaspoons minced fresh thyme or
lemon thyme leaves
12 to 16 oil-cured black olives, pitted or not
(as preferred)
About 2 tablespoons lemon juice
½ teaspoon kosher salt
About 1 teaspoon minced fresh rosemary or
oregano leaves
Pepper

1. Cover onions with boiling water; let stand while
you shell favas. When beans have been shelled, drain
onions. Trim their tips and roots, then peel. If peeled
onions are wider than an inch, halve them.

2. Heat 2 tablespoons oil in heavy skillet large
enough to hold all ingredients closely. Add onions and
garlic and toss over moderate heat until browned in
spots, about 5 minutes. Add favas, water, sugar, and 1
teaspoon thyme. Cover and simmer gently, stirring
often, until beans are tender, about 15 minutes.

3. Stir in olives, another tablespoon of olive oil, 1
tablespoon lemon juice, and salt. Cover and cook to
blend flavors and plump olives, about 5 minutes longer.
Uncover. If any liquid remains, simmer momentarily
to evaporate. Stir in rosemary and additional thyme,
oil, salt, pepper, and lemon juice to taste. Remove
garlic.

4. Transfer to serving dish and serve hot, warm, or
at room temperature. Or cool, cover, and chill. Return
to room temperature or reheat gently to serve, seasoning again.

Serves 4

Pros Propose

Most chefs are purists about favas, serving them with just a few additions. Salty cheese is the usual foil, as in **Grilled Pecorino with Fava Bean Salad** from Fortunato Nicotra: Blanch favas and peel while still warm. Toss with olive oil, fresh mint, and garlic. Grill ½-inch slices medium-hard pecorino cheese until just colored on each side. Put warm cheese on plate; spoon over favas.

Chef Jody Adams has served her version of **Salad of Fresh Favas and Pecorino** for years, refining it to the present combination. Mix blanched, skinned favas with lemon juice, grilled and halved red onion rings, olive oil, and arugula; season. Top with three types of pecorino and serve with red wine biscuits.

For an appetizer spread, **Pistachio and Fava Puree,** unpeeled beans are flavored, enriched, and colored with pistachios: In food processor, pulse toasted, skinned pistachios to a coarse consistency. Crush blanched fava beans; add olive oil, minced garlic, and Pernod. Mix in nuts and a little grated romano. Chill and spread on fennel slices (from *The Vegetarian Compass* by Karen Hubert Allison).

For **Fava Bean Ragoût with Crostini,** chef Scott Bieber serves crusty bread over, not under, the beans: Gently cook very fine dice of fennel, leek, and garlic in olive oil until translucent. Add blanched, skinned favas and rosemary-thyme bouquet, cover with cold water, and simmer until very tender. Spoon onto plates; top with long slices of baguette that have been brushed with olive oil, baked, and swiped once with a garlic clove. Drizzle with the finest olive oil. For a main course, prepare favas as above, but half-cook. Add a fine julienne of savoy cabbage, then complete cooking. Top with poached Alaskan cod.

Another fish-and-fava pairing features more intense seafood flavors. For chef Wayne Nish's **Poached Black Sea Bass with Fricassee of Favas:** Soften shallot and garlic in olive oil. Add blanched, skinned favas and light fish stock to barely cover. Cook a few minutes, until tender. Add a touch of mixed herbs (parsley, chives, basil, and tarragon). Add a portion of black sea bass with skin, a squash blossom, and a sprinkle of sea salt. Cover and cook through.

A spring classic, **Pappardelle alla Romana,** is interpreted simply by chef Nicotra: Soften thin-sliced leeks and garlic in oil. Add raw peas and toss a moment, then add blanched, sliced baby artichokes and blanched,

skinned favas. Simmer gently until juicy. Add vegetable stock to moisten ("this is a favorite vegetarian entree"). Toss with whole-wheat pappardelle. Add mint and grated pecorino, "which are always the best finish for favas."

If you have access to small, young favas, cook them in the pod for a messy and delicious stew that suggests okra and spinach. For **Stewed Favas, Leeks, and Lemon:** Cut trimmed, halved leeks into ½-inch slices. Remove tips from fava pods; then remove "strings" from both sides of each pod with a paring knife or peeler. Cut pods into sections between the bean bumps. Simmer leeks in olive oil to soften slightly. Add favas, lemon juice, salt, and water; cover tightly, and simmer until very soft, from ¾ to 1½ hours. Stir now and then, adding water if mixture sticks. If too soupy, uncover and simmer briefly. Serve at room temperature with olive oil, lemon juice, and seasoning. Sop up juices with pita or lavash (from *Uncommon Fruits & Vegetables: A Commonsense Guide*).

Soybean, Green (*Glycine max*)

Also vegetable soybean,
fresh soybean, edamame or
eda mame (Japanese)

Fresh green soybeans in the pod have only recently come to the attention of Americans, through Japanese restaurants, where they are called edamame (ed-ah-mah-may) and served as nibbles before a meal: The small, flattened pods are briefly boiled, salted, then slurped (or politely plucked) to extract the firm, buttery seeds.

Resembling plump, petite limas, these beans of Chinese origin were developed in Japan especially for eating at the green shell stage. They are green-seeded variants of the same yellow-and-black field soybean that is transformed into tofu, miso, tempeh, fermented black beans, soy sauce, soymilk, and other building blocks of Far Eastern cuisine. Dramatically different from that mature starchy legume, this form is as vivid as fresh favas—and the same apple green.

green soybeans   length: 2-3 inches

What astonishes is how long it has taken for us to recognize the delights of the young green pods, given that soybeans have been a major crop in the United States since the 1950s, according to the breeder Thomas Carter, who specializes in soybeans for his work with the Agricultural Research Service of the USDA in Raleigh, North Carolina. "Before 1915, soy was a minor forage crop in the United States," he says, "and then oil was discovered—in the bean! This led to the switch from a forage to a seed crop. By 1930 soy production was 50 percent for seed, and by 1950 the change was nearly complete."

Green soy production is in its infancy in the United States. "Of the seventy million acres of soybeans we have in this country, just a few hundred are given over to edamame," says Thomas Carter. But he and other breeders (and chefs) see great potential. Part of the appeal may be sweetness. According to James R. Myers, a bean geneticist at Oregon State University, "One of the characteristics of a good edamame variety is the sugar level in the seed. It is sweeter than other beans— almost as sweet as English peas." Carter thinks we may someday grow fresh soy in greenhouses, year-round, as the Japanese do.

Until you've nibbled these toothsome tidbits, it may be difficult to believe that plain boiled beans can be so special, but they are: Boil al dente, rinse to cool slightly, then sprinkle with coarse salt. Or shell the beans and add to tofu dishes, composed salads, or rice or seafood dishes; or toss in butter with another vegetable or two. Treat more or less as fava beans, skinned or not. Shelling is easily accomplished after a brief boil.

Basic Fresh Green Soybeans

Delicious and healthful, this simple snack or appetizer is a snap to prepare and thoroughly rewarding. Serve a warm platterful and let guests pop the beans from the pods to nibble with wine or beer like salted nuts— without the high fat content.

Alternatively, shell the beans and add them to composed salads or warm grain dishes. Or put together a summery sauté to brighten grilled poultry or fish: Cook the prepared beans in butter with corn kernels, then add fresh tomato dice and minced chives and heat through.

1 pound small green soybeans in the pod
Coarse salt

1. Rinse pods well. Drop into a large pot of boiling water. Return to a boil over highest heat. Boil until beans are just tender and have lost their raw taste, 3 to 5 minutes.

2. Drain and cool slightly under running water; drain again. Sprinkle generously with salt.

3. Serve at room temperature, with a separate dish for discarded pods.

Serves 4 to 5 as an appetizer or snack

Pros Propose

From traditional Japanese treatments to newfangled American "succotash," fresh soybeans are finding their way into the vegetable repertoire. For the authentic, chef Masaharu Morimoto purees soybeans in a thin, smooth **Green Edamame Sauce:** Shell, blanch, and skin beans as you would favas. Press through a fine sieve. Mix with dashi (stock). Thicken with kuzu starch if needed. Serve over fish or steamed silken tofu. His **Fish Fillet with Green Edamame Crust and Sauce** "is not for Japanese tradition," says Morimoto, who calls it "my green dish." To prepare, toss blanched, skinned edamame (save some for garnish) and olive oil on a sheet pan. Bake in moderate oven until dried. Crush to particles. Combine with bread crumbs, ground coriander, garlic powder, and shredded potato. Spread a thick layer on fish fillets. Brown the coated side in hot butter: Turn and cook to just color. Serve with Green Edamame Sauce seasoned with shoyu. Garnish with chopped reserved beans.

Warm Salad of Santa Barbara Shrimp and Green Soybeans from chef Jean Joho has touches of France, California, and the Far East: Blanch soybeans and remove from pods. Sauté unpeeled shrimp in hot grapeseed oil. Remove and shell. Return shrimp to pan with soybeans, and toss to blend juices. Add hazelnut and walnut oils and sherry vinegar. Stir in a hint of fresh marjoram, chives, and parsley, and scoop onto a bed of tiny frisée.

Green soybeans and garlic transform an old favorite into **Edamame Succotash,** which chef Matt Costello developed for local growers in Washington state: Combine cold milk and peeled garlic cloves in saucepan and bring to a boil. Cool. Drain garlic; discard milk. Puree garlic, adding enough heavy cream to make a thin sauce. Boil, then shell green soybeans. Combine with equal quantities of cooked fresh cranberry beans and raw corn kernels. Add the garlic cream to cover and cook until tender. Stir in sliced green onions. Spoon vegetables around roast pork or chicken and use the cream as a sauce.

Chef Daniel Bruce, who oversees a formal dining room, serves **Roasted Fresh Green Soybeans** at home: Toss fresh soybean pods in bowl with olive oil, salt, and garlic. Spread in a single layer in a roasting pan. Bake in 350°F oven until cooked through, about 15 minutes. "Serve on a platter and let everyone help themselves. It's a great way to get kids to dig into their vegetables. They love eating with their fingers and pulling the beans out with their teeth."

Barbara Kirshenblatt-Gimblett, scholar and food adventurer, chooses green soybeans as the centerpiece for one of her purist presentations, **Jade Platter:** Blanch and shell soybeans. Cut peeled jícama into dice the same size as beans. Dress with lime juice, chives, salt, and mint or holy basil or cilantro. Mound in the center of a platter. Surround with boiled, peeled, sliced, and fanned chayote halves. Dress peeled, boiled, and sliced lotus with pickled ginger, umeboshi, and mirin. Set in between chayote "fans."

Beans, Snap (*Phaseolus vulgaris*)

Also green beans, string beans

Including **common snap (green, yellow, purple)**, **filet** or **French**, **Italian flat** or **Romano**, **Dragon Tongue** and **Tongue of Fire**, **Dutch flat pole**

See also: **YARD-LONG BEAN,** page 718

Snap beans look so different from one another that they confuse cooks who are not familiar with the whole range. But if you know and like any one, do not hesitate to try the others. They are surprisingly similar in the kitchen. All those pictured here are young forms of the common bean, *Phaseolus vulgaris* (see also Common Bean, page 56), harvested before the seeds (beans) develop appreciably. It is the tender green (meaning immature—not green in color)

pods that are eaten at this stage of growth. Although "string bean" is a term still applied, few snap beans today have the tough filaments that earned the name.

These New World beans are colorful, lively, fresh-tasting, and easy to enjoy. Round, flat, long, short, skinny, or fat, they can be purple or yellow as well as green. Some are variegated. Some are meaty, some crisp. Some are dense, some juicy. The flavor of all is distinguished by three primary components, according

top, left to right: green (Blue Lake), yellow French, green French; *bottom, left to right:* green (Daytona), purple, purple French

length: 3-6 inches

to James R. Myers, a geneticist at Oregon State University: a "beany" or astringent taste, a flowery or fragrant aspect, and sweetness. The balance is what determines the totality, but there is less individuality than one might expect from such diverse hues and forms.

Green snap beans are best known. There are endless numbers of cultivars, from slim and trim to long and plump (like the touted Blue Lake). Most are stringless. For my taste, they are best when boiled. Simmered in a small amount of liquid, covered, they are less vivid and crunchy, but very flavorful. Steamed, they have less verve, an olive cast, and a slightly tinny taste. Microwaved, they have a texture that is both flaccid and tough.

Yellow snap beans or wax beans are much like green beans, crisp and meaty, but they tend to be paler in flavor. They look charming presented in combination with other snap beans. Their coloring makes them perfect for pickling: They do not fade in vinegar as green and purple beans do.

Purple snap beans have a velvety, midnight purple exterior and cook to a dark matte green. No acid or base chemical fiddling or special cooking techniques will hold the purple—at least not any I've tried in my role as a mad kitchen scientist. Purple snap beans are much like green beans once cooked, with as much variation. Although I am not a fan of raw beans, I make an exception here—in small doses—to take advantage of the visual effect. Thin-slice the beans and add them to mixed green or composed salads. The dramatic dark nuggets, which are pleasantly firm, also make a tasty garnish—almost like nuts. Cook as green beans.

Filet or French beans or haricots verts are a different style of common green bean that was traditionally favored in France and is now grown internationally. The solid pods must be picked tiny (which means early and often) or they very quickly turn stringy and fibrous.

top, left to right: Dragon Tongue, green Romano, yellow Romano; *bottom, left to right:* Tongue of Fire, Dutch flat pole bean
length: 4–10 inches

Obviously, they are more difficult and expensive to produce than the stringless American types, which are more patient on the vine and hold longer in storage. But filet types are more concentrated in flavor and texture than American snap beans. Boiled, they develop an even, velvety finish and a sweet, uniform meatiness.

Yellow and purple filet-style beans are also available. The yellow type seems to cook to a slightly deeper flavor and color than American snaps and to hold its firm consistent texture.

Italian flat beans, Roma, or Romano-type are not rounded like conventional snap beans but are more flattened, yet still plumpish. Whether green, yellow, or purple, they are meaty and easy to like. Fine on their own, they also blend well into braises, soups (minestrone, of course), and other mixed dishes. Juicy, tender, and toothsome, they are gentle and appealing, but not highly flavorful (although the green may be more so than the yellow).

Other beans that are sometimes sold at the snap or green stage are the beautiful and memorably named **Dragon Tongue** and **Tongue of Fire.** The first, sometimes grouped with yellow or wax beans, looks and tastes just about the same once cooked. I mention this so that you are not surprised by the disappearance of the painterly violet splashes, which is inevitable when Dragon Tongue is cooked. Similarly, the Tongue of Fire loses its rosy scribbles when subjected to heat, turning a monochromatic middle green with a middle flavor. However, the youngest pods of both can be enjoyed raw, in moderation: Angle-cut in thin slices and include in composed salads and mixed into vegetables; or sprinkle as a garnish.

Dutch flat pole bean, an unusual cultivar called Festival (Rijk Zwaan seed company), is so great—in both size and flavor—that I had to include it, although it is rare in the United States. Imported from the Netherlands (by the New York-based distributor Baldor, in this case), it is a greenhouse-grown *Phaseolus vulgaris* with flat, tender pods about 10 inches long, about 16 to the pound. Juicy, bright, and sweet, these beans have more "old-fashioned" flavor than all the others I sampled. Only the very tips, which have a parchment lining, must be trimmed. The pod can be cut into triangles, rectangles, diamonds, or pretty diagonals; or the whole pod can be blanched and used as a wrapper. A singularly delicious and waste-free vegetable.

BASIC USE: Snap beans are well represented in cookbooks. If you don't have favorites for vegetables, I refer you to the excellent guides by Marian Morash and Sylvia Thompson (see the Bibliography) for both growing and cooking.

It is important to recognize that non-green types may not cook up in the colors you anticipate. Purples and reds become green.

The length of time you cook snap beans has more effect on the finished dish than other factors. For some, al dente suits just fine (see Basic Snap Beans). For others, soft and slurpy is preferable (see Semi-Southern Snap Beans with Bacon). For others, medium welldone is best (see Pros Propose).

SELECTION: Domestically, summer is peak season—but green beans are available year-round. All snap beans should snap. If they are limp and do not break crisply, forget them. Once the bean is opened, check to be sure the seeds are tiny. Common green beans can be long or short, plump or slim, but should be crisp, uniformly green and have few or no visible seed bumps. Select yellow types with a tinge of green—younger than those that are uniformly pale yellow. Filet beans (haricots verts) are somewhat shorter, straighter, and much thinner than others—never as wide as common snap beans, or they're tough. They are characteristically less sharply snappable than American types, being less juicy. They may also be less sweet when sampled raw; their flavor develops in cooking. Flat Italian types can be broad and long, but not fat, which signals overmature seeds.

STORAGE: Snap beans are best eaten as soon as possible, but they can be refrigerated up to a week: Enclose in a paper bag or paper towel, then wrap in a plastic bag. Filet beans hold for a day or two.

For foodservice, store in a well-ventilated area, away from moisture. Keep in the original opened or ventilated box in the cooler. If there is any feeling of heat from the box, open it up. Or spread the beans on trays to chill.

PREPARATION: Cut off the stem ends. If the beans are straight, you can line them up and slice the ends off en masse. If the beans are curved or twisty, you'll need to snip the stems individually. There is no need to remove the tips of most beans, which are tender. Some very large ones and some filet beans may be tough: Taste and check. Check for "strings," too, though these are very rare in today's varieties: Zip off, if necessary.

Small beans look best and cook most evenly left whole. Cut larger beans at a diagonal in widths to suit the presentation. Or cut wide flat beans, such as the Dutch green bean, the Italian types, or the Tongue of Fire and Dragon Tongue, into triangles, rectangles, or diamonds, depending upon the shape and size.

Basic Snap Beans

Having microwaved, steamed, simmered, and boiled snap beans, I vote for the last, which have the brightest color, most uniform texture (including a slight crunch), and freshest flavor. If you like your beans more "well-done" and don't mind a little less color, simmer in a small amount of water, covered, until done to taste.

For variety, add toasted sliced nuts, or roasted sesame seeds and a drop of soy sauce, or minced fresh dill, chervil, or tarragon and snipped chives to the hot oil- or butter-coated beans.

> 1¼ pounds snap beans (any kind)
> Butter, nut oil, Asian (dark) sesame oil, or
>   olive oil
> Lemon juice
> Salt and pepper

1. Cut off stems, then trim beans as needed. There is no need to remove the tips of most beans—taste and check. Sample "strings," which are rare with today's varieties. Zip these off if necessary. Leave beans whole if small, or halve diagonally, or cut into slim or wide diagonals to fit the form of the bean and the meal.

2. Drop beans into a big pot of boiling water with plenty of salt. Boil 1½ minutes, then begin tasting for doneness—a completely subjective matter. I like them when the raw taste disappears but a barely perceptible crunch remains; others like them better nearly raw; and others like them cooked thoroughly tender. Drain when they're a tad less done than you like them.

To serve hot: Toss just-drained hot beans in a warmed dish with the best butter you can find and salt and pepper.

To serve warm: Toss the drained beans in a dish with oil. Season with lemon juice, salt, and pepper.

To serve cold: When beans are barely tender, drain.

Refresh in ice water. Drain, pat dry, and refrigerate. Dress to serve.

Serves 4

Semi-Southern Snap Beans with Bacon

Traditional Southern cooks (and others in many countries) take a dim view of the crisp school of vegetable cookery. To properly infuse beans with requisite pork richness, simmering must be lengthy—in the neighborhood of two hours. Obviously, these beans do not have the verve of bright green vegetables. But what they *do* have is smoky, sweet, and salty savors that mellow and mingle in a slurpy, unctuous, noodly soft tangle. (They also provide intense "pot likker" for soup; or cook cubed potatoes in it and serve with the beans.)

My compromise version is not for Southerners (who need no Yankee recipes for beans), but for the food-curious who might want to sample an old favorite in a new way. Non-authentic elements include: shorter cooking time, crisped bacon pieces (lardons) instead of soft salt pork, chillis, and a dash of sherry vinegar.

If you garden or shop at farmers' markets, this is a good recipe for big, sturdy beans of any variety or color (or several): green or yellow Romanos, purple pole beans, Dragon Tongue, Tongue of Fire. For chillis, most will suit, but Chipotles (which are smoked Jalapeños) are particularly tasty. Sherry vinegar is nice and sprightly, but others will do fine.

> 6 to 8 ounces smoky slab bacon, cut into
>   3 pieces
> 2 quarts water
> 3 or more whole dried chillis
> 1½ pounds large snap beans
> About 1 tablespoon kosher salt
> About 2 teaspoons sugar
> Pepper
> Sherry vinegar

1. Combine bacon, water, and chillis in heavy large pot and bring to a boil. Boil gently, covered, until water

is well flavored—about an hour. Taste broth as it cooks; remove chillis if desired.

2. Meanwhile, cut stems from beans. Cut off tips only if tough.

3. When broth is flavored to taste, remove 2 of the bacon pieces (reserve these) and the chillis. Add beans and 2 teaspoons each of salt and sugar to broth. Simmer, partly covered, until beans are soft but not falling to pieces, about 45 minutes or more, stirring often. Taste and add salt and sugar to suit.

4. While beans are cooking, cut the 2 bacon slabs into strips about ⅛ inch wide. Brown in a skillet over low heat until crisped. Transfer to paper towels to drain.

5. When beans are soft and flavorful, lift out gently to a heated serving dish. Strew with bacon. Grind over pepper. Sprinkle with vinegar. Serve hot.

Serves 4

Pros Propose

In the American South snap beans are familiar in long-simmered form, seasoned with bacon or ham. In South Carolina, John Martin Taylor cooks **Pole Beans and New Potatoes** in a slightly different way—with only enough water to steam potatoes atop the beans. He writes, "In the Lowcountry pole beans are any number of varieties of snap beans that are larger than everyday green beans. Kentucky Wonders are a favorite variety." To prepare: String beans, as needed. Peel and halve an equal weight of small new potatoes. Spread beans in a heavy saucepan. Top with potatoes and a small ham hock: add a little water. Cover and simmer until potatoes are done, about ½ hour (from *Hoppin' John's Lowcountry Cooking*).

Green beans cooked with pork are as common in the north of Germany as they are in the southern United States—with the interesting addition of pears. In older recipes, small unpeeled pears are typical. Current ones, such as this from *The New German Cookbook,* call for sliced pears, which "soften and, when tossed with the beans and kettle liquid, emerge as a sort of sweet-sour sauce," write Jean Anderson and Hedy Würz, who serve the dish in modern style as a main course with "husky whole grain bread and a dessert of mixed citrus sections." For **Green Beans, Pears, and Bacon:** Boil a little water in a large heavy saucepan. Reduce heat; add snap beans of bite-size pieces. Cover with an equal weight of small firm pears that have been peeled, halved, and sliced. Top with lean bacon cubes. Sprinkle with dried summer savory and pepper. Simmer 45 minutes, covered. Serve flecked with parsley.

Chef Amaryll Schwertner, in keeping with her heritage, prepares **Wax Beans Hungarian-Style,** lightly bound with roux and seasoned with paprika: Boil bite-size lengths of wax bean in salted water about 5 minutes; drain. Gently cook minced onion, parsley, and garlic in butter; sprinkle with flour and stir briefly to cook smooth without browning. Thin with stock (authentically, goose broth) and simmer to make a mild sauce. Season with sweet paprika or minced dill and sour cream. Add a touch of sugar and lemon or vinegar. Cook briefly.

Chef Schwertner is also fond of small, young **Dragon Tongue Beans with Walnuts and Garlic:** Combine blanched and still-warm beans with caramelized garlic cloves, walnut vinegar, olive oil, and tender, fresh green walnuts, if available (if not, soak mature walnut halves in water several hours, then skin). Season with French sea salt.

In the Republic of Georgia, known for both dried and green bean preparations, the combination of garlic, walnuts, and snaps figures in a very different **Bean Salad with Herb and Walnut Paste:** Grind walnuts, garlic, dried coriander, and powdered marigold petals to a paste. Combine in a bowl with minced onion, chopped fresh coriander, and basil. Boil bite-size pieces of Romano-type beans in a little water, covered, until tender. Drain, pat dry, and blend at once with the paste. Add salt and red wine vinegar; let stand an hour. Serve with radish slices (from *The Classic Cuisine of Soviet Georgia* by Julianne Margvelashvili).

India's repertoire of snap beans is extensive. The vegetable is usually cooked directly in a karhai (Indian wok) with other ingredients—not blanched first as in most Western recipes. As in many countries, soft-cooked is the norm. An exemplary dish of **Fried Fresh Green Beans with Coconut** is lightly thickened with legumes: Heat plenty of ghee. Add black mustard seeds and split, hulled urad dal (black gram); stir briefly to color. Add chopped onions, minced ginger, salt, pepper, and green beans sliced crosswise into paper-thin rounds. Stir in ground hot pepper and cook, tossing, for 5 minutes. Add grated fresh coconut and minced coriander leaves. Reduce heat, cover, and cook about 10 minutes longer. Season with lemon juice (from *The Cooking of India* by Santha Rama Rau, Michael Field, and the Editors of Time-Life Books).

Purple Passion is the name given this fanciful—yet purist—platter from creative cook Barbara Kirshenblatt-Gimblett: Trim stem ends of yellow wax and green beans; cut into 1-inch lengths. Boil separately until firm-tender. Drain, refresh, and pat dry. Toss with pomegranate molasses and salt. Heap on a large platter to form a high cone. Surround with sliced carambola (star fruit) and big juicy blackberries. Cut purple perilla (shiso) into fine chiffonade and strew over beans; top cone with shiso leaves.

For the quintessential and casual, Sylvia Thompson can't be beat. To prepare **Filet Beans with Tomato Ribbons:** Blanch tiny beans; cool. Wrap in a towel and chill. With a fingertip, scoop seeds from big, flavorful, meaty halved red, yellow, and/or orange tomatoes. Whirl halves smooth in a food processor; blend with olive oil, mild vinegar, and salt. Place a soft lettuce leaf on each plate. Arrange beans in a bundle on each. Spoon puree in a ribbon over the center, letting some fall on the leaf. Grind over pepper. Decorate with a fat edible yellow blossom (from *The Kitchen Garden Cookbook*).

For the ultimate in haricots verts, as these slimmest of snap beans are usually called (whether from France, Kenya, or the United States), finish them with "black diamonds." For **Haricots Verts aux Truffes:** Blanch small beans in plenty of salted water. Drain and refresh in ice water; drain. Just before serving, dry in a towel. Blend vinaigrette with minced shallot and crème fraîche. Toss with beans; season. Arrange Bibb lettuce leaves on each plate; set a mound of beans in the center. Surround with julienned fresh black truffle. Add chervil sprigs (from *The Natural Cuisine of Georges Blanc*).

At the beautiful California restaurant Terra, **Fried Haricots Verts with Anchovy-Garlic Mayonnaise** are served as an appetizer: Prepare batter from eggs, pastry flour, a touch of Parmesan and olive oil, water, and a hint of garlic; refrigerate. Blanch small haricots verts, keeping them crisp. Refresh in ice water and drain. Prepare mayonnaise flavored with garlic and anchovy. Coat beans with batter. Drop one at a time into oil heated to 360°F. When golden, drain on towels. Place on a baking sheet in low oven; salt lightly. Spread mayonnaise on plates, set a large radicchio leaf on each, and mound beans in these. Surround with yellow and red cherry tomatoes. Sprinkle with parsley and Parmesan; garnish with lemon wedges (from *Terra: Cooking from the Heart of Napa Valley* by Hiro Sone and Lissa Doumani).

Chef Charlie Trotter conducts a small symphony of vegetables in his typically eclectic and refined manner. For **Ragoût of Baby Bok Choy, Haricots Verts, Yellow Wax Beans, and Dragon's Tongue Beans with Japanese Cucumber Sauce:** Braise whole Japanese cucumbers in butter, water, salt, and pepper, covered, until tender. Add whole baby bok choy and cook a few minutes. Add blanched haricots verts, wax beans, and Dragon's Tongue beans; cook a few minutes. Slice cucumbers into 2-inch pieces; quarter each. Puree raw Japanese cucumbers; press through a sieve. Warm the resulting puree and whisk in herb oil. Set bok choy on each plate. Top with cucumber strips and beans. Spoon around cucumber sauce and hot cooking liquid. Add chopped chervil (from *Charlie Trotter's Vegetables*).

Beech Mushroom, Honshimeji (*Hypsizygus tessulatus*)

Also Clam Shell

The three names above belong to one mushroom with complicated commercial origins. (If nomenclature interests you, read on; if not, skip to the next paragraph.) When the cute, sturdy fungus first appeared in the United States over a decade ago, it was marketed as yamabiko honshimeji and hon-shimeji. Since then "the general name 'Shimeji' has been assigned to about 20 species, causing widespread confusion amongst amateur and professional mycologists," Paul Stamets writes in *Growing Gourmet and Medicinal Mushrooms.* "Scientific articles have attempted to clarify what is the 'true Shimeji' which Japanese call Hon-Shimeji," and which is now known to be a species of *Lyophyllum.* The confusion is understandable "because young specimens [of *Lyophyllum*] . . . look very similar to *Hypsizygus tessulatus,* known in Japan as Buna-shimeji or the Beech Mushroom."

"Beech mushroom" is the name chosen by Phillips Mushroom Farms in Kennett Square, one of the country's largest specialty growers. All beech mushrooms in the marketplace are cultivated, not gathered from the wild—so do not be tempted to call them wild or accept them as such on a menu. "Wild" as they may be in the sense of far-out, they are grown under strict laboratory conditions, not murmuring pines.

Whether pure white or golden-tan, beech mushrooms have smooth, small, thinnish caps with sharply defined ivory gills and thick, tender stems. Gourmet Mushrooms, in Sebastopol, California, has trademarked its strains as the Brown Clam Shell and Alba Clam Shell. Other growers and importers sell *Hypsizygus* as "hon-shimeji." (For the record, the goofy "honeyshmeggie" I noticed on a distributor's list fits no mushroom!)

Although there is variation from grower to grower, generally speaking the mushroom retains its sprightly bounce and clean hue when cooked quickly over high heat. Its flavor is mild with a hint of herbs and nuts (I don't find any clam, although some do); its texture is fleshy and juicy, with a crisp edge. Sautéed, both types gild prettily. If there is any problem with the species, it is an unpredictable tendency to bitterness—from slight to pronounced.

Alba Clam Shell and Brown Clam Shell   ⅓ actual size

BASIC USE: Beech mushrooms can be prepared in the same way as common white buttons (*Agaricus* species) but require less cooking time. Best suited to dishes that play up their charming form, clear color, and light crunch, they shine in fairly simple preparations.

To cook, toss with oil, salt, pepper, and a dash of acid to coat lightly. Roast in a hot oven until tender, a matter of 3 to 5 minutes; or, for an earthier savor, slow-roast at lower heat. Sauté quickly over high heat in a minimum of oil or butter. Chill cooked beech mushrooms to mix into vegetable, meat, seafood, or pasta salads. Stir-fry with vegetables, seafood strips, or both. Stew in brown sauce or cream sauce to serve with poultry, grains, noodles, potatoes, or polenta. Simmer briefly in clear soup. Prepare perky pickled mushrooms, for which the tidy shape and firm flesh are well suited.

SELECTION AND STORAGE: Look for solid specimens with a minimum of heavy base. There should be no trace of dampness. Firm and dry by nature, these mushrooms last longer than most. Refrigerate them in their original containers. If there is any condensation, place a bit of paper towel in the package to absorb it.

PREPARATION: Cut off the thickest part of the base or growing medium to separate the stalks, which should be kept intact. Cultivated in a sterile medium and packed in covered boxes, they need no cleaning.

Salad of Shrimp and Beech Mushrooms

Brightly colored and swiftly assembled, this Asian-accented salad makes a lovely lunch or supper dish. The lightly bitter mushrooms balance the shrimp's sweetness and offer a pleasing springiness. For variety, thin-slice any red radicchio (page 517) to replace the Belgian endive or combine with it. I find shrimp much more appealing warm or at room temperature than cold, but you may want to chill yours.

> 1 pound beech mushrooms (Clam Shell, honshimeji), white or brown
> 1 bunch water cress
> 2-inch knob of ginger
> 3 medium scallions (green onions)
> 4 small Belgian endives or red endives
> 5 tablespoons peanut oil
> ¾ to 1 pound shelled medium shrimp (1 to 1¼ pounds in the shell)
> ½ teaspoon kosher salt
> 2 tablespoons rice vinegar

1. Trim mushroom bases to separate stems. Pull apart all mushrooms. Trim, rinse, and spin-dry water cress. Peel and mince enough ginger to yield 2 tablespoons. Cut apart light and dark parts of scallions, then slice thin. Cut Belgian endive lengthwise into thin slices.

2. Set wide skillet over high heat. Add 1 tablespoon oil. Add mushrooms and toss to brown lightly, about 3 minutes. Spread on plate.

3. Reduce heat to moderate. Add 1½ tablespoons more oil to pan. Stir in ginger, light part of scallions, shrimp, and ¼ teaspoon salt. Cook until shrimp is just barely done, 2 to 3 minutes. Off heat, toss with scallion greens. Scrape onto plate with mushrooms.

4. Dissolve remaining ¼ teaspoon salt in vinegar. Add remaining 3½ tablespoons oil. Toss with cress and endive. Arrange on plates. Top with shrimp and mushrooms.

Serves 4 as a light main course, 6 as a first course

Farfalle with Beech Mushrooms, Peppers, Onions, and Anchovies

Attractively burnished, savory, and sweet, the assertive seasoning sauce produces a pasta dish that is far from ordinary. Although anchovies are a strong presence, they do not overpower as you might think. Cooking times for the mushrooms will vary depending upon their density—check often.

> ½ pound beech mushrooms
> 1 small red onion
> 1 medium-large red bell pepper
> One tin (2 ounces) oil-packed anchovy fillets (12 to 16 fillets)
> ½ pound imported Italian farfalle (butterfly pasta)
> ¼ cup balsamic vinegar
> 3 tablespoons full-flavored olive oil
> 1 tablespoon minced garlic
> Pepper

1. Trim mushroom bases. Pull apart stems to separate mushrooms. Cut stems into 1- to 2-inch pieces. Dice onion. Cut pepper into small dice. Drain anchovies, reserving oil. Quarter each fillet.

2. Boil farfalle in a large pot of salted water until al dente.

3. Meanwhile, heat vinegar in heavy wide non-aluminum skillet. Add onions and cook over fairly high heat, shaking occasionally, until vinegar evaporates—4 to 5 minutes. Reduce heat to moderate. Add olive oil and garlic and stir 30 seconds. Add bell pepper, raise heat, and toss. Add mushrooms and cook, stirring often, until gleaming and tender, about 5 minutes. Remove from heat.

4. Put anchovies and 1 tablespoon reserved oil in a heated serving bowl. Stir with fork to separate pieces

(or they will clump on the pasta). Drain pasta, then toss with anchovies. Add mushroom mixture and pepper. Serve at once.

Serves 2 as a main course, 3 to 4 as a first course

Pros Propose

Chef and author Patrick O'Connell finds "Clam Shell's elfin looks just right for the delicate colors and flavors of a luxurious veal dish," **Loin of Veal with Ravioli and Clam Shell Mushrooms:** Sear seasoned butt tenderloin in olive oil; finish roasting in oven. Slice medallions and arrange interspersed with ravioli filled with mousse of country ham and Fontina, and white Clam Shells sautéed in smoking-hot pan. Sauce with a reduction of veal and red wine seasoned lightly with herbs.

Chef Laurent Gras favors honshimeji for **Sole Goujonettes with Jura Wine and Mushrooms**, an ambitious but quiet dish, "because it adds great texture, but it is very feminine and will not hurt the extraordinary wine, which is the main story": Prepare calf's-foot jelly with chicken stock; strain. Slow-roast chicken legs with mirepoix to brown lightly. Add garlic cloves and honshimeji stems and cook gently—do not brown. Add Jura wine (Arbois), sole bones, and prepared stock. Simmer an hour, skimming; strain. Stew sole trimmings with butter; then add clarified stock and reduce. Add butter. Strain sauce. To serve, cook honshimeji caps in butter and a little Arbois. Boil more Arbois in pan; add Dover sole goujonettes. Add sauce and cook through. Arrange on plates with the mushroom caps. Serve polenta made with mascarpone and Parmesan on the side.

Chef Anne Gingrass says that "with its looks and texture, the Clam Shell makes a great accent mushroom, especially in simple dishes like **Salmon Baked in Parchment**": For each serving, make bed of halved baby carrots, leek slices, brown Clam Shell mushrooms, and celery slivers on parchment. Top each with a salmon fillet. On this, place a pat of compound butter seasoned with tarragon, parsley, chervil, chives, lemon juice, zest, and vermouth. Seal and bake.

White Clam Shell mushrooms are highlighted in chef Kenneth Oringer's **Hotpot of Squab with Mushrooms**: Prepare broth with roasted squab bones, turnips, carrots, celery, and onions; strain. Blanch pearl onions and baby carrots; drain. Glaze in vegetable stock. Arrange in shallow bowl. Set a roasted squab half on each. Surround with steamed white Clam Shell mushrooms. Pour around stock and add chervil and thyme.

Beets and Beet Greens (*Beta vulgaris*)

Including **Chioggia, cylindrical, golden,** and **white**

Beets have come up in the world. Nestled beneath foie gras, accented with truffles, or stirred into risotto, the formerly lowly roots now grace the most elegant tables.

Until recently, beets were considered little more than a useful winter food in the United States, where they were boiled, canned, and not much more. A generation of chefs without wartime prejudices and with an international repertoire have been subjecting them to culinary scrutiny. With this rise in status, new uses, cooking techniques, and cultivars (old and new) have emerged.

Our common table or garden beet (called beetroot in England, to distinguish it from other types that follow) is but one of an extremely variable species, which includes foliage or leafbeets, Swiss chard, sugar beets, and mangel (mangold or mangel-wurzel), a fodder beet best known in Europe, which may weigh in at 100 pounds.

It is difficult to believe that these sturdy edibles share the same botanical classification with the perfect golden teardrops or miniature magenta eggs of haute cuisine. But these gems are no newborn "designer vegetables," as is sometimes stated. Although all beets are comparatively new to cultivation, their colors and sizes have been around for centuries—black, burgundy, rose, brick, yellow, ivory; minute to massive, round to tapered and cylindrical.

Several non-traditional types are making occasional appearances in farmers' markets and specialty shops: Chioggia ("candy stripe"), cylindrical, golden, and white. Although they share many features, there are some distinguishing characteristics.

Chioggia (pronounced kee-oh-ja) or candy-stripe

white (Albino), cylindrical (Formanova), and striped (Chioggia)   ⅙ actual size

baby red, baby and standard golden or yellow
                    ⅙ actual size

beets, from the Italian region of that name, are dramatically two-toned concentric circles of ruby and white when raw. When cooked, their rings turn to orange and rose or to uniform warm rose—there's no predicting which. Like golden beets, they do not bleed and are therefore useful in dishes where contained color is desirable. If unusually large, they may be pale and pithy.

Cylindrical beets, whether miniature or medium size, are unbeatable for ease and speed of preparation, for appearance, and even for flavor—at least those sampled thus far. Once cooked, the skin slips smoothly from the dark burgundy flesh—as rich and lustrous as that of the finest round reds, and with flavor to match. When sliced, this tidy cylinder obligingly falls into perfect rounds, neat as a carrot. Formanova and Cylindra are two cultivars that have been specified in the market, but there are others as well.

Golden or yellow beets have orangy or rosy skin but generally cook to a deep yellow. Sweet and mild, they sometimes lack the rich flavor of the red, but they make up for it in neatness: They do not bleed onto the work surface, food, or your hands. They look particularly sunset-gorgeous in concert with beets of other colors. From grape to grapefruit in size, the largest may be paler-fleshed and more flabby than smaller ones.

White or albino beets—with the exception of their luxuriant greens—have been a disappointment. The ones I have cooked on several occasions have been small and parsnip-like, drab in color, uneven in texture (fibrous at the wider end; flabby and breakable at the tip) and impossible to peel. Although the savor was sweetly earthy and full, I cannot imagine why one would choose these unless it is "to have fun with them!" as chef Jeff Tomchek does. "So many customers tell me they don't like beets, but when I sneak in the white ones, they ask me—without fail—what the delicious vegetable is. And I say, Heh, heh, heh—beets, and make a convert."

(Although fresh vegetables are the focus of this book, it is worth noting that vacuum-packed whole cooked beets, a European staple, have been sighted in American markets. They are a dandy convenience item, far better than canned for use in combination salads or purees. Some are even better, as solid as the real thing.)

Beet greens are part of all good beets, but they behave like another vegetable entirely. Earthiest of cooking leaves, they keep a *goût de terroir* that is all their own: intense, mineral, tonic. I find the taste such a perfect complement to the sugariness of beets that I almost always cook them together. Should you wish to cook them separately, treat them as you would their relative, Swiss chard (page 645).

BASIC USE: Grate peeled raw beets to add textural interest to salad and salsa. For composed salads, cook beets only until they lose their rawness (not their crunch); chill in cold water, peel, then cube or julienne before combining with smoked meat or fish, grains, fruits, nuts, celeriac, fennel, or firm bitter greens. Add a tart, sharp dressing. Enhance with fresh herbs—cilantro, lemon thyme, tarragon, chives, mint, parsley, dill, basil.

Bake beets for maximum flavor, sweetness, and ease of peeling. Steam whole beets over water aromatized with orange peel, anise or fennel seeds, cardamom, cinnamon stick, tarragon, marjoram, or thyme; when tender, peel beets and strain and reduce cooking liquid; add salt, butter, and the peeled and sliced beets to liquid. Complement cooked beets with strong flavors—whether biting (horseradish, chilli, ginger, mustard greens), bitter (chicories, water cress), acid (balsamic or fruit vinegars, citrus fruits), spicy (Sichuan pepper, curry, caraway), or salty (olives, capers, anchovies).

For hot or cold clear soup, simmer vegetable or fish broth with chunks of bruised ginger and lemon grass (or enclose whole spices and chilli in a cloth) until seasoned; add grated and peeled or julienned beets and simmer until tender. Remove aromatics; season with sugar and lime juice. For thick, smooth soup, there is no need to peel beets: simply cook as directed in the recipe, then puree and strain.

"Pickle" baby beets to use as a condiment or salad element: Prepare as for baked beets, then simmer red wine and vinegar with sugar, sliced shallots, cloves, cinnamon stick, anise seeds, and peppercorns, covered, until well flavored. Add beets; bring to a boil. Cool, then chill in liquid.

Beet greens are a subject unto themselves. Slim-stemmed ones need only brief steaming, which renders them tender and succulent. Larger ones take well to braising, especially with Asian touches—coconut milk, sweet spices, fermented black beans, chilli oil, and oyster sauce. As a side dish, combine beet greens with sharp and mild greens for a quick sauté-braise. Beet greens add a new dimension to chunky vegetable soups and pasta or bean dishes. Include some beet greens in vegetable stocks, to which they lend body, depth, and a winy tinge. Separate large leaves and stems to use separately: Work the leaves into recipes for greens; cook the stems à la grecque or braise with garlic and chilli.

SELECTION: Available all year, "bunch beets" (beets with greens) are fresher than those with no tops. One can tell just how fresh by the perkiness of the leaves. But beets can be fine even with droopy greens, as long as they are solid and free of cuts and discoloration.

Unfortunately, freshness is all you can see. When it comes to sweetness, flavor, texture, and interior color, chefs and growers do not make recommendations—nor can I. These can be determined only by tasting parboiled beets. It is fair to say that beets of medium size *usually* have the most reliable consistency, well-developed sweetness, and full flavor and that *some* large ones tend to be woody; but others may be large and tender, while some tiny beets may be tasteless or fibrous. Fortunately, beets are not often problematic.

STORAGE: If you won't be cooking greens and beets together, cut them apart, wrap in plastic, and store separately—the beets in the coldest area and the greens in another. Although one grower likens beets to corn in terms of storage ("the longer from the ground, the less sweet"), I find them to be miraculous keepers. Purchased in fine form, they last for months. Cooked, peeled beets store well in a closed container in the refrigerator for days, so cook extra.

Greens do not store well. Plan to cook them within a few days.

PREPARATION: Cut off and reserve greens, leaving about 2 inches of stem. Scrub beets with a vegetable brush to rid them of sand, especially at the "neck." Wash greens several times, lifting them from the water to rid them of debris that sinks to the bottom. It is best to peel beets after cooking. Some professional cooks don disposable gloves or finger cots and put parchment on the work surface to lessen the cleanup. Red beets just do make a mess; light-colored ones don't.

Baked Scented Beets and Greens

This is my favorite way to cook beets—and as a bonus, cleanup is minimal. Once baked, they retain their satiny sheen and deep flavor for several days—so be sure to cook extra. Serve hot or at room temperature with a gloss of nut oil and a sprinkle of fruity vinegar, or incorporate into more complex dishes, hot or cold. Red or Chioggia and gold beets together are particularly pretty.

2 bunches small-medium beets with greens
  (8 beets)
4 whole star anise "flowers" or 1 teaspoon
  anise or fennel seeds
1 tablespoon butter
Lemon juice

1. Preheat oven to 375°F. Trim off beet greens, leaving 2 inches of stem; reserve. Set each beet on a square of foil large enough to enclose it. Break star anise in half and place a piece on each square (or if using anise or fennel, divide among packets). Crimp each packet tightly shut.

2. Set beets in roasting pan. Bake until tender when pierced through with knife tip or cake tester, about 40 to 60 minutes.

3. Meanwhile, rinse greens in several changes of water.

4. Cool beets or not, as convenient. Keeping them wrapped up, gently squish each beet, sliding the skin back and forth so that it loosens. Open foil and, still holding beet with it, slip off skin and stem. Discard with spices. Halve beets.

5. Set greens on a rack in a steamer over boiling water. Cover and cook until tender, about 5 minutes. Meanwhile, heat beets in a pan with butter.

6. Toss greens with lemon juice. Arrange in a ring on serving dish. Nest beets in center.

Serves 4

Beet, Water Cress, and Kiwi Salad

Beets for cold dishes and hot dishes are best cooked to different stages. The firm, crunchy texture and distinct earthy sweetness of short-cooked beets delight in the former—and come as a rude surprise in the latter. If you can locate small cylindrical beets, cook twice as many and slice into rounds to alternate with the kiwi slices. This festive, colorful salad suits smoked poultry, tongue, or fish—whether on the side, or tossed in as julienne to make a main dish.

> 3 medium red, golden, or Chioggia beets, trimmed
> 1 large bunch water cress
> ½ teaspoon kosher salt
> 2 teaspoons grated ginger
> 1 teaspoon Dijon mustard
> 2 teaspoons honey
> 2 tablespoons lemon juice
> 1 tablespoon cider vinegar
> 2 tablespoons peanut oil
> 2 large kiwis (3 to 4 ounces each)
> Green part from 1 scallion (green onion), thin-sliced

1. Drop beets into boiling salted water; boil until they can just be pierced through but are not tender, about 10 minutes (figure on less time for narrow cylindrical ones).

2. Meanwhile, trim, rinse, and spin-dry water cress. Chill.

3. Drain beets. Cool in cold water. Peel. Cut into slices. Stack a few at a time and cut into strips ½ inch wide. Chill.

4. Blend salt, ginger, mustard, honey, lemon juice, and vinegar. Whisk in oil. Peel kiwis. Halve lengthwise, then slice crosswise into thin semicircles.

5. Arrange cress on platter. Top with beets, then kiwi slices. Whisk dressing, drizzle over. Scatter scallion greens over.

Serves 4

Cool Pureed Beet Soup with Chilli-Cilantro Swirls

A stunning soup for a special dinner: tart and fruity garnet puree punctuated by nippy parrot-green seasoning sauce. Straining is a bit of a nuisance, but it eliminates the need for preliminary peeling and creates a velvety feel in the mouth.

> 1½ pounds red beets (5 medium; weighed without tops)
> 1 medium-large leek
> ½ pound plum tomatoes
> ⅓ cup peeled, coarse-chopped ginger
> ¼ cup white rice
> 1 quart cranberry juice
> About 1 teaspoon kosher salt
> 3 cups water
> 1 large mild chilli, such as Poblano or Anaheim
> 1 small hot chilli, such as Jalapeño or Serrano
> 2 medium scallions (green onions)
> 1 cup tightly packed sliced cilantro (coriander) leaves
> ½ cup yogurt
> 1 tablespoon raspberry or other fruit vinegar

1. Trim, scrub, and slice beets. Trim roots and darkest top leaves from leek. Halve lengthwise, slice thin, and rinse in several changes of water. Slice tomatoes.

2. Combine beets, leek, tomatoes, ginger, rice, cranberry juice, 1 teaspoon salt, and water in a pot. Bring to a boil. Reduce heat and simmer, covered, until beets are very soft, about 1 hour.

3. Transfer mixture to food processor or blender, in batches, and puree to a smooth consistency. Press through a medium-mesh sieve to eliminate skins and seeds. Season. Cool, then cover and chill.

4. Seed and slice both chillis. Trim and slice scallions. Combine with cilantro, yogurt, and vinegar in blender or processor. Whirl to a puree. Add salt, if desired.

5. Ladle chilled soup into wide shallow bowls. Drizzle swirls of the green mixture over this (for a marbled effect, drag knife tip straight across in parallel lines, alternating directions as you go).

Serves 6 to 8 as a first course

Penne with Beets and Their Greens and Pecans

I don't object to pasta tinted party pink, but others do. For them, golden and Chioggia beets should be the varieties of choice for this luscious meal-in-a-bowl, as they won't stain surrounding food as "regular" reds do. Even non-vegetarians enjoy the light yet satisfying dish, which calls for few ingredients but tastes complex. Unlike pasta sauces of uniform consistency, which can be monotonous, this offers different flavor and texture combinations with each bite.

If you have a large steamer, it is easy to boil the beets and steam the greens together. Set the greens on a rack over the boiling beets, and they'll both cook in about the same time. When the two have finished cooking, boil the pasta.

2 bunches small golden, red, and/or Chioggia
   beets with perky greens
1 to 2 tablespoons fruit vinegar, such as raspberry
½ pound imported Italian penne rigate
2 tablespoons pecan, walnut, or olive oil
1 small garlic clove, minced
⅛ teaspoon chilli flakes
Salt and pepper
¼ cup toasted, coarse-chopped pecans

1. Trim off beet stems and greens; reserve. Scrub beets. Drop into boiling water to cover by an inch or so. Boil until not quite tender, about 10 minutes—but timing varies. Drain. When cooled slightly, slip off skins under running water. Quarter beets. Toss with vinegar to taste.

2. Trim and wash beet greens. Cut stems into thin slices. If leaves are large, cut into wide slices; if not, leave whole. Set on rack over boiling water and steam until soft, about 10 minutes—but timing is variable.

3. Cook penne in large pot of boiling salted water until just tender.

4. Meanwhile, heat 1 tablespoon oil in large skillet over moderate heat. Add garlic and chilli flakes and toss. Add greens and heat through. Season.

5. Drain pasta and toss with remaining 1 tablespoon oil. Add hot greens and toss. Divide between two heated shallow bowls. Top with beets and nuts.

Serves 2

Hot and Aromatic Beet Stem Appetizer or Condiment

The stems on bunched beets often stay in fine shape even as the leaves become bedraggled. Cooked, the juicy stalks of red beets turn a warm garnet and add a dramatic touch to a meal as both flamboyant hue and forceful flavoring. (Stems from any beets can be used, but red ones are more fun.) Serve them as part of an appetizer salad or as a condiment/relish with an Indian meal. For a deliciously garish grain salad, toss with cooked quinoa, kamut, or wheat grains.

¾ pound beet stems (from medium red beets)
1 cup water
1 large garlic clove, halved
1 tablespoon sugar
1 or 2 small dried chillis
½ teaspoon fennel seeds
½ teaspoon coriander seeds
¼ teaspoon kosher salt
1 tablespoon olive oil
3 tablespoons cider vinegar or wine vinegar

1. Trim leaves from stems; discard or keep, as condition dictates. Cut stems on a sharp angle into 1½-inch diagonal lengths.

2. In medium non-aluminum skillet, combine water, garlic, sugar, 1 chilli, fennel, coriander, salt, oil, and vinegar. Simmer, covered, for 5 minutes. Taste for "heat." Add another chilli or remove the first, as desired.

3. Add beet stems to liquid. Simmer, covered, until very tender but not mushy, stirring several times and tasting for desired degree of hotness. Cooking time varies with size and toughness of stems, but 25 minutes is usual.

4. Remove garlic and chilli. If liquid has not reduced to just a few tablespoons, simmer gently to evaporate. Cool and chill.

Makes about 1½ cups

Pros Propose

"Although crisp, sweet, and juicy when raw, beets are rarely served that way in the U. S.," writes Susan Herrmann Loomis. "I first ate them raw on a French farm, where they were finely grated and tossed in a simple vinaigrette. Immediately seduced, I have served them this way dozens of times since." For **Raw Beet Salad:** Prepare dressing of balsamic vinegar, pepper, salt, olive oil, paper-thin shallot slices, and cumin seeds. Toss with finely grated raw red beets. Let stand 15 minutes or more. Scoop the mixture onto leaves of lightly dressed Oakleaf lettuce, torn small (from *French Farmhouse Cookbook*).

Visually dramatic **Clusters of Leeks with Beet Vinaigrette** are pictured in *The Natural Cuisine of Georges Blanc,* a work rich in refined and innovative vegetable recipes. To prepare: Puree cooked beets and vinegar. Strain through fine sieve. Add mustard, salt, and pepper, then whisk in mild oil. Cut cooked, well-drained whole slim leeks into ¼-inch coins. Set them in a single layer to form a triangular shape (to resemble a grape cluster). Spoon the beet sauce around: Decorate with celery leaves.

Juicers have made waves in the restaurant business—as here, to create a clear, strong base for chef René Fieger's **Chilled Beet Consommé:** Run beets through juicer: Combine with an equal quantity of water. Bring to a boil with fresh thyme, lovage, parsley, ginger, garlic, horseradish, cider vinegar, pepper, sugar, and salt. Remove from heat; cool. Strain and chill. Garnish with grated raw beets, a fine julienne of celeriac and apple, and fromage blanc with chives.

Raw beet juice is the sauce base for a fish dish from chef Jeff Tomcheck: **Walleyed Pike with Beet Jus:** Juice beets, then cook down with ginger juice and lemon juice. Sauté pike fillets. Warm reduced beet *jus,* stir in butter, and spread on plates. Dot with drops of French sweet almond oil and set pike on top.

Tomchek makes his **Tabbouleh with Golden Beets** to avoid staining the wheat grains: Soak medium-grain tabbouleh in hot vegetable stock. Drain and spread out to dry. Mix with cooked, diced golden beets, preserved lemon, flat-leaf parsley, cilantro, mint, and shaved pickled garlic.

Rozanne Gold's stunningly simple *Recipes 1-2-3 Menu Cookbook* includes **Roasted Beet Soup with Pickled Beet Greens,** a lesson in economy: Cut greens from leafy beets. Cut leaves from stems, wash, and chop. Cook briefly with water, wine vinegar, salt, and peppercorns. Cool, then cover and refrigerate several hours, or more. Coarse-chop stalks. Cook in a little water until tender; reserve. Bake beets with some water in pan, turning, until very tender; when pierced. Cool briefly, then peel and cut into wedges. Combine in food processor with stems and cooking liquid and process to a thick puree. Add vinegar, salt, pepper, and buttermilk. Chill. Thin and season as needed. Garnish with greens.

Chef Laura Dewell used to prepare this "very old Soviet Georgian dish, which serves as relish," at Piros Mani in Seattle. For **Beets in Dried Cherry Sauce:** Bake tiny beets and bay leaves, covered, in a low oven until tender. Cool, then peel. Gently cook minced onions in butter. Add unsweetened dried tart cherries and water; simmer gently until very soft. Puree, adjusting liquid. Add chopped Italian parsley, cilantro, salt, and vinegar. Spoon over beets. Serve at room temperature.

Belgian Endive *(Cichorium intybus)*

Including **red Belgian endive**
(See also European names in text below)
See also: **ENDIVE**, page 264

Belgian endive displays a split personality, both in the kitchen and in its growing habits. Its role as a satiny salad leaf is only half the story, for it is equally enjoyable as tender cooked vegetable—a starring act in Europe, though only rarely in the United States.

Slow acceptance may be due to its slight bitterness—a positive characteristic for most of the world's cooks but a trait with little honor in America. Happily, exposure to foreign flavors through travel and constant restaurant growth has improved attitudes toward non-

sweet foods in recent years. Dashing radicchio (page 517), a comparatively bitter relative of Belgian endive, is now a restaurant regular, raw and cooked.

A dual identity is inherent in the cultivation of Belgian endive as well as in the kitchen. Its pearly leaves are the offspring of homely chicory root, originally grown for the manufacture of a coffee substitute (or flavoring, as in the New Orleans-style brew). Tiny chicory seeds are field-sown and gradually develop large parsnip-like roots beneath fluffy beet-like leaves. The mature roots are harvested, cleaned, and then re-

Belgian endive and red Belgian (or California) endive

length: 4–5 inches

planted indoors in heated soil, which, combined with humidity and darkness, causes a tight torpedo-shaped head of pale leaves to sprout. After growing several weeks, the now-official Belgian endive is cut from the root, trimmed, washed, dried, wrapped in waxed tissue to protect it from dirt and light, and boxed for market. (The big roots become animal feed.)

Alternatively—and exclusively, in the United States at present—the trimmed roots are set in cold-storage bins to prevent sprouting, withdrawn as needed, and transferred to trays filled with water and nutrients in dark, warm, humid growing rooms (much like those where mushrooms are cultivated) where the furled heads develop hydroponically. If production figures from America's primary grower signal a trend, these heads are creating a boomlet: In 2000, California Vegetable Specialties in Rio Vista recorded shipments of 1,600 ten-pound boxes per day—the quantity shipped during all of 1983.

At the same time, imports from Belgium and the Netherlands, the major European suppliers, remain stable, and cultivation on a smaller scale takes place in other European countries and parts of South and Central America. But the primary area of commercialization has always been the vicinity of Brussels, where the first well-documented experimentation with the plant took place in the city's botanical garden in 1850. During the rest of the 19th century, as techniques were improved and standardized, Belgian endive production grew to a sizable industry that spread from its local base to France and the Netherlands.

Perhaps the vegetable's relatively late appearance on the international scene accounts for its main problem: its *name!* What Americans call Belgian endive and the French call endive (pronounced ahn-deev) or chicorée (shee-ko-ray) is not true endive (which we know as escarole or broadleaf endive in the United States). The British call it Belgian or Brussels chicory, French-speaking Belgians dub it chicon, and Flemish-speaking Belgians call it witloof (white leaf)—the name I'd choose to clear up the nomenclature mess.

Red Belgian (or California) endive, an elegant newcomer to the marketplace, is the offspring of Belgian endive and radicchio di Treviso (page 517), a slim, tulip-like red chicory; it is not simply Belgian endive of a different hue. Red endive is generally smallish, pleasantly bitter, and a bit rough-textured. The spears are garnet-tipped, with the interior leaf color more intense than the exterior. It glows in salads, above all. The lovely stuff grown by California Vegetable Specialties is being marketed as red California (not Belgian) endive—to add to the muddle over names.

BASIC USE: Happily, Belgian endive is far easier to cook, eat, and enjoy than to cultivate or refer to correctly in print.

Raw, the smooth leaves enliven a crudité platter, whether bunched upright in glasses with other spears and strips or arranged on the platter in a starburst pattern, a dip in the center. For hors d'oeuvres, spoon or pipe filling onto individual leaves; or cut small heads of wine-tipped endive crosswise into "crackers" that resemble furled roses. For toppings, blends based on smoked fish or meat, avocado, soft cheese, or fish eggs work well.

Add Belgian endive to green salads for a contrast in color, texture, and flavor. Or choose it as a primary component to highlight another ingredient: ham, seafood, avocado, citrus, beets, blue cheese, etc. Toss with herbed or citrus vinaigrette or creamy dressing. For variation, julienne-cut endive and other crisp vegetables, toss them with creamy dressing, and serve as a slaw.

Cooked Belgian endive is surprisingly sturdy despite its delicate appearance. In fact, it really can't be overcooked. Traditionally, it is given a preliminary braising in the oven or on a stove-top, then finished in a variety of ways. Untraditionally, it can be sliced and very quickly sautéed. For basic techniques, see page 87.

SELECTION: Look for tissue-packed Belgian endive. When exposed to light, the leaves turn green and become bitter. Choose tight, crisp, solid heads. European chefs recommend "chiconettes" (the smallest heads), which arrive during the winter. But endive is available year-round and is typically of good quality. Although large heads are popular, small ones are better suited to most recipes because the shapely leaves can be kept whole.

Less than optimum Belgian endive is fine for cooking. Even the most negligent produce department can't destroy it completely. Pull off limp or browned outer leaves and proceed with the recipe.

STORAGE: Keep endive very cold, preferably in the high-humidity "crisper" of the refrigerator. Remarkably resilient, fresh Belgian endive will last 2 weeks if purchased in good shape.

PREPARATION: Growers say that washing is optional if endive is well wrapped in its protective tissue. But I prefer to give the outer leaves, at least, a quick rinse. If you'll be cooking the endive whole, cut off the tip from each head, dip head into water, and slosh around to clean inside without removing leaves.

For salad, very small whole leaves are prettiest; simply remove from base, cutting as needed to release them. For a large head, halve lengthwise, wedge-cut the core to remove it, then slice the head across or diagonally into strips. Rinse and spin-dry the leaves.

To ready whole heads for cooking, pare the base and cut an X into each. Or cut a conical plug from the base. Or halve lengthwise, then cut out a triangular wedge from the base.

To Cook Belgian Endive: The Basics

Whichever method you choose, Belgian endive is likely to respond kindly. It is a surprisingly hardy and forgiving vegetable, despite its fragile look. In fact, unless you forget it in the oven, it is not likely to be overcooked.

To oven-braise: Arrange cored, whole medium heads in a single layer in a buttered casserole. Add a little lemon juice and water, salt, pepper, and butter. Cover endive surface with parchment or buttered waxed paper trimmed to fit the casserole closely. Bake at 325°F until very tender—about 1½ hours. Uncover and bake until endive is golden and liquid is syrupy. Or add a little cream to finish cooking, or top with cheese.

To stovetop-braise: Combine water or vegetable broth, citrus juice, tarragon or dill, and a little sugar in wide non-aluminum skillet. Bring to a simmer. Add cored medium endives and cook gently, covered, until tender—about 45 minutes. Cool in liquid. To serve, remove endives and boil juices to syrupy consistency. Stir in a little butter, cream, or nut oil and fresh herbs. Return endive heads to pan and heat through. Top with toasted pine nuts, pistachios, or almonds.

To grill or broil: Brush halved heads with mustard-shallot or other flavorful vinaigrette, or with seasoned oil. Cook 5 to 10 minutes per side, depending upon size, adjusting rack so that leaves cook through without scorching.

To sauté: Toss sliced leaves quickly over high heat in oil or butter, sprinkling with sugar, salt, pepper, and a spritz of citrus juice. Cook just until leaves lose their raw crunch. Serve at once. (In this case, overcooking *is* to be avoided—crisp texture is the point.)

Salad of Belgian Endive, Water Cress, and Strawberries

Pale bittersweet spears played up by a thick, smooth, fruity (but not sweet) dressing are an unusual and effective combination. The vivid sunset pink dressing can be made well ahead and refrigerated, as convenient. Grapeseed oil is my choice for the mildest, cleanest taste. Although relatively expensive, it is well worth having on hand for dishes where delicacy and lightness are paramount.

> **1 hearty bunch water cress**
> **5 small Belgian endives**
> **1 pint strawberries (preferably small)**
> **1 tablespoon strawberry or raspberry vinegar**
> **¼ teaspoon sugar**
> **¼ teaspoon kosher salt**
> **⅛ teaspoon white pepper**
> **2½ tablespoons mild vegetable oil**
> **(preferably grapeseed)**

1. Trim, rinse, and spin-dry water cress; separate into tidy sprigs. Separate endive leaves and halve each diagonally. Rinse, hull, and slice strawberries. Reserve scant ½ cup. Arrange remainder with cress and endive leaves on four plates.

2. Combine reserved strawberries with vinegar, salt, sugar, and pepper in blender or food processor. Whiz to a smooth, light, fluffy puree. With machine running, gradually add oil. Taste and adjust seasoning. Whirl to blend.

3. Spoon dressing over salads and serve at once.

Serves 4

Broiled Curried Belgian Endive with Peanuts

For this dish, do not trim the base of the endives as is customary, or the heads may fall apart during cooking. Hot Madras-style curry powder underscores endive's sweetness; or choose a milder style, as your taste dictates. Roasted peanut oil adds richness and depth. If it is not on hand, substitute 1 tablespoon vegetable oil plus 1 teaspoon Asian (dark) sesame oil. For variety, mint and basil can replace the cilantro.

6 medium Belgian endives
1½ tablespoons peanut oil (preferably roasted)
¾ teaspoon kosher salt
¾ teaspoon curry powder
¼ teaspoon sugar
2 teaspoons lime juice
2 tablespoons roasted, salted peanuts
¼ cup lightly packed cilantro (coriander)
1 tablespoon thin-sliced scallion
    (green onion) tops

1. Cover broiler pan with foil; oil lightly. Preheat broiler. Halve endives lengthwise. Brush cut sides well with 1 tablespoon oil. Blend salt, curry, and sugar; sprinkle over halves. Arrange on pan, cut sides up.

2. Broil endives until fairly tender and lightly browned, 5 to 7 minutes. If necessary, lower pan to prevent burning. Turn halves. Paint with remaining ½ tablespoon oil. Broil until soft, about 5 minutes longer, lowering pan if necessary to prevent overbrowning before endives are cooked through.

3. Arrange halves on serving dish. Drizzle with lime juice. Chop peanuts and cilantro together. Sprinkle over endives, with scallion greens. Serve hot or at room temperature.

Serves 4

Saffron-and-Citrus-Scented Belgian Endive

Muted marigold, with a silky, sauce-like consistency (potato is the light thickener), this melty mélange rounds out grilled fish or poultry or steamed shellfish,

acting as both vegetable and seasoning. Do not undercook the leaves, which mellow as they soften.

1 tiny potato
1 cup water
1½ pounds Belgian endives
⅔ cup fresh orange juice
¼ teaspoon grated orange zest
¼ teaspoon kosher salt
⅛ teaspoon white pepper
Big pinch of saffron threads
About 1 tablespoon butter

1. Grate potato to yield 2 tablespoons very fine shreds. Combine with water in large heavy skillet. Simmer, covered, 5 minutes.

2. Separate Belgian endive leaves. If large, halve crosswise. Add to skillet with orange juice, zest, salt, pepper, saffron, and 1 tablespoon butter.

3. Cook over moderate heat, stirring often, until endive softens somewhat, about 10 minutes. Lower heat and continue cooking until endive is very soft and translucent, about 15 minutes longer, stirring occasionally. If mixture sticks, add a little water.

4. Add seasoning and butter as needed. Serve hot.

Serves 4

Pros Propose

Swiss-born chef Gray Kunz upholds the classics as he continues to break new ground in the United States. About **Creamed Belgian Endive,** he recollects fondly: "We used to make this such a long time ago, in Switzerland. It's one of those simple, amazing dishes that's just right and shouldn't be lost because of food fashions." To prepare: Toss trimmed whole endives with sugar, salt, and lemon juice to coat well. Drop into boiling cream and stock. Return to a boil at once. Cover with parchment and bake in hot oven until succulent and richly coated, at least an hour. Kunz advises keeping a close watch, because "it is important to keep heat high or the endive darkens—and equally important to beware of over-caramelization."

A not-quite-traditional recipe was served in Brussels, land of the vegetable of honor, by chef Jan Raven when he was executive chef at the Royal Windsor Hotel. For **Caramelized and Raw Belgian Endive:** Melt plenty of butter in very large pan. Fill with separated leaves, sprinkle with sugar, and cook very slowly (about an hour) until caramelized. Cool. Toss together raw endive and apple julienne with cream and mustard. Arrange on plate with sautéed rabbit. Top with caramelized endive leaves.

In a modern mode, Gray Kunz developed **Belgian Endive with Truffles** for Lespinasse, in New York City: Toss together bias-cut Belgian endive leaves, salt, pepper, sugar, lemon juice, corn oil, and Madeira. Melt butter in skillet over high heat; stir in endive. Cover and boil 2 minutes. Uncover; reduce liquid. Add truffle juice, thin-sliced fresh black truffles, and butter. Serve at once in deep plates garnished with sautéed whole endive leaves and chervil.

Chef and author Joyce Goldstein used to serve this sprightly **Salad of Endive, Radicchio, Mint, and Blood Orange** at Square One, her celebrated restaurant in San Francisco: Boil lemon juice with chopped mint. Steep briefly, then strain. Add olive oil, orange juice, red wine vinegar, chopped mint, sugar, salt, and grated orange zest. Toss with small radicchio leaves, spears of red and white Belgian endive, and whole mint leaves. Top with blood orange segments.

Another favorite San Francisco chef, Hubert Keller, suggests this simple method for preparing Belgian endive in volume, whether at home or in a restaurant: Simmer trimmed whole endives in salted water with lemon juice and sugar. (Place a damp towel on top to keep heads submerged so they'll cook evenly). When soft, drain, then press out as much liquid as possible. Sprinkle lightly with sugar. Let cool. To serve, heat gently in butter until golden, or heat up with other cooked vegetables.

Chef and author Yamuna Devi gives a contemporary Indian touch to a vegetable that is in no way traditional to the Asian subcontinent, in **Belgian Endive with Cilantro Sauce:** Combine vegetable stock, bay or curry leaves, parsley sprigs, and lime juice in skillet. Cover and simmer 10 minutes. Add cored whole endives, cover, and simmer until tender. Remove endives and boil stock to reduce considerably. Add half-and-half and minced cilantro and warm through. Spoon over endives. Sprinkle with pistachios (from *Yamuna's Table*).

Barbara Kafka, always an original, devised this pale, elegant first course, **Scallop and Endive Soup:** Remove connective muscles from sea scallops. Combine the muscles with chopped shallots, dry white wine, and water. Simmer 15 minutes, uncovered. Strain, discard solids, and return broth to pot. Boil, then add Belgian endives cut into ½-inch pieces. Return to a boil, then add scallops and plenty of fresh tarragon. Stir once to separate scallops. Stir in cream. Dissolve cornstarch in additional cream and stir in a little hot soup. Add to pot, cover, and bring to a boil. Uncover and simmer briefly (from *Soup, A Way of Life*).

Bitter Gourd, Bitter Melon (*Momordica charantia*)

Also balsam pear, foo gua and variations (Chinese), karela and kaveli (Indian), kho-qua (Vietnamese), ampalaya (Philippine), and balsamina (Spanish Caribbean)

Most North Americans find it difficult to imagine that bitter anything can be a hit anywhere—not to mention over half the globe. But the numerous names above (all encountered in markets in the New York City area) suggest that an aggressive personality can be a popular one. We have only recently discovered the appeal of strong "disagreeable" flavors in the form of fresh chilli, a food virtually unknown in this country outside the Southwest until some dozen years ago. In 1982, when I wrote an article about New Mexican food, the test kitchen staff at the magazine would hardly dare nibble the nasty hot peppers—now an American passion.

Bitter melon, like chilli, has a distinct flavor profile and, like chilli, it seems to create a craving. Once enjoyed (few people chomp Jalapeño happily on the first sampling), the craving is satisfied by nothing else—because nothing else resembles it.

When I visited markets in New Jersey, Vietnamese cooks informed me that "best vegetables are strong or bitter" (chillis and bitter gourd rank high) and "bad ones are no taste" (potatoes do not rank at all). Native to the Old World tropics, chiefly Africa, bitter gourd is now established in China, the Philippines, Malaysia, Vietnam, Latin America, Australia, and India—above all—where a gamut of varieties is cultivated (two are pictured).

"In India, we have a deep passion for bitterness,"

bitter gourd or bitter melon: Chinese type (*left*) and Indian type (*right*)   length: 4-8 inches

says Madhur Jaffrey, an authority on the foods of the East, and India in particular. "Even as a child I remember longing for bitter flavors, not sweet ones—and I still do." Bitter melon is a passion in the Philippines (and Hawaii, where Filipino immigrants settled), particularly in the vegetable dish pinakbet. Versions, seemingly infinite, differ—except for the bitter melon, eggplant, and okra that support this dish. Order it when you find it, as I had the good fortune to do at Cendrillon, in New York City. But I would no sooner dare offer a recipe for it than for authentic ratatouille! The restaurateur Longteine de Monteiro, coauthor of *The Elephant Walk Cookbook,* loves the gourd but is uneasy about serving it in her restaurants in the Boston area. She was disappointed to discover that the gourds grown here are far less bitter than what she knew in Cambodia.

Lacking equivalents to bitter gourd, the closest comparisons I can come up with are quinine drinks and citrus pith. The taste is cool and cleansing; the aroma, bracing and grassy. The texture, which varies with size, is generally supple and lightly crisp. Bitter gourd is usually apple green, fairly smooth-skinned, deeply and unevenly furrowed, and about the size and shape of a cucumber. The smaller type common in Indian markets is pointed, mottled ivy green, and extremely warty.

BASIC USE: Technically, you can do just about anything with bitter gourd that you can with zucchini: deep-fry, sauté, stir-fry, braise, steam, bake. Madhur Jaffrey suggests frying as an introduction: "Scatter crunchy bits over fish, as a flavoring accent. As with okra, you begin with crisp, until you develop a taste for it, then move on to not-so-crisp."

Bitter gourd balances intense flavors with aplomb: chilli, garlic, tamarind, ginger, sweet soy, miso, fermented black beans, fish sauce, dried shrimp, curry paste; all match up, singly or as an ensemble. The gourd is a fine foil for sweet vegetables (hard squash, corn, sweetpotatoes), for starches (rice noodles, cornmeal, millet), and for fatty pork or duck or coconut. The easily hollowed gourds make a natural case for rich stuffing.

SELECTION AND STORAGE: Although bitter gourd bruises easily and spoils rapidly, it is available year-round in the stores that sell it—another indication of its popularity. Choose bright, blemish-free gourds—the darkest, smallest, and firmest in the bin. Refrigerate, individually wrapped in paper toweling, then in plastic bags or an airtight box. Kept this way, they'll last 4 to 5 days. Kept any other way, they're dead in a day or two.

PREPARATION: To trim, run a swivel peeler along the ridges to smooth them just slightly (they have a crunchy texture and make a nice presentation); or scrape lightly to remove the dark skin only, not the ridges. Seeds can be removed or not, as taste and size dictate. To remove, cut slices and pop out both seeds and pith with your finger, leaving a green ring; or halve lengthwise and scoop clean. For gourds to be stuffed, halve crosswise, then, working from the wide end, carefully ream out the core of seeds and pith. Stuff the resulting tubes. Cook as is, or slice crosswise into 1-inch rounds.

DE-BITTERING: If you don't like bitterness, don't eat bitter gourds. I have salted, drained, and blanched them; blanched them in baking soda; blanched them without salting—and salted them without blanching. I have cooked them straight. The result? Once they are mixed with other elements (and it is a rare soul who eats bitter gourd alone), distinctions are meaningless. One exception is purely visual: blanched with baking soda (1 teaspoon to 2 quarts water), bitter melon turns bright emerald.

Potatoes, Bitter Gourd, and Peas in Sweet-Spiced Coconut Sauce

This combination of aromatics and coconut milk suits many vegetables, but bitter gourd adds unique base notes to the creamy mixture. Together, coconut and bitter gourd tame spices and heat, so the chillis and ginger become comparatively mild.

It's not handy to use half a box of frozen peas, but more is too much. When you buy the box, squeeze it to be sure the peas are individually frozen, not melted into an icy block. Without defrosting, pour out half and return the rest to the freezer. Freeze half the coconut milk too. Or double everything and have a party! For a vegetable meal, pair the dish with almond-raisin pilaf.

2 medium bitter gourds (6 ounces each)

About 1½ teaspoons kosher salt

¾ teaspoon turmeric

1½ pounds potatoes (preferably
    yellow-fleshed)

1½ tablespoons peanut or corn oil

½ cup sliced shallots

2 or 3 small fresh chillis, such as Jalapeño,
    seeded and diced small

½ teaspoon fennel seeds

1½ to 2 tablespoons coarse-grated or
    minced ginger

1 teaspoon ground coriander

½ teaspoon ground cumin

½ cup water

Half a 10-ounce package of frozen peas

1 cup coconut milk (about half a
    14-ounce can)

1. Peel bitter gourds lightly, leaving ridges. Halve lengthwise. Scoop out seeds if very large; smaller seeds can be left for nice crunch. Cut into ½-inch slices. Toss with 1 teaspoon salt and ½ teaspoon turmeric. Set aside for ½ hour or more, as convenient.

2. Meanwhile, peel potatoes. Cut into ¾-inch cubes. Drop into a pot of boiling salted water and cook until barely tender, 3 to 5 minutes. Lift out with strainer and set aside.

3. Squeeze gourds to press out juice. Rinse. Return pot of water to a boil. Add gourds and boil until barely tender, a few minutes. Drain.

4. Heat oil in heavy saucepan over moderate flame. Add shallots and cook until lightly browned, about 5 minutes, stirring often. Add chillis, fennel, and 1 tablespoon ginger; toss briefly. Stir in remaining ½ teaspoon turmeric, the coriander, and cumin. Add water, potatoes, bitter gourds, peas, and coconut milk. Simmer, covered, until all elements are tender and flavors blend, about 5 minutes.

5. Stir in more ginger and salt to taste. If necessary, uncover to cook to desired consistency.

**Serves 4 to 6 as a side dish,
2 to 4 as the main part of a vegetable meal**

Rice Noodles Sauced with Beef, Bitter Gourd, and Black Beans

At once homey and exotic, this dish runs a gamut of flavors and textures—delicious and a bit messy. Normally, I wouldn't consider half a pound each of starch and meat sufficient for four, but the rice noodles absorb sauce and expand fluffily to yield twice the volume of wheat ones. Chewy morsels of beef and gourd are melded by a surprise ingredient—dark beer, more effective than stock in this context.

½ pound thin dried rice noodles (vermicelli)

2 medium bitter gourds (6 ounces each)

2 or 3 large garlic cloves

3 tablespoons fermented black beans

2 tablespoons peanut oil

Optional: ¼ to ½ teaspoon chilli flakes

½ pound fatty ground beef or pork
    (coarse-ground, if possible)

2 tablespoons soy sauce

2 teaspoons brown sugar

1 cup dark beer

1. Soak noodles in hot water while you prepare the sauce.

2. Peel bitter gourds lightly, leaving ridges. Halve lengthwise. Scoop out seeds if very large; smaller seeds can be left for a nice crunch. Cut into ¼-inch dice. Combine in pot with plenty of water and salt. Bring to a boil and cook until tender, a few minutes. Drain.

3. Mince together garlic and black beans.

4. Heat wok or large pan over moderately high heat. Add oil, then black bean mixture and optional chilli, tossing. Add beef and stir-fry until lightly browned, about 2 minutes. Add soy, sugar, gourds, and beer. Reduce heat. Cover and simmer a few minutes to blend flavors.

5. Drain noodles. Add to wok and cook until most liquid evaporates—3 to 4 minutes—tossing gently to avoid breaking noodles. Add soy and sugar as desired. Serve hot.

Serves 4 as a main course

Bitter Gourd and Sweet Squash with Aromatics

Intense and unadorned, this is a love-it-or-leave-it dish—for a love-it-or-leave-it vegetable. A dense, very sweet squash variety is essential to offset the gourd's bitterness—and, in fact, the two vegetables are best popped in the mouth at the same time for flavor balance. Choose small bitter gourds, whether Chinese or Indian type.

> 1¼ teaspoons cumin seeds
> 1 tablespoon coriander seeds
> ½ teaspoon anise seeds
> 1 pound very small bitter gourds (5 Chinese or 10 Indian type)
> ¾ teaspoon kosher salt
> 2 tablespoons butter
> 1½ tablespoons vegetable oil
> 1 small sweet hard squash (about 1½ pounds), such as kabocha type or Buttercup
> 1 large onion, cut into ½-inch dice

1. Toast cumin, coriander, and anise in very wide skillet (preferably non-stick) over moderately low heat, shaking often, until fragrant and lightly browned. Crush or grind to a medium-coarse texture in suribachi, mortar, or spice mill. Set aside.

2. Very lightly peel gourds—just a slight once-over, to maintain the green underskin and ridges. Cut into ¼-inch slices. Sprinkle with ¼ teaspoon salt.

3. Melt 1 tablespoon butter with ½ tablespoon oil in same skillet in which you toasted spices. Over moderately low heat, brown gourd on both sides, adjusting heat so it cooks slowly—in about 15 minutes. Transfer to dish.

4. Meanwhile, quarter squash lengthwise, then halve each piece crosswise. Remove seeds, peel, and cut into slices ¼ inch thick, trimming so that each piece is about 2 inches long. Toss with ¼ teaspoon salt.

5. Heat remaining 1 tablespoon butter and ½ tablespoon oil in same pan. Add squash, tossing to coat. Cover and cook until not quite tender—3 to 4 minutes (do not cook through, or squash will turn mushy). Uncover. Cook until nicely browned, 5 to 10 minutes, raising heat as needed and tossing. Add to dish.

6. Add remaining ½ tablespoon oil to pan. Add onion and stir over moderate heat to brown lightly, about 5 minutes. Return vegetables to pan. Add spice mixture and remaining ½ teaspoon salt. Cover and cook a few minutes to mingle flavors. Serve hot.

Serves 4

Pros Propose

"**Stuffed Fried Bitter Melon** may be my favorite dish," reflects Madhur Jaffrey, whose mother prepared it this way: Halve small gourds lengthwise, scrape clean, salt, and set at an angle to drain. Rinse, dry, and fill with onions fried until dark brown, ground fennel, chilli, cumin, mango powder, and salt. "Wind them round with lots and lots of thread to keep closed. Fry in shallow oil, turning and turning to brown well."

Chef and author Neelam Batra is of the non-salting school. "Most recipes advocate peeling and using salt to drain the bitter juices from this melon, but I don't find it necessary," she writes in *The Indian Vegetarian*. "Another way in which I vary from traditional cooking is that I bake it instead of deep-frying it." For her **Bitter Melon with Pickling Spices**: Slice small bitter melons, drizzle with mustard oil, spread on baking sheet, and bake until golden. Grind together seeds of coriander, cumin, fenugreek, fennel, and nigella. Brown thin-sliced onions. Add the spice mixture and turmeric and toss. Add small wedges of potato, salt, and water. Cook gently, covered, until liquid evaporates and potatoes are tender. Add bitter melon and salt. Cook briefly, covered, to blend flavors. Add tamarind powder, tomato wedges, and minced cilantro.

Bitter melon is usually spiced, but **Thai Bitter Melon Curry** is more fragrant than most, with its wide range of aromatics: Stir-fry Thai red curry paste; blend in coconut milk. Add minced lemon grass, galangal, shallots, red chilli, sliced mushrooms, rehydrated dried bean curd pieces, 1-inch slices seeded bitter melon, soy, sugar, and salt. Cook until melon is just tender (from *Thai Vegetarian Cooking* by Vatcharin Bhumichitr).

Noodles, especially fresh soft types, are one of the best vehicles for introducing bitter melon. In *The Taste of China,* Ken Hom "marries the tangy flavor of bitter melon with pork and the airy lightness of . . . delicate noodles" in **Minced Bitter Melon with Rice Noodles:** To prepare, slice, halve, seed, and finely chop bitter melon. Blanch 2 minutes; drain. Stir-fry minced garlic in peanut oil. Add ground pork and cook. Add soy sauce, sugar, salt, chicken stock, bitter melon, and fresh rice noodles. Stir-fry until noodles are heated and most liquid has evaporated.

In *Lord Krishna's Cuisine,* Yamuna Devi writes that "no Bengali meal is complete without a bitter dish," and that Bengalis "assert that bitter melon dishes aid digestion, cleanse the blood and encourage a failing appetite." Devi has found **Bitter Melon Chips with Coconut** to be irresistible even to newcomers: Trim off bitter melon tips. Slice gourds crosswise into rounds ¼ inch thick. Sprinkle liberally with salt. Weight and let stand at least ½ hour. Rinse, drain, and pat dry. Heat mustard oil or peanut oil in large skillet (heat mustard oil until it reaches the smoking point, "which makes the pungent oil docile"). Add gourd and stir-fry until crisp and red-brown, 10 to 15 minutes. Off heat, add ground turmeric, paprika or hot pepper, grated coconut, lime juice, and salt. Serve hot or at room temperature.

Blewit, Bluefoot (primarily *Clitocybe saeva*)

Also pied bleu and pied violet (French)

The scientific names of these mushrooms are hopeless. The fluctuating genera—*Clitocybe, Lepista,* and *Tricholoma* (and even more mix-and-match species)—have been changed so many times in recent decades that mycologists usually refer to the mushrooms by their common name, blewit, which has stuck for hundreds of years. Bluefoot, an American marketing name, is a direct translation of the French pied bleu; blewit is conjectured to be a contraction of "blue hat" or a corruption of the French bleuet (cornflower).

Cultivated blewits have recently entered the American marketplace from France, where they are raised year-round. Several edible species of blewit grow in forests and in fairy rings on meadows across North America but are rarely harvested—although they are traditional favorites in France and England, where the lilac wood blewit (*Clitocybe nuda*) is preferred. However, it is the fawn-capped, violet-stemmed field blewit (*C. saeva*) that is cultivated.

Although I have foraged and phone-hunted for wild blewits, I have found only the cultivated ones, which I understand to be far milder. Exceptionally dense, heavy mushrooms, their barely beige indented caps are solid, satiny, and taut. The gills are beige with hints of lavender, and the solid "trunk" looks as if its base had been splotched with French violet ink. Melded twins or even triplets are common. Lightly earthy, fleshy, with a slightly farinaceous flavor, the cultivated blewit is low on aroma—unlike its wild counterparts, which are extolled (or reviled) for their gaminess.

BASIC USE: Chef Philippe Bertineau likes the "woodsy character of the cultivated bluefoot and its solid texture, which is never watery." He finds it ideal to blend with softer mushrooms because it adds so much body and substance. Or he braises blewit slices: Cut ¼-inch slices through trimmed stem and cap. Cook gently in butter with a sprig of thyme and a garlic clove; add a little water, cover, and cook briefly to extract the juices. Uncover; continue to cook on moderate heat just to evaporate juices, not to brown; fleck with parsley.

½ actual size

Or sauté chopped stems with aromatics to soften and brown, then deglaze pan with wine. Add caps, cover, and simmer to cook through; add herbs and seasoning; or add cream and reduce. To roast: Toss caps with nut oil or melted butter and a drop of vinegar or lemon, salt, or soy. Spread on a heated sheet pan. Bake in a hot oven until tender throughout and crisp on the edges, 4 to 5 minutes. Or grill large marinated caps; or stuff and bake.

SELECTION AND STORAGE: Cultivated blewits are available whenever they happen; I can determine no timetable. Bright coloring indicates freshness; the purple fades with age—and with cooking. Caps are choice, stems less so; choose accordingly. Although quite sturdy in general, the mushroom has brittle gills that decay quickly; sniff for spoilage. Refrigerate, uncovered, in a single layer, for no more than a few days.

PREPARATION: Cultivated blewits are exceptionally clean and need only the slightest trimming. Cut off the chewy stems and chop for soup, stuffing, stock, sauce, or stew; or braise with the caps. Halve or quarter caps or cut into eighths. Or keep whole for grilling, roasting, or baking.

Sautéed Blewits with Aromatics

Blewits cooked this way are at once meaty and earthy. Serve alongside veal or lamb chops, for a main course. To offer as a first course, cook off only a little liquid and finish with a touch of sour or sweet cream. Serve over toast points.

1 pound blewits
1 large shallot
2 tablespoons olive oil
Optional: 4 juniper berries, minced
About 1 ounce prosciutto or firm dry-cured
    ham, minced (¼ cup)
Pepper
¼ cup dry sherry or dry Marsala
Salt
About 1 tablespoon lemon juice
3 to 4 tablespoons minced parsley

1. Clean blewits with soft brush. Cut off stems and chop small. Cut caps into quarters or eighths if large; halve if small. Mince shallot.

2. Heat olive oil in skillet wide enough to hold mushrooms in overlapping layer. Add optional juniper, ham, shallot, chopped blewit stems, and pepper. Cook, tossing, to soften and brown slightly, about 5 minutes. Add sherry and simmer until most of liquid has evaporated.

3. Add blewit caps; toss. Cover and simmer over moderately low heat to cook through and exude juices, about 5 minutes. (Can be prepared an hour or two before serving.)

4. To serve: Reheat gently if necessary. Season with salt, pepper, and lemon juice. Toss with parsley.

Serves 4 as a side dish

Salad of Roasted Blewits, Belgian Endive, and Arugula

Blewits' meaty, smooth texture is nicely underscored by crisp bittersweet endive and nippy, soft arugula; but other solid largish mushrooms with sturdy stems and meaty caps (such as cremini) also suit this context. If available, small radicchio di Treviso leaves make a stunning substitute for (or addition to) Belgian endive.

¾ pound blewits
Handful of parsley sprigs
1 medium shallot, halved
¼ cup white wine
¼ cup water
Salt and pepper
1 bunch arugula
2 or 3 medium red or white Belgian endives
3 tablespoons olive oil
1½ tablespoons sherry vinegar
½ tablespoon shoyu (Japanese soy sauce)

1. Cut off mushroom stems flush with caps. Chop stems, parsley, and half the shallot. Combine in small saucepan with wine, water, and a pinch each of salt and pepper. Cover tightly and simmer gently ½ hour.

2. Heat oven to 450°F. Set foil-covered baking sheet on top shelf. Meanwhile, trim, rinse, and spin-dry arugula. Rinse and trim endives. Slice larger leaves into crescents; leave smaller ones whole.

3. Blend 1 tablespoon olive oil, ½ tablespoon vinegar, and shoyu; toss with caps. Mince remaining ½ shallot. Mix with remaining 1 tablespoon vinegar and 2 tablespoons oil.

4. When stems are cooked, drain in strainer. Press out and reserve juices, and return to saucepan. Boil to reduce to 2 tablespoons. Add to shallot mixture.

5. Spread mushroom caps on heated baking sheet, gill side up. Bake until tender throughout and crisp on the edges, 4 to 5 minutes.

6. When mushrooms are cooked, toss dressing with greens. Arrange on plates. Cut caps into ½-inch strips and arrange over all. Grind over pepper and serve.

Serves 4 as a first course or salad course

Bok Choy, Pak Choi and relatives

(*Brassica rapa*, primarily Chinensis Group)

Including **seedling, Canton, Shanghai, Taiwan, choy sum types;** and **tatsoi** and **yau choy**

See also: **CHINESE CABBAGE,** page 195

Mild, juicy, and accessible, the closely related leafy greens collectively called bok choy are as difficult to identify by name as they are easy to eat.

Just what *is* bok choy? "Bok choy [is] sometimes referred to as Chinese cabbage," writes A. Zee in his delicious cultural-culinary journey, *Swallowing Clouds,* raising the first problem: interchangeable names. Since both originate in China, perhaps translation will clarify? Zee then illustrates that the character "choy" (Cantonese, also romanized as "choi") means "vegetable," and the character "bok" (or "pak") means "white." There you have it: white vegetable! Add "sum" (meaning "heart") and you see what's needed to get you everywhere and nowhere in defining bok choy.

Will scientific nomenclature come to the rescue? Unfortunately, when it comes to the genus *Brassica,* to which everything we know as bok choy and Chinese cabbage belongs (along with hundreds of other plants), scientists disagree. Although most concur on the species *rapa,* each vegetable has a subspecies or subgroup or two to argue about as well. No answer there.

"Once you decide to put anything on paper about *Brassica,*" says Paul Williams, head of the Crucifer Genetics Cooperative at the University of Wisconsin in Madison, "you're leaving footprints in the snow for all to see and to step on. Scientists and produce marketers and seed companies function—if you can call it that—independently when it comes to *Brassica* names." Rather than add my footprints, I have borrowed names from Paul Williams; from Peter Crisp, director of Innovar Plant Breeding in Norfolk, England; and from Joy Larkcom, author of *Oriental Vegetables.*

The general term "bok choy" embraces several growth stages of the same plant: seedling, "baby," mature, and flowering. Confusion arises because each stage may look like a distinctly different vegetable. The term also designates scores of varieties of bok choy, the bulk of which fall into these general groups: large white-stemmed (the most common type), dwarf white-stemmed, and green-stemmed. A type called Taiwan bok choy looks like baby Chinese cabbage and stands alone. (For the purpose of grouping, please know and forget that bok choys are also referred to as Chinese celery cabbage, Chinese white cabbage, and mustard cabbage, and by other confusable names.)

Bok choy seedlings or shoots or bok choy miu (and "chicken feather" in China, according to Joy Larkcom) are the smallest market form of the plant—just a few leaflets to a cluster. They may be one of several types (Shanghai, Canton, etc.) and so may look

bok choy seedlings   length: 3-7 inches

different from one another. But all are juicy, mild, all-edible, and pleasing to munch raw and cooked.

PREPARATION: Pick over and remove bruised leaves. Cut a slim slice from the base of each cluster. Very gently swoosh leaves in several changes of water. Spin-dry for salad or for stir-fry.

TO COOK—OR NOT: Stir-fry or sauté very briefly, or stir into broth; or enjoy raw in a delicate salad mix.

Canton or dwarf is the type of bok choy common in Chinatowns in the United States. A short and squat form of the vegetable, its stalks are very plump, pearly-white, bland, tender, and gushingly juicy. The dark, curled leaves resemble Swiss chard but taste clearly cabbagey. Cooked just right, this bok choy is light, re-freshing, and almost airy; overcooked, it is dull mush.

"Baby" bok choy is a term used for both the dwarf type and small, immature plants of larger varieties. In culinary terms, anything that applies to "dwarf" ap-plies to "baby."

PREPARATION: Halve lengthwise; or quarter, if large. With leaf tips down, plunge into water, dunking energetically to reach the sandy depths. Repeat until base of stalks is clean. If you plan to cut up bok choy for a recipe, cut stalks apart for easier cleaning.

TO COOK: For best all-around flavor and texture, drop into boiling salted water, cook a minute or two, and drain. Then heat in oil or butter to barely color. Or oven-braise in broth, butter-topped, in a moderate oven for ½ hour. Or steam.

Mature bok choy is the full-grown, leggy (10 to 20 inches) vegetable common in Western supermarkets. Its relatively slim stalks are satiny, its curly leaves are spruce green. Although they may resemble Swiss chard, they taste nothing like it, having a mild, juicy sweetness that suggests cabbagey romaine.

PREPARATION: If necessary, trim the base (if in good shape, slice fairly thin and cook it with the stalks). Discard blemished leaves. Separate stalks as you would celery. Rinse thoroughly, checking base of stems. Slice leaves from stalks (the tiny heart can be left whole). Cut wide stems lengthwise, then into diagonals, cross-wise strips, or dice. Tear leaves bite-size or cut into chiffonade.

TO COOK: For most dishes, cook stems and leaves separately, as the latter take only seconds to soften. Stir-fry, adding the leaves and some liquid to finish cooking the stems. Make simple soups by combining stock, shreds of meat, ribbons of bok choy leaves (halve

Canton or dwarf bok choy   **length: 6-8 inches**

mature bok choy   **length: 16 inches**

Shanghai or green-stemmed bok choy   length: 6-10 inches

Taiwan or Fengshan bok choy   length: 9-10 inches

lengthwise, stack, then cut in very thin slices), and a snippet of ginger; then simmer for 5 minutes. Or oven-braise with broth and butter for a melting uniform texture.

Shanghai or green-stemmed bok choy, graceful and relatively small, is increasing in popularity, thanks to its sculptured shape, jade hue, mellow cabbage flavor, and easy cookability (stems and leaves are cooked together). Although other green varieties are sold, "Shanghai" was the first introduced to the West and seems to have lent its name to the lot.

PREPARATION: Keep whole, if tiny; or halve lengthwise. Dunk vigorously into plenty of water, spreading leaves to dislodge the sand that hides between layers. Repeat; check carefully.

TO COOK: Steam a few minutes for uniform translucent green color, light texture, sweetness, juiciness, and a shapely form. Or blanch briefly in salted water with a little oil for a quintessential Chinese jade gleam. Serve as is, or drain and reheat in butter, meat juices, oil, or all three. Or braise with broth and butter, covered, in a moderate oven for ½ hour or so. Do not stir-fry.

Taiwan or Fengshan bok choy looks like a tiny cylindrical Chinese cabbage composed of just a few soft, lettuce-like chartreuse leaves. Very juicy and mild with a bare hint of cabbage, the delicate, pliable leaves turn brilliant when cooked. Although tissue-thin,

they hold their shape without tearing, making perfect wrappers.

PREPARATION: Trim base to separate the leaves, then wash gently, paying attention to the sandy lower part.

TO COOK: Use as a bed when steaming seafood. Stir ribbons into soup. Blanch by boiling or steaming, then drain; heat in butter.

Choy (or choi) sum is an impossible term! Consultation with a dozen scientists and native Chinese culinary specialists leads to three distinct meanings—defended by various supporters with unswerving assurance:

(1) Choy sum, as shown in the photo on page 100, is a small, branching, white-stemmed, yellow-flowered plant similar to—but not the same as—bok choy; it is called choy sum at any stage of growth, flowering or not.

(2) Choy sum, meaning vegetable heart, refers to the tender central flowering stalk and small leaves of *any* plant in the choy clan.

(3) Choy sum is neither of the above but the same plant as yau choy (see page 101), which goes by the name choy sum in southern China, particularly Hong Kong.

PREPARATION: For the first two meanings (anything but yau choy), the goal is the same: to divide the plants into fairly equal-size pieces, whether by cutting diagonal sections or dividing into branchlets or "baby choylets." Cut leaves as large as possible to maintain

choy (or choi) sum

length: 9–12 inches

tatsoi or rosette bok choy

¼ actual size

yau choy (or yu choy or yu choy sum), mature and seedling forms   length: 5-6 and 11-12 inches

the pretty natural form while still permitting polite eating. Cut the relatively heavy central stems into thin slices, or give them a little extra cooking time. Rinse several times, as sand hides in the interstices.

TO COOK: Blanch by boiling or steaming, then cook briefly in oil or sauce. Or stir-fry, then cover to cook through; add a touch of cornstarch dissolved in liquid to finish cooking.

Tatsoi or rosette bok choy is also called wu ta cai and tai koo choi in Chinese markets; tatsoi and tasai are Japanese variants, according to Joy Larkcom. Peter Crisp includes this with the Narinosa Group of the *Brassica rapa,* rather than Chinensis. The pretty plant is also unattractively called flat cabbage—to describe its horizontal growing habit. Whether it is flat or an alternative upright bouquet form, it has celery-green stems topped by darker green, succulent, smoothish-to-puckered leaves (depending upon the variety). Like other bok choy, it is harvested in many sizes. In the United States, where it is usually called by the Japanese name, tatsoi, it is the glossy lollipop leaf in mesclun mixes—juicy, crisp, cabbagey. It is tougher and stronger-tasting than other bok choy. Cooked, it mellows.

PREPARATION: When leaves are sold loose, they need only be rinsed lightly. For smallish heads, halve or quarter, then plunge into plenty of water to dislodge soil that clings to the leafstalks. Repeat as needed. Cut large heads into clusters or individual leaves.

TO COOK—OR NOT: Mix tiny leaves with salad greens and enjoy them raw. Steam or boil to barely wilt, then stir-fry. Or add to soup. Tiny bunches need no preliminary blanching but do need a little liquid to finish cooking.

Yau choy or yu choy or yu choy sum (also yau tsoi, you cai, and similar romanizations, according to Joy Larkcom) is one of those rolling brassicas. It may belong to the Chinensis, the Oleifera (edible oilseed rape), or the Utilis Group, depending on the expert consulted and the day of the week. Wherever it finally stops in the taxonomic roulette, yau choy remains a delicious and substantial vegetable in the wok. When mature, its fairly long (10 to 12 inches), yellow-budded, kelly green stems are dense and fleshy, similar to Chinese broccoli (page 190), but more slender and leafy. Cooked, the stems are bright deep green, uniformly tender, sweet, and meaty; the leaves develop an earthy taste more assertive than that of other bok choys, but not bitter.

Yau choy is one of the vegetables included in the "choy sum" confusion mentioned in the entry of that name (page 99). In *Bruce Cost's Asian Ingredients,* Cost explains that "Yow choy sum or yow choy" is "the ubiquitous green of Hong Kong, where it's called simply *choy sum,* or 'flowering green' (the same term that's used for bok choy sum around Guangzhou and in Guandong Province, and also by most Chinese vegetable dealers in this country.)"

PREPARATION: If small, do no more than trim a tad from the base. If large, cut bite-size pieces: Slice stalks into 2-inch diagonals, halving the stem lengthwise if wide.

TO COOK: Blanch by boiling or steaming; then stir-fry or sauté. The two-step method makes all the difference. For the "babies," simply stir-fry or sauté very briefly, or stir into broth.

All the distinctions notwithstanding, there are a few generalizations that can be made about bok choy and company.

BASIC USES FOR BOK CHOYS: "The differences in bok choys are largely visual," says caterer and author Rosa Lo San Ross. "Chinese love the way each looks, so the goal is to preserve the original shape." Only large bok choy is meant to be cut up. "Leave others whole or halve, then braise or steam." Serve plain or as bouquets around seafood.

It is surprising to discover that bok choys are not enhanced by stir-frying, which is the usual recommendation in the culinary literature. Direct high heat brings out bitterness, and makes them watery and fibrous. But if they are blanched beforehand, or cooked with a little liquid, they are juicy and tender. Experiment: It's the difference between delicious and dull.

Blanching makes bok choy shine—literally and figuratively. Chef Susanna Foo keeps a pot of buttered stock simmering for the miniature Shanghai and choy sum she favors as garnishes. She removes outer leaves for stuffing, keeping the vegetable heart, which she blanches just before serving, replenishing the butter as the evening goes on.

Bok choy loves oyster sauce. More than half the chefs with whom I discussed the vegetable suggested using the sauce as a finishing touch. Joseph Schultz says that the sugar, acid, salt, and touch of starch are just the complements needed. (Others he recommends are sweet tomatoes or red bell peppers, tart lime or vinegar, and salty ham or fermented black beans.) He advises, however, "Remember that ingredients in oyster sauce range from fine to foul. Read the label and go for the fewest ingredients and highest price—more oyster and less goop."

Assemble tasty, simple soups in minutes with stock, meat shreds, slivered bok choy leaves, and a snippet of ginger; simmer 5 minutes. Add soft tofu dice during the last minute of simmering. Dice stalks for a celery-like contribution.

For softer stalks cooked in the Cantonese style: Using ½ teaspoon baking soda for each quart of water, boil briefly to get the puffy authentic texture. Fry for a moment in oil, then coat lightly with a delicate egg, crab, or cream sauce.

SELECTION AND STORAGE: Most types of bok choy are available all year at Oriental markets, farmers' markets, and some specialty supermarkets. Seedling forms and Taiwan bok choy are available intermittently. Keep unwashed bok choy in a perforated plastic bag in the vegetable crisper for no more than a few days; it wilts much more rapidly than head cabbage.

Simplest Bok Choy, Buttered and Cheese-Dusted

A brief simmer in water to which oil and/or butter has been added transforms bok choy. Choose vase-shaped Shanghai type or small, pearly-stemmed Canton, or the heart (*sum*) of either. Select heads of equal size so they cook evenly. For variety, toss with minced fresh dill and chives instead of cheese.

> 4 to 6 "baby" Shanghai or Canton bok choy or
>   8 to 10 bok choy hearts (to equal 1¼ to
>   1½ pounds)
> 1 teaspoon kosher salt
> ½ tablespoon corn, grapeseed, or safflower oil
> 1 tablespoon butter
> ½ cup grated Gruyère or Comté cheese

1. If individual bok choy weighs 4 ounces or more, halve lengthwise; if smaller, leave whole and cut a deep slit in the base. With leaf tips down, plunge into water, dunking energetically to reach sandy depths. Repeat until bases of stalks are clean.

2. Arrange bok choy in very wide deep skillet. Add water to just cover. Add salt and oil. Cover and bring to a boil. With tongs, turn over vegetables. Continue simmering, uncovered, until just barely done to taste, usually 4 to 5 minutes.

3. Holding lid against pan, carefully drain off all liquid. Return pan to moderate heat; shake to dry bok choy somewhat and distribute evenly. Add butter and continue cooking and shaking pan until heads are lightly golden, turning once.

4. Transfer to heated serving dish or serve from pan, first sprinkling with cheese.

Serves 4

Bok Choy Stems Stir-Fried with Almonds

Pale, nacreous stems of relatively large (mature) bok choy can be delicious if neatly cut, seasoned lightly, and cooked with care. Do not be tempted to overseason the mild, juicy stalks. Monitor carefully to prevent under-cooking or overcooking. Save the dark, strong leaves to mix with other greens in braises or for soup or stuffing.

> **2 pounds white-stemmed mature bok choy**
> **1 teaspoon cornstarch**
> **½ teaspoon sugar**
> **½ teaspoon kosher salt**
> **2 teaspoons water**
> **2 teaspoons lemon juice**
> **⅓ cup blanched, roasted, and salted almonds**
> **1 tablespoon peanut oil**
> **2 teaspoons minced ginger**
> **1 teaspoon minced garlic**

1. Cut apart bok choy stems at base. Slice leaves from stems (reserve for another use). Rinse stalks well, halve lengthwise any wider than 1¼ inches. At an angle, cut into slices 1 inch wide. (You'll have about 6 cups.) Blend cornstarch, sugar, salt, water, and lemon

juice; set aside. Chop almonds medium-fine. Have other ingredients ready.

2. Set wok over moderately high heat. Pour oil into pan around edge. Add stems and toss until slightly soft-ened but still crunchy, about 2 minutes. Add ginger and garlic and toss 30 seconds. Reduce heat slightly, cover, and cook until stems are almost tender throughout, about 2 minutes.

3. Uncover. Stir cornstarch mixture and add, toss-ing. Continue tossing a minute or so, until surface of bok choy is slicked and stalks are cooked through. Add nuts and toss. Serve at once.

Serves 4

Choy Sum Stir-Fried with Ham and Ginger

Like celery, bok choy and choy sum add crunch and color. But it's quite a challenge to focus a dish on the vegetable alone. Although easy to cook, it is difficult to cook *just* right.

Here's why it took twelve tests to find a simple, ef-fective stir-fry: Choy sum's texture was uneven when cooked entirely uncovered or covered—it needed both; high heat resulted in a scorched taste; multiple in-gredients hid the choy character; sauced, the satiny sur-face of the stalks turned slippery; ingredients with defined texture undermined the contrasting leaf and stalk textures; bright colors washed out the pretty greens; when pieces were small, the form of the plant was lost; when large, they were ungainly to eat.

The winner follows: pearly, juicy-crisp stalks and chewy-soft dark leaves accented by rosy, salty, firm, ham bits and fresh ginger shreds—delicate seasoning for a vegetable whose message is freshness, lightness, and textural contrasts. The bit of cornstarch prevents "weeping" and adds gloss; it does not make a sauce.

> **1½ pounds choy sum (see Note)**
> **1 teaspoon cornstarch**
> **1½ tablespoons dry sherry**
> **1½ tablespoons peanut oil (preferably roasted)**
> **About 4 ounces firm ham, cut into very small dice (1 cup)**
> **1 tablespoon peeled, coarse-grated ginger**

1. Rinse choy sum. Cut outer stalks and leaves into 1½- to 2-inch pieces. Leave smaller interior leaves, buds, and small stems whole. Cut central ribbed stalk into ½-inch slices. Rinse all again and spin-dry. Blend cornstarch and sherry.

2. Have remaining ingredients ready. Heat wok over moderately high heat. Add peanut oil. Add ham and ginger and toss for 1 minute. Add choy sum and continue tossing until leaves are almost wilted, 2 to 3 minutes; do not brown.

3. Cover pan; cook until stalks are tender, about 2 minutes, tossing twice and re-covering. Add cornstarch mixture and toss until glazed and shiny, about 1 minute. Serve at once.

Serves 4

Note: Canton, baby, or mature bok choy can be substituted for choy sum. To prepare, cut apart leaves and stalks of cleaned vegetable. Cut stalks at an angle into 1½-inch lengths (halve mature bok choy stems lengthwise if large). Slice leaves into large bite-size pieces.

Tatsoi Wilted in Mustard Dressing

Crisp pale stalks topped with ivy green glossy leaves are quick to prepare and just the right note to complement seafood. The color is as vivid as the mustardy tang of the tatsoi, a taste echoed by the lightly sharp dressing.

4 small tatsoi heads (about 1 pound)
2 medium scallions (green onions)
2 tablespoons lemon juice
1 teaspoon Dijon mustard
¼ teaspoon kosher salt
3 tablespoons olive oil

1. Trim tatsoi bases to separate leaves. Rinse in several changes of water, inspecting carefully for grains of sand. Spin-dry.

2. Cut apart scallion bulbs and greens. Mince bulbs. Thin-slice greens. Combine bulbs with lemon juice, mustard, and salt, stirring to dissolve salt. Blend in oil.

3. Pour dressing into a very wide skillet set over moderate heat. Add leaves and turn to coat with dressing (tongs are most efficient). Cook until leaves almost wilt but stems retain crunch, about 2 minutes. Add scallion greens and toss.

4. Arrange tatsoi on a rectangular plate, lined up like asparagus. Pour over any dressing that remains in pan.

Serves 4 as a side dish

Sautéed Yau Choy with Walnuts

Juicy, firm, and sweet with a clean green flavor, this adaptable vegetable is more substantial than most bok choys, but not as forceful as most dark leafy brassicas. Versatile, it is open to interpretation in roles hot, at room temperature, and chilled; plain and fancy. Walnuts are a fitting companion, but pecans, peanuts, or almonds also match, as do garlic, chilli, carrots, onion, and ginger.

Prepare the dish in advance through step 3, if preferred, then refrigerate. Sauté at serving time.

½ cup walnuts
About 1¼ pounds yau choy
About 1 teaspoon kosher salt
1½ tablespoons walnut or peanut oil
1 small garlic clove, minced
Pepper

1. Heat oven or toaster oven to 350°F. Spread walnuts in pan and bake until crisp and toasty, 8 to 10 minutes. Chop coarse.

2. Trim base of yau choy stalks slightly; rinse. Arrange in a single layer in large skillet. Add water to barely cover and salt. Bring to a boil over highest heat and cook until yau choy is not quite tender, about 2 minutes.

3. Drain (no need to wash skillet). Set yau choy on cutting board. Squeeze leaves to remove water. Cut stalks and leaves into bite-size pieces.

4. Return skillet to moderate heat. Add walnut oil and garlic and toss for a moment, until garlic is fragrant but not browned. Add yau choy and toss to fin-

ish cooking, about 2 minutes. Add nuts and toss another 30 seconds. Season. Serve hot or at room temperature.

Serves 4

Pros Propose

Stephen Wong, restaurant consultant and author, bases his recipes on traditional Chinese and international perspectives. For **Basic Bok Choy Shoots:** Toss shoots just a moment in hot pan with plenty of oil. Drain pan and set on high heat. Return shoots to pan with a little garlic and a touch of stock. Season with sugar and fish sauce. Serve at once. For **Basic Shanghai Bok Choy with Garnishes,** the finishing touches are multicultural: Remove outer leaves from medium Shanghai bok choy and save for another use. Halve and blanch heads; drain. Heat through in clarified butter. Top with flying fish roe (tobiko), fried shallots, or crisp bacon bits; or coat with velouté sauce and dot with salmon roe.

Chef Paul Wildermuth features a raw "slaw" that he serves as a relish with barbecued meats or noodle dishes. For **Spicy Bok Choy Salad:** Thin-slice bok choy leaves. Cut stems lengthwise into narrow strips. Toss with salt. Let wilt ½ hour. Rinse and dry. Combine with red pepper julienne, hair-thin Thai chilli strands, sliced mint and Thai basil, slivered ginger in syrup, toasted sesame seeds, rice vinegar, salt, and pepper. Serve freshly made as soon as assembled.

Peripatetic chef and author Ken Hom adapted a northeastern Chinese seaweed dish for **Crispy "Seaweed"** from bok choy leaves: Wash and spin-dry leaves. Cut into chiffonade. Spread on baking sheet. Dry 20 minutes in a low oven. Cool. Deep-fry in small batches in peanut oil; drain on towels. Toss with salt, sugar, and toasted pine nuts (from *Ken Hom's Chinese Kitchen*).

Choy Sum with Eggplant–Black Bean Sauce was a very popular dish for chef Joseph Schultz: Cut twice as much choy sum as eggplant into largish pieces, dividing tougher and tender parts. Stir-fry Chinese fermented black beans with garlic, ginger, and slivered red chilli. Add thin-sliced slim Chinese eggplant and sear.

Add sugar, stock (enough to cook eggplant to sauce-like softness), and tougher choy parts; cook briefly. Add tender parts and cook through. Add salt and distilled vinegar. Top with fried garlic chips.

With tiny tatsoi, Sylvia Thompson tosses a forceful little salad of **Rosette Pak Choi, Sweet Basil, and Nasturtium:** Combine small whole leaves of tatsoi with half as much fresh basil leaves, sliced in half, and a handful of nasturtium flowers and leaves. Dress lightly with nut oil mixed with rice vinegar (from *The Kitchen Garden Cookbook*).

Colorful **Stir-Fried Shrimp with Tatsoi** makes a quick main course: Cut apart tatsoi head, keeping leaf-stalks whole; rinse thoroughly. Heat wok. Add light sesame oil and minced garlic and ginger. Toss in peeled, deveined medium shrimp and stir-fry to just turn pink; transfer to bowl. Add more oil, garlic, and ginger, then red bell pepper julienne and minced scallion, and toss. Add tatsoi and stir-fry to barely wilt. Transfer to bowl. Blend tamari, mirin, Asian sesame oil, vegetable or seafood stock, and arrowroot; stir in wok until clear. Add shrimp and tatsoi and toss to combine (from *Greens Glorious Greens!* by Johnna Albi and Catherine Walthers).

Stephen Wong reminds us that for "tatsoi, like most brassicas, the goal for Chinese cooks is to maintain the look and flavor of the plant—not to cut it into unrecognizable pieces or hide it in sauce." For **Tatsoi Sauté:** "Simply halve or quarter the tatsoi bunch at the base, without detaching the leaves. Do no more than stir-fry for a moment with garlic, salt, and pepper."

Chef and author Susanna Foo divides yau choy, peels the stems, and serves the tips raw in her non-traditional **Yau Choy with Pasta and Dried Tomato:** Cut central bud with small leaves from yau choy; reserve for garnish. Peel central stalk; chop with leaves. Briefly stir-fry with garlic. Add cooked cavatelli, sun-dried tomato strips, and enough stock to cook through and moisten the whole. Garnish with reserved raw buds.

Bruce Cost prepares more traditional **Yau Choy with Black Vinegar:** Cut off and discard bottom few inches of yau choy stems. Cut remainder into 2-inch lengths, leaves and all. Mix Chinese black vinegar, sugar, salt, Shaoxing wine, and water. Stir-fry fine julienne of ginger and the prepared yau choy in lard or peanut oil until wilted. Add vinegar mixture and stir briefly. Cover, reduce heat, and steam briefly. Remove cover, raise heat, and stir until most liquid is absorbed, another 2 minutes or so. Stir in slivered country ham (from *Bruce Cost's Asian Ingredients*).

Yau Choy with Miso Dressing, from chef James Chew, makes a good buffet dish at room tempera-ture—somewhat in the style of Japanese ohitashi: Steam trimmed yau choy. Refresh in cold water; drain. Press dry on towels. Cut into neat 2-inch lengths and arrange in a block. Drizzle with dressing of red miso, minced shallot, lime juice, and canola and sesame oils.

Bottle Gourd (*Lagenaria siceraria*)

Also calabash, hu lu gua and similar names (Chinese),
lauki and dudhi (Indian), upo (Philippine)

Including **cucuzza** and **tennerumi**

Note: Although this gourd is sometimes called serpent gourd,
that name properly applies to another genus, *Tricosanthes*.

Cucurbits—a colloquial catchall term used to signify members of the *Cucurbitaceae* or gourd family (which includes some 800 species)—are as often as not notable more for their usefulness than their distinctiveness. Mild, versatile, and adaptable, the bottle gourd, for example, appears in daily meals from India to Italy, China to Mexico.

Although Americans new to it may think of it as an odd newcomer, the bottle gourd "has a longer documented history of use, in both the Old and New Worlds, than any other plant" according to the authors of *Cucurbits,* R. W. Robinson and D. S. Decker-Walters. In another renowned study, *The Gourd Book,* Charles Heiser devotes 157 pages to what he calls simply *the* gourd. "Its greatest use has been as a bottle or container . . . and for that reason alone . . . [it was] one of man's most important plants before the invention of pottery," Heiser writes. But it has also been used for "food, floats, musical instruments, medicine, artistic endeavors, and as an almost indispensable item in man's attire."

About "man's attire": Bottle gourds have served for centuries as protectors of mankind's manhood in the tropics—and to judge from a notice in *The Cucurbit Network News* (a Miami-based publication that perhaps not all my readers subscribe to) may also do so in the United States: "Our recent offering of penis gourd [a type of bottle gourd] seeds was well received; we distributed seeds to 22 *TCN* members. On what we hope is a non-related matter, Peter Waterman holds the world record for the longest gourd . . . at 110⅝ inches."

The Italian food authority Lidia Matticchio Bastianich has childhood memories of another nonedible use for bottle gourds: "My grandfather would pick the largest and let them dry completely in the sun. . . . He would then tie two gourds at their stems with a rope,

¼ **actual size**

leaving slack of about 1½ feet. We used this as a lifesaver, having a gourd float from each of our underarms."

And, yes, people do *eat* bottle gourd! What's noteworthy about it is its fiberless flesh, which remains satiny and uniform whether hot, warm, or cold. Relatively smooth-skinned, pale lime green smaller specimens, cooked briefly, are reminiscent of firm chayote, or of cucumber and zucchini, although firmer and milder. Immature gourds are cooked like summer squash in India, China, Africa, and South America, to name several vast areas. In Japan, the flesh of a type called Yūgao is cut into strips and dried to become kamypo, an ingredient ubiquitous in the cuisine. Older gourds are also eaten, although primarily in candied form.

There is such diversity in the size and shape of the bottle gourd that each country, and even each region, claims it as a local specialty. When a friend pointed out his favorite "Italian squash" (cucuzza) at the Union Square Greenmarket in Manhattan, he could hardly have known that it was a form of the same gourd we had picked up in Chinatown.

Cucuzza (*Lagenaria siceraria 'Longissima'*), also called zucca lunga or Hercules war club, is a bottle gourd best known in parts of Italy and among people of Italian descent. This is also true of its greens, called ten(n)e-rumi. "The young cucuzzi are eaten around Naples, in Sicily, and in Sardinia," says the Italian food authority Giuliano Bugialli, "but rarely anywhere else in Italy. 'Cucuzza' is a slangy word for zucca, which just means squash." The greens and the plushy, fuzzy leaves and chewy buds are also cooked, with the gourd or separately. A traditional squash preserve called zuccata—or, in Sicilian, cucuzzata—is made from mature cucuzza.

BASIC USE: Shredded raw bottle gourd, bland and light-textured, adds billowy body to raita made with yogurt and herbs. Sautéed or braised like summer squash (but for a longer time), bottle gourd can be delicious, provided it receives a flavor boost of aromatics—without which it tastes like overgrown zucchini. Or enjoy its juicy texture in saucy and soupy dishes. Having microwaved, steamed, and sautéed the squash solo, I can say that all such methods should be avoided.

The fleshy greens are mild but with a tendency

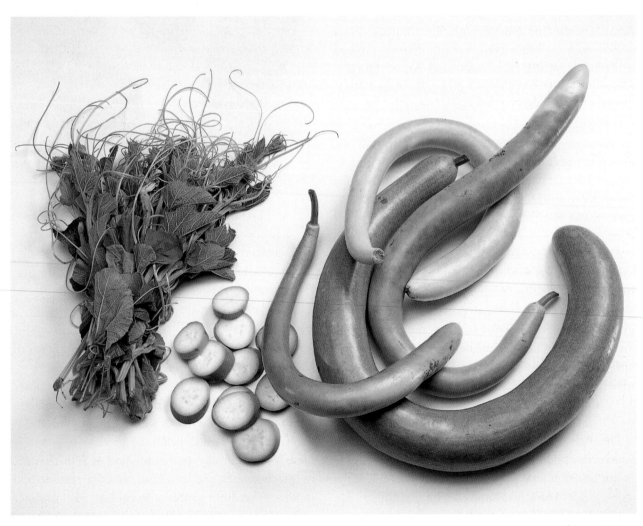

cucuzza   ¼ actual size

toward bitterness: Taste and blanch or season accordingly. Chop and add to soups or mixed vegetable stews, cooking only briefly.

SELECTION AND STORAGE: Bottle gourd can be found most of the year—with the exception of the Italian type, which is usually a summertime special. Gourds may be slim and straight, bottle-shaped and bulbous, snaky or yoke-like—and everything in between. As long as they are comparatively small, green, heavy, and hard, they are good, whatever the form. This is true, as well, of the Mae West shapes: Even though they are round and full, if selected carefully they will be no more pithy than narrow forms.

Both gourds and greens languish quickly. Do not plan to refrigerate for more than a day or two, paper-wrapped.

PREPARATION: The youngest and slimmest (usually cucuzza-type) need no peeling. Others should be pared lightly to retain some green, or peeled with a heavy hand if the skin is tough. If small, slice as zucchini. For larger gourds, halve, quarter lengthwise, pare away seeds and pith, then cut slim bite-size pieces.

To prepare greens, cut off and reserve the leaves, buds, and their attached stems; rinse, bunch together, then slice thin. Discard stalks and attached tendrils (however cute, they are inedibly tough).

Bottle Gourd Raita with Mint

A refreshing recipe based on one from Rashmi Aggarwala, who formerly taught Indian cooking in The New School's Culinary Program in New York City. Bottle gourd lends more textural effect than flavor, creating a light, airy salad or salsa. There is no reason to stop at raita's traditional role as a cooling side dish for super-spicy Indian dishes. It also adds freshness to chili con carne or sweet-hot barbecue.

Flavors develop as the mixture rests—but no more than a few hours, or the clean taste and texture vanish. Choose the yogurt that suits your style, from low-fat to full-fat; non-fat has a chalky edge and tends to separate.

1 pound bottle gourd
About ½ cup packed mint leaves
2 to 3 cups yogurt
About ½ teaspoon ground cumin
About ⅛ teaspoon ground hot pepper
Salt

1. Lightly pare bottle gourd to remove only the thinnest top layer of skin. Grate by hand or in food processor, using light pressure to make fairly small shreds. Forcefully squeeze a handful at a time to remove juice. Place shreds in a bowl.

2. Rinse mint leaves and spin-dry; slice thin. Add ¼ cup to gourd shreds, with 2 cups yogurt, ½ teaspoon cumin, ⅛ teaspoon hot pepper, and salt. Taste and adjust seasonings, using a bit less than you might think necessary (flavors will develop slightly as raita stands). Cover and chill about an hour.

3. Taste and stir in additional yogurt, mint, and seasoning to taste.

Makes 2 to 3 cups, to serve 6 as a side dish

Bottle Gourd (or Cucuzza) in Spiced Fresh Tomato Puree

What's special about bottle gourd cooked this way is its smooth flesh—like melting melon, but with crunch. Sweet spices perfume fresh tomato puree, which in turn is scented with a mince of coriander leaves—all lending flavors to the bland squash, which absorbs them discreetly. Between salad and cooked vegetable, the dish makes a useful buffet item. Or serve alongside grilled seafood or poultry, or as part of a vegetarian meal, with quinoa or rice.

2 pounds firm, slim bottle gourd
   (or cucuzza)
1 medium-large onion
3 tablespoons corn (preferably unrefined),
   sunflower, or peanut oil
1 teaspoon anise seeds
1 tablespoon ground coriander
   (preferably coarse-ground)
½ teaspoon ground cumin
¼ teaspoon fine-ground white pepper
1 tablespoon grated ginger
1 teaspoon kosher salt
1 pound plum tomatoes
¼ to ½ cup minced cilantro (coriander) leaves

1. Peel gourd. Quarter lengthwise. Cut out any seeds and attached spongy pith. Cut gourd into slim bite-size triangles. Dice onion.

2. Heat 2 tablespoons oil in wide casserole or sauté pan over moderately low heat. Add anise seeds and stir a moment. Add onion and cook until slightly softened, stirring occasionally. Add coriander, cumin, pepper, and ginger. Cook about 2 minutes, stirring.

3. Add gourd and salt. Cook until juices are released and pan is deglazed, about 5 minutes. Raise heat to moderate and continue cooking until gourd is slightly golden and most liquid evaporates, about 5 minutes longer.

4. Meanwhile, peel tomatoes (see Note, page 10) and chop. Press through food mill to puree and remove seeds.

5. Add tomato puree to pan. Adjust heat to a gentle simmer. Stir often until slices are translucent and sauce thickens, about 10 minutes.

6. Cool to lukewarm; or chill, if preferred. Fold in remaining 1 tablespoon oil and cilantro.

Serves 4 to 6

Summery Cucuzza with Basil and Tomato

A mild mélange of fleshy leaves, crunchy squash bits, and fresh tomato dice brightens grilled chicken or fish steaks. Or make a meal in a bowl: Spoon the moist mixture over ricotta-filled ravioli or a soft cheese-laced polenta to act as sauce and vegetable. However you present the dish, add the tomatoes just before you serve it, or they will lose their plump vigor and turn the sauce watery.

1 pound cucuzza greens (tennerumi)
¾ pound very slim cucuzza (1 or 2 gourds)
2 tablespoons flavorful olive oil
2 tablespoons butter
1 large onion, diced
3 garlic cloves, minced or sliced
1 teaspoon kosher salt
½ teaspoon sugar
Pepper
1½ cups water
1 pound plum tomatoes
¼ to ½ cup thin-sliced basil leaves

1. Break or cut off all leaves, buds, and their attached stems from the stalks of the cucuzza greens;

rinse. Discard stalks and tendrils. Bunch together greens and cut into very thin strips.

2. Taste gourd to determine if peeling is needed (which is unlikely for small ones). Quarter lengthwise and slice thin.

3. In sauté pan or wide casserole, heat 1 tablespoon olive oil with butter. Add onion and garlic; cook over moderately low heat to soften slightly. Add greens, gourd, salt, sugar, pepper, and water. Bring to a boil. Reduce heat and simmer, uncovered, stirring often, until tender and just a few spoons of liquid remain, about 10 minutes.

4. Meanwhile, peel tomatoes (see Note, page 10, if necessary); cut into ½-inch dice. Add to vegetables. Bring to a boil, stirring. Off heat, stir in remaining 1 tablespoon olive oil and ¼ cup basil. Season and add more basil to taste. Serve at once.

Serves 4

★For an additional recipe, bottle gourd can be substituted for fuzzy gourd in Shrimp and Fuzzy Gourd in Spiced Coconut-Buttermilk Sauce, page 295.

Pros Propose

Bottle gourd has its detractors and its devotees. Giuliano Bugialli likes **Fried Cucuzzi**—only. "It's firmer and less seedy than zucchini. You salt and drain it—or, even better, you dry it out a little in the sun, like in Italy. Flour, fry, and serve with salt and lemon wedges."

Italian restaurateur Tony May recalls, "I did not like it, no matter which way Mother used to make it!" But he does like **Cucuzza with Broccoli di Rape,** the way he makes it: Slice, flour, and roast the gourd in a cast-iron pan until gold. Spread over this broccoli raab sautéed in olive oil and garlic, "for just the right bittersweet combination."

Madhur Jaffrey, authority on Indian food, *did* like her mother's bottle gourd: "I've enjoyed ghia—what we call it in northern India—since I was two," she says. "**Spiced Stir-Fried Ghia** was my mother's favorite vegetable: She peeled and diced it, stirred it into popped cumin with turmeric and chilli powder, then cooked it soft with diced tomatoes. Or she would cook the dice in a lentil puree and season it with tamarind and chillis. The only way I hate bottle gourd is boiled, because that's what we had when we were sick."

But **Boiled Bottle Gourd Soup** is a "universal panacea, a dish that performs magic, much in the same way as the legendary chicken soup," writes Aung Aung Taik in *Under the Golden Pagoda: The Best of Burmese Cooking*. It is a far cry from the plain boiled soups spooned out to Western invalids: sautéed onion, turmeric, paprika, mashed garlic, and shrimp powder flavor the gourd as it cooks.

The vegetarian Indian repertoire offers the most elaborate recipes for bottle gourd, such as this from Julie Sahni—which she calls **Snake Squash Stuffed with Spicy Potatoes in Tomato-Herb Sauce**: With apple- or zucchini-corer, scoop out central pulp from peeled narrow gourds. Mince pulp. Stir-fry in oil. Add ground cumin, ground ginger, and mango powder, tossing. Add mashed boiled potatoes and minced green chillis and stir-fry 5 minutes. Add a little molasses. Stuff squash with mixture. Set in baking dish that holds them snugly. Pour over tomato puree seasoned with onion, garlic, fresh ginger, and cilantro. Cover with foil. Bake until tender, 30 to 45 minutes. Let rest briefly. Transfer squash to platter; cut into 1-inch diagonal slices. Pour over sauce and top with cilantro (from *Classic Indian Vegetarian and Grain Cooking*).

Breadfruit *(Artocarpus altilis; also A. communis and A. incisus)*

Also fruta de pan, árbol de pan, and panapén (Latin American);
fruit à pain (French West Indian)

diameter: 6-8 inches

I f you chance upon this green bruiser in an out-of-the-way shop, where it may be idling in a barrel of water, or huddled stickily in a bin with its peers, you may wonder about it. Breadfruit is included here primarily to satisfy the curiosity of the intrepid food explorer.

For those hungry for history, few subjects provide such a wealth of myths, tales, paintings (Gauguin's are the best-known), and poems as this tree, which is a source of shelter, food, medicine, fiber, timber, and latex. But the oft-told true story of breadfruit's trip to the New World, among the most dramatic in the history of plant introduction, may have an edge over fiction. (And that the towering tropical tree is kin to figs and mulberries is science fiction to me!)

First, there is Captain Cook's initial expedition (1768) to the Pacific with the naturalist Joseph Banks, whose discoveries so vividly informed the Western understanding of the fauna and flora of the South Pacific —breadfruit included. Banks's belief in the usefulness of the plant convinced King George III of its potential as a foodstuff for slaves in the British Caribbean. As a result, in 1789, the king appointed William Bligh to transport breadfruit from Tahiti to the West Indies on the ship he commanded, HMS *Bounty*. The rest, as they say . . . Put to sea by his crew (along with the thousand breadfruit seedlings) in this infamous mutiny, Bligh survived to fill another ship with breadfruit—which arrived in Jamaica in 1793. It was not until some time after the slaves' emancipation in 1838, however, that breadfruit became part of the West Indian diet.

For those eager to cook and eat breadfruit, I can go just so far. It would be best to have a personal guide to help in the selection, so dynamic is the subject. Its tropical character (breadfruit is considered native from Malaysia to Micronesia) eludes capture in temperate climes. Depending upon its stage of maturity, what you taste can vary as much as the descriptions of the blind men examining an elephant. A breadfruit can be as solid as a tree trunk, dry and starchy; a slightly riper one can be tender, rather resinous. A still riper one can be rich and sweet, creamy and yeasty. Another will change from cannonball to alcoholic mash in a weekend. Anyone tasting breadfruit for the first time is likely to contend that it is an acquired taste (and texture), or more accurately, several tastes and textures.

BASIC USE: Cook breadfruit (do not eat it raw) in different ways at different phases of ripeness. If you're north of the equator, chances are you'll be cooking green, hard breadfruit. Technically, you can cook it as you would potatoes; but don't expect potato-like results. Boil, bake, fry, roast, steam, or simmer for soup.

Cook green breadfruit straight and serve it *piping* hot (otherwise, it will be inedibly waxy—like starchy tropical roots and tubers) with highly seasoned stews and meats with peppery sauces. Although it can be peeled and boiled, I find that the flavor and texture develop fully if whole breadfruit is roasted in the peel at 375°F (about 1 hour for a smallish one), then peeled (or wrapped in a towel up to 30 minutes) and served sliced into wedges. The result is an extremely dry (bread-like), firm starch that is slightly nutty, fruity, and altogether unique.

However green breadfruit is cooked, it can then be sliced and deep-fried, or combined with a creamy or cheesy or coconutty (and spicy) sauce and then baked to heat up and to let the breadfruit absorb the sauce—which it does, like a sponge.

However you cook or sauce breadfruit, use *much more* liquid than you would for other starches. Its absorbency is formidable. Dress warm slices *generously* with vinaigrette.

When slightly ripe, just a touch tender, and scented, breadfruit can be cooked in any of the ways above except frying; but it is then quite different: The raw pulp resembles both eggplant and partly baked bread. Cooked at this later stage, the texture is comparable to starchy potato plus plantain, but stickier. It has a slightly musky, fruity flavor but is still bland.

Fully ripe breadfruit is sweet, tacky, and sometimes runny, like ripe cheese or creamy pancake batter. In the tropics it figures in a wide variety of desserts and baked goods.

SELECTION: Breadfruit in markets in the United States (with the exception of Hawaii, where it is common—and an ancient crop) is bright green, not ripened (ripe breadfruit is yellowish-green or mottled with brown), and seedless. It appears erratically, usually in Caribbean markets, where it is subject to import regulations that vary with molds and insects. The fruit, which ranges from 1½ to 6 pounds, is sold whole, often from a bucket or drum of water, which prevents overripening and staining.

Choose breadfruit that feels extremely dense and solid, not spongy. If you want to keep it for a few days, select a fruit that is all green and has uniformly colored and comparatively flattened "scales" that are more or less the same size, not small and large ones of varying tones, which indicate immaturity. For some dishes, you may want to seek out fruit that is yellowing or mottled with brown and *evenly* tender (like an avocado that is not quite ripe). To ripen green breadfruit, enclose in a paper bag with a greenish apple or banana to speed the way with an ethylene boost.

Fruit that is dented or darkened in spots or has hard or knotty areas is subject to rapid spoilage. The gummy latex speckling on most breadfruit is normal. The interior should be cream to beige, not green or brown.

STORAGE: Breadfruit is not a keeper. Store for as short a time as possible. To retard spoilage, which occurs quickly, store the whole fruits in water, refrigerated or not—but no more than a day or two.

If you want a tender fruit for a recipe, hold at room

temperature until the degree of ripeness you want is reached (which happens with alarming rapidity—or never). Once it is at the stage you want, breadfruit can be refrigerated for a day—two at most.

Green breadfruit freezes well. Peel slices and drop into acidulated water, drain, and freeze directly (but expect some darkening). Or blanch in salted boiling water for a minute, cool in ice water, drain, then wrap tightly and freeze.

PREPARATION: For hard green fruit: Quarter lengthwise, cut out the core, then pare off the skin. Rinse pieces and place in acidulated water (this can be refrigerated up to a day). When ready to cook, cut smaller, as the recipe requires. For riper, softer fruit, score the peel, then pull off gently; the core can be removed like a plug.

Warm Breadfruit and Ripe Plantain Salad with Avocado

Maricel Presilla shared this recipe from her forthcoming book about the foods of Latin America—a book that is likely to become the classic reference on the subject. To turn the salad into a hearty main dish, she adds salt cod, which is traditionally paired with the starchy staples of the Caribbean. For the following fish-less form, warm cubes of sweet yellow plantain and ivory breadfruit are accented with onion, tomato, green onion, and roasted peppers, then bathed in a garlicky cilantro dressing—just the right sharp counterpoint. Serve warm or at room temperature as a luncheon main course, or a side dish to seafood or grilled meat. Or chill, if more convenient; but return to room temperature to serve. If you buy breadfruit at a Latin American market, you'll also find the inimitable little fragrant chillis, ajíes dulces, for the dressing.

1 medium red bell pepper
5 medium plum tomatoes
1 medium white onion or 1 small sweet onion
2 medium scallions (green onions)
1 firm, green smallish breadfruit
   (about 2 pounds)
2 yellow-to-brown plantains
6 ajíes dulces or ½ Italian frying pepper
   (Cubanelle)

2 or 3 garlic cloves, peeled
¼ cup packed cilantro (coriander) leaves
½ teaspoon ground cumin
¼ teaspoon ground pepper
¾ teaspoon kosher salt
¼ cup cider vinegar
½ cup olive oil
Optional: thin-sliced Spanish green olives or
   capers
1 Florida avocado (see page 38)
Cilantro (coriander) sprigs for garnish

1. Peel pepper (see Note). Cut into ¼-inch dice. Peel and seed tomatoes (see Note, page 10). Cut each into six wedges. Halve onion lengthwise. Cut into thin vertical slices and separate slivers (to make 1 cup). Trim and thin-slice scallions. Combine diced pepper, tomatoes, onion, and scallions in a wide shallow serving dish.

2. Rinse, quarter, and core breadfruit. Cut into 1-inch slices and peel closely. Cut into 1-inch cubes, dropping into a pot of salted water as you work. Bring to a boil. Cook until fork-tender, about 20 minutes. Drain.

3. Meanwhile, halve plantains crosswise. Slit peel lengthwise on each ridge, then pull down at an angle to remove. Cut plantains into 1-inch segments, dropping into another pot of salted water. Bring to a boil, reduce heat, and simmer until tender, about 10 minutes. Drain.

4. Prepare dressing: In food processor combine ajíes dulces, garlic, cilantro, cumin, pepper, salt, vinegar, and olive oil. Whiz to a smooth puree.

5. Combine half the dressing with breadfruit, folding it in until it is absorbed. Pour remaining dressing over vegetables in serving dish. Add breadfruit and optional olives, and mix gently. Halve, peel, pit, and cut avocado into 1-inch slices. Arrange over salad. Garnish with cilantro.

Serves 4 as a main course, 6 as a side dish

Note: If you don't have a favorite way to peel peppers, try this: Set each one directly in a high gas flame and turn frequently until pretty well blackened all over. (If you don't have a gas stove, halve, seed, flatten, and then broil peppers with skin side as close as possible to the heat.) Wrap each pepper in a wet paper towel. Let stand 15 minutes or longer, as convenient. Loosen skin by gently rubbing towel back and forth, then slide off towel and skin together. Scrape off any residual skin with knife. Halve; remove core and seeds.

Baked Breadfruit "Cream" Soup

If you favor old-fashioned potato cream soup, eggnog, blancmange, and almond milk (even evaporated milk!), you may well be charmed by this mild, rich, pinkish-ivory soup that is—unbelievably—cream-free. While experimenting with breadfruit, I discovered that when it is roasted for several hours, it is transformed from a bland starchy substance to something akin to sweet plantain and semisoft cheese. It becomes so oily, in fact, that it must be modified with liquid to cut the fat.

The investment is in baking time, not labor, and the fruity, yeasty aroma that wafts from the oven is as appealing as brandied bread pudding. Note, however, that breadfruit is shockingly variable. The dish depends upon the ripeness and flavor of the main ingredient, not flavorings, which are few and serve to underscore the subject.

> 1 smallish breadfruit (about 2 pounds),
>   slightly ripe (green mottled with beige)
> 1 quart flavorful vegetable broth
> A few handfuls of celery leaves or fennel tops
> ¼ teaspoon celery seeds or fennel seeds
> 2 to 3 cups milk
> About 2 tablespoons brandy or rum
> 2 to 3 teaspoons kosher salt
> About ¼ teaspoon fine-ground white pepper
> Optional: sugar
> Optional: grated nutmeg and chives

1. Rinse breadfruit and wrap loosely in foil. Set in a baking pan in oven; turn to 375°F. Bake until breadfruit is very easily pierced with a knife tip—which can range from 1 to over 3 hours, depending upon the degree of ripeness and richness of the breadfruit. Remove from oven when done—but don't worry about overcooking.

2. Halve breadfruit and cool until it can be easily handled.

3. Meanwhile, combine broth with celery or fennel tops and matching seeds in heavy medium-large pot. Boil, covered, to extract flavor—15 to 30 minutes or so. Strain out solids. Return broth to pot.

4. Quarter, core, and peel breadfruit, then cut into thin slices. Add to broth with 2 cups milk, 2 tablespoons brandy, 2 teaspoons salt, and ¼ teaspoon pepper and bring to a simmer. Lower heat, cover, and barely simmer to blend flavors and further soften breadfruit, about 15 minutes.

5. Transfer solids to food processor (do not cool first). Add as much cooking liquid as machine can process without overflow. Puree until very smooth, then add remaining liquid gradually, working in batches if necessary. Whiz until super-smooth. Add additional milk as needed for desired consistency. Add salt, brandy, pepper, and optional sugar to taste. Serve hot with optional grating of nutmeg and a few snips of chives.

Serves 6 as a first course

★Traditionally, breadfruit is cooked interchangeably with plantain, taro, yam, and yuca. I have not tested the recipes with breadfruit, but I think that it could replace them in:

Hot and Gingery Collard-Plantain Soup, page 492
Mashed Taro, Sweets, and Potatoes, page 657
Almond-Topped Yam Gratin, page 716
Yuca in Picante Citrus Sauce with Olives, Peppers, and Onions, page 729

Pros Propose

Breadfruit is one of those traditional foods cooked simply, in time-honored ways: boiled, baked, and fried. Interpretations are likely to come from "outsiders." Mogens Bay Esbensen, born and trained in Denmark, was a chef in Thailand before he moved to Australia, where he wrote *A Taste of the Tropics,* a book about tropical and subtropical fruits. Esbensen prepares dessert fritters, scones, cheesecake, and pie from sweet-ripe breadfruit. Green to slightly ripe breadfruit figures in chowder, cream soup, and these **Breadfruit Fish Patties with Mustard Crust:** Peel breadfruit and cut out core. Dice flesh and steam until soft. Drain; coarsely puree in food processor. Add flaked cooked fish, minced onions, eggs, and seasoning. Form into small cakes. Dip into flour, then beaten egg, then a mixture of bread crumbs and freshly ground yellow mustard seeds. Shallow-fry until golden. Serve with lemon wedges or curried coconut sauce.

Sandra Allen, who teaches about the foods of Brazil, showed me the trick of blanching breadfruit to modify its inherent pastiness. For her **Cream of Breadfruit Soup:** Blanch quartered, peeled, cored, and cubed breadfruit for 2 minutes. Drain. Gently cook sliced white of leek in butter. Add breadfruit and grated fresh ginger. Add chicken broth and white pepper and cook until breadfruit is soft, about 35 minutes. Press soup through a food mill, then a sieve. Return to pot, add cream to taste, and reheat. Garnish with toasted, chopped macadamia nuts.

According to *Charmaine Solomon's Encyclopedia of Asian Food,* in Sri Lanka, wedges of peeled breadfruit are boiled with turmeric and salt to color and flavor them, then served with a sambal of ground chillis and onions, with grated fresh coconut—a simple and effective side to just about any broiled, grilled, or roasted seafood or meat dish. Coconut milk is a frequent cooking medium for breadfruit, as in the author's **Breadfruit Coconut Curry:** Dilute coconut milk by half with water and combine in saucepan with grated onion, grated ginger, crushed garlic, split fresh green chillis, ground turmeric, strips of pandan leaf, cinnamon stick, curry leaves, and salt. Simmer to blend. Add peeled thick unripe breadfruit slices and cook until soft.

Broccolini, Asparation

(hybrid of *Brassica oleracea,* Botrytis Group and *B. oleracea,* Alboglabra Group)

Also baby broccoli, mini-broccoli

If you were seeking a pharmaceutical to deliver hope to the respiratory system, you might check out something with a name like Asparation. It seems unlikely that you'd go shopping for a vegetable—but that is the cultivar name for a recently developed broccoli hybrid. Perhaps Broccolini, a name trademarked by one of its growers, is closer to the mark.

Happily, this slim, elegant little vegetable is far more appealing than its names. It requires no trimming to speak of, lasts admirably, cooks in minutes, looks charming on the plate, and tastes like crisp, delicate broccoli without the cabbagey note. Bright green, crunchy, and smooth, it is rewarding hot, cold, or at room temperature.

Asparation, the seed name, is the "invention" of Sakata Seed, a company based in Yokohama that has made numerous valued introductions in the United States. Because more than three-quarters of its lineage is broccoli, the plant is officially thus registered. But the remaining quarter derives from the plant variously and confusingly known as Chinese broccoli (page 190) and Chinese kale or gai lan, which contributes conspicuous crunch and special sweetness.

Relatively expensive, so-called baby broccoli is a labor-intensive crop—and the care with which it is grown dramatically affects the end product. According to Bruce Sanbonmatsu, a co-owner of Sanbon, the family-run company in El Centro, California, that began planting the vegetable in 1994, "it's an unusually sensitive crop. It can look just fine when it's harvested, but if you haven't given it just what it needs—just the right amount of water, fertilizer, love, and attention—it won't be tender and delicious."

Although the plant can grow quite large, only its side shoots are harvested. "You break off the first main shoot by hand, then harvest the forced shoots that are produced," explains Sanbonmatsu. "What we'd like to see is a way to change this from a super upscale product to just a plain upscale one. That, and a single name for the product, whoever is growing it." The name Broccolini was given to the same Sakata seed by its other grower, Mann Packing Company in Salinas, California.

length: 6-7 inches

BASIC USE: Aspabroc was the original name of the seed. Mercifully, that name has disappeared. But you can take a clue from this compound name for its culinary use. Broccolini is as pretty as asparagus, as versatile as broccoli, and the crème de la crème of "plain" green garnish vegetables. Dress it as you would asparagus, in lemon vinaigrette or hollandaise or maltaise sauce. The broccoli side takes kindly to Asian touches, whether in a warm peanut sauce, an oyster sauce blend, a sesame dressing, or Japanese gingered dipping sauce. Sweet, salty, and smoky flavors are good allies—ham, honey mustard, smoked duck breast.

Because the pretty broccoli "palm treelets" are expensive and very good alone, serve them whole, as an appetizer or accompaniment to something cooked simply, such as grilled salmon, pan-seared sea scallops, or calf's liver. Or they can be slant-cut like asparagus and stir-fried. Or blanch the angled stems and toss with slim same-size penne, butter, and Parmesan; or stir cheese or cream sauce into pasta, then top with the Asparation florets.

Broccolini is equally delicious steamed or boiled until crunchy-tender, 2 to 3 minutes. To serve as part of a cold vegetable platter, blanch for half the time. Do not microwave.

SELECTION: Available year-round. Broccolini should be a rich green, like broccoli, with no trace of yellow. The only visible "warning sign that quality is off may be lighter color—which can mean tough, bitter stalks," says Sanbonmatsu. In my experience, size is also significant. If the vegetable looks like small broccoli, it is too large. To be properly tender and sweet, it should be almost unrecognizably slim and delicate.

STORAGE: Shelf life is absolutely amazing. I have refrigerated stalks in ventilated plastic for 2 weeks without harm. (If you see even the smallest suggestion of splitting or curling at the stem base, however, you know the product has been on the shelf for several weeks.) Once, when I left town unexpectedly, I trimmed Broccolini stems, plunked the bouquet in water, and put a plastic bag over it. A week later, it was fine.

PREPARATION: The batches I worked with were exceptionally tender right to the base of the stem. They needed no more than rinsing. Some Broccolini I've spied in supermarkets looked as if it could do with a stem trim.

Basic Broccolini (Asparation)

As elegant as asparagus, as crunchy as broccoli stems, as quick to prepare as—nothing else: simply heat and eat, more or less. Serve the hot or warm vegetable with no more than salt and lemon or melted butter or nut oil. Dress it up with whipped cream flavored with nutmeg, or a more traditional cream sauce. Or serve cold with shallot vinaigrette or saffron mayonnaise or a light mustard or peanut sauce.

> 1 bunch (about ½ pound) Broccolini
>   (Asparation), rinsed
> Coarse salt
> Lemon or orange wedges

To serve hot or warm: Set stalks on steamer rack over boiling water, cover, and cook until crunchy-tender, 3 to 5 minutes, depending upon size. Or cook in boiling salted water about 2 to 3 minutes. Serve with salt and citrus wedges on the side.

To serve cold: Cook as above, but only until raw taste disappears—about half as long. Texture should be firmer and crisper than when it is to be served hot. Cool, then chill. Serve with dressing.

Serves 2 as a side dish

Broccolini (Asparation) with Asian Orange Dressing

This dainty brassica is set off by rich traditional French sauces (such as hollandaise or vinaigrette) or by Asian ones based on soy and sesame. The hybrid that follows, lightly creamy in texture and caramel in color, derives its juicy body from pureed onion, yet tastes more of sesame and orange. Serve Broccolini alongside pork, beef, or seafood, or as part of a vegetable meal, with grains. Or offer as a first course topped with oranges and roasted chopped cashews.

> 3 tablespoons corn oil
> 1 tablespoon Asian (dark) sesame oil
> 1 tablespoon balsamic vinegar
> 1 tablespoon shoyu (Japanese soy sauce)
> ¾ teaspoon grated orange zest
> 2 tablespoons orange juice
> 1 very small white onion (or ½ medium onion),
>   cut into small chunks
> About 1 pound Broccolini (Asparation)

1. Combine corn oil, sesame oil, balsamic vinegar, soy sauce, orange zest, and juice in blender or small food processor. Whirl to blend. Add onion and whiz until smooth. Continue processing until fairly pale and creamy—not just until it is pureed.

2. Rinse Broccolini and trim if needed. Set on a steamer rack over boiling water. Cover, and steam until crunchy-tender—3 to 5 minutes, depending upon size.

3. Arrange stalks in serving dish. Spoon neat bands of dressing over all. Serve hot or warm.

Serves 4 to 6 as a side dish or first course

Broccoli Raab (*Brassica rapa,* Ruvo Group)

Also rapini, cime di rapa, broccoletti, and broccoletti di rape (all Italian)

length: 8 inches

A love affair with Italian food and a growing awareness of the health benefits of a crucifer-rich diet have increased the popularity of a diverse group of greens with "broccoli" in their common names. The affair has been so ardent that we may forget that "regular" broccoli—not just broccoli raab—is a relative newcomer to the United States. It seems that we have the same two enterprising Italian immigrants to thank for the widespread availability of both.

In 1927, the D'Arrigo brothers, "who knew broccoli from the old country," became intrigued with "the idea of marketing a new and different vegetable," explains Margaret D'Arrigo, vice president of business development for D'Arrigo Brothers Company—and daughter of "Andy Boy," the boy whose face still smiles from the bright pink labels that helped establish the identity of the company and of broccoli as we know it. Broccoli quickly outgrew the Italian commu-

nity to which it was first marketed and has become a primary American green.

Broccoli raab, which took longer to put down roots, is more closely related to turnip than to broccoli—but its names are many and maddening: broccoletti, rapini or rappini (both from *rapa,* turnip), cima di rapa (turnip top), ruvo kale, turnip broccoli, and Italian turnip. (For reasons of etymology as well as pronunciation, broccoli *raab* is preferable to broccoli *rabe,* which is sometimes used.)

"Broccoli" as we apply the word, exists only in America. In Italy, the word means "little sprouts" and has been used for centuries to describe, among other things, sprouts on cabbages and cauliflowers left in the field. It is not clear when what we call broccoli was introduced to cultivation, because "broccoli" referred to several vegetables, making distinctions hazy.

But Margaret D'Arrigo knows when broccoli raab

was introduced to cultivation in the United States: "My grandfather found the wild plant growing all over California fields and remembered it from Italy. He began a breeding program in the 1930s and ultimately developed varieties with juicy stalks, many buds, and small leaves"—a combination that appealed to Americans more than the Italian type, which is more like its turnip-top kin: leafy, rough, and bitter.

Even modified, broccoli raab is a bitter blast to a sweet-loving American palate. If you chance on it, imagining it to be mild as broccoli, you will be shocked, for it packs an assertive wallop. But if you meet it head-on, expecting a mustardy bite, you may be happily surprised. Until recently, broccoli raab was enjoyed primarily in Italian and Chinese communities, where bitterness ranks high as a flavor principle. Finally, though, the vegetable has become widespread, thanks in large part to its affinity for pasta and garlic—two American passions. Whatever the reasons for its continuing presence, it is most welcome in the American vegetable repertoire, which has few bitter representatives.

BASIC USE: Nothing quite compares to this aggressive green, which adds zest to bland foods—such as potatoes, pasta, and fresh white cheese—and holds its own with big flavors such as chilli, garlic, and ginger. Its intensity is sustained in dishes that are hot or chilled, but it is too harsh and fibrous to serve raw.

Cook broccoli raab more or less as you would broccoli, remembering that it is considerably more pungent and cooks through more rapidly, becoming soft *suddenly*. Do not wander far from the stove—whether you boil, steam, stir-fry, braise, sauté, or microwave the green. If you find the flavor too intense, try blanching the broccoli raab in salted water; then drain, dry, and go on with the recipe as directed.

SELECTION: Broccoli raab is available all year, but its quality is best during cool seasons. As with all brassicas, sniff first! There should be no hint of over-the-hill cabbage. Choose broccoli raab with thin stalks and just a few open flowers. Avoid bunches that are too wet, too dry, or yellowing.

Most telling is the stem base: The cut area should be green and smooth, with no separating fibers and no white core. Sylvia Thompson describes this undesirable material in *The Kitchen Garden:* "When kept too long in storage after harvest, sugar in broccoli turns to

lignin . . . a material that's one-fourth the composition of wood! There's nothing you can do to make lignin tender."

STORAGE: Remove the twist tie or rubber band that holds the bunched stalks together, or the center ones may spoil. Refrigerate for as short a time as possible, wrapped lightly in a damp paper towel, then enclosed in perforated plastic. Broccoli raab is more perishable than its looks suggest.

Ethylene gas, formed during ripening, adversely affects green leafy vegetables, causing yellowing and hastening decay and drying. Avoid storage near fruit that continues ripening after harvest, such as apple, avocado, banana, pear, melon, plum, and most tropicals.

PREPARATION: Broccoli raab rarely needs more than a slight trim of the base; the whole stalk is usually edible. However, at certain times of the year the stalks may be more fibrous. Taste, and trim off as much as needed to reach a relatively tender level. Wash in several changes of water, lifting out pieces so debris settles.

I used to cut apart the leafy parts and stems to cook separately, but in recent years the types on the market have been uniform.

Micro-Quick Hot-Sweet Salad of Broccoli Raab and Carrots

I'm not a big fan of microwaving, but in this case, it preserves both vegetables' deep color and nutrients as it speeds cooking. The honey and sweet sherry accents temper the bitter broccoli raab for a side dish that's fast, fresh, pretty.

1 hearty bunch broccoli raab (1 pound plus)
About 1 pound fairly thin medium carrots
  (weighed without tops)
1 tablespoon sweet sherry or sweet vermouth
1 tablespoon cider vinegar or balsamic vinegar
1½ tablespoons honey
½ teaspoon kosher salt
⅛ to ¼ teaspoon ground hot pepper
2 tablespoons peanut or corn oil
1 tablespoon Asian (dark) sesame oil

1. Cut a slice from broccoli raab base and taste to determine toughness. If fairly tender, trim only ½

inch or so from stalks; if tough, trim more. Wash vegetable in several changes of water, lifting out so debris settles. Without drying, spread in microwavable serving dish. Cover with plastic wrap and cook for 2 minutes. Toss, then continue cooking until not quite done, 1 to 2 minutes more. Pierce plastic and allow to cool.

2. Peel carrots. Place in microwavable dish. Cover with plastic wrap. Cook just until carrots lose their raw crunch but are *not* cooked through—1½ to 2 minutes. Pierce plastic and cool slightly.

3. In a small dish, mix sherry, vinegar, honey, salt, and hot pepper to taste, stirring to blend. Add peanut and sesame oils.

4. Line up broccoli raab stems on cutting board. Cut apart from tops (the florets and leaves). Squeeze tops dry, then blot with towel. Cut into very thin shreds; return to dish. Slice stems on a sharp angle to form long oblongs ⅛ inch thick; add to dish. Cut carrots the same way and add to dish. Toss with dressing. Season. Chill.

Serves 4

Two-Gingered Broccoli Raab

You'll discover new dimensions of broccoli raab when you balance its bite with ginger—both fragrant fresh and crunchy crystallized—and modify its earthiness with turmeric. The brilliant ocher spice also serves to keep color bright despite covered cooking, which usually turns greens olive drab. Don't save this just for Asian moods; it's at ease with pork roast, lamb chops, beans, and, especially, grains. Serve over aromatic rice as a main dish, topped with roasted cashews.

You can use any candied ginger, but if you're going to invest in it (and it is a lasting and useful pantry item), look for a brand from Australia, the source of remarkably fiber-free, bright-flavored ginger products.

>About 1¼ pounds broccoli raab
>   (a large bunch)
>1 tablespoon olive oil
>1 tablespoon thin-sliced garlic
>1 tablespoon minced fresh ginger
>½ teaspoon turmeric
>½ teaspoon kosher salt
>¾ cup water

2 tablespoons medium-dry sherry or Madeira
1 tablespoon butter
1 tablespoon fine-minced crystallized ginger

1. Rinse broccoli raab. Sample a slice from bottom of a heavy stalk. If very fibrous, trim ends well; if not, simply shave a slice from each stem base. Stack stalks and cut into 1-inch pieces.

2. Set large skillet over moderate heat. Add olive oil, garlic, and fresh ginger. Cook, tossing, until garlic is slightly colored, about 2 minutes. Add turmeric, salt, and water.

3. Add broccoli raab, tossing to wilt slightly. Cover pan and simmer until stalks are almost tender throughout, from 4 to 15 minutes, depending upon the variety and season.

4. Uncover, raise heat, and add sherry and butter. Continue tossing until liquid concentrates to a near-glaze. Scoop into a warm dish. Sprinkle with crystallized ginger. Serve hot or warm.

Serves 4 as a side dish

Pasta with Broccoli Raab and Olives

Everyone who likes broccoli raab loves it with pasta. My simple staple version cooks conveniently in one pot, in stages. It is heavy on greens, which soften to a near sauce-like consistency during the final cooking with pasta—a technique that deepens and distributes flavor evenly. Spinach pasta improves the drab look of long-cooked greens. Nicely variable, the recipe lends itself to many final fillips: a splash of sherry or balsamic vinegar, or a scattering of tiny garlic croutons, toasted walnuts or pine nuts, or tomato dice tossed with fresh basil. Or stir in chopped anchovy when you combine the greens and pasta. The usual finish of grated cheese, however, does not suit.

>1 bunch broccoli raab (about 1 pound)
>½ pound small curly Italian spinach pasta,
>   such as gemelli or rotini
>About a dozen oil-cured black olives
>1 to 3 garlic cloves
>2 tablespoons olive oil
>¼ teaspoon chilli flakes

Salt and pepper
Lemon wedges

1. Set a large pot of water to boil. Cut a slice from broccoli raab base and taste to determine toughness. If fairly tender, trim about ½ inch from stalks; if tough, trim more.

2. Drop broccoli raab into boiling water and add a handful of salt. Cook until tender—begin tasting at about 3 minutes. With long tongs or strainer, lift out vegetable, then drain.

3. Add pasta to the boiling water in which broccoli raab cooked. While pasta cooks, slice or chop broccoli raab. Pit and slice olives. Mince garlic.

4. Add olives to pasta during the last few minutes of cooking. When pasta is just al dente, scoop out and reserve 1 cup water. Drain pasta in colander. Add 1 tablespoon oil and toss.

5. Combine remaining 1 tablespoon oil, garlic, and chilli flakes in the pasta pot over low heat. Cook until garlic softens and barely begins to color, stirring often. Add greens and half the reserved pasta water. Raise heat and simmer, partly covered, until greens absorb flavors and soften, about 3 minutes.

6. Add pasta and remaining water. Boil gently, stirring often, until most liquid evaporates—just a few minutes. Season. Serve with lemon wedges.

Serves 2 as a main course

Pros Propose

Chef Jody Adams serves broccoli raab as often as broccoli, but she prefers it as a seasoning vegetable, rather than as a side dish. For **Penne with Mussels and Broccoli Raab:** Heat olive oil and garlic in large pot. Add mussels and white wine; steam mussels open. Add cooked penne, blanched broccoli raab cut into 2-inch lengths, roasted red pepper strips, and chilli flakes. Season with balsamic vinegar and parsley.

Shellfish with broccoli raab suits chef Michael Romano's taste too. For maximum flavor, he sautés the green before adding liquid. For **Scallops with Broccoli Raab and Dried Tomatoes:** Sauté cut-up broccoli raab in garlic-infused oil to wilt. Add a little water and cook until tender. Toss with marinated dried tomato halves. Top with seared scallops and rosemary-lemon vinaigrette.

A rustic classic of Apulia highlights just two ingredients, dried fava beans and bitter greens—whether dandelion, chicory, or zesty broccoli raab. For **Pureed Favas and Broccoli Raab:** Soak dried favas, drain. Boil briefly in fresh water; drain. Cover with cold water; peel. Cook in salted water until mushy. Puree through food mill, incorporating milk-soaked bread and olive oil. Boil broccoli raab until tender. Drain well, then sauté in garlic oil. Spread fava puree on dish, cover with greens, and drizzle with olive oil.

The French-American dishes chef and author Daniel Boulud devised for his New York City café were turned into written recipes by Dorie Greenspan for the *Café Boulud Cookbook*. For his simple, unusual **Broccoli Raab with Honeyed Grapes:** Boil trimmed broccoli raab in salted water until tender. Drain, refresh, and squeeze dry. Heat chilli flakes in olive oil. Add broccoli raab and slivered canned piquillo peppers (or strips of seeded plum tomato) and toss to heat through. Transfer to a heated dish. Wipe out pan and heat a little honey in it. Add ground cumin, then sliced seedless grapes, and stir just until lightly glazed. Spoon over greens and sprinkle with toasted, slivered almonds.

Chef and author Susanna Foo creates her own brand of East-West flavors. Although most Chinese greens are usually blanched initially, she finds broccoli raab more flavorful braised. For **Curried Brown Rice with Broccoli Raab:** Sauté diced onion in olive oil until golden. Stir in diced red bell pepper, celery, curry powder, and pepper. Add chicken stock, coconut milk, and salt. Stir in washed, drained short-grain brown rice. Bring to a boil, stirring. Cover and cook until soft. Meanwhile, heat additional chicken stock, add chopped broccoli raab, then tomato dice. Simmer until greens are tender. Serve on the rice (from *Susanna Foo Chinese Cuisine*).

Like Susanna Foo, chef Mark Allen believes blanching broccoli raab diminishes its flavor, so he cooks it in stock. For **Broccoli Raab–Stuffed Chicken with Tomato Sauce:** Cook trimmed whole broccoli raab stalks slowly in chicken stock with lightly cooked garlic and shallots; drain well. Spread boned chicken breast skin side down and pound flat. Top with prosciutto. Place broccoli raab on top. Roll up and tie. Brown in oil, then bake. Serve with sauce of slow-cooked roasted tomatoes, black olives, and capers.

Broccoli Romanesco
Also Romanesco cauliflower, Roman broccoli

Broccoflower
Also Cauli-Broc

(Both are *Brassica oleracea,* Botrytis Group)

If you assume that the vegetables in these photographs are cauliflowers—not broccoli, as their names suggest—you are probably correct, according to the majority of vegetable classifiers. Other classifiers think that broccoli and cauliflower have enough overlapping characteristics to wear both names. There would be fewer problems if we could just stick with scientific nomenclature. The common names for the green cauliflowers, for reasons related to marketing and translation from the Italian (see broccoli raab, page 119) have landed them in the broccoli bin, under "B"; still, cauliflower is what they are.

There are a fair number of green cauliflowers, from smooth and rounded to studded and peaked, although only a few crop up in North American markets. Broccoflower, a widely marketed brand name for Alverda or Brocoverde cultivars and crosses thereof, is close to "regular" cauliflower in form. According to Gene Mero, a breeder at Petoseed in Saticoy, California, who specializes in such plants, "Broccoflower originated with a green cauliflower grown in the Macerata area of Italy. It is definitely not a broccoli-cauliflower cross as is often written."

Romanesco cauliflower, one of nature's more spectacular creations, has a conical chartreuse head arranged in ornate turrets which suggest that it might be part starfish, part wedding cake. Mero laments that "although it can be found in California, it is rare in the United States because it is so difficult to grow outside its home turf."

Peter Crisp, director of Innovar Plant Breeding in Norfolk, England, who was active in developing Ro-

broccoli Romanesco   diameter: 6-7 inches

Broccoflower   diameter: 7-8 inches

manesco, describes that turf: "Geographically, the Romanesco cauliflower is a traditional crop on the Mediterranean coast roughly in the region from Rome to Naples" and just one of many interesting and similar strains. In particular, "on the Adriatic coast there is another type called the Jesi, which has white (or creamy) curds with the spiral shape of the Romanesco." David Astley, a breeder at Horticulture Research International in Warwick, England, illustrates the name problem when he observes that even in Italian, "the Romanesco form is labeled as *Cavolo Broccolo* [sprouted cabbage], while the di Jesi form is *Cavolfiore* [cauliflower]."

I find the Romanesco considerably more subtle and elegant in flavor and form than most Broccoflowers, with a delicate nuttiness and an appealing nubbly texture. Broccoflower varieties, while they can be mellow and attractive when very fresh, tend to be more cabbagey—less buttery and nutty.

Both styles of green cauliflower are generally smaller, lighter in weight, and less crisp and dense than our common white cauliflowers, with a crumbly curd. Their flavor (like that of white cauliflower) is dramatically dependent upon freshness.

BASIC USE: Green cauliflower can be cooked whole or cut into florets for very different effects. Above all, beware of overcooking. Cauliflower quickly changes to mush, so do not stray far from the stove. Despite recommendations to boil cauliflower, I find that it can become watery (an exception is the brief blanching of florets for cold dishes). Steaming, microwaving, and baking preserve the vegetable's texture better; for enhanced flavor, cook by one of these methods, coat with sauce, then roast in a moderate oven.

When it comes to seasoning and saucing, I'd go gently to preserve the quiet cauliflower demeanor: Season with lemon juice and delicate herbs, such as chervil, dill, tarragon, coriander, mint, or parsley; anoint with cream, butter, or cheese; top with toasted almonds, pistachios, or pine nuts. For more forceful treatment, choose salty and acid complements: olives, anchovies, dry cheeses, capers, citrus, vinegar, tomato. Or finish with spices or aromatics, such as black, white, green, or pink peppercorns; sansho (prickly ash powder), ginger, or chives.

SELECTION: Green cauliflowers are at their peak from late summer through winter, although you may find them during a good part of the year on the West Coast. Choose carefully for optimum quality—which disappears long before looks. The gentle, sweet side is lost before discoloration begins. Sniff deeply: There should be no trace of stinkiness, which turns into the harshness of elderly cabbage when the cauliflower is cooked. Taste, if possible. Heads are usually sold by the piece, not by the pound. Since size does not affect quality, it pays to pick the largest. Look for a tight, comparatively crisp bouquet with no loose or yellowing buds.

STORAGE: Keep very cold for as short a time as possible. Place a damp piece of paper towel on the curd, wrap the head in perforated plastic, and refrigerate stem end up (condensation on the curd causes discoloration and decay).

PREPARATION: Most green cauliflower requires only a quick rinse. If purchased from a farm stand, soak ½ hour, curd side down, in salted, acidulated water to draw out hidden creatures.

To cook whole, cut off large outer leaves (small ones need not be removed). Pare off any heavy stem base. For florets, simply break the vegetable into equal-sized bunchlets to suit your dish. If any stems are unusually heavy, it is best to peel them.

Steamed Whole Romanesco with Pine Nuts and Peppercorns

Romanesco's startling chartreuse turrets fade, when cooked, to a more respectable willow green. Too beautiful to deconstruct, this elegant head is best left whole for presentation. Quiet adornments keep the vegetable as star. If green peppercorns are not in your pantry, crushed pink ones (not true peppercorns, but so-called) add a sweet dimension; or fine-ground white pepper lends heat. Broccoflower can be substituted, but the dish will be less distinctive.

2 tablespoons pine nuts
1 head broccoli Romanesco
 (1 to 1½ pounds)
Salt
2 tablespoons butter
½ to 1 teaspoon freeze-dried green peppercorns

1. Toast nuts in preheated 325°F oven until golden, about 8 minutes; set aside to cool. Turn oven to lowest setting and warm a serving dish.

2. Trim heavy stem base and leaves from Romanesco. Set stem end down in heavy pot in ¾-inch boiling salted water. Cover tightly and cook over moderate heat until tender throughout, 7 to 8 minutes. Salt sparingly.

3. Meanwhile, in small skillet, heat butter with peppercorns over low heat until liquid turns pale golden.

4. Set Romanesco in dish; pour over peppercorn butter. Sprinkle with pine nuts. Serve hot.

Serves 4

Micro-Steamed Romanesco (or Broccoflower) with Provolone, Parsley, and Croutons

Luminous pale green florets are strewn with a confetti of dark parsley leaves, toasty little croutons, and shreds of firm ivory Provolone. The recipe is freely adapted from one in *Verdura* by Viana La Place, who has an inspiring way with vegetables. She might frown on microwaving, but I find both cauliflower and broccoli florets sweeter and less watery cooked this way than when boiled in traditional fashion.

1 head broccoli Romanesco or Broccoflower
  (1 to 1½ pounds)
Salt and pepper
1 teaspoon minced garlic
2 tablespoons flavorful olive oil
¼ cup minced flat-leaf parsley (or mint and
  parsley combined)
½ cup shredded or coarse-grated imported
  Provolone
½ cup small toasted croutons

1. Trim leaves and heavy part of base from Romanesco. Break into neat bite-size florets.

2. Place in microwavable dish with a few tablespoons of water, or just enough to cover bottom of dish. Cover with plastic wrap and cook until barely tender—not cooked through—5 to 6 minutes (but test often, as ovens vary). Drain well. Season with salt and pepper.

3. Combine garlic and oil in microwavable cup. Cook to just color garlic, about 2 minutes. Stir parsley into warm oil and spoon evenly over florets. Toss gently. Add cheese and croutons and toss. Serve hot or warm (reheat for 30 seconds or so if you like a hot dish).

Serves 4

Chilled Broccoflower with Dilled Yogurt-Radish Dip

What appears to be a whole pistachio green cauliflower is actually cooked, ready-to-eat pieces formed easily into a rounded head. An appealing hors d'oeuvre for the calorie-conscious—and others. Choose whole-milk or low-fat yogurt. My favorite is whole-milk sheep's yogurt.

1 head Broccoflower (about 1½ pounds)
2 teaspoons olive oil
1 cup diced or chopped red radishes
  (about 8 medium-large radishes)
½ teaspoon kosher salt
1 cup yogurt (preferably whole-milk)
1½ tablespoons whole-grain mustard
2 tablespoons minced fresh dill
2 tablespoons thin-sliced scallion (green onion)
  tops
Garnish: whole small radishes with leaves and
  dill sprigs

1. Trim leaves and some stem from Broccoflower. Break into large florets, then into 2-inch bunchlets. Peel any thick stems. Drop into large pot of boiling salted water. Return to a boil, and cook just until the raw crunch disappears—less than 1 minute. Drain. Refresh in cold water; drain well.

2. Coat a 1½-quart rounded bowl (to mimic the Broccoflower head) with 1 teaspoon oil. Pack florets tightly against the sides with stem ends inward. Fill the center with remaining odd bits and pieces. Top with a plate slightly smaller than the bowl's rim and press to compact. Place a weight on top. Set aside.

3. Toss radishes with salt and let stand at least 15 minutes. Drain, then pat dry. Combine with yogurt, mustard, dill, scallions, and remaining 1 teaspoon oil and blend. Cover.

4. Drain any accumulated liquid from Broccoflower. Refrigerate dip and vegetable 2 hours or longer.

5. To serve, drain Broccoflower again. Set serving plate on top, then invert. Garnish with whole radishes and dill. Serve with dip.

Serves 6 as an hors d'oeuvre

Pros Propose

In keeping with the seashell swirls of Romanesco, Sylvia Thompson proposes **Romanesco Broccoli and Seashell Pasta:** Cut Romanesco into equal-size florets. Cook al dente in boiling water. Heat garlic in oil until golden. Off heat, add dried tomato strips, chopped fresh plum tomato, Kalamata olives, capers, dried chilli, and white wine. Add large cooked shell pasta, a little of the cooking water, and fresh oregano; simmer to mingle flavors (*The Kitchen Garden Cookbook*).

Chef and author Carlo Middione deems Sicilian **Pasta Arriminata** ("tossed around") a best-seller for his San Francisco restaurants. To prepare: Cook both white cauliflower and Romanesco or Broccoflower florets in boiling salted water until tender. Sauté smashed anchovies in olive oil. Add saffron, plumped currants, and florets. Cook briefly, adding a little boiling pasta water "just to make it a little swampy, not watery." Add cooked perciatelli or penne; heat through. Serve with grated Pecorino Romano.

Sformato, an eggy, crustless quiche, is customarily made with green cauliflower in parts of Tuscany and Lazio. Chef Odette Fada, from Lombardy, prefers the white for her refined restaurant version of **Sformato di Cavolfiore al Pepe Rosa**—more custard than rustic pie. To prepare: Blanch whole, trimmed cauliflower (reserve cooking water). Drain and break into florets. Sauté in olive oil. Add some reserved liquid, eggs, crushed pink pepper, grated Parmesan, and seasoning. Spoon into small molds and bake in bain marie in very low oven. Meanwhile, very gently cook rinsed and boned salted anchovies in butter until they melt to a sauce. Unmold the warm sformato, spoon sauce over, and serve with toast slices.

★ See also Warm Cauliflower Salad with Raisins, Pine Nuts, and Pink Peppercorns, page 157, in which Romanesco or Broccoflower can be substituted for white cauliflower.

Brussels Sprouts (*Brassica oleracea,* Gemmifera Group)

Including **red Brussels sprouts (Rubine)**

Brussels sprouts behave beautifully if you follow these rules: Buy them small and superfresh (no minor feat). Do not overcook them (stay near the stove). Do not undercook them (taste often). If you ignore these rules, what sprout-haters say about the vegetable will be true. More about this later.

The origins of Brussels sprouts are lost in the mist—the coastal atmosphere in which they flourish. Although "it is assumed that" they developed around Brussels and it is often stated that they "probably first appeared in the 13th century," proof is lacking. E. L. Sturtevant wrote, in *Sturtevant's Edible Plants of the World* (edited by U. P. Hedrick), "Authors have stated that brussels sprouts [note that he does not commit himself to a capital B, which would denote the city] have been grown from time immemorial about Brus-

sels, in Belgium; but if this be so, it is strange that they escaped the notice of the early botanists, who would have certainly noticed a common plant of such striking appearance." Reliable 20th-century botanical texts date the development of Brussels sprouts from the late 18th century and the early 19th century.

When I sent the query "why Brussels?" to *Brassica* wise men worldwide, the most logical response came from Peter Crisp (director of Innovar Plant Breeding in Norfolk, England), as often happens. He stressed the significance of local varietal names and the fact that Chou de Bruxelles Ordinaire and Chou de Bruxelles Nain (Ordinary—called Tall—Brussels Cabbage and Dwarf Brussels Cabbage) were the primary varieties available in France and Britain at the end of the 19th century: "It is worth pointing out that suburban mar-

standard and small Brussels sprouts

½ **actual size**

Brussels sprouts on the stalk   length: 2 feet

ket garden industries were extremely well developed around the major European cities during the 18th and 19th centuries and many of the major vegetable types owe their origins (and names) to these industries—hence 'Paris market carrots,' 'Early London cauliflowers,' 'Hamburg parsley,' and so on."

The evolution of Brussels sprouts in the United States is also misty. Because Thomas Jefferson cultivated everything before almost anyone else, it is likely that his notation about planting the vegetable, in his garden book of 1812, was among the first in the country. For a century, Brussels sprouts were the province of home gardens. Somewhere between 1909 and 1919, depending upon which California farmer is remembering, Brussels sprouts were undertaken as a commercial crop by Italian artichoke growers in San Mateo County. Why? The cool mist of the northern California coast and the vegetable's success in Europe were the reasons given by six farmers who were there at the beginning.

Production acreage quickly stretched south to Monterey County, and the combined strip now produces 98 percent of the Brussels sprouts in the United States. (New York State grows the remaining 2 percent.) A substantial quantity is imported from Belgium, Mexico, and Guatemala, and a minuscule quantity from other countries, notably the Netherlands. The vast majority of all Brussels sprouts in the United States are frozen. Only 15 to 20 percent end up at fresh markets. Most of these are rejects that are too large to meet the standard for frozen Brussels sprouts: ¾ inch to 1⅜ inches in diameter. A small amount is reportedly picked by hand for farmers' markets and restaurants.

Surprisingly, the cultivars grown today are said to be superior in taste to those grown earlier. In the 1960s "one-harvest" varieties that could be mechanically cut were developed, and these did little to please the taste buds, according to growers who remember them. "In the 1960s, we began working with all these hybrids that matured so well and were so much easier to harvest," said one old-timer. "The Japanese perfected crosses for looks and harvesting uniformity—all that mattered for frozen food. But they were bitter, and everyone was turned off." The first hopeful note for the sprouts sounded when "as fresh vegetables made a comeback, development became more refined and the Dutch seeds took over. The current hybrids are mild and sweet and please folks who like sprouts."

There are also purply **red Brussels sprouts, or Rubine** by name, always small or miniature, which flit in and out of distribution. I have not cooked enough of them to report knowledgeably. My limited experience is this: Steamed, they turn deep indigo-violet (not green); boiled, they turn purple-splotched dark to light green; braised in liquid with some acid and fat, they are maroon-green and are most flavorful. Their flavor is not deep or complex, merely pleasant and earthy, and lacking sweetness. The cores are thick and somewhat fibrous and mealy. When being prepared, they bleed blue (onto hands, other vegetables, and plates), so plan accordingly. When marinated in vinaigrette, they become glossy show-stoppers and their flavor rounds out nicely. Deep-fuchsia with green details, they offer spectacular possibilities for presentation.

Where does this leave a person who wants to buy fresh Brussels sprouts for dinner? On shaky ground. Asked about the taste of the different types he was growing, one California farmer shot back: "Taste? We're not here to eat them. We grow them." In two rounds of samplings, three Dutch sprouts (obtained through restaurant distributors) were peerless on all counts. The California sprouts purchased at a local market in New York were agreeable, if overgrown. The small, tight buds sent from a friendly West Coast farmer were wonderfully juicy, sweet, sprightly, and assertive. Samples from south of the border were consistently large and leathery.

My hope is that consumers will pay attention and demand improvements in fresh Brussels sprouts. That hope is based on the changes I've seen in artichokes over the last few years. Growers who once sold only giants have responded to chefs and connoisseurs who want small fresh artichokes and different varieties—now more widely available. Since these are the same people who grow Brussels sprouts, perhaps they will heed the aficionados who pay a premium for the rosebud gems that are available only from Belgium and Holland. Or perhaps the sad reality is that they cannot

red Brussels sprouts (Rubine)   ½ actual size

afford to produce such sprouts, given the cost of land and labor in California—and without government support.

Readers who fancy Brussels sprouts should cast their votes at the grocery store, by paying for quality or complaining about the lack thereof; otherwise, there is a good chance that the fresh vegetable will disappear from the marketplace.

BASIC USE: Tiny Brussels sprouts, if you can get them, are perfect whole, boiled. Although it is aesthetically cruel to cut them up, for my taste they are vastly improved by being halved, quartered, or sliced to cook quickly and uniformly in order to keep their vivid green taste. If you have the patience to separate the leaves, they are delightful quick-cooked.

For the mildest flavor, boil prepared sprouts in plenty of salted water. For more pronounced flavor, steam them, but expect less vivid coloring. In either case, watch carefully lest they turn mushy with overcooking, as they do very suddenly. Nor should they be undercooked. Taste often. Plain-cooked sprouts can be enhanced in many ways (see Basic Brussels Sprouts, Boiled or Steamed, page 130).

Stir-fry or braise sliced Brussels sprouts, tossing to wilt, then adding liquid to soften and cook through.

They can handle assertive flavorings, even more so than cabbage. Do not be shy.

Although Brussels sprouts are served raw on vegetable platters and in salad, those I have tasted are too harsh and tough to eat this way. Gardeners say fresh-picked raw sprouts are different.

Brussels sprouts cooked for use in salad are another story, however—and oddly neglected. They stand up to all kinds of forceful dressings and additions and can be prepared ahead without losing their fine flavor and tooth.

SELECTION: Brussels sprouts are available year-round but are likely to be best during cold times or from cool climes. Market sprouts are generally sold in pint containers and weigh 10 to 11 ounces. There is vast variation in size, ranging from as many as 96 to the pound for minis (usually available to restaurants only) to 60 for small imports to 40 for small domestic sprouts to 24 for medium to about 12 for the largest. These are observed measures, not standards. Whichever you choose, look for sprouts that are all about the same size so that they'll cook through at the same time. In my experience, smaller does mean fresher and sweeter and more tender. Sprouts from ½ inch to 1¼ inches in diameter are the most tender and tasty.

Choose uniformly green, *tightly* furled sprouts with no yellowing, wilting, or mold. They should be very dense, with no impression of airspace within when squeezed. Apart from the obvious yellowing of old age, color is not important. Some types are naturally dark; others are paler. Purple (called red) Brussels sprouts are not as tightly packed or rounded as green ones and are typically smaller.

Brussels sprouts on the stalk are fun to display and have a storage advantage over sprouts that have been cut—provided they are in good shape to begin with. The giant top leaves, if present (unfortunately, the sprouts in the photo are missing this majestic umbrella), can be cooked like kale or collards.

STORAGE: Buy sprouts when you expect to cook them, not in advance. Despite the keeping qualities of cabbage, their close kin, sprouts store poorly. While they do not visibly deteriorate, their flavor rapidly turns heavy and bitter—even just a few days after harvesting. Refrigerate loose sprouts in a plastic container with a sheet of paper towel or in their original containers for as short a time as possible. If you buy a "tree" of sprouts, trim the "trunk" base and plant the tree in a container of water in the coolest place available (the refrigerator is fine, but the height won't fit unless you have a walk-in).

PREPARATION: Pull off any loose or yellowing leaves. Trim bases if they extend below the bud. Keep sprouts whole if very small. I have not found it useful to incise a cross in the root end, but many experienced cooks do this. Halve or quarter small to large sprouts lengthwise. If you want individual leaves, first pare out the core from the base, then separate the leaves, cutting them free. Or, if sprouts are small, just cut off individual leaves. In either case, the central leaves, which are too tight to unwrap, can be thin-sliced. Soak all sprouts briefly in lukewarm water to rid them of hidden insects.

Basic Brussels Sprouts, Boiled or Steamed

Taste Brussels sprouts as they cook. Overcooking and undercooking are equally cruel to the tasty buds. Be vigilant. Because of the size range—I have counted from 12 to 96 (yes—mini-delicacies) to the pound—there is no general timing or accurate number of servings I can provide.

Whole sprouts require slightly more cooking time than cut ones. Steamed sprouts need slightly more cooking time than boiled ones. One dry pint (about 10 ounces) of small-medium sprouts should generously serve two.

About 10 ounces (1-pint container) Brussels sprouts

1. Pull off any loose or yellowing leaves from sprouts. Trim bases flush with bud (to make a ball of leaves without protruding stalk). Keep sprouts whole if smaller than 1 inch or so; halve or quarter larger sprouts lengthwise.

2. Soak in lukewarm water, weighted with a plate to keep submerged, for 15 minutes or so. Drain.

3. Spread sprouts in a skillet to hold them in a single layer, more or less. Pour over boiling water to just cover, and add salt. *Or* set on a steamer rack over boiling water and cover. Boil or steam until just tender to taste—or a touch less if you'll be reheating the sprouts or using them in salad. Start testing at 4 minutes.

To serve hot: Drain thoroughly, then tamp dry with a towel. Toss with butter and season.

To serve cool or chilled: Drain. Spread in a single layer on a towel and cool slightly; then chill, as desired. Alternatively, for brighter color, drop hot drained sprouts into ice water to cool. Then drain and dry well.

Serves 2

Variations for Cooked Brussels Sprouts

- Sauté in brown butter or nut oil. Add toasted sliced pecans, walnuts, or almonds; or toss with the traditional roasted chestnuts.
- Sauté bacon or pancetta. Drain on paper towels and break into bits. Brown sprouts in the fat, then top with reserved bits.
- Boil heavy cream in a skillet with nutmeg, salt, and pepper. Add sprouts and cook just to heat through and coat with cream.
- Add to stews and braises during the last few minutes of cooking.
- Thin-slice and serve as garnish for soups.
- Combine with cooked sliced carrots or roasted bell pepper dice or small cherry tomatoes. Dress with vinaigrette and herbs. Chill.
- Add slices or quarters to stir-fries (sprouts are particularly nice in fried rice and Asian noodle dishes).

Brussels Sprout Slivers Sautéed with Orange and Caraway

Vivid seasoning, defined textures, and quick cooking distinguish not-plain-boiled Brussels sprouts. The chewy green ribbons and rounds sliced from medium to large sprouts liven up grilled or roasted fish or meat. Or pair sprouts with mushrooms and kasha or cracked wheat, for a vegetable dinner. Or try the variation with pasta that follows for a deliciously different one-dish meal.

About 10 ounces (1-pint container) medium-to-large Brussels sprouts
1 orange

1 tablespoon lemon juice
1 teaspoon honey
⅛ teaspoon kosher salt
Large pinch of ground hot pepper
½ teaspoon caraway seeds
2 slim scallions (green onions)
1 tablespoon corn or peanut oil

1. Trim bases of sprouts closely. Stack in tube of food processor on slicing blade and press down firmly to cut into fairly thick slices. Combine in bowl with lukewarm water to cover, and weight with a saucer to submerge.

2. Pare a few strips of zest from orange. Cut into thin strands, then cut into fine confetti—about ½ teaspoon. Halve orange. Squeeze about ⅓ cup juice into small bowl. Add lemon juice, honey, salt, and hot pepper and mix.

3. In wide skillet, toast caraway seeds over low heat, stirring until pungent and crackling. Scoop onto a cutting board; chop. (Set skillet aside.) Trim scallions and slice thin, separating light and dark parts.

4. Drain sprouts. Heat oil in the same skillet. Add zest and light part of scallions and toss. Add sprouts and toss over high heat until wilted, about 2 minutes. Add juice mixture; toss until leaves are tender and juice has evaporated, about 4 minutes. Reduce heat as needed to prevent sprouts from drying out before they are cooked through. Add scallion greens and caraway and toss. Season and serve.

Serves 2

Variation

Pasta with Aromatic Brussels Sprout Slivers

Boil ½ pound butterfly or spiral pasta in salted water until just barely tender. Drain; toss with 1½ tablespoons toasted pumpkin seed or walnut oil. Prepare Brussels sprouts as above, using 4 thin scallions. When sprouts are done, add pasta to the pan and heat through, tossing. Add a few tablespoons of water if needed to moisten. Season, add 3 tablespoons chopped toasted pumpkin seeds or walnuts, and serve hot.

Serves 2

Braised Baby Brussels Sprouts and Baby Onions with Cumin

These bright little orbs of contrasting texture, color, and flavor are not merely cute. They taste just right—and wouldn't if they were larger. *The onions must be the same size as the sprouts* (or slightly smaller) to cook properly. Serve with buckwheat or barley and mushrooms for a vegetarian meal. Add pork or lamb for a meaty one.

Note that the time spent peeling mini-onions is balanced by the time not spent trimming mini-sprouts, which need mini-attention.

> 1 pint baby (pearl, boiler, or mini-) white, red, or golden onions
> About 1¼ pounds (two 1-pint containers) baby Brussels sprouts
> 1 cup vegetable broth
> ¼ teaspoon dried thyme
> ½ teaspoon sugar
> ½ teaspoon kosher salt (omit if broth is salted)
> 1½ tablespoons butter or olive oil
> 1 teaspoon cumin seeds

1. Pour boiling water over onions in a bowl. Weight with dish and let stand 5 minutes. Drain, then cover with cold water. Removing one at a time, cut a *thin* sliver from root end (more, and you lose too many layers). Pull off skin and trim neck. As needed, trim bases of sprouts. Rinse.

2. Combine onions with broth, thyme, sugar, salt, and 1 tablespoon butter in a heavy, lidded pan wide enough to hold the vegetables in a single tight layer. Bring to a full boil, stirring.

3. Add sprouts, reduce heat, and simmer, covered, until just tender, 6 to 10 minutes, depending upon size.

4. Meanwhile, stir cumin seeds in a small pan over low heat until toasty and pungent—not dark and smoky. Transfer to a board and chop.

5. When sprouts and onions are tender, uncover, raise heat, and boil until liquid evaporates, swirling pan. Add cumin and toss. Off heat, add remaining ½ tablespoon butter and toss.

Serves 4

Brussels Sprouts Salad with Roasted Pepper and Walnuts

"These burnished and adorned Brussels sprouts are good, pretty, versatile, and convenient. They can be a first course, vegetable side, or salad—and they'll even survive a day or two in the refrigerator," writes Barbara Spiegel, who cleverly updated a Thanksgiving meal with this untraditional sprouts dish. If you can locate red sprouts, their dramatic fuchsia makes an exotic backdrop for the diced red bell pepper.

> 2 large red bell peppers
> About 1¼ pounds (two 1-pint containers) medium Brussels sprouts
> 1 tablespoon sherry vinegar
> 1½ teaspoons Dijon mustard
> ½ teaspoon kosher salt
> Pepper
> ¼ cup walnut oil
> 1 cup toasted walnut halves or pieces (organic preferred)
> 2 tablespoons snipped chives

1. Peel, seed, and dice bell peppers. (If you don't have a favorite method, see Note, page 114).

2. Trim bases of sprouts and remove any yellowing leaves. Quarter lengthwise. Spread on steamer rack over boiling water, cover, and cook until tender but still slightly crunchy—about 8 minutes. Spread in dish to cool to lukewarm.

3. Combine vinegar, mustard, salt, pepper, and oil in small jar and shake to blend. Add bell peppers to sprouts. Pour all but 1 tablespoon dressing over them. Coarse-chop walnuts; add three-quarters to vegetables. Add chives and toss. (Can be refrigerated at this point.)

4. To serve, add remaining vinaigrette, toss, and sprinkle with remaining walnuts. Serve at room temperature.

Serves 6

Brussels Sprouts with Ginger and Sesame

When boiled, then sautéed, Brussels sprouts are tender, mild, and bright. Ginger and sesame taste so natural with these mini-cabbages that you would think they were all born in Asia.

> About 10 ounces (1-pint container)
>   small-medium Brussels sprouts
> 1 tablespoon sesame seeds
> 1 teaspoon honey
> ¼ teaspoon kosher salt
> 1 tablespoon dry sherry or vermouth
> 1 tablespoon peanut oil
> 1 tablespoon minced ginger

1. Trim bases of Brussels sprouts and remove any yellowing or loose leaves. Halve (or quarter, as size dictates) sprouts lengthwise. Soak in lukewarm water, submerged with a saucer, for about 15 minutes.

2. Drain sprouts. Drop into a large pot of boiling salted water. Cook over high heat until just tender throughout, about 4 minutes.

3. Meanwhile, stir sesame seeds in a heavy skillet (large enough to hold sprouts in a single layer) over moderate heat until evenly tan, a minute or two. Pour onto a plate.

4. Drain sprouts well. Spread on a towel. Stir together honey, salt, and sherry. Heat oil in same skillet, add ginger, and stir over moderate heat until lightly colored. Add sprouts and toss to coat. Add sherry mixture and toss gently about a minute.

5. Transfer to warm serving dish. Sprinkle with sesame seeds.

Serves 2

Tofu and Brussels Sprouts with Chinese Black Beans

Soy savant Lorna Sass devised this toothsome meal-in-a-wok for *The New Soy Cookbook*. Intense fermented black soybeans, orange zest, ginger, sherry, and garlic permeate the absorbent curd cubes (darkening and seasoning them) as carrots and sliced sprouts add color and crunch—a novel and effective use for the buds.

"Pressing tofu is the single most important step in producing a delicious final dish. Pressed tofu offers pleasing resistance to the tooth," writes Sass, and "the watery liquid released by pressing can be replaced with a flavor-packed . . . sauce"—which this surely is, even adapted to my meeker taste buds.

> 1 pound firm or extra-firm tofu
> 1½-inch ginger chunk, peeled and
>   quartered
> 2 garlic cloves, peeled
> 2 tablespoons Chinese fermented black beans
> ¼ teaspoon chilli flakes
> About 10 ounces Brussels sprouts
>   (1-pint container)
> 2 large carrots
> 1 cup vegetable broth or water
> ¼ cup dry sherry
> 1½ tablespoons shoyu (Japanese soy sauce)
> 1 tablespoon peanut oil
> Grated zest of 1 large orange

1. Press tofu: Wrap loosely in several layers of kitchen towel. Set on a plate and top with 1-pound weight. Let stand 15 minutes, then rewrap tofu in a dry section of towel and weight 15 minutes more. Repeat, if desired, or refrigerate, weighted, overnight.

2. With food processor motor running, drop ginger, garlic, and black beans down feed tube. Chop fine, stopping to scrape sides. Add chilli flakes.

3. Trim sprouts; cut into ⅛- to ¼-inch slices. Peel carrots; thin-slice on diagonal. Cut tofu into ¾-inch cubes. Stir together broth, sherry, and shoyu.

4. Heat wok over moderate heat. Add oil and tip to coat wok. Add black bean mixture and toss a few seconds. Add liquid seasoning and boil a moment. Add tofu, cover, and simmer 3 minutes, stirring a few times.

5. Stir in orange zest. Scatter Brussels sprouts and carrot over tofu. Cover, raise heat slightly, and cook until vegetables are crisp-tender, about 3 to 5 minutes. If mixture dries out before vegetables are cooked, stir in a little water. Taste and adjust seasoning.

Serves 3 to 4 as a main course

Pros Propose

Louis P. De Gouy's 1947 mammoth opus *The Gold Cook Book* (1,250 opinion-packed pages) is rich with vegetables that others barely mention in passing, then or now: cardoon, salsify, kohlrabi, Brussels sprouts—for which he supplies six recipes and the startling information that a "New York produce merchant interested the circus midget 'Tom Thumb' in the new vegetable, and for a time the sprouts were called 'Tom Thumb Cabbages.' "

Chef De Gouy served **French Fried Brussels Sprouts** as a garnish for venison, duck, guinea hen, or pork: Boil trimmed sprouts until tender. Drain well. Roll in seasoned flour, beaten egg diluted with milk, and then fine bread crumbs. Fry in deep fat, drain, and serve hot on a folded napkin alongside the meat. There is also a recipe for **Brussels Sprouts Gourmet:** sprouts cooked in chicken stock, combined with béchamel sauce and small seedless grapes, sprinkled with crumbs, and browned under a broiler.

This was the first of what became ten sightings of grapes and sprouts, a recipe I had not even known existed. I found them not only in American, English, and French cookbooks, but this simplest of all, from Belgium—nominal home of the sprouts. According to Juliette Elkon, author of *A Belgian Cookbook,* **Brussels Sprouts with Green Grapes** are cooked in a casserole lined with grape leaves in wine country, along the Moselle River. To prepare: Add very small trimmed sprouts to simmering chicken stock and cook until tender. Add halved and seeded Malaga grapes and cook until done to taste. Add butter, dust with white pepper, and serve at once. English cookbooks suggest this as a first course with fried toast snippets.

Belgium, Great Britain, and the Netherlands are the main sprout-eating countries. But Germany—where the little buds are sweetly called *rosenkohl* (rose cabbage) has its share of recipes as well. **Quark Tart with Brussels Sprouts** is a rich and unusual example:

Brown small slab bacon cubes. Drain on paper. Sauté thin-sliced leeks in the fat to brown lightly. Add boiled, sliced Brussels sprouts and toss. Blend quark (or ricotta and sour cream), heavy cream, a little Parmesan, nutmeg, salt, pepper, and eggs. Add shredded Emmentaler and reserved bacon. Fold together with leek-sprouts mixture. Pour into unbaked pie shell. Bake 10 minutes at 400°F. Reduce heat to 325°F and bake until lightly browned and set. Serve lukewarm (*The New German Cookbook* by Jean Anderson and Hedy Würz).

Chef Jeff Buben cooks diced Brussels sprouts or the separated leaves. He is adamant that the vegetable never tastes good cooked whole. His speedy **Brussels Sprouts Sauté with Bacon** "ranks with the great cabbage classics, however simple it sounds," he says. To prepare: Cook bacon lardons until crisp. Drain off fat as desired. Add diced shallots and diced Brussels sprouts. Sauté briefly. Add "enough chicken stock to just humidify." Simmer a few minutes, until just tender. Season and serve at once—do not wait.

Another swiftly made dish, **Brussels Sprouts and Celery in Walnut Butter,** a flavorful original made with few ingredients, is typical of chef/teacher/author Michele Urvater's recipes: Steam halved Brussels sprouts and diced celery over boiling water until tender. When just about cooked, melt a good quantity of butter in a wide skillet and cook until it browns lightly. Add the vegetables, mustard blended with a little water, and fine-chopped walnuts. Sauté until heated through. Season and serve hot (*Fine Fresh Food Fast*).

"Garnishing is a perfect role for baby Brussels sprouts, which are finally more widely available," says chef Daniel Bruce. "They're the ideal finish for any dish with cabbagey elements included or that could benefit from a cabbage connection. They add just the right small dose of color and flavor." He blanches tiny whole sprouts, refreshes them in ice water, and dries them on towels. To serve, he heats them in butter with toasted caraway, cumin, curry—or whatever suits the dish.

Burdock (*Arctium lappa*)

Also great burdock, gobo (Japanese)

Chances are good that if you've crunched burdock in the United States, it will have been in a Japanese restaurant—either in the form of a firm filament of orange pickle that runs through sushi rolls, or shredded and cooked with carrots in sweetened soy with sesame (kinpira).

Although the plant is naturalized throughout Europe and North America, it is probably Asian in origin, and it stakes its culinary claim in Japan. "It is thought that the Chinese introduced it to Japan as a medicine about 1000 years ago," writes Joy Larkcom in *Oriental Vegetables,* but they do not seem to have eaten it. Nor did burdock make a mark in the kitchens of Europe, although it was common in the pharmacopeia from the Middle Ages, if not earlier.

A minor attempt was made to include it in the French repertoire toward the end of the 19th century, when the seed company Vilmorin-Andrieux added it to a catalogue with this description: "The roots, which grow from 1 ft. to 16 inches long, are boiled and served up in various ways. . . . If eaten when young, as it is by the Japanese, although it cannot be termed delicious, it is certainly not a bad vegetable" (from *The Vegetable Garden,* English edition). This damning with faint praise did not alter the aspect of the French kitchen garden. Although I have read that burdock appears in Scandinavian and British dishes, I can verify its use only in the soft drink "dandelion and burdock."

Despite minimal international enthusiasm, I'd still say that the curious cylindrical yardstick has undeniable charm, if considered as a backup voice—not a lead singer. Cut fine, it offers a unique kind of crunchiness and sweetly earthy undertones. As a flavoring or complementary vegetable, it lends the subtle savor of artichokes and salsify.

BASIC USE: Cut burdock into slivers, julienne, or rough shreds to act as a flavor- and texture-enhancer for braises, grain dishes, or stir-fries. Or cut matchsticks and simmer in sweetened broth with sesame and ginger until tender—about ½ hour; cool in liquid. Fold into composed salads, mixed vegetables, and grain dishes for zesty contrast. If you have a great quantity of burdock, I imagine it would make a subtle pureed soup—but I haven't had the chance to try it this way.

If you pick wild burdock, you'll have another aspect to consider: "For many individuals the tastiest part of the great burdock reposes in its flower stalks," writes Pamela Jones in *Just Weeds*. "These may be already quite tall and more than an inch thick, but the crucial factor is that they are gathered during the formative stage of the flower heads. It is essential to peel off the thick green rind, revealing the . . . tender white pith. This can be cut into 6-inch lengths and prepared like asparagus, to be either steamed or boiled in two changes of salted water with a pinch of baking soda. The delicately flavored pseudo-asparagus can then be served with . . . hollandaise or béchamel sauce."

SELECTION: Burdock is available irregularly year-round in Japanese, Korean, and some natural food stores. Sufficiently scruffy and colorless to be nearly invisible on market shelves, it is, however, usually noticeable by its length—especially the yard-long Japanese varieties. Choose roots that are firm—not floppy—and preferably no thicker than a narrow carrot.

STORAGE: Wrap burdock in wet paper towels, then plastic. Refrigerated, it will stay in good shape for a few days. Or store in a shallow dish of water.

PREPARATION: Choose the method of preparation that suits the burdock and the dish. If the flavorful skin is thin, it need not be peeled, only well scrubbed. (Cleaned, the peel is rusty beige—the color of a scruffy parsnip. Inside, the flesh is a grayish white that quickly browns on contact with the air.) If you peel, do so as you whittle, slice, shred, or sliver the pieces for cooking—not beforehand, or they will brown. To rid them of a possible bitter aftertaste, soak the pieces in salted or acidulated water briefly before cooking.

For dishes in which you'll use larger chunks or slices, precook burdock, or it may be stringy: Combine pieces with cold water and baking soda (½ teaspoon per 2 cups water); bring to a boil, then drain. Cover with fresh water, boil to desired state of doneness, or add to the stew or braise you're preparing for additional cooking.

Burdock, Leeks, and Mushrooms Braised with Wine and Lemon

This quiet complex of flavors suggests artichoke stew, yet the dish is quick-cooking and texturally distinct, retaining burdock's characteristic chewiness. Serve it to garnish crisp-cooked seafood or to add tooth to fluffy quinoa or millet. If the blah beige of burdock bores you, brighten it with a fine confetti of parsley and celery leaves, or try minced lovage, chervil, or fennel.

2 cups water
1½ teaspoons kosher salt
3 tablespoons lemon juice
1 medium-large burdock root (about ½ pound)
1 medium-large leek
2 tablespoons olive oil
½ pound small button mushrooms, thin-sliced
½ cup white wine
½ teaspoon sugar
½ teaspoon grated nutmeg
¼ teaspoon pepper
1 cup vegetable, mushroom, or chicken broth
½ teaspoon grated lemon zest

1. Combine water, 1 teaspoon salt, and 2 tablespoons lemon juice in bowl. Scrub burdock under running water. Peel off rooty bits, nubs, and tips as needed (nibble to determine just how fibrous it is). Grate on julienne or grating blade of food processor, vegetable cutter, or large holes of hand grater. Stir into the lemon water.

2. Trim roots and heavy dark top from leek. Slit leek lengthwise, then cut into thin crosswise slices. Swish around in plenty of water, then lift out. Repeat until no grit remains.

3. Heat fairly large skillet over moderately high heat. Add oil and tip to coat pan. Add mushrooms and toss until they exude liquid. Add leeks and cook until softened, about 5 minutes. Drain burdock and add to pan. Toss until mixture colors lightly, about 3 minutes.

4. Add wine and stir until nearly evaporated. Add sugar, nutmeg, pepper, broth, remaining 1 tablespoon lemon juice, and zest. Simmer, covered, until burdock is tender but still has some bite, about 5 minutes. Uncover and simmer until liquid is reduced to taste, 5 to 10 minutes.

Serves 4

Toasted Barley Baked with Burdock, Shallots, Celery, and Walnuts

This muted and monochromatic dish (in terms of both taste and color) rewards those who appreciate nuance, not big-bang flavors. The seasoning underscores burdock's subtle scent; the chewy barley and chunky walnuts play up its dense, peculiarly pleasing crunch. Try it with roast turkey or chicken.

    1 fairly large or 2 small burdock roots
       (½ pound), scrubbed
    4 medium shallots
    3 medium celery stalks
    1¼ cups barley
    3 tablespoons walnut oil
    ¼ teaspoon anise seeds
    3½ cups water
    1¼ teaspoons kosher salt
    ¾ cup toasted walnuts

1. If burdock skin is thin, there is no need to peel. Taste and decide, checking both ends. Slice into diagonals ¼ inch wide, halving those from the larger end. Place in cold salted water as you go. Dice shallots. Zip strings from celery and dice stalks fine (to make 1 cup).

2. Set oven to 350°F. Stir barley in dry heavy ovenproof pot (to hold all ingredients) over moderately low heat until grains are lightly browned, about 5 minutes. Transfer to bowl.

3. Drain burdock and pat dry. Heat 2 tablespoons oil in same pot. Add burdock, shallots, and celery and toss over moderate heat until lightly browned, about 8 minutes. And anise and toss a minute longer.

4. Add barley, water, and salt. Bring to a full boil, stirring occasionally. Cover and bake in center of oven until tender, about 1 hour. Let stand, covered, 15 to 30 minutes.

5. Chop walnuts coarsely. With a fork, fluff barley into heated serving dish. Stir in remaining 1 tablespoon walnut oil and walnuts.

Serves 6 as a side dish

Pros Propose

Elizabeth Andoh, Tokyo-based journalist and educator, cooks kinpira—**Braised Burdock and Carrot**—the traditional way: Whittle burdock into slivers. Soak briefly in cold water; drain. Cut peeled carrot into similar slivers. Sauté both vegetables in oil over high heat for a minute or two. Add a little sake, reduce heat, add sugar, and stir a minute. Add shoyu; simmer until liquid is reduced and vegetables are golden, about 5 minutes. Serve warm or at room temperature, sprinkled with sesame seeds.

"Cubes of crunchy, woodsy burdock root, tender chicken, smooth konnyaku [a gelatinous yam cake] and colorful sweet carrot . . . in a faintly sweet soy broth . . . with a pinch of fiery hot spices" make up Andoh's **Braised Chicken Cubes and Vegetables** (iri-dori) from *At Home with Japanese Cooking*. To prepare: Cut peeled burdock into ¼-inch cubes; soak in cold water for 5 minutes; drain. Cut konnyaku into ¼-inch cubes. Blanch and drain. Cut chicken and carrots the same size. Sauté burdock in oil until slightly translucent. Add carrots and sauté a few minutes. Add konnyaku and toss. Add chicken. When it whitens, add soy, sugar, and sake. Cook until frothy liquid is reduced. Raise heat and shake pan to glaze. Sprinkle with shichimi togarashi (7-spice mix).

Chef Michel Nischan found that his thoroughly non-traditional **Steamed Gulf Shrimp with Pickled Burdock Salad in Sea Urchin Sauce** had to be changed from an occasional "special" to a regular menu item—a surprise, given the oddity of its ingredients: Press turnip through juicer. Combine juice with rice vinegar, mirin, and cardamom pods and bring to a boil. Pour over red onion rings and a few Habanero chilli slices; cool, then refrigerate. Cut peeled burdock into 4-inch lengths, then quarter each lengthwise. Drain liquid from onions; reserve a little, and combine the remaining liquid and burdock in a saucepan. Simmer until tender. Cool; refrigerate. To serve: Build a triangular "nest" of burdock "logs" on each plate. Fill with a salad of thin-sliced Chinese cabbage, the pickled onion, thin-sliced kumquats, and strips of mint leaves. Press sea urchins through a fine sieve and add some reserved pickling juice. Arrange hot, steamed Gulf shrimp against the nest and drizzle with sea urchin mixture. Serve at once.

Chef Daniel Bruce prepares **Fried Burdock Ribbons** "that curl up and taste sweet and crisp": With a swivel peeler, remove skin from burdock, then continue stripping to make thin slices. Fry quickly and drain. Serve with seafood. He also prepares **Burdock Gratin** "of the old school—because the vegetable is one that really works with béchamel." Peel burdock and cut into manageable lengths. Blanch, then cut thin diagonal slices. Combine with béchamel in baking dish. Top with minced parsley and garlic. Bake until tender.

Cactus Pads, Nopales (*Opuntia* species)

Also cactus paddles (not leaves), nopalitos (Latin American)

Some consider cactus consumption a curiosity, a practice reserved for overenthusiastic devotees of south-of-the-border cuisine or for times of famine. But both wild and cultivated cacti, of the *Opuntia* species in particular, are enjoyed in parts of Europe, the Middle East, India, North Africa, Australia, South and Central America, and the United States. And if you imagine that they are a minor crop, consider that in a typical year in Mexico nearly three times more cactus pads than carrots are produced.

In North America, cactus production and use are still minimal, but the potential for development is considerable. At a meeting of the Professional Association of Cactus Development held in San Antonio, Texas, Peter Felker, then the head of cactus research at Texas A & M University at Kingsville, summarized the plant's virtues: "Cactus represents the most efficient conversion of water to calories on the planet. It is an extraordinarily productive plant and an important food source in semiarid climates." *Opuntia* may also provide unusual health benefits. It has long been part of the pharmacopeia of traditional medicine, and recent studies suggest that it provides short-term reduction of blood sugar in diabetics and also lowers LDL ("bad") cholesterol.

Opuntia develops fruit and vegetable at the same time, each with a distinct flavor, texture, color, and culinary application. The succulent green vegetable parts are cladodes, technically speaking—commonly called pads or paddles (not leaves, as they are often labeled). In Latin America, the whole cactus is referred to as nopal (plural, nopales), as are its pads, the smallest and tenderest of which are called nopalitos.

Nopalitos are an acquired taste—or, more accurately, texture. The flavor of green pepper, string beans, and asparagus with a citric or sometimes sorrel-like sourness pleases many. The simultaneously soft and crisp texture pleases some. The slippery interior juices, however (which are much like okra's), attract or repel—nothing in between.

BASIC USE: Cactus pads are quick and easy to cook and most forgiving. Like okra, they exude a slith-

length of pads: 6-9 inches

ery stickiness that one likes or doesn't like. You will read that it is advisable to cook the pads into oblivion (whether boiled with baking soda, sautéed for a long time, or braised) to eliminate this slipperiness. I think it makes more sense to long-cook green peppers or green beans, which taste similar but far better. Nor am I a fan of raw pads, although they are edible and are served.

I have tried a dozen cooking techniques, and I suggest these basic ones (as well as those in the recipes that follow): For best flavor, color, and texture, sauté bite-size squares, diamonds, or strips in butter or oil for a few minutes. Or blanch sliced pads in salted water, drain, rinse in cold water, then cut to suit; sauté with seasonings and other vegetables. Or steam sliced whole pads over boiling water till al dente, then proceed as above. Generally speaking, nopalitos combine well with eggs, cheese, tomatoes, onions, chillis, cilantro, and oregano.

Chef Rick Bayless recommends grilling whole paddles that have been scored lengthwise, then brushed with oil, lime juice, and salt. Roast over a medium-low charcoal fire for 15 minutes, turning.

Deep-fry cactus "sandwiches," as is done in Mexico: Place a piece of queso fresco between two small cactus pads or strips of larger pads, dip into a light egg-and-flour batter and deep-fry. Serve the crisp appetizers as is; or heat briefly in fresh or dried chilli sauce.

Chances are good that no one has considered the culinary aspects of *Opuntia* as comprehensively as chef Jay McCarthy, the "cactus king," who has devoted many of his years in the restaurant business to cactus cookery. Among his ways with nopales are these: He purees them with spices to use as a substitute for fat in sausages and tamales or to coat foods to be roasted. He prepares a pocket sandwich by slitting the cactus pad, stuffing it with spicy meat, rubbing it with flavored oil, and grilling it until hot throughout. He batters and fries whole small cactus pads, à la chicken-fried steak, to serve with tomato sauce for a vegetarian main course. To add tartness and body to light soups, particularly seafood, he adds sliced cactus pads at the end of cooking and simmers briefly. For lightly liaised quick sauces, he sautés minced vegetables and herbs with fine-cut cactus, then adds seasoned stock and simmers briefly.

SELECTION: Available erratically year-round, cactus pads are most often in the market from early spring through late fall, with the peak season during Lent—when they're a Mexican favorite. If possible, buy spineless nopales, which are grown in Texas but are difficult to come by. Select medium-green, crisp-firm, smallish paddles (very small ones may have a higher proportion of prickers and eyes, which will require longer cleaning time). Avoid pads that are dry, limp, soggy, or apparently fibrous at the base.

STORAGE: Wrap cactus pads in paper, then closely in plastic. Store in the warmest part of your refrigerator (not below 40°F, or damage is likely). If bright and firm, they'll last more than a week.

PREPARATION: If you cannot obtain spineless nopales, proceed as follows: Wearing rubber gloves, scrub pads with a vegetable brush under running water to knock off some stickers and the "eyes" to which they attach. With a swivel peeler, zip off those that remain; then shave the rim of each pad and trim any dry or fibrous areas. (This takes no more time than peeling a cucumber.) Rinse thoroughly to remove any stray prickers and some of the sticky stuff.

Mild Chilli-Cactus Rice

"Mexican rice" with a difference: cactus. When cooked with grains, cactus is lightly tacky and nicely moist. For mild seasoning, I use plain dried, ground chillis (available throughout the West and by mail-order), which provide a sweet-warm vegetable savor, not jolts of heat. If you don't keep this pure chilli powder on hand, substitute 3 to 4 teaspoons blended chili powder (and check out page 189 for information on the spellings) for the combined spices. Serve with grilled sausage, flank steak, or a saucy bean dish—Indian, Mexican, or Italian in origin.

When microwaved, pumpkin seeds crisp up and balloon rather than browning. If raw seeds are elusive, substitute roasted and salted ones and skip step 1.

¼ cup pumpkin seeds
½ pound cactus pads
  (preferably spineless)
1½ tablespoons olive oil
1 large onion, diced
1 or 2 garlic cloves, minced
2 to 4 teaspoons ground mild chillis (also called
  pure mild chile)
½ teaspoon ground cumin
1 teaspoon dried oregano
1½ cups long-grain (not converted) white rice
1½ cups water
1 cup tomato juice
1½ teaspoons kosher salt
¼ cup chopped cilantro (coriander) leaves

1. Spread pumpkin seeds between sheets of paper towel on carousel in microwave oven. Zap a minute or so, until seeds puff and crisp. Set aside.

2. Rinse cactus and cut into ½-inch diamonds or squares. (If not spine-free, first scrub with brush under running water. Zip off "eyes" and rims with peeler or knife, then rinse again.)

3. Heat oil in heavy casserole over moderate heat. Add onion and cook, tossing now and then, until golden. Add garlic and toss briefly. Add chilli, cumin, and oregano and toss briefly. Add cactus, rice, water, tomato juice, and salt. Bring to a boil over high heat.

4. Reduce heat to lowest point, cover tightly, and cook 20 minutes. Remove from heat and let stand 10 minutes. Uncover and toss rice gently with wide fork or rubber spatula, incorporating cilantro. Add toasted pumpkin seeds.

Serves 6 as a side dish

Fresh Cactus-Corn-Pepper Relish

Good for cactus beginners (and for those on a fat-free regimen), thanks to its fresh crunch and bright coloring. Adjust heat and tartness to your level, then serve on grilled or poached seafood or with bean and grain dishes. For those who prefer meat, serve on grilled burgers, London broil, or chicken.

The relish is at its best within an hour or so of preparation. If you want to make it ahead, mix and refrigerate the vegetables, then add the seasonings just before serving. I like the dual scents of basil and mint, but neither is strictly necessary for a good relish.

6 ounces cactus pads (preferably spineless)
1 ear corn, kernels cut from the cob
   (¾ cup kernels)
1 medium-large red bell pepper
1 to 3 small fresh chillis
Salt
About 2 tablespoons thin-sliced mint leaves
About 2 tablespoons thin-sliced basil leaves
1 scallion (green onion), sliced extra-thin
About 3 tablespoons mandarin or orange juice

1. If cactus is not spine-free, first scrub with brush under running water. Zip off "eyes" and rims with peeler or knife. Drop cactus and corn kernels into pot of boiling salted water. Return to a full boil and cook 1 minute. Drain. Cut cactus the same size as corn.

2. Dice bell pepper to match. Combine with corn and cactus (can be made ahead to this point and chilled).

3. Remove seeds and veins from chilli(s). Mince and add gradually to vegetable mixture, tasting. Add salt, mint, basil, and scallion, adjusting quantities to taste. Add juice. Adjust seasonings.

**Makes 2 generous cups,
to serve 4 to 6 as a condiment**

Torta of Nopales, Feta, Dried Tomatoes, and Chiles en Adobo

Eggs are a traditional match for nopalitos—but they are usually scrambled. This savory complex makes much more of the pair. Pumpkin seeds top a golden, spicy torta (or frittata, or baked omelet) studded with crunchy cactus bits, salty feta, sweet dried tomato, and hot-smoky chiles in adobo sauce. Rich, savory—curiously meaty-tasting—this is a hearty crush of flavors in a handsome rustic guise.

Serve with dry sherry before a meal, dotting the platter with small green olives and little radishes with their greens. Or set the slices on a small-leafed mixed salad for a light main dish.

½ pound cactus pads (preferably spineless)
6 to 8 tender dried tomato halves
6 eggs
1 small can chiles en adobo (Chipotles in
   adobo sauce; see Note)
2 scallions (green onions)
About 3 ounces feta cheese, cut into ⅛-inch
   dice (¾ cup)
1½ tablespoons pumpkin seed oil or
   olive oil
1 teaspoon dried oregano, crumbled
1½ tablespoons pumpkin or sunflower seeds

1. As needed, zip off prickers and "eyes" from cactus with swivel peeler, wearing gloves. Pare rims. Rinse well. Cut into ½-inch pieces (to make 1 heaping cupful). Rinse tomato halves and pat dry. Cut into fine dice (to make ¼ cup).

2. Preheat oven to 375°F with rack set in upper level. Whisk eggs just to blend. Add tomatoes. Remove 2 chiles en adobo from can and mince. Stir into eggs with 2 teaspoons adobo sauce, or more if you love picante dishes. (Transfer remainder to jar and refrigerate for another use.)

3. Slice scallions, separating stem and bulb parts. Add stems and feta to eggs.

4. Heat 1 tablespoon oil in heavy ovenproof 9- to 10-inch skillet over moderate heat. Add sliced scallion bulbs, oregano, and cactus. Stir until cactus is slightly softened, about 3 minutes. Scrape cactus to one side.

5. Add remaining ½ tablespoon oil and heat to near-smoking. Pour in egg mixture; cook just to set bottom (edges will bubble and firm up), less than a minute. Spread cactus and pumpkin seeds over the top.

6. Set in upper level of oven. Bake until slightly puffed and not quite set in the center, about 12 minutes. Let stand 5 minutes. Gently loosen with flexible spatula and slide onto a serving dish to cool.

7. Cut with sharp knife or pizza cutter into wedges.

Serves 6 as an appetizer, 3 to 4 as a main dish

Note: You'll need only a few chiles en adobo. If you have some in your refrigerator, there is no need to purchase more.

Pros Propose

Chef Stephan Pyles sees nopalitos as "the last ingredient from Mexican peasant food that has made it to the fine dining table," adding, "I use them less than I'd like to, but more than in recent years because diners are more adventuresome." He prepares a light **Grilled Nopales-Jícama Salad:** Marinate whole trimmed pads in oil, red onion, chillis, cilantro, and lime juice. Grill pads; cut into thin strips. Combine with jícama julienne. Arrange on water cress and endive. Toss with orange vinaigrette and pomegranate seeds.

For a different style, try **Cactus Pad Salad with Fiery Jalapeño Dressing:** Cut trimmed cactus pads into 3-inch-long strips and blanch in boiling salted water until they turn bright green, about 1 minute. Drain and rinse well. Drain again. Whisk together sunflower oil, tarragon vinegar, salt, pepper, ground New Mexico chillis, and seeded and chopped Jalapeños. Cut roasted, peeled red bell peppers into strips the same size; toss with cactus. Add orange segments and toasted pumpkin seeds. Pour dressing over salad and toss (from *Native American Cooking: Foods of the Southwest Indian Nations* by Lois Ellen Frank).

Chef Josefina Howard proposes a bright appetizer, **Nopalito and Cheese Salad,** of tricolor rounds: Boil whole trimmed nopalitos until barely tender. Rinse; cut with round cookie cutter. Marinate in lemon-thyme vinaigrette. Cut rounds of queso fresco the same size as cactus, then arrange with sliced tomatoes.

Mexico City's "Mercado Merced has an aisle devoted to nothing but edible cactus," writes Nancy Zaslavsky in *A Cook's Tour of Mexico.* She adapted this nippy, cheese-topped soup, **Sopa de Nopales,** from Maria Reyes de Rodrigo after a stroll down that aisle: Boil whole, trimmed paddles in salted water with halved onion and smashed garlic cloves for 5 minutes. Drain, rinse, and boil cactus again in fresh water until soft, about 10 minutes. Rinse. Griddle-roast whole tomatoes on a steel pan until charred; enclose briefly in plastic. Toast whole garlic cloves the same way. Peel both; puree in a blender with canned chipotle chiles en adobo. Heat vegetable oil in pot; add puree carefully. Add chicken broth and chopped cilantro; simmer. Chop cactus and add. Simmer 5 minutes. Season. Serve in wide bowls sprinkled with ranchero or dry farmer cheese. Serve with tortillas.

Ingredients from the Old World and the New are blended in chef Jay McCarthy's **Creamy Potatoes with Nopales and Horseradish:** Sauté diced nopales and grated horseradish in peanut oil until just tender. Add nutmeg, cumin, and heavy cream; bring to a simmer. Drain boiled, peeled potatoes; whip smooth. Fold in nopales mixture.

Other chefs interested in trying out cactus on the menu might heed Jay McCarthy's advice. "Introduce it to customers in ways that sound familiar, not far out. **Cactus Fries,** for example, cross cultural boundaries— and expand the repertoire of ethnic Mexicans at the same time," he says. "Later, when people get used to cactus, you can be more creative." To prepare the fries: Make a light tempura batter substituting a little cactus pear puree and sake for water; add ground achiote. Just before frying, cut pads into strips, dip into cornstarch, then into batter; deep-fry.

"Pureed cactus helps retain moisture in roasting foods and lets it brown—like egg wash," explains McCarthy. To prepare **Fish Fillets in Pumpkin-Seed Crust:** Puree cactus with horseradish, Worcestershire, lime juice, and Serrano chillis. Stir in fine-ground pumpkin seeds. Coat mahimahi or another firm fish, then roast.

As a footnote, it is curious that although cactus fruit is typical market fare around the Mediterranean, its pads are not. The only place that food sleuth and author Paula Wolfert found them used was in southern Tunisia, stewed with lamb, onion, hot pepper, and tomato.

Cardoon (*Cynara cardunculus*)

Also cardo (plural, cardi), cardone (Italian)

Stacked against a stucco wall, the shoulder-high bouquets cast shadows across the pale baked earth. Cardoons, their sharp-edged feathery leaves silver in the sun, await shoppers in the Casablanca market—but not for long. The bundles sell quickly, as I have seen in Italy, Spain, and France as well. (I hear that they have invaded the pampas and are cooked in regions of South America, but I don't know firsthand.) I am fascinated to learn which foods are taken for granted—as is this thistle in its native Mediterranean.

Cardoon was probably first described by the Greek philosopher Theophrastus (372–287 B.C.). Its name, conjectured to derive from Latin *carduus* or the later French *chardon,* means thistle. A blooming cardoon is almost indistinguishable from a globe artichoke, its close kin. But it differs from the artichoke in that what is eaten is not the flower but the fleshy stalks, which slightly resemble flattened celery with a suede-like finish. When cardoon is cooked, a subtle bittersweet savor announces its kinship with artichoke and suggests one with celery and salsify—to which it is not related, however.

Of cardoons in the United States, Paula Wolfert writes in *Mediterranean Grains and Greens* that "whenever they appear in markets around Christmas, they're snapped up by Italian-Americans, French-Americans and North African–Americans so fast that you can barely get a crack at them. The demand is there, but the quantity is small." "Small" is an understatement. Cardoons have become nearly extinct, although their fans remain ardent.

In one of those frustrating chicken-or-egg situations that characterize the distribution of non-mainstream crops, cardoon growers contend that there is no market for the vegetable beyond traditional Italian communities. But chefs and culinary connoisseurs maintain that they would love to use the cardoon if they could only get it. Alice Waters, the restaurateur and crusader for local agriculture, who is close enough to North Amer-

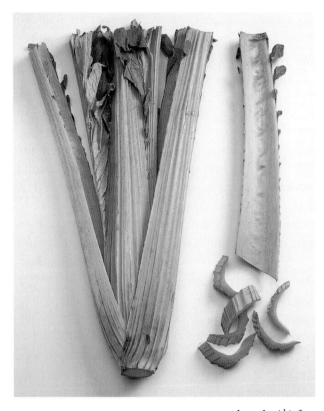

length: 1½ feet

ica's sole cardoon crop (on the central California coast) to find what she wants for her table, wrote in *Chez Panisse Vegetables:* "The season for cardoons starts late in spring, with young stalks cut from plants that have over-wintered. It continues through the summer and fall, when you are more likely to find the hearts of plants that have been started in the spring."

So why do I find cardoons (in the remains of Little Italy in Greenwich Village) in winter only? I asked the few surviving growers, who all said more or less the same thing: Cardoons grow at just about any time in California, but winter is the traditional season for them if you belong to the only group that eats them—Italians. A maddening response!

Setting aside the question of season, there is a question of quality. One week, I find smooth, meaty cardoons—and the next week will bring stringy, pithy specimens. Is there no way to ensure a more uniform product? Are there no special varieties or growing methods? Seed catalogues indicate distinct varietal characteristics. Matt Kramer, the author of *A Passion for Piedmont,* writes that "in Piedmont they distinguish between two types of cardoon: *lunghi* and *gobbi.* The *lunghi,* or long ones, are the regular stalks, conventionally grown. The *gobbi* (literally, humped) are bent over when very young and partially buried to make them more tender."

When I looked into California cardoons, I learned that they are inherited. "No one has any idea of the varieties," said a farmer. "We work with what we found, which we assume is French or Italian." When I asked about growing the tender *gobbi,* I was told that there was no reason to go to the trouble of blanching cardoons. "No one buys them but traditional Italians—and they never complain."

So why do I bother to include them? Because despite my complaints, they are still worth snapping up if you find them. Mostly, I hate to see a valuable and venerable vegetable forgotten.

BASIC USE: Cardoons are served raw in Italy—notably as dippers for the creamy, garlicky Piemontese bagna cauda. But the cardoons I have seen here are far too large and tough to consume raw.

Cardoons are usually precooked to dispel bitterness. Once this is accomplished, they can be treated as artichoke hearts, broadly speaking: Dress with lemon vinaigrette and herbs, or combine with cheese sauce and bake until golden. Stew gently in cream and herbs, simmer with a mirepoix or sofrito containing ham and plenty of onions, or dip large cardoon "cutlets" in batter or crumbs and fry. Add pieces to veal or chicken stew. Potatoes, onions, and mushrooms all have an easy affinity for cardoons. Simmer cardoons in broth, then puree for a subtle soup.

Cardoons are rarely precooked for long-simmered, highly seasoned dishes. Such is the case for the North African tagine and kdra, and Persian khoresh, for which cardoons are cut small and added to the stew during the last hour of cooking.

SELECTION: There is little agreement about cardoons' growing season, but most concur that the vegetable appears in the market in fall and winter. Look for comparatively slim, pale, firm stalks, which are more tender. Very large stalks tend to be pithy and

stringy and need more trimming. If possible, cut a few stalks before you buy a large quantity to be sure they're not hollow.

Browned edges are normal. Cardoons' huge upper leaves are sliced off before packing, and the cut discolors immediately, as with artichokes. Although there is a superficial resemblance to celery, cardoon is never as crisp and bright; it is, rather, more pliant and grayish.

Store cardoons wrapped at the base with damp toweling, then covered with a plastic bag. If in good condition when purchased, they should last for about 2 weeks.

PREPARATION: Separate stalks, cutting apart at the base. Remove very pithy stalks (unless you're making pureed soup). Slice off all the pretty leaves and discard them (they are inedibly bitter—even the delicate inner ones). If large stalks are very stringy, zip off the fibers as you would with celery. Swoosh the lot in a sink filled with water, scrubbing with a brush if stalks are silty. It is usual to rub lemon on cut stalks to prevent browning, but I see no reason for this, since cooked cardoons, acid-treated or not, turn gray-green, and the lemon can be overpowering.

To maintain paleness, stalks are traditionally precooked *à blanc*—in water thickened with flour and acidified with lemon. I prefer to simply cook stalks in a large amount of salted water until tender, drain, place in cold water, then zip off strings and cut to size.

CAVEAT: If you enjoy cardoons, you must be flexible about cooking them. Those grown in the United States are utterly unpredictable in terms of size (2 to 7 pounds per head or bunch), texture (crunchy to limp), bitterness (almost none to extreme), pithiness (ditto), color (mild green to gray-silver), and stringiness (minor to major). Happily, they almost always make fine eating, even if you must turn them into pureed soup.

To Precook Cardoons

Having tried five precooking methods, I vouch for the following, which is simplest and fastest and which produces yielding, juicy, neat non-fibrous pieces, as mild as artichokes. If you have an unusually bitter bunch, you may want to boil it twice, but that is exceptional. I don't know whether it's different tastes or different cardoons, but French and Italian cookbooks recommend 2 to 3 hours precooking for this vegetable, while I have found that less than an hour works fine.

1 small bunch (or ½ larger bunch) cardoons (about 2½ pounds)

1. Trim off cardoon base. Remove all leaves (which are inedibly bitter) and any seriously wilted or damaged outside stalks. Halve remaining stalks crosswise, separate, and wash carefully.

2. Drop stalks into a huge amount of boiling salted water—as for pasta. Boil gently until tender, usually 15 to 25 minutes. When half-cooked, taste; if too bitter, drain and finish cooking in fresh boiling water. Drain, then cool under running water.

3. Return to pot and add cold water to cover. Remove a stalk at a time, then zip off very heavy strings with aid of a paring knife, pulling first from one end of the stalk, then from the other. Cut into 1- to 3-inch pieces, as suits the recipe. Pat dry, unless the next step includes liquid.

Makes about 6 cups

Additions for Precooked Cardoons

Once you have precooked cardoons as above, you can:
- Dress with citrus vinaigrette, chervil or parsley, and chives.
- Toss with olive oil or butter and seasoning; bake in a moderate oven until very tender, then sprinkle with grated Parmesan or Gruyère.
- Combine in a shallow baking dish with white sauce, cream sauce, cheese sauce, or onion sauce (soubise), then bake until bubbling and lightly golden.

Creamy Cardoon and Portobello Gratin

Even unadventurous diners seem to love the succulence of cardoons paired with portobello mushrooms and lightly bound with cream. Although several operations are required, the result rewards with the lusciousness of artichoke hearts—without the leafy fiddling. Serve as a rich side dish, appetizer, or vegetarian entree.

About 2 pounds small slim cardoons or 2½ pounds larger ones
5 medium-large portobello caps (1 pound without stems)
1 cup heavy cream
Salt and pepper
½ teaspoon grated nutmeg or ground mace
2 tablespoons cornstarch
1 cup mushroom or vegetable broth
1 cup coarse-grated firm cheese, such as Gruyère or Comté

1. Follow directions To Precook Cardoons (page 144). Cut into 1-inch slices.

2. Preheat oven to 375°F. Clean portobello caps with soft brush. Trim stems flush if this has not been done already (save for broth). Using ¼ cup cream, brush mushrooms, coating thoroughly. Set gill side up on baking sheet. Bake until tender, 15 to 20 minutes. Season well.

3. Meanwhile, combine remaining ¾ cup cream, nutmeg, and 1 teaspoon salt (omit if broth is salted) in a small heavy pot. Blend cornstarch with 2 tablespoons broth, then add to remainder of broth. Stir into cream mixture. Bring to a slow boil over moderate heat, stirring. Set aside.

4. Cut mushrooms into 1-inch cubes. Combine with cardoons in shallow 2-quart baking dish. Pour sauce over all, blending gently with spatula. Sprinkle with cheese.

5. Bake on upper level of oven until bubbly and browned, about 25 minutes.

Serves 8 as a side dish or first course, 4 to 6 as a main dish

Cardoons and Potatoes in Anchovy Vinaigrette

A softly subtle dish, anchovy and garlic notwithstanding. Bitterish cardoons balance the assertive sauce; mellow potatoes act as buffer. Yellow potatoes, which are almost always more flavorful and waxy than others, make a big difference in the quality of the dish. Lovers of a strong garlic taste will want to use more of the potent raw allium.

About 2 pounds small slim cardoons or
   2½ pounds larger ones
5 medium-large potatoes (1¾ to 2 pounds)
2 tablespoons white wine or 1 tablespoon
   lemon juice
⅓ cup olive oil
1 small garlic clove, peeled
¼ teaspoon kosher salt
¼ teaspoon pepper
1½ tablespoons white wine vinegar
5 oil-packed anchovy fillets, drained and
   chopped (1 tablespoon)
¼ cup minced parsley leaves
Optional: small ripe olives, such as Niçoise or
   Arbequina

1. Follow directions To Precook Cardoons (page 144). Cut into 1-inch pieces. Pat dry.

2. Meanwhile, peel and halve potatoes. Boil in salted water until just tender, 15 to 20 minutes; do not overcook. Drain, then let cool 10 minutes to firm up. Halve lengthwise; then cut crosswise into ½-inch slices.

3. Spread potatoes in wide shallow serving dish. Blend wine and 1 tablespoon olive oil. Mix with potatoes. Spread cardoons on top.

4. Crush garlic with salt and pepper to form paste. Combine in small dish with 1½ tablespoons vinegar; add anchovies. Whisk in remaining oil with fork.

5. Spoon dressing over cardoons. Mix gently with the potatoes underneath, gradually folding in parsley. Adjust seasoning, oil, and vinegar. Do not refrigerate, or texture and flavors will be dulled. Serve warm or at room temperature, with optional olives.

Serves 6 as a side dish

Silky Cardoon Soup

Cardoons blenderize to an elegant, creamy puree—even if the stalks are rather large and scruffy. The soup looks and tastes as if it were made with artichoke hearts—at a fraction of the labor and expense. Like all cardoon dishes, it is low-key and low-color—a greenish greige that benefits from contrast with deep-toned serving bowls. For a bright garnish, scatter snips of chervil over each serving.

3 pounds cardoons
4 medium shallots, sliced (about ¾ cup)
2 or 3 large garlic cloves, sliced
3 sturdy rosemary sprigs (each about
   4 inches long)
2 tablespoons walnut oil (or hazelnut and
   olive oil combined)
1 teaspoon ground coriander
½ cup dry vermouth
About 4 cups mushroom and/or vegetable
   broth
About 3 cups water
3 tablespoons white rice (preferably short- or
   medium-grain)
3 tablespoons rolled oats
2 teaspoons kosher salt
¼ teaspoon fine-ground white pepper
Lemon juice
About ½ cup grated Parmesan cheese

1. Trim base of cardoons and separate stalks. Run knife down sides to remove leaves. If stalks are very large and stringy, zip off some fibers with a knife. Cut into 2-inch lengths (to make 8 to 10 cups). Rinse well. Combine in large pot with water to cover. Bring to a boil, covered; drain.

2. Meanwhile, in small saucepan, gently cook shallots, garlic, and rosemary in oil over fairly low heat to soften but not brown. Stir in coriander, add vermouth, and bring to a boil. Add to cardoons.

3. Add 4 cups broth, 3 cups water, rice, oats, salt, and pepper. Bring to a boil, stirring often to prevent sticking. Reduce heat and simmer, covered, until cardoons are soft—timing varies, but 45 to 60 minutes is usual. Taste during cooking to determine if rosemary should be removed.

4. Uncover soup and cool briefly. Remove rosemary, if still present. With slotted spoon, transfer solids to food processor, then puree until smooth, adding liquid gradually. (Puree in batches, as necessary.)

5. Press soup through medium sieve. Season with salt, pepper, and lemon juice. Thin, if desired, with broth or water.

6. Reheat soup gently. Ladle into bowls. Sprinkle cheese on each.

Makes about 8 cups, to serve 6 as a first course

Pros Propose

The Mediterranean is home to cardoon cookery, as nearly all the following recipes demonstrate. A Provençal classic, **Cardoon in Anchovy Sauce**, comes from *Lulu's Provençal Table* via the sage of the region, Richard Olney: Cut stalks into 3-inch sections, removing strings; halve each lengthwise and place in lemon water. Simmer *à blanc* until tender. Prepare white sauce. Crush garlic cloves and anchovies to a paste; add to sauce. Arrange drained cardoons in earthenware dish. Top with sauce and bake until bubbly.

Chunky **Chickpea and Cardoon Soup** has Sicilian roots: Cook soaked, drained chickpeas in fresh water and salt until just tender. Sauté onion in olive oil; add to chickpeas with thin-sliced blanched cardoons, chopped beet greens, chopped tomatoes, and dried whole chillis. Simmer until thick and tender. Serve with sourdough croutons fried in olive oil (from *Mimmetta Lo Monte's Classic Sicilian Cookbook*).

Roman chef Stefano Riccioletti serves a refined **Timballo di Cardi:** Cut trimmed, "stringed" cardoons into 5-inch sections. Cook *à blanc* until tender. Meanwhile, poach shrimp in vegetable stock, white wine, and chervil. Strain and reduce liquid. Puree cardoons with half the shrimp reduction and eggs. Turn into timbale molds; bake in bain marie. Unmold each into a shallow bowl. Garnish with shrimp; drizzle around remaining reduction and drops of the finest olive oil.

Chef Odette Fada, from Brescia, prepares **Tortino of Cardoons and Gruyère** "for a special, rich vegetarian main course": Cut cardoons into 3-inch sections; remove strings. Simmer *à blanc* until tender; drain. For each portion, lay pieces in a baking pan to form a square. Cover with Gruyère. Repeat. Top with more cardoon, then grated Parmesan and butter slivers. Brown in a hot oven.

Low-key flavors and multiple textures characterize the many Mediterranean dishes developed by chef Catherine Brandel for Chez Panisse and for her inspiring courses at the Culinary Institute of America at Greystone. For **Gratin of Cardoons, Cannellini, and Farro,** blanch trimmed cardoons; zip off strings, slice. Braise in olive oil and salt until soft. Sauté onion, garlic, carrot, Provençal herbs, and chopped tomato. Cook farro (or kamut) until tender, reserving liquid. Add some to tomato mixture to make it soupy. Combine cooked cannellini, prosciutto or pancetta, farro, and cardoons in gratin. Cover with tomato mixture and plenty of olive oil. Bake until crusty.

Chef Loretta Keller has a knack for combining contemporary concepts and traditional flavors, as in her **Warm Salad of Cardoon, Fennel, Radicchio, Cremini, and Fontina**: Cook trimmed cardoon *à blanc;* slice diagonals. Combine with thin wedges of roasted fennel, quartered and sautéed cremini, and slivered radicchio; toss with basil chiffonade. Moisten with vinaigrette of reduced chicken stock, mint, shallots, aged balsamic vinegar, and olive oil. Mound on plates, cover with thin Fontina slices; run under flame. Sprinkle with minced orange and lemon zests, parsley, and garlic.

Paris restaurateur Fatéma Hal simmers her version of traditional Moroccan **Krda of Beef with Cardoons** without precooking: Brown beef cubes, chopped onions, garlic, cumin, ginger, pepper, and saffron in olive oil. Cut cardoons into bâtonnets and soak in lemon water. When beef is half cooked, add cardoons; cook soft. Add lemon juice. Decorate with preserved lemon strips (from *Les saveurs et les gestes*).

A similar Persian **Khoresh of Cardoon and Beef** appears in *New Food of Life* by Najmieh Batmanglij: Brown onions and beef or lamb in oil; add salt, pepper, and turmeric. Add water, cover, and simmer an hour. Sauté soaked 2-inch cardoon pieces in oil; add a large quantity of chopped parsley (3 cups to 1 pound beef) and mint; cook about 10 minutes. Add to the meat with lime juice and ground saffron dissolved in a little hot water. Simmer another hour or so, until all is tender.

Carrots, "Non-Traditional" *(Daucus carota,* Sativus Group)

Including **red, white, purple; baby** or **mini-carrots; carrot greens**

This is a footnote to a familiar vegetable—much abused by growers and retailers. Most carrots in the market today, like mainstream tomatoes and cucumbers, are visual stand-ins for the real thing. Carrots can be (and are, if you do some rooting around) more than just orange crunch. One taste of the genuine article will suffice to restore your memory or alert your senses. The difference is alarming: a true wake-up call. But chances are good that unless you garden, you'll have to go outside standard channels to avoid the mass-produced models. Check out farmers' markets or specialty grocers for organic carrots in an inviting range of colors, shapes, and sizes, the non-mainstream forms that are likely to offer sweetness, scent, and flavor.

There is nothing new about "colored" carrots. William Woys Weaver writes in *Heirloom Vegetable Gardening:* "While the white carrot is native to Europe, the genetic origin of both yellow and violet carrots is believed to be Afghanistan. Both the yellow and violet carrots were mentioned by Arabic writers and moved westward through Iran into Syria, and then into Spain by the 1100s." By the early 1300s, the violet carrot was being cultivated in Italy, but the familiar orange form came along later, probably during the 17th century.

The rose, scarlet, and yellow farm and garden carrots that I have tasted have all been remarkable for their rich flavor—and for their differences. I recommend that you try any you can get your hands on, but I can make no general statements about the disparate lot. There is commercially available one carrot that fits into this non-traditional category. **Beta Sweet** is the trademarked name of the large (and soon to appear as "baby") winy carrot pictured below, which is also sold generically by some distributors as burgundy, bordeaux, and maroon carrot. It came not from Afghanistan but from Texas via Brazil. In 1988, Leonard Pike, director of the Vegetable and Fruit Improvement Center at Texas A & M University in College Station, was evaluating a trial planting of Nantes-type carrots called Brasilia and noticed three slightly maroon specimens. Pike was intrigued by the maroon streaks and the crisp sweetness of the carrots. He began crossing them with his own high-carotene orange breeding lines to develop a sweet, crisp variety with uniform maroon color (a trait that indicates anthocyanins, potent antioxidents that Pike wanted to increase).

At this writing, I have purchased Beta Sweet from five stores in New York City. The very thin skin is wine-dark, the interior brilliant orange. The flavor is usually rich and concentrated, the texture consistent and crunchy throughout, not fibrous. Cooked, the carrots are brazenly bicolor and flavor-balanced. Leonard Pike reports that they are grown by Jimmy Bassetti, of J & D Produce in Edinburgh, Texas, who "isn't as interested in *big* as some growers in the state. He's the son of a New Jersey farmer who cared about flavor and appearance and growing things right. And it really shows."

Baby or mini-carrots can be purple, yellow, orange, white, or red—anything a larger carrot can be. They are cultivars that develop full flavor and color when small and tender. Globular, tear-shaped, cylindrical, or tapered, these plumed petite carrots are charming to behold in the market and just as cute on the plate—especially with their feathery greens intact. Plastic-bagged "mini-carrots" are as likely as not to be older carrots machine-cut ("baby-cut") to resemble little ones. If convenience matters more than taste and nutritional value, they're the ones to buy.

Beta Sweet carrots

length (without leaves): 10 inches

Small carrots are irresistible raw; cute and colorful, they beg to be crunched. But do not stop there, for baby carrots are delightful cooked. And some, which may lack sweetness or seem aggressive when raw, are transformed into balanced beauties when cooked. Color changes, too. A dusky burgundy turns into a bright tricolor when steamed. Leaves that are sharp and oily may soften and mellow—or not. Experimentation is the order of the day with these unknowns.

Carrot greens, too, are interesting in terms of cookability, especially those on small carrots—clearly intended by nature for presentation. Steamed, they keep their color and shape, and taste like a blend of sharp parsley and chrysanthemum (both relatives).

BASIC USE: Larger carrots, whatever their color, can be used like orange carrots. Small carrots were born to show their shape whole or only slightly deconstructed. They are not meant to be pureed or used in volume. The real question is whether to eat a particular cultivar raw, cooked, or both. There is only one way to know: Nibble some raw (try first with skin, then without; some do not need to be peeled); then cook and taste. Then decide what you'll do.

For greens: Cut the feathery parts of baby greens into salads for a vivid aroma, as you would add fennel tops or celery leaves. Steam carrots and their tops as one. Or cook greens separately to serve as a nest for seafood or vegetables. Or stir segments of the greens into broth to add color and rich aroma. Or make soup with the greens (see Pros Propose). Greens vary as much as roots: Taste before you serve.

SELECTION: Small carrots are, for the most, part a spring and summer special. Colored larger carrots and Beta Sweets are available most of the year, but any availability at all will depend on local distribution. It is important to buy organic carrots (and other vegetables, too, but carrots and potatoes above all) so that you don't have to peel them—carrots grown with the usual pesticide cocktail should be peeled. Good baby carrots break easily; they're not meant for storage. If a tip or two is missing, that's a good sign.

Look for fluffy and short—not leggy—greens on carrots you'll cook with tops. Carrots with plumage let you see how fresh they are. But only a taste of the root will let you know about flavor.

STORAGE: Baby carrots should be refrigerated loosely wrapped and used as soon as possible. Larger ones, which can be kept longer, are better stored with the greens cut off and wrapped separately.

PREPARATION: Scrub baby carrots gently with a soft toothbrush, particularly where the greens sprout. They should not need peeling. If you're cooking greens and roots separately, cut apart to wash. Large colored carrots—with the exception of Beta Sweet—are usually improved by peeling. Sample each to determine.

Basic Steamed Baby Carrots

Raw baby carrots can be sweet and crisp and rewarding. But there is more to them. Cooking changes them in most agreeable ways—particularly the fluffy greens. Raw, they are harsh and oily; cooked, they can mellow and soften to become an aromatic complement to the sweet root. Steaming is the best way to maintain the feathery forms and at the same time cook the carrots fully. Dark red mini-carrots seem to be particularly well suited to steaming—both their roots and their leaves.

There can be no strict recipe for such a treatment because the sizes and cultivars vary so. Most important, keep a watchful eye on the babies. Overcooking destroys their special qualities.

Baby (mini) carrots

1. Scrub 1 carrot (or 1 of each variety, if there are several) and set on steamer rack. Cook until easily pierced in the center with a knife. Taste to determine whether the greens should remain or not. (If unsure, leave intact. They look lovely. Diners can cut them off at the table if they don't want to eat them.)

2. If you decide to keep the greens, trim off any long skinny stalks, leaving just the shortest. Scrub carrots gently with a toothbrush if earthy or rooty. Or simply rinse.

3. Arrange carrots on steamer rack. Cover and cook until just tender in the center, from 2 to 5 minutes, depending upon size. Test often to avoid overcooking. Serve at once.

★ For another recipe with baby carrots, see Miniature Mélange, page 219.

Basic Beta Sweet (Maroon) Carrots

Spectacular coloring, thin edible skin, rich flavor, smooth texture: What more can you ask of a carrot? Serve alone as garnish, or mixed with other vegetables, hot or cold. Microwave for maximum color and zip. Although nothing could be quicker and easier, vigilance is a must, or the carrots turn flabby—in seconds. The carrots can also be steamed (less vividly). Sautéing or simmering the raw carrots muddies the color. Reheat in butter for a sweet, warm flavor, then finish with herbs. Or gild in peanut oil and add shiny black sesame seeds for an Asian touch. The slices are brilliant orange with an eggplant-purple edge. Most large red or purplish carrots—not just Beta Sweet—can be cooked in the same way.

> 5 large Beta Sweet carrots (about 1 pound)
> 1 tablespoon butter or peanut oil
> Salt and pepper
> Optional: snipped chives and slivered chervil or
>   parsley leaves; or toasted black sesame seeds

1. Remove carrot greens (save for another use). Scrub carrots with brush under water; do not peel. Halve carrots crosswise at an angle.

2. Set carrot halves on microwave carousel with narrow ends pointing into the center. Cook just until the center of each piece can be pierced with a sharp knife. Test after 2 minutes, then check every 30 seconds thereafter. Remove smaller pieces first as they cook through. (Alternatively, set the halves on a rack over boiling water, cover, and steam until almost done, but not quite, about 5 minutes).

3. Let stand until cool enough to handle. At a sharp angle, cut into slim slices to make neat ovals (can be prepared ahead).

4. To serve, heat butter or oil in wide skillet over moderate heat. Add salt and pepper; toss carrot slices in pan until heated through and brightly colored, a matter of a few minutes. Add optional herbs and season.

Serves 2 to 3

Rosy Microwaved Carrot Salad

Microwaving maintains the brilliant coloring of the Beta Sweet and other large red-purple carrots. The addition of acid brightens it even more: The dark-beet edge and cadmium orange center pinken in the vinaigrette as the peel develops a curiously piney-gingery taste. (If left in the vinaigrette for more than a few hours, the slices turn overall borscht-pink and lose their dual coloring.) Serve as an appetizer with cucumber salad on cress or as a side dish on mixed small greens (especially purple mini-mustard or mizuna); or mix with other cooked vegetables for a composed salad. Or garnish meat or seafood with the bright slices.

> 5 large Beta Sweet carrots (about 1 pound)
> 1 tablespoon lime juice
> 1/8 teaspoon kosher salt
> Optional: 1/2 teaspoon honey
> 1 tablespoon grapeseed or corn oil
> Optional: snipped chives, minced chervil, dill,
>   or parsley

1. Remove carrot greens (save for soup or discard). Scrub carrots with brush under water; do not peel. Halve crosswise at an angle.

2. Set carrot halves on microwave carousel with thinner ends pointing in to the center. Cook just until the center of each piece is easily pierced with a sharp knife. Test after 2 minutes, then check every 30 seconds thereafter. Remove smaller pieces first as they cook through.

3. Let stand until cool enough to handle. At a sharp angle, cut into 1/8-inch slices to form neat ovals.

4. Blend lime juice, salt, optional honey, and oil. Toss with carrots and optional herbs. Chill until serving time.

Serves 2

Pros Propose

"Humble root" does not describe the carrot as presented by chef Roland Liccioni in his **Terrine of Bordeaux Carrots and Lobster:** Scrape Beta Sweet carrots very lightly with knife to remove a tiny bit of skin. Set in baking pan in very low oven and roast until tender, about 2½ hours. Cover bottom of terrine with these whole carrots, then build up the sides with more of them. Fill center with lobster meat cooked in court bouillon. Cover with a layer of more roasted carrots. Add sheet gelatine to tomato water to make a delicate *gelée;* pour into terrine, weight, and chill. Prepare a light cauliflower cream sauce; chill. Whisk whipped cream into sauce. Stir in beluga caviar just before serving with terrine.

Masses of tiny orange carrots find an equally luxurious setting in Chef Charlie Trotter's **Baby Carrot Terrine with Shiitake Salad, Carrot Juice Reduction, and Balsamic Vinegar:** Dip tender roasted baby carrots in carrot-juice aspic and layer to half-fill a terrine lined with plastic wrap. Set aspic-coated roasted shiitake and dill on the carrots, then top up with more aspic-coated carrots. Chill, then wrap in blanched, aspic-coated chard leaves. Chill again. To serve, set a slice of terrine on each place and surround with little heaps of roasted and pickled shiitake slivers and julienned cucumber in gingered yogurt. Dot plate with dill oil, carrot juice reduced to a near-glaze, and 50-year-old balsamic vinegar. Sprinkle with Japanese chilli-spice blend (from *Charlie Trotter's Vegetables*).

In a simpler mode, there are **Braised Baby Vegetables** from Monique Jamet Hooker. She writes in *Cooking with the Seasons* that "baby vegetables are not new to cooking and have the most humble of origins in country gardens everywhere. After planting . . . in early spring, every couple of weeks Maman sent us to thin out the young seedlings. . . . Instead of throwing away the immature roots, we always braised and enjoyed them as another treat from nature's calendar of seasonal delights." To prepare: Arrange some outer leaves of Boston lettuce in a saucepan. Top with whole baby carrots, halved baby turnips, halved baby fennel, and peeled pearl onions. Add butter and a small quantity of chicken stock. Season, cover, and cook over low heat 10 minutes. Add shelled peas, fresh dill, and chervil and toss. Cover and cook 5 minutes. Remove from heat and let rest 10 minutes, covered, before serving.

"I had never heard of eating carrot tops until I met Tom McCombie [the late chef at Chez T.J.'s in Mountain View, California]," writes Rosalind Creasy in *The Edible French Garden*. "I was actually a little skeptical, so before I asked Tom for the recipe, I checked to make sure carrot tops were edible. The reports deemed them safe to eat, and after I tasted and loved them, carrot tops became a must." To prepare McCombie's **Cream of Carrot Top Soup:** Sauté diced large yellow onion and mashed garlic in butter until golden. Add fresh thyme and toss. Add chicken stock, peeled and chopped carrots and potatoes, bay leaf, and seasoning. Simmer 30 minutes. Remove bay leaf; puree soup. Thin with milk or half-and-half to taste. Stir in softened butter and minced parsley. Pick over carrot tops. Blanch in boiling water, adding salt when water returns to a boil. Drain. Puree greens with some pureed soup (3 cups greens to 2 of puree). Fill bowls two-thirds full with carrot soup, then ladle green soup into center. Top with whipped cream.

Cauliflower (*Brassica oleracea,* Botrytis Group)

Including **purple cauliflower/broccoli** and **miniature cauliflower**
See also: **BROCCOLI ROMANESCO** and **BROCCOFLOWER,** page 123

white cauliflower with its pre-market cloak intact

diameter of heads: 7-8 inches

In France, dishes in which cauliflower figures are dubbed "Du Barry," in honor of the countess who was a favorite of Louis XV. Countries where vegetable cuisine reigns, notably India, treat cauliflower as royalty.

But in the United States, cauliflower is barely bourgeois—never aristocratic—primarily because it is carelessly chosen and cooked in ways that fail to enhance its mild sweetness, creamy pallor, and delicate crunch. The unenlightened say that cauliflower is "strong" and compare it to broccoli—a fair comparison botanically,

if not in terms of taste (the two share genus and species). But I'd lay odds that those who consider it strong have never tasted truly fresh or properly cooked cauliflower, an elegant vegetable.

"Training is everything," wrote Mark Twain in *Pudd'nhead Wilson.* "Cauliflower is nothing but cabbage with a college education"—a remark often quoted in nonbotanical contexts. The word "cauliflower" comes from the Latin *cauli-* (stem or stalk) and *flor-* (flower); and cauliflower is indeed an evolved version of broccoli, in which the namesake flower stems have been cultivated to form a tight head, a process of selection that probably began during the 16th century. (Although the closely related—sometimes indistinguishable—vegetables called cauliflower and broccoli became stabilized in the Mediterranean area, their origins are murky.)

Another refinement is the whiteness of the flowery "fleece," usually called "curd," which may also be yellow, orange, pinkish, green, or purple, depending upon the variety, the growing area, climate, and regional preferences. Most colored types have a more pronounced flavor than white cauliflower.

The white or cream cauliflower preferred in the United States requires a fair amount of labor during cultivation. The fleece must be hidden from the sun if it is to retain its tenderness and pale complexion (colored varieties need not be covered—or blanched, technically speaking). To accomplish this, the nest of dusky green leaves is tied in a loose bundle around the budding new head, which continues to grow under wraps until harvest. "Self-blanching" commercial varieties produce conveniently curved leaves that grow around the head and act as a sun-guard. But most farmers blanch by hand, tying up each head, "because even a tiny yellow spot makes a cauliflower unmarketable," explains one grower from California, where the vast majority of the vegetable is produced.

American cooks have not treated cauliflower kindly, to judge from my own review of recipes of the last hundred years. Most commence with a half-hour boiling—enough time to destroy the curd and produce the aggressive cabbagey smells that develop with excessive cooking. Nor has the repertoire gone much beyond boiled and sauced, with detours into pickled, fried, and creamed.

Happily, the recipe field has blossomed with the country's newer immigrants. It has been enriched with the colors, spices, and aromatic herbs of regions where cauliflower is awarded a more prominent place in meals: the Mediterranean, the Middle East, Southeast Asia, the Far East, the Balkans, and India, among others.

Please note: Several vegetables that breeders consider cauliflowers are sold under names that include "broccoli." For ease in locating them, they are listed under their American market names, broccoli Romanesco and Broccoflower on page 123, rather than cauliflower.

purple cauliflower/broccoli   length: 6 inches

Purple cauliflower/broccoli approaches broccoli in form and function but usually has a more delicate nutty flavor. Depending upon which cultivar you have in hand (and which geneticist you have on the phone), the botanical boundaries between purple cauliflower and broccoli are unclear. Some forms are considered broccoli (*Broccoli oleracea,* Italica Group) by some geneticists, cauliflower by others, and a combination by others. Softer than either vegetable, with a more open shape, purple whatever-it-may-be ranges from acid green with violet tips to dusky deep purple throughout. Like most purplish plants, it turns brown to green when cooked. The exception is careful cooking in a microwave, which produces a deep green to purplish head. For this, do not add water. Undercook, then uncover immediately before allowing to rest briefly.

Miniature cauliflower has been embraced by the restaurant trade and has made its way into specialty shops. Elfin white and chartreuse cauliflower and purplish cauliflower/broccoli, weighing in at an ounce or

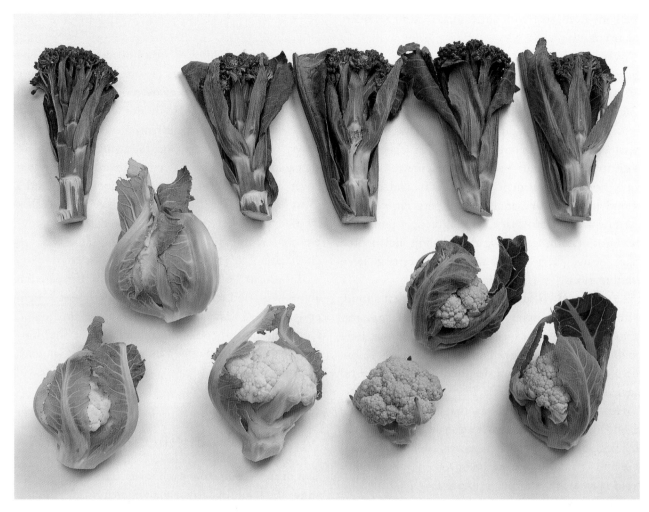

miniature white and green cauliflowers and purple cauliflower/broccoli   length: 2-4 inches

two apiece, are the same varieties as the large ones—but grown in tight quarters.

Some miniatures are delicate and sweet, but some are bitter—usually because they've spent too long on the shelf. "Or it may be growing conditions," says Shepherd Ogden, owner of The Cook's Garden, a seed company in Londonderry, Vermont. "When plants are stressed by being crowded together to be dwarfed, flavor is affected. Unless food and water are increased drastically, harshness results," he says. Sample the costly cuties before investing in a truckload.

Miniature Romanesco types and Broccoflower (see page 123) are more likely to be worth the extra cost, since their unusual forms look distinctive in miniature. Common broccoli or cauliflower may appear no different from florets cut from a large head.

BASIC USE: Cauliflower as raw vegetable often tastes "off"—and is off-putting—because it is too old and too large to nibble nicely. Truly fresh cauliflower tastes nutty and mild and has a pleasing, nubbly texture and crumbly crunch—not chewiness or a squeaky bounce. If you like raw vegetables, seek out a fine head of fresh cauliflower. If necessary, taste a few heads to discover the difference.

Cauliflower can be cooked whole or cut into florets for very different effects. Above all, beware of overcooking—unless you are intentionally cooking pieces to a sauce-like texture. Cauliflower changes quickly to mush, so do not stray far from the stove. Despite recommendations to boil cauliflower, I find that it risks becoming waterlogged when boiled. Steaming, microwaving, and baking preserve the vegetable's texture; for enhanced flavor, cook by one of these methods, coat with sauce, then roast in a moderate oven.

When it comes to seasoning and saucing, you can go gently, to keep the quiet cauliflower demeanor—or assertively, to add punch to its character. For a soft approach, season with lemon juice and delicate herbs, such as chervil, dill, tarragon, coriander, dill, or parsley; anoint with cream, butter, or cheese; top with toasted almonds, pistachios, or pine nuts. For a more forceful treatment, choose salty and/or acid complements: olives, anchovies, capers, citrus, vinegar, mustard, tomato; black, white, green, or pink peppercorns; chillis, ginger, garlic, shallots, fermented black beans, curry pastes, and other aromatic spice combinations.

SELECTION: Cauliflower is available year-round, with the greatest supply in fall and winter. *Choose very carefully* for optimum quality—which disappears long before looks do. The gentle, sweet side is lost before discoloration begins. Sniff deeply: there should be no trace of stinkiness. Taste, if necessary.

Heads are usually sold by the piece, not by the pound. Since size does not affect quality, it pays to pick the largest. Look for a tight, heavy, crisp, white mass with no crumbly or loose buds. Green and purplish types may weigh less and are more loosely shaped—a bouquet-like form rather than dense head.

Avoid all precut "cauliflorets"! Freshness, nutrients, money, and much of the vegetable (pared off as "waste") are all likely to be lost.

STORAGE: Keep cauliflower very cold, for as short a time as possible. Place a damp piece of towel on the curd, wrap the head in perforated plastic, and refrigerate stem end up (condensation on the curd causes discoloration and decay).

PREPARATION: Most cauliflower requires a quick rinse. If purchased from a farm stand, soak ½ hour, curd side down, in salted, acidulated water to draw out hidden creatures.

To cook whole, cut off large outer leaves (small ones need not be removed). Cut off the heavy stem base. Cut a large conical plug from the remaining stem to hollow it.

To cut florets, turn cauliflower stem end up and cut off the heavy base. Slice large branches from the main stem (peel this and slice to cook with florets). Cut branches into small equal-size mouthfuls.

Basic Cauliflower Cookery

To plain-cook cauliflower, steam or microwave to best maintain the light crumbly crispness and milky, nutty flavor. Above all, beware of overcooking. Cauliflower changes quickly to mush, so do not wander away.

To microwave: Wash and trim a small whole cauliflower or a halved large one, following directions for Preparation here. Set in a deep dish with ⅛ inch water, cover, and cook until almost—but not quite—tender (5 to 6 minutes for 1½ pounds trimmed weight). Test by piercing with a knife. Once cooked, let stand, covered, a few minutes. Cook florets the same way, but check after 2 to 3 minutes.

To steam: Following directions for Preparation above, wash and trim a whole cauliflower. Set it stem end down in a heavy pot in ¾ inch boiling salted water. Cover tightly and cook over moderate heat until tender, figuring on about 7 minutes for 1½ pounds trimmed weight.

Miniature Cauliflower Cookery

Boil or steam miniature cauliflower. The results will be about the same, but flavor may be marginally stronger and sweeter if the cauliflower is steamed (or milder if boiled, however you look at it). To keep the mini-idea paramount, mix with other little vegetables, such as tiny carrots.

To cook: Barely trim base of heads (or trim after cooking, keeping leaves intact to protect buds). Rinse. Boil in salted water or steam on a rack until not quite al dente (the cauliflowers will continue to soften after cooking), 3 to 4 minutes. If boiled longer, shape and bud texture are affected adversely. Spread out to cool. To serve, heat in sauce or butter, or toss with dressing and serve at room temperature or chilled.

Creamy Cauliflower Soup

Cream of cauliflower soup is a classic preparation that is too rich for many modern American home cooks. This lightened version is no compromise, even though it is comparatively low in fat. Silky and baby-mild, the shiny puree makes a fine opener for a multicourse meal or a light lunch for lovers of delicate dishes. For a lush finish, add a spoonful of cream and scattering of pistachios to each serving.

1 medium white cauliflower (2 to 2½ pounds)
White part of 1 large leek
1 small baking potato
1 cup thin-sliced tender celery stalks
1 teaspoon kosher salt
3 cups whole or low-fat milk
3 cups vegetable broth
½ teaspoon grated nutmeg
3 to 4 tablespoons lemon juice
Fine-ground white pepper
Optional: 6 tablespoons cream
Optional: chopped pistachios or chervil sprigs for garnish

1. Cut off and discard cauliflower's outer leaves and heavy base. Break cauliflower into large pieces. Cut off stems and chop small. Slice curd thick. Halve leek lengthwise, slice crosswise, then rinse well. Peel and chop potato.

2. Combine cauliflower, leek, potato, celery, salt, milk, broth, and nutmeg in pot. Simmer, partly covered, until vegetables are tender, about 20 minutes. Uncover and cool to lukewarm.

3. With slotted spoon, transfer solids to blender or food processor. Puree until smooth, adding liquid gradually. Return to pot. Add lemon juice, salt, and white pepper, and heat. Ladle into bowls; garnish as desired.

Serves 6 as a first course

Warm Cauliflower Salad with Raisins, Pine Nuts, and Pink Peppercorns

For this tart-sweet mélange of unusual colors and flavors, cauliflower is speedily cooked whole (steamed or microwaved), then cut into wedges while still warm and dressed to serve as appetizer or side salad.

Vibrant green broccoli Romanesco or Broccoflower is a spectacular substitute.

1 medium white or green cauliflower (about 2 pounds)
2 tablespoons pine nuts
¼ cup golden raisins
¼ cup fruit vinegar such as raspberry, strawberry, or pear
¼ cup diced red onion
½ teaspoon pink peppercorns
¼ teaspoon kosher salt
1½ tablespoons olive oil
2 teaspoons capers (preferably tiny nonpareil type)
½ teaspoon cornstarch
2 tablespoons water

1. Trim large leaves only from cauliflower. Cut off heavy stem base. Cut a large conical plug from remaining stem to hollow it. Set cauliflower in ¾ inch boiling salted water in heavy pot that holds it closely. Cover and cook over moderate heat until tender, about 8 minutes. Let stand a few minutes before uncovering. (Alternatively, microwave the cauliflower; see Basic Cauliflower Cookery, page 156.)

2. Meanwhile, toast pine nuts, stirring, in small heavy pan over fairly low heat until golden. Spread out to cool. In same pan, combine raisins, vinegar, onion, peppercorns, salt, oil, and capers. Cover and bring to a simmer over low heat. Stir together cornstarch and water. Add to pan, stirring constantly until mixture thickens and turns clear. Remove from heat.

3. Cut hot cauliflower into 8 wedges. Spoon sauce over, distributing it evenly. Serve warm.

Serves 4

Cauliflower Baked in Spicy Tomato Sauce

Cauliflower baked in a piquant, fragrant sauce until spoon-tender and deep-flavored (no crunchy crudité here), then topped with a dollop of yogurt, becomes a mainstay of a vegetarian meal. If you have not tried cooking the raw vegetable directly in sauce, you'll be pleased with the fuss-free method. Serve with bulgur, millet, or mixed grains for a vegetable meal; or spoon alongside grilled lamb. The soft, saucy dish can be reheated, if advance preparation is more convenient.

1 tablespoon coriander seeds
1½ teaspoons cumin seeds
½ teaspoon anise or fennel seeds
2-inch knob of ginger
1 medium onion
1 large garlic clove
1 tablespoon peanut oil (preferably roasted)
½ teaspoon turmeric
¼ to ½ teaspoon ground hot pepper
1 teaspoon sugar
¾ teaspoon kosher salt
1½ cups tomato juice
1 medium-large white cauliflower
    (about 2½ pounds)
½ cup tightly packed cilantro (coriander)
    leaves
⅓ cup roasted peanuts
Optional: yogurt

1. Set oven to 400°F. Combine cilantro, cumin, and anise seeds in suribachi, mortar, or spice mill. Grind fine. Peel ginger and cut into matchsticks, to equal 1½ tablespoons. Dice onion. Mince garlic.

2. Heat oil in medium skillet. Add onion and garlic and toss over moderate heat to soften slightly, a few minutes. Add ginger, spice mixture, turmeric, hot pepper, sugar, and salt. Toss a minute. Add tomato juice and bring to a boil, stirring. Reduce heat to low, cover, and cook 5 minutes.

3. Meanwhile, trim outer leaves and heavy stem base from cauliflower. Cutting as close to the white curd as possible, slice off remaining stem and branches; chop these small. Spread in 2-quart baking dish. Cover completely with the pieces of curd, making a neat mound. Spoon sauce over this.

4. Cover and bake until very tender, 30 to 35 minutes. Uncover and bake until watery liquid evaporates and top browns lightly.

5. Meanwhile, chop together cilantro and peanuts. Sprinkle over cauliflower and serve hot with optional yogurt.

Serves 4 as a main dish

Butter-Browned Cauliflower Slices with Lemon and Almonds

Cauliflower morsels and toasty almonds mingle in a gentle monochrome of color and taste. Rock-solid, unblemished white cauliflower is essential for the success of the simple dish, a natural partner to veal or poultry. To gild evenly, the slices must be cooked in a single layer with plenty of space for tossing, or they will steam and overcook. To prepare for two, halve the recipe and brown just one skilletful.

1 large white cauliflower (about 3 pounds)
⅓ cup sliced blanched almonds
1 tablespoon butter
1 tablespoon grapeseed, corn, or other mild oil
1 lemon, well scrubbed
¼ cup water
½ teaspoon sugar
½ teaspoon kosher salt
Big pinch of white pepper
¼ teaspoon grated nutmeg

1. Cut off cauliflower leaves. Rinse head. With stem end up, slice large clusters of florets from the central stalk. Cut these into ¼-inch slices (some will crumble). Peel remaining stalks and slice very thin (you should have about 7 to 8 cups in all).

2. Spread almonds in wide pan over moderate heat. Cook, shaking occasionally, until golden, about 5 minutes; remove from pan. Add ½ tablespoon each butter and oil to pan and tip to coat. Add half the cauliflower and cook, flipping the pieces a few times to brown lightly and evenly, about 10 minutes (reduce heat if necessary to prevent burning). Scoop into dish. Repeat with remaining butter, oil, and cauliflower.

3. Meanwhile, grate enough zest from lemon to equal ¾ teaspoon. Squeeze 2 tablespoons juice, mix with water, sugar, salt, pepper, and nutmeg.

4. When second batch of cauliflower has finished cooking, add the first batch to it with the juice mixture. Lower heat, cover, and cook until cauliflower is just tender, about 2 minutes.

5. Uncover, add zest, and raise heat. Toss gently until liquid evaporates. Season, add almonds, and serve.

Serves 4

Note: The dish can be prepared ahead if more convenient: Omit the almonds in step 5. Cool cauliflower in a single layer in a wide dish. Chill, then cover. To serve, reheat as briefly as possible in microwave oven or in skillet. Toss with almonds and serve at once.

★ Cauliflower can be substituted in the recipes for Micro-Steamed Romanesco (or Broccoflower) with Provolone, Parsley, and Croutons (page 125), Steamed Whole Romanesco with Pine Nuts and Peppercorns (page 124), and Chilled Broccoflower with Dilled Yogurt-Radish Dip (page 125).

Pros Propose

While Europe may be the cauliflower's earliest home base, India has given the vegetable pride of place. That country's prolific culinary spokesperson, Madhur Jaffrey, includes several non-traditional recipes in her *World Vegetarian,* including **Benita Kern's Cauliflower with Ginger and Cream,** a fast and rich recipe to liven up any simple repast, Eastern or Western: Combine florets in wide sauté pan with diced fresh ginger, minced green chilli, chopped fresh coriander, a goodly quantity of cream, and half as much milk. Bring to a boil, cover, reduce heat, and cook until cauliflower is almost tender, stirring now and then. Uncover and cook until cauliflower is tender throughout and sauce has thickened.

Whole cauliflower in fiery crimson sauce, a mainstay of classic vegetarian cuisine, was made modern by Julie Sahni in her innovative *Moghul Microwave.* For **Whole Cauliflower with Vendaloo Sauce:** Grind together coriander, cumin, and mustard seeds. Add ground cinnamon, clove, turmeric, and cayenne. Heat mustard oil, minced onions, minced garlic, and grated ginger in covered microwavable skillet; cook until soft. Add spices and fry briefly. Add water, tamarind juice, tomato puree, paprika, sugar, and salt; cover, and cook until thickened. Cut stem from cauliflower. Rub curd with lemon juice and sprinkle with salt. Lay stem side down in microwavable dish, cover, and cook through, about 12 minutes. Let stand 5 minutes. Pour sauce onto platter. Cut cauliflower into wedges and set on sauce. Garnish with fresh green chillis and cilantro.

Viana La Place soft-cooks cauliflower for a "copper-colored sauce [that] evokes the exoticism of Sicily." For **Pasta with Cauliflower and Sun-Dried Tomato Paste:** Boil trimmed, quartered cauliflower in salted water until tender. Remove cauliflower, reserving water. Cut cauliflower into small florets. Soften diced onion in olive oil; add some reserved cooking water and simmer until very soft. Add sun-dried tomato paste and more cooking water. Simmer, covered, for 10 minutes. Add florets, raisins, pine nuts, salt, and pepper. Continue simmering, covered, breaking up cauliflower with a fork and adding water as need to make a coarse, soft, thick sauce. Meanwhile, cook bucatini in reserved cauliflower water (plus additional water as needed). Drain and drizzle with olive oil. Add sauce and toss. Let rest a few minutes, tossing a few times before serving (from *Verdura*).

Cauliflower Mushroom (*Sparassis* species)

Western cauliflower (*Sparassis crispa*) and Eastern cauliflower
(*Sparassis spathulata* or *S. herbstii*)

Poufs of feathery or flattened ruffles, these mushrooms hardly look like what one associates with a mushroom—or cauliflower, for that matter. Resembling pale coral or sea anemones, the "heads" are at once supple, slippery, and crisp. The aroma has a marine edge, but cucumber and cedar also figure in it. Dimensions vary from bath sponge to hassock, and this may account for their supposed variability: The 1- to 2-pounders I have cooked were tender—turning into "egg noodles," in minutes—but I have read that some need long cooking.

However cooked, they have a light, fresh flavor, not dark or earthy: enokitake, oyster mushrooms, button mushrooms, and scrambled eggs with a hint of fennel and almond. The texture is unique and unpredictable. Depending upon size and cooking method, cauliflower mushroom can be silky as pasta or firmer, with a slightly cartilaginous crunch. Although European and Asian species may differ, the ones in North America— the Eastern (pictured) and Western species—are culinarily similar, according to chefs who cook both. I have tried only the Eastern, and only wish I could try them more often!

Eastern cauliflower mushroom   diameter: 4-7 inches

BASIC USE: Cauliflower mushrooms require very little cooking. For maximum visual and textural impact, cook them whole: Daub with flavored oil, then roast briefly at very high heat. Or sauté "florets" in butter with shallots, tossing until they become a tender-crisp mass; then add lemon and herbs. Serve as a side dish, an omelet filling, or an element to combine with other vegetables, such as asparagus or fennel. Some chefs chop the firmer base for stuffing or sauce and save the ruffly tips for consomme or to sauté as a garnish.

SELECTION: Look for cream-to-tan, comparatively crisp specimens from late summer into fall. Do not worry about a few discolored areas, which are easily pared. A cauliflower mushroom usually weighs a few pounds, but I am told that it can weigh close to 50.

STORAGE: Eastern cauliflowers I have known lasted a few days; those from the dry, cool, less bug-infested Western heights are said to last a week or more. Set in a towel-lined basket or pan and refrigerate as short a time as possible.

PREPARATION: "Cauliflower mushroom looks so special you want to keep pieces as large as possible," says chef Anne Rosenzweig. "But be sure they're clean, that nothing you don't want at the table has grown into them. They're blobs that envelop unknown stuff," she warns.

Although they may appear quite clean, cauliflower mushrooms are best subjected to a stiff spray of water (if you have a hose attachment), for debris hides in the folds. Cut apart the ruffly top part and base; spray both parts well to dislodge debris. Break top into "florets" or "sprigs"; pat dry. Chop base small (some are trimmed closely and may have no base). Unusually clean ones can be kept whole for roasting: Submerge in water for 5 minutes; drain, then spray, if possible. Repeat. Pat dry, then allow to air-dry.

Simplest Sautéed Cauliflower Mushroom

Cauliflower mushroom is quite unlike other mushrooms: Light, leafy, slightly crunchy, and mild, it is closer to fine fluffy cabbage than an earthy mushroom. Because it is difficult to come by in New York, I've had less opportunity to experiment than I'd like. But I can vouch for the following fast sauté—unusual for wild mushrooms, which usually require longer cooking. The quick toss makes an intriguing garnish for seafood, a delicate omelet filling, or the element to transform more common vegetables—such as asparagus and braised carrots—into an unusual vegetarian main course.

1 cauliflower mushroom (about 1 pound)
1½ tablespoons olive oil
1 large shallot, minced
Salt and pepper
Lemon juice
3 tablespoons minced parsley leaves

1. Cut apart leafy uppers from branching base of mushroom. Quickly rinse out any debris that may hide in the folds. Pull apart feathery masses into large bite-size pieces, then pat dry. Chop base into small pieces.

2. Set large skillet over moderate heat. Add olive oil and tip to coat pan. Add shallot and toss. Add mushrooms, raise heat to high, and continue tossing until tender-crunchy to taste, about 5 minutes. Season with salt, pepper, and plenty of lemon juice. Serve hot, tossed with parsley.

Serves 4

Butter-Roasted Cauliflower Mushroom with Chives and Nuts

There is just one cooking technique that maintains a cauliflower mushroom's frilly form: high-temperature roasting. Fortunately, the same method also brings out its curious sweet-wild aroma—fruity, nutty, eggy, and altogether sui generis. If you enjoy butter, it is worth investing in the Danish and French products, which have more character than most American ones I've tasted.

1 cauliflower mushroom (about 1¼ pounds)
1½ tablespoons butter
Salt and white pepper
Optional: baby spinach leaves or mâche
2 teaspoons snipped chives
2 tablespoons roasted, salted, and chopped pecans, macadamias, or cashews

1. Preheat oven to 475°F. Trim heavy base from mushroom, if there is any (save for another use). Submerge mushroom in water for 5 minutes. Lift out gently. Turn mushroom over and repeat. If your sink has a hose, spray the crevices to remove soil and forest debris. Set mushroom on a towel and pat dry (or refrigerate, towel-covered, until cooking time).

2. Melt butter in microwave oven or small pan. Choose baking pan to hold mushroom fairly closely. Brush pan with butter and set mushroom in it. Gently brush mushroom all over with butter, reaching into folds. Sprinkle with salt and pepper.

3. Set in center of oven. Bake until edges brown, about 8 minutes.

4. Immediately cut mushroom into 4 wedges. Set on 4 serving plates (on optional greens). Strew chives and nuts evenly over wedges. Serve at once.

Serves 4 as a first course

Pros Propose

Chef Jean Joho prepares **Cauliflower Mushroom Pancakes,** with both cooked and raw mushrooms: Sauté sliced cauliflower mushroom with shallot in butter. Puree, then blend with a little flour, melted butter, and nutmeg; then add chopped raw cauliflower mushrooms. Ladle small pancakes onto griddle and bake. Serve with smoked fish as an appetizer.

Chef Greg Higgins, in the heart of Northwestern cauliflower mushroom country in Oregon, uses the mushroom in a number of ways. For **Japanese-Flavored "Cutlets" of Western Cauliflower Mushroom:** Marinate ½-inch mushroom slabs briefly in sake, Japanese soy sauce, and sweet pickled ginger; then grill to char lightly. When Higgins finds he has a glut of mushrooms, "which happens often and suddenly here," he sets in a supply of **Smoked Cauliflower Mushrooms:** Place slices on lightly oiled trays in a smoker. Leave a day or two, until dried. Add dried slices directly to leek soup flavored with sweet sherry. For a vegetarian entree, reconstitute slices in vegetable stock. Combine with cooked lentils, leek, carrot, and cauliflower; then finish with a bit of feta. (Grind any broken bits of smoked mushrooms for breading.)

Jerry Traunfeld, another chef from the Northwest and author of *The Herbfarm Cookbook,* serves **Sturgeon with Cauliflower Mushroom in Cider Sauce:** Reduce apple cider, verjuice, and shallots; add fish stock. Whisk in butter "as you would for beurre blanc," then add minced chervil. Briefly sauté bite-size cauliflower mushroom pieces in butter, shallots, and seasoning. Strain sauce over sautéed fillets of Columbia River sturgeon. Arrange mushrooms around these.

Classic French techniques distinguish **Cauliflower Mushroom Terrine with Sweetbreads and Foie Gras with a Chanterelle Emulsion,** from Jean-Louis Palladin, chef and author: Cook soaked sweetbreads in bouillon; reserve bouillon. Clean and weight sweetbreads to flatten. Roast whole foie gras with garlic; reserve fat. Cut sweetbreads and foie gras into large cubes. Cut trimmed cauliflower mushroom into large "florets." Sauté in some reserved fat with thyme and garlic cloves. Add florets to cubed meats. Add some bouillon to garlic in pan and simmer until garlic is soft; remove and reserve. Combine broth in pan with bouillon used to cook sweetbreads. Reduce; add gelatine leaves. Pack meat-mushroom mixture into terrine set in larger container. Gradually add the gelatine liquid. Set board and weight on terrine to compress it and squeeze out liquid, then chill. Sauté chanterelles in more reserved fat. Puree with bouillon, reserved garlic, vinegar, and more fat. Strain, then season. Serve terrine slices at room temperature with sauce.

Celeriac, Celery Root (*Apium graveolens*, var. *rapaceum*)

Also knob celery, turnip-rooted celery

Where would the poor russet potato be if it were introduced today? Shunned, no doubt, for its plain brown wrapper and dumpy shape. It may be Americans' current demand for cosmetic perfection that explains celeriac's relative lack of popularity in this country. It is unlikely that the flavor is at fault, for this earthy prize—a pitted and whorled planet with snaggly rootlets—is imbued with herbaceous pungency. Few who sample the parsley- and celery-scented bulb, a variety of branch celery cultivated for its lowers rather than its uppers, remain indifferent.

There are three forms of celery: "regular" stalk celery (*dulce*), leaf celery (*secalinum*), and the gnarly root (*rapaceum*). All are Mediterranean in origin but are now widespread. Although celery root has been available in the United States since the start of the 19th century, it is ignored by most cooks who were not raised with it on the table. "When well grown, these bulbs should be solid, tender, and delicate," wrote the American botanist E. Lewis Sturtevant in 1919, but he noted that "in this country, it is grown only to a limited extent and is used only by our French and German population." Americans of Scandinavian, Dutch, and Hungarian heritage were also part of the welcoming committee.

Those deprived of it at the home front can usually find celeriac in traditional French bistros and brasseries, where the time-honored céléri en rémoulade (celery root in mustard-mayonnaise), still heads the list of appetizers. So popular is the vegetable in France that its full name, céléri-rave, has been abbreviated to céléri, while céléri-branche is used to distinguish what we call celery. Happily, it looks as if modern American chefs have rediscovered this Old World vegetable, to gauge by its increasingly frequent mention on menus in recent years.

BASIC USE

Raw: For a vervy, chewy salad, grate, shred, or julienne peeled celery root (always cut very fine) and toss with sharp dressing. Do not serve at once, but allow at

diameter of root: 5 inches

least several hours of marinating time to tenderize and mellow the dense vegetable.

For a less assertive flavor, toss 1 teaspoon salt and 1 tablespoon lemon juice with each pound of shredded celeriac; let stand about an hour; rinse, drain, and dry well before dressing. For the mildest effect, blanch in boiling salted water, drain, freshen in cold water, drain again, and dry well.

Celeriac tends to dominate in salads, and is best when balanced by fairly strong flavors and defined textures such as water cress, beets, apples, carrots, walnuts, smoked meats or sausages, capers, mustard, anchovies, and onion.

Cooked: Celeriac shines in soup, where it seasons, lends body and complexity, and blends seamlessly with other ingredients. It works particularly well in concert with earthy roots, whether cooked and served in chunks or pureed. Peeled, sliced, or cubed celeriac needs 15 minutes to cook through—more, when used in purees.

Celeriac-potato puree is among the most reliable and rewarding of traditional preparations: Combine peeled, chunked celeriac and potatoes, garlic, salt, and cold water: boil gently, covered, until tender. Drain, reserving liquid. Press through food mill, season with salt, pepper, and nutmeg; add cooking liquid as needed to make a fairly soft puree. Add a little butter, oil, or cream to flavor and enrich the puree.

A boon for stuffing, cubed celeriac combines most of the flavors of poultry seasoning mix in one vegetable. Braised with meat, celeriac acts as bouquet garni while still retaining its own identity. Similarly, the aromatic root adds depth to stews and casseroles made with lentils or beans, potatoes, carrots, leeks, onions, parsnips, sweetpotatoes, or winter squash.

Boiling and steaming are often recommended for cooking celeriac, but I find they bring out the fiber and deaden the taste. Nor do I suggest cooking celeriac whole, which prolongs cooking time and flattens flavor. However you cook it, watch carefully, for it changes rapidly from firm to mushy.

About stalks and leaves: Save these to season broths, soups, and stews, removing when cooking is done. Slice leaves hair-thin and sprinkle as you would celery leaves or parsley.

SELECTION: Celeriac is sold year-round, but is generally at its best from fall through early spring. Locating it may take some searching, for it is often tossed in among other beige rooty things. Celeriac with its celery-like top intact is easiest to spot and usually freshest. Whether they are trimmed or sold with tops, look for roots with the least convoluted shapes, to facilitate peeling and minimize waste. Heft to determine which roots are comparatively heavy. Medium ones are often smoother and harder, which is desirable. Press stalk end to be sure it is not spongy.

STORAGE: Trim stalks and save to perfume soups and stews (use sparingly; they are more potent than celery). Refrigerated, wrapped in plastic, the root will keep for over a week.

PREPARATION: Scrub with a brush. Trim off and discard bottom and top of bulb, roots and all. Quarter bulb, cut out any spongy part, then peel closely. Although many cookbooks warn that peeled celeriac

darkens and must be plunged at once into acidulated water, I do not find this necessary. However, if you won't be using the celeriac for a while and prefer extreme pallor, cover it with cold water plus a little lemon juice. Because celeriac absorbs water, keep the pieces large and the soaking time short.

Salad of Celeriac, Carrots, and Beets

A light and colorful variation on traditional mayonnaise-rich céléri-rave en rémoulade that is fresh, crunchy, and versatile. Both earthy and herbal, the salad serves as first course or side dish, or as condiment to fill out a platter of cold meat for Sunday supper. If you're cooking the beets specifically for this dish, boil them just until they lose their raw taste—but not all their crunch. For variety, substitute unpeeled apples and water cress for beets and carrots.

About ½ teaspoon kosher salt
1 tablespoon whole-grain mustard
1 tablespoon lemon juice
2 tablespoons olive oil
¼ cup whole-milk yogurt
1 medium celeriac (about ¾ pound without tops)
1 small shallot, minced
About ½ pound carrots
¼ teaspoon dried dill
1 tablespoon small (nonpareil) capers (or chopped larger ones)
2 tablespoons minced parsley leaves
4 cooked, sliced smallish beets

1. Blend salt, mustard, and lemon juice in small bowl. Whisk in oil, then yogurt.

2. Peel and quarter celeriac. Cut out spongy core, if any. Cut into coarse shreds with food processor or grater. Transfer to bowl. Add shallot and three-quarters of the dressing. Using your hands, toss and separate the strands to coat well.

3. Peel and shred carrots. Mix with remaining dressing and dill in another bowl. Cover both vegetables and refrigerate a few hours, or more.

4. To serve, toss celeriac with capers and parsley. Arrange beets on serving dish and top with celeriac, then carrots.

Serves 4

Pureed Celeriac and Sweetpotato Soup

This unusual pairing yields a flavor-rich, smooth soup that can be served steaming or chilled (top with a little sour cream). Like many soups, this one develops nuance if allowed to rest overnight.

> 1 tablespoon corn or peanut oil
> 1 large onion, sliced
> 1½ pounds sweetpotatoes
> 2 medium or 1 large celeriac (about 1¼ pounds without leaves
> About 2 teaspoons kosher salt
> ½ teaspoon ground mace or grated nutmeg
> ¼ teaspoon white pepper
> 1 quart water
> About 2 cups whole milk
> Brown sugar
> Medium-dry sherry or sweet vermouth
> 3 tablespoons toasted, chopped almonds or hazelnuts
> Optional garnish: thin-sliced celeriac leaves

1. Heat oil in heavy large pot. Stir in onion, cover, and cook over moderate heat 5 minutes. Uncover and brown lightly, about 5 minutes.

2. Meanwhile, peel and chunk sweetpotatoes. (Trim off celeriac tops, if present, and reserve.) Scrub and casually peel root (bits of skin are no problem in puree). Cut into fairly thick slices.

3. Add celeriac and sweets to pot with 2 teaspoons salt. Cook, covered, 10 minutes, tossing now and then, until lightly browned. Stir in mace and pepper.

4. Add water and 1 cup milk. Simmer gently, covered, until vegetables are very tender—30 to 40 minutes. Cool to lukewarm.

5. Puree mixture in blender or food processor. Return to pot. Add enough milk to reach desired consistency. Reheat. Season with brown sugar, salt, and

sherry. Serve hot, topped with nuts and optional celeriac leaves.

Serves 6 as a first course

Creamy Gratin of Celeriac, Parsnip, and Potato

Autumnal roots, sweet and sturdy, distinguish this useful dish—which, although creamy, does not contain cream. It is easily varied: For a milder taste, use half potatoes and half celeriac; for a more aromatic dish, add shallots and tarragon; for sweetness, include sweetpotatoes; or, for a meaty dish, add cubed smoked turkey or ham. The dish can be made ahead and reheated.

> 1 medium celeriac
> 2 medium parsnips
> 1 medium baking potato
> 1¾ cups vegetable or meat broth
> 1 cup whole milk
> 1 teaspoon kosher salt (omit if broth is salted)
> 1 garlic clove, halved
> 1 tablespoon hazelnut, pecan, or walnut oil (plus some for dish)
> 1 tablespoon flour
> Salt and pepper
> About 2 ounces Comté or Gruyère cheese

1. Trim and peel celeriac, parsnips, and potato. Cut vegetables into ¾-inch pieces. Combine in saucepan with broth, milk, and salt. Simmer gently, covered, until barely tender—about 10 minutes.

2. Set oven to 375°F. Rub shallow 1½-quart baking dish with garlic halves. Brush dish with a little nut oil. With slotted spoon, transfer vegetables to dish. Strain and reserve cooking liquid.

3. Heat oil in rinsed-out saucepan. Add flour and stir and scrape often over low heat until toasty. Gradually whisk in 1½ cups reserved cooking liquid. Boil a minute or two, stirring constantly. Season; pour over vegetables. Grate over enough cheese to cover generously.

4. Bake in center of oven until lightly browned and bubbling, about ½ hour.

Serves 4

Braised Lamb Shanks with Celeriac and Leeks

Lamb shanks and celeriac are made for each other—in terms of both flavor and rugged appearance. No matter how you cook shanks, there is a touch of Neanderthal to the presentation, but the chewy, dense meat is luscious and sweet—particularly served on the bone. If neatness counts more than taste, you can remove the shanks: When the meat is very tender, slice it from the bone and cut into bite-size pieces, then return to the casserole to heat through. Otherwise, serve the bone-in shanks and luscious slurpy vegetables in wide bowls with knife, fork, and soupspoon.

> 4 small lamb shanks, well trimmed
> Salt and pepper
> 2 medium leeks
> 2 medium or 1 large celeriac (1 to 1¼ pounds without leaves)
> 1 tablespoon olive oil
> 2 garlic cloves, sliced
> ¾ teaspoon ground ginger
> ½ teaspoon dried oregano
> 1½ teaspoons kosher salt
> 3 tablespoons barley
> 3 cups water
> 3 to 4 teaspoons Dijon mustard
> Garnish: thin-sliced celeriac or celery leaves

1. Brown lamb shanks under broiler, turning often, until burnished on all sides, 20 to 25 minutes. Drain on paper towel. Salt and pepper generously.

2. Meanwhile, trim roots and dark tops from leeks. Halve stalks lengthwise, then slice crosswise. Rinse and drain. Peel and quarter celeriac; cut into 1-inch cubes.

3. Heat oil in large heavy casserole. Add leeks and toss over moderate heat until slightly browned. Add garlic, ginger, oregano, and salt and stir a minute. Add celeriac and toss a few minutes.

4. Add shanks, barley, and water. Simmer gently, covered, turning shanks now and then, until very tender—1 to 1½ hours.

5. Remove shanks. Stir mustard into sauce a little at a time, tasting as you add. Return shanks to casserole. Sprinkle generously with leaves.

Serves 4

Pros Propose

Northern Europe is not the only area where celeriac plays a significant role. "Celery root and leeks are two gems of the Greek winter garden. Together with avgolemono [the ubiquitous lemon-egg sauce], they make for a luscious combination that appears in many soups and stews throughout Greece," writes Diane Kochilas in *The Greek Vegetarian*. For **Celeriac Avgolemono:** Peel and quarter celeriac. Cut into ½-inch slices, placing in lemon water. Heat plenty of olive oil in large saucepan. Add drained celeriac and cook, covered, a few minutes. Add minced garlic, sliced carrots, and chunked potatoes. Add water to cover and simmer, covered, until all vegetables are tender. Whisk egg yolks until frothy and add lemon juice. Whisk in a little hot broth. Off heat, stir sauce into pot. Serve at once.

At the elegant end of the spectrum celeriac pairs perfectly with truffles —whether in soup, salad, or this **Celery Root Puree with Truffles** from chef Ed Brown: Using three parts celery root chunks to one part potato (cut twice as large as celeriac), boil in salted water until tender. Drain, then dry slightly in oven. Press hot vegetables through food mill directly into saucepan of hot cream and butter ("Never lose the temperature in between, or you wind up with a gluey mess"). Add salt and sliced black truffle.

Julie Sahni's **Celery Root Salad with Celery Seeds** displays an innovative palette of scents and textures, as do so many of her dishes: Toast celery seeds and pine nuts in a dry skillet, shaking, about 2 minutes. Cool. Cut peeled celeriac into ¼-inch-thick bâtons. Drop into boiling water and cook 1 minute. Drain and refresh in cold water. Drain; pat dry. Combine with peeled, cored Asian (or Anjou) pears cut the same size as celeriac, carrots cut the same, minced fresh chilli, balsamic vinegar, and chopped cilantro. Chill. To serve, sprinkle with the toasted celery seeds and toasted pine nuts (from *Savoring Spices and Herbs*).

Celeriac Pancakes with Shallots and Crème Fraîche, from chef Hubert Keller, make a charming winter appetizer: Soak shallots a few minutes in water. Cut off tops and root ends. Roast in dry pan until very tender. Cool. Squeeze from skins. Peel celeriac and baking potatoes. Cut into fine shreds on mandoline. Combine with chives, salt, and pepper. Form small balls and flatten to ½-inch-thick cakes. Brown in olive oil. Drain. Heat the cooked shallots in olive oil with a little sugar, thyme, and seasoning. Top cakes with shallots, drizzle with crème fraîche, and heat under broiler. Sprinkle with chives.

Celery Salt makes sensible use of celery root's aromatic skin. To prepare: Scrub celeriac well. Slice off peel (use flesh for another dish). String on thread, then hang to dry—however long that takes in your part of the world. When dried through, process to a powder with coarse sea salt. Strain through sieve. Store airtight (from *Roger Vergé's Vegetables in the French Style*).

Chef Jean Joho keeps to a minimum of ingredients, as in this perfect pairing of **Chestnuts with Celery Root:** Combine peeled fresh chestnuts and celery root cubes in stock and simmer until tender. Drain. Roll gently in sauté pan with sugar and butter until slightly glazed. Serve with game. And, as a chef's footnote, Joho declares: "There is nothing better than céléri rémoulade on your day off!"

Chanterelle Mushrooms (primarily *Cantharellus* species)

Including **chanterelle (golden), white, African red-capped, yellow-footed, trumpet (funnel), black trumpet, horn of plenty**

With the internationalization of the mushroom market in recent years, quite a few favored fungi are available during a good part of the year. Chanterelles are at the top of the list of favorites, it seems. "There are no longer just seasons, but seasons for parts of the United States, Europe, Africa, and Asia," says Rosario Safina, president of Urbani USA in Long Island City, New York, a major mushroom importer who was receiving African chanterelles when we spoke in midwinter.

Not long ago, wild mushrooms were a strictly local affair. "When we opened 20 years ago, we could only get the occasional chanterelle from amateur mycologists," says David Waltuck, chef and owner of Chanterelle, in New York City. "Now, with mushrooms an industry, foragers concentrate on these and other easily recognized species and you can get them all the time."

These members of the Cantharellaceae (chanterelle) family have been sighted in restaurants and (far less often) retail shops.

Chanterelle or golden chanterelle (*Cantharellus cibarius* and *C. formosus*—the latter applied to the Pacific Coast golden chanterelle) is the most widely available and popular of the wild bunch. Although the term "chanterelle" covers a whole family of mushrooms, it usually refers to this tawny type. Ranging from a gumdrop to a lily in form and shape, the firm, fleshy, warm-gold fungus is usually described as apricot-scented, but my large nose finds cinnamon, hazelnuts, and pepper. When cooked, chanterelles—especially

chanterelle or golden chanterelle   ½ actual size

white chanterelle   ½ actual size

small ones—retain their meaty texture and their pretty color and form.

White chanterelle (*Cantharellus subalbidus*), gathered more on the West Coast than in the rest of the country, resembles the golden chanterelle in all ways but color. Cream to beige, sturdy, firm, and meaty, it has a fine, peppery edge and may taste at least as rich and complex as the golden—at half the price. Raw, it may appear bruised and pale in comparison with the golden, but the flesh gilds to a uniform tan when it is cooked.

African red-capped chanterelle (*Cantharellus longisporus* or *C. symoensii*), although indeed a rarity (at present available to restaurants only), merits inclusion for its astonishing color and aroma. The smooth, tidy, small caps are lobster-red to candy-corn orange; the stems and gills are golden ocher and exquisitely defined. They exhale an overpowering fruity scent that will fill a room in the way a truffle does. Imported from Zimbabwe and other parts of southern Africa

during the winter, they are bound to be a hit if they survive the trip.

BASIC USE FOR GOLDEN, WHITE, AND RED-CAPPED CHANTERELLES: Braise, roast, sauté, or sauté-braise by first cooking gently in liquid, then raising the heat to glaze and brown. Slice raw chanterelles into sauces and soups to release their juice and mingle it with the liquid.

Chanterelles seem to match just about anything. They have an affinity for chicken and other light meats, such as rabbit, veal, Cornish hen, quail, and pheasant—whether as stuffing, sauce component, or side dish. They pair with fish and shellfish, as well as lamb, veal, and organ meat. They are a natural complement to grains (especially millet and buckwheat), pasta, rices, and polenta. Sauté gently in olive oil to add to a warm composed salad.

SELECTION: Golden chanterelles are erratically distributed most of year. White ones are rare outside

African red-capped chanterelle

actual size

the West. For now, red-capped ones come from Zimbabwe, in winter. Choose solid, dry (but not leathery) chanterelles—preferably young, small ones, which are firmer, last longer, and hold their shape when cooked. The more aroma, the more flavorful they'll be.

A note to chefs: If you find great variation in your chanterelles, you may be getting several types—which is fine if you like them all. If you don't, insist on true *cibarius* and *formosus*, especially in light of what one supplier said: "I don't know which chanterelles we're getting any more than pickers do. You need to be a mycologist for that. Chefs all want golden chanterelles, so that's what we call them. The average chef doesn't know what's what."

Value is not the sole issue. "Although golden chanterelles are extremely well-known in the restaurant business," says Gary Lincoff, author of numerous books on mushrooms, including *The Audubon Society Field Guide to North American Mushrooms,* "they have been confused with the poisonous jack o' lantern—which makes a person mighty sick. In fact, that confusion is the most common mushroom problem in the East. Luckily, most chanterelles are from the Northwest, where there are no jack o' lanterns. But it isn't a *bad* idea to learn to recognize the blunt, forked ridges of chanterelles and knife-sharp gills of jack o' lanterns."

STORAGE: Keep in a single layer in a basket in the refrigerator, covered with a cloth—dampened if the mushrooms seem dry, as they often do. While golden and white chanterelles may look perky and healthy for some time, their elegant aroma evaporates after a few days of storage. Once the frilly edges open up, they become flabby and spoil quickly. Delicate little red-capped chanterelles are extremely perishable. Modern self-defrosting freezers ruin them all unless they're used within a few weeks (the old freezers preserved them quite well).

PREPARATION: If unusually clean, merely brush lightly, then trim the stem bases. To remove stubborn soil and forest fragments, most chanterelles must be bounced vigorously in a sieve under cold running water. Spread on thick toweling and pat gently to dry.

Yellow-footed chanterelle, also called **yellowfoot** (*Cantharellus xanthopus*), although closely related to the species described above, requires different handling. Rather delicate, ocher to brown, it "develops earth flavors with notes of thyme," according to chef Greg

yellow-footed chanterelle   ½ actual size

trumpet or funnel chanterelle   ½ actual size

Higgins, who advises no more than quick cooking with a little shallot, salt, pepper, and a splash of white wine. I find these chanterelles maddeningly variable—even for wild mushrooms. Some cook to a melting texture and a sweet-spicy savor, some are watery and bland. Some batches are small, dry and tender-stemmed; some are large funnel shapes with stringy stems.

Trumpet or funnel chanterelle (*Cantharellus tubaeformis*) has more in common with the yellow-footed than with the golden chanterelle. But it is less charming to behold than other chanterelles, with graceless flattened stems and brown caps that tend toward flaccidity. Yet if it is sautéed speedily, its taste is sweetly nutty and chanterellesque, though mild, and the stems are pleasingly firm—not fibrous. The ones that I cooked were French imports, called chanterelles grises.

BASIC USE FOR YELLOW-FOOTED AND TRUMPET CHANTERELLES: Cook quickly. They toughen and lose their flavor when simmered slowly. I have enjoyed these thin mushrooms bubbled in a little cream, where they become silky and nutty; and sautéed in butter, which turns them springy and slightly spicy. Chef Peter Hoffman finds the yellowfoot ideal for soup. "The scale is so delicate you can drop them whole into broth and that's it—they're done. They keep their special sweetness and shape."

For chefs, there is another useful technique not available to home cooks: partial drying. Chef Greg Higgins describes it: "Tear chanterelles into ribbons and spread them on trays under heat lamps. They become chewy, resilient threads of extraordinarily intense flavor. They're not quite crisp—more like sun-dried tomatoes in texture."

SELECTION AND STORAGE: Both yellow-footed and trumpet chanterelles are usually available in fall and winter from domestic and foreign sources. Unless they have been carefully selected and packed, however, they are likely to be so wet or so full of forest detritus that they are not worth buying. Quality packers remove twigs and leaves and fan-dry the mushrooms, if necessary. Don't buy a bundle without scrutinizing it well—and don't pay a bundle for it.

Store them in a wide shallow basket in the refrigerator, uncovered, for a few days at most.

PREPARATION: If yellow-footed chanterelles look dry and clean, simply check through for bad ones and discard, then brush off debris. Snip off the earthy base and halve the largest caps. If rinsing is unavoidable, spritz mushrooms lightly, gently spin-dry, then spread on a soft towel to dry further.

To prepare trumpet chanterelles, trim off the dirty base, halve the stem lengthwise, then cut 2-inch sections. If stems are tender, halve and pick out bits of forest debris; brush-clean. *Do not rinse,* or the lively texture will be lost in the cooking.

Black trumpet (*Craterellus fallax*) and **horn of plenty** (*Craterellus cornucopioides*), although not part of the *Cantharellus* genus to which the mushrooms discussed above belong, are included in the larger chanterelle family and may be called black chanterelles or by their French name, trompettes de la mort. They are conspicuously different in color and shape from the *Cantharellus*.

As is often the case, the colloquial names present intriguing extremes: horn of plenty and trumpet of death. Because of the latter meaning, chef Roland Liccioni uses this species only in mixes, unidentified, "because the French trompette de la mort on the menu scares people off." In contrast, chef Jean Joho has warm associations with them and does list them: "When I hunted as a child in Alsace, my father let me gather

black trumpet   ¾ **actual size**

trompettes de la mort by myself because they resemble no dangerous species. So I'm particularly fond of them."

Gray to black, with a bloom that can be ashy (on *cornucopioides*) or pinkish (on *fallax*), the mushrooms are shaped like irregular petunias. Although the droopiness and thin, rubbery flesh may suggest a wan flavor, this is far from true. The drab aspect belies a bold and curious perfume with hints of smoky tea, banana, violets, and peat. When these mushrooms are cooked, their flavor can be as deep as their color.

BASIC USE: Black trumpets and horns of plenty adapt to numerous cooking methods, dry to wet, short to long; and to serving as a seasoning, garnish, or solo appetizer. If you like them on the crunchy side, sauté briefly with shallots, then add a splash of stock or wine and cook dry. For a juicier texture, first sauté, then add stock, cream, and herbs; braise until tender. To make a rich, dark stock or sauce, simmer raw black trumpets in broth, cream, or water. Use to prepare thick soups, supported by autumnal flavors like chestnut, juniper, and roasted onions, and complemented by other dark flavors, such as wild rice and game. Mince the mushroom trimmings to use as "breading" to coat egg-washed cutlets before sautéeing.

SELECTION: Sniff out fragrant specimens from summer into spring. They should be as clean as possible—which is not very clean. Chef Greg Higgins, whose location in Oregon gives him more choice than most, recommends ones that are "succulent—not dry and leathery—with a pale bloom. If they are uniformly black, they are old and not worth the investment." If they look shiny, they are spoiling.

STORAGE: Spread in a wide, shallow basket and refrigerate, covered with a paper towel (dampen if the mushrooms are very dry). If in good shape, they will last a week. In addition to standard storage methods, these mushrooms may remain unspoiled if refrigerated loosely in a paper bag and simply left alone. If they are fresh and mold-free, they gradually lose moisture but retain their aroma and flavor. Or dry more traditionally: Brush mushrooms clean and spead on a baking sheet in an oven with a pilot light—or more conveniently, in a dehydrator—to remain until crisply dried throughout. *Remember to rinse well before rehydrating!*

PREPARATION: Trumpets almost always need a serious bath. Pick over to remove shriveled or slimy specimens and any stray forest bits. Trim bases, as needed, then tear lengthwise into halves or shreds, as suits the recipe. Drop mushrooms into cold water and swish around vigorously; quickly lift out. Repeat until very little soil sinks to the bottom. (The water will not be completely clear—and you don't want to wash out all the mushroom flavor.) Spin-dry, then spread on a towel.

Roasted Chanterelles and Winter Squash

This "plain" recipe holds little more than what the title tells, yet tastes deeply delicious. The bosky, peppery mushroom juices are the sole source of moisture and mingle mysteriously with the sweet squash. Choose sturdy white chanterelles, which are especially meaty, or large golden chanterelles. The tawny trumpets and saffron squash make a handsome embellishment for pork, duck, chicken, or pheasant. For a vegetarian main dish, add cooked kamut or wheat grains, then stir in butter to bind and gloss.

¾ **pound solid, meaty, large white or golden chanterelles**
1 **chunk (about 1 pound) sweet, dense squash, such as Buttercup or kabocha type**
Butter
2 **tablespoons corn oil (preferably unrefined)**
½ **teaspoon kosher salt**
¼ **teaspoon cinnamon**
Pepper

1. Preheat oven to 350°F. Clean mushrooms with soft brush. Trim stem bases. Rinse quickly if needed. Dry on a soft towel. Cut into 1½-inch chunks, more or less. Scrape seeds and fibers from squash. Cut into 1-inch-wide slices, pare, and cut into 1-inch cubes.

2. Butter a shallow baking and serving dish to hold all ingredients in a double layer. In it, combine mushrooms, squash, and oil, tossing to coat well. Sprinkle with salt, cinnamon, and pepper, tossing to distribute evenly. Cover with foil, crimping it onto the dish.

3. Bake in upper third of oven for 20 minutes. Toss to redistribute. Bake until mushrooms and squash are cooked through but not soft, about 20 minutes more (dish should be juicy).

4. Uncover dish and raise heat to 425°F. Toss gently, then bake until mushrooms and squash are browned and juices have reduced to a glaze, about 10 minutes.

Serves 4 as a side dish

Chanterelles Braised with Corn, Summer Squash, and Carrot

A colorful toss of vegetable dice is braised in a rich stock made from all the trimmings. Summery sweet, the ragoût fills out a meal of roasted poultry or serves as sauce and vegetable for poached cod or broiled salmon. Or, for a vegetarian meal, ladle over polenta.

Use white, golden, or other sturdy chanterelles, which will stay meaty and firm as they absorb the flavorful broth. Delicate species—such as yellowfoot or funnel chanterelles—are too floppy and mild.

¾ **pound chanterelles**
1 **ear corn**
2 **slim yellow summer squash (crookneck, straightneck, or golden zucchini)**
1 **medium carrot**
1 **medium sweet or white onion**
2 **tablespoons butter**
1 **tablespoon corn oil**
1¼ **teaspoons kosher salt**
½ **teaspoon peppercorns**
½ **teaspoon coriander seeds**
¼ **teaspoon dried tarragon**
¼ **cup white wine or 3 tablespoons dry sherry**
2 **cups water**
Lemon juice
About 2 tablespoons snipped chives

1. If mushrooms are unusually clean, merely brush lightly. If not, bounce vigorously in a sieve under cold running water. Trim well; reserve trimmings in a medium bowl. Cut mushrooms into ½- to ¾-inch pieces. Spread on a towel.

2. Remove heavy outer layers of husk from corn; discard. Remove inner husks and silk, chop, and add to bowl. Halve corn; cut off kernels and set aside. Hack corncob into shorter lengths and add to bowl.

3. Slice 1 squash and add to bowl. Pare carrot and add peel to bowl. Rinse and peel onion; add peel to bowl. Cut off one-quarter onion and reserve. Slice remainder and add to bowl.

4. In heavy saucepan with cover, heat ½ tablespoon each butter and oil. Add contents of bowl and cook over moderately high heat, stirring often, until vegetables begin to brown, about 10 minutes. Coarsely crush salt, pepper, coriander, and tarragon in mortar. Toss with vegetables. Add wine and bring to a boil. Add water and simmer, tightly covered, about 20 minutes.

5. Meanwhile, cut remaining squash into ¼-inch dice. Do same with reserved onion. Cut carrot into ⅛-inch dice.

6. Strain broth through sieve, pressing hard to extract all liquid.

7. Heat 1 tablespoon butter and remaining ½ tablespoon oil in wide skillet over moderate heat. Add mushrooms and onion and toss until liquid that is released begins to evaporate, a few minutes. Add squash and carrot and toss a few minutes. Add corn kernels and ½ cup broth and simmer until liquid evaporates, stirring often. Add all but ⅓ cup remaining broth and simmer until vegetables are tender and liquid is slightly syrupy. (If too much liquid remains, raise heat to reduce it to a syrup; if vegetables start to glaze before they cook through, add more broth.)

8. Off heat, season; then add lemon juice. Stir in remaining ½ tablespoon butter and chives. Serve hot.

Serves 4

Crisp-Roasted Chicken Stuffed with Chanterelles

Chanterelles make a rich and fleshy stuffing cum sauce—as do hedgehog mushrooms or morels, as alternatives. If crisp chicken skin is not a delicacy you relish (or if you can find poultry with firm flesh and dry, tight-fitting skin—difficult to do in the United States), skip the drying step. As a substitute for or an addition to cress, curly endive (frisée) and small dandelion greens keep their pleasing bitterness when drenched with warm chicken juices.

    1 chicken, about 3½ pounds
    1½ teaspoons kosher salt
    1 teaspoon ground coriander
    ¼ teaspoon white pepper
    ½ to ¾ pound common or white chanterelles
    1 medium celery stalk with leaves
    1 medium parsley root or carrot
    1 large shallot
    1½ tablespoons butter
    1 bunch water cress, trimmed,
        rinsed, and dried (at room temperature)
    ⅓ cup white wine or dry vermouth
    1 cup rich poultry or veal stock

1. Pull loose fat from chicken. Combine 1 teaspoon salt, coriander, and pepper. Sprinkle one-third inside bird, then pat remainder evenly over it. Set on a rack over a plate (to catch drips, if any). Refrigerate about 24 hours, more or less, turning once.

2. Turn oven to 325°F. Remove chicken from refrigerator while you prepare stuffing. Brush mushrooms clean with soft brush. Trim base of stems. If necessary, bounce around briefly in sieve under running water to remove stubborn soil. Cut mushrooms into bite-size pieces.

3. Mince celery, parsley root, and shallot. Set medium-large skillet over moderate heat. Add butter, then minced vegetables. When they are slightly softened, add chanterelles and remaining ½ teaspoon salt. Stir over moderate heat until mushrooms are nearly cooked, 5 to 10 minutes. Do not sear—stew gently, raising heat only if needed to evaporate some juice once mushrooms are almost cooked.

4. Fill chicken with mushrooms; sew or skewer cavity to close. Fold under wings to hold neck skin;

skewer or sew closed. Set chicken breast side down on an oiled rack in a roasting pan. Roast 45 minutes.

5. Turn chicken breast side up. Roast 30 minutes more. Meanwhile, arrange cress on a platter.

6. Raise heat to 400°F. Roast bird until golden, 15 to 20 minutes longer. Set on carving board to rest.

7. Skim fat, as desired, from pan juices. Add wine, set pan over moderate heat, and stir to evaporate some alcohol, a minute or two. Add stock and boil to reduce by about half.

8. Carve chicken. Arrange on cress. Scoop stuffing into reduced stock and bring to a simmer; season. Spoon over chicken, and serve at once.

Serves 4

★See also recipes for Tawny Hedgehog-Hazelnut Ragoût and Hedgehog Mushrooms à la Grecque (both on page 304), for which golden and white chanterelles can be substituted.

Brandied Yellowfoot Chanterelles

Serve this mild, juicy toss in a number of ways: For an old-fashioned appetizer, spoon over toast points. Or ladle onto steamed, sliced yellow-fleshed potatoes, soft cornmeal mush, or crisp polenta slices. Or offer as a saucy side dish with roasted meat or poultry.

    ¾ to 1 pound fairly clean, dry yellowfoot
        chanterelles
    2 tablespoons butter
    ¼ teaspoon ground cinnamon
    ½ teaspoon kosher salt
    2 tablespoons brandy
    ¼ cup rich mushroom, vegetable, or meat stock
    ¼ cup heavy cream (preferably not
        ultrapasteurized)
    Optional: chervil leaves or minced parsley and a
        little dill

1. Nip off the earthy lower part of each mushroom stem; discard. Brush away stray bits of soil from cap.

2. Set wide heavy skillet over high heat. Melt butter and stir in mushrooms. Sprinkle with cinnamon,

and toss over highest heat just to barely wilt, about a minute. Add salt and brandy and toss briefly to evaporate some liquid. Add broth and cream and boil, tossing, just until slightly reduced, a minute or so.

3. Scoop into a heated dish and sprinkle with chervil, if desired. Serve hot.

Serves 4 as a side dish

Hazelnut-Sautéed Yellowfoot (or Trumpet) Chanterelles

This fresh and sprightly toss suits seafood or chicken, not stronger flavors. Cook it quickly and serve at once; do not reheat. If you don't have roasted hazelnuts on hand, you might want to try the processor husking method, which saves time and fingernails.

> ¾ to 1 pound yellowfoot (or trumpet) chanterelles
> 1 tablespoon butter
> 1 tablespoon hazelnut oil
> About ½ teaspoon kosher salt
> White pepper
> 2 to 3 tablespoons roasted, chopped hazelnuts (see Note)
> 2 to 3 tablespoons minced parsley leaves

1. Nip off the earthy lower part of mushroom stems and discard. Brush away stray bits of soil from cap. (For trumpet chanterelles, trim bases, cut off stems and halve them lengthwise, then cut into 2-inch sections.)

2. Set wide skillet over moderately high heat. Add butter and oil and tip to coat pan. Add mushrooms and toss to coat. Press down to flatten with spatula, then toss again. Repeat a few times just to barely cook through—a few minutes at most. Add salt and pepper with the last toss.

3. Sprinkle with nuts and parsley and toss. Serve hot.

Serves 4 as a side dish

Note: There are many ways to roast, husk, and chop hazelnuts. I prefer this method: Set oven to 450°F. Spread nuts in a baking pan and mist lightly with water. Roast until husks crack and nuts begin to color,

10 to 15 minutes, depending upon how quickly the oven heats. Cool slightly. To loosen and remove husks, whirl briefly in food processor fitted with plastic blade. Separate husks from nuts—although some will be stubborn and can be ignored. Spread nuts to cool. With metal blade in place, chop medium-coarse.

Soup of Black Trumpets (or Horn of Plenty) and Wild Rice

Thick and autumnal, this dark mysterious mixture suggests chestnuts and truffles, making it an ideal opener for a meal of game. Juniper adds an inimitable piney undertone. If you prefer a stronger taste, substitute meat broth for the water. However, I find that black trumpets yield an unusually savory broth on their own.

> ½ pound black trumpet (or horn of plenty) mushrooms
> 3 ounces firm dry-cured country ham, such as Smithfield-type, cubed
> 2 large shallots, halved
> 2 or 3 medium parsnips, peeled and chunked
> 2 medium interior celery stalks with leaves, chunked
> 1 medium potato, peeled and chunked
> 2 tablespoons butter
> 8 juniper berries, chopped, or ½ teaspoon dried thyme
> ½ teaspoon grated nutmeg
> ¼ teaspoon coarse-ground pepper
> 1 teaspoon kosher salt
> ¼ cup medium dry sherry or Madeira
> ½ cup wild rice
> 6 cups water or mushroom or meat broth
> ½ to 1 cup light cream or half-and-half
> 3 to 4 tablespoons brandy
> Lemon juice

1. Pick over mushrooms to remove over-the-hill specimens and stray pine needles or twigs. Drop mushrooms into a bowl of water, swish around vigorously, then quickly lift out. Repeat until very little soil sinks to the bottom (water will not be completely

clear—and you don't want to wash out all mushroom flavor). Spread mushrooms on towel.

2. With motor running, drop ham and shallots into food processor and chop fine. Add parsnips, celery, and potato and chop to medium texture—not fine.

3. Set heavy pot over moderate heat. Add butter. As soon as it begins to brown, stir in chopped vegetables. Continue stirring until lightly golden, about 5 minutes. Add juniper, nutmeg, and pepper; stir another minute. Add mushrooms and salt and stir a few minutes more. Add sherry and cook until nearly evaporated.

4. Add wild rice and water and bring to a boil. Lower heat and simmer, partly covered, until wild rice is tender, or until a few grains "explode." Timing varies, but 45 to 60 minutes is likely.

5. With slotted spoon, transfer about one-quarter of the solids to food processor. Add ½ cup cream and 2 tablespoons brandy and puree until smooth. Return to soup. Add cream, water, salt, brandy, and lemon juice to taste.

Serves 8 as a first course

Sautéed Black Trumpet (or Horn of Plenty) Shreds

Dark, chewy slivers of mushroom resemble swirls of black seaweed. They taste as exotic as they look—but surprisingly mild. A spoonful strewn over white fish fillets, grilled salmon, pale veal scallops, or calf's liver makes a simple dish special. The springy mushrooms barely shrink in cooking, so even a small investment (they are expensive) will make a dramatic difference.

8 to 10 ounces black trumpet (or horn of
    plenty) mushrooms
1 tablespoon nut oil, such as pumpkin seed,
    hazelnut, or pecan
1 tablespoon butter
1 tablespoon minced shallot
2 tablespoon Madeira or dry Marsala
¼ teaspoon pepper
½ teaspoon kosher salt
¼ teaspoon grated nutmeg
3 tablespoons minced fresh parsley
1 tablespoon snipped fresh chives

1. Pick over mushrooms, removing any that are shriveled, sticky, smelly, or very muddy. Pull them apart lengthwise to make strips about ¼ inch wide at the base. Drop into plenty of cold water, swish around, and lift out. Repeat as needed until water is almost clean (it will never be clear). Spin-dry mushrooms, then pat dry on towel.

2. Heat a wide skillet over high heat. Add oil, ½ tablespoon butter, and then mushrooms. Toss until wilted, 2 to 3 minutes. If any liquid remains, boil off most of it.

3. Add shallot and toss a moment. Add Madeira, pepper, salt, and nutmeg. Reduce heat and toss until mushrooms are done to taste and liquid has completely evaporated, a few more minutes.

4. Off heat, add remaining ½ tablespoon butter. Toss with parsley and chives.

Serves 4 as a side dish or garnish

Pros Propose

Chanterelles and corn are a sweet, summery pair. Chef Bill Telepan combines them in a little appetizer stack, fashionably dubbed **Corn and Chanterelle "Napoleon":** Grill whole ears of corn in the husk. Shuck; cut off kernels. Sauté chanterelles in butter. Add vegetable broth and simmer until tender. Add corn kernels and chives; reserve. Prepare pancakes: Blend whole egg, yolks, and heavy cream, then mix into flour, cornmeal, and baking powder. Add blanched chopped corn, snipped chives, and seasoning. Bake small pancakes. Spoon some chanterelle mixture onto each plate and top with a pancake, more chanterelles, and another cake. Skewer with a sprig of savory.

In Oregon, prime mushroom territory, chef Andrew Nordby has his pick of chanterelles. A popular pasta dish is his **Tasso-Yellowfoot Chanterelle Fettuccine:** Brown julienne of tasso or other country ham in butter. Add cleaned whole yellowfoot chanterelles, minced shallots, rich chicken *jus,* and heavy cream. Cook just to mingle flavors. Add cooked spinach fettuccine. Toss until it absorbs some sauce. Add sliced green onions.

Chef Peter Hoffman finishes soups with yellowfoot chanterelles because they cook in seconds and retain their flavor and shape. For **Striped Bass and Yellow-foot Chanterelles in Ginger Fish Broth:** Sear striped bass fillets, then finish cooking in hot oven. Meanwhile, heat gingery fish stock with cooked large white beans. Add chanterelles. Ladle soup into bowls, then add fish. Top with chopped sweet-sour pickled shallots or little onions.

Chef David Waltuck separates chanterelles from their cooking juices to incorporate into a sauce. For **Baby Lamb with Chanterelles:** Stew chanterelles in butter until very juicy. Drain liquid into another pan and reduce. Continue cooking mushrooms until nearly dry. Remove mushrooms and set aside. Deglaze pan and add contents to mushroom liquid. Prepare *jus* from trimmings of baby lamb and mirepoix. Add reduced mushroom stock and tarragon. Reduce, then smooth with butter. Sauté reserved chanterelles with minced shallot in butter and season with lemon. Arrange a grilled lamb rib chop, loin chop, and kidney on each plate. Add the chanterelles and sauce.

Similarly, Waltuck sets black chanterelles apart from their cooking liquid for **Skate with Black Trumpet Sauce:** Stew trumpets in butter, then drain liquid and reserve. Return trumpets to low heat and cook to dry and tenderize. Reduce mushroom liquid, then puree with some of the mushrooms. Finish with butter. Sauté skate in clarified butter. Serve on top of sauce, garnished with trumpets and blanched, sautéed fiddlehead ferns.

Black chanterelles and pale seafood spark the imagination of many chefs, among them Jean Joho. He likes his mushrooms on the crunchy side for **Flageolets and Sea Scallops with Black Trumpet Garnish:** Sauté trumpets in butter with shallots. Add a splash of Alsatian white wine, salt, and pepper. Toss to evaporate liquid. Fold in parsley and chives and arrange on plates with cooked flageolets. Top with grilled sea scallops and fried parsley sprigs.

For a dramatic **Ballotine of Salmon with Choucroute,** Joho spreads a long rectangular fillet of salmon with a layer of classic choucroute, then sautéed black trumpets. He rolls the ballotine tightly in plastic wrap and chills it. To serve, he cuts the ballotine into thick slices and sautés them. Each plate is drizzled with Pinot Noir sauce made with a fish stock base, then garnished with fried celery leaves.

Earthy beets and Swiss chard blend with the bosky flavor of black chanterelles in **Swiss Chard and Black Trumpet Tart** from chef Charles Dale: Prepare tart pastry with the addition of ground almonds. Press into individual tart molds and bake blind. Sauté halved and cleaned black trumpets with shallots. Sauté Swiss chard leaves with garlic. Chop and mix with black trumpets. To this, add nutmeg-seasoned custard base (just enough to bind—not to make a quiche). Spoon into tartlet shells and bake. Serve warm, with sauce of pureed roasted beets.

Chayote (*Sechium edule*)

Also vegetable pear; mirliton (Louisiana and French Caribbean),
chocho and christophine (French Caribbean), cayote (Spanish Caribbean),
faat sau guah and variations (Chinese)

Chayote, like many members of the rambling Cucurbitaceae (gourd family) is known more for its usefulness than its distinctiveness. This versatile, mild-mannered player fits roles from soup through dessert. Its pale flesh is crisp and fine-textured, with a taste and consistency that meld cucumber, zucchini, and a hint of kohlrabi. Roughly the shape and size of a pear, with uneven furrows running its length, chayote may be pale apple-green (the most common form found in the United States), cream, or ivy. It usually has fairly smooth skin but may display a hedgehog array of prickles (not sharp). Those available here generally weigh about ¾ pound.

Chayote is native to this continent, planted by the ancient Aztecs, whose Nahuatl name, chayotli, is the source of its present-day Mexican and most common international market name. The gourd's current range of cultivation seems to confirm its popularity nearly worldwide. It grows on a hardy vine that snakes throughout the Far East, the Caribbean, India, North Africa, South and Central America, New Zealand, Australia, and China. Outside the United States, people consume not only the gourd but its starchy tuberous roots, young shoots, and flowers (as they do those parts of many cucurbits). What's more, growers praise its nectar-rich blossoms as among the finest honey producers.

It is difficult to guess why a simple, charming, unaffected gourd should travel around the world before becoming part of the North American marketplace. It pops up in pockets of Louisiana (as mirliton), Florida, and the Southwest, but only recently, with new Latin American migrations, has chayote become widely available—primarily from Costa Rica.

BASIC USE: Chayote can be cooked pretty much as you would cook tender squash—and more, because it holds up well stuffed or in salads. Being more solid, it requires longer cooking, generally speaking. Its charac-

diameter: 2½-3½ inches

ter, unlike that of summer squash, is best defined when it is parboiled and then sautéed or tossed with oil and broiled. But it can also be sliced and pan-cooked, baked with butter and herbs, cooked in stock and pureed for soup, steamed and then sliced and tossed with vinaigrette and other vegetables, or baked in gratins. In the West Indies, chayote plays the role of apples, in pie—with the same spicing.

In Latin America, chayote is often halved and stuffed with a savory or sweet filling. Although stuffing is traditionally accomplished without peeling, I prefer to peel and partly cook the shells, then bake the stuffed vegetable until tender. Some like chayote raw in salsa or salad (some like zucchini raw, too).

In terms of seasoning, the gourd's mild nature can be lightly enhanced with butter, herbs, and cream; or it can be forcefully augmented with garlic, onion, chillis, and curry pastes. Chayote works well with seafood and ham.

SELECTION AND STORAGE: Supplies seem to be most abundant in winter, but chayote is available year-round, though unpredictably. It can appear in Chinese, Latin American, and West Indian markets or run-of-the-mill supermarkets. Choose solid, blemish-free chayotes that are small or medium-size. Although I have been advised otherwise, I find those with sprouting stem ends to be equal in quality to those without. It's worth picking up a few extra, because they last well. Lightly wrapped and refrigerated, they store for weeks.

PREPARATION: Chayote skin toughens with cooking. It can be removed beforehand, with a peeler; or it can be slipped off after cooking, if that is suitable for the recipe. If you have sensitive skin, you might oil your hands or peel raw chayote under running water, as some people find its slick juice irritating.

You will come across recommendations to discard the central seed—but don't! Keep the seed in place and cook it along with the chayote for a pleasing nugget that tastes like a cross between lima beans and almonds.

Tarragon-Tinged Chayote Cubes

Blanching transforms pale chayote flesh into cool green cubes that mimic honeydew. Full and juicy, yet not watery, the vegetable is as refreshing as cucumber, which it resembles in flavor. The final cooking step and tarragon round out the flavors—don't be tempted to ignore them. Serve with salmon or shellfish.

2 chayotes (about ¾ pound each)
Salt
2 scallions (green onions)
1 tablespoon mild olive oil
¾ teaspoon dried tarragon

1. Peel chayotes. Cut crosswise into slices ¾ inch thick. Cut these into ¾-inch pieces, more or less. Combine in saucepan with cold water to cover. Bring to a boil. Add salt as desired. Boil until almost tender throughout, 4 to 5 minutes. Drain and rinse under cold water.

2. Separate pale and dark parts of scallions. Mince enough white part to make 1½ tablespoons. Toss with chayote and olive oil. Add tarragon, crumbling to powder. Thin-slice enough scallion greens to make 1 tablespoon.

3. Set medium skillet over moderate heat. Add chayote and cook until scallions are cooked through and flavors blend, about 5 minutes, stirring often. Sprinkle with scallion greens. Serve hot.

Serves 3 as a side dish

Broiled Chayote Wedges

Broiling chayote produces concentrated sweetness and crunch but a sad pallor. Add some color and juiciness by broiling tomato halves with the chayote during the last few minutes of cooking.

2 medium-large chayotes
1 tablespoon olive oil
Coarse salt, preferably fleur de sel
Orange or mandarin wedges

1. Preheat broiler with pan set at highest position. Peel chayotes. Halve lengthwise, then cut each half lengthwise into 4 wedges. Toss with olive oil.

2. Set slices on preheated broiler pan. Cook until tender throughout, 5 to 7 minutes. Turn once during cooking, as the pieces become speckled with brown.

3. Serve at once, accompanied by the salt and citrus wedges.

Serves 3 as a side dish

Chayote and Plantain Baked in Creamy Nutmeg Cheese Sauce

Fruity golden plantain and mild celadon chayote nestle in a light, custardy sauce fragrant with nutmeg. Serve with roast chicken or as a vegetable main course accompanied by a Salad of Treviso, Enokitake, Water Cress, and Hazelnuts (page 519). The dish can be made through step 5 and refrigerated to be baked later. For this, add 5 minutes extra baking time, or let the dish return to room temperature beforehand. (For information about plantain, see page 490.)

1½ pounds half-ripe (yellow-skinned) plantains
2 medium chayotes
1 teaspoon corn oil
⅓ cup chopped shallots
2 tablespoons butter
2 tablespoons flour
1¼ teaspoons kosher salt
1 teaspoon grated nutmeg
½ teaspoon white pepper
1½ cups whole milk
¾ cup grated Comté, Gruyère, or
     Parmesan cheese

1. Cut plantains into 2- to 3-inch sections. Slit peel lengthwise on each ridge and pull it off at an angle, unwrapping the flesh. Cut flesh into ¾- to 1-inch pieces. Peel chayotes and cut into pieces about the same size.

2. Drop plantain into boiling salted water. Cook until half done, 2 to 3 minutes. Add chayote and boil gently until almost tender, about 3 minutes longer. Drain.

3. Spread plantain and chayote in shallow 2- to 2½-quart baking dish. Preheat oven to 350°F.

4. Warm oil in small heavy pan over moderate heat. Add shallots and stir until lightly colored, about 2 minutes. Transfer to dish. In same pan, melt butter over low heat; add flour and stir 1 minute. Add salt, nutmeg, and pepper and stir a minute. Add milk, raise heat to moderate, and stir until mixture boils and thickens. Reduce heat and stir a few minutes longer. Add shallots and half the cheese. Remove from heat.

5. Scrape sauce over vegetables, folding it in with a spatula. Smooth top and sprinkle with remaining cheese. Cover with foil.

6. Bake in upper level of oven until bubbling, about 20 minutes. Remove foil and bake until lightly browned, about 15 minutes.

Serves 6

Pros Propose

Raw chayote seems to be gaining popularity in salads and salsas, to judge by recent cookbooks, among them *Bistro Latino* by Rafael Palomino with Julia Moskin. For **Chayote Mango Salsa:** Combine peeled, diced chayote with peeled, diced mango, grated ginger, chipotle puree, and lime juice.

Raw chayote also shows up in *Beyond Bok Choy* by Rosa Lo San Ross—but hardly in typical Chinese fashion. To prepare **Chayote–Snow Pea Salad:** Whisk together yogurt, grainy mustard, and minced garlic; add plum wine, then vegetable oil. Season with toasted and crushed Sichuan pepper and salt. Combine peeled, thin-sliced chayote with julienne of blanched snow peas. To serve, fold black sesame seeds and roasted chopped cashews into dressing, then spoon over vegetables.

Chayote in a contemporary Asian mode—this one cooked—comes from Barbara Kirshenblatt-Gimblett, who writes about food and cookbooks. **Gingered Chayote-Lotus Salad** is composed of chayote that she either boils whole and unpeeled or pressure-cooks on a rack. She writes that "these 'vegetable pears' make perfect 'fans' when cut in half, sliced vertically, and splayed . . . their pale green translucence contrasting beautifully with the faint pink of sliced lotus root that has been steamed and dressed while still warm with the juice from pickled ginger and a very fine julienne of the pickle." Or she combines chayote prepared the same way with black soybeans and boiled fresh green soybeans dressed with lime vinaigrette and garnished with sliced kumquats and fresh coriander leaves.

Restaurant consultant and author Stephen Wong recalls a dish from his childhood in Hong Kong, **Braised Pork and Chayote:** Blend minced garlic and ginger, 5-spice powder, salt, dry sherry, and cornstarch; mix with ½-inch-thick pork tenderloin medallions. Marinate ½ hour. Stir-fry until just golden; set aside. Add rich pork stock to pan, then peeled chayote "fingers." Season with fish sauce, sugar, and white pepper. Cover and simmer gently until tender. Uncover, add pork, and cook over high heat for a minute or two to thicken sauce slightly.

There are numerous recipes for chayote from Mexico, its area of origin—but few please Diana Kennedy, grande dame of Mexican culinary literature, and author of *My Mexico.* "With few exceptions, chayotes are rather insipid, but I was surprised at how delicious they could be when cooked with *natas* (the layer of cream that forms on the top of scalded raw milk)." For **Chayote con Natas:** Gently cook thin-sliced white onion, garlic, and minced Serrano chilli in oil. Add peeled, thin-sliced chayote, pepper, and a little water. Cook, covered, until most water has evaporated but chayotes are still quite firm. Stir in natas or crème fraîche, re-cover, and cook until slices are tender and cream-coated.

Mexican chef and author Patricia Quintana finds many chayote recipes that suit her. **Chayote, Corn, and Cucumber Mélange** "is made with chayotes (or water pears) and fresh white corn, which have been combined in Tabascan vegetable preparations like this one since pre-Hispanic times. The conquistadors introduced cucumbers to Mexico and they now grow in abundance throughout the region." To prepare: Boil quartered, peeled chayotes in water to cover with brown sugar and salt. When tender, drain and refresh in cold water; drain. Cook white corn kernels and peeled, quartered small cucumbers in boiling salted water until tender; drain. Soften minced garlic and white onions in plenty of butter in wide skillet. Add minced very hot chillis, ground allspice, and the vegetables. Heat through, then stir in more butter. Serve garnished with chopped epazote and minced white onion (from *Cuisine of the Water Gods*).

Chicken of the Woods

(*Laetiporus sulphureus* and *Polyporus sulphureus*)

Also sulphur shelf, chicken mushroom

Several mushrooms have inspired comparisons to poultry, but the likening makes more sense in this case than in some others. *Laetiporus sulphureus* is no relative to hen of the woods (*Grifola frondosa*) or fried chicken mushrooms (*Lyophyllum decastes* group), but it does, with a little imagination, suggest lemony chicken—unlike so many foods that are described as chicken-like but aren't.

The wild fungus grows in fleshy, knobby projecting clusters that develop into shell- or feather-like curves. The sueded two-tone mass, bun-to-beehive in size, is soft to sharp orange and butter to ocher; the distinct pores (not gills) on the underside are bright yellow; the interior is subdued. When the mushroom is young, its thick flesh is solid and smoothly uniform, breaking into fiberless golden chunks when fork-cut. But while young specimens are velvety, yielding, and flavorful, older ones—however handsome—can be stiff, fibrous, and allergy-provoking.

BASIC USE: Chicken mushroom has three parts and uses, as chef Odessa Piper describes it: "The delicate tips [shell-like or finger-like parts] can be quick-cooked—simply sautéed in thin slivers for garnish." The largest area, the midsection, cannot be adequately cooked by a sauté. Slice and brown it in clarified butter, add mushroom broth, and simmer until tender, about 20 minutes. Use this in fillings, ragoûts, and just about anything you'd want mushrooms in. The heavy base (and trimmings) can be simmered with celeriac, Jerusalem artichoke, and thyme to make an aromatic broth.

Use chicken mushroom as the broth base and "poultry" garnish for vegetarian risotto. Marinate and roast or grill the tender parts as a main course; or serve over greens for an appetizer. Simmer chunks in a ragoût or pasta sauce. However the mushroom is cooked, the pretty colors will remain true but will darken. With virtually no shrinkage during cooking, the yield is great: What you see is what you get.

width: about 1 foot

SELECTION: Chicken of the woods emerges from summer to fall. Careful choice is crucial. Young ones feel cool, damp, and chamois-like—not stiff. The bright, full "shells" or "fingers" will show marks or exude a drop of juice if pressed. Overmature mushrooms are dry, chalky, and fibrous—and they never become edible no matter how they are cooked.

Chef Jack Czarnecki advises his colleagues that "this is not a mushroom to buy over the phone. You must see it and feel it, or you run the chance of a dead loss 50 percent of the time." Odessa Piper warns that large ones are favorites of wood mites and should be inspected before purchase: "Cut open to check for tracks. The mushroom can look fine outside, then disintegrate overnight."

STORAGE: Refrigerate in a wide flat basket or baking pan covered with a towel. Mist the towel if the mushroom feels dry. In good shape, it can last a few days. For longer storage, chef Daniel Bruce—also a formidable forager, who hunted down the mushrooms for this photo and others—freezes his booty: Trim; cut long thin slices (by hand or on a meat slicer). Sweat in butter. Wrap each slice, then layer, and freeze. ("When recooked, they're as good as fresh.")

PREPARATION: Because it grows on trees, sulphur shelf is rarely dirty, but it may hide splinters, leaves, and twigs; check for these. Rinse if necessary. Trim in three-part fashion (tips, midsection, and base, as Piper suggests); or pare away woody or dry parts, then cut long slices on a meat slicer or small pieces with a knife, keeping the natural shape.

Risotto of Chicken of the Woods

Meaty chicken of the woods becomes both "poultry" main dish and seasoner supreme as it flavors the soupy rice. Be demanding in your selection (page 182), or you will have full-flavored broth and inedibly tough mushroom strips that no amount of cooking can modify. If your broth is salted, use just 5 cups and dilute with 1 cup water. For risotto rice, use the common arborio type—or you might try baldo, carnaroli, or vialone nano.

> 1 to 1¼ pounds tender chicken of the woods mushroom
> 3 small celery stalks with leaves, plus about 3 tablespoons thin-sliced celery leaves
> 1 medium onion
> 6 cups mushroom, vegetable, or light chicken broth (or a combination)
> About 1½ teaspoons kosher salt (omit if broth is salted)
> ½ teaspoon dried tarragon
> About 2 tablespoons butter
> 1 tablespoon olive oil
> 1½ cups Italian rice for risotto
> ½ cup fruity dry white wine
> About 1½ cups grated Parmesan cheese
> Lemon juice
> ¼ teaspoon fine-ground white pepper

1. As necessary, rinse and brush mushrooms to remove debris. Check for insects or holes and cut out affected parts and any woody ones. Cut very slim slices from the tips (to sauté); reserve. Following the natural undulations, cut remainder into bite-size strips. Mince celery stalks and their leaves. Mince onion.

2. Combine mushroom strips in saucepan with broth, 1 teaspoon salt, tarragon, and ½ tablespoon butter. Bring to a boil. Reduce heat and simmer, covered, until mushrooms are chewy-tender, 15 to 20 minutes. Reduce heat to lowest point.

3. Meanwhile, melt 1 tablespoon butter with ½ tablespoon olive oil in heavy pot over medium heat. Add onion and celery and stir a few minutes to soften. Add rice and stir a few minutes. Add wine and stir until evaporated.

4. Add 1 cup of the hot broth and mushrooms. Stir a few minutes, until almost all broth is absorbed, adjusting heat to keep it bubbling. Continue adding broth and mushrooms in ½-cup increments, stirring. As each portion of broth is absorbed, add the next. (If broth seems skimpy toward the end of cooking, add a little water to it.)

5. Meanwhile, in skillet, sauté reserved thin-sliced mushroom tips in remaining ½ tablespoon each butter and oil over moderate heat until browned. Season. Sprinkle the thin-sliced celery leaves over; set aside.

6. After 15 to 18 minutes, the rice should be nicely al dente. Off heat, stir in more butter, if desired, and about ½ cup Parmesan with enough broth to give risotto a slightly soupy consistency. Season with lemon juice, salt, and white pepper.

7. Scoop into warmed dishes and spoon over sautéed mushrooms. Serve remaining cheese alongside.

Serves 4 as a main course, 6 to 8 as a first course

Roasted Chicken of the Woods

Slabs of chicken mushroom resemble baked pumpkin, have a remarkably fleshy consistency and a subtle citrus undertone—and defy categorization. Use only very tender, juicy specimens for this dish or it will became inedibly dry. If you prefer mushrooms browned, grill them over moderate heat or broil, brushing with additional oil to prevent drying.

1 small lemon

1 small orange

3 small shallots

1½ teaspoons minced fresh thyme or
  rosemary

About ½ teaspoon kosher salt

4½ tablespoons olive oil

Pepper

¾ pound tender chicken of the woods
  mushroom

1 quart mixed small salad greens—including
  cress or arugula, or both

2 to 3 tablespoons roasted, salted, and sliced
  pecans or cashews

1. Scrub lemon and orange. Grate enough zest to
yield ½ teaspoon from each. Peel and slice shallots; separate into rings.

2. In dish large enough to hold mushroom slices,
combine zest, shallots, thyme, and ½ teaspoon salt.
Squeeze 1 tablespoon juice from lemon and 2 from orange and add both. Whisk in 3 tablespoons olive oil. To
dress greens, squeeze another ½ tablespoon lemon
juice; mix with a little salt and pepper and remaining
1½ tablespoons olive oil; set aside.

3. Trim mushrooms as needed. Cut into lengthwise slices ⅛ inch thick. Combine in dish with marinade, coating well. Set oven to 450°F. Marinate
mushrooms, turning now and then, while oven heats.

4. Set mushroom slices close together or slightly
overlapping on baking sheet; reserve marinade. Roast 10
minutes. Turn with tongs. Roast until flesh is cooked
through and edges are beginning to color, about 10
minutes. If slices look dry, brush with some marinade.
When cooked, brush with remaining marinade.

5. Toss together greens, dressing, and pecans. Divide among 4 plates. Set hot mushroom slices on
greens (halve diagonally if unwieldy). Serve at once.

Serves 4 as a first course

Pros Propose

Chefs seem to like to incorporate chicken of the
woods into fairly elaborate recipes, particularly rich appetizers and main dishes.

Daniel Bruce cuts long thin sheets that he uses like
pasta. Young chicken mushrooms that grow in knobs
rather than shell shapes can be cut lengthwise on a
meat slicer to make **Chicken Mushroom and Black
Sea Bass "Cannelloni":** Overlap long slices of mushroom on plastic to form wrapper. Set skinned black sea
bass fillet on this "cannelloni." Roll up tightly in the
plastic and refrigerate. To cook, remove plastic, then
brown "cannelloni" in clarified butter over fairly low
heat ("the mushroom gets dry and tough on high
heat"). Finish cooking in a hot oven. Serve over a toss
of roasted, cubed fall vegetables. For sauce, reduce
Champagne; blend with a little butter and cream.
Spoon over fish.

Chef Bruce finds that **Creamy Polenta with Wild
Mushrooms** is a dish he can never take off the menu,
and chicken of the woods is his mushroom of choice in
season: Whisk stone-ground white cornmeal into
scalded milk and butter and prepare polenta. Add
heavy cream to make a soft paste; season. Half-fill individual hexagonal molds with mixture. Thin-slice tender part of chicken mushrooms. Cook gently in butter.
Top up molds with mushrooms. Heat through in oven.
Unmold onto plates. Dot with chicken or veal
demiglace and sprinkle with thyme leaf tips. Thin additional demiglace with cream and dribble a tiny bit
around polenta.

Odessa Piper serves **Strudel of Chicken of the
Woods** as a main dish: Prepare duxelles of button
mushrooms, cooking until thick. Add sweet and dry
sherries and chopped shiitake; cook slowly until dark.
Sauté slices of center section of chicken mushroom in
clarified butter to brown, then add mushroom broth
and simmer until mushrooms are tender. Spread first
duxelles, then chicken mushroom slices on strudel
dough. Roll up and chill. To serve, cut into wide slices
and bake until golden. Serve with carrot-butter sauce,
garnished with small whole carrots, sautéed chicken
mushroom tips, and bitter greens.

Chef Anne Rosenzweig turns a homey egg dish
into a luxury affair in **Matzo Brei with Chicken
Mushrooms and Truffles:** Caramelize plenty of
minced onions in butter. Sauté diced tender tips of
chicken mushrooms in butter with a little garlic. Soak
broken-up matzos briefly in hot water. Drain, squeeze,
and mix with beaten eggs and cooked onions and
mushrooms. Add diced black truffle. Cook over high
heat until eggs just set.

"The orange curves of chicken mushroom remind me of the webbing on duck feet," says chef Michel Nischan, for whom the association inspired **"Confit" of Chicken of the Woods:** Cut "webbed feet" from chicken mushrooms. Spread in roasting pan, cover with mushroom stock, then add smoky bacon fat to coat the surface. Bake, covered, in moderate oven until mushrooms sink into the liquid. Lower heat, uncover, and braise slowly, turning now and then, until stock has evaporated. Transfer pan to burner. Brown mushrooms, being careful not to burn the glaze. Remove mushrooms. Add sliced shallots to pan and toss until soft. Add thyme leaves. Sprinkle shallots over "confit."

Serve with venison or partridge. (Deglaze pan and save juices for another use.)

Chef John Claussen precooks large slices of chicken mushroom to season and soften them. For **Braised Chicken Mushrooms:** Combine center-cut slices with chicken stock, white wine, shallots, fennel seeds, bay leaf, and thyme. Bake, partly covered, until juicy and nicely chewy, about an hour. Combine with vegetables for a side dish, or use as filling. Or drain, then grill for a main dish: Season, coat with olive oil, and grill "just enough to give a smoky edge but not to char, which hides the fungus flavor."

Chickweed *(Stellaria media)*

½ actual size

Although chickweed is diminutive, it is exuberant in its growing habits, taking root throughout much of the planet virtually year-round. "It has been said that there is no part of the world where the Chickweed is not to be found," wrote Mrs. M. Grieve in *A Modern Herbal*. She explained its common name thus: "The custom of giving chickweed to birds is a very old one, for Gerard [the 17th-century herbalist] tells us: 'Little birds in cadges (especially Linnets) are refreshed with the lesser Chickweed when they loath their meat.' " Alan Davidson notes that "a pleasant old English name for chickweed is 'hen's inheritance' " (*The Oxford Companion to Food*).

Chickweed is "a native of all temperate and north Arctic regions, and has naturalized itself wherever the white man has settled, becoming one of the commonest weeds," Mrs. Grieve continued. The tangle of low-lying greens and star-shaped white flowers persists even in Alaska, where "according to a weed control booklet put out by the University of Alaska Extension Service, chickweed is 'the most troublesome annual weed in Alaska gardens,' " write the authors (simply "Alaskans") of *Cooking Alaskan*. The extension service suggests ways to kill off the plant, but "Alaskans" have other plans—"We suggest another way to control it: Invite it in for lunch."

Lunching on chickweed is no hardship, for it is not a starvation weed or a tonic to be forced down. Chef Jean-Georges Vongerichten compares its flavor to fresh corn husks—and so pairs it with foie gras from corn-fed ducks, "to match." Others find it deeper and earthier, more like beet greens. The West Coast chef Bruce Naftaly puts it this way: "As sea urchin roe is essence-of-sea, chickweed is essence-of-green."

BASIC USE: Chickweed is the perfect garnish green, whether as simple sprigs or mixed in salad. Its spinachy depth, juicy bite, and branching shape contrast with soft, pale leaves, making it ideal for punctuation in a salad—not a leading role. Or mellow its grassy edge with the sweetness of apples, pears, corn, or tomatoes; dress lightly with lemon juice, nut or grapeseed oil, and salt. Tuck chickweed into sandwiches as you would sprouts, or fold it into grain or potato salads.

Alternatively, heat chickweed just enough to barely wilt—not more, or it loses its looks and springiness. Stir it into hot cooked vegetables, such as carrots, cucumbers, hard squash, or parsnips.

It may be that large chickweed is good for cooking, as I have read often, but the comparatively small plants I have met up with are not. If you are going to cook it, remember that it shrinks a good deal.

SELECTION AND STORAGE: Although chickweed grows wild most of the year and is also cultivated, it is likely to come to market during the spring and fall. Curiously, leaf size does not seem to affect flavor or texture. Large-leafed sprigs may be tender and succulent and smaller ones less so—and vice versa. Rinse, shake dry, pack in plastic, and refrigerate for a few days at most.

PREPARATION: Unless unusually leggy, chickweed is all edible. Simply rinse, spin-dry, then snip to suit your recipe. If stalks look heavy, taste to check for fiber, then trim if needed.

Salad of Chickweed, Apples, Celery, and Pecans in Tart Cream Dressing

A bouncy bed of small chickweed lends mineral depth to a toss of apples, celery, and toasted walnuts bound with a light, lemony sour cream dressing.

3 to 4 ounces small chickweed (4 cups; or see Variation)
¼ teaspoon kosher salt
1 teaspoon sugar
2 to 3 tablespoons lemon juice
¼ cup sour cream
2 to 3 tablespoons thin-sliced chives
Several small pale inner celery stalks
1 large sweet apple
½ cup toasted pecans, coarse-chopped
Pepper

1. Rinse chickweed. Spin-dry. Mix salt and sugar with 2 tablespoons lemon juice, stirring to dissolve. Add sour cream and 2 tablespoons chives; blend well.

2. Trim off celery leaves (reserve for another use). Cut stalks into ¼-inch squares (about 1 cup). Place in a bowl. Without peeling apple, cut 8 very thin slices for garnish. Cut remaining (unpeeled) apple into ¼-inch dice (1¼ cups). Toss with celery, pecans, and dressing. Adjust lemon juice, chives, salt, and pepper.

3. If necessary, pull apart chickweed into small sprigs. Arrange on plates. Top with apple mixture and toss lightly. Garnish with apple slices.

Serves 4 as a side dish or first course

Variation

For a milder flavor, substitute miner's lettuce (page 386) for half the chickweed. Break off long stems, if any.

Sweet-Spiced Carrots with Chickweed

One of those simple combinations that just plain work: scented carrot slices balanced by deeply earthy, shiny little leaves. Do not cook the chickweed, or it will lose its succulent spring; just barely begin to wilt it in the warm buttery spices. Serve with shrimp or poultry. Accompany with a pilaf of rice or quinoa.

2 to 3 ounces small chickweed (about 3 cups)
1 pound medium carrots
¼ cup water
1 tablespoon lemon juice
¼ teaspoon ground allspice
½ teaspoon ground ginger
1 teaspoon sugar
1 tablespoon butter
¼ teaspoon kosher salt

1. Rinse chickweed and shake dry. Chop into small bits. Peel carrots. Cut thinner ends on diagonal into ½-inch slices. Halve wider ends lengthwise, then slice on diagonal.

2. Combine carrots in medium-large heavy skillet with water, lemon juice, allspice, ginger, sugar, butter, and salt. Bring to a boil.

3. Reduce heat, cover, and simmer gently until carrots are tender, about 10 minutes, shaking pan or stirring fairly often. Uncover and continue cooking a minute or two to glaze, if necessary.

4. Add chickweed, cover, and steam just until leaves begin to wilt, about 1 minute. Toss to mix. Serve immediately.

Serves 4

Pros Propose

Despite being there for the picking, chickweed seems to have found more of a welcome in fancy restaurants than on the plates of gardeners and hikers who might gather it—but who more often banish or ignore it. For example, here is **Foie Gras on Rhubarb with Chickweed** from chef Geoffrey Zakarian: Broil rhubarb strips tossed with balsamic vinegar and brown sugar to barely soften. Toss chickweed in a small metal bowl with hazelnut oil, salt, pepper, and lemon juice. Set in moderate oven "just long enough to change the raw taste—not to wilt the leaves." Place seared foie gras on rhubarb and arrange chickweed alongside. Mingle juices from bowl with rhubarb juice. Spoon around.

Antoine Cedicci, a chef who regularly features wild foods, combines **Chickweed with Beef Carpaccio:** Separate chickweed into small sprigs and arrange on salad plates. Arrange paper-thin raw beef slices over this. For dressing, puree ripe red-fleshed plums with chives, salt, pepper, and olive oil; spoon around.

At Restaurant Jean Georges, another restaurant where wild foods are a signature ingredient, chef Vongerichten offers **Porcini and Walnut Tart with Chickweed:** Caramelize onions with walnuts, then puree. Spread puree on disc of thin puff pastry. Top with porcini slices; brush with garlic oil. Bake. Toss together chickweed with lemon juice and grapeseed oil. Serve alongside tarts.

Billy Jo Tatum's Wild Food Cookbook and Field Guide, first published in 1976, remains a useful guide for foragers. For **Chickweed and Cress with Onion and Sour Cream:** Heat butter and minced wild onions or leeks; stir until soft, not browned. Mix sour cream, lemon juice, and paprika in small skillet over low heat, add onions, and season. Toss chopped water cress, winter cress, and chickweed (twice as much of this as the others) in a bowl. Mix with coarse-chopped hard-cooked eggs. Pour dressing over and toss.

Chillis (*Capsicum* species)

The vast and complex range of chillis deserves volumes. Happily, it now has them. Beginning in 1984 with the publication of *Peppers: The Domesticated Capsicums* by Jean Andrews, there has been a succession of guides and cookbooks, notably her several subsequent volumes and the countless popular articles and books by Dave DeWitt. A few of their relatively recent books are *Red Hot Peppers* and *The Pepper Lady's Pocket Pepper Primer* (both by Andrews) and *Peppers of the World* (by DeWitt and Paul W. Bosland) and *The Chile Pepper Encyclopedia* (by DeWitt). Look to these for *Capsicum* information.

About that word "chilli"—first used in print by Francisco Hernandez (1514–1578), according to Andrews. I have chosen that spelling because most English-speaking people outside the United States (and many within it) use it and because Jean Andrews does: "Not because one name is right and another is wrong, but for the sake of consistency and clarity it would help if . . . *chilli* [were used] for the pungent types; *chili* for the spicy meat dish. . . . *Chile* in italics should refer to a native Mexican cultivar. . . ." (*The Pepper Lady's Pocket Pepper Primer*).

Although vegetables used as spices are not the subject of this book, some names for chilli in dried form require additional description (explanation is impossible). "Chili" is a term for a blend of spices, as well as the dish with meat, beans, or both known as chili.

When chillis are crushed, they travel under numerous aliases in North American markets: chil(l)i flakes, chile flakes, crushed chil(l)is, red pepper flakes, hot pepper flakes, and pepper flakes. I use chilli flakes in this book.

When chillis are ground to a powder (not flaked or crushed), they have another confusing batch of names. The most common is "ground hot pepper," so that is what I call for. Ground hot red (or red hot) pepper is a variant. Cayenne is another name for the same thing, although Cayenne chillis are rarely used and the powder is not produced in Cayenne, French Guiana, as previously.

In the Western United States, chilli (or chile) powder may be described specifically or by its strength: pure ground New Mexican chiles, or ground mild (or hot) chiles, for example.

Simple, huh?

Chinese Broccoli, Chinese Kale

(*Brassica oleracea*, Alboglabra Group)

Also gai lan, kaii laan, jie lan and variations (Chinese)

length: 10-12 inches

Chinese broccoli or Chinese kale is not broccoli or kale as we know them, nor is it truly Chinese in origin. This handsome vegetable is a species apart—and individually, distinctly delicious. And while we are on the subject of misleading names, if you have tasted Broccolini (Asparation), the diminutive offspring of Chinese and standard broccolis, you will recognize its Chinese parent in the similarly smooth, straight, waxy stems and inimitable juicy crunch.

Among the many flowering brassicas that bloom in Oriental markets, this one can be identified by its white buds (although I have read of yellow-flowering types, I have seen only white); by its round, solid jade stems, like narrow broccoli stalks; and by its slightly leathery, decidedly collard-like leaves. The leaves have an assertive collard flavor, but the meaty, succulent stalks suggest the freshest, sweetest kohlrabi and broccoli. When small, the raw buds—sweet, with a cabbagey kick—are delightful in salad.

Brassica experts bump up against a Great Wall when it comes to the origins of Chinese kale. About all they agree on is summarized in these observations by Joy Larkcom, a British authority on Oriental vegetables: "It probably originated in the Mediterranean, possibly sharing a common ancestor with European calabrese [broccoli]. Botanically, it is very close to the famous Portuguese 'Tronchuda' cabbage. It was introduced to China in ancient times."

As a culinary sleuth, what I find most mystifying is

that—as far as I can determine—it did not travel beyond China. How could such a hardy, handy vegetable *not* move around? Its nature seems just as well suited to Italian, Spanish, and Thai dishes as to Chinese. I think I have seen it in other countries. I think I have read about it in non-Chinese texts. Yet each time I imagine I've found a path, I run up against the Wall. I can find nothing outside China—nor can the British plant breeder Peter Crisp, a *Brassica* specialist who also expresses frustration with this seemingly pursuable subject.

It is Chinese immigrants who planted gai lan in the United States and to whom we should be grateful for the presence of this lively, versatile green. With its clover color, juicy crunch, and bittersweet flavor, it is a refreshing addition to the home or foodservice repertoire—one of the most appealing of the brassica bunch.

BASIC USE: Although it is not bitter, Chinese broccoli is suited to roles somewhere between broccoli raab and broccoli: Serve with pasta or chewy grains; pair with sweet foods (winter squash, raisins, carrots), salty foods (olives, sausage, ham), or acids (citrus, balsamic vinegar, tomato). I find Chinese broccoli is best when blanched, then stir-fried or sautéed with seasonings. Alternatively, for a firmer, more concentrated and bitter effect, trim and peel the stems, slice, and stir-fry briefly. Add sliced leaves and a little liquid, and continue tossing until just al dente. Or add sliced stems and leaves to soups and stews for the final 5 minutes or so of cooking. For cold dishes, blanch Chinese broccoli, cool in ice water, drain, pat dry, and refrigerate; slice to suit at assembly time.

SELECTION: Chinese broccoli is available all year, but its quality peaks during cool seasons. Because it may deteriorate internally before it shows its age, take a good long whiff to be sure there is no skunky stink—not even a hint. Choose Chinese broccoli with comparatively thin stalks and just a few open flowers. Be sure to check the stem base: The cut area should be green and smooth, with no fibrous white core. Overgrown specimens taste aggressively earthy.

STORAGE: Keep in the coldest part of the refrigerator for no more than a week, covered with a slightly damp towel in a perforated bag.

PREPARATION: Rinse stalks well, swishing around in a sinkful of water. Thickness and tenderness of stalks vary dramatically. As with asparagus, it is important to taste to determine the need for paring. Very thin stalks don't usually require this. Larger ones, when peeled, can be crunchy and rewarding. Stalks can be left whole or cut before cooking, depending upon the dish.

If cooking will be completed in one operation, separate leafy tips from stems to allow extra cooking time for the latter. If stalks will be blanched and then sautéed later, leave them whole. Or, if stalks are nicely narrow (no thicker than ½ inch), heed the sensible advice of Sylvia Thompson, author of a remarkable duo, *The Kitchen Garden* and *The Kitchen Garden Cookbook:* Stand a bunch of Chinese broccoli stalks on end to even their bottoms, then lay them flat on your cutting board. Starting at the bottom, make slices ⅛ inch thick. As you move up the narrowing stalks, gradually broaden the slices to ¼ inch. Continue to broaden until, when there are only leaves at the top, the slices are ½ inch thick.

Basic Chinese Broccoli, Blanched and Sautéed

Chinese broccoli tastes best if first blanched to retain juiciness and color and to develop sweetness, then sautéed over high heat to seal those in, deepen flavors, and add shine and seasoning. I've tried other methods, but this traditional dual process wins out, underscoring the special crunch and bittersweetness of the vegetable. I enjoy the thick, somewhat chewy leaves, but their collard flavor is not to all tastes. If this means you, buy extra and use the stems alone—as is done in many Chinese restaurants, where leaves figure only in soups and stuffings.

This basic preparation can be embellished with sautéed mushrooms, leeks, Chinese chives, winter squash, or beets; or add sautéed seafood, pork, or chicken to make a main dish.

> 1½ pounds Chinese broccoli
> 2½ tablespoons olive or peanut oil
> 1 to 2 teaspoons minced garlic
> ½ teaspoon sugar
> ½ teaspoon kosher salt
> **Pepper**

1. Rinse Chinese broccoli well, swishing around in a sinkful of water. Taste a piece of the base to see if paring is necessary (as for asparagus). Very thin stalks don't need it, but others usually do. Trim as needed.

2. Drop vegetable into a large pot of boiling salted water. Add ½ tablespoon oil, cover pot, and return to a boil. Uncover and boil until broccoli is not quite al dente, about a minute. Drain and spread on a towel to cool and dry. (Can be prepared ahead and left at room temperature for several hours, or refrigerated, covered.)

3. Slice broccoli into 1-inch pieces, or to suit, separating stalks and leafy parts. Heat wide sauté pan or wok. When hot, add remaining 2 tablespoons oil. Toss stems about 30 seconds. Add leafy pieces and garlic and toss another 30 seconds or so. Add sugar and salt and toss briefly, until just done.

4. Season and transfer to heated serving dish.

Serves 4 as a side dish

Basic Chinese Broccoli, Stir-Fried

When the blanching step is dropped, a firmer, more concentrated effect is achieved. Thus intensified, the flavors work especially well with sweet complements—diced cooked beets, carrots, sweetpotato, winter squashes, parsnips, ham, or sausage, or currants or raisins plumped with a little balsamic vinegar.

½ pound Chinese broccoli
½ tablespoon olive or peanut oil
½ teaspoon minced garlic
¼ teaspoon sugar
¼ teaspoon kosher salt
¼ cup water
Pepper

1. Rinse Chinese broccoli. Peel lower part of stems. Cut off leaves and buds; slice if large. Starting at lower part, cut stalks into thin slices, widening slices as you reach the thinner top part.

2. Set a medium skillet over moderately high heat. Add oil, then stems, and toss to coat. Add garlic and toss. Add sugar, salt, and water. Cook, tossing, until stems are not quite cooked—about 1½ minutes. Add leaves and buds; continue tossing until liquid evapo-

rates and broccoli is still crunchy but not raw-tasting, about 1 minute. Season and serve hot.

Serves 2

Pasta with Chinese Broccoli, Garlic, Chilli, and Lemon

If you like broccoli raab with pasta, you'll love this Chinese-Italian version—stellar in both flavor and nutritional value. For variation, substitute orange for lemon zest and add ¼ teaspoon fennel seeds when you heat the olive oil to sauté the broccoli; or for a meaty meal, serve with browned sweet Italian sausages.

About ¾ pound Chinese broccoli
2 tablespoons olive oil
1 to 2 teaspoons minced garlic (to taste)
½ teaspoon coarse-grated lemon zest
½ teaspoon sugar
¼ teaspoon kosher salt
⅛ teaspoon chilli flakes
About 1 tablespoon lemon juice
½ pound imported Italian whole-wheat linguine

1. Rinse broccoli well in a sinkful of water. Taste to see if paring is needed (as for asparagus). Thinnest ones don't need it, but others do.

2. Drop vegetable into large pot of boiling salted water. Cover pot and return to a boil. Uncover and boil until broccoli is not quite al dente, about a minute. Lift out with tongs or skimmer (do not drain water). Spread on a towel to cool and dry.

3. When cool enough to handle, cut broccoli into 1-inch sections, separating lower stalks and leafy parts. Heat 1 tablespoon oil in large skillet. Add stalks and toss 30 seconds. Add leafy pieces and garlic and toss 30 seconds longer. Add zest, sugar, salt, and chilli flakes. Toss another minute or so, until broccoli is not quite done. Set pan aside.

4. Return water to a boil. Cook pasta until al dente. Drain, transfer to heated serving dish, and toss with remaining 1 tablespoon oil.

5. Meanwhile, reheat broccoli. Toss with linguine, adding lemon juice and seasoning to taste.

Serves 2 as a main course

Chinese Broccoli in Sesame-Sichuan Vinaigrette

Chinese broccoli stems have a pickly crunch par excellence, but their dark green becomes a bit drab in the presence of acid—although far less so than other brassicas. The shorter the marinating time, the brighter the color. Serve with barbecued meats, or mix into grain salads. Or top with peanuts and chillis to serve as a side dish to an Asian meal.

¾ teaspoon Sichuan pepper
¼ teaspoon anise seeds
¼ teaspoon kosher salt
Optional: 1 or 2 small dried chillis
¼ teaspoon minced garlic
2 tablespoons rice vinegar
2 teaspoons honey
1 tablespoon soy sauce or tamari
1 tablespoon peanut oil
1 tablespoon Asian (dark) sesame oil
1 pound Chinese broccoli
3 medium-large carrots
Optional: ¼ cup chopped roasted peanuts

1. In small pan over low heat, stir Sichuan pepper, anise seeds, salt, and optional chillis until fragrant and crisp, about 3 minutes. Transfer to suribachi or mortar; cool slightly. Crush spices fine. Add garlic and crush. Stir in vinegar, honey, and soy, blending well. Add peanut and sesame oils.

2. Rinse Chinese broccoli in a sinkful of water. Cut leaves with their stems from stalks. Halve smaller leaves; quarter larger ones and cut from stems. Peel base of larger stalks. Cut stalks on diagonal into 1½-inch pieces. Peel carrots and halve crosswise. Halve wider top parts lengthwise, then cut all into diagonal slices ¼ inch thick.

3. Drop broccoli into plenty of boiling salted water. Return to a boil, covered. Uncover and boil 1 minute. Add carrots. Return to a boil and cook just until slices lose their raw crunch, less than a minute. Drain and refresh in cold water. Spread vegetables on towel to dry.

4. Combine vegetables and dressing and toss. Serve at room temperature or chilled. If desired, sprinkle with peanuts.

Serves 4

Pros Propose

Authors Bill Jones and Stephen Wong make inventive use of gai lan (Chinese broccoli) throughout *New World Chinese Cooking*. A simple, effective, non-traditional recipe is **Gai Lan in Anchovy Garlic Butter:** Cut slim stalks into 2-inch segments. Sauté minced anchovy fillets and minced garlic in butter to soften. Add gai lan and toss to coat. Add a little chicken stock, cover, and simmer until just tender, about 2 minutes. Season, sprinkle with toasted sesame seeds, and serve hot.

Similarly, Sylvia Thompson stir-fries the sliced vegetable, then moistens it with a bit of stock, but the seasonings change the tone of the dish. For **Chinese Kale with Chinese Chives:** Cut up narrow kale as directed in Preparation (following her method). Stir-fry the stalk pieces in oil until coated and hot. Add broth and cook a minute or so. Add the leaves, thin-sliced garlic chives, and lemon juice; stir-fry a moment. Add oyster sauce and stir-fry briefly. Grind pepper over and garnish with chive buds (from *The Kitchen Garden Cookbook*).

Cold Chinese Broccoli with Grilled Shiitake and Papaya Salsa, a cross-cultural appetizer from Susanna Foo, is typical of the style of her eponymous restaurant. To prepare: Blanch and chill trimmed, peeled Chinese broccoli stalks. Toss in mustard vinaigrette. Paint shiitake caps with olive oil and soy. Grill, then cool. Toss baby greens and chopped water chestnuts with vinaigrette. Top with stalks. Garnish with salsa of diced papaya, minced Jalapeño, lime juice, and cilantro. Top with shiitake caps.

Irene Khin Wong, a New York City caterer, finds the vegetable well suited to advance preparation. Blanched, it holds its firm bite and bright hue for hours. For simple **Chinese Broccoli and Rice Salad:** Separate peeled stems from leaves. Blanch both separately; drain. Dice stems; halve leaves crosswise. Toss stems with dressing of soy, cider vinegar, garlic, sesame oil, salt, sugar, and chilli flakes. Mix the stems into rice salad. Arrange on platter. Garnish with the leaves and a sprinkling of toasted sesame seeds.

Chef James Chew punctuates an Asian pasta-and-greens dish with rich fried pork and shallots. For **Chinese Broccoli with Crisp Pork:** Stir-fry cilantro roots, garlic, and shallots in peanut oil. Add diagonal lengths of Chinese broccoli and toss to cook slightly. Add rice noodles, Thai oyster sauce, fish sauce, and palm sugar; then finish cooking broccoli. Add a little diced deep-fried pork and toss. Top with crisp-fried shallots.

Chew serves **Asian Greens in Thai Dressing** as an appetizer or, with crabmeat, as a lunch entrée: Blanch gai lan. Slice thin. Mix with baby tatsoi and mizuna leaves. Toss with dressing of minced lemon grass, white and coconut vinegars, peanut oil, garlic, shallots, chilli, fish sauce, and lime juice. Garnish with enoki mushrooms and avocado slices.

Chinese Cabbage (*Brassica rapa,* Pekinensis Group)

Also napa, celery cabbage, Chinese leaves; da bai cai, bok choy, wong bok, and numerous other variations (Chinese); hakusai (Japanese)

Note: The name Chinese cabbage is also used for bok choy, page 97.

Of all the bewildering brassicas that cluster under the umbrella "Chinese cabbage," those pictured are probably the types most readily recognized in the United States.

Oddly enough, for a vegetable with such a confused terminology, this really *is* a cabbage—although the word "cabbage" sounds heavy and rustic for a plant with a satin sheen and pastel tint. Also, Chinese cabbage really *is* Chinese. It "did indeed originate in China, the earliest record in Chinese literature being in the fifth century A.D. No wild Chinese cabbage has ever been found. It was probably a cross, which occurred naturally in cultivation, between the southern 'pak choi' and the northern turnip," Joy Larkcom writes in *Oriental Vegetables.* She adds that contemporary varieties are primarily Japanese hybrids, although the vegetable didn't reach Japan until the 1860s and breeding didn't begin until the 1920s.

Two types of Chinese cabbage are common in the West: a stocky barrel with crinkly veined leaves (usually called napa or wong bok), and a slim cylinder with smoother leaves (usually Michihli). Both are generally compact and tight-headed and can weigh from as little as 2 pounds up to 10. Although similar, the mild, juicy, lightly radishy cabbages are somewhat different: Napa is comparatively fluffy, light, and delicate; the Michihli type is generally darker, firmer, crunchier, and juicier. A third type, which has a loose-leaved, more lettuce-like head, is rarely seen in the United States.

A familiar sight in markets, but still exotic, Chinese cabbage was among the first greens from the Far East to take root in America, during the late 19th century. Its popularity continues to grow, if we can judge from production statistics. Acres of Chinese cabbage harvested here (primarily in California and Florida) increased from 8,824 in 1992 to 12,393 in 1997 (the most recent United States Department of Agriculture census) and are still expanding.

Why is Chinese cabbage in these pages if it is so

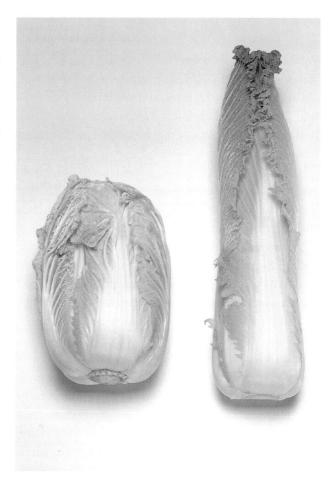

napa type or wong bok (*left*) and Michihli type (*right*)
length: 10 inches (*left*) and 18 inches (*right*)

popular that everyone knows about it? Because not everyone knows about it. Even though it is widely available and recognized, few cooks except those on the West Coast and in other areas settled by Asians seem to know how to use it. It languishes in the produce aisles of supermarkets all over America—and this is a large part of the problem, for it is not a keeper. Unlike European cabbage, it is fairly delicate. It does not excel as a substitute in recipes for the latter, as is often suggested, because it is too bland and juicy. Although it is easy enough to enjoy at a certain level, getting the most out of it, getting to the heart of it, can be difficult. Suggestions follow.

BASIC USE: Whether raw or cooked, Chinese cabbage is at least as much about texture as it is about flavor. Savor it all through its textural gamut: from raw-crisp to salted half-crisp to blanched-tender to stir-fried crunchy-tender to long-cooked silky-soft.

Raw, the white ribs can be sliced or coarsely shredded for salads and slaws and cut into strips for raw vegetable platters; salt or blanch the leaves to soften slightly. Chinese cabbage is a base for kimchee, the chewy, hot, garlicky Korean condiment. In Japan and China, as well, simple salted and spiced pickles made from Chinese cabbage—whether vinegary-sweet and fresh or nippy and long-fermented—are part of most meals.

Ribbons of Chinese cabbage leaves can be added to broth during the last few minutes of cooking. Dice the crisper narrow stalks for a celery-like contribution. That celery-like quality of the cylindrical cabbage also suits fried rice or mixed vegetable dishes: toss ribs in hot oil about 2 minutes; add a bit of broth to soften, then add leaves and toss another minute or so. As necessary, boil off excess liquid. Chicken fat, duck fat, butter, or nut oil stirred in at the last minute lends richness and blends flavors.

Best of all, simmer Chinese cabbage in thick stewy soups. Joseph Schultz, founder of India Joze restaurant in Santa Cruz, California, points out that Chinese cabbage is the mainstay of hotpots throughout Asia: "It's the secret ingredient that makes Oriental soups taste the way they're supposed to. It's a no-risk flavor additive that turns fleshy and soft if long-cooked but never gets gassy and sulfury like Western cabbage. Its sweetness mellows and adds bulk as its cooks, and you can keep adding more for crunch, if you like."

Chinese cabbage also responds to long, slow braising, becoming tender and flavorful as it absorbs the cooking liquid: Cut wide chunks or quarter lengthwise (or use the hearts only, reserving outer leaves for another dish). Cook slowly in a rich, meaty seasoning liquid—particularly one with ham or duck.

SELECTION: Chinese cabbage can be found year-round in Asian and many Western markets. Generally speaking, the difference between cabbage in the two markets is the difference between a clean, crisp, juicy, vegetable and flat, foolish Styrofoam. Although the cabbage may not look over the hill in Western markets, it rarely has the sheen, solidity, and succulence I've seen in the Asian. Look for tightly packed, firm heads, with no dried tips. Chinese cabbage should generally be fairly crisp, but when somewhat limp it has a different flavor that is appealing in lightly cooked dishes.

Neither the rounded barrel form nor the slender cylindrical form is "better," as you may read. The two are simply different. Select by tasting both, then choosing the form, texture, and color that fit the recipe: For example, if you want leaves to lie flat, as in a spring roll filling, choose the cylindrical. For a light-textured salad, choose the drier, fluffier napa type.

STORAGE: If the cabbage is fresh, it should keep, tightly wrapped in plastic in the vegetable drawer of the refrigerator, for about 2 weeks. If it's to be used in salads, store no more than a few days.

PREPARATION: Trim the base. For most dishes, separate the leaves from the central core (which is delicious and should be sliced and enjoyed, not discarded). Wash leaves fairly casually, but checking for smudges of soil. For dishes in which you'll be cutting the cabbage lengthwise, don't separate the leaves but simply wash the head. How you cut the cabbage depends on what guise it will take. Halve it, quarter it, or cut it lengthwise into sixths for braising. For stir-frying, salads, or soups, cut the separated leaves into julienne strips, wide ribbons, or squares.

Chinese Cabbage Slaw with Clementines and Sesame

Chinese cabbage shreds offer refreshing texture with a mild taste. Delicate and fresh, this salad must be served as soon as it is assembled, or it will become watery. Serve it after roast pork, duck, or spareribs.

Sichuan pepper, also called anise pepper or Chinese pepper, is not related to true pepper. Sampled straight, it tastes bitter and numbing—not biting or hot. Its forceful aroma suggests menthol, eucalyptus, and cedar but alters surprisingly when heated and blended. For a different effect, substitute ½ teaspoon fennel seeds and ¼ teaspoon white pepper.

About 1½ pounds Chinese cabbage

2 tablespoons sesame seeds

1 teaspoon Sichuan pepper (preferably without seeds)

1 teaspoon kosher salt

3 Clementines or other small mandarins

1 teaspoon honey

1 teaspoon grated ginger

2½ tablespoons rice vinegar

2 tablespoons peanut oil (preferably roasted)

Chilli oil

¼ cup minced cilantro (coriander) leaves

3 tablespoons thin-sliced scallion (green onion) tops

1. Cut cabbage into 8 wedges, then cut on the diagonal into thin slivers. Rinse and spin-dry. Chill in a serving bowl.

2. In small heavy skillet, toast sesame seeds, stirring often, over moderately low heat until pale tan, about 5 minutes. Transfer half to suribachi or mortar; reserve remainder. Wipe out skillet. Over low heat, stir Sichuan pepper and salt until fragrant and crackling, a few minutes. Add to suribachi.

3. Scrub one Clementine. Grate zest, then add to suribachi. With pestle, crush mixture to even consistency. Add honey, ginger, and vinegar, mixing thoroughly. Add peanut oil and blend. Add chilli oil to taste.

4. Cut rind and pith from all Clementines. Halve fruit crosswise, slice thin, then halve slices.

5. Toss cabbage, cilantro, and scallion greens with dressing. Top with Clementines and reserved sesame seeds. Serve at once.

Serves 4

Hotpot of Chinese Cabbage, Bean Threads, Tofu, and Shiitake

An Asian hybrid that illustrates the reticent charms of Chinese cabbage, which acts as lightener, binder, texturizer, and mild sweetener—yet is nearly invisible. Barely cook it to retain a slight crunch, or, if you prefer softer shreds, cook longer with more broth. Enjoy the contrasts of chewy shiitake, crepey cabbage, slippery noodles, and tender tofu for a main course or part of a vegetable meal. Improvise, adding soaked dried seaweed, fresh mushrooms, bean sprouts, diced red pepper, or lotus root. If piquant is your preference, substitute sesame-chilli oil for the plain toasted type. The sizes of packages of bean threads vary slightly; choose one close to ¼ pound.

8 firm, fat dried shiitake (Chinese black mushrooms)

4 cups boiling water

2 medium scallions (green onions)

About 2 tablespoons fish sauce

1 teaspoon Asian (dark) sesame oil

1 tablespoon cornstarch

½ teaspoon white pepper

2 tablespoons dry sherry, Madeira, or rice wine

1 pound firm tofu (bean curd)

About ¼ pound mung bean threads (noodles)

3 star anise "flowers"

About 4 cups vegetable or chicken broth

About 1 pound Chinese cabbage (1 very small or ½ medium)

3 to 4 tablespoons white wine or cider vinegar

2 to 3 teaspoons sugar

3 tablespoons fine-sliced basil or cilantro (coriander) leaves, or both

1. Break stems from mushrooms (save for making stock). Rinse caps. Combine in small bowl with 1 cup boiling water and weight down with saucer.

2. Thin-slice scallions, separating light and dark parts. Prepare marinade: In dish large enough to hold tofu, combine light scallion parts, 2 tablespoons fish sauce, and sesame oil. Blend cornstarch and pepper, stir in sherry and add to dish. Cut tofu into bite-size pieces. Toss gently in marinade, using rubber spatula. Continue to toss occasionally while you prepare other ingredients.

3. Pour remaining 3 cups boiling water over noodles in medium bowl. Add 1 star anise. Soak noodles 5 to 10 minutes, until bouncy-tender, turning and stirring occasionally to submerge. Drain; then discard star anise. With scissors or knife, cut noodles into 3- to 4-inch lengths.

4. Drain mushrooms, reserving liquid. Thin-slice caps. In large pot, combine mushroom liquid, remaining 2 star anise, 3 cups broth, and mushrooms. Bring to a boil, then cover and reduce heat. Simmer until mushrooms are tender and broth tastes of star anise—about 10 minutes. Remove star anise, if desired. (Can be prepared ahead to this point.)

5. Trim base of cabbage to separate leaves, then rinse. Stack leaves and slice thin on diagonal (to make about 5 cups). Add to pot, raise heat, and stir until cabbage wilts into broth. Add noodles, tofu with its marinade, 3 tablespoons vinegar, and 2 teaspoons sugar. Cook gently, stirring occasionally, until cabbage is tender to taste and flavors blend—a few minutes.

6. Adjust fish sauce, sugar, vinegar, and/or broth as necessary. Stir in basil and scallion greens. Serve hot, with soupspoons and chopsticks.

**Serves 4 as a main course,
6 to 8 as a first course**

Chinese Cabbage with Mushrooms, Noodles, and Almonds

Soft, sweetish cabbage, chewy noodles, and crunchy almonds make a comfy, homey supper or side dish for pork or chicken. Good old-fashioned butter melds textures and flavors; oil won't do the trick.

> **About 1¾ pounds Chinese cabbage (preferably napa type)**
> **½ pound wide egg noodles (preferably thick-cut)**
> **3 tablespoons butter**
> **½ pound small button mushrooms, quartered**
> **1 teaspoon sugar**
> **1 teaspoon kosher salt (less if broth is salted)**
> **2 teaspoons cornstarch**
> **3 tablespoons dry sherry**
> **⅔ cup ham, poultry, beef, or vegetable broth**
> **Green part of 2 small scallions (green onions), thin-sliced**

> **½ cup roasted, salted, and coarse-chopped almonds or cashews**
> **3 tablespoons thin-sliced cilantro or dill**

1. Trim base and separate leaves of cabbage. Rinse. Stack and halve or cut in thirds lengthwise, then cut crosswise into ½-inch slices. If central core remains, thin-slice.

2. Drop noodles into boiling salted water and cook until tender; drain.

3. Meanwhile, heat 1½ tablespoons butter in very wide skillet. Add mushrooms and toss over moderately high heat until lightly browned. Add 1 tablespoon butter, the cabbage, sugar, and salt. Toss over very high heat until juices have evaporated and cabbage has browned slightly, 4 to 5 minutes.

4. Blend cornstarch, sherry, and broth. Add to skillet and bring to a boil, stirring. Add noodles and remaining ½ tablespoon butter. Stir over low heat to mix well and heat through. Stir in scallion greens. Scoop into a dish, top with nuts and cilantro, and toss.

**Serves 3 as a main dish,
5 to 6 as a side dish**

Pros Propose

American chefs display Chinese cabbage in a wide range of styles, from almost-Japanese to Chinese with American touches to French with Chinese touches (with foie gras at the forefront).

Joseph Schultz, founder of the pan-Asian restaurant India Joze, offers a salad of salt-tenderized **Chinese Cabbage-Hijiki Slaw:** Thin-slice Chinese cabbage. Mix with plenty of coarse salt; let wilt 10 minutes. Rinse and spin-dry. Blend rice vinegar, soy sauce, white pepper, sugar, and fine-shredded ginger. Toss with the cabbage and a small amount of briefly soaked, well-drained hijiki. Add sesame oil, cilantro, and toasted sesame seeds.

Stephen Wong, Vancouver-based author and restaurant consultant, uses Chinese cabbage in a near-traditional dish. **Cabbage Slivers Flavored with Mushroom and Shrimp:** Sauté soaked, fine-diced dried shiitake (Chinese black mushrooms) and minced dried shrimp in butter. Add thin-sliced, cross-cut cabbage, and toss to wilt. Add chicken stock and simmer, covered, until cabbage is tender and liquid is absorbed. Stir in a little butter. Serve with fish.

Stepping farther from tradition, Wong (and his co-author Bill Jones) includes maple syrup in **Shanghai Noodles with Shredded Chinese Cabbage, Walnuts, and Spicy Bean Paste:** Toast walnut pieces 5 minutes in moderate oven. Drizzle with maple syrup, then sprinkle with salt and pepper, and continue baking until lightly browned; set aside. Soak fresh Shanghai noodles in boiling water 5 minutes; drain (or substitute spaghetti, cooked al dente). Stir-fry sliced onion, shredded Chinese cabbage, and minced garlic in vegetable oil until they begin to color. Add spicy bean paste thinned with water and sweet soy sauce. Add noodles, season, and heat through. Top with the walnuts (from *New World Noodles*).

Chinese cabbage leaves serve to protect and moisten the valuables in **Napa-Wrapped Roasted Squab with Foie Gras,** a dish from multicultural chef Erling Jensen: Brown whole squabs in hot oven to half-cook. Cool. Top each with a thick foie gras slice. Wrap in blanched napa cabbage leaf. Set in pan, return to oven to just cook through, a few minutes. Serve at once, in their green packets.

Chinese Celery (*Apium graveolens* var. *secalinum*)

Also cutting celery, leaf celery, soup celery, smallage; qin cai and kan tsai (Chinese)

There are three distinct forms of cultivated celery (*Apium graveolens*), although there is disagreement about their scientific names. The crunchy, thick-stalked form (usually called the *dulce* variety) is most common in North America. The gnarly-bulbed celery root, *rapaceum* is a second form. The slender-stalked, leafy type pictured here is the form closest to wild celery.

As is often the case, Joy Larkcom sums up the basics in her invaluable *Oriental Vegetables,* making a further distinction between Chinese and cutting celeries. "Chinese celery probably evolved from a wild form of Asian celery. It bears a remarkable resemblance to the 'leaf,' 'green,' 'cutting,' or 'soup' celery still grown in Europe as a herb—itself not far removed from the wild European celery. Both are hardier and generally more robust than the long-stemmed trench celery and self-blanching celery, which have usurped them as table vegetables in Europe and America." It is curious that the old form of celery should be maintained in America only as "Chinese celery," but in any case, unless you grow it yourself, you can now find it exclusively in Oriental markets, as far as I can determine.

If the familiar celery of crudités (formerly part of what Americans called a relish tray) is about crispness and juiciness, this older form certainly is not: Its stalks are skinny, fibrous, and somewhat limp. The abundant leaves look and taste like flat-leaf parsley, a relative. The vegetable's value lies in its aromatic punch (*graveolens,* the name of its species, means strong-smelling), which can transform a simple dish into something exotic.

BASIC USE: Think of Chinese celery as cooking and "ingredient" celery rather than crunchy "eating" celery—although these roles overlap. In cooking, the fibrous, thin stalks, off-white to light green, act as both vegetable and aromatic seasoning, whether sliced and stir-fried, chopped and simmered in stews and soups, or pureed. Chinese celery lends pungency and depth to mild foods, such as chicken, white fish, bean curd, noodles, or beans. At the same time, its strength of

length: about 2 feet

character stands up to assertive flavors, such as sausage, mussels, pork, citrus rind, onions, seasoned tofu, and fermented black beans. Chop Chinese celery stalks very fine to use as a seasoning—like scallions or parsley—in salads or cooked dishes.

SELECTION AND STORAGE: Chinese celery is available year-round in Oriental markets. It is never as crisp and firm as "regular" celery, but it should not appear truly limp. Look for relatively clean, uniformly green leaves; avoid it if the leaves are yellowing, wet, or slimy. Chinese celery is quite perishable. It will last no more than a few days, refrigerated in a paper bag or perforated plastic.

PREPARATION: Remove any yellowing or damaged leaves. Trim roots and separate stalks. Wash in several changes of water, lifting out so debris sinks (the celery can be quite muddy). Either chop to mix into a stir-fry or uncooked dish, or slice for recipes in which the celery will be cooked with liquid. It is not possible to zip off the "strings" the way you can with "regular" celery; the flesh is too thin and the fibers are too thick. If the leaves will serve as final raw herbal seasoning, cut them from the stems and slice very thin.

Hot and Fragrant Mussels in Chinese Celery Broth

Chinese celery provides background depth, aromatic foreground, and discreet crunch. Herbal and briny, this quick-to-prepare dish can have the heat turned up if you love chillis. Some cultivated mussels are so un-briny that you may have to add salt. Taste and check.

½ pound Chinese celery
2 tablespoons olive oil
1 tablespoon thin-sliced garlic
⅓ cup thin-sliced shallots
2 or more small green chillis, seeded and sliced
1¼ cups light white wine
¼ cup lime juice
4 pounds cultivated mussels, rinsed

1. Trim roots from celery. Wash stalks in several changes of water, lifting out so debris sinks. Trim off and reserve a cupful of the prettiest leaves for garnish. Cut remaining stems and leaves into extremely thin slices.
2. Heat oil in wide non-aluminum pot or deep pan large enough to hold all ingredients. Add garlic, shallots, and chillis and toss a few minutes over moderate heat. Add celery and toss over high heat another minute or two. Add wine and boil to evaporate some alcohol, 2 minutes.
3. Add lime juice and mussels. Bring to a boil. Cover, shake to mix ingredients, and boil until all mussels open, 2 to 3 minutes.
4. Transfer mussels to four wide bowls. Scatter reserved celery leaves on top. Ladle broth over, avoiding any sand that may have settled in the bottom of the pot.

Serves 4 as a main course

Creamy Soup of Chinese Celery and Leeks

For this gentle but rich-scented soup, "throwaway" parts of celery, leek, and cilantro are first simmered to make a fragrant broth. The vegetables are cooked in the broth until soft and mellow, and then a raw mince of the same vegetables is added for another layer of flavor and subtle crunch.

About 1¼ pounds Chinese celery
3 medium leeks
2 bunches cilantro (coriander), preferably with roots
2 quarts water
1 tablespoon mild vegetable oil
¼ cup white rice (preferably medium- or short-grain)
2 teaspoons kosher salt
¼ teaspoon fine-ground white pepper
Lemon juice
About 6 tablespoons heavy cream or 3 tablespoons sour cream

1. Prepare broth: Trim celery base to separate branches. Wash in several changes of water. Cut off leaves and place them in soup pot. Cut dark green parts from leeks; slice, wash these well, and add to pot. Cut off cilantro stems and roots (if any), reserving leaves for later. Scrub roots and stems; rinse and chop; add to pot. Add water, cover, and boil gently to extract flavors, 20 to 30 minutes. Strain broth, pressing on solids.
2. Meanwhile, trim leek roots. Halve stalks lengthwise, then slice crosswise. Wash well and drain. Chop fine confetti from enough Chinese celery stalks to yield ¾ cup; set aside. Slice remaining stalks.
3. Heat oil in same pot. Stir in leeks and sliced celery. Cook over moderate heat until they just begin to color, 5 to 10 minutes. Add the reserved broth, rice, and salt. Bring to a boil, stirring. Simmer, uncovered, until rice is soft—about 20 minutes. Meanwhile, rinse cilantro leaves. Spin-dry. Chop enough to make ¾ cup.
4. Transfer soup to blender or food processor and puree. Return to pot, stir in pepper and chopped celery, and return to a simmer. Season generously with lemon juice. Gradually add minced cilantro, tasting.

5. Ladle into bowls. Drizzle a tablepoon of cream over each, or liquefy sour cream with a tablespoon of water and divide among bowls.

Serves 6 as a first course

Gingery Rice Noodles and Chinese Celery

Pale rice noodles are bathed in a fresh green sauce and punctuated with crisp celery, sesame seeds, and sweet pickled ginger. This rather dainty dish need not be confined to an Asian repertoire. It will turn plain-cooked seafood or poultry into a lively meal. Black sesame adds drama to the pastel mix, but toasted white seeds are fine. I like this at room temperature, but it can be served warm or cold. Packet weights vary for rice noodles; use about ½ pound.

> About ½ pound medium or thin dried rice noodles (vermicelli)
> 3½ tablespoons peanut or vegetable oil
> 1-inch ginger chunk, peeled
> 1 small garlic clove
> 2 medium carrots, peeled and chunked
> About 2 tablespoons fish sauce
> About 3 tablespoons lime juice
> 2 tablespoons sweet pickled ginger
> 1 or 2 small fresh hot chillis, seeded and deveined
> 2 medium scallions (green onions), dark and light parts separated
> ⅓ cup cilantro (coriander) leaves
> ½ pound Chinese celery
> 2 tablespoons sesame seeds (preferably black)

1. Cover rice noodles with boiling water in medium bowl. Let stand, turning occasionally, until tender and opaque, about 10 minutes. Drain, return to bowl, and toss with ½ tablespoon peanut oil.

2. Meanwhile, with motor running, drop fresh ginger and garlic into food processor. Mince fine. Scrape out and reserve. Chop carrots in processor to medium coarse texture; scrape out and reserve.

3. In processor, combine 2 tablespoons fish sauce, 3 tablespoons lime juice, 1 tablespoon pickled ginger, chilli, light part of scallions, cilantro, and 2 tablespoons oil. Puree to smooth consistency, scraping side often. Pour over noodles. With tongs or two forks, twist and toss noodles to coat evenly with dressing.

4. Trim celery base and separate stalks. Rinse well in several changes of water. Cut off leaves; bunch and slice as thin as possible. Cut stalks into ⅛-inch slices. Thin-slice scallion greens. Thin-slice remaining 1 tablespoon pickled ginger.

5. In medium-large skillet, stir sesame seeds over moderate heat until tan (or, if black, until toasty), about 3 minutes. Scoop into dish. In same skillet, heat remaining 1 tablespoon oil over moderate heat. Add garlic-ginger mixture and toss. Add celery stalks and toss to soften slightly, about 1 minute. Add carrot and toss a moment, just to remove raw crunch. Add scallion greens and half the celery leaves, tossing.

6. Add vegetable mixture to noodles, tossing and twisting with tongs. Add remaining celery leaves, sesame seeds, and sliced pickled ginger, tossing to mix well. Season with fish sauce and lime juice if needed. Serve warm, at room temperature, or chilled.

Serve 4 to 6 as a side dish

Pros Propose

"Celery has unfortunately and undeservedly acquired a bad reputation in Chinese-American cooking, because it is used simply as a filler in so many dishes . . . but the vegetable has better uses," writes chef Ken Hom in *Easy Family Recipes from a Chinese-American Childhood*. He records this favorite from his mother, **Simple Stir-Fried Celery with Shrimp Paste:** Swirl peanut oil in a heated wok. Add chopped garlic and scallions and stir-fry. Add 1-inch slices of Chinese celery and stir-fry a minute. Add rice wine, shrimp paste, and sugar; fry another minute. Add a little stock or water and toss until celery is tender. Season with sesame oil. Serve at once.

For a luxurious one-dish Chinese meal, Stephen Wong combines **Beef and Prawns with Chinese Celery and Lychees:** Marinate thin-sliced beef in oyster sauce, cornstarch, and sherry. Stir-fry hot bean paste, minced ginger, and sliced onions in oil. Add beef and brown, turning just once. Add shrimp and stir-fry to just turn pink. Scoop into dish. Add plenty of sliced Chinese celery and a little stock to pan, cover, and cook until just tender. Return beef and shrimp to pan, with a little juice from canned lychees, and toss to heat through. Off heat, add halved lychees. Serve at once (from *HeartSmart Chinese Cooking*).

While the Chinese do not serve celery raw, Westerner Sylvia Thompson does, in her **Salad of Oranges, Lemons, and Leaf Celery:** Combine rough-chopped Chinese (or leaf) celery, olive oil, a sprinkling of sugar, salt, and pepper. On individual salad plates, arrange paper-thin slices of unpeeled thin-skinned oranges and Meyer lemons. Spoon the leafy dressing over these. Cover and refrigerate for a few hours before serving (from *The Kitchen Garden Cookbook*).

Celery and Coconut Salad comes from "the eastern Turkish Mediterranean coast, the home of a number of refreshing fruity salads devised to calm the palate after the local spicy food," writes Ghillie Başan, author of *Classic Turkish Cooking.* Although she calls for "reg-ular" celery, the recipe is more likely to have included leaf celery on its home turf: Blend together thick yogurt, lemon juice, and garlic crushed with salt. Toss with minced Chinese celery stalks and freshly grated coconut. Garnish with sliced celery and mint leaves.

Aglaia Kremezi proposes a simple soup from Cyprus in her in-depth guide, *The Foods of the Greek Islands.* Prepare it with Chinese celery, which is much like the wild celery of Greece, selino. For **White Bean Soup with Wild Celery and Lemon:** Combine soaked, drained dried white beans with halved onion and water to cover generously. Simmer until beans are about half-cooked. Add sliced onion, chopped Chinese celery, and salt. Simmer until beans are tender, adding water if needed. Add plenty of lemon juice and pepper; simmer until beans are just barely covered with broth. Transfer a small quantity to a blender and puree, for thickening. Return to pot and cook briefly. Discard onion halves. Add flavorful olive oil. Top with chopped flat-leaf parsley and serve.

Chinese Garlic Stems (*Allium sativum*)

Also garlic flower stems, green garlic, suan tai (Chinese), shen sum (Korean)

length: 12-14 inches

I am going to reveal one of those "hot" tips that the food media invent daily, but this one is true: There is a vegetable poised to take over the United States! If ever there was a healthy "new" edible destined to delight contemporary foodies, this is it. Redolent of garlic, crunchy, sweet, and juicy, it requires no more than slicing to ready it for cooking; it takes just minutes to cook; it looks bright and fresh on the plate; and it's low in calories (like all greens, of course). The hitch is that I seem to be one of only a handful of people who can locate it or identify it. But now that you've seen the photo, perhaps you can, too. (Do not be misled by *curled* garlic at farmers' markets and fancy groceries, which can be inedibly fibrous. Chinese garlic stems are straight and tall, not curled.)

To find these delectable stalks, you'll have to keep your nose twitching in Chinese markets come summertime when the bunches first arrive. There is little but scent to signal the specialness of these foot-long, solid (not hollow) greens that resemble smooth, pencil-slim asparagus. The garlicky aroma wafts faintly—though ferociously if the stalk is snapped or cut. Raw, the vegetable has an almost unbearably strong bite; but cooked, it is sweetly tamed.

From what I can learn in the markets, garlic stems are exported from China in summer and fall. (But just might they be grown in California in the fall?) American garlic growers I spoke with said that such a tender stem could not be grown and insisted that I must be asking about garlic chives (page 297). Two British horticulturists with experience in China thought otherwise. Joy Larkcom wrote that "in China, garlic flower stems are a side product of garlic bulb production, using strains known to produce flowering stems. The bulbs are cultivated in the normal way, the flower stems being cut in early summer when green. They are harvested very carefully so the bulb is not damaged and can be left to mature."

Peter Crisp, director of Innovar Plant Breeding in Norfolk, England, responded to my query this way: "The 'stem garlic' you ask about is a true garlic. Around Beijing I saw this being marketed as an autumn crop. I don't know exactly how it is produced, but cloves of particular varieties of garlic are grown to give flowering scapes up to 18 inches long. These are harvested and sold as bundles. . . . My guess is that they are expensive to produce, and that there may be a fair bit of technology in their production. I was sufficiently impressed with them to try to produce them in UK—without success."

BASIC USE: Garlic stems are too strong to use raw, but they need only a moment's cooking to be gentled and just a little more to become almost mellow. For salads, blanch 1 minute in boiling water, chill in ice water, then drain and dry. Thin-slice and toss in composed vegetable, grain, meat, or seafood salads to act as onion, garlic, and crunchy green vegetable wrapped into one.

Boiled a mere 2 minutes, the stems turn uniformly tender, extremely sweet, evenly green, and plump, with a succulent snap reminiscent of asparagus. The flavor is garlicky but tempered. Cut 1-inch diagonals and reheat gently in butter or oil to serve as topping for pasta or beans or polenta, or to mix with other vegetables.

Or brown boiled, sliced garlic stems over high heat, then cover pan and cook on low heat, shaking often, until very tender and concentrated in flavor, about 10 minutes. Although the color fades, the flavor is heightened.

Add slant-cut "quills" to soups or braises during the last few minutes of cooking, for color, crunch, and a fresh allium aroma.

Where *not* to use these handy green flavoring vegetables? They slip in anywhere that you want a hint of garlic with the crunch of green, in hot, cold, or room-temperature dishes.

SELECTION: Grab these juicy stems whenever you find them! In Chinese markets in the New York area, they have appeared on and off from July through October. Ideally, they should be a clear, regular green, with no yellow. But if they are pale or yellowing at the base, they are still worth the purchase. Buy a little more than the recipe requires and trim off more. They may be a bit less bright in flavor, but they'll still be fine.

STORAGE: Remove ties and wrap bunch loosely in a sheet of paper towel, then enclose in plastic. Refrigerated up to 2 weeks, the stems remain virtually unchanged. Do not allow them to become too moist or too dry.

PREPARATION: The stems should be supple and moist, but some are fibrous at the base. Mine were tougher in the late fall, but this may have been a coincidence. Snap off any woody sections from the base, if necessary. If flower heads are present (see bunch on left in photo), cut off and discard.

Pasta with Garlic Stems and Basil

This juicy green allium, which has little of garlic's aggressive aspect (as is evident from the equal weight of penne and garlic stems!), plays vegetable and seasoning in a fresh pasta toss. Choose pasta that mimics the pretty, slim slices, such as narrow quills (penne), or another form of the same length, such as gemelli. For a variation, omit the lemon and toss the hot pasta with halved small cherry tomatoes (at room temperature, not chilled).

½ pound Chinese garlic stems
½ pound imported Italian pasta (preferably penne)
About 3 tablespoons full-flavored olive oil
¼ to ½ cup thin-sliced basil leaves (or parsley and basil)
Lemon wedges
Salt and pepper

1. Bend bottom portion of each garlic stem (like asparagus) to snap off where it breaks naturally (tender ones may not need trimming). Drop trimmed stalks into a large pot of boiling salted water. Boil until not quite tender, a minute or two. Lift out with tongs (save water for pasta). Drain and blot on towel. Cut into long diagonal slices ¼ to ½ inch wide.

2. Drop pasta into the boiling water. Cook until just tender.

3. While pasta boils, heat wide skillet over moderate heat. Add 1 tablespoon oil and tip to coat pan. Add garlic stems and toss to brown lightly, 3 to 4 minutes. Set aside.

4. Drain pasta. Toss in heated serving bowl with 1 tablespoon olive oil. Add garlic stems, half the basil, a big squeeze of lemon, and salt and pepper. Toss. Taste and add more oil, basil, lemon juice, salt and pepper as needed to achieve a bright flavor balance.

Serves 2 as a main course, 4 as a first course

Braised Tofu, Garlic Stems, and Dried Black Mushrooms

Assemble a copious vegetarian meal of meaty mushrooms, creamy tofu, and crunchy garlic stems bathed in a light gingery sauce. There are many grades of dried Oriental mushrooms (also called Chinese, forest, and black) from pale to dark, skimpy to pudgy, light to ponderous. All are forms of *Lentinula edodes,* called shiitake in Japanese. Whether you use Chinese or Japanese strains, opt for those with thick, fissured caps, which give luscious fleshiness to vegetarian dishes. Save the stems (which are too tough to eat) to flavor broth.

1 pound firm tofu (bean curd)
8 medium-large dried shiitake (Chinese
　　black mushrooms)
3 cups vegetable or chicken broth
½ pound Chinese garlic stems
1 tablespoon cornstarch
1 tablespoon rice vinegar
About 1 teaspoon kosher salt
　　(omit if broth is salted)
2 tablespoons peanut oil
1½ tablespoons minced ginger

1. Rinse and drain tofu. Place in a pan of boiling water and return to a full boil. Transfer tofu to a flat plate, top with another plate, and let drain while you prepare other ingredients.

2. Break off shiitake stems (save for another use). Combine caps with broth in small pot. Bring to a boil,

then set aside, covered, to rehydrate, 15 to 30 minutes. When mushrooms are puffed, simmer until very tender (timing varies considerably, from 5 to 20 minutes, depending upon type).

3. Bend bottom portion of each garlic stem to snap it off where it breaks naturally (tender ones may not need trimming). Cut on a sharp diagonal into sections about 1 inch wide. Drain tofu and cut into ¾-inch cubes.

4. Lift mushrooms from broth; slice thin. Measure broth; if necessary, add water to make 1¾ cups. In small cup, blend ¼ cup broth with cornstarch; add vinegar and salt.

5. Set fairly wide skillet over moderate heat; add oil. Add ginger and garlic stems and toss until fragrant. Add mushrooms, broth, and tofu. Simmer just until garlic is tender, about 5 minutes. Add cornstarch mixture and bring to a boil, stirring. Season.

Serves 4 as a main course

Salad of Green Beans, Chinese Garlic Stems, and Olives

This light and crunchy salad looks as if it were made entirely of green beans—but a sniff reveals the garlic stems, which appear to be almost identical. The fragrance of crushed fennel seed adds a sweet note, and slivers of oily black olive contribute their winy richness. Shreds of Belgian endive lighten color, texture, and flavor.

6 ounces Chinese garlic stems
½ pound green beans (see Note)
10 oil-cured black olives
½ teaspoon fennel seeds
½ teaspoon freeze-dried green peppercorns
　　or ⅛ to ¼ teaspoon white pepper
½ teaspoon kosher salt
1 tablespoon rice vinegar
2 tablespoons olive oil
1 medium Belgian endive

1. Bend bottom of each garlic stem to snap it off where it breaks naturally (tender ones don't need trimming). Drop into a large pot of boiling salted water.

Boil until not quite tender, a minute or two. Lift out (save water for beans) into ice water. Drain and pat dry.

2. Trim stems from beans. At an angle, cut beans into 1½- to 2½-inch lengths, approximately, as size of bean dictates. Boil in the reserved water until barely al dente—not tender—3 to 5 minutes, depending upon size. Drain and cool in the ice water. Drain and pat dry.

3. At an angle, cut garlic stems to match beans. Combine in bowl.

4. Pit olives, then cut into very thin lengthwise strips. Combine fennel, peppercorns, and salt in suribachi, mortar, or spice mill; crush to medium-fine texture. Combine with vinegar, then whisk in oil. Add to bowl and toss to coat. Chill.

5. To serve, halve endive lengthwise and cut into thin strips. Add to salad and toss. Season, and add oil and vinegar if needed.

Serves 4

Note: Choose green beans of the same thickness as the garlic stems. For skinny stems, pair with slimmest French haricots verts; for comparatively sturdier stems, select "regular" green beans. Or, if contrasting colors are more to your taste, use yellow wax beans or other pale snap bean types to set off the green garlic.

Chrysanthemum Greens (*Chrysanthemum coronarium*)

Also edible or cooking chrysanthemum, garland chrysanthemum, chop suey vegetable, shungiku and kikuna (Japanese), ssukat and variations (Korean), tung hao and variations (Chinese)

⅓ **actual size**

Decorative chrysanthemums in several species and many forms brighten gardens across the temperate zone. The edible chrysanthemum species (*coronarium*) originated in the Mediterranean, then spread throughout Europe into Africa and Asia, but "strangely it has only been adopted as a vegetable in China, Japan, and south-east Asia," writes Joy Larkcom in *Oriental Vegetables*.

Chyrsanthemum greens have begun to appear in North America in areas where Asians have settled, making a vivid contribution to the greens repertoire. Little bunches of sharply serrated or broader, rounded leaves (and an in-between form), they resemble the decorative chrysanthemum in look and scent: a crush of tomato plant, pine, and autumn foliage. Muted spruce with a fuzzy feel and decoupage design, the tender, juicy leaves fit unobtrusively into the popular mesclun, but their flavor is anything but soft-spoken. Complex and aromatic, they are prickly-pungent and intensely bitter. (The petals as well as the greens are eaten in the East, but I have not seen them sold fresh in the West.)

BASIC USE: Traditionally, in the East, chrysanthemum is served in soup, sukiyaki, and other brothy dishes; or it is boiled and cooled to be served as a vegetable salad or condiment.

Non-traditionally, in the West, the fragrant leaves are ideal to add punch to salads, provided they are used sparingly—in the way of small Japanese red mustard or dandelion leaves. Thin-slice the stems and keep the leaf tops whole.

For less intensity, cook the greens. Add to stir-fries or braises or soups—for mere moments. For my taste, chrysanthemum's finest hour is as a final fillip for clear soup: Mere seconds in contact with the leaves will transform the simplest broth into a complex of scents and savors. Or prepare one of the assertive Korean condiment dishes, for which the powerful greens are well suited: Blanch and cool the leaves, squeeze them dry; mix with soy sauce, sesame oil, minced scallion, hot garlic paste, and toasted, crushed sesame seeds; add black pepper, rice vinegar, and sugar.

SELECTION: Chyrsanthemum leaves are erratically available in Oriental markets throughout the year.

Strictly speaking, shungiku is a spring chrysanthemum and kikuna an autumn one, but I see several forms year-round in the United States: slim and serrated, rounded and broad-leaved, delicate nosegays or fairly bushy bouquets. Despite variations in size and shape, I have noticed little difference in flavor or texture. Small and large leaves have been surprisingly similar.

Choose bunches with thin, evenly green stems, preferably with roots. There should be no yellowing or wetness. The overall look is lively but not crisp; the greens have a naturally droopy aspect. If there is a choice, select the smallest in order to maintain the whole leaf form, which looks prettier than cut-up pieces.

STORAGE: Untie the bunches, wrap the roots in damp toweling, and enclose the whole in plastic. The greens look hardier than they are. Refrigerate no more than a few days.

PREPARATION: Trim roots and heavy stem bases, if any. Drop greens into plenty of water; swish around and lift out. Repeat as needed. For salads, spin-dry, then cut stems into small pieces and keep leaves whole, unless unusually large. For cooked dishes, cut or not, to suit the recipe.

Sylvia Thompson, whose invaluable garden cookbooks are often cited in these pages, writes that if you grow your own chrysanthemum, you may have the advantage of their foot-long stalks. She trims them where they grow thicker than a pencil, then thin-slices to cook with the leaves.

Chrysanthemum Greens and Frisée with Tomato-Onion Dressing

For lovers of bittersweet flavors, here is a bright salad of spruce green chrysanthemum foliage, pearly frisée (curly endive), fuchsia onion, and scarlet tomato dice. A fine foil for game or red meat.

1 bunch small chrysanthemum greens
   (about 3 ounces)
1 medium head frisée (about ½ pound)
3 or 4 medium-large plum tomatoes
1 medium-large red onion
3 tablespoons cider vinegar

2 teaspoons brown sugar
¼ teaspoon kosher salt
⅛ to ¼ teaspoon hot pepper sauce
½ teaspoon Worcestershire sauce
¼ cup olive oil

1. Trim and discard roots, if any, from chrysanthemum. Cut greens into 2-inch pieces. Wash and spin-dry. Cut base from frisée and remove any tough or dried leaves. Rinse and spin-dry. Tear into bite-size pieces. Peel tomatoes (see Note, page 10). Cut into ½-inch dice. Do same to onion.

2. In a non-aluminum skillet, combine vinegar, sugar, salt, hot pepper sauce, and Worcestershire and bring to a boil. Add onion and toss over moderate heat until it softens slightly and vinegar has nearly evaporated, 2 to 3 minutes. Add tomato dice and boil until juice just begins to exude, a minute or so. Do not overcook—the vegetables should retain their shape and texture. Remove from heat, season, then set aside.

3. Heat oil in wide skillet over high heat. Add frisée, then chrysanthemum. Toss vigorously until just heated—not wilted—about 1 minute.

4. Immediately divide among serving plates. Top with tomato mixture. Serve at once.

Serves 4

Aromatic Shrimp and Chrysanthemum Soup

In the East, chrysanthemum is often paired with seafood—and a taste of this simple dish tells why. Pungent, perfumy, but mellowed, the tender green gives aromatic depth as it balances briny sweetness.

10 to 12 small-medium shrimp in the shell
4½ cups seafood, vegetable, or poultry broth
2 cloves
1-inch knob of ginger
2 slender scallions (green onions), trimmed
4 to 5 ounces small chrysanthemum greens
¼ teaspoon kosher salt
⅛ teaspoon white pepper
1 medium-large carrot
1 lemon, well scrubbed

1. Peel shrimp, placing shells in a medium saucepan with the broth and cloves. Slice ginger and light part of scallions. Add to pan. Bring to a boil, stirring occasionally. Reduce heat and simmer, partly covered, for 15 minutes.

2. Meanwhile, trim roots or heavy base, if any, from chrysanthemum. Wash greens in several changes of water. Pull leaflets from stems; set aside. Slice stems. Cut larger leaves into 1-inch pieces.

3. Strain broth (there should be 3 to 3½ cups; add water if needed). Lay shrimp on cutting board. Halve horizontally, then discard veins. Toss shrimp with salt and pepper.

4. Peel carrot, then shave into fine ribbons. Thin-slice scallion greens. Remove 1-inch strip lemon zest; cut into finest "needles," to make 1 teaspoon.

5. Bring broth to a boil in rinsed-out pan. Stir in carrot and greens; return to a boil. Immediately add shrimp, scallion greens, and zest. Turn off heat and stir. Let stand 1 minute. Ladle at once into small bowls, dividing the solids evenly.

Serves 4

Pros Propose

Although chrysanthemums are native to the Mediterranean, one rarely finds them in recipes outside the Far East. However, they do show up in the Greek mélange of boiled greens known as **Horta**: Trim tough stems from leaves (mixed leaves, or chrysanthemum alone). Boil leaves in salted water until tender, then drain and press dry. Chop, fluff slightly, and toss with a dressing of red wine vinegar, olive oil, and seasoning. Serve warm or at room temperature.

The greens are blanched for **Chrysanthemum Leaf and Water Chestnut Salad,** but the sweet water chestnuts against the astringent leaves produce an entirely different effect: Drop stemmed, rinsed leaves into plenty of boiling water. Turn off heat; stir until thoroughly wilted. Drain, then rinse in cold water. Squeeze leaves dry with hands. Chop and combine with peeled, chopped fresh water chestnuts, light soy sauce, salt, sugar, and sesame oil (from *Bruce Cost's Asian Ingredients*).

In Japan, a slightly different blanching technique gives the stems extra cooking (from *Good Food from a Japanese Temple* by Soei Yoneda): Trim stems only very slightly. Holding the plants by their leafy parts, immerse stems in boiling water for about 30 seconds, then release into the water and boil another minute; drain, rinse, and squeeze dry. Cut large pieces and mound in little dishes to serve with a sauce of soy and yuzu (or lemon) juice; garnish with fine shreds of crisp nori. Or toss the cooked greens with a dressing of toasted ground sesame seeds, soy, sake, sugar, and salt.

For an equally pure dish of a different stripe, **Salad of Chrysanthemum and Tomatoes,** chef Amaryll Schwertner blanches the leaves in salted water, then drains and refreshes them in ice water. She then chops the drained leaves and tosses them with halved tiny cherry tomatoes and olive oil, then scatters over sea salt.

Chef Schwertner puts the leaves into a modern Mediterranean mode with her **Eggplants Stuffed with Chrysanthemum:** Brush small globe eggplants with oil; bake in a wood-burning oven until nearly tender. Halve, scoop out some pulp, and chop; combine with onion sweated in olive oil. Combine with chrysanthemum leaves sautéed in olive oil, browned coarse bread crumbs, and chopped flat-leaf parsley. Season and replace in eggplants. Bake until hot and browned. Or serve tepid with vinaigrette.

In a traditional vein, **Glutinous Rice Dumplings in Chrysanthemum Leaf Soup** "is one of those heavenly meatless soup-like meals so loved by the Chinese. The dumplings are faintly sweet, and the chrysanthemum leaves also have a sweet, fragrant flavor" (from *Florence Lin's Complete Book of Chinese Noodles, Dumplings and Breads*). To prepare: Soak dried black mushrooms in warm water until soft; reserve liquid. Remove and discard stems; shred caps fine. Prepare a soft dough of sweet rice flour and hot water. Knead very smooth; break small pieces and roll balls; set on plastic-lined tray. Stir-fry mushroom shreds in oil for a minute; add fresh chicken broth and mushroom soaking liquid; boil. Add rice balls; within 2 minutes they should float. Add trimmed chrysanthemum greens and return to a boil. Serve at once.

Collards, Collard Greens (*Brassica oleracea*, Acephala Group)

See also: **KALES,** page 335

length of bunch: 18 inches

Collards (the term is usually plural, like grits) are a form of kale, an ancient plant of Eurasian origin that represents the oldest cultivated form of cabbage—and is still much the same as it has been for two millennia. Thick-leaved, dense, and cabbagey in flavor, collards are sturdier and stronger than most kales. Taxonomy confuses rather than helps define them, for kale and collards share a classification. (Acephala, meaning headless, is the designation that separates most kale and collards from other cabbages, for the two grow in loose bouquet form—not a tight head.) The great American botanist Liberty Hyde Bailey hoped that future generations could improve upon his classification, which he described in his revision of

the *Manual of Cultivated Plants* (1949) as "a name of somewhat indefinite application, perhaps to be discarded as a systematic category when the cult. races have received greater study." But it is still in place.

Latin *caulis* (stem) is the root of a group of words for cabbage: Dutch kool, German kohl, and English cole, kale, and collards (from colewort, meaning cabbage plant). Collards are so called only in the United States, as far as I can determine—but why and when that began I cannot say for sure. In 1774, when Thomas Jefferson planted the seed in his gardens at Monticello, it was as coleworts. *The Compact Edition of the Oxford English Dictionary* (curiously, American dictionaries seem unconcerned with collards' origins) defines "collard" or "collart" as a dialect of the American South, a phonetic corruption of the word "colewort," meaning "a variety of cabbage that does not heart." The dictionary's first citation of "collart-leaves" is in 1755, and by 1807 there was "collard." But when Fearing Burr published his *Field and Garden Vegetables of America* in 1863, both names were still used: "Colewort, or Collards."

Collards arrived in this country with slaves, although whether directly from Africa or via Haiti is not clear. Their culinary connection with the southern United States is strong but by no means unique. Collards are cooked (under other names) in countries around the Mediterranean and in Africa, Asia, and Latin America.

BASIC USE: In parts of the South, collards are cooked pretty much the same way they have been since they were introduced: boiled until tender with some piggy part—a delicious duo. They can be cooked slow and long (all night in parts of the South) to yield a soft, mellow mass. Or they can be simmered in broth for 15 to 30 minutes for a texture that is medium-firm, like sautéed cabbage. Or thin-sliced leaves can be cooked very briefly, for a greener flavor and chewier texture. Mix collards with softer leaves (spinach or curly mustard) for a more melting texture and complex taste.

Blanch collards for a milder, more tender leaf to use as a wrapper, like grape leaves; or slice and incorporate into stuffings. Season delicately or forcefully, since collards have plenty of taste of their own but can support a wide range of vivid additions: garlic or onions, mustard, ginger, anchovies, curry or sweet spice mixes, oyster sauce, Chinese chilli-bean paste, fermented black beans, and sweet-tart seasoning sauces. Accent collards with crisp garnishes such as fried croutons or crumbled bacon.

SELECTION: Collards are most abundant, flavorful, and tender during the coldest months, although they are available nearly all year. Choose comparatively small, deep-colored bunches with leaves that feel cool and slightly damp. Avoid dried, browned, yellowed, or coarse-stemmed plants. In the market, collards should be kept cold, not displayed in a warm area.

STORAGE: Keep collards very cold, or they may acquire a pronounced elderly cabbage taste. Wrap in ventilated plastic. Store for a shorter time than their sturdy looks suggest.

To avoid yellowing, store collards far from climacteric fruits (fruits that continue to ripen after harvesting). The presence of ethylene gas, a product of ripening, causes a loss of chlorophyll and protein and hastens drying and decay.

PREPARATION: Small leaves can be left whole or sliced into ½-inch pieces. If collards are large, strip stems from leaves and discard; stack leaves and halve lengthwise, then cut into ½-inch strips. Generally, most stems will soften if cooked more than 10 minutes or so. Dunk leaves into plenty of water and lift out so that the grit sinks. Repeat until the sink no longer feels sandy. Do not be tempted to stop at one washing.

Collards with Sweet Spices and Corn Bread Topping

Mellow and warming, soft collard pottage is topped with puffy yellow biscuit-dumplings. Serve for a cozy vegetarian main course or as starch and vegetable accompaniment to roasted pork, ham, chicken, or turkey. Although the results taste long-cooked, the actual cooking time is only half an hour.

2 to 2½ pounds collard greens
2 quarts water
1 tablespoon kosher salt
2 tablespoons butter
1 large onion, chopped
1 teaspoon ground ginger
1 teaspoon ground cumin
¼ teaspoon ground cardamom
¼ teaspoon ground cinnamon

TOPPING

¾ cup yellow cornmeal (preferably coarse stone-ground)
½ cup flour
1½ teaspoons baking powder
1 teaspoon sugar
½ teaspoon kosher salt
½ teaspoon grated nutmeg
1 egg
1 tablespoon corn oil
Optional: hot pepper sauce

1. If collards are large, strip stems from leaves and discard. Stack leaves and halve lengthwise, then cut crosswise into ½-inch strips. If collards are small, simply cut both stems and leaves into ½-inch slices. Rinse collards in several changes of water.

2. Bring water to a boil in large non–aluminum pot about 10 inches in diameter. Add salt, then collards, and return to a boil. Boil gently, stirring now and then, until tender. Timing varies, but 15 minutes is usual. Drain, reserving liquid. Chop collards quite fine.

3. Melt butter in same pot over low heat. Add onion and cook until softened, about 5 minutes. Add ginger, cumin, cardamom, and cinnamon. Stir a minute or two. Add collards and 1 quart (see Variation below) reserved cooking liquid. Simmer gently for a few minutes. (Can be prepared ahead to this point.) Because mixture will thicken as it cooks with the topping, add more cooking liquid (reserve ½ cup for topping) if you prefer a more soupy than stewy texture. Turn off heat.

4. To make the topping: Whisk together cornmeal, flour, baking powder, sugar, salt, and nutmeg in mixing bowl. In a small bowl, beat egg and oil to blend. Stir in ½ cup of the reserved cooking liquid. Pour into dry ingredients, mixing with a fork to barely blend. The batter should resemble thick applesauce; add more cooking liquid if needed.

5. Bring collards to a boil. Drop batter by tablespoons (about 10) over greens, leaving spaces between. Cover pot and boil gently for 10 minutes. Uncover and boil a few minutes longer, until dumpling tops become nearly dry to the touch.

6. Serve hot, accompanied by hot pepper sauce, if desired.

Serves 3 to 4 as a main dish, 6 to 8 as a side dish

Variation

Spiced Collards as a Side Dish

To serve as a vegetable dish without topping, follow the recipe through step 3, adding just 1 cup of the reserved cooking liquid ("pot likker" in the South) instead of 1 quart.

Serves 4

Collard Ribbons with Sesame

If you're a fan of collards, you'll appreciate the chewy assertiveness of the short-cooked vegetable as much as the mellowed softness of the long-simmered—and be surprised by the smoky meatiness of this vegetarian dish. I like this firm form as a partner for whole grains, such as kamut, wheat, or buckwheat. Round out the meal with steamed Buttercup or kabocha type squash.

About 2 pounds collard greens
2 cups water
1 tablespoon molasses
¾ teaspoon kosher salt
1 tablespoon peanut oil
2 teaspoons Asian (dark) sesame oil
¼ teaspoon chilli flakes
1 garlic clove, minced
About 2 teaspoons sherry vinegar or
    cider vinegar
1½ tablespoons toasted sesame seeds

1. Strip stems from collard leaves and discard. Rinse leaves in several changes of water. Stack leaves 5 or 6 at a time and halve lengthwise, then cut across into ¼-inch strips (to make about 10 packed cups).

2. Combine collards in very wide deep skillet with water, molasses, salt, and peanut and sesame oils. Bring to a boil, twisting greens with tongs or turning with spatula until wilted. Cover and boil until collards are tender but still chewy—about 15 minutes.

3. Uncover and add chilli flakes and garlic. Raise heat and boil, stirring often, until liquid has evaporated, about 5 minutes.

4. Season, adding vinegar gradually. Sprinkle with sesame seeds. Serve hot.

Serves 4 as a side dish

Variation

Spaghetti with Collard Ribbons and Sesame

Follow recipe through step 3, but do not evaporate all the juices. While collards cook, add ½ pound imported Italian whole-wheat spaghetti to boiling salted water and cook until not quite al dente. Drain pasta, then add to collards. Over low heat, turn and twist with tongs until liquid is absorbed and collard strips are evenly distributed. Season well, adding vinegar. Sprinkle with sesame seeds.

Serves 2 as a main dish

Bittersweet Braised Pork and Collards in Dark Beer

Collards are meant to be stewed: Impossible to overcook, they soften and absorb meat juices without losing their defined personality. Pork has the right sweetness and fattiness to mellow them—but not if from some fashionably lean pig. Look for a cut with marbling, and do not trim off all the creamy, flavor-carrying fat. Orange juice and dark beer add nuances to a modern pork-and-greens one-dish meal that is at once homey and unusual.

Millet or quinoa (pan-toast either one before cooking) makes a fluffy foil. Like most stews, this one can be prepared ahead and reheated. I haven't yet experimented, but I imagine this dish would also be delicious with lamb shoulder or beef chuck.

2 pounds small-medium collard greens
2 pounds pork for stew, cut into 1-inch cubes
2 tablespoons flour
1½ teaspoons kosher salt
2 tablespoons bacon fat, lard, or peanut oil
1 large onion, diced
2 garlic cloves, chopped
One 12-ounce bottle dark or amber beer or ale
¾ cup orange juice
¾ cup water
1 tablespoon brown sugar
¼ teaspoon chilli flakes
3 tablespoons cider vinegar, malt vinegar, or wine vinegar
Optional: coarse-grated orange zest

1. Preheat oven to 350°F. Wash collards in several changes of water. Slice both stems and leaves into ½-inch pieces. Toss pork in a bag with flour and ½ teaspoon salt to coat evenly.

2. Heat fat in very wide sauté pan over moderate heat. Brown pork, turning, until well colored. Transfer pieces to 4-quart casserole.

3. Add onion to pan and sauté until lightly browned. Add garlic and toss. Add collards and stir until completely wilted, a matter of a few minutes. Add beer, juice, water, sugar, chilli flakes, vinegar, and remaining 1 teaspoon salt; bring to a boil.

4. Pour over pork, stirring to mix. Bring to a boil. Cover and bake until very tender, about 1½ hours, stirring several times. Sprinkle with optional zest.

Serves 4 to 6

Collard Rolls on Roasted Red Pepper Sauce

Lorna Sass's vegetarian recipes are fresh and innovative, not health food-y. This vibrant example is adapted from *The New Vegan Cookbook*. Forest-green packets filled with nubbly grains and nuts are set on a scarlet pool of sweet pepper puree studded with white beans. As you marvel at the leaves' striking veins and tenderness, you will wonder why collards are not regular wrapping greens. To ready this time-consuming dish, it is best to have cooked grains on hand (they freeze well) and to prepare the sauce in advance.

RED PEPPER SAUCE

3 large red bell peppers, roasted, peeled, and chunked (see Note, page 114)
2 tablespoons olive oil
1¾ cups cooked navy beans (or one 15-ounce can, drained)
About ½ teaspoon kosher salt
About 1 teaspoon balsamic vinegar

COLLARD ROLLS

1½ pounds collard greens (or at least 20 leaves, of varying sizes)
1¼ teaspoons kosher salt
1 tablespoon vegetable oil
1½ cups fine-chopped leeks
½ cup fine-diced celery
½ cup fine-diced carrot
Pepper
2 cups cooked pearl barley

2 cups cooked short-grain brown rice (or
    additional 2 cups barley)
½ cup hazelnuts, toasted, husked, and chopped
    (see Note, page 175)
½ tablespoon hazelnut oil
⅓ cup loosely packed chopped dill
2 to 3 tablespoons lemon juice

1. Prepare sauce: Combine peppers, olive oil, ¾ cup beans, and ½ teaspoon salt in food processor. Whirl to a puree. Transfer to saucepan and add the remaining 1 cup beans. Taste, season, and add balsamic vinegar. Bring to a boil. If sauce lacks finished flavor or seems thin, continue cooking briefly (can be made ahead).

2. Cut off collard stems. Trim any leaves longer than 10 inches. Thin-slice enough stems to make 1 cup (discard remainder or save for soup).

3. Choose a pot large enough to hold leaves without bending. Pour in enough water to cover them generously. Bring to a boil with ¾ teaspoon salt. Press in leaves. Boil, covered, until just tender—5 to 10 minutes. (To test: With scissors, snip off a small piece near the stem end. Err on the side of undercooking, or leaves may tear.)

4. Drain collards in colander set over a bowl; reserve broth. Run cold water over the leaves, turning once or twice.

5. Heat oil in same pot. Add leek and stir over moderate heat to wilt. Add celery, carrot, sliced collard stems, ½ cup collard broth, the remaining ¾ teaspoon salt, and pepper. Simmer, covered, until vegetables are cooked through but still firmish—8 to 10 minutes. Add more broth if mixture becomes dry.

6. In food processor or blender, whiz 1 cup barley with ½ cup broth to coarse puree. Add to vegetables in pot, with remaining 1 cup barley, the rice, nuts, nut oil, and dill. Season. Add lemon juice.

7. To assemble rolls: Flatten a leaf on work surface, with smoother side up and mid-rib running left to right (i.e., horizontally). Patch any tears with pieces of another leaf. Mound ¼ to ¾ cup filling (depending on leaf size) just below and along length of mid-rib. Flip leaf edge close to you over filling and continue rolling (mid-rib will run along the length of the roll). Set on microwavable or ovenproof platter, seam side down. Prepare all rolls.

8. To serve, heat rolls in microwave (or in low oven, loosely covered with foil). Reheat sauce, then spoon onto plate. Set rolls on the sauce.

Serves 5 to 6 as a main course

★ For an additional recipe, see Hot and Gingery Collard-Plaintain Soup, page 492.

Pros Propose

Herewith a sampling of collards' many far-flung ports of call.

Ethiopia may be the place where collards (there called gomen) are cooked in the most diverse and complex ways. **Ethiopian Spiced Collards with Buttermilk Curds** is one such. Prepare spiced butter: Melt butter, then boil. Add chopped onion, garlic, and ginger, then stir in turmeric, cardamom seeds, cinnamon sticks, whole cloves, and nutmeg. Cook over low heat until milk solids on bottom are golden and butter on top is transparent; strain off clear butter. Prepare buttermilk curds: Beat buttermilk to 160°F. Ladle curds into cloth-lined sieve. Once drained, wrap curds in cloth, squeeze, and weight until firm and compact. Crumble curds into a bowl and blend with some spiced butter, ground cardamom, white pepper, and salt; refrigerate. Fine-chop stripped collard leaves. Boil in salted water until tender; drain, then squeeze dry. Pound chopped chillis, ginger, garlic, and ground cardamom to a paste; add a little boiling water. Rub through fine sieve onto collards, extracting all juices; discard pulp. Add some spiced butter and grated onion, and toss to coat. Marinate briefly at room temperature. Serve with a mound of the buttermilk curds (*African Cooking: Foods of the World*).

From Kenya comes easy and appealing **Collard Greens with Lemon Sauce**: Cook stemmed, slivered collards in a little water, covered, until just tender, about 10 minutes; drain. Sauté chopped onion and minced chillis in oil until softened. Add peeled, chopped plum tomatoes and simmer briefly. Add collards. Blend lemon juice, flour, and a little water. Add to vegetables and stir until raw taste disappears and mixture thickens (from *Kwanzaa* by Eric V. Copage).

Chillis, dried and fresh, figure in **Collard Greens**

Cooked in Broth. In *Madhur Jaffrey's Cookbook,* she writes that the "method of cooking these greens is Kashmiri in inspiration, though I have made some changes such as using olive oil instead of mustard oil and using broth instead of water": Combine chicken broth, garlic, fresh green chillis, dried hot chillis, and olive oil; bring to a boil. Add trimmed collards, cut into 1-inch strips. Cover and cook until greens wilt. Lower heat and simmer until collards are tender to taste. Raise heat, uncover, and cook rapidly until most liquid has evaporated.

Jamaicans, who enjoy their fair share of collards, add ground allspice, ginger, and Angostura bitters to an otherwise similar dish. Chef and author Didi Emmons has her own take on collards in a **Jamaican Rice Mix-Up,** a kind of fried rice Caribbean-style: Bake halved butternut squash cut side down until tender. Cool, peel, and cut into large pieces. Lightly brown chopped onions in corn oil. Add minced fresh ginger, garlic, allspice, and curry powder; toss a few minutes. Add cooked long-grain white rice; toss briefly. Add stemmed, thin-sliced collard leaves and toss until wilted. Add cooked black beans, toss, and season (from *Vegetarian Planet*).

Hopping back to Europe, there is **Caldo Verde,** perhaps kale and collards' finest hour. "If Portugal has a national dish, it is . . . this lusty green soup which originated in the Minho Province but now bubbles on stoves everywhere regardless," writes Jean Anderson in *The Food of Portugal.* The soup is defined by hair-thin strips of a juicy collard-like kale called couve tronchuda (and Galician or Portuguese cabbage) that are cooked in thin potato puree. Or it may be more complex, as is Jean Anderson's version: Sauté minced onion and garlic in olive oil until translucent. Add thin-sliced potatoes and sauté briefly. Add water, cover, and boil until potatoes are mushy. Meanwhile, brown thin-sliced chouriço or other garlicky dry sausage. With potato masher, crush and puree potatoes in the pot. Add sausage; simmer 5 minutes. Add stemmed collards, cut into finest filaments, and simmer, uncovered, until just tender. Add olive oil and seasoning.

Southern chef Jeff Buben returns us to the American home front—with French underpinnings (duck confit) in **Duck with Collards:** Blanch stripped collard leaves in boiling water seasoned with three parts sugar to one of salt. Drain, then cut ribbons. Heat in duck fat from confit, with some of the julienned duck, onion slivers, and minced garlic. Add a sachet of bay leaves, thyme, and peppercorns, with duck stock and a drop of wine vinegar. Simmer, covered, until collards are just tender—not mushy—and liquid is absorbed. Sear (raw) duck breast and slice. Fan over collards. Serve with duck *jus* seasoned with honey, vinegar, and thyme.

In a more traditional vein, chef Mike Patton long-cooks **Cream of Collards Soup:** Combine trimmed medium-size collards with bacon, onion, garlic, ham hocks, water, and light chicken broth; simmer until very soft and browned. ("I'm from Virginia, where they put up collards at night and let them cook until morning," says Patton.) Remove meat and puree collards and liquid. Add some heavy cream. Serve with polenta croutons and browned lardons.

Sarah Belk has three delightful newfangled collard recipes in *Around the Southern Table:* collard and black-eye pea soup with cornmeal croustades, collard greens with warm walnut vinaigrette, and **Sautéed Collard Greens with Dijon Mustard and Sour Cream.** To prepare the last: Strip stems from collards. Rinse and stack leaves (halve lengthwise, if large). Cut into 1-inch-wide strips. Boil in salted water until just tender; drain. Melt butter in non-aluminum skillet. Add chopped onion and cook gently to soften. Add collards; toss. In small bowl, combine sour cream, mustard, and ground hot pepper. Add to greens and cook, stirring, until liquid has evaporated, a few minutes.

Corn, Baby (*Zea mays*)

Also miniature corn, mini-corn (Thai cookbooks refer to it as
candle corn, an apt description I have not seen elsewhere)

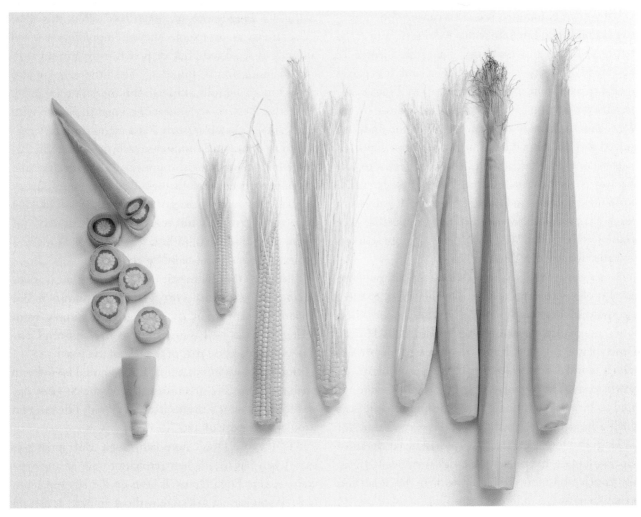

½ **actual size**

This entry is a mini-mention, for corn and its uses are well known. Fresh baby ears are a mere blip on the corn chart, but different enough from larger forms to warrant attention on their own.

"Baby corn" refers to tiny ears picked just as the silk appears. Fresh, they taste as you might imagine: like the essence of mild corn with a green vegetable underpinning. (You eat the tender cob along with the minute kernels.) Those I've cooked averaged about a dozen ears to the pound in the husk, which yielded about ¼ pound trimmed "cornlets" 2 to 4 inches long and ½

inch in diameter. These infants may be field corn (the starchy kind used for dried grain products and animal feed), which can be sweet and juicy at a literally tender age. Or they may be sweet corn cultivars.

"There are two labor-intensive systems for harvesting baby corn. The first has a dual purpose, with the top ear retained for either grain production or market sweet corn and the lower ears picked by hand before pollination for baby-corn production," the geneticists Walton C. Galinat and Bor-Yaw Lin wrote in an article in *Economic Botany* (1988). "The second system is based on almost twice the density of planting with all ear shoots being harvested as baby corn." Since most varieties produce one to three ears per stalk, and since these must be gathered by hand, the economics of such a crop are pretty poor. Baby corn has always been produced commercially in countries where labor costs are very low—until recently, only in the Far East.

Baby-corn commerce is a 20th century phenomenon, according to Dr. Chokechai Aekatasanawan at the National Corn and Sorghum Research Center of Kasetsart University in Pakchong, Thailand. It began as a local market item in Taiwan, then moved into commercial production and processing for export to the West and to Asian countries. In 1969 the industry moved to Thailand, which is now the largest exporter.

Everyone who tastes fresh baby corn seems to like the way it looks, crunches, and tastes. But given the prohibitive cost of hand harvesting, there doesn't seem much chance for cultivation on any considerable scale in the United States. What comes fresh to our markets is primarily from Central America.

A few growers persevere with the crop, although no one I spoke with expects to profit. They grow to meet the demands (primarily chefs') for the product. Bob Jones, general manager of Chef's Garden in Huron, Ohio, planted 120 cultivars in order to determine which worked best in his area. "We finally narrowed down to six. The Japanese was the easiest, because it's bred to be small and holds best—meaning that it stays small a longer time, giving a three-week window for picking. But four local sweet corns had by far the most superior taste—and only a three-day window. It's a really touchy business. Ten miles down the road you would be growing different corns."

John Llano, a co-owner of San Diego Specialty Produce, has been farming baby corn in San Diego County and Baja California for over a dozen years. "It has become very competitive, with Mexico, Costa Rica, Texas, Florida, and other places growing now. There is no way to make up the money it costs to produce. All we do is fill time windows that others can't—late spring and early fall. But now the windows of opportunity are looking more like peepholes."

BASIC USE: Steam husked and trimmed ears until barely tender, a matter of a few minutes. (You can boil it if you prefer, but some of the flavor will be washed away. Do *not* microwave, no matter what anyone says!)

Depending upon the size and recipe, you can leave the ears whole, halve them, slice them diagonally, or cut into rounds: All look charming. Serve them in prominent, even starring, roles.

In the Far East, baby corn is stir-fried with other vegetables and seafood or poultry. Pickling is also traditional, but I find that it hides the delicacy. *Charmaine Solomon's Encyclopedia of Asian Food* offers this idea: "Use them as an edible skewer, moulding a small amount of seasoned pork or prawn paste around each and steaming for 10 minutes." The little ears are also perfect in spring rolls, although this use isn't traditional.

In the Western style, heat the corn in butter with other small vegetables, such as asparagus tips, baby carrots or turnips, small summer squash, or Broccolini. Include baby corn in light summer salads with the same vegetables plus mini-tomatoes. Top a quiche or savory vegetable tart with spokes of baby corn. If you like the corn raw, serve it with vegetable strips for dips (or steam and chill first). Whole or halved ears make a beautiful garnish, especially for clear soups.

SELECTION: Domestic baby corn is in markets during the traditional corn season, late summer. But restaurants can count on a continuous supply from spring to fall, as well as intermittent arrivals from Central America a good part of the rest of the year.

Bob Jones advises that the "leaves should be soft and pliable and the silk greenish and a bit sticky—not dry or browned, which means it's a week old. The cut end should not be discolored."

STORAGE: Don't store baby corn. Bob Jones says that "corn has the highest respiration rate of any vegetable except English peas. It heats up, literally—you can feel it if you leave it in a crate without chilling. It uses up nutrients and the sugar goes first." If you must postpone cooking it, keep it in the husk and refrigerate in a basket or paper bag.

PREPARATION: To unwrap the ear quickly, though messily: Score the husk lengthwise with fingernail or knife, then pull off a batch of layers at a time. This makes sense if the ear is very small and hiding deep in the husks (squeeze and palp to determine). The look will be raggedy.

To ensure neat results, one-at-a-time husk removal is necessary, if painstaking. If you remember to pull each leaf in the opposite direction from the preceding one, the unfurling will be easier. When you reach the final tissue-thin layers (you'll feel the kernels or see them), stop. Cut off the furled tip just above the little cob. The gauzy leaves and corn silk taste fine; they need not be removed unless you prefer the look and texture of the cleaned ear or unless the corn has a superabundance of silk. Cook an ear as a test, if you're not sure.

Basic Baby Corn

Cute but time-consuming to prepare, these doll-size ears are best reserved for garnishes or dishes that don't require many of them. The laborious part is cleaning, not cooking—which takes minutes at most.

It's difficult to imagine a dish that would *not* be made charming by these natural grace notes, but they are particularly right with seafood, in bisques or broths (sliced in crosswise rounds), baked atop a tart or quiche, sautéed with other mini-vegetables, or as part of composed salads based on grain or poultry. The cooked ears can be presented whole, halved or thick-sliced on a diagonal, or sliced into rounds. They are cute whole in rice paper–wrapped spring rolls.

12 to 16 ears baby corn

1. Remove husks: To do this quickly but messily, score each ear lengthwise with fingernail or knife, then pull off a few layers of husks at a time. To ensure a neat result, one-at-a-time husk removal is necessary. If you remember to pull each leaf in the opposite direction from the preceding one, unfurling is easier.

2. When you reach the final tissue-thin layers (you'll feel the kernels or see them), stop. Cut off the furled tip just above the little cob. The thin leaves and corn silk taste fine—they need not be removed unless you prefer the look of the cleaned ear.

3. Set ears on a rack over boiling water. Cover and steam 2 to 6 minutes, depending upon size of ears and thickness of any remaining husks. Sample one before removing all the ears.

4. Serve whole, if very small. Or halve on diagonal, halve lengthwise, or cut into crosswise slices. Serve hot or warm.

Serves 4 as a garnish

Herbed Miniature Corn and Petite Okra

Miniature corn and okra podlets look and taste truly delightful together—and cook in the same amount of time. The finest okra (and nothing less will do for this simple recipe), like the finest corn, is at its best steamed: bright, sweet, and succulent. If corn is tiny, use 36 ears; if larger, use 18 ears, and halve them diagonally.

18 or 36 ears baby corn
1 pound very small okra
1½ tablespoons butter
A pinch each of salt, sugar, and pepper
1½ tablespoons snipped chives
2 teaspoons minced tarragon or
    2 tablespoons minced parsley

1. Husk corn as in Preparation. Halve diagonally if large.

2. Rinse okra. Pare off caps without cutting into the pods.

3. Set corn and okra on rack over boiling water. Cover and steam until just barely tender, 3 to 5 minutes. Do not cook okra until soft; it should be slightly al dente for maximum flavor and color.

4. Transfer vegetables to a heated dish and mix gently with butter, salt, sugar, and pepper. Then delicately toss with chives and tarragon (or parsley). Serve at once.

Serves 4 to 6

Miniature Mélange

A very cute (some might say precious) fairy-feast garnish to fancify plain-cooked fish or fowl. Preparation is time-consuming, but the dish can be made ahead and heated at the last minute. Do not cook the vegetables until tender—just half-cook them, or a bit more, timing from 2 to 5 minutes for most. Gauge the number of squash and carrots by size: If tiny, use twelve of each; if larger, use six, then halve or quarter.

12 ears baby corn

6 or 12 miniature carrots

6 or 12 miniature zucchini and/or yellow
    squash or miniature pattypan squash

12 pearl (small boiling) onions

1 tablespoon sliced flat-leaf parsley leaves

1 tablespoon sliced chives

1 teaspoon fresh tarragon leaves

1 tablespoon butter

Salt, sugar, and white pepper

1. Trim ears as described in Preparation. Scrub carrots (peel only if skin is tough or bitter). Scrub and trim squash. Rinse onions.

2. Set onions on rack over boiling water. Steam, covered, until half-tender. Carefully trim root ends, then slip off skin.

3. Steam other vegetables in batches or together, as convenient. As each finishes cooking, place on towel. When slightly cooled, halve corn diagonally. Halve or quarter carrots and squash, as suitable.

4. Mince together parsley, chives, and tarragon. Melt butter over moderately low heat in skillet large enough to hold all ingredients in a single layer. Add vegetables and sprinkle with a little salt and pepper. Cook gently, shaking pan and turning vegetables carefully, until slightly colored. Serve hot, sprinkled with herbs.

Serves 4 as a garnish

Pros Propose

Chefs I spoke with limit baby corn use to garnish, which is a shame—but understandable, given the price. The culinary literature on the subject is sparse and made up primarily of stir-fries.

Baby Corn with Snow Peas is Roger Vergé's lovely Western take on a Chinese pairing. To prepare: Cook husked ears in water with a little milk for 2 minutes. Drain. Trim and string snow peas. Melt butter in large skillet. Add snow peas, a bruised garlic clove, thyme sprig, sugar, and salt. Sauté over high heat a few minutes. Add corn and toss to heat through. Remove garlic and thyme (from *Roger Vergé's Vegetables in the French Style*).

"This recipe is a splendid example of the new cooking of Hong Kong," writes Ken Hom in *Fragrant Harbor Taste*. "Western asparagus and Southeast Asian baby corn have been absorbed into the Cantonese tradition" in **Stir-Fried Asparagus with Corn:** Cut asparagus into ½-inch rounds. Blanch husked baby corn in boiling water; drain. Heat a wok; add peanut oil. Stir-fry asparagus 1 minute. Add chicken stock and salt and cook 2 minutes. Add baby corn and continue to stir-fry until liquid evaporates. Add a little sesame oil and serve at once.

In Southeast Asia, aromatic meat or fish paste is molded around baby corn (or sugarcane) to make a handy hors d'oeuvre, such as **Young Corn Cobs with Steamed Fish:** Mince (or process) white fish fillets with white pepper; set aside. Pound to a paste (or process) chopped garlic, coriander roots, chopped galangal, sliced lemon grass, and fish sauce. Blend well with the fish, minced red chillis, and minced scallion. Divide mixture into even portions and press each firmly around a husked corn cob, keeping the ends uncovered. Set on an oiled steamer, cover, and cook 8 to 10 minutes. Serve with dipping sauce or salad (from *Charmaine Solomon's Thai Cookbook*).

Cremini and Portobello Mushrooms

(*Agaricus bisporus*)

See also the many names below

Cremini mushrooms—also marketed as Crimini, Baby Bellas, Golden Italian, Roman, or Classic Brown mushrooms—are also, as you may already know, juvenile portobellos (about which more later). They are, as well, the same as white or button mushrooms (or champignons, to the restaurant trade), but a different strain. "What's old is new": This mushroom is a reintroduction of the brown mushroom that was common in the United States before the white strain was isolated and developed during the mid-1920s. It differs from the white in its cocoa coloring, more solid texture, and richer flavor.

As for the name "cremini" . . . I give up! Crimini means "crimes" in Italian (although one company claims that it means "brown"). An Italian writer calls the mushrooms cremosini, but three knowledgeable Italian chefs assert there is no such word. A distributor says that he saw the mushrooms in Milan in 1980—simply called funghi cultivati—and named them Roman Mushrooms when he brought them to the United States the next year. An American grower subsequently "introduced" them as Golden Italian. As the popularity of portobello mushrooms grows—and it is growing very rapidly—it seems likely that related names, such as the recent Portabellini, will rise to replace or join the others in the criminal confusion.

The chubby cremino (if that is the singular; no one can be sure), properly encouraged by environmental conditions, will metamorphose to a portly portobello (also portabella), a name as difficult to document as cremini. I asked dozens who work with mushrooms, here and in Italy, about the name. The marketing director of a mushroom farm told me, "It was named after Portobello Road in London, where they sell fashionable things, you know." An importer said, "Until ten years ago, the mushroom was cappelaccio in Italy. Then it was renamed after a TV show called Portobello—because it sounds better." Another importer told me that "portobello is known only in northern Italy, where it is

cremini   diameter of caps: 1½-2 inches

called capellone." To one authority, capellone means "big hat." To the director of an Italian trade board—and a dictionary—it means "hippie." Two northern Italian chefs had never heard of capellone or cappelaccio. The most outlandish derivation came from an Italian distributor: "Well, you know that champignon comes from the word for Champagne, and that a Champagne cork looks like a round port—and that's how we get porto bello—beautiful port."

Whatever its provenance, the portobello or portabella (depending on the brand) has upgraded America's view of "vegetarian," whether it appears on pizza, grilled on baby greens, or in the exalted role of "A Portabella Mushroom Pretending to be a Filet Mignon with a Roasted Shallot and Tomato Fondue," at the elegant Inn at Little Washington, Virginia.

BASIC USE: Cook cremini in all the ways you would white "buttons," but expect a denser consistency (even when thin-sliced) and deeper savor. They taste particularly meaty when brushed with nut oil or

portobello   **diameter of caps: 4-6 inches**

herb- or garlic-infused olive oil, then roasted or grilled. Broad, handsome portobello caps are also at their best oil-seasoned, roasted or grilled, then thin-sliced. They are a natural for stuffing, as well, providing a neat, large container to be filled. Chop and incorporate the huge, meaty stem into the stuffing, or save it for soup, sauce, stock, duxelles, or seasoning. Note that the deep-brown gills of older portobellos will darken any preparation. If this is not desirable, scrape them out with a blunt knife to use in sauce or as a garnish.

SELECTION: Cremini and portobelli are culti-vated year-round, but the latter are vulnerable to viruses and occasionally disappear from the market for a while. For both, choose plump, solid, firm, dry mush-rooms with no shriveling or slipperiness. If in doubt,

sniff: An earthy, vegetable smell is right; a sourish or animal smell is not.

Select small cremini with closed caps when you plan to cook them whole; they hold their shape neatly. Larger ones are fine for slicing, dicing, and chopping. (An intermediate size, Portabellini, has a closed cap, like cremini, but is larger.) Maturing cremini with opening caps and darkening gills may have more flavor, and their juices will be darker; plan accordingly.

Portobello's open cap should reveal gills that are dry and shapely—not damp or dented. As the mushroom ages, the gills turn from pinkish-taupe to chocolate. Older mushrooms, recognizable by a loss of sheen as well as by darkened gills, are fibrous and taste muddy.

Typically, portobello caps are 4 to 6 inches in diameter. The comparatively newly named and marketed Baby Portabella is smaller and has a smoother texture and milder flavor (more "veal" than "beef"). For best keeping, choose whole mushrooms, usually packed in open cases. Caps alone are less prone to breakage but more expensive—and they lack the useful stems. Do not consider sliced caps—a waste of money, freshness, and flavor.

STORAGE: Unlike most mushrooms, cremini seem to last particularly well in "breathable" plastic retail packs—over a week, if they are in good shape to start.

For portobello mushrooms, remove wrapping, if any. Spread mushrooms in a basket or tray, cover with a towel, and refrigerate. Do not moisten or set objects on top. Mushrooms need circulating air, so don't crowd them. If very fresh, they may last 5 to 6 days.

PREPARATION: If cremini will be cooked with liquid, rinse quickly in a colander, then blot on towels. If they will be roasted or sautéed, it is better—though time-consuming—to clean them with a soft brush only. For portobello mushrooms, hold each one upright, tap the top to dislodge any growing medium that lurks, then flick gills clean with a *soft* brush. People usually twist, then break off the stem, but I find this risks cracking the cap. I prefer to hold each upright and gently cut the stem flush with the cap.

Nutty Roasted Cremini

Juicy and chewy, whole mushrooms tossed with crunchy nuts are a pleasing change-of-pace side for a roast. Plump cremini (the smaller they are, the cuter they look and the more manageable the mouthfuls) are just right for the job. Roast in a hot oven after you've removed a turkey or chicken to rest before carving. Nut oil and spices accentuate the flavors rather than adding contrasting notes. (If needed, see Note, page 175, to roast, husk, and chop hazelnuts.)

> 1½ pounds small cremini
> About ½ teaspoon kosher salt
> 1 teaspoon Chinese 5-spice powder or ground
>   fennel or anise
> 1 tablespoon sherry
> 2 tablespoons hazelnut oil
> ⅓ cup roasted, husked, and coarse-chopped
>   hazelnuts
> Pepper

1. Set oven to 450°F; place rack in upper third. Clean mushrooms with a soft brush or, if necessary, rub with damp towels. Trim stems flush with caps.

2. In a large bowl, combine ½ teaspoon salt, spice powder, and sherry, blending well. Add oil. Add mushrooms and toss to coat as evenly as possible. Spread mushrooms in a roasting pan that will hold them in a single layer.

3. Roast until cooked through and browned—10 to 15 minutes. Toss nuts with mushrooms, adding seasoning. Serve hot.

Serves 4 to 6

Penne with Aromatic Cremini-Tomato Ragoût

Cremini retain their appealing shape and texture when simmered, making them good candidates for a hearty sauce to cloak polenta or pasta. Orange and mint alter the familiar tomato-mushroom pairing while the generous quantity of mushrooms changes the sauce from seasoning to vegetable accompaniment. Eden or Muir Glen canned tomatoes are particularly good. If you're drinking red wine, add a splash to the sauce.

> 1½ pounds cremini
> 1 large onion
> 1 or 2 garlic cloves
> One can tomatoes (14 to 16 ounces)
> 3 tablespoons olive oil
> 1 teaspoon grated orange zest
> 1 teaspoon kosher salt
> 1 can tomato puree or sauce (about 8 ounces)
> ¼ teaspoon chilli flakes
> ¼ to ½ cup chopped mint leaves
> 1 pound imported Italian penne rigate

1. Rinse cremini lightly in a colander, then dry on soft towels. Thin-slice half of them. Halve or quarter the remainder, as size dictates for neat eating. Chop onion. Mince garlic. With scissors, snip tomatoes in can into smallish pieces.

2. Heat 1½ tablespoons olive oil in large heavy saucepan. Add onion, garlic, orange zest, and salt; toss over moderate heat until onions are lightly colored, about 5 minutes. Raise heat, add cremini, and sauté

until juices are released, then nearly evaporate—about 10 minutes.

3. Add tomatoes, tomato puree, and chilli flakes. Cover and cook over low heat, stirring often, until flavors blend, about 15 minutes. Stir in 2 to 4 tablespoons mint, to taste. (Can be made ahead.)

4. Boil pasta in plenty of salted water until al dente; drain. Toss with remaining 1½ tablespoons oil and a big spoonful of sauce. Top with remaining sauce and sprinkle with mint to taste.

Serves 4 as a main dish

Broiled Portobellos on Soft Parmesan Polenta

Savory portobello caps are the "meat" of this vegetarian main dish, their chewy flesh sliced into thin strips like flank steak. For polenta lovers, microwave ovens are a boon, making the cornmeal dish fast, fussless, and foolproof (albeit less luscious than when long-cooked). The recipe yields a soft mush. If you prefer solidity, reduce the liquid by ½ cup and cook the polenta a few minutes longer.

Please note that broilers differ so dramatically that there is no way to provide uniform directions: You must know your own. The goal is to cook through and crisp the mushroom caps—not to sear or steam them.

4 large portobello mushrooms
   (5 to 6 inches across)
2 tablespoons olive oil
1 small garlic clove, minced
2 teaspoons shoyu (Japanese soy sauce)
1 tablespoon lemon juice
1 cup coarse stone-ground cornmeal
2 cups water
2 cups vegetable, mushroom, or chicken broth
About ¾ teaspoon kosher salt (omit if broth is salted)
½ cup grated Parmesan cheese
Pepper
2 tablespoons thin-sliced chives
2 tablespoons chopped parsley leaves
1½ tablespoons toasted pine nuts

1. Holding each mushroom upright by its stem, tap tops of caps to dislodge dirt from gills. Carefully cut off stems flush with caps (reserve stems for another dish). Clean gills with a soft brush.

2. Combine olive oil and garlic in a cup; cover and microwave 30 seconds at 50 percent power. Add shoyu and lemon juice. Stirring mixture often, brush caps all over with it. Cover broiler rack with foil. Preheat broiler.

3. Whisk together cornmeal, water, broth, and ¾ teaspoon salt in a 2- to 3-quart microwavable container. Cover and cook (at full power) until water *just begins* to boil and cornmeal starts to thicken (do not wait until water has boiled, or clumps may form). My 850-watt oven takes about 7 minutes, but timing varies with power. Carefully uncover, avoiding steam. Whisk vigorously to smooth. Without re-covering, continue cooking until raw tastes disappears, about 6 to 8 minutes, stirring every 2 minutes. Let stand 5 minutes (can be made ahead and reheated; you may need to add water to loosen). Stir Parmesan into polenta. Taste and season.

4. Meanwhile, broil mushrooms gill side down until just crisped. Turn gently. Continue broiling until thoroughly tender. Lower or raise heat and/or broiler pan level so that mushrooms cook through and crisp but do not burn. Transfer to a cutting board. Sprinkle with salt and pepper. Cut into long slices on the bias.

5. Ladle polenta into four wide shallow bowls. Overlap mushroom slices in spokes or fan shape on each. Drizzle with accumulated juices. Sprinkle with chives, parsley, and pine nuts. Serve at once, with forks and knives to cut mushrooms.

Serves 4 as a main course

Baked Stuffed Portobello Caps

Large portobellos fairly cry out for dramatic whole-cap presentation. Here, a simple mince of the stems, herbs, and bell pepper adds flavor and color and prevents the caps from drying out as they bake. Serve with crusty bread as an appetizer, or to accompany grilled meat or fish.

1 teaspoon minced garlic
3 tablespoons olive oil

¼ teaspoon chilli flakes
6 portobello mushrooms (about 4 inches in diameter)
1 teaspoon kosher salt
½ cup fine-diced red bell pepper
1 tablespoon minced parsley leaves
1 teaspoon minced thyme leaves
¼ teaspoon coarse-ground pepper
Arugula, baby mustard, or mizuna leaves

1. Combine garlic and oil in small skillet. Cook over low heat to flavor oil but not to brown garlic, about 5 minutes. Add chilli flakes. Remove from heat.

2. Holding each mushroom upright by its stem, tap tops of caps to dislodge dirt from gills. Carefully cut off stems flush with caps. Clean gills with a soft brush. Paint caps sparingly with half the garlic oil—first outside, then inside. Set gill side up on a baking sheet. Sprinkle with ½ teaspoon salt; set aside to marinate.

3. Peel mushroom stems, then cut into fine dice. Combine in a bowl with bell pepper, parsley, and thyme. Add the remaining garlic oil, salt, and pepper. Let stand an hour or so, until somewhat juicy, tossing occasionally.

4. Preheat oven to 450°F. Divide stuffing among caps, spreading evenly. Set baking sheet on upper rack in oven. Bake until mushrooms are tender throughout—10 to 15 minutes. Serve hot.

Serves 6

Pros Propose

Chef Nora Pouillon cuts matching "checkers" of rutabaga and mushroom to layer in **Grilled Portobello-Rutabaga Napoleons:** With 2- to 3-inch cutter, cut rounds from grilled portobello caps. Cut discs the same size from steamed rutabaga; toss gently with vinaigrette. Sandwich alternating rounds in ring molds that fit tightly. To serve, unmold and drizzle with dressing of goat cheese pureed with garlic, lemon juice, and olive oil. Arrange on frisée; garnish with tiny dice of root vegetables.

Portobello "Pizza," from chef Tom Gray, makes use of a similar circular scheme: Toss portobello caps with balsamic vinegar, garlic, thyme, and olive oil. Roast in moderate oven, covered, until no longer pale in the center, about 20 minutes. Set on perforated pan to drain (collect the juices as a base for dressing for a mushroom salad). Top each cap with a neat round slice of mozzarella. Brush with pesto. Top with roasted pepper. Warm just until cheese is melted. Sprinkle with oregano.

Chef Joseph Schultz, who has always been fascinated by the cooking of ancient Rome, combines flavors of that era in **Cremini with Artichoke Hearts in Red Wine–Coriander Reduction:** Sauté quartered cremini and diced onion in olive oil until glazed. Add red wine, parboiled artichoke hearts, garlic, pepper, and a touch of red wine vinegar. Cook down to concentrate flavors and evaporate moisture. Serve dusted with toasted crushed coriander seeds.

Chef Brian Whitmer prepares a dark savory broth of portobello stems in which he arranges fans of roasted caps on cornmeal crostini. For **Roasted Portobello with Crisp Polenta:** Slowly brown sliced portobello stems in minimal oil until dark. Add sliced leek and celery, then vegetable stock, and simmer an hour. With hand mixer, whiz to break up vegetables. Continue cooking briefly; strain. Toss portobello caps with oil, rosemary, and garlic. Spread on baking sheet, cover with foil, and roast in hot oven until well cooked. Spoon fall vegetable ragoût into shallow bowls. Top each with a crisp-fried polenta rectangle, then sliced and fanned portobello caps. Add a little butter to the broth and ladle around.

Portobello Fries are a regular winner for chef Rick Hackett: Cut portobello caps into ½-inch strips. Dust with flour and dip into a wash of egg beaten with cream, then into Japanese bread crumbs (panko). Deep-fry and serve immediately.

Cresses

Including **water cress (cultivated and wild), upland cress, garden cress, winter cress, nasturtium (Indian cress)**

See also multiple names under each cress

cultivated water cress (*top*), upland cress (*center*), and wild water cress (*bottom*)

¼ actual size

This entry has two primary goals: To remind readers that water cress is not the sole such kicky little cress; and that it is not for salad alone. Water cress is different and delicious when cooked—as it often is in countries other than the United States.

Cress is a common name for more than a dozen sharp, pungent small-leafed plants from various families, a handful of which I've gathered here for description. Water cress, because it is the most widely cultivated and cooked, is first.

Water cress or watercress (*Rorippa nasturtium-aquaticum* and *Nasturtium officinale*) delivers a big flavor punch in its perky leaves, befitting its membership in the family often called mustard (also brassica and crucifer). That punch is the reason given for the scientific name *Nasturtium*, from *nasum tortus*, meaning "twisted nose," a description that the Roman naturalist Pliny attributed to its pungency. Whatever that explanation means, nasturtium is also the *common* name of a familiar and unrelated plant (page 229) that is also called cress!

Water cress has been valued as a food and medicine since ancient times, at the very least since the 4th century B.C., when the Greek historian Xenophon recommended it. Two thousand years later, Nicholas Culpeper's popular *Herbal* advised: "Water-cress pottage is a good remedy to cleanse the blood in the spring . . . and consumes the gross humours winter hath left behind: those that would live in health should use it freely. If any fancy not pottage, they may eat the herb as a salad." They still do both in England, Culpeper's country.

"Water cress soup is the favorite cleansing tonic in South China," says Cecilia Chiang, founder of the legendary Mandarin restaurants in Beverly Hills and San Francisco, "and beef stir-fried with water cress is a perfect match, but in a salad? Never!" Water cress is always cooked in China, but it brightens salads as well as soups and stir-fries in Thailand, Vietnam, Indonesia, and Japan, among other Eastern lands.

Of Eurasian origin, water cress now flourishes throughout the temperate zone. In North America, people of Asian origin are the largest group of water cress consumers, according to Andrew Brown, marketing manager for B&W Quality Growers, headquartered in Fellsmere, Florida (which claims to be the world's largest water cress producer). "I'd guestimate that about 50 million bunches—roughly 150 million pounds—are purchased each year in the Eastern United States and Canada and that one-third of that is by Asians," Brown says.

"Watercress will, the Chinese believe, cool one's system and thus provide wanted interior balance," writes Eileen Yin-Fei Lo (*From the Earth*). The cooling aspects

left to right: garden, upland, and curled micro-cresses

⅓ actual size

of the vegetable were also admired in early English herbals. Perhaps the cooling aspect results from the plant's habitat—slow running water, whether mountain stream or irrigated field. It is the "water" in "water cress" that provides its special succulence and distinguishes it from land cresses.

For **wild water cress** (the same species as the cultivated, which has naturalized), water is the problem. Pollution of streams, whether from industry or animals, is prevalent. Unless you are sure of your source of water or your forager, stick with the truly fine cultivated product. In any case, even though wild water cress may have a deeper, sharper flavor than the cultivated, it is remarkably similar—except that it has tougher stems and is potentially dangerous.

Upland cress or land cress (*Barbarea verna*) does grow on dry land, not in water. Confusingly, it is also known as American cress, despite its Old World origins; winter cress (also the name of another cress, below); Belle Isle cress; and scurvy grass. Its flavor is close to that of water cress but more refined and focused, less diffuse. The initial taste is mild but develops to a lingering sharpness, like water cress intensified. The elegant look is due in part to its diminutive dimensions and comparative fragility. For some reason, the slender-stalked, spoon-shaped leaves are grown for

market in micro, mini, and petite sizes, not to the fuller size of water cress. In the wild and the garden, it grows larger and stronger and tastes just fine. What comes to market is too delicate to cook. Enjoy it raw.

Garden cress or pepper cress (*Lepidium sativum*), although a single species (of African origin), is represented by a jumble of common names, leaf shapes, and sizes. Turid Forsyth and Merilyn Simonds Mohr, authors of *The Harrowsmith Salad Garden,* write that "garden cresses are such a large group that they can be subdivided again into four basic types: common cress, curled cress, broadleaf cress, and golden cress." Other gardening guides give different names as well.

Garden cresses are harvested tiny, as sprouts. They will be known to many as half of British mustard-and-cress, a venerable and justly celebrated duo. What all types of garden cress have in common is a hot-sweet peppery bite distinct from water cress. They taste more like leafy condiments (quite like fresh horseradish) than greens. Whether micro-wisps or blotter-planted seedlings, they pack a wallop. These little powerhouses are clearly meant to be enjoyed as a salad or garnish; they are too tiny to cook (although they wilt agreeably atop hot dishes).

Winter cress (*Barbarea vulgaris*), also called yellow rocket, does look like rocket (see arugula, page 26)

winter cress

²⁄₃ **actual size**

nasturtium leaves (Indian cress)   diameter: 2½–5 inches

crossed with water cress, which is what it tastes like too; but it is more forceful. "This dry-land cress, also called bitter cress, poorman's cabbage, and yellow rocket," writes Mark F. Sohn in *Hearty Country Cooking,* "is a green, and you can prepare it like turnip greens or collard greens. It grows up to two feet tall and in the southern Appalachians, it can be gathered all winter."

Gathering is the most usual way to obtain it (preferably smaller than 2 feet, however, unless you like ferociously bitter greens). Although winter cress can be found in seed catalogues, it is more often foraged, and even more often ripped out of gardens, where it is considered a weed by many. If those many cooked the deep-flavored water-cressy leaves, they might think again. Any dish that includes cooked water cress will be even better with winter cress. To be eaten raw, it must be picked when it is *minute* and mixed with milder leaves. It can be found in some farmers' markets and through specialty produce suppliers—rarely. But if foraging is part of your life, this is quite a treat, being the first wild green of the year.

Nasturtium (*Tropaeolum majus*), also called Indian cress and Peruvian cress, does originate in South America (one of those rare plants whose common name makes sense). It is the only non-crucifer cress in this entry, but it certainly tastes as if it came from the same group. The plant was introduced to Europe from Peru in 1684 and has since supplied the South of France and environs with the yellow-to-scarlet flowers that most assume are native.

When John Evelyn combined the botanical and colloquial nasturtiums in his *Acetaria: A Discourse of Sallets* (1699), this one was his clear favorite: "Cresses, Nasturtium, Garden Cresses; to be monthly sown: But above all the Indian, moderately hot, and aromatick, quicken the torpent Spirits, and purge the Brain."

Nasturtium was previously marketed as cress in the United States. William Woys Weaver writes in *Heirloom Vegetable Gardening* that the "Philadelphia botanist

John Bartram propagated and sold it in the 1760s under the name Great Garden Cress and probably grew it much earlier."

Nasturtium leaves appear in the market, but less often than their delectable flowers (off limits for this volume on vegetables). The large, uniform leaves pictured here come through restaurant suppliers. Should you spot blooms without leaves at a farmers' market, ask the grower to bring along the leaves next time. They have a vibrant bite and last longer than flowers. The "heat" of the leaves increases with the heat of the growing area, as is the case for all such greens. But no matter how nippy, all turn surprisingly tame once dressed or combined with other foods.

BASIC USE: What not to do with this charming array? Some reminders—and these are by no means the complete panorama of possibilities—may help your creative juices flow.

• Do not disdain cress sandwiches, which are among the finest of simple foods. "Nothing can challenge the perfect combination of good bread, salty butter, and peppery crisp cress," writes Jane Grigson (*Jane Grigson's Vegetable Book*). "Don't go for the genteel triangular mouthfuls—use proper slices and plenty of watercress [or any other cress except winter] so that it bursts cheerfully out at the sides." Avocado is a luscious (nutritionally correct) New World substitute for butter.

• Tiny cresses are perfect ready-made garnishes: Strew over soups or composed salads, wreathe around fish or meat, sprinkle on grain dishes, tuck tufts into canapés, cluster atop seafood dishes.

• Cut a fine chiffonade of nasturtium leaves to sprinkle over tomatoes, beans, eggs, potato salad, goat cheese—anywhere you would strew small cresses.

• For salad, complement cresses with salty and/or sweet ingredients: feta or ricotta salata, smoked meat or fish, fruits—such as citrus, apple, grapes, and pears—or beet, carrot, and tomato. Counter the forceful flavors with bland ones: potatoes, white beans, raw button mushrooms, tofu, creamy fresh white cheese, and rice.

• Arrange cresses as a bed for hot grilled meat, poultry, or fish, which agreeably wilt the leaves with their warm juices. Or top with grilled eggplant, squash, and tomatoes for a vegetarian meal.

• For cooked dishes, cresses' bitterness balances bland, sweet, and salty ingredients: potatoes, beans, tofu, rice,

pasta, corn, green peas, sugar snaps, sweet pepper, olives, anchovies, sharp cheeses, soy and tamari, fermented black beans, and smoked meat.

• For a quick sauce, puree cress with buttermilk or yogurt and seasonings. Whip up a speedy bright green spring soup by pureeing cress with scallion, fresh herbs, and broth, then adding buttermilk.

• Barely wilt water cress or winter cress in stir-fried dishes; stir into pasta and heat through over low heat; add to steamed fish as it finishes cooking. Avoid reheating cress dishes, which become extra-bitter.

• For clear soups, simmer water cress or winter cress stems with broth to flavor it; strain. Then stir in seafood or poultry bits to match the broth, then add the leaves at the last. For thick soups, cook cresses with potatoes or beans, then puree.

SELECTION: We seem to be enjoying more and more water cress, for it has recently become a year-round crop. Water cress usually matures in about 6 weeks and is harvested by hand. A second growth and harvest follow this, and sometimes a third, each crop progressively thicker-stemmed. Beginning in Pennsylvania and moving south as winter approaches, harvesting winds up in Florida, which, with California, produces the bulk of the crop in the United States.

Choose only water cress that is in top form. It spoils quickly and tastes nasty when it is over the hill. Look for rich greens with no trace of yellow. Cress displayed on ice is best. Sniff to be sure there is no hint of the old radish smell that afflicts elderly crucifers. If the bunch is bound with a band (paper cones are best, but rare), check beneath it for slipperiness.

Upland and garden cresses and their kin grow like small trees from plugs of sandy soil or blotter paper; or they are clipped and tumbled in plastic containers. All should be perky and smell peppery, not fishy or old radishy. None should be slippery or yellowing.

STORAGE: For water cress, remove the band, if any. Discard any slippery greens. Set stems in a jar of water, cover leaves with plastic, and refrigerate. Alternatively, trim stems as needed; swish in cool water and lift out. Drain, then spin-dry. Pack into plastic bags and refrigerate. Keep little sprouts and seedlings in their packing. Store water cress and seedlings no more than 4 or 5 days.

PREPARATION: How you trim water cress stems depends upon their coarseness, which varies considerably with variety, weather, and time of year. Chew before you cut. Some stems are delicate and tender; some are so tough that the leaves should be stripped and the stems discarded. If you have the patience, stripping rather than cutting makes for a more tender, uniform effect for garnishing leaves. For cooked dishes, virtually all stems can be included.

Do not rinse garden and upland cress and nasturtiums until you are ready to serve them. Be very gentle, so as not to bruise the leaves. Spin-dry or blot dry.

Water Cress and Orange Tabbouleh

This unusual form of the popular Middle Eastern green and grain salad has more herbal variety and punch than the original. Water cress gives textural definition, sharp flavoring, and a tonic bitter freshness to the soaked wheat grains, while orange adds sweetness and color, and its aromatic zest.

    1 cup medium or coarse bulgur wheat
    1 large bunch water cress (or nasturtium
        leaves; see Note)
    1 medium bunch mint
    1 medium bunch dill
    3 or 4 medium green scallions (green onions),
        sliced
    3 small oranges, well scrubbed
    1 teaspoon kosher salt
    ¼ teaspoon ground cinnamon
    Optional: ⅛ to ¼ teaspoon ground
        hot pepper
    1 lemon
    2 tablespoons full-flavored olive oil
    ½ cup lightly toasted walnuts
    1 small head romaine lettuce, rinsed and dried

1. Combine wheat with boiling water to cover by several inches. Soak until grains are plumped and no longer hard, 15 to 30 minutes. Pour into a sieve and press to drain. Leave in sieve and, every now and then, fluff and bounce to dry out as you prepare the other ingredients.

2. Sample cress stems; if fibrous, trim as needed. Rinse cress and spin-dry. Reserve some sprigs for garnish. Thin-slice lower cress stems; slice upper parts about ½ inch wide. Strip leaves from mint and dill; discard stalks. Rinse and spin-dry leaves. Bunch and slice leaves, then mince together with scallions. Toss with cress. (You should have about 1 quart.)

3. Grate zest from 1 orange. Halve and juice the orange. Combine juice, zest, salt, cinnamon, and optional hot pepper. Halve lemon. Squeeze juice from one half and add to orange mixture. Slice the other half for garnish.

4. Toss together wheat, half the juice mixture, and 1 tablespoon olive oil. Add the chopped greens, remaining juice mixture, and remaining 1 tablespoon oil; toss. Chill 1 hour or more, as convenient.

5. Taste and season. To serve, cut peel and pith from remaining 2 oranges. Section by cutting between membranes to release sections; then halve. Chop walnuts. Save smallest romaine leaves for garnish. Stack and slice enough remaining leaves to make 2 cups thin ribbons. Toss with wheat mixture, oranges, and nuts. Garnish with cress, the small romaine leaves, and lemon slices.

Serves 4 to 6

Note: If you have nasturtium leaves, cut into very fine strips, and substitute about half as much as water cress.

Rotini with Water Cress, Sweet Pepper, Pine Nuts, and Garlic

A pleasingly chewy texture (from both braised and raw cress), bright coloring, speedy preparation, and an attractive sweet-bitter balance make this a useful meal-in-a-bowl. If rotini (corkscrew) pasta is not easy to come by, use farfalle (butterflies). For variation, substitute ½ cup grated Parmesan for the pine nuts.

    1 bunch water cress
    1 red bell pepper
    1 tablespoon full-flavored olive oil
    1 tablespoon minced garlic
    1 cup vegetable or chicken broth
    ½ pound imported Italian rotini pasta
    Salt and pepper
    1½ tablespoons toasted pine nuts

1. Cut apart and separate water cress leaves and stems. Examine leafy parts and snap off any stems to add to stem pile. Slice stems thin; keep leaves whole. Cut bell pepper into small dice.

2. Heat oil in medium skillet over moderately low heat. Add garlic and stir until barely golden—not browned. Add red pepper and toss. Add broth and cress stems. Raise heat, and boil a few minutes to reduce liquid by about half, stirring often.

3. Meanwhile, boil pasta in plenty of salted water until almost al dente. Drain and return to pot.

4. Add cress mixture to pasta. Toss a few minutes over moderately low heat until most liquid is absorbed. Season. Off heat, stir in cress leaves and toss.

5. Serve in shallow bowls, sprinkled with pine nuts.

Serves 2 as a main course

Gingery Water Cress–Topped Tofu

A good last-minute dinner for a busy day: Bean curd poached to puffy tenderness is smothered in a chewy tangle of gingery stir-fried water cress. If you aren't near a good Asian or natural foods market for the real thing, buy packaged, refrigerated tofu rather than the bland shelf-stable types. Medium-to-firm is easiest to handle.

   1 bunch water cress
   2 scallions (green onions)
   1 block medium-firm tofu (about 10 ounces)
   ⅔ cup vegetable, mushroom, or chicken broth
   2 teaspoons shoyu (Japanese soy sauce) or
       tamari sauce
   1 teaspoon Asian (dark) sesame oil
   1½ teaspoons cornstarch
   ½ teaspoon sugar
   1 tablespoon peanut oil
   1 tablespoon very fine ginger julienne
   2 teaspoons toasted sesame seeds

1. Taste cress stems and trim as necessary. Cut cress into 2-inch lengths. Rinse, then spin-dry. Spread on towel. Trim scallions and cut apart dark and light parts; thin-slice both.

2. Cut tofu crosswise into 3 pieces. Arrange in skillet to fit closely in a single layer. Add broth, soy, and sesame oil. Bring to a simmer. Reduce heat, cover, and poach gently 15 minutes. With slotted spoon, transfer tofu to serving dish (save cooking liquid). Dice or slice.

3. Toss cress in bowl with cornstarch and sugar. Heat wok or large sauté pan over moderately high heat. Add peanut oil and tip to coat pan. Add ginger and pale part of scallions and toss 30 seconds. Add cress and toss until barely wilted. Add reserved cooking liquid and bring to a boil, stirring. Add scallion greens and sesame seeds.

4. Spoon over tofu and serve at once.

Serves 2 as a main dish

Sesame Noodles with Radishes and Garden or Upland Cress

Red radishes and cress sprouts tossed with a silky tangle of fine, pale Japanese noodles make a light main dish—especially useful at a buffet, barbecue, or picnic, where room-temperature food is a boon. Or serve as both starch and vegetable for broiled fish or poultry.

Whether sold loose or growing upright like a miniature forest, these cute mini-greens pack quite a punch. Garden cress (pepper cress) is nicely nippy, but just about any sprouted cress (or mustard or radish) will sharpen the mild noodles. If the dish seems bland to you, turn up the heat with a spritz of hot pepper sauce. If your peanut oil is pale (not roasted), add 1 teaspoon Asian (dark) sesame oil.

   2 tablespoons sesame seeds
   ¼ teaspoon fine-grated lime zest
   About 2 tablespoons lime juice
   3 tablespoons peanut oil (preferably roasted)
   About 2 tablespoons shoyu (Japanese soy sauce)
   1 teaspoon honey
   ½ pound somen (thin Japanese wheat-flour
       noodles)
   1 medium-large carrot
   About 2 cups loose cress (or radish) sprouts
       (2 ounces), or 2 containers of growing sprouts
       (about 4 ounces each)
   About ½ cup diced red radishes

Thin-sliced green part of 1 medium scallion (green onion)

1. In small pan, stir sesame seeds over low heat until tan, about 5 minutes. Crush 1 tablespoon of seeds in suribachi or mortar. Blend in lime zest, 2 tablespoons lime juice, peanut oil, 2 tablespoons shoyu, and honey. (Alternatively, combine these ingredients in a blender and whirl to crush seeds.) Reserve remaining seeds.

2. Drop somen into a large quantity of boiling water. Boil, stirring frequently, until tender, about 2 minutes. Drain. Rinse and drain again. Combine in a serving bowl with sesame dressing. Toss to coat strands thoroughly. Keep at room temperature.

3. To serve, pare carrot, then zip into thin curls with a vegetable peeler. Add to noodles with three-quarters of the sprouts and ½ cup radishes. Toss gently with your hands to combine evenly. Taste and add more sprouts, radishes, shoyu, and lime juice as needed. Sprinkle remaining sesame seeds and scallion over salad.

Serves 4 as a main course, 6 as a side dish

Chilled Pureed Winter Cress (or Garlic Mustard) Soup

Winter cress and garlic mustard (see page 411), separately or together, work wonders for simple leek and potato soup. Add a dose of nettles (see page 417) for even more springiness. Cool and tangy, the celery-green soup, flecked with deep green, tastes fresh and leafy.

I find that assertive greens offer the most complexity and vividness when some are cooked and some are pureed raw and stirred in later to brighten taste and color. The intensity of wild foods varies dramatically: Adjust balance by taste, not by the numbers.

¼ pound young winter cress and/or garlic
    mustard (4 cups)
1 pound potatoes
1 medium leek
1 tablespoon olive oil
2 small celery stalks with leaves, sliced
3 to 4 cups light vegetable broth or water
1 teaspoon kosher salt (omit if broth is salted)
½ to 1 cup whole-milk or low-fat yogurt

1. Rinse cress several times. Peel potatoes. Cut into ½-inch slices. Trim and discard roots and darkest top parts of leek. Halve stalk lengthwise. Then slice crosswise. Wash in several changes of water.

2. Heat oil in heavy pot over moderately low heat. Stir in leek and celery and cook, stirring often, until slightly tender, about 5 minutes. Add potatoes, half the cress, 3 cups broth (or water), and salt. Simmer, covered, until potatoes are soft, about 20 minutes. Let cool slightly or completely, as convenient.

3. With slotted spoon, transfer solids to food processor. Puree until smooth, then gradually add cooking liquid. Season. Cool, then chill.

4. Save a dozen cress leaves for garnish. Puree remainder with ½ cup yogurt to smooth texture. Stir into soup. Add additional broth (or water), salt, and yogurt to taste. Chill well.

5. Serve in small bowls garnished with cress leaves.

Serves 4 as a first course

Cucumber, Green Bean, and Nasturtium Salad

This beautiful, essence-of-summer salad comes from Barbara Spiegel, who prepares it with teeny-tiny nasturtiums she grows on Cape Cod—smaller than any you'll find in the market. Taste as you add the leaves. As with arugula or other nippy greens, "heat" varies considerably. The cucumber crunch suits the al dente bite of the beans; the nasturtium becomes an integral part of the whole, not a mere garnish.

1½ tablespoons rice vinegar
1 teaspoon kosher salt
1 tablespoon chopped fresh tarragon
    leaves
¼ cup mild vegetable oil, such as grapeseed
    or safflower
3 medium unwaxed cucumbers
    (about 1½ pounds)
1 pound slim green beans, preferably
    haricots verts (filet beans)
⅓ to ½ cup thin-sliced nasturtium
    leaves
16 or so small nasturtium blossoms

1. For vinaigrette: Combine vinegar, ½ teaspoon salt, tarragon, and oil in a jar and shake to blend well. Set aside.

2. Peel cucumbers, then halve lengthwise; scoop out seeds. Cut slices about ⅛ inch wide. Sprinkle with remaining ½ teaspoon salt; set aside.

3. Trim beans (halve, if long). Cook in boiling salted water until just barely tender, about 3 to 4 minutes. Drain, then refresh in ice water. Drain well, then combine in medium bowl with two-thirds of the vinaigrette.

4. Drain cucumbers; pat dry. Toss with nasturtium leaves and remaining vinaigrette. Mix with beans. Top with blossoms.

Serves 4

Nasturtium-Leaf Butter

Bright pistachio-lime green, this deeply nasturtium-flavored butter—its texture lightened with sour cream—holds plenty of pungent leaves. Quick to make, thanks to a food processor's power, it jazzes up the plainest canapés or sandwiches and fancifies simple poached or broiled fish. Or toss with hot blanched haricots verts, cooked baby carrots, or steamed potatoes.

> **¾ cup packed sliced nasturtium leaves**
>   **(about 20 large leaves)**
> **8 tablespoons (1 stick) salted butter, at room**
>   **temperature**
> **1 tablespoon lemon juice**
> **2 tablespoons sour cream**
> **Green part from 1 medium scallion**
>   **(green onion), sliced**

Combine all ingredients in food processor fitted with metal blade. Whiz until bright and smooth. Pack into small crock and refrigerate.

Makes about ¾ cup

Variation

Nasturtium-Leaf Butter Pats

To prepare butter pats to serve atop grilled steaks or hamburgers, veal chops, or fish steaks, omit the sour cream. Form the butter into a cylinder on a sheet of waxed paper. Roll up paper and close ends. Freeze. To serve, cut discs from the frozen log and set one on each portion of meat or fish.

Pros Propose

Cress is familiar in salads, but this one is a little off the beaten track, as are most recipes from Viana La Place. For **Old-Fashioned Potato and Nasturtium Salad:** Simmer medium new potatoes until just tender. Drain; cool slightly, then cut into small dice. Combine potatoes in a bowl with plenty of chopped nasturtium leaves, chopped dill pickle, capers (or pickled nasturtium buds), and minced garlic. Add olive oil, red wine vinegar, and seasoning, and toss gently. Mound on a platter, top with parsley, then "use scissors to cut nasturtium petals into strips, working directly over the salad and letting them cascade over the top" (from *Unplugged Kitchen*).

Soups are cooked cresses' forte, whether broths, thick pottages, or silky creams. Asian soups are quick to prepare and of a similar style, whether Chinese, Thai, or Vietnamese—the nationality of this **Watercress-Shrimp Soup:** Remove shells from medium shrimp and combine shells with pork or chicken broth. Simmer about 5 minutes. Devein shrimp. Pound thin-sliced shallots to a paste in mortar. Add shrimp, fish sauce, and pepper. Pound lightly to flatten shrimp and incorporate flavors. Remove shells from broth. Add shrimp mixture and cook 1 minute. Add water cress cut into large pieces (or whole, in authentic style) and stir to wilt. Season and serve (from *Simple Art of Vietnamese Cooking* by Binh Duong and Marcia Kiesel).

"Watercress is used extensively in Alsace, where it is a common crop," writes chef Hubert Keller (*The Cuisine of Hubert Keller*), who remembers appreciating its peppery flavor there even as a child. His **Watercress, Bay Scallop, and Potato Soup** is adapted from the famed frogs' legs soup of his mentor, Paul Haeberlin. To prepare: Gently cook minced onion and thin-sliced white of leek in olive oil until soft. Add vegetable broth, a little diced potato, and seasoning. Cook until soft. Add chopped tender stems and leaves of water cress (equal in volume to broth) and simmer 5 minutes. Add a touch of cream; simmer a moment. Whiz until smooth in blender. Season and reheat. Meanwhile, season rinsed, well-dried bay scallops. Sauté a minute in hot olive oil. Set scallops in shallow bowls, ladle in soup, and garnish with cress.

"In rural areas, wild watercress (called creasies, field cress, pepper grass, 'cressies,' or 'creasy greens') are found along slow moving streams and around the edges of lakes," writes Sarah Belk in *Around the Southern Table*. For a contemporary approach to Southern greens, cultivated cress is "sautéed with radicchio and served warm, sprinkled with homemade pepper vinegar, a milder version of the fiery Dixie condiment of vinegar infused with Tabasco peppers." For her **Sautéed Watercress and Radicchio with Pepper Vinegar:** Steep hot pepper flakes overnight in distilled white vinegar (2 teaspoons per ½ cup). Strain. Melt plenty of butter in skillet over fairly low heat. Add well-trimmed water cress and separated leaves of small radicchio. Cover and cook a few minutes, tossing occasionally, until wilted but still crisp-tender. Serve hot, with pepper vinegar on the side.

Crosne (Chinese), Japanese Artichoke

(*Stachys affinis* and *S. sieboldii*)

Also choro-gi (Japanese)

Why is this crisp, pearly little tuber called crosne (pronounced crone)? Is it Chinese, and if so why is it absent from Chinese culinary texts? Ditto for the Japanese. Why artichoke?

I can answer only the first question with assurance. Crosne is the market name in the United States for the tiny tuberette pictured, which is usually imported from France with that name. But why from France if it is Oriental? Twenty pages of the fascinating history by Paillieux and Bois, *Le potager d'un curieux* (second edition, 1892), tell all. In brief: These authors, whose plant introductions changed the gardens and farms of Europe, received *Stachys* rhizomes at the Botanical Garden in Paris in 1882 from an important collector of Chinese plants, Dr. Bretschneider. Paillieux was wildly enthusiastic, rented land near his own garden, and began serious production of the vegetable, a member of the mint family (Labiatae). "Convinced that the words *Stachys affinis* could not be pronounced by our cooks, I gave the little tubers the name of Crosnes, which is that of my village," he explains. Voilà! They were officially introduced as Crosnes du Japon (why, when they came from Peking, I cannot say) but crosne later became the usual name.

The vegetable flourished beyond the town, too, thanks to a far-reaching marketing and distribution campaign by Paillieux. From 1887 on, the plant became increasingly popular throughout Europe, where it is still cultivated (though not nearly as widely as in Paillieux's time). Chinese artichoke was the name adopted in England, according to Paillieux. The reference is probably to the native American sunchoke or Jerusalem artichoke (page 631), which crosne resembles in flavor, and which has nothing whatsoever to do with Jerusalem or artichokes. It was introduced to the United States in 1890 under a name destined to disappear: "One of the leading promoters of the vegetable in this country was the seed firm of V. H. Hallock & Sons in Queens, New York," writes William Woys Weaver in *Heirloom Vegetable Gardening*, "which adver-

actual size

tised this 'wonderful new food' . . . [as] Vegetable White Bait." About the same time, in Italy, "M. Bullo . . . proposed the name Tuberina for the plant, which has the merit of being easy and short," noted Paillieux. A trifle silly, perhaps, but the name is closer to reality than what we have. Too bad it didn't take.

Chef Roland Liccioni and other chefs with a French culinary background are disappointed not to find crosnes growing in the United States. "I have a passion for them," Liccioni says, "so I began growing them at home in Mettawa (near Chicago) about 10 years ago. They resist the cold very well and grow like crazy." He considers the results superior: "When they grow in the soil here, they are beautiful and pale, just as they should be. In France, they grow them in sand and they are not as pale or tasty. I'd use them more, but people in Illinois seem to want them only as garnish."

As for discovering how crosne is cooked in its native China and Japan, Paillieux and Bois didn't fare any better than I. "We do not know how the Chinese prepare them for the table," they report. (To add to the confusion, the *New Columbia Encyclopedia* of 1975 claimed that the native North American Jerusalem artichoke is the vegetable popular in China.) For Japan, they found only this: "Choro-gi has tuberous roots which resemble caterpillars; they are conserved, to be eaten, in plum vinegar." They seem to be rare in Japan at present, according to chef Masaharu Morimoto: "When I did a television program in Japan, people did not know any more what are chorogi. I had to explain. Now it is only for New Year and very few persons use it."

BASIC USE: Crosne's unique appearance, juicy crunch, and lightly earthy, nutty flavor make it a natural garnish. I prefer it cooked to the point where it no longer tastes raw but has not lost its crunchy edge—whether boiled, steamed, sautéed, or roasted. Sauté in butter and/or nut oil to garnish poultry, veal, seafood, or vegetable dishes—particularly dark-green or orange foods, which make a handsome backdrop for the twirly crosne pieces. Or blanch, chill, and marinate.

Paillieux and Bois made the following suggestions in 1892. On the basis of present experience, I support them all: One does not peel crosnes; it is enough to scrub them carefully. If they stay too long on the fire, water penetrates and they become pasty and bland. Cook them as you would fresh green beans. They are delicious as a garnish for veal ragoût. They are excellent fried; cook a day before, chill, then batter-dip and fry the next day. One also eats them au gratin.

SELECTION AND STORAGE: Look for pale, firm crosnes during the winter. They are perishable and expensive, but a little goes a very long way: 4 ounces equals about 40 of the odd squiggles (like swirled seashells or pointed grubs, depending on your frame of reference). The paler the fresher; but they're fine eating as long as they are hard. Refrigerate in a basket or open container up to a week.

PREPARATION: Discard any flabby tubers. Rinse crosnes, then spread on a towel; sprinkle liberally with coarse salt. Twist and rub to remove most of the skins, as you would nut husks. Or sprinkle wet tubers with salt in coarse-mesh sieve and rub to remove the skin. Rinse; trim any loose rootlets.

Basic Sautéed Crosnes

This is a simple, savory way to prepare curious little crosnes, which are most appealing in small portions, especially as a garnish for poultry, seafood, or veal. Or serve as a more generous side dish by mixing with other vegetables, such as miniature carrots, snow peas, or asparagus slices. Or arrange crosnes as decorative crunch atop winter squash puree or braised chard or spinach.

About 10 ounces crosnes
Kosher salt
1 tablespoon butter
1 tablespoon lemon juice
½ teaspoon sugar
Optional: chervil or dill sprigs

1. Discard any flabby crosnes; rinse remainder. Spread on towel and sprinkle generously with kosher salt. Twist and rub tubers in towel to scrape off skin, as you would nut husks. (Alternatively, salt wet tubers in coarse-mesh sieve, then rub and scrub against side to scrape fairly clean.) Rinse. Trim any rootlets.

2. Melt butter over moderately low heat in skillet large enough to hold crosnes in a close single layer. Add the tubers and a few spoonfuls of water. Cover and simmer until they just lose their raw crunch, about 4 minutes.

3. Uncover, raise heat slightly, and add lemon juice, sugar, and ¼ teaspoon salt. Toss over moderate heat to glaze crosnes lightly, about 2 minutes. Finish with optional herb sprigs.

Serves 4 as a garnish or side dish

Marinated Crosne and Cherry Tomato Salad with Dill

Perfect picnic or buffet fare, petite crosnes are barely cooked, then marinated in a delicate vinaigrette. They emerge delightfully crisp, pale, and pearly from their bath. Substitute tarragon or chervil for dill, if desired. For a meaty approach, add very thin strips of smoked ham or turkey and increase the amount of dressing. Mirin is found in Japanese and natural food shops and some supermarkets.

¾ pound crosnes
Kosher salt
2 small scallions (green onions)
2 tablespoons rice vinegar
½ teaspoon dried dill
2 tablespoons mirin (syrupy Japanese rice wine)
2 tablespoons corn oil (preferably unrefined)
1 pint grape tomatoes or small cherry tomatoes
Optional: fine-snipped fresh dill
Bibb lettuce for serving

1. Rinse crosnes. Spread on towel and sprinkle generously with a handful of coarse salt. Twist and rub tubers in towel to scrape off skin, as you would nut husks. (Alternatively, salt wet tubers in coarse-mesh sieve, then rub to scrape fairly clean.) Rinse. Trim loose rootlets.

2. Drop crosnes into plenty of boiling salted water. Return to a boil and cook until they barely lose their raw crunch, a minute or two. Drain, then refresh in cold water. Drain and spread out to dry and cool.

3. Cut apart light and dark scallion parts. Mince light parts. In a small bowl, combine with vinegar, ¼ teaspoon salt, dried dill, and mirin, blending well. Add oil and whisk to emulsify. Transfer crosnes to bowl and pour over the dressing. Chill a few hours.

4. To serve: Halve tomatoes, thin-slice scallion greens, and add both to crosnes with optional dill. Season, then spoon onto lettuce leaves.

Serves 4

Pros Propose

Fricassee of Périgord Truffles and Crosnes is one of those rare dishes that result when a few perfect ingredients come together in the hands of a purist. Chef Jean Joho serves the black and white tubers thus: Blanch cleaned crosnes in salted water to barely cook. Melt butter in small pan and add whole black truffle and crosnes. Cook, tightly covered, over very low heat just to develop the perfume and flavors—no more. Remove truffle. Quickly slice and return to pan, shaking to mix. Add a touch of butter, season, and serve at once.

Chef Joho goes from the sublime to a conversation piece that beats maguey worms in mezcal—but somewhat resembles them. For **Pickled Crosnes for Martinis:** Combine white wine vinegar, bay leaf, garlic cloves, mustard seeds, thyme, tarragon, salt, pepper, and fennel seeds ("go light on the seasonings"). Boil, then pour over cleaned crosnes in a quart jar. Chill 3 months or so before serving.

The New Year's dish chef Morimoto mentioned earlier is **Pink Pickled Chorogi on Black Soybeans:** Blanch cleaned chorogi (crosnes) just until barely tender. Marinate in rice vinegar, salt, sugar, and red shiso (perilla) leaves overnight in refrigerator. Boil black soybeans until tender, then simmer with sugar, soy, and dashi. Serve in a little bowl with the pickled chorogi on top.

Anita Lo served this dish at the Korean-inspired Mirezi restaurant in New York City when she was the executive chef. Both fresh and pickled crosnes play parts in **Mackerel Tartare with Crosnes:** Heat red wine vinegar with a little sugar and salt and pour over crosnes. Let cool, then refrigerate overnight. Briefly blanch fresh crosnes just until starchy taste is gone. Slice into rounds and mix with fine-diced sushi-quality mackerel. Season with lemon, olive oil, chives, tarragon, capers, and a touch of mustard. Mold into the center of each plate, then garnish with some pickled crosnes and a few drops of lemon-mustard vinaigrette.

Cucumber

Including **American pickling, American slicing, Middle Eastern, Oriental, European greenhouse** (all *Cucumis sativus*)

Also **Armenian cucumber** (*Cucumis melo,* Flexuosus Group)

Why cucumbers? (Doesn't everyone know about cucumbers?) Because the time is ripe for a cucumber revolution. Refuse to buy pumped-up, tasteless, seedy blimps with greasy, thick, nasty skin masquerading as cucumbers! Tomato lovers have rallied and restored some valuable forms of the fruit to the market. If some readers are too young or inexperienced to have enjoyed the clean crunch and sweet grassy perfume of this refreshing cucurbit as it is meant to be, they can (albeit with some effort) find examples of the real thing at farmers' markets and Asian groceries (Japanese, Middle Eastern, Indian, etc.).

Different types of cucumbers are favored in different parts of the world and named after those parts, broadly speaking. The plant breeder Todd C. Wehner, a professor of horticultural science at North Carolina State University, says that the major types grown for fresh markets worldwide are described as European (or Dutch) greenhouse slicers, Middle Eastern slicers, Oriental slicers, American slicers, and American picklers—

top row: European greenhouse, American pickling, Middle Eastern slicing
bottom row: Oriental (Japanese) slicing, American slicing, Oriental (Korean) slicing

⅓ actual size

informal but comprehensible catchalls for a huge number of cultivars that can be similar or distinct. For brevity, I'll drop the slicing and pickling, except in the case of American cucumbers, which are marketed in those two forms.

American slicing cucumbers are the ones to boycott. They have cultivar names that sound like racing cars and recreational vehicles: Speedway, Panther, Dasher, Daytona, Turbo, Early Triumph, Whopper, Thunder, etc. Maybe the greasy wax usually applied is to help them move with the speed of lightning. Obviously bigger, heavier, and meaner than other types, they are also flavorless and soggy—whether because of the way they are grown or because of the cultivars themselves, I do not know. Of the dozen I sampled, most were just water and crunch. If other types are not available, you can peel and seed these for soups and beverages.

A report from Todd Wehner notes that of the major commercial varieties grown in the world today, "all cucumber types have thin-skinned fruits except for the American slicer, which was bred for a thick skin for good keeping ability and protection during shipping."

American pickling cucumbers are usually relatively short, thick, and warted with pale striping and skin that may be light to dark. They appear in a range of uneven sizes and shapes, some blocky, some pointed, some curved. Their uniformly solid crunch, evenly distributed juiciness, and fresh, lightly sweet flavor have made them the preferred choice in America for those who care. They are still used for pickling, but in recent years they are also "being used for fresh consumption in the United States because their fruits are smaller and thinner-skinned than American slicer fruits," says Wehner.

Although they are sometimes called Kirbys, this is a misnomer. A cucumber called Kirby Stays Green (and other names) was introduced in 1920 by I. N. Simon & Son in Philadelphia and registered under the name of its developer, Norval E. Kirby, a company employee. Susceptible to disease, it disappeared from the market in the mid-1930s, but the name remained, particularly on the East Coast, and is used to signify pickling-type cucumbers in general.

European greenhouse cucumbers (also called Dutch greenhouse or hothouse cucumbers) are the super-long, smooth, dark ones sold in shrink-wrapped plastic sheaths. Extremely thin-skinned, straight, virtu-

ally seedless, and waste-free, they taper at the tip, sometimes to a nipple shape that seems to mock their neat uniformity. Very smooth, barely ridged, totally wart-free, they are perfect physical specimens. More often than not, they also have a fine consistent crunch and a refreshing, mild-sweet flavor, although some tend to be bland. For presentation and reliable good taste, these can't be beaten.

Middle Eastern cucumbers are also called Beit Alpha types, after the original cultivars, which probably came from Israel in the early 1900s. Those pictured have a typically multicultural American background: They were labeled "Persian cucumbers" and grown in Baja California (Mexico). Whatever their pedigree, Middle Eastern–type cucumbers are almost always exceptional. Thin-skinned and smooth, they are lightly ridged, slim, relatively small, and fairly straight (with a few curvy ones), tapered toward the bud end. Superficially, they look like small versions of the European greenhouse types—although they are raised in both greenhouses and fields. The slightly green, sweet flesh is evenly crunchy, uniformly juicy (not watery), and fine-textured. The flavor is refreshing, charming, truly cucumber.

Oriental cucumbers, the uniquely crunchy slivers at the heart of the best kappa-maki, those purest of sushi rolls, have been developed for their concentrated crispness and deep flavor. They exist in a dramatic range of lengths, colors, and gradations of flavor from mild to bitter. Most are long, narrow, and warted (both of those pictured are on the plump side) and may have conspicuous dark or light spines, which are easily brushed off. Examples I've found in Korean markets have been light-colored—a mottled pistachio-cream— while those in Japanese markets have been uniformly green, smoother, and straighter. In all Oriental cultivars sampled, the skin (more defined than in the Middle Eastern types) and flesh are smoothly integrated; there should be no need to peel. The green flesh has a pickly crunch and an even distribution of juice. The flavor is rich, slightly earthy, and not sweet at all—but delicious, matching the fresh green scent.

Armenian cucumber (*Cucumis melo,* Flexuosus Group), also known as serpent or snake melon, is a different species from cucumber (grouped botanically with melon), although it looks and acts like a cucumber. Not a common grocery item, it is, however, intriguing enough to warrant mention in case you

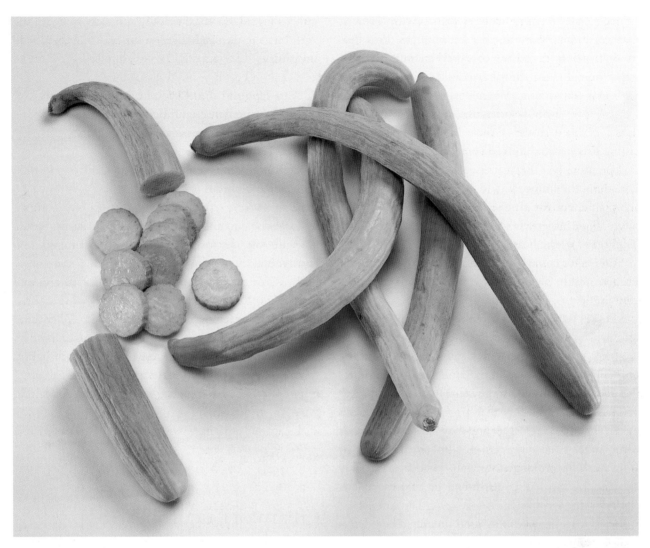

Armenian cucumber   ½ **actual size**

should come across it—most likely in an Indian or Middle Eastern grocery. "It was introduced from Armenia into Italy in the 1400s along with the true cantaloupe and raised off and on by European horticulturists since then," writes William Woys Weaver in *Heirloom Vegetable Gardening,* adding that "American gardeners in the past seem to have grown it more for display purposes than eating."

This is a shame, for while the curious chartreuse crescents and coils, downy and ribbed, are charming to behold, they do make good eating. Cut, the ribs form scalloped slices and the raw flesh is pale and very crisp. The almost nonexistent matte skin has an indescribable flavor like that of no other cucumber, as if it had imbibed the smell of an Indian grocery store. (Or could this be the plastic bags I carried it in?) A touch waxy, the flesh is very mild, with a light citric finish and a dis-

tinct sweetness. A pretty natural garnish in shape, size, and color (although those pictured are a moment beyond their finest hour).

BASIC USE: Cucumbers for salads and pickles are well known and need no elaboration in this book. A few reminders about raw cucumbers: Use as you would citrus slices to perfume and brighten mixed drinks, wine punch, lemonade, limeade, plain water, or sparkling water. Puree with yogurt and fresh herbs for quick cold soups. Puree with buttermilk or yogurt and ice for refreshing drinks, sweet or savory.

Most of all, don't forget warm or cooked cucumbers, which are still news, even to some accomplished cooks. Two revelations stand out in my memory: In 1961, when I was cutting my culinary teeth, *The New York Times Cook Book,* edited by Craig Claiborne, appeared. Page 376 of my copy is stained with turmeric from an Indonesian dish, atjar ketimun (see Pros Propose), that introduced me to wilted cucumber and to Asian aromatics. In 1968, Julia Child's *The French Chef Cookbook* was published. Her Potage aux Concombres became one of my favorite first courses for company meals. Thickened with Cream of Wheat (farina) and tasting primarily of cooked cucumbers, it has stood up to repetition over the years (see a variation, this page). For soups, the European and American cucumbers are acceptable; but for sautés, the Eastern types are infinitely superior—their color, flavor, and crunch are heightened by the heat.

Sources for cooked cucumber recipes follow in Pros Propose, just in case you haven't yet explored this delicious subject.

SELECTION: Most cucumbers are available year-round, primarily from Mexico and Florida. Summer is the peak season for the widest range of types and the only time I have seen the Armenians. Cucumbers should be solid from stem to stern, with no soft spots or shriveling. Avoid any that are turning yellow; this means they are overmature and may have begun to become watery and pithy. Do not buy cucumbers that are waxed (for prolonged storage). They are invariably tasteless cultivars. And you should be able to eat cucumber skin.

STORAGE: Cucumbers spoil quickly. They dehydrate rapidly and deteriorate if kept too warm or too cold (below 45° F). Buy them from a store where there is regular turnover. Keep for a few days at the very most. Wrap in a paper towel, enclose in a plastic bag, and store in the warmest part of your refrigerator.

PREPARATION: The peel and seeds are edible and good in most properly grown cucumbers except American slicing types. Taste each cucumber to determine individually whether the skin is too bitter or tough or the seeds too large or too hard to suit your taste and the recipe.

Sautéed Eastern Cucumber Slices

Oriental, Middle Eastern, and Armenian cucumbers demonstrate their bright coloring, sweet and green flavor, and solid crunch when merely sliced, salted, and quick-sautéed. Both the look and taste suggest the very best of cuke and zuke—a superior quick-cooked side dish for seafood, poultry, veal, or pilafs.

¾ **to 1 pound slim Oriental, Middle Eastern, or Armenian cucumbers**
½ **teaspoon kosher salt**
1 **tablespoon butter**
Optional: chervil leaves, snipped dill, and/or chives

1. Rinse cucumbers. Cut into ¼-inch slices. Sprinkle with salt and toss. Let stand 15 to 30 minutes, as convenient.

2. Rinse slices in sieve, bouncing so all are well rinsed. Spread on towel. Pat dry.

3. Melt butter over moderate heat in skillet large enough to hold slices in a single layer. Add cucumbers and toss often, shaking the pan until slices are lightly speckled with gold and raw taste disappears, about 3 minutes or so, or somewhat longer for the Armenian type.

4. Sprinkle sparingly with optional herbs. Serve hot.

Serves 2 to 3

Cream of Cucumber Soup with Herbs

This soup was inspired by Julia Child's Potage aux Concombres, from *The French Chef Cookbook,* which taught me the pleasures of cooked cucumber soup. I've substituted vegetable broth, wine, and water for chicken stock; fresh herbs for dried; scallions for shallots; oil for butter; and light cream for sour cream—but the recipe is much the same, and just dandy. The use of farina (Cream of Wheat) as thickener instead of the traditional potatoes means a fresher cucumber taste.

Serve the soup chilled or hot. For chilled soup, add basil after the soup has cooled (basil loses its charm when heated). For hot soup, you can add dill directly to the hot liquid.

2 **to 2½ pounds cucumbers**
1 **bunch scallions (green onions)**
1 **tablespoon grapeseed or other mild vegetable oil**

3 cups vegetable broth
1 cup water
1 cup dry white wine
2 teaspoons kosher salt (omit if broth is salted)
¼ cup quick-cooking farina (Cream of Wheat)
¼ cup tightly packed dill leaves, plus some for garnish, *or* ½ cup tightly packed sliced basil leaves, plus some for garnish
About ¾ cup light cream or half-and-half
White pepper

1. Reserve the smallest cucumber for garnish. If using European greenhouse or Middle Eastern cucumbers, there is no need to peel. For others, taste and determine degree of bitterness and toughness (remember that the peel will soften with cooking) and peel as desired. Halve lengthwise. Scoop out seeds only if large or tough. Cut into 1½-inch lengths. Trim and slice enough scallions to make 1½ cups.

2. Warm oil in medium pot over moderately low heat. Stir in scallions and cook briefly to wilt, not brown. Add cucumbers, broth, water, wine, salt. Bring to a boil. Stir in farina. Simmer, partly covered, until cucumbers and farina are very soft, about 20 minutes. Remove from heat.

3. *To serve hot:* Cool slightly, then puree with dill until as smooth as possible in food processor. Gradually add cream to taste. Season. Reheat and garnish with thin-sliced reserved cucumber and dill.

To serve cold: Pour into a bowl and cool in sink of cold water. Puree soup with basil in a food processor until very smooth. Gradually add cream to taste. Overseason slightly. Chill thoroughly. Before serving, thin with water if needed. Season. Garnish with thin-sliced reserved cucumber and hair-thin basil slivers.

Serves 6 as a first course

Cucumber-Ginger Refresher

This granita of cucumber and ginger shreds is not a vegetable dish per se, but a special course to serve alone. It was prepared at the Jakarta Hilton International by Detlef Skrobanek when he was executive chef. The pale green icy mass is so sharply refreshing it will wash away the pervasive shallots, garlic, coconut milk—even chillis—of the Spice Islands to make way

for another course. (The recipe appears in another form in *Dining in Grand Style,* a book I wrote with Dieter Hannig and the chefs of Hilton International.)

About 1¾ pounds cucumbers (European greenhouse work well)
About ¼ cup lime juice
About ¼ cup sugar
About 1½ tablespoons peeled fine-grated, fresh ginger

1. Peel, halve, and seed cucumbers as necessary. Cut two-thirds of them on shredding blade of food processor, pressing *very* lightly to make fine shreds. Transfer to stainless steel bowl.

2. Switch to the all-purpose blade and puree the remaining cucumbers. Press in a sieve set over a bowl to extract juice; discard solids. Add water to juice if needed to make 1 cup.

3. Add the liquid to the cucumber shreds, with ¼ cup lime juice, ¼ cup sugar, and 1½ tablespoons ginger. Let stand 2 hours at room temperature.

4. Taste and adjust lime, sugar, and ginger. Cover, then set in coldest part of freezer. When mixture begins to solidify (timing will vary considerably, with the freezer; begin checking after an hour), stir with a fork. Repeat several times during freezing to break up crystals and produce a snowy texture.

5. Serve at once, or cover tightly and freeze up to 24 hours. To serve if frozen hard, soften in refrigerator about ½ hour, breaking up crystals with a fork three or four times, or until mixture has a snowy texture—on the verge of slush. Serve at once.

Serves 4 to 6

Summer Cucumber and Tomato Pasta, Ambient Mode

"Room temperature" has never seemed a pleasant culinary term, especially during a New York City summer. Therefore: ambient mode. This colorful toss, neither hot pasta nor salad, but somewhere between, emphasizes cucumber crispness and tomato softness. Heightened with fresh herbs, the flavors blend and mellow as the pasta cools and absorbs the vegetable juices that well up on contact with the hot strands.

Prepare in individual bowls to distribute the ingredients and allow for custom herbal treatment.

FOR EACH PERSON

About ¼ pound thin-skinned cucumber
2 tablespoons diced red onion
¼ teaspoon kosher salt
1 tablespoon champagne vinegar or rice vinegar
About 5 ounces red or yellow cherry tomatoes
1 to 1½ tablespoons flavorful olive oil
1 teaspoon minced lemon thyme, thyme, or savory leaves *or* 1½ tablespoons thin-sliced basil leaves
¼ pound imported Italian thin spaghetti or fine linguine

1. Cut cucumber into julienne strips, ¼-inch dice, or small thin triangles to make about ¾ cup. Combine with onion, salt, and vinegar in bowl; toss. Let stand at least 15 minutes, then drain in strainer for 5 minutes.

2. Meanwhile, quarter tomatoes (to make about ¾ cup). Toss in individual serving bowl with 1 tablespoon oil and ¾ teaspoon thyme or 1 tablespoon basil. Let stand while you prepare pasta.

3. Boil pasta in salted water until slightly more tender than al dente; drain.

4. Meanwhile, add cucumber to tomatoes; toss. Add drained hot pasta and toss. Let stand 15 minutes or more, tossing now and then to redistribute. Season and add remaining herb and/or oil, as desired.

Pros Propose

Fresh cucumber salads, salsas, and cold soups are fairly familiar and easy to turn up in cookbooks. Recipes for heated or cooked cucumber are less common, and therefore the focus of this section.

Atjar ketimun, **Cucumbers in Turmeric,** the dish mentioned earlier that piqued my budding culinary curiosity about Southeast Asia and cucumber, appeared in *The New York Times Cookbook,* edited by Craig Claiborne. To prepare: Cut peeled, quartered, seeded cucumbers into bite-size lengths. Salt heavily. Refrigerate 1 hour or more. Rinse, drain, and pat dry. Sauté minced shallots, garlic, and ginger in peanut oil until soft. Add ground almonds, turmeric, salt, and sugar. Then add a generous amount of vinegar and simmer 10 minutes. Pour over cucumbers. Mix well and refrigerate at least an hour.

In her fresh contemporary recipe collection, *Savoring Spices and Herbs,* Julie Sahni includes this simple and effective **Glazed Cucumbers with Sesame:** Trim cucumber tips. Peel, halve, scoop out seeds, and cut 2-inch lengths. Cut each into ½-inch thick sticks. Toss in butter and seasoning over moderate heat. When opaque, about 4 minutes, sprinkle lightly with water. Cover and cook until soft, about 4 minutes. Uncover, raise heat, and shake until pieces are glazed. Sprinkle with toasted sesame seeds.

In China, diced cucumbers are salted before stir-frying for a similar toss. To prepare **Cucumbers Stir-Fried with Diced Pork:** Peel, halve, seed, and dice cucumbers. Sprinkle with salt and let stand 15 minutes. Rinse and pat dry. Cut pork into dice of the same size. Stir-fry until whitened. Add chopped green onion, fresh ginger, and brown bean sauce; stir-fry 1 minute. Add cucumber, light soy sauce, rice wine, and chicken stock; stir-fry another minute. Add sesame oil and serve at once (from *China the Beautiful Cookbook* by Kevin Sinclair).

From France, Richard Olney's **Skewered Scallops and Cucumbers with Dill** is light and simple—unless you count the coral roe butter, which is nearly impossible to make in the United States, where scallops are sold without their peach-colored eggs. To prepare: Peel small firm cucumbers and cut into ½-inch sections. Blanch 1 minute in heavily salted boiling water; drain. Marinate cucumbers and scallops (halved horizontally if very thick) in lemon juice, olive oil, and minced fresh dill for about an hour. Alternate on skewers. Grill over intense heat, basting with marinade. Serve with beurre blanc if coral butter is lacking (from *Simple French Food*).

More often, cooked cucumber dishes contain thickening of some kind, whether flour, eggs, cream, or all three. *The Cuisines of Germany* by Horst Scharfenberg includes traditional **Braised Cucumbers,** lightly flour-thickened: Cut peeled, halved, seeded cucumbers into short segments. Combine with vinegar, sugar, and salt: Marinate 2 hours. In saucepan, combine enough beef stock to cover cucumbers with allspice, sugar, and vinegar. Add cucumbers and cook until they begin to get tender. Meanwhile, cook diced bacon to render fat;

remove and reserve pieces. In fat, sauté minced onion until translucent. Add a little flour, stirring until browned. Add some of cooking liquid, then add cucumbers and cook until tender. Garnish with reserved bacon.

Soups are probably the widest recipe category for cucumbers, although more are raw than cooked. In Finland, traditional flour and egg thickenings are added to creamy **Cucumber Bisque:** Cook peeled and chopped cucumbers and onions in butter until softened. Add chicken broth and simmer until vegetables are tender. Whiz to a puree. Melt butter in same pan and stir in an equal amount of flour; add pureed soup, stir, and cook until thickened. Blend egg yolks and cream; whisk in. Cook over lowest heat to smooth, about 5 minutes. To serve, stir in diced raw cucumber, seasoning, and parsley (*The Finnish Cookbook* by Beatrice A. Ojakangas).

In Estonia, a very similar recipe is served cold with herbs. For **Estonian Chilled Cucumber Soup:** Prepare soup as above, and add a large quantity of chopped dill to the cooked cucumbers and onions. Substitute sour cream and dry sherry for the sweet cream. Stir in grated lemon zest. Cool, then chill. Garnish with dill (from *Please to the Table: The Russian Cookbook* by Anya von Bremzen and John Welchman).

At the opposite pole is American haute cuisine: modern, clean, and purely Charlie Trotter. To prepare emerald **Chilled Clear Cucumber Soup with Watermelon, Apple, and Jícama:** Cut peeled European greenhouse cucumber into 1-inch pieces. Hollow with a round cutter to make cups. Combine removed pulp and more peeled cucumber in blender; puree, and season. Pour into sieve lined with several layers of cheesecloth. Refrigerate until all liquid has drained. Blanch the cucumber cups in water 1 minute; drain and cool. In bowl, combine julienned raw cucumber and green apple. Toss with yogurt, lemon juice, and shichimi togarashi (7-spice powder). Place 2 cucumber cups in each shallow soup bowl. Fill with julienne mixture. Surround with tiny dice of watermelon, avocado, jícama, and tomatillo. Ladle in cold cucumber broth, sprinkle with dill, then add a little dill oil and pepper (*Charlie Trotter's Vegetables*).

Dandelion (*Taraxacum officinale*)

Including **wild** and **cultivated dandelion**

Dandelion Chicory (*Cichorium intybus*)

Including **Catalogna, Red-Ribbed,** and **Puntarella chicories**

wild dandelions

½ **actual size**

Dandelion

Somewhere along the line, the two distinct plants named at the top of this page both became "dande-lion" in the market. **Wild dandelion** (*Taraxacum officinale*), a native of Europe and Asia, now settled throughout the temperate zone, has been used for food and medicine since ancient times. Given the geographical

cultivated dandelions   ½ actual size

range of wild dandelion, it is odd that the culinary side has been developed almost exclusively in the Mediterranean. From that area comes the common name dandelion, through Latin to French, dent-de-lion (lion's tooth), arguably due to the leaf's sometimes sawtoothed appearance.

Pamela Jones writes in *Just Weeds* that European immigrants deliberately introduced dandelion to the New World for its established tonic properties and also "encouraged the good-natured workhorse of a weed to excel in yet another occupation, as a food source for bees. Even today," she continues, "dandelion ranks high among honey-producing plants, thanks to its bounteous stores of pollen and nectar. In fact, with what is surely an angel's patience, it has been observed that no fewer than ninety-three kinds of insects help themselves to the dandelion's lavish larder."

Well-known to all gardeners and some cooks, this old-time wild green makes occasional spring visits to farmers' markets and to the most elegant restaurants, where—ironically—humble weeds have finally been restored to the table. Wild dandelion looks and tastes rather different from what is cultivated. The appealing little crowns have a strong earth-mineral scent and a flavor that is more forceful but also more complex and balanced. The leaves are tougher; they must be picked early in spring when they are petite and tender and look enchanting, too—like a swirly cock's tail.

Cultivated dandelion is difficult to recognize in the market because growers also call certain chicory "dandelion." A longtime farmer from New Jersey (where most dandelion is raised) told me that true dandelion is grown only in the spring for "special ethnic markets in Chicago and New York and other places where people like that traditional taste." The varieties planted are "just kinds from the old country" and two commercial cultivars called Thick-Leaved and Arlington. They are all generally larger, milder, and more tender than their wild relative—and do, in fact closely resemble some of the following chicories.

Dandelion Chicories

This group is also known generally as catalogna-type, Italian dandelion, and asparagus chicory; and, specifically, for the names of distinct cultivars, Cicoria Catalogna, San Pasquale, Red-Ribbed, Puntarella, and more. Although most American "dandelion" growers cultivate San Pasquale and Catalogna chicories, they *call* these dandelion. Although similar to cultivated dandelion, they are not exactly the same.

Catalogna, Catalonia, or Catalan chicory is the one that tastes and looks like what we usually associate with dandelion—and what often *is* "dandelion" in the markets: comparatively large, deeply cut dark green leaves with slim white ribs and a distinctly bitter bite. Recently, however, several catalogna types have been raised hydroponically or in smaller sizes (or both) to be more tender and mild than traditional types. These are clearly meant for salad mixes, not cooking, and that is where they excel. Note the range of California-grown catalognas in the photo, from the larger braising size on the far right to intermediate sauté size to small salad size.

Red-Ribbed Catalogna (called "Red Dandelion" in the market) is stunning, useful, and one of the few red leafy things that keep their crimson when cooked. The organically grown catalogna, with deep green leaves and ruby stems, is more flavorful, firm, and bitter (pleasantly so) than the hydroponically grown kind and is especially good in a quick sauté. The paler, slimmer, milder hydroponic version is light and lovely raw, in salad.

BASIC USE: When spring-new, wild dandelions are vervy, a touch mushroomy, and a bit tannic and make a memorable contribution to salads, both cold and warm. When small and relatively tender, all culti-

dandelion chicories or Catalogna: Red-Ribbed (*left*) and 4 sizes of green   ⅕ actual size

vated dandelions and dandelion chicories excel in salads, too. They are enhanced by heated dressings, which soften the slightly fibrous texture of the leaves and mellow their bitter edge. The bitterness can be balanced with roasted nut oils, fruit or sherry or balsamic vinegars, and cheese with sharpness and acidity—such as blue and goat. Or mitigate the bitterness with citrus fruit or beets, time-honored partners.

As dandelions and chicories grow larger and more fibrous, they are better braised, generally in combination with milder greens than in salads. Old-fashioned pork is still the best seasoning, whether in the form of bacon, hocks, country ham, or prosciutto ends. Braise as you would other greens, but for a shorter time. Timing varies; but cultivated dandelions and chicories do not seem to improve with very long cooking, so season for a more immediate impact.

Stir sliced dandelion or chicory into soups or legume dishes during the last half-hour or so of cooking to add depth, contrast, and chewiness. Cook chopped dandelion with rice or grains for textural interest and a bitter-green flavor.

For mildest taste, blanch leaves first, then refresh, chop, and proceed with cooking: Simmer in cheese or cream sauce, combine with sauce for a gratin, or add to layered pasta dishes.

SELECTION AND STORAGE: Wild dandelions are most abundant and delicate in early spring, before their flowers appear. For most cultivated dandelions and chicories, the paler and smaller the leaves, the more tender they are. Choose firm greens with thin stems, preferably attached at the base. Avoid flabby specimens that are yellowing or browning.

Wild dandelions last longer if rinsed and soaked briefly in lukewarm water, allowed to dry slightly, then packed airtight with a paper towel on top and bottom. Cultivated types and chicories will benefit from this treatment if they look limp. Otherwise, store in ventilated plastic for no more than a few days.

PREPARATION: For all dandelions and chicories, slice off any roots, then cut apart and trim any heavy parts of the stems, as needed. (Hydroponic and organic Red-Ribbed chicories may not need to be trimmed.) Dunk into plenty of water and swish around. Lift out gently and repeat until no grit remains in the sink.

Cut into manageable pieces to suit the recipe. Spin-dry for salad.

length: about 1 foot

Puntarella (or puntarelle, the generic plural for the shoots) is a type of catalogna chicory, but it is prepared in ways that are so different from the others that it is treated separately. Catalogna chicories have several forms: slim and opened up, or barrel-like with leaves that are pale and fairly smooth-edged, or wide, dark, and deeply notched—and anything in between. Lucio Gomiero, a co-owner of European Vegetable Specialties Farms in Salinas, says that "puntarelle is the Roman name for what is cicoria de Galantina in Puglia—its home region, where I buy my seeds. In late fall and winter, it sends up shoots—puntarelle—that are crisp and juicy." (In summer, the shoots grow tall, bolt, and become tough and inedible.) Puntarelle's unusual crunch, deep bittersweet savor (especially cooked), and intriguing looks make them a welcome addition to the category of greens.

BASIC USE: Traditionally, applications for puntarelle are specialized: They are thin-sliced in a Roman salad with anchovy-garlic dressing or served as a complement to Pugliese dried fava puree. Try them "straight"—separated into individual "spears" and offered along with mild olives, marinated mushrooms, and dry sherry to open a meal.

I love this chicory braised, when it develops considerable depth of flavor and a gamut of rich textures, none of them "crispy." (When did that word displace the perfectly good "crisp" on menus?) For a lazy pasta meal: Cut the leaf-stems bite-size; slice the shoots into crosswise rings, leaving tips whole. Add leaves to boiling pasta (sturdy, short shapes) during the last 6 to 7 minutes of cooking; add puntarelle during the last 3 to 4. Drain, toss with a little scallion and olive oil; sprinkle with crumbled fresh goat cheese.

SELECTION AND STORAGE: Look for Puntarella from November through January, more or less. Choose carefully: Because the heads superficially resemble dandelion or Catalogna, you must rudely spread the slim, pale-stalked leaves to check for the presence of the hidden pointlets. If the opened head reveals only leaves at its core, you do not have puntarelle—although the chicory may be delicious. What you *should* see is a mass of chubby, twisted, hollow shoots, each topped with leafy twirls; the whole may range from the size of an apple to a small cauliflower. Or sometimes the shoots may be nearly as large as broccoli stalks; these are less desirable but still good. Check to be sure there is no sign of softening or browning.

Store in the refrigerator, tightly enclosed in plastic. The shoots perish and/or toughen very quickly. Do not keep for more than a few days.

PREPARATION: Snap or cut the leaf stems from the base, leaving the center complex of shoots intact. Rinse outer leaves, cut bite-size, and spin-dry. Cut apart shoots, trimming the hard base of each as needed. To serve shoots raw, rinse and soak in ice water until serving time; for slightly curled snippets, cut thin strips about 2 inches long before soaking. For cooking, cut the shoots crosswise into 1-inch rings; or if short, halve lengthwise to maintain the curious crayfish-like form.

Salad of Dandelions, Frisée, and Bacon with Croutons

A modification of a classic bistro appetizer in which smoky bacon dice play sweet and chewy foil to bitter dandelion or chicory leaves (the Red-Ribbed is striking here) and pale, crunchy frilly frisée (curly endive). The French original is topped with poached egg, which many Americans consider an unthinkably rich garnish. I am not among them.

½ pound small dandelion or dandelion
   chicory
½ pound frisée
1 or 2 small scallions (green onions)
6 ounces lean slab bacon
About 2 tablespoons olive oil
1 French bread (baguette) about 10
   inches long
1 or 2 garlic cloves, halved
2 tablespoons balsamic vinegar
1 tablespoon white wine vinegar
¼ teaspoon kosher salt
Pepper
Optional: 4 soft-poached eggs

1. Cut apart dandelion stems if necessary. Swish in a sink filled with water; lift out gently so debris sinks. Repeat as needed. Cut into manageable pieces. Spin-dry. Cut apart frisée. Rinse. Cut into bite-size pieces and spin-dry. Combine both in salad bowl. Trim scallions and thin-slice.

2. Preheat oven to 350°F. Pare off and discard bacon rind, then cut bacon into ½-inch dice. In wide skillet, cook over moderately low heat to render fat and turn bacon brown but not brittle. Transfer to dish. Pour out and save fat (do not wash pan); measure ¼ cup. Add 2 tablespoons olive oil (if less than ¼ cup fat is rendered, make up the difference with more olive oil).

3. Cut off and discard bread crust, then cut slices ½ inch thick. Arrange on baking sheet. Bake until firmed but not crisp—3 to 4 minutes. Rub both sides generously with halved garlic (to scent, not to coat with pulp). Cut into ½-inch dice. Toss with 2 tablespoons of the reserved fat. Spread on baking sheet and bake until golden, 10 to 15 minutes.

4. Mix both vinegars and salt. In small saucepan, heat remaining ¼ cup fat until hot but not smoking. Drizzle over greens, tossing to coat evenly. Add bacon to pan and reheat. Add to greens. Add vinegar mixture to pan and bring to a boil. Drizzle over greens, tossing well.

5. Divide among salad plates. Top with croutons, scallions to taste, and pepper. Add optional eggs and serve at once.

**Serves 4 as a first course or light supper
or lunch main course**

Basic Braised Dandelion or Dandelion Chicory

Any of the sizable so-called dandelions are usually best when simmered in a hot bath: The bitter-green savor seems to mellow and deepen with a little liquid. Catalogna chicory even a foot long may be tender and succulent as baby bok choy when cooked this way instead of being sautéed (but, being of the very variable chicory clan, it may also wind up solid and chewy). I particularly like the Red-Ribbed variety cooked this way. Serve with sausages, pork chops, or roasted poultry, and baked sweetpotatoes. For a vegetable meal, serve with roasted squash and wheat or rice pilaf.

> About 1½ pounds dandelion or dandelion
>   chicory
> 2 tablespoons pork, duck, or bacon fat;
>   or olive oil
> 1 teaspoon minced garlic
> About ½ cup ham, pork, duck, turkey,
>   mushroom, or vegetable broth
> ½ teaspoon sugar
> Salt and pepper
> Optional: sherry vinegar or cider vinegar, or
>   hot pepper sauce

1. Cut apart dandelion stems if necessary. Swish in a sink filled with water; lift out gently so debris sinks. Repeat as needed until no grit remains. Cut into bite-size pieces.

2. Melt fat with garlic in large skillet over moderate heat. Add greens, ½ cup broth, and sugar and bring to a boil. Reduce heat, cover, and simmer 5 minutes.

3. Uncover and continue cooking until greens are tender and almost all liquid has evaporated. (Timing can vary from a few minutes to 25, depending upon the texture of the leaves.) If liquid evaporates before leaves are sufficiently tender, add more broth.

4. Season. Add optional vinegar or hot sauce.

Serves 4

Dandelions with Red Pepper and Ginger

"Dandelions can be exceptionally bitter or just-right bitter, and it seems unpredictable. I've had the best (surprisingly large) from the supermarket in early fall and the worst (small) from a friend's well-tended garden in summer," wrote trusted recipe developer Barbara Spiegel. "Somehow, the sweetness of the pepper, and heat and sharpness of the sherry vinegar and ginger, adapt to enhance the greens when they're mild, and mellow the bitter when they're harsh."

Barbara cooks the full-length greens until fork-tender, then cuts them on the plate. You can slice them into 2-inch lengths before cooking, if neatness counts. She serves grilled tuna with the bright orange and green vegetable duo.

> 1 very large red bell pepper
> 1 tablespoon olive oil
> 1 tablespoon minced ginger
> 1¼ pounds dandelion or dandelion
>   chicory
> ½ teaspoon kosher salt
> 1 to 2 tablespoons sherry vinegar
> 1 to 2 tablespoons medium-dry sherry

1. Clean and chop red pepper. Warm oil in heavy non-aluminum skillet over moderate heat. Add red pepper and ginger and stir occasionally until pepper softens and releases its juices, a few minutes.

2. Meanwhile, cut apart dandelion stems as necessary. Wash greens in several changes of water, lifting out gently so debris sinks.

3. Without drying greens, add them to pan. Cover and cook 15 minutes. If greens seem dry, add a few spoonfuls of water.

4. Stir, reduce heat to low, and cook, covered, 10 to 30 minutes, depending upon how firm or tender the dandelions are—and how firm or tender you like them. Season with salt, vinegar, and sherry. Serve hot.

Serves 4

Dandelion Frittata with Smoked Mozzarella

Bittersweet, chewy greens and a generous helping of smoky cheese are bound with egg to form a flat golden cake that can be served hot or at room temperature, as a main course, appetizer, or part of a picnic or tapas-style meal. The high proportion of dandelion makes this a very vegetably dish; if a more omelet-like texture is preferred, halve the quantity of greens. Enjoy for brunch or supper with a tomato and herb salad, whole wheat baguette, and light red wine.

1 pound dandelion or dandelion chicory
½ teaspoon hot pepper sauce
3 cups water
7 eggs
½ cup lightly packed crumbled rustic white bread (crusts removed)
2 teaspoons kosher salt
¼ cup thin-sliced dried tomatoes
2 teaspoons minced garlic
5 to 6 ounces smoked mozzarella, cut into tiny dice (1 cup)
1 tablespoon olive oil

1. Cut apart dandelions as needed. Swish in plenty of water, lifting out gently so sand sinks. Repeat as needed. Drain and cut into bite-size pieces.

2. Preheat oven to 400°F. Blend pepper sauce with 1 tablespoon water. Add to eggs in mixing bowl, beating just to blend. Stir in bread.

3. Boil 3 cups water in wide saucepan. Stir in salt, then greens, tomatoes, and garlic. Boil until greens are fairly tender, about 5 minutes. Drain in sieve over bowl, pressing hard to extract liquid (reserve for another use).

4. Whisk eggs to break soaked bread into small bits. Add mozzarella and greens and mix. Set large oven-proof skillet over moderate heat. Add oil and tip pan to coat. Scrape in egg mixture and cook a minute to firm underside.

5. Set pan in upper level of oven. Bake until not quite set on top, about 15 minutes. Gently loosen frittata with spatula and slide onto serving plate. Serve hot or at room temperature, cut into narrow wedges.

Serves 4 as a main dish, 8 as an appetizer or hors d'oeuvre

Puntarella Picante with Olive-Anchovy Dressing

A swirl of Puntarella parts (shoots, stems, and leaves separated for textural play) suggests a bouquet of wild greens on the plate. Sharp, hot, and salty seasonings add punch to the mild chicory.

Select a head with an abundance of short shoots, which look and taste best in this dish. The yield from each head varies with the ratio of shoots to leafy greens, making it impossible to predict the number of servings or exact quantity of dressing needed. Dress gradually, holding some back if there is too much, or adding a little oil and vinegar for more.

About ¼ cup full-flavored olive oil
½ tablespoon minced garlic
⅛ teaspoon chilli flakes
½ tablespoon minced fresh thyme, marjoram, or oregano leaves
About 2 tablespoons red wine vinegar
2 or 3 oil-packed anchovy fillets
8 oil-cured black olives, pitted
½ tablespoon capers
Salt and pepper
1 head Puntarella chicory (about 1 pound)

1. Heat ¼ cup olive oil, garlic, chilli, and ½ teaspoon thyme in small non-aluminum pan over low heat until garlic softens. Add 2 tablespoons vinegar and simmer to evaporate slightly and blend flavors—a minute or two.

2. Meanwhile, chop together anchovies, 4 olives, capers, and remaining 1 teaspoon thyme. Add to pan. Season. Remove from heat.

3. Cut or snap leaf-stems from Puntarella base, leaving interior shoots intact. Cut leaves casually from stems (neatness doesn't count). Wash and spin-dry. Wash stems, spin-dry, then thin-slice. Arrange in center of salad plates. Cover completely with leaves.

4. Cut apart shoots, trimming any hard base parts as you go, then rinse. Cut off 1½-inch-long tips and halve lengthwise. Slice the remaining part of shoots crosswise into ½-inch rings. Rinse.

5. Arrange shoots decoratively on the dark leaves, making a radiating pattern of tips, if desired. Chill or not, to taste.

6. Heat dressing. Spoon over salad, adjusting amount to suit. Slice remaining 4 olives and sprinkle over. Serve with forks and sharp knives to make tidy work of the crunchy shoots.

Serves about 4 as a first course

Braised Sweet-Sour Puntarella

The crispness of raw Puntarella makes a refreshing chomp, but when it is cooked, the vegetable becomes multi-dimensional, with elements of escarole, asparagus, and broccoli raab. The look is rustic and simple, but the complex textural gamut runs from lush and fleshy to softly crunchy—with flavors to match.

> 1 head Puntarella chicory (1½ to 2 pounds)
> 2 tablespoons olive oil
> 2 medium onions, diced
> 1½ tablespoons tomato paste
> ½ teaspoon kosher salt
> About 1 cup water
> ½ tablespoon capers (preferably small;
>   if large, chop)
> Pepper
> 1 to 2 teaspoons balsamic vinegar

1. Cut leaf-stems from Puntarella base, leaving interior shoots intact. Wash leaf-stems well, especially at the base; thin-slice or chop small. Cut apart shoots, trimming off hard base parts as you go. Slice into 1-inch lengths, or thereabouts, keeping tips whole. Rinse.

2. Heat oil in wide pan over moderate heat. Add onions and cook until well browned. Meanwhile, mix tomato paste, salt, and water. Add to onions. Stir in chopped leaf-stems.

3. Simmer, tightly covered, until Puntarella is tender, not crunchy, stirring now and then. Timing varies; 15 minutes is average, but more or less is not unusual. If mixture threatens to scorch, add a spoonful of water.

4. Stir in capers. Spread shoots over greens. Cover and simmer until shoots are as tender as cooked broccoli stems or asparagus, stirring now and then. Timing varies: Start tasting for doneness at 4

minutes, but expect longer. Off heat, season. Gradually add vinegar, tasting.

Serves 4

Pros Propose

Wild foods have always been at the heart of the celebrated cuisine of Sinclair and Frederica Philip's Sooke Harbour House in British Columbia. The **Spring Dandelion Salad with Pacific Rock Scallop Roe** features examples from sea and soil: Blend hazelnut oil with red wine vinegar and whole-grain mustard. Being careful to avoid sections of roe that cover the dark bile pouches, remove bright roe from large scallops. Toss dressing with early small wild dandelion leaves. Sauté scallop roe with a touch of minced garlic in clarified butter for bare seconds. Place on salad; serve at once.

Wild dandelions figure in chef Odette Fada's Italian background and are something she likes to prepare annually in the United States. For simple **Traditional Easter Wild Dandelion Salad:** Rinse salted anchovies, remove the bones, then press through a sieve. Mix with lemon juice, olive oil, and pepper. Pour over "super well washed" dandelions. Cut hard-cooked eggs in segments; arrange all around.

In Italy, where Puntarella is served almost exclusively as a salad, each household seems to have its own recipe. For Lidia Matticchio Bastianich's **Puntarelle and Anchovy Salad:** Soak small dried white beans overnight. Snap leaves from Puntarella; blanch until tender; drain and halve. Cut shoots from Puntarella base into strips ¼-inch wide. Soak in ice water for at least an hour. Drain beans; cover with cold water; simmer until tender. Mix equal parts olive oil and red wine vinegar with seasoning. Combine the cooked greens and beans with half the dressing. Drain and dry shoots. Toss with minced anchovies and remaining dressing. Serve the two mixtures side by side on salad plates (*Lidia's Italian Table*).

In California, Chef Amaryll Schwertner departs from tradition with her **Eastern Mediterranean Salad:** Soak Puntarella strips ½ hour in salted ice water, "which leaches out a bit of the bitterness and renders them more palatable for the average palate." Toss with purslane sprigs, cucumber, fried capers, olive oil, and lemon juice. Serve with crisp flatbread.

Chef Schwertner also offers a light soup of **Puntarelle in Brodo** in the fall: Prepare game stock, preferably from pigeon and quail. Cut Puntarella leaves into pieces. Cut hollow points across into rings. Blanch both in salted water, then refresh in cold water and drain. Heat in the stock. Serve topped with poached egg and accompanied by grilled bread.

Creamy pureed favas with wild chicory is a traditional dish that has captured the imagination of American chefs, according to Nancy Harmon Jenkins in *Flavors of Puglia*. She uses dandelion instead of the wild Pugliese cicoriella for **Dried Fava Beans with Bitter Greens:** Soak favas overnight. Drain (skin if not peeled). Top up with water and simmer, covered, until melted to a soft puree. Skim often as favas boil, then stir constantly as they soften, adding boiling water if needed to prevent scorching. Cook well washed dandelion chicory in the water that clings. Drain and dress with olive oil; season. Pile puree on one side of plate, greens on the other. Serve with thick rustic bread slices fried in olive oil.

Italian-born Chef Stefano Riccioletti, now in New York, says that "in Lazio, wild chicories are Sunday food. Everyone used to take an afternoon walk in the country, pick the greens, and return starving. We'd make salad or pasta as soon as we came in the door." He suggests the duo of **Tonnarelli con Puntarelle** because you "cut the greens in slivers to resemble and mix with the pasta, like paglia e fieno." To prepare: Remove leaves. Cut Puntarella core into fine strips on a mandoline. Steam, heat in olive oil with garlic cloves and rosemary sprigs. Cook gently to absorb flavors, then remove seasoning. Toss with fresh tonnarelli. Grate over pecorino romano, "the symbol of Roman culture, a sharp, full flavor that creates the balance."

Eggplant (*Solanum melongena*)

Also brinjal (Indian and Caribbean), aubergine (some Caribbean),
berenjena (Latin American)

Eggplant, like chilli—another member of the vast nightshade family—exists in an astonishing array of colors, shapes, sizes, and textures. But for eggplant, unlike chilli, I know of no significant popular books to help me address a subject that requires a volume to explain its complexities.

Eggplant is common enough that I need not describe its usual market types or the fundamentals of its cookery. But a touch of history is needed to account for its amazing diversity. Eggplant is one of the few Old World species of a family famous for its New World edible forms (along with one smokable form, tobacco): chillis and bell peppers, tomatoes, and potatoes. Eggplant is no more typically purple and pear-shaped (America's main market type) than it is green and egg-size, or ivory and scimitar-slim, or raspberry-striped and oval. Nor is eggplant Italian, as Americans might have assumed until recently.

white: Dutch baby white (*round*), and Tango (*elongated*), darkest purple: Dutch baby purple (*left*), and Santana (*upper right*), green: Lime Green (*elongated*), and Kermit (*small round*), long violet: Machiaw; striated reddish-purple: Spanish type (*far right*)

¼ actual size

top row: Bambino, Megal, Neon; *bottom row:* Lilac Bride, Little Fingers, Rosa Bianca, Ova   ⅓ actual size

The earliest written accounts of eggplant, in Sanskrit and Chinese, date from the beginning of the Christian era, according to Marie-Christine Daunay, a geneticist and eggplant specialist at the Centre de Recherche Agronomique d'Avignon in Monfavet, France, who cites Indo-Burma and China as its original areas of growth. It was introduced to Japan in the 8th century and to Europe in the 13th; thereafter, distinct regional forms began to develop. At the start of the 16th century, eggplant came to North America—with that name, an indication that the purple pear-shaped type was not the first ashore.

There is a reason for the "egg" in eggplant. John Gerarde's *Herball* (first published in 1597) describes the fruit as "great and somewhat long, of the bignesse of a Swans egge, and sometimes much greater, of a white colour, sometimes yellow, and often browne." The first plants to reach the American colonies were grown as ornamentals, not for consumption, and looked like eggs.

The bosomy maroon fruit (a berry, botanically speaking) that became the norm in our markets arrived later. While this is still the primary type, the conservative market is changing again, finally, to our culinary advantage. A sampling from a list of 66 eggplant seeds now sold in North America reveals some colorful options: Black Egg, Japanese Early Purple, Neon, Oriental

White, Pinky, Turkish Orange, Thai Green, Violetta di Firenze, Hmong Red. This gamut is a happy consequence of an influx of East Asian, South Asian, and Middle Eastern immigrants who have brought with them wondrous eggplant forms and a wealth of recipes.

Unfortunately, it is not possible to group the eggplants in any meaningful way. Although *Solanum melongena* is defined in botanical terms, its many cultivated variations have not been classified. Marie-Christine Daunay and a group of European scientists have recently assembled to put some order into the situation, but the job has just begun.

I regret that there is just one general statement I can make about eggplants that is accurate across the board: Cooking changes the hues and forms drastically, from a glowing garden of Eden to a compost heap. The brilliance of the uncooked fruit does not translate to the cooked one. All but the red-orange types (not treated here), turn some shade of dun or greige.

Nevertheless, with the hope of adding some delicious unfamiliar types to your repertoire, I'll tell you what I've learned in the process of cooking 40 cultivars and try to distill what some wise cooks have to say. But short of describing every cultivar individually, the best I can do is ignore many worthy characters and focus on a few semi-accurate groups and partly true basics.

Oriental-type eggplants are represented primarily by slim, tapered, or pointed elongated fruits, in the style of Little Fingers, Lilac Bride, and Machiaw. They are among the most dependably mild, tender-skinned, creamy-fleshed, and quick-cooking eggplants in the market, whether miniature or full-grown. The lavender-blushed white, amethyst, and red-violet eggplants are usually called Chinese and are especially delicate and low in seeds. The darker violet to inky-purple cultivars are usually called Japanese and may be firmer and heavier. They usually have sweet skin and flesh and tend to maintain their color better than other types. Light-bodied and creamy, they can be cooked all ways but keep their form and flavor best when baked. For dishes that require even slices, they are as neat as cucumbers.

Small deep purple eggplants may be Oriental, but they may also be other types. Round or pear-shaped and variously called Japanese, Indian, Italian, and baby eggplants, they have proved highly variable. Some are similar to their larger counterparts. Some have finer skin and flesh and interesting nuances of flavor and texture. Some are bitter, unyielding, and undesirable. The potential for bitterness and hardness is minimized or eliminated by a simple process: First salt moderately and sugar lightly, then drain briefly. Then bake, covered, until soft.

Green-skinned eggplants come in as many shapes and sizes as other eggplants. Contrary to what you might expect from green (which is associated with unripe fruit) they are sweet, not bitter. The elongated ones (see Lime Green in the photo) are comparable to Oriental types in flesh and skin tenderness but may be meatier and fuller-flavored. Although these eggplants are associated primarily with Southeast Asian cuisines, some tasty cultivars were developed in the United States, such as the egg-shaped Applegreen from New Hampshire and the Louisiana Long Green. They can be cooked in all ways but are particularly good broiled. The skin turns bronzy and melds with the soft flesh.

Round green-skinned, lime-size eggplants (not grape-size and bunched—a type not treated here) are usually called Asian or Thai. They are mild and sweet, but be warned: They have nothing else in common with the long greens. Dense and fairly thick-skinned, they are also extremely seedy—though nicely so. The pockets of sesame-like seeds are not bitter but mild and crunchy, offering unusual textural contrast, especially when blended with a soft or creamy stuffing. The American cultivar, repellantly dubbed Kermit (the name of a popular frog puppet on television), is meaty and flavorful with hints of mushroom and artichoke. This is one of the few vegetables that benefit from microwave cooking, primarily because the color does not turn drab. But whether microwaved, steamed, braised, or sliced and sautéed, these solid citizens remain plump, undeflated, and sweet.

White-skinned eggplants, common in Southeast Asia, come in all the shapes and sizes of other eggplants. They are usually firm, heavy, and dense, with a characteristically thick skin that may need to be removed. Cooked, the flesh is sweet and meaty and mild (sometimes bland). It doesn't keep its ivory pallor but turns beige or pale-gray—but it holds its shape well. Use these eggplants steamed, broiled, or baked when you want a close-grained, fleshy result.

Striped or purple-blushed European eggplants are pictured here as Spanish and Rosa Bianca. Listada de Gandia seems to be the most esteemed of the striped (and may be the same as Rosa Bianca, but the experts do not agree). It is often called French or Italian in seed catalogues, but it is neither, says Marie-Christine Daunay: " 'Listada de Gandia' is a Spanish variety (Gandia is a town) purple or white with pink or purple stripes . . . and another Spanish variety 'Zebrina,' white with pink to purple stripes, is cultivated in the French West Indies." Similar eggplants are also popular in Greece, she notes. In New York City, I find such eggplants in Latin groceries with a choice of competing country names: Spanish, Puerto Rican, Dominican, or French. Quite large, creamy-textured, and fairly low in seeds, they are pleasant and bland, if a bit tough-skinned. They are, perhaps, less charming than the Oriental types and greens but more charming than the typical market purples.

Rosa Bianca (also Bianco), a seductively rounded fruit with a fine reputation of long standing, proved no more interesting than the above, in four tests. But from the praise Rosa Bianca, Listada de Gandia, and other striped cultivars elicit from seasoned gardeners, I suspect that market fruits are very different and that perhaps these types are not suited to commerce.

The size and fullness of both make them good candidates for stuffing, slicing and rolling with filling, and baking whole to smoosh to a puree—since the skins are not tasty.

Italian-American eggplant types, typically dark, large, and pear-shaped or bell-shaped, are the "regulars." Purchased from "regular" markets, and tested as a "control" alongside all the above types, they have proved insipid, fibrous, and tough-skinned by comparison. All the others had softer, tastier flesh and more edible skins. This may be due to problems that arise with large-scale production rather than the specific cultivars.

Small red, orange, and ochre eggplants (*Solanum aethiopicum* and *S. macrocarpon*) are available to gardeners but are rarely seen in the market. They can be deep and rich in flavor, mild and sweet, but are characteristically seedy and sometimes bitter. The last two traits are appreciated for some Asian, African, and Middle Eastern dishes but thus far have been difficult to justify to most American palates.

SELECTION: There is supposedly a "trick" to choosing eggplants, based on the superior quality of round-bottomed "females." However, eggplants are not male or female, and rounded bottoms are an expression of type or cultivar, not sex.

Eggplants are available year-round, primarily from Florida. They are likely to develop their fullest flavor from summer into fall, when they are grown in the open field. In spring and winter, they may be greenhouse products. Select fairly heavy fruit: Heft a few of the same size to compare. High solid content signifies even, stress-free cultivation with sufficient heat and moisture. Choose eggplants that are smooth, taut-skinned, and strikingly shiny, not dull. Although the stage of maturity preferred for consumption varies with nationality (the Japanese prefer soft eggplants, for example), the fruit available in the United States is generally firm. When pressed, the flesh should dent, then return to its shape (though softer Chinese and Japanese varieties may not rebound). Bronzed or pitted areas, which may result from chilling—to which eggplants are highly sensitive—bode bitterness. The fuzzy green cap (calyx) should be tightly intact and free of mold.

STORAGE: Eggplants store miserably. They are highly perishable (those grown in heat even more so than cool-climate types). If possible, don't refrigerate; keep in a cool place in a plastic bag for no more than 36 hours. For longer storage, keep in a paper bag in the warmest part of the refrigerator—but be aware that browning and textural breakdown occur with cold. Most eggplants deteriorate below 50°F.

PREPARATION: Small eggplants just need to be rinsed and to have the cap (calyx) trimmed. Few must be peeled, but the recipe and your taste will dictate this. Test larger ones if they seem tough. Also, test for wax by scratching with a fingernail; if the eggplant is waxed, peel it—and complain to the grocer. The skin of some white eggplants, too, may need to be peeled because it is thick, though not bitter. Check each eggplant before attacking it with knife or peeler.

SALTING: Eggplant is traditionally salted to rid it of bitterness. While salt does draw out moisture—and this step is helpful in recipes where you want a firm result or slices that absorb less oil—salting is not predictably useful in eliminating acridness. Often, it merely adds unneccessary salt and prolongs the preparation time. Bitter eggplants stay bitter even if salted, unless they are also covered and slow-baked with a little liquid—and even that is not a sure remedy.

Broiled Eggplant with Cilantro-Mint Sauce

Firm, narrow eggplants form neat ovals when sliced at an acute angle for this quick, pretty, multi-national dish. Keep a close watch to prevent the slices from burning before they turn creamy. If they darken quickly, move the pan farther from the heat.

1 large garlic clove, minced
2½ tablespoons olive oil
1 tablespoon soy sauce
1½ pounds elongated Oriental-type eggplants
1 cup lightly packed cilantro (coriander) leaves
½ cup lightly packed mint leaves
⅓ cup crumbled feta cheese (about 1½ ounces)
2 to 4 tablespoons yogurt
½ teaspoon sugar
Optional: ¼ teaspoon hot pepper sauce
½ cup roasted, salted, and chopped pistachios or walnuts

1. Preheat broiler. Blend garlic, olive oil, and soy sauce. Cut eggplants at a sharp angle into ¾-inch slices, to make ovals. Or for very skinny eggplants, simply halve each one lengthwise. Cut a deep crosshatch pattern into each slice or half.

2. Spray or brush a baking sheet with water. Arrange eggplant slices on pan, pressing them close together. Paint with oil mixture until it is absorbed.

3. Combine cilantro, mint, feta, 2 tablespoons yogurt, sugar, and optional hot sauce in a food processor or blender. Whiz to a light, smooth puree, adding yogurt as necessary. Taste and adjust flavors.

4. Set eggplant in broiler (if halved, place cut sides up). Cook until tender and lightly charred, about 5 minutes (do not turn over).

5. Arrange on platter; spoon over half the sauce. Sprinkle with nuts. Pass remaining sauce separately.

Serves 4

Eggplants Baked with Gingered Red Pepper Puree

Narrow, lightweight lavender Oriental-type eggplant is the most dependably sweet and tender type for this and other recipes, Eastern or Western. Prepared roasted peppers are a handy shortcut to a bright sauce that moistens and seasons the eggplant.

White part of 1 medium scallion (green onion)
1-inch ginger chunk, peeled
1 or 2 small fresh red or green chillis
1 large red bell pepper, roasted and peeled (see Note, page 114) or 4-ounce jar roasted red peppers
½ tablespoon honey
½ teaspoon kosher salt
1 teaspoon rice vinegar
1 tablespoon vegetable oil
3 narrow Oriental eggplants (about 6 ounces each)
1 tablespoon sesame seeds

1. Preheat oven to 375°F. Slice scallion and ginger. Seed and slice chilli(s). Drain and rinse jarred peppers, if using. Combine scallion, ginger, chilli(s), and bell pepper in food processor with honey, salt, vinegar, and oil. Puree until smooth.

2. Carefully and evenly halve eggplants lengthwise. Deeply score a diagonal crosshatch pattern (at ½-inch intervals) to cut through flesh nearly to skin. Press the sides of the eggplant to open the cuts. Spoon sauce into them, then spread remainder on top.

3. Set halves in a baking pan or dish just large enough to hold them in a single layer. Pour in a shallow slick of water—just to cover bottom of pan. Cover pan with foil. Bake until eggplants are very tender, ½ hour or more.

4. At the same time, spread sesame seeds in a small pan. Set in oven and bake until tan, about 5 minutes. Set aside.

5. Arrange eggplants on a platter, sprinkle with sesame seeds, and serve hot.

Serves 4

Small Dark Eggplants with Green Olive–Red Onion Dressing

Small dark eggplants tend to be more bitter than other types. The following salt-and-bake technique yields mild, creamy results predictably—or as predictably as any eggplant recipe can. The topping is rich, complex, and somehow mysterious, although the components are not unusual: a mince of tart olives, red onion, and tomato mellowed with a large dose of toasty coriander seeds and freshened with mint. Offer the little boats as a first course, side, or salad. Or serve with rice or wheat pilaf and yogurt-cucumber salad for a vegetable meal.

> 4 small dark oval eggplants (5 to 7 ounces each)
> 1 teaspoon kosher salt
> 2 teaspoons sugar
> 1 tablespoon whole coriander seeds
> ¼ teaspoon ground cinnamon
> ⅛ teaspoon ground hot pepper or ¼ teaspoon black pepper
> 2 tablespoons red wine vinegar
> 3 tablespoons pitted, chopped green olives (Picholines are nice)
> ¼ cup fine-diced red onion
> ¼ cup olive oil
> 3 tablespoons diced mini-tomatoes (currant, grape, or tiny cherry)
> ⅓ cup thin-sliced mint leaves

1. Rinse and halve eggplants. Score fairly deep crosshatched diagonals an inch apart in the flesh. Sprinkle each half with ⅛ teaspoon salt, then ¼ teaspoon sugar. Let stand 15 minutes, or longer, while you preheat oven to 400°F.

2. Set halves cut side down in a baking pan that holds them closely. Pour in water to not quite cover pan bottom. Crimp foil tightly over all. Bake until eggplants are very tender when pressed but not collapsed, 20 to 35 minutes, depending upon variety.

3. Meanwhile, toast coriander seeds in small pan over moderately low heat until they begin to crackle and color, a few minutes. Pour into mortar or spice mill; add cinnamon and pepper. Crush to a medium-coarse texture. Combine in small bowl with vinegar, olives, and onions. Stir in oil. Add tomatoes and 1 tablespoon mint.

4. With spatula, lift eggplants onto serving platter, skin side down. With large spoon, depress flesh slightly to hold dressing, leaving a ½-inch margin. Spread dressing to cover each half evenly. Sprinkle with remaining mint. Serve warm or at room temperature.

Serves 4

White Eggplant Slices Steamed with Black Beans and Orange Zest

Pungent, dark, nubbly seasoning transforms mild, smooth eggplant. Steaming ensures a creamy texture, softens the somewhat sturdy white skin, helps prevent darkening, and provides a speedy non-traditional cooking method.

Serve hot, with rice pilaf and roasted poultry (or not, for a vegetarian meal). Double the recipe (prepare in batches) to offer as part of a buffet meal, at room temperature. Or chill and serve with a sprinkling of cilantro, as a salad course.

> 2 slim white eggplants (about 8 inches long, about 6 ounces each)
> 1 teaspoon Asian (dark) sesame oil
> 2 teaspoons corn or peanut oil
> ⅛ teaspoon kosher salt
> 1 tablespoon rice vinegar
> 1 tablespoon Chinese fermented black beans
> 1 small orange, well scrubbed
> 1 tablespoon extra-thin-sliced scallion greens

1. Slice eggplants on sharp diagonal into slices as long as possible and ½ to ¾ inch thick (about 12 slices). Score deeply. Set on wide steamer rack (such as bamboo). With fork, whisk together both oils, salt, and vinegar to emulsify. Spoon onto slices, smoothing over the surface to coat.

2. Chop black beans *very* fine. Remove a few thin strips of zest from orange with swivel peeler. Stack and cut crosswise into hair-thin strips. Then cut into fine confetti to yield 1½ teaspoons. Sprinkle first the beans, then the zest over eggplant.

3. Set rack over boiling water, cover, and steam until slices are creamy-tender, about 10 minutes. Remove rack from steamer. Sprinkle slices at once with scallion greens. Transfer to platter.

Serves 4

Microwaved Thai Eggplants Filled with Taramosalata

Cute golf ball–size eggplants, green or white or with a pattern of both, take well to microwaving, I am surprised to report. Although these 1- to 2-inch globelets can be dense with seeds, they are crunchy and mild, not bitter. Creamy cod roe spread (taramosalata, a widely available Greek preparation), balances the crispness. Should fish not be your favorite, substitute curried mayonnaise and use the same herbs. Offer small knives and forks for tidy service.

> 10 Asian or round baby green or white
>   eggplants (about 1½ ounces each)
> Lemon or lime juice
> 2 tablespoons snipped chives
> 2 tablespoons minced parsley and/or cilantro
>   (coriander) leaves
> ¼ teaspoon dried dill, crumbled to powder
> ¼ cup prepared taramosalata
> Optional: very fine parsley mince

1. Slice caps from eggplants and discard. Place eggplants in microwavable dish with a paper towel on top. Cook at approximately 50 percent power (850 watts is full power for my oven) until just tender throughout. This will take 6 to 10 minutes, depending upon size. Check often so that the eggplants do not overcook and collapse.

2. Uncover and cool, then chill.

3. With melon ball cutter, remove most seeds and pulp from eggplants and reserve. Sprinkle shells lightly with lemon juice. Chop pulp, then combine with chives, parsley, dill, and taramosalata. Season with lemon juice.

4. With small spoon, fill shells, mounding mixture smoothly. Chill until serving time.

5. Garnish with optional minced parsley.

Serves 4 as an hors d'oeuvre

Fragrant Broiled and Pureed Eggplant

This recipe suits any large eggplants—ones with a large proportion of flesh to skin. Season, broil until smoky and squishy, drain, and puree. Do not trim off the stems, which act as handles during preparation.

Serve as a salad course, accompanied by olives, sliced tomatoes, and breadsticks or toasted pita triangles. Or thin puree slightly to offer as a dip with raw fennel and other vegetable strips. Allow to mellow overnight before serving. Mince feathery fennel tops to sprinkle over the dip.

> 3 large garlic cloves
> 1 teaspoon ground coriander
> ½ teaspoon ground cumin
> ¼ teaspoon ground anise, fennel, or allspice
> About 2 tablespoons flavorful olive oil
> 2 or 3 eggplants of equal size (to total about
>   2½ pounds)
> 1 teaspoon sugar
> ½ tablespoon kosher salt
> About ⅓ cup whole-milk yogurt or a smaller
>   quantity of thick drained yogurt to taste
> Black pepper or ground hot pepper to taste

1. Preheat broiler. Cut garlic into long slivers or slices. Combine in cup with coriander, cumin, anise, and ¼ teaspoon oil; mix well. With knife tip, cut deep slits in eggplants. Holding slits open with knife, insert garlic. When garlic is used up, rub eggplants with any remaining spice mixture.

2. Place eggplants in a baking pan as far from broiling element as possible. Broil, turning once, until skin wrinkles and blackens and eggplants collapse—about 20 to 30 minutes, depending upon size of eggplants and type of broiler.

3. Remove from heat, cover, and let stand about 10 minutes. Holding stem of one still hot eggplant, gently remove skin with a small knife. Discard skin along with stems. Place flesh in a strainer to drain as you peel remaining eggplant(s).

4. Combine eggplant flesh, sugar, and salt in food processor and pulse to barely mix. Pulsing, gradually add yogurt to taste, then add remaining oil. Do not puree until smooth—some texture is nice. Scrape into

a bowl. Add pepper and adjust seasoning. Refrigerate overnight.

5. Season before serving, preferably at room temperature.

Serves 4

Pros Propose

Italian dishes based on eggplant are common, but not this one, in which chocolate is the mellowing influence. Michele Scicolone writes that the ingredient is not unusual in southern Italian recipes, and compares this **Spiced Eggplant** to the sweet-sour caponata of Sicily: Cut purple eggplants into 1-inch dice. Toss in colander with salt: weight for an hour. Rinse and drain, then combine in pot with raisins, semisweet chocolate, sugar, cinnamon, olive oil, red wine vinegar, and water. Simmer, covered, until tender. Stir in lemon zest and chopped walnuts. Serve at room temperature on toasted bread (from *A Fresh Taste of Italy*).

In *The Cooking of the Eastern Mediterranean*, Paula Wolfert supplies a wealth of unusual eggplant recipes—but how to choose among Deep-Fried Eggplant Fans with Red Cabbage Salad, Stuffed Eggplants with Tomato Pomegranate Sauce, Rainbow Trout Fillets with Eggplant, and more? **Eggplants Stuffed with Walnuts** demonstrates a useful Georgian frying-steaming method that reduces the oil needed without sacrificing taste and texture: Halve baby eggplants lengthwise; sprinkle with fine sea salt. Set cut side down on towel and weight with plates for 20 minutes. Rinse, squeeze out moisture, and pat dry. In food processor, combine walnuts, chopped garlic, hot Hungarian paprika, ground marigold petals (or turmeric), and salt. Process to an oily puree. Add water and process to blend. Transfer to bowl. Add rice vinegar, chopped red onion, chopped celery, basil, and cilantro leaves, then pomegranate seeds. In large non-stick skillet, heat a small amount of olive oil. Add eggplants cut side down, cover tightly, and cook until golden and tender, about 15 minutes. Drain on paper towels. Press an opening in cut side and mound walnut mixture in each eggplant half.

In neighboring Turkey, "aubergines are halved and put into the still-hot ovens, once all the bread has been baked. The warm, softened halves are then filled with a cool mint-flavoured yogurt and eaten like a melon with a spoon," writes Ghillie Başan in *Classic Turkish Cooking*. To prepare: Bake slim small eggplants in a moderately hot oven 15 minutes. Slit lengthwise, keeping attached at base to form "wings." Place skin side down on baking sheet and bake until soft. Meanwhile, blend thick creamy yogurt with lemon or pomegranate juice, garlic crushed with salt, and chopped mint. While still hot, slit eggplant flesh, and press to form "boats." Fill with yogurt. Eat at once.

Small eggplants that are first charred, then peeled and fried figure in the cuisines of Italy, India, and here, in a recipe from the Philippines for **Eggplant "Fans" in Batter**: Prick small dark pear- or bell-shaped eggplants in several places (do not remove caps and stems). Place directly in gas flame, using stems to turn until charred all over (alternatively, broil close to heat). Keeping caps attached, peel, rinse, and pat dry the eggplants. Flatten each into a fan shape. Heat vegetable oil for shallow-frying in wide skillet. Salt each eggplant, then dip gently into beaten egg and place flat in pan. Fry until crisp on each side. Drain on paper towels and serve hot, as is, or with vinegar-garlic sauce (from *Madhur Jaffrey's World-of-the-East Vegetarian Cooking*).

Chef Neela Paniz finds that soaking eggplants in water banishes bitterness. For her **Sweet and Sour Small Eggplants**, trim stems but not caps from small round or egg-shaped eggplants. Cut a crosswise slit halfway through each at blossom end. Soak in water at least half an hour to open slits and remove bitterness. Meanwhile, blend plenty of ground coriander, cumin, and cayenne. Add turmeric, mango powder, and salt. Drain eggplants. Press and rub about ½ teaspoon spice mixture into each slit. In wide skillet, slowly and evenly brown eggplants in oil. Meanwhile, grate halved tomatoes to a pulp on coarse holes of grater, discarding skin. Add to eggplants, with salt. Cover, and simmer until eggplants are tender but still hold their shape, 15 to 30 minutes. Garnish with chopped cilantro and serve hot (from *The Bombay Cafe*).

In Thailand, Laos, and Cambodia, the small round Asian eggplant is part of salads, stir-fries, and, here, of **Khmer Chicken Soup with Eggplant,** Westernized with American hot peppers: Soak dried New Mexico chillis. Drain, seed, and devein. Combine in blender with sliced lemon grass, peeled and chopped galangal, shallots, garlic, turmeric, deveined kaffir lime leaves, and shrimp paste. Grind to a smooth paste, adding water as needed to help pulverize and blend. Heat oil in soup pot; add coconut milk and cook briefly until oil separates. Add the spice paste and stir a moment. Add strips of skinned and boned chicken breast and cook 5 minutes. Add chicken broth, sugar, fish sauce, and salt. Bring to a boil. Add halved small Asian eggplants and tamarind juice. Simmer 10 minutes. Add basil leaves (from *The Elephant Walk Cookbook* by Longteine de Monteiro and Katherine Neustadt).

The equally assertive flavors of Sichuan—ginger, garlic, chillis, and Sichuan pepper—penetrate eggplant that has been steamed until creamy. The rich dish "makes a very good centerpiece for a vegetarian meal, as there is nothing mild or shy about its taste," write Jeffrey Alford and Naomi Duguid in *Seductions of Rice*. For **Eggplant with Spicy Sesame Sauce:** Steam whole Oriental eggplants until well softened. Cool slightly. Halve lengthwise. Then, cut into 3-inch diagonals. Combine minced garlic and ginger, salt, sesame paste, vegetable stock, soy sauce, cider vinegar, chilli oil, Asian sesame oil, and roasted and ground Sichuan pepper in food processor or blender. Process until smooth; transfer to bowl and stir in minced scallion. Combine eggplant with sauce to just coat. Serve the remainder on the side.

Endive (*Cichorium endivia*)

Including **curly endive (curly chicory, frisée)**
and **broad-leaved endive (escarole, batavian)**

See also: **BELGIAN ENDIVE,** page 85

This vegetable is not mixed up; its names are. Endive (pronounce the word any way you like; it will be correct) is one plant that has two primary forms: the first with curly, feathery leaves; the second with broader, more flattened leaves. Each form can be grown from mini to massive, and from creamy-pale to deep green. But all sizes, shapes, and colors are *Cichorium endivia,* which is endive, correctly speaking, in the United States of America and in Britain. (In France, endive, pronounced ahn-deev, refers to what we call Belgian endive, a misnamed chicory.) Incorrectly speaking, a jumble of conflicting common names creates a salad daze in the marketplace.

Market names are not the only problem. Most American growers are benighted about proper cultivation of endive for salad (although it has been grown in the United States at least since the beginning of the 19th century). Literally, you might say they're not benighted enough, for if they really kept their heads in the dark (the endives', not their own) we would be able to enjoy the large, lustrous leaves that are raised for European tables; hearts kept hidden from light to subdue bitterness and maintain tenderness and crispness. Why excluding light is a tradition there and not here is a mystery. At any rate, what grows here usually has a small percentage of pale leaves and a large proportion of tough, coarse green ones. Fortunately, these green ones are just dandy for cooking, which is the best thing to do with them.

Curly endive—also, maddeningly, marketed as **chicory** or **curly chicory**—is the term for the sturdy "garden variety" green in the upper part of the photo, as well as the general term for all curly-leaved endives. Assertively bitter, this bushy, dark head tends to be fairly tough and chewy, but is mellowed and tenderized with cooking or when wilted by hot dressing.

Frisée or chicorée frisée (French for curly chicory), also called Italian or French curly chicory, is the petite, pale, expensive curly endive (see lower part of photo) produced by blanching. It has an opened, flattened shape and springy, slim, incised leaves of ivory to apple-green. Bittersweet and tender, its dramatic decoupage enlivens almost any combination of greens.

To blanch frisée, "the endive is covered and pressed to keep it from light when it is about three fourths grown," explains Minos Athanassiadis, president of Underwood Ranches in Somis, California. "Some cover it with boards, others with cups, but whatever you do, the intrusion makes the plants susceptible to problems and difficult to maintain until the right paleness and tenderness are achieved. Costs are proportional to the time the plant spends in the ground, and cultivating time for frisée is more than twice that for baby lettuce."

Endive, broad-leaved endive, escarole, scarole, and **batavian** are names applied to the large, comparatively flat-leaved head shown on the next page. While it is like lettuce in form, it is not lettuce; rather, it is thick

curly endive or curly chicory (*top*), 1 foot across
frisée or chicorée frisée (*bottom*), 4-6 inches across

and solid, with firm leaves that have the characteristic flavor of endives and chicories. The dark leaves are chewy and bitter, but the pale heart is succulent and only lightly bittersweet. The light and dark parts can be cooked together or separated, and the white part can be served raw.

BASIC USE: When cut into very fine strands, both curly and flat endive add lively body and bitterness to a salad of julienne vegetables or mixed greens. When wilted slightly with hot dressing, they are tender and tasty. They are lovely soup ingredients, giving both depth and sweetness to broth and cooking to an almost leek-like softness. Braise both in the manner of bitter greens for a change of pace—and relatively quick cooking.

The delicate frisée form is essentially a salad and garnish leaf, but one with an unusually wide range of capabilities. The seemingly fragile openwork is surprisingly resilient, making the leaves an interesting underpinning for hot or cold game, poultry, or seafood. The pale inner leaves of escarole can also be served this way.

SELECTION AND STORAGE: Choose heads that are damp and cool, not dried out or wet. Endive browns naturally at the base, where it is cut, but should not be brown elsewhere. Escarole should exhibit a full heart with plenty of white that is "heading up," that is, not outspread, but tightening to form a solid core—otherwise, it may be bitter.

Frisée "has no secrets—it's all out in the open," says Minos Athanassiadis. "Choose the palest for best value. Some growers trim each head right down to the blanch line; others leave more of the green leaves. Frisée should be priced accordingly." Since the vegetable lasts well, you should be able to choose from fine specimens, which may hail from Italy or California. To avoid costly waste, check for firm, tender leaves with no browning.

Store in plastic bags, up to a few days. To crisp up endive or extend its storage time: Trim the base to separate the leaves, then soak 2 minutes in lukewarm water. Shake dry, then pack into plastic containers with a piece of paper towel on top; refrigerate.

PREPARATION: Trim base to separate leaves. Remove any leaves that are very coarse or yellowing. Rinse well, paying particular attention to the silt that hides in the narrow channels where the leaves attach to the base. If any are gritty, run your finger down the remaining leaves to be sure they're clean. For salad, spin-dry. To cook, proceed with cutting directions, or pack and refrigerate.

endive, broad-leaved endive, escarole, scarole, or batavian   diameter: 9-12 inches

Escarole-Lentil Soup with Olives, Garlic, Lemon, and Parsley

Escarole turns juicy, melting, and mild when wilted, then simmered. Unlike most stewy soups, this one cooks quickly and needs no overnight mellowing period. The deep and winey olive broth has a meatiness akin to stock. I am a fan of tiny Black Beluga lentils, an unusually dark and flavorful cultivar, which I like to mix with the common green or brown ones. The French Verte du Puy is also pleasingly firm.

    1 to 1¼ pounds escarole
    2 to 3 celery stalks
    1 medium carrot
    2 to 4 garlic cloves
    3 tablespoons olive oil
    ¼ to ½ teaspoon chilli flakes
    1 cup lentils, picked over and rinsed

3 tablespoons pitted, coarse-chopped
oil-cured black olives
3 cups vegetable or meat broth
4 cups water
½ cup chopped flat-leaf parsley leaves
½ teaspoon coarse-grated lemon zest
Salt and pepper
Few tablespoons of red or white wine

1. Trim base of escarole and separate leaves. Wash in several changes of water, paying special attention to white base, where soil collects. Cut into very thin strips (to yield 8 to 10 cups). Dice celery. Chop carrot. Chop garlic; set aside 1 teaspoon for finish.

2. Warm 2 tablespoons olive oil in soup pot over moderate heat. Stir in celery, carrot, garlic, and chilli flakes. Cook to color vegetables slightly, a few minutes. Add escarole and toss until wilted.

3. Add lentils, olives, broth, and water. Simmer, partly covered, until lentils are tender, about 35 minutes.

4. Combine parsley, lemon zest, and the reserved garlic on cutting board and mince fine. Stir into soup, with salt and pepper. Stir in remaining 1 tablespoon olive oil and wine to taste.

Serves 4 as a main course

Curly Endive and Potato Salad with Hot Bacon-Caraway Dressing

A Sunday supper meal-in-one: potato salad with bacon pieces, bitter endive tempered by a heated dressing, and a scattering of hard-cooked eggs. Caraway and cider vinegar add pungency and acidity. If you can find them, small pink-skinned, yellow-fleshed potatoes are usually the most flavorful and look cute in their jackets. Other yellow-fleshed types are fine too, but white ones may lack the savor and "muscle tone" needed to hold their own against forceful curly endive.

1¼ pounds small potatoes
1 medium head (8 to 10 ounces) curly endive
(not small, pale frisée)
About 6 ounces sliced bacon
3 tablespoons olive oil

½ cup cider vinegar
1 tablespoon sugar
1 tablespoon Dijon mustard
½ teaspoon caraway seeds
2 medium shallots, diced
3 hard-cooked eggs, coarse-chopped
Pepper

1. Scrub potatoes with brush. Combine in heavy pot with cold water to cover by a few inches. Bring to a boil and add a handful of salt. Boil until just tender, about 15 minutes. Drain. Cool until easy to handle. Quarter potatoes or cut into 1-inch pieces, as shape dictates. Place in large serving bowl.

2. Trim endive base to separate leaves. Dunk into water, swish around, and lift out. Repeat as needed, checking for grit that may cling at stem bases. Spin-dry. Cut into 1½-inch pieces. Spread over potatoes.

3. Cook bacon in skillet over moderately low heat until it renders fat and crisps. Transfer slices to paper to drain. Pour fat from pan, reserving 3 tablespoons; discard remainder and the browned solids. Set skillet aside. Combine fat with olive oil. Cut bacon into 1-inch pieces.

4. Add vinegar, sugar, mustard, caraway, and shallots to the skillet. Bring to a boil, stirring. Add oil mixture, blending well. Immediately pour over chicory and toss. Add bacon and toss to mix well. Top with eggs, then grind over pepper. Serve at once.

Serves 4 as a lunch or light supper main dish

Salad of Cooked and Raw Escarole with Garlic and Herbs

The raw and the cooked in an unusual textural play that incorporates all parts of the endive. The dark, chewy leaf tips are cut thin; sautéed with garlic, rosemary, and lemon zest; and then strewn over the pale, raw crunchy hearts, which have been drizzled with mustard-lemon-thyme dressing.

1 large or 2 smaller heads escarole
(to total 1½ to 2 pounds)
1 lemon, well scrubbed

½ tablespoon Dijon mustard
1 teaspoon minced fresh thyme leaves
5 tablespoons olive oil
Salt and pepper
½ tablespoon minced garlic
1 teaspoon minced fresh rosemary leaves
Optional: 2 small navel oranges, peeled,
    sectioned, and diced

1. With large knife, cut darker ruffly escarole leaf tips into very thin strips, leaving only the paler heart(s). Rinse the strips and spin-dry. Carefully cut the heart into 8 equal pieces, or quarter each heart if using smaller heads. Gently wash, keeping leaves joined. Pat dry, then set 2 pieces on each salad plate.

2. Grate zest from lemon; reserve. Halve lemon and squeeze enough juice to measure 1½ tablespoons. In cup, combine mustard, lemon juice, and thyme. Whisk in 3 tablespoons oil. Season. Spoon over hearts.

3. Heat remaining 2 tablespoons oil in wide skillet over high heat. Add garlic and toss until slightly colored. Add leaf strips, lemon zest, and rosemary. Toss until leaves *just begin* to wilt.

4. Immediately distribute hot escarole strips over hearts. Grind over pepper. Distribute optional oranges over all. Serve at once.

Serves 4

Pros Propose

Curly endive of the sturdy sort needs to be relaxed with heat of some kind. For example, at the Trellis restaurant in Williamsburg, the menu includes **Warm Frisée Salad with Potatoes:** Dress frisée with balsamic vinegar, whole-grain mustard, and olive oil. Surround with slices of blanched, grilled Idaho potato, and top with chunks of hot crisped bacon. For their leaner **Warm Frisée Salad with Tuna:** Dress frisée with vinaigrette based on pureed roasted red bell pepper. Top with hot tuna slab and surround with roasted red and yellow pepper strips.

"Curly endive is hardly ever served as a cooked vegetable in North America—we presume because people don't know how good it is," wrote Paola Scaravelli and Jon Cohen in *Cooking from an Italian Garden* in 1984—

and it still appears to be true. To cook **Indivia alla Romana:** Discard toughest outer endive leaves: rinse remainder. Boil or steam until tender. Drain, squeezing out water; rough-chop. Heat olive oil and chopped garlic in skillet. Add a little tomato sauce or chopped plum tomatoes, minced mint leaves, chopped capers, and seeded, minced fresh chilli. Cook just until sauce begins to thicken, 5 to 10 minutes. Add endive and seasoning and simmer until the mixture is well blended, about 5 minutes.

Carlo Middione, author of *La Vera Cucina,* likes curly yellow endive raw, with no more than oil and vinegar, and he also loves it cooked. For **Endive with Prosciutto and Garlic:** Trim 1 large head curly endive and tear into narrow sections, pulling apart from the stem end. Boil in salted water until tender. Drain, wrap in a towel, and squeeze dry. Heat olive oil and add chopped garlic, then chopped prosciutto and endive. Mix well and season. Cook a few minutes to blend flavors. Serve as a separate vegetable course, with bread, or alongside roast pork or chicken.

Frisée as raw salad leaf needs little explanation, but here's a fresh look from chef Charles Saunders. "Frisée makes an electric-looking salad because it sticks up dramatically and keeps its shape, which is why I choose it to build **Caesar Frisée.**" Arrange leaves in a bowl, pointing upward. Drizzle with garlic dressing, top with shaved dry aged Jack cheese, and add focaccia croutons.

Chef and author Joyce Goldstein puts escarole into her **Caesar Salad Pasta** in *Back to Square One:* Heat olive oil in skillet. Add chopped garlic and anchovy, then strips of escarole; wilt just slightly. Add bread crumbs, lemon zest, and grated Parmesan and toss. Add hot cooked spaghetti and pepper. Transfer to bowls and top with more crumbs and cheese.

Charles Saunders wraps cheese in escarole leaves as an appetizer. To prepare **Escarole Cheese Packets:** Blanch large, fairly flat endive leaves. Gently tap the heavy bases to flatten and soften fibers. Wrap eggroll-style around soft white cheese, such as mozzarella. Paint with oil and grill briefly over wood fire. Serve warm with sauce of dried tomatoes, balsamic vinegar, and olive oil.

"In Sicily a whole head of escarole is stuffed with a typically Arab-Sicilian mixture: raisins, pine nuts, and breadcrumbs," writes Clifford A. Wright of **Scarola Ripiena:** Blanch whole escarole heads briefly in boiling salted water. Drain in colander. Prepare stuffing of bread crumbs, anchovies, pine nuts, garlic, capers, and soaked and drained golden raisins. Set each head on its stem base, then open carefully. Push stuffing gently into the center of each head. Fold leaves back to their original position to enclose stuffing. Set in oiled pan. Pour over olive oil and chicken broth; season. Cover and cook about 15 minutes. Halve lengthwise to serve (from *Cucina Paradiso*).

Chef James Chew likes escarole leaves in his **Asian Bitter Green Salad** because they keep their character alongside other defined textures and flavors. To prepare: Tear pale escarole into small pieces and toss with sprigs of water cress and leaves of fresh mint, cilantro, and Thai basil. Add finest strands of red chilli and shallot julienne. Toss with dressing made from sweet garlic-chilli sauce and lime juice.

For softened—rather than texturally defined—endive, the leaves can be tenderized by marinating. This curious "tired salad" comes via two culinary originals: chef and author Viana La Place and one of her favorite cooks, Simonetta, the Italian fashion designer whose couture house in Paris flourished during the 1960s. In La Place's *Unplugged Kitchen,* she offers Simonetta's **Salade Fatiguée,** a salad that must be "drunk with its dressing." To prepare: Tear escarole and romaine hearts into small pieces. Combine in bowl with water cress sprigs, sliced Belgian endive, chopped fennel bulb, thin-sliced radishes, and thin-sliced mushrooms. Crumble over Roquefort. Drizzle with olive oil, lemon juice, salt, and pepper, and let rest an hour before serving.

Enokitake, Enoki (*Flammulina velutipes*)

Also enokidake, enoki mushroom, winter mushroom

Everything about enokitake is perky and pale. Even its name—a romanized form of the Japanese *enoki* (Chinese hackberry), a tree on which the mushroom *(take)* grows—sounds light. Enokitake is about as far from the wild as fungi get. It is therefore surprising to learn that in the natural habitat, "*Flammulina velutipes* is easily told by its velvety brown stalk, sticky cap, cheerful color, and growth on wood," according to David Arora, who (in *Mushrooms Demystified*) calls it velvet foot or velvet stem, from its species name, *velutipes*.

I have not seen it in the forest, but many people have, for it grows not only in the United States and Japan but throughout a good part of China, Siberia, Asia Minor, Europe, Africa, and Australia, according to S. T. Chang and P. H. Miles in *Edible Mushrooms and Their Cultivation*. (And more fungophiles than I realized must enjoy the cultivated mushroom. What I incorrectly assumed to be a mere garnish was ranked fourth in worldwide production of mushrooms, Chang and Miles report, with China and Japan the main producers.) Clearly, the gumdrop-topped bean sprouts shown above, cultivated enokitake, have little in common with the sylvan—at least to the naked eye. They do not even grow on wood; they grow on sawdust combined with rice bran and corncob meal, according to Jim Angelucci, general manager for Phillips Mushroom Farms, a primary specialty mushroom grower in the United States. The sweetly grainy aroma of that blend penetrates the growing room in Kennett Square, Pennsylvania, where enokitake puff up like soufflés from collared bottles (which keep the skinny stems straight) in a brightly lit, unusually cold environment, the mushroom's preferred man-made habitat.

This dramatically different version of *Flammulina velutipes* was tamed and trained by the Japanese, whose culinary style—a style dependent upon dramatic presentation with few ingredients—it suits very well. For visual impact, nothing else looks quite like this creamy, diminutive, long-legged, tiny-capped mushroom. And its oddly unmushroomy flavor fits in with other gentle Japanese flavors; mild, a bit yeasty, fruity, and acid. The texture, comparatively crisp, is equally unfungal, more vegetable.

BASIC USE: Perhaps the best way to think about enokitake is as a sprightly little vegetable, not a mushroom. Its delicacy, mildness, and form make it, above all, a graceful garnish for just about any food imaginable.

For the most part, enokitake is enjoyed raw: trimmed, then separated into small clumps or individual strands. Toss with light salad ingredients—feathery leaves, tart-sweet fruit, mini-vegetables. Tuck into sandwiches or spring rolls, like sprouts. Roll inside thin slices of ham or salmon for a first course.

Add to hot foods, just before serving: Float in consomme, enclose in crêpes or omelets, stir into broth. Tie enokitake bundles with blanched scallion greens and cook briefly in Japanese broth dishes, such as nabemono and sukiyaki.

SELECTION: Enokitake grown in the United States and Japan have become increasingly available in recent years, although they are not exactly common. They are sold on and off most of the year. Japanese imports, more expensive than the domestic product, are usually larger, more uniformly sized, and individually differentiated: more like tiny lollipops than tangled thread-thin sprouts. They are easier to handle and have far less waste. Try to locate enokitake packed in clear boxes, rather than shrink-wrapped in plastic packets—often unhelpfully opaque. The boxes protect the delicate mushrooms better and let you see what you're buying. Look for bright-white mushrooms that are relatively dry in appearance. They should not look at all watery or flabby, and there should be no sign of browning on the caps. (The growing medium attached to the clump of joined stems is usually beige.)

STORAGE: Refrigerate in the original container, unopened. Enokitake should last at least a week if purchased in good shape. Keep space around the packages to prevent bruising and allow airflow.

PREPARATION: Enokitake are grown in a sterilized environment and do not need rinsing. Some people prefer to rinse and dry the mushrooms, however. Trim off the base and growing medium. For vacuum-packed enokitake, cut 2 inches from the base without removing the mushrooms from the bag. Then slip off the bag and separate the mushrooms into clumps or individual stems.

Creamy Salad of Enokitake, Apple, and Water Cress

For a festive first course for a winter meal, these seemingly disparate elements join cheerfully in a crunchy Christmas tricolor salad. Enoki mushrooms are often sold prepacked in containers of various sizes, which is why a weight range is given below.

¼ cup lime juice
2 teaspoons sugar
½ teaspoon kosher salt
¾ cup sour half-and-half or sour cream
7 to 8 ounces enoki mushrooms
2 smallish Granny Smith apples
1½ tablespoons snipped chives or
    thin-sliced scallion (green onion) tops
1 bunch water cress
3 tablespoons fine-cut dill
¾ cup halved, thin-sliced round red radishes

1. Stir together lime juice, sugar, and salt. Blend in sour cream.

2. Trim off enoki base. Separate most stems (it is not necessary to pull them all apart) and halve crosswise. Halve and core apples (do not peel). Slice, then cut into matchsticks.

3. Season dressing. Toss half of it with the apples. Toss enoki and chives with about three-quarters of the remainder. Refrigerate apples and enoki.

4. Trim water cress, then break into sprigs. Rinse and spin-dry.

5. To serve, divide cress among plates. Top with apples. Sprinkle with dill and radishes. Divide enoki over this. Spoon over remaining dressing.

Serves 4 to 6 as a first course

Gingered Broth with Enokitake, Ham, and Cucumber

Whip up an elegant, low-fat first course in ten minutes. To maintain the textural contrasts, be very careful not to overcook. Choose serving bowls that will play up the cream, pink, and green ribbons. If you have access to a Japanese or Korean market, pick up crunchy Oriental cucumbers. If you can't find these or Middle Eastern or pickling types, use half of a European greenhouse cucumber.

3½ to 4 ounces enoki mushrooms
2 small unwaxed cucumbers (Oriental, Middle
    Eastern, on pickling type)
About 2½ ounces thin-sliced cooked ham
4 cups fat-free seafood, vegetable, or chicken
    broth
About 2½ teaspoons hair-thin ginger julienne
1 to 2 tablespoons dry sherry
Salt

1. Cut base from enoki, then separate most stalks. Without peeling, cut cucumbers into matchsticks (about 1 cup). Cut ham into strips the same size (to make about ½ cup).

2. Bring broth to a boil with 1 teaspoon ginger in medium saucepan. Add cucumbers, enoki, ham, 1 more teaspoon ginger, and 1 tablespoon sherry. Return to a boil over high heat. Taste and add ginger, sherry, and salt, as desired.

3. Distribute broth and solids evenly among small serving bowls. Serve immediately.

Serves 4

Pros Propose

Even when used in small quantity and most simply, enoki mushrooms make a distinct statement. Chef Anita Lo combines them with strands of like size and shape—but dramatically different color and texture—in **Hot-Sour Soup with Enokitake:** Prepare Chinese chicken broth with ginger, garlic, and scallions and bring to a boil. Season with distilled vinegar, Chinese black vinegar, pepper, and soy sauce. Thicken with cornstarch slurry. Add rehydrated hair-thin wood ear strips and rehydrated, halved lily buds, then heat through. Add enoki mushrooms and scallion ribbons. Serve at once.

Restaurant consultant and author Stephen Wong developed **Salmon Roulades with Enoki Mushrooms** to demonstrate the mushroom's special charms: Thin-slice salmon fillets, then cut into 2 × 4-inch rectangles. Marinate briefly in lightly beaten egg white, ginger juice, cornstarch, and salt. Blanch scallion greens (1 per roll). Refresh in cold water; drain. Trim enoki; divide into as many bundles as salmon slices. Roll salmon around enoki, keeping caps exposed, then tie each roll with scallion. Arrange on oiled plate. Microwave, covered with plastic, for 2 minutes. Loosen plastic and let rest 1 minute. Meanwhile boil chicken stock, soy sauce, dry sherry, sesame oil, and sugar. Spoon over fish and serve at once (from *HeartSmart Chinese Cooking*).

Chef Nora Pouillon's modified **Vietnamese Spring Rolls** also take advantage of the mushroom's slim straightness and small size: For each roll, lay a large spinach leaf on a spring roll wrapper. Top with cooked rice noodles, enoki mushrooms, shredded carrots, and grilled halved shrimp. Roll up and serve with soy-citrus dipping sauce.

For **Enokitake Slaw,** Pouillon tosses the fine-stemmed mushrooms with even finer pea shoots in a spicy dressing: Mix trimmed pea shoots with enokitake and thin-sliced pickled ginger. Add pickled ginger juice, lime juice, salt, pepper, cilantro leaves, and sliced Thai chilli. Serve as a salsa with steamed fish.

For **Light Bean Soup with Slender White Mushrooms and Bean Curd,** Elizabeth Andoh writes that enokitake's "delicate, almost floral bouquet is beautifully balanced . . . by the mellow fermented bean paste" (from *An American Taste of Japan*): Season dashi with soy sauce, rice wine, and salt; heat. Add well-drained ½-inch tofu cubes and cook a moment. Add trimmed enoki and cook 30 seconds. Ladle a few spoons of broth into a little shiro miso (white fermented soybean paste) and blend well. Add to soup and heat gently; do not boil. Sprinkle with chopped mitsuba (trefoil) or scallion green.

Fairy Ring Mushroom (*Marasmius oreades*)

Also fairyring, mousseron, Scotch bonnet

Fairy rings surprise with a flavor far more pronounced than one might expect from something so small: nutty, toasty, with a bitter-almond edge. Alan Davidson writes (in *The Oxford Companion to Food*) that "they are traditionally the mushrooms which are added to English steak and kidney pies," certainly no place for shy violets.

"But it is the French who make a big deal of them, who really love the big flavor of those mini-mushrooms," says the chef, restaurateur, and mycophile Jean-Louis Palladin. "Where I grew up, in Condom, people would pursue them like crazy. They take up little airplanes to hunt them. You'd spot a big area of green *mousse* [moss] and know where to find mousserons."

Curiously, the fairy ring mushroom is barely known in American markets and restaurants, and when it is, it is by the French word mousseron. This is odd because: (a) Although the mushroom is imported from France, it flourishes throughout North America. (b) Mousseron is a partial name. In France, it is generally modified as mousseron d'automne, faux mousseron, mousseron de Dieppe, petit mousseron, mousseron des prés, etc. "Mousseron" alone is likely to refer to a hefty *Tricholoma* that we call St. George. (Chef Eric Ripert knows fairy ring by the picturesque French name bouton de guêtre, or gaiter-button.) I vote for the restoration of the charming name fairy ring to better suit this cute tutu of a mushroom.

If fairy ring does not show up frequently in commerce, it is, nevertheless, well known to North American foragers. "Veil-less and scale-less, without freckle, speckle, or spine, the delectable fairy ring mushroom is one of suburbia's best-kept secrets," writes David Arora in his engaging *All That the Rain Promises, and More.* . . . Because it grows on lawns, in parks, and in cemeteries, a "*Marasmius* hunt is not so much an escape from civilization as an entry into it, a social event (unless you stick exclusively to cemeteries). It means getting to know your neighbors, offering to remove 'the blemishes from their premises,' encouraging them not

½ **actual size**

to spray pesticides, discussing global warming." So at the very least, consider fairy ring as a conversation piece if not a pièce de résistance.

BASIC USE: Whether the mini-mushrooms are served as a sauce or a garnish, the point is to let them stew gently in butter or cream until they mellow and turn silky and the juices become syrupy—which happens quickly. Spoon over fish fillets, scallops, veal, or breast of pheasant or chicken. Finish with seasoned butter. Or add beaten eggs to the cooked mushrooms and stir until custardy, for a luscious little supper scramble. Or add the caps to broth and cook briefly.

SELECTION: Fairy ring mushrooms pop up (in circles called fairy rings) on grassy areas throughout temperate North America, Europe, and Asia in all but the coldest weather. When they come to market depends on foragers, distributors, and transportation systems—but early summer to fall is most usual. Look for dry ones, as the thin flesh is soggy if recently rained on. Now and then they are bland or bitter, but no one seems to know how to detect either problem before cooking.

STORAGE: Spread in a basket or on a towel on a baking pan and cover with paper towels. Refrigerated this way, fresh ones will keep a few days. If they dry out, spray the towel. For long storage, fairy rings desiccate—and rehydrate—quickly and neatly. To prepare, first clip off and discard stems. Dehydrate the old-fashioned way, as chef Ripert does: "Run a string through the caps and hang in a dry place. They hold their flavor amazingly well and long." Or set on a sheet pan in a turned-off oven with a pilot light, leaving the door ajar; keep them there overnight, or until dried throughout and crisp.

PREPARATION: Fairy ring stalks are too tough and bitter to use. In my experience, it is necessary to cut them off with a knife or tiny scissors (which can get closer to the cap without breaking it, whereas the pressure from knife cuts can break it). If caps are large, halve or quarter them. To rid them of forest debris, rinse quickly in a bowl of water and lift out quickly. Check the knobbed caps if they look puffed or have tiny holes; insects hide in the domes.

Basic Fairy Ring Mushrooms (Mousserons)

Tiny caps simmered to shiny softness become a rich vegetable-cum-sauce. Spoon the intense (sometimes slightly bitter, like almonds), buttery garnish over roasted or sautéed white-fleshed fish fillets, veal scallops or roast, or breast of pheasant or chicken. Or increase the herbs and fold the mixture inside an omelet. Allow the fairy rings to stew gently in their juices—do not sear.

> 6 to 8 ounces fairy ring mushrooms
> 1 tablespoon butter
> ¼ teaspoon kosher salt
> 1 teaspoon lemon juice
> Pinch of sugar
> 1 to 2 teaspoons minced chervil or parsley leaves
> 1 to 2 teaspoons thin-sliced chives

1. If mushrooms are very small, cut off stems and leave caps whole. If more than a dainty mouthful, first halve or quarter caps, then cut off stems. Quickly dip in and out of bowl of water. Drain.

2. Heat medium skillet with tight-fitting cover. Add half the butter and sizzle over moderate heat. Add mushrooms, salt, lemon juice, and sugar, then toss. Cover, reduce heat, and simmer gently until juices turn syrupy, stirring now and then, about 5 to 8 minutes.

3. Off heat, add remaining butter. Season. Add 1 teaspoon each chervil and chives. Taste and add more as desired.

Makes about ¾ cup, to serve 2 as a garnish or side dish

Fairy Ring Mushrooms with Spring Peas in Cream

Shiny and succulent caps, deeply mushroomy, are brightened and sweetened by fresh peas. Although rich, the dish is not heavy, the cream plumping and smoothing the vegetables rather than becoming a thick sauce. Spoon alongside halibut, cod, or scallops.

> About ½ pound fresh peas in the pod
> ½ pound fairy ring mushrooms
> ¼ cup heavy cream
> ¼ teaspoon kosher salt
> ¼ teaspoon grated nutmeg
> 1 tablespoon thin-sliced chives

1. Shell peas (to make about ½ cup). If mushrooms are very small, snip off stems and leave caps whole. If more than a mouthful, halve or quarter caps, then cut off stems. Quickly dip in and out of a bowl of water.

2. Heat cream, salt, and nutmeg in medium skillet with tight-fitting cover. Add mushrooms and toss. Cover and simmer gently until cream and juices thicken slightly and mushrooms are soft, about 8 minutes; do not hurry the cooking.

3. Add peas and raise heat. Cook, uncovered, stirring, until cream is thick (but not reduced to a glaze) and peas are tender—a minute or two. Add chives, then season. Serve hot.

Serves 2 to 3 as a side dish

Pros Propose

Fairy rings at their simplest become delicate **Mousseron Garnish** in the hands of chef Laurent Gras: Trim and rinse caps, then dry on towels. Melt butter in heavy saucepan, add mushrooms, and simmer briefly, covered, until liquid reduces to coat the caps. Add chives, more butter, fleur de sel, pepper, and lemon—"but no more."

Chef Philippe Bertineau prefers a slightly more intense **Mousseron Sauce:** Gently cook caps in butter with diced shallots. Deglaze pan with red wine vinegar and reduce. Add just enough chicken stock to make a loose sauce. Cook briefly to blend, then add butter and chives. Pair with white fish or seafood.

Veal Chops with Mousserons "is the ideal use for these little mushrooms," says Jean-Louis Palladin: Dust thick veal chops with seasoned flour and pan-sear. Add caps, and season. Cover pan and cook in oven until veal is just done. Add "just a drop of veal *jus* and butter. The natural juices, thickened by the little bit of flour, make a fabulous sauce—simple and filled with flavor."

Chef Jimmy Schmidt likes his mushrooms with veal too, but he calls them by their American name and gets them locally. He also sears the caps in fat and does not discard the stems—departures from European tradition that he attributes to the quality of Michigan mushrooms. For **Roasted Veal with Fairy Ring Mushrooms:** Separate caps and stems. Cook shallots until soft. Add stems and white wine and reduce to nearly dry. Add cream and deep-fried rosemary needles ("fry at 310°F—not more—in olive oil to tame the bite and to flavor the oil"). Reduce cream slightly, puree, strain, and season. Heat butter until rich brown in non-stick skillet. Fry caps briefly, to crisp and cook through; drain. Add to sauce with more fried rosemary. Serve over roasted rack of veal seasoned with rosemary and roasted garlic.

Fennel

Florence Fennel
Common Fennel, page 280

Fennel is generous. All parts of the several forms of this aromatic plant are eaten—seeds, foliage, and stalks—particularly in lands around the Mediterranean, its home ground. Common fennel, cultivated and wild, is all stalks and feathery greenery. Fresh or dried, it is a familiar ingredient in southern Europe, whether in sauces, soups, or beverages or as seasoning. The bulbous vegetable type, Florence fennel, is the one that has captured America's attention, after many years of relative obscurity. But if we have finally discovered the pleasure of the raw vegetable, we still have much to learn about other aspects of the multifaceted plants, notably their cookability and the many uses of the versatile greens.

Florence Fennel

(*Foeniculum vulgare,* var. *azoricum*)

Also fennel, finocchio (Italian), bulbing fennel

In 1824, Thomas Appleton, the American consul in Florence, sent seeds of the city's vegetable to Thomas Jefferson with this glowing report:

> The Fennel is beyond, every other vegetable, Delicious. It greatly resembles in appearance the largest size of Sellery, perfectly white, and there is no veg-

left to right: Florence fennel in trimmed market form, with full greens, and baby

⅕ actual size

etable, equals it in flavour. It is eaten at Dessert, crude [see Basic Use] and with, or without Dry Salt, indeed, I preferred it to every other vegetable, or to any fruit. I think they will all thrive in your climate; the experiment may compensate the Labour.

Although seeds did travel beyond Jefferson's peerless experimental garden at Monticello, it is just recently that fennel has become widely available in the marketplace, probably thanks to America's ever-growing fascination with Mediterranean food. It is in Northern California, our most Mediterranean region in both climate and cuisine, that fennel has flourished in the field and in restaurants (where the baby form pictured here is most likely to appear).

The crisp, sweet-scented vegetable has its culinary and horticultural roots firmly planted in Italy, where the chubby "bulbing" type (not a true bulb, but thickened leaf stems) has been grown since the 17th century. "Finocchio" is the general Italian word for all fennels, but outside Italy it is used to signify this bulbing type. Finocchio is a word you may see in American markets (there is even "finocchio fennel"), as well as the misnomer "anise," which fennel simply is *not*. While fennel and anise are members of the same family, the Apiaceae (also called Umbelliferae), they are no more closely related than other aromatics in the group, which include dill, parsley, caraway, and coriander.

There is another market problem in addition to misidentification: the guillotining of the plant's pungent, aromatic greens. Look at the splendid stuff! Smell it! Who started the foolish plumage purge? A recent American report about "a new specialty vegetable for the fresh market," evaluates each variety for its bulb, the "greens being understood to be less desirable." As an afterthought, the authors conclude that "the possibility of marketing both the bulb and the fresh-cut foliage from the same plant of finocchio fennel remains an intriguing yet unexplored possibility." Unexplored where? Everyone who enjoys fennel includes the foliage—unless it has been hacked off.

BASIC USE

Raw: For a sublime starter, serve iced fennel wedges with crumbly fresh Parmesan and iced dry sherry or extra-dry (vergine) Marsala. Or offer fennel with other raw vegetables to serve with dips or to swizzle a cock-

tail. Lay prosciutto or smoked salmon over a bed of paper-thin fennel slices; grind pepper, coriander, and fennel seeds over all.

For a light salad, thin-slice fennel bulb and arrange with bell peppers, Asian radish, pear, orange, or apple; dress with lemon, olive oil, and snipped fennel tops. Add fennel to hearty grain salads to lighten and freshen. Substitute fennel for celery in any meat or seafood salads.

About Appleton's fennel "as Dessert, crude": One of the finest ways to end a meal is with fennel strips, soft goat cheese, figs, and cool vin santo. Or follow the beautiful suggestion of M. Audot, editor of the horticultural journal *Bon Jardinier*, whose notes on the gardens of southern Italy (1839–1848) are cited in *Le potager d'un curieux* (Paillieux and Bois): "The most general usage is to serve it at dessert with fruits; it thus decorates the table, planted in a glass bowl and raising like plumes its fine and elegant foliage; one eats it without any seasoning."

Cooked: First, a word about cooking fennel in general. Fennel's characteristic taste is usually compared to licorice and anise, but it is lighter and less cloying than either—and it becomes more delicate when cooked. Moreover, there is wide variation in the intensity of the perfume from one head to another. To amplify it, add a small quantity of crushed fennel seeds or fennel and/or anise-based liquors such as Ricard and Pernod to the recipe.

Parboil fennel slices and marinate in herbed vinaigrette; or cook slices in a seasoned court bouillon, à la grecque. Or brush thick slices with seasoned oil and grill them.

Bake fennel: Brown quartered bulbs and minced trimmings in oil and butter; moisten with wine and broth; cover and bake until tender. Or layer fennel slices in a casserole with potatoes, broth, milk, and cream. Top with crumbs or Parmesan or both; bake until tender.

Stir-fry or sauté fennel slivers or dice with shallot, onion, or garlic and just about any thin-sliced or diced vegetable you can imagine. Serve as a side dish, or use to stuff poultry, vegetables, or whole fish to be baked, adding a binding of eggs, crumbs, or both.

For silky soup, simmer fennel with water, milk, rice, and a pinch of fennel seeds until soft. Puree, then strain. Transform fish chowders by adding fennel instead of celery.

And for an unorthodox use: Fennel "improves the taste of bad wine," wrote Giacomo Castelvetro in 1614. "Our villainous Venetian wine-sellers solicitously offer innocent or simple-minded customers a piece of nice fennel to eat with their wine, or a few nuts, insisting that otherwise they might do themselves harm by drinking wine on an empty stomach" (from *A Brief Account of the Fruit, Herbs & Vegetables of Italy.* translated by Gillian Riley).

About fennel tops: If your finocchio has its fluffy feathers intact, as it should, use it as **common fennel** (page 280), adding some fennel seeds or fennel-based liquor to enhance the flavor.

SELECTION: Fennel is available year-round, but its peak is generally from early fall into spring. Choose hard, pearly (not dull) fennel. Select squat, rounded bulbs for volume and juiciness. Choose flattened, elongated symmetrical types for richer flavor. The outer layer should not be dried, split, or browning at the edges. The tops should sport fluffy green fronds which add flavor, color, and texture (if the fronds have been removed, *complain*).

STORAGE: Despite its hardy look, Florence fennel does not store well. Refrigerate, plastic-wrapped, for no more than a few days.

PREPARATION: Cut off greens, if any; wrap and refrigerate. Trim off stalks and tough outer layers; reserve to flavor stocks or roasting fish or poultry (insert in the cavity). Pare out some of the core.

For fennel to be braised, halve or quarter the trimmed bulbs. To sauté or stir-fry, thin-slice or dice these. To make thick slices, do not trim the core, which holds together the finger-like projections of stalk. For neat crudités, unwrap bulb layers and slice each one into strips—crisping briefly in ice water, if desired.

Fennel, Orange, and Green Olive Salad with Lemony Dressing

Crisp and juicy with a bright salt-sweet balance, this salad is a natural for grilled fish or poultry, or to accompany grain entrees. Pastis, the generic name for the fennel- and/or anise-flavored apéritifs of France, is most widely available in the United States under the Ricard and Pernod labels, but there are others. Choose tangy cracked green Provençal or Greek olives, herbed or plain.

16 medium green olives
1 or 2 lemons
About 1 tablespoon Ricard, Pernod, or orange juice
¼ teaspoon kosher salt
¼ teaspoon white pepper
2 tablespoons full-flavored olive oil
⅓ cup fine-diced red onion
2 medium Florence fennel bulbs with tops (about 1½ pounds)
2 medium-large navel oranges

1. Pit and thin-slice olives. Scrub 1 lemon and grate ¼ teaspoon zest. Squeeze lemon(s) to yield 3 tablespoons juice. Blend juice, zest, Ricard, salt, and pepper. Add oil and whisk to emulsify. Combine with onion and olives.

2. Cut off fennel tops and mince as desired for seasoning. Cut off stalks (reserve for another use). Quarter fennel bulbs lengthwise. Remove any heavy fibrous layers and trim tough part of core. Thin-slice crosswise on food processor slicing blade or vegetable slicer. Toss with minced tops. Arrange on salad plates.

3. Cut peel and pith from oranges. Slice each one into very thin rounds, then quarter to form wedges. Arrange around fennel. Spoon dressing over all, dividing olives and onions evenly.

Serves 4

Gingered Fennel Toss

An easy, last-minute side dish that's surprisingly special, given the few ingredients and speed of preparation. Use fresh, juicy ginger and taste as you add: Ginger's "bite," like fennel's aroma, varies considerably. Instead of ginger, you can substitute ½ to 1 teaspoon grated lemon zest.

2 medium-large Florence fennel bulbs with tops (1½ to 2 pounds)
Fresh ginger
1 tablespoon butter
¼ teaspoon kosher salt

2 tablespoons dry sherry
½ teaspoon sugar
2 tablespoons water

1. Trim off and reserve fennel tops. Cut off stalks (reserve for another use). Cut each bulb lengthwise into 4 equal pieces. Remove outer layer if heavy or dryish. Cut each quarter crosswise into very thin slices.

2. Using vegetable peeler, first peel ginger, then shave enough slivers to equal 1 generous tablespoon. Cut into very thin strips.

3. Melt butter in large heavy skillet over moderately low heat. Add fennel and toss to coat, then add salt. Toss frequently until fennel is somewhat tender but not cooked through, about 5 minutes.

4. Add 2 teaspoons ginger slivers, the sherry, sugar, and water. Cover and cook 2 minutes. Uncover and toss until fennel is tender and lightly browned, 3 to 4 minutes, adding more ginger to taste.

5. Mince reserved tops as desired. Sprinkle over fennel and serve hot.

Serves 4

Creamy Fennel Soup

Although this subtle, elegant puree is creamy, there is little (or no) cream in the recipe. It is easily made ahead for a dinner party, to be served chilled or hot. To serve hot, prepare with the butter; for the chilled, use the vegetable oil. Because the moisture content of fennel varies, add the milk gradually, so as not to thin the puree excessively.

1 very large or 2 medium Florence fennel
   bulbs with tops (1½ pounds)
1 large leek
1½ tablespoons butter or mild vegetable oil
1 medium-large floury potato
1 tart-sweet apple
About 1½ teaspoons kosher salt
6 cups unsalted vegetable or light poultry broth
1 tablespoon cornstarch
¼ to 1 cup whole milk, as needed
About 2 tablespoons Pernod, Ricard, or
   other pastis

Lemon juice
White pepper
Optional: 6 tablespoons heavy cream

1. Cut off and reserve feathery fennel tops. Zip strings from outer layers of bulbs and stalks, as you would from celery. Thin-slice all fennel bulbs and stalks. Trim roots and darkest leaves from leek, and discard. Slice leek lengthwise, then across into thin slices. Wash in several changes of water.

2. Melt butter in large pot. Stir in sliced fennel and leek. Cook over moderate heat until softened, about 10 minutes.

3. Meanwhile, peel and slice potato. Core, peel, and slice apple. Add both, 1 teaspoon salt, and broth to fennel. Simmer, covered, about 30 minutes, or until vegetables are very soft.

4. In blender or food processor, puree soup until smooth. Strain back into pot through medium sieve (or, for thicker soup, omit straining).

5. Blend cornstarch and ¼ cup milk. Add to soup and bring to a simmer, stirring. Simmer 1 minute, stirring constantly. Add more milk as needed for desired consistency. Add pastis to taste. Season with lemon juice, salt, and white pepper. (To serve chilled, cool, uncovered, then cover and refrigerate.)

6. Mince fennel tops to taste. Ladle soup into bowls, then drizzle each serving with 1 tablespoon cream, if desired. Sprinkle with fennel tops.

Serves 6 as a first course

Fennel and Shrimp Risotto

Subtle flavors reward the patient cook who prepares this special risotto. First broth is simmered with the "discards"—fennel stalks and shrimp shells—then it is slowly incorporated into the rice for a creamy but comparatively low-fat version of a commonly rich dish. While arborio is the most familiar of Italian risotto rices, baldo, carnaroli, and vialone nano are all interesting.

Because risotto demands attention, I serve it as a main course, with other foods that require little or no work: Begin with olives, radishes, and grissini; follow the risotto with a salad of arugula, frisée, and Bibb lettuce. For dessert, serve biscotti and candied ginger and citrus peels, with espresso.

> 1 large Florence fennel bulb with feathery tops (1¼ pounds)
> 1 carrot, sliced
> 2 celery stalks with leaves, sliced
> 1 bay leaf
> ½ teaspoon fennel seeds
> 3 cups water
> 4 cups vegetable, veal, or chicken broth (preferably unsalted)
> ½ pound medium shrimp in the shell
> Salt and white pepper
> About 2 tablespoons sour cream
> 2 medium shallots
> 1 tablespoon butter
> 1½ cups Italian rice for risotto
> 1 tablespoon olive oil
> ½ cup dry white wine
> Lemon juice

1. Cut off and reserve feathery fennel tops. Remove stalks and heavy outer layers and chop. Combine in pot with carrot, celery, bay leaf, fennel seeds, water and broth. Peel shrimp, reserving shells. Halve shrimp by splitting down the back, then season; reserve. Add shells to pot.

2. Simmer broth ½ hour. Strain into clean pot. Salt lightly (omit if broth is salted). Blend 2 tablespoons broth with 2 tablespoons sour cream; set aside.

3. Meanwhile, separate fennel bulb into layers; slice into matchsticks. Mince shallots.

4. Melt butter in a heavy pot over moderately low heat. Add shallots and stir a minute or so. Add fennel, cover, and cook over low heat until not quite tender, about 10 minutes, stirring now and then. Meanwhile, set broth over low heat and maintain at just below a simmer.

5. Add rice and oil to fennel and cook over moderately low heat 2 minutes. Add wine and stir until liquid evaporates. Add simmering broth ½ cup at a time, keeping it at a lively simmer, and stirring until each addition is nearly absorbed before adding the next. When rice is almost done, after 16 to 18 minutes, stir in shrimp and ½ cup more broth. Stir until shrimp is just cooked, about 2 minutes.

6. Off heat, stir in the sour cream mixture and salt, pepper, and lemon juice to taste. Add more broth and sour cream, as desired. Scoop into warmed dishes. Mince fennel tops and sprinkle over.

**Serves 3 to 4 as a main course,
6 to 7 as a first course**

Pros Propose

With typical panache, minimalist Rozanne Gold assembles a maximally original dish from three ingredients. For **Fennel Wafers with Poached Eggs:** Remove fennel stalks and reserve fronds. Cut bulb into thin vertical "wafers," slicing through the core to hold layers together. Spread on foil-covered sheet. Coat each slice with grated Parmesan. Bake at 425°F until crisp and golden. Arrange 4 or 5 wafers on each plate and top with a poached egg, minced fennel fronds, and pepper (from *Recipes 1-2-3 Menu Cookbook*).

Another minimalist, always fresh in his approach, is the luminary Jean-Georges Vongerichten. To prepare his **Fennel and Apple Salad with Juniper:** Trim stalks from fennel bulb, keeping fronds for garnish. Quarter and core Granny Smith apple (do not peel). Slice fennel crosswise as thin as possible, preferably on a mandoline. Slice apple equally thin. Toss with lemon juice, olive oil, salt, and pepper. Crush juniper berries with knife, then mince. Stir into salad and let sit 5 minutes before serving. Sprinkle with minced fennel tops (from *Jean-Georges*).

At the other end of the spectrum is oozingly rich **Pancetta-Wrapped Roasted Fennel in Cream** from *Regional Foods of Southern Italy* by Marlena de Blasi: Coarse-chop fennel stalks and fronds. Combine in pot with water to just cover. Trim and halve bulbs. Add to pot, cover, and bring to a simmer. Poach until bulbs begin to soften; then remove them (save broth for another use). Sauté as many pancetta slices as fennel halves in olive oil; drain and reserve drippings. Wrap each fennel half in pancetta, securing with a toothpick. Arrange in single layer in baking dish. Sprinkle with chopped black Sicilian olives. Combine heavy cream, crushed anise and fennel seeds, white wine, and pepper. Pour over fennel. Sprinkle with grated pecorino and fine bread crumbs. Drizzle with reserved pan drippings. "Roast the fennel for 40 minutes, or until it has drunk in nearly all the liquids, a good burnished crust has formed from the cheese and the bread crumbs, and bits of lightly charred pancetta are poking through it all."

Common Fennel

(*Foeniculum vulgare* var. *dulce*)

Also sweet fennel, leaf fennel,
wild fennel

Including **bronze fennel**
(*Foeniculum vulgare* 'Rubrum')

This is no dainty herb to simply snip, but foliage to roll in, take armfuls of, and cook with. It is used in volume as a vegetable.

Whether it is pushing through cracks in the sidewalks, poking uninvited into polite gardens, climbing over sere hillsides, or cultivated in neat rows on commercial herb plantations, on a warm day you can smell common fennel from a block away. The powerful penetrating aroma (along with a taste to match) is what first sets it apart from Florence fennel.

The wild fennel of the Mediterranean (which D. J. Mabberley dates to the 13th century B.C. in *The Plant-Book*) is similar to the escaped garden fennel of the American West Coast, as anyone knows who has been surprised by the perfume while walking along a country path in Provence or a busy street in San Francisco. The fennel of herb plots and that of wild hills seem to differ primarily in luxuriance. Both are composed of skinny, non-bulbing stalks and covered with feathery leaves that are far more intense in flavor and perfume than Florence fennel.

Bronze fennel, except for a variation in color, is much the same. Shiny, dense, fluffy plumes cover stalks that broaden and lighten in color at the base but do not bulb like Florence fennel. The greens range from medium to very deep with hints of purply brown—not really bronze. Although this plant is highly aro-matic, like green common fennel, its forceful flavor is not sweet but slightly harsh, even overwhelming when raw—and smoothly rounded and mellow when blanched.

BASIC USE FOR COMMON, BRONZE, AND WILD FENNELS: When raw, the soft young feathery greens are almost too powerful but can be used in very small quantity, as a seasoning herb, like dill. Once they are cooked, their flavor becomes soft and balanced: Chop feathery tops and fine stems to add to sautéed vegetables—such as cucumber, summer squash, or shell beans—during the last few minutes of cooking. Stir into soups as they finish cooking. Add raw to stuffing mixtures for fish or poultry to be cooked. For fragrant green rice, combine the chopped tops with raw rice and cook as usual. Blanch and puree with scallions and yogurt, then liaise with olive oil for a fresh-tasting sauce to serve over seafood or vegetables; or spoon a ribbon into thick bean soup or fish stew, or drizzle over bean and grain salad.

SELECTION: Take any you can find!

STORAGE: Feathery fennel lasts remarkably well. I have refrigerated it in a ventilated plastic bag and found it fragrant and flavorful weeks later.

PREPARATION: For common and bronze fennel, just cut to suit the dish at hand. For wild fennel, which may be leggy, strip the thin stems and fluffy greens from the tough stalks (reserve for bouquet garni).

bronze fennel bunch   length: 2 feet

wild fennel tips

length: 3-5 inches

Common or Bronze Fennel Puree with Pasta

Much more than a seasoning pesto, this puree is both green vegetable and deep-flavored sauce for lovers of pastis, anise, licorice, and the like. Boiling tames the ferocious flavor, rendering it mellow and buttery—much like creamy, mild Pernod. For variation, garnish with halved cherry tomatoes.

    1 pound common or bronze fennel stalks
    2 or 3 garlic cloves, peeled and halved
    About ½ teaspoon minced garlic
    Salt and pepper
    1 pound imported Italian pasta of
       just about any type
    About ⅓ cup full-flavored olive oil
    About 2 tablespoons dry vermouth or
       white wine

1. Bring a large pot of water to a boil. If bases of fennel stalks are tough or dried, trim off and discard. Separate feathery fronds from stalks and reserve. Slice stalks, then drop into the boiling water with plenty of salt. Boil until tender, about 10 minutes.

2. Meanwhile, rough-cut fennel fronds (to make about 6 tightly packed cups). When stalks are tender, add fronds to water, cover, and return to a boil. Uncover, add halved garlic cloves, and boil, stirring often, until greens are quite tender, about 5 minutes. (If using bronze fennel, do not be surprised if the water turns navy-purple.) Drain.

3. Refill pot and bring water to a boil. Add salt and cook pasta.

4. Meanwhile, transfer well-drained fennel to food processor. Puree, scraping sides often. Add minced garlic to taste and plenty of salt and pepper—to overseason. Gradually whirl in ⅓ cup oil. Add vermouth to taste, then more oil, salt, and pepper as needed.

5. Mix puree thoroughly with pasta, using tongs to coat well. Season.

Serves 4 as a main course

Feathery Fennel-Yogurt Sauce

This pale green sauce with darker flecks has the texture of thick buttermilk and a clean, fresh flavor. Serve it over hot or chilled poached salmon or shrimp, or steamed vegetables (such as carrots, squash, or potatoes). Or spoon into thick bean soup or fish stew, or drizzle over bean and grain salads.

1¼ cups tightly packed common or
    wild fennel greens
1 large scallion (green onion), trimmed
    and sliced
½ teaspoon kosher salt
White pepper
1 tablespoon olive oil
1 cup yogurt, whole-milk or low-fat
    (not fat-free)

1. Drop fennel into boiling salted water. Return to a boil; drain.

2. Combine fennel in a food processor or blender with scallion, salt, and pepper. Add the oil and one-third of the yogurt and process to chop fine. Pour into dish and whisk in remaining yogurt.

3. Chill to serve.

Makes 1 generous cup, to serve 4

Cucumbers with Feathery Fennel

Barbara Spiegel, whose recipe ideas figure in this and my earlier cookbooks, set out to develop a seafood-fennel recipe but then decided a vegetable dish would be more useful, "because just about any seafood will be enhanced by the subtle, aromatic, crunchy combination of cucumber and fennel." Try this dish with scallops, shrimp, or grilled salmon and you'll find seafood is more than enhanced by fennel and cucumber—it cannot be improved! (As evidence: *The Oxford English Dictionary* defines fennel as "a fragrant perennial umbellifer . . . cultivated chiefly for its use in sauces eaten with salmon, etc.")

1 pound cucumbers (3 medium)
1 teaspoon kosher salt

2 cups tightly packed common, wild,
    or bronze fennel tops
2 or 3 large shallots
2 tablespoons fruity olive oil
Optional: 1 tablespoon Pernod, Ricard, or
    other pastis

1. Peel cucumbers and halve lengthwise; scoop out seeds. Cut into ¼-inch slices and toss with salt. Drain in sieve about ½ hour, tossing occasionally. Pat dry.

2. Meanwhile, rinse and dry fennel. Chop to medium-coarse texture. Mince shallots, to yield ½ cup.

3. Set large sauté pan over moderately high heat. Add olive oil and shallots. Stir frequently until shallots are translucent, a few minutes. Add cucumbers. Stir until they are cooked but still somewhat crunchy, about 3 minutes.

4. Add fennel. Taste, then add optional liquor if flavor is not pronounced enough. Toss just to "melt" fennel, less than a minute.

5. Serve hot or at room temperature.

Serves 2 as a side dish

Pros Propose

Wild fennel's best-known use may be in the traditional Sicilian **Pasta con le Sarde:** Boil wild fennel until tender; drain. Chop. Soften minced onions in plenty of olive oil; add the fennel, smooth tomato sauce, pine nuts, currants, anchovy fillets, and nutmeg. Simmer 15 minutes. Add cleaned sardines and cook until they break up. Toss cooked perciatelli with saffron steeped in hot water. Mix with half the sauce, then spoon over remainder. Garnish with cleaned sardines that have been dipped in semolina flour and fried in olive oil (from *The Heart of Sicily* by Anna Tasca Lanza).

"Here in Berkeley, we gather tender green wild fennel tops on the way to work, for this and other Sicilian-inspired dishes," writes Alice Waters in the *Chez Panisse Café Cookbook*. On the West Coast, the pasta con le sarde gets a more complex treatment as **Baked Pasta with Sardines and Wild Fennel:** Scale, gut, and fillet fresh sardines. Season flesh, drizzle with oil, then refrigerate. Boil penne rigate until not quite done; drain. Toss with oil. Boil wild fennel tops 3 minutes;

drain, saving some cooking liquid. Sauté onion and diced Florence fennel bulb in olive oil. Add toasted, crumbled saffron and salt and cook until fennel is tender. Add chopped garlic, pounded anchovies, and chilli flakes and cook briefly. Meanwhile, puree wild fennel tops with enough cooking liquid to make a pesto. In large bowl, mix pasta, plumped and drained golden raisins, toasted pine nuts, fennel-onion mixture, and pesto. Add seasoning, olive oil, and fennel liquid as needed. Turn into a gratin dish. Tuck sardines into the pasta and drape a few on top. Drizzle with oil and bake until pasta is lightly browned, about 15 minutes. Serve with lemon wedges and parsley.

There is also a quick and easy approach to seafood and fennel—an aromatized marinara—from chef Bruce Naftaly. For **Mussels and Fennel in Tomato-Herb Broth:** In food processor, blend homemade tomato paste, garlic, shallots, and plenty of fennel greens to a coarse puree, scraping sides often. Mix in

saucepan with butter and Riesling. Add mussels and steam until they open. Serve at once.

A few ingredients, thoughtfully combined, distinguish the dishes of Italian chef Odette Fada. Her **Fennel-Stuffed Rabbit** illustrates: Bone rabbit, open out, and pound flat. Season and spread with ground, seasoned pork fat. Top with a thick layer of chopped wild fennel greens. Roll and tie. Roast, brushing often with olive oil. Slice and serve warm as a main course, or cold with a green salad as an appetizer.

Raw fennel stalks and greens, both wild and cultivated, are the flavorful (and frugal) base for **Fennel Vinaigrette** from West Coast chef Nancy Oakes and her chef de cuisine, Pamela Mazzola: Chop Florence fennel bulb and cucumbers in food processor with wild fennel stalks (reserve fronds). Add garlic and rice vinegar. Puree until fine, then strain through coarse sieve. Return to processor. With motor running, add olive oil. Season. Chop fennel greens and add.

Fenugreek Greens, Methi (*Trigonella foenum-graecum*)

Also methi saag (Indian)

½ actual size

International sources indicate that fenugreek, a leguminous plant native to western Asia and southeastern Europe, is cultivated in much of the world: Africa, the Middle East, South America, the Mediterranean, China, and the Asian subcontinent. But if you're looking for the fresh vegetable in the United States, it is only this last source that counts. If you want fenugreek greens, you must look primarily in Indian or Pakistani groceries and ask for them by their Hindi name, methi (pronounced met-hee).

The genus *Trigonella* means little triangle, "in reference to the triangular shape of the small yellowish-white flowers," writes the former spice producer Frederic Rosengarten, Jr., author of *The Book of Spices*.

"The species epithet *foenum-graecum* means 'Greek hay'—the Romans who got the plant from Greece, where it was a very common crop in ancient times, gave it this name." The association with hay holds in other senses, too. Fenugreek is a fodder crop and a relative of clover; and Rosengarten notes that "mildewed or 'sour' hay is made palatable to cattle when fenugreek herbage is mixed with it."

Fenugreek is best known for its seeds. Of curious form and stony hardness (they were preserved in Tutankhaman's tomb), they are the distinctive aroma that defines curry powder, if you ask this nose (minus fenugreek, the bouquet of spices is just that, not what we call curry). Oddly, extract of fenugreek is also the source of maple flavoring. (How can real fenugreek be imitation maple?)

But the fresh greens (not the dried ones, a related species that is a popular Indian aromatic) are the subject under examination here. This introduces the dangerous topic of bitterness, a characteristic of the greens (moderate, not aggressive), and often treated as a threat to American taste buds. I mention it up front to allow those who wish to leave the room to do so now. Those who enjoy bitterness for the way it gives backbone to the mild, counterposes sweetness, cleanses the palate, and heightens the sense of taste may wish to know that tender fenugreek leaves also offer hints of celery, fennel, spinach, and split pea (they are legumes, after all), and that the cooked texture is similar to that of water cress.

BASIC USE: Too bitter to be served "straight," fenugreek works wonders on all manner of starchy and sweet vegetables when added toward the end of cooking, to simmer and release its suggestive scents. Add the chopped leaves to potatoes, carrots, lentils, wheat kernels or kamut, sweetpotatoes, parsnips, or beans when they're nearly done; cover and steam just moments to permeate. Traditionally, fenugreek is chopped into bread doughs or combined with chickpea flour for fritters. When the leaves are being cooked, the addition of even a very small quantity of ground turmeric boosts the color to a vivid parrot green.

SELECTION: In Jackson Heights and Jersey City, methi has been available most of the year. If it is like other bitter greens, the bitterness may increase when it is grown in hot weather, but I haven't yet been able to prove that to my satisfaction. Look for leafy—not stemmy—plants that are comparatively small. The leaves should be uniformly green, not darkening or yellowing. Fenugreek is sold bunched (6 to 8 ounces is usual), with its very sandy tough roots attached. If it isn't labeled and you're not sure, take a sniff: the curry-celery smell should let you know.

STORAGE: Cook as soon as possible. Methi is extremely perishable, blackening and rotting like basil. Remove the band from around the bunch, spread out the plants, and remove any darkening or mushy leaves. Return the greens to a plastic bag, with a piece of paper towel to absorb condensation. Refrigerate a few days at most, turning the bag to prevent moisture from collecting in one area.

PREPARATION: Cut roots and any heavy stem bases from plants. If plants are small, that should be enough. If large, strip small stems and leaves from the main stalk, which should be discarded. Dunk into water, slosh around, and let sand sink. Lift out and repeat with fresh water. Fenugreek can be very gritty and require many baths.

Fenugreek-Scented Potatoes

Small potatoes browned in butter and scented by the vapor of fenugreek leaves develop a warm curry-maple taste. The plant's unique bitterness is tempered by cooking, but if you prefer even less, add a squeeze of lemon. The recipe, based on a traditional dish of New Delhi, was described to me by Rashmi Aggarwala, formerly at the Culinary Center of New York at The New School.

½ **pound fenugreek greens (1 large bunch)**
1¼ **pounds very small potatoes (preferably**
    yellow-fleshed)
1 **tablespoon vegetable oil**
2 **tablespoons butter**
1 **teaspoon kosher salt**
½ **teaspoon pepper**
1 **teaspoon ground coriander**
¼ **teaspoon turmeric**
Optional: lemon wedges

1. Cut roots and heavy stems, if any, from fenugreek; discard. Wash greens in *many* changes of water,

lifting out so debris sinks. Chop medium-fine. Scrub and trim potatoes. If no more than 1¼ inch in diameter, halve; if larger, cut into ¾-inch pieces.

2. Heat oil and 1 tablespoon butter in wide pan over moderately high heat. Add potatoes and cook, tossing often, to brown lightly, about 10 minutes.

3. Add fenugreek, tossing until greens wilt, about 2 minutes. Add remaining 1 tablespoon butter, cover pan, and cook over low heat until potatoes are very tender, about 10 minutes. Check often to avoid scorching; if necessary, lower heat and add a little water.

4. When potatoes are cooked through, uncover and raise heat to moderate. Add salt, pepper, coriander, and turmeric and toss briefly to coat. Serve hot or warm, with optional lemon wedges.

Serves 4 as a side dish

Curried Cucumbers with Fenugreek Greens

Crunchy crescents of cucumber turn bright yellow-green in this quick sauté. Sweet-salty and ever so slightly curried, they are subtly altered by the light bitterness of chewy chopped fenugreek leaves, which suggest pea vines with power. A natural complement for seafood and jasmine rice.

> 2 pounds cucumbers, preferably not waxed (6 medium)
> ½ tablespoon kosher salt
> 2 teaspoons sugar
> ½ pound fenugreek greens
> 2 large shallots
> 2 tablespoons peanut or other vegetable oil
> 1 teaspoon curry powder
> ¼ teaspoon white pepper or ⅛ teaspoon ground hot pepper
> A few drops of mild vinegar
> Optional: chopped salted peanuts or toasted coconut

1. Peel cucumbers and halve lengthwise; scoop out seeds. Cut into ¼-inch slices and toss with salt and sugar. Drain in a sieve about ½ hour, tossing often, while you clean the fenugreek.

2. Cut roots and heavy stems from fenugreek; discard. Wash greens in *many* changes of water, lifting out so debris sinks. Chop medium-fine. Mince shallots.

3. Drain cucumbers and pat dry. Place large sauté pan over moderately high heat. Add oil and shallots. Stir frequently until shallots are translucent, a few minutes; do not brown. Stir in curry powder and pepper.

4. Add cucumbers, raise heat to high, and stir often until cooked but still somewhat crunchy, about 2 minutes. Add fenugreek. Toss just to "melt" slightly, less than a minute. Season with vinegar. Serve hot, with optional nuts.

Serves 4 to 5 as a side dish

Pros Propose

Cooks in many lands add fenugreek seed to their meals, and recipes exist to prove it. But greens are rarely mentioned. Although I am told that they are cooked in Ethiopia, Yemen, Egypt, and Cyprus, among other countries, I cannot find solid verification or recipes. India is what tells the tale, and what follows.

Rashmi Aggarwalla cooks **Methi with Carrots:** Peel and thin-slice slim carrots. Warm corn oil over moderate heat. Add whole cumin seeds and turmeric and stir a moment. Add carrots and salt. Toss to coat well. Cover and cook gently until carrots are not quite tender, shaking often to prevent sticking. Add cleaned, fine-chopped methi; toss to wilt, less than a minute. Serve hot.

Aggarwalla also makes a paste of the leaves to season fish fillets. For **Monkfish in Fenugreek Pesto:** Brush fillets with oil. Season with ground chilli, salt, pepper, and turmeric. Wilt chopped fenugreek greens in olive oil. Scoop into food processor and chop to a coarse paste. Spread on both sides of fillets. Sauté in plenty of olive oil.

I prepared **Rice with Fenugreek** before I learned that it was a traditional dish in Sri Lanka, Malaysia, and India. The Indian versions are all I have found in print—similar and delicious. To prepare: Wash basmati rice in several changes of water, then soak in water to cover by about an inch for ½ hour. Heat vegetable oil and cumin seeds, tossing briefly. Add minced onion and cook until golden. Add minced garlic, a little turmeric, and about the same amount of minced fenugreek leaves as rice. Add the rice and its soaking water, then salt. Bring to a boil, stirring. Cook, partly covered, over moderately low heat until surface looks dry and steam holes form. Cover, reduce heat to lowest level, and cook about 5 minutes. Let stand for about 15 minutes. Fluff into a warmed dish to serve.

Fenugreek Fritters (methi vada) are "traditionally made with chickpea flour, but this version is innovative and appetizing. It is crunchy and remains so with keeping. Serve it as a snack with a sweet chutney," writes Monisha Bharadwaj in *The Indian Spice Kitchen*. To prepare: Mix fresh fenugreek leaves, cornmeal, ground turmeric and cayenne; whole cumin, ajowan, and sesame seeds; and grated ginger. Add water to make a thick batter. Heat corn oil for shallow-frying in a skillet. Drop little balls of batter into it. Fry until brown. Turn, cover, and cook over low heat until done. Serve hot.

Fiddlehead Fern (primarily *Matteuccia struthiopteris*)

Also fiddlehead greens

A fiddlehead is not a special kind of fern but the coiled (crosier) form of any new fern that has not yet unfurled. Ostrich fern (*Matteuccia struthiopteris*), pictured here, is the species usually collected in Canada and the mainland United States (in Hawaii, *Diplazium esculentum* is common). Of Asian origin, ostrich fern is one of more than twenty species that regularly figured in the diet of early American Indians, according to the ethnobotanist Barrie Kavasch, author of *Native Harvests*.

In 1966, ostrich fern was described as "a Canadian specialty and gourmet vegetable" that is "found in quantity in the St. John River Valley in New Brunswick" (*The Laura Secord Canadian Cook Book*, prepared by the Canadian Home Economics Association). It doesn't seem to have progressed much since then, which is odd given its far-reaching natural distribution and the percolating interest in wild foods. In the United States, Vermont and Maine are prime terrain, and the ferns emerge on riverbanks as far south as

Virginia, as far north as Newfoundland, and west over almost half the country.

Ferns are part of the green vegetable repertoire in many parts of the world, from northern climes to the tropics. New Zealand, "with almost 200 native ferns, many of them very common . . . is sometimes called 'The Land of Ferns.'" Andrew Crowe writes in *A Field Guide to the Native Edible Plants of New Zealand*. "One fern—bracken [*Pteridium aquilinum*]—was the most important wild source of plant food of the Maori, and the shoots of many other ferns were also eaten." Bracken fern (warabi in Japanese) is popular in Japan and Korea, as is cinnamon fern, zenmai (*Osmunda cinnamomoea*).

Although consumption of these and of the royal fern (*Osmunda regalis*) is an old practice, particularly in the Far East, experts now advise strongly against it. "There is considerable evidence that they are a cause of cancer of the stomach and esophagus," says John Mickel, senior curator of ferns at the New York Botanical Garden, who recommends eating only young ostrich fern.

When small and fresh, ostrich fern suggests asparagus, artichokes, green beans, and mushrooms but has a chewy texture all its own. Chef Jean-Georges Vongerichten says that "fiddlehead ferns taste like a walk in a moist forest, especially paired with their seasonal companions, morels." Other chefs, less charmed, consider the curled shape to be the plant's most appealing trait.

BASIC USE: Fiddleheads should not be consumed raw. They are at their best after boiling, which retains texture and color as it helps banish bitterness and compounds associated with gastric problems. According to John Mickel, problems (which are uncommon) do not occur if the vegetable is cooked for 5 minutes or longer.

Treat cooked fiddleheads more or less as asparagus: Drizzle with lemon butter, cream or cheese sauce, hollandaise or maltaise. Add blanched fiddleheads to a creamy ragoût as it finishes cooking. Or serve fiddleheads at room temperature, with a sprinkling of shoyu and sesame seeds, as is done in Japan. Boil fiddleheads, refresh in cold water, drain, then toss with a light mustard vinaigrette (just before serving—or the color turns nasty); or add them to a composed salad.

Curiously, although fiddleheads lose their charming appearance when chopped or pureed, they seem to develop flavor. If you have a wealth of them, puree the cooked ferns and fold into a quiche or soufflé base, then garnish with whole cooked ferns and miniature vegetables, such as pattypan squash and round carrots.

SELECTION: Nature will determine the fiddlehead season. In each locale the shoots sprout for about 2 weeks, then unfurl to inedible plumes. In southerly areas, fiddleheads may emerge in early April. As warmth increases, growth shifts northward, with the final Canadian crops appearing as late as July. Choose fiddleheads that are jade, bouncy, small, and firm—not flabby.

STORAGE: Fiddleheads do not store well. Although they do not visibly spoil, they quickly lose their fresh taste and elastic tone. Wrap tightly in plastic and refrigerate no more than a few days. Freezing is often recommended, but I find frozen ferns fibrous and fishy.

PREPARATION: Trim the base of each fern to leave only a small tail beyond the circumference of each circular shape. Some fiddleheads will require cleaning;

some will not. Those that do will need to have the fuzzy brown covering or scales removed by being rubbed between your palms. All should be well rinsed.

Basic Boiled Fiddlehead Ferns

Having steamed, poached, braised, microwaved, and boiled fiddlehead ferns, I find the last method best retains texture and color, and it eliminates the bitterness that sometimes unbalances the flavor. Ferns cooked with baking soda have a more uniform but somewhat soft texture, no trace of bitterness, and slightly brighter coloring. The choice is yours. Both methods yield pretty, pliant ferns ready to sauce, sauté, or dress for salad.

1 pound fiddlehead ferns (1 to 1½ inches in diameter)

Method 1

1. Trim base of each fern if necessary, to leave only a short tail beyond circumference of each round shape. If furry brown covering remains on ferns, rub it off. Rinse briskly under running water.

2. Drop ferns into a large pot of boiling salted water. Boil until tender throughout—about 5 minutes—testing often; if they are undercooked, their full flavor will not develop. Drain well.

Method 2

Proceed as above, but boil ferns in 2 quarts water to which you have added 1 tablespoon kosher salt and ½ teaspoon baking soda. Cook for a shorter period of time, about 3 to 4 minutes.

Serving Suggestions for Basic Boiled Fiddlehead Ferns

- Serve freshly cooked with butter, chives, and parsley.
- Serve freshly cooked with about ¾ cup hollandaise, maltaise, cream or cheese sauce.
- Refresh boiled ferns in ice water; drain (can be refrigerated). To serve, melt 2 tablespoons butter in large skillet. Sauté ferns until heated through. Sautéed morels make a fine addition.
- Refresh boiled ferns, drain, and blot dry. Toss with ¾ cup vinaigrette.

Serves 4 to 6 as a side dish or garnish

Sunny Springtime Luncheon Salad

Fiddleheads, golden squash, little potatoes, eggs, and cress in dill-mustard sauce make a pretty picture. The bouquet of rounds upon rounds—yellow, green, and white—tastes best lukewarm or at room temperature. The appealing textures change if chilled—and the pistachio ferns turn sickly green if dressed in advance. For a meaty meal, serve thin slices of ham alongside.

½ pound fiddlehead ferns
4 eggs
2 small golden zucchini or yellow summer
    squash (4 to 5 ounces each)
12 fairly small yellow-fleshed potatoes
    (1½ pounds)
1 small shallot, minced
½ tablespoon Dijon mustard
2 tablespoons lemon juice
¼ teaspoon kosher salt
2 tablespoons olive oil
1 tablespoon mild oil, such as corn or safflower
1 tablespoon white wine or dry vermouth
¼ cup minced dill
1 bunch water cress, trimmed, washed, dried,
    and separated into sprigs
Pepper

1. Trim and cook fiddleheads as for Basic Boiled Fiddlehead Ferns.

2. Combine eggs and plenty of water in a medium pot. Bring to a boil. Add a handful of salt and the squash. Boil gently, turning several times, until a dent is left in the squash when pressed, about 5 minutes. Lift out with tongs, then drop into cold water. Lift out eggs. Tap gently to crack shells all over. Place in cold water.

3. Meanwhile, combine potatoes with water to cover by a few inches in another pot. Add about 1 teaspoon salt per quart of water. Bring to a boil. Cook until potatoes are just barely tender throughout, about 15 minutes.

4. Dry squash; cut into ⅛-inch coins. Combine in bowl with fiddleheads. Peel eggs and set aside.

5. Drain potatoes and cool briefly on cutting board. Meanwhile, prepare dressing: Blend shallot, mustard, lemon juice, and salt. Gradually whisk in both oils to emulsify.

6. Slip off potato skins; cut potatoes into ⅛-inch slices. Combine in bowl with wine and 2 tablespoons dill, and turn gently with spatula until wine is absorbed. Drizzle over 2 tablespoons dressing, folding gently to mix.

7. Arrange potatoes on platter with cress around them. Toss fiddleheads and squash with 2 tablespoons dressing. Distribute over potatoes. Slice eggs into rounds. Arrange around and over vegetables. Spoon a dab of dressing onto each egg slice and sprinkle with dill. Grind pepper over all.

Serves 4

Braised Veal and Mushrooms with Fiddlehead Ferns

Veal slow-cooked with mushrooms and aromatics concentrates to a deeply savory stew. The warm meaty flavor is freshened by the green coiled ferns, added at the last minute. (Don't be tempted to serve them separately—they are far more delicious combined.) The bit of cream acts as liaison and adds unexpected lightness and nuttiness.

Theoretically, two pounds of veal should serve six, but it simply did not satisfy more than four gourmands. Note that cooking time can vary considerably, so it makes sense to plan on the longer time, then simply remove the stew from the oven if finished early. Or make ahead, minus the fiddleheads, then reheat and stir in the blanched ferns.

2½ tablespoons flour
1 teaspoon kosher salt
2 pounds stewing veal, cut into 2-inch pieces
1½ tablespoons olive oil
1½ tablespoons butter
2 medium shallots
2 small celery stalks
½ cup dry white wine
½ pound white button mushrooms
    (preferably small)
1 pound small fiddleheads
About 3 tablespoons heavy cream
About 2 tablespoons minced tarragon

1. Preheat oven to 300°F. Mix flour and salt, then toss with veal to coat. Heat oil and butter in large skillet over moderate heat. Add veal and brown lightly on all sides. With slotted spoon, transfer to flameproof casserole just large enough to hold all ingredients.

2. Meanwhile, mince shallots and celery. Add to fat in pan, with wine. Cover and cook over low heat until softened, about 5 minutes. Scoop over veal. Halve mushrooms, or quarter if large. Press into casserole to fit closely around veal. Heat over moderately high heat until sizzling.

3. Cover casserole and place in center of oven. Bake until veal is very tender, stirring once or twice. Meat is ready when it can be easily pierced with a fork—start checking at 1¼ hours, but do not be surprised if it takes as much as an hour longer.

4. While veal cooks, prepare ferns as in Basic Boiled Fiddlehead Ferns.

5. When veal is tender, stir in 3 tablespoons cream, 1 tablespoon tarragon, and fiddleheads. Taste, season, and add cream to taste. Sprinkle with additional tarragon.

Serves 4

Fiddlehead Custards with Baby Vegetable Garnish

An odd characteristic of these ferns is that they seem to develop flavor when chopped, pureed, and otherwise beaten up—which is a shame, considering their charming look when whole. If you have a windfall and wish to try for yourself, cook up these fancy little unmolded custards with a pretty spring vegetable garnish. Use whichever small vegetables are freshest: tiny turnips, baby yellow squash, marble-size golden beets, red radishes. Cook until tender, drain, and cool; then sauté in butter to heat through.

About 10 ounces small fiddlehead ferns
12 baby carrots
12 miniature turnips or large red radishes
1 medium shallot
½ cup lightly packed parsley leaves
2 tablespoons butter
½ teaspoon kosher salt
1 tablespoon flour
½ cup lightly packed grated Gruyère or Comté cheese
3 eggs
¼ teaspoon white pepper
1¼ cups whole milk
Melted or softened butter for molds
Optional: tiny chervil or dill sprigs for garnish

1. Preheat oven to 350°F. Trim ends of ferns. Rinse briskly under running water, rubbing together to remove loose brown bits. Scrub and trim carrots and turnips, leaving an inch or so of green stems.

2. Cook carrots in a very large pot of boiling salted water until not quite tender, a minute or so. Lift out and drop into ice water. Add turnips to boiling water and cook until just tender, a few minutes or so. Meanwhile, slip skins from carrots. Lift out turnips and chill in ice water. Drain and halve or quarter. Halve carrots. Spread both on towel.

3. Drop fiddleheads into the same pot of boiling water. Boil gently until just cooked through, about 5 minutes. Drain and chill in cold water. Drain and dry. Reserve 24 of the smallest and prettiest ferns.

4. In food processor, mince shallot and parsley. Add remaining fiddleheads and chop fine. Melt 1 tablespoon butter in medium skillet; add salt and minced vegetables. Stir over moderately low heat until shallots are softened and juices have cooked off, about 5 minutes.

5. In processor bowl, blend flour, cheese, eggs, and pepper. Add vegetable mixture and pulse to mix. Blend in milk.

6. Choose 12 timbale (or dariole) molds or muffin tins of about ⅓-cup capacity (preferably non-stick). Fit a round of waxed paper in the bottom of each, then butter the mold and paper. Divide custard mixture among molds. Set in roasting pan and pour in hot water to reach halfway up side of molds.

7. Bake until slightly puffed and just set in the center, 30 to 35 minutes. Let stand 15 minutes.

8. Run thin-bladed knife around edge to free each custard. Unmold (or cover lightly and leave up to 2 hours before serving): Invert 2 onto each serving dish (or, if using a muffin tin, invert all onto a cutting board, rapping sharply to release).

9. Heat remaining 1 tablespoon butter in skillet and toss reserved ferns, turnips, and carrots over high heat

to warm. Season and arrange around and on top of custards. Garnish with optional herbs.

Serves 6 as a first course

Pros Propose

A sauce I like for plain-cooked vegetables, **Nutmeg Cream,** suits fiddleheads nicely: Whip heavy cream and salt until slightly thickened. Gradually add nutmeg. Stir in a little lemon juice. Whip until quite firm. Scoop into cheesecloth-lined sieve. Cover. Chill an hour or two before spooning over hot boiled ferns.

Chef Fernando Divina's **Salad of Fiddleheads and Wild Rice** includes truly wild, not cultivated, rice, to match the wild fiddleheads: Simmer rice until kernels open slightly; drain and cool. Dress orach (see page 451) and baby mustard with hazelnut oil, lemon, and seasoning. Toss boiled ferns and rice with the same. Mound rice mixture and greens separately on salad plates.

"Fiddleheads . . . and wild asparagus push their heads up through the damp spring forest floor just around the 'Fishing Opener' that falls on Mother's Day in Minnesota," write Beth Dooley and Lucia Watson in *Savoring the Seasons of the Northern Heartland.* "At Lucia's Restaurant we serve this light and pretty entree for Mother's Day brunch, along with parslied new potatoes." For **Baked Walleye with Asparagus and Fiddleheads:** Cut foot-square sheets of aluminum foil; butter liberally. On each, place 1 fish fillet, 2 asparagus spears cut into 1-inch pieces, and 2 fiddlehead ferns. Sprinkle with snipped chives, squeeze over lemon juice, and season. Fold closed and bake in moderate oven about 12 minutes.

Chef, forager, and hunter John Manikowski devised **Flaming Red Pepper and Fiddlehead Flan** for his *Wild Fish and Game Cookbook:* Sauté roasted, peeled, and chopped red pepper and onions until soft; puree. Boil milk; lower heat and gradually add beaten eggs, whisking. Off heat, add pepper puree; season. Place small fiddleheads in buttered ramekins. Fill with the custard. Bake until firm in center. Cool briefly, then unmold.

Fuzzy Gourd (*Benincasa hispida*)

Also fuzzy melon, hairy squash (or melon or gourd), little winter melon;
tsee gua, mo qwa and variations (Chinese)

See also: **WINTER MELON,** page 702

First-time shoppers for this slightly prickly character sometimes confuse it with forms of bottle gourd. Although it can look superficially similar, it *is* fuzzy, while bottle gourd is smooth. More important for the cook, its culinary personality is distinct, ranging between zucchini and cucumber enhanced with a lemony edge. The two types I have seen in New York City suggest both vegetables: One is slightly belled, lighter green, and dappled (left in photo); the other is stocky, cylindrical, exceptionally juicy, firm, and sweet.

Surprisingly, the fuzzy gourd is not confused with winter melon; even though it is the same *Benincasa hispida,* it can look dramatically dissimilar at different stages of growth. Some authorities consider fuzzy gourd to be a young form of winter melon; others consider it a distinct cultivar. According to *Cucurbits* (by R. W. Robinson and D. S. Decker-Walters), the cultivars "have evolved locally and vary among geographic regions. Seed companies offer several cultivars distinguished by their fruit characteristics. Those with names like 'Fuzzy Squash' or 'Chinese Fuzzy Gourd' belong to *B. hispida* var. *chieh-qua.*" The mature fruit of this variety is small, comparatively cylindrical, and fuzzy, while other varieties become large, round, and waxy when mature. But the young fruit of both types is similar. (For those who are interested: "The genus name was given to it by an Italian botanist, Gaetano Savi, in 1818, to honor Giuseppe Benincasa, an Italian patron of botany," writes Charles B. Heiser in *The Gourd Book,* "while its species name, *hispida,* means rough-hairy.")

Believed to have originated in Southeast Asia, *Benincasa hispida* has been cultivated in China for over two millennia, according to Robinson and Decker-Walters, who write that it is also grown in other parts of Asia and in Latin America and the Caribbean. Depending upon local customs, the gourd is consumed raw,

length: 5-12 inches

cooked, or pickled while the young leaves, vine tips, and buds are cooked and eaten as greens.

BASIC USE: In the United States, the fuzzy gourds in the market are comparable to summer squash in terms of culinary versatility. Peeled and cooked, the refreshing cucurbit retains its texture—stir-fried, braised, or in soups. Shredded and sautéed, it keeps an appealing suggestion of crunch and a lightly tart finish. Or sauté peeled chunks with aromatics, then braise briefly in broth and coconut milk; add seafood or chicken bits for the last few minutes. When cut into thick slices or lengths, fuzzy gourd is ideal for stuffing. It stays firm and bright—unlike zucchini, which tends to become flabby. Fuzzy gourd is at ease with seasonings of the Far East or Mediterranean—or just about anywhere else.

SELECTION: Look for relatively small, rock-solid squash with no pitting or bruising. If the dark, blocky types are avilable, they are most firm, sweet, and tasty. For any type, the shinier the better. The paler form is available year-round; the dark, only intermittently.

STORAGE: As perishable as zucchini, fuzzy gourd will last up to a week if each fruit is first wrapped in paper towel and then all are enclosed in a plastic bag and refrigerated.

PREPARATION: Scrub with a brush under running water. To keep maximum color, scrape off only the outer layer of skin with a knife, rather than paring deeply. Or use a swivel peeler and apply the lightest pressure possible.

Sautéed Shredded Fuzzy Gourd

Although fuzzy gourd resembles zucchini superficially, it does not shrink much or become flaccid in the same way, but retains its texture and citric edge—here underscored by lime. Lime is just one flavor that suits the versatile vegetable: Grated ginger also fits fine. Or omit the shallot and substitute a little garlic, then finish with fresh basil, lemon thyme, or mint and chives. You might add another shredded vegetable, such as carrot, or julienne of ham.

2 pounds small, firm fuzzy gourds
2 medium shallots
2 tablespoons butter
1 tablespoon vegetable oil
½ teaspoon kosher salt
Lime juice
Pepper
Minced dill

1. Scrub fuzzy gourds. Cut off stem and base. Pare lightly. Using shredding blade of food processor, press down firmly on fuzzy gourd and shallot to cut into coarse shreds. (Do not drain or dry.)

2. Heat butter and oil in very large heavy skillet. Add gourd, shallot, and salt. Toss over moderate heat until tender—about 10 minutes—adjusting heat so that gourd does not brown, but just cooks through without drying out.

3. Add lime juice and season. Toss with dill and serve hot.

Serves 4 as a side dish

Fuzzy Gourd with Pork and Cellophane Noodles

Stephen Wong, Vancouver-based food and wine consultant, author, journalist—and gracious gentleman—shared this recipe and others throughout the book. The green gourd rounds make ideal stuffers, for they retain their firmness, fresh flavor, and color. Snippets of cellophane noodles keep the juicy filling tender and light textured.

When I ran out of fresh ginger, which the original recipe calls for, I substituted beni shoga (Japanese salt-pickled ginger), which looked and tasted delightful. Although knife and fork are not traditional, I find them to be imperative for these gourd hassocks topped with noodly nests and slicked with a nippy, slightly sweet sauce.

½ pound boneless pork (preferably
   a bit fatty)
2-ounce package (or skein) cellophane
   noodles (bean threads)
2 fuzzy gourds (each about 8 inches long
   and 2½ inches in diameter)
¼ teaspoon kosher salt
1 egg white
2 teaspoons cornstarch
1 teaspoon Asian (dark) sesame oil
1½ tablespoons minced salt- or sweet-pickled
   ginger or fresh ginger
2 tablespoons chopped cilantro (coriander)
   leaves
2 tablespoons Chinese oyster sauce
1¼ cups flavorful pork or chicken broth
⅛ to ½ teaspoon chilli flakes
4 large fresh shiitake

1. Cut pork into 2-inch pieces. Place in freezer while you prepare other ingredients, about 45 minutes. Soak noodles in hot water until soft, about 10 minutes. Drain well. Chop into 1-inch pieces.

2. Peel gourds lightly. Cut into 1-inch slices (or 16 pieces). With melon ball cutter, scoop out half the flesh

and seeds from each to make a shallow circular "bowl," leaving a neat ¼-inch rim.

3. Chop pork medium-coarse in food processor. Scrape into bowl. Whisk together salt, egg white, and cornstarch; add sesame oil. Mix with the pork, half the noodles, the ginger, and the cilantro.

4. Spoon a scant tablespoon of meat mixture into each gourd slice and flatten. Dip meat side of each piece into remaining noodles to coat top.

5. Combine oyster sauce, stock, and chilli flakes in skillet large enough to hold all slices in single layer: Bring to a boil. Place gourd slices in pan, noodle side up. Simmer 5 minutes, covered. Baste, re-cover, and cook 5 minutes longer.

6. Meanwhile, remove shiitake stems. Halve caps, then slice very thin. Add to pan, stirring into broth. Cover and simmer 5 minutes longer.

7. With slotted spoon, transfer slices to platter. Spoon mushrooms and sauce (which should have reduced to just a few spoonfuls) over slices. Serve hot.

Serves 5 to 6 as a first course

Shrimp and Fuzzy Gourd in Spiced Coconut-Buttermilk Sauce

I love coconut milk but often find that dishes cooked with it become too oily and heavy for my taste. Here, coconut shreds are blended with buttermilk (a refrigerator staple for me) and a shrimp and coriander broth for a sauce with a light feel. Abundant, creamy yellow, sweetly aromatic with a hint of white pepper heat, it mingles with the pale green gourd for a pretty shrimp-studded vegetable dish. Scented rice is all that's needed to make a meal.

¾ **pound medium shrimp in the shell**
2 **cups water**
1 **medium bunch cilantro (coriander) with**
  roots intact if possible
½ **teaspoon white peppercorns**
1 **teaspoon fennel seeds**
1 **teaspoon coriander seeds**
1 **teaspoon kosher salt**
1 **teaspoon sugar**

½ **teaspoon turmeric**
¾ **pound slim fuzzy gourd(s)**
1 **large white onion**
1 **tablespoon butter**
⅓ **cup (unsweetened) shredded coconut**
1 **cup buttermilk**
1 **tablespoon cornstarch**

1. Rinse shrimp and remove shells. Place shells in small pot with the water. Cut off coriander roots, if any, and scrub well under running water. Add to pot. Separate leaves and reserve. Chop stems and add to pot. Bring to a boil, lower heat, and simmer, partly covered, about 20 minutes, while you prepare remaining ingredients.

2. Combine pepper, fennel, coriander seeds, salt, sugar, and turmeric in spice mill or clean coffee grinder; grind fine. Trim ends from gourds and pare lightly. Quarter lengthwise, then cut into ¼-inch slices. Peel and dice onion.

3. In heavy 3-quart casserole, melt butter over fairly low heat. Stew onions gently until almost translucent. Add spice mixture and coconut; toss a minute or so. Add gourd and remove from heat.

4. Strain shrimp broth and return to pot. Boil to reduce to ¾ to 1 cup. Add to vegetables. Simmer, covered, until gourd is translucent and just barely tender, 5 to 10 minutes.

5. Meanwhile, gradually stir buttermilk into cornstarch. Bunch together cilantro leaves and slice thin. Add buttermilk mixture to pot and bring to a simmer over moderate heat, stirring until thickened, about 1 minute. Add shrimp and cook until barely done, another minute or so.

6. Off heat, gradually add cilantro leaves, tasting for correct balance.

Serves 4 as a main course

Pros Propose

Fuzzy gourd's favored role is as soup ingredient, as the following ideas illustrate. Author and chef Ken Hom recalls that when he was a child in San Francisco, fuzzy gourd was not yet a regular item in the market, but a rare treat. When it did arrive, he looked forward to playing with the fuzzy vegetable before his mother peeled it for **Chicken–Fuzzy Gourd Soup:** Cut chicken breast into thin strips and toss with egg white, salt, and cornstarch. Marinate 20 minutes or so. Peel gourd and cut into 1-inch cubes. Salt and drain for same amount of time as marinating. Rinse and blot dry. Blanch chicken slices 2 minutes in boiling water. Drain. Season chicken stock with soy sauce, rice wine, sesame oil, and sugar. Add gourd and cook until tender. Add chicken and sprinkle with thin-sliced green onions (from *Easy Family Recipes from a Chinese American Childhood*).

For chef and author Longteine de Monteiro, the "soul food" that "exemplifies Cambodia's healthful rural fare" is **White Fish Soup with Young Winter Melon:** Simmer small wedges of fuzzy gourd in chicken broth seasoned with galangal, garlic, prahok (fermented fish paste), tamarind juice, fish sauce, and sugar. Add catfish strips and cook through. Top with cilantro, basil, or mint and thin-sliced red bell pepper. Serve with rice (from *The Elephant Walk Cookbook*).

Eileen Yin-Fei Lo also prepares soup from the gourd and steams it in hollowed gourd halves. In a less traditional mode, she cooks up **Hairy Melon Pancake:** Combine peeled and julienned fuzzy gourd, sliced scallions, water chestnut julienne, grated ginger, rice wine, sesame oil, soy sauce, flour, and baking powder. Moisten with vegetable stock. Spread to form an 8-inch cake in hot oiled wok. Brown both sides. Serve hot (*From the Earth: Chinese Vegetarian Cooking*).

Garlic Chive, Chinese Chive (*Allium tuberosum*)

Also gau choy and variations (Chinese), nira (Japanese)
Including **common green, yellow,** and **flowering forms**

Garlic chives do not taste, look, or cook like what we call chives (*Allium schoenoprasum*), although there are superficial similarities. They are another species (*A. tuberosum*) that tastes garlicky, is flat (not tubular), and is cooked as a vegetable in the lands where it is grown (that is why it is in this book)—unlike "regular" chives, which serve as seasoning. To further distinguish itself, the variable vegetable comes to market in three distinct and attractive forms, as you see: green-leafed, blanched (yellow), and as budding stems.

Sampled (or sniffed) raw, all forms are strong indeed; far more garlic than chive, yet with an underlying green vegetable taste and a certain sweetness. But the raw vegetable is not the point. With the slightest cooking, the sharp allium bite mellows to a soft savor.

The **common green form** is quite tender but a bit less so than the more succulent and expensive pearly **yellow form** (gau wong), which is the same garlic chive grown under wraps—plastic sheeting, a clay pot, or anything else that keeps out the light. Yet the two are similar when cooked, save for the striking difference in color. **Flowering chive** (gau choy fa and gau choy sum) is distinct from both and is by far my fa-

garlic chive or Chinese chive: green, yellow or blanched, and flowering (*left to right*)   length: 10-13 inches

vorite. Its sturdy stem may seem stiff as a reed, but it cooks to the tender, juicy consistency of haricots verts or asparagus, with a light garlic edge.

Forms of the plant have been cultivated for centuries in China, Japan, and parts of Eastern Asia, to which garlic chive is probably native. Some are best for their abundant green leaves, some for blanching, some for the flower stems. The Japanese have developed some of the most popular cultivars, but I have not been able to locate Japanese users—although Richard Hosking in *A Dictionary of Japanese Food* mentions that garlic chive is included in dumplings, soups, ohitashi, and stir-fries.

Those impossible stir-fries of garlic chives! The bane of my kitchen! When I followed traditional Chinese stir-fry recipes, I found myself picking out clumps of nasty-tasting chives. I know they have been cooked this way for centuries, but after half a dozen unpleasant tests I returned to my own previous cooking methods and was once again charmed by garlic chives: steamed whole, simmered in broth, stirred into thick soups, and cooked gently with moist vegetables—but not stir-fried. A loverly bunch of recipes follows.

BASIC USE: Garlic chives in any form need only the briefest cooking. I find them sweeter and plumper when cooked in liquid or steamed than when subjected to direct high heat. Add 1-inch lengths to scrambled eggs as they cook, using a much larger volume than you would of "regular" chives. Traditionally, they are cooked in soups, stir-fried with meat or seafood or soft noodles, and stuffed into spring rolls and dumplings. To incorporate them raw, as seasoning, use a very light hand.

SELECTION: Green garlic chives are available all year, usually bunched. Generally speaking, the thicker and larger, the more strident. Check the center of the bunch to be sure the leaves within aren't slippery and spoiled. Have a good sniff: What you smell is what you get. For blanched chives, which are somewhat milder, the paler the yellow, the more tender and succulent—and expensive. For flowering chives (not literally flowering: there should be pointy buds, not open flowers), the stems should be taut enough to snap at the base.

STORAGE: If garlic chives are bunched, remove the fastener. Open up the bouquet and take out any stems that feel slippery. Place chives in a paper bag, then a plastic one. Close tightly. Blanched chives are naturally limp and delicate and spoil quickly; don't keep more than a day or two. The green keep longer, the buds much longer.

PREPARATION: Trim an inch off the base to be tidy. No more should be necessary if chives look fresh. Rinse.

Steamed Flowering Garlic Chives with Ginger Butter

This simple, unorthodox treatment rewards with beauty, ease of preparation, and a surprisingly sweet demeanor. The bright green bundles, which suggest miniature asparagus in both appearance and taste, brighten main dishes from steamed seafood to roasted lamb—and just about anything in between. For a vegetable meal, serve with grilled mushrooms and buckwheat (kasha) or aromatic rice. If you don't care to buy additional chives to bind the bundles, slim scallions halved lengthwise will do the job. Employ chopsticks or a sharp knife with your dinner fork for tidy service.

1 bunch flowering garlic chives (about
    5 ounces)
4 flat garlic chives (leaves) or regular chives
2 tablespoons butter
2 teaspoons fine-grated ginger
1 teaspoon shoyu (Japanese soy sauce)

1. Trim an inch or so from base of chives. Rinse. Divide into 4 bunches, the flowers aligned at one end. Cut each bunch in half crosswise, then combine the two halves, mixing to distribute the buds evenly. Tie each bunch with a garlic chive, wrapping it around twice before knotting.

2. Set bundles on rack over boiling water. Cover and steam until tender throughout and somewhat limp, about 5 minutes.

3. Meanwhile, combine butter and ginger in small skillet or microwavable container (cover the latter). Heat *just* until butter melts and becomes pale and creamy, not oily. Stir in shoyu.

4. Set hot chive bundles on plates and spoon over the warm, clinging sauce. Serve immediately.

Serves 4

Shredded Yellow Squash with Garlic Chives

Mild and versatile, yet far from ordinary, this simple toss pairs familiar New World squash with Old World Chinese chives. The result is prettily yellow-green, tender, light-textured, and subtly seasoned. The bright twirl of matching textures suits pan-fried fish or veal, broiled fish fillets, or roasted pork tenderloin, among other dishes.

> 2 pounds firm, narrow yellow summer squash
>   or golden zucchini
> 1¼ teaspoons kosher salt
> About 2½ ounces green garlic chives
> 1 tablespoon butter
> ½ tablespoon olive oil
> About ½ teaspoon grated nutmeg
> Optional: lime juice

1. Scrub squash; trim ends and cut into 2-inch chunks. Pack into food processor fitted with shredding blade and press down firmly to make comparatively large shreds (about 8 cups). Place in large colander and gradually add salt, tossing. Let stand 5 to 10 minutes, as convenient, tossing occasionally.

2. Meanwhile, trim base of garlic chives. Cut chives into 1½- to 2-inch lengths (about 1½ cups).

3. Squeeze squash, a handful at a time, to extract as much liquid as possible.

4. Heat butter and oil in very wide skillet over moderate heat. When sizzling, raise heat to high and add squash, chives, and ¼ teaspoon nutmeg. Toss 2 to 3 minutes. Taste and add more nutmeg, as desired (it varies considerably in strength). Continue tossing and pressing shreds against pan until tender and slightly browned, about 5 minutes longer. Season, adding lime if desired. Serve hot.

Serves 4 as a side dish

Mussels, Flowering Garlic Chives, and Fennel in Wine Sauce

This Mediterranean and Chinese mix was suggested by a recipe from Stephen Wong, author and restaurant consultant. A lovely balance of bright colors, mellow and forceful flavors, and contrasting textures: tender mussel meat, crunchy bell pepper and fennel slivers, and the strong-sweet savor of flowering chive stems. I like to serve the soupy dish in bowls, topped with a scoop of rice, gumbo style. If you prefer a thicker sauce to coat the mussels closely, reduce the broth to 1 cup. For this, serve on flat plates with rice on the side.

> 1 medium bulb Florence fennel with tops
>   (about 1 pound)
> 2-inch chunk of ginger
> 1 onion
> ½ teaspoon fennel seeds
> About 1 cup white wine
> ½ cup water
> 1 bunch flowering garlic chives
>   (about ¼ pound)
> 1 small red bell pepper
> 2 pounds cultivated mussels, rinsed
> 1 tablespoon cornstarch
> 1 tablespoon olive oil
> About 4 cups cooked white rice, preferably
>   jasmine or basmati type

1. Cut stalks from fennel bulb. Strip off and reserve feathery greens. Chop stalks. Remove and chop coarse outer layer of bulb. Place in heavy pot large enough to hold mussels. Slice ginger and onion. Add, with fennel seeds, 1 cup wine, and water. Bring to a boil. Cover, reduce heat, and simmer to extract flavors, about 15 minutes. Strain. Add wine to equal 1 cup if needed.

2. Meanwhile, cut fennel bulb into matchsticks. Trim base of chives. Reserve 4 stalks for garnish. Cut remainder into 2-inch lengths (for about 1½ cups). Cut pepper into matchsticks. Mince reserved fennel greens.

3. Combine wine-broth and mussels in the pot. Bring to a boil, cover, and cook, shaking occasionally, just until all mussels open, about 3 minutes. With slotted spoon, lift mussels from broth into a bowl. Slowly

pour broth into a container, being careful to avoid sand that lurks at the bottom. Add wine as needed to make 1½ cups.

4. Shell all but 12 mussels. Dissolve cornstarch in a little broth, then blend with remainder.

5. Heat oil in the rinsed-out pot over high heat. Add fennel, sliced chives, and bell pepper. Toss to soften just slightly, about 2 minutes. Add the shelled mussels and broth and stir until broth thickens, about 1 minute.

6. Ladle into shallow bowls. Sprinkle with fennel greens. Set a scoop of rice on each. Divide reserved mussels and chive stalks among bowls.

Serves 4 as a main dish

Salad of Soba Noodles, Garlic Chives, and Sprouts with Wasabi

A swirl of slippery buckwheat noodles, chewy chive strands, and crunchy sprouts makes a good summer buffet dish at room temperature or slightly chilled. While cool and light, it is forceful in flavor and can stand on its own as a main dish or serve as a side for grilled salmon or pork. Packages of soba noodles vary in size; precise weight is not important. Choose yellow or green garlic chives—or both. I marginally prefer the yellow chives for their resemblance to the sprouts and their slightly more resilient texture, which blends more evenly with the noodles.

¼ cup rice vinegar
3 tablespoons shoyu (Japanese soy sauce)
1 tablespoon grated ginger
2 teaspoons wasabi powder
½ teaspoon sugar
¼ teaspoon kosher salt
About 2 tablespoons warm water
1 tablespoon vegetable oil
1 tablespoon Asian (dark) sesame oil
2 tablespoons sesame seeds
7 to 8 ounces garlic chives (green, yellow, or both)
One 12- to 13-ounce package Japanese buckwheat (soba) noodles
¾ pound bean sprouts, preferably mung

1. Combine vinegar, shoyu, and ginger; set aside. Blend wasabi, sugar, salt, and 1 tablespoon warm water, then add more water as needed to make a pourable mixture. Whisk in both oils.

2. In small skillet, stir sesame seeds over moderately low heat until tan; set aside. Trim, rinse, and halve garlic chives. Cut enough into 1-inch pieces to make ¼ cup.

3. Drop noodles into a large pot of boiling water. Return to a boil, stirring. Boil gently until noodles are just barely tender, 2 to 4 minutes. Meanwhile, rinse sprouts and place in colander in which you'll drain noodles. When noodles are just cooked, stir in the halved chives and return to a boil. Drain in colander. Run under cold water to cool.

4. Toss noodles with vinegar-soy mixture, then wasabi dressing. Divide among bowls. Top with reserved sliced chives and sesame seeds.

Serves 4 as a main dish, 6 to 8 as a side dish

Soup of Bean Thread Noodles, Garlic Chives, and Spiced Tofu

A soupy, slurpy hotpot for a wintry afternoon. If you're in a hurry or prefer not to prepare the flavored tofu, purchase ready-made seasoned, pressed tofu, available in most natural food stores. Tawny and firm, it is labeled variously as hot Chinese, Thai, spiced, and so forth. If you bake your own, choose either of the blends of sweet aromatics called garam masala (an Indian mix) or 5-spice powder (a Chinese one). Like most thick, noodly soups, this is best tackled with spoon and chopsticks.

About 2 tablespoons shoyu (Japanese soy sauce)
2 teaspoons garam masala or 5-spice powder
Optional: ⅛ teaspoon ground hot pepper
1½ tablespoons minced ginger
1 tablespoon peanut oil (preferably roasted)
1 pound extra-firm tofu (bean curd)
About ¼ pound bean thread noodles (package sizes vary)
¼ pound green and/or yellow garlic chives
1 tablespoon cornstarch
1 tablespoon rice or cider vinegar
4 cups vegetable or chicken broth

1. Preheat oven to 375°F. In bowl large enough to hold tofu, combine 2 tablespoons shoyu, garam masala, optional hot pepper, 1 tablespoon ginger, and oil. Cut tofu into ½- to ¾-inch cubes. Toss with soy mixture. Spread on greased or non-stick baking sheet. Bake until a thin skin forms and cubes are well browned, about 35 minutes, tossing gently several times with spatula. (Can be prepared ahead and refrigerated.)

2. Meanwhile, combine noodles with boiling water to cover. Let stand until tender but still springy, about 5 minutes. With scissors, cut into 3-inch pieces, more or less. Drain; then rinse in cold water. Trim chives and cut the same length.

3. Blend cornstarch with vinegar and ½ cup broth; add remaining ½ tablespoon minced ginger. In saucepan, combine tofu and remaining 3½ cups broth. Bring to a boil over high heat, then reduce heat and simmer gently until tofu is slightly puffed, about 2 minutes. Raise heat to high. Stir in garlic chives, noodles, and cornstarch mixture. Return to a boil, stirring constantly. Season with vinegar and shoyu. Serve at once, in bowls.

Serves 4

Pros Propose

Soup with flowering garlic chives, shrimp with yellow chives, and noodles with green chives, from Vietnam, China, and Cambodia.

For **Bean Curd and Chinese Chive Buds Soup:** Combine thin-sliced pork shoulder with a touch of nuoc mam (Vietnamese fish sauce) and pepper. Let stand ½ hour. Combine with chicken broth and bring to a boil. Reduce heat and skim until foam no longer appears. Add salt, sugar, and fish sauce; simmer 5 minutes. Add 2-inch lengths of flowering chives and 1-inch cubes of soft bean curd. Return to a boil and remove from heat. Serve at once (from *The Foods of Vietnam* by Nicole Routhier).

For **Yellow Chive Shrimp:** Blend soy sauce, oyster sauce, sugar, cornstarch, and seafood stock. Heat wok, add peanut oil, and stir in minced ginger. Add large shelled shrimp, spread in single layer, and cook 1 minute. Add shaoxing wine and toss 30 seconds. Mix in julienne of water chestnuts. Form a well in the center, stir sauce mixture and pour into it. Scoop shrimp and water chestnuts onto sauce, then mix well. Add yellow chives cut into 1-inch pieces and blend well (from *The Chinese Way* by Eileen Yin-Fei Lo).

For **Rice Noodles with Chilli Sauce and Garlic Chives:** Soak dried rice noodles in warm water 10 to 15 minutes; drain. In blender, combine soaked, seeded, and deveined dried New Mexico chillis with garlic cloves, shallot, and water; puree to a paste. Heat vegetable oil in large skillet. Stir in the paste and cook 1 minute. Fold in the noodles, reduce heat, and cook gently 4 to 5 minutes, mixing well with chopsticks; add water as needed to prevent sticking. Add mung bean sprouts and Chinese chives cut into 2-inch pieces. Cook 2 minutes or so. If desired, top with strips of thin omelet (from *The Elephant Walk Cookbook* by Longteine de Monteiro and Katherine Neustadt).

Gyromitra, False Morel (*Gyromitra* species)

Including **snowbank false morel, conifer false morel, edible false morel, snow mushroom, brain mushroom,** and **gyromitre** (French)

Do not eat or serve this mushroom or any mushrooms that resemble it.

Gyromitra species can be life-threatening. I hate to say this. I have cooked them, eaten them, and spoken with celebrated chefs who still serve them. At present they are sold in Europe (usually as gyromitre) and North America (under the umbrella term "false morel"). They are considered a seasonal sine qua non by many international connoisseurs. But please, even if you have cooked, gathered, distributed, or consumed *Gyromitra* species in the past: reconsider.

For simplicity, I have chosen to quote one person on the subject, but other experts share his opinions. John Trestrail, retired chairman of the Toxicology Committee of the North American Mycological Association, is, at this writing, managing director of Spectrum Health Regional Poison Center in Grand Rapids, Michigan, which handles the majority of *Gyromitra* poisonings in this country.

Because poisonings have been reported in the East and Midwest (according to *The Audubon Society Field Guide to North American Mushrooms*), I asked Trestrail if he could comment about species outside his area as well. There was not a second's hesitation: "There are more deaths in Europe from *Gyromitra esculenta* than anywhere else. There are no completely safe species. All *Gyromitra* contain a compound that breaks down with water to become MMH (monomethylhydrazine), a toxin that simply should not be consumed."

Mycologists from France, Italy, and other parts of North America agree—though with qualifications too complex to discuss here. French sources state that until the isolation of the poison in 1967, many believed that the traditional long cooking or blanching detoxified *G. esculenta*. But subsequent experiments (and deaths) proved these techniques unreliable. Trestrail says that it is possible to boil off *some* of the toxin, but even fumes can be hazardous when inhaled.

What lulls mycophiles into complacency or disbe-

½ **actual size**

lief about gyromitra is the unusual "all or none" effect of MMH. Each individual has a different specific threshold for the toxin. Once the threshold is crossed, the victim suffers symptoms; there is no gray area. To add to the risk, the amount of toxin varies wildly from mushroom to mushroom. "The question is what throws the switch for each individual. We have worked on people who eat the mushroom year after year and are suddenly affected," says Trestrail. "One *cannot* predict when the meal being eaten may be the very one which will precipitate a toxicological crisis." He sums up the matter unequivocally: "Persons who decide to continue this gastronomic gamble should have the number of their regional poison centers engraved on their eating utensils."

Hedgehog Mushroom
(*Hydnum repandum* and *Dentinum repandum*)

Also sweet tooth, pig's trotter, pied de mouton (French)

Tiny spine-like soft teeth cram the caps of this species, taking the place of gills and giving the mushroom its odd dental labels, both vernacular and scientific. Unlike some other members of the tooth fungus (Hydnaceae) family, which may have spines soft and long enough to be called beards, waterfalls, or fur, these tiny stalactites are barely visible.

Its spines excepted, hedgehog is not a distinctive mushroom. Although chanterellesque in appearance and culinary possibilities, it is less fragrant and flavorful—but certainly appealing. Buff- to tawny-capped, with pale stems, hedgehogs are firm and fully packed. They are collected from the wild in North America, Europe, and China, not farmed. The cooked mushrooms taste like chanterelles blended with cultivated button and oyster mushrooms—and have none of the sweetness which the common name suggests and which some people expect to find. In fact, sweet tooth tends toward bitterness, which usually dissipates with simmering and a touch of added sweetness or richness in the form of nuts, cream, ham, butter, or alcohol.

¾ **actual size**

BASIC USE: Braise, roast, or sauté-braise hedgehog mushrooms, keeping in mind that they tend to be dry and do best in the same creamy, buttery, or saucy preparations as chanterelles. Or marinate the raw mushrooms in a court bouillon, à la grecque. Slice raw hedgehegs into sauces or soups (creamy and not) to exude and mingle their juices with the liquid as it cooks. Hedgehogs complement a wide range of light meats—such as rabbit, veal, Cornish hen, quail, and pheasant—whether as stuffing, in a sauce, or as a side dish. A sauce or ragôut of hedgehogs makes a tasty topping for rice, grain, or polenta. Hazelnuts, almonds, and cashews bring out the nutty aspect of the fungus and lend textural contrast for vegetarian entrees. Hedgehogs can be substituted in recipes that call for white or golden chanterelles.

SELECTION AND STORAGE: Hedgehogs are harvested from fall to spring in North America. Look for caps that are dry to the touch but not dried out. Small hedgehogs are easiest to handle. Large ones tend to be brittle and form jagged slices when the spines break. Look for comparatively pale, evenly colored specimens with spines intact, indicating freshness. The teeth should be fairly clean—because they're impossible to brush! Although stems can be trimmed and tops brushed clean, teeth break off and look messy. Refrigerate in a single layer, topped with a light towel. Being winter mushrooms, they tolerate cold well and will last a week or so.

PREPARATION: Although hedgehogs are at their best if simply brushed clean, you may have to swish them around in cold water to get out pine needles and leafy bits. Clean caps with a soft brush and trim stubborn bits of soil from the stems. If caps are broader than an inch or so, cut mushrooms bite-size.

Tawny Hedgehog-Hazelnut Ragoût

Hazelnuts bring out the chanterelle side of these little golden fungi. Because the mushrooms are expensive—unless you pick your own—it makes sense to give them a starring role. Set them on a backdrop of soft polenta, just the right foil for the thick, nutty, sauce-stew. Golden chanterelles can be added or substituted.

If you don't have roasted hazelnuts on hand, see directions on page 175 to roast, husk, and chop the nuts.

About ¾ pound hedgehog mushrooms
2 large shallots
1½ tablespoons flour
2 tablespoons hazelnut oil
½ teaspoon kosher salt
¼ cup Madeira or medium-dry sherry
About 2 cups mushroom, vegetable, or
   poultry broth
White pepper
½ cup hazelnuts, roasted, husked, and chopped
   medium-fine
Soft Polenta (page 224)

1. Clean mushroom caps with soft brush (or rinse if necessary). Trim stubborn bits of soil from stems. Cut mushrooms into 1-inch pieces, approximately.

2. Cut shallots into fine dice. Combine with flour and ¾ cup mushrooms on chopping board. Mince very fine, tossing to incorporate flour.

3. Heat fairly wide skillet over moderate heat. Add hazelnut oil and tip to distribute. Add shallot mixture and toss to coat. Reduce heat and stir a few minutes to color, being careful not to overbrown flour. Add mushroom pieces and salt; toss a minute or two. Add Madeira, scraping to loosen flour. Raise heat and cook, stirring, to evaporate liquid.

4. Add 1 cup broth, then simmer to thicken and blend flavors, about 15 minutes. Gradually add remaining broth as needed to attain a somewhat thinner consistency than desired final result. Continue simmering until thickened and blended to taste, 5 to 10 minutes. Add pepper. (Can be prepared ahead and refrigerated.)

5. To serve, add hazelnuts to sauce and bring to a boil, stirring. Thin, if necessary; season. Ladle over polenta in wide shallow bowls.

Serves 6 as a first course, 4 as a main course

Hedgehog Mushrooms à la Grecque

Mini-mushrooms marinated in a mild court bouillon do not lose their shape or pleasing bounciness. Choose small specimens for the best effect—but larger ones will do if they are trimmed and sliced about ¼ inch thick. Serve this fresh salad-y dish as part of an antipasto mixture, with olives, artichoke hearts, and shrimp. Or toss with poultry or ham dice and serve on greens, as a lunch salad.

1 tablespoon coriander seeds, lightly crushed
¼ teaspoon peppercorns (preferably white),
   lightly crushed
1¼ cups vegetable or chicken broth
1¼ cups light dry white wine
2 teaspoons kosher salt (less if broth is salted)
2 bay leaves
½ teaspoon dried tarragon
½ teaspoon dried summer savory or thyme
¾ pound small hedgehog mushrooms
   (or golden chanterelles)
3 small-medium shallots
¼ cup lemon juice
¼ cup olive oil
Minced parsley, tarragon, and chives

1. In saucepan, stir coriander and peppercorns over moderate heat until crackling and fragrant, about 3 minutes. Add broth, wine, salt, bay leaves, tarragon, and savory; bring to a boil. Reduce heat and simmer, covered, until liquid is flavorful—about 15 minutes.

2. Meanwhile, clean mushrooms: Trim bases and scrape off conspicuous soil. Dunk into sink filled with cold water and swish around, then lift out. Spread on towel, then blot dry. If small (caps about an inch in diameter), leave whole. If larger, halve, quarter, or cut into ¼-inch slices. Slice shallots. Intersperse mushrooms and shallots in wide-mouth heatproof jar of 4- to 5-cup capacity.

3. Add lemon juice and oil to court bouillon and return to a boil. Pour slowly over mushrooms and stir to mix in seasoning. Refrigerate, uncovered, stirring occasionally, until chilled. When cold, cover tightly. Serve after a day, or within a week.

Makes 1 quart

*See also recipes for golden and white chanterelles, pages 172–174, for which hedgehog mushrooms can be substituted.

Pros Propose

For the simplest route to pure mushroom flavor, chef Paul Bertolli simmers hedgehogs in their own juices: Toss sliced mushrooms in hot pan with butter and oil. Add salt and pepper, then reduce heat and cook gently, without stirring, to release juices. When juices accumulate, add minced shallots, then lemon juice. Simmer until liquid is reabsorbed and/or evaporates. Serve at once, sprinkled with herbs, if desired.

Anything but simple, **Eggplant Tart, Hedgehog Fricassee, and Almond Tea** is a complex of refined flavors derived from multiple cooking techniques, as is typical of chef Laurent Gras. To prepare: Toss small hedgehog caps with lemon juice, olive oil, and salt; refrigerate several hours. Steep sliced almonds for an hour in a sugar-salt syrup. Drain. Bake in low oven until caramelized. Prepare almond "tea": Toast raw almonds in dry pan to brown. Add butter and hedgehog stems and sauté briefly. Add diced eggplant, rehydrated dried yellowfoot chanterelles, and chicken stock: cook very gently for 1 hour. Add a little brown butter, then strain "tea" through fine sieve. Add cornstarch slurry to merely gloss—not thicken. Peel slim dark Japanese eggplant and cut into 1-inch slices. Steam 5 minutes. Season with olive oil and salt, then grill just to color and flavor. Sauté fresh (not the marinated) hedgehog caps in duck fat. Arrange rounds of eggplant in shallow bowls to form "tarts." Cover with a layer of the sautéed caps, then the marinated ones. Spoon "tea" around tarts. Sprinkle with caramelized almonds.

Hedgehogs make a fine subject for a traditional à la grecque pickle, as they retain their shape and color. For chef Philippe Boulot's **Roasted Stuffed Quail with Hedgehogs à la Grecque**: Prepare court bouillon of equal parts chicken stock, olive oil, and white wine, seasoned with chopped shallots, thyme, toasted coriander seeds, salt, and pepper. Add whole small hedgehogs to the hot bouillon. Cool, then refrigerate overnight to pickle. Roast more hedgehogs in pan with oil, salt, and pepper in hot oven. Chop (by hand) to coarse texture. Combine with twice as much pork stuffing. Fill boneless quail with mixture. Roast to 160°F. Spoon room-temperature à la grecque mushrooms onto a bed of frisée, then top with warm quail.

Apples, apple brandy, and cream are hedgehogs' partners in an unusual appetizer from Normandy, home to all of them. For **Compote of Apples and Pied-de-Mouton in Calvados**: Brown quartered hefty hedgehogs in butter. Add Calvados, and flame. Cover and simmer until tender. Soften minced onion in butter. Add cider and reduce until almost dry; then add the mushrooms and cream. Cook to desired thickness. Meanwhile, cut peeled tart apples into eighths. Cook in butter in non-stick pan until golden. Add to mushroom mixture and warm through. Serve in individual casseroles, with a glass of sparkling cider (from *Toutes les bases de la cuisine aux champignons* by Frédéric Jaunault and Jean-Luc Brillet).

Hen of the Woods (*Grifola frondosa*)

Also maitake (Japanese)

Whether foraged or farmed (as in the photo), this fluffy fungus is highly variable but almost always delightful. Autumnal and faintly gamy or garlicky in aroma, the nutty flesh is firm, a bit crumbly. Even cooked, it has a leafy, wild look and a dynamic tone—tender with an al dente bounce. Cultivated forms, weighing from ½ pound to 1½ pounds, are milder and considerably daintier than the wild, which can weigh from 3 to a reported 100 pounds per clump.

The "hen" is an aggregate of branched clusters of small, overlapping irregular "feathers" whose pale bases are compressed in a nearly solid mass. These leafy caps (the species name, *frondosa,* means leafy) are taupe, greige, or smoky brown, with light colored undersides.

It is this underpart only that relates in a distant manner to another mushroom named after poultry, chicken of the woods (see page 182), for both species are poly-pores—fungi with pores instead of gills or teeth.

Maitake, a Japanese name, translates as dancing mushroom, a more appealing picture than the avian images that for some odd reason abound in English. The mushroom is grown in great quantities in Japan and now is being exported to the United States in ex-perimental shipments for further development. The sample maitake I have cooked were smooth-capped, uniformly rounded, and aromatic, with an impressive array of "feathers" and minimal base area—meaning no waste at all.

The first record of maitake cultivation is in a tale

from the 11th-century Japanese text Konjaku Monogatari, according to Paul Stamets (*Growing Gourmet and Medicinal Mushrooms*). He writes that *Grifola frondosa* is "indigenous to the Northeastern regions of Japan, the temperate hardwood regions of China, and Europe where it was first discovered"; to deciduous forests in Eastern Canada; and to the Northeastern and Mid-Atlantic United States.

Production in the United States is minimal, primarily because the mushroom itself fruits unpredictably, according to Don Phillips, president of Phillips Mushroom Farms in Kennett Square, Pennsylvania, an elder statesman of the industry: "It's an unstable producer, sometimes yielding plenty, sometimes nothing." He makes no promises, but production has increased and stayed up in recent years.

BASIC USE: Generally speaking, the mushroom's spongy, chewy flesh benefits most from gentle cooking with liquid. Braise pieces with olive oil, garlic, stock, and pancetta; or stew in cream and brandy or Madeira, then serve the meaty sauce over polenta, pasta, or grain. The cultivated mushrooms can also be quickly sautéed and tossed with herbs or toasted nuts for a side dish with an intriguing texture and a woodsy fragrance. Or cut into clumps, swab with seasoned oil or fat (duck or goose confit is perfect), and roast at a high temperature.

SELECTION: Look for fluffy "feathers" and comparatively little heavy core—although it is edible and good. The scent should be woodsy and sweet, with no hint of sourness or fishiness indicating spoilage. Check the edges of the thin caps for signs of decay. Daniel Bruce, a forager and chef, says the wild hen of the woods that appears in the fall is thicker, meatier, and earthier. Cultivated hen of the woods is available erratically all year but fairly difficult to find.

PREPARATION: For the cultivated mushroom, tear the big pouf into thin branching fronds, paddles, and swirls, dividing it from the base, rather than cutting it. Or cut or break into larger clumps. If any growing medium adheres, trim or brush it off. If the center is chunky and solid, cook it first, then add the caplets for a finishing touch.

The wild mushrooms need considerable cleaning. Daniel Bruce suggests this approach: Flip over the "hen" and trim away soil and bits of wood, pine needles, and twigs. Split large pieces, cutting from the heavy base toward the tips so that you can "check out any inhabitants of the wild mushroom condominium, which may be many. Spray with bursts of water, then spread on towels to dry." At the end of the season, when the mushroom may be comparatively dry, it can be soaked briefly to rehydrate.

To break down for cooking, cut small wedges or strips from the base to the tips so that you display the "branches and leaves" in the same way you would cauliflower florets.

Creamed Hen of the Woods with Thin Egg Noodles

When heated, these polypores develop a nutty, woodsy aroma and flavor and an al dente consistency—provided cooking is relatively long and gentle. (Count on doubled intensity and firmer texture if you've landed the wild fungus.) The few elements create a subtle sauce that is rich tasting but only lightly creamy. For a more unctuous effect, use ¾ cup cream and cook it down a little more.

½ **pound hen of the woods**
1 **cup rich mushroom, vegetable, or**
    chicken stock
½ **cup heavy cream**
¼ **to ½ teaspoon Worcestershire sauce**
Salt and pepper
½ **pound dried narrow egg noodles**
Minced parsley leaves

1. Trim any very tough dark bits from mushroom as needed (most or all is usually edible). Break mass into bite-size pieces, cleaning with a soft brush. (For wild specimens, see cleaning instructions in Preparation above.)

2. Combine mushroom pieces with broth in saucepan that holds them closely. Simmer, covered, until almost tender—this can take from 5 to 20 minutes or so, depending upon the specific mushroom.

3. Uncover, add cream, and simmer very gently (do not hurry the process) until flavors develop and blend and cream thickens very slightly, about 20 minutes. Add Worcestershire, salt, and pepper to taste. Remove from heat.

4. Cook noodles in boiling salted water until tender. Drain, then return to pot. Heat creamed mushrooms. Toss with noodles over lowest heat. Sprinkle with parsley. Distribute among heated plates.

Serves 4 to 6 as a first course

Sautéed Cultivated Hen of the Woods with Parsley and Walnuts

Cultivated hen of the woods varies in intensity, sometimes comparing favorably to its wild kin, sometimes lacking its depth. But it is reliably flavorful, needs minimal cleaning, and cooks rapidly. Add instant mystery to a meal with the addition of the chewy dark "feathers." Serve as a first course or vegetable side dish.

> ¾ pound cultivated hen of the woods
> 1 cup lightly packed curly parsley leaves
> ¼ cup toasted walnuts
> 3 tablespoons olive oil
> 1 large shallot, chopped
> ½ teaspoon kosher salt
> 1 teaspoon minced thyme leaves
> Pepper

1. Trim any moist, very dark, or heavy, corky bits from mushroom if necessary. Separate into clumps about ½ inch wide at the base, pulling apart at the natural separations. Mince half the parsley; set aside. Chop the remainder together with the walnuts to medium-fine texture.

2. Heat oil in fairly large skillet over moderate heat. Add shallot and toss a few minutes to color and soften. Add mushrooms and salt and toss a few minutes. Cover; continue cooking until mushrooms are not quite cooked through, about 3 minutes. Lower heat if mushrooms begin to scorch.

3. Add minced parsley and thyme; toss, uncovered, to blend flavors and cook through completely, about 3 minutes. Add parsley-walnut mixture and toss. Season with pepper. Serve hot.

Serves 3 to 4 as a first course or side dish

Roasted Maitake

The large pouf of small, smooth-topped caps that make up the cultivated Japanese maitake is best when simply roasted at high heat with a generous glaze of oil or fat (duck or goose is particularly right in its gaminess). Other cultivated hen of the woods will do fine as well, but may be less presentable. These tidy "florets" look like small trees or branching coral.

> 1¼ to 1½ pounds maitake (hen of the woods)
> 3 tablespoons duck or goose fat or olive oil
> 4 garlic cloves, peeled
> Salt and pepper

1. Heat oven to 450°F, with two racks set close to the center. Break or cut mushroom(s) into large clumps (1½ to 2 ounces apiece) so that each extends fully from caps to base of stem. You want chunks, not slices that may break into individual mushrooms.

2. Select two baking pans that will hold mushrooms in a single layer with space in between. Divide fat between them. Set garlic on fat. Place in preheated oven until you smell the sizzling garlic.

3. Tip pans to distribute fat. With tongs, hold mushrooms and quickly swab pieces to coat. Sprinkle with salt and pepper (do not omit salt—it draws out moisture that ensures even cooking and prevents burning).

4. Roast until maitake is browned underneath, about 8 minutes. Turn gently with tongs or spatula; salt and pepper lightly. Return to oven, switching pan positions. Roast until browned and al dente—tender at the thickest part of the base, about 5 minutes longer. Timing will depend on density. If caps seem to be scorching, lower heat slightly.

5. Transfer mushrooms to paper towels to blot fat, if desired. Serve hot, with additional salt and pepper.

Serves 4 to 5 as a side dish

Braised Hen of the Woods over Soft Polenta

Hen of the woods has a meatiness and a complexity that suit starchy accompaniments. This dish even looks like meat stew, making it a good choice to serve as a main course for "mixed company" (vegetarians and non-). I like the mushroom pieces chunky-chewy. For a saucier effect, cut into small dice. Timing may vary, with wild mushrooms needing more cooking than cultivated. Try the microwaved polenta: It is fuss-free and good, if less developed in flavor than the traditional long-stirred.

5 medium garlic cloves (unpeeled)
1 medium carrot
1 large celery stalk
2 medium shallots
3 tablespoons full-flavored olive oil
1 teaspoon fine-chopped rosemary
¼ cup red wine or dry sherry
¾ to 1 pound hen of the woods
1 cup flavorful chicken, meat, or
   vegetable broth
1 teaspoon kosher salt (omit if broth
   is salted)
¼ teaspoon pepper
Soft Polenta (page 224)
½ cup grated Parmesan cheese

1. Bring garlic to a boil in small pot of water; drain. Peel. Boil and drain a second time. Slice.

2. With food processor motor running, drop vegetables into the feed tube in this order: carrot, celery, and shallots, chopping fine. Heat oil in heavy saucepan large enough to hold all ingredients. Add minced vegetables and stir over moderately low heat until lightly colored and softened, 7 to 8 minutes. Add garlic and rosemary and toss a few minutes. Add wine.

3. Meanwhile, trim any tough or very dark bits from mushrooms as needed (most or all of cultivated is usually edible; to clean wild hen of the woods, see Preparation, above). Break into 2-inch clumps.

4. Add mushrooms to pan and toss. Add broth, salt, and pepper. Cover and simmer 5 minutes. Continue to cook gently, partly covered, until mushrooms are flavorful and tender—about ½ hour (longer for some wild ones), tossing occasionally. Do not hurry process. Liquid will be nearly evaporated and mushrooms slightly firm. Season. (Can be made ahead, cooled, and chilled.)

5. Ladle polenta into four wide shallow bowls. Spoon mushrooms over each. Serve at once, with cheese alongside.

Serves 4 as a main course

Pros Propose

Chef Daniel Bruce prepares a rich **Local Hen of the Woods Cream Soup** with the savory East Coast mushroom: Cut tips of wild hen of the woods into julienne. Prepare stock using the heavy base. Sauté julienne in butter to brown slightly; deglaze with Madeira. Add mushroom broth; simmer until tender, about 20 minutes. Add heavy cream and minced fresh thyme and simmer briefly. Fold in chopped baby spinach leaves and cook to just wilt. Gloss with butter.

The caps and base are also treated separately by chef Lee Hefter. For **Wild Striped Bass with Hen of the Woods, Lobster, and Brussels Sprouts in Mushroom Broth:** Clean and chop mushroom base; reserve feathery caps. Gently simmer base in butter with garlic. Add mushroom stock to cover and cook gently to extract all flavor and reduce. Strain and emulsify with olive oil. Sauté mushroom tops with parsley and butter. Add Brussels sprout leaves and bits of lobster. Place a mound of the mixture in each bowl. Top with sautéed striped bass. Spoon mushroom broth around.

Cultivated maitake are common in Japan, where they have long been farmed. Raw, they are the base for an unusual **Maitake Shoyu Sauce** from chef Masaharu Morimoto: Combine raw maitake, dashi, and shoyu. Whiz in food processor until as smooth as possible. Use as sauce for white fish sashimi.

Japanese ingredients dominate **White Miso and Maitake Broth** from chef Michael Otsuka: Choose small cultivated hen of the woods. Trim some of base, then tear lengthwise strips. Brown over moderate heat in clarified butter, watching carefully so mushrooms brown and crisp but do not scorch. Drain on paper towels. Add to mushroom broth. Stir in white miso dissolved in water. Finish with sesame oil and shichimi togarashi (7-spice chilli mix).

Chef Otsuka's **Duck Breast with Yuzu Sauce on Maitake and Spinach** incorporates the sautéed mushrooms in a different way: Caramelize sugar, then add orange juice to liquefy. Season with rice vinegar and yuzu juice. Add poultry *jus* and dried blueberries soaked in crème de cassis. Prepare mushrooms as in recipe above. When crisp, fold in baby spinach leaves to just wilt. Serve as a bed for duck breast dry-marinated in 5-spice powder, then seared, roasted, sliced, and fanned. Spoon sauce around. Dust edges of warmed plates with 5-spice powder and serve at once.

Hericium species

Including **Pompon Blanc**™ or **bear's head** and **wild** *Hericium* **species**

Pompon Blanc

diameter: 3-4 inches

I am sorry about the heading above, but there is so little agreement on common and species names that I can offer only the genus, *Hericium*, as a sure thing. The cultivated and wild forms of a mushroom are always distinct, but farmed *Hericium* is so different from wild as to be unrecognizable and to require different care and handling. Hence, the two-part entry that follows.

Pompon Blanc and **bear's head** are two market names for cultivated *Hericium erinaceus*, a mushroom that is more likely to be available than any of the wild *Hericium* species. Paul Stamets, author of *Growing Gourmet and Medicinal Mushrooms*, gives these names as well: lion's mane, monkey's head, old man's beard, satyr's beard, pom pom, and yamabushi-take (which he

translates as "mountain-priest mushroom"). Most, if not all (depending upon your interpretation), refer to the soft white glissade of "teeth" (in lieu of gills) that distinguishes this species as well as others of the genus *Hericium*.

The trim little Pompon Blanc pictured here (there are also larger cultivated bear's head mushrooms with longer spines), looks and feels like a powder puff crossed with mozzarella. Rounded, spongy, almost furry in texture, each pouf weighs about 2 ounces—a far cry from the giant, shaggy wild ones. Jacky Robert (then chef at Ernie's in San Francisco, and who has long been chef at Maison Robert in Boston) takes credit for naming it Pompon Blanc in the 1980s, when Gourmet Mushrooms of Sebastopol introduced it. Although available in limited quantities since that time, it continues to be a novelty, with only spotty distribution.

This is not surprising, for the mushroom (except for Gourmet's product) is highly variable and so unlike most mushrooms that it confuses even dedicated fungophiles. It can be fresh, light, a bit bitter, with a suggestion of artichoke—a curiously yeasty, spongy delicacy like bubbly tofu. Or it can be inedibly bitter, wet, chewy, and thoroughly nasty.

BASIC USE: Brush the whole mushroom with melted butter and roast in a hot oven until there is only a little resistance in the center, a matter of 10 minutes or so. The little golden pillow looks charming presented on a bed of tiny greens, for each diner to tackle individually. Or sauté: Cut ¼-inch slices (they are pretty and uniform) and sauté in oil and butter, turning carefully, until just gilded on both sides. (Do not overcook, or the interior will get soggy.) Blot to absorb some of the considerable fat the mushroom soaks up.

SELECTION AND STORAGE: Buy only the driest, palest specimens. In my limited experience, the tiny-toothed small poufs (see photo) are the best. Freshness is not the only factor, unfortunately. I have tasted superficially fine specimens that proved inedible. Refrigerate swiftly and cook ASAP. This is not a keeper!

PREPARATION: Nothing to do: Just heat and eat.

I would like to caption this photo more specifically (it's probably *Hericium coralloides*), but the changing classifications make this dicey. In *Mushrooms Demystified,* David Arora, after meticulously noting revisions and overlaps of the *Hericium* species *abietis, coralloides, ramosum, americanum, weirii,* and *erinaceus,* bursts out in exasperation: "Since all of these Hericiums are equally edible, their exact identities needn't concern you—at least, they don't concern me!"

I can tell you a little about the mushroom pictured so that if you find it in a market (preferably not one where it is draped forlornly over tropical fruit, as it was in a fancy foolish New York City food shoppe where I spotted it), you might chance the pleasure of its curious company.

My limited experience follows: The 1½-pound mass of stout ivory, cottony stems and tufted "teeth" looked and felt more like a sea plant than a mushroom. Barely trimmed and quickly cooked, it was fresh and delightful, a wild creature for adventurous eaters, who will be

rewarded with . . . what? Animal, vegetable, or mineral? The fleshy stem parts resemble tender scallops, and the delicate spines are more like shredded crabmeat, yet neither tastes like either or like any other mushroom I know. Light, fleshy, a bit acid, a bit sweet—and truly unique. Experts tell me this sample looks a little old and damp, but I found that the massive fungus tasted fresh and lovely.

BASIC USE: I haven't explored this difficult-to-come-by mushroom in depth, nor have I found chefs who have, but I can recommend this technique: Toss bite-size pieces in a sauté pan with butter and salt. Reduce heat and simmer, covered, until tender (a few minutes). Raise heat to evaporate the large quantity of accumulated liquid. Add cream or butter and toss, then finish with a mere touch of tarragon, chervil, or chives. Spoon the mushroom over delicate sprigs of green.

SELECTION AND STORAGE: You'll have little choice with this late summer-fall mushroom. As long as it smells pleasant, it's worth trying. Cook it as soon as possible, for it is highly perishable. If you must keep it, spread on paper toweling in a basket and refrigerate.

PREPARATION: Nip off any browning or yellowing tips. If, miraculously, the mushroom is clean (or if

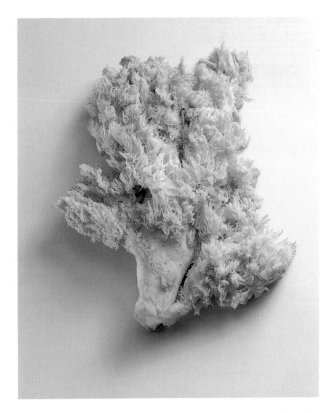

wild *Hericium*   length: 12 inches

you don't mind a touch of forest), ignore the following: Pull off the tufty smaller branches, tearing them into large bite-size pieces. Coarse-chop the central stem and branches. Dip these all into water and lift out quickly. Repeat, if needed, until little debris sinks to the bottom.

Golden Slices of Pompon Blanc on Mixed Greens

Pompon Blanc or other cultivated bear's head mushrooms must be cooked quickly at a high temperature or they become soggy. Oven-seared slices look like sautéed chicken, taste like juicy tofu, and make an unusual opener. Or, for a vegetarian meal, omit the greens and serve as main-course "cutlets" for two accompanied by bright, crunchy vegetables, such as sugar snap peas and carrots.

1 tablespoon lemon juice
Big pinch of white pepper
Optional: 1 garlic clove, halved
3 tablespoons olive oil
¾ to 1 pound small cultivated *Hericium*
3 cups cleaned baby tatsoi or mizuna leaves
   (about 3 ounces)
1 Belgian endive, trimmed and cut into
   ¼-inch slices
Fleur de sel or other crisp sea salt

1. Set oven to 475°F. Combine lemon juice, pepper, optional garlic, and oil.

2. Gently cut mushrooms into ½- to ¾-inch slices. Lay on baking sheet.

3. Whisk dressing. Reserve 1½ tablespoons. Brush half the remainder on the slices. Turn and brush the other sides and edges to coat.

4. Bake until underside of mushrooms is golden, about 5 minutes. Sometimes the top will brown too. If not, flip gently with spatula and bake until browned underneath. Timing varies, but do not overcook: The interior will be tender when both sides are golden.

5. Meanwhile, toss greens with reserved dressing. Arrange on four plates. Set hot mushrooms on salad and sprinkle generously with crisp salt. Serve at once.

Serves 4 as a first course

Warm, Creamy Wild Hericium Salad

This indescribable wild creature is for adventurous eaters—not because it tastes "weird" or strong, but because it is unlike other foods. It is light and luscious in texture, mild and fresh in flavor, with little earthiness about it—and, for all I know, tastes different every time it is cooked. Experiment!

About ¾ pound wild *Hericium*
1 tablespoon butter
½ teaspoon kosher salt
2 to 4 tablespoons heavy cream
Minced fresh tarragon leaves
Lemon juice
Nutmeg
1 bunch water cress, rinsed, dried, and
   trimmed into sprigs
Optional: minced chives and lemon slices

1. Nip off and discard any brown or yellow tips from mushrooms. Pull off tufty smaller branches and tear into large bite-size pieces. Chop central stem and branches. If miraculously clean, do not wash. More likely, you will need to dip quickly in and out of water, repeating until clean.

2. Melt butter in medium sauté pan over high heat. Add mushroom and salt, cover, reduce heat, and simmer until tender, about 5 minutes (it will be juicy).

3. Uncover and raise heat briefly to evaporate juices. Reduce heat and add cream: Use the smaller amount to cook down to a glaze or, for a creamy-soft effect, stir in the larger amount and heat through.

4. Add tarragon, lemon juice, and nutmeg a little at a time, tasting often to balance the delicate flavors.

5. Arrange cress on plates. Spoon mushrooms on top. Serve warm, with optional chives and lemon.

Serves 4

★See also recipe for Parasol Mushrooms Baked Under Crunchy Crumbs, page 467, for which sliced cultivated or wild Hericium can be substituted.

Pros Propose

Small cultivated *Hericium* is the subject here, not the wild thing. "The problem with these pretty mushrooms is they soak up so much fat," says chef Michael Otsuka. To prevent this, sauté small slices in non-stick skillet with a bare slick of fat until colored but not cooked through. For **Salad of Pompon Blanc and Fingerlings:** Toss roasted potatoes and frisée with dressing of champagne vinegar, grapeseed oil, and olive oil. Toss with sautéed mushroom slices.

Several chefs identify a flavor note of crabmeat and lobster in the mushroom and underscore it with the real thing. Chef Randy Kliewer serves a pure, clean **Lobster Broth with Pompon Blanc and Nameko:** Season Pompon Blanc and set on dry baking sheet in high oven. Bake just until the edges color, not until mushroom softens inside. Slice. Quickly sauté nameko (see page 414) caps ("they add just the right slippery contrast to the spongy Pompon"). Add both mushrooms to clarified lobster broth infused with saffron and tomato.

Chef Mark Franz finds the texture of lobster an ideal match. For **Roasted Pompon Blanc with Lobster Gnocchi:** Brush Pompon with olive oil; season. Roast in moderately hot oven until slightly crisped outside. Set on gnocchi studded with lobster bits and tarragon and spoon light shellfish sauce over all.

Fish as well as shellfish suit this mushroom. For **Fillet of Sole with Hericium and Tangerine Peel:** Lay fillets on pieces of oiled parchment. Sprinkle with white wine, melted butter, salt, and grated tangerine zest, then rub to coat evenly. Cover with thin-sliced red bell pepper, then *Hericium* slices. Enclose in the parchment and bake in 450°F oven 10 minutes (from *A Cook's Book of Mushrooms* by Jack Czarnecki).

Honey Mushrooms (*Armillariella mellea* and *A. tabescens*)

Meaty, earthy honey mushrooms flourish in abundance (in Europe and Asia, as well as the United States) in a perplexing range of colors, shapes, and sizes; but "for all practical purposes, the complex of nearly identical species makes for excellent eating," says Gary Lincoff, an educator and author of the *Audubon Society Field Guide to Mushrooms.* Lincoff's counterpart on the West Coast, David Arora, writes in *Mushrooms Demystified* that honey "is among the most variable and cosmopolitan of the fleshy fungi, and in its innumerable guises will confound you time and time again." What honey mushrooms have in common is rewarding comestibility but extreme perishability and, as Lincoff stresses, a need to be "cooked through and through—not sautéed, not stir-fried—unless you want to risk gastrointestinal upset."

Whether caramel, cream, or canary when raw, honey mushrooms usually turn shiny cocoa to licorice when cooked, while the interior stays comparatively pale. Solid caps and scaly stems soften to a succulent, muscular, scallop-like texture, and the flavor is deep and sweet. Some taste like cremini gone wild; others have the richness of roasted liver, and a look to match; still others taste like a golden omelet.

BASIC USE: This is a mushroom with firm presence—not to be hidden or slipped into sauce but served in a primary role. Serve it as an accent to meat or game. Feature it in a frittata, ragoût, or risotto. Braising plus sautéeing is my choice of cooking method: Toss with hot butter, or oil (or both) and salt. Cover, reduce heat, and cook until juicy and tender. Uncover and cook gently until glazed, about 10 minutes longer. The chef and forager Daniel Bruce advises that "ringless honey mushrooms have thin stems that lend themselves to presentation in whole form—but they must be primo buttons, just a day or two out of the soil."

SELECTION: Youth is paramount. The Italian name for the mushrooms, chiodini (little nails), describes the optimum form. "It's important to get these as buttons or just as they start to open, because they spoil quickly, turn squishy, and get worms in the gills,"

says chef Bruce. Mushrooms picked in clusters are safest and freshest.

STORAGE: Honey mushrooms perish more quickly than you can imagine. Refrigerate in a wide basket and cook at once—if not sooner.

PREPARATION: Trim base of mushroom stems. As their condition dictates, brush mushrooms clean, or rub with damp towel, or rinse; then spread to dry on a towel. Leave small buttons whole. If mushrooms are large, cut stems diagonally into bite-size sections and halve or quarter caps.

About blanching: European cooks often boil honey mushrooms in salted water for 5 minutes before sautéing. I tried this, drained the mushrooms, trimmed the stalks (which at this point looked like fat squid), then sautéed in butter with shallots. The mushrooms turned chocolate brown and kept their shape, shine, and juicy

ringless honey (*top*) and honey mushroom (*bottom*)

length: 3–6 inches

crunch. They had a sweeter if milder flavor than when sauté-braised.

Glazed Honey Mushrooms with Spinach Leaves

Chef Daniel Bruce, a formidable forager (he had collected 100 pounds of porcini the day I spoke to him about honey mushrooms), finds spinach an ideal partner for honeys—and now, so do I. This is one of those perfect pairings that pull together flavors and textures as they preserve the individual characteristics of the partners. Plump, glossy mushroom chunks are accented by soft spinach in a side dish for sautéed liver or kidneys, broiled steak, roasted lamb, or game—or a nut-studded vegetarian pilaf of brown rice or buckwheat.

½ pound small honey mushrooms, preferably
   unopened buttons
½ tablespoon mild oil, such as grapeseed or
   corn
1 tablespoon butter
¼ teaspoon kosher salt
2 to 3 ounces cleaned small spinach leaves
   (1 generous cup)
Pepper

1. Trim base of mushroom stems. As condition dictates, brush mushrooms clean, or rub soiled spots with damp towel, or rinse, then spread to dry on a towel. Slice stems into 1- to 1½-inch sections. Leave caps whole, halve, or quarter to make pieces the same size.

2. Heat oil and ½ tablespoon butter over moderate heat in heavy skillet that will hold mushrooms closely in a tight single layer. Add mushrooms and salt and toss. Lower heat slightly, cover, and cook, shaking pan often, until mushrooms are juicy and tender—about 5 minutes.

3. Uncover and continue cooking gently until mushrooms are glazed and cooked through and only a little liquid remains—5 to 10 minutes.

4. Add spinach leaves. Toss until not quite wilted—about 30 seconds. Remove from heat and add remaining ½ tablespoon butter, shaking to distribute evenly. Season and serve at once.

Serves 2

Frittata of Honey Mushrooms and Red Pearl Onions

Swarthy, handsome mushrooms and caramelized onions decorate a thin frittata flecked with parsley and cheese. Rings of red pearl onion blend beautifully with the shiny mushrooms—but 1 cup red onion dice can be substituted if small red onions are elusive.

The frittata, with its rich flavors and textures, has character enough to be served over a zesty blend of wild leaves or pungent cultivated greens and herbs. For 6 to 8 servings, figure on 7 cups aromatic greens. Toss with a dressing of lemon juice, nut oil, and olive oil. Cut frittata into very thin strips and drape over the salad. Garnish with tiny currant or cherry tomatoes.

8 to 10 ounces honey mushrooms, preferably
   unopened buttons
2 tablespoons butter
½ teaspoon kosher salt
About 5 ounces red pearl onions, peeled
   (see page 439)
1 tablespoon sherry or Madeira
6 eggs
2 tablespoons minced parsley
¾ cup coarse-grated Gouda or Gruyère cheese
   (about 1½ ounces)
½ tablespoon mild oil
Pepper

1. Trim base of mushroom stems so none are longer than 3 inches. As needed, brush mushrooms clean, or rub with a damp towel, or rinse, then dry on a towel. Halve each lengthwise unless very small.

2. Melt 1 tablespoon butter over moderate heat in large skillet (preferably non-stick) with ovenproof handle. Add mushrooms and ¼ teaspoon salt, tossing to coat. Reduce heat, cover, and cook, shaking pan often, until mushrooms are juicy and tender—about 5 minutes.

3. Uncover and cook gently—do not sear—until mushrooms are dark, glazed, and well cooked, 5 to 10 minutes. Scoop into a dish.

4. Meanwhile, cut onions into ⅛-inch slices and separate rings. Heat remaining 1 tablespoon butter in same pan. Add onions. Brown over moderate heat, shaking often, about 10 minutes. Add sherry and stir until evaporated. Scoop onions into a dish.

5. Turn on broiler. Whisk eggs to blend. Add remaining ¼ teaspoon salt, parsley, and half the cheese. Return skillet to moderate heat (rinse out if sticky). Add oil. When hot, pour in egg mixture. When sides set, lift with spatula to let liquid run underneath. When half-cooked (still liquid on top), remove from heat.

6. Scatter onions on top, grind over pepper, and sprinkle with remaining cheese. Scatter mushrooms over and press gently with spatula. Slide pan under broiler 3 to 4 inches from heat. Cook just until barely set, a minute or so.

7. Let rest about 10 minutes, until edges of frittata separate from pan. Run flexible spatula around edge, then slide onto flat plate. Serve hot, warm, or at room temperature, cut into wedges.

Serves 3 as a main course, 6 as an hors d'oeuvre, 6 to 8 with salad

Pros Propose

When Chef Odessa Piper long-baked honey mushrooms ("because my forager warned me that they need extra thorough cooking"), she found they "developed a truly honey-like complexity." To prepare **Baked Honey Mushroom Caps:** Remove stems from smallish honeys and use in stock. Toss caps with melted butter, salt, and pepper. Set gill side up on parchment-lined baking sheet. Bake in a moderate oven "to wick off moisture but not to caramelize" until fork-tender—about 40 minutes.

Chef Jean-Louis Palladin pairs honey mushrooms with veal. For **Rack of Veal Stuffed with Honey Mushrooms with Thyme Sauce:** Sauté small, closed honey caps in oil to brown well. Cut slit through center of veal rack to form pocket. Put mushrooms in pastry bag and pipe into pocket. Rinse caul fat, squeeze dry, and wrap twice around veal; secure with twine. Season. Heat oil in roasting pan and place large quantity of thyme sprigs in the center. Set veal on this, then brown on all sides. Roast bone side down at 500°F until thermometer registers 135°F. Let stand 10 minutes. Remove caul and slice veal. Serve with sauce made from veal stock and thyme, a tart of straw potatoes (*pommes paillasson*), and honey mushrooms (from *Jean-Louis: Cooking with the Seasons*).

Broiling is another way to fully cook and concentrate the flavor of honey mushrooms. Daniel Bruce chooses it for **Risotto of Lemon-Scented Honey Mushrooms with Madeira Essence:** Toss trimmed mushrooms with fine-grated lemon zest, olive oil, salt, pepper, and clarified butter. Spread on baking sheet. Broil mushrooms near heat, turning them and adjusting distance from heat so they cook through but juices do not scorch. Prepare risotto with mushroom broth. To serve, stir juices from broiled mushrooms into risotto, with butter and Parmesan. Arrange mushrooms on top with a cluster of sautéed spinach leaves. Drizzle Madeira essence (Madeira cooked down to a syrup) around edges of bowls.

Horseradish Tree, Drumstick (*Moringa oleifera*)

Also sajuna and murungaikkai (Indian), malunggay and variations (Philippine)

length: 10-14 inches

This native Indian plant is not a relative of horseradish or drums—both names that were given to it by the British. The tree is, however, a bit of a curiosity. It comes from a family, Moringaceae, with just one genus, *Moringa,* which makes it unusual by botanical definition. Its mustard-sharp leaves, flowers, immature seeds, and biting root (the explanation for its English name "horseradish") are all edible. The long, slender, ribbed pods (the "drumsticks") are the only part I have found in the Indian and Pakistani groceries in New York and New Jersey where I shop. For some reason, whenever I examine them, shoppers talk to me;

that is also unusual, for these are markets where I am habitually ignored or viewed with overt mistrust. I have not discovered why these vegetables make friends.

Although horseradish tree is grown in parts of Southeast Asia, the West Indies, South America, and Florida, it is basically an Indian plant, cultivated primarily in Bengal and Assam. It is not a staple but a regional specialty. In North America, it is truly an oddity, and it is not likely to become more commonplace in your home, if only because it is probably the messiest vegetable ever tackled at table. Traditionally, it is cut into lengths, stewed in a spicy bean or lentil puree (dal), and fished out to be eaten with the fingers. Each piece must be split, then pulled between the teeth, like artichoke, to scrape off the soft succulent pulp and tender seeds that nestle in it. The rewards are greater in volume than with artichoke, and although there is a hint of artichoke flavor, the taste and texture are closer to pureed beans and okra.

BASIC USE: In India, drumsticks are usually cut into sections, parboiled, then cooked in spicy sauce until soft. I prefer to cook the vegetable in broth, from which it is more tidily retrieved and which lets the subtle flavor of the pods come through.

It is simplest to cut 2-inch lengths and simmer them in seasoned stock until tender, a matter of 5 to 20 minutes, depending upon size. You can eat them hot, or drain, then marinate in sauce or dressing to serve at room temperature. Or half-cook the pods, then stir into simmering stews or soups for the last 10 minutes of cooking.

SELECTION: Look for medium pods (in terms of both length and width) that are comparatively smooth and uniform—like the ones in the photo. They should not be bulging with seeds or very skinny. A relatively bright green with few or no brown patches signals freshness. All drumsticks have a rather dry and drab aspect compared with legumes in the pod, which they resemble. I have found them most often in late summer but also at other times throughout the year.

STORAGE: Wrap pods in paper towel, enclose in a plastic bag, and keep no more than a few days in the warmest part of the refrigerator.

PREPARATION: Rinse pods, cut off and discard tips, then slice 2-inch lengths—at which point you'll release the bracing horseradish scent.

Horseradish Tree Drumsticks à la Grecque

Those who like to work their way through whole artichokes or suck on crab legs will enjoy this yummy, messy 100 percent non-traditional dish. To savor the soft-cooked interior, split each piece of pod lengthwise, then scrape off the pulp and creamy seeds with your teeth. If you like a nippy finish, add a generous pinch of chilli flakes to the cooking liquid. Finger bowls are a must!

> 2 cups vegetable broth
> ½ cup light dry white wine
> 1 to 2 tablespoons lemon juice
> ½ teaspoon kosher salt
> ½ teaspoon coriander seeds
> ¼ teaspoon dried thyme
> ¼ teaspoon fennel seeds
> 1 pound horseradish tree drumsticks
> 2 tablespoons olive oil
> Optional: minced parsley and/or cilantro (coriander) leaves

1. In a large skillet, combine broth, wine, 1 tablespoon lemon juice, salt, coriander, thyme, and fennel and bring to a boil. Cover, reduce heat, and simmer 5 minutes.

2. Slice tips from drumsticks. Cut pods into 2-inch sections. Add to broth. Simmer, covered, until tender inside, about 5 minutes. (To test, split open a pod and taste the interior; it should be soft and fleshy.) With slotted spoon, transfer to serving dish.

3. If necessary, boil liquid to reduce to about 1 cup. Add olive oil. Pour over drumsticks. Cool to room temperature. Taste; season with lemon juice and salt.

4. Serve at room temperature or chilled, with or without herbs.

Serves 4

Pros Propose

Traditionally, horseradish tree drumsticks are cooked in the following ways. I have not been able to locate "new-style" recipes.

For **Drumstick Vegetable Curry**: Boil drumstick sections until tender; drain. Grind chopped onion, garlic, ginger, green chillis, and dried coconut to a paste. Fry mustard seeds and asafoetida until seeds stop popping. Stir in besan (chickpea flour) and fry until very aromatic. Add water, salt, chilli powder, turmeric, and tamarind concentrate. Bring to a boil. Add garam masala, ground cumin, and drumsticks. Cook until thickened. Sprinkle with cilantro (from *The Encyclopedia of Asian Food and Cooking* by Jacki Passmore).

For **White Drumstick Curry:** Pare any dry patches from drumsticks with vegetable peeler. Dilute coconut milk with water and combine in saucepan with turmeric, sliced onion, chopped garlic, grated ginger, fenugreek seeds, curry leaves, pandan leaves, and salt. Add drumsticks and simmer until soft, about 20 minutes. Add more coconut milk and season (from *Charmaine Solomon's Encyclopedia of Asian Food*).

For **Drumstick Rasam:** Cook red or yellow lentils in water until soft; set aside. Heat red chillis, asafoetida powder, coriander seeds, peppercorns, and a touch of yellow split peas for a few minutes. Process to a fine paste with grated fresh or dried coconut. Boil drumsticks until tender. Drain, reserving water. Combine water with tamarind pulp and soak 15 minutes. Strain into saucepan. Add ground turmeric and drumsticks; simmer briefly. Add the spice paste, lentils, and water as needed for desired consistency. Toss mustard seeds, cumin seeds, halved red chilli, and curry leaves in ghee in hot pan. When seeds splutter, add to cooked dish (from *Dakshin: Vegetarian Cuisine from South India* by Chandra Padmanabhan).

Huitlacoche, Cuitlacoche (*Ustilago maydis*)

Also corn smut, corn soot, corn mushroom

Some think that the looks of the curious corn-and-fungus combination pictured should deter culinary aesthetes, but it has numerous devoted fans. You will need to fight your way to the head of the line to taste it—should you have the good luck to locate it at all. Then you may need to overcome an aversion to its names before sampling the luxury that most Americans who know it call corn smut.

The word the Aztecs used to describe it has even less appealing connotations, says Maricel Presilla, an authority on Latin American foods, who consulted her dictionaries of ancient and modern languages: "The Nahuatl word *cuitlacochin* translates mildly as 'bad ear of corn,' but it is based on *cuitlatl*, which means dirt, tumor, abscess, and excrement. *Cochi* means to sleep, but the connection is not explicit."

Whether the fungus, *Ustilago maydis*, enters the corn spontaneously or is introduced through inoculation by a farmer, it develops darkly inside the kernels, swelling them to grotesque shapes and gross sizes. The inky result is dense and pasty, but much milder and sweeter (once cooked) than its ominous appearance suggests. In fact, the sweet-corn skin and soft interior have a gentler, more vegetable flavor than some paler mushrooms.

Huitlacoche-engorged ears of corn, from gray to red to blue to black, line market stalls throughout the rainy season in Mexico, where the delicacy is best appreciated (and I have been told that it sells out on arrival in the Paris market as well). "I thought that in New York I'd have a hard time selling this weird black 'Mexican truffle,'" says Josefina Howard, chef and founder of Rosa Mexicano, "but it is unbelievably popular—universally accepted in a way I've never seen with any other exotic food. Honestly, people clean their plates. They never send it back. They call to see if it's on the menu. I must use 100 pounds a week—unless I can't get it, which happens more and more, I'm sorry to say."

The potential for popularity is considerable, to judge from chefs who work with huitlacoche. The problem is not finding a more appealing appellation

½ **actual size**

but simply finding huitlacoche at all. According to *Rick Bayless's Mexican Kitchen*, "only a few specialty farmers have been farsighted enough to perceive that there is a market for the stuff." Low demand is always cited as the reason for low (or no) production, but high labor costs seem more likely: Tricky to harvest, the ears must be hand-picked at the right point so that the bulging kernels will not burst, then transported in a way that keeps them in good shape.

Although Native Americans celebrated corn in many forms and did incorporate corn smut into rituals, few tribes are known to have eaten it—or to have recorded eating it—with any regularity. The Hopi, who call it nanha, are an exception, writes Betty Fussell in *The Story of Corn*. But if "older Hopi savored the fungus, few younger ones have tasted it, and today children use it to blacken faces in a game of tag."

BASIC USE: Huitlacoche is almost always chopped and cooked as a preliminary to its primary role as a filling: for omelets, crêpes, empanadas, tamales, tacos, ravioli, lasagne, or stacked tortillas. Because huitlacoche is quite dense and may be grainy, it benefits from the addition of contrasting and lightening textures and flavors—whether in the form of crisp, tart, or sweet vegetables; sharp sour cream; or pale fish or meat. Seasoned and thinned, it becomes a sauce to spoon over seafood, chicken, polenta, or beans, or to swirl into soups.

SELECTION: If you can find them in the summertime, whole ears are freshest and fullest. Rick Bayless, whose restaurants in Chicago celebrate traditional Mexican foods, says that "small farmers are holding on to the delicacy for their favored customers. Mine comes from a local organic farmer who grows it on four varieties of corn—all similar, all good." Select the fullest kernels, avoiding any broken or cracked ones. If a kernel is open, dust and sand can penetrate it.

If you find frozen huitlacoche at a Mexican market or a specialty distributor, do not hesitate to buy it, provided the kernels look plump. It freezes admirably.

STORAGE: Spread fresh kernels on a pan in a single layer (they bruise and crush easily). Refrigerate, lightly covered with a towel, for up to a week or so. Or freeze kernels, tightly wrapped. There is little loss in texture or taste.

PREPARATION: For fresh whole ears, remove husk and silk. Cut kernels as close to cob as possible in one sure movement. Or, for whole (untraditional) kernels, pull them from the cob. They'll have bits of cob and silk attached, but the textures and flavors are appealing. Using a soft brush, flick any debris from kernels. Or rinse and dry gently. Then chop coarsely, or not, as taste and recipe dictate.

Precooking: "Traditionally, huitlacoche is precooked, whether or not it will be further cooked," says Bayless: Sauté onion, add a bit of garlic, chilli, and chopped tomatoes. Then add the cleaned, chopped kernels and epazote and cook 15 minutes to blend flavors.

Untraditionally, I prefer the plain fungus flavor and the whole kernels: Heat huitlacoche in oil over moderate flame; reduce heat, add a little salt, and cook gently for 15 minutes, until the texture lightens slightly, the kernels darken, and any bitterness dissipates. If desired, chop at this point.

Huitlacoche Sauce over Polenta

"Polenta" is the word we now use in North America to refer to the former cornmeal mush, a gift of the Americas—not Italy—that attained celebrity with its use by Italians. Now we need Mexican huitlacoche to teach us about the pleasures of what we grimly refer to as "corn smut," which grows anywhere corn does.

The following warm, thick, sweetish charcoal porridge is utterly mysterious—your guests will have no idea what it is made of. The looks suggest a dark chilli sauce or refried black beans, but the flavor is all its own. If you're using frozen huitlacoche, defrost just long enough to break apart the kernels. If you don't have chiles chipotle en adobo or Chinese chilli sauce, add 2 teaspoons pure mild chilli powder when you stir in the spices.

2 tablespoons corn oil (preferably unrefined)
1 medium onion, chopped
1 teaspoon ground coriander
½ teaspoon ground cumin
⅛ teaspoon ground cloves or allspice
1 large tomato, diced
½ teaspoon kosher salt
2 medium ears corn
2 cups fresh or frozen huitlacoche (½ pound)
1 cup vegetable or poultry broth
⅓ cup chopped cilantro (coriander) leaves
1 to 2 teaspoons adobo sauce from canned
    chipotles en adobo or Chinese chilli sauce
About 2 tablespoons lime juice
About ⅓ cup heavy cream
Soft Polenta (page 224), made with 1¼ cups
    cornmeal

1. Heat oil in medium saucepan over moderate heat. Stir in onion and cook until softened. Add coriander, cumin, and clove; stir a moment, until fragrant. Add tomato and salt. Simmer a few minutes, until juicy. Reduce heat and simmer, stirring often, until most liquid has evaporated, about 5 minutes.

2. Cut kernels from corn. Add to pan, with huitlacoche and broth. Simmer gently, uncovered, 15 minutes, stirring occasionally.

3. Transfer half the huitlacoche mixture to blender or food processor. Add half the cilantro and 1 teaspoon adobo sauce. Puree mixture. Return to pan. Simmer gently, stirring, to heat through. Gradually add lime juice, tasting. Adjust seasoning.

4. Heat polenta, adding a touch of water if needed to smooth. Spoon into heated shallow bowls, forming an indentation in the center of each serving. Fill to overflowing with huitlacoche sauce. Drizzle a tablespoon or two of cream over each and sprinkle with remaining cilantro.

**Serves 4 as a main course,
8 as a first course**

Pros Propose

Chef and author Josefina Howard maintains a wide selection of cuitlacoche dishes (she prefers the "c" spelling of the Nahuatl, like most Mexican cooks) at her New York restaurants: skewered Serrano chilli and scallops on cuitlacoche cream sauce, cuitlacoche ravioli in Poblano cream, cuitlacoche cream soup with epazote, fried chicken breasts filled with cuitlacoche, and even a smooth swirl of sweetened thin cornmeal and cuitlacoche for dessert. For her **Cuitlacoche Crêpes, Gratinéed:** Sauté chopped onion and garlic in butter and olive oil; add cuitlacoche, Serrano chilli, and salt and cook until liquid evaporates. Add crème fraîche and epazote. Spoon onto thin crêpes and roll up. Set 2 rolls on each plate; top with mascarpone and Manchego cheeses. Glaze under heat. Top with epazote.

Cooked and raw huitlacoche figure in chef Richard Sandoval's menu. For his popular **Huitlacoche-Mashed Potatoes:** Sauté onion; add huitlacoche, Serrano chilli, and cilantro. Cook briefly. Press boiled potatoes through sieve. Heat while mixing with butter, milk, and seasoning. Stir in huitlacoche until darkened and well flavored.

For Sandoval's **Grilled Corn Soup with Huitlacoche Dumplings and Vinaigrette:** Cut kernels from corn grilled in the husk. Puree with cream and stock. Sauté onions, huitlacoche, epazote, and roasted Arbol chillis. Seal this filling in wonton skins. Poach in water, then add to corn puree. Drizzle with vinaigrette made of raw huitlacoche pureed with sherry vinegar, lemon juice, salt, pepper, and olive oil.

Zarela Martinez prepares a more traditional **Huitlacoche Soup,** a rich brew that she serves in demitasse cups as an appetizer: Cook sliced onion and minced garlic in lard until softened. Add roasted, peeled, and diced Poblano chillis; cook briefly. Add huitlacoche and dried epazote or fresh cilantro leaves. Simmer 5 minutes. Cool slightly. Puree in food processor until smooth, adding chicken stock as needed. Return to saucepan and bring to a boil. Add more stock to achieve the consistency of thin cream soup. Add heavy cream, bring to a boil, and simmer briefly (from *Foods from My Heart*).

Avocado Stuffed with Cuitlacoche: Coat peeled avocado halves with vinaigrette. Heat butter and olive oil, add grated white onion, pureed garlic, finely chopped cuitlacoche, chopped epazote or cilantro, and minced Serrano chillis. Simmer slowly until thick. Cool. Arrange avocados on lettuce, and garnish with slices of queso fresco and tomato. Spoon in cuitlacoche and top with epazote leaves. Serve with Mexican rice (from *The Taste of Mexico* by Patricia Quintana).

Japanese Greens:
mizuna, mibuna, komatsuna

"Japanese greens" is the roof under which I'm grouping a trio of leafy vegetables that would otherwise remain homeless—that is, unclassifiable for the purposes of this book. Although authorities agree that they are all of the genus *Brassica* and nurtured in Japan, their species, origins, and close relatives remain debatable. But these mustardy-cabbagey greens share culinary characteristics and personality traits that put them on common ground.

Mizuna (also mizu-na, mizuna mustard, kyona) is slowly moving beyond Japanese groceries, home gardens, and restaurants to farmers' markets, specialty produce stores, and a few supermarkets. Packing plenty of flavor in their pretty, incised leaves, the smallest specimens have a mild and refreshing nip; the largest have a potent bite.

Like Japanese purple mustard, which is included in the best miniature mixes, mizuna entered the United States on a salad ticket. Also like the mustard, mizuna (pronounced with equal emphasis on all syllables), is Chinese in origin, although it has been cultivated for centuries in Japan and is generally considered a Japanese vegetable. Elizabeth Andoh, a Tokyo-based authority on Japanese food and culture, says that it is common in the Kansai area (around Kyoto and Osaka), which explains its other common name, "kyona," meaning "leafy green from Kyoto." Its scientific names are not so straightforward. Taxonomically, it slips in and out of subgroups and even species but usually stops at *Brassica rapa* Nipposinica or Japonica Group. This is, however, a discussion I'll forgo.

BASIC USE: Mini-mizuna is just fine all on its own. Chef Chris Hastings says, "There is nothing like small mizuna as a garnish. It's the most perfect foil for

length (of bunches): 10-12 inches

all kinds of meat and fish, holds its shape and color, works great as a propper-upper, and tastes wonderful and fresh without overpowering or getting lost." Arrange the graceful feathery shapes as a wreath for composed vegetable or fish salads, or as a bed for grilled seafood, poultry, or barbecued pork or beef. Or toss mizuna with milder leaves in mixed salads.

Larger mizuna is best cooked, however briefly. Although it loses its mustardy edge, it keeps its bitter-green tang, its deep color, and its pretty cut-leaf shape. Boil or steam it, then cut bite-size pieces; serve hot or tepid with olive oil and lemon, sesame oil and shoyu, or pickled ginger. Or add sliced mizuna to stir-fries with some liquid, cover, and cook until tender.

According to Elizabeth Andoh, mizuna is traditionally pickled in salt brine or cooked in nabemono (one-pot casseroles) or soups. Or it is served as ohitashi: blanched, cooled in seasoned dashi, and garnished with bonito flakes.

SELECTION: Mizuna is available year-round, erratically. It is sold in sizes from micro to mini to large dan-

delion, either attached at the base in a loose head or cut apart into individual leaves. Like dandelion, it should be moist, cold, and fully green, without a hint of drying or yellowing. There is as much variation in tenderness and bite as in size—so taste. For raw dishes, choose small-leafed mizuna. Use heartier heads for cooking.

STORAGE: Refrigerate in plastic. Loose cut leaves keep about a week. Untie bunched heads and open up for storage.

PREPARATION: Remove soft or yellowed leaves. Small leaves need no more than to be rinsed and dried. For heads or bunches, trim a few inches from the base to separate the stalks. As needed, cut into 1½-inch sections. Wash well, dunking in several changes of water. Spin-dry for salads.

Mibuna (also mibu-na and Japanese mustard) floats among classifications as mizuna does and usually winds up in the same places. It is similar in other ways, too (including its pronunciation; as with all Japanese words, there is equal emphasis on all syllables). However, mi-

mibuna

length: 8–10 inches

buna is milder and juicier than mizuna with tender, pearly stems and thin sorrel-shaped leaves that taste gently sweet and just barely piquant.

Joy Larkcom writes in *Oriental Vegetables,* "Mibuna ('mibu greens') is one of the most recent vegetables to break through the bamboo curtain. It appears to be closely related to mizuna—though no one is sure. Like mizuna, it is regarded as a Japanese vegetable, with a long history of cultivation in Mibu, in the Kyoto prefecture."

BASIC USE: In my limited experience, mibuna excels as a raw ingredient only. It adds brisk flavor and succulence to just about any leafy salad. It makes a sprightly, attractive garnish, too. Its liveliness fades with cooking.

SELECTION AND STORAGE: Theoretically, mibuna is available year-round, but it is difficult to find— I have not seen it outside Japanese groceries and an occasional farmers' market. Fresh mibuna *looks* fresh. It droops quickly. Wrap it in plastic and refrigerate for no more than a few days.

PREPARATION: Rinse gently and lift out of the water so that the grit sinks. Blot with a towel or spin-dry. If mibuna is sold in bunches or with roots attached, cut off a few inches to separate the stems.

Komatsuna (also mustard spinach or tendergreen) does have a classification: *Brassica rapa,* Perviridis Group, but the country's great botanist and horticulturist Liberty Hyde Bailey, who decided reluctantly to group it with *rapa* species, wrote at the time (1930): "I am none too well satisfied with this disposition of it . . . [but] one hesitates to make a new species of it unless further evidence accumulates." It remains there still.

Although komatsuna (the name refers to its main area of use, Komatsu) is to be found primarily in Japanese markets, it had—and still has—another life in gardening circles, as Tendergreen. (If the quirky saga of a barely attainable vegetable does not fascinate you, please go directly to the recipes, page 328.)

Bailey also wrote that Tendergreen "was first offered under this name in the catalogue of Van Antwerp's

komatsuna

length: 6-9 inches

Seed Store, Mobile, Alabama, in 1929, to take the place of spinach, turnip greens, kale, and mustard greens . . . [and has been] sold recently by other dealers as Mustard spinach, Komatsuma mustard, Koatsuma mustard, Japanese mustard." The Van Antwerp catalogue—which I have, thanks to the L. H. Bailey Hortorium at Cornell University—shows photos of Tendergreen that are clearly the plant pictured above. According to the catalogue, "Tendergreen is the first entirely new vegetable introduced in America in the last half century, and will . . . revolutionize the markets of this country. . . . Tendergreen is destined to become America's most popular vegetable green for table use, also for canning factories. . . . [It is] superior to Spinach, Turnip greens, Mustard or Kale in flavor, eating qualities, mineral content, and is far easier to grow." And in case anyone missed the point, it then promises again that "Tendergreen unquestionably will, within a few years be America's most popular vegetable."

Hyperbole didn't do the trick, for here I am trying to describe Tendergreen—or komatsuna or mustard spinach—more then seventy years later. That is a shame, because it is a lovely vegetable, easy to like and easy to grow. Large, thick, tender, oval leaves on slim juicy stalks attach at the base, spinach fashion. Both raw and cooked it suggests exceptionally mild, very juicy spinach crossed with bok choy (a close relative). But komatsuna is not bok choy or mustard or spinach, or a cross of the last two, as its mustard-spinach name suggests. It is its own vegetable, and a fine one.

BASIC USE: Slice raw leaves and stems into mild, light salads. Stir-fry briefly, thickening with cornstarch. Simmer in soup.

Traditionally, komatsuna is treated like ohitashi: blanched; seasoned with dashi (stock), soy, and mirin; and garnished with toasted sesame seeds or bonito flakes. Or the blanched greens are dressed with sesame sauce or served in clear soup.

SELECTION AND STORAGE: The komatsuna in the photo is perfect—and that is the only way I've ever seen it. Somehow, Japanese growers have a knack for cultivating picture-perfect produce. The vegetable is erratically available year-round at Japanese markets. I have not seen it elsewhere, but I've been told that it is sold at farmers' markets in the West. As with mizuna, large leaves are suited to cooking, smaller ones to salads. But for komatsuna, unlike mizuna, size is mainly a question of preference; the plants I have tested, small and large, are equally tender.

PREPARATION: Trim base to separate leaves. Dunk into water several times. There is no need to separate stem and leaf, which are both tender, except for ease of eating. To stir-fry, cut 2-inch diagonals.

Mizuna with Molasses and Peanut Dressing

This shiny, sweet-salty, chewy, and crunchy combination draws on staples allied with the American South—molasses, peanuts, and cider vinegar—but substitutes Japanese mizuna for the usual curled mustard greens.

The heated dressing slightly tenderizes the greens and creates a juicy setting for croutons. For a Southern touch, prepare dense and crunchy croutons from corn bread: Cut unsweetened corn bread into ½-inch dice and bake in a low oven until tawny and crisp.

¾ pound small, feathery mizuna
1 small red onion
1¼ cups croutons
¼ cup cider vinegar
2 scant tablespoons molasses
¼ to ½ teaspoon hot pepper sauce
2 teaspoons shoyu (Japanese soy sauce) or tamari
3 tablespoons corn oil (preferably unrefined)
¼ cup roasted, salted, fine-chopped peanuts

1. Trim base of mizuna as needed. Cut into 2-inch sections, more or less. Wash pieces well, dunking in several changes of water. Spin-dry. (Do not refrigerate.)

2. Cut onion into ¼-inch dice. Place croutons in serving bowl. Top with mizuna.

3. In small skillet, combine vinegar, molasses, pepper sauce, shoyu, and onion. Bring to a boil, stirring. Add oil and return to a boil.

4. Pour dressing over greens. Immediately toss to coat. Add peanuts and toss. Serve at once.

Serves 4 as a first course or side salad

Buckwheat Noodles, Mizuna (or Mibuna), and Radishes with Tart Tofu-Mizuna Dressing

Cool and satisfying on a summer's eve: taupe soba noodles, sharp emerald mizuna, and scarlet radishes are dressed with a thick, smooth, lemony dressing. Choose the smallest mizuna so the pretty lacy leaves (not stems) can star. Or substitute mibuna. The weight of soba noodle packages varies—use whatever is close to ¾ pound. If roasted peanut oil is not in your pantry, substitute 1½ tablespoons vegetable oil plus 2 teaspoons Asian (dark) sesame oil.

    1 cup silken (soft) tofu (about ½ pound)
    1 large bunch round red radishes
    ¾ pound delicate mizuna or mibuna
    ⅓ cup sliced scallion (green onion) tops
    1 tablespoon Dijon mustard
    ¼ teaspoon kosher salt
    ¼ cup lemon juice
    1 teaspoon grated lemon zest
    2 tablespoons peanut oil (preferably
        roasted)
    12- to 13-ounce package Japanese
        buckwheat (soba) noodles
    1 tablespoon shoyu (Japanese soy sauce)
    1½ tablespoons toasted sesame seeds
        (preferably black)

1. Cut tofu into small pieces. Place in fine strainer to drain while you prepare other ingredients, about ½ hour. Set large pot of water to boil. Cut off radish leaves. Rinse radishes. Slice enough to equal ½ cup, then dice the remainder.

2. Remove soft or yellowed leaves from mizuna. Trim any comparatively heavy stems. Cut remaining stems and leaves into 1½-inch sections. Wash well, dunking in several changes of water. Spin-dry. Chill or not, as desired.

3. Measure 1 cup tightly packed mizuna. Combine in food processor with all but 2 tablespoons scallions, mustard, and salt. Chop fine. Add drained tofu, lemon juice, zest, and 1 tablespoon peanut oil. Whirl until smooth, scraping sides a few times. Serve or refrigerate, as convenient. (Can be refrigerated overnight.)

4. Drop noodles into boiling water. Return to a boil, stirring. Boil gently until barely tender, 2 to 3 minutes. Taste frequently to avoid overcooking. Drain, then rinse to cool. Drain.

5. To serve, divide remaining mizuna among wide shallow bowls. Toss noodles, diced radishes, and reserved scallions with remaining 1 tablespoon peanut oil and shoyu. Divide among bowls. Spoon over dressing. Top with sliced radishes and sesame seeds.

Serves 3 to 4 as a main dish

Gingery Salad of Mizuna (or Mibuna), Apple, Celery, Chives, and Sesame

Refreshing, light, and low in fat, this salty-sweet-tart toss is a good partner for broiled or grilled fish. For a vegetable meal, serve with stir-fried tempeh or tofu. Cut the apple and celery extra-fine so they will be dispersed evenly throughout the leaves. Dress the salad when ready to serve, not beforehand, or it will become watery.

    2 tablespoons sesame seeds
    7 to 8 ounces delicate mizuna (or mibuna)
    1 medium very crisp apple (not waxed)
    2 celery stalks
    1 tablespoon fine julienne of sweet pickled
        ginger
    2 to 3 tablespoons distilled white vinegar
    2 to 3 teaspoons fish sauce
    2 to 3 teaspoons Asian (dark) sesame oil
    ½ cup chives cut into 1-inch lengths

1. Stir sesame seeds in small pan over fairly low heat until tan and fragrant, about 5 minutes. Reserve.

2. Remove any soft or yellowing leaves from mizuna. Trim off any relatively heavy stems. Rinse and spin-dry (you should have 6 to 7 packed cups). Refrigerate in large bowl. Zip strings from celery. Cut enough fine 1-inch julienne to equal 1 cup. Refrigerate. Without peeling, cut apple into julienne the same size. Refrigerate.

3. Mix together ginger, 2 tablespoons vinegar, and 2 teaspoons *each* fish sauce and sesame oil.

4. To serve, add celery, apple, and chives to mizuna, tossing. Add dressing and toss. Taste and add fish sauce, vinegar, and sesame oil as needed. Add sesame seeds, toss, and serve immediately.

Serves 4

Basic Cooked Mizuna

Large mizuna is best cooked—albeit very briefly—in the way of other mustards and of dandelions. Like these, it loses its nip when heated, but becomes juicy and develops a different taste—more generic bitter green. Unlike these, it maintains its deep-green color and sharp-edged cut-out shape.

1 pound large mizuna

Trim a few inches from the base of each clump of stems to separate them. Slosh mizuna around in plenty of water and lift out so that debris sinks to the bottom. Repeat as needed.

To boil: Drop into boiling salted water to which you've added a spoonful of oil. Boil until just tender, about 1 minute. Drain. Leave whole, or bunch together and cut into bite-size pieces.

To steam: Spread on steamer rack. Cover and cook over boiling water until just tender, 4 to 5 minutes. Cut stems into thin pieces and leaves into wider strips.

To serve: Season the cooked room temperature greens with olive oil, lemon, and shoyu or salt. Or combine with toasted walnuts, walnut oil, and a touch of sherry vinegar. Or sprinkle with hot sesame oil.

Serves 4 as a side dish

Komatsuna, Apple, and Grape Salad with Almonds and Dill

A refreshing, pretty first-course salad that's unusual but not far-out. What pleases particularly is the textural range: soft leaves, juicy stems, crisp apples, slippery grapes, crunchy nuts. Surprisingly, the delicate greens do not get watery after being dressed, but hold up bright and tidy.

½ pound komatsuna
2 tablespoons peanut oil
2 tablespoons corn oil
½ cup thick-sliced or coarse-chopped whole (unblanched) almonds
¾ teaspoon kosher salt
½ teaspoon sugar
1 teaspoon ground ginger
¼ cup lemon juice
1 large Golden Delicious apple
1 cup seedless grapes (about 5 ounces)
¼ cup sliced (½-inch pieces) chives
¼ cup thin-sliced dill

1. Trim base of komatsuna to separate leaves. Dunk into several changes of water as needed. Spin-dry.

2. Heat peanut and corn oils in very small skillet or small pot (so that oil is as deep as possible) over moderately low heat. When surface wavers, add almonds. Fry gently until golden—1 to 2 minutes. Pour at once into a small sieve set over a cup. Toss almonds with pinch of salt.

3. Add salt, sugar, and ginger to drained warm oil; mix, then gradually whisk in lemon juice.

4. Stack 4 to 5 komatsuna leaves with their stems aligned. Cut off leaves and reserve (cut smaller, if desired). Slice stems into ½-inch pieces; place in a bowl.

5. Quarter and core (unpeeled) apple. Cut one half into ½- to ¼-inch dice. Add to komatsuna stems. Halve grapes; add half of them to stems and apple. Add half the chives and half the dill. Add half the dressing and toss. Chill ½ hour, or as convenient.

6. Halve remaining apple crosswise, then cut into paper-thin slices. Toss with remaining dressing. Arrange komatsuna leaves on four plates. Spoon chilled salad into center. Surround with apple slices and reserved grapes. Top with the remaining chives and dill, then almonds.

Serves 4

Komatsuna and Carrots in Tart-Sweet Sauce

A colorful side dish that is Chinese in feeling, but not authentic. If fermented (also called Chinese or salted) black soybeans are not part of your pantry, they should be. These potent little seasoning bombs cost little, last forever, and transform a dish from simple to multidimensional. For microwave blanching, large carrots work best.

About 1 pound komatsuna
1 hefty carrot or 2 smaller ones (½ pound)
½ cup vegetable or poultry broth
1 tablespoon shoyu (Japanese soy sauce)
2 tablespoons distilled white vinegar
2 teaspoons brown sugar
1 tablespoon cornstarch
1½ tablespoons peanut oil
1 tablespoon minced ginger
1 tablespoon chopped fermented black beans
2 to 3 teaspoons minced garlic
2 to 3 tablespoons thin-sliced scallion (green onion) tops

1. Trim base of komatsuna to separate stems. Wash well, drain, and spin-dry. Slice into 1-inch diagonal strips.

2. Peel carrot and quarter lengthwise (or halve, if using 2). Place in microwave oven. Cook until barely tender, about 1½ minutes. Cut into very thin diagonal slices.

3. Combine broth, shoyu, vinegar, and sugar in a small cup. Remove 2 tablespoons and mix with cornstarch in another cup. Line up all ingredients by the stove.

4. Heat wok over high heat. Spoon oil around rim and tip pan to coat. Add ginger, black beans, and garlic, tossing a few times. Add carrots and toss another minute. Add komatsuna and toss 30 seconds. Add broth mixture and simmer until greens are just tender, a minute or two. Add cornstarch mixture and stir to thicken. Scoop at once into heated dish and top with scallions. Serve hot.

Serves 3 to 4

Pros Propose

When luxury ingredients need a leafy base to present them in flavorful style, mizuna is a good choice. To prepare chef Michael Otsuka's fancy opener, **Smoked Sturgeon and Buckwheat Blini on Mizuna and Meyer Lemon Cream:** Coat mini-mizuna lightly with dressing of Meyer lemon zest and juice mixed with crème fraîche, shallot, and chives. Set hot blini on this and top with dressing. Serve each with a strip of fennel-rubbed smoked sturgeon and dollop of osetra caviar.

Chef Bill Fuller serves **Seared Scallops on Wilted Mizuna:** Prepare vinaigrette by reducing orange, lemon, and lime juices by half. Cool, then add the same juices in fresh form, with rice vinegar and shallots. Puree in blender. Gradually add blended canola and olive oils and a little sesame oil. Sear seasoned scallops in cast-iron pan; set aside. Add touch of oil to pan and toss mizuna a bare few seconds with a drop of rice vinegar; do not allow to cook. Arrange scallops on greens and drizzle with vinaigrette.

New Year's Rice with Chestnuts and Mizuna, although clearly Japanese in its purity, is not a traditional dish. Victoria Wise, author of *The Vegetarian Table: Japan,* explains that "it's an unusual preparation in that the rice is flavored . . . and chestnuts are added during cooking rather than paddled in after the rice is steamed." She also substitutes brown rice for the customary white and adds mizuna. (Altogether more heretical than one might guess at first glance.) To prepare: Soak 1½ cups short-grain brown rice in water for ½ hour. Drain and combine with fresh water, peeled chestnuts, sake, and sea salt; bring to a boil. Cover and cook over lowest heat 40 minutes. Turn off heat; let stand about 20 minutes. Meanwhile, blanch coarse-chopped mizuna. Refresh in cold water. Drain and squeeze dry. Spread over hot rice.

When Anita Lo was executive chef at Mirezi, a Korean-inspired New York restaurant, she served **Salad of Grilled Baby Octopus with Sweet Onion and Mizuna:** Dress very small mizuna leaves with yuzu (Japanese citrus) juice and oil. Top with grilled red onion slices and blanched, marinated, and grilled baby octopus. She also offered a traditional Korean-style greens side dish of mizuna: Blanch trimmed leaves in salted water to barely wilt. Drain and refresh in cold water. Squeeze dry. Toss with soy sauce, sesame oil, ground chilli, and garlic. Serve with pickled and salted vegetables alongside.

The typical Japanese method of blanching greens, steeping them in stock, and then seasoning to serve is used for **Komatsuna Ohitashi.** Chef Kazuhiro Okochi prefers komatsuna to the more familiar spinach "because it doesn't shrink and has a nice bitter edge." To prepare: Make stock with bonito flakes, kombu (kelp), shoyu, and mirin; cool. Cut apart komatsuna leaves and stems. Drop stems into boiling water; return to a boil. Add leaves and bring back to a boil; drain. Steep in stock a few hours, or overnight. Drain; cut into bite-size pieces. Top with shredded dried bonito.

Sylvia Thompson, who grows and cooks everything, likes komatsuna leaves pan-seared until they begin to brown. For **Toasted Komatsuna:** Cut apart leaves and stems; chop stems. Toss both in large skillet with any water that clings. Continue to turn and toss until leaves on the bottom turn brown and begin to stick to pan, about 3 minutes. Scoop onto a board; chop. Drizzle with flavorful oil of any kind and lemon juice. Add ground ginger, salt, and white pepper. Sprinkle with toasted sesame seeds. Serve at room temperature with noodles drizzled with sesame oil (from *The Kitchen Garden Cookbook*).

Jícama (*Pachyr[r]hizus erosus*)

Also yam bean, dou shu and sha got (Chinese), chop suey yam and
chopsui potato (Hawaiian), singkamas (Philippine)

"What kind of word was 'useful' to use on the air?" fumed a talk-show host with whom I had been discussing jícama. "Useful?!! These babies are supposed to be *dynamite, outrageous!*" he raged, pointing an accusing finger at the slightly scruffy, tan lobed tubers I had arranged in a shallow basket on camera.

As packed produce aisles overflow and vegetables compete for customers' attention, it has become customary to expect unfamiliar vegetables to deliver out-of-this-world taste. People hope to be transported heavenward at the first bite or even at first glance. If all vegetables were measured by these criteria, imagine the fate of such modest—yes, useful—earthlings as zucchini and potatoes in this day and age.

Jícama (pronounced HEE-kama), the Mexican word most often used in North America to describe this vegetable, is a member of the Fabaceae (Leguminoseae) family. As proof of its membership, the jícama—a native of Central America—develops pods on its twining vines. The pods account for one of its most common English names outside the United States—yam bean—but that name in no way suits the part we eat (pictured). When the crisp, juicy tuber is first sampled, the earth may not move, but its taste generally provokes another bite, then a smile. The mild sweetness and distinct crunch are equally appealing whether jícama is raw or cooked. The ivory flesh resembles water chestnut in color and texture, but is less sweet—more bland. Jícama fits in easily with seafood, meat, poultry, rice or noodles, fruit, other vegetables—you name it.

Even if jícama does not qualify as a red-hot trend-setting vegetable, it is established and popular in a good part of the world, including the United States. According to the Plant Protection and Quarantine Division of the Animal and Plant Health Inspection Service, 12,604,754 kilos of jícama were imported in fiscal year 1988–1989. For 1998–1999, imports nearly doubled, to 23,450,985 kilos.

All jícama sold in the United States is imported. Although American growers and distributors claim that it

diameter: 4-5 inches

would thrive in parts of California, Florida, Georgia, and Alabama (where it is cultivated in home gardens), its primary commercial source, thus far, is Mexico.

Jícama's culinary history begins with Mexico, but the vegetable has also spent three centuries in the East, starting in the Philippines, where it was introduced by the Spanish. In Mexico, jícama is traditionally served raw, as a refreshing snack, usually sharpened with chilli, salt, and lime. Or it lends crunch to spicy salsa (pico de gallo); or it is blended with orange or tomato dice and cilantro. In Thailand, the chilli is accented with fish sauce. In Vietnam, decoratively carved jícama is pickled with carrots or shredded into spring rolls. In Indonesia, it is part of the lively fruit and vegetable relish, rujak, a salsa-like refresher. In the Philippines, it fills lumpia and plays a regular role in so many dishes that "it has been used in the folk religious drama called the *sinakulo* as the 'apple' with which Eve was tempted in the Garden of Eden," writes Doreen Fernandez in *Tikim: Essays on Philippine Food and Culture.*

Jícama is now cultivated in scattered areas of China, Japan, Malaysia, Indonesia, Vietnam, Thailand, Burma, and India, and in parts of South and Central America and the West Indies—a broad enough base to let jícama be considered useful, I would say.

BASIC USE: Jícama—raw or cooked; cut into slices, sticks, cubes, or rounds; or shredded—fits into a meal from hors d'oeuvres through dessert and also makes a fine snack. Because jícama does not discolor, soften, or lose its crunch, it is well suited to garnishes or crudités. Or cube for salsa or relish, include in marinated vegetable salads, or prepare as a quick pickle.

Few know the charms of cooked jícama—which can be more interesting than the raw vegetable. Stir-fry or braise quickly with pork, seafood, or poultry and colorful, juicy vegetables; or cook with vegetables alone. Accent this bland but always crisp vegetable with chilli, tart-sweet sauces, or sharp and salty seasonings. Jícama absorbs sauces without softening. Even paper-thin slices keep their fresh vegetable sweetness and pleasing crunch when cooked through.

SELECTION: Jícama weighing from about ½ pound to as much as 6 pounds is sold year-round, but it is best from fall through spring. Selection is crucial: Old tubers are fibrous and tasteless. No matter what the size, take care to select relatively unblemished tubers with a slight silky sheen; ones that look smooth and young compared with their companions. Nick the skin to determine that it is quite thin and to be sure that the flesh is juicy. Thick-skinned, dryish jícama may be stringy and starchy instead of crisp and sweet. Invariably, I find the best specimens in Far Eastern markets.

STORAGE: Store whole jícama in the refrigerator, unwrapped. Uncut, in good condition, it will keep about 2 weeks. Once it has been cut, cover the cut side with plastic, refrigerate, then use within a week.

PREPARATION: Always peel jícama. Halve, quarter, or cut the tuber into as many lengthwise chunks as are easily handled for peeling. With a paring knife (a vegetable peeler won't do the trick) pull the skin from the sections, taking with it as much fibrous underlayer as will come off easily. Pare off remaining fibers, as needed. The fresher the vegetable, the more easily and completely the skin pulls free.

Jícama takes well to all manner of processor blades or slicing tools, as well as to decorative cutting, should you be inclined.

Sweet-Hot Fruit and Vegetable Dice in Tart Dressing

Refreshing and fat-free, this pastel relish is at once hot and sour, sweet and salty, acid and aromatic. Crisp fruit and vegetable bits in a brisk seasoned vinegar (a kind of South Seas salsa) make a fine foil for curry, barbecued meat, spicy tofu, or fried fish. Charentais, Galia, or another orange-fleshed, smooth-skinned melon makes the sweetest statement, but good cantaloupe will do the job.

2 limes
1 tablespoon honey
¾ teaspoon kosher salt
4 cloves
¼ teaspoon ground hot pepper
1 large garlic clove, quartered
⅓ cup rice vinegar
¾ pound jícama
2 small unwaxed cucumbers
1 small or ½ medium orange-fleshed
    melon
¼ medium pineapple
About 3 tablespoons thin-sliced mint or cilantro
    (coriander) leaves

1. With zester, remove thin strips of skin from one-quarter of 1 lime (alternatively, remove zest with swivel peeler and cut into hair-thin strips). Combine in small saucepan with honey, salt, cloves, and hot pepper. Add garlic and vinegar. Bring to a full boil. Cool.

2. Quarter jícama. Pull off skin and underlayer with paring knife. Pare away remaining fibers. Cut into ½-inch cubes.

3. Peel cucumbers, quarter lengthwise, then cut out seeds. Cut crosswise into ¼-inch slices. Cut melon to match. Pare pineapple and cut to match.

4. Toss fruits and vegetables with dressing. Halve and squeeze limes. Gradually add juice, sampling as you go for the right balance—about 3 tablespoons. Season.

5. Chill 1 hour or more. To serve, remove cloves and garlic. Toss with mint.

Serves 4 to 6 as a side dish or condiment

Stir-Fried Chicken, Jícama, and Carrots with Ginger

Although jícama is usually served raw, it can be more interesting when cooked and seasoned, as in this light but substantial one-dish meal. Chicken thighs are more juicy and savory to my taste, but if white meat is your preference, substitute breasts and cut down on the cooking time. For variation, sprinkle with toasted sesame seeds or chopped peanuts. Serve with aromatic rice, quinoa, or millet.

2 pounds chicken thighs (5 or 6 thighs)
½ tablespoon cornstarch
1 teaspoon brown sugar
2 tablespoons Scotch or bourbon
2 tablespoons soy sauce
2 teaspoons Asian (dark) sesame oil
1 pound jícama
3 medium carrots
2-inch chunk of ginger
2 scallions (green onions)
2 tablespoons corn or peanut oil

1. Remove skin, fat, and bones from chicken. Cut meat into thin strips about 2 inches long.

2. Combine cornstarch, brown sugar, and whiskey in a dish that will hold the chicken, stirring to blend. Add soy sauce and sesame oil. Add chicken and toss. Cover and marinate 15 to 60 minutes, as convenient.

3. Quarter jícama. With paring knife, pull off skin with as much of the fibrous underlayer as will come off easily. Pare off remaining fibers. Cut into bâtons about ¼ inch thick and 1½ inches long.

4. Peel carrots. Slice ⅛ inch thick on the diagonal. Peel ginger; cut into finest julienne, to equal 1½ tablespoons. Thin-slice scallions, separating light and dark parts.

5. Heat wok or wide skillet over moderate heat. Add 1 tablespoon oil. Add chicken strips. Cook until

nearly done, about 3 minutes, tossing occasionally and pressing against pan. Transfer to dish.

6. Add remaining 1 tablespoon oil to pan. Add white part of scallions and ginger; toss. Add jícama and carrots; toss 1 minute. Cover and cook until vegetables lose their raw crunch, about 2 minutes. Return chicken to pan, add scallion greens, and toss a few seconds to mix.

Serves 4

Spicy Beef and Jícama

Juicy, meaty, crunchy, hot-sweet, and spicy, this dish will please even first-time jícama tasters. A bowl of rice or noodles rounds out the meal. For those who like as many vegetables in a meal as I do, steamed or sautéed cabbage or mustard greens complement too.

1 tablespoon plus 2 teaspoons cornstarch
2 teaspoons brown sugar
¾ teaspoon curry powder
¼ teaspoon ground hot pepper
2 tablespoons dry sherry
1 tablespoon soy sauce
1 tablespoon cider vinegar
1¼ cups beef broth
1¼ pounds jícama
1 garlic clove
1-inch chunk of ginger
Optional: 1 fresh red chilli
2 tablespoons peanut oil
1 pound ground beef chuck
¼ cup chopped mint or cilantro (coriander)

1. Blend cornstarch, sugar, curry, and hot pepper in small bowl. Stir in sherry, soy sauce, and vinegar. Add broth.

2. Quarter jícama. Pull off skin with paring knife, taking as much of the fibrous underlayer as will come off easily. Pare off remaining fibers. Cut ¼- to ½-inch cubes of jícama. Mince garlic. Peel ginger and chop enough to make 1 tablespoon. Seed, devein, and mince chilli if using.

3. Heat wok over high heat. Pour in 1½ tablespoons oil and tip to distribute. Add jícama and toss until lightly browned, about 4 minutes. Transfer to dish.

4. Reduce heat to moderate; add remaining ½ tablespoon oil to wok. Add garlic, ginger, and optional chilli and toss briefly, until fragrant. Add beef, breaking it up and tossing to just cook through, about 2 minutes. Add jícama. Stir cornstarch mixture and add, tossing constantly until thickened.

5. Scoop into heated dish, sprinkle with mint, and serve hot.

Serves 4

Pros Propose

Crunchy jícama and creamy avocado, both native to Central America, have a definite affinity, more so in the presence of sweet and acid ingredients—here combined in one fruit, pineapple, another American original. For **Pineapple, Jícama, and Avocado Salad:** Cut jícama and pineapple into ½-inch dice. Combine in bowl with Hass avocado cut into 1-inch dice. Add thin-sliced red onion and chunks of softened cream cheese. Blend a little juice from the pineapple with vinegar, olive oil, minced parsley, cilantro, and seasoning. Add to bowl, with toasted pecan halves and toss gently, to keep cheese and avocado intact (from *Seasons of My Heart* by Susana Trilling).

From Mexico to China, via Philadelphia's reigning Far Eastern interpreter, chef Susanna Foo. For **Noodles with Sesame and Jícama:** Boil fresh thin noodles until al dente. Drain and toss with corn oil. Cool and refrigerate. Blend sesame paste, soy sauce, vinegar, Chinese chilli sauce, and sugar to a paste. Add vegetable broth to thin. Add crushed roasted peanuts. Toss with the noodles. Arrange in bowls, making an indentation in center of each. Fill with mandoline-cut jícama strands, ribbons of egg crêpe, slivered coriander, and toasted sesame seeds.

Chef Vincent Guerithault combines jícama with bell peppers and diced chillis in several dishes on his American Southwest-and-French-based menu, among them a **Tricolor Vegetable Sauté with Grilled Chicken (or Quail) and Sherry Sauce:** Sauté julienne-cut jícama a few minutes in olive oil; set aside. Sauté julienned red, yellow, and green bell peppers and yellow chilli. Center jícama on plates and top with grilled chicken breast or whole grilled quail. Surround with the peppers. Serve with sauce of reduced sherry vinegar, chicken glaze, and olive oil.

Tuna Tartare and Jícama Ravioli is from chef Hubert Keller, who specializes in light and elegant fare. Use equal weights of jícama and tuna (or substitute raw beef or salmon). Cut peeled jícama crosswise on mandoline to form irregular rounds. Arrange in single layer on baking sheet, sprinkle with salt, and cover with another layer of jícama. Continue until all slices are salted (this tenderizes them and makes them less brittle). Refrigerate, covered, 1 to 24 hours. Cut sushi-quality tuna into small dice. Refrigerate. Combine enough Dijon mustard, olive oil, shoyu, minced shallot, minced cilantro, lemon juice, salt, and pepper to season the tuna very lightly; toss with the cubes, then refrigerate. Lay half the jícama slices on work surface. Place a teaspoon of tuna mixture in middle of each. Set second slice on top and press edges together to seal. With fluted 3-inch cookie cutter, cut out "ravioli"; discard trimmings (from *The Cuisine of Hubert Keller*).

Kales (primarily *Brassica oleracea,* Acephala Group)

Including **curly, Tuscan, ornamental,** and **Russian types**

See also: **COLLARDS,** page 211

Tuscan Black, Blue Scotch, Nagoya Red, and Champion may sound like Olympic teams, but they are forms of *Brassica oleracea,* Acephala Group—probably the most venerable cultivated representative of the Old World cabbages. Latin *caulis* (stem) is the root of a group of words for cabbage: Dutch *kool,* German *Kohl,* and English cole, kale, and collards (from colewort—meaning cabbage plant—a word still current in parts of the world). *Acephala* (headless) is the designation that separates (most) kale and collards from other cabbages, for the two grow in the form of a loose bouquet, not in a tight head.

Kales are showing up in novel forms and far from their traditional setting in the southern United States. At first, the different shapes and colors appeared in miniature: relatively tender and feathery, the petite leaves blended cheerfully into the everblooming field of salad mixes. Then, they grew up into imposing magenta ruffles, spruce plumes, and lime-striped ivory rosettes. However, these bigger plants, although eye-catching, proved inedible raw and turned drab and tough when lightly cooked. How to handle the bouncy bunches? Advice ensues—first for kale in general, then particulars about each type.

SELECTION: Kales are most abundant, flavorful, and tender during the coldest months, although they are available most of the year. Choose comparatively deep-colored bunches with moist, small to medium leaves. Avoid dried, browned, yellowed, or coarse-stemmed plants. Although kale should not be flabby, it is best when not too crisp. It should be displayed chilled.

STORAGE: Wrap kale in plastic or an airtight container and keep very cold—near freezing if possible—or it may acquire a pronounced elderly cabbage taste. Although kale will not look spoiled, it should not be refrigerated more than a few days or it loses its fresh green flavor.

To avoid yellowing, keep kale far from climacteric fruits (ones which continue to ripen), such as apple, avocado, banana, peach, pear, plum, tomato, and most tropical fruits. The presence of ethylene gas, a product of ripening, adversely affects greens, causing a loss of chlorophyll and protein and hastening drying and decay.

To extend storage or revive leaves, trim base of stems, drop kale into plenty of lukewarm water; soak 5 minutes. Shake dry, leaving a little moisture on the leaves. Pack into an airtight box in the coldest part of the refrigerator. This treatment revitalizes even the tiredest specimens and extends the storage time of good ones for many days.

Curly kale—its familiar frilly, dark, thick leaves shaped like a mammoth bunch of parsley—is a fairly common sight in Canadian and U.S. markets, yet it is woefully underused except by people who grew up with it on the table: those of Northern European stock. Kale earned its devotees and its culinary traditions in the colder European climes. Settlers from these lands introduced it to the New World not very long ago.

Kale needs no explanation in Scandinavia, Germany, the Netherlands, and above all, in Scotland, where "to come to kail" meant an invitation to dinner, with or without the green. There, kale is pureed and served with oatcakes, layered with potatoes, stirred into barley soup, or cooked, then chopped and thickened with toasted oatmeal and cream to make a rich pottage. The kale grown in the United States still announces its origins: Scotch Dwarf Green Curled, Scotch Dwarf Blue Curled, or Scotch Tall Green Curled kale.

If they are minuscule, raw curly kale leaves—lightly chewy, colorful, quite assertive—make excellent salad mixers. When cooked, mature leaves (usually bottle green, but there are also dusky bluish types) develop a well-rounded, sweetish "best of the brassicas" taste and a springy texture more delicate than is typical for the cabbage group. Despite its comparative delicacy, however, curly kale maintains much of its volume when cooked; it does not shrink and soften as many greens do.

BASIC USE: Whether steamed, boiled, or blanched and sautéed, kale can be cooked until meltingly soft in traditional style, or until crunchy-tender in the newer mode. For strong flavor, braise in stock. Use as a base for a creamed gratin, a layered pasta, or a thick puree. Cook with beans, barley, or potatoes for hearty soups; or make pureed soup with the same ingredients, enriched with cream. Braise curly kale to stuff pork, tortelli, or sturdy savory pies. For milder flavor, steam it; for the mildest effect, blanch first, then use in all the same ways.

For bright color and fresh flavor, to serve as a simple side dish, blanch kale in just a small amount of water;

curly kale

length: 10-15 inches

Tuscan kale   length: 10-15 inches

this helps preserve color, texture, and flavor. Although many vegetables lose their character when precooked, this is not true of kale. After blanching, sauté in olive or nut oil, butter, bacon, or pancetta. Season with olives, garlic, chilli, cumin, caraway, fennel, anise, or toasted sesame oil.

Small, tender kale microwaves nicely to a bright green: Strip stems, slice leaves, overfill cooking container; top with hot water, and zap a few minutes. Drain thoroughly, then dress with lemon vinaigrette. Larger leaves turn leathery with microwaving.

PREPARATION: Kale leaves that are very small or will be long-cooked need not be stripped from the stems; merely cut off the base of the stems, then slice leaves to suit and wash as below. For larger leaves or shorter cooking: Either hold a stem with one hand and run a knife along each side to cut off the leaf halves; or hold the folded leaf halves together and pull them free of the stem. Drop into plenty of water and slosh energetically. Lift out, so that the debris sinks. Repeat until clean. Drain.

Tuscan kale is just one of many names for the ostrich-plumed dark beauty also called black kale, cavolo nero, lacinato kale, Tuscan black palm kale, and combinations of these names. (Although it is also marketed as "dinosaur" or "dino" kale, I refuse to say those aloud.) The plant was developed in Tuscany, as the word "Tuscan" indicates, probably during the 18th century.

Sadly, the glossy, curled leaves with their puckered pattern retain little of their glamour when cooked, but they must be cooked if edibility is the goal. Ruthlessly strip out the flat stems, stew the leaves long and slowly, and they will reward you with a dense, meaty, forest-primeval color and savor—as full and distinct as broccoli raab, but not bitter. Or blanch the trimmed leaves, then cook briefly for a concentrated, vivid, dark flavor and a chewy texture . . . usually. Occasionally, kales sold under the names above have round, not flat, stems and are milder and far more tender than what I have just described. Taste and see.

BASIC USE: Tuscan kale has an affinity for richness—whether oil, cheese, or pork (in the form of pancetta, bacon, or sausage)—and for starches, such as cornmeal, chestnuts, whole wheat, buckwheat pasta, barley, and beans. Seasoning can be nil (the kale has plenty of character of its own) or forceful: chilli (fresh, dried, or smoked), anchovies, garlic, citrus rind, or spice seeds (fennel, anise, cumin). Use Tuscan kale as you would curly kale, but reserve it for leading roles, given its high price and the time required to strip it clean.

Slow-cook Tuscan kale in broth (like collards, the longer the better). Or blanch it and cook it briefly: Boil in lots of water until al dente, stirring to keep the leaves submerged; then drain, tear into large bite-size pieces, and cook gently in fat, seasoning, and a little liquid, tossing to absorb flavors. Do not dry out or sear.

PREPARATION: With the exception of the type of kale mentioned above, which has a round stem and can be stripped from base to tip like curly kale, Tuscan kale needs special treatment. The entire central flat stem of each leaf must be carefully cut out; it will not soften with cooking. If you tear it hastily, you'll find strings in your teeth. Take the time to scissor or slice carefully against the stem to remove it. Or strip each leaf half by first delicately pulling down on its pointed top; then pull against the grain to yank off its bottom half. Repeat on the other side. (This sounds more complicated than it is.) Perhaps very small leaves do not require this preparation, but in my experience, all have needed it.

Ornamental or flowering kale (also Salad Savoy, a marketing name) ranges from merely pretty to stunning. Frilly, delicately serrated leaves in pastel hues branch from a central stalk to form a lacy, old-fashioned wedding bouquet. The fluffy form is ideal for filling out table displays, wreathing around bowls, and supporting iced dishes (or even fishes), since the hardy leaves are not damaged by freezing temperatures.

ornamental kale (purple)   diameter: 10-12 inches   ornamental kale (cream)   diameter: 10-12 inches

But until recently, eating the plants best known for beautifying shopping malls has not been rewarding. In 1985, when I was working on *Uncommon Fruits & Vegetables: A Commonsense Guide,* I tried flowering kale raw, steamed, boiled, sautéed, braised, and salted—and wound up with leathery leaves. But now, things seem to be changing for the better. Steamed, the ruffly leaves turn translucent and tender and eminently edible—especially the cream and purplish types. Salt-softened, the leaves are colorful, tasty, and tender enough to eat raw.

BASIC USE: Simply steam and serve as a bed for poached or steamed seafood or with a selection of other vegetables: Spread leaves on a rack over boiling water; cover and cook briefly until tender. Or steam seafood and kale together for a quick, elegant dish.

For salads and slaws, flowering kale must be tenderized. Salting and weighting intensify the color and soften the leaves. Strip stems from leaves; stack leaves and cut diagonally into very thin strips. (Leave tiny leaves whole.) Toss with kosher salt. Top with a plate and weight; let stand 15 minutes. Toss strips again, then replace the weight. Let stand another 15 minutes. Drain; rinse thoroughly; then spin-dry. Toss in a citrus or gingery vinaigrette to further brighten color and mellow flavor and texture.

PREPARATION: Remove the leaves from the central stalk or stalks. Strip or cut the stalk or stem from each leaf. (There's no need to do this with the tiniest leaves, which can be left whole.) Rinse.

Russian Red and similar cultivars—Siberian, Ragged Jack, White Russian, Red Ursa, Winter Red—belong to a different species, *Brassica napus,* Pabularia Group, according to kale breeder Frank Morton of Shoulder to Shoulder Farm in Philomath, Oregon, who says that they are often misclassified. The silvery-green or blue-gray leaves resemble a cross between an oak leaf and a turnip top and look distinct from the frillier ornamental and curly kales. In the cultivars with "red" in their name, the stalks and veins turn magenta to ruby in cold weather; but they exhibit little of this coloring when grown in warmer conditions (as was the Russian Red kale in the photograph, unfortunately).

Like other vegetables that glow garnet when raw, red kales turn evergreen (glossy and handsome, with traces of purple) when cooked. And the mature leaves,

Russian Red kale length: 12-16 inches

although lacy, are tough to the tooth. Succulent and sturdy, Russian Red kale has a forceful flavor profile.

BASIC USE: Choose Russian Red for its thick, juicy, chewy leaves. Meaty and assertive, it holds its own in a vegetable meal or provides companionship to grilled sausages, pork, or turkey. It excels, in particular, as a chewy accent vegetable combined with grains, roots, meat or game, or dried fruits and nuts. Blanch in salted water, drain, then sauté with the same additions that you would use with curly or Tuscan kale. Sweet-sour combinations seem to work well. At their tiniest, the leaves are perfect as garnish or in salad.

PREPARATION: It is absolutely necessary to strip the mature stems, which do not soften when cooked: Hold a stalk in one hand, stem base upward, and grasp the wider lower leaf base with the other hand. Pull stem slowly downward to remove it completely. Turn the stem in the opposite direction; with the free hand, using a downward motion, strip off remaining leaves. Rinse leaf pieces. Because leaves are sparse and stem waste is significant, buy more than other kales.

Baked Curly Kale with Potatoes, Olives, and Garlic

This savory rustic mix is baked rather than simmered to better retain the distinct textures. Small yellow-fleshed potatoes are my favorite, but they are hard to find. If you use larger ones, you may prefer to peel them. Vegetable devotees may want no more than grilled tomatoes to fill out the meal; others might serve an assertive grilled fish (such as mackerel or sardines), roast lamb, or sausage of any nationality.

> 1½ pounds curly kale
> 1½ pounds small yellow-fleshed potatoes
> About 20 oil-cured black olives
> About 3 tablespoons olive oil
> 2 large garlic cloves, chopped
> ½ cup water
> ¼ cup dry vermouth
> Pepper
> Lemon wedges

1. Preheat oven to 350°F. Wash kale in plenty of water, lifting out gently so debris sinks. Drain. Strip out heaviest stems; do not bother to remove smaller ones. Bunch or stack kale and cut into ½-inch slices. Scrub potatoes. Halve, then cut into ¼-inch slices. Halve and pit olives.

2. Heat 2 tablespoons oil in large casserole. Add garlic and stir over low heat until lightly colored. Add potatoes and toss. Add kale, olives, water, and vermouth. Bring to a boil.

3. Cover tightly, set in oven, and bake until potatoes are just barely tender, about 40 minutes, shaking or stirring occasionally.

4. Add olive oil to taste. Serve hot or at room temperature (my preference), with pepper and lemon.

Serves 4 as a side dish

Curly Kale, Noodle, Soybean, and Shiitake Hotpot

Lorna Sass, who has refreshingly reinterpreted vegetarian cooking in her many books, is a kale devotee, as demonstrated by this recipe (adapted from *The New Soy Cookbook*) and others. Kale ribbons add verve to a nourishing, slurpily satisfying, tightly packed mélange of rice noodles, shiitake snippets, and black soybeans. For this speedy hotpot, neither dried mushrooms nor noodles are soaked, and canned beans are welcome.

The disparate elements are bound by the magic of miso, the fermented soy seasoning of Japan. Sass recommends both barley and sweet white misos, available in natural food stores and Oriental groceries, as are the translucent rice noodles or vermicelli (variously called mi fen or mai fun, sen mee, pancit bihon, or bun, depending upon their provenance). Barley miso alone will work, but the duo adds depth. If you have another kind, use it instead, tasting and adding gradually.

> 6 cups water (or part soybean cooking liquid, part water)
> 1 medium carrot, peeled and diced fine
> 1 tablespoon plus 1 teaspoon minced ginger
> 8 to 10 dried shiitake (Chinese black mushrooms)
> 1 small bunch curly kale (about ¾ pound)
> 1 cup hot water
> 3 to 4 tablespoons barley miso
> 2 tablespoons sweet white miso
> 1½ cups cooked drained black soybeans (or one 15-ounce can, preferably Eden brand)
> 3 to 4 ounces dried rice noodles (vermicelli)
> Sesame chilli oil or chilli oil

1. Combine water, carrot, and 1 tablespoon ginger in soup pot and bring to a boil. Meanwhile, break stems from shiitake caps (save for stock). Chop caps into tiny bits. Rinse and add to pot. Simmer, covered, while you prepare kale.

2. Keeping kale in its bunched form, slice off and discard stems. Cut leaves into very fine strips (you should have about 5 very tightly packed cups). Immerse leaves in water and swish around. Lift out, leaving debris. Repeat if necessary.

3. Bring soup to a boil. Add kale, pushing it into the water. Boil, stirring often, until almost tender, about 5 minutes. Meanwhile, blend the hot water with the two misos.

4. Add soybeans and rice noodles to soup, stirring to separate strands. Boil gently until noodles are tender, about 2 minutes.

5. Reduce heat; stir in half the miso mixture and the remaining 1 teaspoon ginger. Taste and continue adding miso until seasoned to your liking. Add chilli oil. Serve with chopsticks, soupspoons, and napkins.

Serves 4

Tuscan Kale with Lemon, Garlic, and Fennel

This quick blanch-and-sauté method produces kale with bounce and beauty (the pretty veined patterns remain intact) if less depth of flavor than long-cooked, but the aromatic seasonings make up for the loss. Serve as a side to lamb, sausage, beef, or poultry. Or include in a vegetable meal (winter squash or sweetpotatoes make good partners), where the assertive leaves hold their own in a meaty role.

> 1½ pounds Tuscan kale
> 1 or 2 garlic cloves, sliced
> ¼ to ½ teaspoon chilli flakes
> ½ teaspoon fennel seeds
> 3 tablespoons flavorful olive oil
> 1 lemon, well scrubbed

1. Strip kale leaves: With scissors or knife, slice carefully against each stem to remove it completely, (each leaf will be halved). Or strip each leaf half by first delicately pulling down on its pointed top, then pulling against the grain to yank off its bottom half. Repeat to remove the other side of the leaf from the stem.

2. Drop leaves into a large pot of boiling water. Add salt and return to a boil. Cook until al dente, about 8 minutes, stirring often to keep leaves submerged. Meanwhile, combine garlic, chilli flakes, and fennel seeds on cutting board. Chop to fine consistency.

3. Drain kale thoroughly in large colander, bouncing to rid leaves of water. When cool enough, tear leaves into large bite-size pieces.

4. Combine olive oil with garlic mixture in wide skillet. Turn heat to low and cook until garlic colors, stirring now and then. Add kale, raise heat to moderate, and continue stirring and tossing (tongs maneuver best) until seasonings are absorbed, about 5 minutes. Do not dry out or sear—kale tastes best moist. Grate zest from half the lemon over kale. Cut remaining half into 4 wedges and serve one with each portion.

Serves 4 as a side dish

Soup of Tuscan Kale, Beans, and Farro with Citrus Scents

This sturdy soup, thick with chewy grains and fleshy kale, is perfumed with a last-minute burst of orange, lemon, rosemary, garlic, and parsley, which dramatically alters its character. As in many dishes, anchovy plays a silent background role—not a fishy foreground one. Italian farro, an ancient wheat form, cooks swiftly to tender, plump kernels with clinging bits of fine husk. Mild, sweetish, with a pleasing bounce and stickiness, it differs from spelt, its North American counterpart, which is firmer and more wheaty tasting. If farro is not available, substitute barley. Cut the kale into small pieces, or it will make messy eating.

> ¾ cup dried beans (preferably light-colored)
> About 7 cups vegetable, mushroom, or light
>   meat broth
> 2 teaspoons fresh rosemary leaves
> 3 oil-packed anchovy fillets
> 3 garlic cloves
> ¼ cup olive oil
> 1 large onion, chopped
> 1 large carrot, chopped
> 1 pound Tuscan kale
> 2 teaspoons kosher salt
> ¾ cup farro (or barley)
> Pepper
> Coarsely grated zest of 1 small lemon
> Coarsely grated zest of 1 small orange
> ¾ cup coarse-chopped parsley leaves

1. Soak beans overnight in water to cover by several inches. Drain.

2. Combine in small pot with water to cover by a few inches. Simmer, covered, until just tender, not soft—timing depends upon the beans chosen. Drain and reserve liquid; puree in food processor or blender with half the beans. Combine with broth as needed to equal 8 cups.

3. Mince together 1 teaspoon rosemary with anchovies and 2½ garlic cloves. Combine with olive oil in soup pot over moderate heat. Add onion and carrot and stir until soft, about 5 minutes.

4. Meanwhile, trim kale: With scissors or knife, slice carefully against each stem to remove it completely (leaf will be halved). Or strip each leaf half by first pulling off its top, then pulling against the grain to yank off its bottom half. Repeat to remove the other side of the leaf from the stem. Stack and slice as you proceed, cutting into 1-inch strips.

5. Add kale to pot, with salt, tossing until completely wilted. Add reserved broth mixture, farro, and beans; bring to a boil.

6. Reduce heat, cover, and simmer until kale and farro are tender, about 25 to 45 minutes. Taste and season with salt and pepper.

7. To serve, combine and mince fine the remaining 1 teaspoon rosemary and ½ garlic clove, the orange and lemon zest, and parsley. Sprinkle over hot soup.

Serves 6 as a main course

Steamed Magenta or Ivory Decorative Kale

Determined to overcome my prejudices against this primarily pretty veggie, acquired when I first tried to cook it in 1985, I tried again. The ruched leaves turned tender and toothsome when steamed—at least the predominantly cream-colored and purplish types. Some things do get better. Green-edged varieties turned olive drab and did not soften (some things don't). Serve as a beautiful bed for seafood, poultry, or a medley of small, buttery root vegetables.

¾ pound predominantly cream or magenta
　　decorative kale
Butter or citrus-infused oil

1. Remove leaves from central stalk or stalks of kale. Tear or cut stems from all but smallest leaves and discard.

2. Spread leaves on steamer rack over boiling water. Cover and cook until tender and almost translucent, 8 to 10 minutes. Gloss with butter or oil and serve hot.

Serves 2 as a side dish

Gingered Colorful Kale and Apple Slaw

Kale leaves are salt-tenderized instead of being cooked, to prevent the loss of their brilliant color and charming parsley frills. Well-rinsed, they are then bathed in vinaigrette to further soften and to sharpen color and flavor. Serve the gingery, vivid slaw at a picnic (cupped in the outer leaves) or as a refreshing intermediate course during a rich meal. Look for the smallest, brightest kale heads in one or several colors.

1 to 1¼ pounds small decorative kale heads
2 tablespoons kosher salt
2 tablespoons rice vinegar
1½ tablespoons fine-diced red onion
2 teaspoons honey
1 tablespoon mild oil, such as corn or safflower
½ tablespoon Asian (dark) sesame oil
1 large apple
1 tablespoon very fine ginger julienne

1. Separate kale leaves from central stalks. Cut central stems from leaves (the tiniest leaves can be left whole). Stack leaf halves and cut into very thin diagonal strips.

2. Combine kale strips with salt in large bowl, tossing. Set a plate on leaves, top with a weight, and leave 15 minutes. Toss, then replace weight. Let stand another 15 minutes. Drain, then rinse thoroughly in several changes of water. Spin-dry.

3. Combine rice vinegar, onion, honey, and corn and sesame oils, blending well. Cut apple (unpeeled) into thin slices, then julienne strips. Toss with dressing, kale, and ginger. Chill until serving time.

Serves 4

Russian Red Kale with Cranberries and Red Onion

Succulent kale leaves sweetened with dried cranberries are a pleasing Old and New World cross. Unfortunately, the promise of "red" is deceptive, for the color greens in cooking. But the pinky punctuation of vinegared red onion and the berries brighten the whole. The rugged kale can play a role in an all-vegetable meal, or accompany grilled sausages, pork, or turkey—smoked or not.

1½ pounds Russian Red kale
2 quarts water
1 tablespoon kosher salt
½ cup dried cranberries
2 tablespoons olive oil
2 medium red onions, cut into ½-inch dice
3 tablespoons red wine vinegar

1. Strip kale: Hold a kale stalk in one hand, stem base upward, and grasp the wider lower leaf base with the other hand. Pull stem slowly downward to remove it completely. Turn stem in the opposite direction. With your free hand, using a downward motion, strip off remaining leaves. Rinse leaf pieces.

2. Boil water in very wide sauté pan. Add salt, then kale, prodding until it wilts sufficiently to sink into water. Cover and boil 5 minutes. Add cranberries, re-cover, and simmer until kale is tender, a few minutes more. Drain (reserve liquid to make soup or polenta).

3. Dry pan. Set over moderately high heat; add 1 tablespoon oil. Add onions and sauté until lightly browned, 4 to 5 minutes. Add vinegar and toss to evaporate completely. Transfer to a dish.

4. Return pan to high heat; add remaining 1 tablespoon oil. Add drained kale and cranberries and toss a minute or two to heat through. Add onions and toss to mix. Serve hot or at room temperature.

Serves 4

Pros Propose

From the United Kingdom to India, kale has deep culinary roots—often twirled around potatoes, which enhance the greens in truly special fashion. Among the most venerable treatments for the two is Irish **Colcannon**. Ashley Miller, author of *The Potato Harvest Cookbook,* chooses Russian Red kale for her modern adaptation: Steam potatoes until tender; cool and peel. Steam stemmed Red Russian kale for 5 minutes. Drain, squeeze dry; chop fine. Sauté chopped leeks in butter until tender. Reduce heat, add kale, and cook about 10 minutes more. Sauté thin-sliced onion halves in butter until browned. Mash the potatoes, adding milk. Beat in kale and leek; season. Reheat, turn into dish. Form an indentation in the center; fill with browned onions.

Neelam Batra, author of *The Indian Vegetarian,* recommends flowering or curly kale for her spicy **Kale with Diced Potatoes:** Fine-chop trimmed kale leaves in processor. Heat mustard oil until it smokes; add coarsely ground fenugreek seeds, slivered garlic, minced ginger; add chopped onions and cook until golden. Add chopped fresh tomatoes and cook until liquid evaporates. Add garam masala and yogurt; cook until absorbed. Add chopped kale, diced potatoes, and a little water. Raise heat, cover; cook until kale wilts. Reduce heat, cover and cook until potatoes are tender. Garnish with scallion whites and black pepper.

Cream is the mellowing agent for assertive Tuscan kale in a recipe from *Rogers Gray Italian Country Cookbook* that is uncharacteristic for the vegetable and country. For rich **Conchiglie al Cavolo Nero:** Remove kale stems and cut leaves into 3 or 4 sections. Blanch in salted water; drain and dry. Simmer heavy cream and whole garlic cloves until soft; puree. Heat olive oil, sliced garlic, and crumbled dried chillis in a skillet until garlic colors. Add kale, stir and season. Add cream and boil briefly, until kale is coated and sauce thickened. Add grated Parmesan. Mix with hot shell pasta.

Recipes from the New World, and particularly the New South, feature kale of the curly kind—just lightly cooked. "Unlike spinach, kale keeps its shape after cooking, so it is suitable in salads," write Johnna Albi and Catherine Walthers, who spice it up for **Cajun Kale Salad:** Cook shucked corn ears in water to just cover; cool and cut kernels from cobs. In reserved cooking water, cook stemmed kale cut medium-fine until just barely tender. Drain; spread to cool. Toss kale, corn, diced red and green bell peppers, minced Vidalia onion, minced garlic, and a blend of paprika, cayenne, black pepper, allspice, thyme leaves, and white pepper. To serve, add lemon juice and olive oil (from *Greens Glorious Greens*).

Barely cooked kale also appears in sweet-and-smoky **Arkansas Kale and Bacon Salad:** Brown lardons. Deglaze with pickled beet juice. Add garlic, salt, pepper, and stripped curly kale leaves, torn small. Toss to soften slightly, about 5 minutes. Transfer to serving plates, top with cubed pickled beets, onion slices, and sliced hard-cooked egg (from *Farmhouse Cookbook* by Susan Hermann Loomis).

Virginia food and wine writer Sarah Belk King uses traditional curly kale in an updated **Buckwheat Pasta with Kale and Goat Cheese:** Blanch stemmed kale ribbons in salted water; drain and squeeze dry. Gently cook shallots in butter; add small squares of thin-sliced Smithfield ham. Stir in cream; set aside. Mash fresh goat cheese with more cream and add to kale with a little Parmesan. Return to heat; simmer a moment. Mix with freshly cooked pizzoccheri.

Last and foremost, kale of every type is a soup staple. A time-honored Tuscan porridge, **Farinata de Cavolo Nero,** calls for Tuscan kale—naturally. To prepare: Drop stemmed leaves into heavily salted water; boil until tender. Drain, reserving water. Drop kale into ice water; drain, then chop. Boil reserved water; sprinkle in polenta (1 cup to 6 cups water), whisking constantly. Add kale; set in another pot of water or double boiler. Cook until creamy and thick, about 45 minutes. Sauté chopped garlic in olive oil until barely colored. Stir into farinata just before serving. Top each bowl with olive oil and pepper (from *Red, White & Greens* by Faith Willinger).

Barbara Kafka writes that "the descendants of many Portuguese sailors and fishermen still live in Provincetown, Massachusetts, and make foods based on Portuguese originals," such as **Kale and Clam Stew,** derived from caldo verde, perhaps the best known of kale soups. To prepare: Cut stemmed curly kale in 1-inch pieces. Wilt in a tall, narrow soup pot over low heat. Add pork or ham stock, diced bacon, and smashed garlic. Simmer until tender. Add firm potatoes cut into ¼-inch slices. Simmer until almost tender. Add small scrubbed clams, hinged side down. Cover, boil, and cook until clams open. Shuck and return to soup. Stir in pepper (from *Soup, A Way of Life*).

Kiwano (*Cucumis metuliferus*)

Also horned cucumber, African horned cucumber, jelly melon

Aptly dubbed hedgehog gourd in some texts, this fruit gets short shrift from me (and from a broad sampling of chefs, who came up with one use, as a dessert garnish). More a curiosity than a comestible, this strange cucurbit was an African horned cucumber until the 1980s, when it was rechristened and trademarked Kiwano for export from New Zealand. (Many goods from New Zealand are marketed with a kiwi prefix.)

Whatever the virtues of this piggy bank–satellite gourd, edibility is not an obvious one (although it would prevent dehydration in the Kalahari Desert, near which it originated). Cut open the barbed, rubbery orange skin and you'll have a refreshing whiff of grassy cucumber. Suck the Jell-O-green blobs that encapsulate the many seeds to sample its tart taste. But just try to do anything else with it that involves eating!

I have pulped and juiced and seeded the Kiwano. I have frozen its juice, whipped it, blended it with liquor and with yogurt, made vinaigrette and other sauces with it, and even microwaved and baked the whole fruit in an attempt to discover some uses for it. But I still find the seeds inedible, the pulp flimsy and astringent, and the price exorbitant. The emerald juice (which does whip up somewhat, egg-white style) seems the most likely candidate for recipes, but I was able to strain just 3 tablespoons from a ½-pound fruit that cost $4. I rest my case for the time being.

BASIC USE: Conversation piece or one-time tasting diversion.

length: 4-6 inches

SELECTION AND STORAGE: Select evenly orange fruit for maximum sweetness (which is minimal, at best). The New Zealand crop runs from spring to summer; the California crop, from summer to winter. If you do figure out what to do with Kiwano, you're in luck, because it will last for months at room temperature (we are advised not to refrigerate it).

Kohlrabi (*Brassica oleracea*, Gongylodes Group)

"What did you do to this kohlrabi?" asked a food writer, chomping up more than her fair share of the snack I had set out. "I cut it up," I replied. "Didn't you cook it or sweeten it or something? I don't remember it tasting this way."

Whenever I serve kohlrabi, people notice, and are pleasantly surprised. But it appears that unless you're from Hungary, China, Germany, or India (a curious culinary gamut) you probably haven't tasted it. Why, I can't imagine. It has been in the United States since the beginning of the 19th century (if not earlier) and it's as easy to enjoy as the best summer cukes. If there was ever a "try it, you'll like it" vegetable to simply sample straight and plain, this is it.

What prevents it from being popular? Is there some hidden prejudice? Is the name off-putting? The word is not inviting, but it shouldn't be a deterrent. "Kohl" is from Latin for stem, then German for cabbage; and "rabi" is from rapa, turnip. But kohlrabi is not a cross of the two; it tastes more like broccoli stalks, water chestnut, and cucumber. (Speaking of names, "*gongylodes* refers to a type of small red turnip resembling the purple kohlrabi and common in C. Asia, where its Kashmiri name is gongolou," Alan Davidson tells us in *The Oxford Companion to Food*.) Does the strange shape confuse people? Kohlrabi is an enlarged above-ground stem (not a tuber) from which spring collard-like leaves, but the whole has a fairly familiar cruciferous look.

What seems clear is that if you didn't grow up with kohlrabis (kohlrabi sounds plural, but isn't) in the kitchen, you don't know what to do with them. So here's the answer, basically.

BASIC USE

Raw kohlrabi is juicy, refreshing, and versatile. I like it best peeled, sliced, or cut into half-moons or sticks and served on a vegetable platter with dips or a smear of soft cheese, such as fresh goat cheese or creamy blue, my favorite accompaniment.

⅙ **actual size**

Cut dice or julienne to toss in vegetable, grain, or meat salads. Grate or shred kohlrabi for slaws to mix with dressings that are sweet, spicy, sour, or aromatic. Use it like sunchoke or jícama.

For a slightly sweeter, more concentrated flavor, blanch kohlrabi for salads and vegetable platters instead of serving it raw: Peel closely (keep small bulbs whole, halve medium and larger ones). Boil in salted water just until the raw taste disappears, about 3 to 4 minutes. Cool in ice water, drain, and pat dry.

Cooked kohlrabi can be crisp or soft, depending upon your taste. Traditional European recipes are often elaborate (stuffed, creamed, crumbed), but I prefer the sweet delicacy when it is sparingly seasoned and sauced.

Steam or boil whole or halved peeled kohlrabis until tender to your taste, about 15 to 30 minutes. (Although it is often written that the flavor is best retained when kohlrabi is cooked with the skin, I find it less tasty this way and more of a nuisance to clean.) Serve with light cream or cheese sauce, flavored butter, or vinaigrette.

Sauté or stir-fry slices, strips, dice, or shreds with aromatics such as shallots or onion, marjoram, thyme, nutmeg, or ginger.

Cook leaves as you would tender kale or collards—but strip off the tough stems entirely. Blanch leaves until tender, then drain, chop, and heat in oil or butter with seasonings.

For soups and braises, cook both leaves and bulbs (correctly speaking, swollen stems, but this is confusing). Add peeled small whole or medium-size halved or quartered kohlrabis to braised dishes and stews for the final 15 to 25 minutes or so of cooking. About 10 minutes before the dish is done, add the stripped leaves, cut small.

To stuff kohlrabis: Peel, parboil, then hollow; stuff with blanched and chopped leaves and hollowed-out stem parts and rice, or with bread crumbs and chopped meat. Braise, then thicken the braising liquid to serve as sauce over the stuffed vegetable. This is particularly useful with larger bulbs.

SELECTION: Kohlrabi is available erratically all year and abundant during the summer. Select from Ping-Pong-ball- to baseball-size depending upon how you'll use it. Tiny kohlrabi is not tastier or sweeter than medium-size, in my experience; in fact, it may be less so. Choose the smoothest globes, with no cracks—which indicate dryness and probable pithiness. The leaves, if present, should be firm and green, with no sign of yellowing. Kohlrabi in Asian markets, which is generally medium to large, has its leaves removed, for no reason I understand.

All "baby" kohlrabi I have tried has had more waste than edible parts, but I am told that if you grow your own, it need not be peeled. If that is true, it is worth cultivating the ravishing violet, which, once peeled, looks just like the green. It may be a coincidence, but all purple types have tasted less sweet and juicy to me than green types.

STORAGE: Cut apart leaf-stems and globes. Wrap separately in perforated plastic and refrigerate. Leaves last a few days; the crunchy parts last for weeks.

PREPARATION: Cut the leaf-stems from the globes. Wash leaves well in warm water. Strip off tough stems. Pare all skin and any fibrous layer from the bulbs. Try not to be disappointed when you remove the regal purple, which is only skin-deep. I like peels

and leaf-stems as a strong-sweet contributor to vegetable stocks, but some don't.

Sautéed Kohlrabi Shreds

If you haven't already done so, add kohlrabi to your list of quick-cooking anytime vegetables. Shredded in a processor, it takes minutes to sauté to crisp-tender, and it follows just about any flavoring lead. Spices, herbs, and aromatics all work.

> 4 medium kohlrabis (about 1½ pounds with tops)
> 1 tablespoon olive or peanut oil or butter
> Optional: 1 teaspoon minced ginger
> Optional: 1 small shallot, minced
> Salt and pepper

1. Remove kohlrabi leaves, if any, and reserve for another use (see recipe following). Peel kohlrabis thoroughly, removing any fibrous underlayer. Halve bulbs. With grating blade of food processor in place, push down firmly on cut sides to make large shreds.

2. Heat oil in wide skillet over moderate heat. Toss kohlrabi shreds, with optional ginger and shallot, over moderate heat until tender to taste, a matter of a few minutes. Season.

Serves 2

Variation

Kohlrabi Shreds with Bacon and Caraway

Cut 3 slices bacon across into thin strips. Cook gently in skillet until browned. Drain on paper towel. Add kohlrabi to fat with a pinch of caraway (or chopped fennel) seeds. Cook as above. Season, then sprinkle with bacon bits.

Basic Kohlrabi Leaves

Kohlrabi leaves are not to be ignored (unless you buy the vegetable in a Chinese market—in which case there won't be any). Blanched and sautéed, the leaves have a smooth, fleshy feel, spinach color, and flavor like Swiss chard crossed with bok choy. Since they are rather skimpy (the leaves from one small bunch serve one person), it makes sense to fill out a recipe with leaves from either one of these similar greens. Sautéed sliced mushrooms are a welcome addition.

¾ to 1 pound kohlrabi leaves (or a combination of kohlrabi and chard or bok choy leaves)
1 to 2 tablespoons butter, goose or bacon fat, or olive oil
Optional: 1 medium shallot, minced
Salt and pepper

1. Strip kohlrabi stems from leaves. Rinse leaves well. Drop into a large pot of boiling salted water. When water returns to a full boil, stir, then boil until just tender (this will vary with your taste and time of year), from about 2 minutes to as long as 10.

2. Drain leaves well, pressing out moisture. Keep whole, or slice or chop to suit. (They can be left for hours at room temperature; or refrigerate until needed.)

3. To serve, melt butter in a skillet over moderate heat. Add optional shallot and toss a minute; add leaves and sauté until hot through. Season and serve hot.

Serves 2

Crisp Peppery Kohlrabi-Carrot Slaw with Dill and Anise

Bright and clean tasting, this simple slaw freshens a buffet or picnic—and won't lose its crunch. Once salted, kohlrabi strips stay firm (they can even be prepared a day in advance). Two Umbelliferae or Apiaciae (parsley family members), dill and anise, subtly sweeten the mix. To make pretty ribbons in place of shreds, zip a swivel peeler across the carrots in short strokes.

6 medium kohlrabis (2 pounds without leaves)
1 tablespoon kosher salt
1¼ teaspoons anise seeds
1 teaspoon coarse-cracked or crushed pepper
3 tablespoons grapeseed, corn, or safflower oil
2 medium garlic cloves, sliced
4 medium carrots
2 tablespoons rice vinegar
3 to 4 tablespoons snipped dill

1. Peel kohlrabis. Cut into slices ⅛ inch thick, then cut these into very thin strips. Toss with salt in sieve set over a bowl. Let stand 30 minutes or more, as convenient, tossing occasionally.

2. Meanwhile, set small heavy skillet over low heat. Add anise seeds and stir until fragrant, about a minute. Remove ¼ teaspoon and reserve. Add pepper and shake often until anise darkens, 3 to 4 minutes. Add oil and garlic. Stir just until garlic begins to color—a minute or so. Cover and let steep while kohlrabi drains.

3. Shred carrot, using food processor or vegetable slicer, pressing firmly to make large shreds.

4. Drain kohlrabi. Rinse lightly, then spin-dry. Strain oil; discard seasonings. Combine oil, reserved anise, and vinegar; blend. Toss with kohlrabi and carrots. Chill at least ½ hour, or until serving time.

5. Sprinkle with dill, toss, and serve.

Serves 4 to 6 as a side salad

Balsamic-Tinged Kohlrabi

Lightly browned, juicy kohlrabi dice taste like artichokes and cucumbers, for no reason I understand. Barbara Spiegel, who devised this simple, tart-sweet sauté-braise, likes the delicacy of the dish without the leaves. For an earthier dish with kale-like undertones, prepare the variation with the greens included.

To serve four, double the ingredients and use a very wide skillet to hold the kohlrabi dice in a single layer.

4 medium or 3 medium-large kohlrabis (2 to 2½ pounds with tops; 1½ pounds without)
1 tablespoon olive oil
¼ teaspoon kosher salt
½ cup water
1 tablespoon balsamic vinegar
Pepper
1 tablespoon snipped chives

1. Cut leaf-stalks from kohlrabis; reserve for another recipe (or see variation). Trim and peel globes thoroughly, removing all fibrous underlayer. Cut into ¾-inch slices, then dice (to make about 2¼ cups).

2. Heat oil in skillet large enough to hold dice in a single close layer. Add kohlrabi and toss over moderately high heat to brown lightly, 6 to 7 minutes. Sprinkle with salt; add water, and bring to a boil. Cover and simmer over low heat until just tender, stirring now and then, about 10 minutes.

3. If any liquid remains, uncover and toss over moderate heat to evaporate. Add vinegar and pepper and toss until kohlrabi is slightly glazed, about 2 minutes. Add chives and toss. Season and serve hot.

Serves 2

Variation

Balsamic-Tinged Kohlrabi on Its Leaves

Strip leaves from stems. Rinse leaves well. Stir into a pot of boiling salted water; boil until tender to taste, 2 to 10 minutes. Drain leaves well, pressing out moisture. Chop. Prepare kohlrabi as above. When done, scoop into a dish. Heat ½ tablespoon olive oil in skillet. Add leaves and toss to heat through. Spread in serving dish. Distribute cubes on top.

Serves 3

★*See also* Black Radish–Noodle "Stoup" with Meatballs, page 529, in which kohlrabi can be substituted for black radish.

Pros Propose

Sweet and simple, this maple dressing for kohlrabi won Mary Jirik a ribbon at the Barre Farm Show, recounts Ruth Cousineau, author of *Country Suppers.* To prepare **Kohlrabi Salad with Mary's Prize Dressing:** Combine pure dark amber or Grade B maple syrup, salt, cider vinegar, canola oil, dry mustard, and poppy seeds, whisking to blend well. Toss with peeled, coarsely shredded kohlrabi. Add sectioned navel oranges. Arrange on romaine lettuce leaves.

Sweet salad in a wholly different style is served at weddings in north Vietnam, according to *Madhur Jaffrey's Far Eastern Cookery.* For **Vietnamese Kohlrabi Salad:** Cut peeled kohlrabis into fairly fine julienne strips. Cut carrots into strips the same size. Mix both with salt; let stand 15 minutes. Squeeze out moisture and pat dry. Mix vegetables with distilled white vine-

gar, sugar, and ground hot pepper. Adjust seasoning. Add shredded mint and coriander leaves, then coarsely chopped roasted peanuts. Garnish, if desired, with fine chilli threads.

Corinne Trang, author of *Authentic Vietnamese Cooking,* grew up eating foods in the style of southern Vietnam, where her family lived. The spring roll common in American restaurants, cha gio, is one such example. While visiting Hanoi in the north, she enjoyed nem ran, a spring roll in which grated kohlrabi replaces the familiar carrot. For **Northern Vietnamese Spring Rolls:** Chop rehydrated cellophane noodles and cloud ear fungus. Mix well with ground pork, minced onion and garlic, grated kohlrabi, egg, salt, and pepper. Fill dampened small triangular rice papers with the stuffing; roll up tightly. Deep-fry until golden. Drain. Set each on a lettuce leaf, add mint leaves, and roll up. Serve with dipping sauce of fish sauce, lime juice, sugar, water, sliced garlic, and Thai chilli.

No country offers as many recipes for kohlrabi as India, where the vegetable was introduced by the British Raj, according to Julie Sahni. Keeping pace with modern times, her *Moghul Microwave* includes **Kohlrabi, Tomato, and Chick-Pea Soup:** Heat oil; stir in ground cumin, ground coriander, turmeric, and cayenne and cook until spices begin to brown. Add peeled, thin-sliced kohlrabis, cooked chick-peas, chopped tomatoes, tomato paste, and water or stock. Mix, cover, and cook until soup is boiling rapidly and kohlrabi is tender, about 9 minutes. Add salt and roasted, ground cumin. Top with chopped coriander. (Although most recipes in Sahni's book are best in the microwave, this is also fine for the stove top.)

Neelam Batra's recipe from *The Indian Vegetarian* includes the leaves. For **Spicy Kohlrabi:** Cut peeled kohlrabis into ½-inch dice. Shred stemmed leaves. Heat crushed bay leaves in oil in non-stick pan. Stir in chopped garlic, minced Serrano chillis, ajowan (carum) seeds, ground coriander, cracked black pepper, and turmeric. Add leaves; cook, stirring occasionally, 5 minutes. Add diced kohlrabi and cook briefly. Add water and simmer, covered, until tender. Add lemon juice and cook until liquid evporates. Sprinkle with garam masala.

Chef and author Marian Morash lightens a traditional Western European dish of meatballs with mini-kohlrabis. For **Swedish Meatballs with Kohlrabis:** Blend ground beef and pork, minced onion, egg, fresh bread crumbs, minced parsley, Worcestershire sauce, milk, and seasoning. Form 1-inch balls. Brown in butter and oil; reserve. Add flour to pan and cook briefly. Add paprika, salt, and pepper; whisk in beef broth, then sour cream. Return meatballs to sauce, with peeled tiny kohlrabis. Cover and simmer until tender, about 20 minutes (from *The Victory Garden Cookbook*).

The varied origins of American haute cuisine are apparent in this chef's recipe from vegetable connoisseur Charlie Trotter. For his elegant **Kohlrabi Broth with Glass Noodles, Lotus Root, and Savoy Cabbage:** Run kohlrabis through juicer. Simmer until the solids mass, then strain broth through fine-mesh sieve.

Brown thin-sliced kohlrabis in butter for garnish. Cook Japanese transparent noodles (harusame) al dente: Refresh in ice water. Gently cook fine chiffonade of savoy cabbage in butter with a little rice vinegar until tender. To serve, plunge noodles into boiling water; drain, then toss with sesame oil and season. Center some cabbage in each bowl. Twist some noodles into a spiral with a fork and set on cabbage. Arrange kohlrabi slices around. Set hard-cooked, peeled, and halved quail eggs on these. Ladle hot kohlrabi broth into each bowl and add a touch of sesame oil. Place thin-sliced deep-fried lotus on noodle mounds (from *Charlie Trotter's Vegetables*).

Lamb's Quarters (*Chenopodium album*)

Also goosefoot, pigweed, fat hen, wild spinach
Including **magenta lamb's quarters**

This tasty, thick-leaved green travels under the various names above and a few other animal-linked names, as well as some notably unappetizing British ones: muckweed, dungweed, and dirty dick. Happily, the vegetable itself is as delightful as its names are off-putting. Because goosefoot and pigweed are names shared by numerous other plants of the genus *Chenopodium,* it makes sense to stay with lamb's quarters if the green you mean is the one whose top leaves are pictured here. By the way, it is no relation of lamb's lettuce (mâche or corn salad).

"Spinach-like," a description often applied indiscriminately to wild greens, does fit this plant—which is a relative of spinach. Like spinach, it can be eaten raw or cooked. Raw, it tastes quite different from cooked, with a suggestion of peanuts, grass, and, oddly, fruit. Cooked, the slightly waxy, fleshy, flavorful leaves have an earthy, walnut-like savor and, although green and spinachy, lack that vegetable's iron tang.

There are fifty *Chenopodium* species in the United States, ten of which were introduced unintentionally from such diverse places as Europe, Asia, Latin America, and Australia, according to Charles B. Heiser, Jr. (*Of Plants and People*). Until recently, *Chenopodium album* was a name used to designate native American species, but it is apparently difficult to tell the species apart at this point. Native Americans made good use of the dusky, bloom-powdered blue-green leaves, pink-

lamb's quarters (tips of plant): wild (*left*) and cultivated magenta (*right*)

½ actual size

streaked stems, leaf-like buds, and countless little seeds—all edible and choice—that are either *album* or a close relative. Cultivated and wild forms, both of which tend to be rangy and rather scruffy once grown beyond a foot or so, taste remarkably similar when cooked at almost any stage.

A bright cultivated form, **magenta lamb's quarters,** makes a splendid raw accent leaf, but when cooked it loses its glowing color and tastes less distinctive than other types. A larger species, *Chenopodium giganteum* (pictured on the right), also produces a purplish form—the cultivar name is Magentaspreen—which is similar when very young and small, the only way I have tried it.

BASIC USE: Combine small leaves of raw lamb's quarters with a variety of mild greens; dress with nut oil and roasted nuts. Like spinach, lamb's quarters cooks tender in moments, then goes through a less lovely intermediary stage before melting into velvety lusciousness—whether in soups, sauces, stews, or buttery Indian purees. For seasoning, treat it as you would spinach, going from a mere gloss of butter or oil to citrus to garlic to hot and spicy.

Here are the basic cooking methods: Boil a few minutes for tender, mild leaves that are bright spinach-green and slightly slick. Steam on a rack a minute or two longer for a slightly firmer, more meaty, chewier result, with more pronounced flavor and a slight bitterness. Or sauté-braise for more assertive flavor and texture.

SELECTION AND STORAGE: For those who gather it in the wild, lamb's quarters is one of the early spring tonic greens. Both wild and cultivated lamb's quarters seem to arrive erratically from April to October.

For minimum waste, choose small-stalked plants, but expect even sturdy ones to cook agreeably tender. How much you need will depend upon the size of the greens. Delicate springtime specimens need no trimming; thus, one pound can feed four. When plants are large and heavy-stemmed, you'll need twice that amount. Store unwashed, plastic-wrapped, for up to a week.

PREPARATION: Early spring plants and small cultivated ones need nothing more than a rinse. For others, everything that pulls off the main stalk will cook up just fine: stems, leaves, seed heads, flowers, branch-lets. Discard the stalk and dunk all the rest into plenty of water. There is no chance of oversoaking, because water simply slips from the leaves, as off a duck's back.

Basic Lamb's Quarters: Three Ways

However you choose to cook these meaty leaves, they'll taste deep green and earthy, reminiscent of spinach—but minus the iron bite. The quantity you need will depend upon the size of the plants. Tiny spring tips need no trimming—thus, 1 pound can feed 4 people. But you'll need twice that when plants are large and heavy-stemmed. The following recipe is for a size in between. If you have preserved lemons, mince some, then stir into the cooked leaves with their oil.

1½ pounds medium lamb's quarters
Fruity olive oil, hot pepper oil, herbed oil,
    or garlic oil
Coarse salt and pepper
Lemon or orange slices

1. Strip everything from main stalks of lamb's quarters: flowers, seeds, leaves, branches. Discard stalks and rinse all the rest.

2. Then, choose one of these three options for the cleaned greens:

To boil: For the most tender, mild, and fleshy result, with leaves that are brightly spinachy green and slightly slick. Drop into boiling salted water. Cook just until tender, about 1 to 2 minutes. Drain.

To steam: For a slightly firmer, more meaty and chewy result, with more pronounced flavor and slight bitterness: Set on steamer rack, cover, and cook until tender—about 3 minutes—tossing once with tongs.

To sauté-braise: For the most assertive flavor and texture: Toss in skillet with just enough water to moisten and a little olive oil. Cook over moderate heat until tender, about 2 minutes. Raise heat to cook off moisture, leaving only oil.

3. Season with the oil of your choice, salt, and pepper. Garnish with citrus slices. Serve hot or at room temperature.

Serves 4

Creamed Spring Lamb's Quarters

Thick lamb's quarters' leaves turn pillowy soft in cream. Serve as a rich side dish with roast chicken or lamb. Or, for devoted lovers of greens, enrich with more cream and serve as a first course over crisp thin toast. While not glamorous, the plushy mass is as luscious as the finest creamed spinach, with complex mineral undertones.

If tender tips are not in season, the later, leggier plants will taste fine but require more trimming: Increase the quantity of greens and remove all the long primary stalks.

> 1 pound tender lamb's quarters
>   (primarily top parts)
> 2 cups water
> About ½ teaspoon kosher salt
> About ⅔ cup heavy cream
> Parmesan cheese
> Pepper

1. Dunk lamb's quarters into water and lift out. Spring greens are tender and require no trimming: Simply break into 1½-inch sprigs.

2. Combine greens in non-aluminum skillet with water and ½ teaspoon salt. Bring to a boil. Cover, reduce heat, and simmer gently, stirring occasionally, until stems are tender, about 8 minutes (timing varies—check often).

3. Uncover skillet and raise heat to evaporate most liquid. Add ⅔ cup cream, reduce heat, and simmer gently, stirring often, until most of it is absorbed, a few minutes or so. Adjust consistency, adding more cream, if desired.

4. Grate over cheese, gradually stirring it in to taste. Season and serve hot.

Serves 4 as a side dish or first course

★See also recipe for Orach with Balsamic Vinegar and Currants, page 452, for which lamb's quarters can be substituted.

Pros Propose

Theme dishes and wordplay figure in chef Odessa Piper's menus, such as this little lamb riff, **Carpaccio of Lamb with Lamb's Quarters.** "I couldn't resist the double entendre or rightness of the colors and flavors," says Piper, who prepares the dish thus: "We take tenderloins from the tiny local lamb, cut a nubbin, then gently press it paper-thin—to about 3 inches. Overlap a few on a big plate. Combine very light truffle oil and balsamic and toss just a whisper with magenta lamb's quarters and baby arugula, then place in the center. Drizzle a spoonful of dressing on the lamb and grate over it a touch of hard sheep's cheese—what else?"

For "great gorgeously green soup, there is nothing like this wonderful wildling," says foraging chef Bruce Naftaly. To prepare **Lamb's Quarters Soup:** Combine celery root with chicken stock and cook until soft. Add plenty of trimmed lamb's quarters; cook until tender. Puree and strain. Season with salt, pepper, and nutmeg. Garnish with chickweed snips and chives.

Jean-Georges Vongerichten, a natural minimalist, serves a chilled **Gazpacho of Lamb's Quarters with Shrimp:** Marinate shrimp in thyme and olive oil. Blanch leaves and tender stems of lamb's quarters in boiling water. Drain and refresh, then squeeze dry. Combine in food processor with ice cubes, grapeseed oil, and soaked, drained white bread. Puree until smooth, adding water for correct consistency. Chill. Grill shrimp and serve them hot on the iced soup.

"Quelites" is a generic term for Mexican greens, but it is often used for lamb's quarters—sometimes called quelite cenizo (ashy green). Chef and author Rick Bayless writes that in Toluca, where he first tasted tacos of quelites, "they think of this rustic earthy taco as old-fashioned (poor people's) food. I think of it as some of the best food on the face of the earth" (*Rick Bayless's Mexican Kitchen*). For **Tacos de Quelite:** Wrap corn tortillas in towel and steam over boiling water 1 minute. Turn off heat; let stand 15 minutes. Meanwhile, boil stemmed lamb's quarters until barely tender. Drain and spread to cool. Chop. Cook thick-sliced white onion in olive oil until browned. Add chopped garlic and stir. Add greens; cook a few minutes longer. Season. Scoop into warmed dish and sprinkle with crumbled queso fresco. Let guests fill the warm tortillas with greens and a favorite salsa (Bayless's is made from tomatillos and Serrano chilli).

Chef Diane Forley prepares her south-of-the-border ingredients in more fusion fashion. For **Slow-Cooked Green Tomato with Pozole, Peppers, and Lamb's Quarters:** Bake halved green tomatoes in very low oven until dense and concentrated in flavor. Combine cooked white corn pozole, chopped red bell peppers, scallions, and tomato dice with lemon and lime juice and zest and chilli oil. Marinate briefly. To serve, add leaves of lamb's quarters to "relish" and heat just until they wilt. For each serving, spoon relish into a green tomato half until juices overflow into the bowl. Set another half against it.

Leek (*Allium ampeloprasum,* Porrum Group)

See also: **RAMP,** page 534

Giant bunches of leeks burst from net bags and grocery baskets, part of the regular shopping list in much of Europe and the Middle East. American cooks without ties to those areas are likely to slice a few tired leeks into winter soups—and that's about it for this neglected vegetable. We have relegated this ancient, noble allium to the role of a mere seasoning; elsewhere, it plays leading roles—for good reasons: It is big, handsome, and versatile, and it cooks to a silky mellowness that makes it one of the most subtle of the onion group.

But Elephant, King Richard, Titan, and Winter Giant—a few of the names of seeds available to gardeners in the United States—hardly suggest the delicacies for which the leek is celebrated: vichysoisse (iced leek and potato cream soup), flamiche (Belgian leek quiche), and leeks vinaigrette, to name a few. The rather threatening connotations of these names suggest that the leek's solid, masculine appearance and its forceful raw aroma override its more feminine culinary personality. This seems unfair to a plant that, although superficially robust, becomes tender and mild after even a brief blanching. Leeks seem to confuse cooks who have not been raised with them in the kitchen. They see the large size and think "strong." They see stiff, sturdy leaves and don't realize that leeks will turn softer than Belgian endive or lettuce.

The only way to know this gentle giant is to cook it. This has been done for a very long time indeed—so long that no one knows where the wild plant originated, although the Mediterranean is likely. Leeks were cultivated by the ancient Egyptians, Romans, Greeks, Welsh, and Scots, among others. The ancient Romans were particularly partial to leeks, to gauge from a first-century cooking manual, translated as *The Roman Cookery of Apicius* by John Edwards, which includes 17 recipes for leeks. Among them are leeks stewed with shell beans in white wine, beets and leeks in raisin sauce, leeks and celery poached with honey and pepper, leek sauce with pepper for braised meats, fish fillets with leeks and coriander, and leeks with truffles.

The venerable Welsh cawl (meaning soup) has leeks

length: 10-18 inches

as its sole constant, and other "all day on the fire" soups made with leek abound in national variations, with classic pot-au-feu as satisfying today as it was during the Middle Ages. Contemporary Greeks, like the ancients, bake leeks in pies, chop them into stuffings, smooth them in soups, and poach them in what may be the best known leek preparation, à la grecque (a term that has come to us via the French), in which whole leeks are simmered in an aromatic broth that is then reduced and poured over the leeks.

BASIC USE: Leeks—whether whole, chunked, sliced, or eventually pureed—excel in braises and soups. They provide complexity, sweetness, and body, more so than onion.

Cooked in parchment or foil (oven-steamed), leeks are truly special—different from any other way you may have tasted them: unusually savory, concentrated, and of a uniform, melting consistency.

Poaching displays leeks' mild, leafy, lettuce-like side. Steamed whole or in julienne strips, leeks look satiny and taste extremely mild, almost bland—suitable for those who prefer only a hint of leek.

Small whole leeks (fairly difficult to find, at least on the East Coast), boiled or steamed tender, well dried and oil-brushed, turn smoky and juicy on the grill.

Stir-fried, sautéed, and deep-fried leeks have a one-dimensional caramelized onion flavor and a chewy (sometimes fibrous) texture.

SELECTION: Leeks are available year-round, with peak availability from late fall to spring. There is little choice in the United States. Tender spring leeks are rarely part of our repertoire unless you live in a growing area where they are sold in farmers' markets. Market leeks average about ½ pound apiece, but there is wide variability. Smallness and paleness, both of which signal tenderness, are important for leeks that will be cooked whole.

Look for leeks with taut upright green tops. Avoid leeks with bulging bulbs. Most important, bend the pale lower part of the stalk to be sure it has "give"; if it does not, chances are good that it has a woody core and will never soften during cooking.

STORAGE: Wrap leeks in a slightly damp paper towel, then plastic; keep in the vegetable crisper up to a week. They are fresh, uncured vegetables that do not have the staying power of onions or garlic.

PREPARATION: Cleaning is critical. With one exception, there is no being polite about ablutions: Leeks must be ruthlessly slit or sliced and their innards rudely rinsed. A hidden mud layer ruins a dish. Here are the approaches.

Traditional: Trim off roots without cutting into the bulb; cut off dark green leaves (save for soup). Insert a knife through the bulb end an inch or so above the base. Slice lengthwise toward the leaf tip to halve the stalk, keeping the base intact. Plunge up and down in a sinkful of water, opening up the layers and sloshing vigorously, then examine each down to the base. Repeat until pearly. Then, either slice crosswise, leave whole, or tie with string to maintain the shape.

For small, skinny leeks (this is the polite wash): Trim roots and green tops. Cut a lengthwise slit halfway through shaft, leaving base intact. Hold leek upright under running water and gently pull apart layers to let water run between them. Shake off water and drain on towels.

Unorthodox: Unless the leek is to be cooked whole, it is much simpler to trim the roots and very ratty leaves. (Dark green leaves turn tender if cut small and well cooked; there is no reason to remove them.) Slice across to the width desired, dump into plenty of water, then drain. Repeat a few times. The slices do not absorb water or lose flavor, and the process is faster and easier than slitting.

Herbed Carrot and Leek Chunks, Oven-Steamed

When leeks and carrots are moistened with minced mushrooms, sealed in packets, and baked in their aromatic juices, a new richness emerges. Quickly assembled, the colorful, tender mélange is peppery, sweet, and woodsy. Pop into the oven while a roast rests, or bake alongside whole fish. Very simple, very special.

2 tablespoons hazelnut, walnut, or olive oil
2 medium leeks
4 medium carrots
¼ pound white (button) mushrooms
½ teaspoon dried thyme
½ teaspoon sugar
½ teaspoon kosher salt
⅛ teaspoon pepper

1. Preheat oven to 400°F. Cut four 12-inch lengths of aluminum foil. Spread 1 teaspoon oil on each to coat half.

2. Trim off roots and dark green leaf tops from leeks. Slice lengthwise toward leaf tips to halve each leek. Plunge up and down in a sinkful of water, opening up the layers to slosh clean, then examine each down to the base. Repeat until soil-free. Lay cut side down and slice across into 1-inch lengths. Divide evenly among foil squares, arranging on the oiled part.

3. Peel carrots; cut into 1-inch diagonal slices. Distribute among the leeks. Mince mushrooms very fine. Toss with thyme, sugar, salt, and pepper. Add remaining 2 teaspoons oil and mix well. Divide evenly over the vegetables. Fold over foil and form half-moon packets, crimping edges tightly, as if making turnovers.

4. Set packets on baking sheet. Bake in center of oven 20 minutes, or until tender. Serve hot.

Serves 4

Cock-a-Leekie Soup

This celebrated old recipe of the British Isles is common across the Atlantic, and we would do well to know it on the American side. This adaptation of the substantial classic needs only a crusty dark loaf and plenty of ale to make a warming meal. The prunes lend a winy, mysterious taste and creamy feel to the dish—not the sweetness you might expect—and the leeks deepen in flavor and become silky.

2 parsnips
2 quarts chicken broth (or a mixture of chicken and vegetable broths)
3 celery stalks with leaves, sliced
2 bay leaves
1 (whole) chicken, about 3½ pounds
2½ pounds leeks (5 medium leeks)
½ cup pearled barley
½ tablespoon curry powder
1 teaspoon ground allspice
1 teaspoon kosher salt (omit if broth is salted)
12 pitted prunes, halved
About 2 teaspoons Worcestershire sauce
½ cup minced parsley and celery leaves

1. Peel and slice 1 parsnip. Combine with broth, celery, and bay leaves in pot large enough to hold all ingredients. Boil gently, covered, 15 minutes. Meanwhile, peel and dice the other parsnip.

2. Add chicken to broth and return to a boil. Reduce heat and barely simmer, covered, ½ hour, turning once. Transfer chicken to cutting board. Remove vegetables from broth; discard. Skim fat.

3. Meanwhile, trim roots and damaged or very tough leaves from leeks. Halve leeks lengthwise, then cut crosswise into 1-inch slices. Wash in several changes of water. Add to broth, with diced parsnip, barley, curry, allspice, and salt. Simmer, covered, until barley is tender and leeks are meltingly soft, about 40 minutes.

4. Meanwhile, skin and bone chicken. Cut meat into small pieces.

5. Add chicken to soup, with prunes. Simmer until prunes are puffed and soft, usually just a few minutes if using the usual moist-style ones. Add Worcestershire to taste. Season. Stir in parsley and celery leaves.

Serves 6 as a main course

Lemony Leeks and Potatoes Baked with Mint and Dill

This homey dish works best with yellow potatoes. If you have saffron on hand, add it for depth and color—but it isn't *absolutely* necessary. Serve with roasted lamb or grilled chicken. For a vegetable meal, accompany with goat cheese, olives, fennel strips, and radishes.

1½ pounds leeks (3 medium leeks)
3 tablespoons olive oil
1 teaspoon kosher salt
1½ pounds small potatoes, preferably yellow-fleshed
¼ teaspoon white pepper
1 teaspoon dried mint
1 teaspoon dried dill
1 cup hot water or vegetable broth
2 tablespoons lemon juice
Big pinch of saffron, crumbled
⅓ cup dried bread crumbs
Optional: lemon wedges

1. Preheat oven to 375°F. Trim roots and heaviest dark tops from leeks. Halve leeks lengthwise, then cut into 1-inch slices. Rinse in several changes of water; drain well.

2. Heat 1 tablespoon oil in heavy skillet. Add leeks and ½ teaspoon salt. Cook over moderate heat, stirring often, until leeks are softened, about 5 minutes. Meanwhile, cut potatoes into ½-inch slices.

3. Spread half the leeks in a 2-quart baking dish. Combine potatoes, remaining ½ teaspoon salt, pepper, ½ teaspoon *each* mint and dill, and ½ tablespoon oil; toss. Spread half over the leeks. Cover with remaining leeks, then top with remaining potatoes. Combine water, lemon juice, and saffron and pour over. Cover tightly with foil.

4. Bake in upper part of oven until vegetables are tender, about 1¼ hours. Meanwhile, mix crumbs, remaining ½ teaspoon *each* dill and mint, and remaining 1½ tablespoons oil, tossing to blend well.

5. Uncover dish and flatten mixture with spatula. Sprinkle evenly with the crumbs. Raise heat to 425°F. Bake until crisp and browned, about 15 minutes. Serve hot, warm, or at room temperature.

Serves 4

Leek Terrine with Horseradish Cream

With little fat, few ingredients, and minimal input of labor, you can assemble a fairly fancy presentation based on small leeks. These should be about the same size as the carrots so that they all line up and stack neatly.

> 9 small leeks (about 1½ pounds)
> 2 cups vegetable broth
> 1 cup light dry white wine
> 1 teaspoon kosher salt
> 1 teaspoon coriander seeds
> 4 medium carrots, peeled
> 1½ packets (about 3¼ teaspoons)
>   granulated gelatine
> ⅓ cup water

HORSERADISH CREAM

> About 1 tablespoon lemon juice
> 1½ tablespoons prepared horseradish
> ½ teaspoon sugar
> ½ cup sour half-and-half or sour cream
> Salt and white pepper
> 2 tablespoons chervil leaves or snipped dill

1. Trim leeks to about 10 inches. Insert knife about 1½ inches from root end, pull toward leaf end to halve each leek, keeping the base intact. Trim roots, without cutting into base. Swish leeks in water, gently separating layers to clean.

2. In very large skillet, combine broth, wine, salt, and coriander; bring to a boil. Add leeks and carrots, cover, and simmer gently until tender-soft (*not* al dente), about 25 to 30 minutes, turning several times with tongs.

3. Transfer vegetables to plate. Sprinkle gelatine over the water and let stand at least 2 minutes. Meanwhile, measure broth. Strain, if the crunch of whole coriander seeds doesn't appeal to you. Boil liquid to reduce to ¾ cup. Pour boiling broth over gelatine, stirring to mix.

4. Line a lightly oiled 9 × 5-inch loaf pan or baking dish with plastic wrap, allowing it to hang over all edges. Spoon in a little of the gelatine mixture. Arrange 3 leeks and a carrot on this, their bases at the same end. Spoon over more gelatine. Repeat, with bases at the other end, then add more gelatine. Repeat, with bases in opposite direction.

5. Chill until set, several hours or more. When set, fold plastic over top to cover.

6. Prepare cream: Blend 1 tablespoon lemon juice, the horseradish, and sugar. Gradually stir in sour cream. Adjust seasoning. Chill.

7. To serve: Lift terrine out of pan by picking up the plastic and set on cutting board. With very sharp serrated knife, cut into 8 slices. Set on individual plates with a scant tablespoon of cream and sprinkle of chervil or dill on each.

Serves 8

Leek Top and Ginger Broth with Vegetable Garnish

This is a handy, fat-free way to use up leek trimmings. Consider it a general guide, not a strict recipe. Cilantro or parsley stems are a pleasant addition, but not necessary. Add other aromatics: bits of celeriac, parsley root, parsnip, carrot, or dried mushrooms. Toss in shrimp shells for sweetness. Ignore the garnish and use the broth as a soup base; or freeze it for future soup-making.

> About 1 quart leek greens/trimmings
> 1 quart water
> ¼ cup sliced ginger (no need to peel)
> 2 celery stalks with leaves, sliced
> Sliced cilantro (coriander) or parsley stems
> About 1 teaspoon kosher salt
> 1 to 2 tablespoons lime juice
> 2 ounces snow peas
> 4 red radishes

1 small unwaxed cucumber (Oriental, Middle
    Eastern, or pickling type)
Greens from 1 scallion (green onion)
2 tablespoons whole cilantro or mint leaves

1. Slice leek greens. Rinse in several changes of water. Combine in pot with water, ginger, celery, cilantro stems, and ½ teaspoon salt. Simmer, covered, 30 to 45 minutes, to extract flavor. Strain out solids. Add lime juice and salt to taste.

2. Meanwhile, zip strings from snow peas. Cut pods into thin diagonal strips. Slice radishes into paper-thin rounds. Cut cucumber into tiny dice. Cut scallion green into hair-thin strips.

3. Bring broth to a boil. Stir in snow peas and cook just until tender, a minute or so. Add radishes, cucumber, scallion, and cilantro. Bring to a boil. Serve hot.

Serves 4 as a light first course

Pros Propose

The classic leek preparations—leek and potato soup, leeks vinaigrette and à la grecque—are well represented in cookbooks. Then there is *truly* classic à la grecque, **Leeks the Classic Way**, "a popular *mezé* since the days of Homer," writes Rosemary Barron in *Flavors of Greece*. Half-slit trimmed thin leeks and gently wash, keeping intact. Combine olive oil, crushed coriander seeds, bay leaves, and cracked pepper in wide skillet and simmer until fragrant. Add leeks, turning to coat. Blend aged red wine vinegar with half as much aromatic honey. Add, with currants. Gently simmer, covered, until leeks are just tender. Cool. Season and sprinkle with parsley.

Thickened yogurt sauce over leeks is as common in the Middle East as vinaigrette in France. To prepare **Leeks with Yogurt Sauce**: Simmer water, lemon juice, peppercorns, salt, coriander seeds, chopped scallions, and parsley in wide pan. Add partly slit, cleaned leeks and simmer, covered, until tender, about 20 minutes. Cool in liquid. Blend yogurt, egg yolks, lemon juice, salt, and pepper in heatproof bowl. Set over simmering water. Stir often until thickened, 10 to 15 minutes. Add pepper, fennel seeds, sumac powder, and

Dijon mustard. Drain leeks on towel. Arrange on plate and spoon over sauce (*Middle Eastern Cookery* by Arto der Haroutunian).

France has other classic leek dishes, such as **Leeks in Red Wine.** Susan Herrmann Loomis writes that "this rich and beguiling dish is as much a part of the history of the Périgord as are the caves of Lascaux and the walnut trees that dot the landscape. Simple, made with the most basic of farm ingredients, it forms part of the gastronomic memory of every Périgord farm family" (from *French Farmhouse Cookbook*). To prepare: Brown strips of slab bacon in large pan. Remove and reserve. Pour out fat; add goose fat or olive oil. Add ¼-inch slices of white of leek (at least 1 large leek per person) and small onions, halved and sliced. Cook until limp. Sprinkle with flour and stir until golden. Add red wine to cover. Boil, then remove from heat. Immediately flame to evaporate alcohol. Simmer gently until sauce is thick and leeks are soft. Add the bacon. Make 4 wells in the mixture; break an egg into each. Cook, covered, until eggs are done to taste.

Leeks in a rarefied French mode are the province of *The Natural Cuisine of Georges Blanc*. A simple and visually dramatic dish, it is typical of the chef's spare approach to haute cuisine. For **Clusters of Leeks with Beet Vinaigrette:** Puree cooked beets with vinegar. Strain through fine sieve. Add mustard, salt, and pepper; whisk in light oil. Cut cooked, well-drained slim leeks into ¼-inch coins. Set in a single layer on each plate to form a triangular shape (to resemble a grape cluster). Spoon sauce around; decorate with celery leaves.

Belgian Mashed Potatoes with Leeks (Stoemp met Prei) are as squooshy and rich as Blanc's dish is austere. Combine cubed potatoes with cold water and salt and simmer until tender. Drain; press through food mill. Meanwhile, cook halved, sliced light and white parts of leek in butter to wilt. Add heavy cream, chicken broth, salt, and nutmeg. Simmer, covered, 15 minutes. Drain, saving liquid. Boil liquid until thickened and flavorful. Mix with leeks and potatoes. Season and add cream and butter to taste (from *Everyone Eats Well in Belgium Cookbook* by Ruth Van Waerebeek).

Faith Willinger includes this lively **Penne Sauced with Leeks and Lemon** in her colorful collection of Italian recipes, *Red, White & Greens:* Slice a small piece of trimmed halved leek into hair-thin half-rings; toss with lemon juice and reserve. Boil halved trimmed leeks in salted water until soft. Remove with slotted spoon (reserve water). Refresh leeks in cold water; drain well. Puree in processor with minced lemon zest, chopped parsley, olive oil, and enough cooking water to make a light, smooth sauce. Season and pour into saucepan large enough to hold pasta. Cook penne in reserved water until three-quarters done. Drain, reserving some water. Add penne to sauce, with reserved marinated leek. Cook until pasta is tender and coated with sauce, adding more cooking water as needed. Add grated Parmesan and toss to melt. Serve at once.

American chef Daniel Bruce's unusual **Summer Leek Terrine** is made from layered strips of leek rather than the hard-to-clean cylinders. Cut roots and some white base from very large leeks; trim off as little green as possible. Cut apart dark and pale parts. Halve each cylinder lengthwise. Soak the two parts separately, sloshing and changing water until leeks are perfectly clean. Boil greens in salted water until tender. Refresh in cold water, drain, and pat dry. Simmer pale part in pink grapefruit juice, olive oil, and seasoning until tender; drain. Choose a terrine the same length as leeks. Alternate light and dark layers, seasoning and sprinkling with minced chervil and parsley. Pour in light vegetable aspic. Weight and refrigerate overnight.

Lettuce, Stem; or Celtuce

(*Lactuca sativa*, Augustana Group and Asparagina Group)

Also Chinese lettuce, asparagus lettuce, woh sun (Chinese)

length: 15-18 inches

On a rainy Saturday in November on Flushing's Main Street, these rusty-looking lettuces were being snatched up by hordes of shoppers as quickly as the bins could be refilled. "Chinese people love this," an elderly woman told me as I watched her heft four large "trees" into her bright pink grocery bag. She said she was going to make a salad with sweet-sour dressing. Because greens are rarely eaten raw in China, I assumed this to be a Western adaptation; but in the authoritative *Vegetables in South-East Asia,* Herklots described "a race of lettuce which originated in China in which the edible part is the thickened soft stem, which grows to 3 feet or more

becoming thick and tender. It has long been cultivated in China under the name woo chu. The tender young leaves are used in salads or as greens and the succulent stem is peeled and sliced and eaten raw, or cooked." However, most of China's crop of stem lettuce goes into Shanghai pickles (called "lettuce pickle" in Chinese groceries), according to *A Popular Guide to Chinese Vegetables* by Dahlen and Phillipps.

This subspecies of the plant we call lettuce is similar to lettuce, but with the priorities changed, as mentioned above: The thick, juicy central stem, the main subject, is crisp and pale as cucumber, with the texture of broccoli stem and the flavor of lettuce. The leaves are less significant; their flavor and texture suggest Boston and romaine lettuces, but stem lettuce is less sweet and refined than either of those.

In an odd turnaround, the plant breeder Peter Crisp, who developed a cultivar for the British market, discovered that there was more interest in using stem lettuce as a "baby leaf" for salads because of its "upright growth, and good flavour and texture at an early stage" (and a desire to throw everything into a salad bowl instead of cooking it, if you ask me).

A British grower, John Organ, writes (in *Rare Vegetables for Garden and Table*) that "this form of lettuce was first listed by American seedsmen in the 1890's under the name of Asparagus Lettuce. In 1942 Messrs. W. Atlee Burpee Co. of Philadelphia reintroduced celtuce, seed of which was sent to them in 1938 from Western China, near the Tibetan border, by the Rev. Carter D. Holton, then a missionary." The name "celtuce" is a creation of American marketing—the muddling force behind many common names—coined to describe the "celery- and lettuce-like qualities of the plant." The vegetable is decidedly not a cross between celery and lettuce, as is sometimes written, nor does it have any similarity to celery as I know it.

William Woys Weaver believes that stem lettuce was here earlier than the 1890s. It "came to the attention of American horticulturists in the 1850s and was grown by a small circle of specialists since that time," he writes in *Heirloom Vegetable Gardening*. "It was introduced to them by the Mennonite plant collector Jacob B. Garber (1800–1886) of Lancaster County, Pennsylvania," who obtained it from a collector in Illinois. According to Weaver, Garber was the one who figured out which parts were choice.

BASIC USE: Although both stem and leaves are edible, the stem is prime, in my opinion. After separating the two parts, the stem must be pared deeply before using, raw or cooked. The stems can be neatly cut into circles, semicircles, cubes, julienne strips, or diagonals to be served raw, as part of a vegetable platter or a composed salad, as you might use kohlrabi, cucumber, or jícama—although the taste and texture are different.

Or cook the prepared stems: Simmer in soup or stir-fry until they lose their raw crunch, a few minutes at most. They still retain a lovely crunch and turn a pretty celery green.

Use the leaves in mixed salad. Cut larger ones into thin strips. Or cook the leaves. Small, pale ones need only be barely wilted in a stir-fry or sauté; they keep their flavor and crunch and do not get floppy. Use large leaves as wrappers for foods to be braised or steamed; or cut into ribbons to stir into broth or stir-fry.

SELECTION: Choose long, well-trimmed (naked) stems with fairly perky upper leaves. Do not be daunted by brown leaf scars, which are normal. Discoloration occurs as soon as the leaves are removed.

STORAGE: Refrigerate no more than a few days, plastic-wrapped. If the leaves look limp and you want to use them for salad, they are easily revived: Trim from stalk and soak 1 minute in a lukewarm bath. Shake off most moisture, enclose in an airtight container, and refrigerate. For longer storage of the whole plant: Trim base of stem without removing leaves. Soak 5 minutes in lukewarm water. Shake off water; wrap in a paper, then plastic, and refrigerate.

PREPARATION: Snap leaves from stem. Wash in several changes of water. Spin-dry. Separate smaller upper and larger lower leaves for different purposes in most dishes.

Pare off the bitter, pale fibrous covering from the stem. Only the pale green interior is edible. Then cut circles, half-circles, dice, julienne strips, thin diagonal slices, or anything that suits the dish.

Salad of Stem Lettuce and Clementines

Fresh-tasting and bright, this emerald and orange salad suits grilled fish or roasted pork or duck; or serve after a tofu main dish.

**2 medium heads stem lettuce
    (1 to 1½ pounds each)**
1 small bunch cilantro (coriander)
2 scallions (green onions)
**4 small-medium Clementines or other small
    seedless mandarins or tangerines**
¼ teaspoon kosher salt
½ tablespoon lemon juice
**1 tablespoon mild vegetable oil, such as
    grapeseed or canola**
2 tablespoons olive oil

1. Remove leaves from lettuce stems. Choose a few handfuls of the smallest ones; rinse, spin-dry, then chill. Refrigerate remaining leaves for another use. Pare off all fibrous pale (and bitter) peel from stems. Cut stems crosswise into ⅛-inch-thick slices (about 2 cups).

2. Nip off enough cilantro leaves to make ¼ cup, very tightly packed. Rinse and spin-dry. Slice enough scallion greens to make ¼ cup lightly packed (reserve white part for another use). Scrub 1 Clementine and grate ¼ teaspoon zest.

3. Combine zest, salt, and lemon juice in blender or small food processor. Halve the zested Clementine and squeeze juice. Add 1 tablespoon to blender, with cilantro and scallions; whiz to a puree. With motor running, gradually add the oils. Process to a creamy dressing.

4. Blend half the dressing with the lettuce stems. Refrigerate (can be prepared as much as a day ahead). Add remaining Clementine juice to the dressing. Chill.

5. To serve: Pare remaining Clementines, trimming off all pith. Slice thin. Arrange in ring on one large or four salad plates, with lettuce stems in center. Tuck reserved small leaves around. Spoon remaining dressing over Clementines.

Serves 4

Sauté of Stem Lettuce and Shrimp

Tender pink shrimp and juicy celadon stem slices, matched in size and curve, make a pleasing pair. While the few elements are not sauced, the leaves provide enough moisture to prevent sticking. This fast, fresh, understated main dish needs no more than a bed of aromatic white rice. Use smooth, tender young ginger if available, doubling the quantity.

> About ¾ pound medium shrimp in the shell
>   (or ½ pound peeled)
> ½ tablespoon cornstarch
> 1 tablespoon medium-dry sherry or Madeira
> 1 teaspoon Dijon mustard
> 1 medium scallion (green onion), cut into
>   very fine slices

> 1 stem lettuce (about 1½ pounds)
> 1 tablespoon vegetable oil
> 1 teaspoon hair-thin ginger strands
> ½ teaspoon sugar
> ¼ teaspoon kosher salt

1. Peel shrimp. Blend cornstarch and sherry. Add mustard. Toss with shrimp and scallion. Set aside at room temperature.

2. Pull off lettuce leaves. Rinse, then spin-dry. Selecting small, pale leaves, cut enough into 2-inch pieces to make 2½ well-packed cups. Refrigerate remainder for another use. Peel lettuce stem thoroughly; halve lengthwise. Cut crosswise into ¼-inch slices.

3. Heat oil in a pan wide enough to hold shrimp and stems in a single layer with room to spare. Add ginger and toss a moment. Add stem slices, sugar, and salt and toss until slices just begin to lose their crunch.

4. Add shrimp and spread in a single layer. Reduce heat a bit and cook, turning once, until pink on both sides—about 2 minutes. Add sliced leaves and toss just until they barely begin to wilt, about 1 minute.

Serves 2

Pros Propose

I have not discovered stem lettuce outside Chinese cuisine—except in the kitchen of Sylvia Thompson, cook and gardener nonpareil, who seems to grow *every* vegetable that Southern California's climate can. For her **California/Chinese Celtuce Salad:** Cut peeled stem lettuce into julienne strips. Pull a zester along carrots to make long wisps, or shred fine. Combine both with thin-sliced green onions. Blend peanut oil, low-sodium soy sauce, orange juice, rice vinegar, and toasted sesame seeds. Pour over vegetables and toss well. Chill until serving time (from *The Kitchen Garden Cookbook*).

Stem Lettuce and Chicken are typically stir-fried in China: Remove, rinse, and spin-dry lettuce leaves. Peel lettuce stem and cut into julienne. Thin-slice boned and skinned chicken breasts. Marinate briefly in soy sauce, cornstarch, and rice wine. Stir-fry minced ginger in vegetable oil. Add chicken and toss to whiten. Add lettuce stem and stir-fry a few minutes until tender. Add leaves and toss to barely wilt. Season with salt, pepper, and sugar. Add a touch of chicken stock.

According to Ken Hom, stem lettuce is found primarily in the north and west of China, its leaves cooked in soups, its stems pickled or used in spicy stir-fries. For **Stem Lettuce with Cloud Ears:** Soak cloud ears to rehydrate. Rinse, drain, and reserve. Peel stem lettuce and cut into thin diagonal slices. Stir-fry chopped fresh ginger, garlic, and scallions a moment. Add cloud ears and lettuce stems; stir-fry 1 minute. Add chilli bean paste, rice wine, light and dark soy, sugar, and salt. Stir-fry 1 minute; moisten with water. Cook until tender, a few minutes longer. Add roasted, ground Sichuan pepper (from *The Taste of China*).

Lobster Mushroom *(Hypomyces lactifluorum)*

Hypomyces lactifluorum is exceptional for several reasons: its brilliant hue (see its gill side at the upper right in the photo), its sole common name, and the fact that it is not a mushroom. It is a sandpapery mold-like fungus that covers mushrooms. It grows throughout North America (apparently not in Europe) and parasitizes certain *Russula* and *Lactarius* species. David W. Fischer and Alan E. Bessette, authors of *Edible Wild Mushrooms of North America,* observe that "the mushrooms known to serve as host species are normally unpalatable," which is "rather odd, when you think about it: something that's edible only if it *does* look moldy!" Although old field guides "recommend caution to those who would sample mushrooms parasitized by this colorful and unusual species . . . there is no evidence whatsoever to justify this concern," stress Fischer and Bessette—as do other experts.

Its oddities notwithstanding, lobster mushroom (the polite name for both the encapsulating fungus and its prey), is among the most popular of the wild bunch, to judge by chefs' comments. Crisp, solid, cinnabar-edged slices are curiously unmushroomy and intrigue even those who do not usually fancy fungi. Chef Greg Higgins, who has long worked on the Pacific Coast, says that "in the Northwest, the lobster has big name recognition and big appeal." He attributes the appeal to "that ridiculous name, which makes a mental-culinary association with lobster, to diners' curiosity about all wild mushrooms, and to the fact that people just plain seem to love the lobster mushroom!"

It is likely that color and texture are the attractions (the rough-textured surface may be flaming or rusty to brilliant red; the interior is smooth white), because this mushroom is surprisingly bland—like cremini with a hint of woods and bitterness. Its size depends upon the host, as does its shape, but it is most often trumpet-like. Ranging from an ounce to a pound, the mushrooms barely shrink or change color when cooked: They remain firm and resilient, and darken and brown only slightly.

BASIC USE: Lobster mushrooms are firm and dry. They need fat and moisture in cooking. Braise or simmer in soups. Stir into risotto. Dice and sauté-braise

⅓ **actual size**

for stuffing, for topping, or to add to ragoûts. Young, moist specimens can be sliced, marinated, and grilled. "Lobster mushrooms really make the grade on vegan menus," says chef Higgins. "They take in so much flavor without getting lost."

SELECTION: Lobster mushrooms appear from midsummer into the fall. Higgins checks their condition this way: "Squeeze the stems hard. If there is any 'give' or you hear a crunchy noise, the mushroom is decayed or eaten. If you're not sure, cut it in half. They usually have nothing wrong, but when they're wormy, they're totally wormy." It is usual for the cap tops to be scruffy (see photo) while the undersides are uniform and orange—somewhat like coarse, deep orange chanterelles with blurred gills.

Gary Lincoff, author of numerous mushroom guides, advises that lobsters from the Pacific Northwest, although abundant and large, may be woodier and tougher than the smaller, less copious East Coast ones. I have found large and small to be equally tough or equally tender. For a more colorful presentation, choose small mushrooms, which have a larger proportion of orange per slice.

PREPARATION: Clean attentively. Use a strong spray of water to loosen sand (some lobster mushrooms grow along the coast) and debris, which can be considerable. Some caps need to be scrubbed with a toothbrush, then dried on towels. Quarter or halve caps to check for insects; pare away infested parts and dark or woody areas, then cut colorful slices (for a starring role) from the bright, pretty gills and thin-slice or dice the interior pale part. Halve stems lengthwise, then bias-cut half-moons.

Lobster Mushroom Risotto

For a special vegetarian dinner, this is the mushroom to use. Crisp, meaty, with paprika-red edges, the slices are oddly unmushroomy and most likable. The broth turns a saffron hue from the mushrooms, which in turn prettily tints the rice. For risotto rice, arborio type is most common, but baldo, carnaroli, and vialone nano are all worthy.

> About 1 pound lobster mushrooms
> 3 inner celery stalks and leaves
> 2 medium shallots
> ¼ teaspoon dried dill
> ¼ teaspoon dried tarragon
> ¼ teaspoon dried thyme
> 6 cups unsalted or lightly salted mushroom
>   and/or vegetable broth
> About 1½ teaspoons kosher salt (reduce if
>   broth is salted)
> 2 tablespoons butter
> ¼ teaspoon white pepper
> 1 tablespoon walnut or olive oil
> 1½ cups Italian rice for risotto
> ⅓ cup Madeira or medium-dry sherry
> Lemon juice
> About 3 tablespoons fine-slivered
>   celery leaves

1. As necessary, rinse and brush mushrooms to remove debris. Halve or quarter; check for insects or holes and cut out those parts and any darker or woody ones. Cut large bite-size slices from brighter gill and stem sections, following the natural form. Cut paler parts into ¾-inch dice. Mince celery stalks and leaves. Mince shallots.

2. Combine mushroom slices in saucepan with dill, tarragon, thyme, broth, 1 teaspoon salt, and ½ tablespoon butter. Bring to a boil. Reduce heat and simmer until mushrooms are almost tender, about 10 minutes (but timing varies). Maintain below a simmer.

3. Meanwhile, melt 1 tablespoon butter in heavy pot over medium-low heat. Add shallots and minced celery and stir a few minutes to soften. Add mushroom dice, ¼ teaspoon salt, and white pepper; cover, and cook over low heat until mushrooms are almost tender, about 5 minutes, stirring now and then. Uncover, raise heat slightly, and stir until slightly golden.

4. Add oil and rice and stir about 3 minutes. Add Madeira and stir until evaporated. Add 1 cup broth and mushrooms, and stir a few minutes, until broth is almost absorbed, adjusting heat to keep it at a good bubble. Continue to add broth and mushrooms in ½-cup increments, stirring often. When a portion has nearly been absorbed, add the next. In 15 to 18 minutes, the rice will be just nicely al dente (if at this point the broth looks skimpy, add a little water to it).

5. Off heat, stir in remaining ½ tablespoon butter, with enough broth to make a slightly soupy consistency. Season with lemon juice, salt, and pepper. Scoop into warmed dishes and sprinkle with slivered celery leaves.

Serves 4 as a main course,
6 to 8 as first course

Pros Propose

Fernando Divina used to run through bushels of local lobster mushrooms at his restaurants in Oregon, prime mushroom territory. With small, moist specimens, he prepared **Grilled Lobster Mushrooms:** Clean mushrooms and split to examine the deep pockets that can hide forest bits; then cut into ½-inch slices, following the mushroom's natural form. Marinate in olive oil with rosemary and blanched garlic cloves. Grill over a moderate fire a few minutes per side. With large lobster mushrooms, Divina prepared **Tamales de Hongo:** Gently stew diced mushrooms in corn oil; add onion, then epazote ("which grows thick along our shoreline"). Cook slowly until tender. Cool. Place on masa dough (made with duck confit fat) on corn husks. Top with epazote and close husks. Steam. Serve with a light tomatillo sauce as a first course, or with a rich duck-stock sauce and roasted duck for a main course.

Chef Jerry Traunfeld also marinates small mushrooms, but he roasts and then chills them "for a change-of-pace appetizer with a distinctive texture." For his **Lobster Mushrooms Vinaigrette:** Cut mushrooms into bite-size rectangles. Toss with olive oil, garlic, and thyme, then marinate briefly. Roast until edges brown slightly, about 5 minutes at 450°F. Cool. Toss with thyme mustard, sherry vinegar, and fine olive oil. Chill overnight. Serve with purslane or pepper cress snips and slices of grilled brioche.

Chef Greg Higgins prepares an elaborate dish of local Pacific ingredients: **Columbia River Sturgeon with a Reduction of Corn and Lobster Mushrooms.** To prepare broth: Gently stew onions, lobster mushroom peelings, and shrimp shells in oil. Grill corn; cut off kernels, catching juice. Add juice, corncobs, and water to broth pot. Simmer, strain, then reduce. Gently cook slices of lobster mushroom in oil with shallots and garlic. Add some reduced broth and cook until tender. Rub thick square cuts of sturgeon with coarse-ground toasted juniper, fennel seed, coriander, white pepper, and salt. Sear under broiler, then finish cooking in oven. Set sturgeon on small corn puddings. Add butter to heated reduced broth, season with salt, pepper, and lemon juice, and spoon around fish. Arrange lobster mushroom slices and corn kernels around, with small sliced tomatoes tossed with olive oil.

Loofah, Angled (*Luffa acutangula*)

Also angled luffa, ridged gourd, Chinese okra, silk squash, tori or toray (Indian), see gua and variations (Chinese), patola (Philippine)

However exotic in appearance and name, this curious cucurbit is as mild and fresh-tasting as a simple summer squash. Slim and lightweight, tapered and graceful, it is decorated with sharp ridges that develop as the fruit matures, becoming rough and leathery with age. Young loofah has a texture and flavor between zucchini and cucumber and a clear, uniform emerald color. When it is quick-cooked, the flesh turns soft and pale green while the edges remain lightly crisp.

Probably native to India, loofah remains popular there and throughout much of the Far East. R. W. Robinson and D. S. Decker-Walters write in *Cucurbits* that "immature fruits of the domesticated varieties . . . are harvested when about 10 cm long, and then are boiled, peeled or intact, and used in curries. . . . Leaves are also edible and used as greens, and mature seeds are sometimes roasted."

Another loofah species, *Luffa cylindrica* or smooth loofah, is occasionally available at the same Asian markets that offer the angled type. Outside, it resembles an overblown zucchini; inside, a wet marshmallow. It hefts like a plastic bag filled with jelly and blackens on contact. Culinarily, I have thus far found it inscrutable; and in fact, according to *Cucurbits,* it is better known as "sponge gourd, because its mature fibrous endocarp is often used for that purpose. These 'environmentally friendly' sponges have become very popular in the USA, which imports millions of them each year" from Korea, China, Guatemala, and Colombia.

BASIC USE: Angled loofah can be stir-fried, stirred into soup, hollowed and stuffed, or stewed in rich sauces. Sauté diagonal slices with rehydrated shiitake strips, ham slivers, dried tomato snippets, or other firm foods that supply textural and color contrast. Fill lengths of hollowed loofah with stuffing, steam them, then slice across to serve with sauce. Chef and author Longteine de Monteiro says that loofah (ronon in her native Cambodia) is typically simmered in soup with bamboo shoots and preserved fish. Although associated

length: 10–14 inches

with Asian cuisines, loofah takes kindly to Western herbs and seasonings—the ones you'd choose for cucumber, zucchini, or yellow squash.

SELECTION AND STORAGE: Knowledgeable selection is critical with loofah, which loses its charm when it is too large or anything but perfectly fresh. Choose gourds that are relatively small, hard, and evenly green. De Monteiro recommends the heaviest ones. They are extremely perishable and must be used quickly. To store, wrap in toweling, then enclose in airtight containers or plastic bags—for no more than a few days.

PREPARATION: To prepare for cooking, rinse, trim ends, then select your style: For a soft interior and crunchy (if slightly rough) edges, use a swivel peeler to zip off the "fins," leaving thin green strips of peel. For uniformly pale green and soft-textured squash, remove all the peel. For most dishes, cut sharply angled slices ¼ to ½ inch thick. Halve those on the "bell" (thicker end) so that the pieces are more or less the same size and will cook evenly. To prepare for stuffing, cut 2- to 3-inch lengths and hollow carefully with a zucchini or apple corer.

Sautéed Angled Loofah and Shiitake

Chewy shiitake strips and silky squash ovals are paired for a light side dish for seafood or poultry, or to complement a mixed noodle or grain dish for a vegetable meal. Don't "economize" on skimpy dried black mushrooms (aka shiitake, Chinese, or Oriental mushrooms). Buy the fat, fleshy high-quality ones sold in fine Asian markets. If thin ones are all you can find, use a dozen of them.

8 thick dried shiitake
2 tablespoons peanut or corn oil
1 pound angled loofah (3 medium loofahs)
½ teaspoon kosher salt
½ tablespoon minced garlic
Optional: Japanese "plum" (ume) vinegar
    or balsamic vinegar

1. Break off shiitake stems (reserve for another use). Put caps in 2-cup measure. Pour over boiling water to half-fill. Stir in ½ tablespoon oil. Set a dish or cup inside to submerge caps. Let stand until hydrated throughout—at least ½ hour (timing varies with thickness), or as long as convenient. Drain. (Reserve liquid for soup or broth.) Cut caps into thin strips.

2. With swivel peeler, remove "fins" from squash (or remove all peel for a softer effect). On sharp diagonal, cut into ¼-inch slices; toss with ½ tablespoon oil.

3. Set large sauté pan over moderately high heat. Add remaining 1 tablespoon oil. Add mushrooms and toss to brown slightly, about 2 minutes, sprinkling with salt. Reduce heat somewhat, add garlic, and toss. Add loofah and cook until tender, tossing often, 3 to 4 minutes.

4. Season, adding a touch of vinegar if desired. Serve hot.

Serves 4 as a side dish

Angled Loofah and Peas in Aromatic Coconut Milk

Mild and creamy, sweetly scented, this easy-to-assemble dish can be sauce and vegetable for poached fish or grilled poultry, or topping for mixed grains when a vegetable meal is preferred. Pale green loofah absorbs the coconut milk as it softens and turns translucent; the barely cooked peas retain their shape and bright color.

About 1 pound small angled loofah
    (approximately 4 loofahs)
½ pound fresh peas (½ cup shelled peas)
3 slim scallions (green onions)
½ cup vegetable or chicken broth
1 cup coconut milk
½ teaspoon kosher salt
1 teaspoon anise seeds, ground or crushed
Optional: big pinch of saffron
2 tablespoons slivered cilantro (coriander)
    or mint leaves

1. Cut tips from loofahs. With swivel peeler, zip off all the ridges, leaving the green between. Slice slimmest parts into ½-inch rounds. Halve the rest lengthwise and cut into ½-inch slices. Shell peas. Slice scallions thin.

2. In heavy saucepan, combine loofahs, scallions, broth, coconut milk, salt, anise, and optional saffron. Stir, cover, and bring to a boil. Uncover and simmer gently, stirring a few times, until squash is tender, about 10 minutes.

3. Raise heat and boil until liquid thickens a bit. Stir in peas and cook another minute or two. Add cilantro. Season.

Serves 4

Shrimp-Stuffed Angled Loofah with Tart Sauce

Lightweight and elegant, this pretty pink and green presentation makes a fine starter for a multicourse meal. Since chances are good that you'll be in an Asian market for the loofah, pick up fresh water chestnuts there as well.

1 tablespoon thin-sliced ginger

3 scallions (green onions), white and green parts
  sliced and separated

1¼ teaspoons kosher salt

3 tablespoons dry or medium-dry sherry

1 tablespoon cornstarch

1 egg

¼ teaspoon white pepper

1 teaspoon grated lime zest

½ pound shelled shrimp

1 cup peeled, sliced water chestnuts
  (fresh or canned)

4 comparatively straight loofahs (1½ to 2 inches
  in diameter and about 1 foot long)

SAUCE

½ cup tomato puree (seeded, strained tomatoes)

⅓ cup lime juice

About 1½ tablespoons sugar

About 1 tablespoon mild vinegar

1 tablespoon cornstarch

¼ cup dry or medium-dry sherry

⅓ cup water

2 teaspoons butter

1½ teaspoons grated ginger

Optional: minced cilantro leaves and
  thin-sliced scallion greens

1. Combine sliced ginger, white part of scallions, salt, sherry, cornstarch, egg, pepper, zest, and half the shrimp in food processor. Whirl to a fine puree. Scrape into a bowl.

2. Place water chestnuts and scallion greens in processor; chop fine. Add remaining shrimp and pulse to a coarse texture. Add to bowl and blend thoroughly. Chill. (Can be prepared a day ahead.)

3. With swivel peeler, zip fins from loofahs. Trim stem ends and halve each crosswise. With zucchini or apple corer (see Note), remove central pith, leaving a thin layer of flesh. Stuff with shrimp mixture.

4. Set loofahs on steamer rack over boiling water. Cover and steam until filling is firm and squash just tender, about 10 minutes.

5. Meanwhile, prepare sauce: Combine tomato puree, lime juice, 1½ tablespoons sugar, 1 tablespoon vinegar, cornstarch, sherry, water, butter, and 1 teaspoon ginger in small pan. Cook over fairly low heat, stirring often, until mixture boils up and thickens. Add remaining ½ teaspoon ginger and stir a moment longer. Taste and add vinegar, salt, and sugar as needed.

6. To serve, cut each loofah section into 4 or 5 slices. Spoon ¼ cup hot sauce onto each individual serving plate. Divide slices among the plates. Sprinkle with optional cilantro and scallion.

Serves 6 as a first course

Note: If you don't have a corer and want to make "boats" instead of slices, prepare this way: Halve each loofah crosswise, then lengthwise, and scoop out a trough in each with a grapefruit spoon or melon ball cutter. Mound filling in boats. Steam, slice as desired, and serve as above.

Pros Propose

"The unique property of silk squash is that it becomes quite sweet and soft, whether cooked alone, with chicken, or vegetables, and whether it's stir-fried or made into soup," writes Eileen Yin-Fei Lo. For her **Silk Squash and Fresh Mushroom Soup:** Stir-fry sliced ginger with salt. Add lightly pared loofah cut into angled ¾-inch slices and halved small mushrooms; stir-fry briefly. Add vegetable stock and water, cover, and cook until squash is tender. Raise heat and season with rice wine and sesame oil (*From the Earth*).

Another Chinese recipe, **Green Loofah with Prawns,** although slightly more elaborate, still lets the mild-mannered gourd speak for itself: Marinate prawns in ginger, soy sauce, sugar, and sherry. Stir-fry and set aside. Cut peeled loofah into ¼-inch diagonals and stir-fry until soft. Add sliced water chestnuts and bamboo shoots. Return prawns to wok with oyster sauce, white pepper, and cornstarch slurry; bring to a boil. Add roasted cashews (from *Every Grain of Rice: A Taste of Our Chinese Childhood in America* by Ellen Blonder and Annabel Low).

Crunchy dried cloud (or wood) ears provide just the right textural contrast to the soft squash in **Stir-Fried Cloud Ears and Luffa:** Soak small cloud ears in cold water until softened and expanded; drain. Trim hard spots. Cut peeled loofah into 2-inch sections, then cut lengthwise into ¼-inch-thick slices. Blend thin soy sauce, rice wine, sesame oil, sugar, white pepper, and salt; reserve. Heat oil in skillet; add sliced ginger and shredded scallion and toss. Add more oil and loofah and stir-fry 30 seconds. Add cloud ears and reserved seasoning mixture and toss just until tender (from *The Wisdom of the Chinese Kitchen* by Grace Young).

Similarly stir-fried, but assertively Cambodian in seasoning, is chef Longteine de Monteiro's **Pork and Loofah:** Stir-fry smashed garlic. Add pork slices, fish sauce, and sugar; toss briefly. Add peeled loofah, angle-cut into 1-inch pieces, and cook until soft. Add scallions and plenty of pepper.

Lotus, Lotus "Root" (*Nelumbo nucifera*)

Also Asian lotus, renkon (Japanese), leen ngau (Chinese)

The lovely lotus, native to a wide swath of Asia, is celebrated extensively in the painting, sculpture, religion, and mythology of India, China, and Egypt, as well as the culinary arts of those and other countries. Fresh and dried, whole and ground, the elegant aquatic plant is a generous one, edible from its bulbous base to the very stamen of its pink or white flowers.

Fresh stems, young leaves, and petals are used raw and cooked in Southeast Asia; dried mature leaves become a wrapping for parcels to be steamed or baked—notably the mud-packed beggar's chicken of China. Seeds are snacked on fresh or sugar-crystallized, ground to a paste to fill confections, or cooked into sweet soup. The tuberous underwater parts are sliced into chawan mushi, a popular Japanese savory egg cus-

tard; folded into vegetable patties (kofta), bean dishes (dal), and fritters in India; and soy-glazed in Korea.

Although leaves and stems appear occasionally in American markets, the only part sold fresh with any regularity is so-called "lotus root," a confusing term indeed. Botanically, the genus *Lotus* refers to some 100 species of the family of Leguminosae—not one of which is the plant in question: *Nelumbo nucifera* (formerly classified with the water lily family, *Nymphaeaceae,* but now belonging to the *Nelumbonaceae*). This edible portion is not a root but a rhizome (thickened stem) from which the true roots grow.

However theoretical the taxonomy, the sausage-shaped links themselves are solid and real. Cut apart and pared, the beige, woody flesh is crisp and pleasingly tacky. When sliced, the rhizomes, which are pierced with internal tunnels, reveal a remarkable petal pattern. Mild and delicately earthy, they suggest jícama and water chestnut.

BASIC USE: Surprisingly versatile, lotus suits dishes from soup through dessert, as a decorative element, thickener, or conveyor of crunch and light sweetness. Boiling seems to be marginally more effective than steaming—which takes longer and does not prevent darkening. Blanch slices to include in composed salads, to use as garnish, or to toss into stir-fries. Stir into clear soups to add a light slickness and visual appeal. Braise slices in stews or with roasts. For sweets, cook in light syrup to add to compotes of soft fruits such as lychee, mango, cherry, or citrus.

SELECTION: Lotus "root," usually imported from China, is sold in Asian markets. Because it is imported, its seasonality is dictated by its provenance. Local markets may be able to advise you about availability. Some stores manage to have it nearly year-round.

Choose pale, relatively blemish-free links with no pitting and little or no darkening (but don't worry about mud and a few spots, which are normal). Size does not seem to affect tenderness, so select what suits the dish. Narrow links usually make prettier, more manageable slices. Look for lotus with cut ends that are juicy and sticky, not dried.

STORAGE: Refrigerate lotus in damp paper towels. Or immerse in water. Either way, it should last 1 to 2 weeks, if fresh when purchased.

When lotus will be used as garnish or in salads (not in cooked dishes), it can be stored thus: Drop slices into boiling, salted water; boil 1 minute. Drain, run under cold water. Toss with lemon juice. Refrigerate, tightly covered, for up to a week.

PREPARATION: Cut apart links. Trim off "necks" and bristly roots, if any. Scrub with vegetable brush. Pare skin with swivel peeler. For most dishes, you'll want to cut thin slices by hand, processor, or mandoline. Despite warnings to the contrary, I find lotus less susceptible to browning than most potatoes. But if you'll be preparing lotus in advance, keep slices pale and moist by storing them in water.

Salad of Lotus, Oranges, Avocado, and Water Cress

Creamy avocado contrasts with crisp lotus rounds, and sweet oranges with bitter water cress, in a salad that looks as good as it tastes. Pear or raspberry vinegar is nice here, but any gentle fruity vinegar will suit. Lotus that is narrow in diameter makes the best presentation, as slices can be kept whole. Serve alongside seafood or pork.

About ½ pound lotus
2 medium navel oranges
¾ teaspoon kosher salt
3 tablespoons fruit vinegar
Optional: sugar
Fine-ground white pepper
⅓ cup delicate olive oil (or mix olive oil with grapeseed or corn oil)
1 medium-large avocado (preferably Florida type; see page 38)
2 bunches water cress, trimmed, rinsed, and separated into sprigs

1. Cut apart lotus links. Trim off "necks" and bristly roots, if any. Scrub with vegetable brush. Pare skin with swivel peeler. Cut into thin slices (if lotus is of large diameter, first halve lengthwise). Drop into boiling salted water. Boil just until raw taste disappears, about 1 minute. Drain and refresh in cold water. Drain and spread on a towel.

2. Scrub 1 orange. Coarsely grate zest; put into a small jar. Pare all peel and pith from both oranges. Halve oranges lengthwise, then cut into thin crosswise slices, saving any juice. Add juice and vinegar to zest, then add sugar and pepper to taste. Add oil and shake to blend. Toss half the dressing with lotus. Cover and chill until serving time (can be refrigerated overnight).

3. Halve, pit, peel, and thin-slice avocado. Toss cress with remaining dressing. Arrange on plates. Arrange orange, avocado, and lotus over all.

Serves 4 as a first course or side dish

Sweet-Spiced Pork Loin Braised with Lotus Rounds

Lotus is a fussless and fabulous foil for pork roast, emerging crisp and golden from the braising bath. Purchase the loin untied so that you can trim the fat and season the meat deeply. For maximum seasoning power, marinate several days. The petal-like shape of shiny star anise "flowers" magically mimics the pattern formed by the channels in the lotus. It is an inimitable addition to the spice shelf—and lasts and lasts.

    2 teaspoons kosher salt
    2 star anise "flowers"
    4 bay leaves
    1 teaspoon peppercorns
    3 garlic cloves, minced
    1½ tablespoons brown sugar
    2 tablespoons brandy
    2 tablespoons vegetable oil
    3¼-pound boneless pork loin, *not* tied
    2½ pounds lotus (about 4 links)
    1½ cups fresh orange juice
    1 bunch mizuna or water cress, trimmed,
       rinsed, and dried

1. In spice mill, grind together salt, star anise, bay leaves, and pepper to fine consistency. Combine in small bowl with garlic, brown sugar, brandy, and 1 tablespoon oil.

2. Trim most fat from meat and stab all over with skewer. Set on large sheet of parchment or waxed paper. Coat evenly with spices. Tie with string to make compact cylinder. Wrap in paper, then aluminum foil. Refrigerate 1 to 3 days, as convenient.

3. Set oven to 325°F. Remove wrappings from loin and pat it dry. In heavy non-aluminum casserole large enough to hold lotus and meat, brown pork over moderate heat in remaining 1 tablespoon oil.

4. Meanwhile, cut apart lotus links. Trim off "necks" and bristly roots, if any. Scrub with vegetable brush. Pare skin with swivel peeler. Cut into rounds about ⅛ inch thick.

5. Drain fat from meat. Surround pork with lotus. Add orange juice. Cover and set in oven. Cook about an hour, basting once or twice, until meat registers 155°F on a thermometer (timing will vary depending upon thickness). Transfer to board and cover with foil. Allow to rest (up to an hour) before carving.

6. To serve, slice pork and arrange on warm platter. Heat lotus in pan juices. Arrange slices around meat; surround with greens. Spoon over juices.

Serves 6

Pros Propose

"Crunchy, sweet, and possessing the beautiful look of a wheel spoke with dewdrops, [lotus] is revered by Chinese Buddhists for its purity of flavor and color in spite of birth in a muddy bog," writes Barbara Tropp in *China Moon Cookbook,* which includes these **Lemon-Pickled Lotus Rounds:** Blanch thin-sliced peeled lotus; drain. Refresh in ice water, drain, and chill. Combine rice vinegar, sugar, chilli flakes, salt, pepper, lemon zest strips, and ginger julienne in a non-aluminum pot. Bring to a boil. Arrange lotus in wide-mouthed jars. Fill with hot brine. Cool. Cap and refrigerate a few days or more before serving as pickles.

Lemon and ginger season a very different contemporary Japanese salad, **Lotus Root Flower with Sweet Lemon-Ginger Dressing:** Briefly soak thin-sliced peeled lotus root in vinegared water. Drain, then simmer in lightly vinegared water with mirin until slightly wilted but still crunchy. Drain. Arrange on a platter dotted with peeled, seeded, and chopped Fuyu-type persimmon and cooked black soybeans. Tuck perilla (shiso) leaves around the edge. Blend minced ginger, lemon juice, and mirin; pour over. Serve, or mellow for a few hours (from *The Vegetarian Table: Japan* by Victoria Wise).

Chef Susanna Foo serves a non-traditional **Lotus Salad with Chinese Vinaigrette:** Soak go chi (dried red wolfberries) briefly in water to swell. Drain; rinse. Bring berries to a boil with water, and orange and lemon juices. Off heat, add brandy. Cool, then refrigerate. Prepare dressing with the wolfberry mixture, rice vinegar, olive oil, fresh coriander, chervil, salt, and pepper. Pour over blanched, lemon juice-sprinkled lotus slices. Serve the pinkened slices over bitter greens and Belgian endive.

Chef Foo also prepares traditional **Rice-Stuffed**

Lotus, "which may seem plain, but lotus releases a subtle flavor into the rice," she explains: Soak glutinous (sweet) rice in water for about 4 hours; drain. Trim and peel lotus. Using a chopstick, stuff the lotus tunnels with rice. Set on pan and sprinkle with sugar water. Steam until tender to taste, at least an hour. Slice.

For **Crisp Lotus Garnish Slices,** Foo dries thin slices on towels for at least ½ hour, then deep-fries. Chef Gray Kunz suggests an alternative that is low-calorie and long-lasting: Flatten thin-sliced lotus between professional flexible baking sheets (to prevent curling), then dry out thoroughly in low oven. Store airtight.

Pumpkin and Lotus Root Stew is a warming main dish from *New World Chinese Cooking* by Bill Jones and Stephen Wong: Soak dried Chinese black mushrooms in boiling water to just cover. When rehydrated, drain (reserve liquid), remove stems, and halve caps. Cook chopped bacon in wok until slightly crisp; drain off most fat. Add chopped shallots, minced garlic, the mushroom caps, 1-inch pumpkin cubes, and sliced lotus and stir-fry 2 minutes. Add chicken stock, reserved mushroom liquid, dark soy sauce, and oyster sauce. Boil, cover, and cook until pumpkin is tender, about 10 minutes. Add 2-inch lengths of scallion. Stir in cornstarch slurry to thicken.

Mâche, Corn Salad *(Valerianella locusta* and *V. olitoria)*

Also corn-salad, lamb's lettuce, field salad, fetticus

"Mâche" is the word you'll see in fancy groceries and on menus, but that term is a recent French import. If you plant these greens in your garden or find them in a farmers' market, they will be called corn salad or lamb's lettuce. (Some restaurateurs say they put "mâche" on the menu because diners expect sweet corn when they read "corn salad.") I would like to write about this plant's numerous varieties (many still available through gardening catalogues) and charming names (none of which make it a relative of lamb's quarters or any true lettuce). But what is presently in markets is limited in form and nomenclature, so I'll stay with that.

Temperate Europe, which is corn salad's general area of origin, is still its primary area of popularity. A tender green of velvety texture and gentle flavor, it was described by the English diarist John Evelyn in his *Acetaria: A Discourse of Sallets* (1699): "the tops and Leaves are a Sallet of themselves, seasonably eaten with other Salleting the whole Winter long, and early Spring." Corn salad was once a common cold-weather salad leaf in the United States, too; then it all but disappeared until it was rediscovered by Americans traveling in France, the Netherlands, Belgium, and Germany—from where it is exported.

Small-scale growers in the United States have taken it up again now; and imports appear erratically (see the French nosegays on the left in photo). Although there are many choices of seed, including some with delicious and distinct flavors, the bunches we grow here are mainly mild, offering more a sense of soft succulence and green freshness than a defined savor.

BASIC USE: Corn salad is a charming salad and garnish leaf. Treat it kindly, and it responds sweetly and prettily. For a simple salad, dress it with a blend of peanut (or walnut) oil and corn (or grapeseed) oil and a modicum of acid (sherry or champagne vinegar, or citrus juice). Toss the smooth, petal-like leaves at the last minute, or they wilt. Mâche with julienned beets

mâche or corn salad: French import (*left*) and American-grown (*right*)

½ **actual size**

and celery in vinaigrette (salade Lorette) is traditional in the French culinary repertory—and as fine a combination now as ever. For garnish, tuck rosettes or individual leaves around quiches or omelets, rice dishes, and cooked vegetable or potato salads. Thick or large leaves make a plushy bed for poultry or a roast (lamb's lettuce *is* good with lamb loin) and soak up the juices.

SELECTION: Choose bright, lively bunches with roots. Avoid wet or yellowed leaves. In Europe, mâche is both a field-grown and year-round greenhouse crop. In the United States, it is greenhouse-grown, but you can find some field-grown greens in California, and occasionally elsewhere.

As a shopper with nationalist preferences, I would like to recommend the American product. But so far, imports have been superior: more succulent, complex, with a surprising floral flavor and a hint of black truffle. Domestic corn salad that I have sampled has been too small and underdeveloped in flavor; it looks charming and has a pleasing texture but is bland. If you garden, this is a vegetable to consider seriously, from all reports.

STORAGE: Do not store this delicate creature. Refrigerate, plastic-wrapped, as briefly as possible.

PREPARATION: Trim rootlets. Swish leaves around in lukewarm water, then lift out gently. Repeat until no grit remains. If field-grown, mâche may need many very gentle washings (it bruises very easily), for soil and sand hide in the base. Blot dry on soft towels.

Salad of Mâche, Belgian Endive, and Violets with Walnuts

As beautiful a salad bouquet as you can imagine, with a lilting taste to match. If flowers are not to be found, leave them out—but don't expect the same charm.

¼ teaspoon kosher salt
¼ teaspoon sugar
¼ teaspoon grated orange zest
1½ tablespoons orange juice
¼ teaspoon ground fennel seeds or crumbled dried tarragon
1 tablespoon champagne vinegar or white wine vinegar

White pepper
2 tablespoons walnut oil
2 tablespoons grapeseed or corn oil
About ¼ pound mâche (corn salad)
4 small Belgian endives
½ cup toasted walnuts
2 to 3 teaspoons thin-sliced chives
1 dozen or more violets or small pansies

1. Combine salt, sugar, orange zest and juice, fennel, vinegar, and pepper, stirring to dissolve crystals. Whisk in both oils.

2. Trim rootlets from mâche; gently swish around in water, then lift out. Repeat as needed until no grit remains. Blot on soft towel. Cutting from the base, trim cores from each endive head. Separate leaves. Rinse and spin-dry. Chill mâche and endive.

3. To serve, arrange 3 or 4 endive spears on each plate; thin-slice remainder crosswise. Coarse-chop nuts. Toss sliced endive, nuts, mâche, and chives with dressing. Spoon onto plates. Top with violets.

Serves 4

Mâche and Bibb Lettuce with Butter Dressing

An unusual butter-dressed salad that is nearly acid-free—and thus a boon to fine white wine.

About 3 ounces mâche
2 Bibb lettuces (about ¼ pound each)
2 teaspoons lemon juice
¼ teaspoon kosher salt
¼ teaspoon sugar
¼ teaspoon grated nutmeg
1 teaspoon snipped fresh tarragon
4 tablespoons unsalted butter
1 garlic clove

1. Trim rootlets from mâche. Gently dunk leaves up and down in lukewarm water, then lift out. Repeat until no grit remains. Pat dry on soft, thick towel. Separate Bibb lettuce leaves, rinse, and spin-dry, then cut to suit. Combine mâche and Bibb in a serving bowl. Do not refrigerate.

2. In a small bowl, combine lemon juice, salt, sugar, nutmeg, and tarragon. Combine butter and garlic in a small heavy pan over lowest heat. When butter is slightly golden, not browned, skim off foam and remove garlic.

3. Whisk butter gradually into the lemon juice mixture. Immediately pour over the leaves and toss. Serve at once.

Serves 4

Salad of Mâche, Beets, and Radicchio

Not the traditional French mix of julienned beets, celery, and mâche, but not far from it. The soft mâche, bitterish radicchio, and sweet beets make an interesting side for baby chicken or veal. A handful of toasted pecans or pine nuts adds crunch, if you're in the mood.

¼ **teaspoon kosher salt**
2 **teaspoons balsamic vinegar**
2 **teaspoons wine vinegar**
1 **small shallot, minced**
2 **tablespoons olive oil**
2 **tablespoons corn oil**
About 5 **cooked small red beets**
About ¼ **pound mâche**
1 **small head radicchio di Verona or Chioggia**
   (about 5 ounces)
Optional: ⅓ **cup toasted pecans or**
   2 **tablespoons fresh chervil leaves**

1. Combine salt, both vinegars, and shallot. Whisk in both oils. Cut beets into julienne to make about 1 cup. Combine half the dressing with the beets. Refrigerate.

2. Trim rootlets from mâche. Gently dunk up and down in water, then lift out. Repeat until completely clean. Pat dry on towels. Chill.

3. Cutting from base, trim core from radicchio. Separate leaves and cut into bite-size pieces or strips. Rinse and spin-dry. Chill.

4. To serve, toss mâche and radicchio with remaining dressing. Arrange on four plates. Arrange beets in center. Slice optional nuts and sprinkle over; or top with chervil.

Serves 4

Pros Propose

Mâche is for salads and garnishes. There is not much to add to that, except to remind those unaccustomed to "plainness" that in France, the lovely green is enjoyed alone. Susan Hermann Loomis, who lives in Louviers, in Normandy, prepares her **Salade de Mâche** thus: She blends salt, pepper, and a touch of sherry vinegar in a salad bowl, then whisks in olive oil. She stirs in a little paper-thin shallot and a tumble of rinsed and dried mâche rosettes, which she tosses gently with the dressing and serves *immédiatement*. (She writes in her *French Farmhouse Cookbook* that "shallots are essential in a mâche salad. They enhance its delicacy as much as garlic snuffs it out. To me this salad is magic—it's so green, tender, and perfumed.")

Mallows (*Malva, Althaea,* and *Hibiscus* species)

Including **common mallow, marsh mallow,** and **whorled mallow** (ah-ook in Korean)

The family Malvaceae counts an intriguing number of disparate plants among its members; notably cotton, okra, hibiscus, hollyhock, and marsh mallow, all established in the United States, wherever their original homes may have been.

Marsh mallow (*Althaea officinalis*) surprises most Americans, who wonder what a squishy confection called "marshmallow" could have in common with a European shrub that clusters around salt marshes, damp meadows, and tidal rivers. Plenty, at one time; and little to nothing, now. The confection we know as marshmallow was formerly made from the plant's roots—and still is in some culinarily civilized corners of Europe. All mallows exude a soft mucilage; in the case of marsh mallow, this was the base of the candy that took its name in English.

But our subject here is the softly crumpled, serrated, scalloped leaves of several mallows, not their roots. These greens, renowned in ancient Greece and Rome, are still part of Middle Eastern, Far Eastern, and some European cuisines in both wild and cultivated forms. The greens have also become established in Mexico, where they were introduced by Europeans. And mallow is "believed to have been one of the most important vegetables in ancient China, and cultivated clumps are common in the field today," writes the plant authority Joy Larkcom in *Oriental Vegetables.*

"The main native oriental species are the flat-leaved *M. verticillata* and *M. crispa,* which has crisply puckered leaves," according to Larkcom. *Malva verticillata* (for which I have no photo, but which is recognizable as a relative of the leaves shown) first caught my eye at a Korean market in Flushing, in New York City, where it was being sold in big spinach-like bundles called "ah-

common mallow (*left*) and marsh mallow (*right*)

ook," as the patient vendor repeated to me numerous times. He told me to "cook in soup." That is the way every Asian vegetable seller tells Westerners to cook greens, and they rarely do—but I did. I loved the melting, mellow leaves and now cook them whenever I can find them.

Cooking is what they need, in my opinion. In the United States, for some reason, greens are at present considered first as a salad subject, then as a cookable vegetable—which would go far to explain why mallows are absent from the Western mainstream marketplace. Although small raw leaves are pretty in a geranium-like way (see the spriggy leaf tips at the left in the photo), all species, while appealingly soft to the touch, are fuzzy to downright hairy and even stringy when raw. Cooked, they are another story. Leaves and small stems turn meltingly soft and slick, with an unusual billowy body. The flavor is gentle, freshly green, with little of the earthy or mineral aspects of many wild plants.

BASIC USE: For soups or sauces, add sliced stems to sautéed aromatic seasonings or directly to broth; cook until tender, about 5 minutes, then stir in leaves and cook another 2 to 5 minutes. Serve as is, or puree and serve the exceptionally smooth, bright green soup hot or iced. Or stir leaves into pasta, grain, or vegetable stews as they finish cooking. Or cook the greens like spinach, squeeze dry, chop, and use as a base for dips or in layered pasta or grain dishes.

SELECTION AND STORAGE: I have found mallows in spring and fall markets, but I hear that they may be available in Korean markets much of the year. Take what you can find—whether wild or cultivated, leafy or leggy, miniature or larger. As long as they are relatively dry, green (not yellow), and fresh-smelling, mallows are fine. Limpness is common and natural to the plant. If it has been bunched, open up the bouquet to expose the interior leaves before refrigerating. Store in a plastic bag for no more than a few days.

PREPARATION: Rinse in as many baths as needed to eliminate sandiness. Shake dry. For the smaller common mallows, separate stems and leaves. Thin-slice stems and cut leaves bite size. (Very skinny stems will soften and need not be cut apart.) For the larger marsh mallow, the stems will not soften with cooking and must be stripped, as with mustard or kale. Tear leaves bite size.

Chilled Pureed Mallow Soup

The subtle green flavor of this soup will reward purists. Lovers of big tastes may find it plain—meaning that it tastes like what it is: a gentle leaf. Oatmeal merely underlines the intrinsic shine and body of the puree; it does not add flavor or texture.

½ **pound bunched mallows**
2 **medium leeks**
1 **tablespoon butter**
1 **carrot, sliced very thin**
1 **quart water**
About 1 teaspoon kosher salt
2 **tablespoons old-fashioned oatmeal**
    (rolled oats)
¼ **to ½ cup sour half-and-half or sour cream**
Pepper

1. Wash mallows in several changes of water, as needed. Cut leaves from stems; set aside. Thin-slice stems. Trim roots and darkest leaf tops from leeks. Halve leeks lengthwise, then cut crosswise into thin slices. Wash well, checking for grit. Drain thoroughly.

2. Melt butter in heavy pot over moderate heat. Add mallow stems, leeks, and carrot. Cook, stirring often, until mixture begins to brown, 7 to 8 minutes. Add water and 1 teaspoon salt. Bring to a boil and stir in oats. Boil gently, partly covered, until vegetables are soft, about 15 minutes.

3. Meanwhile, slice mallow leaves. When vegetables are soft, add leaves to soup. Simmer until tender, about 5 minutes. Cool briefly.

4. Transfer to blender or food processor and whiz to a smooth puree. Scoop ¼ cup sour half-and-half into mixing bowl. Whisk in puree. Add more half-and-half to taste, if desired. Season with salt and pepper.

5. Chill well before serving.

Serves 4 as a first course

Orzo "Risotto" with Shiitake and Wild Mallows

Soft, thick, juicy mallows, a generous helping of fresh shiitake, and chewy orzo pasta combine to make a luscious, slippery dish with a muted pine undertone. If you use mallows that are leggy and large (whether wild or cultivated) you'll need about twice as much to yield 4 cups leaves. If you're preparing fresh vegetable broth for this, add the shiitake and mallow stems; if not, save them for another broth batch. I prefer the wheaty color and flavor of Greek orzo.

3 to 6 ounces young mallows (to yield 4 cups lightly packed leaves)
6 ounces fresh shiitake
1 medium shallot
About 4 cups mushroom and/or vegetable broth
6 ounces orzo pasta (preferably Greek)
2 tablespoons butter
About ½ teaspoon grated lemon zest
Grated nutmeg
Salt and pepper

1. Strip stems from mallows; rinse leaves. Remove shiitake stems. Slice caps thin. Mince shallot.

2. Bring 2½ cups broth to a boil in heavy medium-large pot. Stir in orzo and return to a boil. Boil gently until tender, about 10 minutes. (If orzo begins to stick, add water; absorption rates vary.)

3. Meanwhile, heat heavy medium skillet over moderate heat. Add 1½ tablespoons butter. Stir in shallot and toss to soften slightly. Add shiitake and sauté until lightly browned, about 6 minutes. Season with lemon zest, nutmeg, and salt and pepper. Add ¾ cup broth and mallow leaves. Stir and toss until leaves are wilted and tender, about 2 minutes.

4. Add contents of pan to orzo. Add broth as needed to make a slightly soupy consistency. Stir in remaining ½ tablespoon butter. Serve at once, in wide bowls.

Serves 2 as a main course

Pros Propose

"Stir into soup" may be good advice for cooking mallows, but it is difficult to learn unless you find someone to tell you that. Curiously, for greens that are widely used, they remain largely within traditional—unwritten—channels. Although they are often cited as part of the mixture of boiled greens that make up the Greek *horta*, I find no specifics.

Recipes from North Africa are among the few I've seen that recommend more than boiling up and serving. Mallows are featured in the appetizing array of aromatic cooked salads that may open a meal in Tunisia and Morocco. Beqqula or bekkoula, a common Arabic name for the green, is usually served up in a **Spiced Salad with Preserved Lemon:** Combine 4 parts mallow leaves with 2 of parsley and 1 each of cilantro and celery leaves. Chop, then wash well. Steam in a heavy pot with any water that clings and with whole garlic cloves. When the greens are easily mashed, peel and crush the garlic with salt. Return to the pot with sweet paprika, hot pepper, peanut oil, and olive oil. Stir over low heat to evaporate liquid. Add lemon juice, preserved lemon peel, and oil-cured olives. Stir briefly. Season. Decorate with more lemon and olives. Cool to serve (from *La cuisine marocaine* by Latifa Bennani-Smirès).

Another traditional Moroccan recipe, **Barley Grits (Tchicha) with Mallows,** appears in several books, including *Les saveurs et les gestes* by Fatéma Hal: Rinse and drain barley grits (available in natural foods markets); set in top part of couscoussier or steamer. In lower part, combine chopped onion, olive oil, chopped mallows, chopped green pepper, minced garlic, pepper, and paprika; add water to cover. Spread barley grits on top, cover, and steam until fluffy. Arrange grits on dish and toss with butter. Spoon over the mallow mixture and juices.

Matsutake, American (*Tricholoma magnivelare*)

Also white matsutake or pine mushroom

"Matsutake (matsu = pine; take = mushroom) is the collective Japanese common name for a group of similar mushrooms formed by closely related *Tricholoma*" species, write Yun, Hall, and Evans in *Economic Botany*. American matsutake, which they classify as *T. magnivelare,* and which grows primarily in the Pacific Northwest, is a relative of Japanese matsutake, a seasonal prize second only to Alba and Perigord truffles in the category of luxury fungi.

The Japanese passion for matsutake was the impetus for the American "discovery" of this species—for reasons that have as much to do with economics as with cuisine. "Large-scale commercial mushroom harvesting in the United States is concentrated on matsutake, morels, chanterelles, boletes, black Oregon truffles, and hedgehogs—to list them in order of their greatest to least cash value per harvest," says David Pilz, a botanist at the Forestry Sciences Laboratory of the United States Department of Agriculture in Corvallis, Oregon. "Japan is the main market for American matsutake, followed by Asian communities in the U.S. and Canada."

The lucrative Japanese market has proved a boon for some, a disappointment for others, and a hazard for still others. Forest disputes in matsutake territory are no fantasy; although they are often sensationalized by the press, it is true that more than one forager has been killed and others have reported life-threatening run-ins. Fernando Divina, formerly the chef-proprietor of Fiddleheads Restaurant and Bella Coola Cafe in Portland, Oregon, picked his own wildlings for years, as his distinctly local menu attested. "But the climate has changed," he recounts. "I was collecting with my wife and child when we were pinned down under gunfire as we got too close to someone's patch. We were absolutely terrified. I'll leave foraging in subalpine regions to those braver than I am and stick to the safer coastal meadows and valleys."

What is matsutake's magic? Connoisseurs mention a powerful spicy aroma which, regretfully, I have not encountered. Perhaps I am too far from the source or perhaps my samples were not superior. Matsutake I

diameter of caps: 2-4 inches

have cooked has been more memorable for its texture—like fiberless white asparagus—than its aroma. The aroma has been subtle and fleeting: pine-tinged, peppery, with a touch of mint. The flavor has been gentle and balanced, with a cereal sweetness.

Having failed to discover the secret of matsutake, I asked connoisseurs for particulars. What I discovered is that either matsutake itself or people's response to it varies dramatically. Oregon-based chef Greg Higgins, who has featured the American species on his menu for years, loves "the amazing cinnamon-musk-pheromone pungency." Chef Anne Gingrass tastes a "rounded, elegant, and soft flavor, with citrus and sherry notes." Gary Lincoff, author of mycological reference works, describes a "special cedary scent, wafted from an ice cave. Matsutake cleans your senses the way menthol does." Elizabeth Andoh, an authority on Japanese food finds a "dark, woodsy, green fragrance—far more intense in the Japanese than American mushrooms." I hope you have a chance to explore for yourself.

There is, perhaps, another reason for matsutake's appeal. The authors of the article in *Economic Botany* explain that "matsutake at the 'button' stage are elongated with a bulbous end" (if you've seen it, you'll know that it's not just rather phallic—it *is* a phallus); and "consequently, 'matsutake' became the enigmatic word for the male organ and the word was not used in polite company."

The closed number one grade, astronomically priced American matsutake was not available for the photo because, as one distributor said, "it all goes to Japan." Yun, Hall, and Evans write that "while smell, taste, flavor and color are important attributes, shape is by far the most important factor controlling the value of matsutake." Richard Hosking notes in *A Dictionary of Japanese Food*, "There is a certain ribaldry about young men and women going hunting for *matsutake*, since it is quite phallic in shape, and the chances of getting lost in the woods of red pine where it grows are quite high."

BASIC USE: To my taste, nothing beats unadorned matsutake, simply broiled (see recipe, this page) or baked in parchment: Slice ¼ inch thick, dab with a touch of soy, wrap, and bake in a moderate oven for about ½ hour. Or cube matsutake and simmer with short-grain rice, which fills the grain with flavor and maintains the pallor and firmness of the mushroom. In short: Roast, steam, grill, or cook en papillote or broth. I find that sautéing hides the mushroom's special qualities. Simmer peelings and any tough stems for stock.

Richard Hosking writes that one celebrated use of matsutake is in dobinmushi, a clear soup made in miniature pottery or china teapots: "It is a famous autumn specialty of Kyoto and usually contains matsutake, chicken, mitsuba, and ginnan [gingko]. The juice of sudachi [a tart citrus] is squeezed into the dashi, which is drunk from little cups. The other ingredients are fished out with chopsticks and eaten. One of the great delicacies of Japan."

Chef Greg Higgins finds that the Japanese repertoire matches the American species, too: "Western ingredients—particularly dairy—are not suitable. Rice, dashi, and fermented soy products are what matsutake

needs—or to be grilled dry." Keep matsutake the focus: "They are so expensive, and such concentrated flavor bombs, that they should be the main part of a dish."

SELECTION: Matsutake are fall to winter mushrooms. They should be heavy, rock-solid, and aromatic. Those that are closed or have turned-under caps are freshest. Squeeze each stem to check for "give"—which means that insects lurk within.

Restaurants buy by grade with prices to match. Number one grade is the premium (hugely pricey) satin-fleshed, closed-cap form. Number six is opened-out flat, may be broken, or may have browning gills—but it can still taste fine in a multi-ingredient dish. Choose a grade according to your use and your budget. "Pricing is driven by Asia. If their season is poor, U.S. prices are out of sight," says chef Higgins. "If they're available, then all grades are usually to be had."

STORAGE: Store in a basket, in a single layer, covered with a towel. Because matsutake are so dense, they do not spoil quickly, but they may lose their fresh aroma if kept for more than a few days.

PREPARATION: If clean, just rub matsutake with a damp towel. While some may look clean, embedded grittiness is common. More typical mushrooms (like those in the photo) need serious cleaning and trimming. Rinse and even scrub with a vegetable brush to remove grit or soil; scrubbing will not harm the very solid mushrooms. It is prudent to peel the stems, which may be fibrous; save the trimmings for stock.

Note that when sliced, neither caps nor stems discolor, even after hours. They remain solid fleshy white.

Broiled Matsutake

Matsutake in its opened-out stage (less pricey than other phases) makes an impressive, if still fairly extravagant, appetizer. Allow one quarter-pounder per person—or more for healthy appetites and healthier budgets. Do not be tempted to cook the caps on high heat, or they will char on the outside before being cooked within. Serve this simple dish with an elegant sake—to admirers of quiet flavors.

4 matsutake (each cap about 4 inches
  in diameter)
2 tablespoons sake
1 tablespoon shoyu (Japanese soy sauce)

1 tablespoon mild oil, such as grapeseed or corn
Small mizuna or tiny oakleaf lettuce leaves

1. Preheat broiler to 400°F (see Note). Cut stems gently apart from mushroom caps, taking care not to break caps. Trim stem bases. If muddy or obviously tough, peel stems, then halve lengthwise. Clean gills with a soft brush. If caps are muddy, rinse and scrub lightly with vegetable brush; or peel if hopelessly dirty.

2. Combine sake, shoyu, and oil. Brush all parts of mushrooms with this, repeating until all is absorbed. Let stand 15 minutes or so.

3. Place mushrooms on preheated broiler pan close to heat, gill side down. Broil until lightly browned and slightly crisped—not charred—about 10 minutes. Turn over and cook to the same stage, about 5 minutes.

4. Serve hot, on mizuna leaves.

Serves 4 as a first course

Note: My old-fashioned broiler is the type that supplies the heat to the oven: When I set the oven to 400°F, the heat is right for the mushrooms. If your broiler unit is separate, adjust as necessary to prevent scorching the matsutake.

Variation

Broiled Matsutake and Asparagus with Ginger-Orange Sauce

Those who prefer bolder flavors and a more generous presentation will be better served by this version with a dipping sauce.

¼ cup orange juice
2 tablespoons sake
2 tablespoons shoyu (Japanese soy sauce)
½ teaspoon honey
½ to 1 teaspoon fine-grated ginger
¼ to ½ teaspoon fine-grated orange zest
1 pound medium asparagus

1. Mix together orange juice, sake, shoyu, honey, ginger, and zest, using the smaller amounts of the last two. Taste and add more, if desired.

2. Prepare Broiled Matsutake above. While mushrooms are marinating, trim asparagus. While matsutake is in the broiler, cook Basic Microwaved Green Asparagus (see page 36). Leave whole or cut into 2-inch diagonals.

3. Divide hot cooked asparagus and matsutake among four plates, each supplied with its own tiny dish of dipping sauce.

Serves 4 as a first course

Pros Propose

Northwestern chefs, who share terrain with the American matsutake, have the most experience with it. Chef Greg Higgins says that he now "knows enough to stick with the Japanese, who know matsutake best, and consequently do the least to it." For **Grilled Matsutake in Broth:** Prepare dashi and steep matsutake trimmings in it. Slice small matsutake lengthwise through cap and stem. Cook on a dry grill. Transfer to strained dashi; add fine scallion threads. "Serve under a cloche, so the sexy aroma is saved for guests, not the dining room," says Higgins.

West Coast chef Anne Gingrass follows a Japanese path to savory egg custard (chawan mushi)—then adds California embellishments. For **Steamed Matsutake Custard with Warm Frisée-Shallot Salad:** Separate matsutake caps and stems. Simmer chopped stems with chicken broth and sherry. Add kelp (kombu), bonito flakes, and ginger, then strain. Whisk in eggs, pour into custard cups, and top with thin matsutake slices; steam. Meanwhile, wrap reserved caps in foil with salt, lemon juice, sherry vinegar, and butter. Bake until tender. Combine the cooking juices with olive oil, sherry, thyme, and lemon for vinaigrette. Cut the caps into small pieces. Mix with frisée, caramelized shallots, and parsley leaves. Set custard on plates with salad. Top each with soft-cooked quail egg.

Washington State chef and author Jerry Traunfeld thinks sweetness brings out hidden aspects of the mushrooms. For **Sea Scallops with Matsutake, Delicata, and Pear Cider Sauce:** Brown slim Delicata squash wedges in butter. Add pear cider and cook until glazed and tender. Thin-slice small, tight matsutake, brush with grapeseed oil and season. Roast at 400°F until edges color. Sear sea scallops. Deglaze pan with pear cider and shallots, then whisk in butter. Add lemon juice and season. Arrange scallops, squash, and matsutake on warm plates and spoon over sauce.

Chef Traunfeld bakes mini-**Matsutake and Leek Soufflés with Chervil Butter** for a first course: Heat milk and add chopped matsutake stems. Steep at least ½ hour. Strain; discard stems. Braise sliced leeks in butter with a little chicken stock until soft and liquid has evaporated. Whisk in flour and infused milk. Bring to a boil. Off heat, whisk in egg yolks, to make a soufflé base. Meanwhile, slice caps, brush with grapeseed oil and season. Roast in 400°F oven, in single layer on baking sheet, until edges brown slightly. Chop and add to soufflé base. Fold in whipped egg whites. Spoon into buttered and crumbed cups and bake. Serve with beurre blanc blended with a generous amount of fresh chervil.

Chef Alex Lee employs a restaurant technique for his **Warm Matsutake with Greens and Parmesan**: Film each salad plate with the best olive oil. Set a bruised garlic clove and thyme sprig on each. Spread ⅛-inch matsutake slices over this, season, and brush with oil. Cover with several layers of plastic wrap. Set on a rack on the stove top near a flame, but not over it. "In about an hour, it will be tender and juicy, but not really 'cooked,' " explains Lee. Drain off the juice and accent it with salt, lemon juice, and olive oil. Toss with imported mâche and delicate frisée. Arrange mushrooms and Parmesan shavings over greens.

Simplicity of the kind described by West Coast chef Greg Higgins is expressed on the East Coast by chef David Waltuck, who says of his **Matsutake in Papillote**: "This may sound too simple to even be called a recipe, but that's what makes it just right for matsutake." To prepare: Wrap small halved matsutake in parchment with a touch of mushroom glace, butter, lemon, and chives. Bake in a hot oven and "open at the table, for customers to inhale."

Miner's Lettuce (*Montia perfoliata*, formerly *Claytonia perfoliata*)

Also winter purslane, claytonia, Cuban spinach or lettuce, Spanish lettuce

³⁄4 actual size

This adorable, delicious salad green does, indeed, show up toward the end of winter, as one of its names promises—in contrast to true purslane (page 513), a summer arrival. Cuban spinach and Spanish lettuce, alternative common names, designate once disputed places of origin. But if the birthplace remains debatable, there is now agreement that this plant is native to the Americas—even though it is more widely appreciated and cultivated in Europe.

Maricel Presilla, a Cuban-born authority on Latin American foods, says that miner's lettuce is called verdolagas de Cuba to distinguish it from the several greens generically dubbed verdolagas (such as purslane). She reports that it has fallen out of use except in the most rural areas of the country, where it is part of "typical Cuban salad: greens, avocado and/or tomato, and olive oil, vinegar, and salt." Occasionally it is stirred into "colonial stews, as a thickener, like okra, because it has some of the same mucilaginous quality."

"Lettuce" is about as unlikely a description as you could come up with: The juicy, pea-green, cupped elfin lily pads perched on skinny stalks have a unique look and a flavor rather like mâche accented with spinach. They resemble lettuce not in taste or appearance but only in the common characteristic of being best in salads.

Indian lettuce is another name that appears in some field guides—such as *Edible and Useful Plants of California* by Charlotte Bringle Clarke. Clarke writes that American Indians "ate the tender fleshy leaves raw or cooked and made a tea of the plant." It is "one of our few native plants introduced to other countries. It has been taken to Europe where it is cultivated under the name Winter Purslane."

Addressing the term "miner's," William Woys Weaver explains in *Heirloom Vegetable Gardening* that "the vegetable received considerable attention during the days of the California gold rush, when it served as a cheap and readily available source of greens for the miners. Unfortunately, the name carried with it the implication of a rough-and-ready emergency food, not an elegant green for proper Victorian tables. This may have helped prejudice many Americans against it in the nineteenth century, especially since it was a common 'weed.' "

Chefs and devoted shoppers in farmers' markets now pay a pretty penny to have the tender leaflets grace their salads and garnish delicate dishes—the jobs it does best.

BASIC USE: Mild, softly succulent miner's lettuce suits the roles played by mâche (see page 376). Individual leaves, scattered separately or gathered into a loose bouquet, make a tasty garnish for canapés, seafood, eggs, veal, and just about any simple savory dish. In a salad, miner's lettuce fits in tastefully with other petite greens, herbs, and especially with edible flowers, whether tiny whole ones or petals from larger ones.

Relatively larger leaves, slightly more earthy and sturdy, can take a little heat: Stir into cooked vegetables at the last minute, tuck into an omelet, or toss with warm potato salad. If you have a goodly quantity, make a little bed for poached fish fillets and spoon a warm, buttery sauce over all.

I have read that larger leaves cook up nicely, but I have not seen any approaching large in the market. Unless you're gathering basketfuls in the wilderness, it seems a waste. They're cute and tasty raw.

SELECTION: Look for miner's lettuce in early spring, then expect erratic appearances into the summer. Choose bright, lively, comparatively small specimens. Although it is cultivated (or springs up and is helped along) in other countries, I know of only wild miner's lettuce in American markets, thus far—and very little of that.

PREPARATION: Sample, then decide. Some batches are mild and fiber-free, some are more earthy and fibrous. If the stems are juicy and tender, cut them up and add to the dish; if not, discard. The buds and flowers can be mild and pleasant or inedibly bitter: Taste, then keep or nip off. For most presentations, long stems should be snipped off so that just the terminal leaves and a little tail remain (as in the photograph).

Salad of Miner's Lettuce, Enoki, Belgian Endive, and Grapes

Here's the prettiest nosegay of a salad for an elegant dinner party. As first course or refreshing intermezzo, this mélange of miniatures sparkles: a toss of bright white enoki mushrooms, fresh green miner's lettuce leaves, translucent grape slices, and pearly endive crescents glisten in their tart dressing. It is not for bold palates, but for lovers of subtlety and simplicity. Enoki mushrooms are sometimes loose-packed—in which case, buy ¼ pound—but more often prepacked in 3.5-ounce packets.

> 2 small Belgian endives
> 3½ to 4 ounces enokitake
> 6 ounces seedless green grapes
> 2 to 3 ounces (2½ cups) lightly packed
>   miner's lettuce leaves (see Preparation)
> 1 tablespoon lemon juice
> 1 tablespoon sherry vinegar
> ¼ teaspoon kosher salt
> Pinch of fine-ground white pepper
> 3 tablespoons delicate olive oil

1. Cut cores from Belgian endives. Halve heads lengthwise. Cut crosswise into ½-inch slices and divide into individual crescents.

2. Trim several inches from enoki base. Separate stalks, more or less, keeping short ones intact and halving longer ones. Combine in a bowl with endive.

3. Stem and slice grapes. Add to bowl along with miner's lettuce.

4. Combine lemon juice, vinegar, salt, and pepper, stirring to dissolve salt. Whisk in oil to emulsify. Pour over salad and toss gently. Serve at once, on large plates.

Serves 4

Pros Propose

Miner's lettuce is best raw, so there is not much need for culinary description. Herewith a few ways to incorporate the leaflets.

Chef Todd Humphries's **Warm Goat Cheese Salad with Miner's Lettuce and Poached Rhubarb** is a "little earthy, a little tart, a little creamy, and sweet-salty." To prepare: Peel firm red rhubarb. Boil trimmings with water and sugar to make poaching liquid; strain. Cut thin rhubarb slices on bias. Boil poaching liquid again and pour over slices. Use some of the liquid to make a vinaigrette with champagne vinegar and nut and olive oils. Toss with miner's lettuce. Warm goat cheese, set on croutons. Spoon rhubarb over goat cheese and miner's lettuce.

Three ingredients balance in a deceptively simple conceit from Jean-Georges Vongerichten, **Pasta with Miner's Lettuce and Crayfish**: In each serving bowl, toss hot fresh bow-tie pasta with crayfish and very hot crayfish *jus*. Add miner's lettuce and toss well, "so the earthy water cress taste comes out with the heat."

A hot bacon dressing is just what's needed to wilt little leaves of miner's lettuce and add a touch of smokiness. For easy and effective **Wilted Miner's Lettuce**: Snip miner's lettuce into bowl. Brown bacon. Drain and crumble. Add vinegar, salt, and pepper to fat in pan and bring to a boil. Pour over miner's lettuce and serve at once, topped with sliced hard-cooked egg and the bacon (from *How to Prepare Common Wild Foods* by Darcy Williamson).

Morels (*Morchella* species)

Also merkel (in parts of the United States) and morille (French)

wild morels

¾ **actual size**

Morels, the earliest spring mushrooms, are cause for celebration in many regions of the United States, particularly the Midwest, where they are most abundant. In Appalachia, too, they are greeted with festivities, but under a local name—molly moochers. Curiously, in an otherwise mycophobic country, this is one mushroom that appears to have slipped past the censors. Why, I cannot say. But I can say that the way morels are commonly cooked in the United States—by deep-frying in batter—manages to mask if not eliminate most of their mushroomier aspects.

The flavor of morels is less intense than that of many wild mushrooms: They may be nutty and slightly smoky, or merely mildly earthy and pleasing in a mushroomy way. It is their texture—thin flesh whorled and pitted in ways that create a play of softness and some crunchiness—that is most distinct. (But this distinctiveness is not to everyone's taste. Lidia Matticchio Bastianich, an authority on Italian food, says tartly: "I don't like the way they squirt sauce back at you when you bite them.")

Morels are not limited to North America. They flourish in most temperate parts of the world, including Europe, China, India, and Turkey, where they are sold dry and fresh. Several species cluster under the heading "morel." Of these, the yellow or golden morel (*Morchella esculenta*) and the white morel (*M. deliciosa*) are usually considered the most choice. These pale types are also more desirable in that they are associated with fewer gastric complications than black morels, a complex of several dark-ribbed species, which upset some diners, particularly in conjunction with alcohol.

Cultivated morels, a luxury long under development, are now available year-round. On the plus side, they are miraculously clean (labor-free and waste-free); on the minus side, the dozen chefs I queried found them relatively tasteless, as have I.

BASIC USE: Berry- to brioche-size, rounded and fat to narrow and conical, honeycombed and hollow, morels are seemingly designed to hold creamy sauces and savory juices, which they simultaneously flavor and absorb. The simpler the sauce, the better, as the mushroom fragrance is easily overpowered. Larger morels, halved, make fine little boats for stuffing. Small or sliced morels become a luscious stuffing for veal or poultry, obligingly soaking up seasoning and juices.

To cook morels, simmer in liquid for fullest flavor: Cook gently in stock or cream or both, reducing juices slowly. For variation, add blanched asparagus, fiddleheads, or peas to the simmering liquid when the morels are partly cooked. Serve over polenta, or toss with pasta and butter. For a frittata, sauté raw sliced morels lightly, then add the egg mixture and bake. Prepare risotto or pilaf with morels. Or bake sliced morels in a tightly sealed dish with sliced potatoes, sunchokes, or blanched celery root to absorb the flavorful juices.

SELECTION: Wild morels, primarily a domestic crop, still put in firmly seasonal appearances during early spring and summer. Choose comparatively dry, tender specimens with a sweet earth aroma—but with no hint of sourness or an animal smell. Check them very carefully for insect infestation: Even a few stray critters can turn them into crumbs by morning. Chef Jean Joho spreads morels in a well-spaced single layer on white towels to best observe the emergence of wildlife. Cultivated mushrooms need not be checked.

STORAGE: Refrigerate morels in a basket for no more than a few days. If damp, cover with a paper towel; if brittle and dry, mist the towel. For long storage, morels are easily dried: Halve, brush clean, then spread on a sheet pan and leave in an oven with a pilot light until dry and crisp. Or dry in the sun, if you have the option. They will retain their scent and savor, and sometimes even improve.

PREPARATION: Trim off the bases, as needed. Unless cultivated or miraculously clean, morels require a good going over. Halve them or slice rounds, checking each for soil and insects. Brush clean if exceptionally dirt-free. Usually you'll need to rinse in several baths until no grit remains in the sink. Dry on soft towels.

Note: The thimble morel (*Verpa bohemica*), although sold on the West Coast, is poisonous to some people. With its open thimble-like cap, it is distinct from the closed *Morchella* form. The brain-shaped false morel (see Gyromitra, page 302) should never be eaten.

Golden Potato-Morel Casserole

To keep every drop of flavor, bake morels, covered, with petite potatoes to soak up the juices. Small yellow-fleshed potatoes, which have a waxy texture and rich flavor, are a must for the success of this simple dish, which looks casual but tastes elegant. Roast chicken or Cornish hens at the same time, then set on a bed of cress, and you have a lovely dinner.

> 1¼ pounds tiny (1- to 1½-inch diameter)
>   yellow-fleshed potatoes
> 5 to 6 ounces morels
> 2 tablespoons minced shallots
> 1 tablespoon hazelnut oil
> 1 tablespoon corn oil
> ½ teaspoon grated nutmeg
> ½ teaspoon kosher salt
> 3 tablespoons white wine

1. Turn oven to 375°F. Scrub potatoes with brush. Cut into ⅛-inch slices. Trim off mushroom bases and chop. Slice caps into ½-inch rounds (wreaths). Rinse morels *quickly* in strainer, bouncing lightly. (If you have cultivated morels, do not rinse.) Repeat, as needed.

2. Combine potatoes, morels, shallots, hazelnut and corn oils, nutmeg, and salt in 8-inch round shallow earthenware dish or similar baking dish. Toss to mix. Drizzle over wine and toss again.

3. Cover closely with foil and seal tightly. Bake until potatoes are very tender and most liquid has been absorbed, about 45 minutes.

Serves 4 as a side dish

Morels and Asparagus in Cream over Fresh Pasta

Springily pretty, a delicate dish of cream-steeped morels, crisp asparagus bits, and soft pasta. The effect is distinctly more vegetably than creamy, as the liquid is absorbed by the linguine, leaving just a smooth trace. If you prefer a saucier feel, add more cream or ignore the reduction part of step 5. If you have cultivated rather than wild morels, there is no need to slice them unless they are too large for bite size. The asparagus and mushroom trimmings and cooking liquid are the flavorful base for the sauce.

½ pound morels (preferably small)
½ pound medium-small asparagus
½ teaspoon dried tarragon
½ teaspoon kosher salt
1 medium shallot, minced
½ cup heavy cream
½ pound fresh linguine, tagliatelle, or fettuccine

1. Trim morels (save trimmings). Halve or slice, as size dictates. Rinse trimmings and place in small saucepan. Rinse morels; spread on towel. Bend each asparagus spear at the base end to snap off the tough part; chop this and add to saucepan. Peel asparagus and add peelings to pot. Add 2 cups water, tarragon, and salt. Simmer, covered, to extract flavor, 20 to 40 minutes, as convenient. Strain liquid into medium skillet.

2. Slice asparagus at an angle into 1-inch pieces. Add to liquid in skillet and simmer until not quite tender, about 3 minutes. With slotted spoon, lift out asparagus; set aside.

3. Add shallot to pan. Boil liquid to reduce to ¼ cup. Add cream and morels. Cover and simmer gently until tender—10 to 15 minutes.

4. Boil pasta in plenty of salted water until just al dente—a matter of a few minutes. As it finishes cooking, add the asparagus (in order to reheat). Return to a boil, then drain.

5. If desired, uncover morels and boil for a few minutes, to thicken sauce *slightly* (it should not be thick but liquidy). Add asparagus and noodles to sauce. Stir gently over low heat to blend and absorb sauce. Taste, season, and serve hot.

Serves 4 as a first course, 2 as a main course

Frittata of Wild Morels and Spring Peas

Barbara Spiegel, mentioned often in these pages for her creative, casual recipes, sent this one with a reminder about the usefulness of frittatas (hot, warm, or at room temperature) for feeding last-minute (or anticipated) guests, at breakfast, lunch, or dinner. "If I have eggs, the rest will follow from pantry, refrigerator, or small summer herb garden, and the results are inevitably pretty and cheerful—sunny yellow with bright bits and pieces that nicely and naturally float to the surface." This one is particularly attractive, with its primavera peas and intricate morel forms highlighted by the yellow egg backdrop. Sliced, blanched asparagus is equally delicious with the morels, as are cooked, sliced fiddlehead ferns.

6 ounces morels
1 to 1½ tablespoons olive oil
1 to 1½ tablespoons butter
¾ teaspoon kosher salt
1 pound peas in the pod (to yield about 1 cup)
4 ounces soft fresh goat cheese
6 eggs
3 tablespoons fine-chopped flat-leaf parsley
Pepper

1. Trim morel bases as needed; slice mushrooms into rounds. Slosh around in bowl of warm water and then lift out. Repeat if needed until water is clean. Dry on soft towel. (Do not wash cultivated mushrooms.)

2. Melt 1 tablespoon each oil and butter in 11- to 12-inch skillet (preferably non-stick) with ovenproof handle over moderately high heat. Cook morels, stirring occasionally, until tender, about 5 minutes. Sprinkle with ¼ teaspoon salt, and set skillet aside.

3. Shell peas. Cook in plenty of boiling salted water until just barely cooked through, a minute or two. Drain; reserve.

4. Preheat broiler. In large bowl, break up cheese with fork. Add eggs, remaining ½ teaspoon salt, parsley, and pepper; blend. Stir in morels and peas.

5. Return skillet to moderate heat. Add remaining ½ tablespoon each butter and oil as needed. When sizzling, pour in egg mixture. Lift with spatula and tilt, letting uncooked mixture run beneath. Slide pan

under broiler in its lowest position to finish cooking until just barely set, not browned, about 2 minutes. Remove from broiler.

6. Let frittata rest 5 to 10 minutes, until edge separates from pan. Slide onto a plate. Serve hot, warm, or at room temperature, cut into wedges.

**Serves 3 as a main dish,
5 to 6 as an appetizer or cocktail nibble**

Pros Propose

Spring morels and asparagus are meant for each other—season, color, texture, and flavor. **Sautéed Morels with Asparagus and Santa Barbara Prawns,** a typically unfussy treatment from chef Jean Joho, exemplifies this: Gently cook shallots and peeled asparagus. Add vegetable stock, and braise until soft. Puree. Sauté prawns, blanched asparagus diagonals, and halved morels in olive oil. Deglaze pan with dry white wine. ("That's it," says Joho. "The juices from morels and asparagus blend perfectly with seafood.") Spoon puree alongside.

Chef Sylvain Portay combines **Roasted Jumbo Asparagus with Parmigiano, Morels, and Poached Egg** for his springtime appetizer: Peel jumbo asparagus, blanch, and refresh in ice water. Trim morel stems. Halve large caps; leave small caps whole. Rinse thoroughly; dry well. Sauté in olive oil and butter, then simmer gently in their juices, about 15 to 20 minutes, until reduced. Add minced shallots and butter. Season and add lemon juice. Roast asparagus with oil and butter in hot oven. Toss with Parmesan. To serve, spoon morels over asparagus and top each serving with a poached egg.

Morels and cream have a special symbiotic relationship: the cream adds succulence to the tender, thin morel flesh as the mushrooms infuse the cream with their tasty juices. Simple old-fashioned stews such as **Pheasant Ragoût with Morels and Chives** bring out the special texture and sauceability of the mushrooms. To prepare: Brown quartered pheasants in butter in casserole. Add quartered shallots. Sprinkle with flour, tossing to coat. Add minced garlic and white wine and scrape to deglaze, then simmer to reduce. Add medium morels, chopped chives, and enough chicken stock to cover. Cover and simmer until meat comes easily off the bone. Remove pheasant. Simmer sauce to reduce a little. Add cream and simmer until thickened to taste. Arrange pheasant on platter and pour over sauce (from *Cooking with the Seasons* by Monique Jamet Hooker).

Patrick O'Connell, chef and co-owner of the celebrated Inn at Little Washington, Virginia, is in prime morel country. "One of the main reasons we love this place so is that we're surrounded by morels. It's heaven in springtime." He serves morels on a pizza with Fontina and country ham, in risotto with shrimp and Parmesan, and his favorite way, in **Fettuccine with Morels, Cream, and Country Ham:** Heat olive oil and butter in wide pan and add cleaned, halved fresh morels ("as many as you can get your hands on"). Toss over high heat to crisp slightly. Add minced shallot and a mere touch of garlic. Add half the sautéed mushrooms to boiling cream and simmer until cream thickens to coat a spoon. Stir in a little Parmesan, nutmeg, salt, and pepper. Mix cooked fresh pasta with sauce. Cut very thin slices of country ham into ribbons. Divide pasta among heated bowls, top with the remaining mushrooms, the ham, and snipped chives or chive flowers.

A range of intriguing close textures defines **Morels with Yellow Corn Grits and Okra,** a comparatively simple dish for chef Charlie Trotter: Bake well-cleaned large whole morels, covered, with thyme sprigs, olive oil, salt, pepper, and water 30 to 40 minutes. Drain and strain juices. Reduce by one-third. Halve morels lengthwise. Fill with hot yellow corn grits. Warm blanched whole okra, then slice, season, and arrange on plates. Top each with 3 stuffed morel halves and 1 plain half, add a thyme sprig, and spoon over morel juice (from *Charlie Trotter's Vegetables*).

Mushrooms

"Mushroom," like "vegetable," is an inexact term that cannot be defined except in context. Here, the context is simply culinary. With the exception of *Gyromitra,* all the following are edibles (strictly speaking, not plants—since they do not manufacture their own food) and are worth pursuing and enjoying far beyond the confines of this book. Of the many references listed in the bibliography, two on wild mushrooms are indispensable: *The Audubon Society Field Guide to North American Mushrooms* by Gary Lincoff and *Mushrooms Demystified* by David Arora.

Information about the selection, handling, and cooking of mushrooms cannot be reasonably generalized as that for some squash and beans can be. Porcini, enokitake, and truffles have nothing in common beyond the fairly meaningless rubric "mushroom." Thus they are treated separately and listed individually by common names. If you do not find the mushroom you are seeking here, please consult the Index of Vegetables by Their Common and Botanical Names.

bear's head:
see Hericium

beech mushroom or honshimeji, page 76

black trumpet:
see chanterelle mushrooms

blewit or bluefoot, page 95

cauliflower mushroom, page 160

chanterelle mushrooms (including black trumpet, golden, horn of plenty, South African red, trumpet or funnel, white, and yellowfoot), page 168

chicken of the woods,
page 182

Cinnamon Cap:
see nameko

cremini and portobello, page 221

enokitake,
page 269

fairy ring or mousseron,
page 272

gyromitra or false morel,
page 302

hedgehog or pied de
mouton, page 303

hen of the woods or
maitake, page 306

Hericium species (including
Pompon Blanc), page 310

honey mushrooms,
page 314

honshimeji:
see beech mushroom

horn of plenty: *see*
chanterelle mushrooms

huitlacoche or cuitlacoche,
page 320

lobster mushroom,
page 365

matsutake, American,
page 382

morels,
page 389

nameko and Cinnamon
Cap, page 414

oyster mushrooms (including black, blue, common, king or
Trumpet Royale, pink, white or angel trumpet), page 454

parasol,
page 467

Pompon Blanc:
see Hericium

porcini or cèpes,
page 495

portobello: *see* cremini

puffballs,
page 509

shiitake,
page 568

truffles (including black or
Périgord, Chinese and
Himalayan, Italian white or
Alba, Oregon black,
Oregon white, summer,
Tuber brumale, Tuscan or
bianchetto), page 672

Trumpet Royale or king
oyster: *see* oyster
mushrooms

wood ear and cloud ear,
page 706

Mustard Greens

Ask someone in Atlanta to describe mustard greens, and you'll get one picture. Ask someone whose family came from Peking, and you'll get another. Someone with roots in Southern China, however, might give you the same description as an Indian from the Punjab—or from Jackson Heights, Queens. And a young chef from Cleveland sees them as "spicy purple microgreens." Mustard greens have many personalities.

Technically, the term "mustard greens" refers to a single species of Old World plants, *Brassica juncea,* which is thought to have originated in the Central Asian Himalayas and then spread to China, India, and the Caucasus, according to Joy Larkcom, an expert on Oriental vegetables. But taxonomists identify as many as 17 subgroups or subspecies that can differ sharply in heat, flavor, and appearance. It hardly seems possible that the array belongs to just one species: Lime green to burgundy, smooth to prickly, nippy to fiery, chewy and fibrous or smooth and lettuce-like—mature *Brassica juncea* plants have few common characteristics. And when harvested at the micro or the mini stage, they may not even resemble the grown-up versions.

It is at this petite stage that mustards now play small but powerful roles in mixes for salads, stir-fries, or braises. Little as they are, mustard greens can pack a wallop, combining the pungency of horseradish, the bite of arugula, and the bitterness of broccoli raab. Such tastes still take some getting used to in parts of the United States, where mildness and sweetness are customary. Outside the southern United States—where mustard greens are a traditional food—it is largely in Africa, India, Southeast Asia, and the Far East that these vegetables meet up with stewpot, karhai, steamer, wok, and crock.

Thanks to new Americans from these lands, many of whom depend on a daily dose of mustard greens, we can now choose from a wide selection. As interest in foods from these places increases, so does cultivation of their vegetables—along with endless confusion about their regional, romanized, and conflicting names. So please, keep your eye on the mustard greens pictured, not the variable market names.

BASIC USE: Mustards are really not interchangeable—that is why this entry is so lengthy. But a few generalizations can be made. Raw, small-to-medium, thin-leafed mustards add a hot, radishy bite and vivid color to salads; the inclusion of mild greens and dressing that is heated or sweet (or both) somewhat subdues the bite.

Stir ribbons of any kind of mustard leaf into hot soup just before serving for depth and brilliance. Or stew mustard greens with starchy vegetables, mild greens, or apples and pears, then puree for a creamy soup or sauce. For assertive flavor and maximum aroma, fold slivered leaves into rice, stir-fries, or braises at the end of cooking. For a more earthy, gentler effect, cook the chopped mustard along with potatoes, beans, or grains. For most recipes that call for American curled mustard, large-leaf Japanese mustards can be substituted—and vice versa.

SELECTION: Mustards are available pretty much year-round, with peak volume from December into May. During hot weather, expect erratic supplies and increased "heat." Avoid yellow or dried leaves. Large and small leaves generally cook to the same tenderness; but for use raw, small are preferable. With the exception of wrapped-heart types, considerable volume is lost to stripped stems and shrinkage during cooking. Buy accordingly.

But above all, *taste* when you choose mustards.

Every batch, every bunch of mustard varies—from as mild as bok choy to searingly sharp, from semisweet to inedibly bitter.

STORAGE: Keep mustards cold—at 34° to 40°F with high humidity, advises Adel A. Kader, a professor of postharvest technology at the University of California at Davis. Enclose in ventilated plastic to prevent sulfur-containing volatiles from collecting and creating an unpleasant odor. Do not store near fruits that continue to ripen after harvesting (apple, avocado, banana, pear, plum, and most tropicals), because the ethylene gas produced in ripening causes chlorophyll loss (yellowing) and potential for spoilage. For restaurant storage, keep away from fans, which dry out the leaves.

SUPERSTORAGE: Mustard lasts for quite long periods if treated this way: Cut a slice from the base of the head or stalks, depending upon the type. Soak in lukewarm water for 2 to 4 minutes (shorter for thin-leafed types, longer for thicker). Shake partly dry. Pack into ventilated bags or boxes with a sheet of paper toweling. Flip containers every few days to avoid concentrated condensation. Purple and wrapped-heart types last up

to 2 weeks; small gai choy lasts 4 to 5 days. Others are in between. For a quick but shorter lift, mist mustards before you refrigerate them.

CUTTING THE MUSTARD: Chiffonade, which ensures even distribution of flavor throughout a dish, is the kindest cut of all for most mustards that are to be served raw or briefly cooked. To cut chiffonade: Stack a few cleaned leaves (or halved leaves, if they have been stemmed) and roll into a cylinder. Holding tightly, *thin*-slice through the roll to make fine coiled strands.

Southern or American Mustard

Also curled mustard, Southern curled mustard

This familiar leaf belongs to the *Brassica juncea* subgroup Crispifolia, meaning curled leaf, another collo-

Southern or American mustard

length of bunch: about 15 inches

quial name. American (although not originally) mustard is by far the most common type sold in the United States, above all in the South, where it may simply be known as "greens." Like most mustard greens developed in the United States, Southern Giant Curled mustard and the several similar cultivars that are the major market varieties have fairly large, frilly, parrot green leaves that are quite soft and thin, with a slight fuzziness. The flavor is radishy, herbal, and distinctly sharp and hot, but less so than that of some Asian types.

Traditionally associated with soul food, curled mustard probably arrived with African slaves. Since its introduction, it has most often been cooked one way: boiled many hours with fatty parts of the pig until soft and sweetly pork-imbued.

PREPARATION: Discard dried, very coarse, or yellowing leaves. Wash mustard in tepid water, swishing vigorously. Lift out gently so that debris falls to the bottom. Drain and repeat until no sand remains.

Most curled mustard must be stemmed: Hold a leaf folded in its natural position. With the other hand, slowly pull the stem end toward the leaf tip to zip off the fibrous "backbone." For leaves to be used as wrappers, do not strip stems: Slice them flush with the leaf base, then cut a notch to remove any tough stem that might resist rolling. "Mini" mustards need only a rinse—the stems need not be removed.

TO COOK: Cook three different ways for three different tastes.

(1) Barely wilt: Toss with hot dressing or sauce, or fold mustard chiffonade into hot beans, grains, or pasta to retain maximum aroma, color—and sometimes breathtaking sharpness. Or pour boiling water over whole trimmed leaves to soften for wrapping.

(2) Short-cook: Boil a few minutes in broth or water for greens that are bright, juicy, and tender but low in bite and scent; or steam 4 to 5 minutes for tender leaves with a bit more flavor and heat.

(3) Long-cook: Earthy bitterness and depth develop in greens that are slow-braised; but bite, perfume, and color dissipate.

(Note also that Southern or American mustard can be substituted in recipes and recipe ideas that feature giant-leaf Japanese mustard.)

Mustard Greens, Spinach, and Avocado with Sweet Dressing

Boiling-hot dressing softens the mustard greens' bite (in terms of both taste and texture) and rich avocado further tames it in this vivid, unusual salad. Seek small-leafed greens, which are perkier and less fibrous than large ones in most cases.

½ pound small Southern curled (or Japanese)
    mustard greens
½ pound small spinach leaves
1 medium California avocado
    (about ¾ pound)
1 small-medium red onion
3 tablespoons cider vinegar
3 tablespoons currants or raisins
1 teaspoon Worcestershire sauce
¼ teaspoon (or more) hot pepper sauce
½ cup tomato juice
1½ tablespoons vegetable oil
½ teaspooon cornstarch blended
    with 1 tablespoon water
Salt

1. Discard dried, wilted, or yellow mustard leaves. Wash mustard in plenty of tepid water, lifting out so that debris sinks. Repeat until no sand remains. Do same to spinach. Spin-dry both greens. Strip stems from mustard. Trim spinach. Stack or bunch leaves and cut into very thin slices. Transfer to a serving bowl.

2. Halve, pit, and peel avocado. Cut into small dice. Peel and dice onion.

3. Combine vinegar, currants, Worcestershire, and hot sauce in small non-aluminum pan and bring to a boil, stirring. Let stand off heat 5 minutes, then add onion, tomato juice, oil, and cornstarch mixture. Bring to a boil, stirring. Taste and season.

4. Pour over greens and toss at once. Add avocado, toss, and serve immediately.

Serves 4

Mustard Green Pilaf with Oranges and Olives

Mustard greens add a chewy consistency and herbal edge to the toasty rice—but they lose their bright color. For fresher color and a much sharper flavor, reserve half the mustard, cut it into fine chiffonade, and incorporate the raw shreds when you add the orange and nuts. Use tart, assertive green olives, such as Greek or Spanish style, not mild French or American types.

> ½ pound Southern curled mustard greens
> 1½ tablespoons olive oil
> 1 garlic clove, minced
> ½ teaspoon cumin seeds
> 1 cup long-grain aromatic white rice
> 1 cup orange juice
> ½ teaspoon grated orange zest
> 1 tablespoon lemon juice
> ½ teaspoon kosher salt
> 1 tablespoon honey
> ¾ cup water
> 3 tablespoons sliced green olives
> 1 orange, sectioned and diced
> 3 tablespoons roasted, chopped cashews, almonds, or sunflower seeds

1. Discard any dry or yellowed leaves, then wash mustard in several changes of water. Strip off stems. Without drying leaves, chop fine. Cook mustard in non-aluminum pot, covered, over low heat, stirring often, until just softened—about 5 minutes.

2. Meanwhile, heat oil in heavy medium saucepan over moderate heat. Add garlic and cumin and stir. Add rice and cook, stirring often, until golden, about 6 minutes.

3. Combine orange juice and zest, lemon juice, salt, and honey in a bowl, stirring to blend. Add to rice, with greens, water, and olives. Bring to a boil, stirring. Reduce heat to lowest point, cover and cook 20 minutes. Without uncovering, remove from heat; let stand 15 minutes.

4. Fluff rice into a dish, incorporating orange dice and nuts.

Serves 4

Pros Propose

Southern curled mustard is by no means limited to the American South. Chef Neela Paniz prepares this mighty hot **Spicy Greens in Mustard Oil** at her Bombay Cafe in Los Angeles: Heat mustard oil in wok (or karhai) until it loses its yellow color. Add brown mustard seeds and cover. When sizzling stops, add several dried Árbol chillis and brown lightly. Gradually add stemmed, chopped mustard greens and peeled, chopped broccoli raab, tossing in more as each addition wilts. Salt and cook gently, covered, until vegetables become a coarse, tender puree, adding water as needed.

A French-style **Mustard Green Gratin** comes from chef Jeffrey Weiss: Cook roasted garlic cloves in heavy cream until reduced by half. Add stemmed, blanched mustard greens and cook until soft, about 20 minutes. Transfer to baking dish and cover with shredded Gruyère and fresh bread crumbs. Brown under broiler.

Confit of goose is as natural in French New Orleans as are the adopted mustard greens. For **Baby Mustard Green Salad with Goose Confit**, chef Jamie Shannon simply warms pieces of confit, seasons them with a little cane vinegar, and then arranges them on tiny curled mustard leaves and mild lettuce.

For a more traditional Southern approach to greens, Shannon cooks **Braised Mustard Greens:** Cook bacon to render fat. Add onions, garlic, pepper, and salt. Gradually add stripped, chopped mustard greens, adding more and more layers as they cook down, to fill pot. Add cane vinegar. Without adding more liquid, cook until tender. "You want to be eating greens, and more greens, not bacon, and not other flavors," says Shannon, who serves onion-and-crumb-crusted fried rabbit and iron-skillet corn bread with the greens.

Southern staples get a Southeast Asian lift in **Glazed Pork with Sweetpotato Soufflé on Braised Mustard Greens,** from chef Jeff Weiss: Marinate tenderloin in reduction of pineapple juice with guava, Jalapeño, and star anise. Roast, basting with marinade. Gradually add stemmed mustard to light chicken stock seasoned with kaffir lime, ginger, and galanga, adding more greens until pot is filled. Cover; oven-braise until tender. Spoon greens and some liquid into deep dishes. Top with sweetpotato soufflé and fanned pork slices.

Humble hocks are refined in pureed **Mustard-Potato Soup with Ham Croutons** from chef Chris Hastings: Prepare ham broth with mirepoix, chillis, tomatoes, chicken stock, and ham hocks. Remove hocks and shred meat, mixing with roasted garlic to the texture of rillettes. Gently cook onions and garlic in oil. Stir in stripped large mustard greens, adding more gradually as they wilt down. Add cubed (unpeeled) new-crop potatoes and the broth. Cook until greens are tender. Puree soup, which should be slightly thick. Spread rillette mixture on toasted baguette slices and float on soup.

Chef Jerry Traunfeld claims no traditional roots. His dish is in a class by itself. For **Hot-Smoked Salmon with Mustard-Green Butter Sauce:** Brine salmon with salt and sugar. Pat dry. Smoke over dried basil stems. Pack shredded mustard leaves into a warmed blender, half-fill with warm very thin beurre blanc, and puree until smooth. Serve at once (or the color turns drab) with the heated salmon. Top with purple mustard chiffonade and mustard blossoms.

Wrapped Heart Mustard

Also dai gai choy and variations (Chinese), Swatow mustard or cabbage, heading mustard

This is the mustard that appears most often in Asian and Oriental markets—fortunately, for it is a versatile and luscious green, as I hope you'll agree the four recipes illustrate. Various forms of the ribbed, vaguely romaine-like leaves swirl into long flattened heads. Usually, their ruffly tops have been chopped and one sees only a thick cluster of tightly furled pale leaf-bases edged with darker green (central and right heads in photo). Raw, the mustard is ferocious and is traditionally tamed by salt-pickling (as for kimchee). Cooked, its fleshy stalks and leaves turn bright jade, bittersweet, and juicy.

PREPARATION: Trim the base to separate the leaves; drop them into water. Halve the cores (hearts) and rinse. Check each leaf for grit where it attaches to the stalk. For most dishes, cut ribs and leaves into fairly large triangles or squares, following their natural forms; or thin-slice on the diagonal. Alternatively, to cook small whole hearts (see pair in photo, right), trim the bases and cut off upper leaves; dunk the hearts into water, top down, and slosh to dislodge grit.

TO COOK: This mustard should be cooked through, but I prefer a few minutes to the hours often recommended. Unlike most greens, this barely shrinks in cooking. For mildest flavor, brightest color, and tenderest texture: blanch, slice, and stir-fry. For more tooth and bite: Stir-fry raw sliced stalks, then add leaves; moisten with liquid, cover and cook a few minutes; thicken lightly with cornstarch. Add pork, seafood, or beef to any of the above. For hearts alone, simply blanch with a little oil, salt, and sugar.

Gorgeous Green Mustard Hearts

A simple treatment produces spectacular results: juicy, bittersweet art nouveau swirls of mustard stalks gleam like polished jade on emerald leaf ribbons. Although culinary traditions of both West and East are ignored (we do not condone the use of baking soda to brighten and tenderize greens; the Chinese do not serve sliced leaves with the hearts or use olive oil), the dish seems to fit menus from around the world. Sautéed shrimp and brown rice suit nicely. Before shopping, check the photo (center pair) to identify the right form.

6 small partly trimmed wrapped heart mustards (about 6 ounces each)
2 quarts water
4 teaspoons sugar
4 teaspoons kosher salt
1 tablespoon olive oil
½ teaspoon baking soda

1. If necessary, remove any yellowed leaves and cracked stems from mustard. Trim a small amount from bases, being careful not to cut apart the leaves (these are

now "hearts"). Slice leafy tops into ½-inch-wide ribbons. Rinse well; drain. Wash hearts in several changes of water, sloshing gently to clean hard-to-reach crannies.

2. Select a deep sauté pan or skillet that will hold the hearts in a close-fitting single layer with the water. Combine water, sugar, salt, olive oil, and baking soda in the pan; cover, and bring to a boil.

3. Uncover, add hearts, and boil until barely tender, 1½ to 2½ minutes, turning with tongs after 1 minute. Lift up hearts from base end, letting water drip back into the pan. Set on cutting board.

4. Drop ribbons into the boiling water, return to a full boil, then drain at once. Spread on a warm serving platter. Halve hearts. Arrange over ribbons, leaving spaces between. Serve at once.

Serves 4 to 6

Wok-Braised Wrapped Heart Mustard

This venerable dish, described to me by Chinese cooking authority Stephen Wong, need not be confined to Asian meals—but *do* cook it in a wok to prevent the mass of greens from flipping onto the stove. The bright, bitter stems and resilient leaves fit any meal at which you might serve braised or sautéed broccoli raab, dandelions, or escarole. The ginger doesn't add an Asian note but merely highlights mustard's natural nip. Choose heads (or trimmed hearts) with minimal leaves and big fleshy stems for maximum meatiness and juiciness.

1½ pounds partly trimmed wrapped mustard
1 garlic clove
1-inch chunk of ginger

wrapped heart mustard: full, trimmed, and hearts

length: 6-16 inches

1 tablespoon mild vegetable oil
Optional: 2 tablespoons minced firm
  dry-cured ham
¼ cup broth (ham, vegetable, mushroom,
  chicken, or beef)
1 teaspoon cornstarch, dissolved in
  1 tablespoon water
Salt and pepper

1. Trim bases of mustard and separate leaves. Wash thoroughly, checking carefully for grit. Drain. Cut apart ribs and leafy parts. Cut ribs into 2-inch segments on the bias. Cut leaves crosswise into 1-inch strips. Mince garlic. Peel ginger and cut into fine julienne. Have the other ingredients wok-ready.

2. Set wok over moderate heat. Add oil, optional ham, garlic, and ginger and toss. Add mustard stems and stir-fry until bright green, a minute or two. Add leaves and toss to coat with oil.

3. Add broth. Cover wok and simmer until greens are just barely tender, about 3 minutes, tossing a few times. Stir in cornstarch mixture and toss a moment, until sauce thickens. Scoop into a warm dish. Season. Serve hot.

Serves 4

Variation

If you prefer milder and softer ribs—and an even brighter green—blanch them before stir-frying. Drop into boiling salted water and return to a rolling boil. Drain and dry. In step 2, simply toss to coat with oil, then add leaves and proceed.

Fried Rice with Wrapped Heart Mustard, Red Pepper, and Eggs

Festive colors, lively textures, and flavor that is equally appealing hot and at room temperature make this dish a good choice for company meals. In fifteen minutes, the mixture molds into a smoothly rounded cake that holds its shape neatly even after being cut. The juicy dai gai choy tastes bitter and hot—deliciously so—but if your taste runs to mild, substitute Canton or Shanghai bok choy for half the mustard.

If you have 3 cups leftover rice (that's what packs into the usual take-out container), the cold grains work even better. If fried rice is new to your repertoire, you may be pleased to discover how moist, fresh, and light it can be, compared with most restaurant versions. As usual for Chinese dishes, prep is time-consuming, cooking is speedy.

1 cup long-grain white rice (not converted)
1¾ cups water
About 1 pound wrapped heart mustard
1 bunch scallions (green onions)
1 red bell pepper
3 tablespoons shoyu (Japanese soy sauce)
Optional: 1 to 2 teaspoons Chinese chilli sauce
  or puree from chiles chipotles en adobo
3 eggs
2 teaspoons Asian (dark) sesame oil
2 tablespoons vegetable oil
1 to 3 large garlic cloves, minced
2 tablespoons fine-diced ginger

1. Combine rice and water in a heavy 1- to 2-quart saucepan with close-fitting cover. Bring to a rolling boil, stirring occasionally. Reduce heat to lowest point, cover, and cook 15 minutes.

2. Without uncovering, remove pot from heat and let stand 15 to 30 minutes, as convenient. With a fork, separate the grains, fluffing into a bowl to cool.

3. Trim off and discard base and any browned leaf edges from mustard. Pull leaves apart and wash carefully in several changes of water. Cut into thin diagonal slices, separating leafy top parts and heavy stems. Cut pale parts of scallions into ¼-inch slices; thin-slice greens. Cut pepper into ¼-inch dice. Blend shoyu and optional chilli sauce.

4. Combine eggs and sesame oil in small bowl, blending with a fork. Heat wok over moderate heat. Pour in ½ tablespoon vegetable oil, then add eggs and scramble quickly, until just barely set. Scoop into dish; set aside. Wipe out wok with paper towel.

5. Return wok to moderate heat. Add remaining 1½ tablespoons oil. Add garlic and ginger and toss. Add mustard stems, raise heat to high, and toss for about a minute. Add red pepper, pale scallion slices, and mustard leaves. Stir-fry until vegetables are lightly cooked but still quite crunchy, about a minute.

6. Add rice and half the scallion greens, stir-frying until slightly browned, 2 to 3 minutes. Add shoyu and eggs, tossing and chopping eggs with spatula or spoon to form small bits. Remove from heat.

7. Pack mixture very lightly into 2-quart bowl; pat surface flat. Cover with towel and let stand about 15 minutes to blend flavors.

8. Remove towel, set serving dish on top, and invert. Sprinkle remaining scallions over and around. Serve hot, warm, or at room temperature.

**Serves 4 as a main dish,
6 to 7 as part of a Chinese meal**

Stir-Fried Shrimp and Cashews over Wrapped Heart Mustard

This dish is adapted from a chicken stir-fry developed by Yu Wen-Shen and Huang Hsien some years ago at the Hilton International Taipei. The mustard has an assertive radishy edge that is balanced by the sweetness of cashews and shrimp. Although it is seasoned forcefully, the egg binding mellows the dish, making it milder and silkier than most stir-fries. Save the leaves to sliver into egg drop soup—whether Chinese-style or alla romana.

1¼ pounds medium shrimp in the shell
2 tablespoons soy sauce
2 teaspoons cornstarch
1 egg
2 medium heads partly trimmed wrapped heart mustard (1½ to 2 pounds)
1 or 2 small fresh chillis, preferably red
2 medium-large scallions (green onions)
2 large garlic cloves
2 tablespoons peanut oil
Salt and pepper
2 tablespoons Chinese rice wine or dry sherry
1 tablespoon distilled white vinegar
½ cup roasted cashews

1. Shell shrimp and devein. Stir together 1 tablespoon soy sauce and 1¾ teaspoons cornstarch; add egg and whisk to blend. Add shrimp, tossing to coat. Marinate while you prepare the other ingredients.

2. Set a large serving dish in oven and turn it to lowest setting. Separate mustard leaves. Trim off most of the leafy part (save for another dish), keeping only the ribs; rinse these very thoroughly. Cut into triangles, about 2 inches on a side. Drop into boiling salted water and cook until just crisp-tender, about 2 minutes. Drain and refresh in cold water. Drain and spread on towel.

3. Cut chilli into hair-thin strips. Trim scallions and cut on sharp diagonal into 2-inch slices. Slice garlic. Drain shrimp in sieve.

4. Heat wok over moderate heat. Pour 1 tablespoon oil around rim. Add mustard and toss to heat through. Sprinkle with salt and pepper. Arrange in the heated serving dish. Set in oven.

5. Combine chilli, wine, vinegar, and remaining 1 tablespoon soy and ¼ teaspoon cornstarch. Pour remaining 1 tablespoon oil into wok. Add scallions and garlic and toss briefly over high heat. Add shrimp and toss until not quite cooked through. Add wine mixture and toss a minute. Add cashews and toss.

6. Immediately scoop over greens. Serve hot.

Serves 4

Pros Propose

Fragrant Butter-Laced Pureed Mustard Greens is the soul food of the Punjabi Sikhs of Amritsar, according to Julie Sahni in *Classic Indian Vegetarian and Grain Cooking,* and like southern soul food, it is eaten with corn bread. To prepare: Combine fresh chillis, asafoetida (or onion), and a little cornmeal in a pot and bring to a boil. Add chopped wrapped heart mustard and spinach and simmer, covered, until very soft, about 1 hour. Puree. Add cornstarch slurry and cook until smooth. Lightly brown shredded ginger and thick-sliced garlic in butter or ghee. Transfer puree to a shallow dish, gently drizzle over the butter, and stir lightly to lace puree with butter streaks.

Although wrapped heart mustard is traditional in Indian cooking, chef Floyd Cardoz's contemporary creation is hardly that. For **Seared Duck Breast with Mustard and Hoppers:** Braise duck legs in stock seasoned with mirepoix, ginger, cumin, garlic, coriander, pepper, and star anise. Strain liquid; reserve. Shred duck meat. Soften shallots, ginger, and garlic in corn oil. Add ground versions of the same spices as above. Cook briefly. Add thin-sliced mustard stalks and ribs; toss a minute. Add chopped leafy parts; cook lightly. Add chickpea flour to thicken. Add shredded duck. Prepare crêpes (Sri Lankan "hoppers") of fermented rice flour and coconut milk. Roll up the mustard-duck mixture in these. Serve with reduced braising liquid and seared, sliced duck breast.

Eileen Yin-Fei Lo, Chinese cooking authority, always blanches wrapped mustard—perhaps because of her experience in China, where it is far more bitter, she says. Swatow cabbage, another one of the confusing array of colloquial names for the mustard, is the one she prefers. To prepare **Stir-Fried Beef and Swatow Cabbage:** Thin-slice mustard ribs and stalks on diagonal. Blanch in boiling water with a little sugar and baking soda; drain. Briefly marinate thin strips of London broil in cornstarch, ginger juice, Shaoxing wine, oyster sauce, soy sauce, white pepper, and sugar. Stir-fry minced garlic and ginger in oil. Add beef and toss to partly cook. Add mustard and toss to heat through. Thicken with cornstarch slurry.

Spicy Mustard Soup, Somewhat Indonesian comes from the eclectic Sylvia Thompson (*The Kitchen Garden Cookbook*): Combine chicken broth, quartered and thin-sliced onion, chopped garlic, turmeric, and seeded, chopped small chillis. Bring to a simmer; add mustard greens—the leaves coarse-chopped, stems thin-sliced. Simmer, uncovered, until greens are tender. Shortly before serving, stir in corn kernels and cooked black beans and cook until corn is just tender. Add diced tomato, ground coriander, and lime juice. Season. Serve with rice on the side.

length: 8-10 inches

bamboo or leaf mustard   length: 10-14 inches

Bamboo or Leaf Mustard

Also juk gai choy and variations (Chinese), small gai choy, and stickleaf mustard

The names listed are likely matches for the vegetables pictured according to a group of confused experts (myself included). But when you do see this ubiquitous Oriental market mustard, the bunch alongside will probably look different enough for you to wonder about its identity—as we all do. It may be darker or

lighter romaine green, multi-branched or single-stalked, wide-stemmed or slim-stemmed, ribbed or not, leafier or less so. It is always smaller (juk means small) than dai gai choy (dai means large).

But whichever name it wears or doesn't wear, the mustard should be something like this: The stems are comparatively narrow and rounded or celery-shaped and almost as juicy and mild as bok choy; the slightly ruffled, fairly narrow leaves are thin and lettuce-like but taste mustard-sharp. Taste before you use it, as with any mustard: Some bunches are mild, some strong. In my experience, the paler and plumper the stalks, the milder the taste.

PREPARATION: If stalks join at the base, cut them apart. Wash well, for grit lurks between them. Cut whole stalks and leaves into 1½-inch lengths. Do not plan on keeping more than a few days. The mustard wilts quickly.

TO COOK: Bamboo mustard positively shines in soup. In a few minutes, the stalks cook to juicy and buttery-bittersweet as the leaves soften silkily. Or braise briefly in a tart-sweet sauce. Or blanch momentarily, then heat through with stir-fried seafood or pork. The most delicate specimens can be sliced raw into salad.

Quick Pick-Me-Up Bamboo Mustard and Noodle Soup

The tonic effect of chicken broth is well known in the West and East. Here, the two worlds meet easily in a ten-minute preparation that combines the typically Jewish additions of egg noodles and dill with the typically Chinese ginger and mustard cabbage. The stalks turn tender and juicy, while the leaves melt into the broth, and both parts become a brilliant green. A soup that feels familiar but not ordinary, it is doubly equipped to cure what ails you—or just to enjoy as a quick lunch or first course. If the soup stands a while before being served, the noodles swell and take over; add another cup of broth to rebalance if needed.

5 cups flavorful chicken broth
½ teaspoon dried dill
½ teaspoon kosher salt (omit if broth is salted)
2 teaspoons hair-thin ginger julienne
About ½ pound bamboo mustard
About 3 ounces skinny, short dried egg noodles
  (if long, break them)
A few tablespoons Chinese rice wine,
  medium-dry sherry, or Madeira

1. Combine broth, dill, salt, and ginger in a pot and bring to a boil.

2. Meanwhile, trim ends of mustard stalks. Halve leaves lengthwise. Cut leaves and stems into 1-inch sections. Drop into water and swish around to clean. Lift out, and repeat if necessary.

3. Add noodles to broth: Boil until slightly tender, a minute or so. Add mustard pieces and boil until tender, 1 to 2 minutes.

4. Stir in wine to taste, a tablespoon at a time. Serve at once.

Serves 4

Gingery, Juicy Sweet-Sour Bamboo Mustard

For a lively change-of-pace vegetable that's nothing fancy—but hardly everyday—toss together these ingredients and simmer until the mustard loses its crunch. The sweet-tart mélange makes a good sauce and vegetable for broiled or pan fried meat or seafood. Don't rush the cooking by raising the heat, or the mustard will not cook through.

1½ to 1¾ pounds bamboo mustard
½ pound ripe tomatoes, coarse-chopped
  (peeled or not, to taste)
1½ tablespoons minced ginger
¼ cup raisins (dark or golden)
1 to 2 tablespoons brown sugar
1½ tablespoons mild vegetable oil
½ teaspoon kosher salt
1 small garlic clove, minced
1 teaspoon cornstarch
1 tablespoon distilled white vinegar

1. Pull apart mustard bunches by separating stems. Rinse thoroughly in several changes of water. Line up stalks. Trim bases as needed, then cut mustard crosswise into 1- to 1½-inch pieces.

2. Combine mustard with tomatoes, 1 tablespoon ginger, raisins, 1 tablespoon brown sugar, oil, and salt in a deep wide non-aluminum skillet or sauté pan. Stir over high heat until greens are wilted.

3. Reduce heat to moderately low. Stir often until stalks are tender, roughly 10 minutes. Taste and add sugar if needed. Add garlic and raise heat to moderate. Continue cooking until little liquid remains, another minute or two.

4. Blend cornstarch, vinegar, and remaining ½ tablespoon ginger. Stirring constantly, add to pan and return to a boil. Serve at once.

Serves 4

Pros Propose

Lighter textured than most mustards, the bamboo type invites ingredients of a similar nature, such as those in **Fresh Rice Noodles with Bamboo Mustard, Shrimp, and Chicken** from chef Ken Snapp: Cut mustard leaves and base into 2-inch pieces. Blanch quickly. Refresh in cold water. Stir-fry shrimp and chicken strips with garlic until almost done. Add soft fresh wide rice noodles, tossing. Stir in diced tomatoes, the mustard, fish sauce, sweet soy, and lime juice. Serve at once.

Fresh rice noodles are also a silky backdrop in **Mustard and Pork Noodle Soup,** a traditional dish interpreted by restaurant consultant Stephen Wong. To prepare: Marinate pork slices in cornstarch, Chinese rice wine, salt and pepper. Boil chicken stock, ginger, and chopped Tianjin preserved vegetable. Stir in the pork and bamboo mustard, cut into 1-inch pieces. Add fresh rice noodles and a dash of sesame oil. Serve at once.

World explorers, photographers, and cookbook authors Naomi Duguid and Jeffrey Alford discovered the following aromatic stew in Luang Prabang, in Laos.

Unlike most recipes for bamboo mustard, this one is long-cooked to a soft mass. For **Pork Stew with Bamboo Mustard:** Heat pork fat or oil. Add minced garlic and chopped shallots and toss until golden. Add lean pork shoulder cut into strips and stir-fry until no longer pink. Add 2-inch strips bamboo mustard, fresh dill, sliced garlic chives, and shredded kaffir lime leaves. Add water to almost cover, then simmer, partly covered, until soft and stewy. Add fish sauce, thin-sliced green onion, and pepper. Serve with rice.

Red-in-Snow Mustard

Also green-in-snow mustard, hseuh li hung and variations (Chinese)

This mustard is called red-in-snow in books on Chinese food; thus one can only wonder at the blatant

red-in-snow mustard

length of bunches: 12-14 inches

greenness of the loosely bunched, sharply serrated leaves, which resemble (but are not) a mizuna-dandelion cross. In *Florence Lin's Complete Book of Chinese Noodles, Dumplings, and Breads,* the author explains that "the name should, of course, be green-in-snow, but since the Chinese love red, they put that color in the name." One still wonders . . . but I can find no other explanation.

Like wrapped mustard, red-in-snow is traditionally "blanched, then fermented with salt and vinegar for the very popular sour mustard pickle used in soups and stir-fries," says the Chinese food authority Eileen Yin-Fei Lo. She advises blanching the leaves to add to soups or stir-fries. But from what I have sampled from New York's Chinatown, I cannot imagine why red- or green-in-snow is not used fresh—all the time, all over. The raw or lightly cooked mustard offers a unique balance of deeply sweet, herbal, and cabbagey, with a glowing spiciness that grows slowly in the mouth.

I was not surprised to learn that red-in-snow is popular on the West Coast, where vegetables are often established before they become part of the East Coast garden. A grower based in Seattle, Koua Lee, owner of Mai Choy Produce, says, "I sell it to people at home and in restaurants, and they all love it. It is very popular in the farmers' market especially."

PREPARATION: Trim the base of each little loosely bunched head to separate the stalks. Remove coarse or yellowing leaves. Rinse well. If small and tender, cut stems flush with leaf and cook whole or halved leaves. If large, strip stems and use leaves only.

TO COOK—OR NOT: For small, very fresh specimens, try a salad that includes crisp, sweet elements—such as apples or grapes—and smoked meat. Or steam for a few minutes to tenderize the stems, then gloss with butter or sesame oil. Or serve the hot greens with a peanut, sesame, or mustard dressing. Or cook in soup, like bamboo mustard.

Steamed Red-in-Snow Mustard

Barely cooked, this full-flavored mustard becomes tender and bright green. The bitter, sharp, aromatic elements are modified but not mellowed—a treat for mustard lovers and vegetable purists, but not for everyone. Bracing and cleansing, the simple presentation makes a good backdrop for pork, duck, shrimp, or scallops. Or serve as a side to coconut-enriched curries or rich, spicy vegetable stews.

1 pound fairly small red-in-snow mustard
Butter, olive oil, or Asian (dark) sesame oil

1. Trim base of each mustard bunchlet to separate stalks. Remove any unusually coarse or yellowing leaves. Rinse trimmed leaves well.
2. Spread on rack of large steamer over boiling water. Cover and cook until just tender, 2 to 3 minutes, turning once with tongs to redistribute.
3. Transfer to towel to blot dry. Immediately transfer to heated serving dish and gloss with butter (or your oil of choice). Serve hot.

Serves 4

Variation

Red-in-Snow Mustard with Sweet Sesame Dressing

1½ tablespoons white sesame seeds
¼ teaspoon grated lemon zest
2 tablespoons lemon juice
1 tablespoon peanut oil (preferably roasted)
1 tablespoon shoyu (Japanese soy sauce)
1 tablespoon orange or lemon marmalade
2 teaspoons fine-grated ginger
1 tablespoon water

In small pan, stir sesame seeds over low heat until tan, about 5 minutes. Place 1 tablespoon in suribachi or mortar and crush fine. Blend in lemon zest, juice, oil, shoyu, marmalade, ginger, and water. (Alternatively, combine the ingredients in a blender; whirl to blend and puree as smooth as possible.) Spoon over the hot mustard. Sprinkle with remaining sesame seeds. Serve at once.

Giant-Leafed Mustard

Also Japanese mustard,
purple mustard, red mustard,
aka takana (Japanese)

Giant-leafed mustards, as the purple-green leaves pictured here are often called, are, ironically, represented primarily by miniatures in the United States. The naturally huge beauties (the bunch on the left is medium-size), harvested when tiny, are most familiar as the punchy little two-tone leaves (bordeaux backed by shamrock—pictured on the upper right) that sharpen so many salad and braising mixes.

Although there are all-green forms of these puckered leaves, the most common are maroon or bronzed purple, or green-tipped or veined with oxblood. As with most red- and purple-leafed vegetables, the coloring comes with chilly growing conditions: If plants are field-grown in cool areas, the red tones deepen; in warmer areas or greenhouses, redness may not develop. For this reason, greenhouse-raised purple micro-mustards are nearly all green (see the fluffy pile on the lower right).

Chinese in origin, these mustards have been adopted by Japan, as some of their names indicate: Osaka Purple, Miike Giant, Aka Takana, Aka Chirimen. Mini-forms nothwithstanding, the full-grown specimens can be really big (although their texture remains quite tender) and *really* hot—hotter than other mustard greens in the market.

"Aka takana is especially known on the southern island of Kyushu, where other plants can't live in the

giant-leafed (Japanese) mustard: large and trimmed (*upper and lower left*), miniature and micro (*upper and lower right*)

length of bunch: 12-14 inches

poor volcanic earth," explains chef Masaharu Mori-moto. As in China, it is used primarily for pickles, "which are very popular all over Japan, in soups and sometimes wrapped around rice, instead of seaweed," Morimoto says. Seaweed (usually kelp) may also figure in the pickle, as do chillis and the requisite salt.

Asked whether the mustard is ever used fresh, Morimoto replied with a smile in his voice: "Japanese do not like much change. Aka takana is for pickles. You do not try it for something different." But he recalls that it is occasionally boiled, squeezed dry, chopped, and mixed with sesame or mustard sauce to serve at room temperature.

FOR PREPARATION AND TO COOK: Follow directions for Southern or American mustard (page 397). Japanese mustard can also be substituted in recipes for American mustard. Note that whether it is cooked for seconds or hours, purple mustard turns green and the water it cooks in turns navy blue.

Red or Green Mustard Spring Rolls

Oddly enough, Japanese red mustard leaves wrapped around Vietnamese spring roll filling wind up looking like Middle Eastern stuffed grape leaves! Southern curled mustard works equally well, provided the leaves are large. Both types make dandy wrappers, but first must be blanched to become more mellow (although still peppery and bitter) and malleable. Thus transformed, the forgiving "crêpes" can be rerolled, patched, and otherwise handled in ways that dough doesn't permit (but keep some blanched leaves for "bandaging," just in case). Fine-cut raw leaves lend perfume and a sharp, invigorating bite.

Dried rice noodles, also called rice sticks, are packaged in varying weights and sizes with myriad romanized names. Whether mai fun, mi fen, sen mee, bihon, or bun—or a bunch more—what you buy should look like thick white thread.

DIPPING SAUCE

2 or 3 limes
4 teaspoons sugar
½ teaspoon minced garlic

2 teaspoons minced ginger
¼ cup shoyu (Japanese soy sauce)

SPRING ROLLS

About 2 dozen large Japanese mustard leaves
4 or 5 whole star anise "flowers"
About 4 ounces very thin dried rice noodles (vermicelli)
2 medium carrots, peeled
1 tablespoon sugar
1 tablespoon distilled white vinegar
3 tablespoons thin-sliced scallion greens
½ cup roasted, salted, and chopped peanuts
1 cup (not packed) cilantro or basil leaves

1. Prepare sauce: Scrub 1 lime and grate enough zest to equal ½ heaping teaspoon. Halve and squeeze as many limes as needed to yield ⅓ cup juice. Combine zest, juice, sugar, garlic, ginger, and shoyu. Set aside.

2. Fill large pot with water and bring to a simmer. Meanwhile, prepare greens: Slice off each stem flush with leaf, then cut a deep notch in leaf to remove any remaining wide stem that may resist rolling. If very big, cut out stem entirely and separate halves. Reserve 2 leaves.

3. Combine enough water to cover noodles in a pot with the star anise and bring to a boil. Pour over noodles in heatproof bowl. Soak until just tender, about 15 minutes.

4. Meanwhile, immerse a few mustard leaves at a time in the simmering water. Remove with tongs as soon as pliable. Spread on towel, dark side down, notched ends toward you. When all are done, cover with a towel.

5. Cut carrots into 2-inch matchsticks. Toss with sugar and vinegar. Cut 2 reserved mustard leaves into fine chiffonade. Remove star anise and drain noodles, then spin-dry. Chop into 2-inch pieces.

6. Prepare rolls: Divide noodles evenly among leaves, placing in center of each with a margin on both edges. Top with scallions and peanuts. Arrange carrots lengthwise on each roll. Top with mustard chiffonade and cilantro. Fold notched edge of each leaf over filling. Fold the sides over toward the center. Roll up as tightly as possible and set seam side down on a serving dish. (Rolls keep several hours at room temperature,

covered with plastic wrap. For overnight storage, refrigerate; bring to room temperature to serve.)

7. Serve with the dipping sauce, either as a passed hors d'oeuvre or as an appetizer or first course.

Makes about 20 rolls to serve 5 as a first course, more as an hors d'oeuvre

Pasta with Mustard-Green Pesto, Walnuts, and Raisins

A curious and delicious dish for lovers of bitter greens. The mustard leaves, sprinkled with boiling water and pureed, keep their strong herbal scent and sharp flavor—which are then reinforced by the raw mustard filaments. Curly egg noodles can replace Italian pasta. If the nuts need to be toasted, spread them in a pan and bake at 350°F until they just begin to color and their husks split, 8 to 10 minutes. Then rub lightly in a towel to remove loose husks.

> ¼ cup golden raisins
> 1 tablespoon balsamic or sherry vinegar
> 1 tablespoon water
> 6 ounces large Japanese red mustard leaves
>   (at room temperature)
> ½ teaspoon kosher salt
> 1 small garlic clove, sliced
> ½ cup toasted walnuts
> 3 tablespoons boiling water
> 6 tablespoons olive oil
> 1 pound Italian imported pasta shells, farfalle,
>   or twists
> Salt and pepper

1. Combine raisins, vinegar, and water in very small saucepan and bring to a boil. Cover and turn off heat. Let stand while you prepare other ingredients.

2. Cut mustard leaves from stalks, to make 2 halves (or fold leaves in half and pull off stalks). Rinse and spin-dry. Reserve 3 leaf halves for garnish. Discard stalks.

3. In food processor, combine leaves, salt, garlic, and half the nuts. Drip the boiling water evenly over all. Cover at once and whiz to a coarse puree, scraping down sides several times. With motor running, gradually add oil.

4. Cook pasta in boiling salted water until al dente. Meanwhile, cut reserved mustard into thinnest chiffonade. Chop reserved walnuts.

5. Drain pasta well. Toss with pesto. Season. Sprinkle raisins over. Divide among bowls. Top with walnuts and chiffonade.

Serves 6 to 8 as a first course

Spaghetti with Mustard Chiffonade and Goat Cheese

At home, for a quick, casual dinner, I toss together this dish and love it. Be warned: Others may find raw mustard too sharp and coarse. But for our taste, the goat cheese and warmth of the pasta mellow the mustard ribbons just enough to produce a bracing blend of garlicky, pungent, bitter, and herbal elements. Cut the leaves hair-thin, or they will not meld with the spaghetti.

> 6 ounces Japanese purple mustard or Southern
>   curled mustard greens
> ½ pound imported Italian whole wheat
>   spaghetti
> 1½ tablespoons flavorful olive oil
> 3 to 4 ounces fresh, crumbly goat cheese

1. Fold leaves in half and strip off stalks; discard. Rinse leaves. Stack a half-dozen or so at a time, roll into a tight cigar, and cut into super-thin slivers. (You'll have about 2 lightly packed cups.)

2. Drop pasta into plenty of boiling salted water. Cook until al dente. Stir in half the leaves and remove from heat at once. Drain. Immediately toss with olive oil and remaining leaves, mixing well.

3. Divide between heated pasta bowls. Crumble over cheese. Toss and serve at once.

Serves 2

Pros Propose

The following recipes feature Japanese mustard, but recipes for Southern curled mustard will work too. When tiny, the raw leaves make a vivid base for luxury seafoods. Jeffrey Weiss prepares **Tuna Carpaccio on Mustard Greens with Tobiko Vinaigrette:** Sear tuna "loin" in peanut oil. Wrap and chill. Prepare dressing of ginger oil, ponzu (citrus juices), and shoyu. To serve, arrange mini- and/or micro-mustards on plates; surround with tuna slices. Add tobiko (flying fish roe) to dressing, stirring gently. Drizzle over.

Seafood is also the subject of chef Jerry Traunfeld's elegant **Mustard-Wrapped Black Cod with Beet and Lemon Sauce.** To prepare sauce: Boil raw beet juice, white wine, shallots, and lemon juice until almost syrupy; stir in butter. Blanch very large red mustard leaves until stems are pliant. Refresh in cold water; drain. Wrap a seasoned black cod fillet in each leaf. Steam. Serve wrapped fillets with sauce and tiny cooked beet dice.

Not surprisingly, Japanese mustards are complemented by Japanese dressings. To prepare **Mustard Green Rolls with Sesame Dressing:** Grind toasted sesame seeds. Add shoyu, sake, and mirin. Thin with water as needed for a thick dressing. Steam Japanese mustard leaves until just tender. Drain and cool. Spread leaves in a strip across a bamboo rolling mat, about 2 inches from the bottom (gauge ½ pound raw greens for each roll). Fold, then roll, pressing firmly. Twist mat to remove excess liquid. Press to neaten, then unroll. Cut into 1-inch pieces. Top with dressing. Serve at room temperature (from *The World in a Bowl of Tea* by Bettina Vitell).

The austerity of these Japanese mustard rolls is sharply contrasted by **Foie Gras with Mustard Leaves and a Fig Tart,** from chef Michael Otsuka. To prepare: Roast foie gras. Quickly toss very small red mustard leaves in the rendered fat to wilt. Arrange on plates. Place a slice of foie gras and tart of brioche dough baked with a pinwheel of fresh figs on top of each. Nap with a reduction of Banyuls.

Garlic Mustard

(*Alliaria petiola* and *A. officinalis*)

Also hedge garlic, jack-by-the-hedge, sauce-alone

garlic mustard leaves (tips)   1-2½ inches

Garlic mustard, if rare in commerce (an occasional farmers' market or specialty distributor will have it), is not rare in the open woodlands it carpets in spring and fall—nor should it be it the kitchen. In the *Wild Foods Forum,* James A. Duke, elder statesman of the wild, provides international testimonials about its edibility and nutritional value from Great Britain (it is a native of Europe) to Russia to India.

The plant really does seem custom-made for today's culinary fashion, combining as it does the popular perfume of garlic and the kick of mustard in a pretty leafy package: a ready-made pasta sauce. Sauce-alone, a common name for the plant, describes its potential as a complex condiment. Now all we need is someone to pick, pack, and distribute the vervy little leaves.

Like *Brassica juncea,* garlic mustard is a member of the far-reaching Cruciferae family (also called Brassicaceae), although a different genus. Yet both its common name and its flavor ally it more closely with mustard greens than with any other group. In early spring, the serrated, faintly heart-shaped little leaves are as sharply bright in taste and color as Southern mustard, with a bitter undertone and an intense garlic bite. The tender buds are slightly sweeter and even more garlicky. Later in the season, the plant can become inedibly bitter, but I have read that it turns mellow and edible during the winter months.

TO COOK—OR NOT: When small, the tender leaves are a perfect garnish; like the leaves of strong herbs, they look charming and are packed with flavor. They have the effect of nasturtium, garlic, mustard, and broccoli raab combined; all that is needed for an interesting salad is a softening background of mild little lettuces. When the mustard leaves are larger, slice them into a fine chiffonade to disperse the flavor wallop. Like other mustards, this kind loses its bite and fragrance when cooked, but just a touch of heat will gently mute the impact: Fold into hot bean, grain, or pasta dishes at the last minute. For soups, cook half the leaves with the base, puree, then mince the remainder and stir raw into the finished soup. Or add to sautéed vegetables during the last minute of cooking. If leaves are very large, halve and sauté briefly.

Spiced Chickpeas and Pasta with Garlic Mustard

The spicing is subtle and warm, with a Moroccan feel, and the color equally so—a golden orange punctuated by red peppers. Spring mustard garlic needs no trimming, as the leaves will be tender and small—1½ inches or so. If larger, you may want to halve them. Winter cress (see page 228) or nasturtium leaves (page 229) make an equally vivid contrast, used just the same way. If wild leaves are lacking, small-leafed cultivated mustard, slivered very fine, can be substituted.

Canned beans are among the few prepared ingredients I use—and Eden is, thus far, my brand of choice for the unadorned flavor and consistent texture of its high-quality legumes, which are usefully not salted. The chickpeas are particularly impressive (other brands are often chalky or mushy—and always too salty). I like all chickpeas skinned. If you do not mind the tissuey hulls, omit step 2.

¼ pound imported Italian short tubular pasta
    or small shells
1 large onion

1 red bell pepper
1½ cups cooked chickpeas (one 15-ounce can)
2 tablespoons olive oil
½ tablespoon paprika
½ teaspoon ground cumin
½ teaspoon turmeric
½ teaspoon ground coriander
½ teaspoon pepper
1 teaspoon kosher salt
1 cup water
About 3 cups tender garlic mustard leaves,
    rinsed

1. Boil pasta in salted water until about three-quarters cooked, 5 to 6 minutes. Drain and rinse. Meanwhile, cut onion and pepper into ½-inch dice.

2. Pour drained chickpeas into a bowl of water. Gently rub to remove skins. Pour off water and skins, which float; then drain well.

3. Heat oil in heavy casserole over moderate heat. Add onion and cook until slightly softened. Add red pepper and continue cooking a few minutes to soften slightly. Add paprika, cumin, turmeric, coriander, pepper, and salt. Stir until fragrant, about 2 minutes.

4. Add chickpeas, pasta, and water. Simmer gently, covered, until flavors blend and pasta is just tender, about 5 minutes. Stir in half the mustard leaves and allow to wilt. Remove from heat.

5. Slice or chop remaining leaves and sprinkle over dish. Stir the fresh leaves into each portion as you serve.

Serves 2 as a main course, 4 as a side dish

Pros Propose

Substitute garlic mustard in any of the preceding recipes (or Pros Propose ideas) for Southern and Japanese mustards that call for either a chiffonade or for miniature leaves. Typically, garlic mustard is used to make a simple **Garlic Mustard Sauce,** such as this one from ethnobotanist Barrie Kavasch in *Native Harvests:* Combine coarsely chopped garlic mustard leaves with nut oil and ground dried spicebush (or a little allspice) in a heavy skillet. Cook until wilted, about 5 minutes. Serve over fish.

For a more sophisticated treatment, Jean-Georges Vongerichten coats lamb with garlic mustard paste and serves with a *jus* seasoned with the slivered leaves. To prepare **Rack of Lamb with an Herb Crust and Garlic Mustard Jus:** Blend cooked lamb's brains, butter, bread crumbs, and enough garlic mustard to make a dark green paste. Spread on baking sheet lined with plastic wrap and cover with plastic. Refrigerate. Cook rack of lamb. Heat lamb *jus* and add chiffonade of garlic mustard leaves and butter to smooth. Cut a rectangle of the chilled paste to fit over the lamb. Run under broiler to crisp. Serve with sauce.

Nameko
and Cinnamon Cap (*Pholiota* species)

Cinnamon Cap (*left*) and nameko (*right*)

½ **actual size**

Both of the perfect mushroom clusters shown here are cultivated *Pholiota* species. The shiny caramel bouquet at the top right is *Pholiota nameko*. At the lower left is an unspecified *Pholiota* isolate collected in Asia and farmed (and trademarked) by Gourmet Mushrooms in Sebastopol, California—producers of some of this country's finest fungi.

Nameko, "common in the cool temperate highlands of China, Taiwan and throughout the islands of northern Japan," has become "one of the most popular cultivated mushrooms in Japan, closely ranking behind Shiitake and Enokitake," writes Paul Stamets in *Growing Gourmet and Medicinal Mushrooms.* The small, slender-stemmed beauty (which looks like a ceramic mushroom imitating a real one) cooks quickly to a sweet, gentle savor with a hint of chanterelle. It also de-

velops a slurpy and slithery quality that pleases Japanese connoisseurs but makes many Westerners squirm.

BASIC USE: Nameko's viscid coating suits soup-making, above all, contributing a special noodly slick to broths. In Japan, nameko stars in miso shiru, nabemono, and some aemono dishes. It also slips subtly into mild vegetable or seafood ragoûts and braises, as well as some pasta and risotto combinations. But do not sauté this mushroom unless you want a tough, sticky mess.

Cinnamon Cap, firm and tawny, grows in small clumps, like nameko, but its solid, sturdy white stems are scaly and its crème brûlée cap, while a tad tacky, is not nearly as viscid. Cooked, it is quite different: When separated and sautéed, the mushrooms gild to a glossy dark amber, the caps taste toasty and juicy, and the stems become lightly crunchy—but not fibrous or rough, as one might expect from their appearance.

BASIC USE: For a charming garnish of truly cinnamon-capped little beauties, cut apart the little mushrooms and sauté quickly in butter and oil, salting partway through cooking. Or include them in quick braises, light soups, or risotto.

SELECTION: Both *Pholiota* species should be small, firm, and sprightly, with closed or turned-under caps and taut, dry stems. Sniff to be sure there is no hint of sourness. Nameko has a naturally slimy cap, and Cinnamon Cap is slightly sticky.

STORAGE: Refrigerate mushrooms in a single layer in a basket. Do not keep more than a few days. Both mushrooms can be frozen *if* they will be cooked with liquid, in soup, stew, or such; their slippery character is exaggerated by freezing.

PREPARATION: Trim base so that mushrooms separate into individual stalks; or cut into small clusters. If the mushrooms are too large to eat politely, you may want to cut the stems into bite-size pieces and halve the caps.

Ginger–Lemon Grass Broth with Nameko

Slippery and exotic, this glistening mushroom suggests oysters, scallops, and satiny sexual parts. Its tawny hue remains after cooking, as does its defined, neat form. Prepare this light course using a broth that is clear and brisk, based on mushrooms, on a vivid vegetable combination, or seafood and vegetables, or veal and mushrooms. Reserve for amateurs of delicacy and slurp.

    1 stalk lemon grass
    1-inch ginger chunk
    4 cups flavorful clear broth (see suggestions
        above)
    Dry sherry
    Shoyu (Japanese soy sauce)
    About ¼ pound nameko (to yield 1 cup
        trimmed)

1. Pound lemon grass slightly to break fibers and release aromatic oils. Slice thin. Do same to ginger.

Combine both with broth in saucepan. Simmer to reduce to 3 cups, 5 to 10 minutes. Strain out solids. Season discreetly with sherry and shoyu.

2. Cut apart mushroom stems at base. If mushrooms are relatively large, cut stems into 2-inch sections and halve caps. Add to broth. Simmer until cooked through, 1 to 2 minutes.

3. Ladle into small bowls. Serve hot.

Serves 4 as a first course

Sautéed Cinnamon Caps

The trim caramel-colored mushrooms turn slithery when sautéed but retain their toothsome bounce. Asian touches highlight the mushroom's exotic feel without hiding its natural flavor.

    About 10 ounces Cinnamon Cap mushrooms
    1½ tablespoons peanut or olive oil
    About ¼ teaspoon Chinese chilli-garlic sauce
    1 tablespoon shoyu (Japanese soy sauce)
    1 tablespoon minced cilantro (coriander) leaves

1. Trim mushroom bases to separate stems.

2. Heat wide sauté pan over moderate heat. Add oil and tip to coat pan. Add mushrooms and sauté until tender, about 3 to 5 minutes, adjusting heat so that they cook through and brown but are not seared.

3. Add chilli sauce and shoyu and toss to glaze. Serve at once, sprinkled with cilantro.

Serves 2 as a side dish

Pros Propose

Nameko's color and texture slide seamlessly into subtle miso soup, making it the preferred garnish for special occasions. Shizuo Tsuji makes this classic **Miso Shiru** in *Japanese Cooking: A Simple Art:* Prepare first-quality dashi. Soften red (barley) miso with a little tepid dashi, whisking to blend. Gradually ladle into simmering dashi. Add tiny bean curd dice, nameko, and chopped mitsuba (trefoil). Keep at under a simmer just until mushrooms and tofu are hot. Remove from heat. Sprinkle with sansho powder (ground prickly ash seeds).

In her *Encyclopedia of Asian Food,* Charmaine Solomon describes a simple preparation for nameko that seems particularly suitable: Season cooked nameko with vinegar, sugar, and soy; mix with grated daikon. Serve as a topping for chilled tofu.

Chef Michael Otsuka professes a passion for both Cinnamon Caps and nameko, which he uses frequently and interchangeably. In contrast to the miso soup above, his **Nameko in Lobster Broth** could hardly be considered traditional. To prepare: Chop lobster carcasses, sauté in olive oil, and deglaze with white wine and Cognac. Add chicken stock and lemon verbena; simmer briefly. Sauté nameko for a moment, then strain hot lobster stock over them. Finish with cubes of cooked foie gras.

Otsuka uses both Cinnamon Cap and nameko in risotto, as well as for a risotto-style pasta. To prepare **Cinnamon Cap "Risotto"**: Toast orzo in olive oil, boil until al dente, then cook until tender with chicken broth, white wine, Parmesan, and button mushroom duxelles. Stir in Cinnamon Caps sautéed in a little prosciutto fat.

For Otsuka's appetizer **Salad of Cinnamon Caps, Tomato, and Greens:** Sauté trimmed mushrooms in olive oil. Add minced shallots and toss momentarily, then deglaze with white wine. Off heat, toss with diced tomato, snipped chives, and a touch of balsamic. Arrange over tiny frisée and arugula; add a few drops of olive oil.

Nettle, Stinging Nettle (*Urtica dioica*)

Also nettles (singular and plural)

²⁄₃ **actual size**

It is nettlesome to note that a venerable plant of extraordinary usefulness has been awarded no modifier other than "stinging." But the word is apt in one aspect: The irritation resulting from a brush with nettles comes not from prickers but from a substance that contains formic acid, the stuff of stinging ants. Pamela Jones writes in *Just Weeds:* "It is simply impossible to ignore a plant that is capable of feeding, clothing, and healing the human body; a plant that has proved commercially successful . . . [and] been in continuous use for no fewer than 3000 years."

Although nettle was used primarily as a fiber and medicine, this plant of Eurasian origin has also been recorded as a food in the Old World since the days of ancient Rome. Directions for preparing a first-century "frittata" have been translated thus: "Wash well and chop young spring nettles. Add ground pepper, stock, and olive oil; boil. Once cooled, add beaten eggs. Bake in a shallow dish. Serve hot or cold" (from *De Re Coquinaria,* translated by John Edwards as *The Roman Cookery of Apicius*).

But nettles are not just some antique foodstuff that has gone the way of garum. They continue to play a part in the cooking of countries as diverse as Japan, Australia, Iran, Sweden, Great Britain, and Italy—in fact, in virtually all of Europe. In France, nettle (*ortie*) even stars in its own annual celebration, the Ortiefolies.

For most of the present generation of Americans, nettles are just weeds. Yet fortunately, "weeds" have made a comeback in the food business in recent years, as many entries in this book will attest. Bruce Naftaly has featured wildlings on his menu at Le Gourmand, in Seattle, since it opened in 1985. "It may sound silly," he says, "but the romance of gathering is still what delights and excites me as a chef." And the farther we move from nature, the more intriguing nettles and other wild foods become for diners and home cooks, too.

Nettles are easy to find (they grow profusely in a wide range of conditions nationwide) and easy to like. Cooked, they are more saucy and soupy than most leafy greens, melting into a smooth puree. Mild and fresh-flavored, they impart an impression of tonic green springiness more than a defined taste or texture.

BASIC USE: Nettles are first and foremost a soup-maker. Cook them in old-fashioned pottages with leeks and potatoes, then puree for a forest green soup that looks intense but tastes and feels surprisingly light in the mouth. For variety, mix nettles with other, more forceful greens; or enrich them with cream and eggs, or blend in fresh herbs. For garnish, top nettles with a poached egg or slices of hard-cooked egg, or with shrimp, whipped cream, or sour cream.

Sauces are nettles' other forte. To prepare: Blanch nettles, drain, and squeeze dry. Puree with a broth made from fish, poultry, meat, or mushroom stock. Finish with butter, cream, eggs, or all three. Blanch and puree nettles, then stir into pancake or blini batter; or add to pasta or gnocchi dough; or fold into a soufflé base.

Curiously, small raw nettle leaves make an intriguing salad ingredient *if well minced* (mincing removes the sting). They add a fresh hay-like scent and a sweetish green bean–cucumber flavor. Or blend minced nettles into butter with chives; chill and serve on canapés or atop poached or baked fish.

SELECTION: Nettles are most copious in spring-time but continue to leaf if the plants are nipped regularly and new growth is stimulated. (At Chez Panisse, in Berkeley, pasta with fresh nettles was on the winter menu!) It is the new shoots, whether initial small ones or later upper parts, that are deliciously edible. Check quality by *looking* for these—not by touching. Despite what you may read, many people are sensitive to the stinging hairs that cover the plants even when nettles are young and even well after harvesting.

The trimmed yield varies: The leggier the nettles, the more waste you'll have. As a general rule, figure on losing about half in the trimming process. One pound yields about 2 quarts of trimmed leaves.

STORAGE—AND NOT: Nettles perish *very* quickly; try not to store them. If you can't use them within a day or two, blanch and refrigerate or freeze

them. To blanch: Drop the cleaned leaves into plenty of boiling salted water. Bring to a rolling boil and cook 1 minute, stirring. Drain, then drop into ice water. Drain again and squeeze out excess water. One pound of nettles yields about 1 cup blanched, drained, and squeezed leaves, which resemble coarse puree.

PREPARATION: Wearing gloves, strip the leaves and their stems from nettle stalks; discard stalks. Remove any mushy or very dark leaves. Drop nettles into plenty of water, then swish around with tongs—or with gloved hands. Lift out leaves and drain.

Springtime Pottage

Old-fashioned "pottage" seems the right name for this essence-of-spring soup. Why bother to gussy up a good thing, when the time-honored basic works so well? Although the spruce hue and lush body suggest intensity, the soup is surprisingly light in flavor and feel. Stir in cream, if you prefer a richer effect.

Double the quantity of nettles if you want to use just one green. For tangy depth, add wild dock or sorrel (see page 573); for satiny smoothness and shine, add mallows (see page 379). Whatever you choose, figure on a total of 2 quarts lightly packed trimmed leaves.

> **About ½ pound nettles (to yield about
>   4 cups trimmed)**
> **About 4 cups cleaned sorrel (wild or cultivated)
>   and/or mallows**
> **2 medium leeks**
> **2 tablespoons butter**
> **2 large floury potatoes (1 pound)**
> **5 cups water**
> **½ tablespoon kosher salt**
> **Pepper**
> **About 1 tablespoon lemon juice**
> **Sour cream**

1. Wearing gloves, strip leaves and their stems from nettle stalks. Discard any mushy or very dark leaves. Drop nettles into plenty or water, then swish around with tongs or gloved hands. Lift out leaves and drain. Trim and wash other greens, as needed.

2. Cut darkest green parts from leeks. Trim off and discard roots. Halve leeks lengthwise, then slice cross-wise. Wash in several changes of water; drain.

3. Melt butter in heavy pot over moderately low heat. Add leeks and cook gently until soft, stirring now and then; do not brown. Meanwhile, peel potatoes and cut into ¾-inch slices.

4. Add potatoes, water, and salt to pot and bring to a boil. Stir in nettles and other greens. Simmer gently, covered, until greens are soft, about 25 to 30 minutes.

5. Remove from heat. Let cool, if convenient. With slotted spoon, transfer solids to processor and whirl to smooth puree, gradually adding cooking liquid. Add salt, pepper, and lemon juice.

6. Reheat to serve. Meanwhile, blend sour cream with a little water to liquefy. Ladle soup into small bowls and top each with a spoonful of cream.

Serves 6 as a first course

Variation

Chilled Springtime Pottage with Buttermilk

Prepare soup as above through step 5, substituting corn oil for butter and omitting the lemon juice. Cool, then chill. When chilled, gradually stir in buttermilk to taste—about 1 cup should be right. Adjust seasoning.

Shad Roe with Pureed Nettles

Two of the few truly seasonal products left to us arrive in markets together: shad and nettles. Browned and buttery roe is dressed up with silky, moss-green nettle puree. Although some poach shad roe before sautéing, I think it spoils the special texture, which is both creamy and caviar-crunchy. Substitute shad fillets for the roe if you prefer, but increase the cooking time. Either way, steamed small potatoes alongside are a must.

About ¾ pound nettles (or about 6 ounces trimmed)
About 2 tablespoons butter
1 cup vegetable broth or water
About 1 teaspoon sugar
About ½ teaspoon kosher salt
Pepper
3 to 4 teaspoons lemon juice
2 medium-small pairs shad roe (5 ounces each)
2 to 3 teaspoons snipped chives
Lemon wedges

1. Wearing gloves, strip leaves and their stems from nettle stalks. Discard any mushy or very dark leaves. Drop nettles into plenty of water, then swish around with tongs—or gloved hands. Lift out; drain.

2. Melt ½ tablespoon butter in medium saucepan over moderate heat. Add nettles, tossing to wilt. Add broth, 1 teaspoon sugar, and ¼ teaspoon salt. Cover and simmer over low heat until soft, about 15 minutes. Drain and reserve liquid.

3. Puree greens in blender to a very smooth texture, scraping down sides and adding reserved liquid as needed for a thick puree. Season with sugar, salt, pepper, and lemon juice.

4. Salt and pepper shad roe on both sides. Melt remaining 1½ tablespoons butter over moderate heat in heavy skillet that will hold roe closely in a single layer. Place roe gently in pan. Brown on one side—about 2 minutes. Turn carefully, to avoid breakage. Brown until crisp outside but still pink in the center—about 1 minute. Transfer to cutting board.

5. Heat nettle puree (a microwave is good for this) Stir in more butter, if desired. Spoon 2 wide strips of sauce onto each warmed plate. Cut roe sacs apart. Place 2 on each plate across the puree. Sprinkle with chives. Serve with lemon.

Serves 2

Variation

Shad Roe with Nettle Puree and Bacon

Fine-dice enough thick-cut bacon to make ¼ cup (about 1½ ounces). In saucepan to which you'll add nettles, cook, covered, to render fat. Transfer bacon to paper towel. Pour fat into a dish and reserve. Continue as above, using 1 tablespoon bacon fat and 1 tablespoon butter to brown the roe. When you heat the nettle puree, heat the bacon dice. Sprinkle over shad roe, with chives.

Pros Propose

Jean-Georges Vongerichten recollects: "The first day I arrived for work at Paul Bocuse, I was handed gloves and scissors and sent to cut nettles along the railroad tracks. I thought it was one of those jokes you play on apprentices. I did it for two hours every day—and I still like nettles." To prepare Vongerichten's bright, simple **Nettle Butter:** Chop raw nettles very fine with a tiny bit of minced garlic and shallots. Blend with butter and lemon juice to make a compound butter with a high proportion of nettles. Spread on toasted country bread, or put a molded piece on poached fish.

Swedish-born chef Christer Larsson cooks the traditional pureed nettle soup of Sweden, which is garnished with hard-cooked egg. He also prepares a special **Corned Goose (or Beef) with Nettle Sauce:** Combine corned goose or beef with aromatics and mirepoix. Add cold water to cover and simmer until tender; set aside. Degrease stock; cook down just until flavor is correct. Strain. Gently stew shallots in butter; add white wine and reduce. Add stock and blanched chopped nettles. Cook briefly, then puree. Strain. Serve sauce over sliced goose arranged on potato puree and garnished with spring vegetables.

Chef P. G. Gustafsson, who is also familiar with nettles from his native Sweden, uses them in nontraditional combinations in the United States. To prepare **Nettle Sauce for Fish:** Blanch nettles in salted water. Squeeze dry, then puree with a little Jalapeño chilli and fish fumet. Heat with butter. For his **Nettle Blini:** Puree blanched nettles with crêpe batter, using enough to give a deep green color. Bake small pancakes to serve with spring vegetables as a vegetarian main course. For **Nettle Cream Soup:** Thin blanched, pureed nettles with chicken stock; add heavy cream and heat through. Set a poached egg with a smoked salmon rosette on top of it in each wide shallow bowl. Pour around the creamy soup.

For a rich version of a common Scottish soup, a stuffed bird is simmered in oatmeal-thickened nettle broth. In *The Scots Kitchen,* F. Marian McNeill explains how to prepare the Highland and Hebrides version of **Nettle Kail:** "Gather a sufficient quantity of young nettles from the higher part of the wall, where they are clean," begins the recipe. Wash, dry, and chop the leaves. Stuff a cockerel with butter rubbed into oatmeal and seasoned with salt, pepper, and wild garlic or mint. Sew it up. Place in soup pot with cold water and bring to a boil. Add nettles, a handful of oatmeal, butter, salt, and wild onion or mint. Simmer until tender.

Nettles are part of the Italian repertoire—in soup, blended into pasta, or in egg custards, like this **Nettle Flan with Fresh Tomato Sauce** from chef Fortunato Nicotra: Blanch trimmed nettles. Refresh in ice water, drain, and squeeze out water. Combine in food processor with chives and sage; chop fine. Whisk together eggs, salt, pepper, and nutmeg. Add to nettle puree, with grated Parmesan; process until smooth, then add heavy cream. Divide among buttered ramekins. Bake in water bath. For sauce: Chop peeled and seeded ripe tomatoes in processor. With motor running, slowly add olive oil to make thin puree. Strain and season. Cool flans briefly. Run knife around each and unmold. Spoon around sauce.

Chef Jerry Traunfeld, author of *The Herbfarm Cookbook,* is very fond of nettles, which appear in a number of dishes, including this **Stinging Nettle Gnocchi with Morels:** Blanch trimmed nettles. Refresh in ice water, drain, and squeeze dry. Chop in processor. Blend with baked potatoes pressed through a ricer, then mix with egg, salt, and flour to make a soft dough. Roll into ropes; cut into gnocchi. Poach, then toss with butter. Sauté morels in pan with olive oil and salt; stew until dry. Add minced shallot and cook to soften. Add sherry and boil to evaporate. Add chicken stock and mashed roasted garlic. Boil to reduce slightly. Add gnocchi, butter, parsley, and Parmesan.

Traunfeld gathers both wild nettles and mint from around The Herbfarm Restaurant for **Stinging Nettle and Wild Mint Soufflé:** Blanch trimmed nettles. Refresh in ice water, drain, and squeeze dry. Soften shallots in olive oil over moderate heat. Add nettles and heat through. Transfer to food processor, with chopped wild mint leaves, and puree to coarse texture. Prepare soufflé base. Stir in nettles, salt, pepper, and Parmesan. Fold in whipped egg whites. Divide among buttered, crumb-coated ramekins. Bake in water bath.

New Zealand Spinach, Tetragonia

(*Tetragonia tetragonioides,* formerly *T. expansa*)

Also tetragonia, warrigal greens, Botany Bay greens, New Zealand ice plant

¹⁄₃ actual size

I'm going to take the liberty of calling this plant tetragonia, to help dispel any expectation that it will be like spinach. The common names tetragona, tetragone, and tetragonia exist in other languages—and there is a precedent for change. After Captain Cook and his botanist, Joseph Banks, returned to England from New Zealand with the plant, it developed a small following as "Botany Bay greens."

However, Alan Davidson tells us, "Botany Bay was originally going to be called Sting-ray's Harbour, since several large sting-rays had been caught and eaten there. But as Banks recorded in his diary: 'We had with it a dish of the leaves of tetragonia cornuta [as the plant was classified at the time] boil'd, which eat as well as spinage or very near it.' This and other botanical discoveries prompted the change of name" (*The Oxford Companion to Food*).

Tetragonia is not a relative of spinach. It belongs, rather, to the same family as the sparkly ice plant that blankets the California and Oregon coasts: Aizoaceae (also called Tetragoniaceae). It clings to rocky beaches in New Zealand, Australia, many of the Pacific islands, China, Japan, and South America. *A Field Guide to the Native Edible Plants of New Zealand* by Andrew Crowe also notes that tetragonia is used in Indonesia and that "by the 1820s New Zealand spinach was being cultivated in both England and France, and appeared for the first time in American seed catalogues." Records of the New York Horticultural Society of 1827 show that the seed was distributed among its members that year and appeared in seed catalogues the next year.

In 1943, Victor A. Tiedjens wrote in *The Vegetable Encyclopedia and Gardener's Guide* that New Zealand spinach "is much more useful than spinach, because it can be grown all summer in heats which spinach cannot stand, because its open growth collects much less sand and can be washed more easily, and because it is much more easily grown and gives repeated cuttings all summer." As recently as 1980, Waverley Root devoted more space to New Zealand spinach than to kale in his eccentric encyclopedia, *Food*. He mentions that it is sold in regional markets in France but rarely in Paris: "This is the situation almost everywhere in Europe and the United States, where those who want to eat New Zealand spinach usually have to grow it themselves." Twenty years later, it is still easier to find in a home garden than in a market in the United States (or France).

Its thick, attractive arrowhead leaves are firm and springy, with slightly glassy dots on the underside, like ice plant. When cooked, the greens turn creamy, almost unctuous, and the rich texture dominates—not the flavor, which is mild almost to blandness. The plant is clean, has little waste, and shrinks very little in cooking. It will flourish in dry, hot areas where other leafy greens droop and go to seed (though it tastes better when grown in cooler regions); it grows expansively; and it can be cut again and again.

Why does this obliging plant remain a secret? The obvious explanation is that with current blockbuster growing practices, small crops such as tetragonia (and the majority of vegetables in this book) haven't a chance for revival. Yet other old-time greens have crept through the cracks. Perhaps it is the contemporary fashion of tossing leafy greens into a salad bowl (whether they taste good or not) rather than cooking them that has made this vegetable obsolete. Bite into raw tetragonia, and chances are good it will bite you back. At first, it may seem earthy and interesting—but a moment later, it may taste acrid and bitter, its harshness intensifying for minutes after it has been swallowed. It is a vegetable to be *cooked*.

BASIC USE: Boil tetragonia, uncovered, in plenty of salted water to eliminate possible bitterness. When it is tender, a matter of a few minutes, drain well. For a salad course, undercook slightly, drain, and place on a towel to absorb moisture. To serve, toss with oil and lemon. Blanched tetragonia can be substituted in spinach recipes: Include it in a frittata or soufflé, layer it in noodle or grain casseroles, simmer it with cream or cheese sauce, blend it into a vegetarian loaf of rice and

nuts, or sprinkle it with cheese and brown lightly. Add to soups without preliminary blanching, stirring it into bean, grain, or vegetable bases for the last 5 minutes and then simmering uncovered until tender. I've read that small leaves grown in the proper soil make fine salad material, but thus far I have not found a leaf to eat raw.

SELECTION: If you're going to try tetragonia raw, follow Juleigh Robins's advice: "Be discerning in the leaves that you pick for salads. Choose only the young light green leaves and nibble on one to determine their edibility" (*Wild Lime: Cooking from the Bushfood Garden*). Generally speaking, smallish leaves are also a good idea, but not a necessity, for cooked dishes.

STORAGE: Tetragonia keeps very well. Refrigerated in perforated plastic, it lasts over a week, remaining springy and firm.

PREPARATION: Strip off lower larger leaves first, then nip off the top terminal sprig and buds; discard the remaining stalk. Rinse in a change or two of water.

Basic Tetragonia (New Zealand Spinach)

To be served as a side dish, tetragonia needs no more than a brief boil in plenty of water. That accomplished, it can be buttered or glossed with nut oil. Unlike true spinach, which "melts" with cooking, each tetragonia leaf keeps its shape and much of its texture, making for greater volume than most leafy greens. The mildly earthy flavor is enhanced by toasted nuts, sautéed mushrooms, browned shallot slices, or caramelized parsnips or carrots.

1 pound tetragonia
About 1 tablespoon butter or nut oil (pecan, walnut, or hazelnut)
Salt and pepper

1. Strip leaves from tetragonia stalks. Nip off leaves and buds at tip. Discard stalks. Dunk leaves and buds in several changes of water; drain.

2. Drop greens into a very large pot of boiling salted water. Return to a full rolling boil. Boil, uncovered, until very tender but not mushy, about 4 minutes.

3. Drain well, pressing out some liquid. Toss at once with butter (or oil) to taste. Season. Or reheat momentarily in a microwave oven.

Serves 4

Creamed Tetragonia (New Zealand Spinach)

Thick, soft tetragonia absorbs cream while it retains its special succulent density; it does not "deflate" like other greens. Although there is a hint of okra, the general effect is of creamed spinach with more distinct leaves and bouncier body.

1 pound tetragonia
⅔ cup heavy cream
2 medium scallions (green onions), halved
 lengthwise and thin-sliced
¼ teaspoon kosher salt
¼ teaspoon dried tarragon, crumbled to powder

1. Strip leaves from tetragonia stalks. Nip off terminal sprigs and any buds. Discard large stalks. Swish leaves and buds in several changes of water; drain.
2. Drop into a large pot of boiling salted water. Return to a full rolling boil. Drain.
3. Combine cream, scallions, salt, and tarragon in heavy saucepan and bring to a boil. Add drained leaves. Reduce heat and simmer, partly covered, stirring often, until leaves are tender—5 to 10 minutes.
4. Uncover, raise heat slightly, and simmer, stirring often, until cream has reduced to desired consistency and leaves are well coated—a few minutes.

Serves 4

Smoky, Spicy Soup of Limas and Tetragonia (New Zealand Spinach)

For a fast, flavorful main dish, meaty tetragonia leaves and buttery lima beans give body and color to a broth seasoned with Indian aromatics and bacon dice. Familiar-seeming, yet unusual.

½ cup diced lean slab bacon (rind removed)
1 large leek
½ teaspoon cumin seeds
¼ teaspoon turmeric
½ teaspoon ground coriander
¼ teaspoon ground allspice
1 teaspoon brown sugar
5 cups meat or vegetable broth
About 6 ounces tetragonia
1½ to 2 cups (10 ounces) blanched fresh limas
 (or 1 package frozen baby limas)
½ tablespoon kosher salt (omit if broth
 is salted)
12 small cherry tomatoes, sliced

1. Brown bacon in large heavy soup pot, covered. Pour off fat as desired. Trim leek, halve lengthwise, then thin-slice. Wash thoroughly.
2. Add cumin seeds to bacon and stir a minute. Add leek and cook, partly covered, over moderate heat until soft, about 10 minutes. Add turmeric, coriander, and allspice and stir a minute.
3. Add sugar and broth and bring to a boil. Cover and simmer 5 minutes. Meanwhile, strip leaves from tetragonia stalks. Nip off tips and discard stalks. Rinse leaves and tips in several changes of water.
4. Add limas to pot and simmer until almost tender, about 5 minutes. Add the tetragonia and salt and simmer until leaves are tender, about 5 minutes. Season. (Can be cooled and refrigerated.)
5. To serve, heat to boiling. Add water if soup is too thick. Ladle into bowls. Float tomatoes on each.

Serves 4

Pros Propose

Warrigal greens, as tetragonia is called in Australia and New Zealand, hold up well to spices and lap up cream. Both appear in **Curried Warrigal Greens and Pea Soup:** Gently cook onion in butter with curry powder until soft, but not browned. Blend in a little flour. Add blanched, chopped tetragonia, salt, pepper, chopped fresh mint, and green peas. Deglaze pan with white wine. Gradually add milk as needed. Simmer until tender and flavors are well combined. Add cream. Puree. Reheat without boiling (from *Wild Lime: Cooking from the Bushfood Garden* by Juleigh Robins).

From the same source comes a far-removed version of pesto genovese, here seen as **Warrigal Greens and Macadamia Pesto:** In food processor, combine crushed garlic, roasted and chopped macadamia nuts, blanched and chopped tetragonia leaves, salt, pepper, and olive oil. Blend until fairly smooth. Incorporate grated Parmesan. Serve on hot pasta with shaved Parmesan.

Chef Michael Otsuka finds that "the tannic underpinnings of New Zealand spinach create an interesting backdrop for red wines." He prepares the greens simply. For **Sautéed New Zealand Spinach:** Trim leaves from stalks and blanch in salted water. Drain and squeeze lightly to dry. Cook gently in butter to warm through. Season and serve as a base for roasted squab or guinea hen.

Oca (*Oxalis tuberosa*)

Oca, pronounced with the accent on the "o," is one of several names that the plant has in South America, but it is the sole name I've seen in the United States. I would like to offer numerous recipes for this delightful edible and write about it at length, but it is just barely available in North American markets so I'll be fairly brief and hope that the situation changes and we have a regular supply sometime in the near future.

The fresh tuberettes I've tasted here (like the pale pink ones pictured) are crisp and moist, thin-skinned, sour-sweet, fruity-vegetably, starchy-waxy—in short, quite unlike anything else you're likely to have eaten before unless you're from the South American highlands, where several similar tubers originate and thrive.

Oca is easy to prepare, easy to like, and worthy of attention, all the more so because the vegetable grows in a glowing range of eye-catching colors: yellow, pink, violet, red, and striped. Among the many types, there is even greater variation in sugar, acid, shape, and size.

A member of the oxalis (Oxalidaceae) or wood sorrel family (see page 576), oca (the word is derived from the Quechua) has edible tart cloverlike greens, as befits plants in this group. Although it has a superficial physical resemblance to fingerlings, oca is in no way whatsoever related to the potato (which it has been called by marketers). It is, however, ranked second in importance to potatoes as a valuable foodstuff in the Andes, according to a report of the National Research Council, *Lost Crops of the Incas*. The same source notes that it is scarcely known outside the Andes, except in Mexico's central highlands, where it is misleadingly called papa roja (red potato). If potato is not sufficiently confusing, in New Zealand, where the plant has been cultivated for some thirty years, it is called New Zealand yam. Heaven protect the identity of helpless misnamed market vegetables! (Incidentally, oca was introduced in New Zealand in the 1860s by an English immigrant who had collected it in Chile, according to Noel Vietmeyer, scientific editor of *Lost Crops of the Incas*.)

I was surprised to learn from William Woys Weaver's *Heirloom Vegetable Gardening* that oca "entered the United States about the same time that it appeared in England [1829], except that our earliest stock came

length: 4–6 inches

from Chile," while England's came from Peru. "It remained an exotic vegetable among our gentleman gardeners for much of the nineteenth century," says Weaver, who continues to grow and expand upon his crop in Pennsylvania. "Furthermore, the 'shamrock' leaves and the cheerful pink flowers are delightful in salads."

At present, all fresh oca in this country comes from New Zealand and is sold—not surprisingly—at astronomical prices. (This is ironic, given that oca is stigmatized as poor people's food in its homeland.) Whole frozen oca tubers from South America can be found in Hispanic groceries in some areas. I keep hoping that the fresh will soon follow.

BASIC USE: Raw oca, thin-sliced, suits both green and composed salads. The pink-gold rounds have a radish-like look; taste tart, juicy, and slightly fruity; and have a hint of sunchokes.

Oca can be baked to a softish state, sliced and sautéed, or steamed—my vote, since steaming gives the most appealing plumpness and sheen. Unfortunately, I have not been able to put my hands on enough oca to explore it in depth.

SELECTION AND STORAGE: Tubers should be crisp and solid, like sunchokes. The fine light pink oca from New Zealand is the only type I know to be available at present. Try it!

Refrigerate oca, uncovered. The whole tubers maintain their flavor and color admirably when frozen. Defrosted, they are fine for cooked dishes, but not for raw salads.

PREPARATION: Rinse—that's it.

Basic Steamed Pink Oca

Pinky-gold oca turns plump and shiny when steamed. Although I can compare it to aspects of tart apples, fingerling potatoes, and carrots, the sheen, warm color, acidity, and waxy texture make it different from these familiar vegetables. I like oca unadorned or merely butter-slicked as a side to shellfish or poultry. If I had it more often, I'd probably find plenty of other accompaniments and ways to use it.

1 pound pink oca
Optional: butter

1. Scrub oca lightly with a brush under running water. Set on a rack over boiling water. Cover and steam until just barely tender. Timing can vary *considerably*. Begin testing at about 5 minutes. Check often, removing the smaller tubers as they become tender. Like Jerusalem artichokes, they tend to get mushy all of a sudden—so do not wander away.

2. Serve hot, glossed with butter, if desired.

Serves 4 as a garnish or side dish

Salad of Oca, Radish, and Red Onion

This recipe, from one that the author-historian-restaurateur Maricel Presilla collected while assembling her forthcoming book about the foods of Latin America, hails from the highlands of Ecuador. There, it is prepared with ulluco (*Ullucus tuberosus*), another colorful, shiny tuber we would be lucky to add to North American markets. She serves the bright-hued mixture of softly sweet oca rounds and sharp, crisp radish coins at room temperature with grilled meat or fish. For a lovely presentation, find radishes of the same diameter as the oca.

1 pound oca (about 16 tubers)
2 quarts water
¼ cup brown sugar
1 very small red onion
1 bunch round red radishes
1 teaspoon kosher salt
2 tablespoons lime juice
¼ cup olive oil

1. Rinse oca, scrubbing lightly with a brush. Combine with water and brown sugar in medium pot over high heat. Bring to a boil. Reduce heat and simmer until barely tender in the center when pierced with a knife tip, 5 to 15 minutes, depending upon size and type. Drain; cool.

2. Meanwhile, cut onion into fine julienne. Cover with well-salted water and let stand 10 to 15 minutes. Rinse and drain.

3. Trim and wash radishes (save greens for another use, such as Radish Top Soup, page 532). Cut into thin rounds or half-rounds; place in serving dish. Cut oca into ½-inch slices (or leave whole, if you prefer the traditional presentation).

4. Dissolve salt in lime juice. Add olive oil and blend. Add to salad, tossing gently to coat. Serve at room temperature.

Serves 4 as a first course or side dish

Okra *(Abelmoschus esculentus* and *Hibiscus esculentus)*

Also gumbo, gombo, ochro, lady's fingers and others (see below)
Including **red okra**

Succulent and mellow, with subtle suggestions of eggplant, artichoke, and asparagus, okra does not seem a likely object of controversy. Yet exclamations of alarm or adoration erupt at the mere mention of this provocative pod, for a simple reason—its undeniable, un-American sliminess. Consequently, almost anyone writing on the subject in the United States hastens to reassure the reader that the unseemly slitheriness will be eliminated when okra is either soaked in vinegar (or water), fried (or boiled), cooked quickly (or forever), etc. Not so. The clear, sweetish,

viscous, light slick that okra exudes *belongs* and will not vanish. It will always be present to some degree—and it is luscious to those who fancy it.

Alarmists are likely to have been raised far from the tender little vegetable, whereas those blessed with early contact generally remain pro-podders for life. Links with Africa, India, and the Middle East foster a fondness for okra; in the New World, culinary connections with the Caribbean, South America, and the southern United States may do the same.

So rooted is okra in the food lore of the American

large red okra, length: 7-10 inches; small green okra, length: 3-4 inches

South that many people assume it to be native to the region, but it arrived, like watermelon, with African slaves. The handsome plant, which displays showy yellow or rose flowers like hibiscus (its close relative) and bears its tapered pods upright like torches, belongs to the Malvaceae family (see mallows, page 379). The word "okra" derives from a Ghanaian language; "gumbo," another common name for the vegetable (and for the celebrated soup-stew of Louisiana and the Low Country) comes from an Angolan language.

Part of okra's problem has been type-casting in recipes. Deep-fried, Deep-South okra and Creole gumbo, however memorable, do not describe okra's range of culinary possibilities. (A recipe for gumbo from a French cookbook of 1931, *La bonne cuisine aux colonies,* didn't help: Take veal breast, chicken, ham, oyster or mussels, lobster or crab. Simmer 5–6 hours. Add boiled okra to thicken.)

Fortunately, okra's repertoire has been refreshed by an ongoing influx of Indian, Caribbean, South American, and African immigrants. Thanks to this revival, the versatile vegetable can be found in new cookbooks and in an increasing number of markets. Depending upon the community a market serves, okra may be called gombo, from West and North Africa and the French Caribbean; bhindi, from India; quiabo, from Brazil; bamya or bamia, from Egypt, Turkey, and Greece; ochro or lady's fingers, from the English Caribbean; or quingombo, from the Spanish Caribbean.

Red okra can range from crimson to maroon in color, and from a cornichon to a banana in size. It is not a fashionable "invention" at all, but a reintroduction to the market. The three distinct cultivars I've cooked have been exceptionally fleshy, sweet, and flavorful—but no more so than good green okra. The brilliant pods are striking, but be warned that once cooked, they're likely to turn deep olive or spruce green (thoroughly acceptable colors to eat). In seed catalogues and plant histories, I have read about scarlet okra that stays scarlet, but none has landed in my pot thus far.

BASIC USE: To suit okra recipes to your taste, it helps to understand some general characteristics. Much like eggplant, okra is redefined by the ingredients it absorbs, at the same time that it transforms foods cooked with it. Its slippery character is balanced by acid, such as tomato, lemon, and vinegar. Mediterranean and Middle Eastern seasonings enhance it: sweet spices, pungent herbs, aromatic seeds, fresh ginger, garlic, and onion—in moderation. Sweet-sour, sweet-hot, and tart-hot preparations complement it. It is effective in low-fat recipes because it thickens and enriches, adding body and smoothness to a dish without the usual fat and starch liaison—as if it were packaged with its own ready-made sauce. In casseroles or stuffings it can act as a binder. Plain-cooked okra benefits from the same sauces as asparagus and green beans.

In short, okra is remarkably versatile. Choose a technique that achieves the effect you want: Steam whole okra pods for a tender, toothsome, bright green vegetable to serve hot or cold. Marinate chilled, barely steamed whole okra for a salad or garnish. Pickle whole okra for crunchy nibbles or a garnish. Braise whole or sliced okra with other vegetables and/or meat for a soft, slurpy dish, meaty and mellow. Bake okra, covered, with other vegetables to maintain maximum flavor and form. Stew sliced okra in long-cooked hearty soups to smooth and thicken. Simmer thin-sliced okra in clear soups and sauces during the last 10 minutes of cooking to thicken the liquid slightly.

SELECTION: Okra is available nearly year-round, primarily from Florida and Mexico, but it is most abundant during full summer. Pods vary in color, shape, and size, but all should be firm. Avoid dried, stringy, or flabby okra, which may be ropy. Uniform bright color usually signifies freshness. Dark-tipped or streaked okra is good for stews or soup, but only the perkiest uniformly colored pods should be considered for steaming or pickling. Choose carefully: the gentle sweetness and tenderness of okra depend upon super-freshness.

STORAGE: Okra perishes quickly. If purchased in fine shape, it keeps for a few days at most. Store in a paper bag in the upper (usually warmer) part of the refrigerator or at cold room temperature. Temperatures below 45°F damage okra. Keep it dry.

PREPARATION: Wash and dry okra before trimming. For tiny okra, just trim stems or their slight protrusions. If larger okra is to be cooked whole, shave off the cap, taking care not to open the capsule and expose the seeds. When a recipe calls for sliced okra, simply cut off the whole top end, then slice the pod.

Simplest Steamed Okra with Oranges and Nutmeg

The finest okra is at its best steamed: bright, sweet, succulent. But naked simplicity tells all, and only smooth, small unblemished pods will do. Choose another dish if the okra is anything less than lovely. Although a slick of butter is all that is called for in a minimalist presentation, orange and nutmeg add surprising dimensions.

4 small navel oranges, at room temperature
1 pound small okra
1 tablespoon butter
Salt
Nutmeg

1. Turn oven to its lowest setting. Pare rind and all white pith from oranges. Cut into individual segments by slicing between membranes. Place in an ovenproof serving dish.

2. Rinse okra. Pare off caps, without cutting into the pods. Place oranges in oven. Set okra on rack over boiling water. Cover and steam until just barely tender, 3 to 5 minutes. Do not cook until soft—leave slightly al dente for maximum flavor and color.

3. Transfer okra to dish with oranges. Add butter and salt. Grate over nutmeg. Toss gently and serve at once.

Serves 4

Okra, Potato, and Tomato Torte with Fennel and Garlic

Cheery and festive, this savory and colorful cake-like arrangement brightens a buffet table. The okra slices, like fruits on an upside-down cake, retain their pretty shape baked this way. The dish can be prepared hours ahead and only deepens in flavor (no liquids or binders dilute its concentrated juices). But do not refrigerate, or the texture will turn gummy.

¾ pound okra
1 pint cherry tomatoes

1¼ pounds small, equal-size waxy potatoes
    (preferably yellow-fleshed)
2 tablespoons olive oil
½ teaspoon kosher salt
½ teaspoon sugar
1 teaspoon fennel seeds, crushed
¼ teaspoon fine-ground pepper (preferably
    white)
1 teaspoon minced garlic
12 large oil-cured black olives, pitted and
    sliced
Optional: olives and basil leaves for garnish

1. Rinse and dry okra. Cut off and discard caps, then cut pods into ½-inch slices. Halve cherry tomatoes. Peel potatoes and cut into ⅛-inch slices. Preheat oven to 350°F.

2. Paint or spray a 9-inch round cake pan or straight-sided baking dish with olive oil. Line the bottom only with waxed paper, then coat with more oil. Beginning with a circle of okra at pan edge, arrange tight concentric rings, alternating with rings of tomatoes, cut side up. Form a central flower with okra tips.

3. Spread half the potatoes, overlapping, over this. Sprinkle with half the salt, sugar, fennel, pepper, and garlic. Drizzle 1 tablespoon oil over this.

4. Combine remaining tomatoes, okra, and olives on a work surface. Chop coarse, then spread over potatoes in pan and press down very firmly. Arrange the remaining potatoes on this and sprinkle with remaining seasonings and 1 tablespoon oil.

5. Cover tightly with foil. Bake until potatoes are very tender, about 1½ hours. Uncover and let stand 10 minutes or more. Run a knife around the edge, then invert onto a wide serving plate.

6. Serve hot, warm, or at room temperature. Garnish with optional olives and basil.

Serves 4 as a side dish or appetizer

Okra Pickles

I am not a pickle fan. I find most vegetables harshly abused by a vinegar bath. Okra is one of the few whose flavor and texture are upheld and nicely modified—

not lost—in the process. If available, use red okra, which pinkens prettily in vinegar. Serve the pickles with smoked or boiled beef or pork, beans and rice, or sweet dishes of Indian, Southeast Asian, or Japanese descent.

> 2½ pounds very small, bright okra pods
>   (green or red)
> 6 or 12 tiny dried chillis, to taste
> 3 teaspoons mustard seeds, bruised
> 1½ teaspoons dill seeds
> 1½ teaspoons coriander seeds, bruised
> 1 very small red onion, sliced, separated
>   into rings
> 2 cups cider vinegar
> 2 cups distilled white vinegar
> 2 cups water
> ¼ cup kosher salt

1. Rinse okra. Dry on soft towel. Trim stems, leaving a little stub of cap on each and being careful not to pierce caps or pods.

2. Divide spices evenly among 6 sterilized wide-mouth pint canning jars. Pack okra upright in jars, placing tip and stem ends in alternating positions and interspersing onion rings—pack tightly enough to keep pods upright, but do not crush or jam them.

3. In a non-aluminum pot, combine both vinegars, water, and salt. Bring to a boil. Fill jars to within ½ inch of rims. Place a scalded two-piece lid on each, then fasten screw-bands.

4. Set jars on a rack in a deep pot half-filled with boiling water. Add boiling water to cover by 2 inches. Bring to a boil, cover, and boil 5 minutes. Transfer jars to a towel to cool completely. Store about a month before serving.

Makes 6 pints

Spiced Okra and Tomatoes over Toasty Cracked Wheat

Sliced, spiced, and braised, okra is quite different from the whole and perky vegetable, softening to a sauce-like consistency. Tomatoes, chilli, and cinnamon are traditional Middle Eastern enhancements for this stewy style, which I like to freshen with mint and parsley. Fennel, Orange, and Green Olive Salad with Lemony Dressing (page 277) makes a fine foil for this vegetarian main dish.

Technically, bulgur wheat has been precooked whereas cracked wheat is raw, but packaging information does not always make this clear. If you cannot find cracked wheat, substitute coarse-grain bulgur wheat.

> 2 tablespoons olive oil
> 1¼ cups cracked wheat (or coarse-grain bulgur)
> ¼ teaspoon cinnamon
> ¾ teaspoon kosher salt
> 3 tablespoons raisins
> 2½ cups water or vegetable broth
> 1 pound okra, rinsed
> 1 or 2 small fresh green chillis
> 1 medium red or white onion
> 2 medium-large firm tomatoes
> 1 tablespoon balsamic vinegar
> About ¼ cup chopped parsley leaves
> About ¼ cup chopped mint leaves

1. Heat 1 tablespoon oil in heavy saucepan: Add cracked wheat and stir over moderate heat several minutes to toast lightly. Add cinnamon, ¼ teaspoon salt, and raisins. Add 2 cups water and bring to a full boil. Turn heat to lowest point. Cook, covered, for 15 minutes. Off heat, let stand, covered, 15 minutes or longer.

2. Meanwhile, trim caps from okra. Cut pods into ½-inch slices. Seed and mince chilli. Peel and dice onion. Peel tomatoes (see Note, page 10, for directions), then cut into ¾-inch dice.

3. Heat remaining 1 tablespoon oil in heavy medium-large pot. Stir in okra, chilli, and remaining ½ cup water. Simmer, covered, 5 minutes. Add onion, tomatoes, vinegar, and remaining ½ teaspoon salt. Simmer until vegetables are soft and almost saucy, about 5 minutes. Season to taste.

4. In heated dish, toss wheat with 3 tablespoons each parsley and mint, then add more to taste. Spoon okra mixture over each serving.

Serves 4 as a main dish

Salad-Relish of Okra, Corn, Red Onion, and Herbs

Handy picnic fare, this colorful toss is at once salad and relish, tart and sweet, crunchy and soft. It's nice with grilled lamb or beef. Or stuff into scooped-out tomatoes (dice the pulp and add to the mixture). Serve leftover relish to garnish cold soup or in sandwiches.

1 medium red onion
3 tablespoons red wine vinegar
½ teaspoon sugar
½ teaspoon kosher salt
Pepper
½ to 1 teaspoon minced oregano or savory
3 medium ears corn, husked
¾ pound okra
3 tablespoons olive oil
1 tablespoon capers, minced
¼ cup chopped parsley
¼ cup slivered basil leaves

1. Bring a few cups of water to a boil. Cut onion into ½-inch dice and scoop into a sieve. Pour over the water. Combine vinegar, sugar, salt, pepper, and oregano in a small bowl. Add onions and toss.

2. Set corn on steamer rack over boiling water and cook, covered, until tender—about 5 minutes. Set aside.

3. Arrange okra on steamer rack, cover, and cook until not quite tender—about 3 minutes. Drop into ice water, then drain and dry well.

4. Cut corn kernels from cobs. Cut okra into thin slices; discard caps. Drain onion, and reserve marinade; whisk olive oil into this and season. Toss with okra, corn, onion, and capers. Refrigerate for a few hours, or more.

5. To serve, toss with parsley and basil. Taste and adjust seasoning.

Serves 4

Pros Propose

Okra is Africa's "culinary totem. From the bamia of Egypt to the soupikandia of Senegal, passing by the various sauces, gombos and more, this pod is used in virtual continent-wide totality," writes Jessica B. Harris—noting that "the slime that has made it the most maligned of vegetables in this country, outside of the South, is actually thought there to be a virtue." For **Sweet and Sour Bamia:** Wash and dry small okra; top and tail. Heat olive oil in heavy saucepan and fry okra 5 minutes, turning once. Add honey, salt, pepper, lemon juice, and water to moisten. Cover and simmer until tender (from *The Africa Cookbook*).

There are others who admire the slipperiness of okra. "Perhaps no nation revels in the natural tastes and textures of foods as much as Japan," writes Madhur Jaffrey. "Take okra. Most people . . . are at pains to hide its viscous quality. . . . Not so the Japanese," who highlight the reality of its texture—by leaving it alone! For **Okra with Wasabi:** Drop small perfect okra pods into boiling water; cook 2 minutes. Drain, run under cold water, and drain again. Cut into ¼-inch slices and discard caps. Blend wasabi paste with shoyu and mirin. Toss with okra and serve at room temperature or cold, as an appetizer or side dish (from *A Taste of the Far East*).

In Japan, as in the American South, the trio of **Rice, Beans, and Okra** is favored for special occasions. To prepare: Trim okra pods and macerate with salt and rice vinegar for ½ hour or so. Slice and blanch. Drain. Mound hot steamed rice in each dish. Place okra on top and cooked azuki beans alongside.

Far from the distinct elements of a Japanese dish are the blended braises of North Africa. From Morocco comes **Stew of Lamb, Pears, and Okra:** Brown seasoned lamb shoulder pieces in smen (fermented butter) and oil. Add chopped onion, ground cinnamon, nutmeg, and water and simmer until meat is almost tender. Add halved firm pears and cook until just tender. Add trimmed okra; cook until crunchy-tender, not longer. Arrange meat on plate with okra and pears around. Cook down sauce and pour over (from *Les saveurs et les gestes* by Fatéma Hal).

Expect the unexpected from Paula Wolfert, who unearthed this Lebanese recipe for **Broiled Okra with Pomegranate:** Wash and dry okra well. Trim tops and tips. Skewer okra, then brush with a mixture of olive oil, pomegranate molasses, water, lemon juice, and garlic cloves crushed with salt. Grill far from heat source until glazed and browned. Sprinkle with chopped coriander leaves (from *The Cooking of the Eastern Mediterranean*).

Sweet and sour is chef Diana Forley's choice too, for a contemporary adaptation of a traditional Turkish dish, **Stewed Okra with Tomatoes and Apricots:** Soak quartered dried apricots in boiling water. Soften diced onion in olive oil, to just barely color. Add trimmed okra and a little water. Cook about 10 minutes over low heat. Add whole peeled plum tomatoes (twice the volume of okra), the apricots, lemon juice, and ground coriander. Cook until okra is soft.

There are probably more ways to cook okra in India than in any other country. For traditional **Okra Stuffed with Spices**, an aromatic mix is tucked into each little pod: Cut a slit lengthwise in each trimmed pod. Blend ground coriander, cumin, mango powder, garam masala, and salt. Divide among the pods, using a tiny spoon. Brown okra pods slowly in oil in a large skillet, removing once they are deeply colored—about 15 minutes. Toss with browned onion slivers and any remaining spices, then cook briefly to blend.

Jeffrey Alford and Naomi Duguid discovered a spicy, sticky, very different Bengali dish, **Okra with Poppy and Mustard Seeds:** Heat mustard oil in heavy pot over moderate heat. Add minced onions and cook briefly. Add ½-inch okra slices, anise seeds, and salt. Cover and cook gently until okra is tender, about 10 minutes, stirring now and then. Grind white poppy seeds and mustard seeds to a powder. Add water to make a paste. Add to okra, with ground hot pepper and sugar. Stir briefly, then serve hot (*Seductions of Rice*).

Whether in Africa, India, the American South, or, as here, in **Coo-Coo from Barbados,** cornmeal is a constant partner for okra. Although coo-coo appears in just about every book about the islands, it was in Elisabeth Lambert Ortiz's groundbreaking *The Complete Book of Caribbean Cooking* that I first spied coo-coo. On the irresistibly named subject, she writes: "Coo-coo means a cooked side dish, and in addition to corn meal coo-coo there are Conquintay (plantain flour) Coo-Coo, Breadfruit Coo-Coo, Cassava Coo-Coo, an interesting cornmeal and coconut version from Grenada, and one from Trinidad made with fresh sweet corn." All are enhanced by the addition of okra, which binds and mellows the cornmeal: Boil sliced okra in salted water until just tender. Gradually add cornmeal, stirring constantly until thick and smooth. Turn into a greased shallow bowl to mold a neat shape, then invert onto warmed platter. Spread butter on top, and serve hot.

Onions

For the purpose of culinary convenience, I have divided the onions as you would be likely to group them for use in recipes: green, little (including pearls, boilers, cipolline, etc.), and sweet/mild. Standard storage onions are not included, because existing literature on the subject is extensive.

Green Onions

Green Onion (*Allium cepa* or
A. fistulosum and crosses thereof)
Also scallion, spring onion, salad onion

Taxonomically, a green onion is the same species (*Allium cepa*) as a common onion and a "sweet" onion. Or it is a different species, *Allium fistulosum*. Or it is a cross of the two. In case you don't think this scientific description is helpful, just try finding a common one, as I have tried, by showing farmers, distributors, and "just plain folks" in different regions of the country the photo at the top of page 435 and asking for names of the green-topped whatever-they-may-bes!

I asked Bruce Sanbonmatsu, co-owner of Sanbon, a grower in El Centro, California: "Is there a distinction between scallions and green onions?" Without hesitation he replied: "Of course. People from New York and Boston call scallions what most everyone else calls green onions." ("Most everyone else" means people who call them spring or salad or bunching onions.) Sanbonmatsu's reply may be as close to a truth about

common names as I can get—a truth that has taught me to list the provincial New Yorker's scallion *and* green onion in the ingredients lists after extensive cross-country questioning.

In the marketplace, the terms "green onion" and "scallion" generally designate slim, bulbless green onions—despite the fact that in all current American and British dictionaries I consulted, the first definition of "scallion" is "shallot" (page 558).

The terms "spring onion" and "salad onion" are more likely to describe a later stage of the same onions, green-topped with more developed bulbs (see photo, page 434). Both the bulbless and the bulbing forms come from the same seed as common storage onions, planted in tight quarters and harvested very young.

Chef Jan Birnbaum describes them this way: "Spring onions have a real freshness that regular onions don't have. You know they're going to be grown-ups—but they aren't yet. The tear-producing and heat-producing aspects are not as strong, and they're much more tender."

BASIC USE: Definitions aside, green onions are familiar to cooks as raw and cooked seasonings; but to qualify for admission into this book, they must act the part of full-fledged vegetables. Raw, the freshest and slimmest green (or red) spring onions can be served as crudités. Or, for an old-fashioned munch, sandwich between white or black bread slices thickly spread with butter or mayonnaise. Quick-pickle small green onions.

Add trimmed and blanched spring onions to vegetable ragoûts—with mushrooms, fresh shell beans, or baby squash. Trimmed and grilled spring onions can be tucked into tacos, sandwiches, or vegetable plates, or

green/spring onions in various colors and sizes   ⅕ actual size

served under grilled meat or fish: Trim off most greens, then blanch onions if bulb is more than 2 inches in diameter. Then toss with oil and seasoning, and marinate as long as convenient. Grill over a low fire or broil close to the heating element.

SELECTION AND STORAGE: Seek bright, stiff, dark green-leafed onions with no sign of drooping, yellowing, or slime. Roots should be creamy and sturdy, not withered. Avoid onions with pale greens, which indicate hurried growing—and short staying power. Vivid red and purplish varieties are sometimes available in specialty stores and farmers' markets. Keep an eye out for these brighteners. Although "spring" is what these onions are called, varieties are available all year from California and Mexico. Other areas have limited short-term production.

Restaurant note: Properly packed green onions should arrive topped with liner paper and ice. Although special polyurethane bags have supplanted ice for some distributors, chefs and growers tell me that icing is still more reliable. Keep green onions very cold (around 32°F) at high humidity for as short a time as possible.

PREPARATION: Trim roots and slip off a layer or two of onion skin, as needed. Cut off any limp greens.

Bunching Onion (*Allium fistulosum*)
Also Japanese or Chinese or Oriental bunching onion, welsh onion, Japanese scallion; negi, Tokyo negi, naganegi, nebuka (Japanese); da cong or tsung (Chinese)

"Bunching onion" is a term correctly applied to the *fistulosum* species, the bunching onion of the Far East (but it is also used in common parlance for all green

young green onions or scallions: Japanese bunching (*left*), American type (*right*) length: 11-12 inches

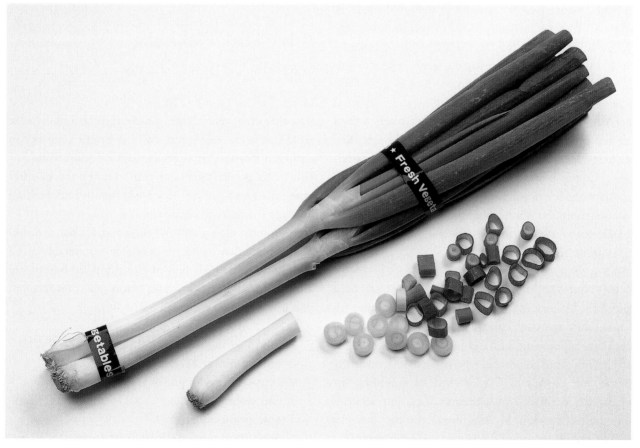

mature bunching onions (called Tokyo negi and nebuka) length: 2 feet

onions). Joy Larkcom observes that "if the long loaf epitomizes the French shopper, the long white-stemmed onion epitomizes the Chinese. Tied to bicycles, peering out of panniers, it is the most ubiquitous of Chinese vegetables" (*Oriental Vegetables*). She dates the bunching onion's appearance in Chinese literature as 100 B.C. and its entry into Europe as during the Middle Ages.

The plant's European name, welsh (lowercase "w") onion, does not refer to leek-loving Wales. It derives from the "Anglo-Saxon *welise* and the German *welsche,* meaning foreign," according to G. A. C. Herklots's classic reference, *Vegetables in South-East Asia,* and "it is grown on a very large scale in China, Japan, and in South-east Asia." The onion is also farmed in California; that is how it gets into the American picture.

When harvested at early stages, common spring onion and bunching onion look almost the same, but the latter has more tubular leaves, which remain tubular when sliced—one reason perfect sushi scallion rings look so tidy. The firmer Japanese bunching onion has an earthy, pungent aroma; the softer "American" type has a greener, sweeter taste. When allowed to mature, a bunching onion does not bulb but simply enlarges.

The aristocrat of the species is the single-stalked, white-shaft form developed by Japanese breeders. Called Tokyo negi in the United States (and nebuka by Larkcom and other specialists), the sleek vegetable is as difficult and time-consuming to produce as fine white asparagus. The pearly tender stalks measure about 2 feet in length and 1 inch in diameter, weigh 4 to 8 ounces each, and cost a pretty penny. Although they are leek-like, their satin sheen and perfectly clean interior set them apart. The ones I have worked with did not have a speck of soil between the layers and so could be cooked intact. While assertive, they are much less so than leeks or storage onions. Cooked gently, they turn translucent, soft, and mild.

BASIC USE: Younger bunching onions are used just like "American" green onions, or scallions. In China, they are well known as "brushes" for Peking duck, in scallion pancakes, and as the melding vegetable of stir-fries. For the nebuka type, the white shank is the prime cut; the green is used only as seasoning for stocks or as garnish. This white part is cut into sections and grilled, cooked in nabemono (brothy one-pot dishes), served in aemono (cooked salads), or prepared as negi make (bundled lengths of stalk wrapped in thin

beef slices and braised in sweetened soy sauce). In nontraditional dishes, this vegetable substitutes for leeks in recipes where its smooth shape and pallor are retained—such as poached and served with vinaigrette, in a clear broth with seafood, or simmered à la grecque.

Chefs will want to experiment with the glossy individual layers as wrappers or "pasta": Trim roots and green tops, then slit each layer and pull off gently. Poach layers in salted water until they become sheer and very tender. (Do not undercook, or they will be tough and fibrous.) Spread rectangles flat to cool; gently pat dry.

SELECTION AND STORAGE: Buy small young bunching onions as you would common scallions. For nebuka, which are available only through Japanese distributors at present, choose brilliant white, straight stalks with solid, dark greens. The interior of the white part should show little or no green when sliced. Keep in a cold part of the refrigerator, topped with a damp towel, for no more than a few days.

PREPARATION: Trim roots and green tops for most preparations.

Party Pink Pickled Spring Onion Slices

Green onions have a tendency to become viscous—a trait that vinegar modifies. Lively and fresh, this quick pickle serves as relish and salsa—a bright note on an antipasto tray or tart vegetable side to smoked fish or cold roast poultry, pork, or beef. Or try the garishly gorgeous combination of snappy onions and melting avocado in salads or sandwiches.

For pretty slices that hold their shape, choose onion bulbs about two inches in diameter—preferably a red variety. Long large shallots or elongated red onions can also be used. Narrow white onions are fine too, but you'll want to add more beet for color.

> 1 pound spring onions without tops (preferably red) or about 1¼ pounds with greens
> 1½ cups cider vinegar or rice vinegar
> ¾ cup water
> 3 tablespoons sugar
> 1 tablespoon peeled, diced beet (or more, if using white onions)

1 teaspoon coriander seeds

½ teaspoon anise or fennel seeds

6 cloves

Optional: cracked green cardamom pods and
    1 or 2 small dried chillis

1. Peel onions as needed. Cut into ⅛-inch slices and separate into rings. You should have about 4 cups.

2. In non-aluminum saucepan, combine vinegar, water, sugar, beet, coriander, anise, cloves, and optional spices. Bring to a boil, covered; boil 1 minute. Stir in onions. Remove from heat. Cool to lukewarm.

3. Transfer to a wide-mouth 1-quart jar. Refrigerate, covered, at least 2 days before serving chilled. (Improves with time—up to about a month.)

Makes 1 quart

Note: "Échalions" (page 558) can be substituted for spring onions.

Broiled Herb-Marinated Spring Onions

Broiled spring onion bulbs are sweet and juicy; their greens, charred and chewy. Broil chicken or fish, set aside to rest under a foil tent, and then brown the onions to serve as a side. Soaking in warm water softens them and helps the marinade penetrate. Slip halved tomatoes under the broiler for the last 5 minutes to round out the meal.

12 to 16 spring onions with bulbs 1½ to
    2 inches in diameter

1¼ teaspoons dried mint, crumbled fine

½ teaspoon dried dill, crumbled fine

¼ teaspoon dried thyme, crumbled fine

1 teaspoon kosher salt

⅔ cup water

1 tablespoon wine vinegar

3 tablespoons olive oil

Crisp sea salt and pepper

1. Slit a layer of the bulb of each onion and pull it off. Trim off most of the dark greens (save for another use), so that each onion measures about 6 to 8 inches in length. Shave roots closely, without cutting into the bulb. Cut a slit ½ inch deep in the bottom of each. Soak in lukewarm water as convenient, changing water several times, until well cleaned. Drain and arrange in a dish in a close-fitting single layer.

2. In a small pan, combine mint, dill, thyme, salt, water, and vinegar. Bring to a boil. Pour over onions. Add oil. Marinate as long as time permits, up to several hours, turning now and then.

3. Cover broiler pan with foil and set close to heat. Preheat broiler. Place onions on foil. Cook through, basting often, until bulbs brown and greens char slightly. Timing will vary with broiler and size of onions, but about 10 minutes is likely.

4. Grind over pepper and sprinkle with crisp salt.

Serves 4

Japanese Bunching Onions à la Grecque—Sort of

This dish belongs to no country: large white Japanese onions (not Japanese in origin) are poached in so-called Greek-style, turn the silver green of ancient Roman glass, and are napped with an almost-French dressing. While similar to leeks vinaigrette, the Tokyo negi (nebuka) are sweeter, milder, more succulent.

Note that although the cooked vegetable is tender, the fibers resist tidy cross-slicing. For neatness, serve with sharp table knives; or slice lengthwise instead of crosswise as you eat.

1 cup water

About 2 tablespoons Ricard or Pernod

½ cup dry vermouth

¼ teaspoon kosher salt

⅛ teaspoon pepper

¼ teaspoon dried thyme

¼ teaspoon dried dill

5 or 6 Japanese bunching onions (Tokyo negi or
    nebuka), each about 4 ounces

1 teaspoon prepared mustard

1 to 2 tablespoons lemon juice

2 tablespoons olive oil

1. In medium-large skillet (to hold the onions in a tight single layer), combine water, 2 tablespoons Ricard, vermouth, salt, pepper, thyme, and dill; bring to a

boil. Lower heat and simmer gently as you prepare onions, or about 5 minutes.

2. Cut off greens where they branch from white stalks; reserve. Trim roots. If some stalks are thicker than others, score and pull off a layer or two so that they are about equal. Cut into 2- to 3-inch lengths, approximately (15 to 20 pieces)—to make neat, equal sections.

3. Add onions to skillet and shake to distribute in a single layer. Cover and keep at just under a simmer (or layers will pop apart) until very tender, turning and redistributing to cook evenly, 35 to 50 minutes. With slotted spatula, transfer to serving dish. (Can be made ahead, cooled, and refrigerated. Bring to room temperature to serve.)

4. If necessary, simmer liquid in skillet to reduce to about 2 tablespoons. Stir in mustard, 1 tablespoon lemon juice, and oil. Season and taste for lemon and Ricard.

5. To serve, slice a narrow section of the reserved greens to make about 1 tablespoon very thin rings. Spoon dressing over onions. Add greens.

Serves 4

Pros Propose

"You want to think of spring onions as true spring vegetables like peas and favas, not as seasoning," says chef Michael Romano, who combines these elements in **Scafeta,** a dish from Puglia: Heat olive oil. Add thin-sliced baby artichokes and thin-sliced golf ball–size green onions (with a few inches of stem) and toss until artichokes begin to get tender. Add dry vermouth and reduce. Add blanched and skinned favas, peas, and stock to just moisten; cook briefly. Add torn Boston lettuce, mint leaves, and pepper and stir. Serve as a condiment or side.

For chef Romano's **Spring Onion Chutney:** Trim tops of small spring onions to 2 inches of green. Heat grapeseed oil; stir in mustard seeds until they pop. Add cumin, kalonji (nigella), and anise seeds; add turmeric and verjuice and reduce slightly. Add sugar, salt, pepper, and onions. Bring to a boil, cover, and bake in moderate oven until tender. If too juicy, remove onions and reduce liquid to a glaze. Serve at room temperature with pâté or roasted poultry.

Chopped spring onions and dill are the simple filling for crisp pastry tubes in a traditional Greek appetizer, **Scallions in Filo:** Chop scallion bunches that have been trimmed of most greens: Toss with olive oil, chopped dill, and seasoning. Spread out a sheet of filo, brush with olive oil, cover with another sheet, and brush again. Sprinkle a wide strip of scallions at one end, then roll up to make a long tube. Cut tubes into 4 diagonal sections, brush with oil, and sprinkle with sesame seeds. Bake until golden and crisp (from *Recipes from a Greek Island* by Susie Jacobs).

Glazed Spring Onion with Bacon Vinaigrette is rich and, perhaps not surprisingly, comes from *Parisian Home Cooking* (by Michael Roberts). To prepare: Trim roots and most of greens from 1-inch-diameter spring onion bulbs: Cut an X in each base. Cook lardons over lowish heat until crisp. Add onions and cook until soft (cover if bacon browns). Transfer to serving dish. Add red wine vinegar and butter to skillet, stirring to melt. Add to onions, with chervil leaves.

Chef Jeff Drew tasted a street vendor's fare in Mexico and worked the components into his **Pork Tacos with Spring Onions and Pineapple:** Trim all but 1½ inches of green from 1-inch-diameter spring onions. Toss with oil, salt, and pepper. Grill along with narrow pineapple wedges. Tuck into tacos with roast pork and serve hot.

Negi No Shiru is a minimalist's dish to offer as an intermezzo in a multicourse meal, which is what chef Robert Gadsby does. To prepare: Wilt fine dice of white part of Japanese bunching onions in butter. Add dashi and bring to a simmer. Skim. Add blanched rings from green part of onions. Add a few drops of the finest olive oil.

For **Halibut with Tokyo Negi Two Ways,** chef Michael Cimarusti braises the white part of the onions and makes a salad of the green: Separate green and white parts of negi. Cut whites into 2-inch lengths. Combine with ½ inch chicken stock, ginger pieces, butter, salt, and pepper. Oven-braise, covered, until tender, about ½ hour. If needed, reduce stock to glaze onions. Arrange onions on plates as base for pan-seared halibut. Brush with glaze of mandarin juice cooked down with star anise and cinnamon stick and finished with ground Sichuan pepper. Cut negi greens hair-thin and toss with a mandarin juice reduction emulsified with olive oil. Arrange with a few mandarin segments around fish.

Cimarusti also serves **Tokyo Negi with Pernod Cream and Oysters** as an unusual brunch dish: Remove green tops from onions. Cut white parts into 3-inch lengths. Braise in white wine with a touch of garlic, shallots, and Pernod until soft. Add cream and oysters. Bake in individual gratins until oysters just puff.

Little Onions *(Allium cepa)*

Also pearl onions, picklers, creamers, boilers, baby onions, mini-onions
Including **cipolline** or **Italian pearl onions**

Distinct as their appearance may be, the golden, silver-white, and fuchsia pearls and teardrops shown here are "all *Allium cepa* and named by size and nothing else," according to the onion breeder Leonard Pike, a professor of horticulture at Texas A & M. "One seed shows up as pearls or boilers and standards and jumbos. The grading machine tells them their names."

Bob Rietveld, co-owner of Magic Valley Growers in Wendell, Idaho, a primary grower of petite onions, reels off these names: picklers (onions less than 1 inch in diameter); pearls (¾ to 1 inch); creamers (1 to 1¼ inches); boilers (1¼ to 1⅞ inches). But "to most customers, they are all just pearl onions anyway," he says. Like green onions, they stay small because they are planted in tight quarters and picked early. But unlike green onions, they are as pungent and storable small as they are when they become large.

They all taste pretty much the same, which means that they can be chosen for shape, size, and color. I have cooked satin-white drops that numbered 35 to the quarter-pound; burgundy bulbs, 22; and golden orbs, 14. All wound up flavorful, balanced, and tender, and each was nicely suited to a particular presentation.

(Irwin Goldman, an onion breeder and an associate professor at the University of Wisconsin at Madison, advises that there is another pearl onion, grown in other parts of the world: "*Allium ampeloprasum,* variety *sectivum,* the true pearl onion, which forms small bulbs that cluster at the base of the plant—like garlic cloves.")

Cipollina means "small onion" in Italian (cipolline is the plural form), but it is usually reserved for a cute,

rounded little onions (pearl, pickler, creamer, boiler, baby, and mini-onions)   diameter: ½–1¼ inches

cipolline (Italian pearl onions)   diameter: 1–2½ inches

button-like onion. "The ones grown in this country come from seeds of Italian origin," says Goldman, "a distinct, flat onion now called Italian Red that arrived with immigrants at the beginning of the 19th century." If you shop in farmers' markets or grow your own, you'll find that some of the prettiest and tastiest little onions still bear Italian seed names, such as Borettano. Whether imported or domestically grown, cipolline are characteristically more complex and mellow than other minis, unusually rich, sweet, and firm-tender.

BASIC USE: Small onions of all types are generally eaten whole, as vegetables—not used as seasoning as larger storage onions are. Their visual and textural aspects are paramount. Once peeled, they can be pickled, braised, sautéed, creamed, gratinéed—you name it. They are the eminent onion for stews. Traditionally a holiday ingredient, they combine conveniently with other wintry edibles, such as cooked chestnuts, Brussels sprouts, and mushroom caps; or with sturdy grains like wild rice and buckwheat. But there is no reason to keep them for cold weather. They are appealing with spring and summer vegetables, too: peas, fiddlehead ferns, tiny carrots, squash, or turnips. Marinated mini-onions make a particularly nice contribution to summer kebabs.

SELECTION: Little onions are harvested in early fall, but they dry well and are available for most of the year. Andy Xitco, co-owner of Arthur Hood, a packing and shipping company in Paramount, California, points out that the onion's fragile skin may break and flake in shipping, but that it protects the onion and should be there, broken or not. "If onions are stripped and shiny, they do not last."

Onions should be sold loose, in open containers or mesh bags—not plastic-wrapped. They should be crackling-dry without a trace of dampness. White onions should show no greening. Cipolline are tender and more perishable than the sturdy round pearls, according to Xitco. If they look bruised or crushed, they will spoil quickly.

STORAGE: Do not refrigerate any little onions. Spread them in a basket and keep in a well-ventilated, preferably cool place (but I have kept little onions for months in a warm city apartment). Sniff them every week or two to check for spoilage. Remove any that are desiccated, moist, or softening.

PREPARATION AND PEELING: Choose one of three following methods to loosen skins: (1) Pour boiling water over onions in a bowl. Weight with a dish to immerse onions; leave for 5 minutes. Drain; cover with cold water. (2) Immerse onions in warm tap water and let stand 30 minutes or more. (3) Put onions in a bowl with water to cover. Weight to keep immersed. Refrigerate overnight.

Then, removing onions from water one at a time, cut a slim sliver from each root end (more, and you lose a layer of onion) and pull skin up and off. Try not to remove onion layers (don't worry about a few rootlets left behind). Trim neck skin, as needed. Although many people advise cutting an X in the base, I have not found this helpful. Alternatively, peel after roasting (see recipe, following).

Basic Roasted Little Onions

Pop whole onions into a hot oven for a mere 10 to 20 minutes and they become succulent, exceptionally mild, roasty-tasting, and easy to peel. Choose relatively large onions—10 to 12 per ¼ pound—which hold their shape nicely. Once cooked, peel them and toss with other vegetables or grains. Or serve as a simple garnish; see below.

FOR EACH SERVING

**10 to 12 small onions of one or many
colors (about 4 ounces)
1 teaspoon butter, olive or nut oil, or duck,
goose, or pork fat
Salt and pepper
Optional: ¼ teaspoon minced thyme or
savory leaves**

1. Preheat oven to 500°F. Spread onions in a roomy pan. Roast until tender—but not squishy—when pierced with a knife, 10 to 20 minutes, depending upon size. Test often, shaking pan to redistribute onions. Remove from oven and cool until you can handle them.

2. With sharp knife, slit each onion skin from root to tip. Gently unwrap and remove skin; trim root, as needed.

3. To serve, choose skillet to hold onions closely in single layer. Combine chosen fat with the onions and seasoning in pan. Shake over moderate flame to heat through and brown slightly. Toss with optional herb.

Cipolline Glazed with Spiced Red Wine

Shiny, burgundy-brown little orbs are richly glazed, sweet, and winy—a gorgeous garnish. One of the few recipes in this book that demands the weight of a red meat or game accompaniment, the onions lend luster to venison, beef, lamb, or squab. Very small onions present the prettiest picture and will adorn more plates but are time-consuming to peel. Larger ones will do fine—but feed fewer diners.

> 1 pound very small (50 or thereabouts) cipolline (preferably red)
> ½ teaspoon bruised juniper berries or cardamom seeds
> 6 cloves
> 2 bay leaves
> ½ teaspoon bruised peppercorns
> 1½ cups red wine
> 1 cup strong veal, beef, or vegetable stock
> 1 tablespoon butter
> 1 tablespoon brown sugar
> 2 tablespoons brandy
> Salt

1. Peel onions in whichever fashion you prefer (see Preparation and Peeling).

2. Combine juniper, cloves, bay leaves, pepper, wine, and stock in heavy non-aluminum skillet large enough to hold onions in a single layer. Boil gently, tightly covered, for 5 minutes.

3. Add butter, sugar, and onions. Cover, reduce heat, and barely simmer (keep heat low, or onion centers will pop out), stirring occasionally, until onions are three-quarters cooked—10 to 15 minutes.

4. Uncover and add brandy. Taste for salt. Continue to cook over fairly low heat (do not hurry the process, or sauce will burn before onions color), stirring, shaking, and turning often until sauce has reduced to a thick glaze and onions are evenly browned, about 10 minutes. Pick out spices, if desired.

Serves 4 to 6

Petite Onions and Potatoes Gilded in Their Juices

Tender baby onions and potatoes bake together in another dish that complements meat, whether roasted pork, lamb, beef, chicken, or turkey. Tuck it into the oven while the meat cooks, then raise the heat to brown the vegetables as the roast "settles" for carving. Choose onions about an inch in diameter, whichever name they go by—pearl, mini-, boiler, baby. Purple or golden onions brighten the look.

> ½ pound mini-onions (about 2 cups)
> 1½ pounds small yellow-fleshed potatoes
> 2 tablespoons duck, pork, or goose fat (fresh or from confit), or butter and/or olive oil
> ¾ teaspoon kosher salt
> Several large thyme, savory, or rosemary sprigs
> Pepper

1. Peel onions (see Preparation and Peeling). Set oven to 375°F.

2. Scrub potatoes with brush. As size dictates, leave whole, halve, quarter, or chunk, to make 1½-inch pieces, more or less.

3. Choose baking dish large enough to hold ingredients in a single tight or slightly overlapping layer. Put whichever fat you favor in the dish and place in oven. When melted, remove. Add potatoes, onions, salt, and thyme, tossing to coat well. Cover closely with foil.

4. Bake until tender, about 35 minutes, shaking dish now and then to redistribute ingredients. Uncover and add pepper. Raise heat to 425°F and roast until slightly golden, about 20 minutes, tossing a few times.

Serves 4 to 6

Variation

> Those who prefer onions deeply browned and slightly crisp should cook them separately: Cook potatoes as above in a slightly smaller dish, reserving half the fat. Melt fat in heavy covered saucepan that will hold onions in a single layer. Add onions and toss with a little salt and sugar. Cook, covered, over lowest heat, shaking pan often, until onions are tender, 15 to 20 minutes. Uncover and brown to taste. When potatoes are tender, add onions and pepper; toss gently. Raise heat and brown to taste.

Pros Propose

In 1950, Elizabeth David's *A Book of Mediterranean Food* opened a sunstruck southern world to the British—in snippets. A sweet-sour onion recipe, **Oignons à la Monégasque** (meaning in the style of Monaco), is described in David's cryptic mode: "Choose small pickling onions. Peel them and put them into a little boiling water. When they are half cooked add olive oil, a little vinegar, 2 or 3 chopped tomatoes, thyme, parsley, a bay leaf, and a handful of currants. They are served cold." Keeping changes to a minimum, I would add: skin and seed the tomatoes; cook the whole gently until the sauce thickens.

Sweet-sour little onions, **Cipolline sott'Aceto**, another classic, is here interpreted by Lynne Rossetto Kasper, who bases her recipe on one from the restaurant Al Castello, where the onions arrive with cured meat and bread fritters. To prepare: Make light caramel syrup. As it colors, add red wine. Once seething stops, add olive oil, red wine vinegar, and seasoning. Add peeled red cipolline; cover and cook gently until tender, but slightly resistant. Off heat, add balsamic vinegar. Cool and adjust sweet-sour balance. Refrigerate in glass storage container for 3 days to 3 weeks. To present, lift onions from liquid and string on long bamboo skewers (from *The Splendid Table*).

While classics are being spotlighted, do not forget **Petits Pois à la Française**, described in 1952 in *Bouquet de France* by Samuel and Narcissa Chamberlain, a book that opened American eyes to the range of regional French cuisine: Place fresh peas in a heavy saucepan on a bed of tender lettuce leaves. Add tiny onions. Season with salt, pepper, sugar, and a bouquet of chervil, parsley, and thyme. Add a lump of butter and boiling water to ¼ the depth of the peas. Cover and simmer until peas are tender and liquid has almost evaporated. Remove the bouquet and lettuce; stir in butter.

Roger Vergé's Vegetables in the French Style is a book that inspires—to a large extent because the recipes are in the chef's personal idiom, not traditional, like **Zucchini and Pearl Onions with Cardamom**: Combine peeled pearl onions in heavy saucepan with olive oil, cardamom seeds, and bay leaves. Add water to cover, salt, pepper, and dried chilli. Cook over high heat 10 minutes. Quarter medium zucchini lengthwise and cut into 2-inch lengths. Dice dried figs, set in a sieve, and run under warm water a few minutes. Add zucchini and tomato paste to onions. Cover and cook 5 minutes. Remove rind and pith from lemons, cut flesh into small dice. Add more oil to pan, and boil to emulsify juices. Add figs and lemons. Serve warm, with chopped fresh peppermint and coriander leaves.

Jean-Georges Vongerichten, an Alsatian with training in Asia, enlivens onions with fresh ginger, a simple and significant modification. For **Gingered Pearl Onions**: Sauté baby onions in butter until lightly colored. Add very thin ginger slices (preferably mandoline-cut) and honey. Toss until browned. Add *jus rôti* (dark broth made with roasted chicken bones and mirepoix) or another flavorful deep-toned broth. Simmer until glazed and tender.

"Sweet" or Mild Onions

(*Allium cepa*)

Onions that are promoted as "sweet enough to eat like an apple" are cultivated widely in the United States: primarily in Hawaii, Washington, California, Texas, Arizona, New Mexico, and Georgia. Add Chile, Peru, Nicaragua, Guatemala, and Mexico (and controlled atmosphere storage) to the domestic production and what was once a regional, seasonal specialty is now a year-round crop.

Whatever they are (an explanation follows), these are not onions that contain more sugar than common ones—and only a marketing maniac would eat them like apples. According to William Randle, an onion flavor researcher at the University of Georgia in Athens, "there are no standards that describe 'sweet onions,' but there are measurements—chemical tests correlated to sensory taste tests from an objective panel." Sugar content is not the key. "A typical storage onion is in the 12 percent range of brix [the measure of sugars]," Randle explains, "while the Vidalia and others of the type are about 8 percent. It is *mildness,* the lack of heat and mouth burn [measured by an analysis of pyruvic acid], that best characterizes the onions." He believes that they should be called mild, not sweet. "As the heat decreases, there is a chance to taste existing sugars. The heat of standard storage onions overrides the sugar."

Vidalia (*left*) and Texas Sweets (yellow, red, and white)

Maui (*left*), Numex (*top*), and Walla Walla (*bottom*)

Sweet Imperial (*top*), and Grand Canyon Sweets (red and yellow)   Diameter all onions: 3-5 inches

Mayan Sweet   (not to scale)

In the promotional literature, almost every onion-growing state claims to be the birthplace of the "original sweet onion." Whatever that may mean, all mild onions cultivated today (with the exception of the Walla Walla) are hybrids of the same two onion types, Grano and Granex, chosen for low heat. Growing temperatures, water application, and the presence of sulfur also affect the heat or bite. In particular, the more sulfur present in the growing environment, the more bite (and, incidentally, the more storage potential) onions develop. Randle notes, "An onion will be least hot if grown under low sulfur conditions, at low temperatures, in well irrigated soils."

These "sweets," as trade groups call them, are mild, exceptionally juicy onions with culinary charms distinct from those of the stronger storage types. Large, with unusually thick rings, they range from a relatively dainty 8 ounces to a whopping 2 pounds apiece. Their outer and inner skins (membranes that separate the layers) are very thin, making for a ragged exterior but a tender interior, free of chewy filaments. Pearly-fleshed and symmetrical, they are best presented raw or lightly cooked in dishes that showcase their texture and appearance.

To me—and to a dozen chefs who shared their opinions with me—mild onions have more in common than not (despite complex chemical flavor profiles and promotional literature touting the uniqueness of each growing region). For all of us, the bite factor outweighed all others: When onions were mild, above all, they tasted no more interesting than watered-down storage onions; when they were biting, their other qualities were difficult to discern.

The most appealing mild onions have a close balance of sharpness, sweetness, and mildness, and some distinctive "personality" traits. Those that most often fit this description were Vidalia, Maui, and Walla Walla. California and Texas onions (red, white, and yellow) were often sharp. Onions from Arizona (red and yellow), New Mexico, Peru, and Chile were balanced but lacked complexity.

BASIC USE: For my taste, mild onions are the only ones to use raw as rings, whether on canapés of seasoned butter, smoked fish, or cheese; or on sandwiches with tomato, roast beef, Cheddar, or herbed flavored mayonnaise. And of course, on burgers.

Dice mild onions for salads, salsas, or relishes, even if you do not normally fancy raw onions; a brief rest in vinegar or lemon will make them even tamer. The mild, crunchy, pale flesh is crisp, brimming with juice—not overwhelming. Chop it fine as a base for dressings, uncooked sauces, or cold soups.

Growing Area	Trade Names	Usual Season
TEXAS	Texas Supersweet, Springsweet, and 1015	March–July
CALIFORNIA	Sweet Imperial, Coachella Sweet	April–September
GEORGIA	Vidalia sweet onion	April–June (controlled atmosphere storage, July–October)
ARIZONA	Grand Canyon Sweet	May–June
NEW MEXICO	NuMex Sweet, Carzalia Sweet	June–August
WASHINGTON	Walla Walla sweet onion	June–August
PERU, NICARAGUA, GUATEMALA	Mayan Sweet	September–April
CHILE	OSO Sweet	December–March
HAWAII	Maui sweet onion	All year (primarily West coast)

If you cook mild onions, do so in ways that will not hide their delicacy. Dip in a beer batter or tempura batter for delectable rings. Or cut thick slices, paint with oil and seasoning, and set on the grill until just lightly marked; do not cook tender.

Roast for a side dish: For each person, rinse and dry a ½-pound onion; set root end down in a baking pan. Bake at 325° to 375°F, as convenient, until tender—not soft—when pierced, about an hour. Cool a bit, peel, and trim root. Pull out a small plug from top and insert some fat (duck, bacon, pork, goose, or butter), salt, pepper, and herbs. Raise heat to 425°F; bake until lightly colored. Serve hot.

SELECTION: Jeffrey Buben, chef and owner of the restaurant Vidalia in Washington, D.C., knows a thing or two about mild onions. His advice: "Watch out for green on the shoulders, which indicates immaturity and sharpness. Onions should be totally dry to the touch with thin (even torn) iridescent skin and rock-solid tops." Buy mild onions close to harvest time, as they quickly lose their fresh charm.

"If you are in the restaurant business, don't just stand at the door and accept onions. You must cut a few, taste them, and see that the core has not deteriorated," says Buben. If you buy in volume, consider a link between chef and farmer: Buben, for example, has 6 acres set aside for him by Plantation Growers in Cobbtown, Georgia. "It is the only way to ensure quality these days," he says. "Sweet onions are no longer regional charmers—they're big business. But you don't want ones that taste that way. When people buy from various farms and repack under their own label, the onions may lack the quality continuity of an individual owner with his name at stake."

STORAGE: Because of their high moisture content, all mild onions are extremely perishable (Maui somewhat less so than others), deteriorating much more rapidly than stored onions. Keep in a *dry,* cool place with good ventilation. A traditional (if unusual) home storage method is to put them in panty hose, tying knots between the onions, and hang them in a cool cellar or garage. Cut off the bottom onions as you want them. Or arrange the onions on wire racks.

In a city apartment, lacking such spaces, I wrap individual onions in paper towels and refrigerate. They last for months and never become as sharp as storage onions—but they do lose the bloom of youth.

PREPARATION: Peel—that's it. The unusually thick layers are well suited to preparing fat rings and neat dice.

Sweet Onion–Lemon Butter Canapés

Dark bread is slathered with lemon-honey butter, chilled, topped with slim onion slices and dill, cut into narrow rectangles, sparked with crisp coarse salt and pepper, and passed as a special hors d'oeuvre—one that demands iced vodka or aquavit. Rich imported butters, usually from France or Denmark, are well worth the extra cost for their satiny texture and deep flavor. Choose a dense, grainy, dark bakery loaf (pumpernickel, 7-grain, or similar) that can be sliced thin.

1 lemon
¼ pound butter (8 tablespoons) at room
   temperature
2 teaspoons full-flavored honey
1 rectangular loaf (about 8 by 5 inches)
   firm dark bread (not sliced)
1 large sweet/mild onion, peeled
3 tablespoons minced dill
Pepper
Coarse sea salt, preferably fleur de sel

1. Scrub lemon. Grate zest. Combine in bowl with butter and honey and whip with wooden spoon until pale and fluffy. Halve lemon and squeeze 1 tablespoon juice. Whip into butter, a teaspoon at a time.

2. With a sharp bread knife, slice crust from all sides of the loaf, trimming to make a neat rectangle. Cut *lengthwise* into slices about ¼ inch thick (8 long rectangles). Lay 4 slices side by side on each of two cutting boards. Scoop a tablespoon of butter onto each slice. With flexible spatula, spread evenly to edges. Chill.

3. Quarter onion, cutting through "poles." Cut lengthwise into thin slices. Arrange 4 slices on each long bread slice to nearly cover, leaving a little space between onions. Sprinkle a stripe of dill down the center of each long slice. Press bread pieces tightly together to make a single-layer rectangle (about 16 by

7 inches) on each board. Cover each with waxed paper. Press down with a rolling pin to flatten slightly. Chill until serving time.

4. To serve, grind over pepper and sprinkle with salt. Cut each long slice into 4 sections, cutting between the onions for tidiness. Halve each if you like small canapés. Serve at once, so that the salt remains crunchy.

Makes 32 or 64 canapés

Sweet Onion-Avocado-Papaya Salsa

The fresh flavors and colors of this relish are just what's needed to liven up a meal of grilled seafood or chicken, or roasted pork loin. The level of sweetness depends upon how sugary both the onions and papaya taste. Adjust seasoning gradually. Serve the salsa freshly assembled. Or complete through step 2, then refrigerate, to finish at serving time.

When choosing papaya, palp for allover tenderness. Do not choose by uniformity of color, or you risk tasteless fruit. Blotchy coloring and pitting are usual. Sunrise papayas or similar orange or pink types are often more juicy and tender than yellow varieties. If you're not familiar with avocado varieties, check out the information on page 38. The usual Hass is not as suitable for salads as the bright green, smoother varieties you'll find in Latin American markets.

> 1 or 2 limes
> ½ teaspoon kosher salt
> 1 teaspoon sugar
> ¼ cup rice vinegar
> ¼ teaspoon chilli flakes, crumbled fine
> 1 medium-small sweet/mild onion (about ½ pound)
> 1 papaya (about ¾ pound), preferably orange-fleshed
> 1 avocado, preferably a Florida variety (about 1 pound)
> ¼ to ⅓ cup slivered cilantro (coriander) and/or basil leaves

1. Scrub 1 lime. With fine grater, remove zest. Halve lime and squeeze juice. If there is not enough to measure ¼ cup, squeeze some from the second lime to make that amount. Blend juice, zest, salt, sugar, vinegar, and chilli flakes in mixing bowl large enough to hold all ingredients.

2. Halve and peel onion. Cut into ¼- to ½-inch dice, separating layers. Add to bowl and toss. Halve, seed, and peel papaya. Cut into ½- to ¾-inch dice. Add to bowl.

3. Taste and adjust seasonings. Halve, seed, and peel avocado. Cut into ½-inch dice. Fold into salsa with cilantro and/or basil leaves. Serve.

**Makes about 3 cups,
to serve 6 as a side dish or condiment**

Variation

Seafood and Sweet Onion-Avocado-Papaya Salad

Blend ¼ teaspoon kosher salt, 1 tablespoon lime juice, and 2 tablespoons olive oil. Toss gently with 1 pound cooked shrimp, lobster dice, or lump crabmeat. Arrange Bibb lettuce leaves on four plates. Mix seafood gently with salsa and spoon over lettuce or mound salsa on lettuce, then arrange seafood on top. Garnish with basil sprigs.

Serves 4

Sweet Onion Condiment/Salad

Lemon zest and honey season a simple toss of pale, juicy onion—a mere nothing to assemble. The tart, fresh mixture is best served as a complement to rich salted fish (such as herring fillets), grilled salmon, barbecued pork or beef, or smoked pork chops—along with small potatoes steamed in their jackets. For a colorful lift, add carrot shreds. Serve as a bed, or strew over the meat or fish.

> 1 lemon
> 1 tablespoon honey
> ½ teaspoon kosher salt
> ½ cup champagne vinegar or rice vinegar
> ¼ teaspoon white pepper
> 2 medium mild onions (about 1½ pounds)
> About 3 tablespoons minced parsley or dill

1. Scrub lemon and remove zest with coarse grater (reserve lemon for another use). In 2- to 3-quart bowl, combine zest, honey, salt, vinegar, and pepper.

2. Peel onions and halve through "poles." Lay cut side down and cut crosswise into ⅛-inch slices (you'll have about 6 lightly packed cups). Add to bowl and toss. Cover and refrigerate an hour, or longer, tossing occasionally.

3. To serve, toss with parsley or dill.

Serves 4

Cool Minted Sweet Onion Soup

Prior to the arrival of tomatoes, bell peppers, and chillis from the New World, cold Spanish soups called gazpachos were not red. The recipe here is typical in its raw vegetables, olive oil, and bread thickening, but atypical in its major ingredients: sweet/mild onion and Iceberg lettuce, which provide both body and liquid. If you ask tasters to identify the ingredients, you may be as surprised by the answers as I was. The components blend so subtly that few will recognize what makes up the pastel pistachio puree.

> 1 large white roll or a few slices of white bread
>   (about 3 ounces)
> ¾ to 1 cup packed mint leaves
>   (preferably peppermint)
> ½ cup packed flat-leaf parsley leaves
> 1 garlic clove, sliced
> 1 large mild onion (1 to 1¼ pounds)
> 2 pickling type ("kirby") cucumbers
> 1 small Iceberg lettuce (1 pound)
> ½ tablespoon kosher salt
> ¼ teaspoon fine-ground white pepper
> 2 to 3 tablespoons champagne vinegar or
>   rice vinegar
> 3 tablespoons mild light oil, such as grapeseed
> 3 tablespoons olive oil, or more to taste
> Fine chiffonade of mint for garnish

1. Remove and discard crusts from bread. Break bread into large chunks (you'll have about 1½ cups), then soak with water to cover. In food processor,

combine ¾ cup mint, parsley, and garlic and mince.

2. Peel onion and cut into chunks; add to processor. Peel, quarter, and seed cucumbers, then add. Cut lettuce into chunks. Add, with salt and pepper. Whiz to a puree, stopping to scrape down the side. (If your processor has a smaller capacity than mine, puree in batches.)

3. Drain water from bread. With motor running, add pieces one at a time until soup is smooth. With motor running, add 2 tablespoons vinegar, then gradually add the two oils. Slowly add water until consistency is slightly thicker than desired (soup thins when strained).

4. Taste soup for seasoning and texture. Add more mint, salt, vinegar, and oil, overseasoning to compensate for chilling. If you like the texture of the soup as is, ignore step 5. For a smoother, thinner consistency (which I prefer), proceed to next step.

5. Push soup in batches through a sieve, pressing to squeeze through most solids. Season again. Chill several hours, or more.

6. Serve in small bowls or cups, sprinkled with mint strips.

Serves 6 as a first course

Sweet Onion and Cottage Cheese Bread Pudding

This savory Sunday supper (or brunch) takes an hour to bake—which gives you time to prepare a Salad of Belgian Endive, Water Cress, and Strawberries (page 87) or sautéed bitter greens to balance the sweetness of the onions in cheese custard. If caraway is not to your liking, substitute ½ teaspoon dried thyme.

> 3 to 4 ounces lean bacon or firm country ham,
>   diced fine
> 2 medium mild onions (about 1½ pounds)
> 1 teaspoon caraway seeds
> 1 teaspoon dried marjoram
> ¼ teaspoon pepper
> 1½ teaspoons kosher salt
> 1 pound cottage cheese
> 2 tablespoons flour
> ½ cup buttermilk
> 2 eggs

7 slices whole-wheat sandwich bread
    (about 9 ounces)
Butter
½ cup coarse-grated Gruyère or
    Comté cheese

1. Place oven racks in center and upper levels. Set oven to 375°F. In large skillet, cook bacon over moderately low heat until evenly browned. Meanwhile, halve and peel onions, then cut into ¾-inch dice.

2. When bacon has browned, pour out most fat from pan. Add caraway to pan, raise heat, and toss until seeds pop. Add onions, marjoram, pepper, and ½ teaspoon salt, and toss briefly, separating onion layers. Remove from heat.

3. Combine cottage cheese, flour, buttermilk, eggs, and remaining 1 teaspoon salt in food processor and whiz until smooth. Cut crusts from bread (save for crumbs). Cut bread into 1-inch squares.

4. Generously butter 2- to 2½-quart shallow baking and serving dish. Combine half the bread and onions in the dish, distributing bread evenly. Spoon one-third of the cheese mixture evenly over all. Spread remaining onions over this. Arrange remaining bread evenly on top, pressing down firmly. Spoon remaining cheese mixture over top to cover completely. Set on a baking sheet. Cover with buttered or oiled foil, crimping to seal.

5. Set in center of oven. Bake ½ hour. Remove from oven, take off foil, and sprinkle the grated cheese over. Set on upper rack and bake until center is puffed and firm and top is nicely browned, about 35 minutes longer. If very crisp topping is desired, set under broiler a minute. Serve hot or warm. (Can be reheated nicely, uncovered.)

**Serves 6 to 8 as a side dish,
4 to 5 as a main dish**

Hoppin' John's Crunchy Onion Rings

John Martin Taylor (aka Hoppin' John), Lowcountry aficionado and frymaster, chooses this way to fry onions—so I do. The recipe, adapted from *The Fearless Frying Cookbook,* begins with this comment: "If you dip onion rings in milk and flour, they'll fry to a golden brown with a crispy coating, but I prefer this thick beer batter. Not only does it remind me of the onion rings from the drive-ins of my youth, it also covers the sweet onion flesh so it doesn't cook too much."

Unless you have a spectacular ventilation system, this is an outside job—preferably outside with an electric outlet. I would rather use a thermostat-controlled wok, skillet, or deep-fryer than the camp stove and thermometer that the more adept Taylor enjoys. He serves the onion rings at summer parties with heavy cloth napkins and beer, "though it seems no one will drink the stuff anymore. They've got to have wine these days."

1¾ cups all-purpose flour (see Note)
1 teaspoon kosher salt
1 can beer (12 ounces), at room temperature
    and flat
2 tablespoons peanut oil
3 or 4 mild/sweet onions (¾ pound each),
    as flat as possible
Peanut oil for deep-frying (have plenty!)
2 egg whites
Salt

1. Combine flour and salt in one bowl, the beer and 2 tablespoons oil in another. Pour all but a few tablespoons of the liquid into the dry ingredients, stirring with a whisk just enough to combine; do not beat. Add remaining liquid if needed, to make a thick but loose mixture—like thick pancake batter. Let stand 1 to 2 hours.

2. Trim ends from 3 onions, then peel. Set each onion with a trimmed end flat on a cutting board and cut like a bagel to make ½-inch slices. Pop out centers (save for another dish). Separate rings. (Slice a fourth onion if you have batter remaining when the others have been fried.)

3. Pour at least 2 inches of oil into whichever frying vessel you've chosen. Heat to 365°F.

4. Meanwhile, beat egg whites until they hold stiff peaks. Lightly fold into the batter. Set a large wire rack on a baking sheet.

5. When oil reaches 365°F, hold an onion ring with tongs and dip into batter to coat completely. Drop into oil. Repeat, adding no more onions than will float without crowding. Fry until golden, about 2 minutes per side.

6. With skimmer or another pair of tongs, lift out rings, letting them drain over the pot. Set on rack. Continue until you have a plateful, then serve immediately. Let diners salt to taste.

**Makes at least 60 rings
(however many that serves is your call)**

Note: Flours in the North (even so-called "all-purpose" flours) are usually harder and heavier in texture than ones in the South, where John makes these. You'll need to adjust the liquid according to your neck of the woods.

Pros Propose

Mild onions are used raw and lightly cooked by those who work with them regularly. "Maui onions are meant to be eaten raw. If you're going to cook onions, you might as well use a generic storage onion," says chef and author Alan Wong. "In Hawaii, we serve them cut into wedges with a bowl of Hawaiian salt or chilli-pepper water to dip into. They are a staple condiment for luau and for grilled fish or meat in general." For his **Maui Tomato-Onion Salad:** Combine julienne of onions with tomato dice. Add minced ginger, garlic, soy sauce, fish sauce, sesame oil, macadamia oil, and minced green onions; toss. Just before serving, add toasted French bread cubes.

Chef Peter Merriman serves raw onion with raw fish, **Poisson Cru,** at his popular Waimea restaurant: Marinate small cubes of marlin with lime juice until cured ("about an hour for locals, 3 to 4 hours for tourists who don't want raw fish"), then drain. Mix with dice of Maui onion and fresh coconut cream. Garnish with tomato julienne.

Merriman also serves a **Maui Onion Relish:** Combine sectioned, diced pummelo (or grapefruit), avocado bits, julienne-cut onions and red bell pepper, and lime juice. Serve with hot and spicy grilled fish or meat.

Boston chef Daniel Bruce says that he pictured himself in the sun, eating outdoors, to come up with the right ingredients for **Grilled Maui Onion and Papaya Salsa:** Toss ½-inch onion slices with oil, salt, and pepper, then grill and halve. Puree pink papaya, cilantro, and lime juice and puddle in the middle of each plate. Arrange grilled onions and papaya wedges around, and accent with cress to counter the sweetness.

"Only sweet onions do the job of sweet onions. Other onions are too harsh for real tomato-onion salad," says New York chef Patrick Vaccariello, who prepares a complicated upscale version "with Vidalias, because they're on my side of the map—as close to regional as I get." For his **Tomato–Vidalia Onion Salad:** Prepare tomato water by wrapping seeds, skins, and scraps in cheesecloth and hanging to drain. Discard the sediment and keep the "water." Combine with sour cream, buttermilk, and basil oil and pour into espresso cups. Cut onions very thin (preferably on a meat slicer). Cut thick slices from beefsteak tomatoes and overlap on one side of each plate. Fluff onions in the center to form a pile. Set espresso cup and spoon on each plate. Drizzle green basil oil on salad and add salt, pepper, and basil sprig.

Walla Walla Onion and Yogurt Salad is based on Indian raita, a relish spooned alongside spicy dishes or sopped up with bread. To prepare: Cut large Walla Wallas into thin slices. Combine with minced ginger and seasoned rice vinegar; let soften and mellow briefly. Pour off liquid. Stir in yogurt, torn basil, and coarse-cut cilantro and spearmint; season. Cover and chill. Before serving, add nasturtium flowers (from *The Herbfarm Cookbook* by Jerry Traunfeld).

Chef Jeff Buben stresses that onions should be only very lightly cooked for his simple **Pan-Roasted Vidalia Onion Slices:** Sear very thick Vidalia rings on both sides in a little olive oil in a cast-iron pan—do not cook through. Deglaze pan with chicken stock and add salt, pepper, and fresh thyme. Serve at once as a bed for hearty fish, such as salmon or rockfish.

To accompany oven-roasted rib-eye steak, Chef Jan Birnbaum serves both **Sweet Onion–Tomato Relish and Fried Onion Rings.** To prepare: Marinate thick Walla Walla slices in champagne vinegar and olive oil. Grill to remove raw taste, but keep crunch. Cool, then cut into ½-inch dice. Mix with tomato dice, parsley, chervil, and lime juice. Dip thin Walla Walla slices in buttermilk, then a mixture of semolina, flour, cornmeal, Parmesan, coriander, cumin, dry mustard, salt, and black, white, and cayenne peppers. Deep-fry rings. Place on the rib-eye steaks with relish on the side.

For his version of fried onion rings, chef Jeff Drew

finds "very picante batter and sweet NuMex onions are a perfect match." For **Chilli-Battered New Mexico Onion Rings:** Prepare batter of pureed Serranos, cilantro, dark beer, flour, and cornstarch. Lightly flour very thick slices of New Mexico Sweets, dip into batter, and fry.

Chef Drew also offers **Stuffed, Roasted New Mexican Sweet Onions** as a side dish or part of a vegetable plate: Roast oiled small sweet onions in their skins at 300°F until just tender. Cut off tops and remove cores (grill to use in sandwiches). Fill with quinoa tossed with golden raisins, chile de árbol, and toasted Spanish almonds.

Chef Matthew Dunn uses another technique for his **Sweet Onions Stuffed with Figs and Walnuts:** Halve peeled Texas 1015s crosswise. Sear cut sides in clarified butter. Add stock and port. Bake, covered, in moderate oven until just tender. Remove core from each half, leaving three layers of "bowl." Chop cores and mix with toasted walnuts, diced fresh figs, and cilantro. Fill onions with this. Serve with grated pecorino as part of a vegetable plate.

Orach (*Atriplex hortensis*)

Also garden orach, mountain spinach, arroche,
orache, French spinach, and butter leaves

Pick up a book about edible plants, and it will tell you that orach has been cultivated since ancient times, was cooked by the ancient Greeks and Romans, and has long been popular in Europe and then in the United States. Then the entry is likely to end more or less on this note: "Sadly, orach disappeared from our garden this century" (*The Vegetable Book* by Colin Spencer). As recently as 1865, the classic seed reference *The Field and Garden Vegetables of America,* by Fearing Burr, Jr., described seven distinct varieties in use, yet few gardeners or cooks today have even heard of orach.

Why do I include orach here, if only foods currently sold in the American marketplace are admitted to these pages? Because there has been a tiny revival of orach—in miniature size—thanks to Americans' mesclun madness. The handsome red varieties (there are maroon, red, and green types) have become a punchy mixed salad component—probably too punchy for most who eat them raw.

To my taste, *Atriplex* (Saltbush) species, whether the garden variety (of Eurasian origin) or related American species, are really best cooked. I may be influenced by one of my favorite vegetable observers, John Evelyn, who wrote in *Acetaria: A Discourse of Sallets* (1699), "The tender Leaves are mingl'd with other cold Salleting; but 'tis better in Pottage." Like its close relative, lamb's quarters, orach does indeed make a fine, deep-toned (purplish, if you use the maroon variety), flavorful soup. Stronger and saltier than lamb's quarters, orach's arrow-shaped leaves (even velvety baby tips) have the force of raw beet greens—they are vivid as a raw accent, and even more winning as a cooked vegetable.

BASIC USE: Raw orach can be combined with milder greens for a mixed salad, but it is overpowering alone. It needs only a minute of cooking to be tamed. Boiled momentarily, the leaves and stems become succulent, meaty, earthy—very like spinach plus beet greens in texture, taste, and color. Red varieties retain a pretty pinkness in the stems—but *only* the stems—and yield rosy juices. If you're cooking pale foods, such as rice or white beans, purply orach will tint them. Seed catalogues offer varieties that are said to remain red-leafed when cooked, but none that I have tried thus far has done so.

Once orach is blanched, use it in recipes as you would spinach, lamb's quarters (page 351), or beet greens (page 79). For soups, combine orach with other leaves for a puree, or add to potato-leek or rustic bean soups and cook briefly, for depth and color.

SELECTION AND STORAGE: Although most orach in the market (which is pitifully little) is cultivated, I have seen it only in the spring and summer. For minimal waste, choose small-stalked plants, but be aware that even sturdy ones will cook to a pleasing tenderness. How much you need depends upon the size of the greens. Delicate stalks need no trimming; thus, 1 pound can feed four. When plants are large and heavy-stalked, you'll need twice that amount. Refrigerate unwashed, plastic-wrapped, for up to a week.

PREPARATION: For small stalks, keep the branches whole; dunk into water to clean. For larger stalks (more than ¼ inch in diameter), pull everything—the leaves, their stems, buds, seedheads—from the central stalk. Discard the stalk and slosh all the rest in plenty of water to rinse clean.

Salad of Orach, Arugula, Water Cress, Onion, and Oranges

When a selection of assertive greens, equally emphatic orange zest, and strong red onion are combined, they mysteriously mellow and lose their individual identities to become an earthy, brilliantly colored whole. Although deep-dark in flavor, the texture is light and the

effect fresh. The weight of the greens is not crucial—it is supplied only to give some idea of the proportions.

> 2 medium navel oranges
> 1 teaspoon sharp mustard, such as Dijon
> 1 tablespoon sherry vinegar
> ¼ teaspoon kosher salt
> 2 tablespoons pumpkin seed or walnut oil
> 1 tablespoon corn or peanut oil
> 1 small red onion (about 6 ounces)
> 1 small bunch water cress (about 3 ounces)
> 1 small bunch arugula (about 3 ounces)
> 1 bunch small or medium orach
>   (about 6 ounces)
> ¼ cup toasted pumpkin seeds or walnuts (to
>   match the oil)

1. Scrub 1 orange. Remove zest with swivel peeler. Cut into hair-thin strands (to make about 2 tablespoons). Drop into small saucepan of boiling salted water. Boil 1 minute. Drain, rinse, and spread to dry.

2. Cut all pith and rind from both oranges. With sharp knife, cut between membranes (do not discard) to remove sections; chill these. Squeeze juice from membranes into small bowl. Add mustard, vinegar, and salt and blend. Add both oils.

3. Peel onion and halve through "poles." Lay cut side down and into very thin vertical slices. Toss with dressing and zest; refrigerate.

4. Trim cress into sprigs. Rinse and spin-dry. Trim roots and stems from arugula. Wash leaves in several changes of water and spin-dry. Pluck orach leaves from stems. Rinse and spin-dry. Stack large leaves (keep small ones whole) and cut into ¼-inch strips. Chill both whole and sliced leaves.

5. To serve, add onion mixture and nuts to greens and toss. Distribute among serving plates. Decorate with oranges and serve immediately.

Serves 4

Orach with Balsamic Vinegar and Currants

Intense, dark, orach's bitterness is balanced by the sweet-tart addition of dried fruit and vinegar and rounded out with olive oil. Although spinach-like, orach's edible stems, buds, and leaves offer more varied textures. For a vegetable meal, serve over large white beans, or couscous with cashews, or polenta slices. Or spoon alongside grilled chicken or lamb chops. Or serve as a salad course, topped with toasted walnuts.

> 3 tablespoons balsamic vinegar
> 1 tablespoon water
> 3 tablespoons dried currants or
>   coarse-chopped raisins
> 1 large garlic clove, peeled and smashed
> Optional: ¼ teaspoon chilli flakes
> 1 pound medium to large orach
> 2 tablespoons olive oil
> Pepper
> Salt

1. In small saucepan, combine vinegar, water, currants, garlic, and optional chilli flakes; bring to a boil. Reduce heat and simmer, covered, 2 minutes. Let stand while you prepare orach.

2. Strip leaves, stems, and any attached florets and seeds from large orach stalks; discard stalks. Drop stripped leaves and other parts into a pot of boiling salted water; return to a boil over highest heat. Boil just until leaf-stems are tender—a minute or so. Drain well, tossing and pressing in a colander to remove water. Blot with towel.

3. Set skillet over moderate heat and add oil. Add orach and toss a minute to coat. Add vinegar mixture and pepper (remove garlic), tossing briefly to mingle flavors. Season. Serve hot or at room temperature.

Serves 4 as a side dish

★See also Creamed Spring Lamb's Quarters, page 353, in which orach can be substituted for lamb's quarters.

Pros Propose

For salads, orach's strong spinach savor and sturdy leaves must be balanced by acid and sugar. "Orach's high mineral taste is nicely countered by citrus," says chef Fernando Divina. For his **Orach and Citrus Salad:** Toss small orach leaves with vinaigrette made from grapefruit and orange juices, blanched grapefruit and orange zests, and hazelnut oil. Add roasted hazelnuts and citrus segments.

The assertive leaves can also be mellowed with a heated dressing, as in **Mâche and Orach Salad with Warm Vinaigrette:** Heat sherry vinegar, olive oil, walnut oil, and minced shallots in small pan. Toss together trimmed orach leaves and mâche with a little olive oil, then add hot dressing and mix. Garnish with sliced button mushrooms, sliced hard-cooked eggs, croutons, and toasted walnuts. Serve at once (*The Cook's Garden* by Shepherd and Ellen Ogden).

Richness—in the form of bacon, butter, cream, or oil—also balances the aggressive side of orach. Chef Divina chooses pork to soften and sweeten the leaves. For **Pan-Roasted Pork with Wilted Orach:** Render bacon (Divina uses boar bacon) with shallots and wild onions. Add medium to large orach leaves. Moisten with pork stock and a little pork glace and cook briefly. Serve with short-brined pork cutlets, seared and then pan-roasted in a hot oven, adding the drippings to the cooked orach. Or serve with a simple pork roast.

Creamed Orach on English Muffins makes a nice old-time brunch dish. To prepare: Steam orach leaves. Drain and chop. Heat butter and stir in orach. When heated, add a little cream, salt, pepper, and mace. Spoon over toasted English muffin halves. Sprinkle with shredded Jack cheese. Garnish with sliced tomatoes (*The Kitchen Garden Cookbook* by Sylvia Thompson).

Oyster Mushrooms (*Pleurotus* species)

Including **common, yellow, pink, white (or angel) trumpet, blue, king, black**

The oyster mushrooms on a menu or at a "specialty" grocery are not wild, no matter what the management may claim. Oyster mushrooms are farmed in more shapes, sizes, and colors than any others, because they are relatively easy to cultivate and they grow fast.

The most common oyster types are beige, soft, and mild. Others go in and out of fashion. The jonquil yellow and salmon or pastel pink oysters stand out when raw. Although less eye-catching, those with tan, brown, dove-gray, and slate caps are usually firmer and tastier. Whites are highly variable. Here's the roll call.

Common oyster mushrooms or **pleurottes** (primarily *Pleurotus ostreatus* and *P. pulmonarius*) form shelves or clusters of fairly long-stemmed, cream-to-taupe,

sharp-gilled caps. These are rounded or spoon-shaped, from gumdrop- to saucer-size. All are comparatively tender and bland when cooked. These species "are by far the easiest and least expensive to grow. For small cultivators with limited budgets, oyster mushrooms are the clear choice for gaining entry into the gourmet mushroom industry," writes Paul Stamets in his manual *Growing Gourmet and Medicinal Mushrooms*.

Unfortunately, of the many oysters now raised worldwide, the ones that are easiest to grow are often shortest on flavor—at least as sometimes grown in the United States. Malcolm Clark, president of Gourmet Mushrooms in Sebastopol, California, laments that "many oyster growers now use straw as the major growth medium, and this can result in loss of flavor,

white trumpet (*bottom*), yellow (*right*), black (*left*), pink, and imported Italian common (*top*)   ¼ actual size

common oyster mushrooms (domestic)   ⅓ actual size

texture, and shelf life. The natural host to the mushrooms is wood of varying yet similar types." The better mushrooms have more defined body and character.

The light taste of common oyster mushrooms is best suited to dishes with few ingredients, simply prepared. I find that searing brings out bitterness. Instead, roast the mushrooms or gently stew them in broth and butter or cream. Or braise with light meats, such as veal, chicken, or pheasant; or cook with seafood.

Pink oyster mushroom (*Pleurotus djamor* and others) "has a shelf life of about two hours," according to the mushroom distributor Hans Johansson. This is so nearly accurate that I have never managed to cook them. I have bought these mushrooms three times, only to find that within 24 hours of purchase they were sufficiently smelly to be tossed out.

Yellow oyster mushroom (*Pleurotus citrinopileatus* and others) has been almost as perishable as the pink in my experience. It has at least held up long enough to be cooked, but the yellow faded—and so did most of the flavor. (I have heard about yellow oysters that are far more rewarding, but I have not located them.)

Yellow oysters do develop a pleasing springiness when roasted: Toss with a little mild nut oil, then roast on fairly high heat until the edges turn tawny, about 8 minutes. Or simmer in coconut milk, cream, or a rich sauce to plump the mushrooms to a uniformly juicy texture. Do not sauté; this underscores bitterness.

White oyster, white trumpet, angel trumpet (*Pleurotus ostreatus kummeri* and others) are not easily

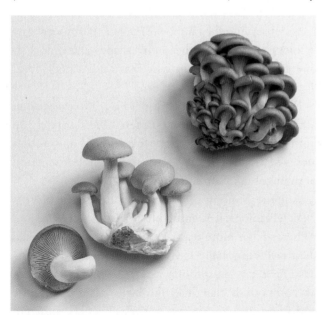

king oyster (*bottom left*) **and blue oyster**   ⅓ **actual size**

recognized as oyster mushrooms, because they may have the shape of their namesake, the trumpet. (They are not related to the black trumpet, page 171.) I have seen two distinct versions: One is pearly and funnel-shaped with thickish central stems. Lightly cooked, each separately harvested lily-like mushroom cooks to mild softness that hints at scrambled eggs. The other version, clusters of creamy, near-translucent overlapping caps, pretty as seashells, cooked up floppy, wet, and nearly tasteless.

For maximum visual impact, serve white trumpets in clear soup: the soft fluted forms wave like sea anemones in the bowl. To prepare: Simmer the whole trumpets (or trimmed separated clumps) in clear broth just to wilt. Or sauté, as garnish: Halve large ones lengthwise and leave smaller ones whole. Sauté gently in butter and grapeseed oil over moderate heat to just barely cook through; stir in a little more butter and a pinch of fresh mild herbs, such as chervil.

Blue oyster, hiratake (*Pleurotus ostreatus* strains) may show up as "shimeji," but that former catchall term for *Pleurotus* species is now considered incorrect (see beech mushroom, page 76). The small satiny, silvery blue-capped, white-stemmed mushrooms are more solid and flavorful than most pale oyster strains (although they usually do fade to taupe, like the others). Hiratake imported from Japan are darker and firmer than what I've see here. In general, blue oysters (there are several strains) taste sweetly shrimp-like, shrink little, and hold their shape and springiness.

Cook briefly, sautéeing a few minutes to brown lightly. Or sauté, then add liquid to cook through and a little cream to glaze. Use as a textural contrast, rather than as a blend-in mushroom. The cute little individuals are a charming counterpoint to chewy greens (frisée), or soft ones (spinach).

Black oyster is a particular strain of *Pleurotus ostreatus* developed by Gourmet Mushrooms. Black oysters—although similar to blue oysters—have round little caps that are satiny charcoal, and their gills are pale gray. Plump, meaty, and moist, but rather fragile, they have a more intense flavor than most other oyster mushrooms.

Sauté over moderate heat, tossing often, for darkly shiny, juicy, fleshy little mouthfuls with a sweet and rich flavor that suggests lobster. Use these rare, expensive little mushrooms as a punctuating garnish, especially for seafood.

King oyster/Trumpet Royale/Royal Trumpet (*Pleurotus eryngii*) is large, heavy, fleshy, and unlike any other cultivated oyster mushroom—although it *is* one, despite its trademark Trumpet Royale (again, it is not related to black trumpet). Although the quality varies, the dense bright-white stalks and creamy tan caps are distinctively thick and solid. The large, plump mushrooms grow in bouquets joined at the base, not in overlapping caps like most oysters.

"Their density seems to hold up to any cooking circumstances," says chef Michael Otsuka. "They're failsafe unless you walk away and let them burn up." Braise or stew, using plenty of liquid to tenderize the solid flesh. Or toss with nut oil and a little lemon juice and roast in a high oven until crisped outside and tender and juicy within. They hold their shape perfectly, turn golden-beige, and become more and more solid, but the flavor remains sweet and rather mild, not intense. When they are roasted whole, you'll want to eat them one at a time—with your fingers, like fried clams. Or cut the stems crosswise into rounds; sauté quickly, until they're juicy and firm as scallops.

SELECTION: Choose comparatively firm, thick, dry oyster mushrooms with a kid-glove feel. Avoid any that are moist or have darkened areas or seriously cracked cap edges (a few cracks are common). Oyster mushrooms growing in clumps are less likely to break and bruise; they also last longer. Because the stems of common oysters (but not king oysters, which have luscious stems) are often inedibly tough, buy them with the bases closely trimmed or you'll be paying for waste. Above all, avoid wetness or stickiness.

STORAGE: Refrigerate in a single layer in a basket, covered with a towel. If mushrooms were purchased in a plastic "clamshell" pack, place a scrap of paper towel on top of the caps to avoid possible condensation and store in the original container. All mushrooms deteriorate in storage, so make it as short as possible. Pink and yellow oyster mushrooms should be used on the day of purchase. Common and white oysters may keep several days if they are firm, full, and solid; but store them far from strong odors, which they will absorb. Blue and black mushrooms last longer. King oysters stand up considerably longer than any other cultivated oyster species.

PREPARATION

For common, yellow, and pink oysters: Brush off any growing compound and slightly trim the stems; or if they seem tough, trim more closely or cut off completely. Break small mushrooms apart into little clumps, or separate into individuals. If relatively small, keep the caps whole, to maintain their pretty form. As needed, break larger ones into bite-size pieces.

For white oysters: Those sold trimmed and singly will need no attention. Clustered ones will require trimming, if stems are tough. Sample and see. Flick clean, as needed, with a soft brush.

For blue and black oysters: The stems are edible and desirable; do not remove. Prepare by cutting apart at the base and trimming as little as possible. Leave caps whole; or halve, as size dictates.

For king oyster: Trim bases just enough to separate. Large ones are best sliced lengthwise to keep their graceful curves. Or tear lengthwise in several strips, like string cheese. Or cut apart cap and stem, slicing the bright-white "trunk" into rounds.

About trimmings: Save all mushroom trimmings for broth. If you won't use them in a few days, freeze. Rinse trimmings and combine in a plastic quart container with water to just submerge; cover and freeze. Repeat whenever you have trimmings, until the container is full. When ready to cook, defrost slightly, then pop out the whole block into a soup pot to mix with other broth ingredients.

Note on raw oyster mushrooms: It is tempting to consider serving the rainbow of oyster mushrooms raw in order to maintain the pretty shapes and colors. If one taste doesn't explain why that's not a good idea, listen to two experts.

Malcolm Clark, a biologist who is a 30-year veteran of the specialty mushroom business: "We absolutely do not recommend that people eat cultivated mushrooms raw. They taste terrible—with the possible exception of shiitake—and can cause indigestion."

Annette Simonson, laboratory director of Northwest Mycological Consultants in Corvallis, Oregon: "There are far more reasons to eat mushrooms cooked than raw—especially if you're in the restaurant business. First, raw mushrooms may contain natural toxins or compounds that interfere with digestion. Some customers may be sensitive to these. Second, sufficient cooking will kill bacteria that can grow even on cultivated mushrooms. And heating helps break down tough fungal cell walls, increasing flavor and digestibility."

Warm Salad of Oyster Mushrooms, Fennel, and Lettuce with Parmesan

A soft salad of graceful oyster mushrooms and red-tipped lettuce is accented with crunchy, saffron-infused fennel. Serve the elegant first course on large plates. Choose any tender, flattened form of oyster mushroom—ones that grow like overlapping shells or leaves, not solid round or button types.

Large pinch of saffron
2 tablespoons lemon juice
½ teaspoon kosher salt
White pepper
6 tablespoons olive oil
1 garlic clove, halved
1 head loose-leaf lettuce, preferably red-tipped
    (about 10 ounces)
¾ pound medium oyster mushrooms
    (any tender flattened type)
1 medium fennel bulb (½ pound)
3-ounce chunk of Parmesan

1. Preheat oven to 475°F. Crumble saffron into lemon juice; add salt and pepper. In small skillet, combine oil and garlic and cook over lowest heat until garlic barely colors, about 5 minutes. Remove garlic. Add juice mixture. Remove from heat.

2. Rinse and spin-dry lettuce: Tear into bite-size pieces; set aside. Trim hard stems from mushrooms (save for stock). Halve caps lengthwise if large; leave whole if small. Trim fennel and cut into fine julienne (about 2 cups). In baking pan that will hold them in a single layer, toss mushrooms with 3 tablespoons dressing. In another pan, toss fennel with 2 tablespoons.

3. Set mushrooms on upper shelf of oven and roast until just cooked through, 4 to 5 minutes. Halfway through, set fennel on same shelf. Cook just until it loses its raw crunch, 2 to 3 minutes.

4. Meanwhile, shave Parmesan into narrow strips with vegetable peeler. Toss remaining dressing with lettuce. Distribute among six plates. Divide warm vegetables over leaves. Top with cheese. Serve at once.

Serves 6 as a first course

Spinach and Blue Oyster Mushroom Salad with Bacon and Walnuts

Tiny firm mushrooms, which give a springy feel to a dish, are cooked in a different way from the soft ones in the preceding salad. For this update of the American mushroom-bacon-spinach classic, satiny little oysters, thick bacon dice, toasted nuts, and mini-greens are tossed in a brisk mustard-balsamic dressing. Trimmed and cleaned small-leaf spinach is sold loose or in bags. Or buy bunched medium leaves, trim well, and cut into small pieces. If beech mushrooms (honshimeji) are easier to find, substitute them for blue oysters.

4 to 6 ounces small oyster mushrooms,
    such as blue (hiratake)
5 to 6 ounces trimmed (or 8 to 9 ounces
    bunched) small-leaf spinach
¼ pound thick-sliced lean bacon
1 teaspoon Dijon mustard
1 tablespoon balsamic vinegar
1 tablespoon lemon juice
Salt and pepper
1½ tablespoons peanut or walnut oil
¼ cup toasted, coarse-chopped walnuts

1. Trim base from mushrooms. Separate into small equal-size clumps or individuals, as size dictates. Rinse, trim, and spin-dry spinach; put in serving bowl.

2. Cut bacon crosswise into ¾-inch strips. Spread in medium skillet and cook over moderate heat until evenly browned. Meanwhile, blend mustard, vinegar, lemon juice, salt, and pepper; then whisk in oil. With slotted spoon, transfer bacon to paper. Drain and reserve fat. Pour sediment from pan (do not wash).

3. Return 1½ tablespoons fat to pan. Over high heat, brown mushrooms, tossing constantly—about 3 minutes. Add to spinach. Off heat, stir dressing into

pan. Pour at once over spinach and toss. Divide among plates. Sprinkle with bacon and nuts.

Serves 2 as a main course, 4 as a first course

Creamy Oyster Mushroom and Potato Gratin

As common oyster mushroom caps bake, they exude their juices, then plump and soften in the creamy sauce. Treated this way, even less than ideal specimens come to life. Serve up with roast lamb and cress for a Sunday supper. Choose mushrooms with a minimum of stem base.

> 2 pounds medium-small yellow-fleshed
>   potatoes (about 10 potatoes)
> 1 pound medium or large oyster
>   mushrooms
> 1½ tablespoons butter
> 2 medium shallots, chopped
> ½ tablespoon kosher salt (omit if broth is salted)
> 1 cup vegetable or mushroom broth
> ⅔ cup heavy cream
> ½ teaspoon grated nutmeg
> ¼ teaspoon white pepper

1. Set oven to 375°F. Peel potatoes. If wider than 2 inches, halve lengthwise. Cut into thinnish slices. Place in 2½- to 3-quart baking dish that will hold all ingredients. Brush mushrooms clean if needed. Trim hard bits, if any, from base. Cut into large bite-size pieces.

2. Melt butter in large skillet over moderate heat. When foaming, add shallots and stir a minute or two to soften slightly. Raise heat and add mushrooms and salt. Toss until mushrooms release juices and soften a little—just a few minutes. Scoop into dish with potatoes.

3. Add broth, cream, nutmeg, and pepper to skillet and bring to a boil. Pour three-quarters over vegetables, then toss together until they absorb some liquid. Cover tightly with foil. Set in upper third of oven.

4. Bake until potatoes are tender, about 25 minutes or so. Uncover and pour over remaining liquid. Bake until golden and slightly crisp, 20 to 30 minutes, basting now and then with cooking liquid.

Serves 6

Stir-Fried Chicken, Oyster Mushrooms, and Almonds

A one-dish meal made special by the character of the mushroom chosen: For a supple feel, choose the large fawn caps; for a juicy, silky effect, try the thinner white or yellow types; for a springy texture, select compact brown, grayish, or bluish oysters. Or try a medley of oyster mushrooms, first removing stems and cutting all the caps to about the same size. Other cultivated mushrooms will work as well: Lovers of the slick and slippery might substitute nameko or Cinnamon Cap; for a bouncy effect, beech (honshimeji) are best.

If you prefer white meat, substitute ¾ pound boned, skinned chicken breast and use ¼ cup prepared broth (this way, the dish cooks very quickly). As with all stir-fries, have all ingredients prepped and close at hand before you fire up the wok.

> 1¼ pounds chicken thighs (¾ pound if
>   boned and skinned)
> ½ tablespoon cornstarch
> 2 tablespoons shoyu (Japanese soy sauce)
> 1 small bunch cilantro (coriander),
>   preferably with roots
> ¾ pound oyster mushrooms
> 1 tablespoon distilled white vinegar
>   (or white wine vinegar)
> 1 teaspoon sugar
> ⅛ teaspoon ground hot pepper
> 2 tablespoons peanut oil
> 1 large garlic clove, minced
> ½ cup roasted almonds or cashews, sliced or
>   coarse-chopped

1. Remove and discard chicken skin. Remove bones and place them in small saucepan with water to just cover. Bring to a simmer, cover, and cook while you prepare remaining ingredients, 20 to 30 minutes.

2. Cut chicken into bite-size strips, adding any trimmings to the pan. Toss strips with cornstarch and 1 tablespoon shoyu; set aside.

3. If cilantro has roots, cut them from stalks and trim, scrub, and chop fine; set aside. Rinse, strip, and chop enough cilantro leaves to make about ¼ cup; dis-

card stems. Trim base from mushrooms. Separate mushrooms into bite-size pieces—clumps or individuals, as size dictates.

4. Strain broth, then boil to reduce to ¼ cup. Add vinegar, remaining 1 tablespoon shoyu, sugar, and hot pepper, stirring to dissolve.

5. Heat wok over moderately high heat. Pour 1 tablespoon oil around rim. Add cilantro roots (if any) and toss. Add mushrooms and toss to brown slightly, about 2 minutes. Transfer to dish.

6. Add remaining 1 tablespoon oil. Add chicken and stir-fry to brown and glaze lightly, about 3 minutes. Add garlic and toss 1 minute. Add broth mixture and toss over high heat to nearly evaporate, about 2 minutes. Add nuts and mushrooms and toss to heat. Remove from stove.

7. Adjust seasoning. Toss with chopped cilantro and serve hot.

Serves 2 generously as a main course

Oven-Crisped Large Oyster Mushrooms

Crisp-edged, fine-gilled golden fans with juicy centers result from a light marinade and a brief turn in a high oven. For this, you'll need large, thick oyster caps (usually imported from France or Italy), which make meaty mouthfuls. Serve as a side to sautéed fish fillets or veal scallops. Or offer as a first course on a bed of mâche or soft baby greens; top with minced toasted hazelnuts, walnuts, or pecans (to match the oil). I think garlic overpowers these delicate mushrooms, but if you want more than a hint, mince the clove.

**12 to 16 large, thick oyster mushrooms
  (to yield about ¾ pound caps)
1 garlic clove, sliced
1 teaspoon minced thyme or lemon thyme
1 tablespoon lemon juice
¼ teaspoon kosher salt
¼ teaspoon hot pepper sauce
2 tablespoons hazelnut, walnut, or pecan oil
2 tablespoons minced parsley leaves**

1. If mushrooms are not trimmed, cut stems flush with caps (save stems for broth). Combine garlic,

thyme, lemon juice, salt, and hot pepper sauce in small bowl. Add oil and mix to blend.

2. With soft brush, paint mushroom caps on both sides with oil mixture, stirring liquid often to keep emulsified. Cover a baking sheet with foil and set in oven. Preheat oven to 450°F.

3. Place mushrooms on the hot baking sheet, gill side down. Bake until crisped on top, 3 to 4 minutes. Turn gently with tongs. Continue roasting until browned and crisped, about 3 to 5 minutes.

4. Set caps on heated dish. Sprinkle with parsley.

Serves 4 as an appetizer or side dish

Black Oyster Mushrooms, Cream-Glazed

Dark, sleek small black oyster mushrooms are more intense in color, flavor, and texture than other oyster mushrooms I've tasted—and much more difficult to come by. Their sweet shellfish aroma is intriguing when just cooked, but fishy if reheated. Serve this rich ragoût as a first course, with no more than herbs and toast points.

**½ pound black oyster mushrooms
1½ tablespoons butter
2 tablespoons minced shallots
¼ teaspoon kosher salt
½ cup mushroom or vegetable broth
¼ cup heavy cream
Lemon juice
Pepper
Optional: minced parsley, chives, and
  chervil or tarragon**

1. Trim base from mushrooms. Separate caps or pull apart into small clumps, as size dictates. If large, halve lengthwise.

2. Melt butter in medium-large skillet; stir in shallots and cook a minute or two over moderate heat to soften slightly. Add mushrooms and salt, tossing. Add broth and toss over moderate heat until liquid evaporates and mushrooms are tender throughout, about 2 minutes.

3. Add cream, raise heat, and stir until cream thickens to coat mushrooms—about 5 minutes. Season with

lemon juice, salt, and pepper. Sprinkle with optional herbs. Serve at once.

Serves 2 as a first course

Braised King Oyster Mushrooms, for Garnish

Handsome and curvaceous, juicy king oyster caps suggest pheasant breast (a fine feathered accompaniment indeed) while the stems resemble firm scallops (another possible complement). I find the mushrooms too solid and fleshy to serve "straight" and prefer to combine them with brightening and lightening vegetables, such as fiddlehead ferns, baby corn, tiny carrots, or sugar snap peas.

½ **pound king oyster (Trumpet Royale)**
    mushrooms
1 **tablespoon butter**
2 **tablespoons minced shallot**
1 **cup mushroom or vegetable broth**
About 1 tablespoon lemon juice
¼ **teaspoon kosher salt (omit if broth is salted)**
Pepper
Optional: minced parsley and/or chervil,
    tarragon, or chives

1. Cut apart mushroom caps from stems. Trim stems only slightly, then cut into thick diagonal slices, or halve lengthwise. If caps are too large to make manageable mouthfuls, halve them.

2. Melt butter in a medium-large skillet; stir in shallots and cook over moderate heat until slightly softened. Add mushrooms and toss.

3. Add broth, lemon juice, salt, and pepper. Simmer over moderately low heat until mushrooms are tender throughout, about 10 minutes. If a less moist dish is preferred, raise heat to evaporate juice, which will quickly become thick and slick.

4. Season with lemon juice, salt, and pepper. Sprinkle with optional herbs. Serve at once, preferably mixed with other cooked vegetables.

Serves 2 as a side dish,
4 when accompanied by other vegetables

Pros Propose

Chef Odessa Piper enjoys layered flavors and words—like **Three-Oyster Chowder,** a play on oyster mushrooms, oyster plant (salsify), and oysters. To prepare: Peel and chop salsify, placing in saucepan with a mixture of half milk and half water blended with a spoonful each of flour and lemon juice. Simmer until tender; drain. Meanwhile, gently cook shallots in butter; add mushroom caps and toss until golden. Add shucked oysters and salsify and season. Deglaze pan with white wine, then add mushroom stock to barely cover. Heat through, then add heavy cream and tarragon.

"Oyster mushrooms need an 'aroma boost,'" says chef Anne Gingrass, who achieves it this way: Sauté shallots and common oyster mushrooms in butter and oil with broken cinnamon sticks in the pan. When browned, season; then stir in parsley, lemon juice, and lemon zest. Let flavors blend off the heat. Serve at room temperature.

Chef Susanna Foo prepares a sauce from the stems of medium common oyster mushrooms, then adds the soft caps to complete **Sea Bass Fillets with Oyster Mushrooms:** Sauté shallots; add chopped stems of oyster mushrooms and toss. Add vegetable stock, cook down, then strain. Thicken with cornstarch and season. Add coconut milk. Briefly marinate sea bass fillets in oil, soy sauce, and vodka. Pan-sear, skin side down. Turn and sear for a moment, then remove. Gently sauté oyster caps; add to sauce. Set fillets in bowls on steamed sliced Chinese cabbage and top with mushrooms and sauce.

Chef Jacky Robert uses stems and caps separately in **Blue Oyster–White Trumpet Consommé:** Chop mushroom stems and boil with water, tarragon, parsley stems, and a hint of rosemary. Strain, then clarify with tomato, carrot, celery, and egg white. Thicken with a touch of potato starch. Sauté caps of both mushrooms in a drop of olive oil with a little garlic. Set in soup bowls. At the table, pour in consommé and top with fines herbes.

At Restaurant Nora in Washington, D.C., where organic foods reign, blue oysters are one of the few specialty mushrooms on the menu—thanks to an organic grower. For plain and simple **Clear Broth with Blue Oyster Mushrooms:** Prepare flavorful dashi, add blue oysters, and simmer until tender. Add cubes of silken tofu, chopped scallion, sake, shoyu, and mirin.

King oyster/Trumpet Royale is a favorite of chefs, including Michael Otsuka, who devised a technique to "bring out the earthiness": Tear apart whole mushrooms lengthwise "into long strips, like string cheese." Sauté in olive oil, then deglaze pan with white wine. Add vegetable broth and simmer gently until mushrooms are well cooked. Drain and blot dry. To serve, sauté until golden, then add to other vegetables.

Chef Beth Collins praises the "buttery, meaty quality" of king oysters in old fashioned veal dishes like **Veal Scallops with Mushrooms:** Slice whole mushrooms lengthwise. Lightly color garlic in oil, then add mushrooms. Deglaze pan with Pinot Grigio. Simmer to evaporate alcohol and cook mushrooms well.

Dredge veal scallops in seasoned flour. Brown in butter and oil, flip, then cook briefly in oven. Remove from pan. Add mushrooms and liquid to pan and reduce. Pour over veal.

Chef Patrick O'Connell offers a pale **Risotto of White Trumpet Mushrooms and Baby Shrimp** as a rich and elegant appetizer: Prepare stock from sautéed oyster mushroom stems, chicken stock, and herbs. Prepare traditional risotto with onions, sautéed white trumpets, rice, and broth. When almost cooked, stir in very small raw shrimp. At the same time, sauté more whole white trumpets to serve on top. Sprinkle with a confetti of Virginia country ham.

Palm Heart *(Bactris gasipaes*; also called *Guilielma gasipaes)*

Also heart of palm, palmito

The palm family comprises 2,650 species, according to D. J. Mabberley *(The Plant-Book),* and most of these bear edible "hearts," the name used for the crunchy-creamy terminal buds (growing tips) from which the new leaves will emerge. They are harvested across the tropics, from the Asian coconut palm to the American palmetto called swamp cabbage (a Florida delicacy not commercially available). While superficially similar, the hearts of these palms differ in size, sweetness, bitterness, tenderness, fibrousness, tendency to discolor, and ability to regenerate.

Fortunately, despite the vast variety, the palm heart sold fresh in the United States is represented by one species, *Bactris gasipaes,* commonly called the peach palm or pejibaye (pronounced pay-hee-bye), generally considered a native Amazonian plant. I say "fortunately" not solely for the sake of a simpler explanation but for the trees and for us. Most edible palms have one heart, which, if excised, kills the tree. ("Rather like murdering a buffalo for its tongue or an elephant for its tusks," one grower remarked.) The market for canned hearts of palm is considerable and growing, particularly in Europe and Latin America. ("At least 100 million [wild] palm trees were being destroyed annually in Brazil in the 1980s" write Nigel J. H. Smith and his coauthors in *Tropical Forests and Their Crops.*) Peach palm does not die when harvested; it sprouts readily, producing several new stems. It has another advantage over other palms, particularly in the United States, a nation that trembles at the sight of browned produce: The hearts do not discolor when sliced but obligingly retain their pallor.

Pejibaye has been cultivated since prehistoric times in South and Central America, and more and more farms have been planted there during the last few decades, mainly in Costa Rica, the present primary source of fresh palm hearts in the United States. Over the past 10 years, the tree has also been planted in Hawaii, and its heart is now distributed on the mainland, mostly to the restaurant trade.

Presently, peach palm heart is sold in two distinct forms. Harvested very young and trimmed to the

quick, small Costa Rican cylinders are dense, uniform in texture, and completely edible. The flavor and consistency of these tidy 1½-ounce ivory columns suggest green (immature) almonds or hazelnuts: lightly legu-

Costa Rican   ⅓ actual size

Hawaiian   ¼ actual size

minous and nutty, lightly sweet, lightly rich. Hawaiian hearts, harvested later and much larger (weighing about 1½ pounds per cylinder), exhibit a lively range of textures, shapes, and flavors, all generally more pronounced than those of the smaller forms. For commercial purposes, these Hawaiian hearts are divided into 3 parts: the wide base; the fully trimmed pure "meat;" and the slender upper shaft in its bamboo-like sheath. Sometimes tightly furled new leaves twist around the tip. These bone-pale, pleated, paper-thin fans make an unusual garnish.

BASIC USE: Traditional uses for palm hearts are difficult to discover. Canned hearts of palm, a very different product, are the norm in cookbooks—even those in the languages of the countries where palms grow. Beyond saying that hearts are stir-fried or used raw in salads and spring roll–type fillings in tropical Asia, and that I know they are cooked in Latin America, I do not have much to report.

Fresh hearts of palm, as far as my experiments have taken me, seem tender, mild, and delicate enough to fit into any part of a meal. Their unique texture—at once crunchy and tender, utterly smooth—makes them welcome in a surprising gamut of dishes. Raw, as a garnish, both embryonic leaves and subtly sweet creamy flesh can be cut into unusual, even fanciful forms. Or combine them in salads with seafood, fruits, and delicate light meats.

Hearts of palm can also be blanched, steamed, sautéed, stir-fried, or long-cooked. Think of them as a combination of bamboo shoot, water chestnut, Brazil nut, and artichoke heart—if you can imagine such a cross-breed. The large sheath-enclosed hearts can also be microwaved, grilled, or steamed in their natural casing, then slipped out, sliced, and sauced.

Chefs accustomed to palm hearts that discolor automatically prepare them *à blanc,* but there is no need to precook this species to maintain its pale color.

SELECTION AND STORAGE: Hearts of palm are available irregularly all year. The small cylinders are packed in plastic and regulation-cut. The plastic should be "breathable," but this is difficult to determine unless you see the holes. Although the hearts look as if they have been blanched, dipped in sulfite, or processed some other way, the growers swear that they are not—and the vegetable is perishable enough to make the claim believable. Check that there is no obvious discoloration (a hint of yellowing is normal) or sour smell. Palm heart should be bright and fresh-scented. Larger palm hearts are not yet sold in retail outlets, although they may be available by mail order.

Store small trimmed hearts no more than a few days in the coldest part of the refrigerator (preferably at 36°F). For longer storage, cook and chill as directed on page 464, To Cook Palm Hearts: The Basics. Or, to keep them for about a week, submerge in water, cover, and refrigerate, changing the water every 2 days. Expect a slight loss of flavor and "muscle tone." Large sheathed sections last much better, up to 2 weeks. For these, growers suggest a temperature of about 50°F.

PREPARATION: There is almost nothing you can do "wrong" in presenting this pristine food. Every smidgen of the meticulously cleaned small cylinders is edible. The choice of cutting technique depends on the dish and your aesthetic. Firm enough to be razored into translucent rounds on a meat slicer or slightly thicker ones on a food processor blade, the vegetable needs no more preparation. Or slide apart the rounds from the slender cylinders into their curious components—rings and crescents and half-moons—as you would shallot slices. Or slice lengthwise to nap with cream sauce; or cut semicircles. Cut into any shape that root vegetables can take; bâtonnets, dice, julienne, brunoise, etc.

The larger hearts can be sliced as above. In addition, the wide base can also be sliced into large discs (this part will not separate into rings). To remove the heart from its sheath, slit the tube lengthwise, then slip out the meat. The pale tubes also make beautiful presentation dishes, like bamboo. If you have the folded leafy upper part as well as the solid cylinders, it can be cut, twisted, and unfolded to make small fans, knots, or ribbons. Work gingerly: The material breaks easily.

Palm Heart, Kiwi, and Shrimp "Cocktail"

Circlets of pale, raw palm heart mingled with emerald kiwi half-moons and topped by shrimp crescents make a simple, elegant, unusual opener. Ripe kiwis should have a little "give." If you find only hard ones, slip them into a plastic bag with an unripe banana and let soften a day or two. Yellow cherry tomatoes (less acid than red ones) are a lovely alternative to kiwi, when in season.

1 tablespoon lime juice
¼ teaspoon kosher salt
2 tablespoons olive oil
8 cooked medium shrimp
One 4-ounce palm heart cylinder (1½ to 2 inches in diameter) or 2 smaller sections, to equal about the same weight
1 tablespoon minced dill, plus sprigs for garnish
1 tablespoon snipped chives
2 medium kiwis

1. Blend lime juice and salt. Whisk in oil to emulsify. Pour over shrimp, then drain dressing into a small bowl. Slice palm heart and add to dressing, with dill and chives; turn gently to coat.

2. Peel kiwi. Halve, then slice thin. Arrange on two plates with palm hearts, interspersing or spreading palm on top, as shape dictates. Top with the shrimp and dill sprigs.

Serves 2

To Cook Palm Hearts: The Basics

Your preference will determine how you cook palm heart. Short-cook for a slightly crunchy, nutty result. Cook longer for a more uniform, mellow, juicier vegetable. I have found this gentle vegetable fresh-tasting and delightful handled in all the following ways. For a perishable delicacy, it is remarkably unfussy when it comes to cooking methods—or no cooking at all.

Figure on 3 ounces of trimmed heart per person for a salad or side dish.

To steam: Set trimmed hearts of palm on steamer rack over boiling water. Cover and cook until tender to taste, 5 to 15 minutes, depending upon size and preference. Cool on a towel. Cover and chill.

To boil: Drop into boiling salted water (lemon is optional). Boil until flavor changes slightly to a cooked taste and texture is somewhat softer, a mere 2 to 3 minutes. Or boil until cooked through and uniform, about 10 minutes. Cool on a towel. Cover and chill.

To simmer and whiten: Combine enough water to cover palm hearts with lemon juice and salt to taste; boil. Add hearts and simmer until cooked throughout, 5 to 20 minutes to taste. Cool in liquid, then refrigerate, covered.

To serve: Once cooked as above, palm hearts can be sliced for garnish. Or coat whole hearts or slices with vinaigrette, then marinate. Or slice and add to salads. Or halve hearts lengthwise, spoon sauce over, and brown in the oven. Or cut into sticks or thick rounds and heat in a skillet with sauce.

Note: Do not microwave trimmed hearts, or they will lose their special texture and sweetness.

Sheath-Steamed Palm Heart with Lemon Butter

Steam Hawaiian palm heart "marrow" in the "bone" for spectacular simplicity. Supple, sweet, and juicy, it suggests a blend of Brazil nuts and asparagus. The natural casing, once cooked, is easily trimmed to form glossy ivory containers in which to serve the sliced rounds of palm heart. Although stems vary in size and weight, about 20 inches long and 2 pounds is typical.

1 Hawaiian palm heart in its sheath (about 2 pounds)
¼ teaspoon kosher salt
1½ to 2 tablespoons lemon juice
2½ tablespoons butter

1. With heavy knife or cleaver, cut stem into 5 equal lengths (if any of them split, bandage with plastic wrap to re-form). Set lengths on steamer rack over boiling water. Cover and steam until the heart is just easily pierced and juicy, about 10 minutes. (Or set spoke-fashion on wide plate on the carousel in a microwave oven. Cook until core is juicy, bubbling, and slightly tender—begin testing at 5 minutes.)

2. When cool enough to handle, slit each casing lengthwise and remove the heart. Cut another lengthwise slit in each tube to remove a portion and form a sled or basket. Cut each length of palm heart into ¼-inch discs and arrange overlapping in its sled.

3. Stir together salt and 1½ tablespoons lemon juice. Microwave butter in small dish to barely melt.

Whisk in juice mixture with fork. Add more juice to taste. Spoon evenly over the sliced hearts.

Serves 5

Variation

Steamed Palm Heart
with Lemon and Nut Oil

Prepare as above through step 2. Blend lemon juice and salt, then whisk in pecan, almond, pistachio, walnut, or hazelnut oil mixed with 1 tablespoon grapeseed or corn oil. Spoon over slices. Top with basil leaves cut hair-thin.

Palm Heart Sautéed in Brown Butter, for Garnish

Slices of palm heart browned in butter taste remarkably like sautéed artichoke hearts plus porcini. Resembling browned shallots or button mushroom slivers in appearance, the little rings and bits transform a simply cooked fish fillet, veal scallop, or chicken breast. (They'd be lovely with sweetbreads, but nobody cooks those these days.) Think of using the snippets as "amandine" or another buttery, nutty garnish.

6 ounces slim cylindrical palm heart(s)
3 tablespoons unsalted butter
Nutmeg
Fleur de sel or other crisp sea salt

1. Cut palm heart into rounds the thickness of coins. You should have about 1½ cups.
2. Melt butter in heavy wide skillet that will hold the slices in a single layer, more or less. When butter foams, reduce heat. Cook until it turns pale caramel.
3. Add palm heart slices. Raise heat to moderate and continue cooking, shaking now and then, until pieces (which will break up into rings and irregular morsels) are lightly browned, about 6 to 8 minutes. Add a generous grating of nutmeg and toss.
4. Scoop into sieve to drain. Set on paper towel to absorb butter. Add salt and toss. Sprinkle over meat or fish of choice and serve at once.

Serves 4 as a garnish

Pros Propose

Chef Jean Joho, who allows vegetables to speak for themselves, says that "heart of palm is most delicious with just butter and salt: Cut bâtonnets and sauté in butter like a beautiful piece of fish. Do not sear it on high heat or steam it on low heat. Just cook golden."

Palm and scallops are subtle pale partners in Joho's appetizer of **Sea Scallops on a Chiffonade of Palm Hearts:** Cut thin rounds of palm heart and slide apart as you would onion rings, separating the irregular rings and crescents and snippets for a "chiffonade." Sauté in butter to gild lightly, not sear. Add a fine mince of chives, chervil, Italian parsley, and dill. Toss a minute. Meanwhile, pan-sear whole sea scallops. Deglaze pan with white wine, a splash each of lemon and orange juice, and a little scallop broth or fish fumet. Reduce and add a touch of butter. Set scallops on palm hearts, spoon sauce around, and garnish with lobster roe.

Most Western-trained chefs prefer to blanch hearts of palm for salad, but Joho thinks this ruins the special texture. To prepare his **Peekytoe Crab Salad with Fresh Hearts of Palm:** Sliver fresh palm hearts and toss with salt, pepper, lemon juice, olive oil, and chives. Blend peekytoe crabmeat with light mayonnaise, a touch of Cognac and orange juice, and soybean sprouts. Form a flat crab cake on each plate, surround with cucumbers, and mound palm hearts on top.

Other chefs cook the hearts—from a few minutes to about half an hour. Roberto Donna boils them in water, lemon juice, and salt for 2 or 3 minutes, then cools and chills them in the liquid until ready for use, as in his simple **Salad of Hearts of Palm with Smoked Salmon:** Slice prepared, chilled palm hearts into thin rounds. Combine with diced tomatoes, chives, lemon oil, salt, and pepper. Top with smoked salmon slices; garnish with thin peeled lemon wedges.

Chef Curtis Eargle, who prepares hearts of palm in many modes, always blanches and marinates them as soon as they arrive on the premises. For his basic **Blanched Hearts of Palm:** Blanch hearts in boiling salted water to cover for a few minutes. Drain (reserving cooking liquid for soup below) and refresh in cold water. Drain and dry. Combine with dressing of champagne vinegar, shallots, salt, pepper, and canola oil. "They'll keep as long as two weeks this way, and they'll be juicy and ready to use as a salad or garnish."

"You can make an awesome velvety soup with the

flavorful blanching liquid, broken pieces of palm—there are always some, since the vegetable shatters easily—and any trimmings," says Eargle. To prepare **Cream of Hearts of Palm Soup:** Soften mirepoix of onions, white of leek, and celery root and trimmings and bits of broken palm heart in butter. Add a little flour and cook briefly. Add the liquid drained from Blanched Hearts of Palm (above) and cook until vegetables are soft. Add milk or half-and-half to taste, salt, pepper, and nutmeg. Strain well. Reheat and serve with thin slices of blanched palm heart.

Chef Eargle also likes to prepare hearts of palm "as Belgian endive in classic style." For **Hearts of Palm au Gratin:** Halve blanched palm heart cylinders lengthwise; arrange in gratin dish. Nap with a medium velouté made with chicken stock and half-and-half. Sprinkle with grated Comté cheese. Brown under broiler and serve in traditional Flemish fashion, with a veal loin or chop.

Although "traditional" is not the province of chef Doug Rodriguez, whose "Nuevo Latino" style is anything but that, his braising of palm hearts in a court bouillon is an Old World tactic. But his appetizer salad, **Royal Palm,** departs from the script after the initial cooking. To prepare: Combine water, white wine, white wine vinegar, peppercorns, bay leaves, and thyme; bring to a boil. Add palm hearts and keep at a light simmer for 25 minutes. Cool in liquid and refrigerate. For dressing: Boil coconut milk with ginger to reduce. Strain and add vinegar, lemon oil, and thin-sliced Jalapeño. Arrange thin-sliced rounds of palm hearts on a bed of water cress and frisée. Spoon over dressing. Garnish with small pieces of dates and toasted coconut.

Parasol Mushrooms (*Lepiota* and *Macrolepiota* species)

Also coulemelle

These meaty, flavorful species are much admired in Europe and well distributed in North America, but few commercial foragers pay them heed. Amateurs seem to seek them out, however—with gusto. Of the American *Lepiota* species (*procera, americana,* and *rachodes*), David W. Fischer and Alan E. Bessette write in *Edible Wild Mushrooms of North America,* "These three *Lepiota* are delicious edibles. The Parasol Mushroom and its shaggy brother are especially prized by those who know them. Strong flavored, large, . . . they're a welcome find for mycophagists."

The parasols that do land in restaurants and specialty shops are usually imported from France (as are those pictured) as coulemelles—just one of many regional names, which also include nez de chat (cat's nose) and tambour (drumstick), for the form some species take before the cap opens. That unopened button is the phase most esteemed by connoisseurs. As the mushrooms mature, the caps flatten out, some to as much as 10 inches. When this happens, the veil breaks, exposing the brittle gills and leaving a thick movable (and edible) ring on the upper stalk—and a very perishable mushroom that can collapse overnight.

Marshmallow-soft, parasols are lightweight breakable fungi that need careful handling. The thick cushiony caps are the prize, as the cocoa stems are too fibrous to eat. As the caps cook, they become very juicy, soft, and earthy, darkening in color and savor.

BASIC USE: The curved caps make fine containers for stuffing, baked briefly in a hot oven. Or simmer sliced or wedge-cut caps briefly with a little liquid, spread them in ramekins, top with buttered crumbs, and bake until golden. Coat small whole caps with crumbs and deep-fry for a succulent amuse-bouche. Paint opened-up caps with seasoned oil; grill over high heat (do not turn or they will break). As with shiitake, the stems are tough and should be reserved for stock.

SELECTION AND STORAGE: Look for these fall mushrooms with their caps still closed or just beginning to unroll. Do not expect to keep them for more than a few days. Once the caps open to parasols, the

¹⁄₃ **actual size**

brittle gills break and spoil quickly. For long storage, slice caps and thread on strings to air-dry; or spread on baking sheets in a pilot-lit oven and leave until crisp.

PREPARATION: Parasol mushrooms are usually dry, clean, and bug-free. Remove any leaf bits, brush caps clean, then twist out stems. Remove and save rings to cook. Sniff stems to be sure they're very fresh if you want to save them for stock; otherwise, discard.

Parasol Mushrooms Baked Under Crunchy Crumbs

Soft, flavorful parasol mushrooms are pan-cooked to release their dark juices, then baked gently in the liquid, covered by a protective layer of buttery crumbs that turns crisp and golden. Divide among four small ramekins to serve as an appetizer, or bake in a single gratin as a side dish to accompany beef, lamb, or game. This method of cooking works well with other soft mushrooms, such as morels or bear's head.

¾ pound parasol mushrooms
1 medium white roll or 2 slices French bread
    (about 2 ounces)
3 tablespoons butter
1 small onion, minced
1 garlic clove, minced
¼ teaspoon dried thyme, crumbled
¼ teaspoon dried tarragon, crumbled
¼ teaspoon kosher salt
Pepper
¼ cup water
1 tablespoon lemon juice

1. Preheat oven to 375°F. Twist stems from mushrooms and discard (keep the rings). Brush caps as clean as possible, rinsing if necessary. Cut small round (unopened) caps into ½-inch slices. Cut opened-up caps into wedges.

2. Break roll into chunks and whirl in blender or food processor to form fine crumbs—about 1 lightly packed cup.

3. Melt butter in large skillet and spoon about half over the crumbs, tossing to coat evenly. Return skillet to moderate heat, add onion and garlic, and toss to soften slightly. Add mushrooms and toss to coat. Add thyme, tarragon, salt, pepper, water, and lemon juice. Bring to a boil. Reduce heat to fairly low. Cook, tightly covered, until juices collect and mushrooms are cooked through, about 5 minutes.

4. Scoop into a shallow baking dish about 9 inches in diameter and spread evenly, flattening. Distribute crumbs to cover the top. Bake until mushrooms are very tender and crumbs are browned, about 30 minutes. Serve hot.

Serves 4

Pros Propose

Parasol mushrooms are a favorite in foie gras territory, where chef Jean-Louis Palladin began his career. For his **Roasted Coulemelles:** Toss parasol caps gently with a little melted foie gras fat, thyme, and whole garlic cloves. Spread in foil-covered pan and roast until juicy and tender. Pour accumulated juices and some garlic into a blender; puree. Pour over mushrooms and serve at once.

American chefs Jimmy Schmidt and Daniel Bruce almost always have foraged mushrooms on their menus. Both like parasol mushrooms with a touch of sweetness. Jimmy Schmidt sets aside the bigger, opened-out mushrooms for **Grilled Parasol Mushrooms and Baby Greens with Red Wine Essence:** Toss caps gently with olive oil, garlic, salt, and pepper. Place on hot grill and cook quickly, without turning (they break easily). Scoop up with spatula and set on salad of small mizuna and mustard leaves. Drizzle over a touch of rosemary-chive oil and red wine essence. (For essence: Combine 1 bottle red wine with ¼ cup honey and boil down to a syrup.)

Daniel Bruce serves **Parasol Mushrooms Stuffed with Spinach and Butternut:** Sauté shallots and spinach in butter, then chop. Sauté Butternut squash dice over high heat until cooked. Add to spinach, season, and add thyme and parsley. Butter and season parasol mushroom caps about 4 inches in diameter. Fill with the vegetables. Place in buttered pan and roast at fairly high heat (preferably in a convection oven) until tender and browned.

Spinach also figures in an old-fashioned creamy brunch dish, **English Muffins with a Florentine Parasol Topping,** a recipe that makes good use of broken or uneven caps—because the mushrooms are diced. To prepare: Sauté diced caps in butter with a little garlic and thyme. Add cooked spinach that has been squeezed dry and chopped; simmer briefly. Add crème fraîche or heavy cream. Season with salt, pepper, and nutmeg. Spread on toasted, buttered English muffins and top with a little more crème fraîche and thyme (from *The Ultimate Mushroom Cookbook* by Peter Jordan and Steven Wheeler).

Battering and frying is a good way to protect fragile foods, but flavor is often limited to the coating. In the case of parasol mushroom, its personality is strong enough to come through the crumbs. For **Breaded Parasol Mushroom Caps:** Blend bread crumbs, flour, salt, pepper, paprika, and minced fresh thyme and parsley in a shallow bowl. In another bowl, blend eggs, a touch of milk, hot pepper sauce, and salt. Heat an inch of oil in skillet. Cut large parasol caps into quarters; keep smaller ones whole. Dip in egg wash, then crumb mixture, coating completely. Fry about 2 minutes per side, until golden. Drain on paper towels (a recipe from Bob Hosh in *Edible Wild Mushrooms of North America* by David W. Fischer and Alan E. Bessette).

Parsley Root, Root Parsley

(Petroselinum crispum, Radicosum Group)

Also Hamburg parsley, turnip-rooted parsley, parsnip-rooted parsley, and others (below)

length (of roots): 6-9 inches

Poor parsley root—snubbed for its pale, unassuming appearance. Its brisk, assertive personality is admired in places where seasons and simmering soups still reign but is not easily discerned by the American shopper, who sees parsley root as a pale carrot.

Parsley root, a native of Europe, has long scented the cooking of Germany, the Netherlands, Poland, Hungary, and Russia—to name just a few countries. It has also been deemed *the* significant indicator of real Jewish chicken soup—at least in the opinion of some strong-minded types. Bert Greene, a beloved food writer, once chided me for neglecting to include "petoushka" among the names for root parsley: "Any-

one who grew up in New York [he did; I did] should know that's its real name and its real purpose in life is chicken soup," he harumphed.

Russian dictionary in hand, I explained that "petrushka," not "petoushka" is the romanized form of the word for parsley (and for Stravinsky's ballet score of the same name and the puppet character, also known as Punch, for which it is named). Greene advised me to tote some of whatever I wanted to call it around Manhattan's Lower East Side and to ask some babushkas who knew better than I what I had in hand. I did, and the unanimous answer from my statistically small sample was: "Petoushka." I cannot find the word written, however. Yiddish dictionaries give "petrishke" and variations. Somehow a special variant seems to have developed in New York City.

Other names for the vegetable include heimischer, Dutch parsley, and Holland parsley—all for fairly explicable reasons. For "heimischer," German dictionaries supply "native" or "home" or "homely." According to Sturtevant's *Notes on Edible Plants* (1919), "Dutch parsley" was used in Germany in 1542 or earlier and known (from its name) to be of "Holland origin." By 1778, Sturtevant says, it was called Hamburg parsley (and at least we know that it did grow there). In the *Gardener's and Botanist's Dictionary* (1771), Philip Miller wrote, "This is now pretty commonly sold in the London markets. . . . This sort was many years cultivated in Holland before the English gardeners could be prevailed upon to sow it. I brought the seeds of it from thence in 1727; but they refused to accept it, so that I cultivated it several years before it was known in the markets."

Sturtevant noted that root parsley grew in American gardens in 1806—and to judge from today's seed catalogues, it still does. It appears with surprising regularity, almost always as Hamburg parsley—a name we don't see in the market.

Parsley root belongs to the vast, fragrant family of Umbelliferae (also Apiciae), many members of which are known for their aromatic uppers, not lowers. (Its feathery leaves are eaten, too, but vary unpredictably from pale parsley flavor to cress-like sharpness.) It is the size of a small to medium carrot, never as large as parsnip (page 473), with which it is forever being confused because of its color and shape. It tastes altogether different. If in doubt, sample: Parsnip is sweet; parsley root is not—its flavor contains elements of celeriac, parsley, and carrot but is more aggressive and aromatic.

BASIC USE: As an aromatic, parsley root adds depth and aroma to braises, stews, purees, and soups, transmitting its fragrance best through liquids. Even a few sliced roots will add an earthy dimension and herbal punch to the plainest dish. Most people prefer its pervasive taste in combination—especially with other roots or tubers.

In purees, root parsley contributes body and complexity. As a reminder to those who have forgotten: Parsley root adds hints of celery, parsnip, celeriac, and parsley to mashed potatoes. Combine scrubbed and sliced root parsley with about twice as much peeled,

chunked potatoes, water to cover, and salt. Cook until tender and drain well. Add butter and hot milk or cream, crushing with potato masher to the desired consistency.

Parsley root can also be cooked by itself: thin-sliced or diced and sautéed, or blanched and creamed or buttered. Or slice long ribbons and deep-fry for garnish.

SELECTION: Although considered a winter vegetable, root parsley is erratically available year-round. Unless you live in a neighborhood with Eastern European connections, you may have to request it—but it is available and is in the distribution network.

Choose uniformly solid, creamy-beige parsley roots that are close in size and sprout luxuriant greens. To minimize labor, choose larger roots for purees or braises, or to cut into dice. For sautés, where you want small slices, choose slim roots.

STORAGE: Wrapped loosely in paper toweling, then enclosed in a plastic bag, parsley root should remain in good shape for several weeks. If you will be keeping it more than a few days, cut apart the roots and greens and wrap separately. Even if the roots darken and become somewhat flabby, they make a fine seasoning for soups and stews.

PREPARATION: Scrub parsley root under running water. Although the peel is tasty, some people prefer vegetables minus their jackets; taste and decide for yourself. Remove the leaves, wash them thoroughly, and dry and enclose in a plastic bag to use as you would leaf parsley (which these are). Keep roots whole, or slice or dice, as you would carrots, according to the particulars of the recipe.

Scented Rice with Parsley Root and Orange "Gremolata"

Prettily flecked with parsley greens and orange zest, and studded with parsley root dice, this highly aromatic pilaf can star in a vegetable meal or play a supporting role with grilled fish or poultry. A variation on Italian gremolata, a parsley-lemon-garlic seasoning best known for its part in osso buco, adds a final flavoring burst of fennel and caraway (both parsley relatives). Because parsley root may have either luxurious or sparse leaves, gauge the quantity you need by aiming at about 3 cups diced roots.

1 to 1½ pounds parsley roots
1 orange, well scrubbed
About 2 cups water or light vegetable broth
1½ tablespoons full-flavored olive oil
1¼ teaspoons kosher salt
1¼ cups aromatic long-grain white rice
1 small garlic clove, minced
¼ teaspoon fennel seeds
¼ teaspoon caraway seeds
¼ teaspoon coarse-cracked pepper

1. Trim leaves from parsley roots and reserve; discard stems. Rinse and chop enough leaves to equal about ⅔ loosely packed cup. Peel roots or not, to taste. Cut into rough ½-inch dice, to equal about 2½ cups.

2. Remove orange zest with coarse grater. Halve and juice orange. Add water or broth to equal 2¼ cups.

3. Heat oil in heavy saucepan. Add parsley root and salt. Cook over moderate heat, stirring often, until nicely browned, about 15 minutes; adjust heat as necessary to prevent scorching. Stir in rice and toss to coat with oil.

4. Add juice mixture and bring to a boil, stirring. Reduce heat to lowest point. Cover and cook 20 minutes. Remove from heat and let stand covered, for 15 minutes.

5. Meanwhile, combine orange zest, garlic, fennel, caraway, pepper, and chopped parsley leaves on chopping board. Mince fine, blending and tossing. Fold into the rice after it has rested. Serve hot.

Serves 6 as a side dish

Variation

Scented Rice with Parsnip and Orange "Gremolata"

For a sweeter but equally delicious dish, substitute parsnip for the parsley root and chopped flat-leaf parsley for the leafy parsley root tops.

Parsley Root–Bean Puree with Bacon and Shallots

Barbara Spiegel used dried cannellini beans when she came up with this creamy, smoky, herbal puree, but many plump, pale varieties will work. Long-soak, quick-soak, or pressure cook (my choice for consistency and speed) beans; or used canned ones *if* they are firm yet creamy, uniform in texture and unsalted, and taste like whichever bean they really are—not generic. Eden is the only brand I have found thus far that fits this description.

Spiegel noted that "these parsley leaves, once separated from the roots, kept almost forever—three weeks, that is—and had a peppery, cress-like edge." Parsley root tops do vary: Some are more aromatic and nippy than others. She suggests serving the puree with duck breast, grilled lamb, or calf's liver—in that order.

About 1½ pounds parsley root
1 large shallot
2 slices bacon
2 cups cooked cannellini beans, with their cooking liquid
1 to 2 teaspoons kosher salt
1 to 2 teaspoons champagne vinegar or other delicate white vinegar
2 tablespoons fine-chopped parsley root leaves

1. Rinse parsley roots. Peel or not, to taste. Cut into ¼-inch slices (to make roughly 4 cups). Peel and mince shallot.

2. In fairly large heavy skillet, cook bacon over moderate heat until very crisp. Transfer to paper towel.

3. Add shallot to fat in pan and cook until golden and softened, about 5 minutes, stirring often. Add parsley root, 1 teaspoon salt, bean liquid, and water (if needed) to just barely cover. Simmer gently, covered, until parsley is tender, 10 to 15 minutes. (Mixture should be no more than a little soupy.)

4. Puree mixture through medium disc of food mill (don't be tempted by the processor, which produces a pasty texture). Stir in vinegar, tasting and adjusting. Taste for salt.

5. Scoop puree into heated serving dish. Crumble bacon fine and sprinkle over. (Can be rewarmed in oven or microwave.) Sprinkle with parsley leaves.

Serves 4 as a side dish

Pros Propose

Chef Antoine Cedicci has a fondness for parsley root, which appears often on his menu in unusual guises—such as the three dishes that follow. For **Polpettine of Parsley Root:** Boil peeled parsley roots with a little potato until tender. Drain and chop. Combine with heavy cream, butter, garlic, Parmesan, and fines herbes. Run twice through a food mill, then a fine sieve. Form into balls and freeze hard. To serve: Deep-fry until golden and serve hot.

Like celeriac, parsley root seems to enhance black truffles' perfume. Although the vegetable is typically used in soup, Cedicci's elegant treatment is hardly typical. For **Pureed Parsley Root Soup with Truffles:** Soften chopped onion in olive oil. Add peeled and chopped parsley root, potato, leek, and celery; cook until soft. Add vegetable stock and cook until vegetables are tender. Puree, then strain. Reheat and season. Serve garnished with sunflower sprouts and black truffle slices—either summer or winter truffle, as the season dictates.

Grated parsley roots and leaves form a protective and flavorful coating for fish. To prepare chef Cedicci's **Parsley Root–Crusted Sea Bass with Lavender Sauce:** Prepare sauce by sautéing shallots and lots of chopped lavender in olive oil. Deglaze pan with white wine. Add fish stock, lemon juice, and tomato paste; boil to reduce to desired intensity. Season, strain, and whisk in butter. Season sea bass fillets. Grate parsley root and combine with minced parsley leaves, a little flour, salt, and pepper; coat fillets with this. Brown on both sides in olive oil. Add a touch of white wine and set in high oven for 5 minutes. Serve with sauce.

Chef Jean Joho prepares parsley root both in soup and with fish, using two distinct approaches. For **Fillet of Black Bass with Parsley Root:** Cut very fine lengthwise slices of parsley root. Gently cook shallots with fine bacon dice, then add parsley root, fresh thyme, salt, and pepper. Cover and cook until parsley is just tender. Serve with sautéed black bass with a garnish of marrow, beurre rouge, and fleur de sel.

Chef Joho's **Parsley Root Soup** is smoothed and garnished with white beans: Gently cook mirepoix (with extra onions) and parsley root. Add soaked white beans and vegetable stock and cook until tender. Save some beans for garnish. Puree remaining mixture until smooth. Garnish with fried parsley leaves, the beans, and julienne of smoked quail.

Chef Diane Forley cooks parsley root two ways, then combines them for a high-class **Parsley Root Hash:** Cut parsley root into cubes ("to cook evenly") and boil until tender. Drain. Puree with butter and cream. Brown small parsley root dice, cooking until tender. Mix with prepared puree, small croutons, and toasted, chopped hazelnuts.

Parsnip (*Pastinaca sativa*)

Herewith another valuable vegetable that is perennially ignored—the more so in our time, when a snappy moniker and flashy looks may get higher scores than usefulness and fine flavor. The name sounds goofy, but no sillier than pumpkin or zucchini, which are both taken seriously. (Parsnip's first syllable comes from Old French *pasnaie,* meaning parsnip; "nip" derives from "neep"—turnip.)

Seeking a more dignified appellation, I explored the etymology of "parsnip." My first discovery was its probable derivation from Latin *pastinaca,* "a two-pronged dibble" (a tool that makes holes in the soil), but dibble does nothing at all to enhance dignity. From the Latin *pastinaca* comes the Russian word for parsnip, *pasternak,* a more serious name. But it seems unlikely that we would adopt the name of a celebrated Russian author to help out a root vegetable.

Then there is parsnip's appearance: fairly frumpy and pallid.

But once we get past these superficial matters, there is parsnip's flavor: complicated, intense, sophisticated— a flavor to be proud of! A relative of carrot, celeriac, and parsley root, parsnip has the sweetness of the first and herbal complexity of the others as well as its own special pungency.

Parsnip has been cultivated in Europe since ancient times but has become less important over the centuries. Alan Davidson suggests historical reasons: "In medieval Europe there was a dearth of sweeteners; sugar was a rare, imported luxury, and honey expensive. Morever the potato, prolific source of starch, had not yet arrived from America. So the sweet, starchy parsnip was doubly useful and became a staple food. . . . As sugar became more readily available and with the gradual introduction of the potato, the standing of the parsnip in Europe waned" (from *The Oxford Companion to Food*).

Parsnip arrived in the New World with the colonists and has cycled in and out of fashion ever since. A possible reason for its lack of popularity in recent decades may be the limited variety and the rich ingredients of American recipes of the 19th and early 20th centuries: For the most part, parsnip was creamed, buttered, fried, and pureed in cream soup. Luscious as they may be,

length: 10-18 inches

these calorie-laden treatments do not bring out the aromatic complexity and sweetness of the root, which are well worth emphasizing.

If we look to a more distant past—to Roman times, when parsnip was common in the kitchen garden—we do find those characteristics heightened. *The Roman Cookery of Apicius* (as edited and translated by John Edwards) includes: parsnips simmered in white wine and olive oil, punctuated with fresh coriander and pepper; parsnips enhanced with cumin and chives; parsnips in a thickened sauce of celery seed, honey, rue, raisin wine, stock, and oil; and vegetable sausage made from boiled parsnips pounded with cooked spelt (an early form of wheat), eggs, nuts, pepper, and stock, then roasted in casing and served up with wine sauce.

Contemporary chefs appear to be heading in this more intense, less creamy direction, as evidenced by the suggestions in Pros Propose (page 476). In fact, modern chefs seem to represent a new rooting section for the unassuming vegetable. Chef Odessa Piper is just one enthusiast: "I'm so crazy about parsnips I use them straight through spring. Here in the chilly Midwest they are appealing just about year-round." Many chefs follow suit, but mostly in secret. Customers like parsnips (and rutabaga) best when they don't see them on the menu. "Serve them as a nameless side dish and customers ask for more," says chef Susan McCreight Lindeborg. "It's a mystery to me."

BASIC USE: Extremely fresh, juicy parsnip is an interesting raw ingredient: Cut fine julienne and combine with other vegetable strips in light lemon dressing.

But it is as a cooked vegetable that parsnip develops maximum flavor and sweetness. For cooked salad, cut parsnip into small strips, blanch momentarily in boiling salted water until no longer raw-tasting; then drain, dry, dress with tart mustard sauce, and combine with other vegetables or chicken, pork, or ham. For soup or as a creamy side dish, cook and mash parsnips with starchy vegetables, such as potatoes, beans, or hard squash.

For gratins, combine parsnip with other thin-sliced root vegetables (turnip, potato, sunchoke) in a wide buttered dish, seasoning each layer; top with broth and bake until tender. For a side-dish vegetable, cook chunks or whole small parsnips in a little butter and fruit juice over low heat, turning often; when tender, raise heat and cook to evaporate juice and caramelize parsnips. Or toss parsnip chunks and other winter roots in seasoned oil; sprinkle with water, then roast, taking care not to scorch. For chewy savory baked goods with a deep flavor and crisp finish, add finely grated parsnip to batter for pancakes, waffles, or muffins.

Offset the sweetness of parsnips with bitter, sour, salty, or smoky tastes (one or several), such as dark leafy greens, capers, citrus juice and zest, anchovies, smoked turkey or fish, or ham. For all parsnip dishes, cut down on or eliminate additional sweetening, as parsnip is seriously sugary.

SELECTION: Parsnip is around most of the year, but quality and volume peak from fall into spring, waning in hot weather. If you have access to farmers' markets or high-quality vegetable shops, you can choose individual roots of equal size; but in other stores they are often inconveniently bagged in an assortment of sizes.

Before you check for quality, be sure that what you have really is parsnip! It is often displayed (and con-

fused) with parsley root (page 469), which is usually identifiable by its long feathery greens. Parsnip is sold bald. This has always puzzled me, since its relatives appear with foliage that is helpful in determining freshness. William Woys Weaver explains that "the leaves of parsnips exude a juice that causes severe skin rashes on many people, one reason why parsnip greens are not sold on the roots displayed in markets" (*Heirloom Vegetable Gardening*). If you're still not sure what you have, nick off a taste: parsley root is pungent; parsnip is decidedly sweet.

Seek sturdy, firm parsnips free of pitting. Although a uniform cream-beige skin indicates the freshest parsnips, some browning is normal. Buy fairly large, squat roots to minimize peeling and maximize meat. Tops should have no hint of a sprouting seed stalk, which signals woodiness within.

Small parsnips are not more tender than large ones. Toughness and pithiness are linked to prolonged storage and the variety cultivated—not to size. The only way to check tenderness and sweetness is to nibble a parsnip raw.

Parsnips flourish in chilly climes, and roots that have spent several months out in the cold are most flavorful, according to growers. You might keep this in mind if there is a farmers' market nearby.

STORAGE: Do not wash parsnips before storing (they are scrubbed before coming to market). Wrap in paper towel, then plastic, and refrigerate in the vegetable crisper—or whichever spot is coldest and most humid. Kept cold and wrapped, they'll last for months.

PREPARATION: Peel parsnips, except in a few cases: If you will be steaming them, the skin slips off easily after cooking. Or, for parsnips that are to be pureed, peeling is unnecessary if they are fairly thin-skinned, fresh-looking, and, preferably, organically grown. For other cooking methods, trim and peel like carrots. Slice off the narrow end in one piece; then halve or quarter the thick end lengthwise to make pieces of about the same size.

To Cook Parsnips: The Basics

Parsnips take well to a variety of cooking methods, which yield very different results. Steaming and roasting are my favorites. Steamed parsnips are plump, uniformly smooth, fully sweet, and flavorful. Roasted, the interior turns creamy as the exterior caramelizes. Whichever method you choose, avoid overcooking; parsnips quickly turn mushy. Gauge about 1 pound for 2 servings.

Steam unpeeled parsnips on a rack over boiling water, covered, until just tender—8 to 10 minutes for medium ones. Let stand a minute or so before slipping off the skins. Cut into pieces of equal size. Heat in a little browned butter or nut oil.

Roast oil-slicked, seasoned parsnip pieces of equal size with a little water in a 400°F oven until tender. Timing can vary from about ½ hour to 1 hour. Turn often, letting water evaporate as parsnips become tender, adding more if they brown before they cook through. If necessary, raise heat to caramelize.

Simmer chunked parsnips in salt water. They will cook quickly and taste almost as good as steamed parsnips, though not quite. This method is best for purees.

Sauté peeled, thin-sliced parsnips for rich flavor and a firm, chewy texture: Cook in a heavy skillet in butter with a touch of oil, tossing until lightly colored and cooked through, 5 to 10 minutes. If they seem dry, cover the pan and allow to steam briefly, then continue to sauté.

Add peeled parsnip chunks to meat or vegetable soups or stews during the last 15 to 20 minutes of cooking.

Do not microwave—unless you want flabby, stringy, spongy, unevenly cooked parsnips.

Creamy, Spicy Parsnip-Carrot Soup

Parsnip and carrot, aromatic relatives in the vast family of Apiaceae (or Umbelliferae) have an affinity for sweet spices, which round out the roots' flavors but do not overpower them. If you prefer a punchier blend than the mild one following, substitute 1 tablespoon hot (Madras-style) curry powder for the selection of spices suggested.

The satiny consistency of the rich ocher soup comes courtesy of oatmeal, a gentle thickener. For warm evenings, serve the puree chilled, thinned with buttermilk, and accented with lime juice and chervil or dill—herbs in the same family as parsnip.

1 large leek
1 pound parsnips
¾ pound carrots
1 tablespoon walnut or hazelnut oil
½ tablespoon kosher salt
1 teaspoon ground coriander
½ teaspoon turmeric
½ teaspoon ground cumin
¼ teaspoon ground cardamom
¼ teaspoon ground hot pepper, or to taste
¼ teaspoon anise seeds
⅓ cup rolled oats (old-fashioned oatmeal)
1½ quarts water
Optional: a few tablespoons of sherry
3 tablespoons sour half-and-half or sour cream
6 tablespoons minced cilantro (coriander) leaves

1. Trim dark heavy leaf tops and root from leek. Halve stalk lengthwise, slice across, then rinse well in several changes of water. Scrub and slice parsnips. Peel and slice carrots.

2. Warm oil in a heavy pot over moderate heat. Stir in leek and cook until slightly softened, about 5 minutes. Add salt, coriander, turmeric, cumin, cardamom, hot pepper, and anise. Stir 1 minute. Add parsnips, carrots, oats, and water. Bring to a boil, stirring.

3. Simmer, partly covered, until vegetables are soft, about 30 minutes. Cool slightly.

4. Transfer solids to blender or food processor. Puree, gradually adding cooking liquid for a smooth consistency. Add sherry if desired. Reheat.

5. Ladle soup into bowls. Top each serving with ½ tablespoon sour cream and 1 tablespoon cilantro.

Serves 6 as a first course

Parsnip, Potato, and Squash Puree with Nutmeg

Parsnip blends seamlessly with other roots and tubers, lending its strength and sweetness to the whole. Squash contributes a peachy tone and smooth consistency (for this small quantity, choose a whole petite squash or mini-pumpkin or a slice from a larger squash). Serve as an alternative to mashed potatoes—but one that successfully reheats, unlike mashed potatoes.

2 large floury potatoes (about 10 ounces each)
About 6 ounces orange-fleshed winter squash
4 fairly large parsnips (about 6 ounces each)
4 large garlic cloves, peeled
1 teaspoon kosher salt
1 to 2 tablespoons butter or nut oil
Nutmeg

1. Peel potatoes, squash, and parsnips (if parsnip skin is very thin, do not peel). Cut all into fairly equal chunks.

2. Combine in a saucepan with garlic and salt and add water to almost cover. Simmer, partly covered, until vegetables are soft, about 20 minutes. Set aside 1 cup of the cooking liquid.

3. Pour contents of pan into colander to drain. Transfer to a mixing bowl. Using a potato masher or ricer, make a fairly smooth puree.

4. Scoop puree back into pan. Beat in a little reserved cooking liquid, smoothing and fluffing with a whisk over low heat. Add more liquid as necessary for desired consistency. When heated through, whisk in butter. Grate nutmeg over puree to serve.

Serves 4

Maple and Vinegar-Glazed Parsnips

These firm, caramelized roots, their flavor and sugar concentrated, call for a counterpoint of bitter greens, such as dandelion, kale, mustard greens, or broccoli raab. Turkey, pork, or sausages are natural partners. Or for a vegetable meal, roast mushrooms with herbs to accompany the parsnips and greens. If you lack pure maple syrup, substitute 1½ tablespoons honey mixed with 2 teaspoons water.

2 pounds medium parsnips (preferably of
   equal size)
1½ tablespoons corn or peanut oil or melted
   duck or goose fat
1 teaspoon kosher salt
½ cup water
2 tablespoons pure maple syrup
1½ tablespoons balsamic vinegar

1 tablespoon cider vinegar
Optional: lemon juice
Pepper

1. Preheat oven to 400°F. Peel parsnips. Cut off 2 to 3 inches from the wide end of each and halve or quarter this to make pieces of fairly equal size. Cut remaining parts into pieces of equal length.

2. In a roasting pan large enough to hold them in a single layer, toss parsnips with oil and salt to coat well. Set pan on burner over moderate heat, add water, and bring to a simmer.

3. Place in oven and roast until tender, turning every 10 to 15 minutes, until easily pierced with a fork. Timing varies considerably, from 30 to 60 minutes, depending upon the condition of the parsnips; add a little water if they appear to be drying out.

4. When fork-tender, drizzle parsnips with maple syrup and both vinegars; toss gently. Roast until deeply browned and glazed, turning once or twice—about 10 minutes. Taste and add lemon juice if too sweet. Serve hot, generously peppered.

Serves 4

*For an additional recipe, see Scented Rice with Parsley Root and Orange "Gremolata," page 470, in which parsnip can be substituted for parsley root.

Pros Propose

Traditional American recipes for parsnips were often high in cream, butter, eggs, and other mellowing influences, and called for soft-cooked roots. Recent recipes play up the vegetable's defined personality.

Raw parsnip adds power to a **Crunchy Root Slaw** from chef Susan McCreight Lindeborg: Peel and shred raw parsnips on mandoline. Combine with julienne of celeriac, chayote, and red onion. Dress with grapeseed oil, shallot, lemon juice, capers, and chives. Marinate briefly. Serve with smoked fish.

Chef Lindeborg's simple side dish, **Orange-Sautéed Parsnips** is just that: Cut sturdy parsnip bâtons. Blanch and cool. Sauté in butter with orange juice and blanched, chopped zest. Cook down to a light glaze. Season with lemon juice. Serve with lamb or poultry.

The roots also play a straightforward role in Deborah Madison's **Parsnips with Brown Butter and Crumbs:** Cut peeled parsnips into even lengths. Halve or quarter thick ends as needed to make pieces of equal size. Steam until al dente. Cook gently in brown butter until colored. Add lemon juice, salt, toasted bread crumbs, minced tarragon, parsley, and chives (from *The Savory Way*).

Wisconsin's winter keeps parsnips at the ready well into spring, and this pleases chef Odessa Piper, a devotee, who can then pair **Spring Parsnip Bisque with Green Pea Swirl:** Gently cook chopped onions and parsnips in butter. Add water and salt and cook until soft. Puree; add milk and dill. Prepare fresh green pea puree. Ladle first parsnip puree, then pea puree into each serving bowl. Swirl to form yin-yang pattern. (In winter, Piper serves pea-less parsnip soup adorned with deep-fried salted ribbons of burdock root.)

Decorative swirls of browned **Parsnip Crisps** "are not just visual garnish, they have flavor," says chef Rick Moonen. To prepare: Shave fairly large parsnips lengthwise into wide strips. Deep-fry at 350°F until just golden. Drape over a curved surface (such as tuile or baguette molds) to cool, or wind at once around sharpening steel to make "unicorn horns." Poke these crisps into vegetable purees for garnish.

Similar crunchy ribbons show up with **Seared Scallops and Parsnip Puree** from chef Robert Bagli: Cook peeled, whole parsnips and a few potatoes and turnips in chicken broth until tender. Puree and press through sieve. Dry out in low oven. To serve, fold in whipped cream, parsley, chives, and tarragon. Serve puree with seared scallops and chicken *jus* accented with sherry vinegar. Poke deep-fried long parsnip strips into the puree.

Parsnip is both flavoring and thickener for chef Bagli's rustic but refined **Parsnip-Oxtail Soup with Vegetable Brunoise:** Combine trimmed oxtail and whole parsnips in a perforated pot insert. Fit into larger pot that holds calf's feet, beef shank, chicken, tomatoes, carrots, and onions. Add water and cook until oxtail and parsnip are tender; lift out insert. Continue cooking stock until flavorful. Strain and reduce broth. Bone oxtails and dice meat. Mash parsnips. Add both to broth, with brunoise of blanched winter vegetables.

The fanciest of tubers, the black truffle, has an affinity for the humble Umbelliferae—celeriac, parsley root, and parsnip. With the last, chef Philippe Chin prepares a light **Parsnip and Truffle Ravioli:** Simmer parsnip chunks in salted milk until tender. Puree, then dry over heat, stirring. Add truffle puree. Fill wonton skins with mixture. Steam. Serve in light vegetable broth with truffle slices.

Peas, Sugar or Edible-Podded

(*Pisum sativum,* Macrocarpon Group)

Including **snow pea, sugar snap, pea shoots,** and **pea sprouts**

"Sugar pea," as sweet as a pet name, is a horticulturally correct term for edible-podded peas. It includes those called mangetout (eat-all) in Britain and in France—where they are also known as *pois gourmand* and *pois sans parchemin* (peas without parchment, a reference to their unlined pods). In the United States, edible-podded or sugar peas are represented in the market by what we know as snow peas and sugar snaps. These eat-all types are a botanical subspecies of *Pisum sativum,* our common garden pea, an ancient Near Eastern plant that has been farmed for about as long as anything we know—"cultivated since 7000 B.C. (as long as wheat and barley)" writes D. J. Mabberley in *The Plant-Book.*

Snow pea, ribbon-flat and grass-green, is also called Chinese snow pea (and "sno-pea," a marketing term in the "lite" genre) but it has nothing to do with snow and didn't originate in China—where it is called *hoh laan dau* (or *he lan do*), meaning Holland pea. Grown as early as 1536 by the horticulturally hyperactive Dutch (who have a tradition of spectacular vegetables), the "Holland pea" has a name that indicates its primary center of cultivation and refinement, as does its introduction into France by its ambassador to Holland around 1600.

Although not native to China, "the edible podded pea, also known as the sugar or mangetout, is the main type of garden pea eaten in China and Japan," writes Joy Larkcom in *Oriental Vegetables.* It is also enormously popular in the Far Eastern dishes cooked in North America—the only place where it is called snow pea, for no known reason. "Snow pea" appeared in print for what is thought to be the first time in an article in 1954, in *The New York Times* by Anthony Lewis. He praised the pea and encouraged home gardeners to grow it, since it was not available commercially.

Growers, taxonomists, and agricultural historians have offered no plausible explanations for the name. Cecilia Chiang, founder of the Mandarin restaurants in San Francisco and Los Angeles, gives one that makes as much sense as any: "I believe the Cantonese word *shii dau,* meaning snow pea, was first used in San Francisco about four generations ago by Chinese farmers, who typically came up with their own vegetable names—for no particular reasons."

BASIC USE: Plain or fancy, hot or cold, snow peas require just the barest minimum of cooking. Overcooking destroys their character. For hot dishes, steam snow peas about 3 minutes or boil about 1½ minutes. Or stir-fry or sauté whole snow peas 2 to 3 minutes. Simmer snow peas in soup for 1 minute. Oven-steam snow peas sealed in parchment or foil for 5 to 6 minutes.

snow peas   length: 2-4 inches

Raw snow peas are edible, but not choice. Brief cooking—even when they are to be used for cold dishes—develops their sweetness, flavor, and color. For chilled snow peas, do not string them beforehand; string them after cooking. This is easier—and for some unknown reason, the pods will taste sweeter and fresher. Boil or steam a shorter time than for hot dishes, then spread on a towel to cool to room temperature before refrigerating; or drop into ice water, drain, dry, and refrigerate.

SELECTION: Snow peas are erratically available year-round in Asian markets, fancy groceries, and many supermarkets. Late spring and early summer yield by far the sweetest, most tender, and most flavorful peas. One taste is worth a thousand words. Seek small, translucent, straight-sided snow peas with no more than a hint of pea-bumps. Jane Grigson writes (in her incomparable work *Jane Grigson's Vegetable Book*), "The row of little peas down one side should undulate through the skin, rather than protrude in full-term manner. The stalk ends, with their moth-like traces of withered petals, will also give you an idea of how vigorous or stale they are." Unfortunately, I find that the ends are often snipped.

STORAGE: Snow peas lose flavor and tone when stored; purchase only for use immediately or in the very near future. In peak condition, they'll keep tolerably, refrigerated in a perforated plastic bag, for a few days.

PREPARATION: Snap the stem end and pull it to remove the seam on the thicker side of the pod (the one to which the peas attach). Test the other side of a few pods in case they need double stringing. Although string-free snow peas exist, most must be stripped of their fibrous sutures—which do not soften with cooking. Snow peas can be decoratively cut in many ways for use as a garnish. A simple method is: Cut a neat wedge from the tip and remove, leaving a fishtail pod. Or halve a pod at a sharp angle; tuck the top half into the base with its tip protruding to mirror the other— again making a fishtail shape.

Sugar snap peas, although all-edible like snow peas, are quite different in that they are curved, plump, crisp, and succulent and contain an array of full-grown sweet peas. Sugar snaps are frequently hailed as a new "invention," but their existence is documented in late 17th-century gardening journals, where they are called "sugar pease with crooked pods" or "sickle peas." In 1885, they were described and illustrated under the heading "butter peas" in the invaluable compendium of garden vegetables (which includes 170 pea varieties) by members of the Vilmorin family, proprietors of one of the oldest and largest seed houses in the world. In 1928, "butter sugar" peas were available from the New York State Agricultural Experiment Station at Geneva, New York, and similar peas were introduced later. In 1967, the Agway seed company proclaimed: "Here it is again—the edible podded variety that so many have asked for since it was discontinued 3 years ago."

But not until the 1970s did this pea really take hold, when the breeder Calvin Lamborn refined, championed, and popularized it. Although at the time he was aiming at a non-buckling form of snow pea for the frozen food market, the cross he developed won a gold medal from All-America Selections in 1979 and zoomed to the top of home gardening charts, then went into commercial production. Although the name Sugar Snap is correctly applied to his horticultural variety alone, it has come to mean any pea of the same type, whatever the cultivar.

BASIC USE: In cooking sugar snaps, quick is the trick! Overcooking destroys character. For hot dishes, steam sugar snaps about 4 minutes, or boil them for about 2. Stir-fry sliced sugar snaps 2 to 3 minutes; for whole ones, first blanch 30 seconds in boiling water, then stir-fry just long enough to heat through. Simmer

sugar snap peas   length: 1½–3 inches

sliced sugar snaps in soup for 2 to 3 minutes. Oven-steam foil- or parchment-sealed sliced sugar snaps for 6 to 7 minutes, whole ones for 9 minutes. Braise sugar snaps in spring ragoûts, adding them for the last 10 minutes of cooking.

As with snow peas, sugar snaps can be enjoyed raw, but brief cooking—even when they are meant for cold dishes—develops their charm. When they will be served chilled, string them after cooking rather than before. Again as with snow peas, this is easier—and the peas will taste sweeter and fresher. Boil or steam for a shorter time than you would for hot dishes, then cool to room temperature on a towel before refrigerating. Or refresh in ice water, drain, dry, and refrigerate.

SELECTION AND STORAGE: The best sugar snaps are fat and full, with comparatively petite pods of a uniform shamrock color. Taut texture and a perky, dry stem signal freshness. Flabbiness and dampness indicate prolonged storage, which makes the pods stringy and bitter.

Sugar snaps lose flavor and tone when stored. Refrigerate in a perforated plastic bag and cook as soon as possible.

PREPARATION: Sugar snaps usually need to have the seams on both sides of the pod removed—but some don't require this. Break the stem end, then gently pull the length of the pod to remove both "spines" at once, if possible. If one side balks, zip again, starting at the other tip.

Pea shoots (also called vines, tendrils, or leaves), are the leafy tips snipped from small sugar pea and sometimes from common garden pea plants. (In recent trials, all kinds of peas have entered the pea shoot competition, and many will probably be added to the market.) Previously available only in Chinese markets, as *dau miu,* these twining clusters are now crossing the East-West culinary line. In traditional Chinese cooking, the jade twists are swirled into soup, steamed, or stir-fried with a touch of salt, and sometimes with ginger, sugar, or rice wine. When sufficiently small, these Art Nouveau curls, which have the distinctly green-sweet flavor of peas, add delicate freshness to contemporary salads, Western-style. Joy Larkcom writes that the practice of eating pea shoots "has spread from China to Japan [where they are called tohbyo] and has been introduced to south-east Asia by people such as the Hmongs" (*Oriental Vegetables*).

There's nothing new under the sun: John Evelyn recommended "the Pod of the Sugarpease, when first

pea shoots

½ actual size

beginning to appear, with the Husk and Tendrels" in *Acetaria: A Discourse of Sallets* (1699), as primary "Furniture and Materials" in a salad.

SELECTION: Check the cut ends of shoots, which should look fresh and moist. If dry, they may be tough and taste fishy. Check as well to be sure that old and new batches have not been combined. Shoots should be small enough to require no trimming, or only a bit of snipping. They should be fully green, without any yellow. Rinse, then spin-dry completely.

PREPARATION: If the vines are not trimmed to a delicate size, cut any heavy base from each, then break them into 2- to 3-inch branchlets, following the natural form.

Pea sprouts are the very first stem-and-leaf pairs the pea seed forms. Some, grown in the warm soil of hothouses, are extremely tender, with a faint pea freshness. Water-grown (hydroponic) snow pea shoots—pale, long-stemmed, neatly aligned in a plastic container—are more widely available and less expensive, but less delicate. Both add charm and a nutritional boost, whether in salads, sandwiches, or as garnish. Like all such sprouts, they should be moist but not wet, with no yellowing or slipperiness. Refrigerate and use within a day or two. To prepare, rinse and spin-dry.

Snow Peas with Radishes and Sesame

Radishes add a tulip-red twist and nicely sharp counterpoint to sweet snow peas. With a few minutes of cooking, you'll have a festive dish to perk up steamed or broiled fish or meat. For a vegetable main dish, substitute ¾ cup toasted, chopped almonds for the sesame and spoon over scented rice tossed with mint or cilantro and scallions.

1 pound snow peas
1½ tablespoons white or black sesame seeds
1½ tablespoons peanut oil (preferably roasted)
2 tablespoons dry sherry
½ cup thin-sliced small red radishes
¼ teaspoon sugar
Pinch of ground hot pepper
¼ teaspoon kosher salt

pea sprouts   ½ actual size

1. Rinse peas. Break off stem end of each pea and slowly zip off the thicker side (where peas attach). Snap and pull the other end of a few pods to see if the batch needs double stringing, which some do.

2. In large skillet, heat sesame seeds over low heat, stirring or shaking until fragrant and lightly toasted, about 2 minutes. Scrape onto plate to cool.

3. Raise heat to high. Add oil to skillet, then snow peas, and toss until not quite cooked through, 2 to 3 minutes. Add sherry and toss another 30 seconds, until peas are just barely tender.

4. Add radishes, sugar, hot pepper, and salt and toss to just heat through. Serve immediately, sprinkled with sesame seeds.

Serves 4 to 5

Smoked Salmon and Snow Pea Barquettes

I'm not usually one for fussed-over starters, but snow peas cry out for filling and can be pleasingly plumped to present as an elegant alternative to crudités. The emerald pods are packed with a pureed green pea mixture for doubled pea power. Salmon slivers seal the filling in the little canoes and add a bright and luxurious tone. If kefir cheese is difficult to find, use sour cream or thick yogurt.

½ **pound snow peas**
About 2 slices French or Italian white bread,
    crusts removed
1 cup shelled green peas (fresh or frozen)
½ **teaspoon dried dill**
¼ **teaspoon kosher salt**
¼ **teaspoon sugar**
About 2 teaspoons drained prepared horseradish
About 4 tablespoons kefir cheese, thick yogurt,
    or sour cream
¼ **pound sliced smoked salmon**
Dill sprigs, snipped chives, or chervil leaves
    for garnish

1. Rinse snow peas. Set on rack over boiling water, cover, and steam until they just lose their rawness—less than a minute. Do not cook through. Spread on towels to dry. With small sharp knife, trim off seam to which peas attach—the thicker side of each pod. Chill ½ hour or more.

2. Whirl bread in food processor to make fine crumbs (you should have ½ cup; adjust as needed). Steam green peas until tender; drain if necessary. Add to processor with bread; let cool briefly. Add dried dill, salt, sugar, 1½ teaspoons horseradish, and 3 tablespoons kefir. Puree to a fine paste, scraping side often.

3. Press paste through a sieve to remove skins and to make a smooth, thick cream. Stir in horseradish and kefir to taste; season. Chill ½ hour or longer.

4. Run a forefinger along the inside of each snow pea to open it fully. With butter knife, insert and spread filling in each (you can even up when you finish).

5. Cut salmon into slivers the length of each opening and about ½ inch wide. With sharp knife tip, pick one up and fit over the filling, pressing on it to attach. Chill until serving time—which can be as long as overnight.

6. To serve, decorate with one or more of the herbs.

Makes 5 to 6 dozen barquettes

Lettuce-and-Mint-Braised Sugar Snap Peas

Glossy, mint-infused sugar snaps are produced by a cooking method usually reserved for shelled green peas. A wrapping of lettuce preserves their color and moisture without additional liquid and yields exceptionally full-flavored peas. Boston lettuce leaves work particularly well, but any large-leafed lettuce will do the trick. Enjoy as is, or toss with braised tiny carrots or pearl onions, or sautéed cucumber crescents.

½ **pound sugar snap peas**
About 8 large Boston lettuce leaves
¼ **teaspoon sugar**
1 tablespoon butter
1 bunch mint (the size of a small parsley bunch)
2 scallions (green onions), halved across
Salt

1. Rinse peas, then remove strings: Some may need double-stringing; some may zip free in one move. Break the stem end, then gently pull along

the length of the pod to remove both "spines" simultaneously, if possible.

2. Rinse lettuce leaves and arrange half of them, with water still clinging to the leaves, in a smallish heavy saucepan to hold ingredients snugly. Add sugar snaps, sugar, and ½ tablespoon butter. Rinse mint and scallions, tie in a bundle, and add. Press remaining lettuce over to enclose contents.

3. Turn heat to high. When contents steam, reduce heat to moderately low and cover pan. Cook, shaking several times, until sugar snaps are just tender, 4 to 7 minutes.

4. Remove lettuce covering and mint bundle; discard. Transfer sugar snaps to a warmed serving dish. Toss with salt and remaining ½ tablespoon butter.

Serves 2

Penne with Sugar Snaps, Tomatoes, and Herbs

Pasta quills and pea pods, about the same size and shape, prove to be a charming match of flavor, texture, and color. For variation, serve at room temperature on a springy cushion of pea leaves or water cress, with an additional generous sprinkling of herbs.

> 9 to 10 ounces sugar snap peas
> 10 firm-ripe cherry tomatoes
> ¼ teaspoon sugar
> ¼ teaspoon kosher salt
> 2 tablespoons fruity, flavorful olive oil
> 2 to 3 tablespoons chives cut into
>   ½-inch lengths
> ½ pound slim small penne (imported
>   Italian quill pasta)
> 3 to 4 tablespoons slivered basil leaves
> 3 to 4 tablespoons chopped parsley leaves
> 2 to 3 tablespoons toasted, chopped
>   pine nuts
> Pepper

1. Set a pasta pot of water to boil. Rinse peas, then remove strings as necessary; some may need double-stringing, some none. Some zip free in one move: Break the stem end, then gently pull along the length

of the pod to remove both "spines" at once. Halve each diagonally.

2. Quarter cherry tomatoes. Combine in a serving bowl with sugar, salt, olive oil, and 2 tablespoons chives.

3. When water boils, add a handful of salt. Place sugar snaps in sieve, then dip into boiling water until not quite cooked, about 1½ minutes. Lift out and set aside (they'll continue to cook).

4. Add penne to water and boil until al dente. Drain, add to the bowl with the tomatoes. Add the sugar snaps, and toss to coat. Add 3 tablespoons each basil and parsley; toss. Taste and add salt, pepper, and additional herbs as needed. Toss to coat well. Sprinkle with nuts, toss again, and serve.

**Serves 2 as a main course,
4 as a first course or side dish**

Basic Pea Shoots

When very tiny, pea shoots can be sweetly eaten raw. The tiniest uncooked pea-vine tips are loveliest just because they look so fetching. Once they are a little larger, they take nicely to quick cooking, which tenderizes their fibrous stems—but not entirely.

I find they are more succulent and even textured when cooked with a little water than when seared directly in a hot pan, as is usually recommended. But taste to determine worthiness: Tough tendrils will not be transformed by cooking. Gauge about 3 ounces for each side-dish serving or generous garnish.

> ¾ pound pea shoots
> Salted whipped butter

1. Trim heavy base from each shoot as necessary, then break into 2- to 3-inch branchlets, following the pea's natural form.

2. Then, choose one of the following:

(a) For purists of pea flavor, steam: Set trimmed shoots in dish on steamer rack over boiling water. Cover and cook until tender, about 2 minutes for medium vines. Toss with butter.

(b) Alternatively, barely film skillet with water. Add a little butter and tendrils, bring to a boil, then toss over moderate heat until just tender—less than a minute.

3. Serve immediately.

Serves 4 as a side dish or generous garnish

Variation

Basic Pea Sprouts

For pea sprouts, the very first leaflets (which require no trimming), use only 2 ounces per person. Steam just 1 minute. Or simply stir directly into a warm vegetable or grain dish and allow to soften.

Quick Couscous with Pea Sprouts or Shoots and Corn

Delicate leafies, protected from direct contact with the hot pan by the couscous grains, need only a few minutes to wilt and become tender. The presentation can be plain or fancified: Spoon the mixture into a ring mold or individual serving dishes, patting down lightly. Then invert onto a dish to form neat cakes. Garnish with raw pea sprouts and chervil or dill sprigs, or steamed snow peas or sugar snaps. When you use shoots, which are more fibrous than sprouts, buy an extra ounce or two so that you can trim closely.

> 3 lightly packed cups pea sprouts (3 ounces) or
>   4 lightly packed cups pea shoots (4 ounces)
> 1 medium ear corn (or ¾ cup kernels)
> 1¼ cups water
> ½ teaspoon kosher salt
> 1 tablespoon butter
> 1 cup whole wheat couscous

1. If using sprouts, trim off comparatively heavy bases and any other apparently tough parts as necessary. Cut vines or sprouts into ½- to 1-inch pieces.

2. Slice corn kernels closely from cob. Select a pot with a tight-fitting lid. Combine corn and water in it and bring to a boil. Cook until just barely tender—a minute or two. Off heat, stir in salt, butter, couscous, and pea sprouts or shoots. Cover immediately. Let stand 10 to 15 minutes, as convenient.

3. Using a wide-tined fork, fluff mixture into a serving dish, separating grains well. Serve warm.

Serves 4 as a side dish

Variation

Couscous with Pea Sprouts, Sesame, and Lemon

Bring water to a boil with salt. Off heat, stir in couscous and pea sprouts. Cover at once. Let stand 10 to 15 minutes. Fluff with wide-tined fork, adding ¼ to ½ teaspoon Asian (dark) sesame oil and a few teaspoons of lemon juice. Serve warm or at room temperature.

Salad of Pea Sprouts, Pear, Belgian Endive, and Ham Julienne

A charming salad, mild-mannered but with a pleasant sharpness beneath the light cream coating and a faint pervasive fruitiness. Refreshing, pretty, and quick to assemble.

> 4 ounces pea sprouts (4 cups)
> 1 teaspoon minced shallot
> ¼ teaspoon kosher salt
> Pinch of sugar
> 2 tablespoons lime juice
> 2 tablespoons mild light oil, such as grapeseed
> 2 tablespoons heavy cream
> 1 ripe Bartlett pear
> ¼ pound Westphalian-style or baked ham,
>   sliced thin
> 2 medium Belgian endives, trimmed and rinsed
> 2 tablespoons chives cut into 1-inch lengths

1. Rinse and gently pat dry or spin-dry pea sprouts. Refrigerate.

2. Combine shallot, salt, sugar, and lime juice. Whisk in oil, then cream. Halve and core pear, then cut into thin julienne strips about 1½ inches long. Toss with 2 tablespoons of the dressing; set aside.

3. Cut ham into very thin strips about 1½ inches long. Halve endives lengthwise, then cut crosswise into thin slices at an angle. Separate into strips. Toss sprouts, endive, ham, and chives with remaining dressing. Add pear and toss gently.

4. Distribute among plates and serve at once.

Serves 4 as a first course

Pros Propose

Elizabeth Andoh presents snow peas in a pure and clean Japanese manner in **Steam-Baked Ocean Perch with Lemon and Snow Peas:** Sprinkle fillets of ocean perch or redfish (with skin) with sake and salt. Set 2 thin lemon slices on each square of aluminum foil and place fillet on top, skin side up. Arrange more lemon on each. Cut trimmed snow peas into thin diagonal strips; scatter on top. Bring edges of foil together and crimp to seal each packet. Set in a steamer and cook 8 minutes. Serve sealed, for each diner to unwrap at the table (from *An Ocean of Flavor*).

Imaginative and subtle, **Sugar Snap Peas with Brown Butter and Sage** couldn't be simpler: Melt butter in sauté pan and add a goodly volume of fresh sage leaves. Raise heat; when butter begins to brown, toss in trimmed sugar snap peas, salt, and pepper. Sauté just until "they surrender their fresh watery crispness but are still crunchy," stirring and turning all the while (from *Chez Panisse Cooking* by Paul Bertolli with Alice Waters).

Essence of Pea Soup from chef Catherine Brandel, a puree that begins with a stock made from "discards," reinforces the special flavors, rather than textures, of the different peas: Gently cook onions in butter with thyme and bay leaf; add water, pods of green peas, oversize pea shoots, and imperfect sugar snaps. Cook to extract flavor, then strain. Add shelled peas, sliced sugar snaps, and tender chopped pea shoots to stock. Cook briefly, then puree. Strain through coarse sieve to extract fibers but not pulp ("the soup will be fairly thin and intensely wildly green"). Heat, then top with crème fraîche.

"Pea shoots . . . are called 'mustaches of the dragon' by the Chinese, who have a penchant for giving their foods lyrical names," writes Susan Costner in *Mostly Vegetables.* A moment's heat is all that's needed to get the most out of shoots, which have an affinity for toasty grains. To prepare **Mustache-of-the-Dragon Wheatberry Pilaf:** Sauté shallots and garlic in oil until soft. Add wheat grains, tossing. Add a little wine and cook to evaporate. Add vegetable broth; cook, covered, until stock is absorbed, about an hour. Add fresh tarragon leaves and coarsely chopped pea shoots, tossing just until wilted. Season and add chives.

A delicate dish of **Roasted Red Snapper with Pea Shoots and Lemon Vinaigrette** comes from chef Kerry Heffernan: Prepare dressing of egg yolk, lemon juice, and grapeseed oil that has been infused with lemon grass and lemon rind. Gently wilt pea sprouts with a touch of water, then add butter. Arrange around pan-roasted snapper. Drizzle dressing around. Garnish with blanched green onions and small potatoes.

Poached Eggs in a Nest of Pea Sprouts is charming and original—like all of *The Kitchen Garden Cookbook* by Sylvia Thompson: Melt butter and whisk in a mixture of vegetable stock, cornstarch, and lemon juice to make a fairly thick sauce. Add plenty of pea sprouts and mingle with sauce to warm through. Arrange a nest of sprouts on each plate, set a soft-poached egg in the center, and serve with toasted sourdough bread.

A pretty, easy salad of contrasting flavors and colors comes from chef Jesse Cool. To prepare **Beet Salad with Pea Sprouts:** Toss together cooked golden and Chioggia beets in a reduction of beet juice seasoned with balsamic vinegar and a nip of chilli. Fluff pea sprouts all around and dot with bits of French feta.

Perilla (Green Korean) (*Perilla frutescens*)

Also kkaennip (Korean), called "sesame leaf" or "wild sesame"

Note: Perilla also refers to a different strain of this plant that is called shiso in Japanese. Highly scented, it is used as an herb rather than a vegetable.

leaves: 3½-5 inches

What is this aromatic leaf doing in a book about plants used as vegetables rather than flavorings? Just what it is supposed to be doing: being a vegetable.

The more familiar purplish form of this member of the mint family (Lamiaceae and Labiatae) is called shiso in Japanese—but should correctly be called aka shiso (red shiso). It is well known as a sushi seasoning and for the scent and color it gives to pickled ginger slices and ume, called "Japanese plums" (which happen to be apricots). The Japanese have cultivated perilla for centuries, but it is probably native to China—although it is apparently missing from contemporary Chinese cuisine.

Kkaennip, the exquisitely serrated larger-leafed green Korean strain pictured here, tastes different and is used in different ways. Resinous, pungent, with a savor of licorice and sage, it is much harsher and less aromatic than shiso, but bracing and intriguing—in the assertive way of chrysanthemum leaves (see page 208).

Green Korean perilla is sold in two distinct forms: as individual leaves (usually folded into a small, beautiful triangular bundle), to be served as a wrapper for meat or as a garnish; and in big bunches, to be cooked or made into kimchee-type salted pickles. In stores with English signage, these are labeled "sesame leaf," as they are in cookbooks. The only explanation I can find for this weird misnomer is that the seeds of perilla are roasted and used like sesame seeds, whole and ground.

BASIC USE: For Korean meals, perilla is folded around barbecued beef (this is also done in Vietnam), combined with other leaves in salads, salted and pickled, and steamed and dressed with sesame-chilli sauce to serve as a condiment.

Perilla's potential as a salad leaf is considerable. Choose small whole leaves (or cut chiffonade of larger ones) for brilliant color, beautiful form, and pungency. But its powerful punch must be balanced carefully with milder greens and dressings that meld and mellow.

The traditional use as a wrapping need not be limited to barbecued beef. The leaves are perfect picker-uppers for cocktail fare (spicy shrimp, smoked fish) or as packets for seviche or escabeche.

Although steaming is customary, I find that steamed perilla becomes fibrous and looks blotchy, so I suggest blanching it in boiling water. Mild, brilliant green, and as elastic as thin balloons, the tissue-thin leaves can act as dumpling skins or rice paper: Just drop them into boiling water; return to a boil, scoop out, then spread flat on towels to dry. Or wrap and steam seafood packets or cooked chestnut with ham or bacon.

SELECTION: When perilla is bunched, look for comparatively slim stalks and fairly small, bright, uniformly green leaves that are closer to the size of mint leaves than squash leaves (the usual range). The large leaves folded into packets, which are relatively expensive, should be flawlessly clear (since they are used for presentation) with no trace of aging or spotting. I have found the vegetable virtually year-round, but only in Korean markets.

STORAGE: Remove tie from bunch, redistribute stalks, then wrap in damp paper towels, then a plastic bag. Refrigerate for no more than a few days. Wrap the individual leaves the same way, but use within a day or two.

PREPARATION: Remove tie from bunched leaves. Trim off stem bases, leaving 2 to 3 inches of thin upper stalk and the leafy tops. Dunk greens into plenty of water and lift out gently so debris sinks. Spin-dry if you'll be using perilla raw. The individual leaves need to be rinsed very delicately and patted dry.

Shrimp in Perilla Packets

The first mystery is what leaf wafts the exotic aroma. The second is what hides inside, like a party favor (shrimp fit the form perfectly). It would be less trouble to serve the leaves raw, as is done in Asia, but the flavor is far too fierce for most Western palates. Blanching rounds it out, while the hint of pastis (fennel- or anise-flavored aperitif) highlights the herbaceous leaves rather than adding a new note. Serve the hot morsels with a chilled rosé.

1 tablespoon Ricard, Pernod, or other pastis
1 tablespoon olive oil
¼ teaspoon minced garlic
¼ teaspoon white pepper
¼ teaspoon kosher salt
1 teaspoon lemon juice
16 small shrimp, shelled
16 fairly large green perilla leaves, stems cut off

1. In a dish, blend pastis, olive oil, garlic, pepper, salt, and lemon juice. Add shrimp and toss to coat.

2. Spread perilla leaves in skillet or wide heatproof dish. Pour over boiling water to cover by a few inches. Lift out with slotted spoon and open each leaf flat on paper towels.

3. Place a shrimp on each leaf to match the curve on one side. Distribute any remaining marinade among the packets. Fold each leaf over to cover the shrimp, like a turnover. If leaves are much larger than shrimp, first fold each leaf tip over the shrimp, then fold in half.

4. Set packets in a steamer, cover, and cook 1½ minutes. Remove from heat. Skewer each packet with a toothpick. Set on a tray and serve at once.

Makes 16 hors d'oeuvres, to serve 3 to 4

Picante Perilla "Salsa"

This garlicky, hot, and aromatic condiment can serve as seasoning or side dish, at room temperature or chilled. Toss the bracing chrysanthemum-like greens with warm short-grain brown rice, bulgur, or with cold soba noodles. Or sprinkle over roasted or grilled seafood, beef, or pork, to jazz up a simple meal.

1 hearty bunch green perilla (6 to 7 ounces)
1 large garlic clove
¼ teaspoon kosher salt
¼ teaspoon chilli flakes
½ tablespoon peanut oil
½ tablespoon Asian (dark) sesame oil
½ tablespoon shoyu (Japanese soy sauce)
1 teaspoon balsamic vinegar

1. Trim off base of perilla stems, leaving about 3 inches of upper stalk and the leafy tops. Dunk greens into plenty of water and lift out gently so debris sinks. Nip off and thin-slice enough leaves to yield 3 tablespoons; reserve.

2. Drop perilla into a large pot of boiling salted water. Return to a boil over highest heat and boil until leaves just lose their raw bite but are still intensely aromatic, about 1 minute. Drain, run under cold water and drain again. Press dry. Slice thin and put in a serving dish.

3. Crush garlic, salt, and chilli to a paste. Combine with peanut oil in tiny skillet over low heat. Stir often until garlic barely begins to color and oil is orangy—a few minutes. Off heat, stir in sesame oil, shoyu, and vinegar.

4. Mix dressing with cooked leaves and reserved raw strips, tossing well. Taste and adjust seasoning. Serve at room temperature or chilled.

Makes about ⅔ cup, to serve 2 as a main-dish complement to starches, or 4 as a condiment

Scented Salad of Perilla, Cucumber, and Sweet Ginger

When musky, sharp Korean perilla meets the bite of ginger and tartness of lime, the result is more mellow and balanced than you might guess. Cucumber provides crunch, juiciness, and a mild contrast. The full, bright flavors are a refreshing bed for grilled seafood or a complement to grain dishes.

Packets of individual "sesame leaves" offered at Korean markets are convenient for this quantity. Or buy bunched whole stalks and pick off and slice enough leaves to make 1 cup. The same stores that stock perilla will carry the tasty, small Oriental cucumbers. If they prove elusive, substitute small dull-skinned pickling

("kirby") types—and buy a little more. You'll need to peel these, quarter them lengthwise, and cut out most seeds, then cut into julienne.

1 pound slim Oriental or Middle Eastern
    cucumbers (4 to 6 cucumbers)
½ teaspoon kosher salt
1½ tablespoons sweet-pickled ginger slices
1½ tablespoons lime juice
1½ tablespoons mild vegetable oil
1 packet large Korean perilla leaves
    (about 10)

1. Cut cucumbers into narrow strips about 1½ inches long (about 2½ cups). Toss in sieve with salt. Let drain 20 to 30 minutes. Spread on towel and pat dry. Chill until serving time.

2. Stack ginger and cut into hair-thin strips. Blend lime juice and oil; mix with ginger. Cut stems from perilla leaves and discard. Stack leaves, halve along center stem, then cut into ¼-inch-wide strips (to make about 1 cup).

3. To serve, toss perilla and cucumber. Add dressing and toss quickly. Serve at once.

Serves 4

Variation

Salad of Perilla, Cucumber, Ginger, and Smoked Salmon

Serve this salad of pale and deep green strands garnished with peachy smoked salmon strips as a first course for a summer dinner party.

Cut about 3 ounces smoked salmon slices into strips about ½ inch wide and 2 inches long. Prepare salad as above and divide among four plates. Arrange salmon over salads. Serve at once.

Pros Propose

Myung Ja Kwak, chef at two New York Korean restaurants—just slightly traditional—developed a cold vegetable-noodle appetizer for both, **O-Bok Salad with Noodles:** Blend dry mustard, roasted perilla seeds, soy sauce, sesame oil, sugar, rice vinegar, and water. Toss with shreds of cabbage, carrot, romaine, and green perilla. Mound over small heaps of cold soba noodles mixed with sesame oil. Garnish with kiwi or tomato slices.

Traditional **Seasoned Perilla,** a ubiquitous condiment at Korean meals, is made for both restaurants, and recorded by Jenny Kwak, the chef's daughter, in her book, *Dok Suni:* Combine soy sauce, sesame salt, minced scallion and onion, crushed garlic, chilli flakes, sesame oil, and brown sugar, blending well. Layer between washed and dried perilla leaves, stacked in bowl. Refrigerate up to 4 days.

Chef Morgen Jacobson prepares a very different version of **Preserved Perilla** but serves it the same way: Rinse umeboshi (perilla-seasoned salted Japanese apricots) under running water to remove some salt; pit them. Combine with white (shiro) miso, garlic cloves, ginger juice, rice vinegar syrup, low-sodium shoyu, and lime juice to make a loose paste. Blanch large trimmed perilla leaves in well-salted water and chill in salted ice bath. Dry well on towels. Layer leaves, brushing generously with the paste. Refrigerate a minimum of 3 days. Serve as a relish for seafood.

Two appetizer salads come from chef Anita Lo. For **Steak Tartare with Perilla and Daikon:** Freeze beef eye of round. Slice thin on meat slicer. Cut into strips and season with wasabi, soy, salt, and pepper. Arrange on julienne of perilla leaves and daikon. For **Tomato and Perilla Salad:** Cut chiffonade of perilla. Mix with skinned, seeded, and diced red-ripe tomatoes, a touch of oil, soy, salt, and pepper. Mold in the center of a plate. Ring with a mixture of soy, wasabi, and oil. Decorate with halved tiny multicolor tomatoes.

Plantain (*Musa x paradisiaca*)

Also cooking banana; plátano and plátano macho (Latin American)

People in the Northern Hemisphere are likely to look at this photo and think, "Sweet fruit." But people in the Southern Hemisphere would be more likely to think of plantain as a staple starch. Plantain is cooked, much like potatoes, wherever it grows.

Questions about use are easily answered. Not so the questions raised (and not answered here) by a botanical description: Plantain is classified as *Musa x paradisiaca* (as are most bananas), a perennial herb, the fruit of which is a berry. The berry is called both banana and plantain (and by similar names) in many parts of the world, but depending upon the locale, the meanings may be reversed.

Plantain looks like a palm tree but isn't: The "trunk" is made of the bases of spirally arranged, tightly overlapping broad leaves that form at ground level. The real stem is a large underground rhizome with massive roots. The "trunk" supports a mass of constantly emerging, shreddy upper leaves; then a florid phallic stem; and then clusters ("hands") of fruit. When the fruit is picked, the plant is cut down or dies back (or both). It develops suckers that form a new "trunk" and the cycle repeats—sometimes for as long as 50 years.

The fruit is complicated, too, for each phase of ripeness has different characteristics and culinary possibilities: When the skin is green to nearly yellow, plantain is solid and starchy, like yuca or a dense waxy potato; when the skin is yellow to mottled brown, plantain has a slight fruitiness and a more tender but still firm texture; when brown to black-ripe, the golden flesh is creamy and sweet but holds its shape when cooked, unlike banana.

Banana and plantain have been so thoroughly absorbed by Latin American countries that many people think they are native to the New World. Yet this is a Southeast Asian plant, which landed in South America in the early 16th century and was not commercially available in the United States until the late 19th century. Plantain has become a symbol of assimilation in Latin America, says the historian Maricel Presilla, who

likens it to the immigrants who "surrendered to the realities of weather and geography and reached for substitutions. . . . Soon the substitutions, the foods of the land, and the brand new creations become comforting. This is the moment of creolization or *aplatanamiento* ["plantainization"], when the alien, like the . . . plantain, becomes native, a familiar sight and flavor in the all-inclusive pot of the New World" (from the introduction to *Latin Ladles* by Douglas Rodriguez).

But if plantain found a permanent home in Latin America, it has remained somewhat alien in North America. Although new immigrants from Asia, Africa, India, the Caribbean, and South and Central America—all areas where plantain is commonplace—have put their starchy staple into mainstream markets, plantain is rarely explored by those who did not grow up with it at home. Its deliciousness deserves recognition

plantain: green, yellow, and black-ripe   ¼ actual size

beyond chips and tostones, however. Perhaps the following information will encourage the timid.

BASIC USE: Think of plantain as a vegetable-fruit with the virtues of a waxy potato and banana, and you'll have an idea of its potential.

Green plantain, hard and starchy, is best thin-sliced and fried as chips or tostones—those thick twice-cooked rounds that are wildly popular wherever you find them. (No need for a recipe here. They're in just about any cookbook that includes recipes from the Spanish Caribbean.) Puerto Rico has a wide repertoire of plantain recipes, and pasteles (similar to tamales) are one of its most complex expressions: One type is made from grated raw plantain and yautía (page 722), seasoned with a rich sofrito made with plenty of achiote oil, then plumped with diced meat, chickpeas, and olives; wrapped in banana leaves, and long steamed to be served with spicy sauces.

Yellow-skinned plantain can be treated as above. Tostones made from it will be lightly sweet and softer inside than tostones made from green plantain. Yellow plantain is good pan-fried in rounds, diagonals, strips, or chunks. Or add it to soups: Rinse and thick-slice, then boil in a salty, spicy broth or pottage for about 20 minutes. When cooked, lift out with tongs, cool briefly, then zip off the peel. Cut to bite size, then replace in soup and reheat. Or simmer yellow plantain in stews—whether meaty and chilli-spiked; Pacific style, with coconut milk and seafood; or Indian, with sweet spices and mixed vegetables.

Brownish plantain can be cooked in all the same ways, but it will have a creamier, less waxy consistency and a light banana scent. It is more tender than yellow plantain, but nowhere near as soft as a banana. Rinse, chunk, and boil in salted water, then zip off the peel, slice, and eat, with or without butter or sauce. Or mash boiled plantain. Traditionally the mash is combined with crisp salt pork and garlic, but olive oil, coconut milk, and butter broaden the horizons. Or rinse plantain, slit the skin, and bake to serve like a potato; or peel and slice the baked plantain, then reheat with sauce.

Black-ripe plantains are the sweetest, creamiest, and easiest to introduce to beginners. Just rinse, trim tips, cut 2-inch slices, and boil until tender, about 10 minutes; then drain, peel, slice, and butter, or mash with seasoning. Slice peeled ripe plantain lengthwise and sauté in butter or oil; line a pie plate with the slices, fill with ground meat or vegetable stuffing, cover with more sautéed slices, and bake until browned for a luscious "crust."

SELECTION: Choose plantain to suit the way you want to cook it: rock-hard green to tender black. It will be edible as long as it is not moldy or cracked. If you don't regularly find plantains in your market, it pays to buy an oversupply, for they cost little, ripen slowly, and last a very long time. Do not worry about browning or blackening; that's the way plantains look. Occasionally, one will harden and dry instead of ripening; chuck it out.

STORAGE: Kept at room temperature, green or yellow plantain ripens *slowly* (sometimes over weeks) through every phase and (as noted above) keeps a good while. Plantain to be used green should be refrigerated, if you don't expect to cook it in a few days. Store yellow to black plantain at room temperature, well ventilated. Cook black fruit within a few days.

Like bananas, ripening plantains emit ethylene gas that affects other fruits and vegetables. Store them separately.

PREPARATION: Ripe plantains can be peeled like bananas. Underripe plantains are stubborn and require alternative procedures: Rinse fruit and slice off tips. Cut into 2 to 4 sections, then slit the thick, stiff peel lengthwise along its ridges. Remove peel in strips, starting at a corner and pulling slightly crosswise, rather than down the length of each. If the fruit has been chilled too long, or is very green, the underlayer may stick, and it then must be completely pared away.

For many dishes, it is easiest to peel after cooking: Cut 2-inch chunks; boil in water or in the soup or stew you're cooking. When done, remove with tongs, cool as needed, and strip off the peel. Cut plantain into ¼-inch slices; or quarter slices for bite-size wedges.

Basic Ripe Plantain, Four Ways

Ripened from yellow-brown to black-skinned, plantain comes into its own: Fruity, lush-textured, semi-sweet, it is more versatile and subtle than sweetpotato.

If you've never cooked plantain before, just boil it. It's a revelation: rich, soft, honeyed, and sunny gold, a remarkable treat in 10 minutes. Microwaved, it is similar, but a bit more stolid, less puffed and creamy. Pan-fried, it is buttery, brown-gold, and dessert-like. Baked, it is tender, but not as rich as when cooked the other ways, making it a fine foil for sauces. However you cook it, figure on about 1 pound for 2 people.

To boil: Cut tips from yellow-brown to black plantain. Cut into 2-inch lengths. Drop into boiling water and boil until tender and evenly golden and moist throughout (there should be no starchy pale yellow areas), about 10 to 15 minutes, depending upon ripeness. Drain.

When slightly cooled, slip off skins. Slice and arrange fruit, overlapping, in shallow dish. Serve hot, as is; or sprinkle with citrus juice and salt. Or drizzle with meat juices, curry or chilli sauce, or spicy gravy, or dot with butter; reheat. Or mash plantain, season as you would sweetpotatoes, and reheat; or mash and add browned chopped onions.

To microwave: Cut tips from yellow-brown to black plantain. Cut into 2-inch lengths. Set in microwavable dish and add ½ inch water. Cover and microwave until creamy-tender and semi-translucent, with no starchy yellow areas, about 6 minutes, turning once. Drain. Proceed as for boiled plantain.

To pan-fry: Peel yellow to brown plantain as directed. Cut into long ¼-inch-thick slices on the diagonal. Heat corn oil (or half oil, half butter) in wide skillet, preferably non-stick. Sauté slices in single layer over moderate heat until deep gold on both sides—3 to 4 minutes per side. Lower heat if necessary so that the inside is cooked tender when the outside is well gilded. Season with salt and pepper—or try toasted and crushed coriander or cumin seeds, or ground sumac, or just about any spiced salt you fancy. Serve as you would pan-fried potatoes, but expect a lightly sweet edge and drier texture.

To bake: Rinse and dry brown to black-ripe plantains, figuring on 1 medium plantain for each person. Cut off tips and make a long slit in each. Set slit side up on foil-covered pan and bake at 375°F until creamy-tender, about 40 minutes. Peel, halve, and serve as you would boiled potatoes—preferably with sauce or gravy. Or cut into thin diagonals, season, drizzle with melted butter, and reheat in oven. Or cut thick diagonals; sprinkle with lime juice, olive oil (or annatto oil), and ground hot pepper, then heat through in oven. Or cut into rounds and reheat in spicy sauce or tomato-meat sauce.

Hot and Gingery Collard-Plantain Soup

To warm a wintry evening, try this tropical meal-in-a-bowl instead of cabbage and potato soup. Thick collard leaves turn soft and succulent and pinky plantains, firm as small waxy potatoes, lend a fruity flavor as they thicken and sweeten the broth. A bonus: The soup is unusually quick-cooking for one of this hearty type and needs no time for mellowing.

> 1½ **pounds collards, well washed**
> 1½ **pounds yellow-ripe plantain**
> 2 **tablespoons corn oil or mild olive oil**
> 2 to 4 **Jalapeño chillis, seeded and chopped**
> 4 **large garlic cloves, sliced**
> ¼ **cup peeled, chopped ginger**
> ½ **teaspoon turmeric**
> 2 **teaspoons kosher salt**
> 2½ **quarts light vegetable or chicken broth**
> 2 **tablespoons brown sugar**
> **Optional: dried coarse-grated or sliced coconut**
> **Wafer-thin half-rounds of orange (with peel)**

1. If collards are large, strip stems from leaves and discard. Stack leaves and halve lengthwise, then cut into ½-inch strips. If small, simply slice both stems and leaves into ½-inch pieces.

2. Cut off plantain tips. Cut plantain into 3-inch lengths; slit peel lengthwise along its ridges. Remove peel in strips, starting at a corner and pulling slightly crosswise, rather than down the length of each. Halve plantain pieces lengthwise, then cut crosswise into ½-inch slices.

3. Warm oil in soup pot over moderate heat. Add Jalapeño, garlic, and ginger, and stir a minute. Add turmeric and blend. Add collards and salt; cook, tossing to wilt, about 5 minutes.

4. Add plantain, broth, and brown sugar. Bring to a boil. Simmer until plantain is tender, 20 to 30 minutes, stirring occasionally. Meanwhile, toast optional coconut in heavy pan over low heat until golden, stirring often. Cool.

5. Season soup. Ladle into wide bowls. Place 2 or 3 orange slices on each. Serve with optional coconut.

Serves 4 as a main course

Plantain and Pork Fried Rice

Jim Fobel, cookbook author and artist, has a knack for developing casual dishes with unusual twists. One day, while enjoying the traditional Latin trio of plantains, pork, and rice, "inspiration struck," he says, "like one of those cartoon lightbulbs that turn on in the head: Why not combine them in Chinese-style fried rice?"

Jim suggests that you "consider making this the day after you've sent for Chinese take-out," adding that a "2-cup carton that has been packed full of cooked rice will yield about 3 cups of rice after chilling and separating the grains." The dish tastes just right with a salad of orange, avocado, escarole, and radishes.

1 large ripe (partly black) plantain
½ pound pork loin
1 medium onion
1 large garlic clove
4 medium scallions (green onions)
2½ tablespoons vegetable oil
2 teaspoons minced ginger
About 3 cups cold, cooked long-grain
  white rice
About 2 tablespoons chopped cilantro
About 2 tablespoons soy sauce
About ½ teaspoon Asian (dark) sesame oil

1. Trim plantain tips. Cut plantain into 2- to 3-inch lengths. Slit skin on each piece lengthwise, then remove, pulling slightly crosswise rather than down the length of piece. Cut into ½-inch slices, then cut into ½-inch dice, more or less. Cut pork into pieces the same size. Halve onion through "poles," then cut lengthwise into slices. Mince garlic. Slice scallions thin.

2. Heat large non-stick skillet or wok over high flame. Add 1 tablespoon oil and pork; stir-fry until browned, about 2 minutes. Add plantain; brown on one side without stirring, about 1 minute. Then toss and cook until browned on all sides, another minute or two. Transfer to a plate; reserve.

3. Return pan to heat, add ½ tablespoon oil, the ginger, and garlic; stir-fry a few seconds. Add onion and cook a minute. Add remaining 1 tablespoon oil. Sprinkle in rice and toss 1 minute.

4. Add pork and plantain, tossing. Add scallions and 2 tablespoons cilantro. Sprinkle with 2 tablespoons soy sauce and sesame oil, tossing. Taste for seasoning, adding soy, cilantro, and sesame oil, as desired. Scoop onto a platter and serve hot.

Serves 2 to 3 as a main course

★For additional recipes with plantain, see Chayote and Plantain Baked in Creamy Nutmeg Cheese Sauce, page 179, and Warm Breadfruit and Ripe Plantain Salad with Avocado, page 114.

Pros Propose

Maricel Presilla, Cuban-born historian, author, and restaurant consultant, devised this **Escalibada** (roasted plantain, peppers, and onions in vinaigrette) for Victor's Cafe in New York City. "Here's a good example of a traditional Catalan dish made criollo by the addition of plantain," she explains. To prepare: Puncture yellow plantain in several places, coat with olive oil, and roast over a wood fire until it just about bursts. Peel, slice diagonals, and coat with oil, then brown them over the fire. Toss with bitter orange juice, oil, garlic, strips of roasted onion, and strips of roasted bell peppers (in three colors). Serve at room temperature, alongside beef. Or sprinkle with mild blue cheese and gratiné for an appetizer.

Tortilla de Plátanos Maduros, another gift from Maricel Presilla, is a golden, dense, savory cake that tastes like what it is: essence of ripe plantain. To prepare: Slant-cut peeled black-ripe plantains to make slices ¼ to ½ inch thick and 3 inches long. Deep-fry at 325°F until golden but still soft inside. Drain on paper; cool. Combine with beaten eggs. Spread mixture in hot olive oil in wide non-stick skillet. Cover and cook over lowest heat until eggs are not quite set, about 15 minutes. Invert onto plate, return to pan, and brown other side, uncovered. Slide onto serving plate. Cut thin wedges to serve hot, warm, or at room temperature, whether "plain" or with a tart salsa verde, or chunky tomato salsa, or Pesto Picante (page 724).

I am particularly fond of plantains simmered in soup, where they resemble soft, fruity potatoes. **Savory Lentil Soup with Pineapple and Plantains** from Oaxaca is also attractive for its use of pineapple. To prepare: Partly cook lentils in pork or chicken stock. Blacken whole tomato on griddle; cool. Toast peppercorns, cumin seeds, cloves, whole allspice, and stick cinnamon until browned and scented, about 3 minutes; cool. Puree tomato and spices in blender, then strain. Soften chopped onion in oil, add chopped garlic and stir. Add tomato mixture and cook about 10 minutes over moderate heat. Add to lentils, with sugar, thyme, oregano, chile de árbol, and bay leaf. Cook, covered, until lentils are almost done. Add 1-inch fresh pineapple cubes and quartered ripe plantain slices. Cook until tender, about ½ hour (from *Seasons of My Heart* by Susana Trilling).

Creamy plantain puree topped with spiced chicken cubes from Miami restaurateur Norman Van Aken is a soup of contemporary character despite its traditional-sounding name, **Little Havana Chicken and Plantain Sopa:** Coat boneless, skinless chicken breasts with toasted, ground cumin seeds and peppercorns; then salt. Coat with annatto or olive oil. Wrap and refrigerate 1 hour, or more. Sauté sliced black-ripe plantains in olive oil and butter with salt, sugar, and hot pepper until browned. Add diced white part of leek, red onion, celery, carrot, garlic, and seeded, minced Habanero chilli. When browned, add saffron, a large quan-

tity of cilantro leaves, and orange juice; cook 2 minutes. Add chicken stock. Simmer until vegetables are soft, about 15 minutes. Stir in heavy cream and reduce soup to taste. Puree in food processor until smooth. Strain through medium sieve. Cook chicken in non-stick pan. Let rest briefly, then cut into bite-size dice. Ladle soup into bowls; top with the chicken (from *Norman's New World Cuisine*).

Plantains with Coconut and Chilli moves to an Asian context: Cook peeled green plantain chunks in boiling salted water until soft, about ½ hour. Drain and mash. Add grated fresh coconut, thin-sliced shallots, seeded and sliced chillis, and thick coconut cream. Season with salt and lime juice. Serve with rice (from *Charmaine Solomon's Encyclopedia of Asian Food*).

Even simpler is **Fried Ripe Plantain Strips** from Minerva Etzioni, who explained that each family in Mexico City has its own version of even the simplest dishes. In her mother's kitchen, fried ripe plantain received an unusual final fillip—a dip in lightly sugared water, to retain the natural juiciness and dispel grease: Halve peeled, fully ripe plantain crosswise and cut lengthwise into slices ¼ inch thick. In batches, pan-fry in single layer in vegetable oil until just golden on both sides. Immediately dip each piece into a little boiling water in which you've dissolved a small amount of sugar; set on baking sheet lined with paper towels. Keep warm in low oven while you fry the remainder.

Porcini (*Boletus edulis*)

Also cèpe (French), cep, king bolete, bolete

Note: The mushrooms are commonly referred to in the plural, porcini (pronounced por-CHEE-nee). The singular is porcino.

¹⁄₃ actual size (*top and bottom*)

Until quite recently, dried Italian porcini and French cèpes were the only forms of *Boletus edulis* sold—and these are the names that have stuck to the fresh forms now available, although the fungus is no more exclusively Italian or French than Polish or Chinese. There are also many other delicious members of the genus *Boletus*—and even more in the several related genera that make up the complicated Boletaceae. But because these are not in the market and this is not a book about foraging, I'll stick to what is sold as "porcini."

"*Boletus edulis* is not truly a single mushroom but a complex of forms, and can look quite different from one patch to another," says Gary Lincoff, author of *The Audubon Society Field Guide to North American Mushrooms* and other books. I've seen fat double hassocks from Oregon with chestnut caps as crisp as apples. I've cooked leggy bone-pale specimens from South Africa, springy and sweet-scented. I've savored huge, tawny porcini from Italy. But whether chocolate or cream, chubby or strapping, tacky or dry to the touch, they will all be distinguished by a spongy tube-mass that replaces the gills, a bulbous shape, fishnet-patterned stalks, and a uniquely luscious savor and smoothness.

These most prized of forest treasures capture the imagination of mycophiles in more lands than many people realize. They occur naturally in a wide variety of habitats throughout China, Europe, North America, and other parts of the Northern Hemisphere. They have also been introduced, albeit inadvertently, via certain trees with which they have a mycorrhizal relationship (the root systems share nutrients), to parts of the Southern Hemisphere, notably southern Africa, according to Lincoff.

This internationalization being the case, I suggest that unless origin and species are being differentiated, we adopt the market term "bolete" to de-ethnicize and generalize this mushroom complex. And if we're fortunate, that could open woods and markets to a

wider range of bolete species, as worthy of delectation as the *edulis,* as foragers and feinschmeckers know well.

BASIC USE: *Boletus edulis* is one of the few wild mushrooms that can be enjoyed raw. Thin-sliced and tossed with the finest olive oil, a hint of lemon, and a touch of chives, it is crisp, subtle, and elegant.

When cooked, the mushroom's unique perfume blossoms, the caps turn creamy, and the stems become tender and lightly crunchy. Although searing is the American mode of the day, I think this method destroys the delicate flavor and consistency. Better to pan-cook very slowly, or to simmer (then cook off liquid, if desired), or to roast. In Gascony, where the word "cèpe" originated, the mushrooms are slowly braised in sauce. In Italy, where they are often speedily grilled or sautéed, they are protected by plenty of olive oil and some moisture—such as tomato cubes or minced herbs and onions.

In cooking whole caps or thick slices, an emollient bath does wonders: warm olive oil (or use part nut oil) with a smashed garlic clove over low heat. Score both sides of the mushroom *lightly,* then paint lavishly with the seasoned oil and allow to rest while you heat the oven or grill. Roast in a preheated pan on high heat. If grilling, let the flame die down, then roast the mushroom caps near the coals, turning once. Season and serve hot .

Porcini cook to perfection in parchment. It prevents them from becoming too wet or too dry as they simultaneously bake and steam in an environment that magically preserves their haunting flavor and satiny suppleness.

However you cook these gems, keep it simple, or the point is lost. Accompany with pasta, rice, cornmeal, eggs, potatoes, mild fish, veal, pheasant, or other gentle foods. The meaty yet smooth flesh—like filet mignon in texture—speaks eloquently for itself.

SELECTION: With the exception of winter, boletes may show up erratically during much of the year, from many countries. They should be almost as solid as potatoes. Ideally, the sponge layer of minuscule tubes beneath the cap should be relatively pale and dry. If it is darkening and mushy (but not nasty-smelling), it is overmature; but the mushrooms can still be fine if the sponge is removed.

Boletus edulis is a favorite of both bugs and people. "Scrunch a few stems," advises chef Jean Joho. "If they give, they're eaten inside." The firmest, most bug-free boletes in the United States are from high-altitude areas, such as the Rocky Mountains; but chefs say that the flavor is usually fuller in boletes from France, Italy, Spain, and Yugoslavia.

For use in restaurants, cut a few in half before you buy them to check for infestation, advises Joho—who also recommends taking a taste: "If you don't like the flavor raw, you won't like it better cooked."

STORAGE: Chef Joho suggests overnight refrigeration on a towel-covered tray to "keep them dry and to get a bug count. They'll come out, if they're there. A few is no big deal, but if there are lots, forget them." Change the towel daily, and good boletes will last about a week. For longer storage, Lidia Matticchio Bastianich, whose restaurants are legendary, reminds us that "porcini dry perfectly. At home we cut up the September crop, which has peak flavor, and hang the slices to dry on thorn bushes. But if you like, they can be dried in a dehydrator or vacuum-packed and frozen, cooked or raw."

PREPARATION: Flick off clinging earth with a soft brush, then check the base for insects (cut these out; the rest of the mushroom will not be harmed). Clean caps and stems with a damp towel. If very earthy, rinse quickly and dry on soft towels. Pare as needed. If the sponge layer is greenish, smelly, or very sticky, discard it.

Caps are often detached from the stems so that they can be grilled alone—but the stems are as delicious as the caps, so I see no need for this. Simply cut mushrooms vertically, through cap and stem, in thick slices. For broken, irregular, or thin-stemmed specimens, you will do best to separate the two, then slice to the thickness desired.

Pale and Pristine Salad of Porcini and Belgian Endive

Boletes are one of the few wild mushrooms safe to eat raw—and they are exquisite. For this light first course, olive oil and lemon coat crisp julienne of endive and look-alike mushroom stems. Fine slices of cap lightly scented with mint are arranged over the julienne and topped with rich, resinous pine nuts: a subtle play of textures and tiny flavor bursts hidden in quiet pallor.

Only the freshest, rock-hard *Boletus edulis* will do here. Avoid any with insect holes or elderly sponge layers. Similarly, only the finest extra-virgin olive oil suits the ensemble.

About 1 tablespoon lemon juice
¼ teaspoon kosher salt
Big pinch fine-ground white pepper
About 2½ tablespoons fine, fruity olive oil
4 small *Boletus edulis* (about 10 ounces total)
4 small Belgian endives (about 3 ounces each)
2 to 3 teaspoons hair-thin chive slices
2 to 3 teaspoons minced mint leaves
2 tablespoons lightly toasted pine nuts

1. Blend 1 tablespoon lemon juice, salt, and pepper. Whisk in 2½ tablespoons olive oil.

2. Clean boletes as needed: Either rub with wet paper towel or, if earthy, rinse quickly and dry at once. Pare stems (save these and any other parings for sauce). Break apart stems and caps. Trim cap edges and sponge layers as needed.

3. Rinse endives. Cut cores from 2 heads and separate leaves. Arrange on four plates. Trim remaining 2 endives, halve lengthwise, and cut into very thin julienne strips about 1½ inches long.

4. Cut bolete stems into strips about the same length and about ⅛ inch thick. Combine both julienne in bowl with chives and half the dressing. Toss gently. Taste and adjust seasoning, oil, and lemon. Spoon onto leaves.

5. Cut caps into thin slices; toss delicately with remaining dressing and mint. Taste and season. Arrange on plates. Strew with nuts.

Serves 4 as a first course

Porcini (or other Boletes) Baked in Parchment

Some time-honored culinary techniques and materials cannot be improved upon by modern ones. Barbara Spiegel, who tried this recipe, put it this way: "I was utterly thrilled to observe the distinction between mushrooms cooked in parchment and aluminum foil when I compared them. You genuinely bake (steam a little) in parchment; in foil, you steam (bake a little). Parchment

works infinitely better and I shan't be cavalier about using foil as I have in the past." Accept no substitutes: Only parchment preserves the special texture of porcini and other boletes, which all benefit from the cooking method.

FOR EACH PORTION

¼ pound *Boletus edulis* (or other firm boletes)
1½ teaspoons olive oil or melted butter
½ tablespoon minced shallot
Salt and pepper
Sprig of thyme, rosemary, or summer savory
Optional: small garlic clove

1. Preheat oven to 425°F. Clean mushrooms with damp towel; or rinse if absolutely necessary and dry at once. If sponge layer is smelly or sticky or tastes bitter, discard it. Pare stems as needed. Cut smaller mushrooms lengthwise into ¼-inch slices through cap and stem. If large, separate caps and stems and slice.

2. Spread 1 teaspoon oil on lower third of parchment square (size is not important, but about 12 to 15 inches square is handy), leaving 2-inch margin at bottom. Sprinkle with shallot, then cover with mushroom slices. Drizzle with remaining ½ teaspoon oil; season. Add herb and optional garlic.

3. Fold over top of paper to meet bottom, make two narrow folds at the edge, then crimp to form a half-moon "turnover." Set on baking sheet in upper third of oven. Bake ½ hour.

4. Serve at once, in packet.

Sautéed Porcini (or other Boletes) with a Touch of Herbs and Tomato

Chef Jean Joho gets to the heart of ingredients. At his high-flying Chicago dining room, Everest, he serves this "plain" dish to complement veal tenderloin, pheasant, or rabbit. It can also be savored alone, as a first course. The cubing step is useful for broken or otherwise imperfect boletes, so that they will cook neatly and evenly. Gently sautéed, the cap pieces turn meltingly soft, while the stems stay slightly springy. The touches of tomato, garlic, and herbs are mere accents:

Do not increase the seasoning, or the mellow mushroom's character will be lost.

> ½ pound *Boletus edulis* (or other firm
>   *Boletus* species)
> 2 medium plum tomatoes
> 1 tablespoon plus 1 teaspoon flavorful,
>   fruity olive oil
> 1 teaspoon butter
> ¼ teaspoon minced garlic
> ¼ teaspoon minced rosemary leaves
> ¼ teaspoon minced thyme leaves
> ¼ teaspoon kosher salt
> Pepper
> ½ tablespoon thin-sliced basil leaves
> ½ tablespoon thin-sliced flat-leaf parsley leaves

1. Clean mushrooms with damp towel; or rinse if absolutely necessary and dry at once. If necessary, remove sponge layer. Pare stems as needed. Cut mushrooms into ½- to ¾-inch cubes (about 3 cups). Peel, seed, and mince tomatoes (see Note, page 10).

2. Heat 1 tablespoon oil and the butter in medium skillet over moderate heat. When butter foams, add mushrooms, garlic, rosemary, thyme, salt, and pepper. Toss to coat well. Cook, stirring constantly, until mushrooms are not quite tender—about 3 minutes.

3. Add tomatoes and continue cooking until juicy and tender, about 2 minutes longer. Off heat, stir in remaining 1 teaspoon oil, the basil, and parsley.

**Serves 2 to 3 as a side dish or garnish,
2 as a first course**

Roasted Bolete Slices

A toss in hot seasoned oil followed by high-heat roasting preserves the delicacy of *Boletus* mushrooms (there is no burned taste from direct heat). Purists will appreciate the subtle underscoring of the mushroom's natural flavor that comes from crushed juniper berries and hazelnut oil, edged with a touch of sweet-acid balsamic. Lovers of big flavors should stick with other recipes.

> 4 juniper berries
> 1 small garlic clove
> ¼ teaspoon dried thyme

> ¼ teaspoon kosher salt
> ½ tablespoon balsamic vinegar
> 1 tablespoon hazelnut oil
> 1½ tablespoons olive oil
> Pepper
> 4 smallish *Boletus* mushrooms (about ¾ pound)
> Optional: fleur de sel or other crisp sea salt

1. Heat oven to 475°F. Using a suribachi or mortar, crush juniper, garlic, thyme, and salt to a paste (remove any hard bits of juniper that remain). Add vinegar and blend, then add oils and pepper.

2. Brush any earth from mushrooms. If sponge layer is sticky or smells "off," trim or remove. Rinse or pare stems as needed. Rub caps clean with damp towel or rinse if absolutely necessary. Cut smaller mushrooms into ¼-inch slices through cap and stem. If large, separate caps and stems and slice.

3. In wide ovenproof skillet, heat the seasoned oil mixture over lowest heat until sizzling. Add mushrooms and toss gently to coat evenly. Set pan in oven and cook until juicy and tender throughout, about 10 minutes. Serve at once, with crisp salt and additional pepper.

Serves 2 as a side dish or first course

Pros Propose

Chef Jean Joho is particularly partial to raw boletes, as in this subtle, pale duo, **Cèpe and Palm Heart Salad:** Thin-slice trimmed cèpes. Season with salt, pepper, lemon juice, and "the most elegant extra-virgin olive oil you have." Add a hint of chervil, chives, and parsley and mix gently. Toss thin-sliced raw hearts of palm with more of the same dressing and arrange on plates. Press mushrooms lightly into individual ring mold, then unmold onto palm hearts. Circle with mâche leaves. Alongside, dab a teaspoon of peeled, diced tomatoes cooked lightly in olive oil.

According to chef Roland Liccioni, boletes respond well to a non-traditional cooking method: steaming. He makes a **Porcini Carpaccio** by thin-slicing the mushrooms, steaming them a few minutes, and tossing with warm haricots verts and truffle dressing.

Gentle, slow cooking results in tender textures and

essential flavors in chef Sylvain Portay's **Sautéed Dover Sole with Cèpes in Natural Juices:** Remove cèpe stems and reserve for another dish. Clean caps with damp towel; slice thick. Combine in wide pan with butter, olive oil, unpeeled garlic, salt, pepper, and just enough light chicken stock to moisten. Simmer, covered, for 20 minutes. Season and add butter. Sauté sole fillets. Spoon cèpes on top and finish with coarse-cut flat-leaf parsley.

Layered close textures and flavors expressed as variations on a theme characterize the thoughtful dishes of chef Laurent Gras, such as **Porcini Risotto:** Prepare classic risotto. When rice is half-cooked, stir in cubed porcini stems and continue cooking. Meanwhile, sauté thick-sliced porcini caps and unpeeled garlic cloves in duck confit fat until golden. When rice is cooked, fold in butter, then mascarpone, then Parmesan, to finish. Spoon risotto into shallow bowls with the sautéed caps and a touch of veal *jus.* Top with thin-sliced raw unseasoned porcini slices.

If a foraging expedition (or forager) rewards you with a healthy supply of boletes of any type, try this rustic casserole of **Baked Porcini and Potatoes:** Arrange peeled potato slices in an oiled baking dish, distributing peeled garlic cloves throughout. Season and drizzle with olive oil. Cover with an equal weight of porcini sliced to the same thickness. Cover with torn large basil leaves, then drizzle with oil. Cover tightly and bake until tender (from *Recipes from Paradise* by Fred Plotkin).

Potato (Specialty Types) (*Solanum tuberosum*)

Called baby, mini-, and gourmet potatoes

Including **fingerling, colored,** and **new potatoes**

The potato is hardly new to North America—it was introduced in the 18th century. But this is still relatively recent, and the route by which the potato arrived is certainly unusual: It came the long way round via Irish immigrants, rather than directly from its native South America. Today, there is a notable trend toward petite potatoes that are *not* all-purpose: a wide array of colorful, smallish varieties that entered through the restaurant door and have since moved into the home. Like mesclun (the mix of baby greens first popularized in France and Italy), many of the present "new" potatoes are old favorites in European markets.

Like potatoes sold in Europe—and unlike sturdy spuds of the American generic type—these specialty potatoes usually come with name tags, whether they are rejuvenated old varieties ("heirlooms"), familiar varieties properly identified, or brand-name products of marketing campaigns. Consequently, once you've sampled an All-Blue, German Butterball, or Ruby Crescent, you can find it again, rather than root around in the meaningless terrain of "round reds" or "long whites."

Fingerling potatoes are among the more distinctive groups you're likely to see. The informal term has come to describe narrow little tubers, whether finger-like, crescent-shaped, or just wiggly and small. (Although "fingerling" describes anything tiny, this word of German origin commonly refers to fish, not potatoes.) Generally speaking, fingerlings are predictably petite, pricey, and uncommonly tasty and firm—ideal for steaming, boiling, baking, and salads.

Fingerlings and other market newcomers often wear bright-colored skins, a major selling point. Unfortunately, these tell little about a potato's interior. Do not be seduced by mere appearance: indigo, fuchsia, and other eye-catching wrappers may lead you down the garden path (read the thumbnail varietal sketches for the inside story). Nor do ravishing colors in the raw necessarily mean rainbows on the plate, once a potato is cooked.

Blue-fleshed potatoes, the most novel of the specialty types, vary considerably. Although commercial sources tend to lump purple and blue potatoes together as if there were only one, there are many, each with its own idiosyncracies. Some are mealy, some moist; in cooking, some fade, others intensify in color. A baby blue chosen to brighten a salad, for example, may turn cement gray when boiled, while a lavender potato may deepen to violet.

Pink-fleshed types are also highly variable, although they are generally more moist. You may read that vinegar in the cooking water holds the color, but it does not. It slows cooking, produces an uneven texture, reddens blue hues, and merely concentrates pink on cut surfaces.

Golden- to tan-skinned potatoes with yellow flesh, whether starchy or waxy in texture, frequently offer superior flavor. Their firm consistency, pronounced flavor, and sweetness make them best bets.

New potatoes are an abused and misunderstood category. I see red nearly every time I order them in a restaurant, because that is what arrives: small red potatoes. "Small and red" does *not* mean new. "A new potato is one that has tender skin and has just been harvested from a plant with still-green foliage, unlike mature potatoes, which are harvested when the vine dies," explains Jim Gerritsen, a co-owner of Wood Prairie Farm in Bridgewater, Maine. New potatoes are the delicate first crop of any potato variety. Some may be small, but others are the same size as mature, stored potatoes. With the exception of new-crop potatoes, others are cured, that is, held in a humid environment for about 2 weeks at 50° to 60°F to heal cuts and bruises and toughen the skin. The temperature is then lowered gradually to suitable storage conditions at which potatoes may remain for up to 9 months without appreciable loss, according to growers. Improperly stored, they shrink, darken, and develop soft spots. Once stored, a potato is not new—no matter how small, what color, or how thin-skinned it is. Perhaps new potatoes might be better served by the name fresh-harvest or first-crop potatoes.

to be taken with a handful of coarse salt. For ease of visual reference, they are divided into fingerling, blue- to purple-skinned, rose- to red-skinned, and golden- to tan-skinned. Not all those described are pictured.

About Sampling Potatoes

Potatoes are more obviously affected by growing conditions than any other vegetable I know. A Rose Gold grown on an organic farm in Maine may have no more than its name in common with one grown on a "regular" farm in California; flavor, texture, skin quality, size, and even color may differ. Thus, the following descriptions are only partially accurate, no more. Still, in the interest of expanding horizons, here are thumbnail varietal sketches (with some crossover names), all

Fingerlings

Austrian Crescent: Oblong tubers with smooth, pale tan skin; yellow-cream flesh steams to pleasing, waxy consistency but skin tends to be bitter. Boil, steam, use (peeled) in salad.

French Fingerling: Smooth, plump uniform oblong; thin rosy skin and yellow or pink-splashed flesh. (According to Sandi Aarestad, owner of The Potato

fingerling potatoes: (*clockwise from midnight*) Ruby Crescent, French Fingerling, Red Thumb, Peanut, Russian Banana, La Ratte, Ozette; (*center*) Purple Peruvian and Austrian Crescent   length: 1½–4 inches

Patch in Halstead, Minnesota, if this tuber is allowed to develop slowly and fully, it turns pink.) When steamed or boiled, the skin is pink-gold and flesh satiny, waxy, and moist with a buttery balanced flavor. Baked, it has a sweet-dough scent; the flesh is less silky but has a creamy, flaky texture and similar flavor.

La Ratte (Larote, La Reine, La Princesse): Tapered, elongated French favorite; satiny pale gold skin, very fine-textured yellow flesh. Steamed, it is sweet, mild, waxy, silky, and creamy; it has a rich flavor, between earthy and sweet. Bakes equally well, with full flavor, light creamy flesh, and nice vanilla aroma. Cook all ways.

Ozette (Anna Cheeka's Ozette): Narrow, knuckly, with tissue-thin pale gold skin and yellow flesh. Steamed, it is slightly nutty, pleasantly floury and waxy, and pale, clean with a pretty look. Baked, it is less attractive; skin toughens a bit, and flesh compresses somewhat—but flavor is good. Said to have come directly to North America with Spanish explorers who brought it from Peru and traded it with the Makah-Ozette tribe of the Olympic Peninsula. Haida, Kasaan, and Ozette all may be the same potato.

Peanut (Swedish Peanut, Mandel, Butterfinger): Smoothly formed crescent, kidney shape, or teardrop; buff skin with light russeting; yellow flesh. Leguminous (yes, peanut-like) flavor, especially steamed; quite dry and starchy for a fingerling. Baked, it is smooth, even, nutty, and sweetish. Cook all ways.

Purple Peruvian: *See* Blue- to Purple-Skinned group.

Red Thumb: Smallish tubers, oblong, chubbier than other fingerlings. Pinky-brown skin steams to a bright, pretty luster and flesh turns pink; earthy flavor, with slight sweetness. Boil, steam, bake.

Rose Finn Apple (Rose Fir): Long, narrow, knobbly oblong; pink-buff satiny, thin skin; yellow flesh. An elegant, versatile, rewarding potato. The flavorful flesh is both waxy and creamy, drier than some. Rarely requires peeling. Cook all ways.

Ruby Crescent: Tapered or wavy oblong with thin, peach-colored skin and yellow-cream flesh. Steams and bakes equally well to a complex blend of earthy, sweet, and milky. Waxy, moist, consistent texture; skin is a bit tough. Prepare all ways—except as salad; it tastes fishy when cold.

Russian Banana (Banana): Narrow, tapering, quite smooth; tan-cream skin, buttercream flesh. Rich, re-fined old-fashioned potato flavor. Firm, fine-textured when steamed, baked, or boiled; also good in salad. Steamed has silkier texture; baked is sweeter. Color remains close to same as raw.

Blue- to Purple-Skinned

All-Blue: Smooth, midnight blue, fairly thin skin; deep purple flesh. Steams to deep lavender with pale rim; moist, light, fine, soft flesh. Bakes to dark lavender-violet; tender, even texture; skin stays deep blue; well-balanced taste and texture. Most versatile of the blues tasted; can be cooked many different ways. Dress with vinaigrette to sharpen color and use as salad accent, in small bits.

Blue Pride: Dark violet russeted skin; white flesh (seed catalogues mention blue splashes; I've not seen these). Steamed, the skin turns gray-brown; waxy white flesh has mild, balanced flavor. Baked is comparable, but skin is sweeter.

Caribe: Large, rounded; silvery-violet skin; white flesh. Steamed, it may range from creamy-waxy, smooth, with sweet delicate flavor to merely ordinary. Baked has a pleasant one-note effect; mashed has a light, fluffy consistency, both floury and moist. Note that the skin offers no advantages: It tastes metallic and turns grayish.

Purple Chief (Kerry Blue): Large, smooth, typical baking potato form; stunning indigo-grape skin, cream flesh with a violet perimeter. Best baked—light, creamy, almost fluffy. Good mashed, too. Steamed is light, starchy-mealy, fresh. Note that the brilliant blueness vanishes, leaving only a blue-gray trace in the skin.

Purple Peruvian (Peruvian Blue): One of the first specialty potatoes to arrive in the United States, in the 1970s. Knobbed, deep purple-navy irregular rounds and teardrops; flesh is pale at perimeter, deepest purple in center. Cooked, the flesh turns violet to indigo; skin remains dark. Starchy-creamy texture balance; flavor bland to earthy. Bake for a pleasant mealy texture; or boil or steam. Peel for salads.

Purple Viking: Medium-large, rounded; the smooth skin has a stunning marbling of deep purple and magenta; white flesh. Steamed, skin and dull white

blue- to purple-skinned potatoes: (*top, left to right*) Blue Pride, All-Blue, Purple Chief; (*bottom, left to right*) Caribe, Viking Purple, Purple Peruvian   length: 1½-3 inches

flesh taste earthy, thin; smooth texture. Baked, the potato has more balance and sweetness, but pale flavor. Note that the striking skin turns purplish brown to brown.

Seneca Horn (Cow Horn): Elongated, smooth, tapered crescent; intense violet skin; white flesh. Steamed, the skin turns silvery lavender; dull white flesh is floury, flaky, dry, without sweetness. Baked, the potato looks crumpled, but flavor is sweeter and more developed; starchy and, oddly, more moist than steamed. Looks more exciting than it tastes.

Rose- to Red-Skinned

All-Red (Cranberry Red): Rounded or oval; deep magenta skin with pinkish lavender flesh. Moist, soft, mild. Steaming brings out a melt-in-your mouth creaminess. However cooked, the flesh turns lavender-pink, to varying degrees. Not a mere novelty, but a pleasing potato.

Desiree: Medium-size, symmetrical oval; thin, pale golden-pink skin; cream flesh. This European favorite is best steamed; it turns pearly alabaster, its flesh waxy, satiny, and sliceable. Pure delicate flavor with a high note—like sparkling wine. Flavor has remarkable staying power. Cook all ways.

Early Ohio: Chunky oblong with peach-colored skin and white flesh. Midwestern favorite of the 19th century, with a friendly, old-fashioned flavor, particularly when baked.

Early Rose: Oval to rounded; pale apricot-pink skin; creamy flesh. Steams best, to palest peach; flesh is lightly tinted, with rich consistency, mild; pleasant skin. Baked, the flesh is less delicate but has fine balance. An improvement on most white-fleshed rose-skinned varieties.

Fontenot: Recently introduced, this round, russeted potato has bright pink skin and white flesh. Steamed, the skin turns candy bright; flesh is waxy, not

rose- to red-skinned potatoes: (*top, left and right*) Fontenot and Huckleberry; (*center, left and right*) All-Red and Red Gold; (*bottom, left and right*) Rote Erstling and Early Ohio   length: 1½-3 inches

starchy. Baked has a sweet honeyed scent, tasty skin, waxy flesh; skin looks dumpy.

Huckleberry: Oval; rosy skin; pink-streaked white flesh; cooked, the skin stays rose and the flesh pinkens. Flavor unexciting. Steam or bake.

Red Cloud: Medium, rounded; pink, fairly smooth skin; fine-textured, ivory flesh. Steamed, it keeps shape, character, and well-balanced long-lasting flavor; holds up nicely for braising. Baked has a creamy, sweet, rich flavor and firm texture that is

at once waxy, starchy, and crumbly. Cook all ways.

Reddale (Red Dale): Medium-large, neatly rounded; pink-rose, smooth skin; cream flesh. Bake, braise, or prepare as gratin for mild flavor and potato-chip aroma; an even, slightly mealy, but moist texture. Boil for salads. Steamed is less successful—too wet.

Red Gold: Medium-large, rounded; pink skin with distinct gold sheen; yellow-cream flesh. Steamed, the sheen remains and the flesh is deliciously waxy-tacky; skin is thin and edible. Cook all ways.

Rose Gold: Small, rounded; pale pink-gold, slightly rough skin; yellow flesh. Steams beautifully—tender skin and silky, waxy texture; golden flesh with delicate flavor. Keeps its shape and flavor for braises, roasts, and salads. Baking develops the starchiness, firmness, and sweetness, and deepens the gold color.

Rote Erstling: Oval; light beet-red skin; cream flesh. Steamed, the flesh turns warm yellow, light, fluffy, and creamy—all at once. Baked, the flesh, color, and flavor dumb down and get dense.

Golden- to Tan-Skinned

Bintje: A Dutch heirloom that may be the most widely grown yellow-fleshed potato in the world. Medium, round-to-oblong; pale-gold thin skin that toughens slightly when cooked, though its appearance remains similar to the raw. Steamed or baked Bintje has a firm, waxy-starchy texture and a warm, balanced flavor; baked, it becomes firmer and starchier.

Butte: Oblong, russeted tan skin; white flesh. Steamed, the fluffy flesh has a surprisingly rich baked potato scent and flavor. Baked, it is pleasingly mealy, unless very small.

Carola (Carole): Small to large, round to oval; smooth tan skin; fine yellow flesh. Steamed, it is golden, with a warm, creamy-smooth texture and sweet scent; also fine for salads (peeled). Baked is golden-skinned, rich yellow, at once moist and flaky, smooth and fluffy; balanced, rich flavor and sweet-dough aroma. Thin, chewy skin. Cook all ways.

Concord: Very smooth medium oval; creamy tan skin; yellow flesh. Steamed, the flesh turns creamy and waxy and is fairly mild. Baked, it is bland and damp.

Charlotte: Small to medium oblong; smooth, thin, pale golden skin; yellow-cream flesh. Baked, it has a lasting, warm, sweet flavor and tender skin. Steamed, it is satiny-soft and flavorful, but skin is less pliant.

German Butterball: Medium, rounded, smooth; very pretty thin pale gold skin; yellow flesh. Bakes and

golden- to tan-skinned potatoes: (*clockwise from top*) Concord, German Butterball, Carola, Yukon Gold, Charlotte
length: 1½–2½ inches

steams to a unique rich gold; both starchy-flaky and moist, with a mild, earthy flavor and supple skin.

Island Sunshine: Round, medium, solid; tan skin, golden flesh. For my taste, this is what everyone says Yukon Gold is—and isn't. Steamed, it has hearty flavor; brilliant yellow, bright clean skin; and a fine, flaky-powdery feel in the mouth. Baked, its full yellow color and rich flavor are rewarding, but its texture is less distinctive. Try it every way.

Onaway: Rounded; tan skin; cream flesh. Steamed, it turns creamy, soft, and mild. Baked, the flavor is slightly more concentrated, but simple, and its texture slightly waxy and moist.

Yellow Finn (Yellow Finnish): Medium-small, with slightly rough, pale gold, thin skin and bright yellow flesh. Baked, it is most appealing, with a solid, smooth, creamy texture and old-fashioned potato flavor; or braise or cook with a roast. Steamed, it is bland and damp.

Yukon Gold: Medium-large, round; yellow-tan skin; yellow flesh—and a huge variation in the samples. Baked is best, a good replacement for the usual "round whites." Some Yukon Golds have an attractive balance of starchiness and waxiness, rich yellow flesh, a warm aroma, and sweet even flavor (and skin, too). Some are at best ordinary on all counts. Some are remarkable for their defined flouriness, steamed or baked. Others are damp and unappealing. The color is buttery, but the flavor is not—although it is often described as such. All in all, very confusing!

BASIC USE: Most petite potatoes are at their best prepared whole and simply: Steam, boil, or bake. I love a finish of crisp salt grains and sometimes a gloss of the best butter. Complex flavors, complicated cooking techniques, or too many accompaniments hide the charms of sweet little spuds. To discover each variety's characteristics, it helps to adopt an experimental attitude: Steam little russeted potatoes that look like "bakers"; adopt a baking-potato approach for purple fingerlings; roast pink-skinned potatoes that are typecast as "steamers."

Cooking techniques affect a potato's color and texture as well as its flavor. The trade-offs are up to you. Microwaving preserves color but degrades *all* other qualities, in my (strong) opinion. While steaming maintains good color, the skin tastes more acrid steamed than baked. Boiling bleaches color more than steaming, for the most part. I find that in boiling pota-

toes it is best to start cooking in *cold*—not boiling—salted water for a more creamy, uniform texture. With few exceptions, potato skins are sweeter and tastier when baked or roasted, but they look more crumpled and browned.

Little potatoes of almost all varieties excel in salad: Steam, slip off skins, then toss with a little wine and/or vinegar, salt, and olive or nut oil and optional herbs. Serve warm or at room temperature, not chilled. Varieties with pink, blue, purple, and yellow flesh are particularly pretty, as the acid in dressing usually heightens their coloring.

For the smallest of small potatoes, particularly thin-skinned fingerlings, nothing beats butter-baking with a sprig of rosemary (see Perfect Butter-Baked Petite Potatoes, page 507).

SELECTION: Potatoes are generally a summer and fall crop, but timing varies with the region. "Gourmet" varieties are available in specialty shops, at farmers' markets, and through mail-order companies; a few vie for supermarket space. The very small percentage of true new-crop potatoes appears several times during the year, depending upon the location. These tubers are conspicuously scruffy and soil-coated, because "the very thin skin makes them difficult to harvest without tattering and feathering," according to the grower Jim Gerritsen.

In most potatoes, flaking skin, uneven color, and "dirtiness" are signs of freshness, not inferiority. Potatoes coated with a dusty layer of soil are likely to be in better condition than clean, shiny ones; soil protects the skin and helps keep it dry.

Choose rock-hard potatoes, with no softening or sprouts. Avoid potatoes with holes or cuts, which hasten spoilage by letting bacteria penetrate. Stay clear of green-tinged potatoes *(and stores where they are sold)*; these potatoes may contain solanine, a bitter alkaloid poisonous to some people and good for none.

Although I know of no visual clue to determine which potatoes take the longest time to cook, my experience indicates that this trait is a hallmark of quality. Comparatively lengthy cooking time signals a high percentage of solid matter—not water—and thus a potential for full flavor and uniform, firm texture. Quick-cooking potatoes are often insipid and flabby, however they are cooked.

Buy organically raised vegetables in general, and potatoes in particular. Fungicides, pesticides, and other undesirables concentrate in the skin, which then is usually consumed.

STORAGE: Unless you have a root cellar, do not stock up. Small, thin-skinned potatoes are more delicate than is generally understood, and they sprout and spoil fairly quickly. (New-crop potatoes are even more perishable—closer to zucchini than to other potatoes.) Keep potatoes in a cool, dark place—but not in the refrigerator, where they will darken and develop a high sugar content. If potatoes are in good shape, they'll last for a few weeks at room temperature in brown paper bags with plenty of breathing room.

PREPARATION: Small potatoes are generally cooked whole, with the peel. They need no more than a thorough brushing and scrubbing under running water. A soft toothbrush works well on small knobby tubers, such as fingerlings.

Basic Petite Potatoes: Boiled or Steamed

It may seem odd to offer a recipe for plain potatoes, but there are, surprisingly, many ways to cook them. I like these two best. In general, steaming preserves the tone and appearance somewhat better, but both methods are honorable.

Most important, select potatoes of equal size so that they cook through in the same time. The texture is always more consistent when potatoes are kept whole rather than cut to matching size. How much constitutes one serving is a subject for combat. I gauge about ½ pound. Some think that's piggy—some think that's paltry.

Small potatoes of equal size
Kosher salt

SUGGESTED ACCOMPANIMENTS

Fleur de sel or other crisp sea salt
Wonderful butter
Crème fraîche or sour cream
Sturgeon or salmon eggs or other "caviar"
Fruity olive oil and snipped chives
Creamy blue cheese
Crumbled queso blanco or other fresh cheese

Taramosalata (cod roe spread)
Aïoli (garlic mayonnaise)
Common or Bronze Fennel Puree with Pasta (page 281) or pesto genovese (traditional basil pesto)

1. Clean potatoes with a vegetable brush, scrubbing assertively and rinsing well. If they are not close in size, cut the largest ones to match the smallest.

2. Combine potatoes in heavy pot with *cold* water to cover by a few inches. Add salt, gauging about 1 teaspoon per quart. Bring to a boil. (Alternatively, to steam: Set potatoes on rack over plenty of boiling water. Cover.)

3. Lower heat so that water boils gently and cook until potatoes are tender in the center when pierced with a knife tip, usually from 15 to 25 minutes, depending on size and density. Test often.

4. With skimmer, transfer potatoes to a towel. Do not pour into a colander, which risks smashing them. (If steaming, lift them out on the rack.) Either place directly in a warmed serving dish or let cool slightly, then peel (slice as well, if desired). Serve with any of the suggested accompaniments.

Perfect Butter-Baked Petite Potatoes

If you add just one recipe to your potato repertoire, make it this foolproof one-size-fits-all. No matter the shape or variety, all mini-spuds seem to take a shine to it. In fact, several varieties cooked together are most appealing. The juices concentrate and the flesh becomes tender within, chewy without, as the skins soften and sweeten. Butter quality is of paramount importance: Invest in the richest and most flavorful, whether from a domestic dairy or imported from France or Denmark.

If you are pressed for time, cook the potatoes in a single layer in a heavy pan on top of the stove instead of baking them. They will be more moist, slightly less brown, but delicious nevertheless.

1½ pounds very small potatoes
1½ tablespoons butter
½ teaspoon kosher salt
Several large rosemary sprigs
Optional: black or mixed peppercorns

1. Turn oven to 375°F. Scrub potatoes ferociously with brush to remove all soil, rootlets, and other undesirables. As size dictates, leave whole, halve, quarter, or chunk to make 1½-inch units.

2. Choose a baking dish large enough to hold potatoes in a single tight or overlapping layer. Place dish with butter in oven just until butter has melted. Add potatoes, salt, and rosemary: toss to coat. Cover closely with foil.

3. Bake until thoroughly tender (no al dente centers), about 40 minutes, shaking dish now and then to redistribute potatoes. Uncover dish, raise heat to 425°F and roast until potatoes are lightly browned, about 20 minutes, tossing a few times. Grind over pepper.

Serves 4

Pros Propose

Humble little potatoes demand rich complements: butter, cream, and truffles, to name a few. Cream in two forms enriches **Warm Potato Salad with Crème Fraîche,** from *Chez Panisse Vegetables* by Alice Waters and the Cooks of Chez Panisse: Boil new-crop Bintje potatoes in skins until tender; drain. When cool, cut into ¼-inch slices. Combine fine-diced shallots in small pan with heavy cream and salt and pepper. Cook gently to soften, but not to reduce cream. Off heat, stir in crème fraîche. Add potatoes, season with sherry vinegar, and warm gently.

Cream is the medium of choice for Lydie Marshall, teacher and author. Her **Creamed Potatoes with Peas** couldn't be simpler: Steam small peeled Yukon Gold or Yellow Finnish potatoes until tender. Meanwhile, boil half-and-half with tarragon sprigs. Add fresh peas and simmer until tender. Discard tarragon, add potatoes, and heat through (from *A Passion for Potatoes*).

Chef Hubert Keller, who specializes in elegant all-vegetable meals, pairs potatoes with the "other tuber," *Tuber melanosporum,* in **Truffled Potatoes:** Slice rounds of peeled yellow-fleshed potatoes. In olive oil–coated earthenware terrine, toss the slices with a touch of minced garlic, onion, carrot, celery, leek whites, thyme, and julienne of black truffle. Add vegetable broth and white wine to barely cover. Set lid on top and seal with rope of paste made from flour, water, and oil. Bake 45 minutes at 400°F. Break seal and serve from terrine.

Using another exalted tuber, *Tuber magnatum,* chef Wayne Nish prepares **Baked Eggs with White Truffles and Potatoes:** Oven-bake eggs individually in small skillets in olive oil. Set each egg in a small serving bowl. Top with quartered marble-size baby potatoes sautéed in butter. Sprinkle with snipped purple basil, dill, and chervil. Shave white truffle over all.

A decidedly more rustic tone is set by **Shepherd Potatoes,** an "out-and-out favorite" of Diana Kennedy's, from *My Mexico.* Kennedy describes tiny Mexican potatoes that travel under several aliases: "*gueros* (blondes), *locos* (mad), or *silvestres* and *cimarrones* (both meaning wild)." To prepare: Heat olive oil in heavy pan. Add potatoes and salt and cook until skins begin to wrinkle, stirring occasionally. Add minced white onion, garlic, and Serrano chillis, tossing. Add chopped cilantro and lime juice and toss briefly. Add a little water, cover, and cook gently until liquid is absorbed and potatoes are tender.

San Francisco chef Reed Hearon serves **Halibut and Potatoes in Saffron:** Halve or slice tiny Yellow Finnish potatoes. Cook in an intense saffron fish broth. Drain, then bake with halibut, a little broth, olive oil, tomatoes, bay leaves, and thyme.

Lydie Marshall's recipe for **Potatoes with Shellfish** is as restrained and as flavorful: Steam mussels, then clams; set aside. Strain their broth, add olive oil, red wine vinegar, and shallots; then reduce by half. Steam Ruby Crescents; peel, slice, and toss with parsley and vinegar. Heat the shellfish broth and pour over shellfish and potatoes (from *A Passion for Potatoes*).

Chef Waldy Malouf's **All-Potato Plate** is a favorite for a Pinot Noir tasting dinner. It is made up of baked Yukon Golds scooped from the skin and pureed with horseradish, shallot, and olive oil; whole small Bintjes roasted with garlic cloves and rosemary; steamed Ozette fingerlings tossed with tomato dice and tomato oil; and a salad of purple potatoes on mixed greens with a light vinaigrette and shredded fresh white cheese.

Puffballs (*Calvatia* and *Lycoperdon* species)

Puffballs are represented by several species that range in size from a mini-marshmallow to a beach ball. "Giant puffball" is a term applied to all large puffballs in general, as well as a single species, *Calvatia gigantea* (also called *Langermannia gigantea*). The puffy dappled buns pictured are *C. cyathiformis* (called purple-spored) smaller but similar in character to the giant. Puffballs, which are common in the temperate zone in both the Northern and Southern Hemispheres, rarely make it to the market. Nature lovers who do not ordinarily forage pick them (probably because they are easy to spot and to identify), and quite a few chefs snatch them up. But I was still surprised to read in *Edible Wild Mushrooms of North America* (by David W. Fischer and Alan E. Bessette) that the puffball "is probably the world's best-known edible wild mushroom."

With a sensuous kid-glove exterior and tofu-mousse-like white interior, the creamy giant puffball and its relatives appeal to those who love mushrooms and many who don't—which may account for their popularity. Since they absorb like sponges, they can taste like garlic and butter, if that's what you fancy.

purple-spored puffballs   **diameter: 2-2½ inches**

giant puffballs   **diameter: 6-8 inches**

gem-studded puffballs   **diameter: ½-1½ inches**

The petite *Lycoperdon* species, also called common puffballs, appear on the table as pear-shaped (*Lycoperdon pyriforme*) and gem-studded (*L. perlatum*) puffballs. These miniature hassocks and chefs' hats pack more into their airy lightness (an overflowing pint weighs about 4 ounces) than one might expect: pungent and earth-scented, they have as much character as charm.

BASIC USE: Bake, sauté, or grill thick-sliced medium or large puffballs. Chef Greg Higgins cuts ½-inch slices with a salmon slicer (or bread knife), lays them on an oiled sheet pan, brushes with oil, and roasts in a moderately hot oven until tan: "The tender and delicate cutlets can be placed as is on top of risotto or pilaf made with vegetable stock for a great vegetarian entree, or finished on the grill." Or drizzle with a thin vegetable coulis and sprinkle with toasted almond slivers. Sauté like veal cutlets: Dredge in seasoned flour, dip into eggs, then crumbs, then brown in butter.

For small species, deep-fry: Dip into egg and milk, then into superfine crumbs, and deep-fry for a crunchy-creamy appetizer. Or toss in butter and gild slowly in a pan. Serve as a garnish for risotto, mild poultry, or veal; or blot to remove excess butter and float in broth. The little white balloons look like pearl onions and deflate fairly quickly, but they have a delightful texture, popping in the mouth to reveal the creamy interior.

SELECTION: Giant puffballs show up intermittently in all but the cold seasons. If firm and uniformly white within (there should be no hint of color), they are edible. They should sound hollow when thumped and bounch back when pressed. Check for traces of insects.

Miniature puffballs are likely to arrive in summer to late fall. Their interior must be creamy, with no sign of yellowing.

STORAGE: Refrigerate both large and small species in an uncovered basket. Large ones, picked in good condition, will last up to a week. Small ones are extremely perishable but can be dried easily and maintain fine flavor. To dry them, trim bases and spread on a sheet pan. Set in turned-off oven with pilot light until dried throughout (or use a dehydrator). Cool and pack airtight.

PREPARATION: Puffballs, large and small, are among the few mushrooms you can spray with water; the skin—if it is not broken—protects the interior. Trim the puckered base ("neck"). Set on a towel to dry.

Salad of Roasted Puffball Slices with Pears and Endive

Large golden slices of giant puffball look somewhat like French toast—and taste a bit similar too. Bosc pear julienne and Belgian endive crescents in hazelnut-lemon dressing offer sweet, bitter, and crisp accents for the mild, soft, eggy puffball.

> 2 tablespoons lemon juice
> ½ teaspoon kosher salt
> 1 teaspoon minced shallot
> Pinch of white pepper
> 1½ tablespoons hazelnut oil
> 2 tablespoons melted butter
> 2 medium Belgian (or red) endives
> 1-pound giant puffball (7 to 8 inches in diameter)
> 2 medium Bosc pears
> 2 tablespoons chopped chervil (or slivered basil)

1. Turn oven to 475°F. Blend lemon juice and salt in small dish. Transfer half to a second dish. Add shallot, pepper, and oil to one dish; add butter to the other. Core endives and rinse. Halve lengthwise and cut into thin crosswise slices. Place in a mixing bowl.

2. Rinse puffball, rub off soil, and trim base. Pat dry. Halve with very sharp knife. Trim a thin slice from each "cheek." Cut puffball into ¾-inch slices (about 16). Arrange closely on large baking sheet. Stir butter mixture and paint slices very sparingly with it, using just half. Flip slices and paint evenly with remainder.

3. Bake slices until golden and center is creamy, about 10 minutes.

4. Meanwhile, quarter and core pears. Cut 2 quarters into thin lengthwise slices. Arrange a "spray" on each plate. Cut remainder into julienne. Toss with endive, chervil, and all but ½ tablespoon shallot dressing. Arrange on the plates.

5. With spatula, flip hot slices onto plates, dividing evenly and overlapping. Brush with remaining dressing. Serve immediately.

Serves 4

Sautéed Giant Puffball Dice with Dill and Tomato

Large puffball dice seasoned with garlic-lemon oil and gilded in a dry pan wind up looking more like fried mozzarella than mushrooms. The puffy pieces are tossed with tomato dice and dill for a touch of moisture, color, and herbal freshness.

2 tablespoons olive oil
1 large garlic clove, halved
2 strips lemon zest
½ teaspoon kosher salt
2 teaspoons rice vinegar
1-pound giant puffball
1 pound ripe tomatoes
Pepper
About 3 tablespoons minced dill

1. Combine oil, garlic, and zest in small microwavable dish. Cover with paper towel and heat on low power until very fragrant, about 2 minutes. (Alternatively, heat over lowest heat in tiny pan on stovetop.) Dissolve ¼ teaspoon salt in vinegar and add to oil.

2. Rinse puffball and rub off soil. Trim base and pat dry. Halve with very sharp knife. With cut side down, cut into 1-inch slices, then into cubes. Place in a very large bowl.

3. Strain oil, reserving solids. Gradually add oil to puffball, tossing constantly to coat well. Mince 1 teaspoon reserved garlic (or more to taste) and ¼ teaspoon lemon zest.

4. Peel tomatoes (see Note, page 10). Halve and squeeze out seeds. Cut into ½-inch pieces. Toss with remaining ¼ teaspoon salt in sieve; let drain. Set a large serving dish in oven. Turn heat to lowest setting.

5. Heat large non-stick skillet over moderately high heat. Add half the puffball dice and cook, tossing, until nicely browned and creamy inside, about 6 minutes; reduce heat if cubes brown too quickly. Transfer to dish in oven. Repeat browning with remaining puffball. Add to dish in oven.

6. Add minced garlic, lemon zest, and tomatoes to pan and cook just to soften slightly and get juices bubbling, about 2 minutes. Scoop onto puffballs, add dill, and toss to distribute evenly. Serve hot.

Serves 4 as a side dish

Pros Propose

Chef Michel Nischan serves little pear-shaped puffballs in a witty dish, **Seared Nantucket Scallops with Puffballs,** that has diners peering at their plates to figure out which is which: Slice a snippet from each "cheek" of puffball so the sides are flat; then cut into 2 or 3 thick slices. Pat slices with paper towel dipped in grapeseed oil steeped with chopped roasted almonds and seasoned. Sear slices in dry pan; move to the side. Add scallop slices and cook very briefly, letting juices mingle with puffballs. Quickly layer both on warmed plates and decorate with purslane. Serve hot.

Nischan uses the same technique for giant puffballs in his **Wild Green Salad with Puffballs and Chestnuts:** Cut thick slices of giant puffball. Pat with towel dipped in lemon-scented extra-virgin olive oil; season. Sear in dry pan over moderate heat to brown lightly; remove and set aside. Add more oil to pan and heat roasted, sliced chestnuts. Add a dash of balsamic; set aside. Crumble goat cheese over lamb's quarters, mizuna, and small mild greens. Add olive oil to pan, add greens, and toss. Set mushroom slices in center of large plates and arrange greens and chestnuts around.

It seems that puffballs are especially favored in warm salads. Chef Daniel Bruce adds pleasing smokiness to his **Wood-Grilled Giant Puffball and Cider-Tossed Cress Salad:** Cut puffball into ¾-inch slices. Combine olive oil, silver thyme, a hint of garlic, sage, salt, and pepper and brush slices lightly on both sides. Cook on wood-fired grill, flipping to cook both sides. Set slices on large plates and top with salad of mixed cresses tossed in dressing of apple cider and cider vinegar, salted fine-chopped shallots, and olive oil. Scatter dried apple chips and toasted nuts over. Serve warm.

For **Browned Puffball Slices with Herbed Salad,** chef Alex Lee sautés the slices as cutlets: Choose puffballs the size of small cantaloupes. Cut into ¼-inch slices. Dredge in seasoned flour, then eggs, then panko (Japanese bread crumbs). Sauté in brown butter. Add capers, diced lemon, tomato confit, chopped olives, and confetti of basil and flat-leaf parsley. Serve with a small herb salad on top.

For restaurants, foie gras appetizers are de rigueur these days. Daniel Bruce, who gathers his own mushrooms, says that "tiny pear-shaped puffballs are most charming when they float on clear consommé." For **Consommé with Caramelized Puffballs and Foie**

Gras Croustades: Prepare consommé from assorted game bird carcasses and parts. Clarify. Brown trimmed puffballs in clarified butter in a non-stick pan with salt and white pepper ("do it quickly, or the little sponges absorb too much fat"). Drain on towel. Sear and roast foie gras. Cut into slices, set on grilled baguette slices, and sprinkle with minced herbs. Set puffballs on consommé. Serve croustades alongside.

Chef Anthony Ambrose follows the luxury route with a technique that may interest other chefs: baking whole puffballs in plastic until they are creamy and puffed, soufflé-like. To prepare **Puffball in Foie Gras–Lillet Sauce:** Choose tennis ball–size puffballs. Coat with olive oil, salt, pepper, and rosemary. Wrap tightly in plastic. Bake in 300°F oven until expanded and interior reaches 105° to 110°F. "Since puffball is unfamiliar, I pair it with a foie gras and Lillet sauce for a sure draw," he explains. Puree raw foie gras. Whip into a near-glaze reduction of Lillet and shallots. Add chervil and pinch of turmeric; strain. Remove wrapper from puffball. Serve at once (it collapses like a soufflé), with the sauce.

Purslane *(Portulaca oleracea)*

Also pussley, pursley, verdolagas (Latin American)

½ **actual size**

"I learned . . . that a man may use as simple a diet as the animals, and yet retain health and strength. I have made a satisfactory dinner off a dish of purslane *(Portulaca oleracea)* which I gathered in my corn field," wrote Henry David Thoreau in *Walden* (1854), "yet men have come to such a pass that they frequently starve, not for want of necessaries, but for want of luxuries."

What would Thoreau make of a dish of purslane that fetches fifteen dollars on a present-day menu? Once frugal fare, wild foods are now stars in sumptuous dining rooms. "Necessaries" have become luxuries. The odd turnaround has reintroduced foods lost to the tempo of the times. Purslane is now being gathered and cultivated in North America after roughly

a century of neglect, thanks in large part to haute cuisine.

Purslane was not neglected by some of the continent's earliest inhabitants. "Purslane was one of the most important wild plant foods for the Ancestral Puebloans and probably for their predecessors as well," write William W. Dunmire and Gail D. Tierny in *Wild Plants and Native Peoples of the Four Corners.* "Shiny black purslane seeds have been recovered from prehistoric hearths . . . at Salmon Run on the San Juan River, . . . at Chaco Canyon, Mesa Verde, and Canyon de Chelly and almost every other Ancestral Puebloan site that has been analyzed for ancient food consumption."

So ancient and widespread is purslane's culinary history worldwide that it makes more sense to call it a lost-and-found vegetable than a wild one. The plant has not been forgotten in India—its probable birthplace—Africa, Australia, China, Europe, or Central America, so it is not in danger of disappearing from the table, even if North Americans forget about it again.

"Garden purslaine, being used as a salad herb, is so well known that it needeth no description," wrote Nicholas Culpeper in his popular book *The English Physician, or Herball* (first published in 1653, it went through many editions). In 1699, John Evelyn said in *Acetaria: A Discourse of Sallets* that purslane "being eminently moist and cooling [is] generally entertain'd in all our sallets, mingled with the hotter Herbs: 'Tis likewise familiarly eaten alone with Oyl and Vinegar."

Yet here we are, after 300 years of fickle fashion, in need of a description—which follows: Perky purslane has oval, juicy-slippery, medium green or yellow-green leaves (more like pads) and a mild, fresh flavor brightened by a tart finish. Wild purslane (it grows naturally in most organic gardens, so "wild" seems an exaggeration) and cultivated purslane can be quite different (see Selection). At its best (usually wild), purslane has a sorrel tang and hint of tomato; mediocre purslane (usually cultivated), can be bland and slimy but still looks cute.

BASIC USE: Sprigs of purslane make a charming and tasty garnish. Tuck into sandwiches, tacos, and spring rolls; or set atop canapés. Chop purslane to fold (as you would celery) into mayonnaise-based salads: chicken, egg, tuna, potato, or shrimp. As in past centuries, purslane shines in green salads—particularly in concert with an assortment of small, flavorful leaves. Purslane benefits from the company of tomato, onion relatives, parsley, dill, mint, coriander, and citrus, among others. Blend with herbs and oil or sour cream or buttermilk for a dip or dressing. For soups, cook purslane stems with broth to add a little body and slickness, then stir in the leaves to just heat through. Steam or sauté for a minute or two to bring out its earthy side—which is just the right underpinning for fish. Do *not* microwave.

SELECTION: Both cultivated and wild purslane have delights and disadvantages. Texture and taste are highly variable: You must sample purslane to know whether it is tender, taut, flabby, fibrous, fresh, tart, bland, or boring—or various combinations thereof.

Wild purslane is a summer crop. At the start of the season, it is small-leafed, thin-stemmed, delicately fleshy, lightly mucilaginous—and entirely edible. It tastes refreshing, citric, and distinct. At the end of summer, its heavy, pink-streaked stems become too tart and fibrous to eat, but the leaves, now of varying sizes, can be succulent and sapid. (The zillions of tiny black seeds that rain from the plant—and look disconcertingly like cockroach eggs—are edible and good.) Whether young or old, wild purslane has a tangly growing habit and picks up dirt, plants, and whatnot. It requires considerable trimming and washing to be table-ready—unless an excellent purveyor has done the job.

Cultivated purslane is primarily a summer crop, but it shows up erratically at other times as well. It may be green-leafed (see photo) or yellowish (a popular cultivar). The plump stems are tender. Waste is minimal to nil. The flavor is always less assertive than that of noncultivated purslane, and the leaves are sometimes overblown and oversized—not tart and trim.

STORAGE: Spread in a basket and refrigerate. Purchased fresh, purslane lasts for a week. Authorities recommend blanching and freezing, but my cultivated greens turned into a disgusting gray-green mass of no redeeming value when blanched.

PREPARATION: Wild purslane usually requires a good deal of cleaning: Cut off roots, if any. Early season purslane is all tender and edible, except the heaviest stalks (sample to find out). Later in the summer, most stems become too fibrous. Snip branchlets from the heavy main stems. Rinse gently; lift out to leave debris behind. Cut into bite-size sprigs. Dry for use in raw preparations.

Cultivated purslane is usually as edible as water cress. Sometimes the lower stems must be removed, sometimes they are tender. Cut into manageable pieces, rinse, and blot dry for salads.

Purslane Dressing or Dip

Crisp snippets of citric purslane stud this creamy, herbal sauce. Serve it with an array of blanched and raw vegetables and bread sticks as an hors d'oeuvre; or spoon over poached salmon. To turn the dip into dressing, puree to a finer texture and add a little more sour cream. Serve with cooked beets, carrots, summer squash, or other mild vegetables for a salad course or side dish.

¼ pound purslane (without roots)
2 scallions (green onions), sliced
1 or 2 small green chillis, seeded
¾ cup tightly packed cilantro (coriander) leaves
½ teaspoon kosher salt
About ⅓ cup sour cream
About 2 tablespoons lemon juice

1. Rinse purslane. Cut off any heavy stalks as needed. Combine in food processor container with scallions, chillis, cilantro, and salt. Chop medium-fine.

2. Add ⅓ cup sour cream and 2 tablespoons lemon juice and whiz to desired texture. Adjust tartness and thickness with additional sour cream and lemon juice, if desired.

Makes about 1½ cups

Purslane and Citrus Salad

Tart and cleansing, this unusual salad makes double use of purslane: as pureed dressing and as salad green. The dressing is bright pistachio, thick, and flecked with crunchy bits. The fat little leaves, slightly slippery, provide colorful contrast to the citrus slices.

½ pound purslane (without roots)
⅓ cup tightly packed peppermint or
    spearmint leaves
¼ teaspoon kosher salt
Optional: 1 small green chilli, seeded
1 tablespoon lemon juice
3 tablespoons olive oil
1 navel orange
1 very small grapefruit
1 very small red onion

1. Rinse purslane. Cut off and discard any heavy stems. Cut remainder into bite-size sprigs (about 1 quart, using cultivated purslane). Place 1 cup in food processor container, with mint, salt, and optional chillis; mince. Add lemon juice and olive oil and whiz to a smooth puree. Chill dressing and sprigs.

2. Cut rind, pith, and membrane from orange and grapefruit. Halve orange, then slice thin. Cut between grapefruit membranes to section out flesh. Peel, halve, and thin-slice onion; separate layers.

3. Arrange chilled purslane sprigs on platter, then oranges and grapefruit. Top with onion. Spoon dressing over all in a pretty pattern.

Serves 4

Tart Purslane-Coriander Broth with Lemony Fish

No need for stock making here, thanks to bottled Chinese oyster sauce, which gives depth to the briefly simmered aromatics. Widely available, the sweetly smoky seasoning is at its best when made of few ingredients—oyster being the first. The purslane stems lend a little body and slickness to the broth. The leaves add decided crunch and color—but will turn gray if allowed to cook: Just stir into the hot soup to wilt a bit. Find cilantro with its roots attached. They scent the soup more assertively than stems alone.

1 bunch cilantro (coriander), with roots intact
1 quart water
6 ounces purslane (without roots)
3 medium scallions (green onions), trimmed
2 celery stalks (preferably with leaves)
Optional: 1 small fresh or dried chilli
1 lemon, well scrubbed
About 2 tablespoons Chinese oyster sauce
4 to 6 ounces boned and skinned firm
    white fish fillet
Salt and pepper
About 3 tablespoons lime juice

1. Cut stems and roots from cilantro. Wash them well (stems need scrubbing with a brush) and combine in saucepan with water. Rinse purslane. Trim off most stalks and add to pan. Break remaining leafy sprigs into 1-inch pieces as necessary; reserve.

2. Cut paler parts from scallions; slice and add to pan. Slice celery; add with optional chilli. Strip half zest from lemon; add to pan, with 2 tablespoons oyster sauce. Simmer, covered, 10 minutes.

3. Meanwhile, chop enough cilantro leaves to yield 2 tablespoons. Grate remaining lemon zest and combine with chopped cilantro. Sprinkle fish with salt and pepper, then pat cilantro mixture onto both sides.

4. Remove chilli, if used, from broth. Pour contents of pan into sieve set over bowl and press to extract all liquid. Add 2 tablespoons lime juice to broth. Taste and add oyster sauce and lime juice. Return to saucepan.

5. Heat broth. Meanwhile, cut fish into small dice. Add to broth and cook just until almost opaque, 1 to 2 minutes, depending upon thickness. Stir in purslane sprigs and remove from heat.

6. Ladle into small bowls and serve at once.

Serves 4 as a first course

Pros Propose

Salads are the most popular purslane category, thanks to the vegetable's special slippery crunch and the cooling properties that make it a favorite in hot climes. Barbara Kirshenblatt-Gimblett was inspired by the purslane salads she tasted in Jerusalem to evolve her own summer medley: "The palette is forest green, burgundy red, and white; the texture crisp and succulent; the flavor peppery and tart, with an aromatic hit of mint or perilla or red basil, depending on what is on hand." For **Colorful Middle Eastern Salad:** Combine trimmed, coarse-chopped purslane with dice of unpeeled greenhouse cucumber, daikon, sweet onion, fennel, and purple bell pepper. Arrange with sliced red mustard, sunflower sprouts, preserved lemon bits, and sliced perilla or purple basil. Dress with fruity olive oil and lemon juice.

Sweet-earthy beets and crisp-sour purslane make a fine pair. Chef Todd Humphries, who has the wonderful trial garden at the Culinary Institute of America at Greystone to pick from, combines baby golden and Chioggia beets for **Roasted Beet and Purslane Salad with Tarragon Vinaigrette:** Toss beets with a little water and olive oil in a baking pan; cover and roast until tender. Peel, then cool. Quarter. Toss beets with tarragon vinaigrette and a few haricots verts. Toss purslane sprigs with same dressing and set on top. Serve at room temperature.

Like salicornia (page 548), purslane is the perfect subject for frittata. Surrounded by the egg mixture, it is protected as it barely cooks to just the right texture. For his **Purslane Frittata,** chef Jean-Georges Vongerichten uses only the small wild plants. The larger cultivated purslane becomes too flabby when cooked. To prepare: Gently cook chopped shallots in butter. Add coarse-chopped small purslane sprigs and toss to just barely wilt. Add beaten eggs and bake in oven until not quite set.

Cooked purslane is a familiar vegetable throughout Mexico, where it is called verdolagas. For **Isaac Uribe Romo's Purslane with Potatoes in Green Sauce:** Simmer husked, rinsed tomatillos until they change color. Drain and cool. Sauté chopped onion, garlic, and chillis. Combine in blender with tomatillos and puree. Sauté cooked potato dice in olive oil with thick-sliced onion. Add the sauce and chopped cilantro; simmer to blend. Add purslane (about the same weight as potatoes) and cook 2 minutes. Serve at once (from *Meatless Mexican Home Cooking* by Nancy Zaslavsky).

Radicchio *(Cichorium intybus)*

Including **Chioggia, Verona, Treviso,** and **Castelfranco types**

Radicchio (pronounced rah-DEEK-eeyo) is the Italian word for all members of the chicory clan, whether green, cream, red, striped, or marbled. But in restaurants and markets in the United States and Canada, the term "radicchio" has come to signify predominantly red-leafed varieties: You could easily think it means "red."

Five Northern Italian varieties, each named for its growing region, are preeminent. By far the most common, **Chioggia** (or rosa di Chioggia), has become synonymous with "radicchio" in the United States: Rounded, compact, Chianti-colored, its chewy-crunchy, characteristically bittersweet leaves tend more toward the bitter. Similar, but far less common, is **Verona,** a more elongated head of exceptionally bright color. **Early Treviso** resembles a small ruby-clad romaine with nacreous ribs. The slender pearl and garnet shoots of hard-to-find **Late Treviso** (I couldn't find it for the photo) swirl like the tail feathers of a tropical bird; their flavor is like assertive Belgian endive. Equally

radicchio: Castelfranco (*top left*), Verona (*bottom left*), Chioggia (*top right*), Early Treviso (*bottom right*)   ¼ **actual size**

uncommon is the mildest and tenderest **Castelfranco,** a softly crumpled rose of wine-speckled cream or yellow, the most lettuce-like of chicories.

Whether Bordeaux or ivory, all radicchio begins as green leafy clusters. Some gradually turns red and changes shape; some doesn't. All resist reddening without sufficiently cold temperatures. Charmingly inconsistent, chicories go their own way no matter how you try to tame them into categories or predictable forms.

This may be why the people who have made an art of raising radicchio—the farmers of the Veneto—still send us a goodly percentage of our crop. When the glamorous redheads arrived from Italy in the 1970s, a number of optimistic American growers tried their hand at cultivation, but few stayed with it. Finally, however, this tricky chicory has taken root in California—on about 4,000 acres. In fact, the world's largest grower of radicchio is European Vegetable Specialties Farms, in Salinas. It was started in 1988 by two Italians, Lucio Gomiero and Carlo Boscolo, who teamed up with local growers and now tend their crops in both countries. The growing area has increased to follow California's climatic shifts through the seasons, and the men have even come to favor the somewhat less bitter products of California—made especially attractive by the potential for year-round production (in Italy, the crop is limited to winter).

That we have embraced radicchio at all seems to me proof positive of the American passions for things Italian, red, and raw. It is unlikely that the bitterness Europeans find so attractive is the major selling point in the United States.

I asked Dennis Donohue, vice president of marketing for European Vegetable Specialties, why radicchio is so popular. "The color red and the rise of the fresh-cut industry," he replied immediately. "About half our radicchio goes to processors for salad mixes," because radicchio retains its firm texture and glowing color longer than lettuces.

Salad may be important commercially, but that is just the tip of the Iceberg (lettuce). "What is most amazing about radicchio is its flavor when cooked, as Italians know," says Donohue, who doesn't need to convince me, or many chefs in the United States. We just need to convince those who eat with their eyes only that brown is beautiful. As the garnet cooks to a warm tobacco color, the leaves develop a sweet, mellow flavor and a supple texture. Most memorable dishes are made from cooked food that's brown, not red.

BASIC USE

Raw: Radicchio is the salad-bowl and garnish leaf par excellence; firm Treviso or small Chioggia leaves enhance a platter of crudités as dipping or cupping tools. Radicchio keeps its firm texture, hue, and flavor when it is sliced into simple mixed greens or complex combinations of cooked meat, fish, pasta, beans, and grains. Whether dressed with sharp or mild and creamy flavors, it is best mixed with other leaves, for its bitterness can be overbearing and monotonous. Or use whole leaves as baskets to hold salads for buffets and picnics. Save Castelfranco for delicate salads.

Cooked: Sauté slivered leaves briefly in olive oil, then fold into pasta or beans or sautéed vegetables. Cut solid radicchio heads into wedges (or halve small heads), coat with seasoned olive oil, then grill until softened but not limp. Stirred into thick soups and stews and cooked slowly, radicchio (even when less than prime) imparts a depth, earthiness, and rich dark color especially welcome in vegetarian meals. Blanch large radicchio leaves and make packets of fish fillets, then steam. Or enclose cheese or highly seasoned foods in blanched leaves, oil lightly, then grill for appetizers.

Most recipes for flat-leaf endive (escarole), Belgian endive, and curly endive (chicory or frisée) are suitable for radicchio.

SELECTION: Radicchio is available year-round. The Italian imports, however, are primarily a winter crop. Generally speaking, warmer weather produces radicchio that is greener and more bitter.

Although radicchio keeps very well, it is difficult to find in good shape—thanks to shopkeepers who drown it, keep it indefinitely because it's slow to show age, and then pare down obviously old heads, presenting them as fresh.

To avoid "new" old heads, look for large plants, which are less likely to have been trimmed down and also have proportionally less core and a better trimmed yield. Choose relatively heavy, dense ones, hefting to compare. They should feel not spongy but solid—almost like red cabbage. Avoid wetness, which hastens breakdown. Browning at the stem end is normal. A few browned outer leaves can be removed, but the inner layers should be in good shape.

STORAGE: For optimum quality, keep radicchio in plastic at the coldest refrigerator temperature for no more than a week. When it will be cooked, radicchio can be held longer. Although bitterness seems to increase in storage, the leaves will look fine for weeks.

PREPARATION: If you will be cutting heads into wedges or slices for grilling or roasting, do not remove the core, but trim the base slightly. For other cooking methods, remove the core, cutting from the base. Break off leaves and trim as needed. Rinse and spin-dry. Wrap and chill for salad. Slice into small pieces as needed, not beforehand. To crisp tired leaves, soak for 2 to 3 minutes in lukewarm water, shake dry, then chill in an airtight container until serving time.

Salad of Treviso, Enokitake, Water Cress, and Hazelnuts

Bright, curved Late Treviso "petals," if available, set a dramatic tone maintained by long-stemmed, bright-white enokitake (see page 269, if you're not familiar with the little mushrooms). Chopsticks are my utensil of choice for this and other salads made of small slippery bits (you will never use a fork again once you've discovered how efficient they are). If enokitake are elusive, substitute julienned white button mushrooms tossed with lemon juice. To toast and husk hazelnuts, see Note, page 175.

> 2 tablespoons sherry vinegar
> ½ teaspoon honey
> ¼ teaspoon kosher salt
> Pepper
> 3 tablespoons hazelnut oil
> 1 tablespoon peanut oil
> 1 bunch water cress
> About ½ pound small Treviso heads
>   (Late or Early variety)
> ½ cup toasted, husked hazelnuts
> 3 to 4 ounces (or 1 packet) enoki
>   mushrooms

1. Combine vinegar, honey, salt, and pepper; whisk in both oils.

2. Trim and discard any heavy cress stems. Rinse and spin-dry cress, then break into equal bite-size sprigs.

3. Cut bases from radicchio and separate leaves. Rinse and pat dry on towel. Slice half the leaves into narrow bite-size strips, and keep the remainder whole (or halve, if large).

4. Combine cress and sliced radicchio in serving bowl. Chop hazelnuts medium-coarse and add. Trim enough off the enoki base to separate most stems, then add mushrooms to bowl. Add dressing and toss gently. Tuck radicchio spears around bowl's edge. Serve at once.

Serves 4

Risotto of Radicchio

Lorna Sass, author of several fine books on pressure cooking, reintroduced risotto to my busy life several years ago when she won me over to her speedy method, which not only eliminates tedious stirring but produces grains of a luscious consistency. (To prepare by the traditional method, proceed through step 2, then see Note.)

Because the moisture content of radicchio is high, this earthy-sweet risotto needs less broth than others, and its texture is lighter. Like all cooked radicchio dishes, the coloring is brown, not bright. Use any imported Italian rice for risotto: arborio, baldo, carnaroli, or vialone nano.

> About ½ pound Chioggia radicchio
> 2 tablespoons olive oil
> 1 large red onion, diced
> 2 large garlic cloves, minced
> ½ teaspoon dried thyme
> 4 oil-packed anchovy fillets, chopped
> 1½ cups Italian rice for risotto
> ½ cup fruity dry red wine
> 1½ tablespoons balsamic vinegar
> Pepper
> About 3½ cups mushroom, meat, or vegetable
>   broth (or a blend)
> About 1 teaspoon kosher salt (omit if broth is
>   salted)
> About 1½ cups grated Parmesan cheese

1. Cut conical core from radicchio. Quarter head and slice thin, as for slaw. You should have about 4 lightly packed cups.

2. Heat oil in pressure cooker over moderate heat. Add onion, garlic, thyme, and anchovies; sauté 1 minute. Add rice and toss another minute. Add wine and stir to evaporate. Add 3 cups sliced radicchio, vinegar, and pepper and toss a few minutes to wilt.

3. Add 3 cups broth and ½ teaspoon salt. Lock lid in place; bring to high pressure. Cook 5 minutes. Run lid under cold water to release pressure. Open lid.

4. Return pot to heat. Stir a few minutes until rice is done to taste, adding more broth as needed to create a fairly loose consistency. When cooked to taste, stir in remaining sliced radicchio, salt, and about ½ cup cheese.

5. Serve immediately in warmed shallow bowls, with more cheese and a pepper mill alongside.

**Serves 4 as a main course,
6 to 7 as a first course**

Note: To prepare risotto in standard fashion, follow directions through step 2, halving the amounts of garlic and thyme and using a heavy medium pot. Meanwhile heat broth—increase it to 5 cups—and keep at a bare simmer in a separate saucepan. Add broth ½ cup at a time to the rice mixture, adjusting heat and stirring so that liquid simmers briskly but rice does not stick or burn; stir until each portion of broth is absorbed before adding the next (to total about 20 minutes cooking time). Then continue with recipe, adding radicchio, salt, and cheese.

Sweet-Sour Wilted Radicchio with Red Onion

Maroon-to-brown shreds with a sweet-hot tang suggest red cabbage with more depth and without the crucifer taste. Use whichever types of dark red radicchio are available. Even rather tired specimens will do just fine here. Chewy, crunchy, and smoky, the bittersweet blend complements venison, pork, roast duck, ham, and other rich meats. Or serve as part of a vegetable meal with wild rice, chestnuts, and roasted or grilled meaty mushrooms.

1 large red onion
2 garlic cloves
1 to 3 small fresh chillis, preferably red
About ¾ pound dark red radicchio
¼ cup cider vinegar
½ teaspoon kosher salt
1 tablespoon honey
3 tablespoons peanut oil

1. Quarter onion and thin-slice lengthwise. Mince garlic. Seed and thin-slice chillis. Rinse radicchio and trim bases. Cut heads into very thin strips (you should have 5 to 6 cups).

2. Combine vinegar, salt, and honey, blending well. Add 2 tablespoons oil. In very wide sauté pan, heat the remaining 1 tablespoon oil over high heat. Add onion and toss to brown slightly, about 3 minutes. Add garlic and chilli and toss another minute. Add the vinegar mixture.

3. Add radicchio and toss once or twice to coat—do not wilt or cook down (the leaves will continue to cook off the heat). Remove from heat and continue tossing a moment. Serve immediately.

Serves 6 as a side dish

Angel Hair Pasta with Clams and Radicchio

Threads of bright uncooked radicchio soften when tossed with hot pasta but keep their rich hue. They not only add welcome color but complement the sea-sweet flavor and help separate the pasta strands, lightening the overall texture. Those who love an overflowing bowl of pasta but don't want to double their starch intake will enjoy the "volumized" effect.

If you can find small Manila clams, substitute a larger quantity of these juicy little gems and cook for a shorter period of time.

1 medium head red radicchio (5 to 6 ounces)
About 2 dozen small littleneck clams, scrubbed
½ cup white wine
½ cup water

½ pound imported Italian angel hair pasta
   or spaghettini
2 tablespoons olive oil
2 garlic cloves, minced
Optional: ⅛ to ¼ teaspoon chilli flakes
Salt and pepper
½ cup minced flat-leaf parsley leaves
Lemon juice

1. Rinse radicchio and trim base. Cut into extremely thin long strands. You should have about 2 cups.

2. Combine clams, wine, and water in deep sauté pan or wide heavy pot. Bring to a boil, cover, and cook at a low boil until all clams open, about 3 minutes. Check on their progress, removing smaller clams if they open first.

3. With tongs, transfer clams to a bowl. Slowly pour broth into a container, leaving any sand behind. Rinse out pan. Remove clams from shells, holding them over the broth container to catch drips.

4. Combine olive oil and garlic in rinsed pan. Cook over low heat until garlic turns very pale golden, then add optional chilli flakes. Add broth and simmer until liquid reduces slightly and flavors blend. Add clams and set aside.

5. Boil pasta in large pot of salted water until almost al dente; drain. Add to broth and stir over low heat until most is absorbed, a minute or two. Season with lemon juice, pepper, and salt. Add radicchio and toss just to warm—*not* to wilt—intermixing strands of the pasta and radicchio. Add parsley. Divide among bowls.

**Serves 2 as a main course,
4 as a first course**

Pros Propose

Radicchio grower Lucio Gomiero prepares a traditional appetizer of **Marinated Treviso Radicchio,** barely vinegar-blanched so that the colors stay bright: Cut heads of Early Treviso lengthwise into quarters. Boil bay leaf, peppercorns, and salt in three parts water to one of vinegar. Blanch wedges in this, a few at a time. Blot dry, squeezing gently. Drizzle lavishly with olive oil, then refrigerate overnight. To serve, bring to room temperature, season, and slice (or not, as desired). Garnish with chopped hard-cooked egg.

Restaurateur and chef Gianni Fassio laments, "In America, radicchio is seriously misunderstood because cooks are so often more color-conscious than taste-conscious. Treviso, in particular, tastes best cooked, whether plain-grilled, in soup, or in risotto." True to his word, he cooks it several ways. For a plain and simple **Radicchio Soup:** Gently cook radicchio strips, onions, and garlic in oil. Add beef stock and barley and cook until tender. Serve with Parmesan. For **Radicchio Grilled with Gorgonzola:** Halve or quarter Treviso, paint with oil, then grill. Cool and spread with Gorgonzola. To serve, melt under broiler "for a simple, perfect sweet and bitter match."

Gorgonzola is also favored by chef Maria Helm in a more elaborate preparation: **Grilled Radicchio, Red Onion, Gorgonzola, and Toasted Walnut Pizza:** Prepare pizza dough with chopped fresh thyme and rosemary. Toss quartered Chioggia radicchio with olive oil, salt, and pepper. Grill lightly to just wilt. Cut into ¼-inch strips and toss with sugar, balsamic vinegar, and olive oil. Roll dough thin, prick with fork, and brush with oil. Top with thin-sliced red onions, the radicchio, and Gorgonzola. Bake in hot oven until crust is crisp. Top with toasted walnuts and chopped parsley.

Radishes (*Raphanus sativus*)

Asian or Oriental Radish
Black Radish, page 527
Table Radish or Small Radish, page 530

What's black and white and red all over? Multicolored, multipurpose, multicultural radishes. But say "radish" to Americans of English or French descent, and what probably pops to mind is a cheery little crimson ball or a scarlet-tipped white oval. For some others—of Korean or Japanese heritage, for example—the word is more likely to conjure up images of tapered white cylinders or stubby green oblongs. People of Russian or Hungarian descent might picture turnip shapes, dark as charcoal. And the radish-loving Chinese might envision a half-dozen types, including softball-size globes with flesh of shocking pink (at right) or lime. Although all *Raphanus sativus* started out in the Old World, it has been cultivated and modified so extensively over such a vast area for so many centuries that its original birthplace and form are not known.

Here in the American melting pot we can find a bright bouquet of all types. Whether for crudités or to be cooked, whether in warm months or cold, the radish repertoire is burgeoning.

Beauty Heart Asian radish   diameter: 2-3 inches

Asian or Oriental Radish

(*Raphanus sativus,* Longipinnatus Group)

Also daikon (Japanese), mooli
(Indian), moo or mu (Korean),
lo bok (also lo pak) or
luo boh (Chinese)

Throughout Asia, radishes are a serious staple, no mere nibble. In China, they are often cooked; in Korea, they are usually pickled. In Japan, they are enjoyed raw, cooked, and pickled—as they are in India, Thailand, Vietnam, the Philippines, and Malaysia, among other countries.

In the United States, Asian radishes are represented in greatest number by the long white daikon—and this Japanese generic name is the one used most often. Although the daikon weighs about 1 pound in our mainstream markets, it can reach 60 pounds and still be juicy and tasty. The Japanese do not limit their relishing of radishes to this white type; they have perfected a range of beautiful varieties, from torpedo- to turnip-shape. But for anyone who has not yet experimented with the full culinary range of radishes, the smoothly tapered daikon is a good place to begin. Flexible and forgiving, requiring little labor, and widely available, it yields gracefully to all stages of preparation, from raw through the softest long-cooking.

white Asian radish (daikon)　　　　　　　　　　　　　　　　length (uncut): 21 and 16 inches

green-skinned Asian radish (moo)　　　　　　　　　　　　　length (uncut): 9 and 4 inches

Koreans (who consume every stage, size, variety and part of a radish, from leaf to root to pod, in their ubiquitous pickle, kimchee) generally choose jade-topped squat types over the long daikon. Stubby green-skinned, white-tipped varieties are typically very solid and extremely juicy, with sweeter flesh than the all-white daikon.

Chinese varieties may be green, pink, red, white, or colors in between. They usually resemble fat carrots, although a rounded turnip form is also common. Green-skinned radishes and green-fleshed radishes are both considered exceptionally delicious by connoisseurs.

Most distinctive of all is a red-meat or red-heart radish (see photo, page 522). The red-fleshed, green- or pink-skinned radishes stand apart from other Asian radishes in use (primarily raw) and looks. What I've met up with in restaurants and markets has been dubbed "watermelon radish"—a name that seems to have stuck, although there is no such name in the seed books. This innocent-looking radish, roughly the size and shape of turnip or kohlrabi, hides a flamboyant interior of borscht-pink or paler rose shot with radiating fuchsia veins. Not only stunning, it offers unusual sweetness and crunch for a sturdy winter root. At a farmers' market in California it was labeled red daikon, and in the Midwest I have heard it called Beauty Heart. The latter name is probably closest to the truth, for a red-meat radish of Chinese origin, xin li mei (also romanized as shin-rimei), translates roughly as "in one's heart beautiful."

BASIC USE

Raw: Peeled, sliced Asian radish excels as a crudité "cracker," especially topped with fish roe, tapenade, or other salty spreads. Slivered, diced, grated, or sliced, Asian radish is coolly refreshing in salads with fruit, vegetables, fish, or meat. Grated, it can serve as a simple dressing for broiled fish or meat. Chopped and mixed with hot spices, yogurt or sour cream, and cilantro, it makes a fine salsa or raita. Shredded, salted, drained, and rinsed, radish becomes a chewy filling for savory breads and pastries in India and the Far East. And no vegetable is as beloved by vegetable-carvers world-wide, particularly in China. Should you divide a large radish, part to be used raw and part cooked, keep the stem end to use raw; it is sweeter.

Cooked: Asian radishes develop the mild juiciness of young turnips when cooked. Diced and added to soup at the last moment, they swiftly become tender and mild, imparting depth to the stock—particularly in the company of mushrooms. Radish chunks added to stews and braises (like turnips in traditional lamb stew) season and sweeten while they absorb some of the cooking liquid. Roast thick radish bâtons alongside pork or chicken. Simmer radish and potatoes, then puree for a subtle, light-bodied soup. When quickly stir-fried, radish slices, strips, or cubes taste lightly turnipy. "In Chinese cuisine," says chef and author Susanna Foo, "radish is well known for its special way of adding sweetness as it removes undesirable fishiness, so it often accompanies seafood." She prefers the white Japanese type for braising and the squat green Korean or Chinese types for salads.

Radish greens: Do *not* discard any greens that are in good shape; they are all worth saving and cooking as much for their flavor as for their nutrient value. If you won't be cooking them with the radishes, reserve for braising along with other bitter greens, or add to stuffings for meat or ravioli, or include in fried-rice mixtures or bean dishes.

SELECTION: Large white and greenish Asian radishes are in the market year-round. Fall and winter radishes are most flavorful and mellow; spring and summer ones are slightly hotter but weaker in flavor. Choose *very* firm, smooth roots with a luminous sheen, not matte opacity (a sign of age in radishes as well as people). Smaller is not necessarily better: Quality can be consistent whether a radish is 1 or 4 inches in diameter, 8 or 18 inches long. If possible, choose roots with greens, which not only are delightful cooked but indicate the freshness of the vegetable.

Red-fleshed radishes are at their best from fall into late winter, after which they become pithy and dry. Andrew Brait, a co-owner of Full Belly Farm near Davis, California, had been growing these flavorful beauties for eight years when I met him at the Marin County Market for my first taste. He sells them bunched with their leaves, "which always tell the tale when it comes to freshness." His advice is to "look for pinkness at the taproot to be sure of a colorful interior." He finds those no larger than a tennis ball to be most reliable in quality but adds that grapefruit-size radishes can also be fine. "The skin should be fairly smooth, without deep cracks—which show over-maturity. If they're sold without greens, check the crown to be sure they're not putting energy into growing seed stalks."

STORAGE: Large Asian radishes, despite their sturdy appearance, do not store well. Wrap and refrigerate greens and radishes separately. Store radishes just a few days if you'll be serving them raw. For cooking, a week's refrigeration is fine. "But there is a better way," says chef Anita Lo. "When I worked at Bouley [in New York], they buried daikon in soil for long keeping. We had truckloads delivered from farmers upstate, and we filled little garbage cans with earth—and just dug the radishes in."

Radish greens are highly perishable. Keep a few days, at most.

PREPARATION: The condition of the radish skin, which varies with type, growing environment, and handling, will determine what preparation is required. Some daikon may want no more than a scrubbing with a brush. Generally, the colored varieties need to be peeled more deeply than white ones. Radish greens demand serious washing; they should be sloshed around vigorously in several changes of water, then lifted out so that silt and sand sink to the bottom.

Basic Asian Radish Sauté

This simple prototype is to remind newcomers to Asian radish that it can be cooked with little effort for a quick side dish. If herbal flavors better suit your meal, omit the ginger and orange and toss in 2 teaspoons each of minced dill or cilantro and snipped chives.

> ¾-pound slim white or green-tinged
>   Asian radish
> 1 small navel orange
> 1 tablespoon vegetable oil
> ½ teaspoon sugar
> ¼ teaspoon kosher salt
> 1 teaspoon hair-thin ginger julienne

1. Scrub radish, then peel lightly. If very narrow, cut across into thin slices; if too wide for tidy mouthfuls, halve lengthwise, then cut into slightly thicker half-moons. Scrub orange, then grate about ¼ teaspoon zest. Cut a few slices for garnish.

2. Heat skillet or wok over moderately high heat, then add oil. Add radish and toss over high heat to coat. Add sugar and salt. Reduce heat to moderate and toss 2 minutes. Add ginger and orange zest and toss

until radish loses its raw crunch, 2 to 3 minutes longer.

3. Transfer to a warm serving dish. Garnish with orange slices.

Serves 2 as a side dish

Sautéed Red-Heart Radish

A spectacular side with the benefits of both cooked and raw radish, this quick sauté looks and tastes remarkable. Shredded and sautéed, the radish has a less flamboyant appearance but retains much of its al dente deliciousness. Moist—not wet—the meaty, sweet vegetable agreeably accompanies roasted pork, duck, turkey, ham, or chicken. Its rosy hue makes even the most ordinary dish seem festive.

> 1 pound red-fleshed Asian radishes
> 1 tablespoon butter
> ¼ teaspoon kosher salt

1. Trim tops, if any, from radishes and save for another use. Trim and discard tips. Peel radishes. Slice on the shredding blade of a food processor. You'll have about 2 cups.

2. Melt butter in fairly wide skillet. Add radishes and toss over high heat until well coated. Reduce heat and add salt.

3. Cover and cook gently until radishes no longer taste raw, about 5 minutes, stirring several times to prevent sticking. Add a few drops of water if radishes look as if they might scorch. Do not sear, since browning changes the flavor.

4. Season and serve hot.

Serves 4 as a side dish

Buttery Asian Radishes with Their Greens

Big white radishes stewed gently with their sharp greens become mild and juicy. Sweet carrot confetti forms a crisp complement. The speedily assembled side dish suits quick-cooked seafood or meat. Use whichever type of large radish is available—moo, daikon, or lo bok. If greens are not attached, buy them separately. About 1 pound radish to ½ pound greens is a nice balance—but just about any proportion will be pleasing.

> 1½ pounds large Asian radishes with greens
> 1 tablespoon plus 1 to 2 teaspoons butter
> ¼ cup water
> ¼ teaspoon kosher salt
> 1 or 2 medium carrots, minced (to make ½ cup)

1. Separate radish tops and roots. Discard any yellowing leaves and heavy stalk bases. Rinse greens well in several changes of water. Chop quite fine. Peel radishes deeply (reserve peel for Spicy-Hot Radish-Skin Condiment with Orange Zest, following). Quarter lengthwise, then cut across into ½-inch slices.

2. Combine radishes, greens, 1 tablespoon butter, the water, and salt in large skillet. Bring to a boil. Reduce heat, cover, and simmer until radishes are tender, about 10 minutes, stirring occasionally.

3. Add minced carrots. Cook, tossing, to evaporate most liquid, if necessary (if mixture is particularly juicy, raise heat to cook quickly, so carrots will not lose their punctuating crunch). Taste for seasoning. Off heat, add remaining butter to taste.

Serves 4 as a side dish

Spicy-Hot Radish-Skin Condiment with Orange Zest

Save up daikon skins in the refrigerator whenever you pare radishes so you'll have enough for this unlikely condiment. Hot, sweet, and bitter, the dense skin has an appealing crunch that is quite different from the juicy flesh. Serve a spoonful of the vibrant mixture, hot or chilled, to accent roasted pork, grilled chicken, and bean or grain dishes.

> 2 cups daikon radish peel (6 to 7 ounces)
> 1 or 2 oranges, well scrubbed
> 2 teaspoons Asian (dark) sesame oil
> ¼ teaspoon kosher salt
> ¼ teaspoon ground hot pepper
> Optional: toasted sesame seeds and/or sliced cilantro (coriander) leaves

1. Rinse radish skins thoroughly; drain. Spread on cutting board so that they lie flat. Cut into thin diagonals about 1 inch long.

2. Pare off a few strips of orange zest. Cut enough into hair-thin strips to make ½ tablespoon. Halve and squeeze juice from the pared orange. If there is less than ½ cup, squeeze the second orange to make that amount.

3. Warm oil in medium skillet over moderate heat. Add skins and salt and toss until skins begin to color and turn translucent, 2 to 3 minutes.

4. Combine juice, zest, and hot pepper and add to pan. Reduce heat slightly and cook, stirring often, until skins are slightly more tender and juice has reduced to a glaze, about 5 minutes. Serve hot or chilled, with or without sesame or cilantro, or with both.

Makes 1 cup

Cold Buckwheat Noodles with White Radish and Wasabi Dressing

Asian ingredients adapted to a Western mode make a lovely lunch or light supper. Crunchy pale radish and green onion threads twine with buckwheat noodles dressed in lemon sharpened with wasabi. If you lack roasted peanut oil, substitute 1½ tablespoons vegetable oil mixed with ½ tablespoon roasted sesame oil. Soba noodles are packed in several sizes; pick whichever is closest in weight to ¾ pound.

> 1 pound large white Asian radish (weighed without greens)
> 1 package Japanese buckwheat (soba) noodles (12 to 13 ounces)
> ⅓ cup lemon juice
> 1 teaspoon grated lemon zest
> 3 tablespoons shoyu (Japanese soy sauce)
> 2 teaspoons wasabi powder
> ½ teaspoon sugar
> ¼ teaspoon kosher salt
> About 2 tablespoons warm water
> 2 tablespoons peanut oil (preferably roasted)
> ¼ cup thin-sliced scallion (green onion) tops

1. Peel radish or not, as desired. Cut half into julienne strips. Coarsely grate the remainder.

2. Drop noodles into a large pot of boiling water. Return to a boil, stirring. Boil gently, tasting often, until just barely tender, 2 to 4 minutes. Drain. Rinse in cold water.

3. Combine lemon juice, zest, and shoyu; set aside. Blend wasabi, sugar, salt, and 1 tablespoon warm water; then add more water as needed to make a pourable mixture. Add peanut oil and blend.

4. Toss noodles with lemon mixture and grated radish, mixing well. Divide among four bowls. Make an indentation in the center of each noodle mound. Fill with radish strips. Drizzle 2 teaspoons wasabi sauce on each. Top with scallions.

Serves 4 as a main dish

Pros Propose

Elizabeth Andoh, an authority on Japanese cooking, sandwiches **Smoked Salmon Between Daikon Slices** dabbed with wasabi, then halves them for pretty half-moon hors d'oeuvres. Her family (both Japanese and Russian sides) concurs that daikon also suits smoked or salted fish and meat, whether eel or corned beef. She grates the root, squeezes out the juice, blends the shreds with sharp mustard, and serves it as a condiment.

For a simple side dish, chef Alex Lee prepares **Glazed Daikon:** Slice peeled daikon into rounds ½ inch thick. Cook gently with butter, sugar, and ginger julienne. Add chicken or vegetable stock, honey, and sherry vinegar. Simmer until meltingly tender and glazed.

Red-Heart Radishes in Daikon Vinaigrette, from chef Bruce Hill, gives doubled radish power: Puree peeled, chopped daikon with rice vinegar, mirin, shoyu, and a little olive oil to make a rather thick, frothy dressing. Using a mandoline, meat slicer, or thin-slicing blade of a food processor, slice peeled red-fleshed radishes. Then cut into julienne. Toss with the vinaigrette. Serve with fish dishes.

A beautiful presentation, **Seared Scallops with Radish Fettuccine,** is another Bruce Hill creation: Thin-slice peeled green-fleshed radishes and white daikon on meat slicer or mandoline, then cut to form "fettuccine." Blanch in salted water; drain. Toss with butter, chervil, chives, and tarragon and form into nests on plates. Fill with seared scallops. Serve with beurre rosé (beurre blanc made with rosé wine).

Wild Striped Bass with Daikon has long been popular at chef Susanna Foo's restaurant: Fillet fish. Prepare stock with its bones and chunks of daikon; strain. Briefly marinate fillets in vodka, soy sauce, and oil. Stir-fry shallots, diced daikon, corn kernels, and red pepper. Add fish stock and cook vegetables through. Divide among bowls. Set the quicky seared fillets and tiny chrysanthemum leaves on top.

At home, Susanna Foo prepares **Spareribs Braised with Daikon:** Cut apart baby spareribs and sear in heavy braising pan. Add garlic, star anise, brandy, Madeira, and soy sauce. Add unpeeled daikon chunks. Cook, covered, on very low heat until tender, about 45 minutes, adding liquid only if mixture threatens to scorch.

Black Radish

(Raphanus sativus)

This sooty subterranean, as fierce in flavor as it is dark in color, is a favorite in cold climates and was originally grown for winter storage. Its dense flesh permits extended keeping without sprouting or pithiness. Almost as pungent as horseradish, it is very firm and rather dry—a far cry from the small scarlet globes that are served as appetizers. Black radishes grown for the North American market are the shape and size of medium-large turnips, charcoal to cocoa outside and ivory within. Elsewhere, they are equally likely to be cylindrical, rounded, or top-shaped.

Clearly of ancient origin (it has a downright primeval look), this radish has been cultivated longer than any others now in commerce. According to William Woys Weaver (*Heirloom Vegetable Gardening*), it was the mainstay radish of American farmers throughout the 19th century, but it has since fallen out of favor. Now, it is found only in a few markets, usually where there are customers of Central and Eastern European heritage (and more often than not Jewish). Growers in California and New Jersey (just about the only places

black radish   diameter: 2½–5 inches

it is still grown) tell me that the crop is now made up of just one cultivar, Round Black Spanish (also called Noir Gros Rond d'Hiver), and that almost all of it is sold for the Passover and Rosh Hashana holidays.

BASIC USE: Black radish has its own identity and will not suit the roles played by either Asian or table radishes; it is firmer, drier, and more assertive than any of these—closer to horseradish.

Raw: Traditionally, black radishes are enjoyed as a piquant appetizer or condiment: Peel and shred coarsely or slice thin, then salt and drain to mellow; rinse, drain, and dry; bind with sour cream or sweet cream—or with goose or chicken fat—and serve with chewy rye or black bread. Slices to be served "straight" still need a touch of tempering: quarter and slice thin; immerse in water, then refrigerate for hours or even days before draining and serving. The slices will be mellowed but still strong—a nice foil for salted and smoked meat. In moderation, raw, unpeeled, julienne-cut black radish contributes a harsh but pleasing bite and dramatic coloring to slaws and relishes. Or blend minced radish with creamy cheese or smoked fish or liver pâté.

Cooked: Cooked black radishes taste like firm turnips, but their cooking time is less predictable—it depends upon how long they have been stored and how dense the flesh is. Sliced, diced, or shredded, they add a sharpness and cabbagey depth to soups, stews, braises, or stir-fries. Or chop fine to add to ground raw meat or fish mixtures for interesting variations in texture and flavor.

SELECTION: Black radishes are at their peak in winter, although they appear in the market erratically year-round. They are most abundant in fall and early spring, but they remain in fine shape for very long periods. Select very firm, comparatively heavy, dark globes that show no flabbiness, pitting, sponginess, or cracks. Unless you are buying from a farmers' market, the radishes will have had their leaves and rootlets removed.

STORAGE: Nothing is better than a root cellar, where you can keep the radishes buried in earth. If that isn't part of your setup, wrap the unwashed, topped radishes in newspaper or perforated plastic and refrigerate. They'll keep longer than just about anything else you've ever stored—unless they become moist, in which case mold develops. Check now and then for dampness. Black radishes mellow as they store and are fine for grating and shredding after months of storage.

PREPARATION: All black radishes need a good scrubbing with a brush, and then a trim. Peeling is almost always recommended, but I don't see the point of it for many dishes. If the skin is not too tough, I prefer to leave some of it, at least—to prove that they're black radishes.

Sautéed Chicken Livers with Sweet-Sour Black Radishes

Firm, bittersweet radish dice are the perfect foil for creamy pink-centered livers. Banished from nutritionally correct kitchens in recent years, chicken livers are a quick-cooking, richly flavorful, inexpensive treat to enjoy now and then. And thanks to the striking black-and-white radish cubes, this ensemble looks more appetizing than most chicken liver dishes.

¾ pound chicken livers
¼ teaspoon kosher salt
Pepper
4 medium scallions (green onions), trimmed
2 small black radishes (about ½ pound)
1 tablespoon butter
1 tablespoon corn or safflower oil
¼ cup white wine vinegar or sherry vinegar
¼ cup water
About 1½ teaspoons honey

1. Separate liver lobes, remove sinews, and halve again. Sprinkle with salt and pepper. Cut apart pale and dark parts of scallions; thin-slice both. Scrub radishes and cut into ⅛- to ¼-inch dice.

2. In a skillet just large enough to hold livers in a single layer, melt butter with oil over moderately high heat. When foaming, add livers and cook 1 minute. Turn and cook another minute. With tongs or slotted spoon, transfer to a plate; cover.

3. Add radishes and pale scallion parts to pan. Toss to soften a bit, about 3 minutes. Reduce heat. Add vinegar and water and cook, stirring often, until radishes are al dente, about 5 minutes. Add honey to taste. Season.

4. Raise heat to moderate (if necessary, cook to evaporate most liquid). Return livers to pan, with darker scallion parts, and toss to just heat through. Serve at once.

Serves 2 as a main course

Variation

Sweet-Sour Black Radish Toss

Enjoy black radish as an intriguing foil for rich meats—roasted duck, barbecued beef, or foie gras. Or serve with grilled sardines, mackerel, or shad.

To prepare as garnish or side dish for 2, increase the radish to ¾ pound. Melt 1 tablespoon butter in pan, then follow through step 3 above. Toss with half the quantity of scallion greens and serve hot. The recipe can be doubled for 4.

Black Radish–Noodle "Stoup" with Meatballs

When you notice that some of the black radishes you bought in November are still there in January (or even February), make a yummy stew-soup supper of them. Since all sharpness disappears when the radish is cooked, you'll want a hearty broth to back up what become chewy, mild, mystery strands. I had both frozen beef broth and ground beef on hand, so I used them. Lamb or pork would be as good; so would ham (add ham dice instead of meatballs). Considering that the whole job takes under forty-five minutes and needs no mellowing, it's a fine, warming meal. The noodly-vegetably tangle makes for messy eating that is much tidied by the use of chopsticks and deep-bowled soup spoons.

3 medium scallions (green onions)
½ pound ground meat
1 tablespoon cornstarch
2 to 3 tablespoons sake or dry sherry
1 tablespoon shoyu (Japanese soy sauce)
2 medium black radishes (about ¾ pound),
    well scrubbed and trimmed
2 medium carrots
2 quarts hearty meat, mushroom, or
    vegetable broth
3 to 4 ounces skinny, short dried egg noodles
About 1½ tablespoons Dijon mustard
¼ cup chopped fresh dill

1. Trim scallions and cut apart dark and light parts. Mince light parts and thin-slice greens. Mix minced scallions with meat, cornstarch, 1 tablespoon sake, and shoyu.

2. With fine julienne blade or coarse grating blade of food processor or vegetable cutter, shred black radish; set aside. (Peel radishes if you prefer; I don't.) Peel and shred carrots; set aside. With a teaspoon, form about 30 meatballs (there is no need to be super-neat).

3. Combine radishes and broth in large pot and bring to a simmer, covered. Add noodles and bring to a boil. Boil gently, stirring often, until almost tender—about 3 minutes. Add meatballs and carrots. Simmer gently until meat firms up, about 3 minutes longer.

4. Blend mustard with about ¼ cup soup. Gradually stir into soup, adding just enough to taste. Add more sake, tasting. Add half each of the dill and scallion greens and return to a simmer. Ladle into bowls and sprinkle with remaining dill and scallions.

Serves 4 to 5 as a main course

Pros Propose

Jean Joho, whose Alsatian culinary heritage includes radishes of all types, prepares **Foie Gras Sauté with Sweet-Sour Black Radish** (the luxury dish that inspired the humble chicken liver version on page 528). To prepare: Fine-chop unpeeled black radish. Sauté quickly in butter. Deglaze pan with honey and vinegar and serve at once as a base for seared foie gras slices. Equally rich and simple is chef Joho's **Gratin of Black Radishes:** Drop chopped unpeeled black radishes into boiling salted water. Return to a boil and drain. Rub a terra-cotta dish with garlic. In dish, mix radishes with cream, salt, pepper, and nutmeg. Bake, topped with aged Gruyère.

I was so disappointed to discover that much of the dramatic black radish peel needs removing that I devised an aesthetic compromise in *Uncommon Fruits & Vegetables: A Commonsense Guide.* For **Striped Black Radishes:** Select small radishes and scrub well to remove soil and rootlets. Trim tip and stem ends. Carefully remove thin longitudinal strips with a citrus stripper, leaving sharp black stripes between. Cover radishes with cold water and bring to a boil. Add salt and simmer until tender, 15 to 30 minutes. Drain, toss with butter, and serve. For **Striped Radish Slices for Canapés:** Select larger radishes and retain more skin. Undercook slightly, so radishes remain firm when sliced. Drain, refresh in cold water, and dry. Slice into rounds or half-rounds ¼ inch thick.

Chef Anita Lo takes an Asian route with **Spanish Mackerel with Black Radish and Umeboshi:** Briefly marinate mackerel fillets in sake, mirin, garlic, and lemon juice. For each serving, mound a base of prepared sushi rice. Top with thin-sliced salted cucumbers, then black radish julienne. Grill fish and set on top. Sprinkle with lemon zest tossed with salt and lemon juice. Puree pickled Japanese apricots (umeboshi) with a drop of marinade; dot around plate, alternating with fine scallion slices.

Table Radish or Small Radish

Also spring or summer radish, European radish

Bright and pretty, small table radishes, whether round, olive-shape, oblong, or icicle-type, are the most popular and most common group of radishes in this country today. They are also the most recent arrivals, because large winter keepers were the favorites until the 20th century.

Called "spring radishes" in horticultural terms, these politely petite snowy white, pale rose, lavender, or brilliant crimson radishes are ideal for raw vegetable platters, salads, and garnishes. Perhaps the best known

Cherry Belle (*top left*), **White Icicle** (*bottom left*), **Long Red Italian** (*top right*), **French Breakfast** (*bottom right*), **Easter Egg** (*center*)
⅕ **actual size**

of these are the popular Cherry Belle and its numerous round, all-red look-alikes. Then there is Easter Egg—not a single radish, but the group term for a selection of small white, purple, pink, and red radishes grown as a market bouquet. French Breakfast types are white-tipped oblongs with rosy shoulders and short, pert leaves meant to be nibbled along with the root. ("Breakfast"? I don't know of radishes as breakfast food in France—although they are in Japan. However, in *Heirloom Vegetable Gardening,* William Woys Weaver mentions "many old Pennsylvania Dutch relatives who lament the fact that people had stopped serving radishes for breakfast.")

Icicle-types, slim and juicy, are also enjoyed primarily as meal-openers, to whet the appetite. The tapering roots, vaguely carrot-shaped, have white or red skin and white or pinkish flesh. White Icicle, Long Red Italian, and Long Scarlet (or Cincinnati) are names you are likely to see in this category.

BASIC USE: The French nibble delicate pink and white radishes raw, buttered and salted, or served with thickly buttered bread, to open a meal. Americans chomp Cherry Belles as an appetizer with celery and olives. But there is no need to limit table radishes to the role of relish, for they are delicious cooked. Blanched or braised, they are paler and less crunchy but they acquire a mellowness and subtle savor that sweetly complements fish and poultry.

SELECTION: Although grown year-round—primarily in California, Florida, and Guatemala—table radishes are at their peak in cool weather. All types, if grown quickly in a cool climate, will be mildly peppery, crisp, and juicy. Generally, they are tastiest in the spring, with a second season in the fall. In between, quality is iffy. In summer they are likely to be harsh, and the leaves may be mangy. In selecting radishes, one can tell only so much by looking at them. Sampling is the only way to determine "heat" and harshness. Select those with greens that are perky—not waterlogged or dry. Radishes should be free of cracks and feel solid and firm.

STORAGE: For small table radishes, I find this a highly effective method of storing and rejuvenating (if necessary): Take apart bunched radishes and discard damaged leaves. Drop radishes into a sink filled with lukewarm water. Swish gently but thoroughly to dis-

lodge dirt, allowing about 3 to 4 minutes in the water (no longer, or they will absorb too much). Spread to dry briefly (they should remain moist). Pack loosely in airtight boxes and chill. In an hour, you'll have radishes that look fresh-from-the-field and that will stay in shape twice as long as any others (7 to 8 days instead of 3 to 4).

PREPARATION: For small radishes, a thorough rinsing is all that is usually needed. If roots are scraggly, trim them, as well as leaves that are less than lively. Icicle radishes sometimes need paring; taste to find out.

Stir-Fried Cilantro Chicken and Red Radish Rounds

Small table radishes make charming cooked vegetables, softening and mellowing, although they retain some pepperiness. Red ones look cute, but the multicolor Easter Egg bouquet is even more so. Seek out cilantro with its roots intact. Their strong fragrance does not dissipate during cooking, whereas leaves, fragrant as they are, disperse their volatile aromatic oils when heated. Have all ingredients ready and close at hand before you begin cooking, as for any stir-fry dish.

¾ **pound boned and skinned chicken breasts**
½ **pound round table radishes (about 1 inch in diameter), trimmed**
1 **bunch cilantro (coriander) with roots**
3 **thin scallions (green onions)**
1 **tablespoon peanut oil**
2 **teaspoons minced garlic**
Big pinch of ground hot pepper
1½ **tablespoons fish sauce**
½ **cup vegetable or chicken broth**
2 **tablespoons rice vinegar**
½ **tablespoon brown sugar**
Optional: flower-cut radishes for garnish

1. Cut chicken into bite-size pieces. Slice radishes ⅛ inch thick. Cut off cilantro roots, with a bit of stem. Scrub them with a brush, then mince. Rinse leaves and pull from stems. Mince half. Trim scallions and cut into 1½-inch diagonals. Measure out the other ingredients.

2. Heat wok or skillet over high heat; add oil, and tip to coat pan. Add chicken and radishes and stir-fry until meat has just barely whitened, less than a minute. Add two-thirds of scallions, the cilantro roots, garlic, hot pepper, and fish sauce and toss until chicken is not quite cooked through, 3 to 4 minutes. Scoop into a warmed serving dish; set aside.

3. Add broth, vinegar, and sugar to pan and boil briefly to reduce to lightly syrupy consistency. Add chicken and radishes and remaining scallions, tossing to heat through.

4. Scoop into the dish and toss with the minced cilantro leaves. Add whole cilantro leaves to taste and optional radishes. Serve at once.

Serves 2 as a main course

Radish Top Soup

Don't toss out bright radish leaves from any kind of radishes. They make good, old-fashioned soups that taste like mild arugula and gentle turnip tops (both relatives). This pale and pretty green puree made from standard table radish tops should persuade you to keep your throwaways.

> Very fresh tops from 2 large bunches of
>   table radishes
> 3 medium scallions (green onions)
> 2 medium floury potatoes (¾ to 1 pound)
> 1 tablespoon oil
> ½ teaspoon sugar
> About 3 cups vegetable or chicken broth
> Salt and white pepper
> Nutmeg
> 8 to 12 red, pink, and/or purple table
>   radishes

1. Discard yellowed radish leaves, if any. Wash greens in several changes of water, lifting out to leave debris behind (radish leaves can be very muddy). Trim scallions, chop white and light green parts; thin-slice greens. Peel and thin-slice potatoes.

2. Heat oil in medium saucepan over moderate heat. Add radish greens, chopped scallion, and potatoes. Toss until leaves wilt. Add sugar and 2½ cups broth. Simmer, covered, over low heat until potatoes are soft—about 20 minutes.

3. Whiz with immersion blender to a smooth puree. Or transfer to blender or food processor and puree until very smooth. Return to pan and stir in remaining broth, for desired consistency. Season with salt, white pepper, and nutmeg.

4. Pare colored skin from radishes and cut it into thin strips and a few petal shapes. Slice the white interior part into rounds. Heat soup and ladle into small bowls. Garnish with radish pieces and slices and scallion greens to taste.

Serves 4 as a first course

Cranberry-Glazed Long Red Italian Radishes

This unusual ruby garnish or side dish has a sweet-sour savor oddly reminiscent of beets. Serve it to brighten and sharpen roast turkey, chicken, or salmon. If you prefer, you can use round red radishes—but halve the cooking time, more or less.

> ¾ cup cranberry juice
> 1 tablespoon balsamic vinegar
> ⅛ teaspoon ground allspice or cloves
> ⅛ teaspoon pepper
> ½ teaspoon kosher salt
> 1 teaspoon hazelnut, walnut, or olive oil
> 1 or 2 bunches long red radishes
>   (12 to 15 radishes)

1. In medium skillet or saucepan, combine juice, vinegar, allspice, pepper, salt, and oil. Bring to a boil.

2. Meanwhile, trim rootlets and greens from radishes. Rinse radishes.

3. Add radishes to liquid, bring to a boil, and cover. Simmer until tender, about 20 minutes (they take longer than you might imagine).

4. When tender to taste, uncover and simmer to reduce liquid to a glaze, stirring or shaking often as it gets sticky, about 5 minutes. Serve hot.

Serves 2 as a garnish or side dish

Pros Propose

Chef Jean Joho fashions a simple and defined dish of **Oysters with Radish Vinaigrette:** Prepare very fine dice of red radish. Macerate an hour or two in the best white wine or champagne vinegar. Serve with raw oysters, in place of mignonette or other peppery sauces. For **Red Radish Salad,** he tosses julienne of long red radishes with salt, then presses to drain, seasons with pepper, mustard, and vinegar and serves as an element in a raw vegetable platter.

When chef Alex Lee cooks **Spring Radishes with Their Leaves,** he employs a special technique to maintain the freshness of the greens: After washing, he re-bunches the radishes with their leaves intact and ties them with a long string to the pot handle—so that the radishes cook in whatever liquid is bubbling while the greens stay above it. When the radishes are cooked, he unties the bouquet and heats the whole bunch in stock and butter just until the greens wilt.

An **Amuse-Bouche of Stuffed Summer Radishes** charms diners at Odessa Piper's restaurant: Cut off and reserve one-third of each large Easter Egg radish. With melon ball cutter, remove most of flesh from radishes. Cut into tiny dice and add an equal amount of tiny celery dice. Prepare pesto with parsley, pumpkin seed oil, toasted pumpkin seeds, lemon juice, and Parmesan. When pureed, blend with radish-celery mixture. Mound into hollowed radishes and top with reserved caps.

For a refreshing twist on a classic, try chef Waldy Malouf's **Rack of Lamb with Radishes and Mint:** Briefly poach French Breakfast radishes with their leaves in salted water. Drain. Combine bunches of fresh mint in saucepan with vinegar and sugar and bring to a boil. Remove mint and reduce liquid. Add poached radishes. Simmer briefly; remove. Roast rack of lamb. Deglaze pan with mint reduction, then lamb *jus.* Add radishes and heat. Stir in chopped fresh mint.

Ramp, Wild Leek *(Allium tricoccum)*

Also ramson

length: 14 inches (without roots)

When I first wrote about ramps in *Food & Wine* magazine in 1985, there were few to be found outside the forest. After all, urban areas are not home to most wild edibles—and not until recently have swanky restaurants and specialty food shops become showcases for foraged fare. Now, these native American leeks arrive in sophisticated city shops with the first garlicky breath of spring and appear on menus countrywide. Another edible has been restored to American tables by a national passion for novel foods and dining out.

But there have always been people who know ramps from the ground up, because the vegetable grows and is harvested and cooked on their home turf—and the turf is wide. Wild leeks flourish in rich forest soil from Canada through New England to Georgia and as far west as Minnesota; and in the southern Appalachians, their emergence in spring sets off a series of celebrations.

The name "ramp" originated in the Appalachians. The term probably derives from the name of a related species, ramson *(Allium ursinum)*, literally bear's garlic (also called wild garlic), which may in some places also refer to *A. tricoccum*. The "Feast of the Ramson" (just one of many ramp festivities) is held annually in Richwood, West Virginia, the state that has come to represent ramps. A brochure from the Richwood Chamber of Commerce offers this fanciful etymology: "The first sign of the Zodiac calendar is Aries, which ushers in the spring during March and April. Aries is the Arabic word for Ram, the male of the sheep family, stout, rambunctious, and a bit odoriferous! The plant we call the 'Rams' Son' is the first green shoot to show itself in the deep Appalachian woodlands."

Superficially, the most obvious appeal of ramp is visual: lily-like (it is a member of the lily family), its smooth leaves sharply defined, its body slim and tapering, the whole freshly painted in tricolor, it could well symbolize spring itself. At close range (in fact, even across a crowded room) its most startling characteristic reveals itself: the superstrong smell, quite unlike that of any other *Allium*. Although the plant looks as ladylike as lily of the valley, its aromatic punch is far more pronounced and persistent than that of its relative the cultivated leek.

BASIC USE: Although in ramp country the whole plant is apparently munched naked and raw, I suggest you cook it for a first encounter, since cooking turns it sweet and surprisingly mild.

It makes sense to preserve the plant's graceful proportions by keeping it whole or cut in two—not sliced helter-skelter. Use ramps in recipes for bulbing spring onions. Or treat them as you would trimmed, young cultivated leeks, but cook for a much shorter time. Parboil and serve like asparagus—with butter, vinaigrette, or hollandaise sauce, or gratinéed. Braise in cream or stock, either alone or with chicken or rabbit for a simple fricassee. Add the blanched bulbs to quiche or custard; or heat them in butter with other blanched spring vegetables, such as asparagus and new carrots.

SELECTION AND STORAGE: Depending on the weather, ramps appear as early as March or as late as July. Choose ones that are firm, springy, and bright green, with their roots intact. They can be tiny (50 to a pound) or plumply petite (30 per pound). They can be soil-coated or scrubbed clean, but in either case do not clean them further until you are ready to cook them.

To store ramps, wrap damp toweling around the roots. Refrigerate in several layers of *tightly* wrapped plastic zipped into a bag, or everything will reek of leek. If the leaves are fresh and dry, the plants should keep for about a week. If you have a walk-in refrigerator, put the ramps in a bucket with water to cover their roots, and they'll last longer.

PREPARATION: If ramps are quite clean, just trim off the roots and rinse the ramps well. Most will need more care: Slip off the first layer of skin from the bulbs, then trim off the roots. Remove any yellowing or wilted leaves. Rinse in several changes of water, swishing vigorously. How you slice ramps depends on the recipe. For the most part, they are best divided into two: Cut the leafy green tops from the rosy stems where they branch from the central stalk.

Ramps in Walnut Vinaigrette with Orange Zest

Wildly aromatic when raw, these slim leeks turn sweet and mild when tamed by blanching. Sherry vinegar adds just the right note, but wine vinegar with a touch of balsamic works too. Figure on about 9 to 12 ramps per serving for a nice presentation.

3 to 4 dozen ramps (about 1 pound, depending upon size)
1½ tablespoons sherry vinegar
1 teaspoon Dijon mustard
¼ teaspoon kosher salt
2 tablespoons walnut oil
2 tablespoons olive oil
1 orange (preferably organic)
3 to 4 tablespoons toasted, coarse-chopped walnuts

1. If ramps are clean, just trim off roots and rinse well. If not so clean, slip off first layer of skin from bulbs, then trim roots. Remove wilted leaves, if any. Rinse ramps in several changes of water, swishing vigorously. Cut leaves apart from stems where they begin to branch, leaving most red stem on bulbs.

2. Place bulbs in a skillet of boiling salted water. Simmer until thickest part can be pierced easily with sharp knife, 2 to 4 minutes, as size dictates. Lift out with slotted spoon and set on towel.

3. Place leaves gently in the boiling water; boil 30 seconds. Drain and dry on towel. Reserve 12 leaves. Squeeze moisture from the remainder and coarse-chop. Blend vinegar, mustard, and salt. Gradually add walnut and olive oils, whisking to emulsify.

4. Arrange whole leaves prettily around serving dish. Stir a spoonful of dressing into chopped leaves, and spread over whole ones. Arrange bulbs over these. Nap with dressing. Chill until serving time.

5. To serve: Scrub orange and coarse-grate enough zest to equal about 1½ teaspoons. Toss with nuts; then sprinkle evenly over ramps.

Serves 4 as a first course

Ramps Simmered in Cream

Smooth wild leek leaves are cut into ribbons and stewed to a creamy, satiny mass that serves as a bed for the pearly lightly cooked bulbs and stalks. Cooked this way, the greens become a surprisingly sweet sauce. Serve with plain poached or baked fish. Seek out pasteurized (not ultrapasteurized) cream for this luscious, rich dish.

> **About 1 pound ramps (preferably of equal size)**
> **1 cup vegetable broth**
> **¼ teaspoon dried thyme or tarragon, crumbled**
> **¼ teaspoon dried dill, crumbled**
> **½ teaspoon kosher salt**
> **1 cup heavy cream**

1. If ramps are clean, just trim off roots and rinse well. If muddy, slip off first layer of skin from bulbs, then trim roots. Remove yellow or wilted leaves. Rinse ramps in several changes of water, swishing vigorously. Cut leaves apart from stems where they branch from the stalk, leaving stalk and bulb attached. Stack leaves and cut into thin diagonal strips. If bulbs are large, cut a slit in the base of each.

2. Combine bulbs, broth, thyme, dill, salt, and cream in skillet that holds bulbs in a single layer; bring to a boil. Reduce heat, cover, and simmer gently, shaking often, until bulbs are tender when pierced with a knife, 3 to 5 minutes. With tongs, transfer to plate.

3. Add leaves to pan and stir to wilt. Simmer gently, uncovered, stirring often, until leaves are cushiony soft and cream thickens, about 15 minutes.

4. To serve, heat bulbs briefly in microwave or skillet. Spoon leaf-cream mixture into warm serving dish. Arrange bulbs on top.

Serves 4 to 6 as a garnish

Pros Propose

Although *Allium tricoccum* is native to North America, Europe has its own wild spring onions. Italian chefs are particularly well versed in their use, to judge from the many suggestions I received. Lidia Matticchio Bastianich loved **Calf's Liver with Sautéed Wild Leeks** in her native Istria and serves a version at Felidia, her restaurant in New York: Blanch halved medium wild leek (ramp) bulbs. Caramelize sugar in pan. Add the leeks, a little olive oil, and drops of aged balsamic vinegar. In another pan, sear thin-sliced calf's liver. Add to leeks, stirring to combine.

The restaurant also offers **Egg Custard Tart with Wild Leeks, Asparagus, and Morels,** a recipe from executive chef Fortunato Nicotra: Cut apart bulb and stem-leaf parts from small wild leeks; reserve leaves. Simmer both cultivated and wild leek bulbs until soft, then puree. Add eggs, cream, and Parmesan, blending. Bake in small timbale molds. Spoon a little fonduta (melted cheese sauce) into shallow bowls. Top with mixture of sautéed morels, asparagus tips, and sautéed leek leaves. Unmold custards on top.

Another Italian chef, Mario Batali, presents an equally rich dish of **Asparagus, Prosciutto, and Ramps over Soft Polenta:** Cook thick asparagus in boiling water to cover until tender; remove and drain, reserving cooking water. Add quick-cooking polenta to the water and cook until thick. Stir in mascarpone. Sauté sliced garlic, prosciutto julienne, and cleaned small whole ramps in butter until wilted. Add asparagus, lemon juice and zest, and white wine and bring to a boil. Add butter and shake pan to emulsify. Divide the polenta among bowls and top with vegetables (from *Simple Italian Food*).

A lovely simple dish with just two principals, **Sautéed Rabbit with Wild Leeks,** could very well have come from Italy, but the source is American: *Country Suppers* by Ruth Cousineau. To prepare: Sauté trimmed small ramps in olive oil until they begin to color. Remove and reserve. Brown cut-up floured rabbit in same pan in more oil; season. Return ramps to pan with a little water. Cook, covered, turning once, until rabbit breast and saddle are tender when pierced, about 25 minutes. Remove; cook legs a little longer. Skim fat. Return all rabbit pieces to pan and reheat.

Far from rustic simplicity is **Foie Gras Terrine with Sweet-Sour Ramps, Haricots Verts, and Hazelnuts** from chef Todd Humphries: Prepare pickling liquid with champagne or apple cider vinegar, sugar, water, coriander seeds, cloves, and whole allspice. Pour over very small ramps; cool in liquid. Refrigerate in crocks. Make a salad of the pickled ramps, apple julienne, and blanched haricots verts. Toss with a little pickling liquid blended with hazelnut oil. Set slices of foie gras terrine and roasted hazelnuts on top.

Pancakes (farinettes) studded with snails and accompanied by creamy wild leeks are Jean-Georges Vongerichten's unusual contribution to this ramp medley. For **Farinettes d'Escargot with Wild Leeks:** Cook petit gris snails in court bouillon with aromatics. Combine 1-inch sourdough chunks, milk, eggs, salt, pepper, nutmeg, raclette cheese, and parsley to make a batter like mushy oatmeal. Spoon onto griddle to make pancakes. Set 6 snails on each. Bake, turning once. Sauté small wild leeks in butter and cream to barely soften. Serve alongside farinettes, sprinkled with parsley.

Rhubarb (*Rheum rhabarbarum*)

⅓ **actual size**

Imagine that you've spent the winter eating fruits and vegetables rationed from a root cellar and canning jars. Now imagine the first rosy rhubarb of the year, welcome as new grass. Not so long ago, rhubarb held a special place in the culinary calendar as a unique fresh food, the earliest harbinger of spring.

Rhubarb is easy to grow; the crowns—from which the shoots develop, asparagus-like—will produce for decades. In fact, the plant is difficult to eliminate once it takes root. A relative of buckwheat, its flavor earthy and bracingly sour, rhubarb thrives in cold climates—although its glowing color suggests the tropics. But the shocking pink and chartreuse are closer to imperial

Chinese satin than a Caribbean sunset, for rhubarb species originated in Western China, Tibet, Mongolia, Siberia, and neighboring areas.

Rhubarb's traditional role was first and foremost medicinal. The dried root was a popular remedy for a wide range of ills. Rhubarb's monetary value was enormous, according to "Culinary Rhubarb Production in North America" by Clifford Foust and Dale Marshall, the authors of many works on rhubarb: "In 1542 [rhubarb] was sold in France for 10 times the price of cinnamon, and in a 1657 English price list rhubarb sold for 2.7 times more than opium." Shipped from China through Russia to Europe, rhubarb acquired its common and Latin names en route (according to one prevailing theory) from the Greek *rheon barbaron: rheon* referring to a plant from the Rha (the ancient name for the Volga), *barbaron* meaning foreign. The words merged to *rheubarbarum* in Latin and *rheubarbe* in Old French, and so on to its present form.

Garden or culinary rhubarb—as opposed to medicinal rhubarb—also developed in the East, where it was an ingredient in drinks and meat stews. Rhubarb was by no means a minor vegetable; in fact, in one pre-Islamic legend, it is the mother and father of mankind: "for when Gayomart died his seed is said to have fallen into the earth. In the course of time a rhubarb plant grew out of the earth, and from this the first human couple emerged" (from *Zurvan: A Zoroastrian Dilemma* by R. C. Zaehner).

Culinary rhubarb was observed in Italy in the early 17th century but did not take firm root in Europe until surprisingly late: "Rhubarb is almost wholly furnished by the London market-gardeners," wrote Andrew Wynter in *Curiosities of Civilization* (1860). "It was first introduced by Mr. Miatt [sic] forty years ago, who sent his two sons to the Borough Market with five bunches of which they only sold three." In 1931, Mrs. M. Grieve wrote in *A Modern Herbal:* "We hear of a pioneer grower, Joseph Myatt, of Deptford . . . [who] persevered in his efforts to make a market for Rhubarb, raised improved varieties, and a few years after, Rhubarb had become established in public favour as a culinary plant."

Rhubarb's acceptance in Britain was stimulated by one of those anecdotal horticultural "accidents": Foust and Marshall write that "the forcing [production hastened by heat] of rhubarb roots was inadvertently discovered in 1815, when earth thrown up by the digging of a ditch in Chelsea Physic Garden accidentally covered dormant rhubarb crowns. Within a few weeks, succulent rhubarb shoots with eye-catching petioles [leaf stalks] . . . pushed through the moist warm mulch in midwinter, long before field rhubarb was due to appear." Rhubarb continued to grow in popularity as sugar from the Caribbean became widely available and canning and bottling techniques improved. By the end of the century, the rhubarb patch was a standard part of a British garden.

In the United States, rhubarb was introduced to Maine at the end of the 18th century. It spread through New England but did not flourish in the rest of the country until late in the 19th century, when the great plant breeder Luther Burbank developed a mild type with an unusually long season, flamboyant coloring, and a growing habit well suited to much of California. Rhubarb is still grown in the West, primarily in Washington, Oregon, and Michigan. All of Oregon's rhubarb is field-grown, but in Washington and Michigan rhubarb is grown both in the field and (forced) in hothouses. Most rhubarb is frozen for commercial and institutional use; only about one-quarter of the crop is sold fresh.

In the United States, rhubarb has been in and out of fashion, but it has declined distinctly since fuel (which is needed for hothouse production) has increased in price. "Now there are only a few types sold," says Sue Verdi of Verdi's Fresh Farm Produce in the Seattle area. "Following the trend of all farming, small crops are disappearing. Anyone who farms has to go with big crops that sell big—which rhubarb doesn't." Although production is small, a recent upturn may encourage rhubarb fanciers (and supporters of minor crops in general): In 1992, 861 acres were cultivated in the United States; in 1997 (the most recent year for which figures are available) 1,379 acres were cultivated.

Still, growers are not optimistic about rhubarb's future. George Richter, a grower of superb rhubarb and berries, and president of George Richter Farm in Puyallup, Washington, says, "Years ago, before the idea of season was lost through long-distance transport, hothouse rhubarb was *the* new crop of the year. Every piece sold. Seasons don't have the same significance now. Add to that the fact that rhubarb needs sugar and that sugar is on the bad list these days—and rhubarb may be on its way to becoming an endangered species."

But rhubarb's nonsweet role is increasing, at least in high-end restaurants. Although traditionally a pie plant (one of its old names) in the American kitchen, it has been rediscovered as a vegetable (despite a curious ruling of the U.S. Customs Court in Buffalo in 1947, which declared it a fruit, making it subject to a smaller import duty at the time). Fashion is fickle, and rhubarb has gone from overabundant garden plant to a rare, expensive treat. I, for one, hope that fashion changes again soon.

Warning: *Never eat rhubarb leaves, cooked or raw.* Dale E. Marshall (aka Dr. Rhubarb), an agricultural engineer with the USDA at Michigan State University, writes: "Rhubarb as a vegetable for food consists of the leaf stalks or petioles. . . . Fatalities have been recorded from ingestion of the leaves" (from *A Bibliography of Rhubarb and Rheum Species*—a work citing 3,385 references on rhubarb).

What about raw stalks? It seems that some rhubarb fanciers like them straight from the patch. Richard Hall, a food technologist and toxicologist, advises: "Eating raw rhubarb stalks won't bother most people any more than spinach or sorrel, which also contain irritating oxalates. But be sensible. As with everything, the dose makes the poison. A friend at the FDA used to say: 'Our job here is to protect normal people, fools, and some damn fools—but not goddamn fools.' Don't gorge on rhubarb, raw or cooked."

BASIC USE: Think of rhubarb as you would sorrel: for a lush consistency and an acid nip. In savory dishes, rhubarb is usually "melted" into a sauce, soup, or stew, where its soft body, its often stunning pink-to-red coloring, and its tart taste create a unique culinary concurrence. It is a good foil for rich or oily game or fish, such as duck or mackerel. The Pros Propose section gives examples.

SELECTION: Hothouse rhubarb appears as early as January and continues through April. Field-grown rhubarb begins arriving in March and, depending upon the area of the country where it is grown, can continue through summer. Spring stalks are juiciest and most tender.

Fresh stalks are flat, not curled or limp. When stalks that have been pulled—not cut—from the field are available, choose them; they'll dry out less rapidly. Size is no indicator of tenderness. Deep red stalks are sweeter and richer. George Richter recommends checking the bases of late-season stalks for pithiness and both ends of all rhubarb for decay. He also says: "Stalks with leaves attached are preferred in Europe and Canada, but I think the leaves draw moisture and wilt stalks quickly." For restaurants, choose boxes in which stalks are layered with leaves to retain moisture.

The question of field-grown versus greenhouse-grown rhubarb stirs up a hotbed of opinions. Richter prefers "mild and tender hothouse-grown Washington rhubarb, a special dark red rarely grown outside the state." Joe Comella, a representative of the Willamette Rhubarb Association in Oregon, where all rhubarb is field-grown, says that field-grown has "more juice, width, and color, and it is a unique dark red." Chef

Gary Danko likes "tender hothouse rhubarb. While field-grown may have big flavor, it may need peeling and more cooking. I like to just bring to a boil, then let it cook itself off the heat." Pastry chef Michelle Gayer finds hothouse rhubarb "dull, pale, and flabby. I like the clean, strong, sour taste of field-grown." Chef Jerry Traunfeld says that old-fashioned green varieties are often more productive, but "chefs are compelled to use red for presentation." Chef Waldy Malouf likes field-grown rhubarb, "which is redder and firmer." Chef Jean Joho says: "Forget the pretty little hothouse sticks from Holland. They have no taste." I suggest that you compare for yourself and decide.

STORAGE: Wrap rhubarb in ventilated plastic and store it in the coldest part of the refrigerator for no more than a few days. In restaurants, keep rhubarb at just above freezing in the waxed boxes in which it is packed. If it is to be stored more than a few days, mist it lightly and reclose the box. Cooked rhubarb and raw both freeze very well.

PREPARATION: Cut off and discard any leaves. A rinse and a trim from base and tip are usually enough. Peeling is a personal matter: Michelle Gayer peels rhubarb and then incorporates the peelings into a simple syrup. "That way I control how much flavor and color I infuse back into the dish." Chef Eric Maillard says that peeling depends on the specific batch: "The most important step is to taste often. Flavor, acidity, and fiber vary enormously. Some stalks need destringing, some don't. Some are highly acid, some mild." Gary Danko doesn't peel rhubarb but slices it thin "like meat, across the grain, to cut the fibers short." Joho peels, then adds another step: "Cut up and toss in a little sugar—about 1 tablespoon per pound of rhubarb—to remove moisture and reduce acidity. For purees, I leave overnight. When the rhubarb will remain in pieces, 4 or 5 hours is enough." Remember to cook in non-aluminum pots only—or you'll have clean cookware and tarnished rhubarb.

Tart and Shiny Rhubarb— the Vegetable

This recipe showcases vivid color, lush texture, and distinct tartness. Often rhubarb's color pales when cooked. For some quirky chemical reason, though, when it is partially cooked, then allowed to finish softening in its warm juices, its ruby color almost always revives. If baked in stationary sections rather than being tossed in thin slices, the red skin remains smooth and shiny and uppermost, while the paler interior is hidden beneath. But timing is tricky: The dish must be watched constantly and removed from the oven while still undercooked if it is to make a beautiful statement on a buffet table.

Choose deep rose stalks of equal width. Be warned that the tartness is merely mitigated with maple, but not eliminated. The bracing taste suits rich seafood or poultry or pork.

1½ pounds rosy-red rhubarb stalks of equal
    width
3 tablespoons pure maple syrup
1 tablespoon butter
1 tablespoon vinegar (preferably raspberry or
    other fruit vinegar)
¼ teaspoon kosher salt
Big pinch of ground allspice
Big pinch of pepper

1. Preheat oven to 425°F. Trim rhubarb stalk tops and bases. With flatter side down, cutting at a sharp angle, slice several stalks at a time into 1½- to 2-inch lengths; keep pieces together.

2. Choose a rectangular or square baking dish to hold rhubarb in a tight single layer. In a small pan, combine maple syrup, butter, vinegar, salt, allspice, and pepper. Bring to a boil, stirring. With a brush, coat dish with the mixture. Arrange rhubarb in neat rows, rounded side upward, tightly packed and aligned as if the stalks were still whole. Brush with half the remaining butter mixture.

3. Bake 5 minutes. Brush with remaining mixture. Continue baking until rhubarb is not quite done—still slightly firm in the center—2 to 6 minutes longer. Cool.

4. With spatula, move pieces as needed to straighten up the pattern. Serve warm or at room temperature.

Serves 4 as a side dish

Variation

Rhubarb with Pink Peppercorns

For those who relish the aromatic, a finish of pink peppercorns is no mere color conceit: The curious sweet taste is just the right finish to the rhubarb. Delete the allspice from the maple mixture. When you take the cooked rhubarb from the oven, sprinkle over 1½ teaspoons crushed pink peppercorns. Allow to cool.

Chilled Spiced Rhubarb and Red Wine Soup

Ruby with a pink flush, smooth, and full-bodied, this soup is fruity, but not dessert-like. The rhubarb presence is mellow, not assertive, in the gingery, winy blend. Offer the light, elegant, unusual puree as the opener for a multi-course spring or summer meal.

½ teaspoon cardamom pods, lightly crushed
6 whole cloves
2 teaspoons coriander seeds, lightly crushed
1 cinnamon stick, broken
¼ teaspoon peppercorns, lightly crushed
½ teaspoon dried thyme
2 cups fruity, fairly light red wine
About 1½ cups water
1 pound rhubarb
1 Granny Smith apple
1 medium-small beet
2-inch ginger chunk
1½ tablespoons sugar
½ teaspoon kosher salt
About 4 tablespoons pure maple syrup
About ⅓ cup whole-milk yogurt, whisked
    to liquefy

1. In non-aluminum saucepan, combine cardamom, cloves, coriander, cinnamon, pepper, thyme, wine, and 1½ cups water. Bring to a boil. Reduce heat, cover, and simmer until flavors are extracted—about 15 minutes. Strain out spices. Return liquid to rinsed-out pan.

2. Meanwhile, trim and slice rhubarb. Peel and chop or grate apple. Peel and fine-chop or grate beet. Peel and thin-slice enough ginger to make 2 tablespoons. Add these to wine mixture, with sugar and salt.

3. Bring to a boil. Reduce heat and simmer, partly covered, until mixture is very soft, about 35 minutes.

Cool slightly, then whiz to a puree with an immersion blender; or transfer to blender or food processor and puree. Allow to cool. Thin soup with water, if desired.

4. Chill thoroughly, preferably overnight.

5. To serve, gradually stir maple syrup into soup, tasting. Ladle into bowls. Drizzle liquefied yogurt over each. Trace a spiral or crosshatch pattern with knife tip or tines of fork.

Serves 4 as a first course

Pros Propose

Sorrel, gooseberries, tomatillos, and other acid fruits and vegetables are traditionally paired with sweet or rich seafood or meats to balance the sourness. Rhubarb slips naturally into this same role, whether as sauce or final flavor accent.

Nothing could be a richer foil than foie gras, which chef Jean Joho considers the most perfect savory partner for rhubarb. For **Foie Gras with Rhubarb:** Macerate diced rhubarb overnight with a little sugar to firm and mellow. Drain and discard juice. Sauté diced pear in a little butter. Add rhubarb, a little Gewürztraminer, pepper, and a touch of nutmeg and clove. Cover and simmer until rhubarb is soft. Puree, return to pan, and cook down. Top with sautéed foie gras sprinkled with coarse sea salt. Spoon a tiny bit of duck *jus* around.

Bone marrow slices provide the richness for an otherwise vegetarian **Spring Ragôut** from chef Tom Colicchio: Sauté raw pencil-thin asparagus tips and morels. Add blanched ramp bulbs and skinned fresh favas. Stir in rounds of bone marrow, a little stock, and thin-sliced rhubarb. Heat through and serve.

For **Pork Tenderloins with Rhubarb Sauce:** Marinate pork tenderloins overnight in salt, pepper, cinnamon, thyme, allspice, and garlic. Combine rhubarb and brown sugar, and macerate an hour. Brown pork; deglaze pan with balsamic vinegar and stock. Cover and cook gently until pork temperature measures 145°F and meat is tender, about 20 minutes; remove and set aside. Add rhubarb and more stock to cooking liquid and simmer until thick. Strain into pan. Add or-ange zest and fresh thyme. Serve with the sliced pork (from *Pacific Northwest Palate* by Susan Bradley).

Similar in concept but different in flavor is a currant-and-carrot-sweetened stew from chef Laura Dewell, whose former Seattle restaurant, Piros Mani, specialized in Soviet Georgian cuisine. For **Spring Lamb Stew with Rhubarb:** Sauté cubed lamb shoulder and onions in butter and oil until well browned. Add water to almost cover, dried currants, small carrot dice, crushed cardamom seeds, cumin, cinnamon, and clove. Cook, covered, until meat is almost tender. Add sliced rhubarb and cook until soft. Serve over baked rice with onions and pistachios.

For Persian **Chicken with Rhubarb,** the stalks are not blended into the sauce but instead placed on top as a tart finish: Brown skinned chicken legs and sliced onion. Add salt, pepper, turmeric, and water. Simmer, covered, 15 minutes. Cook lots of chopped parsley and mint (1 quart for a 2-pound chicken) in olive oil, stirring to wilt and cook down. Add to chicken, with saffron, tomato paste, and lime juice. Simmer, covered, until chicken is tender. Transfer to casserole. Arrange rhubarb pieces over all. Cover with foil and pierce it. Bake in moderate oven until rhubarb is tender but not falling apart (from *Persian Cooking for a Healthy Kitchen* by Najmieh Batmanglij).

Sweet spices are a common addition to rhubarb— but not to lobster. Here, the syrupy aromatic sauce is offset by rhubarb's sharp acidity. To prepare chef Eric Maillard's **Lobster with Rhubarb:** Simmer syrup made from orange juice, cloves, coriander, cardamom, cinnamon, and honey. Add diced Granny Smith apple and diced rhubarb and cook briefly. Add syrup and ras el hanout (or another complex sweet spice blend) and cook to just soften. Poach lobster in salted water with seaweed for a few minutes. Remove meat from shells. Sauté lightly; set meat on warm rhubarb compote.

For a thin herbal sauce, chef James Walt makes a reduction of rhubarb juice, not stalks. To prepare **Lingcod in Light Rhubarb Sauce with Spring Herbs:** Run rhubarb through juicer. Combine with half as much fish stock and a little maple syrup; reduce to a light sauce consistency. Pan-fry lingcod fillets. Reheat sauce and stir in blanched rhubarb bâtons. Off heat, add tarragon, sweet cicely, and fennel fronds. Set fish on cooked greens and surround with sauce.

Rutabaga, Swede (*Brassica napus,* Napobrassica Group)

Also Swedish, yellow, Canadian, or Russian turnip;
chou-navet jaune (French and French Canadian)

If rutabaga had been born in brassica-proud Asia instead of northern Central Europe, its probable starting place, it might have acquired a name like "golden globe" and been honored as the queen of root crops. Rutabaga is smooth-fleshed, sharp-sweet when raw, mellowed by cooking; it is neatly cuttable into trim bâtons or dice (or fanciful hearts and flowers); it can be pureed in soup or slivered into slaw, grated and gilded as little pancakes, steamed in dumplings, braised with sweet spices, and on and on. There is really just one way *not* to cook it: in lots of water for a long time—the method that is common in many English and American kitchens.

In the United States, rutabaga did not become established until the 19th century, and its image has needed upgrading ever since. For British and American food writers, rutabaga-bashing has been a sport for some fifty years. (In Canada, where most rutabaga is cultivated, it is put to regular and excellent use—perhaps owing to the French influence.) Even some talented food writers vilify rutabaga or serve it up with apologies. Jane Grigson, doyenne of British vegetable writers, pens poisonously, "As a vehicle for butter, with haggis and whisky, it is exactly right. But . . . I conclude that otherwise . . . [rutabaga] is a vegetable to be avoided. The watery orange slush of school dinner was unredeemed by drainage or butter" (*Jane Grigson's Vegetable Book*). Barbara Kafka begins a recipe with "I roasted rutabagas out of a sense of duty" (*Roasting*). Such words are typical of the many people who are then amazed to find that they like the vegetable.

What causes this prejudice? Another food writer, the all-embracing Bert Greene, has suggested scent: "When I was young, kitchen odors—even felicitous ones—were considered declassé," he writes in his delicious cookbook and memoir *Greene on Greens*. "If you were respectable (a word my mother summoned up with righteousness all her life), no one was ever supposed to know what was really cooking in your pots!" (Young Bert subsequently fell for a girl whose "entire apartment . . . was suffused with the most intoxicating

diameter: 3-5 inches

perfume" of "rutabaga braising to a dull tarnished gold in a bath that would give any alchemist joy—onions, red wine, and bits of bacon.")

The name rutabaga does not help the image either—and for many people, image seems to matter more than deliciousness. Some chefs deal with this in a curious way: They keep rutabaga a secret or call it something else. Then, diners who discover it are likely to be charmed. Chef Susan McCreight Lindeborg says: "I don't specify the name on the menu. I just serve rutabagas as unexplained side dishes. Everyone eats them—no questions asked—and says they're heaven." Chef and author Deborah Madison suggests: "Write 'root vegetable.' Whether it's pureed or hashed or whatever, people say: wow, great! They always go for 'root vegetable' on a menu."

Fortunately, American chefs of the present generation seem to be sufficiently gaga for rutabaga to turn the tide, even by telling the truth. Maybe this love affair will carry over into the home.

BASIC USE: Shred or julienne small new-crop rutabagas to serve raw and marinated in salads—they're as sweet, crisp, and as interesting as celeriac. Slice paper-thin for crudité platters, or to stir-fry.

Steam rutabaga sticks or dice just until al dente, or the sweetness will be lost. Or microwave for an easy, sunny, tender side dish: Peel and thick-slice or cube about 1¼ pounds rutabaga (for about 3 servings). Combine with ⅓ cup water in microwavable container; cover and cook until tender, 12 to 15 minutes. Toss with a little thyme and butter. To microwave for puree, add more water and increase cooking time by about 5 minutes.

For mellow stew, braise cubed rutabaga with chunks of pork, beef, or lamb. Or blanch rutabaga chunks, then roast alongside large cuts of the same meats, basting now and then. Steam rutabagas and potatoes together, then mash: Use as a base for croquettes and soufflés. Prepare a creamy puree to bake en casserole. Thin-slice to bake with cream and cheese, au gratin. Caramelize cubes slowly with bacon. Brush wedges with maple syrup or honey blended with nut oil or melted butter, then bake in a fairly hot oven until golden and tender.

SELECTION: Rutabaga is available year-round, mostly from Canada. The volume increases in fall and wanes in spring. Rutabaga sold in the United States is beige to tan with a lilac or violet neck. Choose comparatively heavy rutabagas, which are likely to be juicy. Avoid any with cracks, pitting, or soft areas.

In the fall, around harvest time, it is possible to come across rutabagas that have not been waxed. Later, all rutabaga that I find is defiled by a coat of paraffin, presumably to prevent damage in shipping and dehydration. Growers say that the distributors and retailers who want to extend shelf life insist on the wax: "It's a pain and an expense for us—plus, it's so ugly," said one farmer, who asked to remain anonymous. "And when applied too heavily, wax may cause internal breakdown." Stored under ideal conditions—nearly 100 percent humidity at 32°F—rutabaga lasts for months.

PREPARATION: Cutting up rutabaga is dangerous. You must whack hard to get a knife into the dense flesh—and slippery wax makes this even more risky. Unless you have a guillotine, a heavy cleaver works best. Unwaxed rutabaga can be microwaved for a minute or just until softened enough to cut chunks.

Once chunked, rutabaga is easy to peel with a knife or paring tool. For slim slices, use a mandoline or food processor. Chef Odessa Piper has found that "one of the tricks to rutabaga's successful service is to cut it into shapes—turned, parisienne, bâtons, or pearls for broth." Or cut slices, then press small shapes with a truffle cutter or small cookie cutters. Those skilled in vegetable carving can have a field day with rutabaga.

Shredded Rutabaga and Carrot Sauté with Herbs

Bright, light, and quick to prepare—just what one rarely associates with rutabaga. Because both these root vegetables store well, you can whip up a colorful, fresh-tasting dish on the spur of the moment. Season to suit the rest of the meal: Shredded ginger is a brisk substitute for dill and parsley; or try marjoram or mint. If increasing the recipe, use your largest sauté pan.

½ small rutabaga (½ pound)
1 large carrot (¼ pound)
1 tablespoon vegetable oil
¼ teaspoon kosher salt
¼ cup cranberry juice or apple cider
¼ teaspoon dried dill, crumbled
¼ teaspoon fennel seeds, crushed or chopped
Optional: 2 teaspoons butter
1 tablespoon finely snipped chives or thin-sliced scallion greens

1. Trim and peel rutabaga and carrot. Zip through the shredding blade of a food processor (to make about 3 cups).

2. Heat large skillet over moderately high heat. Add oil and tip to coat pan. Add shredded vegetables and salt and toss to just begin to soften, about 2 minutes.

3. Add juice, dill, and fennel and toss 30 seconds or so, until liquid has nearly evaporated. Reduce heat, cover, and, cook until vegetables are tender but still sprightly, about 2 to 3 minutes. Uncover and toss with optional butter and chives. Serve hot.

Serves 2

Savory Rutabaga Tart

Baked golden slices of rutabaga look like a glazed apple tart: an impressive presentation. With a food processor's thin-slicing blade, the fancy-looking dish takes no time at all to put together (although baking time is over an hour). Serve the savory bittersweet vegetable with roasted turkey, chicken, pork, or duck.

> 1 tablespoon plus 1 teaspoon hazelnut oil
>   (or 1½ tablespoons melted butter)
> 1 tablespoon cornstarch
> 1 teaspoon ground coriander
> ½ teaspoon ground ginger
> ½ teaspoon kosher salt
> 1½ tablespoons water
> 1 tablespoon smooth (not coarse-grain) mustard
> 1 tablespoon pure maple syrup
> 1½ tablespoons cider vinegar or wine vinegar
> 2 to 2½ pounds rutabaga (1 medium or
>   2 small rutabagas)
> Optional: 2 tablespoons fine-chopped roasted
>   hazelnuts

1. Turn oven to 400°F. Line bottom and side of 8-inch cake pan with 12-inch round of foil: Coat with 1 teaspoon oil (or ½ tablespoon melted butter).

2. Blend cornstarch, coriander ginger, salt, and water. Add mustard, maple syrup, remaining 1 table-spoon oil (or butter), and vinegar.

3. Trim ends from rutabaga. Cut into 8 wedges (if using 2 small rutabagas, quarter each). Pare off all skin. Cut into lengthwise slices on the 2-millimeter slicing blade of a food processor.

4. Arrange one-third of the neatest, largest slices in a closely overlapping petal pattern (this will be the top of the tart) to cover bottom of prepared pan. Spoon one-third of cornstarch slurry over them, distributing it evenly. Spread half the remaining rutabaga on top (there is no need to arrange a design—just distribute evenly), then half the remaining slurry. Spread final rutabaga layer on top and drizzle with remaining slurry. Cover with foil. Press down firmly on foil to compress slices.

5. Bake in center of oven 1 hour. Using a pot holder, press firmly on foil to further compress the slices. Bake until very tender when pierced with a knife, about 15 minutes longer.

6. Remove from oven and let stand a few minutes. Remove foil. Set a serving plate on top and invert. Serve hot, with optional nuts sprinkled around the edge. (Can be made ahead and reheated.)

Serves 4 to 6 as a side dish

Mashed Potatoes and Rutabagas with Buttermilk

Buttery-looking and -tasting—but with a fraction of the fat usually assigned to this kind of dish. Another plus is reheatability (not possible with plain mashed potatoes), thanks to the moist rutabaga, which maintains its softly spoonable texture. For variety, add other wintry vegetables, such as celeriac, parsley root, or parsnip. An easy-to-like dish, this may be the one to alter the opinion of rutabaga reluctants. If you reduce or increase the recipe, keep the weight of rutabaga and potato about equal.

> 2 floury (baking) potatoes (about 1¼ pounds)
> 1 rutabaga (about 1¼ pounds)
> 2 to 4 garlic cloves, peeled
> About ⅓ cup buttermilk
> About ½ teaspoon kosher salt
> About ¼ teaspoon grated nutmeg
> About 1 tablespoon butter
> Optional: butter pats

1. Peel and quarter potatoes. Trim, quarter, and peel rutabaga. Cut into pieces about the same size as potatoes. Set vegetables and garlic cloves on a steamer rack over boiling water. Cover and steam until vegetables are quite soft, about ½ hour.

2. Transfer vegetables to mixing bowl. Without simmering, gently heat buttermilk. Gradually add to vegetables, crushing them with masher to desired texture. Add salt and nutmeg, then butter.

3. Reheat, if needed, in saucepan or microwave. Serve hot, with optional butter pats and a dusting of nutmeg.

Serves 4

Golden Rutabaga-Onion Pickle

Quick to prepare with a food processor, this wonderfully crunchy refrigerator pickle is hard to identify but easy to fit into a meal. Refresh a leftover roast with the pink and gold slices, or add a tart snap to seafood, grain, or starchy salads (especially ones with avocado, an ideal match). For variety, add chillis, anise, or caraway to the pickling liquid. For more brilliant color, add a thin-sliced raw small beet.

2 pounds small or medium rutabaga(s)
2 small red onions
¼ cup dried cranberries
10 bay leaves
1 teaspoon peppercorns
1 teaspoon whole allspice
2 cups red or white wine vinegar
2 cups "cran-apple" juice (or 1 cup each apple and cranberry juice)
1 teaspoon kosher salt
Optional: 2 garlic cloves, halved

1. Set a large kettle of water to boil. Quarter rutabaga (or cut into eighths, if large); peel. Peel onions; halve through stem end, then slice into half-rounds on food processor (4-millimeter) blade. Dump into colander and separate layers. Slice rutabaga on same blade and add to colander. In sink, empty boiling water over vegetables, tossing.

2. Wash two wide-mouth 1-quart canning jars in hot soapy water. Rinse with boiling water. While jars are still hot, divide vegetables between them, interspersing cranberries, bay leaves, pepper, and allspice.

3. Boil vinegar, juice, and salt in non-aluminum pot. Pour in to top up jars.

4. Let cool somewhat, then cover and refrigerate. Refrigerate 4 to 5 days or more before serving, shaking occasionally.

Makes 2 quarts

Pros Propose

If the recipe and menu repertoire for rutabaga has been limited in recent decades, it isn't any longer. What *is* limited is the appearance of the word "rutabaga" in the name of the dish, as some chefs choose invisibility on the menu, if not on the plate.

Raw rutabaga is delightfully sweet and crisp (I snack on it as I do radishes). Susan Herrmann Loomis includes it in **Root Vegetable Salad with Anchovy Vinaigrette:** Combine julienne of raw rutabaga, white turnip, and fennel. Toss with dressing of minced anchovies, mustard, sherry vinegar and balsamic vinegar, sugar, and olive oil. Toss red bell pepper julienne with minced fennel fronds and more of the same dressing. Pile mixed vegetables on plate and surround with bell pepper mixture (from *Farmhouse Cookbook*).

The recipe that changed Barbara Kafka's opinion about this often maligned root was **Roasted Rutabaga Wedges:** Cut rutabaga into wedges about 4 inches long and peel. Toss with olive oil in a baking pan. Spread wedges flat side down so that they'll brown. Roast at 500°F until caramelized, flipping halfway through. Sprinkle with coarse salt and malt vinegar (from *Roasting*).

The uses of rye bread as thickener and bacon as flavoring are common to Eastern European soups, but other ingredients in this **Rutabaga Soup** reveal its multicultural heritage—not surprising, since it came from Peruvian-Italian-American chef Felipe Rojas-Lombardi. To prepare: Cook diced peeled rutabaga in boiling salted water until al dente. Drain, reserving liquid. Gently cook chopped bacon, add chopped onions, and cook until soft. Add garlic, ginger, minced fresh chilli, chopped carrot, crushed caraway seeds, and peeled, chopped raw rutabaga; toss briefly. Add beef stock, reserved cooking liquid, and rye bread pieces. Simmer until soft. Cool, then puree. Heat gently with milk, white pepper, and reserved rutabaga dice. Garnish with parsley (from *Soup Beautiful Soup*).

"This soup contains many vegetables, but is defined by rutabaga, which has a sweetness and power unlike any others," says chef Patrick O'Connell, who serves humbly dubbed **Root Vegetable Soup** at his very fancy restaurant. To prepare: Peel and dice or chop Ozark Gold or Golden Delicious apple, rutabaga, Butternut squash, carrot, onion, and sweetpotato. Gently cook all in butter. Add salt, pepper, and chicken stock. Simmer until tender. Puree and strain. Add cream and season. Strain again.

O'Connell also prepares a novel **Rutabaga Rösti** that can be assembled in advance (unlike traditional potato rösti) because baked potatoes don't discolor like the usual raw ones and because rutabaga supplies the moisture lost without raw potatoes. To prepare: Bake large floury potatoes. Peel and grate into a bowl. Grate in raw rutabaga; season. Fry spoonfuls of the mixture in clarified butter until golden, pressing down into neat cakes (O'Connell browns and serves these in individual copper pans).

Chef Michael Romano reports that **Mashed Yellow Turnips with Crispy Shallots** (again, the invisible rutabaga!) is one of those dishes that cannot be removed from the menu at the Union Square Cafe. "It's a recipe from Danny's grandmother [Danny Meyer, co-owner], and it's right up there with spinach and garlic on the best-seller list." To prepare: Slowly fry shallot rings in olive oil and butter until crisp; drain. Boil rutabaga dice in salted water, covered, until tender. Drain well. While hot, puree in a tall narrow pot using an immersion blender, working until very smooth. Reheat with plenty of butter. Top with the shallots.

An elegant **Autumn Galette** from chef Odessa Piper is aptly named. To prepare: Thin-slice equal quantities of peeled rutabaga, parsnip, and potato. Slice unpeeled red apples twice as thick. In buttered tartlet pans, arrange spiral layers of potato and apple, then two layers each of rutabaga and parsnip, seasoning each layer and brushing with butter. As you proceed, sprinkle grated Parmesan on alternate layers, nutmeg on the parsnip, and rosemary and thyme on the rutabaga. Cover with foil and bake in moderately hot oven until tender. Cool slightly, then invert onto plates. Surround with seared winter greens, roasted chestnuts, and roasted lady apples drizzled with a cider reduction.

Salicornia, Sea Bean (*Salicornia* species, mainly *S. europaea*)

Also glasswort, poussepied and poussepierre, marsh samphire
or samphire, chicken claws, sea pickle, pickleweed

⅔ **actual size**

The name game begins neatly enough and winds up in a pretty pickle. *Salicornia,* meaning salty horn, is both the common and the Latin name of the plant pictured, an apt description of its pointy saline "twigs" (less pronounced in this cultivated specimen than in the wild). Glasswort (glass plant) originated with a related species that was used in the manufacture of glass. Sea bean, a recent name used in marketing the plant, is not far-fetched. Chicken claws makes reference to the birdlike form of the jointed branchlets.

Samphire is another story. Two unrelated and very different Old World plants share this common name. One is *Salicornia europaea,* which belongs to the goosefoot family (Chenopodiaceae); the other is *Crithmum maritimum* (also called rock samphire and sea fennel), a fragrant, fleshy member of the umbellifer family (Apiaceae). Both are venerable edibles, notably in England and France, where they grow wild along the seacoast and marshes. The name developed along similar lines, from the French perce-pierre (rock-piercer) and Saint-Pierre (from Saint Peter, who struck deep into the rock). Over the years, these were corrupted in both English and French to such forms as passe-pierre, pousse-pierre, sampier, sampyre, and samphire. Both wound up in old cookbooks as samphire—usually pickled, hence the names pickleweed and sea pickle. Although poussepierre, which is derived from French, is the word you'll see on menus and produce distributors' lists in the United States, I have seen only "salicorne" used for the plant in France.

Salicornia is *not* seaweed, as it is often described, nor

a cactus, which it slightly resembles. It is a succulent salt-tolerant plant that grows wild in North America, Europe, Asia, and Australia. Young and crisp, juicy and salty, it delivers a burst of green and sea savors, notably to vegetable and seafood dishes.

Salicornia is also farm-raised. It is now being grown in Mexico under the proprietary name Seaphire by a company called Planetary Design Corporation, with headquarters in Phoenix, Arizona. The cultivated samples I tasted were uniformly tender, clean, and trim, and tasted as intense as the wild plant.

BASIC USE: Unadorned branchlets of salicornia make a briny, crisp, novel garnish. Add to canapés and sandwiches. Toss sprigs or chopped bits into salads for a fresh saline bite. Or blanch, refresh, and chill; then combine with vegetables, seafood, poultry, or meat in a composed salad.

To judge from culinary history and from processed European products, salicornia makes a fine pickle—but I haven't been able to devise a recipe that pleases me. When salicornia is cooked through (whether sautéed, steamed, or boiled), I think it loses its special succulence and turns salty and fishy; but many think otherwise.

If salicornia is too large or too chewy to nibble nicely, it can still be used as a bed or a stuffing to add sea-fresh flavor to steamed or braised seafood; discard after cooking.

SELECTION: Wild salicornia is sold mainly in the summer. By fall (when it may redden), salicornia develops a tough, fibrous central filament, but (as noted above) it can still be used as a bed for steaming or braising. Select small salicornia that is bright and firm, not flabby, darkening, or slimy. If you gather your own, chef and forager Fernando Divina advises "a grab-and-snap motion. Do not cut it or pull up the whole plants, or you take the life out of them."

Cultivated salicornia (Seaphire) is not widely available, but theoretically it is in season year-round.

STORAGE: Salicornia may take weeks to show signs of spoilage, but it loses its perkiness if kept more than a week. It is easily rejuvenated (and slightly desalinated) by an overnight soak in the refrigerator or a short bath in ice water.

PREPARATION: Depending upon how the salicornia was harvested, it may have little rootlets. If so,

trim them off. If the bases are heavy, trim these. Cut plants into bite-size twiglets. Cultivated salicornia should need no trimming.

Salad of Salicornia, Shrimp, Apple, and Belgian Endive

A sprightly toss of pink shrimp, bitter Belgian endive crescents, and sweet apple slivers is accented with briny salicornia "twiglets." The bright green vinaigrette adds lemony and herbal notes. Plan to chill the components for an hour or more.

> 2 cups water
> ½ teaspoon fennel seeds
> 4 to 5 ounces salicornia
> ¾ pound small shrimp in the shell (about 30 shrimp), rinsed
> About 3 tablespoons lemon juice
> ¼ cup olive oil
> 1 crisp, sweet medium apple
> 2 small Belgian endives
> 3 tablespoons sliced chives
> ¼ cup tightly packed parsley leaves
> ⅛ teaspoon pepper

1. Combine water and fennel seeds in medium skillet. Cover and simmer while you trim salicornia: As needed, remove rootlets and any dark bases from salicornia. Cut plants into 1½-inch sections.

2. Add salicornia to water and bring to a boil over high heat, stirring. Lift out with skimmer (do not drain skillet). Refresh in cold water, drain, and pat dry. Refrigerate.

3. Add shrimp to water in skillet and bring to a simmer over moderate heat, stirring constantly. When shrimp have just turned pink, lift out with skimmer. Let cool. Boil liquid in skillet to reduce to about 2 tablespoons; set aside.

4. Peel shrimp, halve lengthwise, and devein. Toss with 1 teaspoon each of the reduction, lemon juice, and olive oil. Refrigerate.

5. Cut apple into eighths. Core, then cut crosswise into thin slices. Trim Belgian endives and slice crosswise. Combine the remaining reduction and lemon juice, chives, parsley, and pepper in blender or mini-processor. Whiz to a frothy puree. Gradually add the remaining olive oil, to form an emulsion.

6. Toss together salicornia, shrimp, apples, and Belgian endive. Toss with three-quarters of the dressing. Taste and add more dressing as needed. Season. Divide among plates.

**Serves 4 as a first course,
2 as a luncheon main dish**

Frittata of Potatoes, Salicornia, and Dill

A collage of salicornia strewn across a golden frittata rewards with crunch and saltiness. Handy for a buffet, this exceptionally pretty dish tastes good hot, warm, or at room temperature.

**2 small yellow-fleshed potatoes
(6 to 8 ounces)
1 medium onion
2½ tablespoons olive oil
Salt and pepper
3 ounces salicornia
5 eggs
¼ cup packed dill (stripped from stems)
Sliced small cherry tomatoes or halved
currant tomatoes**

1. Peel potatoes. Cut lengthwise into slices ⅛ inch thick. Stack, and cut crosswise into strips the same width. Do the same with onion.

2. Heat 1½ tablespoons oil in wide skillet (preferably non-stick) over low heat. Add onions, potatoes, and pinches of salt and pepper. Cook gently, stirring often, for 5 minutes (do not brown—keep heat low). Cover and continue to cook gently until very tender, about 15 minutes, stirring a few times.

3. Meanwhile, turn on broiler, setting broiler pan as far as possible from heat source. Trim salicornia if needed, removing rootlets and dark bases. Cut into 1-inch pieces. Whisk eggs to blend. Chop dill and add to eggs.

4. When potatoes are tender, add salicornia. Raise heat and stir until salicornia begins to get a little juicy, 1 to 2 minutes. Scoop mixture into eggs and stir gently to mix.

5. Wipe skillet clean. Add remaining 1½ tablespoons oil and warm over moderate heat. Add egg mixture, spreading it evenly in pan. Reduce heat and cook, without stirring, just until barely set (top center should remain liquid). Place in broiler just long enough to firm up the top—not to brown—a minute or so.

6. Loosen frittata with flexible spatula. Slide onto a serving dish. Decorate with tomatoes. Or cut into wedges and arrange tomatoes on each. Serve hot, warm, or at room temperature.

Serves 4 to 6 as an appetizer or hors d'oeuvre

Pros Propose

The frittata recipe above is made from the same ingredients as these pancakes from the Savoie, **Matafans aux Salicornes:** Peel, wash, and dry starchy potatoes. Grate medium-fine; discard half the starchy liquid that accumulates. Mix potatoes and remaining liquid with beaten eggs, flour, a touch of garlic, salt, pepper, and a pinch of sugar. Add trimmed salicornia pieces. Fry tablespoons of the mixture in skillet, turning to brown both sides. Drain on paper. Serve hot, garnished with salicornia tips (from *Herbier Gourmand* by Marc Veyrat and François Couplan).

Another crisp, browned appetizer comes from Mexico, through Japanese culinary channels. Chef Alejandro Heredia serves crunchy **Tempura of Salicornia and Eggplant:** Cut eggplant into julienne the same size as salicornia sprigs. Fry eggplant until golden. Dip salicornia into tempura batter. Fry until crisp. Serve both with a dipping sauce of Guajillo chillis.

Several types of salicornia are gathered in Australia. Juleigh Robins offers a range of recipes in her enlightening *Wild Lime: Cooking from the Bushfood Garden.* For **Steamed Crab with Marsh Samphire:** Steam cleaned blue crabs 5 minutes. Toss grated ginger and crushed garlic briefly in oil in hot wok. Add crabs, cooking a few minutes to blend flavors. Add pepper, plenty of lime zest and juice, and white wine. Cover and cook 2 minutes. Meanwhile, steam samphire (salicornia) a few minutes. Arrange crabs on a platter; surround with the samphire. Serve with lemon, lemon mayonnaise, and finger bowls.

To soften salicornia's sharp saltiness, chef Jerry

Traunfeld, author of *The Herbfarm Cookbook,* blanches it and serves it with rich fish. For **Grilled Salmon with Sweet Onion and Sea Bean Salad:** Toss thin-sliced Walla Walla onions with seasoned rice vinegar and grated lemon zest. Blanch and refresh sea beans (salicornia) twice. Grill skinned, oiled king salmon fillets over low fire. Add sea beans to onions and serve draped over the hot fish.

Another West Coast chef, Fernando Divina, finds tender salicornia to pluck for the better part of the year. At the beginning of the season, he serves the most delicate sprigs in what he calls simply **Citrus Slaw,** "so people won't be put off by the unfamiliar green, which they are always intrigued with—once it's on their plates." To prepare: Combine four parts chiffonade of Chinese cabbage with one part salicornia sprigs. Add orange and lime segments, their juices, and blanched fine julienne of the zests. Add hazelnut oil and toss.

For the simplest of shellfish preparations, Divina offers his **West Coast–Style Salish Mussels:** Soften chopped onion (he uses wild) in corn oil. Add cleaned mussels and chicken stock and cover with trimmed salicornia. Boil gently, covered, just until mussel shells open. Season with lemon juice and slices of lemon and butter. Serve at once.

For the most elegant of seafood-salicornia combinations, Chef Laurent Gras presents **Sea Urchins, Chanterelles, and Salicornia with Lemon Emulsion:** Sauté small whole chanterelles. Blanch salicornia tips. Remove wild Maine sea urchins from their shells. Strain juices from sea urchin. Puree lemon flesh with juices and olive oil to make a very lemony (not oily) sauce. Center a small bouquet of frisée on each plate; sprinkle with minced shallot, salt, and pepper. Arrange sea urchin segments, chanterelles, and salicornia around this. Dab a little lemon emulsion on each element ("to be eaten ingredient by ingredient, not as a mixed salad").

Salsify (*Tragopogon porrifolius*)

Also oyster plant, white salsify

Black Salsify, Scorzonera (*Scorzonera hispanica*)

Also black oyster plant

Salsify is a name for two plants of two different genera, both within the giant family Compositae (also called Asteraceae). Although the use of a single name is confusing, there are botanical and culinary reasons for it. Superficially, the two plants can be described by traits they have in common with other members of the family: The leaves resemble flat chicories and endive; the root looks like burdock (I have seen salsify and burdock mixed up in markets).

The flavor is reminiscent of soft-cooked heart of artichoke with a suggestion of sunchoke, although it is usually compared to the oyster—not a relative!

Although similar, the two roots are by no means the same, as you can see. **White salsify** is pale-skinned, comparatively thin, forked, and scraggly with tiny rootlets. The genus name, *Tragopogon,* means goat's beard and refers to the silky white seed filaments (like the fluff of dandelions—another family member) that

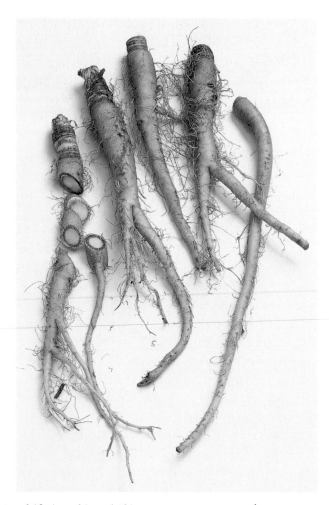

salsify (or white salsify)   ⅓ actual size

scorzonera (also called black salsify)   ⅓ actual size

distinguish plants in the genus. The species, *porrifolius,* means leek-leaved and fairly accurately describes the flat, narrow greens of this plant.

Scorzonera (the correct name, although **black salsify** is common) resembles a muddy brown petrified carrot without the taper. It is usually more regularly shaped, longer, meatier, and smoother than salsify. Its flavor includes a hint of coconut as well as artichoke. The Oxford English Dictionary traces scorzonera to Spanish *escorzon,* "some kind of toad or lizard, deemed venomous," and notes that it was "also formerly called viper's grass . . . [and] was supposed to be good against the bites of vipers and other venomous creatures." Scorzonera was introduced to European culture through Spanish seed (hence *hispanica*), but there seems to be little in the current Spanish culinary repertoire.

Sadly, what is most notable about salsify and scorzonera at present is their absence in the United States. How this came about is a mystery. By the late 18th century the two southern European natives were both cultivated here, and they continued to be standard fare in seed catalogues and markets, and to be mentioned in cookbooks, until . . . poof! They disappeared. Thomas Jefferson mentioned "salsafia" (primarily the white *Tragopogon*) 39 times in his garden records (1766 to 1824) and planted roughly the same amount as of carrots and asparagus. He also noted that over an eight-year period, white salsify was available in the Washington market from June into April, making it one of the most extended crops of the era.

In 1824, Mary Randolph (a relative of Jefferson's) included three salsify recipes in her book *The Virginia Housewife,* with the proviso that "they are a very excellent vegetable, but require nicety in cooking," and summed up with: "They are delicious in whatever way they can be dressed."

Alessandro Filippini, chef at Delmonico's restaurant and author of *The Table* (1891), included "oyster plant" (the term appears to be an American invention of the 1820s) as a matter of course, as did other cookbooks of the time, and mentioned that it was available from September to June in the New York market. He prepared it three ways (with butter and lemon, with poulette sauce, and as fritters), much in keeping with European chefs of the time.

Salsify appeared in most standard cookbooks—for example, *The Original Boston Cooking-School Cookbook* (1896), *Mrs. Rorer's New Cook Book* (1902), and the original *Joy of Cooking* (1931)—until it just stopped (with some exceptions, notably in Pennsylvania Dutch country). Was it wiped out by a salsifian equivalent of chestnut blight or Dutch elm disease? Did marketing "experts" decide that it was old-fashioned? I cannot say. I know that if you want it now you must go to a farmers' market or find imported scorzonera (Belgian, and very good) or grow your own.

BASIC USE: Salsify and scorzonera are virtually interchangeable with regard to techniques and recipe timing, although their taste and texture are somewhat different. Their charm is low-key, so season discreetly. They fit flavorings and recipes for sunchokes and artichoke hearts.

Above all, be vigilant when cooking: The roots change quickly from succulent-tender to mushy. Because they break easily, gentle poaching and steaming are preferable to boiling. Unfortunately, you really can't tell much about the quality of salsify until it's cooked. It should be very tender, a bit tacky, and free of obvious fiber. If roots turn out to be stringy, discard them.

Once cooked, cut salsify to suit and finish in one of several ways: Glaze in melted butter with a touch of sugar and lemon; simmer or bake in a light béchamel or cheese sauce; combine with other root vegetables, sauté in butter, and finish with chervil and chives; bathe in vinaigrette. Dice and combine with cooked veal, turkey, or chicken to make hash or cakes. Or simply mash cooked salsify and stir in a little butter and cream, reheating to thicken and to intensify the flavors.

Add peeled, diagonally cut raw salsify to stews and braises during the last 45 minutes or so of cooking. Or brown salsify first, then braise with fowl or veal. Add to mixed vegetable soups or chowders. Or make a luxurious, delicate all-salsify pureed soup.

Be aware that scorzonera, like sunchoke, falls into the "ill wind" category, and for the same reason: Its primary carbohydrate, inulin, a dietary fiber, is not digested by humans and can thus provoke mild to extreme flatulence. Eat modestly if you don't know your tolerance.

SELECTION: Choose salsify and scorzonera that are medium size and as smooth and even as possible. Large roots may be fibrous and less tasty; very small ones have more skin than meat. Although not as firm as carrots, they should not be flabby. Theoretically, the season is from fall to spring, but I honestly can't figure out what it is.

I have seen white salsify only in local farmers' markets, forked and rooty; but I gather that it can be as uniform as black salsify if properly cultivated. It is sometimes sold with its flowing tops intact (the palest, with their mild endive taste, make a pleasant salad leaf).

At present, almost all scorzonera comes from Belgium. It is sold without greens, often bagged in plastic. If the roots are firm and full, they are generally very good indeed. Those who want domestic scorzonera might consider following the same route as chef Roland Liccioni: "I bring seeds from France to a farmer who grows it for me in Wisconsin. It's similar to the Belgian, but fresher and better."

STORAGE: If salsify is in good shape when you buy it, you can keep it up to 2 weeks in the refrigerator, wrapped in perforated plastic. Just check to be sure it doesn't dry out.

PREPARATION: Scrub with a brush. Peel completely, removing all rootlets and dark spots. (Do not be put off by a sticky exudate; it's normal.) Trim the neck if necessary. Cut off long skinny tips, which tend to be fibrous. If salsify is very wide at the base, cut off the thick part and halve lengthwise. Both salsifies discolor immediately (and also stain your hands) when peeled. Place vegetable in acidulated water as you work; clean your hands afterward with vinegar and salt. Although it is possible to peel salsify after cooking, this can be iffy, resulting in broken, drab roots and too much waste.

To Cook Salsify and Scorzonera: The Basics

Salsify and scorzonera can be steamed or simmered gently. In traditional European kitchens, they are cooked *à blanc* (in water mixed with flour and lemon juice) to maintain uniform paleness. I don't find this necessary, as the color stays pretty much the same with acid alone. But the European method adds tartness and succulence and allows for advance preparation, as the roots can be refrigerated in the liquid for a few days.

About 1¼ pounds scorzonera or 1½ pounds white salsify (weighed without leaves)

To prepare: Scrub roots with brush. Peel completely, removing rootlets and dark spots. Trim neck, if necessary; cut off long skinny tips, which can be fibrous. Leave whole or cut into lengths desired. If salsify is very wide at the base, cut off the thickest part and cut 2 or 3 lengthwise slices. Place pieces in a bowl of lemon water or in the pan of lemon-water or lemon-flour-water in which you'll cook them.

To steam: Drain off water. Place prepared salsify on steamer rack over boiling water. Cover; cook until just tender throughout. Timing varies from about 10 to 30 minutes. Check roots with knife tip and remove when tender. Do not overcook, or they will turn to mush.

To simmer: In non-aluminum saucepan, combine 6 to 8 cups water, ¼ cup lemon juice, and 1 teaspoon salt. Add prepared salsify; bring to a boil. Lower heat to bare simmer and cook until not quite tender. Cool in liquid until tender to taste. If you are going to puree the salsify, cook until truly soft, then drain.

To cook à blanc: In non-aluminum saucepan, whisk ¼ cup flour with enough water to make a paste. Gradually whisk in another cup of water, then pour in 1½ quarts more. Add ¼ cup lemon juice and 1 teaspoon salt, and proceed as above.

To finish: Mash soft-cooked salsify with butter and cream; reheat. Sauté diagonal slices in melted butter with a touch of sugar and lemon or orange to glaze. Simmer slices with cream and herbs. Bathe in vinaigrette and chill. Reheat salsify gently and spoon over any of the cream or egg sauces with which asparagus is served.

Serves 4

Salsify and Celery Salad with Pecans

Salsify not only tastes of artichoke heart but has a similar consistency (when properly cooked), and sometimes even discolors the same way. Don't worry if it looks splotchy. The tone evens out, once salsify is dressed, and looks elegantly cool with the pearly endive and celadon celery. As always with scorzonera or salsify, cooking time is crucial and unpredictable. Keep a close watch to avoid under- or over-cooking.

1 lemon, halved
1¼ pounds scorzonera or 1½ pounds salsify
   (weighed without leaves)
1 tablespoon white wine vinegar
1 tablespoon minced shallot
½ teaspoon kosher salt
2 teaspoons Dijon mustard
2 tablespoons pecan or walnut oil
2 tablespoons olive oil
½ cup pecans or walnuts (to match the oil)
1 cup thin-sliced inner celery stalks with
   leaves
2 medium Belgian endives
1 to 2 tablespoons thin-sliced chives

1. Squeeze juice from lemon; reserve 1 tablespoon. Combine remainder with water in a bowl large enough to hold salsify. Scrub and peel salsify, placing roots in lemon water as you proceed. Preheat oven to 350°F.

2. Remove salsify from water and place on steamer rack over boiling water. Cover and cook until tender throughout. Timing varies from about 10 to 30 minutes. Check roots with knife tip; remove when tender.

3. Combine vinegar, reserved lemon juice, shallot, salt, and mustard; blend. Whisk in nut and olive oils. Set nuts in pan in oven and toast until crisp, 5 to 10 minutes.

4. When salsify is cool enough to handle, cut into sharp diagonals about ½ inch wide. With rubber spatula, blend gently with dressing. Cool to room temperature, tossing gingerly now and then. Add celery. (Can be refrigerated at this point. Return to room temperature to serve.)

5. To serve, core and rinse Belgian endives. Cut about 2 inches from pointed ends. Separate these "petals" and arrange around serving dish. Thin-slice remainder and add to salad, with chives and nuts. Toss and season. Spoon onto serving plate.

Serves 4 as a first course

Scorzonera and Mushrooms in Cream

Scorzonera and salsify subtly suggest artichoke hearts in their complexity—and also in their pallor. The taste is not pale, however, but creamy and nuanced, here faintly underscored by coriander and heightened by lemon. If coriander is not at hand, substitute ¼ teaspoon nutmeg or mace. Do not be tempted to cook the mushrooms with the cream, or the acid will curdle the sauce. Serve over a pilaf of wild and brown rices with almonds, pecans, or pine nuts. Or spoon alongside sautéed veal scallops, baked fish, or roasted pork or poultry.

1 pound scorzonera or 1¼ pounds salsify
   (weighed without greens)
½ pound white button mushrooms
   (preferably very small)
1 tablespoon butter
1 small shallot, minced
½ teaspoon kosher salt
½ teaspoon ground coriander
1 tablespoon lemon juice
3 tablespoons white wine or dry vermouth
¼ cup milk
½ cup heavy cream

1. Scrub scorzonera with brush under running water. Peel, removing rootlets and dark spots. (For white salsify, you may need to trim necks and fibrous tips.) If bases are wide, cut off and halve lengthwise. Set on steamer rack over boiling water. Cover and cook until just tender throughout (there should be no crunch). Timing varies from about 10 to 30 minutes. Check smaller roots first; remove with tongs as they become tender. Let cool. Cut into ¼- to ½-inch-thick slices at a sharp angle.

2. Meanwhile, slice mushrooms fairly thin (if not small, halve first). Melt butter in heavy medium skillet over moderate heat. Add mushrooms, shallot, and ¼ teaspoon salt; toss to soften and release juice, but not to brown. Add coriander and toss. Add lemon juice and wine; raise heat to evaporate liquid. Transfer to a dish.

3. Combine scorzonera, milk, cream, and remaining ¼ teaspoon salt in same skillet. Bring to a simmer. Reduce heat, cover, and cook at just below a simmer until roots are very tender, about 5 minutes. Uncover, raise heat, and simmer to thicken sauce slightly. Stir in mushrooms, to barely heat through; do not simmer. Season.

Serves 4

Rabbit Braised with Scorzonera and Bay Leaves

The gentle flavors of scorzonera and rabbit have a subtle affinity (*firm-fleshed free-range chicken is a fine alternative*). Bay leaves vary in strength depending upon their provenance. Turkish leaves, which I used for this dish, are milder and more diffuse in flavor than those from California (use half the quantity of those). If your rabbit has its innards intact, sauté the sliced liver and kidneys as the dish finishes baking, then stir into the stew.

2 tablespoons flour
1¼ teaspoons kosher salt
¼ teaspoon cinnamon
¼ teaspoon pepper
3-pound rabbit, cut into 8 to 10 pieces
1 tablespoon butter
1½ tablespoons corn or safflower oil
1½ pounds scorzonera (weighed without tops)
1 medium onion, chopped
1¼ cups mushroom, vegetable, rabbit,
    or veal broth
6 bay leaves
2 tablespoons lemon juice
Thin lemon slices

1. Set oven to 350°F. Mix flour, 1 teaspoon salt, cinnamon, and pepper in a bag. Add rabbit pieces and shake to coat evenly.

2. Heat butter and ½ tablespoon oil over moderate heat in an ovenproof sauté pan with cover (or use a Dutch oven). Brown rabbit well on both sides, about 10 minutes. Transfer to a plate.

3. Meanwhile, scrub, trim, and peel scorzonera. Cut into 1½-inch diagonal lengths. Cut thicker pieces into shorter lengths.

4. Add remaining ½ tablespoon oil to pan. Add scorzonera and remaining ¼ teaspoon salt; brown slowly over moderately low heat, about 10 minutes. During the last few minutes, add onion. Add broth, bay leaves, and lemon juice; bring to a boil, scraping pan and stirring.

5. Add rabbit and bring to a boil. Cover pan and transfer to oven. Bake 25 minutes. Turn and redistribute rabbit. Continue baking until flesh is fork-tender, about 20 minutes more.

6. Arrange rabbit in center of warm platter with scorzonera around it. Spoon over the pan juices. Decorate with lemon slices.

Serves 3 to 4

Pros Propose

John Evelyn combined "Viper-grass, Tragopogon, Scorzonera, Salsifex & c." as a single subject in his *Acetaria: A Discourse of Sallets* (1699), and deemed them "best of all stew'd with Marrow, Spice, Wine, & c. as Artichoak, Skirrets, &c. sliced or whole. They likewise may bake, fry, or boil them; a more excellent Root there is hardly growing." Chef Chris Gesualdi prepares a dish that fits Evelyn's era—and even earlier times— **Black Salsify with Red Wine Syrup:** Place peeled scorzonera in acidulated water. Combine red wine, water, sugar, honey, vinegar, bay leaf, and peppercorns; boil briefly. Cool. Add salsify; return to a boil. Lower heat and simmer, keeping salsify submerged, until almost tender. Cool in liquid. Remove and cut into bâtonnets. Reduce red wine to syrup. Serve salsify as a garnish for foie gras, dotting with tiny amounts of the syrup.

Salsify "is another European peasant or poor man's staple that has just started to turn up . . . as a high-priced gourmet novelty in the produce bins of urban America," notes Horst Scharfenberg in *The Cuisines of Germany*. He offers an Old World–style **Black Salsify with Meatballs:** Mix ground veal with eggs, nutmeg, and white bread that has been soaked and squeezed dry. Form little meatballs and dredge lightly in flour. Cook 2-inch lengths of peeled black salsify *à blanc*. Ten minutes before it is done, add meatballs and cook through. Drain, reserving cooking liquid. Melt butter in skillet; stir in flour to make a roux. Add enough reserved liquid to make a sauce. Thicken with egg yolks. Add cream; season with lemon juice. Add salsify and meatballs and heat gently.

"Poor man's" salsify has a distinct affinity for truffles, black and white. Chef Ed Brown adds another present-day luxury item, oysters, to play out the oyster-plant connection. For **Oysters in Salsify Cream:** Blanch salsify; cut into small dice. Cook in heavy cream until the salsify is soft and the cream is thick.

Spoon over warm oysters and top with shavings of white truffle.

Truffles also adorn the spare and elegant **Terrine of Leek and Salsify** from chef Roland Liccioni: Peel salsify and cook *à blanc.* Simmer small leeks in water and salt. Arrange both in a terrine so that the leeks create the "shell" and salsify the center of the block. Press and refrigerate 24 hours. Serve with black truffle vinaigrette.

In contrast to the coolly pale terrine, **Sautéed Scorzonera** seems like another vegetable entirely. Liccioni says, "There is no need to blanch the vegetable first. Black salsify has a very interesting flavor and texture cooked directly in a pan." To prepare: Slice peeled roots very thin. Immediately sauté in olive oil, tossing until tender. Finish with a touch of truffle oil, "which brings out the earthy sweetness of the vegetable."

Chef Diane Forley crisps the exterior of soft salsify to accompany creamy foie gras (humble handmaiden to haute cuisine seems to be this root's role). For **Croutons of Salsify:** Poach scorzonera *à blanc.* Cool in liquid. Drain, dry, and cut into 3-inch lengths. Press 3 lengths together to form "raft." Dip in egg wash and mustard, ground almonds, and bread crumbs; sauté in butter. Serve with foie gras and braised baby leeks.

Chef Daniel Boulud puts scorzonera in a central role—literally—in his **Crisp Rolls of Salsify with Prosciutto and Parmesan:** Cook peeled black salsify in acidulated water until tender. Drain, cool, and dry. Season with pepper. Wrap each root tightly in prosciutto. Brush phyllo dough with butter and sprinkle with Parmesan, nutmeg, salt, and pepper. Set stick of salsify on one edge and roll three times in dough. Trim excess dough, if any. Brush each roll with butter and roll in Parmesan. Bake until crisp in 400°F oven. To serve, cut into angled 2-inch lengths (from *Cooking with Daniel Boulud*).

The oyster connection is played to the hilt in **Oyster Oyster Oyster,** a rich trio from chef Curtis Eargle: Blanch oblique-cut salsify slices, then finish cooking in velouté sauce. Grill 3 large oyster mushroom caps per person and set in individual gratin. Mound salsify in the center; top with 3 shucked Bluepoint oysters. Spoon over hollandaise. Bake in 375°F oven to warm oysters and gild sauce.

Shallots (*Allium cepa,* Aggregatum Group)

and "échalion" or long onion (*Allium cepa*)

Towering banks of pearly pink shallots virtually define the street markets of Southeast Asia, where more shallots are grown than anywhere else in the world. In France, Belgium, and the Netherlands, market stalls overflow with a subtle selection of these bulbs: from gray to red-copper, from grape- to plum-size. Shoppers buy them by the pound, not the ounce, and carry them home in baskets, not in little net sacks like party favors. In the lands where they grow, shallots are served as a vegetable—not only in sauces, their familiar culinary habitat.

In the United States, shallot use has burgeoned over the last two decades. Those who cut their culinary teeth on Julia Child's television show *The French Chef* in the late 1960s will remember that green onions stood in for shallots in her early books, because few shallots were available. Shallots hidden away in fancy shops were tiny and very pricey, and often exploded

French shallots: Jersey Half-Long (*top left*), Jersey Long (*top right*), and Fermor (*bottom*)　　length: 2-3 inches

into dusty gray-green mold when palped. By the 1980s, the vivid little vegetable was much more widely available. Today, shallots are exported from France (our primary source) in rapidly increasing amounts: In 1997, 2,500 tons were sent to the United States; in 1999, that figure had grown to 4,525. Whether the increasing Asian population has stimulated demand or travel to Europe has heightened Americans' awareness of this vegetable's charm, its role is expanding. Bins of satiny shallots are no longer an uncommon sight in supermarkets.

But are they shallots? Probably not all of them are, according to Marcel Le Nard and Gérard Sparfel, shallot specialists at the Institut National de Recherche Agronomique in Ploudaniel and Plougoulm, France, respectively. They summarize the highly complex subject thus: True shallots, which have a distinct, sweeter, more intense, more complex flavor than onions, are grown from a bulb—not from seed—and will continue to multiply this way generation after generation. A "mother" bulb is planted, and from it grow the "daughters."

Other similar *Allium* species are grown from seed: They may be closely sown small onions that superficially resemble shallots, or tightly sown long onions (marketed as "échalions," discussed below), or onion and shallot crosses, or pseudo shallots ("seed shallots"). In France, it is illegal to sell anything but the bulb-propagated form as a shallot. (The esteemed gray shallot, also bulb-propagated, and smaller and stronger than others, is a separate species little known outside France).

A moment's digression about the name: A subspecies of onion (until recently classified as *Allium ascalonicum*), "shallot was described before 300 B.C. by the Greek writer Theophrastus, who called it *askolonion*. In the 1st century A.D. Pliny concluded that it was so named because it came from Askalon (now Ashkelon, in S. Israel)." But this provenance was not correct. "In truth it originated much further east, probably in C. Asia, and reached India before it came to the Mediterranean. The original Greek name has spawned all the modern names, as well as the term

shallots: Asian (*top left*), Dutch Red (*top right*), Dutch Yellow (*bottom left*), Brittany Red (*bottom right*)   length: 1-2 inches

'scallion,' which has been used to mean a shallot, a spring onion, . . . or one of the small bulbs of any bunching onion variety" (Alan Davidson, *The Oxford Companion to Food*). This explains some of the confusion caused by overlapping names.

"*Eschaloigne,* from which échalote [the French] is derived, was probably first used in France in the 12th century," Marcel Le Nard says. Another name for shallots crops up in John Evelyn's *Acetaria: A Discourse of Sallets* (1699): "Scalions, *Ascalonia, Cepae;* the *French* call them *Appetites,* which it notably quickens and stirs up." This charming description that I had seen nowhere else was confirmed by Le Nard, who said that shallots were indeed called *appétits* in the 17th and 18th centuries.

"Colonial Americans called [shallots] 'scallions' or 'scullions,' and so did my grandmother, who preferred the young greens to the minced bulbs," William Woys Weaver writes in *Heirloom Vegetable Gardening.* "I think it was this once-common preference for the tops that caused many people to confuse scallions with bunching onions and to disdain the bulbs as a type of garlic" (see green onion, page 433).

In the United States, French imports are the norm, whether purchased in Chinatowns or gourmet boutiques. They are coppery-skinned, smooth, and tapered and number 8 to 20 per pound, depending upon the cultivar. The Jersey-type shallots (opposite), which Le Nard says were introduced into France from Russia or northern Europe in the 19th century, are represented by two types called simply long and half-long—the shallots you're most likely to find in any American market. Peeled, the flesh has a magenta flush. Roasted until tender, the bulbs are meaty, sweet, and comparatively mild and tender—sometimes too much so for my taste.

Dutch shallots are the next most likely to turn up in the United States. I tasted two small, rounded, and charming types: Yellow ones, petite at 32 per pound, have golden skin and creamy flesh. Coppery red samples, at about 18 per pound, are sturdy, with pink-flushed flesh. Roasted, they make solid, neat, sweet golden or rose packages to serve whole.

Shallots from China fill in seasonal gaps, but I have not (to my knowledge) tried them. Distributors do not speak well of them.

"Échalion," long onion, Cuisse de Poulet du Poitou, and Torpedo Shallot are names I've seen for the sleek allium below, which is . . . what? "It is impossible to give you a definition of an échalion because it doesn't exist," says Gérard Sparfel. "The name is purely commercial, and is in effect a long onion grown from seeds sown at very high density." Growers tell me that the name Cuisse de Poulet (chicken leg or thigh) originally referred to a shallot but may now be used for this onion only.

The large (5 to 8 per pound) handsome imports (mine were from Belgium and France) are shallot-like in form, color, and scent, but their glossy lavender-pink layers are fairly thick and as tough as most common onions—which is what they are. Braised and roasted, they have neither the rounded sweetness nor the melt-

"échalion"   length: about 5 inches

ing, uniform texture of good shallots, but they are pleasant onions. Treat them as such.

BASIC USE: In European cooking, and in France above all, shallots are best known for their roles in sauces—raw and cooked: in vinaigrette or mignonette, beurre blanc, marchand de vin, béarnaise, bordelaise, and other red wine sauces of the Bordeaux area. They are also a constant in Southeast Asian cuisine: as the base for the ubiquitous seasoning pastes, as a deep-fried garnish for noodle and rice dishes (see my non-fat version below), or pickled as condiments. Raw, they are traditionally cut lengthwise to form "natural julienne" that are part of salads, particularly in Thailand. Because the shallot has much thinner layers and a less tough membrane than the onion, shallots are well suited to raw dishes.

Beyond seasoning and garnishing, whole shallots can be cooked like baby onions to produce a more complex, softer, sweeter result. Once peeled, they can be pickled, braised, sautéed, creamed, gratinéed—you name it. Roast to serve with game, chicken, turkey, or pork. Simmer in red wine, then reduce to a glaze to accompany steak or lamb. Braise in broth, cream, and herbs to serve as a sauce and side dish for poultry or to spoon over kasha or whole-wheat pilaf.

SELECTION: Look for the real thing: True shallots grow in clusters (see photo of Fermor cultivar) attached at the basal plate at the root end of the planted (mother) bulb. Once cleaned and graded, the bulbs are separated; thus each bulb shows a tiny pale scar at the base (plate) where it was separated from the "mother." This will *almost* always prove to be a true shallot, according to the specialists.

Shallots are available year-round; there is no need to stock up. They are best when sold loose. Mesh bags are acceptable, but plastic wrapping is not. Shallots should be crackling-dry—without a trace of dampness—and full, solid, and relatively heavy for their size. Avoid any with soft or withered spots, dustiness, mold, or green sprouts. The skin may break and flake in shipping, but it protects the shallot and should be evident, broken or not.

STORAGE: Do not refrigerate shallots. Spread them in a basket and keep in a dry, well-ventilated area, preferably cool. They can last for weeks, but sniff now and then to check for spoilage. Remove any that are desiccated, moist, or softening or that smell overtly oniony.

PREPARATION: Choose one of three methods to loosen skins: (1) Pour boiling water over shallots in a bowl. Weight with a dish to immerse; leave for 5 minutes. Drain; cover with cold water. (2) Immerse shallots in warm tap water and let stand ½ hour or more, weighted. (3) Combine shallots in a bowl with water to cover; weight. Refrigerate overnight.

To peel, remove one shallot at a time from the water. Cut neck skin flush with the bulb, then, with the help of a knife, pull down the thin skin (do not remove layers of flesh) toward the base. Trim roots without cutting into the shallot base (leaving a bit of root won't hurt). Some cooks cut an X in the base, but I haven't been able to rate its efficacy. Sometimes it helps; sometimes it doesn't.

Oven-Toasted Shallot Crisps

Traditional deep-fried shallots add a crisp, zesty finish to creamy or soft Southeast Asian dishes. But frying lacks appeal in my apartment kitchen, where cooking odors (and seemingly oil globules) linger for days. So I oven-toast shallot slices, which turns them crisp as coconut shreds, eliminates the bite, adds a toasted savor, and intensifies their sweetness. There is no need to confine the browned, squiggly crisps to an Eastern menu: Strew them over bitter greens, legume purees, vegetable-noodle tosses, and rice, bean, or tofu dishes.

Choose the longest, largest shallots for ease of peeling and slicing, and for the most uniform rounds.

About ½ pound long, smooth shallots

1. Turn oven to low—225° to 250°F.
2. Peel shallots (do not soak to peel as for other recipes—they should remain dry). Slice fairly thin and as evenly as possible so that the rings will bake through at the same time. Spread on two baking sheets, preferably non-stick.
3. Bake 45 minutes, changing pan positions and tossing shallots every 15 minutes or so to redistribute.
4. Continue baking until slices are evenly golden and dried, tossing often. Timing varies, but 15 to 45 minutes longer is likely. When medium golden—not

brown (or they will taste bitter)—turn off oven. Leave slices in oven to cool down and crisp. They will darken slightly.

5. Cool completely. Packed airtight, they will last for months.

Makes 1 generous cup

Sweet-Sour Glazed Shallots

Few will guess the secret ingredient in the rich, dark sauce that smoothly glosses each shallot: sweet-tart, winy prune juice—woefully under-appreciated in this country, which produces so much. Sharpened with sherry and vinegar, the glaze is as shiny as (and perhaps more subtle than) the traditional meat glaze. Serve with roasted pork or poultry. For a vegetarian version, omit the ham dice and double the nut oil, then serve over bitter greens with buckwheat, kamut, or roasted potatoes.

> 1 pound medium shallots of approximately equal size
> About 1½ ounces country ham (Smithfield-type or prosciutto)
> 1 tablespoon hazelnut, walnut, or olive oil
> ¼ cup dry sherry
> 2 tablespoons sherry vinegar
> Optional: 1 teaspoon minced rosemary
> ¼ teaspoon pepper
> 1 cup prune juice

1. Peel shallots by preferred method (see Preparation).
2. Cut ham (and fat) into tiny dice (to make about ¼ cup). In saucepan that will hold shallots in single close layer, cook ham in oil over moderate heat until crisp, about 5 minutes. Add shallots and cook until golden.
3. Add sherry, vinegar, optional rosemary, and pepper; toss to nearly evaporate liquid. Add prune juice. Simmer, covered, until shallots are just tender, 10 to 20 minutes, depending upon size.
4. Uncover. Raise heat and boil, stirring often, until liquid reduces to a syrup. Season and serve hot (can be reheated).

Serves 4

Caramelized Shallot-Walnut Vinaigrette Sauce

Denser and heftier than other vinaigrettes, this rich brown sauce complements cold roasted pork, turkey, game, or beef. Or spoon a little over hot sautéed calf's liver and potatoes—both thin-sliced. For a vegetable meal, serve to tie together roasted squash slices, braised greens, and mixed grains. Add roasted walnuts to highlight the nuttiness and provide crunch.

> 6 medium shallots (about 5 ounces)
> About ½ cup walnut oil
> ½ teaspoon kosher salt
> ¼ teaspoon cracked pepper
> 3 tablespoons water
> About ¼ cup sherry vinegar
> About 1 teaspoon minced thyme
>   or savory

1. Peel shallots (do not soak to peel; they should be dry). Cut thin, using the 2-millimeter blade of a food processor, or a mandoline or knife.

2. Heat 2 tablespoons oil in medium skillet over moderate heat. Add shallots and salt. Toss often until richly browned, about 10 minutes. Halfway through cooking, add pepper. Add water and stir to evaporate. Remove from heat.

3. In 1½- to 2-cup storage container, blend together ¼ cup vinegar, 1 teaspoon thyme, and ¼ cup more oil. Add shallot mixture. Taste and add oil, salt, pepper, vinegar, and thyme. Cool, cover, and refrigerate. (Use within a few weeks.)

Makes about 1 cup

Baked Creamed Shallots

Glossy cream-coated shallots are an unctuous garnish for chicken, veal, turkey, or pork. Or mix with cooked mushrooms, asparagus tips, or Brussels sprouts to serve as a side vegetable. Some shallots are singles; some come packed two or three to a wrapper. You'll need about 24 to 30 units in all. Choose either large shallots, to separate or cut evenly, or small ones that appear to be singles of about the same size.

> About 1 pound small or fairly large shallots
> About ½ cup heavy cream (preferably not
>   ultra-pasteurized)
> ¼ teaspoon kosher salt
> ⅛ teaspoon ground allspice
> ¼ teaspoon dried tarragon, crumbled
>   to powder
> 2 tablespoons Madeira or medium-dry
>   sherry

1. Set oven to 400°F. Peel shallots by preferred method (see Preparation). Halve large ones or divide into units of fairly even size.

2. Arrange shallots in buttered baking dish to hold them closely in single layer. Cover and bake until about three-quarters done, or still slightly crisp in the center when pierced with a knife—about ½ hour.

3. Meanwhile, combine ½ cup cream, salt, allspice, and tarragon in a small pan and bring to a boil. Add Madeira and return to a boil.

4. Pour cream over onions. Continue baking, uncovered, shaking dish to turn and redistribute shallots every 10 minutes or so, until they are soft but not falling apart and the sauce thickens, about ½ hour. If sauce looks oily, it has separated. Emulsify by adding a bit more cream, a spoonful at a time, until smooth. Season and serve hot.

Serves 4 to 6 as a side dish or garnish

Variation

Baked Creamed Baby Onions

Substitute cipolline or boilers of equal size (about 30 per pound). Prepare as above for a dish that is more firm-textured and uniform, not as melting and fleshy.

*See also recipe for Party Pink Pickled Spring Onion Slices, page 436, for which large shallots or "échalions" can be substituted.

Pros Propose

France is prime terrain for shallot recipes. Wine, not surprisingly, figures in many. Red wine is most common, but Susan Herrmann Loomis offers a simple dish of **Braised Shallots in White Wine** in her *French Farmhouse Cookbook:* Trim shallots and cut an X in each root end. Combine in saucepan with equal quantities of white wine and chicken stock. Add thyme sprigs and bay leaves. Boil gently, shaking now and then, until shallots are tender and liquid has reduced to a few tablespoons—about 25 minutes. Season. Swirl in butter to taste.

Red wine and port are the cooking choices for chef Daniel Boulud's sweet **Shallot Compote,** a jammy reduction that he serves with peppered and seared Arctic char or tuna fillets—a marine steak au poivre with red wine–shallot sauce. To prepare: Combine sliced, rinsed shallots in saucepan with red wine and half as much ruby port. Simmer gently until shallots are soft and most liquid has evaporated, 20 to 40 minutes. Season. Serve warm (from *Café Boulud Cookbook*).

"This recipe has essentially the same flavoring as the classic béarnaise sauce," writes chef Vincent Guerithault about **Roasted Shallots and Tarragon,** which he serves in similar fashion, with beef tenderloin. To prepare: Peel shallots, leaving enough root to keep intact. Blanch 2 minutes; drain. Arrange in baking dish and dot with butter. Roast 10 minutes at 425°F. Blend heavy cream with red wine, chopped fresh tarragon, salt, and pepper; pour over shallots. Roast until shallots are very tender and sauce thickens. If sauce separates, add a touch of water and additional cream (from *Vincent's Cookbook*).

For shallots cooked in the mode of the French Alps, here is an unusual recipe from *Madeleine Kamman's Savoie*. She calls for large "cuisses de dame" (lady's thigh) shallots, cooks them in loads of browned butter (there called cerfuze), and tosses them with dark noodles (taillerins). For **Three-Flour Taillerins with Red Shallot Cerfuze:** Prepare pasta dough from all-purpose flour, rye flour, buckwheat flour, eggs, egg yolks, and salt. Roll out sheets and cut noodles. Heat butter to dark golden, add 1/3-inch-thick shallot slices, and cook until very mellow. Add to boiled, drained noodles and toss. Serve with slivers of Gruyère or Beaufort cheese.

To *Parisian Home Cooking* (by Michael Roberts) for a cute traditional duo, **Glazed Brussels Sprouts and Shallots,** cooked in a different way: Trim sprouts and cut an X in each base. Do the same to shallots. In a skillet that will hold the vegetables in a single layer, combine sprouts, butter, salt, sugar, and pepper. Add water to cover by three-quarters and boil 5 minutes. Add shallots and boil until liquid has evaporated, about 7 minutes. Reduce heat and continue cooking, shaking now and then, until sprouts and shallots are golden.

Jean-Georges Vongerichten has a fondness for shallots and makes them the focus of broth, vinaigrette, seasoned oil, confit, and salad in his restaurants. In the 1980s, while chef at Lafayette Restaurant in New York City, he prepared a pure and simple **Shallot Broth with Flounder:** Melt butter in wide pan; add sliced shallots and salt and cook until deeply browned. Add water and simmer 20 minutes. Add flounder fillets and poach to barely cook. Transfer to deep plates. Add hazelnut oil and chopped marjoram to shallot broth; ladle over fish.

Chef Vongerichten fries shallots in typical Asian style for **Warm Potato Salad with Caramelized Shallots and Watercress:** Combine small potatoes with cold water and salt. Cook until tender. Drain, peel, and slice. Shallow-fry thin-sliced large shallots in grapeseed or canola oil, stirring, until golden, not dark. Drain on towels, blot dry, and sprinkle with salt. Blend grainy mustard, sherry vinegar, and grapeseed oil. Toss gently with potatoes and chives; season. Set on watercress. Top with shallots (from *Jean-Georges*).

Shallots are a common ingredient in the fiery vegetarian sambhars of South India: legume-thickened, tamarind-sharpened soup-stews. For **South Indian Lentils with Shallots:** Simmer soaked split yellow lentils until tender. Add peeled whole shallots and simmer until tender. Add salt, turmeric, and cayenne; set aside. Heat corn oil and add black mustard seeds. When they crackle, add cumin seeds, curry leaves, and asafoetida. Add diluted tamarind paste and stir until thick. Add sambhar powder and cook briefly. Pour over lentil-shallot mixture and garnish with coriander leaves (from *The Indian Spice Kitchen* by Monisha Bharadwaj).

"The elegance of this preparation belies the fact that it's a simple Laotian country dish," writes Bruce Cost of **Chicken with Shallots and Black Pepper:** Cut roasting chicken into small pieces; salt. Shallow-fry peeled whole shallots in peanut oil in wok until browned; drain and reserve. Fry as many trimmed scallions as chicken pieces; drain and reserve. Fry as many red chilli cubes; drain and reserve. In batches, brown chicken. Pour off most fat. Return chicken to wok with coconut milk, water, and shallots; boil. Add fish sauce, cover, and cook 10 minutes. Add chillis and cook, uncovered, until chicken is done and sauce is creamy. Arrange scallions on platter. Pour over the chicken and sauce. Serve with bowls of cracked black pepper and coriander leaves to sprinkle to taste (from *Bruce Cost's Asian Ingredients*).

Shepherd's Purse (*Capsella bursa-pastoris*)

Also naeng-i (Korean), Chinese cress, nazuna (Japanese)

¼ **actual size**

Shepherd's purse (a literal translation of its species name) and I had our first encounter at a raucous market on Flushing's Main Street in Queens, New York City—not on a country lane, as you might expect. Since its name was indicated by the Korean character (and sloppily, as I later found out), I wasn't aware of what I had met until some time later. It took a month to identify the plant, which I dried and pressed, then sent to a handful of helpful experts sprinkled around the globe.

Luckily, shepherd's purse is a distinctive character, easy to recognize: The flat rosettes have solid, dark, glossy purplish-green stems with thick, dentate leaves—rather like dandelion. Now that you've seen its portrait, you may realize that you've tromped on it in gardens and woodlands all over the United States.

From some of this plant's anglicized and romanized names—Chinese cress, water chestnut vegetable, naeng-i, ji cai, nazuna—you can guess that its appreciators are Far Eastern. Yet shepherd's purse came with Europeans on their migrations and took root wherever they settled. George M. Taylor writes in his engaging little book *British Herbs and Vegetables* (1947) that "in gardens near Philadelphia, this plant develops a size and succulence of leaf that is almost incredible if it were not apparent. When properly grown and blanched it is a valuable addition to the list of delicate culinary vegetables." Another plant lost to progressive agriculture! Taylor adds, as I do now: "Why not try a few cultivated plants of the Shepherd's Purse?"

Although shepherd's purse is respected in Europe as an herbal remedy and occasionally enjoyed as a potherb, it is in China (particularly Shanghai) that one finds culinary mentions of it: boiled, stir-fried, and in soups and dumplings.

In the United States, in non-Asian restaurants (if you can find it at all), shepherd's purse is treated as a salad leaf—probably because of its appealing rosette form. I can't imagine that the attraction is the raw flavor. As a member of the vast and branching Brassicaceae family (also called Cruciferae), it has some of the characteristic dry "mouth feel" of broccoli florets and the intensity of cabbage. But once cooked, the little plants turn juicy and tender, with a savor that suggests mild collards with a hint of artichoke.

BASIC USE: For a forceful and attractive salad accent, cut apart shepherd's purse at the base and use the raw "feathers" in a vivid mix; or arrange a few as a garnish to highlight seafood or small whole vegetables. To be eaten raw, it must be tiny (see the rosette in the photo, foreground), gathered in early spring. I prefer the vegetable steamed for a few minutes, then dressed like other dark greens—with lemon and olive oil. Or sauté briefly with smoky, pork-based Southern flavorings or Mediterranean garlic and oil.

SELECTION: Shepherd's purse appears in the spring. I have not been able to determine if it is cultivated in the United States, as it is in Asia.

STORAGE: Sold as individual plants, shepherd's purse lasts nicely for at least a week, refrigerated in a plastic bag with damp paper toweling at the base of the rosettes. If less than sparkling-fresh, it will be completely rejuvenated by a 3- or 4-minute bath in lukewarm water; then shake partly dry, and pack airtight with a paper towel at the top and bottom. Revived, it will keep as well, if not longer.

PREPARATION: The shepherd's purse I have cooked has been spotless, requiring only a rinse, but some needs plenty of dousing. How you trim the plants will depend upon how you use them: Leave whole, or cut apart at the base.

Steamed Shepherd's Purse with Lemon and Oil

So simple it is hardly a recipe. Yet the brief steaming is what makes the case for this vegetable, to my taste. The rosettes become succulent yet firm, with a collard-kale tinge, but softer. Small plants of about the same size will cook evenly and look prettiest.

Figure on 2 or 3 ounces of cleaned shepherd's purse per serving. If it's small and tidy, you won't need more. If it's straggly or dirty, buy about 4 ounces per person to allow for trimming.

6 to 8 ounces shepherd's purse
Olive oil
Lemon wedges
Fleur de sel or other crisp sea salt

1. Rinse rosettes in sink filled with water. If necessary, swish around again until no grit remains.
2. Set on rack of large steamer over boiling water. Steam until plumped and tender, 3 to 4 minutes or so. Blot with towel to dry slightly.
3. Cut plants apart at base (or not), as desired for appearance and ease of service. Drizzle lightly with olive oil.
4. Serve warm, with lemon wedges and salt for each person to sprinkle to taste.

Serves 2 to 3

Shepherd's Purse with Bacon

Another simple treatment for the twirly, tangly strands of shepherd's purse, this one smoky and chewy in the way of Southern greens. Unlike Southern-style greens, however, these are very quickly cooked, not long-simmered.

½ pound shepherd's purse
2 ounces sliced bacon
Optional: 1 garlic clove, smashed
Salt and pepper
Optional: hot pepper sauce

1. Halve each rosette across. If necessary, swish around vigorously in sink filled with water, then lift out. Repeat until no grit remains. Do not dry.
2. Cut bacon crosswise into ½-inch strips. Cook in a medium-large skillet over low heat, covered, until it renders some fat. Uncover and continue cooking

slowly until evenly browned and crisp. With slotted spatula, transfer pieces to paper towel. You should have ½ to 1 tablespoon fat left in the skillet.

3. Add greens and optional garlic to the skillet. Toss with tongs to coat well. Cover and cook over moderately low heat until tender, about 5 minutes, uncovering to toss occasionally. (Cook greens until tender enough to cut and chew easily, but not soft and limp.)

4. Uncover and season. Sprinkle with bacon bits and serve hot, with knives and forks.

Serves 2 as a salad course or side dish

Pros Propose

In traditional Korean cooking, shepherd's purse is treated in these ways, according to Terry Choi, owner of Hangawi restaurant in New York City. For **Shepherd's Purse Condiment:** Combine crushed garlic, chopped scallion, Korean dark chilli paste, sake, sesame seeds, and sesame oil. Add cleaned and separated raw leaves and marinate. For **Shepherd's Purse Soup:** Clean and cut apart shepherd's purse leaves. Stir-fry in sesame oil. Add seaweed stock and simmer. Blend dark Korean bean paste with a little of the soup. Return to pot, with tofu cubes and sesame oil.

Hangawi's **Salad of Romaine, Shepherd's Purse, and Mixed Mushrooms** is not wholly traditional, says Choi. To prepare: Soak shepherd's purse plants (both leaves and trimmed roots) in water for several hours, until the roots soften slightly. Cut apart leaves and dry. Slice stems into rounds. Combine with bite-size pieces of romaine and sliced button and enoki mushrooms. Blend white miso, sesame oil, Korean mustard, honey, and white sesame seeds. Drizzle over salad.

Citrus is just the right complement for the assertive wild plant. For **Blood Oranges and Shepherd's Purse Salad:** Arrange trimmed small shepherd's purse leaves in a star on each plate. Place thinnest slices of blood orange over them. Drizzle with hazelnut oil and sprinkle with a dash of red wine vinegar and salt (from *The Kitchen Garden Cookbook* by Sylvia Thompson).

Shiitake (*Lentinula edodes* and *Lentinus edodes*)

Also Chinese, oakwood, black forest, and black mushroom

Once upon a time, a dark, handsome mushroom lurked incognito in Chinese-American restaurants, magically transforming the simplest soups, stir-fries and braises with its muscular presence. When the dried mystery fungus finally came out of the cupboard in all its fresh glory, nearly 30 years ago, it was with its Japanese name, shiitake (with equal emphasis on the syllables, shee-tah-kay). "Shii" is the tree on which the fungus grows naturally, *Castanopsis cuspidata,* or Japanese chinquapin, one of many members of the vast beech family under and upon which so many marvelous mushrooms happen. The last two syllables (ta-ke) mean mushroom in Japanese, so the word should not be added in English.

So popular is the mushroom in Japan that shiitake soda, wine, cookies, and candies have been added to the national repertoire of shiitake products, according to Paul Stamets, author of *Growing Gourmet and Medicinal Mushrooms,* a book that addresses both the demands of the specialty market and the field of natural medicine—in which shiitake plays a considerable role.

Although shiitake farming is relatively new to the West, the first written record of shiitake cultivation in the East dates from the Sung Dynasty (A.D. 960–1127), according to Stamets, who documents over 1,000 years of its development. It was not until 1986 that shiitake production in the United States reached a level sufficient to be included in reports from the Department of Agriculture—1,203,000 pounds. The amount grew to 8,670,000 pounds in 1998, the most recent year for which figures are available.

Today, shiitake is no longer an unknown hiding in inscrutable menus; the mere mention of shiitake in a dish attracts diners in restaurants across the country. Unfortunately, the name is all that most diners and shoppers know about the mushroom. For if the quantity and availability of fresh shiitake have increased since its introduction, quality and public knowledge have not.

Not all shiitake are created equal—and few cultivated mushrooms exhibit as much variation in quality. Those grown in an environment that approximates the original habitat will be most firm and flavorful. But if temperature and humidity are accelerated to speed growth, as is very often the case, the result may be little more than "soggy Frisbees," as one farmer put it.

In Japan, grades of shiitake are based on numerous criteria; but the United States ranks shiitake on size alone—large mushrooms are prized over smaller ones that may have fuller flavor. The best shiitake (which are selected from hundreds of possible strains) may hint at garlic, pine, and autumn leaves, and are dense, firm, and meaty. Lesser specimens may be mild, lightly earthy, and comparatively soft. Others may be slippery and insipid.

Fresh shiitake from China, a source relatively new to the United States, have arrived in restaurant channels. On the West Coast, where they arrive by ship, they are

shiitake (three strains)   cap diameter: 2-3 inches

at least two weeks old upon docking. Those on the East Coast have come by air and are of course fresher—and more expensive. But those I tasted (on the East Coast), although dramatically thick, full, and glossy, were oddly marshmallowy in texture and "deflated" when cooked. Some chefs love them; others find a "chemical odor." Obviously, the product is too rare to evaluate fairly.

Baby or button shiitake should be pounced upon, if you chance to find them. Very limited in availability, shiitake "buttons" (the name is applied to caps smaller than 2 inches in diameter) are chocolate brown, extremely tender (stems as well as caps) and pungent. The depth of flavor compares in intensity to the finest dried caps.

BASIC USE: Shiitake's natural elegance shines in even the plainest preparations. Silky, swarthy, supple, it elevates vegetable dishes to starring status—whether the mushroom is combined with greens or grains, or served alone as in Japan.

Although shiitake can be cooked in almost any way that you would cook common mushrooms, it is drier and burns easily. For maximum flavor and meatiness, keep caps whole or in bite-size chunks, sauté lightly, then simmer in a little liquid until nearly dry. For thin-sliced caps, sauté on lower heat than usual and cook a little longer. Caps that are to be roasted, grilled, or broiled must be coated with a generous quantity of oil to prevent drying.

Shiitake excels as a vegetarian entrée, alone or with other vegetables. It pairs naturally with flavorful starches, such as cornmeal, brown rice, barley, kamut, or whole wheat, or buckwheat noodles. Pepper, garlic, shallots, chives, rosemary, thyme, savory, ginger, soy sauce, and red wine underscore its complex savor.

SELECTION: Read this! The key to shiitake is careful selection. Buy only the best quality. Thin-fleshed, opened-out specimens are never worth the price of admission.

Choose solid, thick caps, particularly ones that are domed and dappled with a whitish bloom (see group at left in the photo). Above all, curled-under cap margins ensure freshness. Look for a veil over the gills (see uncut mushroom at lower right) "or at least silvery veil filaments which show the mushroom was not rushed, but grown over a correct time period," says Malcolm Clark, president of Gourmet Mushrooms in Se-bastopol, California, who pioneered shiitake production in North America in the early 1970s. Shiitake should be dry but not leathery, with a distinct aroma. The tough stems should be trimmed, but not too short—which cuts shelf life.

When it comes to size, heed Clark's impassioned words: "For some unfortunate reason, the U.S. marketplace wants big shiitake. When allowed to grow large, they are necessarily flabbier because they open. Opened, they release their spores—and like salmon, once they release their eggs, they're goners. You don't want to eat them. They are limp and infection-prone. When I see great big opened-up shiitake, I want to cry."

STORAGE: Refrigerate shiitake in a basket covered with a slightly damp towel. The mushrooms lose their special flavor if kept more than a few days, although their appearance may change little. Freeze for longer storage. To my amazement, I found that high-quality stemmed shiitake caps freeze very successfully, losing just a little tautness after 2 months.

PREPARATION: Clean caps with a damp towel. Cut off all the stem. Either wrap and freeze stems for making stock, or cut them paper-thin and cook until tender in broth, then add to the caps in the dish you're preparing; or mix into vegetables, stew, or soup.

Shiitake with Bacon and Herbs

This useful basic recipe can serve as a model to be varied to suit the meal of the moment: Substitute olive oil or nut oil for the bacon; try thyme or oregano instead of rosemary; add garlic, scallions, or shallots if you're an allium fan. Serve as a side to grilled meat or poultry, along with wheat or buckwheat. Or forgo the meat, and enjoy with grains alone.

½ **pound shiitake**
½ **cup mushroom or meat broth**
Big pinch of crumbled dried rosemary
1 or 2 thick bacon slices, diced
1 medium celery stalk, minced
2 tablespoons dry red wine or dry sherry
Salt and pepper
Minced parsley

1. Cut shiitake stems from caps. Rinse stems and slice very thin. Combine in a small saucepan with broth and rosemary. Simmer, covered, until tender—about 10 minutes; set aside. Clean caps with damp towel. Break into large bite-size pieces or leave whole, as desired.

2. Cook bacon in medium-large skillet over moderately low heat until lightly colored. Pour off as much fat as desired. Add celery; raise heat to moderate, and stir until softened—a minute or two.

3. Add caps and toss a minute, until barely softened. Add broth and stems. Cook over moderately high heat until most liquid evaporates, about 5 minutes. Add wine. Raise heat and toss until liquid has nearly evaporated—another minute or so. Season and add parsley.

Serves 2

Fettuccine with Shiitake, Celery, Garlic, and Lemon

Fresh pasta topped with a generous helping of satiny shiitake and crisp celery is accented with lemon zest and juice for a surprising and subtle effect. For variation, fresh sage adds a different dimension. Wrap shiitake stems and freeze for broth.

> ¾ pound medium shiitake
> 3 tablespoons olive oil
> 1 lemon
> 2 teaspoons Asian (dark) sesame oil
> 2 cups thin-sliced tender inner celery stalks
>   with leaves
> 1 tablespoon minced garlic
> ½ cup full-flavored mushroom, veal,
>   or beef broth
> Salt and pepper
> ½ cup minced parsley leaves
> ¾ pound fresh (not dried) fettuccine or linguine

1. Trim stems from shiitake and reserve for another use. Clean caps with damp towel. Halve, then toss with 1 tablespoon olive oil to coat evenly. Let stand at least 15 minutes. Meanwhile, scrub lemon well, then grate zest. Halve lemon and squeeze 2 tablespoons juice.

2. Heat 1 tablespoon olive oil and 1 teaspoon sesame oil in very large skillet. Add celery and shiitake and toss

1 minute over high heat. Add garlic and toss another minute. Add broth, cover, and cook until caps are tender but celery is still quite crisp—another minute or so. If necessary, uncover and boil a moment longer to evaporate most liquid. Add lemon zest, salt, pepper, and parsley; toss to blend.

3. Cook fettuccine in boiling salted water until barely tender, just a few minutes. Drain and combine in heated dish with mushroom mixture, lemon juice, and remaining 1 tablespoon olive oil and 1 teaspoon sesame oil. Season.

Serves 4 as a main course

Warm Shiitake, Arugula, and Sweet Pepper Salad with Garlic Toasts

A salad starring dark shiitake slivers, supported by bright pepper dice, ham julienne, nippy arugula, and crunchy croutons. Use a firm dry-cured ham such as Smithfield-type, prosciutto, or speck.

> 10 slices French baguette or
>   slim Italian loaf
> 2 garlic cloves, halved
> 4 tablespoons fruity olive oil
> 6 to 8 ounces shiitake
> ¼ to ½ teaspoon kosher salt
> Pepper
> 2 medium bunches arugula
> 2 medium yellow, orange, and/or red
>   bell peppers
> About 3 ounces firm ham, cut into fine
>   strips (½ cup)
> 1 lemon, cut into 8 wedges

1. Preheat oven to 350°F. Arrange bread on baking sheet. Bake until firm but not crisp, 5 to 10 minutes. Lightly rub top of each slice with halved garlic cloves. Brush evenly with 1 tablespoon olive oil; halve slices. Bake until golden, about 5 minutes longer.

2. Meanwhile, cut stems from shiitake (reserve for another use). Slice caps into thin strips. Combine with ¼ teaspoon salt, pepper, and 1 tablespoon oil; toss to

coat evenly. Let stand 10 minutes or more, tossing now and then.

3. Trim and discard arugula stems. Rinse leaves well in several baths. Spin-dry. Arrange on individual plates. Cut peppers into ¼-inch dice.

4. In large heavy skillet, heat remaining 2 tablespoons oil over moderately high heat. Add shiitake and toss until softened, 2 to 3 minutes. Add peppers and toss 30 seconds to heat through. Add ham, toss, and season.

5. Quickly divide warm mixture onto arugula; toss to mix. Place 2 lemon wedges and 5 croutons on each salad. Serve at once.

Serves 4 as a first course or salad

Button Shiitake and Asparagus Stir-Fry

If you are lucky enough to locate hard-to-find little button shiitake, showcase them in a simple dish. The handsome dark caps, tender enough to be cooked with their pale stems intact, contrast sleekly with crisp, grassy asparagus. Powdered sansho, the Japanese name for a type of prickly ash, is not strictly necessary, but it adds an intriguing whiff of lemon, mint, pine—*je ne sais quoi.*

> ¼ **pound button shiitake**
> ½ **pound medium asparagus**
> **3 medium scallions (green onions)**
> ½ **tablespoon shoyu (Japanese soy sauce)**
> **1 teaspoon lemon juice**
> **1 teaspoon honey**
> **Large pinch sansho powder or white pepper**
> **1½ tablespoons corn oil**

1. Trim a sliver from base of each shiitake stem; halve mushrooms. Bend asparagus to snap off bases as necessary. Cut spears into ¾-inch diagonals. Trim, then thin-slice scallions, separating light and dark parts. Blend shoyu, lemon juice, honey, and sansho.

2. Heat wok over moderate heat. Pour oil around rim. Add shiitake, asparagus, and pale part of scallions. Toss until just barely tender, about 3 minutes.

3. Add darker part of scallions and shoyu mixture; toss a moment. Taste, season, and turn into a heated dish.

Serves 3 to 4 as a side dish

Variation

"Regular" Shiitake-Asparagus Stir-Fry

For larger shiitake: Increase shiitake to 6 ounces. Cut off and reserve stems for another use. Quarter and proceed as above.

Pros Propose

Chefs Mark Peel and Nancy Silverton season and roast shiitake to intensify its flavor, then toss with a few leafy ingredients. For **Roasted Shiitake, Mizuna, and Parsley Salad:** Toss stemmed, quartered shiitake with olive oil and rosemary; let stand briefly. Roast until gills brown lightly. Rinse thin-sliced shallots, then blot dry. Combine with shiitake, equal quantities of Italian parsley and mizuna leaves, and olive oil, salt, pepper, and lemon juice (from *The Food of Campanile*).

An unusual appetizer, **Shiitake-Scallop Tempura,** comes from chef Masaharu Morimoto, who considers shiitake especially suited to deep-frying: Dice raw scallops and combine with scallion and minced ginger. Fill shiitake caps with mixture. Dip into flour, then beaten egg, then bread crumbs. Deep-fry. Serve hot with salt, pepper, and lemon wedges.

Quick-pickled raw mushrooms are a color and flavor focus in chef Rob Boone's **Fresh Ramen Noodles with Smoked Salmon and Pickled Shiitake in Miso Broth:** Boil rice vinegar, sugar, Sichuan pepper, star anise, cinnamon sticks, lemon grass, and fresh ginger. Pour over sliced shiitake caps; let pickle an hour or so. Drain liquid (use on another batch of mushrooms). Stir white miso into heated dashi. Add cooked Japanese wheat noodles (ramen), the shiitake, and smoked salmon strips.

Virginia was one of the first shiitake-farming areas in the United States. Chef Marcel Desaulniers has made generous use of the local product in his long-celebrated Williamsburg restaurant, The Trellis. For his **Shiitake Pâté:** Fine-chop caps and trimmed stems. Sauté diced onion in clarified butter. Season and cook until soft. Add mushrooms and sauté. Add brandy and cook to evaporate. Add white wine; simmer 15 minutes. Add chopped spinach, tarragon, and minced garlic; cook briefly. Cool, then chill, then drain. Process softened cream cheese and eggs; add to mixture, with chopped walnuts. Turn into buttered and parchment-lined loaf pan. Cover with foil and bake in water bath. Cool ½ hour before removing foil. Unmold and refrigerate. Serve with toasted walnut bread (from *The Trellis Cookbook*).

Chef Jean Joho, a mushroom enthusiast, usually avoids the farm-raised. "The cultivated mushrooms are like the farm-raised game. They are missing the excitement—except for the good shiitake!" Among the ways he incorporates them into his menu is **Shiitake-Coated Veal Roast:** Sear, then chill veal rib-eye. Coat with a mixture of sautéed coarse-chopped shiitake and minced shallots, garlic, parsley, and chives. Enclose in caul fat, then roast in a very hot oven for 5 minutes. Lower heat and cook until done, about ½ hour.

Sorrels

Including **garden sorrel, sheep sorrel, dock,** and **wood sorrel**

Sorrel is "by nature . . . Acid, sharpening appetite . . . and imparting so grateful a quickness to the rest as supplies the want of Orange, Limon . . . and therefore never to be excluded," wrote John Evelyn in *Acetaria: A Discourse of Sallets* (1699). But it is usually excluded today. The word "sorrel" derives from "sour," which describes a characteristic that all sorrels share and that has limited appeal in the United States.

Americans have historically been fickle about the tart leaves to which much of Europe has remained devoted for as long as salad and soup have existed. Sorrel was planted in American gardens at the beginning of the 19th century and probably earlier. In *The Field and Garden Vegetables of America* (1863), Fearing Burr listed five types of garden sorrel alone and wrote, "It has

been asserted, that, amongst all the recent additions to our list of esculent plants, we have not one so wholesome, so easy of cultivation."

Sorrel is still favored by home gardeners and foragers, but it is an "on again off again" market item. For the moment, it is "on," but precariously, and only in a few fancy groceries and farmers' markets. Chefs' growing interest in foraged foods has sparked some interest in the "free-range" sorrels that pop up nationwide (in every state, according to field guides), but the near future of the market vegetable doesn't look bright.

Cultivated sorrel is now limited to one species, *Rumex acetosa,* known variously as **common sorrel, garden sorrel,** and **broad-leaved sorrel.** Throughout Europe, both this and French sorrel (*R. scutatus*) are still marketed,

cultivated sorrel

length: 7-9 inches

as they used to be in the United States. Large-leaved, tissuey-tender, brightly colored, and tart, common sorrel cooks in a fairly uncommon way: Heated, it melts to a sauce-like consistency in minutes to become a powerful ally for simply cooked fish or meat, which it raises to elegance with the addition of a little cream or butter to soften the sharp edges. Raw, its citric punch adds high notes to a mixed salad.

Wild sorrel is a general rubric for several plants which, like cultivated garden sorrel, are vibrantly acid—and always more intensely flavored than cultivated forms. Some are true sorrels (*Rumex* species), some are not. All have in common appreciable quantities of oxalic acid (as do spinach, rhubarb, and the cultivated common sorrel), which should be consumed in moderation and will be if you eat sorrel in the normal ways in which it is likely to be prepared.

Sheep sorrel or sour grass (*Rumex acetosella*), a diminutive plant made up of fine, narrow arrowheads or shield shapes, is brightly sour, fresh, and clean-tasting—just the right size to use whole in salads made up of miniatures.

Cooked, sheep sorrel turns into an olive drab puree—like its relative, garden sorrel—that is yummy but ugly. Melt it into butter or cream for a suave sauce to nap seafood. In fact, use it like cultivated sorrel but expect a much more subtle, fruity taste. Oddly, sheep sorrel suggests mild *ume* (Japanese "plum"—actually an apricot) vinegar.

"Dock" is a term that embraces several edible *Rumex* species, notably *crispus, obtusifolius,* and *patienta.* **Curly, yellow, or sour dock** (*Rumex crispus*) is so widespread that once you've recognized it, you realize that you've seen it just about anywhere you have traveled in the United States—or elsewhere, from Mexico to Asia. Although related to garden sorrel, it is far more coarse, bitter, and fibrous. Raw, its dark green leaves suggest a blend of acidified beet and dandelion greens—sour, bitter, and earthy. Even tiny, it is a harsh plant that is best blended with mild and sweet saladings or devoted to cooked dishes.

Blanched momentarily, it is transformed. The stems become tender, the leaves turn soft and slippery, and the savor is deliciously sour (no longer bitter). It, too, turns olive drab when cooked. It makes an intense

sheep sorrel

length: 2-3 inches

curly or yellow dock (*left*) and broadleaf or bitter dock

½ actual size

wood sorrel

⅔ actual size

addition to pureed soups, adding deep, tart, tannic, and earthy flavors and a suggestion of tea and rhubarb (a relative).

Broadleaf or bitter dock (*Rumex obtusifolius*) can be used the same way but has more generic grassiness, less depth and complexity. However small, it is crude and lawn-like raw; eat it cooked. **Patience dock** (*Patienta* species), both wild and cultivated, is described in gardening literature as similar to common sorrel, but milder. I have not been able to obtain it.

Wood sorrel, each elfin leaf composed of delicate heart-shaped lobes, suggests clover and shamrock—which most authorities agree that it is. Although called sorrel, this *Oxalis* species is not related to *Rumex* except insofar as it is sour. The fragile greens are suited to raw use above all. The lilting little leaves are a ready-made garnish or a perfect punctuation for delicate mesclun, providing tiny bursts of tartness and a fresh green flavor. Cooking, however, destroys its color, shape, and texture.

BASIC USE

Raw: Sorrel is used raw in moderation, as a seasoning leaf in salads or flavoring in cooked dishes. Garden sorrel, sheep sorrel, and wood sorrel are good for raw use; dock is generally too bitter and harsh. Keep charming small sheep sorrel and wood sorrel whole. Common sorrel should be stripped of its stems and sliced into strips for salad or into a fine chiffonade for seasoning. In salads, the greens provide an inimitable tart lift and bright color. Or garnish seafood, soup, or eggs. Or mash into a compound butter.

Wood sorrel's heart-shaped leaves look particularly fetching and add vivid accents to just about any savory that would benefit from a squeeze of lemon: fish, vegetables, meat, grains.

Wilted: Being wilted by proximity to heat—not raw and not cooked—is a condition that suits all sorrel. Wood sorrel, sprinkled on hot fish, chicken, or veal fillets, sticks and softens to a flavorful finish. Sheep sorrel or fine strips of garden sorrel transform a primavera-type pasta dish: Off the heat, stir in a generous chiffonade of sorrel after all other ingredients have been added to the hot pasta. Or fold into grain or bean dishes once cooking is finished.

Cooked: Sorrel becomes an entirely different culinary element when cooked. It is used primarily as a flavoring puree, a state it assumes naturally the moment it is heated, without sieving or thickening. You can simply simmer the shredded leaves in a tiny amount of water for a few minutes to achieve this, or stir them into melted butter or warmed cream. However you make the puree, count on considerable reduction—even more than with spinach. The concentrated flavoring enlivens pureed soups, root vegetables, or beans. With the addition of a mirepoix or another seasoning, it can be the base for risotto.

Cream, eggs, or both will mellow sorrel puree to a sauce that pairs perfectly with seafood, pheasant, chicken, or veal. Or spoon over an omelet or poached eggs. A thinned puree based on stock or water, thickened with egg yolks, makes a soup that is part of the culinary repertoire of much of the Western Hemisphere (as is potato-sorrel soup). Best known are the Jewish schav and French potage Germiny.

SELECTION: Field sorrels are in season from early summer to fall. Garden sorrel from greenhouses is available year-round, with spring and summer the peak times. Choose leaves that are bright and firm, with no limpness or yellowing and with the slimmest, least fibrous stems.

Refrigerate in a plastic bag with a piece of paper toweling. Garden sorrel, dock, and sheep sorrel will keep up to a week. Wood sorrel should be used as soon as possible.

PREPARATION: Dunk sorrel into a sink filled with water; then lift out gently (the leaves are tender and bruise easily). Dry in a salad spinner or on soft, absorbent towels. For most preparations, you'll need to strip the stems from garden sorrel: Hold each folded leaf in one hand, then simply pull the stem from it with the other hand. Roll or stack the leaves, then cut slivers (chiffonade). Other sorrels need not be trimmed, except as specified in recipes.

When preparing sorrel, use stainless steel knives to prevent discoloration. Avoid aluminum and iron cookware, for the same reason.

Sorrel-Avocado Dressing

Soft, silky, and light-textured, this tangy sauce is quick to assemble and surprisingly versatile. Without olive oil, eggs, or cream, this un-mayonnaise is nevertheless creamy and rich. Spoon it over poached seafood, or fold into meat, fish, or cooked vegetable salads. Sharpen it with hot pepper sauce to serve as a dip for crudités. Thin with additional buttermilk to sauce cooked vegetables, such as asparagus or summer squash. A fully ripe, oily avocado variety is a must.

About 9 ounces common sorrel
   (3 small bunches)
1 medium oil-rich avocado, such as
   Hass or Fuerte
1 teaspoon kosher salt
¼ cup sliced scallion greens
About ½ cup buttermilk
Optional: ¼ cup chopped parsley leaves and
   2 tablespoons sliced chives

1. Bring full kettle of water to a boil. Meanwhile, strip sorrel stems from leaves; discard. Rinse leaves. Pack to measure: You should have about 3 cups.

2. Peel, pit, and chunk avocado; place in food processor container. Mix salt with 1 tablespoon boiling water to dissolve. Add to container.

3. Spread sorrel and scallions in colander in sink. Pour boiling water over them to wilt sorrel thoroughly. Press lightly to squeeze out water.

4. Add wilted greens to avocado, with ¼ cup buttermilk. Puree to smooth light consistency (add parsley and chives if you want a stronger flavor and color). With machine running, gradually add more buttermilk until consistency is as you like it.

5. Chill thoroughly to serve—1 hour, or up to a day or so.

Makes about 1½ cups

Chilled Sorrel and Spinach Soup

Sleek and smooth, this tart soup starts a summer meal with style. The flavor is sprightly and springy, even if the dark olive color isn't—but marbled with cream, the look is anything but drab. Chicken broth is the standard for soups of this kind, but I prefer a clear vegetable flavor. Most recipes recommend stripping sorrel stems, but I find that both cultivated and wild melt softly into the soup. This doubles neatly.

¾ pound small, tender spinach
5 to 6 ounces cultivated sorrel (or 3 to
   4 ounces wild sorrel)
2 medium scallions (green onions)
3½ cups vegetable broth
Salt and pepper
1½ tablespoons cornstarch
Big pinch of grated nutmeg or ground anise
¼ to ½ teaspoon grated lemon zest
Lemon juice
6 tablespoons heavy cream (preferably not
   ultrapasteurized)

1. Cut heaviest stem bases from spinach; discard. Dunk leaves into water, swish around, and lift out. Repeat until water is clean. Do same with sorrel. Bunch both the greens and cut into thin slices. Trim scallions and slice thin.

2. Combine greens and scallions with broth in non-aluminum pot. Bring to a boil, stirring. Simmer until soft, about 5 minutes. Season.

3. Puree soup until smooth with an immersion blender. Or transfer to a blender or food processor and puree. Stir together cornstarch with ¼ cup of the puree. Combine in pot with remaining soup. Bring to a boil over moderate heat, stirring constantly. Add nutmeg, zest, and juice.

4. Transfer to a bowl set in a larger container of ice water. Cool, then chill thoroughly, for several hours or longer.

5. To serve, ladle into bowls. Drizzle 1½ tablespoons heavy cream onto each, then swirl gently with knife tip or fork to form a pretty pattern.

Serves 4 as a first course

Sorrel, Radicchio, and Romaine in Creamy Parmesan Dressing

A creamy, salty sauce mellows and coats tart sorrel, bitter radicchio, and sweet romaine. The dressing yield is about double what is needed for this quantity of "greens" (a range of exceptionally lively hues and varied textures), but that's what one egg makes. You can: double the greens and use all the dressing, to serve eight; halve the egg and make just half the dressing; or refrigerate the unused dressing to spoon over grilled or baked fish or steamed potatoes. If you are concerned about eating nearly raw eggs, skip this recipe.

1 bunch common sorrel (4 to 5 ounces) or
   3 ounces sheep sorrel
1 very small radicchio of any type
   (about 6 ounces)
1 heart of romaine lettuce (about
   6 ounces)
1 large egg (very fresh and organic)
4 oil-packed anchovy fillets, sliced
¼ cup grated Parmesan cheese
1 tablespoon balsamic vinegar
2 tablespoons lemon juice
2 tablespoons snipped chives
About ¼ teaspoon hot pepper sauce
½ cup corn oil or other mild vegetable oil
¼ cup olive oil
Optional: small garlic croutons

1. Swish sorrel leaves in water, lift out gently, and drain. Repeat if needed. Spin-dry. Holding a leaf folded lengthwise with one hand, pull off stem with the other hand. Shred as needed to make large bite-size strips. Or, if using sheep sorrel, leave whole.

2. Separate radicchio leaves and rinse. Spin-dry. Cut larger leaves into diagonal strips ½ inch wide; keep smallest ones whole. Do the same with the romaine. Combine all leaves in salad bowl and refrigerate.

3. Place egg in boiling water. Return to a boil for 60 seconds. Run under cold water. Crack into a small food processor or blender, scraping white from shell. Process to a thick fluff, about 60 seconds. Add anchovies, Parmesan, vinegar, lemon juice, 1 tablespoon chives, and hot pepper sauce. Process to puree anchovies. With machine running, slowly add the oils, to make a pourable mayonnaise. Chill.

4. To serve, thin sauce to taste with a touch of boiling water. Spoon about half the dressing over the leaves and toss. Add the remaining 1 tablespoon chives and optional croutons; toss. (Refrigerate remaining dressing for another use.)

Serves 4

Salad of Frisée and Wild Sorrel with Apricot Dressing

Emerald blades of sheep sorrel or shamrocks of wood sorrel swirled with lacy frisée and minced apricot make a tart-sweet salad to precede a fine cheese tray or rich dessert. Use deep orange California apricot halves, not the plump, paler, candy-sweet imports.

1 tablespoon sherry vinegar
1 tablespoon lemon juice
¼ teaspoon kosher salt
1½ tablespoons walnut or hazelnut oil
1½ tablespoons olive oil
3 tablespoons minced California apricots
1½ to 2 ounces tender wild sheep sorrel or
   wood sorrel (2 cups)
½ pound delicate, pale frisée
2 to 3 tablespoons snipped chives

1. Combine vinegar, lemon juice, and salt, stirring to dissolve salt. Whisk in both oils to emulsify. Stir in apricots.

2. Rinse and gently spin-dry sorrel. Trim base of frisée and separate leaves. Rinse and spin-dry. Tear into bite-size branchlets. Toss with sorrel and chives to distribute evenly.

3. Add dressing to salad, tossing. Serve at once.

Serves 4

Pureed Potato and Wild Dock Soup

Subtle, with a smooth, thick consistency and the look of bright split pea soup, this gentle blend has the familiar appeal of potato soup, but mysterious earthy-tart undertones. For a strong wild taste, set aside a few dock leaves, strip their stems, and cut into very fine chiffonade for garnish.

6 ounces wild dock (any kind)
1 medium onion
2 or 3 celery stalks with leaves

2 medium carrots

1¼ pounds potatoes (preferably
  yellow-fleshed)

1 tablespoon corn oil

1¼ teaspoons kosher salt (omit if broth
  is salted)

4½ cups vegetable or light meat broth

1 teaspoon sugar

¼ teaspoon white pepper

Lime wedges

1. Wash dock in several changes of water, lifting out so any debris sinks to the bottom. Repeat as needed. Bunch tightly and slice (you should have about 4 lightly packed cups). Chop onion, celery, and carrots. Peel potatoes and cut into rough dice.

2. Heat oil in medium soup pot over moderately low heat. Stir in onion, celery, carrot, and salt. Cook until vegetables are softened somewhat—about 5 minutes, stirring occasionally.

3. Add potatoes, broth, sugar, and pepper; bring to a boil, stirring now and then. Simmer, partly covered, until potatoes are tender, 15 to 20 minutes. Add dock and bring to a full boil, stirring. Cool briefly.

4. Puree until smooth with an immersion blender. Or transfer to blender or food processor to puree. Taste, then squeeze in lime juice and adjust seasonings.

5. To serve, reheat gently, ladle into bowls, and garnish with lime wedges and optional chiffonade of dock.

Serves 6 as a first course

Variation

Chilled Potato-Dock Puree

Over-season warm soup with salt and white pepper. Chill thoroughly. Add cold buttermilk to taste, about 1 cup (or more). If necessary, thin with ice water. Adjust balance with lime juice and superfine sugar if needed. Garnish with fine bits of chives and slim lime slices.

Serves 8 as a first course

Pros Propose

Sorrel's significance in France can be illustrated by dishes that appear in just one book, *Simple French Food* by Richard Olney: Sorrel Cream Sauce, Creamed Gratin of Hard-Boiled Eggs in Sorrel, Eggs Stuffed with Sorrel, Gratin of Calves' Brains with Sorrel, Eggs in Aspic with Sorrel Mousse, Creamed Fish Fillets in Sorrel Sauce, Sorrel Soup, Sorrel-Stuffed Zucchini, Sorrel Tart, Sorrel Fritters, and **Sorrel-Wrapped Sardines in White Wine.** For this last: Marinate cleaned sardines in crumbled thyme, oregano, white wine, olive oil, salt, and pepper. Wrap each fish in 1 or 2 large stemmed sorrel leaves. Arrange tightly in a gratin dish and scatter over chopped onions. Spoon over the marinade and white wine to cover the bottom of the dish. Crimp foil over. Bake at 450°F until liquid is bubbling and sorrel clings film-like to fish, about 12 minutes. Remove gratin; let oven cool a bit. Return fish to oven to steep about 10 minutes. Serve hot with a spoonful of pan sauce on each fish.

American chef Jerry Traunfeld melds sharply assertive elements for a side dish that blends Mediterranean flavors, **Spinach, Sorrel, and Mint Sautéed with Anchovies and Shallots:** In large skillet, warm anchovy fillets and minced shallots in olive oil, mashing until blended and softened. Raise heat and gradually add spinach, stirring in more as it wilts. Add sorrel chiffonade, chopped mint, and salt. Toss until liquid evaporates. Season and serve at once.

Traunfeld's *The Herbfarm Cookbook* includes **Smoked Salmon Benedict with Sorrel Sauce,** a delightful twist on the classic brunch dish: Soften minced shallots in butter. Gradually stir in chopped sorrel, adding more as it wilts. Stir just until it melts to a puree, then add cream and season. Place 2 toasted crumpets or 1 halved English muffin on each plate. Set a poached egg on each and top with smoked salmon. Spoon warm sorrel sauce over. Sprinkle with chives.

Philippine-born New York chef Romy Dorotan combines two unusual ingredients (neither associated with the Philippines) for a powerful impact on the eye and tongue. The extremes of **Nori-Sorrel Topping** transform even the plainest seafood: Toss thin toasted nori strips with an equal amount of sorrel chiffonade. Sprinkle on grilled seafood.

"The little hearts created when you pluck off the individual leaves of wood sorrel are too adorable to cook or use as anything but a beautiful garnish," says chef Odessa Piper, who prepares this simple **Wood-Sorrel Butter:** Divide sorrel leaves into lobes and blend with butter, lemon zest, shallot, salt, and pepper. Roll up in a parchment cylinder; chill. Slice into rounds; place a whole wood sorrel leaf on each. Set a pat in each bowl of carrot bisque or another pale, creamy soup.

Chef Jean-Georges Vongerichten uses both common and wood sorrels for his **Slow-Baked Char with Olive Oil and Wood Sorrel:** Blend poached eggs in mixer with garden sorrel. Emulsify with olive oil, then season. Spread olive oil, lemon juice, and wood sorrel on flesh side of Arctic char fillets. Cook skin side down in very low oven. When done, flip over and remove skin. Coat with wood sorrel leaves, then sprinkle with coarse pepper and fleur de sel. Stir more leaves into the sauce, and serve in a sauceboat with the fish.

Squash Blossom, Squash Flower (*Cucurbita pepo*)

Including **baby squash with blossoms**

Pretty as they are, these sunny blooms are more than "mere" flowers. They are flavorful, fleshy vegetables that can play a substantial role at the summer table, not just a decorative walk-on.

Almost any member of the squash genus (*Cucurbita*), whether a summer or winter type, produces edible flowers; but zucchini, which proliferate madly, are a usual source in the United States. Because this is the case, it is curious that North Americans needed Mediterranean menus to direct them to their own backyard. Despite home gardens overflowing with blossoms and a long culinary history in Mexico and the Southwest, we seem to have discovered the charms of squash flowers in French and Italian restaurants.

This book has as its starting point vegetables purchased in the market. But if you are picking the flowers from a garden, you should collect males (leaving a few to continue their work as pollinators) and let the females develop into squash. You should also pick the blossoms in the early morning, according to Thomas C.

Andres, an authority on cucurbits: "They'll wilt on the vine by late morning and will only last that long. But once picked, they can be stored in zip-lock bags in the refrigerator for a few days." In the marketplace, slim-stalked male flowers are preselected. The female flowers are the ones attached to little squashlets.

BASIC USE: In the countries where squash flowers are common fare, they are treated casually, as the versatile vegetables they are—not as single jewels to adorn a fancy dish. At their simplest, sliced and sautéed, they are a colorful and tasty addition to many cooked vegetables—zucchini and other tender squash, fresh shell beans, tomatoes, corn, bell peppers, and chillis. Stir into risotto, pasta, or minestra. Or fold the sautéed blooms, seasoned with shallots or chives, into omelets, crêpes, or quesadillas. Or sauté with strips of ham, poultry, or shrimp, for a light lunch.

Add raw chopped blossoms to egg and cheese mixtures for a frittata, gratin, or tian. Stew gently as the

zucchini squash blossoms

length: 4–6½ inches

base for a light soup, pureeing some blossoms as thickener. Or braise with a mixture of vegetables, as you would ratatouille.

Deep-fry individual flowers in a tempura batter or a similar thin coating for a truly special textural performance, from paper-thin and crisp to soft and meaty.

Squash blossoms are unique natural envelopes. Stuff the agreeably expandable forms with soft cheese, seasoned ground meat, a morsel of seafood, cooked grain, sautéed vegetable dice or purees, or a combination. Once filled, the stuffed party favors can then be poached, tucked into a dish and baked, microwaved, steamed, or batter-dipped and fried. There really is no presentation quite like a plumped squash blossom.

SELECTION: With the increased production from the Southern Hemisphere in recent years, we are seeing more squash blossoms. While home gardeners will always have the freshest choice, summer farmers' markets, restaurant distributors, and fancy shops (often during the dead of winter) carry the flowers with some regularity. Taking into consideration that the petals are naturally soft and somewhat limp, select those that are firmest and brightest.

It may be just a coincidence, but in my experience the male flowers (which exhibit flowers alone; they do not develop squashes) form less perfect pouches for stuffing than females. The blossoms attached to the squashlets take naturally to being twisted around filling and neatly closed. Male petals seem to splay outward, and some have a tendency to open during cooking.

STORAGE: Cook squash flowers as soon as possible. Do not try to store them longer than a day, at most. Keep them spread on a towel-covered baking sheet, topped with plastic.

baby summer squashes with their blossoms

length: 2½–5 inches

PREPARATION: Cookbooks often recommend removing the staminate and pistillate portions (the upright parts within in each blossom), but I see no reason to do this unless you don't like the slight crunch. The same is true of the calyx (the cuplike green base), which is meaty and juicy. Perhaps in some large flowers it is fibrous, but I haven't yet found them. Trim the stems to about an inch.

To clean, open petal tips carefully and dunk the flower in and out of a bowl of water. Or hold the flower open and run a gentle stream of water into it; this facilitates the opening process and eliminates insects. Gently dab on a towel and set to dry. If you will stuff the flowers, open the petals wide and place each rinsed blossom stem end up, like an upside-down umbrella, to dry somewhat. For baby squash with large flowers attached, you may want to trim the blossom tip slightly to make it easier to open and fill.

Baby Squash and Their Stuffed Blossoms with Fresh Tomato Puree

Small squash with their generous blossoms attached are standard issue for the upscale restaurant trade. Recently, they have begun appearing in retail shops and farmers' markets. Most amenable to stuffing, the flowers are best filled with a pastry tube, which makes short, neat work of the job. Microwaving keeps the color and crunch of the baby squashes and maintains the form of the filled pouches. Cooked this way, the blossoms are as bright as fresh ones. Serve as the first course of a long summer soirée.

½ pound (1 cup) whole-milk ricotta
3 tablespoons pine nuts
2 tablespoons minced dill
3 tablespoons minced basil or mint
⅓ cup fine-grated Parmesan
Salt and pepper
About 20 tiny green and yellow squash
    of *equal* size, with blossoms
1 small shallot, sliced thin
1 tablespoon butter
2 fully ripe medium tomatoes (1 pound)
About 2 teaspoons olive oil

1. Scoop ricotta into a sieve set over bowl; drain for an hour or more (or refrigerate overnight).

2. Preheat oven to 325°F. Spread pine nuts in a small pan and bake until golden, about 8 minutes. Cool. Combine drained ricotta, nuts, dill, basil, Parmesan, salt, and pepper (can be refrigerated overnight).

3. Trim squash stems to about an inch if necessary. If petals are very long or twisted, snip their tips to facilitate opening. Hold each flower under a gentle stream of water to open it. Set on towel.

4. Scoop filling into a small pastry bag with a wide opening or tube. Pipe into blossoms, pushing tube deep into base of each. When all are filled, twist petals closed. Place paper towel on microwavable plate large enough to hold blossoms with space between them and arrange blossoms on it. Refrigerate, uncovered, until ready to serve (can be prepared up to a day ahead).

5. To serve, prepare sauce: Cook shallot in butter in medium skillet over low heat until slightly soft, 3 to 4 minutes. Meanwhile, dice or chop tomatoes. Add to pan, cover, and simmer gently until soft, about 5 minutes. Press sauce through a fine food mill or sieve. Stir in 2 teaspoons olive oil, or more to taste. Season.

6. Set plate of squash on microwave carousel. Cook until squashes are not quite crunchy-tender and blossoms are puffed and hot, about 2 minutes (but timing varies considerably among ovens).

7. Spoon a tiny puddle of tomato sauce onto each plate. Arrange 5 squash on each. Serve lukewarm, drizzled with additional olive oil, if desired.

Serves 4 as a first course

Note: If preferred, the squash can be poached instead of microwaved. Bring water to cover squash to a boil in deep wide sauté pan. Add salt, then squash. Reduce heat to a bare simmer. Cook until squash is just tender and filling somewhat firm, about 5 minutes. With slotted spoon, transfer to a towel and blot gently.

Sautéed Squash Blossoms with Mint

This dish has several textures (sumptuous petals, crunchy calyces) and flavors (zucchini, mushrooms, green beans, and a distinct sweetness). Although the blossoms are brilliant cadmium orange, the total effect is sharp light green. Serve as a side dish or omelet filling; or stir into risotto; or spoon over gnocchi or soft fresh pasta. Mint is a pleasing change of pace for squash, but the more traditional dill and basil are equally tasty.

> 6 to 7 ounces medium squash blossoms
>   (about 30)
> 2 slim scallions (green onions)
> 1 small celery stalk
> 1½ tablespoons olive oil
> ¼ teaspoon kosher salt
> 2 tablespoons finely slivered mint leaves

1. Rinse blossoms and blot on towel to dry somewhat. Slice each green stem and calyx (base) into ½-inch slices. Cut petals into wider slices. Trim and thin-slice scallions, separating dark and light parts. Mince celery.

2. Set medium-large skillet over moderate heat. Add olive oil. When shimmering, add light scallion parts and celery and toss a minute. Add blossoms. Toss until slightly wilted, about 2 minutes. Add salt.

3. Cover and reduce heat. Cook until blossoms are tender, tossing and re-covering a few times—about 5 minutes. Add scallion greens and mint; toss.

Serves 4 as a side dish

Deep-Fried Squash Blossoms

All who like squash blossoms love them fried—and no wonder: Lightly coated with batter, the meaty petals, which taste like a pale version of whichever squash they produce (or produces them—chicken or egg?), make an uncommonly appealing appetizer—which is why I have borrowed a recipe from *Uncommon Fruits & Vegetables: A Commonsense Guide,* thinking it unfair to bring up blossoms without frying them. The crisp morsels are best straight from the skillet, but they can be kept briefly on a rack in a low oven. Serve hot with a chilly rosé.

> 1¼ cups cold water
> ¼ teaspoon kosher salt
> 1 cup all-purpose flour
> **About 30 medium squash blossoms**
>   (6 to 7 ounces)

Vegetable oil for deep-frying
Crisp sea salt, preferably fleur de sel

1. Combine water and salt in a bowl. Sift in flour, beating rapidly with a fork to blend. Cover with a towel and let stand an hour or more.

2. Meanwhile, trim squash stems to about 1 inch. Open petals carefully and dunk flowers in and out of a bowl of water. Or hold each flower open and run a gentle stream of water into it. Open petals and place stem up to dry (like an upside-down umbrella).

3. When ready to serve, pour about an inch of oil into a wide deep skillet (preferably electric) and heat to 375°F. Stir batter, coat a blossom thoroughly, and drop into the hot oil. Repeat quickly 4 or 5 times, coating only as many as can "swim" in the oil with room to spare. Fry until golden on one side—about 30 seconds—then flip and fry until golden on the other side.

4. Drain on towels, salt to taste, and serve at once.

Serves 6 generously as an hors d'oeuvre

Pros Propose

Master of haute cuisine chef Alain Ducasse bakes up this rustic dish for personal nibbling: Arrange a fan of whole blossoms in a gratin dish and top with Parmesan slivers and olive oil. Bake until the cheese crisps, then eat with your fingers! Another casual dish called **Scarpaccia de Courgettes** (squashed old shoe) might be described as a savory clafouti. To prepare: Mince baby squash and their flowers, toss with salt, and drain ½ hour. Whisk eggs, flour, water, and milk to make a smooth batter. Rinse squash, squeeze dry, and blot. Mix with minced onion, grated Parmesan, crushed garlic, and seasoning. Add to batter. Turn into an oiled baking dish, to make a cake less than ½ inch thick. Drizzle with oil. Bake in a fairly hot oven until set but soft, about 15 minutes (*Méditerranées: Cuisine de l'essentiel*).

Squash blossom soups exist throughout Mexico. Diana Kennedy, who has probably tried them all, chooses this one as exemplary in *The Art of Mexican Cooking.* For **Sopa de Flor de Calabaza:** Soften minced white onion and garlic in butter in a wide skillet. Stir in chopped squash flowers in generous volume (they will wilt dramatically). Cover and cook over moderate heat about 5 minutes. Blend a cupful of cooked blossoms with chicken broth until smooth. Return to pot with the cooked squash blossoms, more chicken broth, diced zucchini, and corn kernels; cook until tender. Add epazote and salt; cook briefly. Add peeled, diced, and sautéed Poblano chillis.

Tender, sweet crab is an ideal stuffing for squash blossoms. Chef Charlie Trotter assembled this delicacy to garnish consommé of Dungeness crab infused with lemon balm, but it could be served on other light dishes. For **Crab-Stuffed Squash Blossoms:** Stuff blossoms gently with picked crabmeat tossed with lime juice, salt, and pepper. Just before serving, set on a steamer rack over boiling water and cook 2 minutes (from *Charlie Trotter's Seafood*).

"Throughout the Greek islands, zucchini blossoms are stuffed with bulgur, rice, nuts, ground meat and a variety of other ingredients. I prefer . . . a filling of feta and mint, which takes on a complex flavor when the blossoms are dipped in an ouzo-scented batter and fried," writes Aglaia Kremezi. Her interpretation of **Fried Zucchini Blossoms Stuffed with Feta and Mint** follows: Insert a small piece of feta and a mint leaf into each blossom. Whisk together flour, water, egg, ouzo, olive oil, and Aleppo pepper (or crushed chilli flakes) and salt for a batter. Heat olive and safflower oils to 350°F. Dip each blossom in batter to coat. Fry, turning, until golden. Drain and serve hot with mint sprigs (from *The Foods of the Greek Islands*).

Baby Zucchini and Blossoms Stuffed with Lobster and Lobster Salad is the elegant creation of chef Bill Telepan: Prepare mousse with white fish and cream. Fold in cooked lobster and lobster glaze. Pipe into trimmed, rinsed, chilled blossoms; twist closed. Steam until just firm, about 3 minutes. Meanwhile, toss together baby greens, sliced raw baby zucchini, sliced lobster, and sprigs of dill, tarragon, chervil, and parsley. Add vinaigrette made from lobster oil, lobster stock, and red wine and balsamic vinegars. Set warm stuffed blossoms on salad.

For **Fettuccine with Squash Blossoms,** Sylvia Thompson maintains fresh flavor and color by heating—not cooking—the blossoms: Boil fettuccine until al dente. Meanwhile, clean squash blossoms and cut off stems. Cut across into inch-wide rings. Chop plum tomatoes; rough-chop basil and oregano leaves. Toss hot pasta with olive oil and cover. Heat more oil in skillet and soften tomatoes, shaking pan for about 2 minutes. Add basil, oregano, and a generous amount of unpitted small French or Italian olives; warm through and season. Pour over pasta and add blossoms. Toss at once so the hot pasta and tomatoes wilt the blooms (from *The Kitchen Garden Cookbook*).

Squashes, Tender or Summer (*Cucurbita pepo*)

Including
Zucchini
Costata Romanesca
Middle Eastern
Round zucchini
Tatume (and oval types)
Scallop or **pattypan**
Yellow (or **summer**) **crookneck** and **straightneck**
Zephyr
Baby summer squashes

See also: BITTER GOURD, page 90, BOTTLE GOURD, page 107
CHAYOTE, page 178, CUCUZZA, page 108
FUZZY GOURD, page 293, TINDORA, page 664

"Tender squash" is a description more to the point than "summer squash" in today's market—unless you mean "summer" worldwide, for this vegetable is available year-round. "Little squash" is what they're called in the countries that give them the names known in much of the Western world. From zucca, calabaza, and courge (the generic words for squash in Italian, Spanish, and French, respectively) come the diminutive forms: zucchini, calabacita, and courgette. (Thomas C. Andres, editor of *The Cucurbit Network News,* points out that the word "zucca" predates the introduction of *Cucurbita* from the New World and was first applied to the Old World bottle gourd, *Lagenaria.*)

Beyond their relative smallness, what most young *Cucurbita pepo* (among the earliest of New World crops) have in common is tender skin and flesh; mild and nutty or buttery or cucumberish flavor; relatively quick cookability; high moisture content; a lack of mature seeds; and extreme perishability. Traits that winter or hard squash do *not* exhibit are those of summer or tender squash.

Although tender squash is very popular with home gardeners, and seed catalogues offer a beautiful bouquet of old and new varieties, the display at markets is limited. Tender squashes are among the most common

vegetables in this book. They are taken for granted, like cucumbers; they're always there. Also like cucumbers, the standard issue is often tasteless and pulpy. But there are revivals and newcomers worth noticing. The following are ones I've seen in specialty markets and farmers' markets.

"Zucchini-type" squashes, as they are referred to by gardeners and breeders, make up the bulk of the marketplace. But they exist in so many forms and colors that it seems pointless to group them under "zucchini." Culinarily, they have no more or less in common than other types of tender squash.

In discussing the origins of what Americans call "zucchini" in *Heirloom Vegetable Gardening,* William Woys Weaver refers to "the *cocozelle* or Italian vegetable marrow introduced late in the nineteenth century . . . the squash now known as zucchini." He explains that at one time *cocozelle* was used in the Eastern United States for all zucchini-like squash, and that "during the 1920s and 1930s, the term *zucchini* came into general use in California, and in time the rest of the country followed suit."

Zucchini (classic zucchini) is the familiar dark green cylindrical type that defines the word "zucchini" in the United States, if not elsewhere. As a "control" for

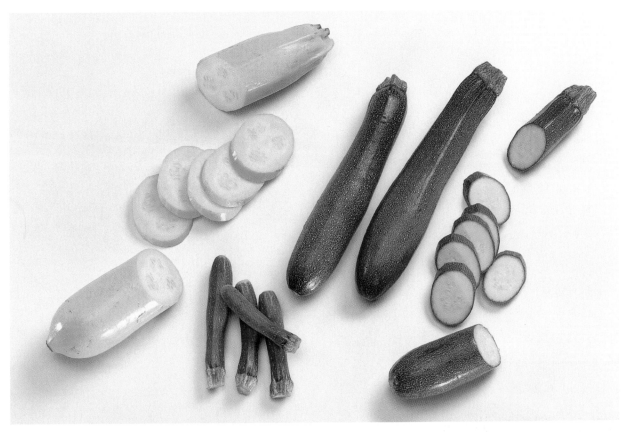

zucchini: golden, classic green, and baby   length: 2½ - 8 inches

Costata Romanesca   length: about 7 inches

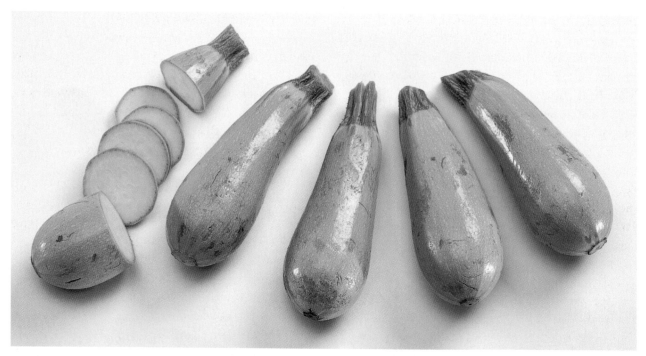

Middle Eastern–type zucchini   length: about 5 inches

round zucchini or globe squash   diameter: 5 inches

tasting all the squashes that follow, I cooked a classic zucchini alongside each. If you do the same, you will begin snatching up Middle Eastern, round, and egg-shaped "other" zucchinis wherever you find them. Mainstream market forms of the "classics" are usually as tasteless as market cucumbers: grown for appearance and durability. **Golden zucchini,** which has many other names, is a spectacularly beautiful squash and, thus far, seems to have more flavor than the green market types. The ravishing skin (which unlike the skin of most other yellow squash is "born" that color; it does not start out green) retains its color when cooked; the flavor is fresh, light, buttery, and simple.

Costata Romanesca (ribbed Roman zucchini) is a mottled, slightly belled squash distinguished by pale, raised ribs that run its length. It is one of the striped and ridged types that are still likely to be called cocoz-elle rather than zucchini. Although more flavorful than the bland commercial zucchini, it is problematic as a market item, for it quickly loses its vigor and savor. When solid and young, it is juicy, refreshing, and summery-sweet, but it quickly turns bland, flabby, and rather bitter. Seek it out at farmers' markets, where it will be freshest. Cook like classic zucchini.

Middle Eastern–type zucchini—also called Lebanese, Egyptian, Cousa, Kuta, and Magda, and by many more names—are typically stocky, pale green tapering cylinders with a thick darker green stem. Smooth-skinned and shiny with unusually solid, crisp flesh, they can be—and usually are—everything you could want from zucchini, and more. Moist (not wet) and flavorful, they brighten with cooking and retain their firm shape and sweet taste when baked, sautéed, steamed, or fried; hot, cold, and at room temperature. Even if their skin looks imperfect (they bruise and scratch easily), their flavor and texture are likely to be fine. Although not widely available in mainstream markets, Middle Eastern types show up at farmers' markets, in specialty groceries, and in neighborhoods with a high proportion of Asian residents. Cook like classic zucchini.

Round zucchini or globe squash, represented in the photo by Eight Ball, appear in varying sizes and shades of green as Gourmet Globe, Apple Squash, Ronde de Nice, and others. Thus far, they seem to be as consistently delicious as the Middle Eastern types. Eight Ball is exemplary for the type: extremely dense and heavy, nearly seedless, and smooth-textured. Cooked, the fiberless flesh acquires a pretty green tinge and becomes juicy, flavorful, and meaty. Bake, steam, sauté, marinate, or grill. Slice small ones into perfect rounds and cook like classic zucchini. Halve larger ones, to hollow and stuff. Cut thick slices, coat with crumbs, and fry like green tomatoes. Layer in casseroles, like eggplant.

Oval or egg-shaped zucchini like **Tatume** are unusual not only for their form but for their extraordinarily dense, smooth flesh. My 5-inch-long sample weighed well over 1 pound—all solid, seamless, virtually seedless meat. While the most tasty and attractive part of most tender squash is the skin and the adjacent flesh, this one is sweet and flavorful throughout.

The type is common in Mexico. "Markets from Mazatlan to Merida are piled high with zucchini, but not the zucchini we know. The vegetable, called calabacita there, has a pale-green complexion," according to *Rick Bayless's Mexican Kitchen*. "The texture is compact, not porous or watery, and the flavor is slightly sweet. Luckily, I've been seeing . . . squash that they call tatume . . . at my farmers' market [in Chicago], so our options are growing." Glenn Drowns, curator for vine crops at Seed Savers Exchange in Decorah, Iowa, says that Tatume probably originated in Mexico and that it is popular in South Texas, but that it is increasingly rare.

Very similar to Tatume is a spectacularly shiny ovoid (and as yet unidentified) squash that I find in markets in Korean communities—parrot green, with patent leather skin. The succulent flesh is firm (without a trace of sponginess or pithiness), full, and flavorful, and turns pale yellow-green in cooking.

Cut beautiful circular slices to layer in a casserole, grill, or bake. Or cut extra-thick slices, hollow the center, prebake, then mound with stuffing and bake through. Fry slices as you would green tomatoes. Or cut thick slices, then cut into neat wedges to sauté.

Scallop or pattypan, also called custard squash or cymling in parts of the South, is represented by some old (early 18th century) and some spanking new squashes, all of which have a characteristic scalloped or crimped pie-like circumference, whether the squash is flattened or bell-shaped. Cream, sunny yellow, pistachio, mottled ivy, and the colors between, they usually

oval zucchini types: Tatume   diameter: 3-4½ inches   "Korean"   diameter: 3½ inches

taste best when small (from a button mushroom to a bun). Solid and smooth-fleshed, they can be buttery and nutty or merely bland. Unless garden-fresh, they are less flavorful than the best zucchini types but can make up in charm what they lack in flavor if prettily presented.

Much of pattypans' appeal is their appearance. Choose small ones and keep them whole, whenever possible. Quarter larger ones or cut into trim pie wedges, using the scallops as a guide. The belled types make neat stuffers: Cut off the conical part and mince and cook briefly for filling; hollow the scalloped "dish" part to fill with stuffing.

Early White Bush (in fact, a creamy celadon) is a very old cultivar, flatter in form than newer ones. Slightly sweet, with a firm, even texture throughout, it has a light summery freshness.

Scallopini, which won an All-America Selections award (the vegetable Academy Award) in 1977, is a zucchini and pattypan cross, and tastes a bit like both, with a touch of yellow straightneck. Uniform in texture, it has minimal seedy areas and cooks evenly. Again, look for small ones. Bake, steam, or sauté.

Sunburst, an All-America Selections winner in 1985, is smooth and creamy, but prone to blandness and big seed pockets if it is larger than petite. The flavor is

of mild yellow crookneck; the glossy Provençal yellow is spectacular. Best when baked or sautéed.

Yellow or summer crookneck and yellow or summer straightneck are squashes that signify summer in American gardening and cookbooks; so much so that they are known simply as "summer squash." But *where* is the crookneck? It has become so rare in the market that I finally settled on a semi-straightneck (in November, from Central America) for a photo. In my experience, warts and crooked necks offer a sweeter, sunnier flavor and a crunchier skin than just about any other summertime squash. The straightnecks that have been selected out from these oldsters seem to be bland in comparison and to have less firm skin and flesh.

In 1807, Timothy Matlack of Lancaster, Pennsylvania, sent Thomas Jefferson the "long crooked & warted Squash—a native of New Jersey, which the Cooper's family have preserved and cultivated for near a century," advising him that "it is our best Squash" (*Thomas Jefferson's Garden Book,* edited by Edwin Morris Betts). Raise your voice and ask for the crookneck before this lovely squash disappears from the market!

Zephyr, a newcomer that has a yellow crookneck as one of its parents, is a hybrid from Johnny's Selected

scallop or pattypan: baby Scallopini (darker green), Early White Bush (pale green), and Sunburst   diameter: 1½-4 inches

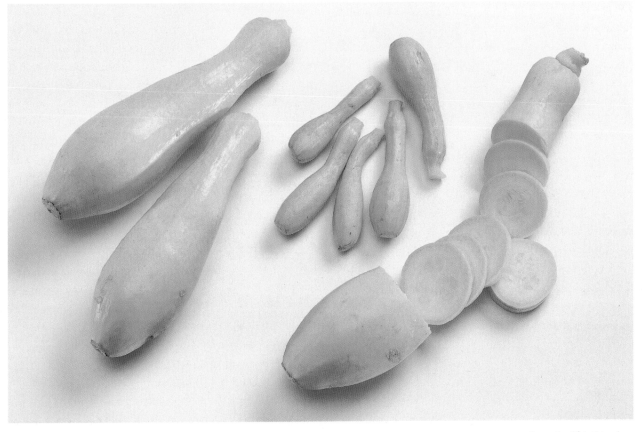

yellow or summer straightneck and semi–straightneck (standard and baby sizes)   length: 2½-7 inches

Seeds. Its other parent was derived from a Delicata and yellow Acorn cross. Unfortunately, all of my samples (including the one in the photo) were picked larger than the size recommended by the developers, so I cannot properly evaluate the product. I can report only that its colors baked to a shiny, deeper brilliance, that it was quite crisp (in fact, brittle), and that it was somewhat sweet but lacked flavor. It seems highly unlikely that a squash with Delicata and yellow crookneck in the mix could be anything less than delightful, so I recommend that you try it for yourself if you find it.

Baby squash or mini-squash can be any squash harvested when very young. The tiny infants are always glowingly pretty—like old-fashioned hard candies or pottery beads. Sometimes they taste good, too; sometimes they have barely any taste. Sample before you buy a large amount. They always look irresistibly cute,

so you might add them to a toss of mixed miniatures even if they're rather insipid.

BASIC USE FOR TENDER SQUASH: Any reliable recipes for zucchini, yellow squash, and scallop squash apply to all the squash above. If you need a basic book about common vegetables, I suggest *The Victory Garden Cookbook* by Marian Morash.

SELECTION: Spring to summer is the best time for domestic squash, but squash are available all year. Choose small to medium fruit with skin that is shiny, squeaky-taut, and free of pitting. Tender squash may be unevenly colored or may look scratched or slightly bruised, but this is no problem unless there is browning or softening. They should be uniformly solid: Squeeze to be sure there is no area that feels flabby or spongy.

STORAGE: Tender squash stores miserably. Wrap in paper towels, enclose in plastic, and refrigerate for no

Zephyr

length: 5-8 inches

more than a few days—preferably less—in the warmest part of your refrigerator.

PREPARATION: These obligingly ready-to-cook vegetables need no more than a light scrubbing with a brush under running water to remove their prickly stubble and any grit. Some need to have their necks and bases trimmed, but just minimally.

Fanned Zucchini with Olive Paste and Oranges

Zucchini is partly sliced, seasoned with olive paste, and fanned to bake neatly: simple, effective, and Mediterranean. Choose whichever cylindrical zucchini matches the colors and moods of the meal: classic dark, paler Middle Eastern, gloriously golden, or mid-green ribbed Roman. Serve as an appetizer, side dish, salad, or part of a room-temperature meal of little dishes (tapas, mezze, whichever).

2 tablespoons black olive paste
2 tablespoons fine dry bread crumbs
2 tablespoons olive oil
6 medium-small Middle Eastern, "classic,"
    Roman, and/or golden zucchini (each squash
    about 6 inches long and about 4 ounces)
A few squeezes of orange or mandarin juice
For garnish: small orange or mandarin sections,
    peel and pith removed

1. Preheat oven to 400°F. Combine olive paste, crumbs, and oil in a small bowl.

2. Without cutting the stem end, cut each squash lengthwise into 4 or 5 slices to come within about an inch of the stem end. Spread open slightly, as you would a fan. Spread olive mixture on the fanned-out slices, dividing it evenly. Arrange in a single layer in an oiled baking dish.

3. Cover dish loosely with foil (do not crimp closed). Bake in upper level of oven until squash is just barely tender, about 15 minutes. Remove foil. Bake until very tender and lightly browned, 15 to 20 minutes more.

4. Cool to lukewarm or room temperature. Squeeze a little orange juice over each squash. Top with the orange sections.

Serves 6

Baked Summer Squash Mélange

Baking concentrates the flavor of mild squash and maintains its texture. This easygoing dish works with any tender squashes, provided they're cut into fairly equal ½-inch slices. Try this if you've run wild at the farmers' market and can't decide how to tackle the multiple variations.

1 pound fairly small yellow crookneck or
    straightneck squash
1½ pounds fairly small zucchini-type squash
    (any kind)
3 small onions
3 medium garlic cloves, sliced
2 bay leaves, crumbled
½ teaspoon dried rosemary, crumbled
½ teaspoon dried oregano, crushed
½ teaspoon pepper
1¼ teaspoons kosher salt
⅓ cup full-flavored olive oil
1 tablespoon red wine vinegar
Tiny fresh basil or mint leaves

1. Preheat oven to 400°F. Cut squashes into bite-size slices about ½ inch thick. Peel onions, slice them, and separate into rings.

2. Oil a baking dish wide enough to hold squash in a single overlapping layer. Spread half the onions in it. Sprinkle with half the garlic, bay leaves, rosemary, oregano, pepper, and salt. Spread squash on top and cover with remaining onions, garlic, bay leaves, rosemary, oregano, pepper, and salt. Drizzle with oil and sprinkle with vinegar. Cover tightly with foil.

3. Bake in upper level of oven 20 minutes. Uncover and toss. Continue baking until squash is just barely tender, 5 to 10 minutes. Do not cook until soft, as mixture will continue to cook once removed from oven.

4. Serve warm, or cool to room temperature. Garnish with fresh basil or mint.

Serves 6

Tatume-Onion Accordion with Diced Tomatoes and Chilli

A dramatic presentation of simple and satisfying flavors. Red onion rounds are slipped into slits cut in sturdy green squash and the whole is cooked until tender on a bed of tomato and chilli dice. Serve hot, warm, or at ambient temperature as a side dish. If the elusive Tatume is not available, use fairly large round zucchini.

2 medium-small Tatume or medium-large
   round zucchini (10 ounces each)
1 medium red onion (8 to 10 ounces)
4 tablespoons olive oil
1 teaspoon kosher salt
2 large tomatoes, peeled, seeded, and diced
   (see Note, page 10)
1 Poblano chilli, peeled, seeded, and minced
   (see Note, page 114)
Optional: chopped fresh cilantro or dill

1. Set oven to 375°F. Halve each squash through "poles." With cut side down, keeping the squash intact at stem end, cut each half into even lengthwise slices ¼ inch wide, to come to about 1 inch from stem end. Halve onion through "poles," then cut lengthwise into as many ⅛-inch slices as there are cuts in the squash. Lay onion slices on cutting board, brush with 1½ tablespoons oil, and sprinkle with ½ teaspoon salt. Slip a slice, cut edge down, into each squash cut.

2. Toss tomatoes, chilli, 1½ tablespoons oil, and remaining ½ teaspoon salt in baking dish that will hold squash fairly closely, then spread mixture evenly. Set squash on top. Brush with the remaining 1 tablespoon oil. Cover with foil and cut a few slits in it.

3. Bake in upper level of oven until squash is almost tender, about 25 minutes (but expect variation). Uncover and baste with cooking liquid. Raise heat to 425°F. Bake until slightly browned and fully tender, about 20 minutes longer.

4. Cool slightly. With spatula, carefully transfer halves to serving dish. Spoon over the tomato mixture and sprinkle with optional herbs.

Serves 4

Scallop Squashes with Herbed Crumb-Cheese Filling

Pattypan squashes are meant to be stuffed. Their shape is sweetly suited to filling, and their mildness is balanced by seasoning and richness. Stay with one kind of scallop squash, or bake a colorful combination of golden Sunburst, ivy green Scallopini, and cream or celery pattypans. Round zucchini can be substituted.

8 yellow, green, and/or white scallop squashes
   (3 to 4 ounces each)
3 quarts water
½ teaspoon dried thyme
2 garlic cloves, halved
½ teaspoon dried rosemary
⅛ teaspoon chilli flakes
5 tablespoons olive oil
1 teaspoon minced garlic
1¼ cups fresh whole-wheat bread crumbs
1 teaspoon kosher salt
Pepper
¼ cup minced parsley
½ teaspoon grated nutmeg
About 3 ounces Emmentaler, Comté, or
   Gruyère cheese

1. Set oven to 375°F. Trim a thin sliver from the bud side of each squash (opposite the stem end). Cut off stems plus about ½ inch of each squash. (If using globe squash, simply halve them.) With a small melon ball cutter, scoop out and reserve the flesh, leaving squash shells about ½ inch thick.

2. In large saucepan, combine water, thyme, halved garlic, rosemary, chilli, and 1 tablespoon olive oil. Boil 5 minutes. Add squash cases and boil until not quite tender, 1½ to 2 minutes. Remove and drain upside down on a rack.

3. Mince reserved squash pulp. Warm remaining ¼ cup oil and minced garlic in skillet over fairly low heat. Add minced squash and cook until tender and lightly browned, about 8 minutes. Off heat, add crumbs, salt, pepper, parsley, and nutmeg; toss. Grate cheese. Add two-thirds to stuffing, blending and seasoning.

4. Spoon filling into squash. Set in an oiled baking dish. Sprinkle remaining cheese over squash. Cover loosely with foil. Bake on upper shelf of oven until tender, about 20 minutes.

5. Uncover squash and bake until browned, about 10 minutes. Serve hot or warm.

Serves 4

Pattypan and Globe Zucchini with Micro-Coddled Eggs

Every now and then, whimsical notions translate into delightful recipes. Bright small squash (not larger ones, which will not cook evenly) serve as colorful cups to protect eggs from toughening as they coddle quickly in a microwave oven. The result is perfectly cooked squashlets *and* eggs, for a truly cute brunch dish. The duo of squash types looks as pretty as marzipan veggies, but one type will be fine if that's what there is.

Note that microwaves move in mysterious ways and not all powers are equal. My oven, at 850 watts, produced consistent results three times for the following recipe. If your oven is either more or less powerful, you will need to adjust timing. But whatever you do, do *not* cook the eggs at full power.

> 2 small Sunburst scallop squash
>   (5 to 6 ounces each)
> 2 small round zucchini, such as Eight Ball
>   (5 to 6 ounces each)
> Salt and pepper
> 1 tablespoon thin-sliced chives
> ½ cup small croutons (preferably whole wheat)
> ¼ cup fine-grated Comté, Gruyère, or
>   Emmentaler cheese
> 4 medium or large eggs
> Butter

1. Scrub squashes with brush. Cut off scallop squash stems. Cut off stems plus about ½ inch from round zucchini. Set squashes cut side down in microwavable dish. Cover and microwave until almost tender, about 6 minutes (but timing varies—check often). Let stand 2 minutes. Uncover and cool as needed to handle.

2. Cut a circular cap from the upturned wide end of the scallop squash. With melon ball cutter or grapefruit spoon, scrape out seeds and flesh to leave a ½-inch shell, approximately. Scoop out zucchini in the same way. Season squashes.

3. Set aside ½ teaspoon chives. Toss together remainder with croutons and cheese. Divide among squash, pressing in firmly. Break an egg into each. With tines of fork, prick each yolk once. Return squash to dish.

4. Re-cover and cook at 50 percent power until whites just turn opaque but are not firm, about 4 minutes (again, timing varies considerably—watch carefully). Let stand 2 minutes, then uncover.

5. Arrange on serving dish. Salt lightly, top each with a sliver of butter and the reserved chives.

Serves 2 to 4

Note: This dish tastes as good warm as hot. If you want to double the recipe, prepare 8 squashes through step 3, then cook in two batches and serve them together.

Summer Squash Shreds with Basil, Sorrel, and Chives

Squash that is shredded, salted, and drained stays crisp-tender, cooks quickly, and keeps its bright hue. Yellow summer squashes have a pleasing firmness, and their coloring complements a wide range of dishes; but tender squash of any type can be used in this adaptable recipe. Clean, fresh, and balanced, the toss of gentle squash, scented basil, tart sorrel, and oniony chives is light and versatile.

> 1½ pounds yellow summer squash (or other
>   tender squash)
> 1 teaspoon kosher salt
> 1 tablespoon olive oil
> 1 tablespoon grapeseed or corn oil
> ¼ cup thin-sliced basil leaves
> ¼ cup thin-sliced sorrel leaves
> 1 tablespoon thin-sliced chives
> Salt and pepper

1. Scrub squashes with vegetable brush. Trim stems if they are unusually long. Using julienne blade of food processor or vegetable cutter, slice squash into very fine

strips. Toss with salt in a sieve or colander. Set over a bowl, top with a plate, weight lightly, and let stand about an hour, tossing now and then.

2. Squeeze squash dry. Fluff with a fork. Spread on paper towels.

3. Heat both oils in a wide skillet over high heat. Add squash and toss until tender and lightly browned, about 5 minutes.

4. Remove skillet from heat. Add basil, sorrel, and chives. Toss to distribute. Season. Serve hot, warm, or at room temperature.

Serves 4

Any-Many Summer Squash "Guacamole"

Creamy and soft, this simple whip tastes and looks as if it were made of avocado dip and eggplant puree, yet it has the lightness and freshness of summer squash. If your garden crookneck or zucchini overproduces or you've been over-enthusiastic at the greenmarket, toss any and all extras into the oven, bake until smooshy, and then puree for a rewarding spread. Serve as a dip for vegetables or bread sticks, as a garnish for cold soup, as mayonnaise with cold meats, or as a canapé spread to be topped with ham, shrimp, or egg slices and sprinkled with herbs. Use big, juicy garlic cloves (but not "elephant garlic"—not a true garlic and not the right flavor); little ones brown too deeply and may burn.

**3 pounds tender squashes of any size
   or shape
About ½ head fairly large garlic cloves
1 large onion (preferably mild/sweet)
1 teaspoon kosher salt
2 tablespoons corn oil
½ cup tightly packed basil or mint leaves
½ cup tightly packed parsley leaves
About 2 tablespoons lemon juice
¼ to ½ cup heavy cream (preferably not
   ultra-pasteurized)
Salt and pepper**

1. Turn oven to 375°F. Scrub squashes with vegetable brush. Halve large squash lengthwise, then cut so they are about the same size as the smallest squash. Spread cut side down in a single layer in an oiled roasting pan.

2. Separate but do not peel garlic and distribute among squash. Quarter and peel onion and add to the pan. Sprinkle with salt, then drizzle over oil.

3. Bake until squashes are very soft, 1 to 1½ hours. Using a brush, baste several times with cooking juices. Remove from oven.

4. When garlic is cool enough to handle, remove skins. Place basil and parsley in food processor. Add the warm vegetables and garlic and whiz to a smooth puree, scraping down side as needed. With motor running, add 2 tablespoons lemon juice, then slowly drizzle in cream, stopping to taste and to adjust the amount for flavor and thickness. Add salt, pepper, and more lemon juice as needed. Chill to serve.

Makes about 1 quart

Variation

Creamless Squash "Guacamole"

Substitute olive oil for the corn oil. Instead of the cream, use ¼ cup olive oil, dribbling it slowly into the food processor. Season as above.

Creamed Baby Squash, Corn, and Chilli

Little squashlets set the scene for a swanky succotash. The backup ingredients round out the mild miniatures, lending depth and sweetness. Use any type of mini-squash, preferably of equal size.

**½ pound "baby" squash (25 to 30 squash)—
   one or several varieties
½ teaspoon kosher salt
½ cup heavy cream
¼ cup milk
¼ teaspoon ground mace
¼ teaspoon sugar
1½ cups corn kernels (cut from 2 or 3 ears)
1 Poblano or Anaheim chilli, peeled and
   diced fine (see Note, page 114)
1 tablespoon thin-sliced chives
Salt and white pepper**

1. Halve squash vertically or horizontally, depending on what best suits the types selected. Sprinkle with salt. Let drain in colander for ½ hour or more. Blot dry with towels.

2. In a saucepan, combine cream, milk, mace, and sugar and bring to a boil. Add squash and corn. Simmer, stirring often, until squash is very tender, about 6 to 8 minutes. Add chilli and toss. Add chives. Season. Serve hot.

Serves 4

Pros Propose

"This sharp, sweet, and salty combination has ancient Roman roots, but it is lighter than the old style, to respect the delicacy of the yellow squash," says Stefano Riccioletti of his **Yellow Squash Cups with Pecorino and Ricotta in Honey-Lemon Dressing:** Cut 1½-inch crosswise pieces of yellow straightneck squash. Scoop out pulp (reserve) to form cups. Sauté the pulp with garlic to barely color. Off heat, add sheep's milk ricotta and pecorino. Steam the cups, then fill with the cheese mixture. Arrange 3 on each plate. Drizzle with dressing of honey, lemon juice, and olive oil.

Chef Riccioletti also prepares an unusual **Zucchini Parmigiana.** "Zucchini is cooked in the style of eggplant in a traditional dish from southern Lazio and northern Campania, where chocolate is typical," he says. To prepare: Cut lengthwise slices of Roman ribbed zucchini. Flour lightly and deep-fry. Layer in baking dish with mozzarella, Parmesan, bittersweet chocolate bits, and basil. Top with Parmesan, then bake.

Zucchini, green and gold, get a light bath in oil and lemon to take off the raw edge. For **Zucchini Carpaccio,** London chefs Rose Gray and Ruth Rogers recommend very young Gold Rush and Ronde de Nice (Tondo di Nizza in Italian): Cut these or other yellow and green zucchini into thin rounds at an angle. Blend olive oil, lemon, sea salt and pepper and toss with zucchini; marinate 5 minutes. Arrange zucchini over trimmed arugula leaves, then top with Parmesan slivers. Grind over pepper and serve at once.

Italian flavors and traditional Chinese cooking methods produce a fresh sauté of **Zucchini or Summer Squash with Fennel Seeds, Lemon Zest:** Sauté ½-inch slices of small squash in olive oil over moderate heat for 3 minutes. Push squash to outside of pan. Add minced garlic, fennel seeds, and more oil to pan center; sizzle a moment. Add minced lemon zest; toss to coat zucchini. Add a little vegetable stock and continue cooking and tossing until just tender. Add minced basil, oregano, or parsley and top with toasted pine nuts (from *Professional Vegetarian Cooking* by Ken Bergeron).

For her **Baked Globe Zucchini Slices with Labne,** chef Amaryll Schwertner uses Tatume squash or large globe zucchini that her distributor calls Persian Globe. "It has spectacular symmetry and texture, and dark speckled green edible skin that makes it one of the most flavorful squashes in the zucchini family." To prepare: Cut thick squash slices, spread on sheet pans, dot with butter, and sprinkle with water and fleur de sel. Cover with parchment, seal with foil, and bake briefly in a 425°F oven until flesh is "chartreuse and translucent, just lightly cooked." Serve at room temperature with labne (a fresh Middle Eastern yogurt-type cheese) and herb salad. Or chill and serve as a salad element, dressed with olive oil, sumac, sea salt, and toasted pistachios or sesame seeds.

Tatume or shiny Korean squash make neat, firm discs on which to mound seasoned topping. The whole is dipped in egg and fried golden for a savory appetizer, **Fried Squash Slices Topped with Beef:** Cut squash across into ¼-inch slices; salt and drain. Mash together minced beef, firm bean curd, soy sauce, beaten egg, minced garlic, and scallion. Dry squash slices; coat lightly with flour. Top with beef mixture, leaving a ¼-inch margin all around. Dip into beaten egg. Fry until golden. Serve with sauce of rice wine, sugar, soy sauce, chopped green onion and garlic, sesame oil, crushed sesame seeds, and black pepper (from *Low-Fat Korean Cooking* by Noh Chin-hwa).

Ronni Lundy, like many Southern cooks, is devoted to cymlings, an old name for pattypans. They should be fairly sturdy (about ½ pound apiece) for this **Pattypan and Leek Buttermilk Soup.** Whether served hot or cold, the soup is meant to showcase the pure flavor of fresh squash and tangy buttermilk. To prepare: Cut trimmed leeks into ½-inch slices and soften in butter over moderate heat. Cut pattypan into ½-inch cubes; add with a modicum of chicken stock and salt. Simmer, covered, until squash skin is easily pierced with a fork, about 15 minutes. To serve hot, add buttermilk to make a soupy consistency and serve at once. Or cool, chill, then stir in the buttermilk (from her *Butter Beans to Blackberries*).

For a more complex chef's soup, ingredients of American origin—squash, chillis, and jícama—are combined in a puree with the look of pumpkin but the lightness of summer squash. For **Yellow Squash and Jícama Soup with Jalapeño, Red Chillis, and Squash Blossoms:** Sweat chopped onion in olive oil to soften slightly. Add yellow squash cut into large dice, peeled and diced jícama, minced Jalapeño, and water. Bring to a simmer, add turmeric; cook until soft, about 40 minutes. Puree smooth in blender. Strain through fine sieve; season. To serve, ladle hot soup into wide bowls. In center, mound thin-sliced squash blossoms, chopped primroses, thin-sliced red chilli, fine-diced jícama, and minced tarragon. Drizzle crème fraîche around and dot with drops of tarragon oil (from *Charlie Trotter's Vegetables*).

Squashes, Winter: Pumpkins and Other Large Types

Including

Banana (Pink)

Butternut

Calabaza

Cheese pumpkin

Cushaw (Green Striped)

Hubbards (Blue and **Golden)**

Jarrahdale

Kuri (Red)

Queensland Blue

Rouge Vif d'Etampes

Valenciano

Turban or **Turk's Cap**

See also: WINTER MELON, page 702

W hat's a pumpkin, anyway? Pretty much anything you want it to be, provided it's a hard-skinned squash. There is no correct response. The group has no botanical (or other) distinction. Local usage dictates. What is considered "pumpkin" changes from country to country and region to region. In the United States, for example, the term generally denotes rounded orange squash carved for Halloween and pureed for Thanksgiving pie—nothing more precise. (By the way, canned "pumpkin" is processed not from this round orange thing but from what North Americans call squash—as in Butternut.) In the British Isles, any one of the list above could be a pumpkin.

"Pumpkin" is a more pleasing word to me than the long-winded term "large hard-skinned squash" so I'll use it from here on to denote that. Pumpkins are not likely to be on your grocery list unless you cook for large groups, and perhaps not even then. Their spectacular looks promise much, but once they are mashed, pureed, or beaten into shape the resulting dish has little connection to the splendid whole squash. Pumpkin

risotto or gratin just won't have the same eye appeal as the Red Kuri or the Golden Hubbard of which it's made. Worse, few pumpkins offer the flavor that their flamboyant exterior suggests.

What to do? First, take care in choosing. Learn to recognize maturity. Unless you pick carefully, you will wind up with vats of baby food puree and nothing more. Then, enjoy the beautiful big cucurbits as decor. They keep for months, and even improve in flavor.

SELECTION: This is the most important part of getting good pumpkins on the table. If you want flavor and not just good looks, heed these guidelines, developed with the help of Andy Grant, owner of Grant Family Farms in Wellington, Colorado, whose organically raised squash are pictured throughout this book; and of Glenn Drowns, curator of vine crops for the Seed Savers Exchange in Decorah, Iowa.
• Although large hard squash are available year-round, they are generally best from fall into late winter. The exception is calabaza, which is cultivated year-round in South and Central America.

• Choose rock-solid squash. Press them as hard as you can to be sure there is no give anywhere. Soft squash is either immature or over the hill. If you can easily nick the skin or scrape it off with a fingernail, the squash is too young.

• Stems should be full, firm, and corky, not skimpy or green, which indicates immaturity. Do not choose pumpkins without stems. Once the stem is removed, the opening that remains—like a wound—permits the entrance of bacteria.

• With a few exceptions the skin should be comparatively dull, not shiny. Avoid wax coating; it masks the skin and becomes ugly and inedible when cooked. Let your market or supplier know you don't want it. Complain.

• Recognize mature coloring. Like other fruit, pumpkin should have no green tinge if the skin is naturally red, orange, yellow, tan, or cream. When there is a light-colored area where the pumpkin lay on the earth, it too should be an orange or warm yellow—not pale or greenish.

• Seek vivid colors at harvest time—generally summer to fall. But later in the year, squash that may fade in storage will be richer in flavor and sweeter.

• Look for winter squash from cooler climates. Many vegetables lack distinction if their growth is accelerated by heat, and this is especially true of hard squash. The cooler the growing area, the slower the development, and the sweeter and more flavorful the squash.

• When buying chunks of large squash—such as calabaza, Banana, and Hubbard—check for flesh that is close-grained, not fibrous, and that appears just barely moist, neither dried out nor watery.

STORAGE: Much of the pleasure of Pumpkins & Co. is their beauty, which can be enjoyed for long periods. Purchased in good shape, they last for months in a well-ventilated dryish area, preferably around 55° to 60°F. While higher temperatures shorten storage time, they do not harm flavor. I kept a dazzling Rouge Vif d'Etampes and a baroque Blue Hubbard (see their portraits) perched on a sideboard and bookshelf for 3 and 4 months in my overheated city apartment—and I was rewarded with soup and puree after the exhibit. Glenn Drowns used a Valenciano as a doorstop in his cool country house for nearly a year before it became dinner.

Do not refrigerate squash unless it is cut open, in which case it should be wrapped in plastic and stored for no more than a few days.

Cooked, pureed squash is one of the finest freezables. Pack it into large containers to serve as a side dish or make into soup. Pack into small containers to stir into soups, sauces, and stews for instant thickening, color, and flavor.

PREPARATION: Smashing pumpkins is (although messy) sometimes the only way to go. Unless you have an ax to cleave them, mammoths are best dropped onto a paper-covered floor. Some large squash, such as Butternut, Banana, and calabaza, can be sliced with a heavy knife or cleaver. Tougher ones need special—and very careful—handling: First knock off the stem, then smack your sturdiest knife into the squash. With a rubber mallet or rolling pin, gently hammer the knife where blade joins handle, until the squash splits. Clean the interior and then cut squash into chunks, wedges, or slices, as convenient. Cook with the rind intact, then peel after cooking if necessary; or pare first, then cut up to suit the recipe.

Alternatively, enlist the aid of a microwave oven if your squash fits into it: Pierce slits on top of the pumpkin in a few places. Cook just until tender enough to cut; this depends upon size and density (4 minutes is average). Cut up and clean as above.

The **Banana** squash (*Cucurbita maxima*) pictured is petite for its kind, weighing in at 15 pounds—with a potential for 100, advises Glenn Drowns. The Creamsicle-peach torpedo is one version of a variety introduced in 1893, according to William Woys Weaver, who writes in *Heirloom Vegetable Gardening:* "The original variety was bluish gray with light orange striping. In storage, this color changes to a creamy pink. After the turn of this century, Aggeler & Musser, a Los Angeles seed firm, selected out three separate colors from the original introduction: a solid bluish gray, a solid yellow, and an orange-pink with flesh-colored stripes." The third is the only one in commercial production, a state of affairs that Drowns laments, for he cherishes the drier and richer Blue Banana. The Pink Banana is favored in the West but rarely reaches the East—which is a shame. Although the Pink may not be as memorable as the Blue, it is a most likable squash: easy to handle, with little waste, and its mild, lightly

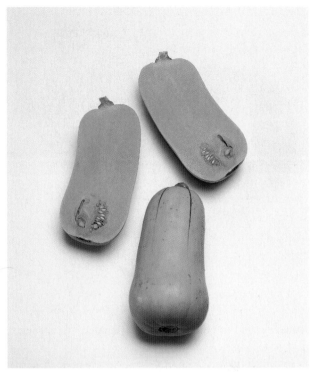

Pink Banana   length: 18-20 inches

Butternut   length: 8-9 inches

sweet flesh tastes fruity and buttery. The texture can be especially creamy—as if butter and cream had been whisked in.

Banana squash is usually sold in big chunks, not in its entirety. It should be moist and fine-grained. Bake or steam (steaming makes it slightly sweeter, but milder), then slice and drizzle with butter and lime or mandarin juice. Or puree as a side dish, or thin for soup or sauce.

Butternut (*Cucurbita moschata*) is not a *really* big squash, but it doesn't fit in with the smaller types. It's all-purpose in the best sense of the word. Long popular (but not that long, for the original Butternut was introduced in 1944) for its ease of preparation and its abundance of melting, fruity flesh, it has stayed put in the fickle squash marketplace. Meaty and moderately sweet, it remains one of the most dependably good squashes available. It also packs in more dazzling golden-orange flesh per penny than any other variety. With its small cavity and easily pared thin skin, there is minimal waste.

Newer Butternut forms bred for small households seem to lack flavor. The market varieties average 2 to 3 pounds, but more mature larger ones may have more

character—one good reason to place Butternut here with the bigger squash. The skin is not agreeably edible. Look for warm, evenly buff skin, a small "ball" end, and a stocky neck.

Bake to concentrate flavors; or slice and pan-fry. Prepare cubed or sliced in casseroles or risotto. Steam or bake and puree; or use to make soups.

Calabaza, Caribbean pumpkin, West Indian pumpkin, and **Cuban squash** (*Cucurbita moschata*) are general names for warm-zone pumpkins. Like "kabocha," the word "calabaza" means no more than squash in the countries that grow it. But in the United States, calabaza, again like kabocha, has become the name for a particular kind of squash—which is, however, so variable in appearance and quality as to seem to be many kinds. Rounded or tending toward pear-shape, averaging 10 pounds, it has mottled skin that may be evergreen, orange, amber, or buff, and speckled or striated; but it is always relatively smooth and hard-shelled when mature. Unlike other pumpkins, it is grown primarily in warmer climates and thus is available year-round. Favored by many Latin Americans and Filipinos, calabaza is likely to be in markets that cater to those populations.

calabaza   diameter: 9-10 inches

Cheese pumpkin   diameter: 10-12 inches

Even more unpredictable in quality than most pumpkins, it may be lightly sweet, fresh-tasting, bright-colored, and of medium consistency (like a fine pie pumpkin) or bland and watery—and everything between. Because the skin coloring is inconsistent, it is difficult to gauge maturity. Buy calabaza in big chunks, so that you can see the flesh. It should be fine-grained (not fibrous), golden to orange (this sample is a little pale), and neither dried-out nor wet, just lightly moist.

Calabaza best suits stews, soups, and purees.

Cheese pumpkin (*Cucurbita moschata*) is an oldie (available by 1815, if not before) and something of a goodie—but not as good as I keep reading and hearing, unless decor and spiced-up pies and soups are your goals. These hefty (10- to 14-pound), warm tan, lobed, flattened pumpkins (there are several Cheese cultivars) have a nostalgic look that suggests real flavor. But cheese pumpkin offers more charm than taste, to this tester. Cooked, the flesh turns a stunning persimmon orange, but I have found it soggy, fibrous, and mild to bland. Drowns says that there is a range in this type, but that few are more than mild and pleasant. Perhaps I have been unlucky.

William Woys Weaver writes in *Heirloom Vegetable Gardening* that "the name of this variety stems from its shape, which vaguely resembles an old wheel of cheese . . . coupled with the very old practice of mak-

ing pumpkin cheese from squashes." For this, the "pumpkins were cooked down to a thick paste, often with watermelon juice, to yield a preserve that was dark brown in color and somewhat sweet, like unsugared apple butter." This is still a good use for the cheese pumpkin, as are amply seasoned soups, pies, and quick breads.

Cushaw (Green-Striped) (*Cucurbita argyrospyrma,* formerly *mixta)* has been a favorite of home gardeners since the early 19th century and is now a regular at farmers' markets. It is prolific and drought- and heat-tolerant, and resists numerous pests. Its hard, prettily striped yellow-white-green skin cuts almost as easily as that of a large summer squash, and its form is friendly. Except for those attributes, I do not know why anyone would choose it over other hard squash. Its utterly bland flesh is wet and coarse. It is wasteful, with almost all the meat in the neck and a bellyfull of pith.

"Hubbard squash" (*Cucurbita maxima*) is a term that embraces a group of medium to monster squash of dependably decent to superior quality. Extremely variable in appearance, they may be bluish, gray, orange, or dark to light green; mottled or not; smooth or warty; and from 5 to 50 pounds. Most are shaped like tears or tops. The green and orange types pictured (at right) are likely market forms.

Green-Striped Cushaw   length: 10-15 inches

New England Blue Hubbard   length: 13-15 inches

The original and celebrated Green (or True) Hubbard first came to Marblehead, Massachusetts, in 1798, probably from South America or the West Indies. It was introduced to the seed trade by J.J.H. Gregory, who named it for Elizabeth Hubbard, who had brought it to his attention. Although the original strain is apparently still available, there are so many crosses that it is nearly impossible to know which you have unless you grow it yourself. Sylvia Thompson writes: "The flesh of the great big warty blue-green melon-shaped Hubbards I've eaten was thick, sweet, and dry although I understand they can be bland and watery."

"Great big" may be one of the reasons for goodness. "For the sake of convenient smaller sizes, they are breeding Hubbards and other great old squash into flavorless extinction," comments Glenn Drowns, who adds that they must be kept in lengthy storage to sweeten properly. I have tasted only Hubbards that were intermediate—in terms of both size and flavor. They were distinguished by bright flesh and a smooth starchiness, but lacked a balancing sweetness. Next year, I'll keep one on my sideboard for spring.

The Golden Hubbard, which is, confusingly, deep orange, is comparatively small (when measured against a Green or Blue Hubbard) but is not one of the new breed, having been introduced in 1898. Bright as candy corn, smooth and medium-bodied, it is fairly sweet, although it may sometimes have a slight bitter aftertaste.

Golden Hubbard   length: 10-11 inches

Jarrahdale   diameter: 13-15 inches

Both the green and orange types shine in soup, puree, stew, or pie. The orange is also tasty—and looks gorgeous—baked, sprinkled with crisp salt (and coarse brown sugar crystals if you have them), and served with a wedge of Clementine or another mandarin. (See also Hubbard (Baby Blue), page 617.)

Jarrahdale or **Australian pumpkin** (*Cucurbita maxima*), while not a regular at the American fall harvest, is an old variety worth inviting to the table. First ask it home to admire its elegantly lobed form and pastel green-gray skin—like finest celadon porcelain, cloudy and deep. You can enjoy it for months, as I did in a warm city apartment, before cooking it.

But it is not just a pretty object. Cut open, the brilliant cadmium flesh, which oozes clear yellow juice, smells grassy and fresh. The rock-solid pulp is copious, surrounding a small cavity packed with neat ropes of tan seeds. Slicing is surprisingly easy because the thin skin is easily pierced—usually a sign of immaturity, like

the shininess of the skin. For this Australian cultivar, however, a thin, shiny skin is normal.

The flavor is light, simple, and pure pumpkin—no sweetpotatoes or chestnuts or anything but gentle winter squash. The texture is very special: Steamed, the flesh melts to the smoothness of a filtered puree, a perfect base for delicate soup, custard, or pie, or to use in batter for bread or cookies. There is no straining or smooshing to be done. Microwaved in chunks, it has a touch more sweetness but does not become as creamy; however, it is totally fuss-free and can be a lovely side dish, mashed with butter or pureed with an immersion blender or in a processor for soup.

Kuri (Red) or **Uchiki Kuri** or **Orange Hokkaido** (*Cucurbita maxima*) is, for some reason, the only orange kabocha-type squash that was allowed to keep its own name in the American marketplace; others are lumped under a catchall name. The British authority Joy Larkcom writes in *Oriental Vegetables,* under the heading "kabocha, the Orange Hokkaido type": "These are 'tear drop' or pear shaped. They have a smooth golden skin, ripening to a beautiful orange, and yellow flesh. They . . . weigh 5–10 pounds. . . . They have been developed from the famous American 'Hubbard' squashes, and in the United States are sometimes known as the 'Baby Red Hubbard.' "

If I were selling these, I would put them in the same bin with the Golden Hubbard—and probably call them all Orange Hubbards. The ones I've tasted have been comparable to Golden Hubbard in all ways, except for the green tip (see the Golden Hubbard photo).

Queensland Blue (*Cucurbita maxima*), like Jarrahdale, was developed in Australia and matures with a fairly shiny skin. It can look like the one below or have the same celadon color as Jarrahdale and a more boxy hassock shape. The fluted Queensland Blue, part drum and part turban, weighs 5 to 10 pounds and arrived in 1932, but I haven't discovered where it has been since. I had my first view last year—and it was long. I admired the pumpkin for several months, like its fellow countryman, before sacrificing it to a meal.

I am baffled by this pumpkin and must taste it again to know it better. For now, here are parts of notes from two tastings, two squash: Baked, the satiny solid smooth flesh turns a uniform orange-gold; it cuts with the richness of avocado and the density of cooked quince. It is not starchy in any way, but thick and moist. Its flavor is curious, unfamiliar—not like any squash I know. It tastes more like an intriguing green vegetable—not sweet, not floury—with an aftertaste of lemon rind. Steamed, it was all the above, but slightly more bland; dense and juicy. The pretty gray-green skin is edible. In sum: So odd that I don't know what to suggest. I need to try samples from several growers to better evaluate it—especially since others who have tasted it have had different impressions.

Rouge Vif d'Etampes, Red Etampes, or **Cinderella** (*Cucurbita maxima*) is the beauty that exemplifies pumpkins with a European look. "W. Atlee Burpee of Philadelphia is credited with introducing this squash to American gardeners in 1883," William Woys Weaver writes in *Heirloom Vegetable Gardening*. "It was cultivated in France almost fifty years prior to that, and proved extremely popular in Paris . . . during the nineteenth century because chefs discovered that it made an excellent base for soups, the flavor being so mild that it did not overpower other ingredients."

Red Kuri or Uchiki Kuri   diameter: 5-6 inches

Queensland Blue   diameter: 8 inches

Rouge Vif d'Etampes   diameter: 11 inches

Fifteen to 30 pounds of (expensive) stunning deep-flame pumpkin, shaped like the quintessential French pottery tureen, have been stunningly disappointing. This may be a cherished heirloom, but four tries from three growers in two years have yielded just one decent use. Baked, simmered, microwaved, or steamed, the deep yellow-orange flesh is basically stringy, soggy, and bland to tasteless (one did have sweetness, but not much flavor). Is Weaver's description of flavor "so mild that it did not overpower other ingredients" charitable, or is the pumpkin different on its French turf?

Here's the one way it worked for me: Bake huge chunks of the pumpkin in a roasting pan until slushy soft (4-pound chunks will take about 1½ hours). Pull off skin. Let cool slightly, then puree without additional liquid for a spectacular orange-gold, lightly creamy soup base that needs help in the flavor department, but none for texture and color.

Turk's Turban or **Turk's Cap** (*Cucurbita maxima*) is an old variety (it was introduced as the American Turban in 1869 but had been sold in the United States long before then) best known as a decorative item. But is it edible? Yes. Is it good? It can be, but fair is more likely. Certainly it is worth the effort to purchase it minus shellac or wax so that you can cook up the yellow, moist, mild flesh to enrich stews, soups, and sauces.

The problem is its sturdy turtle shell. The heirloom gardener and cook William Woys Weaver addresses the problem this way: "The reason it keeps so well is its hard, woody rind, which is very difficult to remove. The simplest way to cook this squash is to cut it in half, scrape out the seeds, and place the halves in glass bowls with about ½ cup of water. Cover the bowls with cling wrap and cook in a microwave oven on high for 15 minutes. The flesh will scoop out like mashed potatoes and can be used as a thickener for soups, especially for split-pea soups."

Turk's Turban   diameter: 6-7 inches

Valenciano (*Cucurbita maxima*) has been selected to represent white pumpkins as a general category. There is nothing new about a white pumpkin per se. What is new is the change from foodstuff to canvas for Halloween faces. In the United States, where redness reigns, cerise apples, scarlet mangos, and sunset peaches take precedence over paler forms that can be more flavorful. It is not surprising that "eating pumpkins" are orange. White pumpkins share no more than skin color (and even that varies from blue-gray to cream). Like squash of any color, white pumpkins are distinct, but they get lumped together unless you are lucky enough to buy from a farmer who provides particulars, so that you can learn which white pumpkins you want to eat again, and which to limit to jack-o'-lanterns.

Valenciano, a lightly lobed, cream-skinned pumpkin with a soft yellow undertone, comes from Argentina (not France, as some sources state). Glenn Drowns obtained it from the USDA Plant Introduction Station in Geneva, New York, and dispersed it in 1983. It appears in several seed catalogues and is grown by some specialty farmers. It is included here to up-

Valenciano   diameter: 10 inches

hold the honor of all white pumpkins for cooking, which seem to be a dying breed. Its unusually dry, hard pale flesh is abundant, dense, and smooth. Cooked, it blooms—even in a microwave oven, which usually brings out fibers and pastiness. Chunks deepen in hue to golden sunshine, while the pulp becomes fruity and custardy, semisweet (apple-like), and mild. Steamed, its consistency is truly satiny, but the flavor is watered down a little.

Basic Pumpkin/Squash Puree

Big squashes are meant to be pureed. You can bake or steam them (I do not generally recommend microwaving except as a preliminary step to soften for cutting), depending upon the variety. Bake the juicy types to concentrate flavor and evaporate excess moisture. Steam starchy dense squash to soften and humidify it. Whichever method you choose, cook until creamy-tender. It's better to overcook than undercook winter squash.

Unseasoned puree can be varied with seasonings or aromatics and butter or cream for a side dish. Or use as an ingredient in other dishes: soups, sauces, stews, pancakes and quick breads, flan, pies. Refrigerate up to a week, or freeze indefinitely.

To bake: Cut squash into 1-pound pieces, approximately. Scrape off seeds and fiber and place cut side down on an oiled foil–covered baking sheet. Bake until very tender; timing can vary from 35 minutes to an hour, depending upon the density of the squash.

To steam: Cut squash into large chunks—½ to 1 pound each, as fits your steamer. Scrape out seeds and spongy fibers. Set on steamer rack over boiling water. Cover and steam until tender; the time varies from 15 to 35 minutes.

To prepare puree: Cool cooked squash until you can handle it, then peel. Press through the medium disc of a food mill. Or whirl in a food processor for a smooth texture. Cool, cover, then refrigerate or freeze.

To mash and serve as a side dish: When cooked squash is cool enough to handle, peel. Scoop flesh into a heavy saucepan. Mash with a little cream, salt, sugar,

and pepper. Cook over low heat, stirring, to evaporate liquid as needed and concentrate flavors, 5 to 15 minutes.

Yield: Figure the cup yield to be the same as the number of pounds; that is, 1 pound of untrimmed squash produces about 1 cup of puree.

Baked Winter Squash and Apple Puree with Nuts

For a holiday feast, try this fuss-free dish—more flavorful and subtle than you might guess from the few and familiar ingredients. The recipe yields two casseroles, but it can be halved to make one.

One 6-pound squash, two 3-pounders,
   or three 2-pounders
6 large baking apples
6 tablespoons butter
Salt and pepper
1 cup pecans, walnuts, or macadamias
1 cup fine dry bread crumbs
2 tablespoons butter, frozen

1. Halve large squash. Smaller ones can be left whole. Set in large roasting pan (if halved, set cut side up and cover each with foil). Turn oven to 350°F and bake squash until tender. Timing varies, but figure on 1½ to 2 hours for the halved large squash and 3-pounders, 1 to 1½ for the 2-pounders.

2. About 45 minutes before you expect the squash to be cooked through, wash the apples, poke a few holes in them, and set in the roasting pan.

3. When everything is tender, remove from oven. Halve the whole squash and set cut side down in colander to drain and cool. Remove seeds, peel, and stems. Remove peels and cores from apples.

4. Raise oven temperature to 425°F. Press apples and squash together through medium disc of food mill into a bowl. Beat in butter and salt and pepper to taste. Spread in two fairly shallow buttered baking/serving dishes.

5. Combine nuts and crumbs in food processor or blender and whirl to medium-coarse texture. Sprinkle evenly over puree. Grate or shave half of the frozen butter over each. (Can be prepared ahead.)

6. Set uncovered dishes in top third of oven and bake until topping is browned, about 30 minutes.

Serves 12 (6 for each casserole)

Crisp Winter Squash Gratin

Easy and straightforward, this useful prototype works best for winter squash of average moisture and solid content, which yield a creamy interior and crusty top. It is not for very dry starchy types (such as Valenciano or kabocha types) or wet ones (Green-Striped Cushaw or Cheese pumpkin). Vary the fat to suit the rest of the meal, substituting melted duck, goose, or bacon fat, or use butter or nut oil.

> 2½-pound chunk of winter squash, such as Butternut or Golden Hubbard
> 1½ tablespoons flour
> ½ teaspoon sugar
> 1 small garlic clove, minced
> ½ teaspoon dried sage, summer savory, or marjoram, crumbled
> 1 teaspoon kosher salt
> Pepper
> 2 tablespoons full-flavored olive oil

1. Turn oven to 325°F. Scrape seeds and fibers from squash. Cut squash into manageable pieces, then peel. Cut into ¾-inch dice (to make about 6 cups).

2. Blend flour, sugar, garlic, sage, salt, and pepper in small dish. Spread squash in well-oiled shallow baking/serving dish of about 2-quart capacity. Sprinkle over flour mixture, tossing squash to coat evenly. Drizzle with 1 tablespoon oil and toss again. Drip remaining 1 tablespoon oil over the top.

3. Cover closely with foil; cut a few slits in it. Set in upper third of oven. Bake until squash is just tender, about 40 minutes. Remove foil and toss squash gently. Raise heat to 425°F. Bake until crusty and browned—about 30 minutes. (Can be reheated.)

Serves 4 as a side dish

Butternut Risotto with Celery and Sage

Risotto is wonderful to eat—and a nuisance to prepare, unless done in a pressure cooker. Lorna Sass introduced me to the risk-free, speedy method in *Great Vegetarian Cooking Under Pressure,* a method that not only eliminates tedious stirring but produces grains of uniform consistency. Arborio rice is the type most commonly sold for risotto, but carnaroli, vialone nano, and baldo are well worth a try. Butternut and Buttercup are particularly appealing, but other fine-textured, full-flavored pumpkin/squash could be used as well. The dice usually keep their shape, while the small bits melt into a sauce.

> About 1½ pounds Butternut or Buttercup squash (½ medium)
> 1 medium-small leek
> Interior celery stalks with leaves
> 1½ tablespoons olive oil
> 1½ cups Italian rice for risotto
> 1½ tablespoons thin-sliced sage leaves
> ⅓ cup dry white wine
> 3½ to 4 cups vegetable broth (or chicken and vegetable mixed)
> 1 teaspoon kosher salt (omit if broth is salted)
> ¼ teaspoon white pepper
> About ¾ cup grated Parmesan cheese
> 1 to 3 teaspoons lemon juice

1. Halve squash as necessary, then clean. Cut into 1-inch slices; peel. Cut two-thirds into 1-inch dice. Chop remainder into small bits. Trim darkest leaves and roots from leek. Halve stalk lengthwise, thin-slice, and then rinse thoroughly. Thin-slice enough celery to equal 1 cup; mince the additional stalks to make ⅓ cup. Set aside some leaves for garnish.

2. Heat oil in pressure cooker over moderate heat. Add leek and sliced celery and sauté 2 minutes. Add rice and 1 tablespoon sage and toss 1 minute. Add wine and stir a moment, until evaporated. Add squash and salt.

3. Add 3¼ cups broth. Lock lid in place and bring to high pressure. Cook 5½ minutes. Run cold water over lid to release pressure. Avoiding steam, open lid.

4. Over moderately low heat, stir in minced celery and pepper. Stir a minute or two, until rice is done to taste, adding broth for a consistency that is slightly soupier than desired.

5. Off heat, stir in remaining ½ tablespoon sage, ⅓ cup Parmesan, and lemon juice to taste. Spoon into four wide bowls and top with additional Parmesan to taste. Slice reserved celery leaves and sprinkle over.

Serves 4 as a main course

Note: To prepare in a regular saucepan: Follow directions through step 2, using half as much sage. Meanwhile heat broth—increase it to 5½ cups—and keep at just under a simmer in a separate saucepan. Add broth ½ cup at a time to the rice, simmering and stirring continuously. Stir until each portion of broth is absorbed before adding the next (about 18 minutes cooking time). Cook until rice is not quite done to taste, then proceed with step 4.

Bourbon-Scented Red Kuri (or Hubbard), Apple, and Cranberry Soup

Red Kuri is just one possibility for this russet-ruby, sweet-tart puree. Any large solid squashes (or chunks thereof) will work: Green or Golden Hubbard, Butternut, Buttercup, Banana, Australian Blue, kabocha, or calabaza. The solid content of the squash will determine the amount of water needed, which varies considerably.

   **About 4 pounds Red Kuri or other
      hard squash**
   2 medium onions
   3 large tart apples
   2 tablespoons butter or corn oil
   3 cups apple cider
   About 3 cups water
   1½ cups cranberries
   About ½ tablespoon kosher salt
   2 to 3 tablespoons bourbon or rum
   Honey or pure maple syrup
   ½ cup whole-milk yogurt

1. Halve squash; scoop out and discard seeds. Cut into 2-inch chunks and peel. Chop onions. Quarter, core, peel, and chop apples.

2. Melt butter in large heavy pot over moderate heat. Add onions and cook until somewhat softened, about 5 minutes. Add cider and 2 cups water and bring to a boil. Add squash, apples, cranberries, and 1 teaspoon salt.

3. Simmer, partly covered, until squash is soft, about 45 minutes (check often—squash timing varies). Cool for about 15 minutes.

4. Puree with an immersion blender. Or transfer in batches to blender or food processor and whiz to a smooth puree. (Can be prepared ahead.)

5. Return puree to pot. Add 2 tablespoons bourbon. Reheat over low heat, stirring often. Soup will be quite thick; add water for desired consistency. Add honey, bourbon, and salt to taste.

6. Liquefy yogurt by whisking with a little water. Ladle soup into bowls. Gently dip a spoonful of yogurt into the center of each. With knife tip, extend to form a star shape.

Serves 6 as a first course

Easy Pumpkin Soup for a Group

The microwave oven minimizes the time and labor required to prepare pumpkins—especially the slippery task of cutting them down to size and paring them. Although squash texture is not usually enhanced by microwave cooking, the method is fine for pulp that will be pureed.

Moist, mild pumpkins make good soup subjects that produce their own natural broth: Pink Banana, calabaza, Cheese Pumpkin, Jarrahdale, and Rouge Vif d'Etampes are a few such. Pumpkins with dry flesh are also good candidates, but they will need more liquid and make starchier soup.

Deep, dark, and powerful roasted pumpkin seed oil, a dramatic seasoning, is sold in fancy groceries nationwide, but unpredictably. Whether domestic or imported, a little goes a long way: Do not be tempted to add more until you've sampled the dish.

8-pound pumpkin/squash

3 tablespoons butter

2 medium white onions, sliced
    or diced

About 2 teaspoons kosher salt

3 tablespoons fine-grated fresh ginger

1 teaspoon ground coriander

4 to 5 cups light vegetable broth

1 to 2 cups low-fat or whole milk

1 lemon

1 orange

Honey

About 5 teaspoons pumpkin seed oil

About ⅓ cup roasted and salted pumpkin seeds
    (pepitas; see following recipe)

1. Cut slits in top of pumpkin in a few places. Microwave at full power just until tender enough to cut—3 to 4 minutes is typical but timing varies considerably. Cut into wedges of equal size, about 1 pound apiece. Scrape out seeds and fiber.

2. Enclose half the wedges in a large plastic bag and arrange on the microwave oven carousel, not touching, skin side down and narrow ends pointing to the center. Close bag. Microwave until pumpkin is tender throughout when pierced with a knife, about 15 minutes—but timing varies. Open bag, being careful to avoid steam. Set aside until cool enough to handle. Repeat with second batch. Pare skin and cut into 2-inch chunks.

3. Meanwhile, melt butter in heavy soup pot over fairly low heat. Add onions and 2 teaspoons salt. Cook gently, partly covered, until onions are tender, about 10 minutes. Add ginger and coriander. Stir a few minutes. Add pumpkin, 3½ cups broth, and 1 cup milk.

4. Bring to a boil, then reduce heat and simmer, covered, until pumpkin is soft, 10 to 15 minutes. Cool slightly.

5. Transfer solids to food processor, working in batches as necessary. Puree smooth. Gradually add cooking liquid and additional broth and milk to obtain desired consistency. Return to pot. Halve lemon and orange and squeeze one-half of each. Gradually add juice, with honey to taste. Squeeze more juice if needed, adding a little at a time. (Can be made ahead, cooled, and refrigerated or frozen.)

6. To serve, warm soup over low heat, whisking often to smooth. Season. Ladle hot soup into bowls.

Dot each with ½ teaspoon pumpkin seed oil and strew with about ½ tablespoon pumpkin seeds.

**Makes about 3½ quarts,
to serve 10 as a first course**

Variations

This is a gentle soup that tastes like pumpkin, not a spiced-up transformation. Its simplicity and sunny smooth canvas encourage considerable variation in the garnish department: Try toasted unsweetened coconut shreds with black sesame seeds, minced candied ginger with a chiffonade of basil leaves, toasted pistachios with cilantro slivers, or a drizzle of thinned sour cream with a sprinkle of sugared fennel seeds (available in Indian shops).

Roasted Pepitas (Pumpkin Seeds)

"Pepita," the Spanish term for the seed, has the right sound for the crisp, salty nutritious cucurbit "nut." I toast only the hull-less types. Seeds that hide in thick, heavy hulls must be cracked open to pry out the minimal rewards, while the slimmer naked seeds can be roasted and enjoyed whole.

To loosen the seeds from their fibrous net, soak the mass in a bowl of water, squishing now and then to loosen the seeds. Skim off floating seeds, then squish some more so that the remaining strands release their hold. Repeat as needed.

To tenderize and season seeds, first boil in salted water, then bake. For mild flavor, toss with corn, safflower, soy, or almond oil. For a slightly more pronounced taste, choose pumpkin seed, olive, peanut, or roasted sesame oil. Because the quantity of seeds will vary, consider the following as a general guide, not a fixed recipe.

1 quart water

2 tablespoons kosher salt

2 cups pumpkin/squash seeds

1½ teaspoons oil

1. Preheat oven to 350°F. Bring water and salt to a boil. Add seeds and boil until fairly tender—about 10 minutes. Drain well.

2. Toss seeds with oil. Spread on a baking sheet or in a wide baking pan. Bake until golden and crisp, 20 to 40 minutes, tossing often.

Makes 2 cups

Pros Propose

Most pumpkins go into soup, which is one of the best places to put them. Two unusual and complex recipes represent the opposite ends of the soup spectrum. This **Double Consommé of Pumpkin**—not what most people have in mind for pumpkin—is chef Jean Joho's contribution. The stunning transformation from gray-blue Hubbard brute to clearest elixir is no mere technical tour de force. The result is sublime. To prepare: Sprinkle cleaned Hubbard wedges lightly with sugar; spray (or paint lightly) with butter. Roast in a moderate oven until soft. In large pot, gently cook a mirepoix of leeks, onions, and carrot. Add the cooked wedges, roasted onion halves, whole garlic cloves, bay leaves, cumin seeds, and vegetable stock. Keep under a simmer for 5 hours. Strain, then cool and refrigerate. When cold, skim off fat. Quarter Carnival squash and blanch briefly. Cool, chill, then chop fine enough to equal about one-fifth the volume of stock. Combine in soup pot with an equal amount of chopped fennel; add egg whites to clarify. Add consommé and bring to a simmer. Lower heat and barely simmer 1 hour. Scoop off solids. Strain through cheesecloth. Season. Meanwhile, prepare flan garnish: Roast Butternut or Buttercup, as for Hubbard above. Scoop out flesh. Process until smooth. Combine with eggs, cream, nutmeg, and seasoning. Pour into tiny ramekins. Set in water bath and bake in very low oven (under 200°F) until set, about 1 hour. Unmold into serving bowls. Pour in consommé. Finish with a confetti of sautéed black trumpet mushrooms.

Caramelized Butternut Squash Soup with Roasted Quince is another example of deeply layered flavors, this in a rich thick puree from chef Morgen Jacobson. He draws out flavor from the squash and quince by high-heat roasting—covered, so the juices concentrate but do not burn. To prepare: Set each whole quince on a square of foil. Rub with vanilla-flavored grapeseed oil, add a drop of Armagnac, and close up foil. Halve and seed squash. Rub with butter and honey. Sprinkle with salt, pepper, and nutmeg. Set on rack in baking pan, cut side up. Pour water into pan and cover with foil. Bake quinces and squash at 450°F until soft. Scrape flesh and juices from squash into food mill and puree. Do same with quince, reserving accumulated juices (save quince seeds and cores for jam). Gently cook onions, garlic, and diced raw quince briefly, then deglaze pan with Armagnac. Add pureed squash. Add light chicken stock and cook to a bisque consistency. Season and add quince puree to taste, with a sachet of lemon zest strips and vanilla bean. Simmer to infuse and blend flavors. Splash with Armagnac. Blend rich yogurt with juice pressed from young ginger, lime juice, salt, pepper, and reserved quince juices. Drizzle yogurt into each bowl and add blanched Butternut cubes and diced, roasted, quince. Pour the soup over.

A rustic soup-stew, **Carbonade of Beef with Peaches in a Pumpkin,** comes from *The Art of South American Cooking* by the late chef Felipe Rojas-Lombardi, whose recipes are always personal, however traditional: Cut beef short ribs into 2-inch pieces. Brown in olive oil; reserve. Peel carrots and onion, reserving skins. Stir flour into the reserved oil in the pan; cook briefly. Stir in enough water for soup and a splash of vinegar. Add thyme, oregano, parsley, chilli, carrot and onion skins, celery tops, garlic, and cumin; simmer ½ hour. Strain. Combine in pot with browned meat (to cover it by a few inches), bay leaf, and salt. Simmer, covered, until meat is tender, then remove. Strain stock; degrease. Sauté diced onion in olive oil until golden; add sherry and evaporate. Add meat, sliced carrots and celery, and stock; simmer 10 minutes. Meanwhile, cut a wide lid from a broad pumpkin (Cheese pumpkin or Rouge Vif d'Etampes looks great). Clean interior, brush with oil, and bake until almost tender. Fill with the soup, an ear of corn, sliced crosswise, and quartered firm peaches. Top with the lid and bake until pumpkin is done, about 20 minutes. Sprinkle with cilantro.

Big pumpkins take time to prepare. This week-long treatment (work time is only a few minutes a day), is based on the traditions that produce candied fruit and other sugar-imbibing preparations, such as marrons glacés. "This condiment is in principle like the mostarda of Cremona, but instead of mustard, it is made sharp with vinegar—once the pumpkin is preserved," explains chef Rémi Lauvand. To prepare **Sweet Pumpkin Pickle:** Choose a large, dense, smooth-fleshed pumpkin of about 20 pounds. Peel and seed. Cut into 2-inch cubes. Spread in wide non-reactive container and cover with sugar—¾ pound for every pound of pumpkin. Let stand 24 hours, to dissolve sugar and draw out juices. Transfer to shallow pot and bring to a boil. Add tarragon sprigs, pepper, and cinnamon sticks. Boil 5 minutes, then cool. Refrigerate 24 hours. Repeat boiling, steeping, and chilling until pumpkin is translucent, about 7 days. Measure and transfer to large non-reactive pot. Add 1 cup white-wine vinegar for every 2 quarts pumpkin. Boil 5 minutes; cool. Transfer to crocks or canning jars and chill. Serve with terrine of foie gras or game dishes.

Salty, sharp fermented black beans are a surprise seasoning for pumpkin, arrived at in the best fusion fashion. Chef Ken Hom writes in *Easy Family Recipes from a Chinese American Childhood* that "in Chicago's Chinatown, with its long, cold Midwestern winters, we were limited to a much narrower range of Chinese vegetables. Out of necessity, we learned to adopt local American vegetables and adapt them to our taste . . . While my American schoolmates were using pumpkins for their Halloween jack-o'-lanterns, at home we were enjoying this treat. It was like having their pumpkins and eating mine too." To prepare **My Mother's Stir-Fried Pumpkin in Black Bean Sauce:** Heat wok; swirl in peanut oil. Add chopped shallots, chopped black beans, garlic, ginger, salt, and pepper; stir-fry 1 minute. Add 2-inch pumpkin chunks, rice wine, chilli bean sauce, light and dark soy sauces, sugar, and chicken stock. Reduce heat, cover, and simmer until pumpkin is soft, about 25 minutes. Raise heat, stir in sesame oil, and serve at once.

"I revere calabaza," says chef and author Maricel Presilla. "For a small restaurant like mine, where we have little storage space, it's a gorgeous display, or it's dinner. It's always ready, always good, available year-round, and never off the menu." For her complex and original **Caribbean Pumpkin and Grilled Pineapple Escabeche with Pumpkin Seeds and Cacao Nibs:** Combine Latin brown loaf sugar with stick cinnamon, lime zest, salt, and water. Boil until syrup lightly coats a spoon. Cool and refrigerate. Strain when ready to use. Combine 1-inch calabaza cubes with water, bay leaf, stick cinnamon, sugar, salt, and whole allspice. Boil until calabaza is tender but not falling apart; drain. Over low fire, grill 1-inch slabs of pineapple about 10 minutes per side. Brush with the syrup, then cook 5 minutes to glaze. Cut into 1-inch cubes. Crush garlic to a paste and heat gently (do not brown) in olive oil with allspice. Add cider vinegar and salt; cook 2 minutes. Toss gently with calabaza and pineapple. Arrange on serving dish, drizzle with more oil, and sprinkle with roasted pumpkin seeds and roasted, ground cacao nibs. Serve as a side to grilled meat or fish, or on romaine as an appetizer.

Maricel Presilla also cooks this homey **Colombian Rice with Caribbean Pumpkin:** Soften minced onion and red bell pepper with bay leaf in olive oil. Add long-grain rice and stir briefly. Add ½-inch calabaza cubes, water, and salt. Cook until water evaporates. Add chopped cilantro and grated queso blanco fresco. Cover and cook over lowest heat until rice is tender.

Chef Sarah Stegner explains that "kuri is one of the savory, not supersweet, squashes, with a rich earthiness that marries well with meat—not sweet meat, the way squash is usually paired, but real meat, like grilled sirloin." For her **Savory Red Kuri Tart:** Prepare a butter tart crust, adding chopped fresh thyme and roasted garlic. Bake blind in rectangular pan. To prepare squash puree: Halve kuri and clean. Brush very lightly with butter and sprinkle with salt and pepper. Cook cut side up (to keep all the intense juices in) in moderate oven. Mash (do not process). Whisk in grated Gruyère, eggs, and cream. Spread in crust. Bake in moderate oven until set.

Squashes, Winter: Small to Medium Types

Including

Acorn

Buttercup

Carnival

Delicata

Golden Nugget

Hubbard (Baby Blue)

Kabocha types

Miniature pumpkins

Spaghetti squashes

Sugar Loaf

Sweet Dumpling

A huge Hubbard may have its place at a Thanksgiving feast, but a Sweet Dumpling does wonders for a workday dinner for two, and a Spaghetti Squash feeds four at Sunday supper. Like watermelon, hard squash has been scaled down so that it no longer needs a whole clan to tote and eat it.

Smaller squashes can have a high profile in a meal, unlike the giants, which must be mashed or beaten to fit into the serving dish and thus lose their distinctive appearance. Smaller squash is more likely to star. While strapping pumpkins of various nationalities can take each other's place in a soup pot, nothing can stand in for a Delicata or Sweet Dumpling.

Before we discuss the particulars, there are important common characteristics of small hard-skinned squash to recognize—the criteria for selection being the most critical.

SELECTION: Choose wisely, or forgo flavor. Like blond and bosomy starlets, squashes that are merely colorful and shapely can be tasteless. Andy Grant, owner of Grant Family Farms, which has raised squash in Wellington, Colorado, since 1965 (and now has 600 organic acres), helped determine these guidelines for selection and storage—and supplied the squash for the photos. Glenn Drowns, curator of vine crops for Seed Savers Exchange, contributed his thoughts, too.

• Choose rock-solid squash. Press as hard as you can to be sure it has no give. Soft squash is either immature or over the hill. Check the skin: If you can easily nick it or scrape it off with a fingernail, the squash is too young.

• Look for firm, full, corky stems (avoid skinny or green ones). Do not buy fruit without stems: removing the stem leaves an opening for bacteria.

• Choose squash with comparatively dull skin. It should be matte, not shiny—shininess indicates either immaturity or wax. Wax masks the condition of the skin and becomes ugly and inedible when cooked. Let your produce supplier know that you don't want it.

• Recognize ripe coloring. As with other fruit, skin with a warm tone such as cream, tan, yellow, orange, or red should show no green cast. When a dark green squash has a spot where the squash lay on the earth, it too should be a ripe color—orange or warm yellow—not pale or green.

• Expect vivid colors at harvest time, generally summer to fall. But note that later in the year, when the squash has been stored and may have faded, it will be sweeter and more concentrated in flavor.

• September and October are the best months to find the widest range. Flavor is finest from that time into late winter. Hard-shelled squash is available year-round, but is often tasteless.

• Check the source of your squash, seeking out colder areas. Squash grown in a cool climate takes longer to develop and will have more flavor and sugar than squash that hurries along in a warm one.

STORAGE: Small to medium hard squashes keep for weeks or more in a well-ventilated, dryish area, ideally around 55°F. Do *not* refrigerate. Higher temperatures shorten storage time but do not harm flavor. Most squash purchased in season can be enjoyed as decor for a month or so, then served up. Delicata, Sugarloaf, and Sweet Dumpling have less storage potential than others in this group. These same squash also turn from cream and green to yellow and orange with long keeping (see Sweet Dumpling photos) but will taste fine if they are not dried out. Once cut, raw squash should be wrapped tightly in plastic and refrigerated for no more than a few days.

PREPARATION: If small squash is to be cooked whole, scrub with a brush, then pierce several slits near the stem. Or cut out a cap to replace during cooking: With a sturdy, sharp knife cut a square cap around the stem, poking into the heart of the squash to cut the fibers, too. Pry out the cap. With a melon ball cutter, scoop and scrape the interior to remove seeds and fibers. Trim fibers from cap.

Or knock off the stem and then halve the squash lengthwise, shaving a sliver from each half to prevent tipping. Or cut into rounds, then trim out the central seedy part with a cookie cutter or melon ball cutter; peel, as desired. To prepare unusually hard squash for cooking, enlist the microwave: Pierce squash deeply. Microwave 2 minutes, or until just barely cuttable. Cut cap, then scoop out seeds and fiber.

Buttercup and kabocha types are best cut into large chunks: With a heavy knife or cleaver, halve or quarter them, as convenient. Clean interior (an ice cream scoop, preferably a smallish one, is perfect for the job). Cut squash into manageable chunks. Cook with rind intact and peel after cooking (or not, as

taste dictates). Or pare decoratively, leaving some skin intact; or peel completely, to suit your preference.

Acorn   length: 5-7 inches

Acorn squash (*Cucurbita pepo*) is the most widely available of small winter squash and one of the most attractive, but it is one of the least likely to be rewarding. At best, commercial cultivars are merely smooth and sweetish; more often, they are bland and fibrous. Glamorous golden and forest green Acorns are typically tasteless, despite their glowing good looks. Some cream-skinned cultivars have come closer to the flavorful green varieties of the past (which were phased out because they were not compatible with commercial sizing requirements). Follow selection guidelines to the letter, and there's a chance of finding goodness. Farmers' markets generally offer more in the way of tasty varieties.

Baking best concentrates flavors and glosses the skin, which is usually edible, unless waxed. Acorn squash averages 1 to 2 pounds.

Buttercup   diameter: 6-8 inches

Carnival   diameter: 4 inches

Buttercup squash *(Cucurbita maxima)*, solid, serious, and superb, delivers what we remember (or imagine) to be quintessential old-fashioned squash flavor. ("Old-fashioned" in this case means dating to 1931, when Buttercup was introduced by the North Dakota Agricultural Experiment Station.) The stocky squash wears an identifying "beanie" that enlarges as the squash matures—and softens if it is over age. Many people (I am one) consider Buttercup the model hard squash. Baked, the fine, dry flesh becomes smooth and tastes of honey, roasted chestnuts, and sweetpotato; the handsome bottle green skin turns as glossy as a leather-bound book. When Buttercup is steamed, those characteristics remain, but in softer style, as the flesh becomes a thick "instant" puree: Just spoon up the seamless plushy mass as is.

Buttercup is truly multipurpose. Bake, steam, prepare au gratin, puree, and make into soup or pie. The skin is edible on some strains, but too tough on others. Buttercup averages 2 to 4 pounds.

Carnival squash and other trademarked names *(Cucurbita pepo)* looks and tastes like what it is: an Acorn and Sweet Dumpling (page 621) cross. Flattened, but similar in size and shape to Sweet Dumpling, it also has its attractive ivy green marbling. The deep yellow, rather loose-knit flesh is sweeter and more flavorful than Acorn's—in fact, much closer to Sweet Dumpling, with its hints of corn and vanilla. The texture is a bit coarse, but not stringy—just chewy. A good substitute for the failing Acorn.

Halve or slice. Bake or steam to serve straight, or as a handsomely decorated, delicious container for grain- or meat-based stuffing. Carnival averages 1 to 2 pounds. Unfortunately, the skin has been inedibly tough on ones I've sampled.

Delicata *(Cucurbita pepo)*, an aptly named squash first introduced in 1894 and popular into the 1920s, has been revived in recent years—although few recognize it as an heirloom and some call it a "designer squash" (a term that makes me gag). Quite petite to just medium, the oblong squash has yellow-ivory skin mot-

Delicata   length: 7-8 inches

Gold Nugget   diameter: 3-4 inches

tled with spruce stripes. The abundant, lightly sweet, butter-yellow pulp is fine and moist with a rounded taste that suggests corn, Butternut, and sweetpotato.

Thanks to its thin skin and handy shape, Delicata has a range of possible presentations. When it is very small, keep part of the pretty skin intact, skimming off stripes with a swivel peeler. Cut out the stem end (make a neat plug to replace during cooking), then scoop out the seeds with a melon ball cutter or teaspoon. Or make little canoes: First knock off the tough stem, then halve the squash lengthwise, then clean out seeds and fiber. Or peel, leaving some green skin, clean the center with a corer, then cut across into scalloped rings.

Reliably rewarding, the flavor is richest when baked; but the texture is also light and lovely when steamed. Delicata generally serves one, but some are large enough for two or three. It weighs from ½ to 2 pounds. Do not expect long storage from this relatively thin-skinned squash.

Gold (or Golden) **Nugget** (*Cucurbita maxima*) appears to be more delicate than it is. This hard-shelled fairy coach has the toughest hide of all the small squashes. The brilliant yellow-orange pulp is moist, rather firm, and very smooth. Its highly variable flavor ranges from buttery and mild sweetpotato to just plain bland squash. Full maturity is essential, or flavor is nil (be sure the skin is dullish, not shiny). Orange- to grapefruit-size, this is one of the relatively new breed of petites, developed at North Dakota State University in the mid-1960s.

Steam or bake. Unless you have a scimitar, Gold Nugget is too dangerously hard, round, and slippery to halve before cooking. It is best cooked whole. Or pierce it, then microwave to soften just enough to cut and clean. It weighs about 1 pound and has totally *in*edible skin.

Hubbard (Baby Blue), another scaled-down squash for smaller families, is a Buttercup and Blue Hubbard cross (*Cucurbita maxima*) and one of the few "baby"

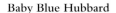

Baby Blue Hubbard   diameter: 4-5 inches

kabocha types: Delica (green) and Gold Debut (orange)
diameter: 5-7 inches

cultivars that retain the thick, dry flesh of real storage pumpkins. (How anyone ever packed those biggies into this little chassis, I don't know.) Typically, it ranges from 3 to 5 pounds. The 2-pound sample pictured is smaller than characteristic, but it tasted just dandy. Baked or steamed, the smooth, starchy, golden-orange flesh happily suggests both its parents. The plump baby holds its shape neatly for stuffing or for serving in wedges. The skin does not make for good eating.

Kabocha types (*Cucurbita maxima and C. moschata*) are numerous and confusing. Kabocha is a generic term for winter squash developed in Japan (including Kuri, page 604). Unfortunately, it is the sole marketing term used in North America to designate all cultivars (rather like using just the word "apple" for Granny Smith, Golden Delicious, Gala, etc.). There are two primary types: drum-shaped green Hokkaido, usually fairly rough-skinned and mottled or striped dark-green to slate; and the globular or pointy smoother orange Hokkaido (derived from American Hubbard).

And then there are all the others between, which look like either or both—and may even confuse you by having Buttercup-style beanies. What you cannot see is what these Japanese squash have in common: deep flavor, honeyed sweetness, and flesh so fine-grained that it can seem more custard than vegetable.

Cut into chunks or slices. (You can incise the skin with decorations, as is done in the Far East.) Roast for a deep, rich, autumnal flavor and a dense, starchy, smooth texture (though the flesh may darken blotchily as it cools). Or simmer in seasoned liquid, then serve hot or at room temperature. Or steam, for a velvety texture.

In particular, steam the orange kabocha types: They blaze to the color of California poppies inside and out, taste fresh and sweet, and are seamlessly creamy. Add a drizzle of butter and a wedge of orange—no more. The average kabocha weighs 2 to 3 pounds, but there are larger and smaller ones. The skin is usually edible.

Miniature pumpkins (*Cucurbita pepo*) are not mere decorations. Think of these pumpkinettes as a quick-

miniature pumpkins   diameter: 3-4 inches

standard spaghetti squash   length: 9 inches

and-easy one-person-anytime dinner delight. They are as delicious as any larger squash, and some are more so. Whether cream or orange, they are likely to be sweet, firm, fully packed, and flavorful. The scalloped and flattened types are drier and sweeter than the rounded types, which have more tender pulp and skin. All weigh from ¼ to ¾ pound. Some have edible skin, some don't. (And once again, these are not "designer" toys, but fruits developed long ago in China.)

White or cream minis (Baby Boo is shown here) bake to a golden beige inside and out, wafting a scent of roasting sweet corn as they cook. The meaty pulp is quite dry and starchy, like a chestnut-sweetpotato cross. Unfortunately, the skin, a gourd-hard shell, is not edible, either baked or steamed.

Orange lobed minis (Jack Be Little, Sweetie Pie, Munchkin, and more) bake or steam admirably, turning a glowing lollipop orange. The skin is more tender and palatable when steamed, but still pretty hard.

Spaghetti squash or **Vegetable Spaghetti** (*Cucurbita pepo*) was growing in various places around the United States before the beginning of the 20th century, but it was not permanently accepted until the Sakata Seed Corporation refined it, and marketing master Frieda Caplan (the formidable founder of

Orangetti spaghetti squash   length: 9 inches

Stripetti spaghetti squash   length: 9 inches

When you select any spaghetti squashes, be aware that the larger the vegetable, the thicker the strands—and, usually, the more flavorful. Bake, steam, or microwave, then top with sauce as you would pasta, or combine with a creamy sauce and bake au gratin, or toss with dressing and serve warm or cool. Spaghetti squashes average 2 to 3 pounds but can be smaller or larger. The skin is not edible.

Sugar Loaf (*Cucurbita pepo*), a warmer-toned, more squat and rounded strain of Delicata, is a comparative newcomer to the market. Its shape is particularly handy for making prettily scalloped slices and halves, but I find its flavor and texture less refined and defined than those of its Delicata parent. The nicely sweet, medium dry, solid flesh suggests good Acorn squash but is lighter.

Bake for firm texture and more pronounced flavor (but skin that is inedible); steam for a softer, lighter feel (and skin that *can*—just—be eaten). Sugar Loaf squash generally weighs about 1 pound, but goes up to 3.

Frieda's, *the* specialty produce company) brought it to America's attention. (It is still not to everyone's taste. As the gardening writer Sylvia Thompson observes: "With every other squash, the aim is to get rid of the fiber in the center. Spaghetti squash is where all those banished fibers went.")

Most think it is just plain fun to cook what looks like a pumpkin crossed with a football, open it up, and unwind an explosion of crisp-tender, golden strands (not clearly visible in the raw squash) from its thin shell. The flavor is lightly sweet, fresh, and mild to bland, a foil for saucing. The marigold-bright orange form has proved comparable in all ways but color.

Stripetti, a cross of Delicata and Spaghetti Squash, is another story—and it has been problematic for me: However I cooked it, the strands broke or turned to mush and tasted sodden and dull. But I don't want to generalize on the basis of just three squash. So I checked with Sylvia Thompson, who prefers it because "the harder shell (from Delicata) makes this a good keeper, and the strands (with Delicata flavor), sweeten with storage."

Sugar Loaf   length: 4 inches

Sweet Dumpling squashes: before storage (green-striped) and after (orange-striped)   diameter: 3-5 inches

Sweet Dumpling (*Cucurbita pepo*), solid and plump, is colored warm cream and striped with ivy green, like Delicata—and, also like Delicata, it changes to butter and orange in storage (see above). The pale yellow flesh is close-textured, fine and dry as a potato, richly starchy with a fresh sweetness and a light corn taste.

Similar squashes were cultivated in the 19th century, but this one was developed in Japan as "Vegetable Gourd" by the same Sakata Seed Corporation that brought us "Vegetable Spaghetti," which became spaghetti squash. "In 1976, the name was changed from Vegetable Gourd because no one was buying it," Glenn Drowns recalls. "And it worked. Everyone and his dog wants it as Sweet Dumpling, even at a higher price."

Steam or bake, stuffed or not, and serve hot, warm, or cold. The skin is relatively tender for a hard-shelled squash and can be eaten. You can partially peel (run a swivel peeler over the squash, leaving the dark green strips in the indentations), or peel completely, or leave it as nature made it. Sweet Dumpling ranges from an apple to a cantaloupe in size and generally weighs about 1 pound.

To Cook Small to Medium Squash: The Basics

Cook hard squash until tender throughout. With the exception of spaghetti squash, it's better to overcook than undercook. Season lightly: most small squashes are delicate and sweet. Sprinkle with a pinch of sage, marjoram, savory, basil, anise, fennel, mace, clove, nutmeg, coriander, or cinnamon—or mix herbs and spices. Sweeten with a modicum of maple syrup, honey, brown sugar, or jelly. Sprinkle hot or warm squash with flavored oil or melted butter and citrus juice. Drizzle mild vinaigrette over warm or cooled slices.

Bake squashes that are fairly bland or moist to concentrate the flavor and caramelize sugars. Bake whole for maximum flavor and the most uniform consistency. Set on a baking sheet in a 350°F oven, allowing a minimum of 45 minutes for 1- to 1½-pound squash and maximum of 2 hours for a solid 3-pounder. Test for doneness by piercing with a knife tip to be sure the interior is creamy. When the squash is done, halve or cut a cap in it. Remove seeds and fiber. Add seasoning, butter, oil, nuts, or cooked stuffing. Reheat, as desired.

Or halve squash before baking. Scrape out seeds and fibers. Set cut side up (to save the juices) on a baking sheet. Season and butter or oil the flesh. Cover with foil. Bake until very tender.

Steam very hard, dry, starchy squashes, as well as spaghetti squash. Set halved, seeded squash cut side down on steaming rack over boiling salted water. (Add aromatics to the water for subtle seasoning.) Cover; steam until tender—15 to 30 minutes, depending upon the variety. Or cut cleaned squash into ½- to ¾-inch rings; steam about 10 minutes. Or steam chunks, allowing 15 minutes for 2-inch pieces. Peel, as desired. Serve with a touch of butter or a wedge of citrus, or drizzle with vinaigrette.

Microwave squash for a spontaneous, quick-and-easy side dish—but do not expect the same quality as baked or steamed. Microwaving mutes flavor and may emphasize fibrous or pasty aspects. Or, every now and then, microwaved squash may be just fine—but this is difficult to predict. Arrange cleaned, seasoned squash (if there are caps, set them askew) in microwavable dish with a slick of water. Cover, cook until tender, then let rest. For 1 to 1½ pounds of squash, cook 5 to 8 minutes; rest 5 more minutes. (For Golden Nugget, first zap 2 minutes to soften; *then* clean, then cook.) For 2- to 3-pound squash, cook 12 to 16 minutes; then let rest for 10 minutes.

Baked Orange-Glazed Acorn or Carnival Squash Rounds

A combination of smallish squash varieties arranged in overlapping slices makes a particularly pretty side dish. Acorn, Carnival, Delicata, and Sugar Loaf work well. If I am using just one, Delicata is my first choice. A small cookie cutter or zucchini corer helps make the presentation tidy. For the marmalade, choose one with fine shreds—not coarse-cut, which won't adhere properly.

3 squashes (1 to 1½ pounds each)
2 tablespoons orange marmalade
2 teaspoons shoyu (Japanese soy sauce)

2 teaspoons lime juice
Pinch of ground hot pepper
½ tablespoon mild vegetable oil
Nutmeg or pepper

1. Preheat oven to 375°F. Cut a thin slice from a long side of each squash to keep it from rolling. Trim ends. Cut crosswise into ¾-inch slices. With small round cutter or corer or melon baller, remove seeds and fibers.

2. Spray non-stick baking sheet (or foil-covered ordinary one) with water. Arrange squash in a single layer. (If squashes are long and narrow, you may end up with more slices and need a second sheet.) Bake 15 minutes. Meanwhile, stir together marmalade, shoyu, lime juice, and hot pepper. Heat slightly if needed to blend.

3. Remove squash from oven. Brush each slice with the oil. Turn over. Brush lightly with marmalade mixture. Return to oven and bake 10 minutes. Brush again with remaining mixture. Return to oven and bake until glazed and tender, 10 to 20 minutes, depending upon type.

4. Overlap slices in a wreath on a warmed serving dish. Season with nutmeg or pepper and serve hot.

Serves 4 to 6

Chillied Buttercup (or Kabocha) Hominy Stew

Chunky with hominy and sweet squash, this soft orange meal-in-a-bowl receives a crisp, aromatic finish of minced green pepper, cilantro, and toasted cumin seeds. "Pure mild ground chile," a staple in the West, is sold in specialty shops elsewhere. Composed of no more than ground dried chillis, its heat depends upon the chilli type. If instead you use the spice blend called "chili powder," reduce the added salt. The convenience of canned hominy makes this a quickie supper, but if you prepare the real thing, the stew will be even more chewy and tasty. (Chilli, chili, and chile all in one paragraph! When will we all get together on this native American indispensable? See page 189 for more on the subject.)

1 Buttercup or kabocha squash
   (1½ to 2 pounds)
2 teaspoons cumin seeds
1 tablespoon peanut or corn oil
1 large red onion, chopped
1 teaspoon kosher salt
½ teaspoon sugar
1 garlic clove, minced
2 to 3 teaspoons pure mild ground chile or
   1½ tablespoons blended chili powder
2 tablespoons flour
2 cups beef broth or strong vegetable broth
2 cups water
1-pound can hominy (preferably yellow),
   drained and rinsed
½ green bell pepper, chopped
½ cup packed cilantro (coriander) leaves

1. Halve squash and scoop out seeds. Cut into 1- to 1½-inch slices. Pare off peel. Cube flesh (you'll have about 1 quart).

2. Stir cumin seeds in large heavy saucepan over moderate heat until fragrant—about 1 minute. Transfer to a dish. Add oil to pan and stir in all but 3 tablespoons onion. Add squash, 1 teaspoon cumin, salt, and sugar. Cook, stirring, until lightly browned, about 5 minutes. Add garlic, ground chile, and flour, stirring to coat.

3. Add broth, water, and hominy. Bring to a boil. Simmer, covered, until squash is just tender, about 15 minutes. Uncover and simmer gently until it is very tender and stew thickens, about 15 minutes longer.

4. Meanwhile, mince together reserved onion, green pepper, remaining cumin, and cilantro to a fine texture. Stir into stew. Season and serve hot.

Serves 4 as a main course

flavor boost. Handy for a buffet, this dish is tasty warm or at room temperature.

2 Delicata or Sugar Loaf squash (about
   1 pound each)
About ¼ teaspoon kosher salt
½ cup cilantro (coriander) leaves
2 tablespoons olive oil
1 medium red onion, diced
¼ teaspoon ground cumin
Pinch of ground hot pepper
Pinch of ground cloves or allspice
2 tablespoons cider vinegar
½ teaspoon honey
2 medium plum tomatoes, chopped small

1. With vegetable peeler, zip skin from squash, leaving what remains naturally in the indentations. Cut off ends. With zucchini corer, remove seeds and pith. Or twist a knife in the center corkscrew-fashion to cut the seeds free, then clean thoroughly with melon ball cutter or teaspoon. Cut crosswise into ½-inch slices.

2. Set rings on rack of large steamer over boiling water. Sprinkle with ¼ teaspoon salt. Cover and steam until tender, about 10 minutes. Transfer to serving dish.

3. Meanwhile, chop cilantro. Warm 1 tablespoon oil in skillet over moderate heat. Add onion (and cilantro roots) and cook to soften slightly. Add cumin, hot pepper, and cloves; toss briefly. Reduce heat, add vinegar, honey, and tomatoes, and toss until juicy—a few minutes at most.

4. Remove from heat. Stir in remaining tablespoon of oil and half the cilantro. Adjust seasoning. Spoon over the squash. Top with remaining cilantro. Serve warm or at room temperature.

Serves 4

Steamed Delicata Rings with Tomato-Onion-Cilantro Dressing

Deep yellow rings are topped with tomato and red onion dice seasoned with cumin, vinegar, and honey and freshened with cilantro leaves. If cilantro's roots are attached, cook them: Cut them off, scrub with a brush, and mince; then sauté with the onion for a substantial

To Cook Gold Nugget: The Basics

However cute this little squash may look, it is *truly* hard-shelled, and dangerously slippery. So unless you're a whiz with a cleaver, ignore advice to halve before cooking. Either cook the little orbs whole, or soften them in a microwave oven so that they can be cut easily. When it comes to cooking, squash that is steamed or baked will be appreciably sweeter and smoother than squash that is microwaved, although it will take much longer to cook. For each person, select one squash of ¾ to 1 pound, which is what most seem to weigh.

To steam whole: Pierce each squash in several places near the top. Set on rack over boiling water. Cover and steam until creamy inside, about ½ hour. Slice off the tops (or halve lengthwise). Scoop out seeds and fiber (a small ice cream scoop is ideal, but a spoon is fine). Season and add butter or cooked stuffing.

To bake whole: Pierce each squash in several places near the top. Set on pan in preheated 350°F oven. Bake until pulp is soft when poked with a toothpick— 45 to 60 minutes. The shell hardens and makes it difficult to gauge doneness, so check carefully. Clean and season as above.

To microwave to clean: Pierce each squash in several places near the top. Cook just until cuttable—about 2 minutes. With pot holder, remove squash from oven, and slice off cap (avoid escaping steam). Clean as above. The squash is now ready for seasoning and stuffing, baking, or steaming (cut side down, if not stuffed). Shorten cooking time if prepared this way.

To cook in microwave: Follow directions for microwave preparation. Set cleaned squash in a microwavable dish with a little water. Cover and bake until just tender, 3 to 5 minutes, depending on thickness of flesh. Let stand a few minutes before serving.

Steamed Kabocha or Buttercup Squash on Greens

Solid, dry-fleshed orange-meat squashes are at their best steamed. Some may become soft and moist; some remain pleasingly dry, rather like chestnuts. Serve with roasted turkey, pork, or lamb, or as a complement to a mixed grain dish for a vegetarian meal. About the peel: Some squashes of this type have edible peels; others are too firm. I hedge my bets and remove stripes from about half the squash. The rest can be easily trimmed by diners if they wish.

1 bunch arugula
1 small bunch small-leafed spinach
2½-pound kabocha or Buttercup squash
1 tablespoon honey
2 tablespoons lemon juice
1 tablespoon shoyu (Japanese soy sauce)
1 tablespoon dry sherry
1 tablespoon butter
Hot pepper sauce

1. Trim stems from arugula and spinach. Wash leaves in several changes of water. Spin-dry. With large knife, slice into ¼-inch strips (to make about 4 lightly packed cups). Do not refrigerate.

2. Scrub squash. Halve with heavy knife. If it resists, place the wide part of the blade of your sturdiest knife next to stem and cut into flesh a bit. With mallet or rolling pin, gently hammer knife where blade joins handle, to cut through. Scoop out and discard fibers and seeds (a small ice cream scoop or grapefruit spoon works well). Cut into 8 wedges. With citrus stripper or small knife, remove about half the peel in a decorative pattern, as desired.

3. Set squash on steamer rack over boiling water. Cover and steam until tender, 10 to 15 minutes; but cooking time may double for very dense or dry squash.

4. Combine honey, lemon juice, shoyu, sherry, butter, and hot pepper sauce in a tiny pan. Warm over low heat until butter melts.

5. Spread greens on platter. Top with hot squash and spoon sauce over.

Serves 4 as a side dish

Kabocha and Fennel over Couscous with Orange

"Kabocha couscous" sounds cute and tastes wonderful, but another sweet, relatively dry squash—such as Buttercup or Baby Blue Hubbard (you'll need just half)—will serve as well. For a tart, creamy variation on this main dish, stir ⅓ cup yogurt into the squash when you serve it.

1½ pounds kabocha squash
1 fennel bulb with fluffy greens
   (about 1½ pounds)

1 medium onion
2 tablespoons butter
1 large garlic clove, minced
About 1½ tablespoons minced ginger
1 tablespoon sugar
1¼ teaspoons kosher salt
½ teaspoon fennel seeds
2 juicy oranges (preferably organic),
    well scrubbed
Big pinch of saffron
Lemon juice
1¾ cups water (for couscous)
1¼ cups whole-wheat couscous (substitute
    white, if preferred)

1. Cut kabocha into large pieces, as convenient (see page 615, if necessary, for cutting directions). Remove seeds and pith. Cut into 1½-inch chunks and peel. Remove and reserve fluffy fennel leaves. Trim off stalks and fibrous layers. Dice bulb; set aside ¼ cup. Chop onion.

2. Melt 1 tablespoon butter in heavy pot; add onion, garlic, and 1 tablespoon ginger. Cook over lowish heat to soften slightly. Add squash, remaining diced fennel, sugar, ¾ teaspoon salt, and fennel seeds. Cover and cook until mixture is just juicy, about 5 minutes. Uncover, raise heat to moderate, and cook until onion begins to brown, about 5 minutes.

3. Meanwhile, rinse, dry, and chop enough fennel fronds to make ¼ cup. Mince the reserved ¼ cup fennel bulb. Grate zest from oranges; reserve. Halve oranges and squeeze juice. Measure and add enough water to equal 2 cups.

4. Add juice mixture to pot, with saffron, and bring to a boil. Cook gently, covered, until squash is very tender, 20 to 30 minutes. Let stand at least 15 minutes. Add remaining ginger to taste, lemon juice, and ½ tablespoon butter.

5. Meanwhile, prepare couscous: Bring water to a boil with remaining ½ tablespoon butter and ½ teaspoon salt. Stir in couscous and return to a boil. Add orange zest and minced fennel and fronds; remove from heat. Cover and let stand 10 minutes.

6. Fluff couscous into a warmed dish, separating grains with a fork. Ladle vegetables over couscous. Serve hot.

Serves 4 as a main course

Best Baked Mini-Pumpkins

Cut off caps, scrape out seeds, season, re-cap, and bake. That's all it takes to give each diner a yummy little pumpkin, custom-flavored. Bake while you roast a pork loin, leg of lamb, turkey, chicken, or duck. Or, for a vegetable meal, serve with braised greens and toasty baked grains. If available, select several white and orange miniature pumpkin types and cook them together to discover your favorite. They should be dull-skinned (not shiny) and free of any coating. As the Cinderella coaches bake, natural oils surface and they turn as glossy and bright as painted and shellacked decorations.

FOR EACH SERVING

1 mini-pumpkin, 6 to 10 ounces
Pinch of ground coriander, nutmeg,
    cinnamon, allspice, or garam masala or
    big pinch of dried savory, sage, or thyme,
    crumbled to powder
Pinch of salt
Pinch of pepper
1 teaspoon butter or nut oil
1 tablespoon prune, apple, cranberry,
    or orange juice
1 teaspoon maple syrup or honey

1. Set oven to 350° to 375°F, as suits whatever else is roasting. With sturdy sharp knife, cut a square (or five- or six-sided) cap around pumpkin stem, poking into the heart of the squash to cut the fibers. Pry out the cap. With melon ball cutter or grapefruit spoon, scoop out and scrape interior to remove all seeds and fibers. Trim fibers from cap.

2. Sprinkle spice (or herbs), salt, and pepper inside and tap to distribute. Add butter, juice, and sweetening. Set cap back in opening, but do not press in fully (or it may slip inside). Place in baking dish.

3. Bake until creamy-soft inside, about 30 minutes for small squash, 45 minutes for larger ones. Test with knife tip—it should slide through easily. Let stand 15 to 60 minutes, as convenient.

Apple-Stuffed Mini-Pumpkins

Neat little fruit-filled squash serve as a side to roasted meat or poultry, or as a vegetarian main dish with whole-grain pilaf.

 4 mini-pumpkins (about 6 ounces each)
 1 teaspoon brown sugar
 1 tablespoon Dijon mustard
 1 tablespoon corn, walnut, or peanut oil
 1 apple
 2 tablespoons minced celery
 2 tablespoons chopped walnuts
 1 teaspoon lemon juice
 ¼ teaspoon dried thyme, crumbled
 ¼ teaspoon dried sage, crumbled
 ¼ teaspoon kosher salt
 Pepper

1. Preheat oven to 375°F. Rinse mini-pumpkins. With sturdy sharp knife, cut a square (or five- or six-sided) cap around each pumpkin stem, poking into the heart of the squash to cut the fibers. Pry out cap. With a melon ball cutter or grapefruit spoon, scoop out and scrape the interior to remove all seeds and fibers. Trim fibers from caps.

2. Blend brown sugar, mustard, and oil. With a brush, paint interior of pumpkins and caps with the mixture.

3. Peel, core, and chop apple. Toss with celery, walnuts, lemon juice, thyme, sage, salt, and pepper. Divide filling among pumpkins. Set caps gently on each without pressing.

4. Place pumpkins in baking dish. Pour in ½ inch water. Cover dish with foil. Bake until pumpkins are tender when pierced with knife, about 1 hour. Do not undercook—the flesh should be creamy.

Serves 4

To Cook Spaghetti Squash: The Basics

Although there are other ways to cook spaghetti squash, I vote for steaming, baking, or microwaving. Whichever you choose, beware of overcooking, which yields soggy, dull squash. Spaghetti squash strands should have a slight crispness when properly cooked.

To steam: Halve squash lengthwise. Scrape out and discard seeds. Halve lengthwise again. Set pieces on steamer rack over boiling water. Cook, covered, until a finger leaves an indentation in the "shell"—20 to 30 minutes. Gently "comb" out the strands with a wide-tined fork.

To bake: Prick whole squash in several places. Bake in a preheated 350°F oven until easily indented when pressed, 35 to 55 minutes. Set on cutting board and halve immediately (or it may overcook). Cool slightly and discard seeds, then pull out strands gently with a fork until only a thin shell remains.

To microwave: Halve squash lengthwise; remove seeds. Set in a microwavable container, season, and then top with a little oil or butter. Cover and microwave 10 to 15 minutes, depending on size. Let rest 5 minutes. Remove strands gently with a fork.

Spaghetti Squash Salad with Sesame and Ginger

Colorful, crisp, sweet-hot-tart, this vegetable salad has an exotic look and taste. Prepare in advance as part of a buffet, or serve chilled, as a course alone. If star anise is not in your larder, substitute 1 teaspoon anise seeds and 2 bay leaves.

 1 spaghetti squash (about 3 pounds)
 4 whole star anise "flowers," broken up
 1 teaspoon kosher salt
 2 small cucumbers (preferably Oriental or
   Middle Eastern types)
 Sliced sweet pickled ginger
 1 large red or orange bell pepper
 2 tablespoons sesame seeds
 1 bunch cilantro (coriander)
 ¼ teaspoon chilli flakes

2 tablespoons sherry vinegar
1 tablespoon rice vinegar
2 teaspoons Asian (dark) sesame oil
1 tablespoon peanut or corn oil

1. Quarter squash lengthwise and scrape out seeds. Boil water with star anise in large steamer. Set squash on steaming rack. Cover and cook until "shell" of squash just dents when pressed, 25 to 30 minutes.

2. Cool squash until it can be handled. Using a wide-tined fork, "comb" all strands from squash "shell" into a colander set over a bowl. Sprinkle with ½ teaspoon salt. Top with a plate and weight. Refrigerate to drain for several hours.

3. Peel cucumbers if tough-skinned or bitter. Halve lengthwise, then slice across. Drain about 1 tablespoon liquid from pickled ginger. Toss with cucumbers and refrigerate. Thin-slice enough ginger to make about 1½ tablespoons.

4. Cut pepper into ¼-inch dice. Stir sesame seeds in small pan over low heat until lightly golden and fragrant. Trim and reserve any cilantro roots for another use. Rinse and spin-dry cilantro. Strip leaves and measure enough to make about 1 cup. Chop.

5. Blend remaining ½ teaspoon salt, chilli flakes, and sherry and rice vinegars. Blend in both oils. Combine drained squash, sliced ginger, bell pepper, 1 tablespoon sesame seeds, the cilantro, and dressing; toss to mix well (can be refrigerated for several hours).

6. Arrange salad in serving dish. Tuck cucumber slices around. Sprinkle with the remaining tablespoon of sesame seeds.

Serves 6

Variation

Microwaved Spaghetti Squash Salad with Sesame and Ginger

If you prefer to microwave rather than steam, halve the spice mixture and combine in microwave dish with ½ cup water. Cover and bring to a boil. Add squash, re-cover, and cook about 10 minutes. Let stand 5 minutes. Use orange or yellow spaghetti squash for this, not the striped.

Herbed Spaghetti Squash with Red Peppers and Walnuts

This bright blend of interesting textures serves as both starch and vegetable accompaniment to a meat or poultry main dish. Or feature it as part of a vegetable meal, alongside broccoli raab or kale, or with whole-grain pilaf. Although spaghetti squash is often suggested for a main dish, I do not feel it has the requisite character or starchiness for the role.

1 spaghetti squash (about 2 pounds)
2 medium red bell peppers
3 tablespoons olive oil
1 teaspoon minced garlic
Big pinch of ground hot pepper
1 teaspoon wine vinegar
Salt
½ cup toasted and coarse-chopped
    walnuts
¼ cup slivered cilantro or
    basil leaves

1. Steam, bake, or microwave squash as directed on page 626, but halve the squash *cross*wise instead of lengthwise.

2. Meanwhile, cut peppers on mandoline or processor blade into extremely thin strips (as spaghetti-like as you can). Warm 2 tablespoons oil in medium skillet over moderate heat. Sauté peppers until just slightly softened. Add garlic and hot pepper and stir a minute. Add vinegar. Set aside.

3. Cool squash briefly. Scoop out seeds. Gently "comb" out all strands with a fork, fluffing into a serving dish.

4. Add peppers, the remaining 1 tablespoon oil, and salt to squash, tossing to blend well. Add half each of the walnuts and cilantro and toss to mix. Sprinkle the remainder over. Serve hot, warm, or at room temperature.

Serves 4 to 6 as a side dish

Sugar Loaf (or Delicata) Baked with Sweet Spices and Cream

An easy and rewarding dish that looks cute too. The very small dose of cream flavors, moistens, and lightly glazes the squash while adding only minimal fat.

2 Sugar Loaf or Delicata squash
    (about 1¼ pounds each)
½ teaspoon kosher salt
½ teaspoon sugar
¼ teaspoon ground mace or grated nutmeg
¼ teaspoon ground anise, fennel, or
    cinnamon
¼ teaspoon ground hot pepper or
    white pepper
6 tablespoons heavy cream

1. Preheat oven to 350°F. Rinse squash. Cut off each stem (or knock it off with a knife handle). Hold each squash upright on this flatter end and carefully slice down with a heavy knife into 2 long halves. With melon ball cutter, remove seeds and fibers. Shave a long sliver from each half to prevent it from tipping.

2. Blend salt, sugar, mace, anise, and hot pepper. Sprinkle evenly into the halves. Drizzle 1½ tablespoons cream into each. Crimp foil over each half and set squashes in baking pan.

3. Bake until very tender, about 40 to 50 minutes. Remove foil; spoon a little cream from each cavity onto the rims to moisten them. Return to oven and bake, uncovered, until lightly browned and bubbling, about 5 minutes.

Serves 4

Steamed Sweet Dumpling Squash with Buttery Citrus-Herb Sauce

Sweet and surprisingly rich—given the mere ½ teaspoon butter per serving—this dish can embellish a casual meal or a Thanksgiving feast. Or substitute 1

mini-pumpkin per person: Halve instead of cutting into quarters, and reduce the cooking time. Or bake instead: Set on a foil-lined sheet and bake in a 350°F oven until tender. For variation, sweeten the butter with maple syrup and sharpen with ginger juice.

1 lemon (preferably organic)
1 orange (preferably organic)
1½ tablespoons sugar
¼ teaspoon dried tarragon, crumbled fine
⅛ teaspoon white pepper
3 Sweet Dumpling or Delicata squash
    (1 to 1½ pounds each)
¾ teaspoon kosher salt
1 tablespoon butter
3 tablespoons thin-sliced mint and/
    or basil leaves

1. Scrub lemon and orange. Grate zest from both. Halve and squeeze juice from both. Measure juice and add water as needed to make 1 cup. Combine with zest, sugar, tarragon, and pepper in saucepan. Boil gently, stirring, until reduced to ½ cup. Set aside.

2. Halve squash lengthwise, slicing slightly off center to avoid the tough "poles." Cut off stems and scoop out seeds. Remove most skin with a swivel peeler, leaving indented green stripes. Halve lengthwise again.

3. Set squash on steamer rack over boiling water, cut sides down. Sprinkle with salt. Cover and steam until tender, 15 to 20 minutes.

4. Arrange squash in wide serving dish, skin side down. Reheat sauce, then stir in butter and 2 tablespoons mint and/or basil. Spoon evenly over pieces. Sprinkle with remaining herbs.

Serves 6

Pros Propose

"A whole acorn squash filled with quinoa is spectacular as a main dish," wrote chef Felipe Rojas-Lombardi in *The Art of South American Cooking*. To prepare **Calabazas Rellenas:** Cut caps from stem ends of 1-pound Acorn squashes. Scoop clean; cut a sliver from each to level bases. Brush interiors and lids with butter; season. Rinse and rub quinoa grains in water. Combine quinoa and plenty of water, and simmer until barely cooked (grains should be semi-translucent); drain. Spread on towel and fluff with fork to dry. Gently cook minced lemon grass core, sliced scallions, ground cloves, nutmeg, white pepper, and salt in butter. Add rum-soaked dark and golden raisins; cook to evaporate liquor. Add chopped hazelnuts and quinoa; cook 5 minutes. Pack into squash; fit lids on top. Arrange in baking pan. Brush with olive oil. Add water to pan and cover with foil. Bake ½ hour. Uncover and bake until squash is soft, about 40 minutes longer.

A completely different tone is set by this spare Japanese-style treatment of **Curried Acorn Squash with Pecans:** Peel squash and cut into 1-inch slices, then into angled 1-inch chunks. Melt butter in skillet and stir in mild curry powder. Add squash, a little water, and salt and pepper. Cover and cook over low heat until tender and all liquid has evaporated, about 10 minutes. Arrange a stack of pieces on each plate and scatter over toasted pecan halves (from *Simple Menus for the Bento Box* by Ellen Greaves and Wayne Nish).

I was surprised to read in Longteine de Monteiro's *The Elephant Walk Cookbook* that Buttercup squash is "exactly the kind we have in Cambodia." She prepares **Stir-Fried Buttercup Squash with Pork:** Cut tenderloin into bite-size squares. Cut cleaned, peeled Buttercup into thin julienne strips. Stir-fry smashed garlic in vegetable oil until golden. Add pork, fish sauce, and sugar. Gently fold in squash and toss until cooked but still slightly crunchy, about 5 minutes. Add 1½-inch scallion lengths and pepper.

Kabocha Soup with Spice-Roasted Pepitas and Lime Crème Fraîche is one of her most popular dishes, says chef Katy Sparks. To prepare: Halve kabochas or Buttercup squashes, clean, and rub with oil. Season and roast until tender in 400°F oven. Gently cook leeks, minced ginger, and minced lemon grass in butter until very soft. Add curry powder and cook briefly. Scoop out cooked squash. Add, with coconut milk and chicken stock; bring to a boil and skim. Add sachet of coriander seeds, orange zest, cilantro leaves, and peppercorns and simmer 1 hour. Cool. Puree in blender until very smooth. Season with honey, cinnamon, salt, and pepper. Prepare spiced pepitas: Shallow-fry raw pumpkin seeds over medium heat until crisp and browned; drain on paper towels. Season while warm with equal parts ground star anise, cinnamon, and pepper. Combine crème fraîche, grated lime zest, and salt and pepper. Ladle soup into bowls.

Garnish each with a spoonful of cream and sprinkle of pepitas.

Baked miniature pumpkins acquire a shine like glazed pottery. Soufflé-filled, they are even cuter. To prepare chef Thomas Moran's **Roasted Mini-Pumpkin Soufflé with Frisée-Roquefort Salad:** Remove caps from pumpkins, clean, and rub insides and caps with butter. Sprinkle with salt, pepper, thyme, and marjoram. Bake in moderate oven until tender but not browned. Scoop pulp from caps and pumpkins. Chop fine with roasted garlic and roasted onion. Prepare soufflé base; blend in the pumpkin mixture, then fold in egg whites. Return to pumpkins. Bake until puffed. Meanwhile, prepare salad of frisée and julienned Granny Smith apples. Dress with apple cider, champagne vinegar, and mild oil. Sprinkle with Roquefort. Set pumpkins on salad and serve as a first course.

Asian aromas enliven mild Vegetable Spaghetti. For **Spaghetti Squash with Kumquats in Orange-Chilli Oil:** Bake whole squash. Halve, seed, and comb out strands. Warm corn oil with fine strips of orange zest over low heat to flavor oil. Add crushed dried chillis, Asian sesame oil, and chopped onion. When onion begins to brown, add the squash, sliced and pitted kumquats, and salt. Toss together and heat through, covered. Garnish with holy basil leaves. Serve with black rice, sautéed red cabbage, and thin-sliced Bosc pears (from Barbara Kirshenblatt-Gimblett, who writes about food and cookbooks).

Aromatics bring out the best in spaghetti squash here too. But chef Morgen Jacobson stresses that they should be minimal so "the refreshing lightness of spaghetti squash is preserved, not hidden." To prepare **Curried Spaghetti Squash Salad with Preserved Lemon, Carrots, and Pistachios:** Steam whole squash: Halve, seed, and comb out strands. Combine with curry oil, small dice of celeriac and carrot, minced shallot and ginger, and dried currants. Remove zest from preserved lemon (which Jacobson makes with one part sugar to three of salt, and whole cinnamon, coriander, and cardamom). Blanch in two changes of cold water. Drain and cut into very tiny dice. Add to squash, with lemon thyme, lemon juice, and toasted pistachios. Season with vinegar and sugar (he uses a syrup of rice vinegar, sugar, and kombu).

A relatively simple **Sweet Dumpling Squash Soup with Crispy Squash** is a surprise from the master of complicated dishes, chef Charlie Trotter: Quarter and clean Sweet Dumpling and cut very thin slices, preferably on mandoline. Spread on non-stick baking sheet, salt lightly, and bake in low oven until slices are golden and dry to the touch (watch carefully—they burn easily). They should crisp as they cool; cook longer if they don't. Cut caps from Sweet Dumplings. Clean, brush interiors with olive oil, and season. Set cut side down in baking pan and add ½ inch water. Bake in moderate oven until tender, about an hour. Scrape out pulp (reserve it), leaving ¼-inch shells. Gently cook chopped onion in butter until translucent. Combine in blender with squash pulp and water. Puree, then press through fine sieve. Reheat and season. Heat squashes in oven. Fill with soup. Set a few crisp squash pieces on top of each and arrange more around the plate. Sprinkle with chopped chervil (from *Charlie Trotter's Vegetables*).

Sunchoke, Jerusalem Artichoke *(Helianthus tuberosus)*

Also topinambour (and variations), sunroot

How ironic that one of the very few North American crops to be introduced to Europe should be based on a South American name, topinambou! And how absurd that the name in England and North America, Jerusalem artichoke, probably derives from a distorted Italian one! Long before Europeans set foot in North America, Native Americans were gathering and cultivating *Helianthus* species (for both seeds and tubers) in many parts of the continent—and using their own languages to describe them. The botanical name, incidentally, is straightforward: *Helianthus* is from the Greek *helios* (sun) and *anthos* (flower); *tuberosus* applies to the tubers produced on the underground root stalks.

The "Jerusalem theory" is: "The tubers, early introduced to Europe, were soon popular in the Mediterranean countries . . . in Italian [as] *girasole* [sunflower]. True to their genius in such matters the English promptly changed it to 'Jerusalem,' " according to the authors of *Edible Wild Plants of Eastern North America*, Fernald and Kinsey—and many others who tell more or less the same story. That droll corruption has not been either documented or discounted. Nor has the other theory—that "Jerusalem" is a deformation of Ter-Neusen (now Terneuzen), a town in the Netherlands where the vegetable was planted early on, according to an herbal published in 1618.

What has been passed down in botanical literature is the fact that the tubers were distributed from the Farnese Gardens in Rome in 1617 under the name *girasole articiocco*. Why artichoke? I can find no other reason than that "the first written notice of the plant by a European appeared in 1605, when Samuel de Champlain mentioned roots with the taste of artichokes which the Indians cultivated. It is generally agreed that this is a reference to *H. tuberosus* and that the observation was made at what is now Nausett Harbor, Massachusetts" (Charles B. Heiser, in his monograph *The Sunflower*).

What about topinambou(r), the name by which *Helianthus tuberosus* is known in many European countries? Talk about truth being stranger than fiction.

⅓ **actual size**

Instead of being named after a *North* American Indian tribe—which would be logical, given its provenance—the plant acquired the Frenchified name for a Brazilian tribe. Accounts vary, but the *Dictionnaire étymologique de la langue française* (Bloch and Von Wartburg) states that the name topinambour was probably given to the plant because it became known in France at the same time that a group of Topinambas (the Brazilian name of the tribe) took part in a celebration at Rouen for Henri II (who ruled from 1547 to 1559).

Other historians agree about the Brazilian tribe but give one King Louis or another—at other times—as the ruler who was being celebrated, and Paris as the city where the members of the tribe were presented. In *Histoire de la nouvelle France* (1618), the historian Lescarbot, who documented Champlain's voyages and may have been responsible for getting *Helianthus tuberosus* to Europe, wrote of the roots, "Some people in Paris, ignorantly call [them] Topinamboux whilst others, more correctly, 'Canada,' for it is from there that they came here. . . . A plague on those who caused the hawkers in Paris to call them Topinamboux." And if all this isn't circuitous enough, our great gardener-president, Thomas Jefferson, noted in 1809 that he had planted "topinambours." This strange etymological and botanical voyage is not yet over.

Then why "sunchoke" in this book? Because I cannot bear to give precedence to the thoroughly misleading "Jerusalem artichoke," although it perseveres. "Sunchoke" arrived in markets through the efforts of the doyenne of specialty produce, Frieda Caplan, who began packaging and selling it in 1965. She credits Will Kinney, an organic farmer in Vista, California, with devising the name. He probably arrived at this sensible promotional name independently, but Charles Heiser writes that around 1950 a Swedish plant breeder investigated the possibility of using a hybrid of Jerusalem artichoke with common sunflower as a sugar crop, and called it Sunchoke.

As a finale to this lengthy etymology: Heiser notes that in 1918 the *Gardener's Chronicle,* an English publication, offered a prize for a new common name for the plant. "Ten persons submitted the name sunroot, which in the estimation of the judges was the best. Probably none of the judges nor the contestants were aware that certain Indians of Virginia already had a name for the plant, *kaischuc penauk,* which means 'sunroot.' " That's the name I'll vote for, too, if anyone gives me the chance.

I wonder if it is because no one has ever known where to look up the vegetable in a cookbook that we are still unsure of how to handle it three centuries after it settled in Europe? In *American Cookery* (1796), this country's first non-British cookbook, Amelia Simmons wrote: "Artichokes—the Jerusalem is best, are cultivated like potatoes (tho' their stocks grow 7 feet high) and may be preserved like the turnip raddish, or pickled." In the index of *Julia Child and Company* (1978), one finds "sunchoke(s), *see* topinambour(s)" and "topinambour (Jerusalem artichoke)."

Every so often, someone writes that this native of North America deserves a fresh look. A look, however, is not the point, for this is not a vegetable that wears a dazzling placard saying "Try me." It is stubby and stumpy, and usually beige-skinned, though it may also

be russet or cream, and long and tapered, or branched and protuberant. Raw, the juicy ivory interior is extremely crisp, like water chestnuts, and tastes sweetly earthy, with undertones of salsify and (dare I say it?) artichoke heart. Sunchokes can also be barely blanched or cooked to a puree, and taste interesting and different at every stage between.

Note on ill winds—and health benefits: The only reason I know not to eat sunchokes is that they can cause flatulence (as do beans, cabbage, and many other foods that people continue to eat). If you don't know your own tolerance, begin by eating a small portion, since "susceptibility varies tremendously, from insignificant in some to devastating in others," according to Stanley J. Kays, a horticultural scientist at the University of Georgia in Athens. He explains that sunchoke's primary form of carbohydrate (inulin), a dietary fiber, "is not digested by humans (hence the gas problem)" but adds that sunchoke "confers a number of significant health benefits, such as reduced blood cholesterol and decreased incidence of colon cancer."

BASIC USE: Raw sunchoke slices have a fresh, clean snap that makes them a fine foil for dips and sauces. They add character and crunch to salads of raw or cooked vegetables, meat, or fish, whether cut into rounds, dice, or julienne. Like jícama, they can be dressed in advance and will remain crisp and pale—at least in my experience. I have often read that they discolor, but this has not yet happened to me.

For the quickest cooking, steam or boil sunchokes until just tender, 5 to 15 minutes, depending upon their size. Serve hot with browned butter, or nut oil and citrus juice, or a creamy sauce, or a light vinaigrette with shallots.

Roast whole tubers for a simple and subtle alternative to potatoes. Slice and bake with cream or cheese sauce. Diced, sliced, or julienned sunchokes can be sautéed quickly or slowly: quickly, on high heat, for a crisp and fairly bland taste; slowly, partly covered, for a nuttier, sweeter flavor. For soup, sauté slices with seasoning, add broth and simmer until soft, then puree with (or without) cream. Grate or shred and combine with eggs and flour to make savory pancakes to accompany roasts and gravy; or serve for brunch with Canadian bacon.

Note that however you cook sunchokes, it is imperative that you check often for doneness as the cooking progresses. A few minutes can mean the difference between crisp-tender and collapsed.

SELECTION AND STORAGE: Although intermittently available year-round, sunchokes are at their best from fall through winter, diminishing in quality when spring arrives. Avoid those that are softening, tinged with green, or sprouting. There are so many distinct types that the only way to know what they are like is to taste them. Of the many I sampled, very small dark-skinned chokes had the most exceptional flavor: hazelnuts + artichoke + chestnuts + celeriac.

If there is a choice, I suggest that you select for flavor, edible skin, and cleanability—in that order. Nibble to find out about the first two criteria (there is no other way). For the last, choose the smoothest, largest, firmest tubers with the fewest hard-to-clean protrusions. Choose tubers of equal size, if possible, so that they will cook in the same time.

Fresh sunchokes in good condition can be refrigerated for about a week wrapped first in paper, then in plastic. If purchased in packages, open up and check the condition of each piece before storing.

PREPARATION: Peel or not, depending upon how edible the skin is and what you think of tubers that are mottled instead of uniformly pale. Fairly thin-skinned tubers should be scrubbed instead of peeled, for maximum flavor. Scrub ferociously with a brush or toothbrush to rid them of stubborn grit.

Peel chokes before or after cooking. If before, drop into a bowl of acidulated water as you peel. To retain the typical French pallor, simmer *à blanc* (see Cardoon, Preparation, page 144). For dishes that will be served cold in salad or which will be reheated, drop the scrubbed unpeeled tubers into boiling salted water; boil to just below the stage desired, then refresh in cold water, drain, and peel.

Basic Roasted Sunchokes

This fuss-free method produces subtle, nutty nuggets and takes less time and trouble to prepare than roasted potatoes. Add it to your regular repertoire for an interesting change of pace. Roast separately, in a baking/serving dish. Or add to a roasting pan with chicken, turkey, lamb, or pork during the last half hour of cooking, tossing to coat with the fat. Let the sunchokes fin-

ish roasting after you've removed the meat to rest before carving.

Warning: Keep an eye on the chokes as they begin to turn tender. They *quickly* change from tender to mush. Remove any that seem to be softening.

About 1½ pounds sunchokes (preferably all the same size)
1½ tablespoons butter and/or hazelnut oil (or meat or poultry fat)
Coarse salt and pepper

1. Scrub sunchokes ferociously with a brush under running water to get at hidden grit; use a toothbrush if there are places you'd miss with a larger brush. If chokes are different sizes, trim them to more or less the same dimensions, keeping them as large as possible.

2. With oven set to 350° to 400°F (depending upon what else you're cooking), heat fat in baking/serving pan or dish that will hold the chokes in a single layer. Roll chokes in fat to coat evenly. Bake until no longer crisp in the center, but not mushy, 25 to 50 minutes—timing varies with how long chokes were stored and their size. Season and serve hot.

Serves 4 to 6

Sunchokes Sautéed with Carrots and Cardamom

Gentle cooking releases the sweet and nutty savors of sunchokes while it keeps some crunch. Carrots supply color and a complementary softness. Serve alongside roasted meat or poultry or as part of a vegetable meal, with braised bitter greens.

¾ pound medium carrots
1 pound sunchokes
2 tablespoons lemon juice
2½ tablespoons butter
2 teaspoons chopped garlic
½ teaspoon ground cardamom
½ teaspoon kosher salt
¼ cup water
Snipped chives and/or chervil leaves

1. Peel carrots, cut into fairly thin rounds, and place in a bowl. Scrub sunchokes forcefully with a brush (or peel if preferred). Halve if they are more than an inch or so wide, then cut into very thin slices. Toss with carrots and lemon juice.

2. Melt 2 tablespoons butter in wide non-aluminum skillet over moderate heat, and stir in garlic. When it is beginning to color, stir in cardamom. Add vegetables and salt, tossing to coat.

3. Add water and bring to a boil. Reduce heat to low, cover, and cook until chokes are tender, about 20 to 25 minutes. Stir now and then, checking to see that some liquid remains; mixture should not dry and brown. Add a spoonful of water if necessary.

4. When done to taste, uncover, season, and stir in remaining ½ tablespoon butter. Sprinkle with herbs and serve hot.

Serves 4 to 6 as a side dish

Sunchokes in Walnut-Mustard Vinaigrette

Nutty flavors bring out the earthy sweetness of raw sunchokes. Walnut oil is suggested here, but pecan or hazelnut is equally delicious. Because the tubers do not become watery, the dish can be assembled hours in advance for a crisp, easily prepared first-course salad.

2 tablespoons sherry vinegar
2 teaspoons Dijon mustard
½ teaspoon kosher salt
Pepper
2 teaspoons minced shallot
2 teaspoons drained, minced capers
¼ cup walnut oil
1 pound sunchokes
⅓ cup minced parsley leaves
1 bunch water cress, trimmed to small sprigs, rinsed, and dried

1. Combine vinegar, mustard, salt, pepper, shallot, and capers. Add oil and blend thoroughly.

2. Scrub sunchokes ferociously under running water, or rinse and peel, as you prefer. Cut into thin strips 1 to 1½ inches long, using a food processor with julienne blade, or a vegetable slicer or knife.

3. Immediately toss with dressing and half the parsley. Mix well. Cover and refrigerate at least an hour, preferably more.

4. To serve, arrange cress on plates. Toss sunchokes with remaining parsley and spoon over cress.

Serves 4 to 6 as a first course or side salad

Light, Creamy Mashed Sunchokes and Potatoes

Just a few ingredients become a subtle, softly spoonable puree. For this dish, it is best to peel the sunchokes for a smooth texture and uniform paleness. Serve as you would mashed potatoes, but expect a juicier consistency and more vegetably (less starchy) quality. A natural for chicken, veal, turkey, or pork. The moisture content of sunchokes varies, so the amount of cream you'll need to add will vary also. If you prefer a low-fat dish, substitute buttermilk for the cream. Or for richness, use cream or butter—as you like it.

1 pound sunchokes
1 pound floury (baking) potatoes
2 to 4 tablespoons light cream or half-and-half
¼ to ½ teaspoon kosher salt
Optional: grated nutmeg or mace
Optional: minced parsley leaves and snipped chives

1. Peel sunchokes. Cut into 1½-inch cubes, more or less. Peel potatoes and cut into slightly larger pieces.

2. Set vegetables on a steaming rack over boiling water. Cover and steam until soft (not al dente), about 20 minutes. Set aside on rack to cool briefly.

3. Combine 2 tablespoons cream with salt in mixing bowl. Add steamed vegetables. Crush with potato masher until as lumpy or as smooth as you like, adding salt, optional nutmeg, and more cream, if desired. Taste and adjust. Spread in microwavable or ovenproof serving dish.

4. To serve, reheat briefly in microwave or regular oven. Sprinkle with optional herbs.

Serves 4 as a side dish

Braised Chicken and Sunchokes with Bay Leaves

Tubby little tubers are treated here as petite potatoes. The rich scent of bay subtly transforms both chokes and chicken in this simple but unusual meal. Don't expect textural uniformity in the Jerusalem artichokes; do expect to relish their various phases from creamy to crunchy. Cook chicken with skin or without (my choice).

> 2 tablespoons flour
> ½ tablespoon kosher salt
> ¼ teaspoon pepper
> 2½- to 3-pound chicken, cut into 8 pieces
> 2 tablespoons olive oil
> 1½ pounds sunchokes
> 1 medium onion, chopped
> 4 bay leaves
> 1 cup white wine

1. Set oven to 350°F. Mix flour, 1 teaspoon salt, and pepper in a bag. Toss chicken pieces in it to coat evenly. Set a large ovenproof sauté pan or Dutch oven over moderate heat. Add oil and tip to coat pan. Add chicken. Cook until both sides are golden. Transfer to plate.

2. Meanwhile, scrub sunchokes with brush under running water. Cut into 1½-inch pieces, more or less. Over moderate heat, brown in fat remaining in pan—6 to 7 minutes, tossing often. During the last few minutes, add onion and remaining ½ teaspoon salt.

3. Add bay leaves and wine and bring to a boil, stirring and scraping. Boil 2 minutes. Return chicken and accumulated juices to pan. Cover tightly. Bake until chicken is cooked through and chokes are tender but not falling apart, about ½ hour.

4. Serve hot, with pan juices and a bay leaf spooned over each portion.

Serves 4

Sunchoke Pickles

To my taste, sunchoke is one of the few vegetables worth pickling (okra, turnips, beets, cabbage, and rutabaga are others). Since there is no reason to reinvent basics, herewith the recipe from *Uncommon Fruits & Vegetables: A Commonsense Guide,* modified slightly. In this version of a Southern classic, the vegetables have a fresh flavor and crisp texture that I prefer to the searing or syrupy styles typical of "artichoke pickles," as they are called in mail-order catalogues and gift shops.

> 3 pounds sunchokes, as smooth and regularly
>   shaped as possible
> Kosher salt
> 2 small onions, sliced into rings
> 4 or 8 tiny dried chillis
> 2 teaspoons mustard seeds, slightly bruised
> ½ teaspoon celery seeds
> ½ teaspoon anise seeds
> 8 allspice berries
> 2 cups cider vinegar
> 1 cup water
> 1 cup distilled white vinegar
> ⅔ cup light brown sugar
> 4 bay leaves

1. Pare skin from sunchokes. Slice ¼ inch thick. You should have about 2 quarts.

2. Place in ceramic or glass bowl and pour in water to cover generously. Pour off and measure the water. For each quart water, add ¼ cup kosher salt, stirring to dissolve. Add to bowl with sunchokes. Cover and let stand 24 hours.

3. Rinse and drain sunchokes. Blot with towel to dry. Divide sunchokes and onion rings evenly among four scalded, dry pint canning jars.

4. Rinse new two-piece canning lids and drop into scalding-hot water. In non-aluminum pan, combine chillis, mustard seeds, celery seeds, anise seeds, allspice, cider vinegar, water, white vinegar, sugar, 4 teaspoons kosher salt, and bay leaves. Boil 5 minutes. Pour hot solution into jars, being sure each has its fair share of herbs and spices; liquid should come to within ¼ inch of rims.

5. Wipe jar rims, cover with the lids, then fasten screw bands. Place on rack in deep pot half-filled with boiling water. Add boiling water to cover jars by 2 inches. Bring to a boil. Cover pot and boil 15 minutes.

6. With tongs, remove jars and set on towel. Cool 1 day. Store several weeks or more before serving, chilled.

Makes 4 pints

Pros Propose

A look through my cookbooks indicates that a prophet is not without honor, save in his own country. Recipes for sunchokes are more plentiful in Italy and France than the United States.

"It puzzles and saddens me to witness the obscurity to which Jerusalem artichoke, one of the finest of tubers, has been relegated. In America it is used only raw, for salads," writes Marcella Hazan in her quintessential *Marcella Cucina*. Chef Odette Fada, who learned to cook sunchokes from her grandmother and mother in Brescia, brought their simple sautés to the elegant New York restaurant San Domenico. She also devised this delicate **Sunchoke and Mint Sauce** ("mint is always best with topinambur") for braised rabbit: Blanch whole sunchokes, then peel. Slice, then sauté in olive oil with shallots and lots of mint. Add vegetable stock; cook until soft. Puree. Add blanched mint leaves.

Matt Kramer writes in *A Passion for Piedmont* that "Jerusalem artichokes are popular in Piedmont," his adopted land, but relatively unknown in the one in which he—and they—were born. His recipe, a lush variation on the bagna cauda, is a specialty of Maria Pagliasso of Arcigola's restaurant, Boccondivino. To prepare **Topinambur con Crema di Bagna Caôda:** Combine enough milk to cover chokes in a pot with a little lemon juice; boil. Add peeled, thin-sliced chokes; simmer until just cooked, but not soft. Drain. Soak whole, filleted salted anchovies; chop to a paste. Heat olive oil in small heavy saucepan. Add minced garlic; cook 10 minutes without browning. Whisk in anchovies and heavy cream. Cook, whisking, about 15 minutes. Toss chokes with sauce in baking dish. Bake, uncovered, in moderate oven until liquid is reduced and creamy, about 20 minutes.

Another rich dish comes from Fortunato Nicotra, chef at Felidia, in New York City, who has several sunchoke dishes on the menu "because I know them from Italy." For **Jerusalem Artichoke Flan with Fontina Crostini:** Boil chunks of leek and whole Jerusalem artichokes until tender. Drain well; puree. Add whole eggs, grated Parmesan, half-and-half, and seasoning; blend. Pour into individual molds, set in bain marie, and bake at 300°F until set. Unmold. Serve on top of toasted country bread coated with melted fontina d'Aosta.

I didn't know that shad or Jerusalem artichokes were to be had in Morocco until I saw this **Tajine of Shad with Topinambours,** then discovered individual recipes for each. To prepare: Blend olive oil, paprika, crushed garlic, and chopped parsley and coriander in an earthenware casserole. Roll pieces of shad in the mixture to season, leaving seasoning in the dish. Peel and quarter topinambours of equal size; add to dish with a little water. Bake, covered, in a hot oven, until half cooked. Add fish and cook until tender, about 15 minutes more. Add lemon juice (from *Les saveurs et les gestes* by Fatéma Hal).

Chef Amaryll Schwertner, of Hungarian heritage, serves a salad that is without apparent national origins and was developed in San Francisco, California—North America, home of the neglected sunchoke! For **Sunchoke, Celery, and Mint Salad:** Cut celery into fine slices on mandoline. Peel large sunchokes. Shave on mandoline. Soak half briefly in ice water. Combine remainder with celery; salt lightly. Drain, dry, and deep-fry the soaked sunchokes. At once, combine with raw vegetables, olive oil, lemon juice, and slivered peppermint.

French-trained chef Roland Liccioni was surprised to find so few dishes based on sunchokes in the United States. He combines them with another American tuberous root in **Sunchoke and Sweetpotato Gratin:** Rub a shallow baking dish with garlic; butter well. Alternate layers of peeled, thin-sliced sunchokes and orange-fleshed sweetpotato, seasoning as you go. Pour in half-and-half to just barely cover. Bake in a moderate oven, uncovered, until tender.

For Madeleine Kamman, it took a move away from her native France to enjoy topinambours. She recalls, "We ate so many Jerusalem artichokes during the Second World War that I took a dislike to them. When they arrived in the eastern United States from California, I gave them a second try, and much to my amazement, loved them. . . ." (*In Madeleine's Kitchen*). For her non-French-style **Topinambours Sautés:** Cut a large chunk of peeled ginger into tiny dice. Set in a sieve and dip into large pot of boiling salted water for 1 minute. Add lemon juice to the water. Add peeled and julienned sunchokes and blanch 1 minute. Drain, refresh in cold water, drain, and pat dry. Cut scallions into thin diagonals. Toss ginger in sauté pan in corn oil. Add sunchokes and toss over high heat until just barely cooked, about 2 minutes. Season and add scallions.

Southern chef Jeff Buben keeps his popular **Jerusalem Artichoke Cream Soup** on the menu a good part of the year. "I buy from a farm in Colonial Beach, Virginia, where they store the tubers in a hay-covered pit through most of the winter," he says. To prepare: Gently cook sliced leeks, onions, and potatoes with sunchokes (to make up about 75 percent of the mixture) in butter. Add chicken broth and simmer until tender. Puree until smooth. Add cream to taste and gloss with butter. For garnish, glaze mandoline-sliced sunchokes in butter and sugar, turning often until golden; add chopped toasted hazelnuts. Sprinkle over soup.

Sweetpotato (*Ipomoea batatas*)

Including **orange-fleshed, boniato, Oriental,** and **moist white types**

There is a luscious world of sweetpotatoes (yes, one word: see below) out there beyond the orange-fleshed, and that is the first reason for this entry. The second is to implore you to believe that none of them are related to yam (see page 711—*please*) or potato (page 500).

I'll start with the second reason, then get to eating. With Latin, it's easy to explain: *Ipomoea batatas* originated in the New World, then traveled to the Old. So did *Solanum tuberosum,* but later. *Dioscorea,* a genus with Old World and New World members, has no connection to either.

With common names, confusion arises and gross simplifications of complicated facts are necessary. First, there is the mixup between sweetpotato and potato: Columbus introduced the sweetpotato to Europe with a Native American (Taino) name, written variously as "batatas" (also the species name), "patate," and other forms that became the word "potato." "Potato" *meant* sweetpotato in Europe until nearly a half-century later, when what we now call the potato, *Solanum tuberosum* ("papa" in its native Quechuan), landed there—*also as* "potato." By way of distinction, *Ipomoea batatas* became the "sweet potato." (Check "potato" in a few dictionaries, including the *Oxford English Dictionary,* and you'll see that *Ipomoea batatas,* not *Solanum tuberosum,* is still the primary definition some 500 years later.) Now you can understand why classifiers use a single word, sweetpotato: this prevents grouping and mixing with potato.

Then there is the confusion between sweetpotato and yam. This has two parts—one historical, one recent. True yams are species of *Dioscorea,* starchy tuberous roots that do not resemble *Ipomoea batatas* and are rarely sweet. The English word "yam," surmised to be of West African origin, came via a word recorded by Portuguese slave traders, inhame (pronounced eenyam). This word was also used in the American South, but erroneously applied to the sweetpotato.

In the 1930s, promoters of Southern-grown sweets hit on the word "yam" for a campaign to set apart their Louisiana product from drier, paler sweets grown in New Jersey, Maryland, and Virginia. (Ironically, although the misnomer "yam" may have helped at the time, it now adds to the mess because the same varieties are grown nationwide.) In sum: Sweetpotatoes, potatoes, and yams are *not* related, despite the shared common names. If Latin is used, the mixup cannot occur.

Outside the United States and Europe (sweetpotato consumption is minimal in both places), *Ipomoea batatas* is not just a minor addition to a fall festival. It is one of the very few food crops considered "major," that is, one that measures above 100 million metric tons per year. Well above 90 percent of sweetpotatoes are grown in Asia—and these are rarely orange. "The moist, orange-fleshed sweetpotato we grow is an exception favored only here and in Australia," says Stanley J. Kays, a horticultural scientist at the University of Georgia in Athens. "Orange color is linked to pumpkin-like flavor, which Americans like, but others don't." He cites the example of a Chinese grower who, pressed to explain why he didn't plant more American sweetpotatoes, answered: "Because they taste like pumpkins, and we'd grow pumpkins if that's what we wanted!"

Sweetpotatoes defy classification with regard to cooking and eating. Skins may be tissue-thin or as thick as cardboard and tinted beige to purple. The flesh may be marigold or mauve and may cook up smooth and creamy or fluffy and granular. Ivory-fleshed when raw, a steamed sweet may turn golden or gray, and may hold a hint of sugar or be truly syrupy. The taste may suggest pumpkin, chestnuts, or vanilla cookies. But if you like sweetpotatoes, sampling your way through the particulars will be an agreeable assignment. Demand names and take tasting notes so that you can request your favorites at farmers' markets and good groceries.

Having said that sweets cannot be grouped, I am now going to group some, because there is no way to take them on one at a time.

Orange-fleshed sweetpotatoes, such as Beauregard, the primary commercial type, and the smaller-volume Jewel and Garnet pictured, are "traditionals" in North American markets. However cooked, they have

orange-fleshed sweetpotatoes ("traditionals"): Jewel (*left*) and Garnet (*right*)   length: 4½-7 inches

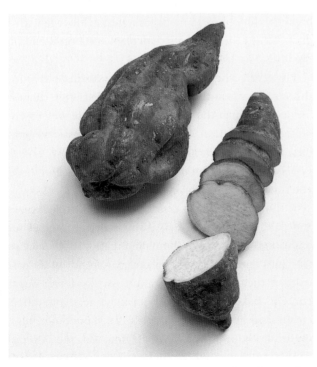

boniato-type sweetpotatoes   length: 8 inches

à soft, sometimes squishy feel in the mouth and a pumpkin flavor. They are always decidedly sweet, but the degree of sweetness "varies with the cultivar, how they are handled after harvest, and the length of time after harvest. As a consequence, sweetness can be quite variable—and a major frustration for consumers," says Stanley Kays. There are also fairly dry orange-fleshed types, but they seem to have all but disappeared from the market.

The sweetpotatoes preferred outside the United States and Canada are white-fleshed and not usually as sweet or soft as those above—but, like them, they are all highly variable. It *is* reasonable to generalize about these burly **boniato** types, which are broadly represented in Latin and Far Eastern markets throughout the United States. A staple in countries from Mexico to Vietnam, they are more versatile than the orange types, fitting as easily as potatoes into savory meals. Aromatic (freshly cut, they suggest violets), less sweet than our orange varieties, they are fluffier and drier—like a blend of "traditional" sweetpotato, chestnut, and a baking potato. They may be rugged and rosy-skinned (as in the photo), or pale and rounded.

Oriental or **Japanese** or **Korean sweetpotatoes** are market catchall terms for various rose-skinned, ivory-fleshed cultivars developed in the Far East. They fall between the drier boniato types and the moist-fleshed whites (discussed below). All those I have tasted have been elegant indeed. Baked, the flesh turns fresh yellow throughout, while the texture is smooth and medium dry (like marrons glacés). The flavor is warm, medium sweet (sweeter than boniato, closer to traditionals). Steamed, the skin slips off neatly, leaving a satiny, creamy cylinder rather like a ripe banana in color and texture and very sweet. It slices sleekly although it feels like puree in the mouth—sweetened chestnut puree. For a side dish, the drier texture of the baked boniato seems more useful.

Pale, moist, soft sweets are generally close to traditionals in texture and sugar but have beige skin and white-to-yellow flesh. They appear erratically at local markets, generally in California, New Jersey, North Carolina, and Virginia. Connoisseurs in North Carolina go out of their way to buy the firm, waxy Nancy Hall with its honey flavor; traditionalists in and around New Jersey seek out the Jersey Yellow and Jersey White. Golden Sweet, Batas, and O'Henry are others that appear in farmers' markets.

The Hayman sweetpotato (pictured) has recently been revived in the Chesapeake Bay area. It is small, unassuming, scruffy, and stodgy. Baked, it develops an overwhelming sweetness but not much flavor or scent. The beige skin is just barely edible; the flesh turns a splotchy yellow-ocher (not "sage" as the literature describes it). Extremely moist—syrupy juice drips from it—the Hayman should please those who like their marshmallows built in. Bake only: Other methods produce a heavy, pasty texture.

Sweetpotato ('uala) was a staple of Hawaii, once cultivated in many forms, but now limited. One variety, Okinawa, known as poni in Hawaii, cooks to a lilac hue and is particularly popular with chefs. Unfortunately, I have not been able to obtain it for sampling.

BASIC USE: For me, there is really just one question: Is the sweetpotato at hand better baked or steamed? A trial is the only way to know. Either way, a sweetpotato makes a rewarding, nutritious snack, breakfast, lunchbox item, or little meal. (I love it with a glass of buttermilk.) More than plain cooking is gilding the lily.

However, others like their sweets embellished. Since this entry is meant to introduce new varieties, there is no need to cover the traditionals, which are well represented in American cookbooks. For all basic vegetables, including this one, go first to *The Victory Garden Cookbook* by Marian Morash, which usually has all you'll need on the subject.

Although I prefer to keep them pure, Oriental types and pale, moist, soft sweets can be used in recipes for traditional sweets. For boniato types, you'll need to take into consideration their comparative dryness, pale color, rather delicate flavor, and usually lower sugar content. Bake, fry, boil, roast, steam, sauté, mash, puree, cream, and combine in custards, flans, puddings, pies, muffins—the works. When frying, do not exceed 325°F; cut them in thick pieces, or they'll burn. When

Oriental-type sweetpotatoes (*top*), length: 6-9 inches
pale, moist Hayman (*bottom*), length: 5-6 inches

boiling, keep them completely immersed in water or the flesh gets spotty. I love the flavor of baked boniato skin, which gets as crusty as a pretzel.

SELECTION: You can't tell a sweetpotato by its cover. Some of the most rich and perfumed wear the dullest coats. If they are solid and dry, try them one and all, pale and gaudy, to find your favorites.

Sweetpotato season begins, not at harvest, but after a curing period of 4 to 8 days to heal splits and firm up skin, and then weeks of storage, "during which the enzymes required for the formation of sugar from starch during cooking are greatly increased," says Stanley Kays. Sweetpotatoes fresh from the field are barely sweet when cooked. Generally speaking, the season starts around mid-November, but properly stored sweets will last into the spring. Heft a few to choose those that are heaviest for their size. Do not buy them from a chilled bin: Refrigeration destroys these tropical tuberous roots.

Boniato, which grows only in the tropical tip of Florida and further south, is picked virtually year-round and is not cured and stored. The thin skin is easily bruised, so the sweetpotato spoils rapidly. Choose rock-hard boniato, checking each root for soft or moldy spots. When grown in pebbly soil, as is Florida's, they develop gnarled forms and blotchy skin, but the flavor is not affected.

STORAGE: Do not stock up on sweets. Buy only what you plan to cook. Store in a basket in a ventilated area, preferably at cool room temperature, for as short a time as possible. Do not refrigerate. Do not enclose in plastic. If sprouts appear, rub them off.

PREPARATION: Scrub well with a brush if you'll be baking them with the skin. For boiling or steaming, simply rinse, then peel after cooking (steamed skin has an unpleasant taste and texture). However sweets are cooked, the question of peeling will depend upon the specific potato. When you peel before cooking, keep them in water to prevent discoloration.

To Cook Sweetpotatoes: The Basics

Most sweetpotato types can be cooked in the following ways. Whichever way you choose, test carefully by piercing with a knife tip to be sure it is completely cooked—creamy-soft—in the very center. Timing is for sweets of about ½ pound apiece.

Steam for the smoothest and creamiest consistency, a rich flesh color, and the shortest cooking time. Quarter scrubbed potatoes, set on a rack; cover and steam over boiling water until very tender, about 20 minutes. Peel. For neat discs, cook potatoes whole, increasing the time. Peel and slice to serve warm, drizzled with butter, lime juice, and a touch of hot pepper sauce; or serve at room temperature with gingered yogurt.

Bake sweetpotatoes in their cleaned skins (no foil, no butter) for deep, concentrated flavor and color, and a firmer, starchier texture. Set scrubbed whole or halved sweets in a pan in a 350° to 400°F oven; bake until very tender in the center, 40 to 50 minutes. (For intense sweetness, according to Stanley Kays, "begin in a cold oven, which maximizes the time for hydrolysis of starch and formation of sugar before the enzymes required to produce sugar are denatured." Increase baking time accordingly.) All baked sweetpotatoes are delicious, but fine boniatos are extra special: The skin bakes crusty-hard and tastes delicious pulled off in chunks, buttered. Because the skin becomes so crunchy, you must test carefully for doneness to be sure the center is creamy-soft.

Boil peeled chunks of boniato and other dryish pale sweets in salted water for gently sweet flavor and texture. (Orange and yellow-fleshed types lose flavor when boiled—unless they are boiled in only a small amount of seasoned liquid to add flavor.) Cook until tender throughout—about 25 minutes. Keep submerged, or the flesh becomes spotty and gray.

Microwave? Never! All sweetpotatoes are compromised if not destroyed by the microwave oven.

Baked Sweetpotato-Apple Puree with Horseradish

A useful, simple-to-make puree that reheats well, thanks to the addition of apple. To complement the fruit's juiciness, use boniato or other relatively dry-fleshed sweets. Figure on 1 medium sweet and 1 apple per person to increase or decrease the recipe. Choose a mix of sweet and tart apples. The hot-sweet bite of fresh horseradish is particularly intriguing, but the puree adapts to other accents with ease: grated fresh ginger, chiles chipotles en adobo, wasabi, lime juice, balsamic vinegar, and umeboshi are among them. For a pretty presentation, pipe the puree through a wide star tube.

> 5 sweetpotatoes of equal size
>   (8 to 10 ounces each)
> 5 medium apples
>   (preferably fairly tart types)
> 10 whole cloves
> 1 to 2 tablespoons butter
> Salt and white pepper
> Grated horseradish, preferably fresh

1. Stab 1 clove into each sweetpotato and each apple. Place all in roasting pan. Set in oven and turn to 400°F. Bake until apples are soft (some will collapse), about 45 minutes, depending upon how long your oven takes to heat. Remove apples and set aside to cool. Continue baking sweets until very soft, around 15 minutes longer.

2. When sweets are finished baking, raise oven temperature to 425°F. Remove apple peels and stems, then take off the sweetpotato skins. Press apples and sweets together through medium disc of food mill. Stir in butter, salt, pepper, and horseradish to taste. Scoop mixture into lightly oiled baking dish.

3. Bake in upper level of oven until slightly browned and bubbling at the edges, 15 to 20 minutes.

Serves 4 to 6 as a side dish

Sweetpotatoes in Curried Coconut Sauce over Kale

Sweetpotatoes make a fine vegetarian main dish, especially complemented by bitter greens. Serve this spicy orange dish with cracked wheat, millet, or quinoa for a complete meal. Pale-fleshed sweets look drab here, so stick with the bright-fleshed varieties. If the dish is made ahead, you may need to thin the sauce, which thickens as it stands.

> 1½ pounds orange-fleshed sweetpotatoes
> 1 or 2 tender celery stalks
> 1 or 2 small fresh green chillis
> 1¾ cups water
> ¾ teaspoon kosher salt
> ½ tablespoon curry powder (preferably hot
>   Madras-style)
> 1 tablespoon minced or coarse-grated ginger
> 1 garlic clove, minced
> ¼ to ¾ cup coconut milk
> 1 pound small, tender curly kale
> Lime wedges

1. Peel sweetpotatoes and cut into ¾-inch dice. Chop enough celery to make ½ cup. Stem chilli, seed, devein (or not, to taste) and mince.

2. Combine chilli, water, salt, curry, ginger, and garlic in a pot and bring to a boil. Add sweets and celery and simmer, covered, until tender, about 15 minutes. Uncover and simmer to thicken sauce somewhat, about 5 minutes. Add ¼ cup coconut milk and cook at a bare simmer about 5 minutes to blend flavors. Taste and add more coconut milk to taste.

3. Meanwhile, strip off and discard kale stems. Thin-slice leaves. Set on a steamer rack over boiling water. Cover and cook until tender, 5 to 10 minutes.

4. Arrange kale on a serving plate and spoon the sweetpotatoes over. Serve hot, garnished with lime.

Serves 4 as a main dish

Roasted Sweets, Fennel, and Onions

Roasting caramelizes the sugary juices in vegetables, bringing sweetness to the surface. Enjoy this hearty dish hot or warm—but not cold, or the sweets will lose their luscious texture. Once the dish is cooked, do not cover, or the vegetables will get mushy. Serve with pork, chicken, or game.

> 3 medium sweetpotatoes (8 to 10 ounces each)
> 2 small-medium fennel bulbs with greens
> 2 large white or red onions
> 3 tablespoons sherry vinegar or red wine
>   vinegar

2 tablespoons full-flavored olive oil
¾ teaspoon kosher salt
½ teaspoon hot pepper sauce

1. Preheat oven to 425°F. Scrub sweets. Peel if skin is pitted or very thick. Quarter and drop into cold water. Bring to a full boil; boil 1 minute. With skimmer, transfer to a lightly oiled large baking dish or roasting pan that will hold all the vegetables closely.

2. Trim off fennel tops and set aside. Quarter bulbs. Drop fennel into the boiling water and return to a boil. Meanwhile, peel and quarter onions. Drain fennel. Arrange with onions in baking dish. Blend vinegar, oil, salt, and hot pepper sauce. Paint vegetables with the mixture to coat evenly, reserving about 1 tablespoon.

3. Set vegetables in oven. Roast until fully tender, about 40 to 60 minutes, turning several times and brushing with the remaining vinegar mixture and pan juices. Meanwhile, chop reserved fennel fronds for garnish, to taste.

4. Serve hot or warm, sprinkled with chopped fennel greens.

Serves 4 as a side dish

Diced Rum-Raisin Sweetpotato Bake

Peeled, cubed, and baked with juice, rum, sweet spices, and raisins or cranberries, sweetpotatoes deserve more than a one-time Thanksgiving appearance. Any type of sweet will work here, but one that turns yellow with baking will have a particularly warm look.

1¼ cups cranberry juice or apple cider
⅓ cup dark rum
2 tablespoons brown sugar
1 tablespoon hazelnut or walnut oil or butter
1 teaspoon kosher salt
½ teaspoon allspice
1 teaspoon ground coriander
¼ teaspoon grated nutmeg
3 pounds sweetpotatoes
⅓ cup raisins or dried cranberries

1. Preheat oven to 375°F. Combine juice, rum, sugar, oil, salt, allspice, coriander, and nutmeg in a small pan. Heat, stirring, until sugar dissolves. Remove from heat.

2. Peel sweets and cut into ¾- to 1-inch cubes. Spread half in lightly oiled 2- to 3-quart casserole. Stir juice mixture and pour half over sweets, then sprinkle with raisins. Spread remaining sweets on top and pour remaining liquid over.

3. Cover tightly. Bake until tender, about 1 hour.

4. Uncover casserole and raise heat to 425°F. Bake, basting several times, until juices are thick and bubbling and top has browned slightly, about ½ hour.

Serves 6 as a side dish

Pros Propose

Although sweetpotatoes are consumed nearly worldwide, there are remarkably few recipes to be found. Outside the United States, they are usually just plain food to be eaten unadorned, boiled or baked, sometimes mashed. In the Caribbean, they may be deep-fried in strips or as chips. If recipes do show up, they are usually for desserts, not vegetable dishes: cakes, pies, flans, and sweet fritters.

A search for recipes—more often than not collected or devised by visiting foreigners—yielded these ports of call.

"I vividly remember the call of the sweet potato man in Taiwan, who used to cruise the alleys of the city in the winter, selling hot baked sweet potatoes," writes Nina Simonds, who followed her calling and developed **Red-Cooked Lamb with Sweet Potatoes:** Sauté smashed ginger slices, sliced garlic, scallion sections, chilli paste, cinnamon sticks, and anise seeds in heavy casserole. Add water, soy sauce, rice wine, and sugar; boil. Add trimmed shoulder lamb cubes; simmer, partially covered, skimming, until just tender. Add sweetpotatoes, peeled and cut the same size as the lamb. Cook, partially covered, until tender. Skim. Remove ginger and cinnamon. Add fresh spinach leaves. Cover and cook just to wilt (from *A Spoonful of Ginger*).

Japan has its hawkers too. "Hot baked sweet potatoes are sold by itinerant peddlars from autumn through spring, and the cry of the sweet potato man is familiar to everyone in Japan," writes Shizuo Tsuji in *Japanese Cooking: A Simple Art*. But for a recipe, it is an outsider, Bettina Vitell, whose Japanese-inspired *The World in a Bowl of Tea* offers **Miso Soup with Sweet Potatoes:** Cut sweets into slices 1½ inches thick. Boil until cooked but still firm; drain. Peel and trim to form diamond shapes. Blend sweet white miso with a touch of red miso in food processor until smooth. Gradually add unseasoned dashi (reserve some). Strain several times through a fine sieve. Heat without simmering. Blend dry mustard with some soup to make a paste; let rest 10 minutes. To serve, thin with more soup. Heat reserved dashi and pour over sweets to warm. Arrange slices in bowls. Pour in soup to come to "shoulder" of sweets. Drop a bit of mustard on top.

From Vietnam, **Crunchy Sweet Potato Nests with Shrimp:** Pound chopped red chilli and sugar to a paste. Add peeled, sectioned limes and pound to blend. Add lime juice and fish sauce; pound to coarse puree. Cut sweetpotatoes into long julienne. Rinse and squeeze dry. Toss with flour. Sprinkle peeled, deveined, and butterflied shrimp with flour. Heat oil for shallow-frying. For each nest, press a handful of sweetpotato shreds into palm of your hand to form a 2-inch-wide oval. Center a shrimp on it and press so it adheres. Fry a few at a time until brown. Flip, press against skillet bottom, and cook until crisp; drain. Serve with lettuce leaves and the chilli sauce (from *Simple Art of Vietnamese Cooking* by Binh Duong and Marcia Kiesel).

"The New Zealand kumara is a purple-skinned and cream-fleshed sweet potato. The flavour is less sweet than many others, which makes it suitable for both savoury and sweet combinations," writes Tui Flower, editor of *New Zealand the Beautiful Cookbook*. The kumara (from the ancient Peruvian kumar—a fascinating etymological trail) looks, tastes, and cooks like the boniato pictured on page 639. To prepare **Orange Kumara:** Boil large boniato in salted water until tender. Cool, peel, and slice thin. Arrange in buttered casserole, overlapping slices with peeled orange rounds. Mix softened butter, brown sugar, a little cornstarch, and salt, then blend in orange juice. Pour over sweets and sprinkle with chopped peanuts. Bake until bubbling.

Brazil is the source of what Elisabeth Lambert Ortiz describes as "one of the most delicious soups I have ever had, whether as *sopa de camote* in Spanish-speaking Latin America or as *sopa de batata doce* in Brazil": Combine peeled, thick-sliced boniato with cold salted water to cover. Boil; reduce heat, and simmer, covered, until tender. Drain and chop. Gently cook onion in butter. Add peeled, seeded, and chopped tomatoes and cook 5 minutes. Puree in food processor with boniato and beef stock until smooth. Pour into pan, and add stock to taste. Heat and season.

For a richer, fancier soup, chef Douglas Rodriguez translates his Cuban heritage into **Sopa de Boniato Frío:** Gently cook onion in oil until translucent. Add diced fresh ginger, peeled and cubed boniato, and chicken or vegetable stock. Simmer until tender. Add mace; cool an hour or so. Puree. Add chilled heavy cream and season. Cover and refrigerate. Deep-fry peeled, thin-sliced long boniato strips. Drain and sprinkle with salt and cumin. Serve with soup (from *Latin Ladles*).

The New Southern Cook by John Martin Taylor treats sweets to a savory finish, rather than the usual "bath of butter and sugar." **Sweet Potatoes with Horseradish,** inspired by chef Frank Lee in Charleston, is Taylor's favorite recipe in this book, and a luscious way to wind up the sweet tour: Peel small slender sweets and slice into ¼-inch discs. Toss with grated fresh horseradish and heavy cream to coat evenly. Scoop into a baking dish, cover with foil, and bake at 400°F until slightly soft, 30 to 45 minutes. Serve at once.

Swiss Chard (*Beta vulgaris,* Cicla Group)

Also chard, spinach beet, leaf beet

Including **rainbow (multicolor) chard**

As of this sentence, I will no longer add "Swiss" to chard. After 25 years of futile probing I can find no significant reason to keep it. Even an international authority on *Beta,* Dr. Brian Ford-Lloyd of the School of Biosciences at the University of Birmingham, could offer no more explanation than that "there is a Swiss national collection of leaf beet [and chard] genetic resources, which I assume means that the crop is of some importance to the Swiss." He also located a mention in *Transactions of the Horticultural Society* for 1822 that a variety planted that year had been grown "from seeds presented by Sir Samuel Young. . . . He found it used as a vegetable on the Banks of the Rhine, and in Switzerland, and has . . . cultivated it very much this season; he speaks highly of its merit." Interesting, but hardly enough to justify "Swiss" chard.

"Chard," from the Latin and French words for thistle—which chard isn't, but cardoon is (see page 143)—will now stand alone. Carde or chard came to mean the stalk or rib of some vegetables, such as chard and cardoon (in French books one still sees warnings not to confuse the two—*cardes* and *cardons,* respectively). *Beta vulgaris* is the common beet, which becomes chard with the appending of Cicla, from *sicula,* referring to both Sicily and a beet variety grown there—in all likelihood chard, the cultivation of which was known in ancient Rome and Greece and probably earlier in the Arab world.

The Swiss mystery is not the only one. Why do Americans prefer the leaves to the stems of chard—if they eat chard at all? At markets in the United States you'll find leaves displayed with stems as skinny as bok

chards: red-stalked, white-stalked, multicolor   length:14-19 inches

choy or hacked off completely. When I checked my library for recipes, American books selected at random called for "Swiss chard with the stems removed" or "stems discarded."

At a vegetable market in Europe you'll find chard with long flat stalks from 3 to 6 inches wide. In 1693, Joannes de la Quintinye (*The Compleat Gard'ner*) observed that "Chard-Beets . . . in the middle have a large, white, and thick . . . Main shoot [that] is the true Chard used in Pottages." Six years later, John Evelyn wrote in *Acetaria: A Discourse of Sallets* that "the Costa, or Rib of the White Beet (by the French call'd the Chard), being boil'd, melts, and eats like Marrow." In 1832, the anonymous author of *Vegetable substances used for the food of man* wrote that "the footstalks and the midribs of the leaves . . . are stewed and eaten under the name of Swiss chard." In 1977, Richard Olney commented that "outside of meridional France, where they are an indispensable element in most stuffings, in many gratins, and in occasional soups, the green leafy parts . . . are usually fed to the rabbits and the ducks" (*Simple French Food*).

I suggest that you eat the mellow stems and the earthy robust leaves both separately and together, for they are a naturally complementary pair. In Portugal and Spain, they are sautéed together in heady olive oil intensified with garlic, and, in Catalunya, further enriched with pine nuts and raisins. In Italy, both parts are layered with beans, tomatoes, and olive oil and baked until tender. In Greece they are stewed with leeks and dill. Cinnamon, cumin, paprika, and hot peppers embellish leaves and stalks throughout the Middle East. In France—primarily Provence and particularly Nice, chard's culinary capital—both succulent stem and leaf are incorporated into daily fare as regularly as spinach in the United States. The pale, broad stalks are simmered in fragrant bouillon that is then thickened and seasoned with pounded garlic and anchovies and presented alone, to star in the way that asparagus do. Or they are bathed in sauce and browned in a gratin. Leaves are folded into terrines, omelets, and soups, pureed in gnocchi, wrapped around pork patties, and even made into a dessert pie.

Rainbow chard, as it is often called in the market, is a multicolor bouquet of chartreuse, candy pink, sunny orange, magenta, cherry, yellow, and white stems with green leaves. It is no "designer" vegetable but a venerable one. In *Sturtevant's Edible Plants of the World* the author comments, "Red chard was noticed by Aristotle about 350 B.C., Theophrastus knew two kinds—the white, called *Sicula,* and the black (or dark green). . . . In 1596, Bauhin describes dark, red, white, yellow, chards with a broad stalk" (the *Phytopinax*). Fearing Burr, in *The Field and Garden Vegetables of America* (1865 edition), includes five types of leaf beets, with green, white, purplish-red, and bright yellow stalks.

Sharon Kaszan, a trials manager at the W. Atlee Burpee company in Warminster, Pennsylvania, explains that the chard now being revived was lost to commerce because it was less productive than white- and red-stemmed types. "But in every field, yellow, orange, and pinky chard comes up. By picking the strong examples, planting and replanting, growers collected enough to make predictable seed in other colors."

The collection we're seeing now started in New Zealand, according to Rob Johnston, Jr., founder of Johnny's Selected Seeds in Albion, Maine. The strains selected by an amateur grower, John Eaton, were bundled into a cultivar called Bright Lights, which in 1998 won a gold medal from All-America Selections, sending it to the top of home gardening charts, then into commercial production. Johnny's maintains and improves the different color stocks at farms in Washington and Oregon and distributes the seed.

BASIC USE: Tiny white or ruby chard leaves contribute color, texture, and earthy flavor to mixed salads—in moderation. But the mature silvery-stalked varieties, relatively mild and earthy, bittersweet, with a suggestion of artichoke hearts, are most widely available. It is best to cook stems until nearly done, then add leaves and continue cooking—whether by steaming, sauté-braising, or boiling (not microwaving). For small to medium chard, steaming and sauté-braising produce fullest flavor. For larger chard, boil in salted water and lemon juice. Serve chard alone or with other vegetables—hot, at room temperature, or chilled, with a squeeze of lemon or balsamic vinegar and a touch of oil.

Chard stalks are particularly nice pickled, or slow-cooked, à la grecque. Or nap with cream or cheese sauce and bake until bubbling.

Incorporate blanched, sliced chard into vegetable or meat stuffings, or into grain dishes. Combine cooked chard with pasta, or stuff into tortelli or calzone. Line a dish with blanched leaves to form "pastry" for a filling of cooked stems and grains or beans or pasta with a custard binding. Enclose blanched and chopped chard stems with stuffing of grain and/or meat in large blanched chard leaves (which are more succulent and easier to handle than grape leaves). Stir thin-sliced leaves and stems into light soup for the last 10 minutes of cooking; for sturdy soup, cook all ingredients together.

For the leaves alone, recipes that work for spinach work for chard, provided that the cooking time is increased. Garlic, onion, smoked meat, olives, raisins, sweet spices, anchovies, mustard, hot pepper, vinegar, lemon juice, and olive oil make good companions.

SELECTION: Although erratically available year-round, chard is in best supply from spring into winter; the high season is June through October. Select wide-stalked bunches with firm, bright leaves. They should not be soggy or yellowed. If produce handlers trim off the stalks, *tell* them that you want to eat them!

If chard has a relatively high proportion of stems, the cooked yield will be larger than if leaves dominate, as stems diminish only slightly but leaves shrink dramatically. Gauge accordingly.

STORAGE: Chard and other leafy vegetables are adversely affected by ethylene gas, which causes a loss of chlorophyll and protein and may hasten drying and decay. Do not store near climacteric fruits (ones which continue to ripen and emit ethylene after harvest) such as apples, avocado, banana, pears, plums, and most tropical fruits.

Wrapped in perforated plastic and kept in the coolest part of the refrigerator, chard will remain fresh for 2 or 3 days at most. Stalks separated from leaves keep a few days more.

PREPARATION: Remove any dried, slippery, or yellow leaves. Dunk chard in a sink filled with tepid water and swish around. Lift out gently so debris sinks. Repeat until clean. Unless chard is baby-size, slice leaves from stalks by running a knife along the stalk held with the curled edges of the leaf upturned. Or snip with scissors to neatly trim the fine upper midrib. If stalks are unusually heavy, zip off "strings" as you would from celery. If stalks are wider than 1 inch (which is desirable), halve lengthwise. Trim bases, then slice to suit the recipe.

Wide-stemmed European chard is traditionally cooked *à blanc* (see Cardoon, Preparation, page 144) to preserve its pallor.

Steamed Chard with Candied Citrus Zest

Snippets of candied peel make a sweetly surprising counterpoint to earthy chard. If you're in a hurry, simply steam the chard, season, and toss with the juices, some grated zest, and oil for a no-frills route that's still a treat. Add minced crystallized ginger, if handy.

1 lemon
1 orange
¼ cup sugar
1 cup water
About 2 pounds chard (any color)
Salt and pepper
2 tablespoons full-flavored olive oil
Lemon juice to taste

1. With a citrus stripper or channel knife, shave thin strips from half the lemon and half the orange; cut into ½- to 1-inch lengths. (Alternatively, remove zest with peeler or knife, then cut into fine julienne.) Drop into small heavy pot of boiling water; drain. Repeat twice more. Combine sugar and 1 cup water in the same pot and bring to a boil. Add zest, reduce heat, and simmer until it is tender and syrup thickens, 10 to 15 minutes. With fork, transfer zest to sheet of foil or waxed paper. Halve and squeeze the lemon. Add juice to syrup; reserve.

2. Follow directions under Preparation for washing and trimming chard. Slice chard stems into ½-inch diagonals (if wider than 1 inch, first halve lengthwise).

3. Arrange stems on steamer rack over boiling water. Cover and cook until tender, about 15 minutes (check often—timing varies). Slice leaves. Add and steam until tender, 5 to 10 minutes.

4. Transfer chard to serving dish. Gradually add lemon syrup to taste, tossing. Add salt and pepper, oil, and additional lemon juice. Serve warm or at room temperature, sprinkled with the zest.

Serves 4

Rainbow Chard, Plain and Simple

"Rainbow" chard, a market name for multicolor cultivars, can be used in any recipe calling for chard, but this one is designed particularly to display the bright stem pieces in their forest of deep green, fleshy leaves. The many hues, which lighten when cooked (yellows and pinks, in particular), hold color better steamed than cooked other ways. Serve at room temperature or chilled. Toss leaves with lemon juice at serving time, not before, or they will turn drab.

> 1 pound multicolor chard
> About 1 tablespoon olive oil
> Lemon wedges
> Optional: Salt and pepper

1. Follow directions under Preparation for washing and trimming chard. Slice stems on an angle into ¾-inch lengths.

2. Arrange stems on steamer rack over boiling water. Cover and cook until tender, checking often: Do not overcook, as color pales with cooking. Remove when just done to taste, usually about 15 minutes. Toss with olive oil to taste. Arrange in center of serving platter.

3. Coarsely slice leaves and place in steamer. Cook until velvety, 5 to 10 minutes. Toss with olive oil. Arrange around stems. Chill or leave at room temperature.

4. To serve, sprinkle with a little lemon juice. Season, if desired. Serve with additional lemon wedges.

Serves 2

Braised Ruby Chard with Middle Eastern Savors

Old World lemon, olives, pine nuts, and capers (plus a touch of the New—chillis) play up darkly handsome greens and their stunning stems, which turn orange-burgundy. Or substitute white-stemmed chard for an equally tasty but less striking presentation.

> About 2 pounds red-stemmed chard
> 2 cups water

> 2 tablespoons lemon juice
> 2 tablespoons olive oil
> 1 tablespoon capers
> 1 tablespoon chopped garlic
> ¼ cup raisins or currants
> ¼ cup pitted, sliced Greek olives (preferably Kalamata)
> ¼ teaspoon chilli flakes
> Salt and pepper
> 2 tablespoons toasted pine nuts

1. Follow directions under Preparation for washing and trimming chard. Cut stems into 1-inch slices. Cut leaves into rough slices.

2. Combine stems, water, lemon juice, and 1 tablespoon oil in large non-aluminum skillet. Simmer, covered, until half-cooked, about 8 minutes. Add capers and half the garlic. Cover and simmer until stems are very tender—usually 5 to 10 minutes longer, but timing varies.

3. With slotted spoon, transfer stems to serving dish and toss with ½ tablespoon oil. Arrange in center of dish.

4. Add leaves to pan, with remaining ½ tablespoon oil, remaining garlic, raisins, olives, and chilli. Simmer, covered, until leaves wilt, about 2 minutes. Uncover and simmer, stirring often, until tender—about 10 minutes. Raise heat to evaporate most liquid. Season.

5. Arrange leaves around stems. Serve warm or at room temperature, sprinkled with nuts.

Serves 4

Chard in Savory Provençal Sauce

Earthy, complex, and balanced, this dish blends multiple seasonings to a mellow, mysterious whole (few recognize the anchovies, which provide a salty edge and meaty richness—but not fishiness). To soften and flavor the stems, they are first braised in flavored bouillon; then the leaves are simply set on top to steam through. If you do not have Ricard, Pernod, or another pastis, substitute ¼ cup dry vermouth and double the amount of fennel seeds. Serve at room temperature as part of a buffet or as a post-pasta "salad" course.

> 2 pounds chard (preferably wide-stemmed)
> 1½ cups vegetable broth (preferably unsalted)
> 2 tablespoons Ricard, Pernod, or other pastis
> ¼ teaspoon kosher salt (omit if broth is salted)
> ½ teaspoon dried thyme
> ¼ teaspoon fennel seeds
> 2 tablespoons olive oil
> 3 garlic cloves
> 3 oil-packed anchovy fillets
> 1 tablespoon capers
> Pepper

1. Follow directions under Preparation for washing and trimming chard. Cut stems diagonally into 1½-inch slices.

2. In sauté pan or wide casserole large enough to hold all ingredients, combine broth, Ricard, salt, thyme, fennel, and olive oil. Slice 2 garlic cloves, add, and bring to a boil. Add stems, cover, and simmer until not quite tender, about 10 minutes (check often).

3. Meanwhile, stack leaves and cut into strips ½ inch wide and 2 to 4 inches long. Raise heat to moderate and spread leaves over stems, tamping down. Cover tightly and steam until tender, redistributing leaves halfway through to cook evenly. Timing varies, but 5 to 10 minutes is usual.

4. Meanwhile, in mortar or suribachi, crush remaining garlic clove with anchovies and capers (alternatively, mince in blender or mini-chopper). Scoop about ½ cup liquid from pan, add to seasoning mixture, and crush or process to blend. Stir into pan and simmer to blend flavors. Adjust seasoning. Serve hot or at room temperature.

Serves 4

Pros Propose

Italy, France, Greece—and New Mexico—are just a few of the places where chard has put down roots. In Italy, it is used widely: in thick soup, pureed in gnocchi, stuffed into tortellini or ravioli, stewed with squid and red wine and tomatoes (calamari in zimino), mixed with eggs and cheese for torta, and in a homey smoosh of soft-cooked **Chard and Potatoes:** Strip leaves from stems; cut stems into ½-inch slices. Halve leaves lengthwise, then cut ½-inch strips. Boil peeled, quartered baking potatoes in salted water for 10 minutes. Add chard stems and leaves; cook until stems and potatoes are soft. Drain. Cook crushed garlic cloves in olive oil until they begin to color. Add the cooked vegetables; stir and crush until liquid evaporates and potatoes are coarsely mashed. Add olive oil, salt, and pepper (from *Lidia's Italian Table* by Lidia Matticchio Bastianich).

Chard leaves act as wrappers in France. In *Roger Vergé's Vegetables in the French Style,* the author laments: "I hate seeing people throw away the green leaves of Swiss chard—as they often do in France, where the broad fleshy stalks are often used on their own" (quite the opposite of what is done in the United States). He uses both in **Stuffed Swiss Chard,** a French take on the Middle Eastern classic: Run a knife along the stalks, separating green and white. Boil sliced stalks in *à blanc* solution until tender; drain and chop. Sauté in olive oil for 5 minutes. Combine with soaked and drained currants, pine nuts, parboiled rice, minced and sautéed onion, and seasoning. Form stuffing into little balls. Wrap each in chard leaf (I'd blanch the leaves first). Arrange closely in baking dish. Sprinkle with olive oil; add a little water. Bake in low oven 35 minutes. Serve hot, sprinkled with pine nuts and raisins.

A deceptively simple combination from Alsatian-born chef Jean Joho is **Chard Stems and Truffles,** in which "each brings out the essence of the other—bittersweet and earthy, soft and slightly crunchy—a fine pair," he says. To prepare: Cook white chard stems in the traditional *à blanc* liquid, then drain and slice. To serve, heat stems in butter, add diced raw black truffles, and toss to heat.

Another simple (but not luxurious) preparation, **Warm Black-Eyed Peas and Swiss Chard Salad** comes from Cypriot chef, Marios Mourtzis, via author Aglaia Kremezi. She writes that she was surprised by the exceptional taste of such a simple dish, by "the clear taste of the chard against the sweet, meaty beans, accented by the sourness of the lemon and fruitiness of the raw olive oil." To prepare: Combine rinsed, picked-over black-eyed peas with water to cover. Boil, cook 5 minutes, and drain. Add fresh water and simmer, covered, until peas are tender, adding water as needed. Add chopped chard stems and salt; simmer 4 minutes. Add leaves cut into 1-inch-wide strips and cook until wilted. Add lemon juice. Drizzle with olive oil and pepper. Serve warm, sprinkled with chopped fresh oregano (from *The Foods of the Greek Islands*).

New Mexico Chard Enchiladas "is an adaptation of the enchiladas I grew up eating in northern New Mexico, where we layer instead of roll our enchiladas," writes Cecilia Rosacker-McCord, who notes that "they're especially delicious with blue-corn tor-

tillas" and authentically New Mexican with fried egg on top. To prepare: Whiz together in food processor chopped tomatoes, garlic, onion, and stemmed, seeded dried New Mexico chillis with enough hot water to make a liquid paste. Sauté chopped onion and garlic in oil. Add chopped chard; cook to wilt. Add tomato mixture and cook until thickened, about 10 minutes. Place tortillas—not overlapping—on jelly roll pan. Cover each with sauce, then sprinkle with grated Jack cheese; continue to make 3 layers, ending with cheese. Bake in 350°F oven until cheese is melted (from *The Gardeners' Community Cookbook,* compiled and edited by Victoria Wise).

Tamarillo, Tree Tomato

(*Solanum betaceum*, formerly *Cyphomandra betacea*)

Also tomate de árbol (Latin American)

½ **actual size**

Imagine that you're tasting baba ghannouj, moussaka, or ratatouille for the first time. You're curious to know more about the main ingredient. The cook brings out a glossy midnight-violet oblong capped with an exotic calyx. How pleasantly surprising that these smooshy dishes come from this sleek beauty!

Imagine the sequence in reverse, and you'll have the tip of the tamarillo problem. Glimpsed in a specialty grocer's basket—or the photo here—the polished surface glows, begging to be bitten into. But tamarillo's peel is more like that of an eggplant (a close relative) than a plum. And symmetry and beauty must be for-

gotten if one is to enjoy the fruit, which is best when pureed. Think of sharp salsa instead of fresh fruit, and you'll be on the right garden path—to the kitchen, to cook it or otherwise prepare it for eating.

Perhaps if tamarillo went by its native "tomato" names rather than an international marketing term, people's expectations would be more realistic. While there are many local variations, nearly all include the word *tomate*. "Although its place of origin is not certain, the tree tomato is generally believed to be native to the Andes of Peru and probably also Chile, Ecuador and Bolivia where it is extensively grown, as it is also in

Argentina, Brazil and Colombia," Julia Morton writes in *Fruits of Warm Climates.* "It must have been carried at an early date to East Africa, Asia, and the East Indies . . . and was popular in Ceylon and the Dutch East Indies before 1903." Subsequently, it has been planted in a large part of the subtropics.

But the major development "as a commercial crop has taken place in New Zealand, where it has become a thriving industry," writes C. A. Schroeder, a professor emeritus of botany at the University of California. " 'Tamarillo' was adopted on January 31, 1963 by the growers of New Zealand as the official common trade name," and was the name under which the fruit arrived in the United States.

Despite its popularity in the Antilles and Central and South America, tamarillo remains a rarity in the United States. Latin Americans and Asians familiar with the fruit from their home countries do not seem inclined to pay the prices necessitated by a trip from New Zealand. People not familiar with it are often baffled by this curious golden- to scarlet-skinned fruit that is at once sour and sweet, fruity and vegetably, dense and juicy. It is decidedly odd.

BASIC USE: Although it has the unusual distinction of working equally well in savories and sweets (which are not included in this book), tamarillo is not a very versatile fruit. For savory dishes, it is generally pureed or chopped—which means that it works in salsas, sauces, soups, and chutneys. Tamarillo looks elegant but is more sturdy than subtle in application. Think of a very meaty, dense tomato, less juicy, with a little bit of eggplant texture and plum flavor, and you'll be close to tree tomato.

Tamarillo is usually best cooked, lightly or long, with plenty of spicing and/or acid. The mellower yellow variety can be good raw, however, as sauce or relish. Or it can be peeled, sliced, lightly sugared, and baked to accompany meat or game.

No matter what you are preparing, tamarillos require sugar and tartness of some kind. Uncooked, they'll need a heavier dose of both.

SELECTION: Tamarillo is erratically available from spring to late fall, almost exclusively from New Zealand. Unfortunately, the golden fruits, which are milder and easier to use, are less widely available—thanks to America's love affair with red. Select smooth, full fruits with no sign of wrinkling at the stem end. If necessary,

let them ripen at room temperature until they yield slightly to gentle pressure and become fragrant. If the stems are green, indicating freshness, the fruit can be stored as long as 3 weeks in the refrigerator. For shorter storage, keep at room temperature.

I have yet to find another fruit or vegetable that freezes as easily and successfully as tamarillo. If you can find it at a good price, buy some for freezing: Enclose the whole fruits with stems in zipper-lock bags and freeze—that's it. I inadvertently left a half-dozen for two years (!!) and they were almost as good as new. If you prefer, they can be peeled, wrapped, and frozen or pureed, seeded, and frozen.

PREPARATION: Tamarillo must be peeled, whether it will be used raw or cooked. I find flame-peeling (even straight from the freezer) simple and tasty. Set fruit directly in flame, turning as needed until it splits and bubbles, a minute or so. For a large quantity, arrange close to broiler on foil-covered pan; broil until blistered and split, turning once. Or pour a kettle of boiling water over a bowlful and let stand for a minute. Drain, then peel from the stem end. To cook the fruit at the same time, simmer 5 minutes, then cool and peel. For just a fruit or two, a swivel peeler works fine. When you prepare red fruits, beware of indelible purple stains. Many fruit must also be pitted, which means being pressed through a food mill. Taste to decide if the seeds are tolerable or not.

Shrimp Cebiche with Golden Tamarillo

If you try just one tamarillo recipe in your life, make it this one from Maricel Presilla, author of a forthcoming book on the foods of Latin America, from which the following is adapted. She developed this "ultimate shrimp cocktail" from one she discovered in the Ecuadorian highlands and now serves in her enchanting restaurant, Zafra, in Hoboken, New Jersey. Tart, fruity yellow tamarillo puree accented with citrus, garlic, chilli, onion, and cilantro envelops shrimp for a cebiche (or seviche or ceviche) unlike any you're likely to have tasted.

Sour or bitter orange, ubiquitous in Caribbean cooking, is found in Latin American markets, particularly Cuban ones, where it is on hand most of the year. If it is not available, other citrus substitutes will do.

To prepare the dish in advance: Cook the shrimp, puree the tamarillo, and prepare the juice, chilli, and onion; then refrigerate the components. Allow to reach room temperature before combining and serving. Although not as lush, the cebiche also tastes good chilled, Yellow tomate de árbol is traditional, but red types suffice.

1 medium red onion
5 cups water
3 teaspoons kosher salt
1 small bunch cilantro (coriander)
1 pound medium shrimp in the shell
     (about 40 shrimp)
5 golden tamarillos (about 1 pound)
½ cup sour (bitter) orange juice or ¼ cup each
     lime and orange juice
2 garlic cloves, minced (or more,
     to be authentic)
Optional: 1 Jalapeño chilli, seeded and minced

1. Cut onion into fine julienne. Combine with heavily salted warm water to cover. Let stand about 10 minutes or so. Drain. Rinse with cold water; set aside.

2. Meanwhile, combine 5 cups water, 2 teaspoons salt, and 3 cilantro branches in a medium saucepan; cover, and bring to a boil. Add shrimp; cook just 1 minute. Drain shrimp. Cool, peel, and devein. Strip leaves from remaining cilantro and mince enough to yield ¼ cup.

3. Drop tamarillos into boiling water. Simmer 5 minutes. Drain and transfer to cutting board. When cool enough to handle, remove and discard stems and peels. Place fruit in blender or food processor and whiz to puree. Press through medium-mesh sieve into a bowl (you should have about 1 cup puree.)

4. Add onion, orange juice, garlic, optional chilli, minced cilantro, and remaining 1 teaspoon salt and stir to blend. Add shrimp.

5. Serve at room temperature, in small bowls. (At the restaurant, toasted huge corn kernels are served alongside.)

Serves 4 to 6 as a first course

Iced Tamarillo Soup

Tart and cooling, this silky sunset soup begins a summery meal in striking style. You can use any tamarillo, but the red-orange ones add a hot pink tinge to the predominant butterscotch-orange. The squash acts as thickener, sweetener, and smoother for the tart tree tomato and produces a mysterious blend that teeters between fruit and vegetable. Don't ignore the yogurt-spice garnish, which pulls everything together.

About 1 pound red tamarillos (5 to 6)
2 tablespoons olive oil
2 medium onions, thin-sliced
½ teaspoon anise or fennel seeds
½ small Butternut or Buttercup
     squash (about 1 pound)
4 cups light vegetable broth
1 tablespoon cider vinegar
1 teaspoon kosher salt (omit if broth is salted)
1 tablespoon honey
1 tablespoon water
1 cup yogurt
Nutmeg
Ground hot pepper

1. Cover broiler pan with foil, then arrange tamarillos on it. Set close to heating element. Broil, turning once, until skins blacken slightly and crack, 5 to 10 minutes, depending upon the broiler. Set aside to cool.

2. Meanwhile, warm oil in saucepan over moderate heat. Add onions and anise and cook to soften onions slightly. While onions cook, peel and seed squash. Cut into thin slices. Add to onions.

3. Stem and peel tamarillos. Slice, then add to pot, with broth, vinegar, and salt. Simmer, covered, until very soft, about 25 minutes. Cool slightly.

4. Puree soup with immersion blender, or transfer to food processor or blender and puree. Press through medium-mesh sieve to remove seeds. Cool and chill.

5. To serve: Blend honey and water; stir into yogurt to liquefy. Taste and adjust sweetness. Ladle soup into bowls. Spoon 3 or 4 puddles of yogurt onto each serving. Drag a fork through the puddles to marble prettily. Grate nutmeg over each, then flick over a tiny bit of hot pepper. Serve cold.

Serves 4 as a first course

Tart-Hot Tamarillo Sauce

For a quick, thick, spoonable condiment, puree peeled tamarillos with a few herbs and seasonings. I like mint as primary flavoring, but find I am in the minority with this aromatic—unless the tasters are Middle Eastern. For variation, substitute lemon and orange for lime juice and add fresh ginger. Serve with baked or grilled fish or poultry or with starchy tubers. Stir into thick soups—such as potato, bean, yautía (page 722), or seafood chowder. Spoon over avocado slices.

> 2 tablespoons fine-diced white
>   or red onion
> 2 teaspoons kosher salt
> 2 or 3 small fresh chillis (to taste)
> 1 pound tamarillos (preferably golden or
>   primarily golden)
> About ¼ cup tightly packed sliced mint,
>   cilantro, or basil leaves
> ½ tablespoon minced garlic
> 1 to 1½ teaspoons honey
> 2 to 3 tablespoons lime juice

1. Combine onion and salt in bowl with hot water to cover generously. Remove stems, seeds, and veins from chillis and slice thin.

2. Pour boiling water over tamarillos and let stand 1 minute. Drain, then remove stems and peels, taking care not to pull off flesh. Press fruit through medium disc of food mill.

3. Combine chillis, ¼ cup mint, and garlic in food processor and mince fine, scraping down side. Add pureed tamarillos. Stir ½ teaspoon honey into 2 tablespoons lime juice. Add, then puree mixture. Transfer to a serving dish.

4. Drain onion in sieve, pressing out liquid. Stir onion into puree. Taste for salt, honey, lime, and mint. Chill, covered, for several hours, or up to 2 days.

Makes about 1½ cups

Pros Propose

There is little to add here. In South America, the tree tomato figures primarily in the types of salsa and sauce recipes already supplied and in syrup, for dessert. New Zealand and Britain focus almost exclusively on sweets: desserts, jams, and sweet sauces. An exception is tart-sweet condiments, such as **Spiced Tamarillos:** Drop tamarillos into boiling water. Let stand 2 minutes, then drain, peel, and halve. Combine white vinegar, sugar, whole cloves, cinnamon stick, and grated lemon zest in saucepan. Boil to dissolve sugar. Add tamarillos and simmer 10 minutes. Pack fruit into jars, pour over vinegar mixture, and chill. Serve with cold meat (from *New Zealand the Beautiful Cookbook,* edited by Tui Flower).

From the same source comes a quick heated sauce to serve over pork chops—as you might fresh apple compote. For **Tamarillo Sauce:** Peel tamarillos as above; thin-slice. Soften minced onion and minced green pepper in oil. Add a little water, brown sugar, and the sliced fruit. Simmer gently 10 minutes. Season and serve hot.

New Zealand food authority Annabel Langbein developed a very different **Tamarillo Hollandaise** to serve with poached or broiled fish, or plain-cooked vegetables. Unusual, and swift to assemble, the soft sauce is made mysterious—and pink—with tamarillo. To prepare: Combine egg yolks, lemon juice, and salt in food processor container. Heat butter over low heat until bubbling but not browned. With processor running, slowly add hot butter. Once incorporated and thick, scrape down side and add peeled, chopped red tamarillo. Process until smooth and pink. (If seeds are large, as is often the case, press tamarillo through coarse sieve before adding.)

Taro, Dasheen, Eddo *(Colocasia esculenta)*

Also cocoyam or old cocoyam, coco, eddoes, colocasia, malanga and malanga isleña (Latin American), satoimo (Japanese), woo tau (Chinese), gabi (Philippine), arbi or arvi and patra (Indian)
TARO LEAVES, page 660

Is it possible to summarize briefly the significance of an Old World plant that has been a staff of life in warm, humid regions worldwide? A plant that has probably been cultivated for 10,000 years—longer than wheat or barley? A food so common that it has hundreds of current names (including some of the American market names selected above)? No, I'm sad to say. Moreover, although the Food and Agriculture Organization of the United Nations lists 44 countries that grew taro in 1999, and the University of Hawaii lists 85 present cultivars, when it comes to mainland North America taro is just another "ethnic vegetable."

Here is the restricted version for the mainland United States: New Americans from the tropics (for the most part), have brought with them a taste for two basic types of taro. One, most often called taro or dasheen (see left and top of photo), is represented by large, barrel-shaped, often shaggy, ringed and ridged corms (not roots). Their exceptionally dense flesh (rather like coconut compressed with potato) may be white, cream, lilac-gray, pinkish, or marbled or speckled with chocolate fibers. The cooked flavor and texture, too, are reminiscent of coconut and potato, with a nice dose of chestnut—dry and sweet.

The second type is represented by the little cormels pictured on the lower right, often called eddoes or Chinese taro (and sometimes designated as a subspecies or variety, *antiquorum*). These are variously shaped like tops, kidneys, and crescents, some sprouting nipple-like pink tips (these are called red-budded taro). Cooked, they are more moist, bland, and slippery than the larger types. They are generally preferred by shoppers with family roots in China, Japan, and parts of the Caribbean—where the cormels are always called eddoes, as they often are by American distributors.

Although taro's culinary history is associated primarily with Asia, the Pacific, the Caribbean, and Hawaii,

diameter: 1-4 inches

Paula Wolfert reminds us that taro was a prevalent starch in the Mediterranean before the potato traveled there from the New World. She writes that it is "still eaten widely in Egypt in a dish called *oulaas,* as well as in Cyprus and along the Turkish Mediterranean coast" (*Mediterranean Grains and Greens*). "Still" signifies a long time in this case, for Egyptian taro was described in the first century by the Roman naturalist Pliny.

Perhaps unfortunately, taro's most publicized role is as Hawaiian poi, a dish that is very much an acquired taste and texture—and differs from just about all other taro preparations. Taro is a national dish not only in Hawaii, but in the Philippines, where it is eaten countrywide. There is little culinary variation (it is almost always prepared with coconut milk and chilli) but some curious specificity. Gilda Cordero-Fernando writes in *Philippine Food and Life,* "Bikolanos cook and eat only the leaves. In Tarlac, the leaves are thrown away and only the stems are eaten. Both stems and leaves . . . are cooked and eaten by the inhabitants of Laguna. In most other provinces, people consume only the . . . tuber, ignoring all other parts." The nuances of taro are fascinating—but I seem to have strayed from the mainland United States. Let's get back to basics.

BASIC USE: The way taro is cooked affects the way it looks, tastes, and feels as much cooking affects a potato: Think of cream of potato soup and potato chips. Although taro does not taste like potato, it has pretty much the same range of possibilities. But any way you cook it, taro smells delicious during the process!

Frying is often the preferred cooking method for taro, for good reason: When fried, it becomes chewy, crunchy, sweet, and full of character; it is not just a bland starch. One of its most celebrated roles is as the spectacular fried "bird's nest" that holds an array of seafood at Chinese banquets. Less grandly, it can be pan-fried or deep-fried in strips or chips. Or grate it and blend with eggs and onions, and fry like potato pancakes or deep-fry for fritters.

Steam or boil taro for a totally different effect—sweet, mild, starchy, soft—to serve with stews or spicy sauces. Or cook it directly in braises and soups, where it absorbs juices without falling apart, and at the same time acts as a flavorsome thickener. If you're cooking taro in liquid, use lots, for it is very dense, dry, and floury. Always plan to serve it freshly made and very hot, or it will be solidly stodgy. Know that whichever color you start with, it is likely to wind up grayish or purplish beige.

Parboil taro chunks to roast with pork and garlic, basting very frequently. Boil and puree taro as a base for soufflés, fritters, or croquettes, or to form a soft pastry for fried dim sum and savory Indian turnovers. But do not plan to simply boil and puree or mash it as you would potatoes: Taro is gluey without additional baking or frying to dry, aerate, or crisp the mixture.

Warning: All parts of uncooked taro contain crystals of calcium oxalate and other irritating compounds. No taro can be eaten raw.

SELECTION AND STORAGE: In Hawaii, there is a choice of types and sizes of taro. Elsewhere in the United States, there is just a choice of large and small. Choose large corms when a more floury, dry, nutty, sweetish effect is desired. Select small ones for steaming and boiling whole.

Large taro spoils quickly; the smaller eddoes last a bit longer. Choose carefully. The corms should be very hard and full with no sign of shriveling, molding, or softness. If possible, slice to check the moist, firm flesh, which should smell fresh and clean (any alcoholic or sour smell is a sure sign of spoilage). If the taro cannot be sliced, nick it with a fingernail to be sure that it is moist, not desiccated.

Store taro no more than a few days, in a single layer in a well-ventilated spot at room temperature (as cool as possible), uncovered.

PREPARATION: Taro can be irritating to the skin. If you are sensitive—or not sure—wear gloves, or peel the corms under water, or coat your hands with oil before you begin peeling. Do not rub your face or eyes if you have taro on your hands.

First trim the ends, then enjoy the unique sweet taro aroma (truly unique, for I can find no comparison). Pare deeply to remove all skin and discolorations. Drop taro into a bowl of water as you proceed. For later use, refrigerate in the water; or drain and wrap in plastic until ready to grate, slice, dice, or chunk for cooking. In Vietnam, taro is traditionally scooped, rather than sliced—a method that works very nicely for soups and stews: Halve corm and scoop out amorphous spoonfuls with a grapefruit spoon or sturdy teaspoon.

Basic Taro, Steamed or Boiled

In most markets where taro is sold there are two sizes. But unless you have grown up with them, you might guess that they are different vegetables entirely (see photo). The "babies," which cluster around a "mother" corm like nursing piglets, are about 3 ounces each, while the mothers can be as large as 3 pounds. Both can be plain-cooked the same way to become the perfect partner to juicy stews or braises, from vegetable curry to pot roast with onion gravy.

Small taro is moist, tender, smooth, and fairly even-colored, but it tends to blandness. Cooked in its skin (which slips easily from the cooked corm), it will be juicier but will look splotchy. Peeled first, then cooked, the flesh is drier, more potato-like, and has a more uniform cream color.

Large taro cooks up drier and more crumbly—almost like chestnuts, but denser. It has more character, sweetness, and nuttiness than the small, but it is sometimes fibrous. Peel before cooking.

Whichever size you cook, serve it *boiling* hot (it can be reheated in a steamer), or it will be waxy and clunky.

1½ pounds small or large taro

To boil: Scrub small taro or peel it. Drop into well salted boiling water. Boil until tender when pierced with a knife, 10 to 15 minutes. If boiled with skin on, let cool enough to handle, then trim ends and slide off skin. For larger taro, peel first, then cut into 4-ounce chunks, approximately. Boil until tender, about ½ hour.

To steam: Scrub or peel small taro. Set on rack in steamer over boiling water. Cover and cook until tender, about 25 minutes. Peel as above, as needed. Steam peeled chunks of large taro about 45 minutes.

Serves 4

Mashed Taro, Sweets, and Potatoes

Romy Dorotan, chef and owner of Cendrillon, a Philippine "fusion" restaurant in New York's Soho, discovered that his customers are so fond of this homey dish that he can't take it off the menu. Although just one of three starches, the taro comes through with its dulcet tones, albeit sotto voce. For variety and an Asian accent, substitute coconut milk for the butter and cream. Choose large taro with its drier texture and more pronounced flavor. It's an appealing way to introduce taro—and to keep it on your menu.

1 large taro (about 1¼ pounds)
1 baking potato (½ pound)
1 large orange-fleshed sweetpotato (¾ pound)
Butter
Heavy cream
Salt and pepper

1. Set large pot of water to boil. Peel taro and cut into slices ½ inch thick. Drop into pot and return to a boil. Add a handful of salt. Boil gently until taro is about half-cooked, approximately 10 to 15 minutes.

2. Meanwhile, peel potato, cut into 4 thick slices and add to pot. Peel sweetpotato, cut into slices of the same thickness, and add to pot. Boil until all vegetables are soft, some 25 minutes longer.

3. Drain well. Crush with potato masher, adding butter and heavy cream to taste. Season.

Serves 4

Lightly Souffléd Taro with Cashew Crunch

When dry, dense large taro is boiled, pureed, and then baked, it is transformed into a puffed and light dish. The aroma of the subtle spices wafts sweetly during baking, suggesting holiday feasts. You might consider serving this dish with duck, turkey, or ham instead of traditional sweetpotatoes (it can be prepared ahead through step 4).

For individual servings, use six 1-cup ramekins and test at 20 minutes. For a fancier, richer finish, spoon sweetened sour cream on top and add a sprinkle of cinnamon.

2 star anise "flowers"
2 cinnamon sticks, broken
8 cardamom pods, lightly crushed
1½ quarts water
1½ pounds large taro
2 teaspoons kosher salt
1 tablespoon butter
3 eggs, separated
White pepper
½ cup fine-chopped roasted cashews or
macadamias
Optional: lightly sweetened sour cream and
ground cinnamon

1. Loosely tie together star anise, cinnamon, and cardamom in cheesecloth, or enclose in a large tea ball. Bring to a boil in the water while you prepare taro.

2. Peel taro and cut into 1½-inch chunks. Add salt to water. Add taro, cover, and boil gently until tender, about 20 minutes. Meanwhile, preheat oven to 400°F.

3. Drain taro, reserving ½ cup liquid. Discard spices. Press taro through medium disc of food mill (do not puree in food processor, or mixture will be gummy).

4. Stir in reserved liquid and butter. Blend in yolks one at a time. Overseason slightly with salt and white pepper (and additional ground spices, if you like a stronger spice flavor).

5. Beat egg whites to soft peaks. Fold into puree about one-third at a time, alternating with cashews. Scoop into a buttered 1½-quart baking dish or six 1-cup ramekins. (You can leave for an hour at room temperature, or refrigerate; if refrigerated, return to room temperature to bake.)

6. Bake in upper level of oven until evenly puffed, lightly colored, and firm in the center—about 35 minutes for the baking dish, or about 20 minutes for the ramekins. Serve hot, with optional sour cream and cinnamon.

Serves 6

Steamed Taro Tossed with Sesame and Greens

Savor the scent of taro as it steams—at once sweetly yeasty, earthy, and nutty. The hot starchy cubes absorb a salty-spicy seasoning sauce and lightly wilt the crunchy chopped greens. Sesame seeds add crispness and richness. Serve with grilled fish or poultry.

1 medium-large taro (about 1½ pounds)
1 tablespoon corn or peanut oil
2 teaspoons Asian (dark) sesame oil
2 teaspoons balsamic vinegar
2 teaspoons mirin
2 teaspoons shoyu (Japanese soy sauce)
Chilli oil
2 tablespoons thin-sliced scallion tops
2 cups chopped water cress or mizuna
1 tablespoon toasted sesame seeds

1. Peel taro. Cut into ¾-inch cubes. Toss to coat evenly with corn oil. Spread on steamer rack over boiling water. Cover and cook until tender and easily pierced. Timing can vary dramatically, but about 20 minutes is average.

2. In mixing bowl, blend sesame oil, vinegar, mirin, shoyu, and chilli oil to taste. Add hot taro (steam the cubes to reheat if they have cooled off). Toss gently with rubber spatula. Add scallions, greens, and sesame, tossing to distribute ingredients evenly. Serve at once, while taro is still hot.

Serves 4

Spicy Taro Chips

Large taro corms fry to the most flavorful, crunchy, and visually striking (feathery brown calligraphic swirls on a golden ground) of chips—provided you have uniform thin slices and a thermostatically controlled fryer. Serve warm, tucked into a napkin-lined basket. If you have only a knife and an iron kettle for tools, stick with packaged taro chips, which can also be delicious—if a tad less so.

1 medium-large taro (about 2 pounds)
1 teaspoon kosher salt
1½ tablespoons distilled white vinegar
¼ teaspoon turmeric
1 teaspoon sugar
¼ teaspoon ground hot pepper
Vegetable oil for deep-frying

1. Halve taro lengthwise, then crosswise. Trim ends and pare off all peel. With thin-slicing (2-millimeter) blade of food processor (or mandoline) apply light pressure to make fine slices from each quarter.

2. Mix salt, vinegar, turmeric, sugar, and hot pepper in a large bowl. Add taro and toss to coat. Separate slices as necessary to coat all sides. Transfer to colander and let stand ½ hour or more, tossing now and then.

3. Spread slices in single layer on paper toweling laid on newspaper. Blot with paper towels. Meanwhile, heat oil in fryer to 350°F.

4. Slip in slices just to cover the oil's surface. Fry, turning once, until evenly golden brown—not just

colored at the edges. With skimmer or perforated spoon, lift onto clean toweling laid on newspaper to drain. Continue until all slices are fried. (If properly dried and fried, these can be stored airtight, but they are best when just made.)

Serves 6 well-behaved nibblers

Spice-Coated "Baby" Taro

While large taro is dry and nutty, small taro (usually called eddo) is moist and slippery—almost to a fault. To counteract this characteristic, it is usually deep-fried. Alternatively, it can be panfried with a crunchy coating. To simplify last-minute preparation, cook the taro in advance, then brown it at serving time. Don't worry about any blotches, which will be hidden by the fragrant spices.

> 1½ pounds small taro of equal size (10 to 12)
> 2 tablespoons vegetable oil
> ½ tablepoon mustard seeds, preferably brown
> ½ tablepoon cumin seeds
> 1 teaspoon ground coriander
> ¼ teaspoon paprika (preferably hot)
> ¼ teaspoon turmeric
> Salt

1. Scrub taro. Drop into salted boiling water. Boil until just barely tender when pierced, about 10 minutes; drain. When cool enough to handle, trim ends and slide off skin. Halve each corm. (Can be prepared ahead and refrigerated until you are ready to brown and serve.)

2. Heat oil over moderate flame in non-stick skillet large enough to hold taro in a single layer with room to spare. Add mustard and cumin seeds. As they spatter and jump, add taro, shaking pan to distribute spices. Reduce heat slightly and cook, shaking pan now and then, until taro is crisp and brown on one side, about 5 minutes.

3. Turn pieces with tongs and brown other side, about 5 minutes, adjusting heat to bronze but not burn. When taro is nearly done, add coriander, paprika, and turmeric, tossing to coat. Add salt, as desired.

Serves 5 to 6 as a side dish

Pros Propose

Stephen Wong updates Chinese-influenced taro for a vegetable entree, **Taro-Stuffed Green Peppers:** Soak dried black Chinese mushrooms in hot water until tender. Drain, reserving liquid, and dice small. Steam peeled, sliced taro until soft. Mash with salt and 5-spice powder. Mix soy sauce, vegetable stock, reserved mushroom liquid, cornstarch, and white pepper. Sauté minced ginger and onions in oil. Add green peas, fine-diced carrots, corn kernels, and mushrooms. Add soy sauce mixture; boil until thickened and most liquid is absorbed. Spoon mixture into quartered green peppers. Mound taro over it to cover; brush with sesame oil. Bake until peppers are tender and taro golden (from *HeartSmart Chinese Cooking*).

Satoimo no Nikkorogashi is an onomatopoetic description of the sound of taro being shaken in the pan as it cooks, according to Elizabeth Andoh, authority on Japanese culture and cuisine. To prepare this dish, which she translates as "Tumble-About Taro": Score small taro of equal size around the "equator" with a shallow cut. Set on rack over boiling water, cover, and steam until a toothpick just passes easily through center (do not overcook). Holding each corm lightly with both hands in a kitchen towel, twist in opposite directions to remove skins. Combine stock, soy, and mirin in pan to hold taro in single layer. Bring to a boil and add taro. Cook over fairly high heat, shaking pan, until liquid nearly evaporates and taro darkens. Sprinkle with a mixture of dried nori flakes and dried parsley.

Chef Paul Wildermuth, who now lives in Chicago but was born in Hawaii ("I still crave poi every day," he says), serves an original dish of **Roasted Taro and Sweetpotatoes:** Peel small taro, and set in milk to keep pale and moist. When ready to cook, drain, dry, and cut into large angled, bite-size pieces. Toss with grated ginger, minced garlic, oil, sugar, and salt. Spread in pan with a little water and roast in a hot oven. When tender, allow all water to cook off and brown, turning. In another pan, roast orange-fleshed sweetpotatoes cut the same size in more of same mixture, with added crumbled chillis. Serve together, with pan-fried large shrimp and mango-chilli sauce.

It is rare to find a recipe that includes both taro corms and leaves—for no reason I can learn—but this appealing **Hawaiian Taro Soup** from chef Alois Raidl makes use of both: Remove stalks and ribs from taro leaves. Cut leaves into thin strips. Scrub corms and cut into large cubes. Steam until almost tender, then peel and cut into small cubes. Heat macadamia nut oil and soften diced onion, chopped garlic, grated ginger, crushed chillis, and whole coriander leaves for 5 minutes. Add chicken broth, coconut milk, and taro leaves. Simmer 20 minutes, stirring often. Add taro cubes and chopped macadamia nuts. Continue cooking 10 minutes or more, until blended. Serve with steamed shrimp and a sprinkling of macadamias.

Taro Leaves

Also callaloo, calalú (see also amaranth, page 7), dasheen bush or bush (West Indian), luau (Hawaiian), elephant ears

As the words callaloo, luau, and elephant ears indicate, taro leaves have an identity distinct from the starchy corm. The two parts rarely share a cooking pot, but they do have common properties—as I learned the hard way.

It is well known that chewing raw or undercooked taro delivers a sharp dose of needle-like calcium oxalate crystals (and other irritants) to the tongue and throat. Having queried the vendors who sold the leaves and perused some twenty books on the subject, I still had found little more advice than "cook like spinach," "boil in two changes of water," "cook until very tender," and "add fat to take away the sting." But years of cooking and eating the corms had made me fairly comfortable about cooking up the big leaves.

Imagine my panic when, with tingling tongue and tightening throat (after having double-boiled the leaves, added 10 minutes to "until tender," *and* cooked them with coconut milk), I belatedly read in Rachel Laudan's thoughtful book *The Food of Paradise* that taro leaves, "like every other part of the plant . . . have to be cooked for 45 minutes to an hour to destroy the calcium oxalate crystals." I lived to tell the tale and retest the recipes, but please hear this: Ignore recipes that call for short cooking; instead, favor the deliciously

length: 12-14 inches

melting consistency—and undeniably drab hue—of *very* cooked leaves.

Having escaped the irritants, you may still find yourself in a callaloo quagmire. "Callaloo" and its variations (callalo, calalú, calilu, caruru, etc.) are words used to describe the leaves of taro, of yautía (see page 722), of various amaranths, and of a soup made from all, some, or none of them. There are more versions of the soup than spellings of the word for it. When recipes call for callaloo, most any leafy greens will make a good soup—but be sure to cook taro leaves long enough.

The word "callaloo" is as tricky to pin down as the soups themselves. Various English and Spanish dictionaries define it only as a tropical American plant but do not supply the usual genus and species or give its origin. André Nègre, in his culinary history *Les Antilles et Guyane à travers leur cuisine,* offers these three possibilities: The term comes from "calao," a word of Carib origin meaning a kind of leafy soup; the term was imported from Africa by the Portuguese and is still used on the Ivory Coast and Dahomey; or, it comes from Oceania, where taro is also called callaloo and is widely used.

BASIC USE: Because the cooking time is necessarily lengthy, taro leaves reduce to a creamy consistency that limits their use to sauce, puree, and soup—but does not limit their lusciousness, because the vegetable excels in these forms.

Traditionally, taro leaves are also used as envelopes, though rarely in dishes that suit most Western kitchens. Primary is palusami, eaten throughout the Pacific islands: Taro leaves are filled with thick coconut cream (and various optional stuffings), enclosed in breadfruit or banana leaves, then long-cooked on hot stones, as in the traditional Hawaiian luau. For Philippine tinumuk (and the similar pinangat), a stuffing of chopped shrimp and young coconut meat is seasoned with minced ginger, garlic, and onion, then bound with coconut milk, wrapped in taro-leaf rectangles and simmered in coconut milk and chillis.

Stuffed dishes in India take a very different form. Taro leaves are spread with a spiced paste made from ground legume flour, then stacked, rolled, and steamed until soft. The rolls are then sliced and fried with more spices. In Southeast Asia, peeled taro stalks are included in soups and are preferred over the leaves.

SELECTION: Where and when you find fresh taro leaves will depend upon the markets in your vicinity. I have been most successful at Caribbean markets—at no particular season. (I most recently found taro leaves stuck in a bucket in a West Indian market between the aisles for videos and religious items.)

The big, heart-shaped leaves are naturally limp and folded (see left of photo) and usually wrapped in plastic to prevent dehydration. They should be uniformly green, and their leaf stalks firm. The half-dozen 1-pound bunches I have cooked were made up of 12 to 20 leaves and stalks. All tasted similar and looked like the photo.

STORAGE: Plastic-wrapped and refrigerated, taro leaves should last for a week.

PREPARATION: Taro leaves can be as irritating to the skin as the corms, so the same precautions should be observed: If you are sensitive—or do not know—wear gloves or coat your hands with oil. Do not rub your face or eyes when you have taro on your hands.

To prepare, trim base of stalks, cut them from leaves, and strip off and discard the thin skin with the help of a paring knife. Cut stalks into thin diagonal slices. Holding each leaf folded with one hand, tear into shreds with the other, following the direction of the veins. If leaves are very large, first halve lengthwise, then shred. If central vein is very thick, slice or discard. Rinse all.

Creamy Taro Leaves in Coconut Milk

"More than any other vegetable, the *gabi* (*linsa* in Bicol, taro in English) plant plays an important role in the daily diet of the Bicolano," writes Honesto C. General, author of *The Coconut Cookery of Bicol* (which is at the southern end of the island of Luzon) in a chapter entitled "The Enduring Romance with Gabi." *Laing,* a traditional dish from the region, was served at Romy Dorotan's restaurant, Cendrillon, in New York City. A thick, rich sauce—more coconut than greens—it was ladled copiously over fat cakes of shredded salt cod and potato. To better suit the vegetable focus of this book, I have doubled the greens and halved the coconut to make a velvety side dish of "tropical creamed spinach."

1½ pounds taro leaves
1 small onion, diced
2 garlic cloves, thin-sliced
1 can coconut milk (13 to 16 ounces)
½ teaspoon curry powder or garam masala
1 cup water
About 2 tablespoons fish sauce (patis, nam pla, or nuoc nam)

1. Trim and slice taro leaves, following directions under Preparation.

2. Combine the sliced taro leaves and stalks, onion, garlic, coconut milk, curry powder, water, and 2 tablespoons fish sauce in a saucepan. Cover and bring to a boil.

3. Reduce heat and simmer gently until leaves are squishy soft and liquid is thickened to a binding element, about 45 minutes. Stir often to prevent sticking as coconut sauce reduces. Add more fish sauce to taste. (Can be reheated.)

Serves 4 to 6

Braised Taro Leaves

Joseph Schultz, founder of India Joze restaurant in Santa Cruz, cooks taro leaves (not stalks) to a concentrated puree, then finishes them in one of two ways: as a savory side dish, or the base for a brunch entree. In either case, the leaves turn buttery soft, mellow, and glum green—the necessary consequence of being long-cooked. Serve the greens with roast lamb or turkey, or as part of a vegetable meal with cracked wheat pilaf and broiled tomatoes. Or see the variation below for the brunch route.

About 1½ pounds taro leaves
2 tablespoons butter
1 medium onion, diced
1 medium red bell pepper, diced small
¼ teaspoon ground hot pepper
2 cups water
About 1 teaspoon kosher salt
1 to 2 teaspoons minced garlic
Lemon or lime juice
Pepper

1. Wearing rubber gloves, strip taro leaves from stalks (discard these). Stack or bunch leaves and cut into long fine shreds. Rinse in several changes of water.

2. Melt butter in heavy pot over moderate heat. Add onion, bell pepper, and hot pepper and stir until onion is fairly soft. Gradually stir in taro, adding more as each batch wilts.

3. Add water and 1 teaspoon salt and bring to a boil. Cover, reduce heat, and simmer 40 minutes.

4. Add garlic. Raise heat and boil gently, uncovered, stirring often, until most water has evaporated, about 10 minutes. Add lemon juice, pepper, and salt.

Serves 4

Variation

Spiced Braised Taro Leaves with Hard-Cooked Eggs

Prepare recipe through step 3. Stir in 1 scant tablespoon tomato paste and ¾ teaspoon garam masala with the garlic in step 4. Spread the finished hot puree in a serving dish. Nest 4 or 5 hard-cooked, halved eggs in the greens. Decorate with halved cherry tomatoes. Serve hot, warm, or at room temperature.

Cream of Taro Leaf Soup

Rich, intense, and mysterious, this smooth soup suggests spinach and sorrel. Like sorrel, the leaves turn a dark khaki with cooking, but when brightened with cream, the velvety puree serves as an elegant opener to a multi-course meal.

About 1¼ pounds taro leaves
2 tablespoons butter
3 medium shallots, sliced
1 medium green bell pepper, chopped
¼ teaspoon pepper
About 4 cups water
1 teaspoon sugar
About 1¼ teaspoons kosher salt
¾ to 1 cup heavy cream
Lemon juice

1. Wearing gloves, pull taro stalks from leaves and discard. Hold each folded leaf with one hand and shred with the other, following the vein pattern. Or stack or bunch leaves, then slice thin. Rinse.

2. Melt butter in a heavy pot over moderate heat. Add shallots, green pepper, and pepper and stir until vegetables are slightly softened. Gradually stir in taro, adding more as each batch wilts.

3. Add 3½ cups water, sugar, and 1 teaspoon salt and bring to a boil. Cover, reduce heat, and simmer 45 minutes. Uncover and simmer 5 minutes.

4. Transfer soup to food processor and puree. Add ½ cup cream and process until smooth. Return to pot and bring to a boil. Reduce heat. Thin with water and/or cream as desired. Season with salt, pepper, and lemon juice.

5. Ladle hot soup into bowls. Drizzle about 1 tablespoon cream on each.

Serves 4 as a first course

Pros Propose

A book that has worn well over the years (since 1940) is *Hawaiian and Pacific Foods* by Katherine Bazore, who covers the particulars of handling and cooking taro leaves (which I failed to notice in time!) and presents simple and sophisticated dishes. **Luau (Taroleaf) Soufflé** evolves from her basic cooking method: Remove stalks from leaves; strip membrane from large vein that remains on each leaf. Combine leaves in pot with a modicum of water, a little butter, and salt. Simmer, partly covered, 1 hour, or until liquid has evaporated and no "sting" remains when taro is tasted. Season; press through coarse sieve. Prepare flour base for soufflé. Fold in the taro puree and egg yolks. Fold in beaten whites, then turn into a buttered dish. Set in pan of water and bake in moderate oven.

In *The Complete Book of Caribbean Cooking* (1973), another book that covers more than many recent works on the subject, Elisabeth Lambert Ortiz gives recipes for callalou from Guadeloupe, St. Lucia, Haiti, Martinique, and Trinidad—all made with taro leaves. The simplest is **Le Calalou** from Martinique: Combine cleaned taro leaves, sliced okra, a chunk of ham, seeded and chopped green chilli, fresh thyme, and chopped garlic, scallions, and parsley with water to cover. Simmer 1 hour, covered. Remove and reserve ham. Beat soup to a puree with traditional wooden *lele* or wire whisk; it should be smooth and light. If desired, chop ham and return to soup. Serve with white rice and optional salt cod.

A Cuban version of **Blue Crab Calalú** from Maricel Presilla, Latin American food authority, is far more complex: Remove stalks and central veins from taro leaves. Stack leaves and cut into thin shreds. Peel and chop stalks. Add both to boiling water, with scallions and parsley sprigs. Boil 2 minutes; drain, then whiz to a coarse puree with chicken stock. Sauté diced slab bacon until golden; add minced garlic and scallions and cook to soften. Add dried thyme, ground allspice, and minced Scotch bonnet chilli, tossing. Add cleaned, halved blue crabs and beer; toss briefly. Add sliced okra, the taro leaf puree, and more stock. Season and cook at least ½ hour. Blend crushed garlic with lime juice and stir into soup to season. Serve with ripe plantain dumplings.

Sweet-Sour Patra is "a dish that delighted me in a vegetarian meal we once ate in Manchester, at an Indian restaurant," wrote the British food historian Jane Grigson—who then pursued the recipe (*Cooking with Exotic Fruits and Vegetables*). To prepare: Soak, strain, and sieve tamarind pulp. Add sugar, chickpea flour (besan), turmeric, coriander, ground chilli, and garam masala to pulp to make a thick paste. Spread trimmed taro leaf with paste, top with another, and continue until you've done 6. Roll up each stack of leaves and tie with string. Steam 45 minutes or more. Remove, cover with cloth, and cool to tepid. Cut into slices and fry until red-brown. Sprinkle with chopped coriander leaves and grated fresh coconut. Serve with lime slices.

Tindora (*Coccinia grandis*)

Also tindori, tindola, ivy gourd

Ivy gourd is the correct English name for this petite cucurbit, but tindora is what you're more likely to see, since it is in Indian, Pakistani, and Bangladeshi markets that you'll find these gourdlettes. Each fruit is a mere 2 inches long and either a uniform lime green or marked with blurred lighter stripes. The pale flesh is packed with gel-coated seeds like a cucumber's, but the gel may be orange if the green fruit is ripening. Exceptionally firm, crunchy, and juicy (not watery), the vegetables suggest dense miniature Kirby-type cucumbers with added slickness, tartness, a grassy freshness, and a touch of bitterness.

Cultivated and wild forms are found in Africa, Latin America, and Australia, where the fruit, leaves, and shoots are all eaten (I have seen only fruits in the United States). I have read that the miniature gourds turn scarlet when ripe (and are then candied and pickled in Java and India), but in five years of foraging in markets I have found only the green form. Although botanical sources indicate that ivy gourd is widely cultivated throughout Southeast Asia, I have been able to locate recipes for India alone. A similar cucurbit called parwal or parval (*Tricosanthes dioica*) is also consumed when tiny and green in India, where it is apparently very popular. I chanced upon it once in Flushing, Queens—and never again.

In short, this is a short entry. But I find the crisp tindora a delightful little package and think it worthy of note. Note also that I cannot determine whether the plural has an "s." Sorry.

BASIC USE: If eaten by itself, the vegetable is almost too crunchy to tell anything else. But it is a fine foil, accent, or complement, whether raw or cooked.

Raw, thin-sliced ivy gourd is a ready-made garnish, a bright and decorative accent vegetable for composed salads, simple seafood dishes, mixed vegetables, and grain dishes—all the foods that match up with cucumbers. Blanched, tindora has the crunch of half-sour pickles and diced celery and, like them, it livens up seafood, chicken, or egg salad. Or slice lengthwise

½ **actual size**

quarters for vegetable platters. Steamed for a few minutes, then cooled and sliced, tindora becomes a perfect partner for shrimp in lemon mayonnaise on a bed of cress. Or stir-fry slices of tindora, adding softer vegetables or seafood as complements.

SELECTION AND STORAGE: Tindora is available just about all year in the Asian markets that sell it. Choose narrow, comparatively small and dark tindora with no signs of yellowing. It should be solid, with no "give" or sponginess. Some varieties are lighter green, some striped, some not; all seem to be similar inside. Refrigerate in a container lined with paper towel. The little gourds will last 5 or 6 days.

PREPARATION: To use raw, rinse, cut off tips (because the peel is heavy) and quarter lengthwise for crudités or composed salads; or slice thin diagonals for garnish. Or blanch whole tindora until just tender to taste—a minute or two—refresh in ice water, drain, and chill to use as an ingredient in salads. Simply trim tips and slice as desired for stir-fries.

Sautéed Tindora with Ginger, Mint, and Cashews

Vivid green oval slices, extremely crunchy, are a perky accent to simple seafood dishes—salmon, shrimp, or fish fillets—in fact, all the foods that complement cucumbers, which tindora resembles. Substitute cilantro or dill (in lesser quantity) for mint, if preferred. Cashews add a sweet richness, but they are not strictly required.

¾ pound tindora
2 narrow scallions (green onions)
1-inch ginger knob
1 tablespoon mild vegetable oil
½ teaspoon kosher salt
2 tablespoons thin-sliced mint leaves
3 tablespoons roasted, salted, and chopped
    cashews

1. Cut tindora crosswise at a sharp angle to form thin (⅛-inch) oblongs. Discard the tips, which have too much skin. Trim scallions and cut into thin diagonals, separating light parts from dark. Cut enough ginger into hair-thin strips to yield 1 tablespoon.

2. Heat oil in medium skillet over moderately low heat. Add tindora, light scallion parts, half the ginger, and salt; toss. Cover and cook, shaking pan often, until tindora loses its raw taste, 3 to 4 minutes.

3. Uncover and sauté until just tender to taste, a minute or two. Add remaining ginger and scallion greens and toss 30 seconds.

4. Off heat, add mint and cashews. Serve at once.

Serves 3 to 4 as a side dish

Variation

Sautéed Shrimp and Tindora with Ginger, Mint, and Cashews

For a quick and pretty main dish, half-cook 1 pound shelled, seasoned small shrimp in 1 tablespoon oil, then remove from pan and proceed with step 1 above. Return shrimp to pan in step 3, when you add ginger and scallions, and continue with the recipe.

Shrimp and Tindora Salad, Quick and Pretty

Shrimp and tindora are steamed just two minutes, cooled, cut into matching pink and pale green slices, tossed with citrusy mayonnaise, then set on avocado dice and cress leaves. If you can find the bright, juicy, low-oil avocados grown in Florida (see page 38), they are sweeter, firmer, and fresher-tasting in this salad than the more widely available rich California types. A tidy, tasty, attractive little opener for a summer meal.

1 or 2 limes (preferably organic)
1 pound shelled medium-large shrimp
    (approximately 32 shrimp)
½ teaspoon sweet or hot paprika
¾ pound tindora (about 30)
⅓ cup mayonnaise
1 scant tablespoon Dijon mustard
⅛ teaspoon curry powder
1 bunch water cress
½ large Florida avocado (or 1 smaller
    California avocado)

1. Scrub limes. Grate fine zest from one. Sprinkle over shrimp, with paprika, tossing to distribute. Spread tindoras on rack of steamer in single layer, leaving room for shrimp (if steamer is not large enough, cook separately). Set over boiling water. Cover and cook 1 minute. Add shrimp, cover, and cook 1 minute longer.

2. Transfer tindora and shrimp to a platter to cool, then refrigerate.

3. Combine mayonnaise, mustard, and curry powder. Halve grated lime and squeeze juice. Add gradually to mayonnaise to taste—about 1 tablespoon; reserve remainder. Refrigerate dressing. Trim water cress and divide into sprigs. Rinse, spin-dry, then chill.

4. To serve, cut tindora into ¼-inch slices, discarding tips. Reserve 4 shrimp. Cut remainder into ¼-inch slices. Toss tindora and shrimp with dressing. Cut avocado into ½-inch dice. Toss with 2 to 3 teaspoons reserved lime juice. If needed, squeeze second lime and add more. Arrange avocado and cress on plates. Top with tindora and shrimp. Halve reserved shrimp lengthwise. Arrange on top.

Serves 4 as a first course

Pros Propose

"Tindola, a delicacy in northern India, is wonderful stir-fried or stewed in a spicy gravy, both of which I enjoyed as a child," Julie Sahni writes in *Classic Indian Vegetarian and Grain Cookery*. To make the **Dry-Fried Tindora with Coriander** that was prepared at her home in New Delhi: Stir turmeric, cayenne, and ground coriander into hot oil. Immediately add tindora that has been quartered lengthwise. Toss to coat and brown lightly. Cover pan and cook about 10 minutes, turning often. Then fry, uncovered, until moisture evaporates and tindora is slightly shriveled, because "the flavor . . . will come out only when it is well fried."

Asian culinary authority Madhur Jaffrey has her own special "fusion" recipe for **Lamb Leg with Tindora:** Choose "many, many tindora of equal size, peel in stripes, halve, then deep-fry until crisp. Toss with salt, pepper, and cayenne, then scatter around a roasted leg of lamb for a truly magnificent dish."

Tomatillo, Tomate Verde

(*Physalis ixocarpa* or *P. philadelphica*)

Also Mexican husk tomato, tomate, tomatito verde, miltomate (for the wild form)

It was not until the United States discovered the joy of Mexican and Tex-Mex dishes in the early 1980s that tomatillo showed up outside a can—or that's what I thought until I read Julia Morton's *Fruits of Warm Climates.* Morton notes that "before 1863, it was thoroughly naturalized and commonly growing in abundance in the far west of the United States, and that some 20 acres were cultivated for the Los Angeles market from 1930 to about 1939 for the Mexican population." Shortly thereafter, in a confusing turn of events (such confusion often accompanies marketing campaigns), "the American Fruit Grower publicized this species under the concocted name 'Jamberry,' as a new fruit introduced by scientists at Iowa State College." Tomatillo was subsequently "introduced" several more times under other names that probably served to muddle its identity even further.

In my experience, this tart queen of salsa and mole remains elusive, except in Mexican neighborhoods and the occasional upscale produce bin. It is a member of the multifaceted and multicontinental family Solanaceae (which includes the potato, bell pepper, eggplant, and tomato, as well as many other, often toxic plants—tobacco among them). Although questions about tomatillo's place of origin and species name have not been settled, Julia Morton states that "the Mexican husk tomato was a prominent staple in Aztec and Mayan economy" and that "the plant abounds in Mexico and the highlands of Guatemala."

The formation of the fruit and its all-enclosing calyx are unusual. You can see the connection to the popular decorative orange Chinese lantern plant, to the widespread American ground cherry (which has many common names), and to the Cape gooseberry (which has even more names)—these all have similar structures. Each rustly-crisp parchment bladder (in Greek, *physalis,* the name of the genus; its species name, *ixocarpa,* means sticky fruit) completely cages the firm berry, which grows to fill it and sometimes tears it open.

diameter: 1–2 inches

The tomatillo, which ranges from an inch in diameter to the size of an Italian plum, resembles a chartreuse cherry tomato but is more lustrous and firm. Although it may be purplish and may ripen to yellow, it is most commonly green.

Its resemblance to a tomato is superficial. It is *not* a green tomato. The confusion with the tomato is largely a mixup of names. Charles B. Heiser, Jr., writes in *Of Plants and People:* "The word *tomate* (from the Nahuatl *tomatl*) is employed for a number of solanaceous fruits in Mexico, with modifiers to distinguish the different kinds of plants. The word alone is used for the domesticated *Physalis* [what we call tomatillo], and the wild plants of the genus are called *miltomate.* . . . The tomato (*Lycopersicon esculentum*) became *jitomate* in Mexico, but when the plant went to Europe the modifier was dropped, and it became *tomate* . . . converted to *tomato* in English."

If tomatillo is not like a tomato, what is it like? It's a

unique character: tart, firm, and fruity. But it's too tart and coarse-textured to eat "straight" except as a thin-sliced accent. Rather, it's a magical culinary medium that becomes a fully realized sauce or soup when pureed with aromatic or fiery flavoring elements, developing a special consistency and a refreshing acid balance that seem like the work of many ingredients and culinary operations.

BASIC USE: Tomatillo is traditionally cooked, but the raw fruit, chopped or diced and used in moderation, adds freshness to vegetable salad, guacamole, and sandwich fillings.

Generally speaking, tomatillo's unique properties are best displayed when it is pureed, whether raw or cooked. Raw, it can be made into dressing or salsa. Cooked, its repertoire increases. The traditional uses for tomatillos are hard to beat: In salsa cruda, the barely cooked fruits are combined with chilli, onion, garlic, cilantro, and variable seasonings for an all-purpose sauce that seems to go with everything that can be dipped or dressed.

Cooked and pureed, tomatillos turn into a sauce to sharpen the focus of tacos, enchiladas, huevos rancheros, and other egg dishes. Blended with herbs, nuts or seeds, and broth, they become the popular salsa verde in which chicken, turkey, fish, or vegetables are simmered to succulence.

Once cooked and pureed, tomatillos can be thinned for a soft, slightly viscid, lusciously slurpy soup, cold or hot.

SELECTION: Look for tomatillos year-round, on and off—with no logic that I can discern. Most come from Central America, with a smaller supply from California. Unless you are in an area with a Mexican population, you may need to push your grocer for them. Choose dry, hard tomatillos with husks that fit the fruit tightly. They should not be damp or darkening or show any trace of mold.

Chef and author Rick Bayless selects small, yellow fruits for rich flavor. If you can find purple varieties, he recommends them highly but notes that the resulting sauce will be brownish, not fresh green.

STORAGE: Tomatillos have remarkable staying power. Spread them in a paper-lined dish or basket in the refrigerator and count on keeping them for several weeks (if purchased in good shape).

For longer storage, cooked tomatillos freeze well. Husk, wash, and stem them. Combine with water to nearly cover; barely simmer until softened but not squishy. Cool, then freeze with their cooking liquid in 1-cup containers, handy for making small batches of sauce.

PREPARATION: Tear the webbed covering and pull upward toward the stem (like pulling an undershirt up over a fat baby's tummy), twisting to remove both husk and stem. Rinse well to remove the sticky coating.

TO PRECOOK: For many recipes, tomatillos are precooked before being combined with other ingredients.

For a soft, saucy effect, simmer in water: Barely cover husked tomatillos with cold water; cook very gently until tender—the time can range from 2 to 15 minutes, depending upon size and thickness. Check often to prevent bursting. Cool in liquid.

For a firmer, drier consistency and a more concentrated flavor, roast in a hot oven: Rinse whole tomatillos. Roast with their husks intact in a pan in a preheated 450°F oven until soft, about 10 to 15 minutes. Check often to prevent bursting. Remove and cool slightly. Pull back and twist off husks. Rinse gently, if desired.

Herbed Tomatillo and Grape Salsa

This soft, fruity (and fat-free) green sauce enhances broiled or fried seafood or roasted chicken or turkey. Sweet and mellow, with herbal tones and a light chilli snap (more, if you go for heat), it is smoother and subtler than relish. Either simmer husked tomatillos or roast them unhusked (for somewhat more concentrated flavor), as you prefer. Should a more assertive and crisp salsa be your goal, prepare the raw variation that follows, for sharper taste and color.

¾ **pound tomatillos**
1 to 3 small green chillis, such as Serrano or Jalapeño, halved and seeded
1 small garlic clove

¼ teaspoon kosher salt
⅓ cup tightly packed cilantro
   (coriander) leaves
¼ cup lightly packed basil or mint leaves
½ cup stemmed seedless green grapes
About 1 tablespoon lime juice

1. Follow directions in To Precook.

2. In food processor container, combine 1 chilli (or more to taste), garlic, salt, and half each of the cilantro and basil. Whiz to mince.

3. Drain tomatillos if needed. Add to container, with grapes and 1 tablespoon lime juice. Whirl to a chunky puree. Taste for heat and tartness, adding lime and minced chilli to suit. Scoop into a bowl. Cover and chill at least 1 hour.

4. To serve, mince the remaining cilantro and basil. Stir into the salsa. Adjust seasoning.

Makes about 1½ cups

Variation

Uncooked Tomatillo and Grape Salsa

Clean and rinse ½ pound tomatillos. Whiz chillis, garlic, salt, and half the cilantro and basil to a fine texture. Add the tomatillos and chop coarsely. Add grapes and pulse to medium-coarse texture. Chill. To serve, mince the remaining herbs and stir into the salsa. Adjust seasoning.

Tomatillo Gazpacho

The sharp color of this cooling puree matches its tartness. Although the refreshing soup tastes as bright as vegetables in the raw, the tomatillos are cooked to round out their flavor, soften their firm hides, and produce a gently jellied consistency. Allow time for the puree to chill thoroughly. For maximum green power, serve in white, pale, or clear glass bowls.

I prefer freeze-dried peppercorns to those packed in liquid. Penzeys Spices (by mail-order from Muskego, Wisconsin) are my favorite source. If you don't relish a "bite," use the smaller quantity of pepper. Or, for a different kind of nip, substitute fresh green chilli.

1 pound tomatillos
2½ cups water
1 teaspoon kosher salt
About 2 teaspoons sugar
1 small white onion
2 medium cucumbers (about 1 pound)
¾ to 1½ teaspoons green peppercorns (to taste)
About ¾ cup lightly packed cilantro
   (coriander) leaves
About ¼ cup lightly packed basil leaves
About 2 tablespoons lime juice
6 small yellow and/or red cherry tomatoes

1. Tear tomatillo husks and pull off toward stem end, twisting to remove husk and stem. Rinse tomatillos well. Reserve the 2 smallest fruits.

2. Place remaining tomatillos in non-aluminum pan to hold them closely in a single layer. Add water and bring to a boil. Reduce heat and simmer until tender (some will break), about 10 minutes, stirring often to submerge. Add salt and 2 teaspoons sugar. Cool, then chill (set in a bowl in ice water, if you do not have time to chill in refrigerator).

3. Peel and quarter onion. Peel, seed, and chunk cucumbers. Combine onion, 1 cup of the cucumbers, peppercorns, and half each of the cilantro and basil in food processor. Whiz to a fine puree. Add the chilled tomatillos and their liquid, the remaining cilantro, basil, and cucumber, and 2 tablespoons lime juice. Whirl to medium-fine puree. Chill soup several hours, or more.

4. To serve: Taste and adjust sugar, salt, lime juice, and herbs. Ladle into small bowls. Cut reserved tomatillos and small tomatoes into very thin slices, and float on soup. Serve at once.

Serves 4 to 6 as a first course

Salmon Poached on a Bed of Tomatillos, Onion, and Chilli

A spectacular and simple dish: Unctuous peachy salmon is set off by a sprightly, tart, muted-green sauce—and plenty of it (if any remains, enjoy on grainy bread with fresh goat cheese). Rice brightened with corn kernels and red bell pepper is a good complement.

2 pounds tomatillos

3 tablespoons full-flavored olive oil

2 small fresh chillis, seeded and minced

1 tablespoon minced garlic

1 cup chopped onions

1 cup minced green bell pepper

1 teaspoon kosher salt

1 teaspoon sugar

Pepper

2 pounds salmon fillets with skin, 1 to
　1½ inches thick

2 to 4 tablespoons snipped fresh dill

1. Tear tomatillo husks and pull off toward stem end, twisting to remove both husk and stem. Rinse fruit. Chop coarsely.

2. Warm 2 tablespoons oil over moderate heat in heavy non-aluminum sauté pan or shallow flameproof casserole that will hold fillets in a single layer. Add chillis and garlic and stir a minute. Add onions and green pepper; cook until soft, about 5 minutes. Add tomatillos, salt, and sugar. Cook, stirring often, until most liquid evaporates—about 15 minutes. Taste and adjust seasoning.

3. Set salmon on sauce, skin side down. Season with salt and pepper and drizzle with remaining 1 tablespoon oil. Bring to a simmer. Reduce heat and cover. Cook very gently, shaking every now and then, until fish is just barely cooked through—about 15 to 20 minutes.

4. Gently turn over salmon with spatula. Remove skin. Coat with minced dill. Serve hot from the pan.

Serves 4 to 5

Pros Propose

Chef Rick Bayless has perfected **Essential Roasted Tomatillo-Serrano Salsa** for his Mexican restaurants in Chicago, which is why I have not offered a recipe for the classic and unbeatable sauce. Here's his method: Spread husked tomatillos on baking sheet and place 4 inches below hot broiler. When blackened and softened, turn and cook other side. Cool completely on sheet. Cook whole fresh Serrano chillis and unpeeled large garlic cloves on a dry griddle until blackened and

soft. Cool. Pull stems and seeds from chillis; peel garlic. Scrape tomatillos and juices into food processor, with chillis and garlic. Pulse to a coarse puree ("the unctuously soft tomatillos will provide the body for the chunky bits of chiles and garlic"). Scrape into a serving dish. Stir in water for a spoonable consistency. Rinse minced white onion in strainer, and shake off moisture. Add to salsa with chopped cilantro. Season with salt and sugar (from *Rick Bayless's Mexican Kitchen*).

Raw tomatillos have different charms: They are tarter, crisper, and bright colored. For **Punchy Tomatillo-Tomato Relish:** Chop cleaned tomatillos. Combine with pulped, seeded, and diced plum tomatoes, minced Jalapeño and red onion, chopped cilantro, and garlic. Add lime juice, tequila, and salt. Cover and chill an hour, or more (up to a few days). Serve with grilled fish, burgers, chicken, or traditional Mexican and New Mexican dishes (from *Chutneys and Relishes* by Lorraine Bodger).

Queso Fundido, "a sort of Mexican cheese fondue," is adapted by chef Mark Miller, who prefers fresh goat cheese to the hard-to-handle stringy authentic types. To prepare: Toast pumpkin seeds in dry pan until puffed and crisp. Combine in blender with epazote, roasted garlic, cleaned tomatillos, a few romaine leaves, cilantro, roasted and peeled Poblano, olive oil, and poultry stock. Puree and season. Cut 3-ounce portions of fresh goat cheese or queso fresco and set each in an ovenproof dish. Brush with olive oil. Broil until bubbly. Pour sauce around cheese and serve with fresh tortillas or tortilla chips (from *Coyote Cafe*).

Chef Zarela Martinez roasts tomatillos in the husk for **Braised Pork Chops with Tomatillo Sauce,** a recipe from Lucila Zarate de Fuentes: Cook tomatillos on hot griddle, turning often to prevent scorching, until softened all over, 10 to 15 minutes. Gently transfer to bowl. Cook small unpeeled onions and large garlic cloves the same way; peel. Remove husks from tomatillos over a bowl, to catch juice. Combine tomatillos, onions, and garlic with a large amount of roasted sesame seeds, a piece of soft (true) cinnamon, pepper, ground cloves, and thyme in blender. Puree. Brown seasoned loin chops in oil; set chops aside. Add puree to pan; boil. Stir in capers, pimento-stuffed green olives, and blanched almonds. Return chops to pan. Reduce heat. Cook, covered, until tender (from *The Food and Life of Oaxaca*).

Corn adds a twist to green sauce Texas-style, in

a recipe developed by San Antonio restaurateur Arthur Cerna, **Chicken and Corn Enchiladas with Tomatillo-Corn Salsa:** Combine diced poached chicken with chopped white onion, minced green pepper, diced tomatoes, olive oil, and a little chicken stock; set aside. Simmer cleaned tomatillos, chopped white onion, minced garlic, and water until soft. Puree and season. Pour half into a small saucepan and add corn kernels; cook until just tender. To soften tortillas, swipe them through tomatillo sauce. Place chicken mixture in center of each and roll into cylinders. Arrange closely in baking dish. Spoon over remaining puree. Sprinkle with shredded Monterey Jack cheese. Top with tomatillo-corn sauce. Bake in moderate oven until bubbly. Sprinkle with cilantro (from *Texas the Beautiful Cookbook* by Patsy Swendson and June Hays).

Truffles (*Tuber* species and *Leucangium carthusianum*)

Including **black truffle, Italian white truffle, summer truffle,** *Tuber brumale,* **Tuscan truffle, Oregon white truffle, Oregon black truffle, Chinese** and **Himalayan truffles**

Fresh truffles are chefs' terrain for the most part. They spoil too quickly and cost too much to be displayed in markets, where customers may or may not buy them before they expire. Truffling in restaurants is another matter. Americans seem *Tuber*-tracked when they dine out these days. Even modest restaurants offer truffled pasta and risotto, and truffle tasting menus have mushroomed in high-end dining rooms nationwide.

What then is this precious and perishable truffle? In the broad sense, as a term used to describe a subterranean fungus, "there are about 2,000 truffles and truffle-like fungi," says Jim Trappe, a professor of Forest Science at Oregon State University in Corvallis and a truffle taxonomist. "In a more confined sense, if you ask about 'true truffles,' as some refer to the members of the *Tuber* genus, there are about 100 species."

In the restaurant business, "true truffles" are generally defined by no more than "black and white," adjectives also understood to mean "French and Italian" or "Périgord and Alba" or, in scientific terms, *Tuber melanosporum* and *T. magnatum* respectively. Always inadequate, this "definition" is now virtually meaningless. Even if the two species were the only ones sold, they are often unearthed outside France and Italy and, more often than not, outside Périgord and Alba. "The expansion of new truffle markets has been the most important change in the business in the last decade," says Rosario Safina, president of Urbani Truffles & Caviar USA in Long Island City, New York, the country's largest truffle importer. "Now, we don't pay for Bulgarian truffles that come long way round through Italy. We get them straight from Bulgaria."

In addition, the field (literally) of truffle cultivation is growing internationally—and, to a minor extent, domestically. Although truffle culture has alternately flourished and failed since the 17th century, according to Jean-Marie Rocchia in his animated, opinionated book *Des truffes en général et de la rabasse en particulier,* interest is lively at present. Rocchia believes that the same passion for the past that has restored farmstead cheeses and heirloom vegetables to France's tables has renewed respect for wild foods like the truffle. With this trend have come improved methods for raising trees inoculated with either *Tuber melanosporum* or *T. magnatum* (which develop on the roots of specific trees). Rosario Safina estimates that "forty percent of truffles from France, Italy, and Spain come from 'helped-along' trees."

Respect for local products is not limited to France. Greg Higgins, a chef in Oregon who has worked in the Pacific Northwest for many years, says that wild regional foods are on an upswing: "The truffle climate has altered tremendously in the last decade. Now, I have fresh Oregon truffles on the menu, and they are sold in our local specialty grocery chain."

The selling of species other than the time-honored duo marks a distinct change in truffle commerce. A half-dozen other species pop up in the American market openly (if minimally), extending the truffle season and increasing availability to those not able to pay the platinum prices of prized *T. melanosporum* and *T. magnatum.*

Because the finest examples of the earth's costliest edibles look like dusty Silly Putty (white truffles) or dung balls (black ones), it pays to have a working knowledge of this subject and to know a reliable purveyor.

How to tell "which are the best truffles? Those of Provence or those of the Southwest? The truffles of Italy . . . ? Those of Spain?" asks Rocchia, who then answers: "I must respond to these questions by saying . . . that they are devoid of sense. There are excellent truffles in the southwest of France as there are in Italy and Spain. There are also execrable ones. Moreover, areas known for the excellence of their production . . . can offer, during some years and when weather conditions are unfavorable, very mediocre truffles."

A quest for the best can mislead. Rosario Safina points out that "*Tuber melanosporum* is the truffle—and it can be just fine in Texas [where it is cultivated] or Bordeaux [as in Périgord] if the temperature and rainfall are right," echoing Rocchia's message. There is no "best" truffle, just as there is no best olive oil or best Burgundy. There is a truffle grown under the best conditions, or best suited to a particular dish, menu, budget, or palate—or best in terms of many other variables that make cooking an exciting and unpredictable undertaking. "Until you are familiar with your own taste in truffles," Safina warns, "go slow. Buy small. Experiment. You can't count on a place name." Only experience teaches the subtleties: Take time to inhale and taste, and learn to recognize which truffles suit you.

Many people fear that inferior truffles are being substituted for the expensive *T. melanosporum* and *T. magnatum*. But when those two are in good shape, they smell and taste like nothing else. Your best defense is to recognize them. Don't look for bargains. Look for quality.

Fresh Truffles: A Down-to-Earth Market Guide

Black truffle or Périgord truffle, the exalted *Tuber melanosporum,* is THE black truffle of truffledom. (As mentioned earlier, despite the appelation "Périgord," it does not grow only in France or limit itself to that region in France.) "Black diamond" is one traditional description that captures the appearance of its distinctive dark-faceted surface—and its price. Its unique bouquet is rich, unaggressive, and highly variable. I have inhaled the scents of violets, roses, and other flowers; of sweet pork, of fresh earth, of cocoa, and—if the truffle was overripe—of cheese, soy sauce, and smoke.

SELECTION: Sniff deeply. If you don't love the perfume, you won't love the truffle. Chef Eric Ripert, who offers *T. melanosporum* in profusion, recommends large truffles that are comparatively hard and heavy with the "diamonds" closely set. The distributor Rosario Safina, on the other hand, finds that "large truffles lose flavor and perfume from being in the ground too long." Thierry Farges, another distributor,

says that black truffles should have a nick cut into them to reveal their ripe interior (and prove their species), especially early in the season.

"Although they're in the market from November, I wouldn't buy them until the end of January," says Ripert. "A ripe one has veins that are bright white and well spaced, and dark gray flesh. If the veins are too close, they have shrunken, dehydrated." Safina agrees: "Everyone wants this truffle too early, before it's mature—when its brownish, not blackish. Charcoal is the right color."

COOKING? Minimal heat releases the scent, which must be enjoyed at that very moment or contained by sealing it in some manner.

Italian white truffle or Alba truffle (*Tuber magnatum*), the grand duke of truffles, hides its power in an innocuous beige blob no more exciting to behold than a mammoth wad of gum. Who would guess that what lurks within the plain wrapper is the priciest fungus on earth? Its cost rests on its rarity (it grows in a limited area of northern and central Italy and in Istria, Croatia) and its stunning aroma. However subjective aroma may be, no one could confuse *T. magnatum* with any other truffle in the market. To my senses, garlic and raunch are what hit first, followed by softer complexities.

Rosario Safina stresses again that conditions—not mere locations—create the product: "You can get a great white truffle from Istria in the right year and a lesser one from Alba in a bad growing year." However, Roberto Donna, a Washington, D.C., restaurant impresario born in Piemonte, remains adamant about what he considers regional distinctions: "I grew up with Alba. I know it and crave it. The perfume is far stronger than others. It almost burns—gives a picante sensation in the nose. Price-wise, it makes sense. You use less, because it is so intense."

SELECTION: Choose dry, very firm tubers. Chef Donna squeezes every truffle before accepting the lot and returns any that feel soft. "Pink spots inside," he instructs, "indicate white truffles at their perfect peak." The interior, pale tan with creamy veins apparent, should be lighter than the exterior.

"It's silly and wasteful to buy early," says Rosario Safina. "The ground is too hot and dry and produces truffles without structure that fracture when cut." He advises holding off until "mid-October unless the weather is unusually wet and cold." Truffle lover Lau-

Oregon black (*top left*)   ⅓ actual size
Oregon white (*top right*)
Italian white or Alba (*center left*)
Tuber brumale (*center right*)
Chinese and Himalayan (*bottom left*)
black or Périgord (*bottom right*)

rent Gras is one of several chefs who prefer the "richer flavor of big truffles—the size of a big peach, about 250 grams is perfect," he says.

COOKING? *Don't cook* is the culinary credo. All you need is a little warmth—not much—to release the aroma.

Summer truffle (*Tuber aestivum*) has become a major player in the truffle trade over the last few years, despite its relatively light perfume. Although its black exterior and impressive size mimic *T. melanosporum,* its interior is pork-pâté beige and white and its flavor is pale. But high quality summer truffles have a nutty, woodsy mushroom flavor and an appealing crumbly, crisp texture. It's this texture that makes them desirable—provided they're used raw in good volume. Chefs usually boost the flavor by adding black truffle oil.

SELECTION: "The summer truffles from France, Italy, Spain—the same places as the *'melano'*—are usu-

ally best in July but can arrive as early as May and last into September," says Thierry Farges. Avoid any that look parched or have a white film; they may be low on flavor. Bigger is better here, since large slices provide more crunch, the special trait of this truffle.

COOKING? Most experts say none at all; others say to cook very slightly, combined with other elements—and certainly with fat, the flavor-transporter.

Tuber brumale, the Latin name, is the one often used in commerce and the only one I know to be correct. Possible common names mentioned in French and Italian texts are black Piedmont truffle, Vaucluse truffle, and violet truffle, but I have not been able to confirm the accuracy of these. The only American market listings I've seen are "black truffle" and "black winter truffle," which are very ambiguous, given that *T. brumale* shows up in season with *the* black truffle, *T. melanosporum.* Spain, France, and Italy have *T. brumale* in abundance, but it is generally canned or otherwise processed before it arrives in the United States. Judging from just a few fresh samples, I would like more. Although *T. brumale* is smaller and looser in texture than *T. melanosporum,* and covered with a black crust, the aroma is similar—if sharper, more woody. The very solid, smooth, and concentrated flesh is grayish, with fine white veins.

COOKING? Some say yes, some no. From my fleeting exposure, I can say that a short bath in buttery broth enhanced its perfume.

Tuscan truffle, spring truffle, or bianchetto (*Tuber borchii,* formerly *T. albidum*) suggests a dark-toned feeble-flavored *T. magnatum.* Massimo Vidoni, director of Boscovivo U.S.A., an importer in New York City, says that this truffle is used regularly in Emilia-Romagna, Lazio, Campagna, and Tuscany because "the eye appeal is similar to the real white truffle, even if the flavor isn't." He points out that "if you look closely at labels, you'll see that this truffle is the one most often canned in Italy."

Tuscan truffles I sampled were not like white truffles but chestnut to tan (and very muddy), with a softish interior divided equally between chocolate brown and white. Distinctly garlicky (although some had a nasty tinge of petroleum), they had a crumbly, nutty texture. Rosario Safina says flatly: "Sometimes they smell lovely—sometimes like gasoline."

SELECTION: Look for Tuscan truffles from January through March. Sniff to be sure they do not have a strong "chemical" smell.

COOKING? Use as you would summer truffles. "You use them raw, casually sliced over sunny-side-up eggs, pasta, crostini—not for big deal dishes," says Massimo Vidoni.

Oregon white truffle (*Tuber gibbosum*) looks much like the Italian white truffle—but the comparison ends there. To Greg Higgins, this and the Oregon black are *the* truffles that define the Northwest. The best white ones, he says, are "sweet-spicy, musky, warm, cedary, with hints of cinnamon, nutmeg, and vanilla."

Unfortunately, the cute ones I tasted, which sliced as neatly as butter, smelled more like bouillon cubes with a touch of petroleum. The flavor was nutty and gaseous; the texture smooth and oddly fatty. But given Higgins's long love affair with *T. gibbosum* and my one-night stand, I'd follow his lead, especially in light of a recent discovery: *T. gibbosum* may comprise three distinct varieties, according to descriptions in an unpublished paper by Charles Lefevre, David Pilz, James Trappe, and Randy Molina, scientists working in Corvallis, Oregon. This might explain the incongruities and lead to harvesting of the preferred types.

SELECTION: Greg Higgins searches out relatively large white truffles, then checks for insect or rodent nibbles. He separates ripe and unripe tubers by scent and look, discarding any that are "shriveled, almost like raisins." Richly perfumed truffles are used at once. Those in good shape but not sufficiently aromatic are packed into a jar with rice to rest on a warm shelf near the stove. "Usually, they're ready in a day or two," Higgins says. For slower ripening, enclose in a paper bag in the refrigerator for a few days. Look for Oregon white truffles in October and November, when they are pale throughout; later, when darker, they are more likely to be gaseous.

COOKING? Higgins serves these truffles raw, to finish a dish; or he steeps them in warm butter or olive oil for sauce. When I heated them in buttery broth, the consistency turned meaty and soft, the flavor more appealing.

Oregon black truffle (*Leucangium carthusianum,* formerly *Picoa carthusiana*) is the only truffle in this group that is not a *Tuber* species—and this is strange, because it may have more of the inimitable black truffle aroma than some true truffles do. In the ripest specimens, enthusiast Greg Higgins sniffs out pineapple, port, mushrooms, rich soil, and chocolate. My large, crusty samples—irregular coal-like lumps of white-veined cocoa flesh—had hints of these, as well as the mild *melanosporum* scent. Neatly sliceable, the texture resembled moist Parmesan and ground almonds.

SELECTION: Choose very hard, dry specimens with no sign of sponginess. Chef Higgins finds that large tubers, which have spent more time in the ground than small ones, are likely to have been nibbled by wildlife. Avoid any batch with an ammoniac scent. If they lack perfume but are otherwise sound, ripen them like the Oregon white truffle.

COOKING? Very slight; or heat by steeping in warm sauce.

Chinese and Himalayan truffles are catchall names for what James Trappe describes as "three distinct *Tuber* species found in South China: *sinense, indicum,* and *himalayense*—which pickers and distributors tend to lump together as 'Chinese truffles.'" This is particularly unfortunate, since flavor and quality vary from one species to another. First marketed in France in 1994, these truffles are now in restaurant channels in the United States at a comparatively low price. To judge from two samples, *T. indicum* is recognizable by its rich brown meat and very fine white veins. My samples looked lusciously chocolate truffly but lacked aroma and flavor and felt dry and dusty on the tongue. A moment in buttery broth only worsened the effect. *T. sinense* also looked richly dark, with large ivory veins. Rather moist, chewy, oily, with a bitter aftertaste, it kept well and sliced elegantly. For good looks, a bit of tooth, and a mushroomy-nutty effect, it seems promising. I could not get *T. himalayense*.

BASIC USE (FROM CHEFS): Because chefs' experience with truffles far exceeds mine, I asked for their advice and gleaned the following.

"To be enjoyed the most, truffles need only be respected for what they are and supported. Don't overwork the plate, garnish it, or try for invention" (Laurent Gras).

"The greatest error chefs make with truffle is not using enough. Stinginess misses the point of its taste and meaning" (Wayne Nish).

"Teach your staff to recognize ripeness in truffles. It takes practice to appreciate the 'barnyardy' tastes—whether of ripe cheeses, truffles, or wines" (Greg Higgins).

"The more you open up the black truffle, the more flavor it pours out. It is as if made of tiny perfume sacs which, when broken, spill perfume. If you grate instead of cut it, you get more flavor, control quantity, and can work *à la minute*. Keep the rest until ready to serve. Do not peel, just grate coarsely" (Eric Ripert).

"Black truffle loves fat, which catches and holds its flavor. Although expensive, truffle likes rustic—not delicate—companions. Even fatty pork is a great flavor conductor for it. In salad, truffle works with celeriac, which elevates its flavor. A hint of garlic does the same. My favorite snack is toasted sourdough with a touch of garlic, goose fat, grated black truffle, crisp salt grains, and mignonette pepper" (Eric Ripert).

"When heating black truffles, use the lowest temperature and the shortest time. Just warm—don't cook—them in duck fat or butter. Serve them the second you finish" (Todd Humphries).

"Black truffle requires heat—even just a little—to release its flavor. I discovered quite by accident that a machine releases the perfume best: One night, I was reverently hand-cutting truffles, noticed the time, panicked, and threw them into the Robot-Coupe. In seconds, as the blades heated up and cut the truffles fine, their aroma filled the room" (Wayne Nish).

"Oregon white truffles, like Italian, are fine to finish a dish. But they can also be steeped in warm butter or oil or included in compound butters, which is the best use for the smallest. Garlic is too strong for them. The most you need is a little shallot and a touch of fresh thyme. Use with lighter fishes, chicken, and, at the most, pork—but not stronger flavors" (Greg Higgins).

STORAGE: My advice to home cooks is to wrap truffles individually in a single layer of paper towel and refrigerate in a loosely packed jar. Change the paper daily and examine the truffles to be sure they are not softening or pitting.

For long-term preservation, do *not* follow the common advice to slice and refrigerate in olive oil, clarified butter, or duck fat. When I experimented with all three, the truffles turned putrid within weeks. (I did not try whole truffles, which are traditionally preserved this way and may keep well.) Sliced truffles and peelings refrigerated in brandy kept for many months and retained a truffly (and brandied) taste.

Storage recommendations from chefs and distributors diverge wildly, making experimentation unavoidable. Eric Ripert says: "Put a tiny bit of rice in a jar to pick up extra moisture, then wrap the truffles in paper

summer truffle   ½ actual size

Tuscan truffle   ½ actual size

towels and close the jar tightly. Store no more than a few days, or the point is lost. Keeping truffles is like keeping an open bottle of perfume."

Thierry Farges swears by this method: "It goes against all rules, but last year we discovered that black truffles last best in zipper-lock bags: We pack one pound to a bag, remove the air, seal, and refrigerate. We repack once a week and keep as long as three without loss of flavor. They do sweat a little, but the taste is fantastic."

Roberto Donna says: "Store white truffles in rice, but only for one day. If longer, change the rice daily. Or better, wrap each truffle in a bar napkin and refrigerate in a sealed plastic box—to keep out humidity and avoid smelling up everything else."

"Do *not* store truffles in rice in a sealed jar," states Rosario Safina. "Keep them in a cardboard box in the walk-in, individually wrapped in paper towels and changed daily. Truffles must breathe, or they sweat and rot. Overnight Pampers do a great job of dehumidifying: Put one diaper on the bottom of the box and one on top. Refrigerated white truffles last 3 to 4 days, black ones up to 2 weeks, and summer truffles 3 weeks."

PREPARATION: The condition of truffles is unpredictable. Although, in theory, imports should be free of earth, they can be dusted with soil or even stuffed with mud (the fissures and holes filled with earth). To remove dirt, use a soft brush for white truffles (which are easily damaged) and a stiff one for blacks (which have a tough hide), easing the dirt out with a knife tip, as needed. Sometimes a spray of water does the trick, sometimes a wet toothbrush.

White truffles, which are usually soft and smooth, need not be peeled. But for black truffles paring is an individual consideration—in terms of both cook and truffle. Some are thick-skinned, some thin-skinned. Some cooks like the granular crunch, some don't. Some cooks mince the peelings for sauces; others say fine truffles need not be peeled. All agree that they should not be cut until service.

Truffled Creamy Potato Soup

Potatoes, leeks, and celeriac are a backdrop to the foreground aroma of fresh black truffle—which is pounded to a paste, sluiced with cream, then stirred into the soup to disperse its scent. The more flavorful the truffle and the more of it, the more vivid the soup—but

it is a quiet one, nevertheless, for subtle palates. For a sweeter variation, substitute well-scrubbed sunchokes for the celeriac and add one tender celery stalk.

1 small leek
1 small-medium celeriac (¾ to 1 pound)
2 tablespoons butter
1 pound potatoes
1¼ teaspoons kosher salt
2 cups water
About 2 cups vegetable broth
White pepper
1 to 2 ounces black truffle (*Tuber melanosporum* or *T. brumale,* or *Leucangium carthusianum*)
About ¼ cup heavy cream

1. Trim dark green tops and roots from leek. Halve stalk lengthwise, then slice crosswise. Wash well in several changes of water. Scrub and peel celeriac (perfect peel removal is not required, unless you object to beige soup). Slice any way you wish.

2. Melt butter in heavy pot; stir in leeks and toss. Add celeriac and toss. Cook over moderate heat to color slightly, about 5 minutes.

3. Meanwhile, peel and chunk potatoes. Add to pot, with salt, and stir briefly. Add water and 2 cups broth. Cover and simmer gently until vegetables are very tender—about ½ hour. Cool briefly, as convenient. (I find all soups benefit from some resting prior to pureeing.)

4. With slotted spoon, transfer solids to blender or food processor container. Puree to very smooth texture, gradually adding liquid. Return to pot and add broth or water as needed for desired consistency. Season.

5. Brush truffle to remove any soil. Rinse and dry if necessary. Taste and peel if needed (refrigerate peelings in brandy). Cut off and set aside a chunk for garnish. Thin-slice remainder. Crush to a fine paste in suribachi or mortar. Add ¼ cup cream, a spoonful at a time, to further smooth the mixture. Stir in about ½ cup soup.

6. Stir truffle mixture into pot. Add more cream, salt, and white pepper, as desired. Barely simmer just to heat through.

7. To serve, ladle into small bowls. Slice reserved truffle over tops. Serve at once.

Serves 6 as a first course

Summer Truffle and Celeriac Salad with Walnuts and Comté

Summer truffle deconstructed tastes like celeriac, nutty cheese, and walnuts–which is why the three play supporting roles to the starring *Tuber*. Sweet-scented, with a bitter aftertaste, this crumbly-crunchy salad is easy to prepare if you have a thin-slicing blade on your food processor or a mandoline. Although I haven't tried it, I think this would also work well with *Tuber brumale* or Oregon black truffles.

¾ pound celeriac (1 small trimmed root)
3 tablespoons lemon juice
¾ teaspoon kosher salt
Pepper
½ tablespoon minced shallot
2 tablespoons walnut oil
2 tablespoons grapeseed or corn oil
Optional: black truffle oil
½ tart apple, halved and cored
3 ounces Comté (or aged Gruyère) cheese
1 or 2 large summer truffles (3 to 4 ounces total weight)
⅓ cup walnut halves, toasted

1. Peel celeriac and cut into blocks about 1 inch to a side and as long as will neatly fit the feed tube of your food processor. Stack together closely in feed tube on thin-slicing (2-millimeter) blade, then cut into thinnest slices. Transfer to bowl and toss with 1 tablespoon lemon juice and ¼ teaspoon salt. Chill.

2. For dressing, blend remaining 2 tablespoons lemon juice, ½ teaspoon salt, pepper, and shallot. Whisk in walnut and grapeseed oils. Add truffle oil, as desired.

3. Slice apple on thin blade. Toss with celeriac. Thin-slice cheese and add to bowl. Thin-slice truffle and add. Add dressing and walnuts and toss gently.

4. Arrange on salad plates. Serve immediately.

Serves 4 as a first course

Belgian Endive, Mâche, and Black Truffle with Butter Dressing

Black truffles (especially *Tuber melanosporum*) warmed in butter exude a sweet perfume. Serve this delicate salad as soon as it is tossed, to take advantage of the scented moment. The greens should not be cold, just barely cool—or the buttery sauce will congeal.

1 to 2 ounces black truffle
   (*T. melanosporum* or *T. brumale,* or
   Leucangium carthusianum)
3 tablespoons unsalted butter
1 tablespoon pecan or walnut oil
About 3 ounces mâche (4 lightly packed cups)
2 medium Belgian endives, rinsed
1½ tablespoons chives cut into 1-inch pieces
1 tablespoon lemon juice
2 teaspoons truffle juice, truffled brandy, or
   brandy
¼ teaspoon kosher salt
¼ teaspoon sugar

1. Scrub truffle lightly under a little running water. Pat dry. In small saucepan, melt butter over lowest heat. Allow to turn golden, but not brown. Skim off foam. Meanwhile, cut a slice from truffle and taste: If skin is gritty or coarse, scrape off (as little as possible; refrigerate peelings in brandy). Thin-slice truffle, then cut into julienne. Add half to butter, with nut oil. Remove from heat.

2. Trim rootlets from mâche if necessary. Gently swish around in bowl of water and lift out. Gently spin-dry, then blot on soft towel. Arrange on four salad plates. Trim base of endives and separate leaves. Stack, then cut into slim julienne on diagonal. Combine in bowl with the remaining truffle and chives.

3. Blend lemon juice, truffle juice, salt, and sugar. Warm butter mixture on lowest heat. Whisk into juice mixture. Pour at once over endive and truffles and toss. Divide among plates. Serve immediately.

Serves 4

Scallops Scented with Black Truffle and Celery

Five minutes of assembly and six minutes in the oven yield a subtle, luxurious first course. Black truffles and scallops have a remarkable affinity, provided the scallops are not cooked to the point where they begin losing liquid. Barely cooked, they offer a soft, satiny sweet counterpoint to the black, nutty truffle slivers.

FOR EACH SERVING

1 tablespoon olive oil
2 tablespoons thin-sliced inner celery stalk
3 ounces sea scallops
Big pinch of kosher salt
2 teaspoons black truffle julienne

Preheat oven to 425°F with baking sheet on center rack. For each packet, fold in half a 12- to 15-inch square of parchment. From this, cut a half heart, then open it out to a full heart. On one half, spread 1 teaspoon oil. Arrange celery on this half. Sprinkle scallops with salt, then set on celery. Toss together truffles with remaining 2 teaspoons oil. Arrange on scallops. Fold over parchment and crimp the packet tightly to close, like a turnover. Set on baking sheet. Bake 6 minutes, until scallops are just barely cooked. Serve each diner a packet to open up and enjoy the scent.

Pros Propose

Eggs and cheese are time-honored transporters of truffles' wealth of aroma. Roberto Donna (and other native Italian chefs) consider traditional **Fonduta** to be Alba truffle's finest hour. "At home in Italy, when you order truffles in season, fonduta simply arrives at your table," he says. To prepare: Trim Fontina d'Aosta, cube, and then soak 24 hours in milk. A few hours before serving, place the container of cheese near a heat source to soften. To serve, warm the mixture—no more—in water bath. Off heat, stir in 1 yolk for every 3 ounces cheese, then return to low heat momentarily. Pour into dishes, slice over "tons of white truffle," and serve with thin white toast.

Egg is the base for a rarefied treatment of a classic rustic dish, **Shirred Eggs with White Truffle Slices,** from chef Wayne Nish: For each serving chill heavy steel blini pan. Coat well with olive oil, break in an egg, and set in 500°F oven for 2 minutes. Slide at once into a porcelain dish ("it slips out easily cooked this way"). Scatter around tiny fingerling potato pieces stewed in butter. Shave white truffles over. Add a sprig each of chervil, basil, tarragon, and parsley.

Potatoes are another favorite ground for truffles, such as this American appetizer, **Potatoes on a Bed of Sea Salt with Truffles:** Bake large russets on a bed of coarse sea salt in 425°F oven, giving them a quarter-turn every 15 minutes until done (reserve salt). Cut off lengthwise "caps"; discard. Hollow out potatoes, scooping flesh into bowl. Mash with soft butter, sliced black truffles, and seasoning. Spoon into potato shells. Reheat slightly. Set potatoes on reserved salt on individual plates. Shave truffle over. Top with melted butter, salt, and pepper (from *Cooking with Daniel Boulud*).

Seafood is also a favorite foil for French black truffles, "but it must be kept simple," warns Laurent Gras. For his **Turbot with Black Truffles:** Press fine-chopped truffles onto one side of turbot fillets. Cook truffle side down in buttered pan in low oven to half-cook. Add a spoon each of truffle juice and shellfish broth to each fillet, and cook through. Arrange fish on plates, truffle side up. Reduce broth to *jus*. Spoon over fillets. Slice raw truffles over and add a touch of olive oil and lemon. ("You have rich fish, rich truffles—cooked, raw, and juice—so don't put anything else on the plate—not a thing!")

Oregon black truffles and fish also deserve a relatively simple treatment, says Greg Higgins, who illustrates with **Sturgeon Studded with Oregon Black Truffle:** Cut sturgeon to make 2-inch squares, 1 inch thick. Cut slits in each and insert truffle "chips." Season and pan-sear, then finish in hot oven. Serve with beurre rouge, made from red wine–shallot reduction, thyme, and fish stock. Finish with truffle butter.

Beggars' Purses with Lobster and Black Truffles, designed to seal in truffle perfume, are a signature dish for Wayne Nish. Cook thin crêpes in 5-inch non-stick pan. Prepare light mayonnaise with olive and peanut oils, vermouth, lemon juice, and rice vinegar. Chop truffles in processor ("use a mini-chop if you're not working in large volume," says Nish, "but do chop in a machine to release the aroma"). Add to minced lobster meat, with mayonnaise. Refrigerate. Fill each crêpe with scant tablespoon filling, form purse, and tie with blanched chive.

Salads made with black or white truffles are increasingly visible on upscale menus. Laurent Gras's version is the purest luxury. For **White Truffle and Porcini Salad:** Intersperse layers of thin-sliced perfectly ripe white truffles and raw porcini with small arugula leaves and sprinklings of fleur de sel, lemon juice, and olive oil. Serve immediately.

Truffle and porcini on a slightly more modest scale star in a salad from chef Fortunato Nicotra. He likes spring truffles (bianchetti) for salads because they have a nice firm texture for shaving, but he finds they need a backup of truffle oil or truffle paste. For **Truffle and Porcini Salad with Smoked Capon:** Toss arugula, shaved raw porcini, and shaved Parmesan with a dressing of truffle paste, olive oil, and low-acid apple vinegar. Top with sliced smoked capon or chicken breast, then with heaps of shaved bianchetti.

Summer truffles are also ideal for composed salads, according to chef Todd Humphries. "They don't have as much flavor as winter, but if you cut them rather thick, use a great quantity, and warm gently, they are delicious." For **Salad of Beets and Truffles:** Cook, peel, and quarter baby Chioggia, golden, and red beets. Toss each type separately with dressing of black truffle oil, champagne vinegar, and truffle juice. Warm summer truffle slices in butter, salt, and pepper and spoon over beets. Crumble over a touch of mild goat cheese.

Not quite salad, **Étouffée of Endive and Truffles** from chef Gray Kunz is in a class by itself: Toss bias-cut Belgian endive with salt, pepper, lemon juice, corn oil, and Madeira. Melt butter, add endive, and cook just 2 minutes, covered. Uncover and reduce liquid over high heat. Add truffle juice, thin-sliced fresh black French truffles, and butter. Meanwhile, quickly sauté whole endive leaves in butter with salt and sugar just until gilded; drain on towel. Spoon truffled endive at once into four dishes, top with sautéed leaves, and garnish with chervil.

Turnips (*Brassica rapa,* Rapifera Group)

Including **Tokyo-type white turnip**
TURNIP GREENS, page 687

This is a refresher course for yet another vegetable that is neglected in much of the United States but is enjoyed throughout the rest of the temperate zone, where it flourishes in a kaleidoscope of colors and forms. Alan Davidson summarizes its geographical distribution: "The turnip spread from the classical world through Asia to N. China, where it had become a common vegetable well before the medieval period in Europe, and it was taken from China to Japan about 1,300 years ago" (*The Oxford Companion to Food*). Today, no refresher course is needed in any of those lands, where it is eaten raw and pickled and cooked in multiple modes.

When we talk about turnips in the United States, we mean pretty much one thing: the radish-shaped, lilac-topped white turnip pictured here. In 1863, when Fearing Burr compiled *The Field and Garden Vegetables of America,* he included 44 turnips, black to rose, cylindrical to round. I am at a loss to explain how we have come to depend upon just one type in the market. Turnips in as many sizes and colors as Burr described still brighten our seed catalogues and home gardens; yet those in commerce are almost all variations on the type at the right.

Perhaps it was turnips wintered-over in root cellars that diminished people's taste for turnips? Or perhaps it was a combination of old turnips and old recipes? Until very recently, recipes suggested a wish to hide turnips, which were typically long-cooked in meat broth and saturated with sauce, or boiled to a tasteless pallor in the French style (or à l'anglaise—depending upon whose side you're on), or boiled and then mashed. Ten American cookbooks in my library (and probably more; I stopped checking) published between 1884 and 1930 contain some form of the following recipe: Simmer peeled, diced turnips in mutton or beef broth or water until transparent (30 to 60 minutes); drain. Rub together butter and flour and mix with cream or milk; bring to a boil with some cooking liquid. Pour over the turnips.

If we were to treat today's fresh turnips this way,

diameter: 2-3 inches

there would be no turnip left in the turnip. Instead, try the following basics.

BASIC USE: Serve turnips raw, on a vegetable platter: Cut sticks, half-moons, or rounds; crisp in ice water. For relish, salsa, or slaw, cut turnips into shreds or julienne, then salt and drain ½ hour. Rinse, dry, then mix with other shredded vegetables, fresh herbs, and tart or sweet-hot dressing or seasoning.

Whichever way you choose to cook turnips, do not overcook—this is what ruins them. They retain sweetness and fresh flavor if *just* tender. They do not turn strong and bitter if overcooked; rather, they get bland and flabby.

Steam small or halved turnips about 15 minutes, or boil about 10. Serve hot with nut oil and coarse salt, or olive oil and lemon, for a simple side dish. Or sauté-braise turnips: Quarter (or turn ovals, if you have the patience; they are just right for this); brown lightly with butter and sugar; salt, cover, and cook very gently until tender.

Stir-fry or sauté turnip shreds, julienne, or small dice about 5 minutes; cook with onions, garlic, carrots, peppers, squash, broccoli stems—almost anything—for color and variety. Toss with fresh herbs.

Add turnips to a stew of lamb, pork, chicken, or beef: Use very small whole turnips, or quarter larger ones. Brown lightly, then add to the stew during the last half-hour of cooking. Because turnips add flavor at the same time as they absorb juices, they contribute nicely to savory stews. Or roast alongside the same meats, allowing about 45 minutes of cooking time.

Prepare soup: Combine turnips with other winter veggies (parsnips, potatoes, carrots) and/or sliced leafy greens. Add water or broth and milk (and rice or oatmeal to thicken, if desired). Cook until tender, then puree. Or simmer turnip dice in chunky meat or seafood chowders.

This summary is just to get the creative juices flowing. There are so many ways to cook turnips! One to avoid, however, is microwaving.

SELECTION: Careful choice is the key to tasty turnips. Poor quality will not improve with cooking. Although sold all year, turnips (most of which are raised in California) are superior during the cool months; they are rarely worth buying during hot weather.

Turnips with greens are freshest—and you can gauge just how fresh by the leaves. Select only hard,

Tokyo-type turnip

diameter: about 1 inch

solid, pearly (not matte) globes. Small to medium turnips are usually sweetest. Avoid dull, slack-skinned, darkening, softish, or lightweight turnips (you must heft to compare) or any that feel spongy at the stem.

STORAGE: Turnips dehydrate very quickly and turn bitter. Today's turnips are meant not for root cellars but for immediate consumption. Store them, plastic-wrapped, in the coldest part of the refrigerator for no more than a few days.

PREPARATION: I regret to say that turnips (with the exception of tiny ones), no matter how smooth and fresh, are better peeled. It is also wise to taste for bitterness, which can ruin a dish. If turnips appear spongy, or if the layer under the skin is fibrous, sample to determine edibility (in fact, it is a good idea to taste all turnips as you pare). High-quality turnips slice as smoothly as potatoes.

The **Tokyo turnip** pictured on the left is fairly new to North American markets.

One tiny turnip can hardly make up for the many lost over the last decades—but if any one could, it might be this pearl of the East, a gem called variously Tokyo White, Tokyo Market, Tokyo Cross, etc., and generalized as Tokyo-type. (Joy Larkcom, the authority on Oriental vegetables, calls all round, white Japanese turnips kobaku-type, but I have not seen that term in the United States.)

Although these turnips can be left in the ground to grow larger, they are generally picked at a dainty 1 inch in diameter, which lands them in the radish bin at times. No matter, for they are delightful raw: bittersweet, nippy, and juicy. Cooked, they mellow to a truly buttery flavor but still retain their special character. Snap them up whenever you find them.

BASIC USE: Serve Tokyo-type turnips raw: slice thin and offer with crisp salt. To cook them whole, as a garnish: Spread cleaned turnips with greens attached on steamer rack over boiling water. Cover and cook until just barely tender, 3 to 6 minutes, depending upon size. Spread on towels to drain. Serve hot with a dish of salt and optional butter and pepper. Or, more practically, cut apart the bulbs and greens and steam separately. Or blanch in boiling salted water—but expect slightly less flavor. Do *not* microwave, unless you fancy gassy, tough-skinned, squishy turnips.

SELECTION: These elegant little specialty items should be in perfect shape: bright and perky greens; pearly turnips. Don't settle for less. Size varies, but 8 to 12 per pound (weighed with greens) is common. Figure on ½ pound per person for a generous portion.

PREPARATION: To cook these turnips whole, nip off any greens that are less than lovely. Scrub each turnip with a toothbrush (especially around the neck, where sand collects). Immerse several times, checking that no grit remains in the water. Or cut apart greens and turnips, pare turnip necks, then scrub under running water. Dunk greens in water, swish around, then lift out. Repeat until no debris remains.

Turnip, Celery, Apricot, and Ginger Slaw

Crunchy raw turnip julienne is salted to "cook" slightly, then tossed with strips of apricot and celery heart in a combination as versatile as it is unlikely. Try the salad as a bright first course alone, as a snappy side for hot or cold seafood or poultry, or as complement to a vegetarian grain entree. Choose deep orange, tart-sweet dried apricot halves (usually from California), not the supersweet plump, whole imported apricots.

About 2 pounds turnips (6 medium turnips, weighed without greens)
½ teaspoon kosher salt
2 tablespoons grated ginger
¼ cup rice vinegar
1½ tablespoons mild vegetable oil, such as grapeseed
2 cups thin-sliced inner celery stalks
⅔ cup thin-sliced California dried apricot halves
2 tablespoons thin-sliced scallion greens
About ¼ cup sliced cilantro (coriander) leaves

1. Scrub and peel turnips. Thin-slice, stack the slices, and cut across into very thin strips. Combine with salt in strainer. Drain 15 to 30 minutes, tossing occasionally. Rinse, then twist in towel to dry.

2. Press ginger in small strainer set over small bowl to catch juice; discard pulp. Add vinegar and oil to juice.

3. Mix turnips in a serving bowl with the celery, apricots, and scallions. Add dressing and toss well. Chill for at least an hour.

4. Taste and adjust seasoning. Toss slaw with cilantro, adding it gradually, to taste.

Serves 4

Mashed Potatoes and Turnips

If this simple, savory (and low-fat) mash is not in your repertory, be sure to give it a try. Steaming retains the turnips' and potatoes' sweetness and flavor and does not waterlog the vegetables as boiling may. Buttermilk adds its special tartness and moistens the puree. And, thanks to turnips' juiciness, the dish reheats well in a microwave, unlike plain mashed potatoes.

About 1½ pounds baking potatoes
   (3 medium potatoes)
About 1¼ pounds turnips (3 or 4 medium
   turnips, weighed without greens)
2 to 4 large garlic cloves, peeled
½ cup buttermilk
About ¼ teaspoon grated nutmeg
About ¼ teaspoon kosher salt
1 tablespoon butter, or more to taste
Optional: snipped chives

1. Peel and quarter potatoes. Peel turnips and cut into slightly larger pieces. Set both on steamer rack over boiling water. Add garlic cloves. Cover and steam until very tender, about 25 minutes.

2. Heat buttermilk over lowest heat without simmering (or it will separate). Dump the steamed vegetables into a mixing bowl. Crush with a potato masher, gradually adding heated buttermilk for preferred consistency. Season with nutmeg and salt.

3. Reheat if needed. Stir in butter. Sprinkle with chives, if desired.

Serves 4

Creamy (Creamless) Turnip Soup

This smooth puree is as adaptable and appealing as French potato-leek soup—but Scottish in origin, as the oatmeal thickening indicates. And a surprising and remarkable thickener it is, offering a richness and shine comparable to heavy cream. Served plain, the soup is pleasingly pale and gentle. Or dress it up with a garnish of minced herbs or salmon roe, caraway croutons, or julienned smoked ham. For a spicy version, stir in curry powder or garam masala with the raw turnips, and substitute meat broth for the vegetable.

1 very large white onion
Several interior celery stalks with leaves
About 1½ pounds turnips (4 or 5 medium
   turnips, weighed without tops)
1½ tablespoons vegetable oil
About ¾ teaspoon kosher salt (omit if broth is
   salted)
2 cups vegetable or chicken broth
1 cup milk
1 cup water
3 tablespoons old-fashioned oatmeal (rolled oats)
2 to 3 tablespoons lemon juice
White pepper
2 tablespoons minced dill and/or celery leaves

1. Chop onion. Slice enough celery to make about 1 cup. Quarter and peel turnips.

2. Warm oil in heavy pot over moderate heat. Add onion and celery and cook gently to soften slightly, about 5 minutes. Add turnips and salt and cook 5 minutes longer, stirring often.

3. Add broth, milk, water, and oatmeal; bring to a simmer. Cover, and simmer until vegetables are soft, about ½ hour. Cool slightly.

4. With slotted spoon, transfer turnips to food processor or blender. Puree until smooth. With motor running, gradually add cooking liquid.

5. Return soup to pot and bring to a simmer. Season with lemon juice, salt, and pepper.

6. Ladle soup into bowls and sprinkle with dill and/or celery. Serve hot.

Serves 4

Variation

Chilled Creamy Turnip Soup with Radishes

Prepare soup using only ½ cup milk, and overseason slightly. Cool, then chill. To serve, stir in buttermilk—about 1 cup. Garnish with ⅓ cup thin-sliced red radishes. Substitute chives for dill.

Turnips with Spinach, Hot Pepper, and Garlic

Salt turnip cubes to firm them up and concentrate flavor, then quick-cook with soft spinach leaves to add moisture and deep green savor. Chilli flakes, garlic, and vinegar add zip to a dish that can serve as a side or first course, either warm or at room temperature. Or toss the cooled mixture with diced sweet red pepper and more vinegar to serve as a salad course.

> 1¼ pounds turnips (3 or 4 medium turnips,
>   weighed without tops)
> 1 teaspoon kosher salt
> 1 pound spinach
> 2 tablespoons olive oil
> 1 large garlic clove, minced
> ⅛ to ¼ teaspoon chilli flakes
> About 1 tablespoon sherry vinegar

1. Trim and rinse turnips. Peel, then cut into ¾-inch cubes. Combine with salt in colander, tossing to coat. Let stand 15 minutes or more, tossing occasionally. Meanwhile, rinse spinach in several changes of water. Trim and discard only the heaviest stems. Thin-slice or chop remainder.

2. Pat dry turnip cubes. Set very large skillet with 1 tablespoon oil over moderately high heat. Add turnips and toss now and then until lightly browned, 4 to 5 minutes. Add garlic and chilli flakes and sauté another minute or so.

3. Spread spinach over turnips, pressing down firmly. Cover tightly, reduce heat to fairly low, and cook 2 minutes. Toss, re-cover, and cook until turnips are tender, 2 to 3 minutes longer. (If too juicy, uncover and boil briefly to evaporate some liquid.)

4. Transfer vegetables to a serving dish. Add vinegar and the remaining tablespoon oil and toss. Serve warm or at room temperature.

Serves 4

Quick Pink Turnip and Onion Pickles

Turnip pickles are an indispensable part of meals in Japan, Korea, the Middle East, North Africa, and areas of the former Soviet Union, but they remain a rarity in the West. This unorthodox composite (including the all-American cranberry) should remedy that, thanks to its ease of preparation, color, and versatility. An assertive munch, the low-cal slices add brightness and a tart-sweet bite to cold meat or seafood, vegetables (avocado, in particular), and grain salads. For variation, add dried chillis and star anise or caraway to the pickling liquid. The beet adds rosiness—a must in Middle Eastern versions and an inviting plus for newcomers to pickled turnips—but is not strictly necessary.

> 2 small red onions
> 1 pound small-medium turnips (about 5 turnips,
>   weighed without greens)
> 1 raw or cooked beet, sliced thin
> 1 cup white wine vinegar or rice vinegar
> 1 cup cranberry juice
> 4 bay leaves
> ½ teaspoon whole allspice
> ½ teaspoon peppercorns

1. Set a full kettle of water to boil. Halve red onions through "poles," and peel. Set cut side down, slice thin semicircles, then separate into layers. Peel, halve, and thin-slice turnips. Combine both vegetables in colander. Pour all the boiling water over them.

2. Combine onions, turnips, and beet in a wide-mouth 1-quart jar with vinegar, cranberry juice, bay leaves, allspice, and peppercorns, distributing the elements evenly throughout.

3. Cover and refrigerate for at least 3 days before serving, chilled.

Makes 1 quart

Steamed Tokyo Turnips Nested in Their Greens

Diminutive Japanese turnips are a bittersweet, beautiful, juicy treat. Steaming brings out the best in them. Serve on a platter to accompany poached or grilled whole fish or roasted meat. Or arrange on individual plates for a pristine appetizer or warm salad course. If possible, choose turnips of equal size so they will cook in the same time. If nasturtium flowers can be had, nothing makes a more vivid finish for the bright-white globes on their dark bed.

1½ to 2 pounds small Tokyo-type turnips
   with greens
About 2 tablespoons fruity olive oil
Crisp sea salt, preferably fleur de sel
Pepper

1. Cut greens from turnip necks; reserve. Pare necks neatly. Scrub turnips with a brush under running water. Immerse greens in water, swish around, and then lift out. Repeat until no grit remains.

2. Set turnips on rack over boiling water and arrange greens over them. Cover and steam until turnips are just barely tender (they will continue to cook off the heat). Timing varies with size and steamer, but 5 minutes is usual. Spread turnips and greens on towel to dry briefly.

3. Cut greens into 1-inch sections, more or less. Toss with about 1½ tablespoons olive oil. Arrange in a wreath or nest on a serving plate. Slice turnips lengthwise into quarters, or halve if tiny. Toss gently with ½ tablespoon oil, or to taste. Nest in the greens. Accompany with a dish of crisp salt and a pepper mill.

Serves 4

Note: If you have only a small steamer, you may need to cook the turnips and greens in separate batches.

Pros Propose

For turnips in familiar guises, turn to French cookbooks for the classic duck roasted with turnips or potato and turnip gratin. (In the Alsatian part of France, turnips salted and fermented in the same way as sauerkraut are traditional—and memorable.) Look for creamed turnip soups in the literature of Western Europe. For pickled turnips, head for the Middle East. Turnips are a regular ingredient in North African couscous, as well. For less traditional uses, consider these.

Roger Vergé's Vegetables in the French Style is not particularly French but filled with Vergé's special interpretations, such as **Turnip Galettes with Cardamom:** Peel medium turnips of uniform shape and slice very thin. Dip in equal parts cornstarch and confectioners' sugar seasoned with cardamom. Place in overlapping petal pattern in heated clarified butter in small crêpe pans or a large non-stick skillet. When golden, turn over. Finish cooking, then salt to serve.

Felipe Rojas-Lombardi's unusual **Pear and Turnip Soup** contains hominy—a hint of his Peruvian origin: Tie a sachet of chopped carrot, green chilli, tarragon, cloves, and allspice. Bring to a boil with enough water to cover the remaining ingredients. Sweat chopped onion in butter; add sweet sherry and evaporate. Add to the seasoned boiling water with peeled, cored, and chopped unripe Bosc pears and pared, chopped turnips. Add salt; simmer until tender. Remove sachet. Puree soup. Sauté drained, cooked white hominy kernels in butter; season with lemon juice. Stir a little cream into the hot soup. Garnish each serving with hominy and mint sprig (from *Soup Beautiful Soup*).

Mario Batali gives the vegetable an Italian twist with **Turnip "Risotto":** Sauté diced red onion in olive oil in a wide skillet until softened. Add diced turnips and cook until opaque. Add hot chicken stock gradually, a ladleful at a time, until turnips are tender. Season; stir in Parmesan and butter. Off heat, add parsley. Serve at once, as an appetizer (from *Simple Italian Food*).

For an Indian treatment, Madhur Jaffrey combines **Turnips with Yogurt and Tomato:** Peel turnips and cut 1½-inch dice. Pierce with a fork. Combine with salt and soured yogurt (left overnight at room temperature) for 3 hours. Strain; reserve yogurt. Brown turnips lightly in large non-stick skillet in peanut oil over high heat; transfer to dish. Add whole cumin seeds to pan; stir in shallot strips and color slightly. Add peeled, chopped tomatoes and ground hot pepper; stir a moment. Add turnips and reserved yogurt. Cover; cook on medium heat, stirring now and then for 10 minutes. Lower heat; cook until remaining mixture clings to the turnip pieces.

Turnips are salted to eliminate moisture and "cook" the flesh for a Japanese salad, **Crisp Turnip with Sesame-Miso Dressing:** Cut peeled turnips into julienne; toss with salt and let stand 20 minutes. Rinse and gently squeeze out liquid. Blend freshly toasted and ground white sesame seeds, sweet white miso, and sake. Add Japanese mustard (or any hot powdered mustard blended to a paste with hot water, then allowed to mellow, covered, for 30 minutes). Add turnips and toss to coat. Top with grated citrus zest, blend, and serve (from *Good Food from a Japanese Temple* by Soei Yoneda).

Turnip Greens

Also turnip tops, turnip salad, foliage turnip, leaf turnip

From where I sit (New York City) turnip greens have become more Far Eastern than Deep Southern. Once a traditional spring green eaten in much of the southerly United States, turnip tops were already pretty much limited to soul food by 1980, when I began to focus on vegetables. Now, I can rarely find them in markets where collards, mustard, and salt pork are still sold. But I do see them in Asian groceries, where they are nearly impossible to distinguish from the various radish greens that are equally popular in the making of kimchee and soup, for which both are often destined.

In the past, when I have written about a familar subject, I have not reviewed the old material until the new was in place. But today, I looked at *Uncommon Fruits & Vegetables: A Commonsense Guide*, and I found this comment under turnip greens: "It will probably be the new Americans from Asia and the Orient, with their myriad modes of saucing, slicing, and spicing, who will put all bitter greens back on the map." Downright prescient—if pretty easily predictable. Strong brassica flavors have never been as popular in the United States as

in the Far East, where vigorous bitterness and bite are preferred. With their harsh heat and rather rough-textured leaves, turnip greens are not a beloved vegetable in America, except to those for whom they mean home. But if the two turnip-green strongholds coexist, perhaps we might see a happy fusion of the bitter-green repertoire in the future.

BASIC USE: Turnip greens are too fuzzy and chewy for the salad bowl, despite the fact that almost everything goes in there these days.

Small, tender turnip greens can be just lightly cooked or wilted, however: For a pleasantly sharp flavor, stir slivered leaves into wok-braised dishes or Asian broths. Or add the greens to long-cooked soups, whether sturdy bean-grain combinations or soups to be pureed, such as potato or root vegetable.

Asian ingredients in general suit turnip greens: sweet and hot spices, fresh and pickled ginger, coconut milk, sesame seeds and oil, soy sauce, miso, and Asian citrus juices.

Blanch turnip greens to mellow their harshness and add succulence to the sometimes too-chewy leaves. Once boiled and drained, they can be treated like dandelion: Bake with cream and/or cheese; sauté with garlic and hot pepper; add to grain or pasta dishes.

SELECTION: Most turnip greens appear in the market minus turnips. Although some cultivars produce good-quality leaves and roots, those grown for foliage alone generally yield larger and thicker leaves. Turnip greens can be found erratically year-round, with peak availability from November through March. Seek fairly thin-stalked plants with no yellowing and no sign of dryness. They should be well chilled and feel moist, not wet. Greens kept in a warm area become bitter, tough, and dry.

STORAGE: Turnip greens, like radish leaves, are more perishable than they look—so don't stock up. Wrap in damp towels, then in a plastic bag, and keep in the coolest place in the refrigerator for no more than a few days. Avoid storage near climacteric fruits (those that continue ripening after harvesting), such as apples, avocados, bananas, pears, plums, and most tropical fruits, which emit ethylene gas that causes yellowing and hastens drying.

PREPARATION: Turnip greens need a good bath. Slosh them in a sink filled with tepid water, then lift

turnip greens   length: 5-10 inches

out so debris sinks. Repeat and check for sand. Repeat as needed. Shake the leaves, then strip from the stems (which are discarded, unless unusually small and tender). When you cook the tops of fresh young turnips—rather than bunched greens—you can usually keep the stems intact: taste to find out.

Nippy Turnip Greens with Olives, Orange, and Cumin

This dark, intense combination, finished with an aromatic flourish, suits grilled lamb or full-flavored fish, such as mackerel, bluefish, or sardines. Or toss the spicy greens with small, sturdy pasta, adding a little of the pasta water to soften and blend the flavors. For variety, substitute mustard leaves or arugula for part of the turnip greens.

1½ to 2 pounds turnip greens
1 orange, preferably organic
12 tender oil-cured black olives
1 or 2 garlic cloves
¼ to ½ teaspoon chilli flakes
¼ teaspoon cumin seeds
2 tablespoons strong olive oil

1. Strip stems from turnip greens and discard. Wash greens in several changes of water until no grit remains.

2. Drop greens into a large pot of lightly salted boiling water. Cook until just barely tender, about 2 minutes, stirring often to keep leaves submerged. Drain thoroughly. Chop to coarse texture.

3. Scrub orange. With zester, remove thin strands from half the orange (or remove zest with peeler, then cut into hair-thin strips). Pit and slice olives. Thin-slice garlic. Combine zest, olives, and garlic on a cutting board. Sprinkle with chilli and cumin and chop fairly fine.

4. Combine the mixture with olive oil in medium-large skillet. Stir over moderately low heat a few minutes, to cook garlic lightly. Add the greens and toss a

few minutes. Cover and cook a few minutes longer to blend flavors. Do not dry out or brown.

5. Cut the part of the orange with peel still intact into 4 wedges. Serve with the greens.

Serves 4 as a side dish

Variation

Nippy Turnip Greens and Chickpeas

Proceed as above, but double the amount of garlic, chilli, cumin, and orange zest and add an extra tablespoon of oil. In step 4, add 1½ cups cooked, drained chickpeas (or other cooked, small flavorful dried beans) with the greens. Omit the orange wedges.

Serves 5 to 6 as a side dish

Creamy Curried Turnip Greens with Coconut

Turnip greens with an Asian edge enrich plain grilled poultry or fish or complement a spice-rubbed version. The greens turn mild and creamy when bound lightly with coconut milk and sweetened with crisp-toasted coconut shreds.

> About 2 pounds turnip greens
> ⅓ cup (unsweetened) dried coconut shreds
> 1 garlic clove, minced
> ½ cup coconut milk
> ½ teaspoon curry powder or garam masala
> ¼ teaspoon turmeric
> ¼ teaspoon kosher salt
> About 1½ cups broth (any kind) or water
> 1 tablespoon cornstarch
> Lime or lemon juice

1. Strip stems from greens; discard. Wash greens in several changes of water until no grit remains. Drop into a large pot of well-salted boiling water and return to a full boil. Drain. Chop or slice fairly coarse (to make about 2½ cups).

2. In a skillet large enough to hold all ingredients, stir coconut shreds over moderate heat until they turn tan, 4 to 5 minutes. Scoop out and set aside.

3. Combine garlic with 2 tablespoons coconut milk in same pan and stir over low heat to soften a bit.

Stir in curry, turmeric, and salt. Add 1½ cups broth and bring to a boil, stirring. Add greens, cover, reduce heat, and simmer until tender to soft, stirring occasionally. Timing varies, but 15 minutes is likely for young leaves.

4. Blend cornstarch with a little of the coconut milk to make a smooth cream, then gradually add remainder. Uncover greens and cook down if there is more than about ½ cup liquid. Add starch mixture. Stir now and then over low heat until flavors blend, about 5 minutes. If necessary, add more broth or water for preferred consistency. (Can be reheated.)

5. Add lime juice to taste, and season. Sprinkle each serving with toasted coconut.

Serves 4 as a side dish

Variation

Creamy Turnip Green–Coconut Sauce

The greens make an interesting sauce to spoon over mixed grains for a vegetarian main dish. Increase the coconut shreds to ½ cup. Double the coconut milk, garlic, curry, and salt. Add ⅛ teaspoon ground hot pepper with the spices. Thin with broth or water if the mixture is too thick.

Pros Propose

Perhaps the best known turnip-top soup is Spain's caldo gallego, similar to the kale-based caldo verde of Portugal—both brews likely to be welcomed in the American South. The Galician soup may begin as long-cooked pork and greens (lacon con grelos), or may contain beef, or vary in other ways, but all forms rely on greens and potatoes, as does this simple **White Bean, Turnip Green, and Potato Soup:** Combine soaked dried white beans with water to cover, cubed Serrano ham, salt pork, chopped onion, and salt. Simmer until beans are almost tender. Add chorizo, shredded turnip greens, and diced potatoes. Cook until tender. Remove sausages and pork. Slice sausages and return to soup (from *The Cooking of Spain and Portugal* by Peter Feibleman and the Editors of Time-Life Books).

Both turnips and their greens figure in a rich, concentrated **"Pot Likker" Soup** from Virginia food writer Sarah Belk King, who updates traditional Southern recipes: Combine chopped turnip greens, bacon chunks, coarsely cut carrots, halved onions, chicken broth, and water to just cover. Tie together a sachet of halved garlic, whole dried chillis, peppercorns, parsley sprigs, thyme sprigs, and bay leaf; add. Simmer, partly covered, for 1 hour, adding water if needed to cover. Drain, reserving liquid. Discard onion and carrot pieces, bacon, and herb sachet. Return liquid to pot and add washed, unpeeled baby turnips (Tokyo-type are fine). Simmer until crisp-tender; remove with slotted spoon. Puree half the greens with half the broth. Return to pot with turnips and the remaining greens; heat. Adjust seasoning and liquid. Top with crumbled bacon.

A soup recipe from the Far East gives a very different picture of turnip greens: Somen noodles in broth, accented with greens and mushrooms, are garnished with candied walnuts. For **Spring Noodles with Turnip Greens and Oyster Mushrooms:** Prepare glazed walnuts: Combine sake, sugar, and shoyu in non-aluminum pan; boil. Add walnut halves and stir over moderate heat until lightly browned and liquid has evaporated. Transfer to a plate; sprinkle with shredded roasted nori. Season dashi with shoyu, sake, and salt; bring to a boil. Add oyster mushrooms cut into ½-inch slices and chopped turnip greens. Simmer briefly to wilt the greens. Divide cooked and drained somen noodles among bowls. Ladle dashi and vegetables over each and garnish with walnut halves. Serve at once (from *The Vegetarian Table: Japan* by Victoria Wise).

In Morocco, vegetables are usually cooked soft and mellow. Turnips with their greens and stems are the melders in **Chicken Kdra with Turnips and Chick-Peas** from Paula Wolfert's early seminal work, *Couscous and Other Good Food from Morocco.* To prepare: Pound garlic cloves with salt and rub into chicken; rinse, and quarter. Rinse, drain, and skin cooked chickpeas. Combine quartered and sliced onions, white pepper, ground ginger, pulverized saffron, turmeric, and butter with the chicken in a casserole. Add chicken broth and bring to a boil. Rinse and chop both leaves and stems from young turnips; cube the turnips. Add all to the pot; simmer 40 minutes. Remove chicken and turnips and simmer sauce to reduce to a thick gravy. Add lemon juice; season. Add chickpeas and heat. Add chicken and turnips; heat through. Add parsley.

Water Celery, Water Dropwort

(*Oenanthe javanica*, formerly *O. stolonifera*)

Also Korean watercress, minari (Korean), seri (Japanese)

length: 18-24 inches

This leafy aquatic plant belongs to the family Apiaceae (or Umbelliferae), which also includes parsley, celery, lovage, and mitsuba (Japanese parsley). Roll them all together and you have the celery-parsley tang and fresh aroma that characterize water celery, grown in East Asia, Southeast Asia, and Hawaii, where it was transplanted by settlers from the Far East.

It is particularly popular in Japan as seri, which "grows along streams and marshes and is best from autumn to spring, although it is picked year-round," ac-cording to *A Dictionary of Japanese Food* by Richard Hosking, who writes that it is used in sukiyaki, soups, and salads, and with chicken. More specifically, he de-scribes it as an element of nanakusagayu ("seven-herb rice gruel"), which is "eaten on January 7 to avoid ill-ness throughout the coming year, being regarded as a medicine. City dwellers can often buy little sets of the herbs in supermarkets."

In most countries that eat water celery, it is both cultivated and gathered from the wild, a practice that strikes terror into the hearts of Western foragers, for whom the genus *Oenanthe* sets off warning bells because of its poisonous species, notably the deadly *Oenanthe crocata* or hemlock water dropwort (also called water hemlock). But there is also a benign native American relative: "The Water Parsley of our Pacific Northwest is another species of Oenanthe (*O. sarmentosa*)," writes Alex D. Hawkes in *Cooking with Vegetables*. "It produces smallish black-skinned tubers which, when boiled, have long been relished by the Indians of the region for their sweet, creamlike texture and flavor."

What you'll find in North American markets is cultivated and safe. The bunches resemble celery plus flat-leaf parsley and vary considerably in size (even more than the photo shows), from some two dozen to eight dozen stalks per pound. The stems, some hollow, some not, range from about ⅛ inch to ½ inch in diameter and have a bamboo-like growth pattern. Oddly, the different sizes take about the same time to cook. The chewy stalks and leaves are green-scented and assertive.

Note: If you have read this far, you are interested enough to be able to bear the news that "water dropwort" is the most common English name for this vegetable. "Water celery" is given first place at the head of the entry because many Americans react negatively (to put it mildly) to "wort," an old word for plant that survives in English vegetable names outside the United States.

BASIC USE: To use water celery raw as a seasoning, chop very fine and add to grain, bean, or tofu dishes. For soups or broth-based dishes, such as sukiyaki, add thin-sliced water celery stalks and leaves for the last minute of cooking. For stir-fries, cut stems into 2-inch lengths and toss until half-cooked before adding the rough-chopped leaves and leaf stems. Or steam: Half-cook stems alone, then add leafy tops and cook until tender; drain and press dry and cut to the size desired. Serve warm or as salad for a succulent, chewy green with a chrysanthemum nip. In Korea, large stalks are blanched to use as ties for seafood bundles, in the manner of small leeks or green onions.

SELECTION AND STORAGE: Check over water celery as you would flat-leaf parsley. It should be moist, not wet, with no leaves that are yellowing or slippery. If there is a choice, select stalks with a minimum of purple base—the tough part. Refrigerate for as short a time as possible, no more than a few days. If bunched, open up to separate the stalks, removing any spoiled leaves. Wrap in plastic.

PREPARATION: Cut off the darkest purple parts, if any. Remove slippery or yellow leaves. Swish in a sink filled with water. Lift out and drain. For most dishes, you'll want to separate the leaves and their stems from the heavier stalks, which take longer to cook.

Water Celery Ohitashi

Presented in the style of Japanese greens, pungent steamed water dropwort stems are crunchy, chewy, and reminiscent of celery and chrysanthemum. The sauce is not traditional, but tart-hot-sweet and gingery. Serve as a side to seafood and rice, or as a first course, plain or embellished with small shrimp. If hot sesame oil is not in your pantry, add a few dashes of chilli oil to Asian sesame oil.

1 pound water celery
1½ tablespoons shoyu (Japanese soy sauce)
1 teaspoon honey
1 teaspoon fine-grated ginger
1½ tablespoons lime juice
1 to 2 teaspoons distilled white vinegar
1 to 2 teaspoons hot sesame oil
1 teaspoon toasted sesame seeds

1. Cut off and discard dark purple bases from water celery, if any. Remove any browned, yellow, or slippery leaves. Swish in a sink filled with water. Lift out and drain. Cut leafy parts from stems.

2. Set stems on rack of large steamer over boiling water. Cover and cook until half tender, 4 to 5 minutes. Add leafy parts and toss. Continue cooking, covered, until quite tender but still crunchy—4 to 5 minutes longer.

3. Meanwhile, blend shoyu, honey, ginger, and lime juice. Gradually add vinegar and sesame oil to taste.

4. Remove water celery from steamer. Cool until you can squeeze it, a handful at a time, to extract as much liquid as possible. Chop fairly coarse. Pack very tightly into four small dishes, molds, or measuring cups, each of about ¼-cup capacity. Chill.

5. To serve, run a knife around edges of dishes to loosen greens. Rap each container sharply on a small plate to unmold. Stir dressing and spoon over tops. Sprinkle with sesame seeds.

Serves 4

Chilled Water Celery and Cucumber Bisque

This delicate puree, herbal and fresh, suggests leek-potato-sorrel soup—and, like it, can be served hot or cold. Milky gray-green, it benefits from a brightening garnish of minced or slivered leaves. In these days of instant everything, plain old *regular* farina (Cream of Wheat) is difficult to locate, so I've compromised on the quick-cooking—but don't use the instant.

> About 1½ pounds cucumbers (3 medium)
> 1 small bunch scallions (green onions)
> 1 tablespoon grapeseed or mild vegetable oil
> 3 cups vegetable or chicken broth
> 3 cups water
> 2 teaspoons kosher salt (omit if broth is salted)
> 1 tablespoon white wine vinegar
> ¼ cup quick-cooking farina
> 8 to 10 ounces water celery
> 2 big handfuls parsley leaves
> ½ cup sour half-and-half or sour cream
> White pepper

1. Cut off one-third of 1 cucumber for garnish and refrigerate. Peel remaining cucumbers and quarter lengthwise. Cut out seeds. Cut into 1-inch slices. Trim and slice enough scallions to make 1 cup.

2. Warm oil in casserole over moderately low heat. Stir in scallions and cook briefly to wilt but not brown. Add cucumbers, broth, water, salt, and vinegar. Bring to a boil. Stir in farina. Simmer, partly covered, until cucumber is soft, about 15 minutes.

3. Meanwhile, trim any dark purple stems and yellowed leaves from water celery. Wash celery well. Separate leaves (reserve about ½ cup for garnish) and stems. Thin-slice stems and add to soup. Simmer, partly covered, until quite tender—5 to 15 minutes, depending upon how fibrous they are. Add leaves and bring to a boil. Add parsley and remove from heat. Cool slightly.

4. Puree soup until as smooth as possible in food processor. When smooth, whiz in sour cream. Over-season slightly. Cool completely. Cover and chill.

5. To serve, seed reserved cucumber and cut into tiny dice. Mince enough reserved water celery leaves to make 3 tablespoons. Thin-slice enough scallion greens to make 2 tablespoons. Taste soup and season. Thin with ice water, if desired. Ladle into shallow bowls and top with cucumber, water celery leaves, and scallions.

Serves 6 as a first course

★See also recipes for Chinese Celery, pages 201–202, for which water celery can be substituted.

Water Chestnut, Chinese (*Eleocharis dulcis*)

Also waterchestnut, ma tai (Chinese)

Not a chestnut—not even a nut—this delicacy needs its botanical name to define it, as several plants claim the name "water chestnut." Without the genus, *Eleocharis,* to help, English-speaking authorities add "Chinese" to the water chestnut pictured in order to distinguish it from the others. According to Frederic Rosengarten's invaluable work *The Book of Edible Nuts,* the characters for "ma tai" mean "horse's hoof," one apt way to describe the distinctive little mahogany corms (not nuts, not tubers, not roots). Because these natives of the Old World tropics require a lengthy stay in a frost-free environment to develop fully, they are imported from warm climates. There has been experimentation with plantings in the southern United States, but little has come of it.

Many Americans are familiar with Chinese water chestnuts in canned form: pleasant, crunchy, and not much else. Fresh, they are another story. Once the scruffy coats are removed, the pale, solid flesh is as dramatically different from the canned as are fresh green beans from processed. Uncooked, the startlingly sweet, juicy tidbits suggest apples, sunchokes, and sugarcane. During cooking, the corms waft the scent of sweet corn.

Like sweet corn, water chestnuts are a popular ingredient in Southeast Asian desserts. In fact, they seem to figure more prominently in recipes for cakes, fruit cups, drinks, and puddings than in savory dishes. Water chestnut powder (or flour), made from peeled, dried water chestnuts, is a light-textured thickening agent available in Oriental markets.

The "other" water chestnuts, of the genus *Trapa,* are also called European water chestnuts and water caltrops, according to Rosengarten. He writes that several species are important staple foods in China, Japan, Korea, and India—and have become naturalized pests in the United States, where they were introduced over a century ago.

One winter, I found *Trapa bicornis* in a market in New York during the Chinese New Year. Shiny as polished ebony, shaped like the horns of oxen, the "nuts" (also called Jesuits' nuts, an etymology I have not—

½ actual size

yet—pursued) were utterly intriguing. With the help of boiling, steaming, nutcracker, cleaver, hammer, and lobster pick, I finally extracted small bits of bland starchy stuff. My colleague Jim Fobel, a strapping man and an able cook, used force and inventiveness to threaten and coerce another batch into submission—without success. If you want to try *T. bicornis,* be sure to cook the corms at length, for they may harbor toxins or parasites or both, depending upon whose information you trust. I give up.

BASIC USE: Chinese water chestnuts can be enjoyed at any stage from raw to long-cooked. Boil, steam, braise, sauté, or chop and add to ground seafood or meat to bake, fry, or use as stuffing. In my experience, there is no reason to be concerned about overcooking.

Add luxury and surprise to a raw vegetable platter with peeled, halved Chinese water chestnuts; or wrap them in salmon or prosciutto. Slice, dice, or julienne into cold or hot salads—Eastern, Western, fusion—with vegetables, fruit, rice, noodles, seafood, or poultry. Even a small quantity will have a lively effect.

Chinese water chestnuts need no precooking when combined with raw ground meat or seafood: Deep-fry for appetizers, or make balls for soup or patties for steaming or frying. Or stuff the mixture into vegetables for steaming. Cut into tiny dice and simply mix in; they'll stay crunchy and separate.

For stir-fries, cut to match the other ingredients, then toss over moderate heat with vegetables, seafood, or tofu, covering briefly or adding a little liquid to finish cooking. Slip snippets into savory custards (like Japanese chawan mushi) and quiches for a crisp accent.

Simmer raw slices briefly in broth-based dishes, such as sukiyaki. For simply perfect soup, follow chef Gray Kunz's advice: "There is no more delicate and delicious binder then fresh water chestnuts. Simply slice them into the finest broth and bring to a boil. Garnish with a handful of sliced greenery and serve."

SELECTION: Chinese water chestnuts are available irregularly year-round, primarily in Asian markets. Look for shiny, heavy, hard, solid corms with no sign of shriveling. They bruise and spoil easily, and thus require careful selection. Press each to check for soft spots, which denote decay. Choose the largest ones, to minimize labor and waste. Buy more than you think you'll need. There is always loss from spoilage and peeling.

STORAGE: Chinese water chestnuts have amazing staying power, kept as follows: Refrigerate, unpeeled, in a jar of water, replacing it with fresh every 5 or 6 days (they have stayed bright and crisp this way for up to 4 weeks). They even "self-clean" and plump up. Although storing them peeled in water is frequently recommended, I find that they lose flavor and spoil.

In restaurants, follow the lead of chef Gray Kunz, who refrigerates them (and most produce) in wicker baskets to allow air circulation: First line the baskets with dry newspaper, then cover the corms with damp newspaper, moistening when it dries.

PREPARATION: Scrub Chinese water chestnuts gently with a vegetable brush. Or, if you have time, soak them overnight and they'll clean themselves.

Once soaked, lift them out, leaving the accumulated mud. Rinse and proceed with peeling; or refrigerate in fresh water.

Peeling water chestnuts is slow work, no matter how you do it. A razor-sharp paring knife or a narrow Asian cleaver does the best job. If you hit brown spots, cut them out; the rest of the chestnut is usually fine. (But sniff to be sure: Spoiled chestnuts smell fiercely alcoholic or sour.) Alternatively, blanch and peel: Boil or steam cleaned corms for 5 to 10 minutes. Refresh in ice water, then peel. There will be less waste this way, but the flesh darkens. Once peeled, halve, quarter, slice, dice, or cut into julienne or tiny dice.

Aromatic Asian Broth with Water Chestnuts and Scallops

This subtle soup surprises. Its pale and polite appearance belies a big bouquet and hot kick. And although scallops and water chestnuts look similar, their textures are shockingly different. Serve as an appetizer for a light supper, followed by Buckwheat Noodles, Mizuna, and Radishes with Tart Tofu-Mizuna Dressing (page 327) or Sesame Noodles with Radishes and Garden or Upland Cress (page 232).

1 bunch cilantro (coriander), with roots
4 cups vegetable, fish, or chicken broth
1 or 2 small dried chillis
1 large stalk lemon grass
About 8 large Chinese water chestnuts
¼ pound sea scallops, halved and thin-sliced
About ¾ teaspoon kosher salt
⅓ to ½ cup coconut milk
2 to 3 tablespoons sliced chives
4 lime slices

1. Prepare broth: Cut stem (with roots) from coriander. Wash well, scrubbing roots with a brush. Slice thin: Combine in pot with broth and chillis. Thin-slice lemon grass, reserving 2 inches of the innermost part of the bulb end; add slices to broth. Simmer, covered, for 10 minutes. Taste during cooking: Remove chillis if desired hotness is reached. Strain broth, pressing hard on solids to extract all liquid (can be prepared ahead).

2. Clean water chestnuts (see Preparation). Peel, halve, and then slice thin.

3. Strip enough cilantro leaves to yield ¾ cup lightly packed; slice if large. Halve reserved lemon grass lengthwise, slice paper-thin, and then mince. Sprinkle scallop slices with ¼ teaspoon salt.

4. Return broth to rinsed-out pot, with ½ teaspoon salt. Bring to a boil. Reduce heat, add water chestnuts, and simmer until raw taste disappears, 4 to 5 minutes. Add scallops, minced lemon grass, and coconut milk to taste. Keeping below a simmer, stir until scallops are barely cooked, about 1 minute.

5. Ladle into bowls, distributing solids equally among them. Add cilantro leaves and chives. Perch a lime slice on each bowl's edge.

Serves 4

Variation

Aromatic Asian Broth with Water Chestnuts and Shrimp

If you prefer pink-and-chewy to ivory-and-slippery, shrimp are a good choice. Substitute 6 ounces small shrimp in the shell for the scallops. Clean them and add the shells to the broth ingredients. Halve the shrimp lengthwise to make thin quick-cooking pink curls. Add at the same point as you would the scallops.

Water Chestnut and Smoked Salmon Hors d'Oeuvre

Smoky, silky salmon slices wrapped around crunchy sweet Chinese water chestnut morsels make a simple, quietly luxurious appetizer.

1 pound large Chinese water chestnuts (about 2 dozen)
3 tablespoons minced dill, and sprigs for garnish
3 tablespoons thin-sliced chives
5 to 6 ounces thin-sliced smoked salmon

1. Either soak water chestnuts overnight (see Preparation) or scrub well with a brush.

2. Either boil water chestnuts for about 6 minutes or steam them for about 10 minutes. Chill in ice water.

Peel carefully with very sharp, thin-bladed knife. Halve each one.

3. Mix dill and chives. Toss with water chestnuts, pressing to coat with the herbs. Wrap each piece in a strip of salmon, cutting the fish to accommodate the number of water chestnut pieces. Fasten each salmon wrap with a dill sprig pierced by a toothpick. Chill until serving time.

Makes about 4 dozen

Variation

Water Chestnuts Filled with Herbed Cream, Salmon-Topped

For a fancier presentation, stuff the chestnuts: With small melon ball cutter, gently cut as large a cavity as possible in each water chestnut half. When all halves are scooped, chill them. Mince the scooped-out parts. Blend with about 3 tablespoons sour cream and 2 tablespoons each minced dill and chives. With teaspoon, form smoothed mounds of filling in chilled water chestnuts. Chill, covered. At serving time, top each with a generous curl of salmon (you'll need only 2 to 3 ounces of smoked salmon for this treatment) or salmon roe.

Stir-Fried Water Chestnuts, Snow Peas, Corn, and Ham

All crunch, sugar, and color, this is an easy dish to make and to like. Serve the simple toss as a main course with scented rice. Or offer the lively mix to brighten grilled seafood or poultry, as you would salsa. What follows is for a duo. You can double or triple to suit your wok and the number of diners.

3 ounces snow peas (as small as possible)
6 ounces Chinese water chestnuts
3 slim scallions (green onions)
1 ear of corn
About 1½ ounces firm country-style dry-cured ham
1 tablespoon vegetable oil
⅓ cup water
Salt and pepper
2 tablespoons minced cilantro (coriander) leaves or 1 tablespoon minced dill

1. Zip out snow pea "backbones" as needed (some don't require this—try a few). Scrub and peel water chestnuts. Halve and slice—not too thin. Trim scallions and thin-slice on diagonal, separating dark and lighter parts. Shuck corn and cut kernels from cob. Cut ham into teeny dice (to make about ¼ cup).

2. Heat wok over moderately high heat. Add oil and tip to distribute. Add light part of scallions and ham and toss. Add water chestnuts and corn, tossing to coat. Add snow peas and toss.

3. Add water. Reduce heat and stir-fry until chestnuts and corn lose their raw taste, 4 to 5 minutes. Raise heat to evaporate liquid if any remains. Season. Add scallion greens and toss.

4. Off heat, toss with cilantro. Serve at once.

Serves 2

Pros Propose

In *Good Food from a Japanese Temple,* a chronicle of seasonal simplicity, abbess Soei Yoneda describes a two-ingredient appetizer served at the New Year, when fresh water chestnuts appear. To prepare **Deep-Fried Water Chestnut and Nori Squares:** Cut nori sheets into small squares. Peel and grate water chestnuts (drain if wet). Spread ⅛-inch layer of water chestnut on each nori square. Slip at once into hot oil, nori side down, and fry, turning, until light golden. Drain on paper, then salt. The abbess informs us: "Best eaten hot. A temple portion is 3 pieces; but it probably will be hard to restrain yourself (and others) from eating more. Does not keep."

Green Beans with Water Chestnuts has Kashmiri origins: Heat skillet over moderate heat and add black mustard seeds. As they pop, add melted ghee or butter. Add ginger julienne, crisp-steamed green beans cut into ½-inch lengths, paprika, ground coriander, and a generous amount of peeled, sliced water chestnuts.

Sauté until hot throughout. Add lime juice, salt, and chopped cilantro (from *Lord Krishna's Cuisine* by Yamuna Devi).

Chef and author Susanna Foo creates culturally unbiased East-West dishes such as **Water Chestnut and Arugula Salad:** Thin-slice peeled water chestnuts. Toss with balsamic vinegar to coat, then with dressing of olive oil, balsamic, and ground dried shrimp. Add cilantro, chives, and tarragon. Arrange over arugula.

For her **Lobster with Corn, Fennel, and Water Chestnuts,** chef Foo starts with traditional Chinese techniques and flavors, then adds Western touches: Prepare stock from crushed lobster shells, heads, bodies, water, and cornstarch. Marinate sliced tail meat briefly in egg white and cornstarch. Blanch claws; remove meat. Toss ginger and garlic in hot oil in wok. Add tail meat; cook briefly. Add peeled, sliced water chestnuts, sliced fresh baby corn, and thin slices of tender fennel, tossing. Add claws and lobster stock; cook to blend flavors and thicken sauce.

Chef Philippe Chin uses water chestnuts with abandon in his **Swordfish with Two-Way Water Chestnuts and Black Beans:** Simmer peeled water chestnuts in water, ginger, salt, and brown sugar until tender enough to crush with a fork. Mash to coarse texture. Add raw water chestnut dice. Sauté tiny dice of tricolor bell peppers and red onion in oil. Add soaked fermented black beans, fish stock, and a touch of soy; set aside. Press water chestnut mixture into ring molds. Then unmold onto plates. Top with grilled swordfish; garnish with pepper mixture.

Water chestnuts provide textural interest in **Stuffed Chicken Slices:** Blend rehydrated, chopped dried black Chinese mushrooms with equal weights of chopped water chestnuts and minced shrimp. Add egg white, pepper, salt, sesame oil, rice wine, cornstarch, and minced scallion. Dust butterflied chicken breasts with cornstarch and mound filling on these. Close up and reshape breasts. Coat with cornstarch; deep-fry in peanut oil. Drain, then slice crosswise. Serve as an appetizer, with roasted Sichuan pepper ground with coarse salt (from *Ken Hom's Chinese Kitchen*).

Water Spinach (*Ipomoea aquatica*)

Also water convolvulus, swamp morning glory, swamp cabbage (not to be confused with Sabal palmetto, also known by that name), ong choy and variations (Chinese and Hawaiian), kangkung and variations (Indonesian, Malaysian, Philippine), pak bung (Thai), rau muong (Vietnamese)

A raft of water-grown vegetables flourishes worldwide. Yet rice, wild rice, and water cress are the only aquatic plants that bob up regularly in kitchens in the United States and Canada. Now water spinach, as the number of names listed above indicates, lands in the grocery baskets of many new Americans. But until recently, this leafy relative of the sweetpotato, a member of the Convolvulaceae, was primarily a mainstay in Asia.

Thanks to its mild flavor, agreeable texture, quick growth habit, and adaptability to different environments, water spinach is as widespread in the cuisines of the Asian tropics as spinach in temperate lands. Introduced to Hawaii by Chinese immigrants in the late 19th century, it has become a staple vegetable throughout the islands as well.

But in the mainland United States, water spinach, which burgeoned with Vietnamese and Philippine migrations in recent years, has an iffy future. The plant's remarkable adaptability to new environments is such that it poses a threat to native species, which it quickly chokes out. Officials in several branches of the Department of Agriculture compare it to kudzu and crabgrass, "useful" plants that grew out of control to became ecosystem killers in areas where they were not naturally contained. Grown primarily in California, water spinach is farmed principally for and by a Far Eastern community that depends on it for diet and income. Its fate is being decided state by state—as it has been for years.

Right now, water spinach is widely available in Asian markets. There are two forms. The main one (see at right in the photo) has firm, tight, tubular, foot-long scallion-green stems and narrow arrow-shaped leaves. The secondary form (at left) has a wider, softer, celery-pale stem. The leaves of both taste mildly spinach-like but have an extra touch of acidity and slipperiness. The stems, which resemble drinking straws (and have inspired still more names—such as "empty-hearted" and

length: 18–20 inches

"hollow-stem" vegetable), are crisp and faintly fibrous with a gentle generic green flavor and a tart tinge.

BASIC USE: Because much of this vegetable's charm derives from the constrasting textures of leaf and stem, it is wise not to follow the usual directions to "use as spinach." Instead, cook the two parts separately, to play up their soft and crisp aspects.

Use water spinach raw or quickly blanched in salads with light Asian dressings. Stir-fry stems with the traditional garlic and fermented bean paste or fish paste seasonings, then add a touch of liquid and the leaves, and toss to wilt. Include in mixed vegetable curries. Steam thin-sliced stems and leaves with seafood. Add sliced stems and leaves to soups during the last few minutes of cooking.

"Water spinach is more delicate than other greens that look similar," advises chef Gray Kunz, who has cooked the vegetable extensively in Asia and New York. "Use it only in light dishes, because it is easily overwhelmed. And like pea shoots, it gets tough and stringy when overcooked. Just wilt and serve."

Alan Wong, whose Hawaiian heritage and several restaurants give him broad familiarity with water spinach, says, "The trick to using water spinach is to precook cut stems by blanching in water with ginger slices and a little peanut oil. The drop of oil coating makes all the difference in the world." Wong compares the hollow stems to penne pasta and sauces them accordingly. "I love the way they release a burst of flavor when you bite them."

SELECTION: The darker type can be found virtually year-round; the paler variety, which is more perishable, appears in the summer. Gray Kunz recommends careful inspection: "Water spinach is sold in large, tight bunches. One must open them to be sure the center is fresh—not slimy and spoiled, which happens quickly. Check under the band for mushiness, which means the greens have been revived in water and are not fresh."

STORAGE: Wrap water spinach in damp newspaper or toweling and refrigerate. Purchased in good shape, it keeps about a week. The less common pale type will last just a few days. If limp, mist lightly.

PREPARATION: With an exception (below), trim like asparagus, by bending the fibrous base and snapping it off. Test individually: Sometimes the whole stalk is good, sometimes none of it. Once trimmed, pull (or cut, for smaller specimens) leaves from stems and set aside. Slice stems to the length desired for a recipe. Dump these into a sinkful of water and slosh gently to coax out hidden mud. Lift out and repeat at least once more. Leaves usually need just one good wash.

Exception: Very thin, firm water spinach is so delicate that it needs no trimming (and there can be too many skinny stems to deal with, anyway). I have found this to be true of the winter crop from California—which has also been exceedingly gritty.

Crisp Water Spinach Salad with Sesame

Colorful and refreshing, this perky salad adds sparkle to a winter or summer meal. Firm water spinach stems and tender leaves are combined with thin carrot and radish rounds in a light Asian dressing for a bright first course. Or serve with grilled seafood or poultry.

> ¾ **pound water spinach**
> 3 **long thin carrots**
> 5 **medium round red radishes**
> 2 **tablespoons white sesame seeds**
> 2 **tablespoons lemon juice**
> 1 **teaspoon honey**
> 1 **tablespoon shoyu (Japanese soy sauce)**
> 1 **teaspoon Asian (dark) sesame oil**
> 3 **tablespoons thin-sliced scallion greens**

1. Nip leaves from water spinach stems. Rinse and spin-dry. Trim stem bases (see Preparation, above). Cut stems into ¼-inch slices. Swish in lukewarm water and lift out. Repeat. Soak 3 minutes in lukewarm water to crisp. Drain, blot dry, and refrigerate, covered, ½ hour, or more.

2. Peel and thin-slice carrots on food processor or mandoline blade. Combine in bowl with ice and water; refrigerate. Thin-slice radishes and refrigerate in another bowl of ice water. Chill 20 minutes or more.

3. In small heavy pan, toast sesame seeds, stirring over low heat until tan, about 5 minutes; reserve. Stir together lemon juice, honey, and shoyu. Add oil.

4. Drain carrots and radishes and blot dry. Toss water spinach leaves with half the dressing and 1 tablespoon sesame seeds. Arrange on four plates. In the same bowl, toss together stems, radishes, carrots, scallions, and the remaining dressing and sesame seeds. Arrange on leaves. Serve at once.

Serves 4

Basic Stir-Fried Water Spinach

Quick, easy, and versatile enough to become a staple, this verdant side dish looks as fresh as it tastes. The tiny crisp rounds of stem remain crisp, while the leaves turn dark and slightly slippery, but not watery. If you like, toss minced garlic into the pan with the stems. A sprinkling of fine-chopped roasted cashews at the last minute makes a sweet, rich addition.

> **1 pound water spinach**
> **1 tablespoon peanut, corn, or grapeseed oil**
> **½ teaspoon sugar**
> **½ teaspoon kosher salt**
> **Optional: lime wedges**

1. Trim base of water spinach if needed (see Preparation). Cut apart or strip leaves from stems. Wash leaves and stems separately, then spin-dry. Cut stems into very thin slices. Slice or chop leaves.

2. Heat wok or wide sauté pan over moderate heat. Add oil and tip to coat pan. Add stems and toss to barely cook through, about 2 minutes. Add leaves, sugar, and salt. Using wide tongs or two spoons, quickly lift and toss to just barely wilt, not cook through—about 1 minute. Serve at once, with optional lime wedges.

Serves 4 as a side dish

Variation

Stir-Fried Water Spinach with Mustard Seeds and Coconut

Set wok or sauté pan in which you'll cook water spinach over moderately low heat. Add ¼ cup unsweetened dried coconut shreds (preferably coarse-cut) to pan and toss often until toasty tan, about 2 minutes. Scoop into a dish and reserve. Add oil to hot pan, then stir in 1 tablespoon mustard seeds. Stir a moment, until they pop and sputter. Add stems and proceed as above. When cooked, sprinkle with coconut and serve at once, with optional lime.

Steamed Black Sea Bass with Water Spinach and Cilantro

Crisp water spinach stems contrast with tender leaves and soft steamed fish in this light, simple dish—which needs no more than scented rice to make a meal. The best coriander has its roots intact. If you find it, trim these and scrub with a brush, then mince and add with the sliced spinach stems. I like roasted peanut oil (Loriva is a widely available brand), which is more intense than oil from raw peanuts. If it is not available, add a soupçon of Asian sesame oil to regular peanut oil.

> **¾ pound water spinach**
> **Salt and pepper**
> **1½- to 2-pound black sea bass, cleaned**
> **1 or 2 lemons**
> **Generous handful of cilantro (coriander) leaves**
> **1½ tablespoons peanut oil (preferably roasted)**
> **Optional: cilantro (coriander) roots**
> **3 slim scallions (green onions), sliced thin**
> **2 tablespoons hair-thin ginger strips (about ½ inch long)**
> **3 tablespoons shoyu (Japanese soy sauce)**

1. Trim base of water spinach if needed (see Preparation). Wash thoroughly. Pinch leaves from stems. Arrange them in a nest on a heatproof dish that can hold the fish and fit into a steamer.

2. Salt and pepper fish cavity. Cut a few lemon slices; slip inside the fish. Tuck in cilantro leaves. Pat fish skin dry, then rub with ½ tablespoon peanut oil. Place fish on spinach leaves. Set on rack over boiling water. Cover and steam until fish just turns opaque throughout, about 15 minutes.

3. Meanwhile, slice water spinach stalks into ¼-inch rings. Halve lemon and squeeze about 2 tablespoons lemon juice. Cut a few lemon wedges as well. Scrub and mince coriander roots, if using.

4. When fish is done, sprinkle with scallions and half the ginger. Spoon shoyu and lemon juice over fish. Immediately heat remaining 1 tablespoon oil in medium skillet. Over high heat, toss stems, the remaining ginger, and cilantro roots to just barely soften, a

minute or two. Spoon mixture over fish and serve at once, with lemon wedges.

**Serves 2 generously
(or more, as part of an Asian-style meal)**

Pros Propose

The repertoire of water spinach is decidedly Southeast Asian, which is not surprising, given its origin in the Old World tropics. At its most basic, water spinach is used as a salad or garnish, the crisp stem being preferred to the leaves. For curly **Water Spinach Stems Vietnamese-Style:** Remove leaves and small stems and reserve for another dish. Set large stems on cutting board and with swivel peeler, zip each into strips. Soak in ice water to curl. To serve, toss with white vinegar, water, vegetable oil, sugar, salt, and pepper.

Stems are blanched for **Shrimp, Spinach, and Sprout Salad** from California chef Helene An, who is of Vietnamese origin: Slice stems lengthwise into narrow strips of desired length; blanch quickly. Drain. Mix with blanched bean sprouts. Blend a touch of shrimp paste with sesame oil, fish sauce, and sugar. Toss some with small cooked shrimp and some with the vegetables. Combine and serve at room temperature.

Helene An also serves her version of a dish popular in much of the Far East, **Beef with Water Spinach,** which includes both stems and leaves. To prepare: Marinate thin-sliced flank steak in oil, garlic, pepper, fish sauce, and egg white for an hour. Blanch convenient lengths of water spinach in boiling water; add leaves, then drain at once. To serve, sear beef in oil in wok. Remove and set aside. Toss chopped garlic in wok until golden; add spinach, fish sauce, and fresh chilli. Arrange beef over spinach.

Stir-Fried Water Spinach may be the most ubiquitous vegetable dish in Vietnam, reports Corinne

Trang (as well as in south and southwest China, where it is seasoned with chilli-fermented bean curd and rice wine, according to Ken Hom). Trang writes that the Vietnamese have a strong preference for the type with "large leaves, thick stems, and a light green color . . . the sweeter and more tender." To prepare: Soak and rinse water spinach. Trim off stems and halve crosswise. Stir-fry minced garlic in oil. Add water spinach and pepper and stir-fry to wilt. Add preserved bean curd or fish sauce. Cover and cook briefly (from Trang's *Authentic Vietnamese Cooking*).

Water spinach (called morning glory in most British texts, where the following recipe originates) is also popular in Thailand. For **Morning Glory in Peanut Sauce:** Coarsely chop water spinach. Blanch quickly and drain. Arrange on plates. Deep-fry bean curd until golden; drain. Slice into long strips, and spread over the greens. Sauté chopped garlic in oil. Add red curry paste, soy, salt, sugar, coconut milk, and ground roasted peanuts; boil. Pour over bean curd (from *Thai Vegetarian Cooking* by Vatcharin Bhumichitr).

For professional kitchens, there is this "fusion" recipe, **Halibut with Water Spinach and Turmeric,** from Troy Dupuy, who served it at Lespinasse in Washington, D.C., when he was executive chef. To prepare: Lightly brown butter. Add trimmed water spinach stems and chilli oil and cook a moment; reserve. Roll halibut fillets around the water spinach stems and lemon thyme leaves; tie each with blanched leek strip. Pour fish fumet into individual buttered gratin dishes. Add fillets, season, and cover with plastic wrap. Set on shelf over flattop to just barely cook through, about 15 minutes. Remove fish. Reduce stock to a glaze. Stir-fry water spinach leaves with butter-crisped chopped shallot. Arrange leaves on plates, then fish; nap with glaze. Spoon around sauce made from minced shallots, garlic, and turmeric cooked with lemon juice and white wine until reduced, then cooked with chicken stock, reduced again, and finished with honey, butter, olive oil, and lemon thyme.

Winter Melon, Wax Gourd *(Benincasa hispida)*

Also ash gourd, white gourd, Chinese preserving melon, dung gua
and variations (Chinese), petha (Indian), kundol (Philippine)

See also: FUZZY GOURD, page 293

diameter: 10-11 inches

This hefty beauty is a mature and dramatically different form of fuzzy gourd—so different that it deserves its own entry. "Winter" may refer to the gourd's frosty finish (and, to my mind, the icy shine of the juicy white flesh), but not to its market season. Or "winter" may refer to the gourd's keeping ability—as long as summer through winter. "Wax" is another way to describe the powdery bloom that develops on the skin of mature fruits.

"Wax gourd" is the more common English word, but for some reason "winter melon," confusing in terms of both season and what Americans mean by melon, prevails in American markets and cookbooks. (In the West, in general, the words "melon" and "gourd" are used interchangeably for Asian cucurbits—whether they are called fuzzy, bitter, or winter.) Despite the name "melon," this is not a sweet fruit to be eaten raw. Although the flesh slightly resembles pearly honeydew, the flavor and scent are more akin to cucumber and summer squash.

"Fortunately, we have a scientific name, *Benincasa hispida,* that is the same all over the world," writes Charles B. Heiser in *The Gourd Book.* "The genus name was given to it by an Italian botanist, Gaetano Savi, in 1818, to honor Giuseppe Benincasa, an Italian patron of botany." Savi called the plant "*Benincasa cerifera,* or 'wax-bearing,' a very good name," Heiser writes, as "the wax has actually been used to make candles." But the species, *cerifera,* did not stick because in 1794 the plant (at the time assigned to another genus) had been given the name *hispida* (meaning "rough-hairy") and "the earliest name given to the plant and names of species follow the rule of priority."

"This species has been cultivated in China for more than 2,300 years and is believed to have originated in southeastern Asia," R. W. Robinson and D. S. Decker-Walters write in *Cucurbits,* but its use is not limited to those areas. According to these authors, wax gourd is also an important vegetable in India, the Philippines, parts of Latin American, and the Caribbean.

Nor does the name "Chinese preserving melon" signify conserving in China alone. The gourd's tender flesh imbibes syrups evenly, whether in the way of pickled or candied watermelon rind—or as recalled by Madhur Jaffrey, an authority on Eastern food: "When I grew up, petha, a specialty of Agra, was the most popular crystallized fruit in India. As a child I hated sweets except for this lovely chewy one, which looked like the rectangular tan erasers we used in school."

BASIC USE: Wax gourd absorbs and retains the flavor of savory liquids as readily as it does preserving syrups. As it absorbs, it develops a satiny, slurpy texture. Cooked for mere minutes, it melts to near transparency and turns jelly-soft. Soup is the gourd's forte, whether it is simmered in small squares with other vegetables or pureed. Or add slices to seafood for the last few minutes of braising, to sponge up flavor and give a sensuous consistency. Or combine cubes with poultry or fish to be steamed.

SELECTION: "Ironically, the best winter melons are summer ones," says Stephen Wong, an author and restaurant consultant based in Vancouver. "Although they're available all year in North America, in China they are understood to have a cooling effect and are served to beat the heat."

Like the large Caribbean pumpkins in Latin American markets, winter melon can be purchased chunked or whole. It is usual to request a hunk cut to order—typically a few pounds. Whole gourds, whether oblong or rounded, may weigh from 5 to 50 pounds. Cut pieces should truly glisten; there should be no dull aspect to the flesh. The skin should show a powdering of waxy bloom, indicating maturity.

STORAGE: Plastic-wrapped chunks can be refrigerated for no more than a day or two, as they quickly lose their fresh scent and luster. Whole winter melons last weeks or even months (some say a year, but I haven't tried this) in a dry, ventilated place, preferably cool.

PREPARATION: When used for their full tonic effect—in Chinese soups, for example—wax gourds need only a good scrubbing, because rind, flesh, and sometimes seeds and leaves (if available) are all cooked. For most Western-style dishes, the gourds are sliced, then seeded (the thick necklace-like ropes of seeds are easily plucked out), then peeled, then cut to edible size.

Winter Melon Soup Seasoned with Mushrooms, Seafood, and Ham

Winter melon soup is soothing, and subtle, a study in close textures and flavors. The gourd softens silkily and becomes a translucent background. A modicum of shrimp bits, scallop slices, firm ham dice, and chewy shiitake nubbins punctuate, but none dominates, and no herbs or spices intrude. For banquets, the gourd becomes the famous "Winter Melon Pond": The whole cleaned and decoratively incised gourd is steamed until tender, while the prepared soup heats inside.

According to Stephen Wong, author and restaurant consultant, his version (from which this recipe is adapted) follows traditional lines . . . which means that every Chinese cook will find it different from the one made in his home.

6 large dried black mushrooms (shiitake)
3 cups vegetable broth
3 cups pork, seafood, or chicken broth
2 ounces pork or chicken (see Note)
¼ pound shelled shrimp
1 teaspoon cornstarch
2 teaspoons water
1 teaspoon fish sauce
½ teaspoon Asian (dark) sesame oil
1 ounce firm dry-cured ham (see Note)
1½-pound wedge of winter melon
¼ pound sea scallops
Salt

1. Break stems from mushrooms; reserve for another use. Combine both broths with the caps in a large pot and bring to a boil. Turn off heat and soak while you prepare other ingredients (or until the caps rehydrate).

2. Cut pork into very fine strips. Chop shrimp. Blend cornstarch, water, fish sauce, and sesame oil; mix with pork and shrimp.

3. Cut ham into tiny dice. Rinse winter melon. Pare off skin in a single piece or two; add to broth. Cut seeds and pith from melon; discard. Cut flesh into ¾-inch dice. Scoop mushrooms from broth and cut into tiny dice. Return to pot, with ham dice.

4. Bring soup to a boil, skimming if necessary. Add melon dice and return to a boil. Reduce heat, cover, and simmer until melon is very tender, just a few minutes. Meanwhile, thin-slice scallops.

5. With tongs, remove melon skin and discard. Return soup to a boil. Add pork-shrimp mixture and scallops. Return to a boil, stirring. Remove from heat and add salt to taste. Serve at once.

Serves 6 as a first course

Note: If it's a nuisance to get a little bit of pork, omit it and increase the shrimp by 1 ounce and the ham by ½ ounce. Use any firm country-style ham, whether from China, Italy, Germany, or the United States.

Cool White Winter Melon Soup with Herbal Swirls

For a completely different take on soup than the preceding recipe, coconut puree freshened with winter melon makes an intriguing first course. The base derives from a recipe of Julie Sahni's in *Classic Indian Vegetarian and Grain Cooking*. But while Sahni's is fiery, this is subdued, with only ginger and pepper for snap. Herbs liquefied with yogurt give bright color and flavor.

    2-pound wedge winter melon
    2½ cups water
    About 1½ tablespoons sugar
    About 1½ teaspoons kosher salt
    1 cup (unsweetened) dried coconut shreds
    2-inch ginger chunk, peeled and sliced
    About ¼ teaspoon white pepper

    1½ cups yogurt (preferably whole milk)
    ⅓ cup tightly packed cilantro (coriander) leaves
    ⅓ cup tightly packed mint leaves
    About 3 tablespoons lime juice

1. Peel winter melon. Scrape out seeds and pith. Cut into ⅛-inch-thick 1-inch squares. Combine in heavy pot with water, 1½ tablespoons sugar, and 1½ teaspoons salt and bring to a boil. Reduce heat and simmer, covered, until melon is tender and translucent, 3 to 6 minutes. Remove from heat.

2. Transfer half the liquid and half the melon to a food processor. Add coconut, ginger, and ¼ teaspoon pepper. Whiz to a fine puree. Return to pot.

3. Cook over low heat until soup simmers, about 5 minutes. Whisk in half the yogurt. Remove from heat. Cool, then chill.

4. Taste chilled soup. Season assertively with lime juice, salt, sugar, and pepper. Combine remaining yogurt, cilantro, mint, and a pinch of salt in blender or processor. Whirl to a fine puree.

5. To serve, ladle into six bowls. Drizzle swirls of the green puree over the soup.

Serves 6

Pros Propose

Soup is winter melon's raison d'être. Usually, this means chicken broth with ginger and winter melon, briefly cooked—whether the recipe is Chinese, Vietnamese, or Thai. For a Thai version, **Chicken Soup with Pickled Limes,** preserved citrus dramatically changes the tone: Chop chicken breasts into 1½-inch pieces (traditionally, bones are not removed). Combine with water and bring to a boil. Reduce heat and add rehydrated Chinese black mushrooms, whole pickled lime, light soy sauce, and black soy sauce. Cover and simmer 10 minutes. Add winter melon cubes, re-cover, and cook 10 minutes more. Add sugar and water to taste; boil. Serve hot, with rice (from *Thai Home Cooking from Kamolmal's Kitchen* by William Crawford and Kamolmal Pootarasksa).

A thick Chinese soup of a wholly different kind is **Mock Bird's Nest Soup.** The authors (Pearl Kong

Chen et al.) of *Everything You Want to Know About Chinese Cooking* write that "the delicate texture of grated winter melons closely resembles . . . bird's nest [which] is expensive and tedious to clean." To prepare: Peel, seed, and puree winter melon chunks until smooth. Pour into a fine sieve to drain: reserve juice. Simmer slivered dry-cured ham in the juice until very flavorful; discard ham. Cook melon puree until translucent. Add chicken stock and the ham broth; boil. Blend water chestnut powder with some of chicken stock; add to soup and stir until thickened. Swirl in egg whites that have been lightly beaten with a spoonful of water. Remove from heat. Let stand a moment. Stir, drizzle with sesame oil, and garnish with chopped ham.

Wood Ear (*Auricularia polytricha*) and
Cloud Ear (*Auricularia auricula*)

Also wood-ear, tree ear, black fungus, ear fungus, Jew's ear, kikurage (Japanese), mo-er and mu-ehr and variations (Chinese)

Note: Growers do not distinguish between these two primary species or other *Auricularia,* which are habitually lumped together under shared names. Strictly speaking, "wood ear" refers to just one species, but the term is used to cover two or three at present.

Wood ear is the name most often applied to this type of fungus, which (with its kin) is associated almost exclusively with the Far East. Unlike many edibles that move from a limited market based on ethnic use to a broader population, wood ears have stayed within the culinary confines of those who have long cultivated them. "Long" in this case is a startling period: "According to records from China circa 600 A.D., this mushroom is heralded as the first species to be cultivated" (Paul Stamets, *Growing Gourmet and Medicinal Mushrooms*).

While wood ear and cloud ear grow wild throughout North America, Europe, Australia, and New Zealand, they are not important. Andrew Crowe writes in *A Field Guide to the Native Edible Plants of New Zealand,* "Though ear fungus was occasionally eaten by Maori [who called it Hakeka] . . . it was not a popular food in New Zealand." But it did develop into an ingredient of significance in the East: in Japan, the Philippines, Indonesia, Indochina, Thailand, and other parts of Southeast Asia. "By the late 1800s, New Zealand had established a significant export trade of ear fungi to China, where they were used both medicinally and as meat on fast days with a mixture of vermicelli and bean-curd," Crowe says. They are still a popular medicine and food in a large part of the East, usually dried.

It is in dried form that wood ears are best known in North America—as the luscious, chewy dark strands that enliven hot-and-sour soup, mu shu pork, Buddha's delight, and other favorites in Chinese restaurants. But they're even more interesting fresh, which is why you're reading about them here. Although dried wood

⅓ **actual size**

ears are astonishing in their ability to rapidly rehydrate to their original size and form, they reveal little of the leafy aroma and soft bounce of the fresh ones.

But it may be bounce that has kept wood ears in culinary quarantine. Their almost cartilaginous crunchiness, cherished in the East, makes most Westerners squirm—though it delights the more adventurous. Slightly gelatinous, this mushroom might just as well have originated in the ocean as the forest (jelly-fish, part of wood ear's Japanese name, is an apt comparison). Nor does the association with ears help in the United States, which is one of only a few countries where ears are not considered a delicacy.

Should you come upon the floppy-firm, whorled "caps" (which can range from a button to a saucer in size), the various species look quite different: licorice to charcoal, translucent and shiny to matte and opaque, slick to granular, the two sides the same or different. Any type is worth the minor investment (wood ear is typically inexpensive) for a small adventure in taste.

BASIC USE: Quick-cooking and mild, these swarthy mushrooms are more about texture and visual drama than flavor—but the flavor is there, just quiet. They work best as lively accents, not starring subjects. Many dishes will benefit from the inclusion of the chewy-crisp, smoky-bosky strips. Mix them with vegetables, grains, noodles, meat, poultry, or seafood in stir-fried dishes, warm salads, casseroles, soups, or braises. There is no possibility of overcooking, for they do not lose their distinctive texture when long-simmered; they only tenderize slightly and absorb the surrounding liquid. If you like a firm, elastic texture, add the sliced mushrooms directly to the dish; for a more tender texture, blanch the slices beforehand.

SELECTION: If mushrooms are sold plastic-wrapped, as is often the case, little choice is possible. If, ideally, they are sold loose, select those that are firm, cool, and damp. Avoid mushy-soft specimens; but do not be wary of a jellyish appearance, which is the nature of the fungus. Sniff: Sourness means they're over the hill. However, this mushroom has a very sturdy nature and lasts well.

STORAGE: Erratically available year-round, particularly on the West Coast, fresh wood ears are very good keepers. In fine form, they'll last a week or two in the refrigerator. They can also be frozen without any loss of character.

PREPARATION: If closed in plastic, unwrap—and do not worry about an unpleasant closed-in aroma, which *should* dissipate. Rinse each mushroom under running water. Discard any that are mushy or gummy. If unusually large knotty areas are prominent, pare them off for a more uniform texture (but all parts are edible).

Chef Gary Palm, who enjoyed working with wood ears in the Orient, then in California, prefers to remove the knots behind each "ear," then soaks the mushrooms briefly in salted water, drains them, and spreads on a cloth-covered pan to dry in the refrigerator.

Wood ears are easily cut into distinctive shapes to dramatize a dish: hair-thin to wide julienne strips, triangles, confetti, or small circles or shapes made with a truffle cutter.

For dishes in which a softer texture is desirable, blanch the whole mushrooms in boiling water for a minute or two, then slice to fit the recipe. This also brings out a pleasant woodsy aroma in the fungus and facilitates the absorption of sauce.

Sautéed Wood Ears, Radicchio, and Arugula

When wood ear mushrooms are marinated and wok-seared, they develop a meaty, smoky flavor and bacon-like chewiness. Tumbled together with firm wine-red radicchio shreds and peppery arugula, they make a striking starter salad. Or serve as a side dish or bed for roast lamb or grilled beef or poultry.

6 ounces wood ears
1½ tablespoons shoyu (Japanese soy sauce)
½ teaspoon minced garlic
2 tablespoons olive oil
1 medium bunch of arugula
1 small head of red radicchio (Chioggia or
   Verona)
2 teaspoons lemon juice

1. Rinse wood ears and trim off heavy knots. Cut into very thin strips about 2 inches long. Toss with 1 tablespoon shoyu, garlic, and 1 tablespoon olive oil. Let stand 15 minutes or more, tossing a few times.

2. Meanwhile, trim arugula. Rinse in several changes of water, lifting out until no grit remains in sink. Spin-dry. Cut into bite-size pieces as necessary (you'll have about 1½ cups). Do not refrigerate.

3. Working from the base, cut out radicchio core. Rinse head. Halve, place cut side down, and slice into thin lengthwise strips. Spin-dry. Blend the remaining

1 tablespoon oil, ½ tablespoon shoyu, and the lemon juice. Toss the radicchio and dressing in a large bowl.

4. Set wok over high heat. Add wood ears and stir-fry, pressing firmly against wok to sear and brown, until dry and crackly—about 3 minutes.

5. Scoop wood ears onto radicchio. Add arugula and toss well. Serve at once, while still warm.

Serves 3 to 4

Cream of Wood Ear Soup

If wood ear mushrooms depend upon their crunch for interest, will a crunchless dish have interest? Obviously, the answer is yes. Although subdued, wood ears contribute a distinct, mysterious flavor to the smooth, rich puree. While the soup is deeply creamy (thanks in good part to oatmeal, for the silken body it provides), the dark wood ear speckles have a faint crispness highlighted by squiggles of sautéed wood ear julienne. Like most pureed soups, this can be prepared ahead, cooled, and refrigerated. Sauté the garnish at serving time.

> 8 to 10 ounces wood ears
> 1 large parsley root or medium parsnip
> 3 medium shallots
> 1 garlic clove
> 1½ tablespoons butter
> Optional: ¼ teaspoon ground cardamom
> ¼ cup dry sherry, or more to taste
> About 4½ cups mushroom, vegetable, or light
>   meat broth
> 2 tablespoons rolled oats (old-fashioned
>   oatmeal)
> 1 teaspoon sugar
> 1 teaspoon kosher salt
> 1 cup light cream or half-and-half
> Pepper
> Lemon juice
> Optional: snipped chives

1. Cut heavy knots, if any, from mushrooms; discard. Rinse mushrooms. Cut enough into hair-thin strips to equal ⅓ cup; reserve for garnish. Coarsely slice remainder. Peel and trim parsley root, shallots, and garlic. Chop all medium-fine.

2. Melt 1 tablespoon butter in heavy saucepan. Stir in chopped vegetables. Cook over moderately low heat until slightly softened, 3 to 4 minutes. Stir in mushrooms and optional cardamom and toss a minute. Add sherry and toss to evaporate.

3. Add 4 cups broth, oatmeal, sugar, and salt. Bring to a boil. Reduce heat, cover, and simmer until vegetables are very soft, about 40 minutes (wood ears will not become truly soft).

4. Transfer to food processor and allow to cool 15 minutes or more. Puree to a very fine texture, scraping down sides. Press through a sieve back into the saucepan. Add cream. Simmer briefly until thickened to desired consistency. Season with salt, pepper, sherry, and lemon juice.

5. Reheat soup, thinning with broth as needed. Melt remaining ½ tablespoon butter in small skillet over moderate heat. Add reserved wood ear strips. Toss until crisp, about 2 minutes. Blot on paper towel. Divide soup among small bowls and sprinkle over wood ears and optional chives.

Serves 4 as a first course

Crunchy, Colorful Vegetable-Noodle Salad with Asian Aromas

A tumble of eccentric textures and colors: curiously chewy charcoal-brown wood ears, magenta cabbage, crisp green cucumber, and soft pale noodles laced with sunny strands of egg pancake. The scents of Sichuan pepper, anise, and sesame oil are exotic, but not far-out. Although the preparation time is lengthy, the result is a complete one-dish meal that can be conveniently served warm, at room temperature, or chilled. If Chinese chilli sauce is lacking, add ¼ teaspoon chilli flakes to the pan as you finish toasting the spices.

> ¾ teaspoon Sichuan pepper
> ¾ teaspoon anise or fennel seeds
> 1 teaspoon kosher salt
> 2 teaspoons sugar
> 1 teaspoon Chinese chilli sauce
>   (or ¼ teaspoon chilli flakes)

3 tablespoons shoyu (Japanese soy sauce)

¼ cup rice vinegar

½ pound wood ears (see Note)

About ¾ pound red cabbage

½ pound Oriental or greenhouse cucumber

2 slim scallions (green onions)

½ pound fine dried egg noodles (thin egg fettuccine or fideos)

1 tablespoon plus 1 teaspoon Asian (dark) sesame oil

2 tablespoons peanut oil

3 eggs

¼ cup cilantro (coriander) leaves

1. Prepare dressing: Toast Sichuan pepper and anise seeds in small pan over fairly low heat until fragrant and beginning to smoke, a few minutes or so. Remove from heat and stir in ¾ teaspoon salt. Grind fine in spice mill or crush fine in suribachi. Mix with sugar, chilli sauce, shoyu, and vinegar, stirring to dissolve crystals.

2. Rinse wood ears and trim any tough "knots." Cut into very fine strips. Do same to cabbage. Cut cucumber into matchsticks. Trim and thin-slice scallions to equal ¼ cup, separating dark and light parts.

3. Drop noodles into a pasta pot of boiling salted water, stirring to separate. Return to a full boil, stirring. Cook until almost tender, about 3 to 5 minutes. Add cabbage and return to a boil; drain.

4. Rinse noodle-cabbage mixture in cold or ice water; drain. Blot dry with towel or spin-dry. Spread in a wide serving dish. Toss with the dressing. Add 1 tablespoon each sesame oil and peanut oil, tossing well.

5. Whisk eggs with remaining 1 teaspoon sesame oil, ⅛ teaspoon salt, and 2 teaspoons water, blending well. Over moderate flame, heat 8-inch skillet. Add ½ teaspoon peanut oil and tip to distribute. Pour in one-third of the egg mixture, tipping pan to coat evenly. Reduce heat and cook just until eggs are no longer wet on the surface. With thin, flexible spatula, slip onto a cutting board, cooked side down. Repeat two more times. Halve each pancake, and slice crosswise into ribbons.

6. In same pan, heat remaining ½ tablespoon peanut oil over moderately high heat. Add pale part of scallions, wood ears, and the remaining ⅛ teaspoon salt. Toss 2 minutes. Off heat, add scallion greens. Add to noodles and toss and twist with tongs to mix well. Add cucumbers and egg strips. Chop cilantro leaves and add. Mix well.

Serves 4 to 6 as a main course

Note: If you want to substitute dried wood ears, they'll work fine for this dish. Choose one of the larger forms (not little flakes). Soak about 2 ounces (about 1½ cups) in boiling water to cover by several inches for 15 minutes or more, until tender throughout. Drain and rinse (you should have about ½ pound, or 2½ cups), then proceed as above.

Pros Propose

Some chefs are using wood ears in ways that are not strictly traditional. Gary Palm developed a fondness for them when he worked in Hong Kong and Korea, and now includes them in Western dishes, where he thinks their potential has yet to be tapped. Among other dishes, he serves red and black **Tomato, Onion, and Wood Ear Tartlets:** Prepare tomato confit by combining sliced tomatoes and onions in baking pan with olive oil, bay leaves, and pepper. Cover with plastic, then foil. Bake 2 hours in a low oven. Cool, then drain. Add sautéed wood ear julienne. Spread filling in pastry-lined tartlet molds. Bake until crust browns. Serve warm.

Soup of Favas and Wood Ears, from Kenneth Oringer, puts the dark mushrooms in a central role on a pale green puree. To prepare: Blanch shelled favas and remove skins. Combine with shallots that have been cooked gently with lemon thyme; puree with vegetable stock. Sauté wood ear julienne in olive oil with garlic, shallot, lemon thyme, chervil, parsley, and tarragon. Deglaze pan with mushroom stock. Mound mushrooms in shallow serving dishes. Surround with the fava puree. Slice spring truffle over.

For **Fried Soft-Shell Crabs with Wood Ear Salad,** Oringer uses the same herbed mushroom mixture at room temperature and combines it with bits of preserved lemon, blanched haricots verts, radishes, frisée, and light olive oil–lemon dressing. This serves as the bed for tempura-fried soft-shell crabs dotted with vinaigrette made from crayfish shells.

"Wood ears are truly a great value. They have an amazing texture and look, but cost next to nothing," says chef Francesco Martorello. He sautés a **Basic Wood Ear Garnish** to accompany pale seafood or poultry, or adds it to filling for spring rolls. To prepare: Julienne fresh wood ears, toss with a little light soy sauce, and marinate an hour or so. Sauté in peanut oil in a hot cast-iron pan to crisp. Serve hot.

Chinese stir-fry dishes with wood ear fungus are familiar in this country, but there are also Thai dishes. For **Cloud Ears with Young Ginger:** Stir-fry garlic crushed with salt in oil until barely colored. Add small cloud ear mushrooms, julienned young ginger, shallot strips, and cleaned small shrimp. Toss just until shrimp is barely cooked. Add fish sauce and sugar and serve at once (from *Classic Thai Cuisine* by David Thompson).

Yam, True Yam (*Dioscorea* species)

Also ñame (Spanish), igname (French)

(See alternative names under separate species)

In the tropical lands where yams grow, they offer more than sustenance; they intertwine with the mythology, medicine, religion, and history of the people who cultivate them. In the hot zones of the Old World, where many originated, they are as essential as corn was to the New World Indians who raised it.

In most of the United States, however, yams are odd nameless tubers—unless you grew up with them elsewhere and know their secrets. In 1999, the United States imported yams from 14 countries—many of which now have an increasing population here. What types arrive is dictated by the demands of newcomers from Jamaica, Nigeria, the Philippines, and a score of countries where yams—not potatoes—mean dinner. Yams that wind up in the New York–New Jersey area, where I live and lug them home, represent a tiny fraction of the tuber's numerous forms. Franklin Martin, this country's primary authority on the subject (who was kind enough to interrupt his active "retirement" to review my information), says that 60 *Dioscorea* species are edible and 10 are prominent.

Yam, ñame (pronounced ny-AH-may), and igname (EEn-yahm) are the generic names most often seen in U.S. markets. The yam is no relative whatsoever of the sweetpotato (see page 638) and is very rarely sweet. Nor is it usually potato-like, a standard description that would lead you to expect the wrong taste. The appearance of yams, as you can see from a mere five examples of well-groomed market produce, is diverse indeed. But what I have just recently come to appreciate is yam's range of flavors and textures. A cushcush yam and a white yam are as different as delicate fingerlings and sturdy russet potatoes (although yams *are* yams, which means starchy and bland and not to everyone's taste). And while we're at cushcush, please realize that there are no "correct" common names to quibble about in the United States. There is only what a yam is called at your market. Few edibles have as many names, forms, and overlaps as *Dioscorea* species.

Rather than generalize, I'll describe what I have found in the New York metropolitan area. Take home whatever you find in your own vicinity, under whatever name you find it, and try this for starters: Peel the yams, cut chunks of equal size, drop into cold water, and bring to a boil. Add a handful of salt, then simmer until truly tender. Eat them at once, *while hot,* with butter, cheese, meat juices, vinaigrette, salsa—or salt alone, if you're a serious comparative sampler.

White yam (*Dioscorea alata*), or ñame blanco, is also called water yam (ñame de agua) and a handful of other names—in my neck of the woods alone. "It is what many people in the world refer to with the word 'yam,' or its translation," says Franklin Martin, who refers to this most widespread of species as wing-stemmed yam. This is the yam I see in any market, whatever its ethnicity, that carries yams. So prevalent and so different are its forms that I have unwittingly cooked four different shapes, thinking they were four

white (*front and right*), African (*upper left*) diameter: 3-4 inches

distinct yams. Fortunately, the tasting notes concurred and set me straight.

A Korean shop owner's sign in New York's Spanish Harlem indicated Colombian yam. Around the corner it was Costa Rican. A Vietnamese acquaintance with whom I shopped in Edison, New Jersey, called it oil yam; but water yam was the name in Jersey City—which gives a fair idea of the accuracy of descriptive names. Like most yams, this one has pale flesh that is crisp and slippery and may froth when cut, depending upon the individual yam.

Boiled or steamed, it is entirely transformed. The crunch turns into a light, loose-knit softness (if the yam has been properly cooked), sometimes just moist, sometimes waxy, sometimes truly creamy. The taste is sweet, delicate, and mild—in a versatile, not bland, way.

Purple yam was labeled ube in a Philippine grocery, and both ratala and kand in an Indian one. It is not common in North America but is worth a detour for its startling color, deliciousness—and the surprising fact that it is the very same species (*D. alata*) as white yam. (What a maddening bunch!) The relatively small (½- to 1½-pound) squared, squat "buns" have thin bark-like skin that shows violet through its flaky patches. Cut, the raw flesh glows lavender-violet—and it turns a rich, mottled, deep red-violet when cooked. Peeled and boiled, the smooth, uniform flesh is almost juicy compared with that of other yams—as if crossed with a sweet rutabaga. Gently sweet, with a touch of smokiness, meatiness, and nuttiness—but really none of these—purple yam is its own curious, moist, fork-tender self.

Cushcush yam (*Dioscorea trifida*), also called mapuey or ñame mapuey (a name that is also loosely applied to other species), igname couche-couche, ñame morado, yampi, ñampi, and on and on, seems to be favored by many (count me as one). Franklin Martin calls it American yam and writes that of the "principal culti-vated species of yam, none is less well known than the American species *Dioscorea trifida* L., or cushcush. Nevertheless, in those areas where it is produced, *D. trifida* is known as the best of the yams because of its flavor and cooking qualities." Yes, indeed!

This small yam may be shaped like an elongated sweetpotato or a mitten or horse's hoof; its skin may be charcoal to purplish, lightly striated but fairly smooth.

Slippery, compact ivory flesh turns to a rosy underlayer just beneath the skin. (There are also dark-fleshed types.)

Whether boiling or steaming, the tubers emit an unexpected and delicious aroma of bacon and eggs. Turning dry, fluffy, and starchy, they melt in the mouth with a texture softer and lighter than other yams (which tend to solidify and become stodgy as they cool). Cushcush suggest slightly sweet, smoky baking potatoes, but with a much finer, drier texture and more character.

African (white) yam (*Dioscorea rotundata*), pictured on previous page, also Guinea yam, ñame guineo, white guinea yam, and Ghana yam, is quite similar to white or water yam, but more solid (and its flesh may be white or yellow). "Although other yam species have been introduced in Africa, in West Africa, the word 'yam' is almost synonymous with *Dioscorea rotundata*," and the closely related *Dioscorea cayenensis*, Franklin Martin explains. "The two species have apparently hy-bridized frequently, and intermediate forms impede exact classification." He notes that the most important use is as fufu, a dish of African origin that also spread throughout the Caribbean. To prepare it, the chunked

purple yams   diameter: 2½-3 inches

Chinese yams (*left*), and cushcush yams (*right*)   length: 14 inches and 6 inches

tubers are boiled soft, drained, "then pounded in a mortar with pestle until a stiff, glutinous dough is formed. The dough is molded into a ball and served. Diners remove portions of the dough with their fingertips and dip them into a stew."

I picked up (with difficulty, at 5 pounds apiece) the neat, symmetrical log-like tuber pictured at a West African market in Manhattan—despite the owner's obvious mistrust of my ability to treat it properly. (An aside to encourage adventurous cooks: Wherever I shop, from the fanciest to the humblest markets, I seem to be the wrong size, color, and style to be trusted with the vegetables I choose. Yet the information for this book and hundreds of articles has been collected in the face of such culinary xenophobia.) Easy to clean, slice, and cook, these are the most potato-like of the yams tested. Waxy, solid, they have a close, even, fiberless texture and a mild starchy flavor with sweet and bitter traces, but not much distinction.

Chinese yam (*Dioscorea esculenta*) or lesser yam, also ñame papa and ñame pequeño (and just ñame, where I found it), is fairly uncommon in the United States. Cluster yam, as Franklin Martin calls it, "is best known near its place of origin, Indochina, and in adjacent islands, but occurs throughout the East." The fairly uniform ones I collected looked rather like long russets except for tufts of disorderly rootlets. The very thin skin can almost be rubbed off. The flesh is typically slick, slippery, and pale, and browns rapidly.

An Indonesian cook who enjoyed Chinese yam all her life had heard about the delights of potatoes and asked to taste typical American types. She was disappointed to find them "so ordinary." That is how I feel about this yam. It is probably one of those all-purpose foods that is taken for granted on its home turf. Boiled and served very hot, it is like a fibrous russet; bland, pleasant enough, somewhat sweet, ordinary. Cooled, it turns dry and hard, like most yams.

BASIC USE: Do not eat raw yams. (There are exceptions, but they are not covered in this entry.) Yams make fine fried chips; or shred for fritters or pancakes. Boil or steam to complement spicy or assertive dishes, such as salt cod, smoked meats, or hot curries. Yams are usually best when drenched in a sauce—spicy, cheesy, picante, or garlicky. Or mash or puree, enrich with eggs and/or cream and butter or coconut milk, and bake to fluff up and dry: in soufflés, in restuffed yams, or as a topping. Generally speaking, yams need moisture to bloom in cooking (most are too dry to bake). To make soup, add peeled and diced yam (cut some small, some larger; the smaller ones will dissolve and thicken the soup) to rich ham or pork stock; cook until the larger dice are tender. Do *not* microwave yams.

SELECTION: Yams are erratically available year-round, primarily in Latin American and Asian markets. I have not found a correlation between size and quality. Yams should be solid and dense, without a trace of softness or mold. Check for cracks and sunken or darkening spots. Sniff to be sure there is no off odor. In the best Latin markets, the vendor will cut a slice from each yam to expose its clean, juicy interior and so indicate value (yams are not cheap). Lacking such help, prick the yam with a fingernail to be sure that it is juicy; if not, reject it.

STORAGE: Yams can be stored in a well-ventilated area, uncovered, at coolish room temperature, for upward of a week. If you want to cook part of a large yam, just hack it off; the latex-like juice will seal the cut area as if cauterized.

PREPARATION: Peeling (or not) before cooking has a dramatic difference on the cooked product. Some yams need only be scrubbed, some should be halved, some peeled. See each recipe for particulars. A very few yams irritate the skin. If you have not handled yams previously, oil your hands or wear gloves. Drop yams into water as you peel to prevent discoloration. Refrigerate if you won't use within an hour or two.

Please note: All generalizations about yams are unreliable. Exceptions are the rule. I apologize for any inadvertent lies.

To Cook White Yams: The Basics

White yam (*Dioscorea alata*) and African white yam (*D. rotundata*) are similar, but the first cooks to a somewhat softer and moister texture than the starchier, waxier African. Although results are as unpredictable as everything else about yams, boiled and steamed yams are similar to each other. Cooked properly, white yam can be surprisingly light (particularly *D. alata*)—almost as if air had been whipped in.

Through some culinary alchemy, yams that have been halved but not peeled cook to a creamier and lighter texture (some even fluff up to double in volume) than yams left whole or halved and peeled.

Boiled or steamed white yams have a flavor that is mild and easygoing, not exciting or dull. Serve with spicy sauces, gravy, meat juices, or one of the suggested toppings.

2 pounds white yams
Crisp coarse salt
Butter, sour cream, or grated cheese

1. If yams are under a pound, simply scrub and halve. If larger, cut into chunks of the same size, about 6 to 8 ounces each.

2. Drop into a pot of cold water. Add a handful of salt. Bring to a full boil. Lower heat and maintain just below a boil until fully tender throughout (not al dente), usually 25 to 45 minutes. Test often—yams must be well cooked, but they disintegrate if overcooked. (Alternatively, steam: Set on rack over boiling water, cut side down. Cover and cook until tender, about the same time.)

3. When tender, the yams can be kept hot in the water (or steamer) for 15 minutes or so. Drain.

4. Offer as is or peel before serving; hot, with butter, and salt, sour cream, or grated cheese. Or peel, mash, and mix with any of the same, then reheat gently.

Serves 4

To Cook Cushcush Yam: The Basics

Mapuey, as this delightful yam is known where I buy it in Jackson Heights, Queens, is the handiest type for individual servings and the best one to enjoy unadorned. Whether it is boiled or steamed (baked, it is too dry), the starchy particles nearly explode into what tastes like a fine-grained baked potato but sweeter, and with more character.

Choose whichever method yields the effect you prefer: If you peel and boil the yams, they will be dry, fluffy, and starchy, with a gentle potato sweetness and lightly smoky edge—but they will be crumbly, with uneven coloring. If you peel and steam them, they will taste much the same but have a more uniform consistency. If you do not peel them, they will have a moist, compact texture and neat appearance—whether they are boiled or steamed.

FOR EACH PERSON

1 cushcush yam (about ½ pound)

To boil: Peel yams (or simply scrub well), placing directly in pot of cold water. Bring to a full boil. Add a handful of salt. Lower heat and boil gently until truly tender throughout, about ½ hour for peeled yams, somewhat longer for unpeeled.

To steam: Peel yams (or simply scrub well). Set on rack over boiling water, cover, and steam until tender, about ½ hour if peeled, somewhat longer in the peel.

To peel cooked yams: Cut off the tips, slit the skin, then unroll and slip it off to reveal lilac-raspberry patches just beneath and fairly smooth flesh, free of cracks.

To Cook Purple Yam: The Basics

Comparison tests are always revealing, but this one proved a real surprise. I tried a second batch to be sure the results weren't fluky. When cooked with its peel, the purple yam was fibrous, wet, bland, and mottled in color, and it lost a good deal of flesh in post-cooking peeling. When cooked without its peel, the flesh was uniformly red-violet and mildly sweet with gentle

smoky, meaty, and nutty hints. It was smooth and juicy in comparison with other yams, and remained moist and soft even as it cooled.

2 pounds purple yams (preferably four ½-pound yams)
Crisp sea salt, such as fleur de sel
Garnish: orange wedges or crème fraîche or sour cream

1. Peel yams. Cut into pieces of equal size, about 4 ounces apiece.

2. Place in cold water and bring to a boil. Add a handful of salt. Lower heat and boil gently until tender throughout but not falling apart, about 25 minutes—but timing varies. Keep a close watch, as the flesh may disintegrate if overcooked.

3. Drain and serve hot, with crisp salt and one of the suggested garnishes.

Serves 4

Afro-Cuban White Yam Puree

Maricel Presilla, author of a forthcoming book about the foods of Latin America, prepares this simple puree with the popular Cuban, Costa Rican, Colombian, etc., white yam. The dish is comparable to mashed potatoes laced with garlic, onions, and bacon dice—but it is different, in the mild, smooshier way of white yam. Do not be concerned if the puree solidifies as it cools—it will reheat and pouf nicely after a brief microwaving. To reheat on the stove, add a little water or milk to soften, then warm over low heat.

About 3 pounds white yam
4 to 6 garlic cloves
1 teaspoon kosher salt
1 medium Spanish onion
½ tablespoon olive oil
About 2 ounces thick-cut bacon
About ½ cup hot milk

1. Peel yam and cut into 2-inch chunks. Drop into a pot of cold water. Bring to a boil. Add a handful of salt. Boil gently, partly covered, until yam is soft, usually 20 to 35 minutes.

2. Meanwhile, crush garlic and salt to a paste. Dice bacon. Cut onion into small dice. Heat oil in small skillet over moderate heat. Stir in bacon and cook until crisp and browned. With slotted spoon, transfer bacon to dish. Add garlic and onion to pan and stir over moderately low heat until lightly browned; set aside.

3. Drain yam. Place in large bowl and crush with potato masher, adding hot milk to smooth slightly. Blend in onion mixture and bacon. Season and serve immediately. Or reheat, adding milk as needed.

Serves 6 as a side dish

Spicy Yam Dice with Toasted Coconut

Cubes of yam are boiled, then pan-fried and topped with toasty spices and coconut for a flavorful treatment that's less fatty than traditional deep-frying. For ease of serving, precook the yam, toast the spice mixture, then proceed with other dinner preparations. At serving time, heat the cubes, *covered,* to steam and soften (if not covered, they will harden). Annatto (achiote) oil aromatizes the dish and burnishes it prettily, but is not obligatory. Serve hot with pot roast and steamed greens. Or include in an all-vegetable meal.

> About 2 pounds white yam of any type
> ⅓ cup dried coconut shreds
> ½ teaspoon cumin seeds
> ½ to 1 teaspoon pure ground mild chilli
> ½ teaspoon turmeric
> ½ teaspoon kosher salt
> 2 tablespoons annatto (achiote), peanut, or corn oil (preferably unrefined)

1. Peel yam. Cut into ½- to ¾-inch slices, then cut into dice (to yield 4 cups or more). Drop into plenty of boiling salted water. Boil until tender, 15 to 20 minutes. Drain in wide colander.

2. Meanwhile, spread coconut and cumin in heavy skillet wide enough to hold yam in single overlapping layer. Stir over low heat until lightly golden, not brown—a few minutes at most. Stir in chilli, turmeric, and salt. Scoop into a dish to cool. Wipe pan clean.

3. Add oil to pan and warm over moderate heat. Add yam, tossing to coat thoroughly. Cover pan and cook, shaking and stirring often until cubes are hot and slightly puffed, about 5 minutes. Sprinkle with coconut mixture, toss, and serve at once.

Serves 4 as a side dish

Almond-Topped Yam Gratin

Yam that has been boiled, then baked is very different from plain boiled—it has pouf and crunch. The texture, made creamy by mozzarella and lightened with soy milk (to heighten the tuber's nuttiness rather than impart a more dairy taste) is like souffléd baked potatoes. Tomato paste adds a peach tone and sweet edge but is not strictly necessary. Serve with bitter greens, with (or without) pork roast.

> 2 pounds white yam of any type
> 2 large shallots, thin-sliced
> ½ pound smoked mozzarella, coarse-grated
> 1 egg
> 2 tablespoons tomato paste
> ¾ to 1 cup soy milk (whole, not light)
> ½ teaspoon white pepper
> ⅓ cup sliced blanched almonds
> ¼ teaspoon coarse sea salt

1. Set a pot of water to boil. Peel yam. Cut into 2-inch chunks, dropping them into the pot as you go. Bring to full boil. Add a handful of salt. Reduce heat and boil gently until tender but not falling apart, 20 to 35 minutes (but timing varies). During last 5 minutes, add shallots. Set oven to 400°F.

2. Drain yam and shallots. Press through medium disc of food mill into a bowl. Stir in grated cheese. In another bowl, whisk egg and tomato paste, then blend in ¾ cup soy milk and pepper. Stir mixture into pureed yam. The texture should resemble soft mashed potatoes. If too stiff, add more soy milk. Season.

3. Spread mixture in shallow buttered baking dish of about 1½-quart capacity. Sprinkle almonds evenly over top, then coarse salt.

4. Bake in middle of oven until center is lightly puffed and firm and nuts are golden, about 35 minutes. Serve hot.

Serves 6 as a side dish, 3 as a main dish

Pros Propose

Recipes for yam are rare, although eating it is not. Yam is plain-cooked in most of the countries where it is common: boiled in chunks, boiled and mashed, boiled and pounded (fufu), or sometimes fried.

An interesting source for yam recipes is India, where meatless dishes star. *Dakshin: Vegetarian Cuisine from South India* by Chandra Padmanabhan offers several methods for cooking yams, two of which follow. For **Coconut Yam Kootu:** Sauté grated coconut in coconut oil to color; set aside. Peel yams and green plantains and chop into ½-inch pieces. Place in saucepan and add water to just cover. Add ground chilli, pepper, turmeric, and salt. Cover and simmer until tender. Meanwhile, pulverize half the sautéed coconut in food processor. Add cumin seeds and blend to a paste. Stir into vegetables and simmer briefly, mashing. Heat more coconut oil, add brown mustard seeds, halved red chilli, and curry leaves and toss. Add reserved coconut, then stir into the vegetables.

For **Yam Chips,** from the same source: Peel and thin-slice yams. Immerse in water, with turmeric. Let stand ½ hour. Drain, pat dry, and spread on towels. Deep-fry. Blend chilli powder, asafoetida powder, and salt and sprinkle over hot chips.

Maricel Presilla co-owns Zafra, a lively restaurant in Hoboken, New Jersey, where she prepares Cuban yams in garlic-citrus sauce, **Ñame con Mojo Agrio:** Crush plenty of garlic to a paste with salt. Blend with strong olive oil in small pan. Stir in small white onions, sliced and separated into rings. Cook over low heat until garlic colors slightly; reserve. Gently boil large chunks of yam until tender. Drain and cut into neat serving pieces. Heat the garlic oil and stir in sour orange juice (or lemon and orange juice mixed). Pour over hot yams and serve at once.

Yam Pie, like shepherd's pie, is made from ground meat topped with mashed and baked tubers—in this case, pork with yam instead of lamb with potato. This version from the Dominican Republic (there are others) calls for the small American mapuey yam, a favorite of author Elisabeth Lambert Ortiz. To prepare: Simmer peeled, sliced mapuey in water with lemon juice, covered, until tender. Drain, then mash with butter and milk. Stir in beaten eggs. Lightly cook ground pork, ham, chopped onion, garlic, and oregano. Add tomato paste, water, Worcestershire sauce, and vinegar. Simmer, uncovered, about ½ hour. Add capers and halved pimento-stuffed olives. Spread half in buttered baking dish and top with half the mashed yams. Add remaining meat, then yams. Brush with beaten egg. Bake until hot and browned (from *The Complete Book of Caribbean Cooking*).

Yard-Long Bean (*Vigna unguiculata,* var. *sesquipedalis*)

Also Chinese long bean, long bean, snake bean; dau gok, chang dou, and variations (Chinese); asparagus bean (a name that also refers to other vegetables), bodi and boonchi (West Indian)

Yard-long beans are *not* simply long green beans. They do not taste like green beans or behave like them in the pan (where they are more likely to be cooked than the pot). They are a subspecies of southernpeas (page 61) harvested young. In a few areas of Asia they are allowed to mature (and produce peas similar to their black-eyed sibling in the American South), but they are usually cultivated for their pencil-slim, flexible, lengthy pods, which are generally picked at about 1½ feet. (The Latin subspecies translates as 1½ feet; *Vigna* refers to a 17th-century scientist—not a vine; *unguiculata* means clawed, but I don't know why that comes up.)

The yard-long bean has been cultivated so long that its origins are unknown, but Africa and Asia are probable. It has been in China since prehistoric times and remains an important crop throughout the country. It is also grown in tropical and temperate parts of the Far East, Africa, the Mediterranean, and the Caribbean.

Whenever I read about these beans, I am compelled to taste another batch to be sure I mean what I say, because my opinion is not the same as anyone else's. "Mild," "sweet," "crisp," "tender," and "as easy to like as any string beans" are words I see again and again, but I don't agree. Yard-long beans are pronounced in flavor, distinctly leguminous, even oily tasting, not sweet. Their texture is dense and solid, not crisp and juicy. These traits make them different and suited to cooking methods that don't usually enhance green beans: stir-frying, deep-frying, and braising. They become nutty, chewy, and firm. The flavor is beany, not greeny, and it intensifies with cooking.

BASIC USE: In Thailand and Malaysia, yard-long beans are served uncooked in salads, but I find them too raw-tasting. However, if cut into tiny bits, like chopped nuts, they are an appealing accent color and texture laced through a grain dish or sprinkled on soft curries.

Yard-long beans are made to be fried: stir-fried, sautéed, shallow-fried, or deep-fried. Frying develops the chewy-crunchy, dryish aspect that makes them so special in Sichuan-style dry-sautéed beans, a familiar restaurant dish. If you prefer the beans juicy, more like green beans, blanch them before stir-frying. I have seen them tied into loose knots, dipped into tempura batter, and deep-fried but haven't tried this myself.

Braise yard-long beans, which retain their firm texture and absorb strong seasonings without losing their identity. Add to vegetable or meat stews and simmer some 20 minutes or more. Spicy, garlicky, or oniony braising liquids, and those based on coconut milk, are a luscious cooking medium for the beans.

Boil or steam yard-long beans for a simple flavor and texture akin to green beans, but less sweet and crisp. Once cooked, marinate beans in a forceful vinaigrette or simmer briefly in an assertive sauce.

Strong and rich foods bring out the best in these beans: fermented fish paste or fish sauce, ginger, salted black beans, garlic, tamarind, aggressive herbs, soy sauce, chilli sauce and chilli paste, roast pork, sausages, smoked or salted meat, salted fish, coconut milk, and plenty of oil and vinegar.

SELECTION: Yard-long beans are available year-round, primarily in Asian markets. Look for very thin, comparatively small beans with no bulging (the seeds or peas should not be developed). They can never be too slim, only too large—and then they're tough and oily. They are fairly floppy by nature, not as moist and crisp as green beans; but they should not look dry, rusty, or truly limp. Avoid yellowing beans—but do not confuse them with the yellowish variety.

There are both dark (more common) and pale green types in the market. Here again, I disagree with the usual evaluations. I find that the paler bean, less vivacious in appearance, cooks up somewhat sweeter, meatier, and more tender than deeper color beans. For quick-cooking dishes I prefer the pale bean; for dishes in which a certain firmness and stronger flavor are desirable, I choose the darker ones.

STORAGE: Yard-long beans do not keep. Wrap in paper towel, then enclose in plastic and store in the warmest part of your refrigerator and use them within a few days, at most. They turn limp and rusty very soon after purchase.

PREPARATION: One yard-long bean equals roughly 5 waste-free stringbeans (no strings attached and all good "meat"). Line up a batch of beans at the stem end. Cut these off, then proceed to slice the beans into desired lengths (generally 2 inches) on the diagonal or straight. Sometimes the other end of the bean will need a bit of trimming, too.

yard-long beans (both pale and dark types)   length: 18-24 inches

Hot and Spicy Yard-Long Beans and Beef

The crunchy chewiness of yard-long beans is best maintained by stir-frying. Crumbly beef (or pork or lamb) bits effectively transport sweet-hot savors to season them—even if ground meat looks untrendy. And while we're being unfashionable, fatty meat does a far better job of flavoring than lean. Pair with cracked wheat or brown rice. Or serve with Fried Rice with Wrapped Heart Mustard, Red Pepper, and Eggs (page 402); if preferred, omit the eggs and add ½ pound thin-sliced mushrooms along with the onions.

½ pound ground beef, pork, or lamb
3 tablespoons shoyu (Japanese soy sauce)
1 tablespoon brown sugar
2 tablespoons whiskey or brandy
1 pound yard-long beans
2 medium onions
2½ tablespoons peanut or corn oil
1 tablespoon minced ginger
½ teaspoon chilli flakes
½ teaspoon fennel seeds (chopped, or crushed in a suribachi)

1. Blend beef thoroughly with 1 tablespoon shoyu. Combine the remaining 2 tablespoons shoyu with sugar and whiskey. Trim tips from beans. Cut beans into 1½-inch diagonal slices. Halve onions through "poles," then slice vertically. Separate layers into strips. Have other ingredients ready to stir-fry.

2. Heat wok over moderately high heat. Pour 1 tablespoon oil around rim. Add beans and toss until most are wrinkled, lightly browned, and tender—about 5 minutes. Transfer to dish.

3. Add another tablespoon of oil to the wok. Add the onions and toss until browned, about 5 minutes. Add to beans.

4. Add remaining ½ tablespoon oil to wok. Stir-fry beef, tossing and pressing flat to brown well—about 3 minutes. Add ginger, chilli, and fennel. Toss another minute. Add shoyu mixture, then reserved vegetables. Toss a few minutes longer, until well combined. Serve hot.

Serves 3 to 4 as a main course

Yard-Long Beans with Fennel and Pepper Strips

Barbara Spiegel lives in lower Manhattan, where Chinatown and Little Italy, formerly separate and well-defined neighborhoods, have gradually melded. For her delightful non-traditional recipe, she combines beans from the Chinese market and fennel from the Italian to produce a dish that somehow seems as Mediterranean as ratatouille. The beans give a special "tooth," a meaty quality, to the mélange, which makes a useful buffet dish, warm or hot. If you do not have the pastis, substitute dry vermouth or sherry.

¾ pound yard-long beans
¾-pound fennel bulb with greens
½ pound red bell pepper
2 tablespoons olive oil
1 teaspoon fennel seeds, crushed
½ teaspoon kosher salt
2 tablespoons Pernod, Ricard, or other pastis
¼ cup water

1. Trim beans. Cut into 2½-inch lengths. Trim stalks from fennel and remove greens. (Reserve stalks for another use.) Cut bulb into narrow 2½-inch strips. Do the same to the bell pepper. Chop fennel greens for garnish.

2. Heat olive oil in very large sauté pan over high heat. When surface shimmers, add beans and fennel seeds. Stir-fry until beans are slightly wrinkled and lightly browned, about 5 minutes.

3. Add fennel and pepper strips to pan. Toss 2 minutes. Reduce heat to moderate. Add salt and toss. Combine Pernod and water; add to pan, cover, and simmer until vegetables are tender, about 5 minutes.

4. Uncover. If necessary, simmer briefly to evaporate liquid. Season. Sprinkle with chopped fennel greens to taste. Serve hot or warm.

Serves 4

Pros Propose

Although yard-long beans are associated primarily with the cuisines of the Far East, they are used in other parts of the world as well. Paula Wolfert writes in *Mediterranean Grains and Greens* that "in the Black Sea town of Amasra . . . whole potfuls of long beans are cooked until tender, then tossed with olive oil and garlic for a dish called . . . 'fresh macaroni-style beans.' " She also cites "dishes in which these long beans are diced as small as grains of rice, cooked until soft, then combined with slow-cooked onions and rice for a regional pilaf." **Sautéed Yard-Long Beans and Walnuts with Garden Greens** should be both "puckeringly sour and hot": Cut slim beans into thirds. Sauté in olive oil. Add salt and a little water and cook briefly, covered. Add coarse-chopped walnuts, ground Aleppo or Turkish red pepper (or both hot and sweet Hungarian paprikas), and mild vinegar or verjuice. Cook, uncovered, until tender. Stir in torn-up lettuce and lemon juice. Serve at room temperature.

In Port-of-Spain, Trinidad, yard-long beans are "generally eaten at lunchtime with roti, a flatbread either plain or stuffed with split peas," according to *Madhur Jaffrey's World Vegetarian*. To prepare **Curry Bodi:** Stir-fry fine-chopped onion, garlic, and chillis in peanut oil to brown lightly. Stir in curry powder, water, then 1½-inch long-bean segments and salt. Simmer until tender and little liquid remains. Add amchar masala (a Trinidadian mixture of ground coriander, cumin, pepper, fennel, brown mustard, and fenugreek) and ground roasted cumin seeds. Toss briefly and serve hot.

Elisabeth Lambert Ortiz notes that in Aruba, yard-long beans are wrapped around skewered foods to secure them for grilling. For **Lambchi and Boonchi** (Lamb with Yard-Long Beans): Marinate lamb cubes in grated onion, hot paprika, curry powder, grated ginger, crushed garlic, salt, lemon juice, and peanut oil. Thread on skewers with blanched, peeled small white onions, bacon squares, green pepper, pineapple cubes, and cherry tomatoes. Twist parboiled yard-long beans around each skewer, tying the ends. Grill until browned, turning gently. Blend mustard, peanut butter, turmeric, soy sauce, Worcestershire and hot pepper sauce to serve alongside (from *The Complete Book of Caribbean Cooking*).

Yard-long beans are called chopstick beans in Vietnam, writes Nicole Routhier in *The Foods of Vietnam*. For **Stir-Fried Long Beans with Shrimp:** Toss halved and deveined shrimp with fish sauce, minced garlic, sugar, and black pepper; marinate ½ hour. Stir-fry minced garlic in oil; add shrimp and toss until pink; set aside. Stir-fry onion slivers in oil until lightly caramelized. Add 2-inch-long bean pieces. Add soy sauce, salt, sugar, and water. Toss until crisp-tender. Add shrimp, 2-inch scallion lengths, and pepper. Serve with rice and nuoc cham (a sauce of garlic, red chilli, sugar, lime juice, rice vinegar, fish sauce, and water).

In the United States, California chef Amaryll Schwertner praises the bean's "unusual ability to absorb flavors, whether it is cooked quickly or simmered until very soft." To enhance this trait, she finds it useful to cut tiny cross sections that "look stunning and unrecognizable—they pique curiosity." For rich **Braised Pork Belly with Long Beans:** Season light pork stock with sliced ginger and good quality sake. Add slices of pork belly, cover with parchment, and gently oven-braise until nearly melting. Add ¼-inch sections of long beans; cook about 30 minutes longer, until tender and flavorful. Serve in small bowls as a starter, or with rice as a main course.

Yautía, Malanga (*Xanthosoma* species)

Also cocoyam, new cocoyam, coco, tannia, tanier, yautía (or malanga) blanca, yautía (or malanga) lila, yautía (or malanga) amarilla, and taro (the names overlap in Latin American and West Indian markets)
Including **white (blanca), lilac (lila),** and **yellow (amarilla) forms**

Note: Malanga isleña—sometimes malanga alone—may also refer to *Colocasia* species (see TARO, page 655), and taro may also refer to *Xanthosoma* species!

Yautía and malanga are the Puerto Rican and Cuban names, respectively, for cormels (not tubers) that have more, and more confusing, international names than you can invent. They're the two most common names in the United States for *Xanthosoma* species and are equally important. To be reasonable and fair, I alternate the names in the text that follows.

Xanthosoma species, native to the American tropics, belong to the same family (Araceae) as *Colocasia esculenta,* usually called taro, a plant of Old World origin. Some forms of yautía and taro resemble each other sufficiently to have resulted in more than a score of common names that overlap both vegetables, hopelessly blurring their nominal identities. That both crops are a staple in much of the Southern Hemisphere, often planted side by side—some for their "elephant-ear" leaves, some for their starchy corms and cormels, some for both—does little to tidy up the tangle.

Here is a curious aside that can be skipped by all but the most devoted plant followers: After *Xanthosoma* was introduced to the South Pacific by botanists in the early 1900s, yet another batch of names arose. "The complexity of the common names given this plant is some indication of its channels of introduction," Gwen Skinner writes in *The Cuisine of the South Pacific,* a most useful reference. "In New Guinea it is called 'Kong Kong [as in Hong Kong] taro' (meaning China taro), in New Caledonia it becomes 'New Hebrides taro,' yet in the New Hebrides it is 'Fiji taro.' In Samoa it is *talo papalaqi* meaning taro of the European." And all these "taros" are what we call yautía or malanga! Another aside comes in a cookbook from Nigeria, where cocoyam is the common name—but for what? "There are several varieties of cocoyam. The main ones are *Xanthosoma sagittifolium* (Tannia) . . . and *Colocasia*

esculentum [sic] (Taro) . . . considered to be an inferior food to other yams." Taro = yautía = yam? Perhaps identification is less meaningful if tuberous starchy things are all prepared pretty much the same way, as in this *Nigerian Cookbook* (by H. O. Anthonio and M. Isoun) and in many other countries where these foods are staples.

The malanga types sold in the United States—some grown here, some imported from Central America—do not look like the taro sold here. (The possible

yautía or malanga: amarilla (*left*), blanca (*top right*), and lila (*bottom right*)   length: 4-10 inches

exception is yellow yautía, pictured opposite, which has the shape of large taro but a very different color.) Most yautía cormels are elongated and tapered, bumpy and crumply, with shaggy, scaly skin that does not quite cover the flesh. They weigh roughly ½ pound to 2 pounds. As with other tropical roots and tubers, the slippery, crisp raw flesh cooks to a starchy "love it or leave it" texture: this one between waxy potatoes and soft legumes. The flavor is more pronounced than most starches of this kind, sometimes nutty and earthy, sometimes lighter and more potato-like, always defined.

Yautía/malanga blanca (*Xanthosoma sagittifolium*) is by far the most common market type in the United States. This is what is generally meant when the term yautía or malanga is used on its own. It varies from lightly earthy and waxy to mild and smooth as creamed potatoes—a distinct and unpredictable textural range.

Yautía/malanga lila or **malanga colorada** (*Xanthosoma violaceum*), or simply lila—in Cuban groceries here—has the same club-shaped exterior and scruffy look as the blanca, but the interior is light gray-lavender. Its texture is heavier than the white, as is the flavor, which has a bacon-like edge. The lavender does not stay when cooked, but turns a putty greige.

Yautía/malanga amarilla (*Xanthosoma atrovirens*) is very different from others you'll find in the United States. It is barrel-shaped, ridged, and dense, and the central "mother" corm is eaten instead of the lateral "baby" cormels that grow around it—the only *Xanthosoma* for which this is the case, according to Stephen K. O'Hair, a root and tuber crop researcher at the University of Florida Tropical Research and Education Center in Homestead. Cooked, the corm is sweet, nutty, warm ocher in color, and extremely dry and dense—too much so to be eaten as a simple starchy vegetable. Maricel Presilla, an authority on Latin American food, explains that the dryness is what makes it ideal for turning into dough. "It is the malanga we use for pasteles, buñuelos, empanadas, tamales, fufu, and other well-known pastries, breads, and desserts."

The young leaves of selected *Xanthosoma* varieties are an important green vegetable throughout the tropics, but I have not seen them sold in the United States. When available they can be used like taro leaves (see page 660), and—also like taro leaves—they are called callaloo (and numerous variations on callaloo) in the Antilles.

BASIC USE: In the countries where malanga is a staple, it is most often plain-boiled. This must be done gently, for the cormels disintegrate easily. Serve with spicy sausages, salty dried meat or fish, or highly seasoned stews—Western or Eastern. Or pour chilli and/or garlic sauce over the hot starch, which absorbs like a sponge.

Yautía excels in fried form. It makes spectacularly crisp, full-flavored chips, or it can be grated to make crunchy fritters or chewy pancakes.

Mash or puree (but do not process) the cooked cormels: Press while still hot through a food mill; thin with milk or cream; then season with allspice, nutmeg, minced and sautéed shallots or onions; then serve piping hot.

Malanga is made for soup. Once it has cooked through in liquid, it begins to soften and dissolve smoothly—as if melting. Slightly sticky and starchy, it melds herbs and spices, smoky meats, and root vegetables. For similar reasons, it makes an interesting contribution to stews, adding flavor, thickness, and creaminess. Be careful not to overcook, or it will disintegrate entirely.

Yellow yautía is handled in different ways from the other types. For the most part, it is boiled, cooled, and pressed through a meat grinder or a sturdy food mill, then blended with additional starches and flavorings to become a dough. Or it may be cut small and included with other starches in boiled stews or soups.

SELECTION: Malanga is available year-round in Latin American and West Indian markets. Select relatively light-colored, hard malanga. There should be no shriveled, softening, or moldy areas. Avoid any malanga with sprouts. Prick with your fingernail: It should be juicy and crisp, like water chestnut—not dry. In the best produce markets, the staff will slice the goods to show you just how fresh they are.

STORAGE: Store uncovered, no more than a few days, at cool ambient temperature and as high humidity as possible—malanga dehydrates quickly. Aficionados tell me that it keeps longer in the refrigerator, but in my experience this has not been true. Try for yourself.

PREPARATION: Scrub under running water. Trim off both ends. Peel thoroughly, placing corms in a bowl of water as you proceed.

Basic Boiled Yautía/Malanga

This is less a recipe than a reminder that if you're going to cook yautía straight, it is best when boiled, and smoother and less dense when the cooking is started in cold water rather than hot. Baked yautía is hopelessly dry and waxy (unless, perhaps, you cook it in ashes, as in the South Pacific). When it is steamed, the color is blotchy, the texture remains a bit heavy, and the cooking time is longer. So: Boil, but gently, lest the cormels break apart. Serve piping hot only. The nippy Citrus Sauce with Olives, Peppers, and Onions (page 729) or the Garlic-Lime Sauce (page 729) suits the yautía well, if you're looking for a topping.

2 pounds yautía/malanga blanca or lila
Salt

1. Scrub corms under running water. Trim and peel thoroughly. Cut into 2- to 3-inch chunks, setting in a pot of cold water as you go.
2. Set pot over high heat and bring to a boil. Add a handful of salt. Reduce heat and keep at a low boil until yautía is soft throughout but not falling apart, usually about 20 to 30 minutes—but timing varies. (If you are not ready to serve the yautía, it can be left in the pot for about ½ hour.)
3. Lift out pieces with slotted spoon into a heated serving dish. Serve at once, with spicy meat gravy, curry, or hot-sharp dressing.

Serves 4

Yautía/Malanga with Pesto Picante

White malanga can be quite creamy and light textured when very hot, but it becomes stodgy and waxy as it cools. Sauce helps retain the lighter texture. This one is vivid green in scent and color and frothy in texture, thanks to green pepper's juiciness. Serve the dish with room-temperature pork or chicken, which both benefit from the sauce. Or garnish the hot vegetable with cherry tomatoes and enjoy as a lunch main course or light supper.

⅓ cup olive oil
1 small green bell pepper, sliced
1 or 2 garlic cloves, sliced
2 to 4 small green chillis, seeded and sliced
1 teaspoon kosher salt
2 tablespoons pine nuts
4 cups lightly packed basil leaves
3 to 4 tablespoons lime juice
2 pounds yautía/malanga blanca

1. Prepare pesto picante: In food processor, combine olive oil, green pepper, garlic, chillis, salt, and pine nuts. Whiz to a fine texture. With motor running, add basil leaves, in batches. When all have been smoothly incorporated, add 3 tablespoons lime juice.
2. Scrub yautía under running water. Trim and peel thoroughly. Cut into 2- to 3-inch chunks, placing in a pot of cold water as you proceed.
3. Set pot over high heat and bring to a boil. Reduce heat and boil gently until yautía is tender throughout, usually 20 to 30 minutes—but timing varies. Meanwhile, taste sauce and add lime juice and salt if needed.
4. When yautía is tender, transfer with slotted spoon to a heated serving dish (or keep hot in the water up to ½ hour). Serve hot, with plenty of sauce spooned over.

Serves 4 as a side dish

Yautía/Malanga-Sweetpotato Pancakes

At once crisp, firm, and chewy, these lightly sweet cakes can serve as appetizer, brunch, or side dish. To serve as a separate dish, top with a favorite chilli salsa or Pesto Picante (above). Or serve as an accompaniment to braised meat or a roast with pan gravy. You'll usually find boniato (see page 639) at the same markets as yautía. If you want to use less fat, cook pancakes in non-stick skillets, but don't expect the same crisp finish.

10 to 12 ounces yautía/malanga
4 to 6 ounces sweetpotato (preferably boniato)
2 tablespoons lemon juice

1 large egg
2 tablespoons grated shallot
1 tablespoon pure mild ground chilli or
   blended chile powder
1 teaspoon kosher salt
About 2 tablespoons mild vegetable oil
1 tablespoon butter

1. Rinse and peel both malanga and sweetpotato and place in cold water to cover. Grate half of each on large holes of a hand grater, and half on the smaller ones (you should have about 2 loosely packed cups). Toss shreds in bowl with lemon juice, coating evenly.

2. In a small bowl, whisk together egg, shallot, chilli, and salt. Stir into the vegetables. Let stand about 15 minutes.

3. Set two fairly large skillets over moderate heat. Add 1 tablespoon oil and ½ tablespoon butter to each. Stir vegetable mixture. Using a scant tablespoon for each cake, drop 8 to 10 mounds into one pan (about half the mixture). Repeat in second pan. Flatten cakes.

4. Reduce heat to moderately low so pancakes cook through without burning, about 4 minutes. Turn, adding a little oil if needed. Cook until nicely browned.

5. Arrange on a heated serving dish and serve hot.

Makes 16 to 20 small pancakes

Fried Yautía/Malanga Chips

All chips attract nibblers, but yautía, with its nutty flavor and dry crispness, is particularly appealing. You'll need a food processor or mandoline to make long thin slices. I like the chips best served hot from the fryer or pan (one with a controlled thermostat), with tropical cocktails: caipirinha, mojito, or daiquiri.

1 pound small malanga/yautía blanca or lila
Mild oil for deep-frying
Fine salt

1. Scrub yautía. Pare thoroughly. Place in cold water until ready to cook. Heat oil for frying to 375°F.
2. Drain and dry yautía. With thin-slicing (2-millimeter) blade in place, cut just enough very thin lengthwise chips to cover the surface of the oil (this can be done with a wide feed tube; if your machine has a small tube, halve yautía first).

3. Place slices gently in oil. Fry until golden on both sides, about 2 minutes. Drain on paper toweling and sprinkle with salt. Repeat.

4. Serve at once, or keep warm briefly in a low oven, if more convenient.

Serves about 4 moderate nibblers

Creamy Pureed Yautía/ Malanga Soup

Ginger and brandy give a lift to the nutty, slightly earthy flavor of this thick, smooth soup. The amount of liquid needed will vary with the type of yautía. Yellow malanga requires the most; white, the least. Yellow and lilac malanga will have more depth and complexity; white will be more mild and gentle. Use a combination if possible. Like most soups—purees in particular—this is improved with mellowing time, but that is not strictly necessary. Serve with a salad of bitter greens, citrus, and red onions for a simple winter meal.

About 1½ pounds yautía/malanga
1 medium leek
1 medium parsnip or 2 medium carrots
3 tender inner celery stalks with leaves
1½-inch ginger chunk
2 tablespoons walnut or hazelnut oil
1 teaspoon kosher salt (omit if broth is salted)
¼ teaspoon dried thyme
¼ teaspoon grated nutmeg
About 2½ cups vegetable or mushroom broth
About 2½ cups beef or ham broth (or more
   vegetable broth)
About 1 cup milk
About 2 tablespoons brandy
White pepper
¼ cup toasted, chopped walnuts or hazelnuts
Garnish: slivered celery leaves

1. Rinse yautía. Peel and cut into 1-inch chunks. Drop into a bowl of water. Trim heaviest part of greens and roots from leek. Halve lengthwise, slice thin, and rinse in several changes of water. Peel and chop parsnip (or carrots). Chop celery. Peel and mince ginger.

2. Heat oil in heavy pot over low heat; stir in leek, parsnip, celery, ginger, and salt. Cook until soft, about 10 minutes, stirring often. Stir in thyme and nutmeg.

3. Add drained yautía and 2 cups of each broth to the pot. Bring to a boil, stirring. Lower heat and simmer, covered, until yautía is soft—about ½ hour, but timing varies. Let cool briefly, as convenient.

4. Puree soup in food processor or blender until very smooth, working in batches if necessary. Return soup to rinsed-out pot. Gradually stir in more broth and milk, adjusting consistency and flavor. Add 2 tablespoons brandy. Bring to a simmer. Taste and adjust liquids and seasoning. Cool, then chill.

5. To serve, bring soup to a simmer. Add broth, brandy, and seasoning to taste. Ladle into bowls and sprinkle with nuts and celery leaves.

Serves 4

Pros Propose

"Viandas" is a catchall term used in the Hispanic Caribbean to include the range of starchy staples that make a meal complete in that part of the world: plantain, yuca, boniato, breadfruit, true yam, taro, and yautía. Maricel Presilla, a Cuban-born historian, chef, and author cited often in these pages, might be considered the queen of viandas, as a review of those subjects in this book proves. **Mariquitas Surtidas,** a combination of these vegetables, fine-sliced and fried to order, served with a dipping sauce, is the starring appetizer at Zafra, the restaurant she co-owns in Hoboken. "But their use at a restaurant can be broader. They can be arranged in a basket, upright, and served like bread sticks, or they can be used as a garnish, or crumbled for a crunchy coating. Because they remain crisp, they can be stored too."

Chef Presilla uses a traditional Spanish enrichment for her creamy **Malanga and Almond Milk Gratin:** Combine blanched almonds with warm water and a touch of honey and salt in food processor and grind fine. Strain through sieve, pressing on solids; discard pulp. Cover peeled, cubed 2-inch malanga cubes with water, add salt, and bring to a boil. Lower heat and simmer until fork-tender. Drain. Press through food mill. Add minced, sautéed Spanish onion, the almond milk, and grated queso blanco fresco. Blend egg, salt, white pepper, and nutmeg and add to malanga. Scoop into buttered baking dish and sprinkle with more grated queso fresco. Bake in 375°F oven until golden.

Rice and Beans and Tasty Things by Dora Romano is a user-friendly guide to the food of Puerto Rico, where complex and labor-intensive dishes are common. Of those that represent the country's culinary heritage, most of the best-known feature yautía, often in concert with other starches (the viandas): sancocho, an elaborate stew of multiple meats and viandas; mondongo, a complicated soup of tripe, viandas, and vegetables; pasteles, viandas-based "tamales" filled with pork, chillis, chickpeas, and green olives; and alcapurrias, viandas-crusted croquettes with a similar stuffing—all recipes that are too long to include here. Little fritters of yautía or taro are common in the Caribbean: Some have baking powder as leavening, some eggs; some are seasoned with parsley and garlic; some are no more than grated vegetables. Romano's **Frituras de Yautía y Queso** are made of rinsed and grated yautía blanca, grated Parmesan, salt, and annatto lard or oil. For each, place 2 tablespoons of the mixture on greased waxed paper and shape neatly. Deep-fry until golden. Drain on paper. Serve as an appetizer or side.

It is curious that so few Latin "fusion" chefs serve the starchy vegetables that distinguish their *patria* (homeland), also the name of the restaurant where chef Douglas Rodriguez established his reputation in New York City. The "sticky starches" (yuca, yam, taro, and yautía) are usually ignored unless fried, because it is thought that "Americans" (whoever they are) won't like them any other way. But Rodriguez, who was born in the United States to Cuban parents, has numerous creamy, sticky, and crisp starches on his menu and in his books. Customers are devoted to his **Malanga–Goat Cheese Puree:** Simmer peeled, cubed malanga in milk to cover until soft. Drain, reserving liquid. Crush with potato masher, adding fresh goat cheese and enough reserved milk for a thick, creamy consistency. Heat and serve garnished with deep-fried long malanga chips.

Yuca, Cassava (*Manihot esculenta* and *M. utilissima*)

Also manioc, mandioca (Brazilian)

Note: Yuca, pronounced YOO-ka, is *not* yucca, pronounced YUK-ka, a genus and common name of a plant in the Agave family; nor are they related.

If you're shopping in North America, you'll probably find this vegetable as yuca; that is why it's under "Y." Elsewhere in the English-speaking world it is cassava. In the Americas, it is most likely to be exported from and purchased by people from Latin America, who call it yuca. According to Maricel Presilla, a historian and authority on the foods of Latin America, "the words 'yuca' and 'cassava' come from the Taino (Arawak), the indigenous people of the Orinoco Basin who settled in the Lesser and Greater Antilles in pre-Columbian times. Yuca referred to the plant and its roots, while caçabi—which became cassava—was the word for the bread, as casabe is today in Cuba, the Dominican Republic, and Venezuela, among others. 'Manioc' comes from mandioca, in the Tupi language of the Brazilian Amazon, which also gives the botanical name *Manihot*."

The historian Sophie D. Coe provides a brief picture of the plant's post-Columbian trajectory in *America's First Cuisines:* From South America, cassava "was taken to Africa by the Portuguese along with maize and westward across the Pacific by the Spaniards, who introduced it into the Philippines, whence it spread into Southeast Asia. Today, Thailand produces a large crop . . . most of which goes into the only manioc product with which those of us who live in northern climes are familiar—tapioca." Thailand is still the largest producer of tapioca, a processed form of cassava that is used as a thickener worldwide.

Tapioca pudding, a milky dessert known to all upstanding American families when I was growing up, is a "love it or leave it" food—like yuca. You will be in sizable company if you like the bland, buttery food. In 1999, 168 million metric tons of cassava were produced in 85 countries (by comparison, 294 million metric tons of potatoes were produced worldwide that year). In the lands where it is a staple, yuca is processed into flour, flakes, refined starch, syrup, vinegar, and al-

length: 10-15 inches

coholic beverages. Fresh, it is usually boiled or fried—as happens with increased frequency in the United States, where consumption is growing with the Hispanic population: In 1990 we imported 18 million pounds of fresh yuca; by 1999 the figure had reached 59.4 million pounds.

The swollen roots, shaped like clubs, bats, or slim sweetpotatoes, have a bark-like covering and flesh as hard and white as coconut. The leaves, a popular green vegetable wherever yuca grows, do not yet make it to these shores, as far as I can tell.

There is nothing quite like yuca. Dense, smooth, so purely starchy that it turns translucent when cooked, yuca has a unique, glutinous sweetness and buttery blandness, whether pureed for creamy Brazilian shrimp sauce (bobo de camarão), simmered with tripe in savory Puerto Rican mondongo, or boiled in the multiple-vegetable stews of Latin America: sancocho, ajiaco, and cozido.

If the main course in cassava countries doesn't feature yuca, accompaniments will: Unleavened casabe, a hard flatbread made of dried cassava meal, absorbs gravies in the Caribbean; toasted cassava meal (farinha de mandioca) is sprinkled over Brazilian dishes; grated fresh cassava is steamed or baked in dumplings and breads that are staples throughout the Pacific and Caribbean Islands.

You may have read that cassava contains lethal doses of cyanide. It can—but this is not true of what comes to market, almost exclusively from Costa Rica and the Dominican Republic. "No special precautions need to be observed when preparing the cultivars that come to the United States," says Stephen O'Hair, the root and tuber crop researcher at the University of Florida Tropical Research and Education Center in Homestead. "Cooking alone will get rid of the very low quantities of cyanogenic glucosides. Only in Africa and Brazil do they grow the high-cyanide types for the special almondy flavor they prefer—and they know how to prepare them."

BASIC USE: Fresh yuca is a variable ingredient, at once distinct and self-effacing. It can fry to inimitable chips or "melt" into thick sauce, be as bland as baby food, or absorb garlic and chilli and still keep its special character.

To cook plain yuca, gently simmer peeled chunks in salted water until tender, about ½ hour. Serve as is (being sure all the tough central cord is removed), or mash coarsely to serve with spicy stews or braises from any part of the world. If you like mashed potatoes, you'll love mashed yuca—which tastes as if the butter has already been added (stir in an actual dab of butter, and it is amplified). Yuca can be reheated in fat or liquid; it doesn't get stodgy like other tropical roots and tubers. Mojo agrio, a Cuban sauce of olive oil, sour oranges, and garlic, is among the best-loved ways to dress up plain yuca.

Cooked, then pureed, yuca has a special texture that makes it amenable to being worked like dough—for both sweet or savory dishes, to be fried or baked. Make pie "crusts" or fritters or crullers.

Add chunks of yuca to meat or vegetable stews during the last half hour or so of cooking. It obligingly thickens and absorbs juices. Fry as chips, as birds' nests, or grated for fritters. For "french fries," parboil yuca and then dry on paper towels before deep-frying. Grate it raw into dumplings, pudding, and bread to be baked, steamed, or fried.

Note: Do not eat raw yuca.

SELECTION: Yuca is available all year. It is variable in quality and tricky to choose. Nothing can be done to improve inferior yuca, which is simply inedible. Look for rock-hard roots that have no stickiness, bald spots, soft areas, mold, or hairline cracks. Choose comparatively cylindrical roots (not sharply tapered ones), which are more easily cut to equal size.

Yuca is almost always heavily coated with wax. Feel carefully for soft spots that may be masked. "Waxing is necessary to prevent dehydration and oxidation, which occur quickly. It is a root, not a storage tuber, and continues to respire," explains Stephen O'Hair. "Within five days of harvesting, dark streaks can appear, and with them, an off taste. I hate to say it, but the only way to be sure yuca is okay is to break the tip to see that there are no streaks or darkening near the skin." It is common in markets where yuca is sold regularly to have the roots cut for you, to show the pure white interior. If just a part of the root is dry or has interior cracks or dark filaments, you can cut it off and discard it and keep the good part.

STORAGE: Although yuca looks hardy, it perishes rapidly, like most tropical produce. Store it in a basket in a well-ventilated area at room temperature (preferably coolish). If it shows cracks, refrigerate it, uncovered. Once cut, refrigerate, wrapped, for a short time. Yuca freezes very well. Peel it, dropping it into water as you proceed. Drain, then wrap tightly and freeze.

PREPARATION: Rinse yuca. With a heavy knife or cleaver, hack 2- to 3-inch lengths. Slit the "bark" lengthwise. Slide a paring knife under it and its pinkish underlayer; pull these off, unwrapping from the white interior; pare off any pinkish parts remaining. Many roots, especially older ones, contain a central fiber that must be removed.

Basic Yuca

Mild, waxy, and sticky, yuca is yummy plain-simmered—if you like the tapioca texture. Serve as a side to vegetable curry, chili, or braised meat. Do not wander far from the stove—if overcooked, yuca becomes a sticky fibrous mass. "Cook until tender" is more subjective than for other starches. Some people like it a touch chewy (never al dente, however), some like it moist and melty. Although it defies traditional methods, I find the roots hold together better if added to boiling—not cold—water (unlike yams and yautía).

About 2 pounds yuca
3 quarts water
1 tablespoon kosher salt

1. Rinse each root. With cleaver or heavy knife, cut into 2- to 3-inch lengths. Slit the "bark" lengthwise, then slip knife under it and the pinkish underlayer, and unwrap and remove both, paring if necessary. Halve each piece lengthwise to remove the inedible central fiber that runs the length of many roots (or halve and remove after cooking).

2. Meanwhile, bring water to a boil; add salt. Add yuca and return to a boil. Reduce to a simmer. After 15 minutes, or when pieces no longer look white, but nearly translucent, test with cake tester or toothpick, which should slip through easily. Expect variation in cooking time (and increase the time if the yuca has not been halved). Yuca is not tidy: Some pieces will separate lengthwise, some will fray, some will resist cooking. If a piece threatens to turn mushy, remove it.

3. When yuca is nearly done (just a little white remains in the center), turn off heat and let stand a few minutes (or up to 30) to finish cooking through. Drain on a towel, and serve hot.

Serves 4

Variation

Yuca with Garlic-Lime Sauce

Cook yuca as above. Prepare sauce while the cooking is finishing: Crush 2 large garlic cloves and 1 teaspoon coarse salt to a paste. Combine in small skillet with ¼ cup strong olive oil and 1 small white onion, sliced and separated into rings. Cook over lowest heat, stirring, until garlic just begins to color. Re-move from heat. Add ⅓ cup lime juice. Drain yuca thoroughly. Separate each piece into its 4 natural sections (2, if it has been halved). Remove central fiber if necessary. Place in warm serving dish. Taste sauce, season, and reheat. Pour over yuca. Serve hot.

Yuca in Picante Citrus Sauce with Olives, Peppers, and Onions

Soft, mild, pale yuca is offset by a tangy and colorful toss of tart green olives, sweet bell peppers, red onions, chilli strips, and citrus juice. Serve as starch-and-vegetable accompaniment to grilled seafood or poultry. Or, for a vegetable meal, add stuffed tomatoes and yellow squash or zucchini. Poblano chilli, which I prefer for its deep color and flavor, can be replaced by another large medium-hot chilli. Although yuca is best fresh-cooked, the dish can also be served at room temperature. Or refrigerate, then microwave to just barely warm the yuca.

2 quarts water
3 bay leaves
½ teaspoon whole allspice
Several small dried chillis (to taste)
1 tablespoon plus ½ teaspoon kosher salt
About 1½ pounds yuca
2 medium red onions
1 red bell pepper
2 Poblano chillis, peeled (see Note, page 114)
⅓ cup strong olive oil
½ cup orange juice
¼ cup lemon juice
3 to 4 tablespoons white wine vinegar
½ cup pitted, thin-sliced green Spanish olives
1 bunch cilantro (coriander) leaves

1. Combine water, bay leaves, allspice, dried chillis, and 1 tablespoon salt in large saucepan and bring to a boil. Meanwhile, cut yuca into 2-inch lengths. Cut a slit down the length of each, then insert a paring knife to help remove "bark" and underlayer. Halve each piece lengthwise, and discard any fibrous cord. Rinse yuca and add to pan.

2. Simmer yuca gently until tender but not falling apart, checking with cake tester or knife tip when it looks more or less translucent. Timing can vary from 15 to more than 30 minutes.

3. While yuca cooks, prepare sauce: Halve onions through "poles," then slice lengthwise and separate into strips. Cut red pepper and chillis into strips about the same size. Heat oil in fairly wide skillet over moderately high heat. Stir in onions, bell pepper, and chillis and toss 1 minute. Add orange and lemon juices, 3 tablespoons vinegar, the remaining ½ teaspoon salt, and olives. Remove from heat.

4. Drain yuca. Halve lengthwise, then cut across into ½-inch slices. Arrange in serving dish. Reheat vegetable mixture. Stir in cilantro. Pour at once over yuca, gently turning pieces to distribute and absorb dressing. Season. Serve warm or at room temperature.

Serves 4 to 6

Variation

Seasoned Boiled Yuca

For lightly seasoned "plain" yuca, simply prepare without sauce, following the recipe through step 2. Serve hot, with meat or vegetable stew—Indian, Ethiopian, Cuban—or a mess o' greens, Southern-style.

Puffed Baked Yuca-Squash Puree

This pretty pale orange puree, smooth and slightly sweet, makes a festive meal with a roast and bitter greens. Or serve larger portions as part of an all-vegetable meal, with broccoli and wheat pilaf. A caveat: Yuca may take as little as 15 minutes of simmering to become soft—or as much as an hour. Baking time will also vary, depending upon how much moisture remains in the puree. Nevertheless, results are deliciously dependable. You can even prepare the mixture ahead, refrigerate, then bring to room temperature and bake.

About 1¾ pounds yuca
1½ cups water

1 cup whole milk
1-pound chunk firm, sweet winter squash
     (kabocha type or Buttercup)
2 or 3 garlic cloves, peeled
½ tablespoon kosher salt
2 eggs
1 tablespoon butter

1. Cut yuca into 1- to 2-inch lengths. Cut a slit down the length of each, then insert a paring knife to help remove the "bark" and underlayer. Quarter each piece lengthwise and remove the fibrous central cord, if present. Combine in heavy medium saucepan with water and milk.

2. Cut squash into 1½-inch chunks. Scrape out seeds and fibers and pare skin. Add to yuca, with garlic and salt. Bring to a boil. Reduce heat to simmer gently until both vegetables are very soft. Timing varies, but 35 minutes is usual. Stir often to keep pieces submerged (but do not add liquid or cover—some liquid should evaporate). Preheat oven to 375°F.

3. Cool vegetables slightly. Transfer to food processor and puree to smooth consistency. With motor running, add eggs and butter and whirl to blend. Scrape into buttered 2-quart soufflé mold or baking dish.

4. Set in upper level of oven. Bake until browned, fairly firm, and puffed in center—an hour or more. Serve hot.

Serves 6 as a side dish,
4 as part of a vegetable meal

Pros Propose

Unlike most cooks, Brazilian food consultant Sandra Allen bakes mandioca to concentrate flavor and sweetness, enclosing the roots in foil to prevent drying once the initial baking has done its job. (The Brazilian name, mandioca, appeals for both recipes that follow: try to say "yuca gnocchi," and you'll hear why.) For **Baked, Mashed Mandioca:** Scrub roots ferociously with strong brush in very hot water to remove as much wax as possible. Bake until mandioca begins to soften. Wrap each in foil. Continue baking until soft. Slip off peels, halve roots lengthwise, and remove cords as needed. Crush slightly with potato masher. Add butter, nutmeg, and cinnamon, then a little crème fraîche.

Mandioca Gnocchi with Cream shows another unusual use from Sandra Allen: Combine peeled yuca with cold water, salt, and bay leaves and simmer until tender. Drain, discard bay leaves, and crush with potato masher. Cool slightly, then add egg yolk, salt, and Parmesan. Gradually add flour, kneading until dough no longer sticks to surface. Roll into ropes and cut into bite-size cylinders. Poach until gnocchi rise to surface of water, then simmer a minute longer. Drain and toss gently with olive oil. To serve, spoon over crème fraîche and Parmesan; bake until bubbling.

Himilce Novas and Rosemary Silva (*Latin American Cooking Across the U.S.A.*) write that "the most popular salad in Nicaraguan restaurants and homes across America" is vigorón, a dish of layered yuca, cabbage, and deep-fried bacon rinds (chicharrones). They have modified the traditional to a **Nuevo Vigorón:** Simmer small yuca chunks with salt and lime juice until tender. Drain, trim, and cut into ½-inch dice. In a large bowl, blend lime juice, salt, and sugar. Whisk in olive oil. Add yuca, paper-thin cabbage shreds (room-temperature), diced tomato, minced red onion and garlic, and minced cilantro. Toss gently and season. Divide among plates. Top with diced Hass avocado and crisp crumbled bacon or chicharrones.

Chillis are yuca's frequent companion. "One of the most original cassava dishes is this Peruvian one where the vegetable is masked by a lively cheese sauce made hot with fresh peppers," writes Elisabeth Lambert Ortiz in *The Book of Latin American Cooking.* For **Picante de Yuca:** In blender, combine queso blanco with chopped large chillis and olive oil; puree to the texture of heavy cream. Boil peeled, sliced cassava in salted water until tender. Drain and arrange on platter. While still hot, pour over the sauce. Garnish with hard-cooked eggs, black olives, and lettuce.

Chef Doug Rodriguez, who has cooked his Nuevo Latino style (also the title of one of his books) in Florida (at YUCA—for "Young Upcoming Cuban-American") and in New York (for yuppies), jazzes up traditional yuca crisps with chilli and citrus rind. For **Lemon-Cayenne Yuca Chips:** Grate zest from lemons (4 for 2 large yuca). Spread on baking sheet and dry overnight in oven with pilot light. Pulverize in spice mill with ground cayenne and salt. Peel yuca and thin-slice on mandoline, placing in water. Rinse and

pat dry. Fry in canola oil at 350°F until golden. Lift out with strainer; drain on paper. While hot, dust with the lemon-cayenne mixture.

Not all yuca dishes come from the Western Hemisphere. In *Indonesian Regional Cooking,* there is a porridge that makes "a very good breakfast or lunch dish," according to the author, Sri Owen. For **Cassava, Sweetcorn, and Pumpkin Soup (Tinutuan):** Boil peeled, diced cassava and soaked white rice 8 minutes. Add diced Butternut squash, corn kernels, and water; simmer until vegetables are tender and soup is thick. To serve, add minced lemon grass core and small spinach leaves; cook a few minutes. Add salt and basil leaves. Simmer 1 minute.

Maricel Presilla (who must be known to readers by this last chapter) says that "yuca is a natural for restaurants, since it is typically prepared ahead." For fries, she simmers, drains, and chills yuca, then cuts it into strips and layers them on sheets between waxed paper ("never plastic!"). These are refrigerated, then deep-fried to order. "You can hold cooked yuca 3 days, and the quality will stay," she promises.

Chef Presilla (she wears many hats) describes her restaurant appetizer **Pollito Mandraque** as "yuca filled with shredded chicken masquerading as drumsticks—a funny, sensible party dish that can be made days ahead, needs no fork (you hold the bone), and doesn't make a mess when you eat it." To prepare: Press cooked, cooled yuca through food mill. Season with the sauce in which you've cooked chicken, adding enough for a pliable dough. Roll small balls, form a depression in each, and fill with the shredded chicken. Shape into a drumstick form, insert a chicken bone ("restaurants have no shortage of these"), and then dip into milk and crumbs. Refrigerate between sheets of waxed paper. Deep-fry to order.

Author Presilla shares her Mexican **Yuca Patties "Los Tuxtlas"** (from her forthcoming book): Soak pan-toasted Chipotle chillis until soft. Drain, reserving some liquid. Puree with chopped garlic, cumin, and reserved liquid as needed. Heat olive oil and stir in the puree. Cook briefly and season with vinegar; reserve. Combine peeled yuca chunks with water to cover, salt, and epazote ("not a stalk or sprig—the whole jungle"). Simmer until fork-tender. Drain and mash while hot. Add grated aged Mexican Cotija cheese and season. Form 3-ounce balls and flatten into 3-inch patties. Fry in olive oil in non-stick skillet until crisp on both sides. Serve with a spoonful of Chipotle puree.

Cakes of a different kind come from Jamaica, where grated yuca is cooked like potato pancakes. "These pancakes, called bammies, are usually served with fried fish, but I serve my version with lime-marinated tomatoes," writes chef Didi Emmons in *Vegetarian Planet*. For her **Big Bammy:** Combine lime juice, thin-sliced garlic and Jalapeño, and olive oil; add cored tomatoes cut into half-rounds. In batches, pulverize yuca dice in food processor. Scoop onto a towel, twist, and squeeze out as much liquid as possible. Mix yuca with beaten egg and chopped onion; season. Heat olive oil in non-stick skillet. Add mixture to pan, patting it out to cover evenly. Cook until golden. Invert onto plate, then heat more oil and brown other side. Slide onto a board and cut into wedges. Spoon over marinated tomatoes.

Bibliography

"Alaskans." *Cooking Alaskan*. Anchorage: Alaska Northwest, 1983.

Albi, Johnna, and Catherine Walthers. *Greens Glorious Greens!* New York: St. Martin's, 1996.

Alford, Jeffrey, and Naomi Duguid. *Seductions of Rice*. New York: Artisan, 1998.

Allison, Karen Hubert. *The Vegetarian Compass*. Boston: Little, Brown, 1998.

Andersen Horticultural Library's Source List of Plants and Seeds. Revised listing of 1993–1996 catalogs. 4th ed. Compiled and edited by Richard T. Isaacson. Chanhassen: Andersen Horticultural Library, University of Minnesota, 1996.

Anderson, Jean. *The Food of Portugal*. New York: William Morrow, 1986.

Anderson, Jean, and Hedy Würz. *The New German Cookbook*. New York: HarperCollins, 1993.

Andoh, Elizabeth. *At Home with Japanese Cooking*. New York: Alfred A. Knopf, 1980.

———. *An American Taste of Japan*. New York: William Morrow, 1985.

———. *An Ocean of Flavor*. New York: William Morrow, 1988.

Andrews, Jean. *Peppers: The Domesticated Capsicums*. Austin: University of Texas Press, 1984.

———. *The Pepper Lady's Pocket Pepper Primer*. Austin: University of Texas Press, 1998.

Arora, David. *Mushrooms Demystified*. 2d ed. Berkeley: Ten Speed, 1986.

———. *All That the Rain Promises, and More . . .* Berkeley: Ten Speed, 1991.

Bailey, Liberty Hyde. *Gentes Herbarum: Occasional Papers on the Kinds of Plants*. Vol. I. *Plantae Chinenses (A Collection of Plants in China)*. Ithaca: Bailey Hortorium of New York State College of Agriculture at Cornell University, 1920.

———. *Gentes Herbarum: Occasional Papers on the Kinds of Plants*. Vols. II and III. *The Cultivated Brassicas*. Ithaca: Bailey Hortorium of New York State College of Agriculture at Cornell University, 1922.

———. *Manual of Cultivated Plants*. 1924. Rev. ed., 1949. Reprint, New York: Macmillan, 1969.

———. *Gentes Herbarum: Occasional Papers on the Kinds of Plants*. Vol. IV. *The Domesticated Cucurbitas*. Ithaca: Bailey Hortorium of New York State College of Agriculture at Cornell University, 1929.

———. *Gentes Herbarum: Occasional Papers on the Kinds of Plants*. Vol. VI. *Species Cucurbitae (Species of Cucurbita)*. Ithaca: Bailey Hortorium of New York State College of Agriculture at Cornell University, 1943.

Bailey, Liberty Hyde, and Ethel Zoe Bailey. *Hortus Third: A Concise Dictionary of Plants Cultivated in the United States and Canada*. Revised and expanded by the Staff of the Liberty Hyde Bailey Hortorium. New York: Macmillan, 1976.

Barron, Rosemary. *Flavors of Greece*. New York: William Morrow, 1991.

Başan, Ghillie. *Classic Turkish Cooking*. New York: St. Martin's, 1997.

Bastianich, Lidia Matticchio. *Lidia's Italian Table*. New York: William Morrow, 1998.

Batali, Mario. *Simple Italian Food*. New York: Clarkson Potter, 1998.

Batmanglij, Najmieh. *New Food of Life*. Washington, D.C.: Mage, 1986.

———. *Persian Cooking for a Healthy Kitchen*. Washington, D.C.: Mage, 1994.

Batra, Neelam. *The Indian Vegetarian*. New York: Macmillan, 1994.

Bayless, Rick, with Deann Groen Bayless. *Authentic Mexican*. New York: William Morrow, 1987.

Bayless, Rick, with Deann Groen Bayless and JeanMarie Brownson. *Rick Bayless's Mexican Kitchen*. New York: Scribner, 1996.

Bazore, Katherine. *Hawaiian and Pacific Foods*. New York: Gramercy, 1940.

Belk, Sarah. *Around the Southern Table*. New York: Simon & Schuster, 1991. Reprint, New York: Galahad, 1997.

Benghiat, Norma. *Traditional Jamaican Cookery*. London: Penguin, 1985.

Bennani-Smirès, Latifa. *La cuisine marocaine*. Casablanca: Société d'Édition et de Diffusion Al Madariss, 1993.

Bergeron, Ken. *Professional Vegetarian Cooking*. New York: John Wiley, 1999.

Bertolli, Paul, with Alice Waters. *Chez Panisse Cooking*. New York: Random House, 1988.

Betts, Edwin Morris, ed. *Thomas Jefferson's Garden Book (1766–1824). With Relevant Extracts from His Other Writings*. Philadelphia: American Philosophical Society, 1944.

Bharadwaj, Monisha. *The Indian Spice Kitchen*. New York: Dutton, 1997.

Bhumichitr, Vatcharin. *Thai Vegetarian Cooking*. New York: Clarkson Potter, 1991.

Biondi, Lisa. *Il cucinafunghi*. Milan: Editrice Erpi, n.d.

Blanc, Georges. *The Natural Cuisine of Georges Blanc.* Translated by Tina Ujlaki and Charles Pierce. New York: Stewart, Tabori & Chang, 1987.

Bloch, O., and W. Von Wartburg. *Dictionnaire étymologique de la langue française.* Rev. ed. Paris: Presse Universitaire de France, 1968.

Blonder, Ellen, and Annabel Low. *Every Grain of Rice: A Taste of Our Chinese Childhood in America.* New York: Clarkson Potter, 1998.

Bodger, Lorraine. *Chutneys and Relishes.* New York: Simon & Schuster, 1995.

Boulud, Daniel. *Cooking with Daniel Boulud.* New York: Random House, 1993.

Boulud, Daniel, and Dorie Greenspan. *Café Boulud Cookbook.* New York: Scribner, 1999.

Bradley, Susan. *Pacific Northwest Palate.* Berkeley: Aris, 1989.

Brewster, J. L. *Onions and Other VegetableAlliums.* Oxon, England: CAB International, 1994.

Brill, Steve, with Evelyn Dean. *Identifying and Harvesting Edible and Medicinal Plants in Wild (and Not So Wild) Places.* New York: Hearst, 1994.

Bugialli, Giuliano. *Giuliano Bugialli's Classic Techniques of Italian Cooking.* New York: Simon & Schuster, 1982.

———. *Bugialli's Italy.* New York: William Morrow, 1998.

Burr, Fearing, Jr. *The Field and Garden Vegetables of America.* 1863. Reprint of 1865 edition. Chillicothe, Ill.: American Botanist Booksellers, 1994.

Canadian Home Economics Association. *The Laura Secord Canadian Cook Book.* Toronto: McClelland & Stewart, 1966.

Castelvetro, Giacomo. *The Fruits, Herbs & Vegetables of Italy (Brieve racconto di tutte le radici, di tutte l'herbe e di tutti i frutti, che crudi o cotti in Italia si mangiano,* 1614). Translated and introduced by Gillian Riley; foreword by Jane Grigson. London: Viking Penguin, 1989.

Centre Technique Interprofessionnel des Fruits et Légumes (CTIFL). *Les spécialités du rayon fruits et légumes.* Paris: CTIFL, 1989.

Centre Technique Interprofessionnel des Fruits et Légumes (CTIFL). *Memento nouvelles espèces légumières.* Edited by Henri Zuang. Paris: CTIFL, 1991.

Chamberlain, Samuel, and Narcissa Chamberlain. *Bouquet de France.* New York: Gourmet, 1952.

Les champignons au fil des saisons. Paris: L'Ami des Jardins et de la Maison, 1984.

Chang, S. T., and P. H. Miles. *Edible Mushrooms and Their Cultivation.* Boca Raton, Fla.: CRC, 1989.

Chen, Pearl Kong, Tien Chi Chen, and Rose Y. L. Tseng. *Everything You Want to Know About Chinese Cooking.* Woodbury, N.Y.: Barron's, 1983.

Child, Julia. *The French Chef Cookbook.* New York: Alfred A. Knopf, 1968.

Child, Julia, and Jacques Pepin, with David Nussbaum. *Julia and Jacques Cooking at Home.* New York: Alfred A. Knopf, 1999.

Claiborne, Craig, ed. *The New York Times Cookbook.* New York: Harper, 1961.

Clarke, Charlotte Bringle. *Edible and Useful Plants of California.* Berkeley and Los Angeles: University of California Press, 1977.

Coe, Sophie D. *America's First Cuisines.* Austin: University of Texas Press, 1994.

The Compact Edition of the Oxford English University. Oxford: Oxford University Press, 1971.

Coombes, Allen J. *Dictionary of Plant Names.* Portland, Ore.: Timber Press, 1987.

Copage, Eric V. *Kwanzaa.* New York: Quill/William Morrow, 1991.

Cordero-Fernando, Gilda. *Philippine Food and Life.* Manila: Anvil, 1992.

Cost, Bruce. *Bruce Cost's Asian Ingredients.* New York: William Morrow, 1988.

Costner, Susan. *Mostly Vegetables.* New York: Bantam, 1996.

Cousineau, Ruth. *Country Suppers.* New York: William Morrow, 1997.

Crawford, William, and Kamolmal Pootarasksa. *Thai Home Cooking from Kamolmal's Kitchen.* New York: New American Library, 1985.

Creasy, Rosalind. *The Gardener's Handbook of Edible Plants.* San Francisco: Sierra Club, 1986.

———. *Cooking from the Garden.* San Francisco: Sierra Club, 1988.

———. *The Edible Asian Garden.* Boston: Periplus, 2000.

———. *The Edible French Garden.* Boston: Periplus, 2000.

Cribb, A. B., and J. W. Cribb. *Wild Food in Australia.* Sydney: William Collins, 1974.

Crisp, Peter. "The Use of an Evolutionary Scheme for Cauliflowers." *Euphytica* 31 (1982): 725.

Crowe, Andrew. *A Field Guide to the Native Edible Plants of New Zealand.* 1981. Reprint, Auckland: Godwit, 1997.

Cucurbit Network. "Bulletin Board." *Cucurbit Network News* 2 (Fall 1995).

Culpeper, Nicholas. *Culpeper's Complete Herbal.* 1653, as *The English Physician; or Herball.* Reprint, London: Omega, 1985.

Czarnecki, Jack. *A Cook's Book of Mushrooms.* New York: Artisan, 1995.

Dahlen, Martha, and Karen Phillipps. *A Popular Guide to Chinese Vegetables.* New York: Crown, 1983.

Dallas, E. S. *Kettner's Book of the Table.* 1877. Reprint, London: Centaur, 1968.

Damerow, Gail. *The Perfect Pumpkin.* Pownal, Vt.: Storey, 1997.

David, Elizabeth. *A Book of Mediterranean Food.* New York: Alfred A. Knopf, 1950.

Davidson, Alan. *Fruit: A Connoisseur's Guide and Cookbook.* New York: Simon & Schuster, 1991.

———. *The Oxford Companion to Food.* Oxford: Oxford University Press, 1999.

de Blasi, Marlena. *Regional Foods of Southern Italy.* New York: Viking, 1999.

De Gouy, Louis P. *The Gold Cook Book.* New York: Galahad, 1947.

Desaulniers, Marcel. *The Trellis Cookbook.* New York: Weidenfeld & Nicolson, 1988.

Devi, Yamuna. *Lord Krishna's Cuisine: The Art of Indian Vegetarian Cooking.* Old Westbury, N.Y.: Bala Books, 1987.

———. *Yamuna's Table.* New York: Dutton, 1992.

———. *The Vegetarian Table: India.* San Francisco: Chronicle, 1997.

DeWitt, Dave, and Paul W. Bosland. *Peppers of the World: An Identification Guide.* Berkeley: Ten Speed, 1996.

Dooley, Beth, and Lucia Watson. *Savoring the Seasons of the Northern Heartland.* New York: Alfred A. Knopf, 1994.

Ducasse, Alain, with the collaboration of Frédérick E. Grasser. *Méditerranées: Cuisine de l'essentiel.* Paris: Hachette, 1996.

Duke, J. A. *Handbook of Edible Weeds.* Boca Raton, Fla.: CRC, 1992.

———. "Garlic Mustard Update." *Wild Foods Forum* 10 (November/December 1999): 9.

Dunmire, William W., and Gail D. Tierny. *Wild Plants and Native Peoples of the Four Corners.* Santa Fe: Museum of New Mexico Press, 1997.

Duong, Binh, and Marcia Kiesel. *Simple Art of Vietnamese Cooking.* New York: Prentice Hall, 1991.

Edwards, John. *The Roman Cookery of Apicius.* Translation and adaptation of *De Re Coquinaria.* Point Roberts, Wash.: Hartley & Marks, 1984.

Elias, Thomas S., and Peter A. Cukeman. *Edible Wild Plants.* New York: Sterling, 1990.

Elkon, Juliette. *A Belgian Cookbook.* New York: Farrar, Straus & Cudahy, 1958.

Emmons, Didi. *Vegetarian Planet.* Boston: Harvard Common Press, 1997.

Esbensen, Mogens Bay. *A Taste of the Tropics.* Ringwood, Victoria: Viking O'Neil, 1988.

Evelyn, John. *Acetaria: A Discourse of Sallets.* 1699. Reprint, New York: Brooklyn Botanic Garden, 1937.

Facciola, Stephen. *Cornucopia II: A Source Book of Edible Plants.* Vista, Calif.: Kampong, 1998.

Fairchild, David. *The World Was My Garden.* New York: Scribner, 1938.

Farmer, Fannie Merritt. The Boston Cooking-School Cook Book, 1896. Reprint [no city]: Hugh Lauter Levin, 1996.

Feibleman, Peter S., and the Editors of Time-Life Books. *The Cooking of Spain and Portugal.* New York: Time-Life Books, 1974.

Fernald, Merritt Lyndon, and Alfred Charles Kinsey. *Edible Wild Plants of Eastern North America.* 1943. Rev. ed., New York: Harper & Row, 1958. Reprint, New York: Dover, 1996.

Fernandez, Doreen. *Tikim: Essays on Philippine Food and Culture.* Manila: Anvil, 1994.

Field, Michael. *All Manner of Food.* New York: Alfred A. Knopf, 1970.

Filippini, Alessandro. *The Table: How to Buy Food, How to Cook It, and How to Serve It.* New York: Charles L. Webster, 1891.

Fischer, David W., and Alan E. Bessette. *Edible Wild Mushrooms of North America.* Austin: University of Texas Press, 1992.

Flower, Tui, ed. *New Zealand the Beautiful Cookbook.* Auckland: Shortland/Weldon, n.d.

Foo, Susanna. *Susanna Foo Chinese Cuisine.* Shelburne, Vt.: Chapters, 1995.

Forsyth, Turid, and Merilyn Simonds Mohr. *The Harrowsmith Salad Garden.* Camden East, Ontario: Camden House, 1992.

Foust, Clifford, and Dale E. Marshall. "Culinary Rhubarb Production in North America." *HortScience* 26 (November 1991): 1360–1363.

Frank, Lois Ellen. *Native American Cooking: Foods of the Southwest Indian Nations.* New York: Clarkson Potter, 1991.

Fried, Michelle O. *Comidas del Ecuador.* Quito: Grupo Esquina, 1993.

Fussell, Betty. *The Story of Corn.* New York: Alfred A. Knopf, 1996.

Galinat, Walton C., and Bor-Yaw Lin. "Baby Corn: Production in Taiwan and Future Outlook for Production in the United States." *Economic Botany* 42 (1988): 132–134.

Garnweidner, E. *Champignons vénéneux.* Paris: Fernand Nathan Éditeur, 1986.

General, Ernesto C. *The Coconut Cookery of Bicol.* Manila: Bookmark, 1994.

Gibbons, Euell. *Stalking the Wild Asparagus.* New York: Alan C. Hood, 1962.

Gold, Rozanne. *Recipes 1-2-3 Menu Cookbook.* New York: Little, Brown, 1998.

Goldstein, Joyce. *Back to Square One.* New York: William Morrow, 1992.

Gómez, Eduardo Sarmiento. *Frutas en Colombia.* 2d ed. Bogotá: Ediciones Cultural Colombiana, 1989.

Gray, A. R. "Taxonomy and Evolution of Broccoli." *Economic Botany* 36 (1982): 397–410.

Gray, Rose, and Ruth Rogers. *The Cafe Cookbook: Recipes from London's River Cafe.* New York: Broadway, 1998.

Greaves, Ellen, and Wayne Nish. *Simple Menus for the Bento Box.* New York: William Morrow, 1998.

Greene, Bert. *Greene on Greens.* New York: Workman, 1984.

Grieve, Mrs. M. *A Modern Herbal.* Edited and introduced by Mrs. C. F. Leyel. London: Jonathan Cape, 1931. Rev. ed., 1973. Reprint, New York: Dorset, 1992.

Grigson, Jane. *Jane Grigson's Vegetable Book.* New York: Penguin, 1981.

———. *Cooking with Exotic Fruits and Vegetables.* New York: Henry Holt, 1986.

Guerithault, Vincent, and John Mariani. *Vincent's Cookbook.* Berkeley: Ten Speed, 1994.

Hal, Fatéma. *Les saveurs et les gestes.* Paris: Éditions Stock, 1995.

Hall, I. R., A.J.E. Lyon, Y. Wang, and L. Sinclair. "Ectomycorrhizal Fungi with Edible Fruiting Bodies. 2. *Boletus edulis.*" *Economic Botany* 51 (January/March 1998): 44–56.

Haroutunian, Arto der. *Middle Eastern Cookery.* London: Pan, 1984.

Harrington, Geri. *Grow Your Own Chinese Vegetables.* Pownal, Vt.: Garden Way, 1984.

Harrington, H. D. *Western Edible Plants.* Albuquerque: University of New Mexico Press, 1967.

Harris, Jessica B. *The Africa Cookbook.* New York: Simon & Schuster, 1998.

Hawkes, Alex D. *Cooking with Vegetables.* New York: Simon & Schuster, 1968.

Hazan, Marcella. *Marcella's Italian Kitchen.* New York: Alfred A. Knopf, 1986.

———. *Marcella Cucina.* New York: HarperCollins, 1997.

Hedrick, U. P., ed. *Sturtevant's Edible Plants of the World.* 1919, as *Sturtevant's Notes on Edible Plants.* Reprint, New York: Dover, 1972.

Heiser, Charles B., Jr. *Nightshades: The Paradoxical Plants.* San Francisco: W. H. Freeman, 1969.

———. *The Sunflower.* Norman: University of Oklahoma Press, 1976.

———. *The Gourd Book.* Norman: University of Oklahoma Press, 1979.

———. *Of Plants and People.* Norman: University of Oklahoma Press, 1985.

Herklots, G.A.C. *Vegetables in South-East Asia.* London: George Allen & Unwin, 1972.

Hollyer, Jim, ed. *Taro Tattler* 4 (June/August 1992). Department of Agricultural and Resource Economics, University of Hawaii.

Hom, Ken. *Fragrant Harbor Taste.* New York: Simon & Schuster, 1989.

———. *The Taste of China.* New York: Simon & Schuster, 1990.

———. *Ken Hom's Chinese Kitchen.* New York: Hyperion, 1994.

———. *Easy Family Recipes from a Chinese-American Childhood.* New York: Alfred A. Knopf, 1997.

Hooker, Monique Jamet. *Cooking with the Seasons.* New York: Henry Holt, 1997.

Hosking, Richard. *A Dictionary of Japanese Food: Ingredients & Culture.* Rutland, Vt.: Charles E. Tuttle, 1996.

Hoyos, Jesús F. *Frutales en Venezuela (nativos y exóticos)*. 1989. 2d ed. Caracas: Sociedad de Ciencias Naturales La Salle, 1994.

Hufford, Mary. "Tending the Commons: Ramp Suppers, Biodiversity, and the Integrity of 'the Mountains.' " *Folklife Center News* 20 (Fall 1998): 3–11.

Isaacs, Jennifer. *Bush Food: Aboriginal Food and Herbal Medicine*. 1987. Reprint, Willoughby, New South Wales: Weldons, 1988.

Jacobs, Susie. *Recipes from a Greek Island*. New York: Simon & Schuster, 1991.

Jaffrey, Madhur. *Madhur Jaffrey's World-of-the-East Vegetarian Cooking*. New York: Alfred A. Knopf, 1981.

———. *Madhur Jaffrey's Cookbook*. New York: Harper & Row, 1987.

———. *Madhur Jaffrey's Far Eastern Cookery*. New York: Harper & Row, 1989.

———. *Madhur Jaffrey's A Taste of the Far East*. New York: Carol Southern, 1993.

———. *Madhur Jaffrey's World Vegetarian*. New York: Clarkson Potter, 1999.

Janick, Jules, and James E. Simon, eds. *Advances in New Crops*. Portland, Ore.: Timber Press, 1990.

———. *New Crops*. New York: John Wiley, 1993.

Jaunault, Frédéric, and Jean-Luc Brillet. *Toutes les bases de la cuisine aux champignons*. Rennes: Éditions Ouest-France, 1998.

Jefferson, Thomas. (See Betts, Edwin Morris, ed.)

Jenkins, Nancy Harmon. *Flavors of Puglia*. New York: Broadway, 1997.

Jones, Bill, and Stephen Wong. *New World Noodles*. Toronto: Robert Rose, 1997.

———. *New World Chinese Cooking*. Toronto: Robert Rose, 1998.

Jones, Pamela. *Just Weeds: History, Myths, and Uses*. New York: Prentice Hall, 1991.

Jordan, Peter, and Steven Wheeler. *The Ultimate Mushroom Cookbook*. New York: Smithmark, 1995.

Kafka, Barbara. *Roasting*. New York: William Morrow, 1996.

———. *Soup, A Way of Life*. New York: Artisan, 1998.

Kamman, Madeleine. *In Madeleine's Kitchen*. New York: Atheneum, 1984.

———. *Madeleine Kamman's Savoie*. New York: Atheneum, 1989.

Kasper, Lynne Rossetto. *The Splendid Table*. New York: William Morrow, 1992.

Kavasch, Barrie. *Native Harvests*. New York: Vintage, 1979.

Kays, Stanley J., and J. C. Silva Dias. *Cultivated Vegetables of the World*. Athens, Ga.: Exon, 1996.

Keller, Hubert. *The Cuisine of Hubert Keller*. Berkeley: Ten Speed, 1996.

Kennedy, Diana. *The Art of Mexican Cooking*. New York: Bantam, 1989.

———. *My Mexico*. New York: Clarkson Potter, 1998.

Khan, Reayat. "*Solanum melongena* and Its Ancestral Forms." In *The Biology and Taxonomy of the* Solanaceae. Edited by J. G. Hawkes, R. N. Lester, and A. D. Skelding. London: Academic Press, 1979.

Kochilas, Diane. *The Greek Vegetarian*. New York: St. Martin's, 1996.

Kramer, Matt. *A Passion for Piedmont*. New York: William Morrow, 1997.

Kremezi, Aglaia. *The Foods of the Greek Islands*. Boston: Houghton Mifflin, 2000.

Kunkel, G. *Plants for Human Consumption*. Koenigstein, Germany: Koeltz Scientific, 1984.

Kwak, Jenny, and Liz Fried. *Dok Suni*. New York: St. Martin's, 1998.

Laessoe, Thomas, Anna Del Conte, and Gary Lincoff. *The Mushroom Book*. New York: DK, 1996.

Lanza, Anna Tasca. *The Heart of Sicily*. New York: Clarkson Potter, 1993.

La Place, Viana. *Verdura*. New York: William Morrow, 1991.

———. *Unplugged Kitchen*. New York: William Morrow, 1996.

La Place, Viana, and Evan Kleiman. *Cucina Rustica*. New York: William Morrow, 1990.

Larkcom, Joy. *Oriental Vegetables*. New York: Kodansha International, 1991.

———. *The Salad Garden*. New York: Viking, 1984. Reprint, New York: Penguin, 1996.

Laudan, Rachel. *The Food of Paradise*. Honolulu: University of Hawaii Press, 1996.

Leibenstein, Margaret. *The Edible Mushroom*. New York: Ballantine, 1986.

Leung, Albert Y., and Steven Foster. *Encyclopedia of Common Natural Ingredients Used in Food, Drugs, and Cosmetics*. 2d ed. New York: John Wiley, 1996.

Lin, Florence. *Florence Lin's Complete Book of Chinese Noodles, Dumplings, and Breads*. New York: William Morrow, 1986.

Linares, Edelmira, and Judith Aguirre, eds. *Los quelites, un tesoro culinario*. Mexico City: Universidad Nacional Autónoma de México, 1992.

Lincoff, Gary H. *The Audubon Society Field Guide to North American Mushrooms*. New York: Alfred A. Knopf, 1981.

Lo, Eileen Yin-Fei. *The Chinese Way*. New York: Macmillan, 1992.

———. *From the Earth*. New York: Macmillan, 1995.

Lo Monte, Mimmetta. *Mimmetta Lo Monte's Classic Sicilian Cookbook*. New York: Simon & Schuster, 1990.

Loomis, Susan Herrmann. *Farmhouse Cookbook*. New York: Workman, 1991.

———. *French Farmhouse Cookbook*. New York: Workman, 1996.

Lundy, Ronni. *Butter Beans to Blackberries*. New York: North Point, 1999.

Mabberley, D. J. *The Plant-Book*. 2d ed., revised. Cambridge: Cambridge University Press, 1997.

Madison, Deborah. *The Savory Way*. New York: Bantam, 1990.

Manikowski, John. *Wild Fish and Game Cookbook*. New York: Artisan, 1997.

Margvelashvili, Julianne. *The Classic Cuisine of Soviet Georgia*. New York: Prentice Hall, 1991.

Markle, G. M., J. J. Baron, and B. A. Schneider. *Food and Feed Crops of the United States*. 2d ed., revised. Willoughby, Ohio: Meisterpro, 1998.

Marshall, Dale E. *A Bibliography of Rhubarb and* Rheum *Species*. U.S. Department of Agriculture, National Agricultural Library. Bibliographies and Literature of Agriculture, no. 62, 1988.

Marshall, Lydie. *A Passion for Potatoes*. New York: Harper Perennial, 1992.

Martin, Franklin. *Tropical Yams and Their Potential. Part 1:* Dioscorea esculenta. U.S. Department of Agriculture. Agriculture Handbook, no. 447. Washington, D.C., 1974.

———. *Tropical Yams and Their Potential. Part 2:* Dioscorea bulbifera. U.S. Department of Agriculture. Agriculture Handbook, no. 466. Washington, D.C., 1974.

———. *Tropical Yams and Their Potential. Part 3:* Dioscorea alata. U.S. Department of Agriculture. Agriculture Handbook, no. 495. Washington, D.C., 1976.

————. *Tropical Yams and Their Potential. Part 4:* Dioscorea rotundata *and* Dioscorea cayenensis. U.S. Department of Agriculture. Agriculture Handbook, no. 502. Washington, D.C., 1977.

————. *Tropical Yams and Their Potential. Part 5:* Dioscorea trifida. U.S. Department of Agriculture. Agriculture Handbook, no. 522. Washington, D.C., 1977.

————. *Tropical Yams and Their Potential. Part 6: Minor Cultivated* Dioscorea *Species.* U.S. Department of Agriculture. Agriculture Handbook, no. 538. Washington, D.C., 1978.

Martinez, Zarela. *Foods from My Heart.* New York: Macmillan, 1992.

————. *The Food and Life of Oaxaca.* New York: Macmillan, 1997.

Massie, I. H., D. Astley, and G. J. King. "Patterns of Genetic Diversity and Relationships Between Regional Groups and Populations of Italian Landrace Cauliflower and Broccoli." Proceedings, International Symposium on Brassicas. Edited by J. S. Dias, I. Crute, and A. A. Monteiro. *Acta Horticulturae* 407 (1996): 45–53.

Mauch, Hans, and Konrad Lauber. *Champignons.* Éditions Payot Lausanne, 1975.

May, R. J. *Kaikai Aniani: A Guide to the Bush Foods, Markets, and Culinary Arts of Papua New Guinea.* Bathurst, New South Wales: Robert Brown, 1984.

McNeill, F. Marian. *The Scots Kitchen.* 1929. Reprint, Bungay, Suffolk: Granada, 1981.

Mesfin, Daniel J. *Exotic Ethiopian Cooking.* Rev. ed. Falls Church, Va.: Ethiopian Cookbook Enterprises, 1993.

Messiaen, Charles Marie, Joseph Cohat, Maurice Pichon, Jean-Paul Lerous, and André Beyries. *Les* allium *alimentaires reproduits par voie végétative.* Paris: Institut National de la Recherche Agronomique, 1993.

Middione, Carlo. *La Vera Cucina.* New York: Simon & Schuster, 1996.

Miller, Ashley. *The Potato Harvest Cookbook.* Newton, Conn.: Taunton, 1998.

Miller, Mark Charles. *Coyote Cafe.* Berkeley: Ten Speed, 1987.

Miller, Mark, Mark Kiffin, and Suzy Dayton, with John Harrisson. *Mark Miller's Indian Market Cookbook.* Berkeley: Ten Speed, 1991.

Molina, Randy, Thomas O'Dell, Daniel Luoma, et al. *Biology, Ecology, and Social Aspects of Wild Edible Mushrooms in the Forests of the Pacific Northwest: A Preface to Managing Commercial Harvest.* U.S. Department of Agriculture General Technical Report PNW-GTR-309. Washington, D.C., February 1993.

Monteiro, Longteine de, and Katherine Neustadt. *The Elephant Walk Cookbook.* Boston: Houghton Mifflin, 1998.

Morash, Marian. *The Victory Garden Cookbook.* New York: Alfred A. Knopf, 1982.

Moreau, Claude. *Guide des champignons comestibles et vénéneux.* Paris: Références Larousse, 1992.

Morton, Julia F. "Cocoyams (*Xanthomsoma caracu, X. atrovirens, X. nigrum*), Ancient Root- and Leaf-Vegetables, Gaining in Economic Importance." *Proceedings of the Florida State Horticultural Society* 85 (1972): 85–94.

————. *Herbs and Spices.* New York: Golden, 1976.

————. "The Chayote, a Perennial, Climbing, Subtropical Vegetable." *Proceedings of the Florida State Horticultural Society* 94 (1981): 240–245.

————. "The Tree Tomato, or 'Tamarillo,' a Fast-Growing, Early-Fruiting Small Tree for Subtropical Climates." *Proceedings of the Florida State Horticultural Society* 95 (1982): 81–85.

————. "The Horned Cucumber, alias 'Kiwano' (*Cucumis metuliferus,* Cucurbitaceae)." *Economic Botany* 41 (1987): 325–327.

————. *Fruits of Warm Climates.* Winterville, N.C.: Creative Resource Systems, 1987.

Morton, Julia F., and O. S. Russell. "The Cape Gooseberry and the Mexican Husk Tomato." *Proceedings of the Florida State Horticultural Society* 67 (1954): 261–266.

National Research Council. *Tropical Legumes: Resources for the Future.* Washington, D.C.: National Academy of Sciences, 1979.

————. *Underexploited Tropical Plants with Promising Economic Value.* Washington, D.C.: National Academy of Sciences, 1984.

————. *Lost Crops of the Incas.* Washington, D.C.: National Academy Press, 1989.

Nègre, André. *Les Antilles et la Guyane à travers leur cuisine.* Caen, France: R. Le Brun, 1977.

Niethammer, Carolyn. *American Indian Foods and Lore.* New York: Collier, 1974.

Noh, Chin-hwa. *Low-Fat Korean Cooking.* Elizabeth, N.J.: Hollym International, 1985.

Novas, Himilce, and Rosemary Silva. *Latin American Cooking Across the U.S.A.* New York: Alfred A. Knopf, 1997.

O'Donnell, Kerry, Elizabeth Cigelnik, Nancy S. Weber, and James M. Trappe. "Phylogenetic Relationships among Ascomycetous Truffles and the True and False Morels Inferred from 185 and 285 Ribosomal DNA Sequence Analysis." *Mycologia* 89 (January/February 1977): 48–65.

Ogden, Shepherd, and Ellen Ogden. *The Cook's Garden.* Emmaus, Pa.: Rodale, 1989.

O'Hair, Stephen K., George H. Snyder, and Loy V. Crowder, Jr., eds. *Taro and Other Aroids for Food, Feed, and Fuel.* Gainesville: Center for Tropical Agriculture, University of Florida, 1983.

Ojakangas, Beatrice A. *The Finnish Cookbook.* New York: Crown, 1964.

Olney, Richard. *Simple French Food.* New York: Atheneum, 1974.

————. *Lulu's Provençal Table.* New York: HarperCollins, 1994.

Oomen, H. A. P. C., and G. J. H. Grubben. *Tropical Leaf Vegetables in Human Nutrition.* 2d ed. Department of Agricultural Research. Communication no. 69. Amsterdam: Koninklijk Instituut voor de Tropen, 1978.

Organ, John. *Rare Vegetables for Garden and Table.* London: Garden Book Club, 1960.

Ortiz, Elisabeth Lambert. *The Complete Book of Caribbean Cooking.* New York: Evans, 1973.

————. *The Book of Latin American Cooking.* New York: Alfred A. Knopf, 1979.

Oster, Gerald, and Selmaree Oster. "The Great Breadfruit Scheme." *Natural History,* (March 1985): 35–40.

Owen, Sri. *Indonesian Regional Cooking.* New York: St. Martin's, 1997.

————. *Classic Asian Cookbook.* New York: DK, 1998.

Pacioni, Giovanni. *Simon & Schuster's Guide to Mushrooms.* American ed. Edited by Gary Lincoff. New York: Simon & Schuster, 1981.

Padmanabhan, Chandra. *Dakshin: Vegetarian Cuisine from South India.* San Francisco: Thorsons, 1994.

Pailleux, A., and D. Bois. *Le potager d'un curieux.* 1892. Reprint, Marseilles: Éditions Jeanne Laffitte, 1993.

Palladin, Jean-Louis. *Jean-Louis: Cooking with the Seasons.* 1989. Reprint, New York: Lickle, 1997.

Palomino, Rafael, with Julie Moskin. *Bistro Latino.* New York: William Morrow, 1998.

Paniz, Neela, with Helen Newton Hartung. *The Bombay Cafe.* Berkeley: Ten Speed, 1998.

Passmore, Jacki. *The Encyclopedia of Asian Food and Cooking.* New York: Hearst, 1991.

Peel, Mark, and Nancy Silverton. *The Food of Campanile.* New York: Villard, 1997.

Pemberton, Robert W., and Nam Sook Lee. "Wild Food Plants in South Korea: Market Presence, New Crops, and Exports to the United States." *Economic Botany* 50 (1996): 57–70.

Persson, Olle. *The Chanterelle Book.* Berkeley: Ten Speed, 1997.

Phillips, Roger. *Mushrooms of North America.* Boston: Little, Brown, 1991.

———. *Wild Food.* Boston: Little, Brown, 1996.

Phillips, Roger, and Martyn Rix. *The Random House Book of Vegetables.* New York: Random House, 1993.

Pilz, David, and Randy Molina, eds. *Managing Forest Ecosystems to Conserve Fungus Diversity and Sustain Wild Mushroom Harvests.* General Technical Report PNW-GTR-371. Portland, Ore.: U.S. Department of Agriculture, Forest Service, May 1996.

Plotkin, Fred. *Recipes from Paradise.* Boston: Little, Brown, 1997.

Popenoe, Wilson. *Manual of Tropical and Subtropical Fruits.* 1920. Reprint, New York: Hafner, 1974.

Purseglove, J. W. *Tropical Crops: Dicotyledons.* 1968. Reprint, Essex: Longman, 1984.

Quintana, Patricia. *The Taste of Mexico.* New York: Stewart, Tabori & Chang, 1986.

———. *Mexico's Feasts of Life.* Tulsa, Oklahoma: Council Oak, 1989.

———. *Cuisine of the Water Gods.* New York: Simon & Schuster, 1994.

Randle, William M. "Onion Flavor Chemistry and Factors Influencing Flavor Intensity." In *Spices: Flavor Chemistry and Antioxidant Properties.* Edited by Sara J. Risch and Chi-Tang Ho. ACS Symposium Series 660. Washington, D.C.: American Chemical Society, 1997.

Randolph, Mrs. Mary. *The Virginia Housewife.* 1860. Reprint, New York: Avenel, n.d.

Rau, Santha Rama, Michael Field, and the Editors of Time-Life Books. *The Cooking of India.* New York: Time-Life Books, 1969.

Riley, John M. *Solanaceae.* Newsletters, 1985–1988. Fullerton, Calif.: California Rare Fruit Growers.

Riley, Murdoch. *Maori Vegetable Cooking.* Paraparaumu, New Zealand: Viking Sevenseas, 1988.

Roberts, Michael. *Parisian Home Cooking.* New York: William Morrow, 1999.

Robins, Juleigh. *Wild Lime: Cooking from the Bushfood Garden.* St. Leonard's, New South Wales: Allen & Unwin, 1996.

Robinson, R. W., and D. S. Decker-Walters. *Cucurbits.* Wallingford, Oxon, U.K.: CAB International, 1997.

Rocchia, Jean-Marie. *Des truffes en général et de la rabasse en particulier.* Avignon: Éditions A. Barthélémy, 1995.

Rodriguez, Douglas. *Nuevo Latino.* Berkeley: Ten Speed, 1995.

———. *Latin Ladles.* Berkeley: Ten Speed, 1997.

Rogers, Ruth, and Rose Gray. *Rogers Gray Italian Country Cook Book.* New York: Random House, 1995.

Rojas-Lombardi, Felipe. *Soup Beautiful Soup.* New York: Random House, 1985.

———. *The Art of South American Cooking.* New York: HarperCollins, 1991.

Romano, Dora. *Rice and Beans and Tasty Things.* Hato Rey, Puerto Rico: Ramallo, 1986.

Rombauer, Irma S. *Joy of Cooking.* 1931. Reprint, New York: Scribner, 1998 (facsimile).

Root, Waverley. *Food.* New York: Simon & Schuster, 1980.

Rosengarten, Frederic, Jr. *The Book of Spices.* Rev., abridged ed. New York: Jove, 1973.

———. *The Book of Edible Nuts.* New York: Walker, 1984.

Ross, Rosa Lo San. *Beyond Bok Choy.* New York: Artisan, 1996.

Routhier, Nicole. *The Foods of Vietnam.* New York: Stewart, Tabori & Chang, 1989.

Royal Swedish Academy of Sciences. *Ambio, a Journal of the Human Environment.* Special report no. 9 (September 1998).

Rubatsky, Vincent E., and Mas Yamaguchi. *World Vegetables: Principles, Production, and Nutritive Values.* 2d ed. New York: Chapman & Hall, 1997.

Sahni, Julie. *Classic Indian Vegetarian and Grain Cooking.* New York: William Morrow, 1985.

———. *Moghul Microwave.* New York: William Morrow, 1990.

———. *Savoring Spices and Herbs.* New York: William Morrow, 1996.

Sass, Lorna. *Great Vegetarian Cooking Under Pressure.* New York: William Morrow, 1994.

———. *The New Soy Cookbook.* San Francisco: Chronicle, 1998.

———. *The New Vegan Cookbook.* San Francisco: Chronicle, 2000.

Scannone, Armando. *Mi cocina, a la manera de Caracas.* Caracas: Edificio Easo, 1990.

Scaravelli, Paola, and Jon Cohen. *Cooking from an Italian Garden.* New York: Holt, Rinehart, Winston, 1984.

Scharfenberg, Horst. *The Cuisines of Germany.* New York: Simon & Schuster, 1989.

Schneider, Elizabeth. *Uncommon Fruits & Vegetables: A Commonsense Guide.* New York: Harper & Row, 1986. Reprint, New York: William Morrow, 1998.

Schneider, Elizabeth, with Dieter Hannig and the Chefs of Hilton International. *Dining in Grand Style.* Rochester, Vt.: Thorsons, 1988.

Schroeder, C. A. "The 'Brazenly Beautiful' Tamarillo." *Fruit Gardener* 28 (September/October 1996).

Scicolone, Michele. *A Fresh Taste of Italy.* New York: Broadway, 1997.

Shetty, Nischit V., and Todd C. Wehner. "Evaluation of Oriental Trellis Cucumbers for Production in North Carolina." *HortScience* 33 (August 1998).

Sijelmassi, Abdeljai. *Les plantes médicinales du Maroc.* 3d ed. Casablanca: Éditions le Fennec, 1991.

Simonds, Nina. *A Spoonful of Ginger.* New York: Alfred A. Knopf, 1999.

Sinclair, Kevin. *China the Beautiful Cookbook.* Los Angeles: Knapp, 1986.

Skinner, Gwen. *The Cuisine of the South Pacific.* Auckland: Hodder and Stoughton, 1983.

Smith, Nigel J. H., J. T. Williams, Donald L. Plucknett, and Jennifer P. Talbot. *Tropical Forests and Their Crops.* Ithaca, N.Y.: Comstock, 1992.

Sohn, Mark F. *Hearty Country Cooking.* New York: St. Martin's, 1996.

Sokolov, Raymond. *Why We Eat What We Eat.* New York: Summit, 1991.

Solomon, Charmaine. *Charmaine Solomon's Thai Cookbook.* Boston: Tuttle, 1994.

———, with Nina Solomon. *Charmaine Solomon's Encyclopedia of Asian Food.* Kew, Victoria: Hamyln Australia, 1997.

Sone, Hiro, and Lissa Doumani. *Terra: Cooking from the Heart of the Napa Valley.* Berkeley: Ten Speed, 2000.

Soyer, Alexis. *The Pantropheon: Or a History of Food and Its Preparation in Ancient Times.* 1853. Reprint, New York: Paddington, 1977.

Spencer, Colin. *The Vegetable Book.* New York: Rizzoli International, 1996.

Stamets, Paul. *Growing Gourmet and Medicinal Mushrooms.* Berkeley: Ten Speed, 1993.

Stearn, William T. *Botanical Latin.* 4th ed. Portland, Ore.: Timber Press, 1992.

Sturtevant, E. Lewis. (See Hedrick, U. P., ed.)

Styles, Sue. *A Taste of Alsace.* New York: Hearst, 1990.

Swendson, Patsy, and June Hayes. *Texas the Beautiful Cookbook.* San Francisco: Collins, 1995.

Taik, Aung Aung. *Under the Golden Pagoda: The Best of Burmese Cooking.* San Francisco: Chronicle, 1993.

Tatum, Billy Joe. *Billy Joe Tatum's Wild Food Cookbook and Field Guide.* Edited by Helen Witty. New York: Workman, 1976.

Taylor, George M. *British Herbs and Vegetables.* London: Collins, 1947.

Taylor, John Martin. *Hoppin' John's Lowcountry Cooking.* New York: Bantam, 1992.

———. *The New Southern Cook.* New York: Bantam, 1995.

———. *The Fearless Frying Cookbook.* New York: Workman, 1997.

Taylor's Guide to Vegetables and Herbs. Boston: Houghton Mifflin, 1987.

Thompson, David. *Classic Thai Cuisine.* Berkeley: Ten Speed, 1993.

Thompson, Sylvia. *The Kitchen Garden.* New York: Bantam, 1995.

———. *The Kitchen Garden Cookbook.* New York: Bantam, 1995.

Thorndike, John. "The Making of the 'Sugar Snap' Pea." *Horticulture* (January 1983): 14–22.

Tiedjens, Victor A. *The Vegetable Encyclopedia and Gardener's Guide.* New York: Avenel, 1943.

Tornabene, Wanda, and Giovanna Tornabene, with Michele Evans. *La Cucina Siciliana di Gangivecchio.* New York: Alfred A. Knopf, 1996.

Trang, Corinne. *Authentic Vietnamese Cooking.* New York: Simon & Schuster, 1999.

Traunfeld, Jerry. *The Herbfarm Cookbook.* New York: Scribner, 1999.

Trestrail, John H., III. "Gyromitrin-Containing Mushrooms—A Form of Gastronomic Roulette." *McIlvaniea Journal of American Amateur Mycology* 11 (1993): 45.

Trilling, Susana. *Seasons of My Heart.* New York: Ballantine, 1999.

Tropp, Barbara. *China Moon Cookbook.* New York: Workman, 1992.

Trotter, Charlie. *Charlie Trotter's Vegetables.* Berkeley: Ten Speed, 1996.

———. *Charlie Trotter's Seafood.* Berkeley: Ten Speed, 1997.

Tsuji, Shizuo. *Japanese Cooking: A Simple Art.* Tokyo: Kodansha, 1980.

Turner, Nancy J. *Food Plants of Interior First Peoples.* Vancouver: UBC, 1997.

Turner, Nancy J., and Adam F. Szczawinksi. *Common Poisonous Plants and Mushrooms of North America.* Portland, Ore.: Timber Press, 1991.

University of California Division of Agriculture and Natural Resources. *Postharvest Technology of Horticultural Crops.* 2d ed. Publication 3311. Adel A. Kader, technical editor. Oakland: 1992.

Urvater, Michele. *Fine Fresh Food Fast.* New York: Irena Chalmers Cookbooks, 1981.

Van Aken, Norman. *Norman's New World Cuisine.* New York: Random House, 1997.

van der Post, Laurens, and the Editors of Time-Life Books. *African Cooking.* New York: Time-Life Books, 1970.

Van Waerebeek, Ruth, with Maria Robbins. *Everyone Eats Well in Belgium Cookbook.* New York: Workman, 1996.

Vergé, Roger, with Martine Anglade. *Roger Vergé's Vegetables in the French Style.* Translated by Edward Schneider. New York: Artisan, 1994.

Veyrat, Marc, and François Couplan. *Herbier Gourmand.* Paris: Hachette Livre, 1997.

Vilmorin-Andrieux, MM. *The Vegetable Garden.* 1885. Reprint of English ed., published under the direction of W. Robinson. Berkeley: Ten Speed [1981].

Vitell, Bettina. *The World in a Bowl of Tea.* New York: HarperCollins, 1996.

Voegeling, François. *La gastronomie alsacienne.* Préface de Emile Jung. Éditions des Dernières Nouvelles de Strasbourg, n.d.

von Bremzen, Anya, and John Welchman. *Please to the Table: The Russian Cookbook.* New York: Workman, 1990.

Vongerichten, Jean-Georges. *Simple Cuisine.* New York: Prentice Hall, 1990.

Vongerichten, Jean-Georges, and Mark Bittman. *Jean-Georges.* New York: Broadway, 1998.

Walsh, Robb, and Jay McCarthy. *Traveling Jamaica with Knife, Fork & Spoon.* Freedom, Calif.: Crossing Press, 1995.

Waters, Alice, and the Cooks of Chez Panisse. *Chez Panisse Vegetables.* New York: HarperCollins, 1996.

Waters, Alice, and the Cooks of Chez Panisse, in collaboration with David Tanis and Fritz Streiff. *Chez Panisse Café Cookbook.* New York: HarperCollins, 1999.

Watson, Benjamin. *Taylor's Guide to Heirloom Vegetables.* Boston: Houghton Mifflin, 1996.

Watt, George. *The Commercial Products of India.* 1908. Reprint. New Delhi: Today & Tomorrow's Printers & Publishers, 1966.

Waugh, F. W. *Iroquois Foods and Food Preparation.* Ottawa Government Printing Board, 1916. Reprint, National Museums of Canada, 1973; Ontario: Iroqrafts, 1991.

Weaver, William Woys. *Heirloom Vegetable Gardening.* New York: Henry Holt, 1997.

Wells, Patricia. *At Home with Patricia Wells.* New York: Scribner, 1996.

Williamson, Darcy. *How to Prepare Common Wild Foods.* Bend, Ore.: Maverick, 1980.

Willinger, Faith. *Red, White & Greens.* New York: HarperCollins, 1996.

Wise, Victoria. *The Vegetarian Table: Japan.* San Francisco: Chronicle, 1998.

———. *The Gardeners' Community Cookbook.* New York: Workman, 1999.

Wolfe, Linda, and the Editors of Time-Life Books. *The Cooking of the Caribbean Islands.* New York: Time-Life Books, 1970.

Wolfert, Paula. *Couscous and Other Good Food from Morocco.* New York: Harper & Row, 1973.

————. *The Cooking of the Eastern Mediterranean.* New York: HarperCollins, 1994.

————. *Mediterranean Grains and Greens.* New York: HarperCollins, 1995.

Wong, Stephen. *HeartSmart Chinese Cooking.* Vancouver: Douglas & McIntyre, 1996.

Wright, Clifford A. *Cucina Paradiso.* New York: Simon & Schuster, 1992.

Yaniv, Zohara, D. Schafferman, and Z. Amar. "Traditions, Uses and Biodiversity of Rocket (*Eruca sativa,* Brassicaceae) in Israel." *Economic Botany* 52 (1998): 394.

Yoneda, Soei. *Good Food from a Japanese Temple.* New York: Kodansha International, 1982.

Young, Grace. *The Wisdom of the Chinese Kitchen.* New York: Simon & Schuster, 1999.

Yun, Wang, Ian R. Hall, and Lynley A. Evans. "Ectomycorrhizal Fungi with Edible Fruiting Bodies: 1. *Tricholoma matsutake* and Related Fungi." *Economic Botany* 51 (July/September 1997): 311–327.

Zaehner, R. C. *Zurvan: A Zoroastrian Dilemma.* Oxford: Clarendon Press, 1955.

Zaslavsky, Nancy. *A Cook's Tour of Mexico.* New York: St. Martin's, 1995.

————. *Meatless Mexican Home Cooking.* New York: St. Martin's, 1997.

Zee, A. *Swallowing Clouds.* New York: Simon & Schuster, 1990.

Zeven, A. C., and J.M.J. de Wet. *Dictionary of Cultivated Plants and Their Regions of Diversity.* 2d ed. Wageningen, Netherlands: Centre for Agricultural Publishing and Documentation, 1982.

Index of Recipes, Recipe Ideas, Chefs, and Cooks

This index includes both complete recipes developed by the author and recipe sketches and ideas from chefs and other cooks. The complete recipes are in standard (roman) type. The recipe ideas are in *italic* type.

Complete recipes are in standard type; *recipe ideas are in italic.*

Complete recipes are in standard type; *recipe ideas are in italic*.

Complete recipes are in standard type; *recipe ideas are in italic.*

Complete recipes are in standard type; *recipe ideas are in italic.*

Complete recipes are in standard type; *recipe ideas are in italic.*

Complete recipes are in standard type; *recipe ideas are in italic.*

Complete recipes are in standard type; *recipe ideas are in italic.*

Complete recipes are in standard type; *recipe ideas are in italic.*

Complete recipes are in standard type; *recipe ideas are in italic.*

Complete recipes are in standard type; *recipe ideas are in italic.*

Complete recipes are in standard type; *recipe ideas are in italic.*

Complete recipes are in standard type; *recipe ideas are in italic.*

Index of Vegetables by Their Common and Botanical Names

The primary entry names appear in capital letters. Latin names are italicized. All others, including transliterated and romanized names, are in standard type.